The Handbook of Phonological Theory

Blackwell Handbooks in Linguistics

This outstanding multi-volume series covers all of the major subdisciplines within linguistics today and, when complete, will offer a comprehensive, critical and authoritative survey of linguistics as a whole.

Already published

The Handbook of Phonological Theory

Edited by

John A. Goldsmith

Copyright © Blackwell Publishers Ltd, 1995, 1996

First published 1995
Reprinted 1995
First published in paperback 1996

Blackwell Publishers Inc.
238 Main Street
Cambridge, Massachusetts 02142, USA

Blackwell Publishers Ltd
108 Cowley Road
Oxford OX4 1JF, UK

Library of Congress Cataloging in Publication Data
The handbook of phonological theory/[edited by] John A. Goldsmith
p. cm. — (Blackwell handbooks in linguistics; 1)
Includes bibliographical references and index.
ISBN 0–631–18062–1 — ISBN 0–631–20126–2 (pbk)
1. Grammar, Comparative and general—Phonology.
I. Goldsmith, John A., 1951– . II. Series.
P217.H27 1995 94-13006
414—dc20 CIP

British Library Cataloguing in Publication Data
A CIP catalogue record for this book is available from the British Library

Typeset in 10 on 12pt Palatino by Graphicraft Typesetters Limited, Hong Kong
Printed and bound in Great Britain by T. J. Press Ltd, Padstow, Cornwall

This book is printed on acid-free paper

Contents

Contributors

Bruce Bagemihl, Department of Linguistics, University of British Columbia, Vancouver.

Juliette Blevins, Department of Linguistics, University of Western Australia, Nedlands.

Diane Brentari, Linguistics Program, University of California, Davis.

Ellen Broselow, Department of Linguistics, State University of New York, Stony Brook.

G. N. Clements, Institute of Phonetics, Paris.

Jennifer Cole, Department of Linguistics, University of Illinois, Champaign-Urbana

Nicolas Evans, Department of Linguistics and Language Studies, University of Melbourne, Parkville, Victoria.

Colin J. Ewen, Vakgroep Engels, Rijksuniversiteit, Leiden.

John Goldsmith, Department of Linguistics, University of Chicago, Chicago.

Morris Halle, Department of Linguistics and Philosophy, MIT, Cambridge, Massachusetts.

James W. Harris, Department of Linguistics and Philosophy, MIT, Cambridge, Massachusetts.

Robert D. Hoberman, Department of Comparative Studies, State University of New York, Stony Brook.

Grover Hudson, Department of Linguistics, Michigan State University, East Lansing.

Harry van der Hulst, Holland Institute of Generative Linguistics, University of Leiden.

Elizabeth V. Hume, Department of Linguistics, Ohio State University, Columbus.

William Idsardi, Department of Linguistics, University of Delaware, Newark, Delaware.

Sharon Inkelas, Department of Linguistics, University of California, Berkeley.

Junko Itô, Department of Linguistics, University of California Santa Cruz, Santa Cruz.

Gregory K. Iverson, Department of Linguistics, University of Wisconsin, Milwaukee.

René Kager, Onderzoeksinstituut voor Taal en Spraak, Utrecht.

Paul Kiparsky, Department of Linguistics, University of Massachusetts, Amherst.

Marlys A. Macken, Department of Linguistics, University of Wisconsin, Madison.

John J. McCarthy, Department of Linguistics, University of Massachusetts, Amherst.

R. Armin Mester, Department of Linguistics, University of California, Santa Cruz.

K. P. Mohanan, Department of English Language and Literature, National University of Singapore, Singapore.

Paul Newman, Department of Linguistics, Indiana University, Bloomington.

David Odden, Department of Linguistics, Ohio State University, Columbus.

John J. Ohala, Department of Linguistics, University of California, Berkeley.

David Perlmutter, Department of Linguistics, University of Rochester, Rochester, NY.

Alan S. Prince, Department of Linguistics, Rutgers University, New Brunswick.

Jerzy Rubach, Department of Linguistics, University of Iowa/Institute of English Studies, University of Warsaw.

Sanford A. Schane, Department of Linguistics, University of California, San Diego.

Elisabeth Selkirk, Department of Linguistics, University of Massachusetts, Amherst.

Donca Steriade, Department of Linguistics, University of California, Los Angeles.

Bernard Tranel, Department of Linguistics, University of California, Irvine.

Jeroen Van De Weijer, Holland Institute of Generative Linguistics, University of Leiden.

Moira Yip, Linguistics Department, University of California, Irvine.

Draga Zec, Department of Linguistics, Cornell University, Ithaca.

Preface

This is a handbook of phonological theory, and is thus neither a textbook nor a collection of research papers. Its goal is to provide its readers with a set of extended statements concerning mainstream conceptions of phonological theory in the first half of the 1990s, and perhaps beyond. The contributors have taken as their charge to bring together the leading ideas in the areas that they describe; in general, their aim has not been to provide new approaches so much as to offer a new synthesis of the ideas that are currently in the field.

This handbook is thus ideally suited for the reader who has a background in phonology but who wants to know more about a particular subarea. A book such as my *Autosegmental and Metrical Phonology* (1990) or Kenstowicz's *Phonology in Generative Grammar* (1993), or the older *Generative Phonology* (1979) by Kenstowicz and Kisseberth, would be more than adequate background for the present volume.

Most of the topics covered in this book need no explanation. It will come as no surprise to see articles on syllable structure, on metrical structure, and on feature geometry. Some topics have not been addressed directly for want of a general consensus at the time the book was constructed. For example, while there has been considerable discussion regarding the correct relationship between constraints on representations and phonological rules, there is no single chapter that focuses on this question. The reader concerned with this issue will find discussions in several of the chapters (especially chapters 1, 2, and 9), and more generally, the reader will find theoretical issues discussed in several chapters, with referencing through the index. A smaller set of issues, however, that might be expected to merit a chapter in this volume do not appear because of unforeseen misadventures and calamities over which authors and editors have no control. In the event, we have tried to make up for the losses with additional details in the chapters that are present.

The final eight chapters have a somewhat different character than the earlier material. They were submitted in response to invitations to write chapters for this handbook which would focus not so much on theoretical issues as on the aspects of particular languages (or language families) which have been particularly important in recent theoretical literature. If it had been possible, I would have liked to extend this section to include a hundred essays of this sort, but editorial limitations have precluded that possibility, and I hope that the reader will not regret the absence of an additional chapter on (for example) the phonology of Native American languages, or South American languages, for they too would have served well here. It simply was not possible to cover all of the areas of the world.

In a book of any size, but especially one of this length, there will have been many people who have helped it along to its completion. The kind people at Blackwell Publishers have put in a great deal of work and enthusiasm, beginning with Philip Carpenter, whose brainchild it was in the first place. Steve Smith and Andrew McNeillie are also to be thanked for their editorial work, as is Ginny Stroud-Lewis as picture researcher. On this side of the Atlantic, Charlene Posner, copy editor extraordinaire, improved the grammar and exposition in ways too numerous to count. Iretha Phillips, here in the Linguistics Department at the University of Chicago, came to the rescue several times when needed. Gail Brendel and Andra Dainora helped greatly with the final production.

The contributors, of course, made this volume a reality. Some contributors went far beyond the call of duty. John Ohala's efforts (unbidden and much appreciated) to help see the bibliography through to its final form have much improved it. Friends, students, and colleagues were helpful in finding errors and suggesting improvements; I would particularly like to thank Diane Brentari and Hisami Suzuki for their aid.

Abbreviations

abl	ablative
abstr	abstract
acc	accusative
adj	adjective
AIAS	Australian Institute of Aboriginal Studies
caus	causative
char	characteristic
CLIII	noun class 3, vegetable class in Australian languages
CNRS	Centre national de la recherche scientifique
COMIT	comitative
conj	conjunction
cons	consonantal
cont	continual (aspect), or continuant (a feature)
COR	coronal
dat	dative
dim	diminutive
du	dual
elat	elative
erg	ergative
excl	exclusive
fem	feminine
freq	frequentive
G	glide
gen	genitive
ICC	Iterative Constituent Construction
IOBJ	Indirect object
incep	inceptive
inch	inchoative
loc	locative
masc	masculine

nas	nasal
NCC	No-Crossing Constraint
nom	nominative
obj	object
OCP	Obligatory Contour Principle
PL	Place
pl	plural
pres	present
propr	proprietive
pst	past
R	root
REDUP	reduplication
sg	singular
SL	supralaryngeal
son	sonorant
SPE	*The Sound Pattern of English*
TB	Tongue Body
TOP	topic
UC	University of California
voc	vocalic

JOURNALS AND PERIODICALS

AIAS	Australian Institute of Aboriginal Studies
AJL	*Australian Journal of Linguistics*
AL	*Anthropological Linguistics*
ALS	*African Language Studies*
AuU	*Afrika und Uebersee*
BLS	Berkeley Linguistic Society
CJL	*Canadian Journal of Linguistics*
CLS	Chicago Linguistic Society
CSLI	Center for the Study of Language and Information
CUP	Cambridge University Press
ESCOL	East Coast Conference on Formal Linguistics
FL	*Foundations of Language*
GLOW	Generative Linguists of the Old World
GLSA	Graduate Linguistic Student Association
IJAL	*International Journal of American Linguistics*
IJSLP	*International Journal of Slavic Linguistics and Poetics*
IULC	Indiana University Linguistics Club
JAL	*Journal of African Languages*
JALL	*Journal of African Languages and Linguistics*

JAOS	*Journal of the American Oriental Society*
JASA	*Journal of the Acoustical Society of America*
JL	*Journal of Linguistics*
JLR	*Journal of Linguistic Research*
JNES	*Journal of Near Eastern Studies*
JOLAN	*Journal of the Linguistic Association of Nigeria*
JP	*Journal of Phonetics*
LA	*Linguistic Analysis*
LB	*Linguistische Berichte*
LS	*Language in Society*
LSA	Linguistic Society of America
Lg	*Language*
LI	*Linguistic Inquiry*
LR	*The Linguistic Review*
NELS	North East Linguistic Society
NLLT	*Natural Language and Linguistic Theory*
OL	*Oceanic Linguistics*
OUP	Oxford University Press
QPR	*Quarterly Progress Report*
RQL	*Revue québecoise de linguistique*
SAL	*Studies in African Linguistics*
SCOPIL	Southern California Occasional Papers in Linguistics
SIL	Summer Institute of Linguistics
SLA	Stanford Linguistic Association
SLS	*Studies in the Linguistic Sciences* (University of Illinois, Champaign)
SOAS	School of Oriental and African Studies
TCLC	*Travaux du cercle linguistique de Copenhague*
WCCFL	*West Coast Conference on Formal Linguistics*
WECOL	See Perlmutter 1991. West Coast Conference on Linguistics
WPL	*Working Papers in Linguistics*

In accordance with current linguistic usage, the abbreviations used for CLS, BLS, ESCOL, and WCCFL volumes is the following. "Papers from CLS 17" abbreviates *"Papers from the 17th Regional Meeting of the Chicago Linguistic Society"*, as "Proceedings of NELS 5" abbreviates *"Proceedings of the Fifth Annual Meeting of the North East Linguistic Society"*.

1 Phonological Theory

JOHN GOLDSMITH

0 Introduction: Phonotactics, Alternations, Contrasts; Representations, Rules, Levels

In this first chapter, I would like to bring together the issues joined and the proposals encountered in the range of papers that follow. These papers discuss a broad range of topics, often cross-referencing each other, usually by way of support, though there is *some* controversy, which I will highlight in the course of in this chapter. The most effective way to bring out the general unity is to step back and formulate the questions that our current theories are intended to answer. I would suggest that the following three questions lie behind most of the work that we find in phonological theory:[1]

1   What constitutes a phonological word in a given language? Many of the things we do in analyzing the phonology of a language are part of the effort to answer this question: we characterize and make an inventory of the sounds in the language, how the sounds can be combined to form syllables and words, what the stress patterns are like in the language, and so on. Conditions on well-formed phonological words have traditionally been called *phonotactics*.
2   What is the nature of *alternations*, that is, the differences in phonological form that we observe in the realization of a morpheme in different contexts? From the phonologist's point of view, what we mean by "context" may be phonological or morphological, and both kinds of context are important in determining the phonological realization of various morphemes.
3   The final question lies at the doorstep of phonemic theory: What phonetic differences are *contrastive* in a given language? – that is, what sound differences can be used to mark a lexical or grammatical distinction? This may be the hardest of the three questions, and I will

devote the greatest attention in this chapter to some of the current suggestions for how this question may be answered.[2]

Most of the everyday work of phonological theory focuses less on these three questions than on the conceptual tools that we employ in order to come to grips with the questions, and it is these tools that change far more rapidly than the questions themselves. The tools can be roughly divided into three groups as well. Phonological theory develops, in the first place, improved types of *phonological representations*; much of the difference in the look and feel of phonology over the past twenty years has come from the rapid changes that have occurred in the degree of articulation found in phonological representations. Second, phonological theory develops conceptions of *phonological levels*, with each level expressing distinct information and allowing distinct representations. Over the course of the development of phonological theory, the differences between the roles played by two or three basic levels in the phonology have always been central. This was true in the development of early phonemic theory, when phonological theory rested on a distinction between a phonetic and a phonemic representation. It is equally true today, when, for example, lexical phonology places certain restrictions on the possibilities of representations in the lexicon, and quite different restrictions on the output of the post-lexical phonology (see Mohanan's discussion of this, as well, in chapter 2 of this volume). Third, phonological theory employs the notion of a *rule*. Of these three, this is the most treacherous term to define in a way that can apply across all phonological theories; perhaps even the hope of achieving a satisfactory common description is unrealistic. But we would not be far off in characterizing phonological rules in the following way: they are the devices employed by the phonological theory to account for the relationship between representations at different levels. Certainly in simple cases this characterization applies in a straightforward fashion; within a structuralist phonemic analysis, a representation at the phonemic level /pat/ and a representation at a phonetic level [pʰatʔ] will be related by the rules of the phonology of the language. The same can be said for an account within classical generative phonology (that of Chomsky and Halle 1968), though in this case the rules are organized so as to apply sequentially, constructing a derivation that links the underlying and the derived representation.

Putting these various notions together provides us with a nine-chambered grid, formed by the three traditional questions of phonological theory along one axis, and the three sorts of tools that are used along the other axis. In the next three sections, I will locate the papers in this *Handbook* along these dimensions, and discuss a few issues that are controversial at the present time.

	Phonotactics	Alternations	Contrasts
Representations	Autosegmental and metrical structure Prososdic hierarchy	Feature geometry and limits on kinds of assimilation Prosodic morphology	Underspecification theory
Levels	Licensing Abstractness Structure-preservation	Issues of stratal organization	Organization of the lexicon
Rules	Metrical theory Harmonic rule application Optimality theory	Equation of phonotactics and alternations: strict cyclicity	Structure-building versus structure-changing operations

1 Phonotactics

The most basic of the traditional goals of phonological theory has been to establish the means of specifying, for any given language, just what a phonologically well-formed word in that language is. This is the question of *phonotactics*: in what ways can the items of phonology be put together to make a well-formed word. We may, after all, wish to express the notion that [blik] is a possible word of English, while [bnik] is not. Among the possibilities that have been considered are the following:

a   A well-formed word is one that is produced by taking an input string created by the morphological component, and applying the phonological rules of the language in the appropriate order.
b   A well-formed word is one that consists of a sequence of well-formed syllables.
c   A well-formed word is one in which all features (or autosegments) are associated to an appropriate skeletal position; all skeletal positions are associated with a syllable; and all syllables are associated with a foot.
d   A well-formed word is one that simultaneously satisfies all the well-formedness conditions of the language (including those given in (c)).

The first answer, (a), is roughly the position of classical generative phonology, that is, the theory proposed in *The Sound Pattern of English* (Chomsky and Halle 1968, hereinafter *SPE*), an account which puts most of the burden of determining phonological well-formedness on the operation of a set of ordered rules. In this conception, there *are* no well-formedness conditions as such; a representation is well-formed by virtue of where it came from, not what it is.

But it has become widely accepted – to the point where we may say it is simply established – that the complete elimination of phonotactics in favor of rule operation misses important generalizations, and the first area studied in this way – and the best-studied one – is that of syllable structure, which is discussed in detail by Juliette Blevins in chapter 6. Well-formed words, it has been argued, consist at the very least of well-formed syllables: answer (b); the ill-formedness of [bnik] is due to considerations of sonority that are intimately involved in the definition of the well-formed syllable.[3]

Further thought and investigation has shown at least two considerations indicating that reducing phonological word well-formedness to syllable well-formedness is only a first approximation. First of all, the phonological material that can occur word-initially is not necessarily the same as what can appear syllable-initially, and the phonological material that can occur word-finally is not necessarily the same as what can appear syllable-finally; in either case, the word-initial or word-final positions may be more restricted or more relaxed than what would be expected if syllable well-formedness told the whole story.[4] Second, syllables with different prosodic prominence (stressed/unstressed syllables have different prosodic prominence) have different possibilities; a well-formed stressed syllable will often have characteristics that would not let it qualify as a well-formed unstressed syllable (English is a typical example of a language with a greatly reduced class of vowel contrasts possible in unstressed position compared to stressed position).

It has proven both helpful and insightful to synthesize these observations by means of a hierarchy of prosodic categories, as suggested by Selkirk, Nespor and Vogel, Hayes and others (see chapter 15 by Sharon Inkelas and Draga Zec on the syntax-phonology interface, and chapter 9 on prosodic morphology by John McCarthy and Alan Prince), stretching from the autosegment at its smallest end, through the skeletal position, the syllable, the foot, and the phonological word (and extending to larger categories than the word as well). Each unit of phonological organization is subject to restrictions governing what elements may (and what may not) make up such a unit. The most familiar case is the way in which segments are composed of skeletal positions associated with features; there are always restrictions (both lower bounds and upper bounds) on which features, and how many features, may associate to a single skeletal position. These restrictions amount to a statement of the segmental inventory of the language. The syllable is subject to well-formedness conditions as well regarding the complexity of each of its components, such as the onset and the rhyme (see chapter 5 by Ellen Broselow and chapter 6 by Juliette Blevins), just as feet are subject to well-formedness conditions on the complexity of syllables in their different foot positions: answer (c).[5]

Are there further well-formedness conditions? In general, the answer is positive. For example, Junko Itô and R. Armin Mester mention in chapter 29 a constraint in Japanese against single (i.e., nongeminate) *p* which holds in native and Sino-Japanese forms; in that dominant part of the vocabulary, only geminate *p*, or *p* following an *m*, may appear. While that additional constraint is best stated in terms that *use* the vocabulary of syllable structure, it is not (at least in any sense formulated to date) a statement about syllable structure per se; it is a statement about a particular combination of features, of syllable structure, and of intersyllable structure. Hence, (d) as a general statement that includes (c) plus other, language-particular generalizations, is the best formulation at this time.

Notions of licensing have been developed by a number of phonologists for several ends, of which the most direct is the need to express the fact that higher-level prosodic categories, such as the syllable, place restrictions on what kind of information can appear within them. A language may permit a segment within the coda of its syllable, for example, without permitting the full range of consonants to appear in that position. Restrictions on what features and segments a prosodic position can license, combined with the requirement that in a well-formed representation, all elements be licensed, results in many cases in the proper statement of what constitutes a well-formed word in the language.[6] David Perlmutter, in chapter 8 on phonological quantity and multiple association, discusses how licensing can account for the odd distribution of geminate obstruents, which in many languages can appear stretched over the coda of a syllable and the onset of the following syllable, even though obstruents may not otherwise appear in coda position in those languages.

During the last few years considerable interest has been generated by the observation that prosodic categories, such as the phonological word, can be subject to a *minimality* condition, i.e., in numerous languages no phonological word may be smaller than the prosodic foot in the language (which, in turn, is frequently bisyllabic). This restriction may override what are otherwise unobjectionable generalizations of the language; this matter is discussed at length by John McCarthy and Alan Prince in their chapter on prosodic morphology (chap. 9), and it arises in Marlys Macken's discussion of language acquisition as well (chap. 22).

The matter of establishing the phonotactics of a language can be approached by analyzing the problem into its component parts, and recognizing that different requirements or restrictions can be placed on representations at different levels in the grammar. It is helpful to bear in mind that the term *level* is used in two ways that may seem distinct, but which share a common origin. On the one hand, the traditional notion of a level derives from having a particular set of tools (syntactic categories, morphological categories, discourse categories, etc.) for analyzing each aspect of an utterance; levels of this sort (syntactic, morphological, discourse, etc.) could, in principle at least, be said to hold "simultaneously" of an utterance. On the other hand, derivational analyses of phonology posit an underlying and a derived representation, and these distinct and apparently incompatible representations are also referred to as belonging to different levels.[7]

In her discussion of underspecification (chap. 4), Donca Steriade explores some cases in which the distribution of phonological information seems to demand two distinct representations in the derivational sense. A typical case of this sort involves one set of conditions regarding where a phonological contrast can appear underlyingly, and a different set of conditions regarding where the contrast can be realized phonetically: a case, say, where nasality can be marked contrastively only on stressed vowels, but where it can be realized phonetically on any voiced segment. She argues that a two-level analysis can be replaced by a single-level analysis in which the notion of licensing is developed and applied.

In earlier versions of generative theory, considerable attention was given to analyses containing abstract segments in the underlying representation which were not part of the surface inventory of segments, that is, employing two different inventories of segments at two different levels. Much of the clamor behind the discussions of these analyses, pro and con, evaporated with the development of autosegmental analyses, in part because the reformulations as an autosegmental account removed the abstractness. That is to say, if an analysis posits a high, back, unrounded vowel that never surfaces in a language with back/front vowel harmony, that vowel is an abstract vowel even if its neighboring vowels assimilate to its [+back] specification. But if we posit a [+back] autosegment as part of a root that associates with affixes, though it fails to associate to one or more vowels in the stem, the autosegment is not abstract, since it *does* quite simply appear on the surface. Such an observation is independent of whether that analysis is factually correct; it does, in any event, cast a new light on what one means when referring to an abstract analysis.

Structure preservation is a concept that pertains to the study of phonotactics at different levels. Structure preservation is the name given to the observation that a large class of phonological rules apply in such a fashion that their output conforms to well-formedness conditions, generally understood to be well-formedness conditions on underlying structure; as a special case of this, these rules do not create any segment types that do not exist underlyingly (see Kiparsky 1982b, 1982c). But in view of the fact that languages generally allow a much wider range of segments on the surface than they do underlyingly, structure preservation is understood to deal with levels that are part of the lexical phonology as opposed to any post-lexical phonological level.[8]

The development of the metrical theory of stress rules, explored by René Kager in chapter 10 and by Morris Halle and William Idsardi in chapter 11, allows for an organization of stress systems in languages of the world that is simple and compact, though richer in important ways than that obtained from metrical theory as it was understood a decade earlier. The greater richness permits a more faithful description of the facts of known languages, while still remaining reasonably close to the abstract structure of earlier metrical theory. James Harris's discussion of stress in Spanish in chapter 32 illustrates the way in which current metrical theories of stress offer important resources for the analysis of languages.

The development of a more elaborate theory of phonological representations has modified our understanding of rules. Early in the development of these theories of representation the argument was made that rule formulations became simpler when we had recourse to such constructs as tiers and syllables, and the simplicity was taken as evidence that these rules represented true linguistic generalizations. Over time, however, the extent of what we could say about what constitutes a well-formed representation grew to the point where the actual rules needed to achieve the well-formed representations grew simpler and simpler; eventually, in a good number of cases, the rules became trivial (of the form "add an association line"), and perhaps no longer what we would want to call rules – that is, particular packages of language-particular information regarding how to shift a representation toward well-formedness – but rather very general principles that would be found in many, many other languages,[9] leading some to question the existence of phonological rules altogether.[10]

A number of different perspectives can be found in the field today. The effort to specify generalizations that are (more or less) true on the surface, and to use these generalizations to simplify language-particular rule formulation,[11] was inaugurated in Sommerstein (1974), echoing the intention of Kisseberth (1970). In some cases, the addition of a group of phonotactics is presumed to lead to a simpler overall grammar because the return on the rule simplification is great compared to the small (formal) cost associated with adding some simple phonotactic statements. This trade-off is motivated for two kinds of cases that seem on the face of it to be closely related: that of rules that fail to apply if their output violates a phonotactic of the language, and that of rules that only apply to structures that violate a phonotactic and in such a way as to create an output structure that does not violate that phonotactic.[12]

A more radical step is taken (and it is one which merges the two cases of phonotactic-driven rule application just mentioned) when the proposal is adopted that the well-formedness of a representation is a scalar (indeed, a quantifiable) notion, not simply a matter of *yes* and *no*. This allows one to propose that a rule applies if and only if its effect is to increase the well-formedness of the representation – or to put the matter in a less dynamic fashion, the rule's effect comes into play if and only if the well-formedness of the output is greater than that of the input. This is the proposal advanced in Goldsmith (1993)[13] under the rubric of harmonic phonology. Other phonologists have explored similar frameworks, emphasizing the hierarchization – that is, the relative violability – of constraints on a language-particular and, in some cases, a universal basis. Noteworthy in this context are Singh (1987), Paradis (1988), and especially the discussion in LaCharité and Paradis (1993) comparing several approaches.[14] A still more radical proposal, that made by Prince and Smolensky (1993) and McCarthy and Prince (1993) under the rubric of optimality theory, discussed in chapter 9 below, places such an emphasis on the character of the output representation that there is no significant role played by the notion of the rule. This optimality approach views the relationship between the input representation (or underlying representation) and the selected output representation as being not subject to language particular considerations except for the relative ranking of the universally given constraints. Associated with each input representation is an extremely large class of candidate output representations, a class so large as to include virtually any representation that may be obtained from the input representation by adding – randomly, so to speak – formal symbols of any kind. Filters are used then to evaluate candidate outputs, and a simple procedure selects the optimal one.

2   Alternations

How do we account for alternations of morphemes in distinct morphological and phonological contexts? The reader of this volume will find none of the contributors worrying about the possibility that phonological theory has been forced to deal with empirical problems that ought rather be taken care of by morphological theory, and this lack of worry is surprising, perhaps, in view of the degree of concern expressed on this score in a survey of phonological theory published about fifteen years ago (Dinnsen 1979). The motto "minimize allomorphy!" remains today's watchword, in the sense that in practice, morphology continues to be concerned with the linear order and constituent structure of words, and with making a choice of which morphemes are to be employed to realize a set of morphosyntactic features in a given sentence; but contextually determined variations in the realization of a given morpheme will to the extent possible be accounted for phonologically.[15]

An important tradition in phonological theory associated directly with generative phonology is the search for formalisms that allow the statement of rules in a simple fashion. It was an oddity of classical generative phonology that rules of assimilation were no simpler in form than rules of dissimilation, and an immediate benefit resulted from adopting autosegmental notation for assimilations, in that the addition of an association line could be easily isolated as one of the characteristics of especially simple phonological rules. The study of feature geometry, discussed in detail by G. N. Clements and Elizabeth Hume in chapter 7, is based in part on a commitment to the principle that the simple character of partial assimilations (assimilation in which more than one, but not all, the features of a segment are involved) is due to a fact about the way in which features are organized representationally. Their commitment to the principle that "rules perform single operations only" leads them ineluctably to the conclusion that an operation that seems to assimilate several features simultaneously is operating on a feature constituent node that in turn dominates a set of features. Thus this innovation can be viewed as an innovation both in our theory of representations and in our theory of rules.

Another striking development in recent work that combines the nature of phonological representation with the treatment of alternations is prosodic morphology, discussed in depth by John McCarthy and Alan Prince in chapter 9. As they observe, prosodic morphology has as its domain a range of processes which fuse together two facets of language that linguistic theory has often attempted to keep apart, phonology and morphology, for in these cases, a morphological process makes crucial reference to one or another prosodic – hence phonological – category.

One of the goals of the development of lexical phonology and related approaches is to elaborate the phonology sufficiently to allow it to deal with the alternations in purely phonological terms. But it is nonetheless all too often the case that different phonological results emerge from what appears phonologically to be the same material (for example, in many Bantu languages, a sequence of a low vowel followed by a high vowel merges to become a mid vowel if the first is in a verb root, whereas elsewhere the vowel quality of the first vowel is lost; similarly, in English, some instances of the unstressed vowel indicated orthographically by –*y* cause a softening of a stem-final consonant [*president, presidency*], while others do not [*flint, flinty*]). K. P. Mohanan explores in chapter 2 the vicissitudes of attempts to analyze these differences solely in terms of derivational levels within the phonology, suggesting that the difficulties encountered in such attempts are likely to be insurmountable.

The development of the theory of lexical phonology brought new life to a traditional question in phonological theory: to what extent can the phonological changes associated with allomorphy be reduced to statements about the phonotactics of the phonological stem and the phonological word? Lexical phonology takes a strong position, essentially identifying phonotactics (or something close to them) with the phonological rules that are responsible for allomorphy. It does this with finesse, to be sure. Post-lexical rules are located in a separate component, sufficient unto itself, and the remaining lexical phonological rules are distributed to the various strata that compose the lexical phonology. These lexical phonological rules[16] apply under two sets of conditions, and thus serve two different functions: they apply to fill in phonological specifications that have been left unspecified underlyingly because of underspecification considerations; we can expect in general that a good deal more than half of the distinctive features[17] would be left unspecified underlyingly in the derivation of a word, and these features will be filled in by lexical rules. But equally importantly (and in practical terms, more importantly), these rules will apply in a structure-changing fashion to modify phonological specifications when they apply across a morpheme boundary, and it is this latter class of modifications that forms what is traditionally understood as instances of alternation. The relationship between these styles of functioning is discussed at length by Jennifer Cole in chapter 3, and it is this relationship, when added to the representational theory of underspecification (discussed below and in chapter 4 by Donca Steriade), that yields a particular theory of alternations, a theory of the phonologicization of alternations, in effect.

3 Contrasts

Phonologists find it crucial to be able to represent differences of sound that can be used in a language to distinguish distinct lexical items or distinct grammatical items and categories. It is necessary to say that the differences of sound are used to refer to either distinct lexical *or* distinct grammatical items because not *all* differences need be distinguished in the formalism – or so traditional wisdom has had it (this, indeed, is the fundamental insight of phonemic theory). *Some* differences, that is, may perfectly well be part of a person's linguistic knowledge (using that term in a pretheoretic way), but fail to satisfy the criterion of being relevant to lexical or grammatical information. For example, while I may tacitly know that imitating an Italian accent involves placing a falling tone on all accented syllables, or that an urban New York accent involves affricating my *t*'s before non-high vowels, this knowledge does not contribute to distinguishing any lexical items, nor any grammatical items, and thus does not enter into a strictly phonological account (though it is linguistic knowledge, and it involves knowledge of sound systems).

In classical generative phonology, all contrastive information was reduced to distinctions involving features; in fact, all contrasts could be reduced to the differences between $+F_i$ and $-F_i$ for some finite set of features F_i. All this has changed in the years since. The advent of lexical phonology (discussed by K. P. Mohanan in chapter 2, Jennifer Cole in chapter 3, and Paul Kiparsky in chapter 21 below) in the early 1980s (see Kiparsky 1982) brought renewed interest in the reasons for which not all phonological differences are equal.

Let us review this problem, which can be expressed simply as the question of how we should treat the difference between two sounds (or phones), x and y, in the phonology of a particular language.[18] The simplest situation we might find is that x and y are allophones in complementary distribution or in free variation. In the former case, we find that there is no phonetic environment in which both x and y appear, while in the latter x and y may occur freely with no lexical or grammatical difference involved. While there may be a sociolinguistic difference noted in the use of x and y, either may be used in any context in which the other is permitted, and in these two cases, we have two phones which are allophones of a single phoneme, in structuralist terminology. In the terminology of lexical phonology, the difference between x and y is post-lexical, and the difference plays no role in the lexical phonology.

A slightly more complex situation involves cases in which the phones x and y are in free variation in a certain context, and in complementary distribution in all the other contexts in which both appear. Once again, x and y would be treated as allophones of a single phoneme in traditional structuralist accounts, or as related ultimately by post-lexical operations in the context of lexical phonology.

At the opposite end of the continuum from these cases of allophones of a given phoneme, we find the case where x and y are everywhere in contrast – that is, in every phonetic context in which x may be found, y may also be found, but in a fashion that produces a word that is grammatically or lexically distinct; and – again, in the simplest case – x and y differ only by the specification of a single feature, F. The contrast between [t] and [d] in English illustrates this case well, and this is a difference that plays a central role in the lexical phonology. But in between these two extreme cases – phones being allophones of a phoneme, and phones being in contrast – loom the more difficult cases. There are at least three sorts of cases that will be familiar to anyone who has worked on the phonology of a natural language; I will refer to these as the *just barely contrastive* situation, the *not-yet-integrated semi-contrastive* situation, and the *modest asymmetry* situation. Let us consider each of these in turn.

Just barely contrastive sounds: x and y are phonetically similar, and in complementary distribution over a wide range of the language, but there is a phonological context in which the two sounds are distinct and may express a contrast. A typical example of this is the case of the "tense" A/lax *æ* in many forms of American English, discussed by Paul Kiparsky in chapter 21.[19] These sounds are largely in complementary distribution, and in free variation in a smaller set of words. In this writer's speech (and simplifying slightly), A occurs before tautosyllabic *m, n,* and *b,* and *æ* elsewhere: we find *sAm, pAn,* but *sæng* (and not **sAng*). However, one sharp contrast exists: the noun *can* with tense A [kAn], and the modal verb *can* with "lax" *æ*. In such cases, it is certainly not true that "anything goes"; a novel word with a lax *æ* before a tautosyllabic *n,* for example, seems quite impossible, and pronunciations such as *mæn, sæm* seem quite impossible, too. Thus while a contrast exists, a stubborn one which will not disappear under scrutiny, the contrast occurs in an extremely small part of the range of contexts in which the sound is found. The contrast is a lexical one, but only just barely.

Not-yet-integrated semi-contrasts: In this case, a language has two sounds, x and y, which may well be in contrast in some environments, but which in a particular environment show a sharp asymmetry, in that x appears in large numbers, while y appears in small numbers in words that are recent and transparent borrowings. In that environment, the contrast may be one that is being built up (perhaps through language contact) or worn down (through the vicissitudes of analogy and grammar simplification). Junko Itô and Armin Mester cite examples from several languages in chapter 29, discussing material from Japanese in detail, and Jerzy Rubach discusses two closely related cases in Russian and Polish, in chapter 31. In English, we might place in this category the contrast between *s* and *š*, used word-initially before a consonant other than *r,* as in words like *stick, shtick, sick, Schick;* while *shtick* is a possible English word (indeed, an existing English word), it remains in the periphery of the contemporary phonology of the language, and is for now a transparent borrowing.

Modest asymmetry cases: This involves pairs of sounds, x and y, which are uncontroversially distinct, contrastive segments in the underlying inventory, but for which in at least one context there seems to be a striking asymmetry in the distribution of the segments, judging by the relative number of words with the one and words with the other, or by some other criterion. The clearest examples of this modest asymmetry are the traditional cases of distribution which involve neutralization and which motivated the class of archiphonemes.

Less clear is the case of a contrast such as vowel length in English in the context of what has come to be known as Trisyllabic Shortening, that is, before two syllables, of which the first must be unstressed. It has long been noted that there are alternations involving vowel length differences in such pairs as *divine/divinity*, and this is no doubt closely related to the fact that even when we look at morphologically simple words, there are many more cases in which a short vowel appears in the context (__σ σ), like *Canada*, than there are in which a long vowel appears in such a context, like *nightingale, stevedore*, or *Oberon*. As we noted above, within the framework of lexical phonology, lexical rules that apply in a derived environment also apply in a nonderived environment as rules that specify the default or expected value of a feature in that environment; again, within the context of lexical phonology, any rule that functions in such a way would be considered in this broad category of "modestly asymmetric" relations between segments.

These five kinds of contrast naturally form a cline of the following sort:

1 Contrastive segments
2 Modest asymmetry case
3 Not-yet-integrated semi-contrasts
4 Just barely contrastive
5 Allophones in complementary distribution

The sense in which these form a cline – a single dimension of variation – is that the phonological system exerts varying amounts of force on the specification of the feature F (the feature that distinguishes the segments *x* and *y* in question). At the bottom, in (5), the specification of F is determined entirely by the grammar – by the essentially unbreakable regulation of the rule of allophony, and thus it is the grammar (as opposed to the specific lexical item) that has complete control over the feature specification. As we turn to the higher cases, the principles of the grammar place weaker and weaker restrictions on F's specification. In (4), the principles regarding the distribution of the values of feature F are almost unbreakable, but in a relatively small phonological and/or lexical class, a phonological contrast exists. In (3), an undeniable contrast exists, but it is one that acts like it is at the limit of what is permissible, and there is a strong tendency to push the one feature value to the other value, so as not to offend the native sensibilities of the language in question. When we turn to (2), we find a featural difference in which some asymmetries may be seen – for example, in statistical proportions – but nothing else suggests an asymmetry between the values of F, and finally, in (1), there are no perceptible differences between the functioning of the two values of the feature F, and there is no pressure, synchronic or diachronic, giving rise to a preference for one feature value or the other.

All of these cases are familiar and important to the phonologist. How are they distinguished from each other in current phonological theory? By and large, it is the case of "allophones in complementary distribution" that is kept qualitatively distinct from the other four, while among the other four cases (contrastive, modestly asymmetrical, not-yet-integrated semi-contrasts, and just barely contrastive) the differences are largely minimized, and all are treated as "lexical contrasts."

3.1 *Underspecification Theory*

The questions we have been discussing have been addressed in recent years as in large measure a matter of phonological *representation*. Underspecification theory, the subject of chapter 4 by Donca Steriade, has been concerned with determining whether, and to what extent, feature distinctions should appear in a phonological representation not as a choice between +F and –F, but rather as a choice between +F and no marking at all. In her contribution here and elsewhere, Steriade is at pains to distinguish what she calls trivial (or inherent, or permanent) underspecification from nontrivial underspecification; if a feature is allowed to take on only one value (+, say) at every level in the grammar (and this sort of case is not controversial), its underspecified character is trivial (though determining that this is the case may not be an easy matter). Such features are called privative, or monovalent, and the consequences for the treatment of phonological representations of such features is discussed in detail by Colin Ewen in chapter 17 and by Sanford Schane in chapter 18. Perhaps the most fruitful area of research on this issue has been that of vowel harmony systems, where asymmetries between the behavior of the two values of the harmonic feature have been studied in detail, as Harry van der Hulst and Jeroen van de Weijer report in chapter 14. Only if the feature is restricted to a single value at a deep level of representation, and finds itself expanded to two values at a more superficial level, is a feature nontrivially underspecified, in Steriade's terminology.

A great deal of work has been invested over the past ten years regarding the fashion in which underlying specifications of featural differences and contrasts are to be represented formally, with an emphasis on whether and when a feature must be treated as a privative, monovalent feature. The reader will find several different positions taken regarding radical underspecification theory in the chapters that follow. Paul Kiparsky offers the strongest defense, while Donca Steriade presents a compelling case against it. Let us consider some of the issues that are involved.

There are questions that lie behind this disagreement that go even beyond the character of underspecification theory. Kiparsky's investigation of featural underspecification brings one to a conclusion that we might summarize in the following way: what we have traditionally referred to as "lexical diffusion" is nothing more nor less than our observation of the grammar of the language attempting to balance off the relative complexity of rule statements and of lexical entries, the two major components of the grammar. The argument is subtle, and worth reviewing in some detail.

Kiparsky proposes, first of all and in line with widely understood principles of lexical phonology, that in any particular phonological context, there will be, for any given feature F, an expected, or unmarked, value; this will be either +F or –F. Whether the unmarked value is +F or –F depends very much on the phonological context C, and if the unmarked value of F in context C is +F, then the marked value will be –F. How are the decisions made as to what is the appropriate context to consider, and which value should be chosen to be the unmarked value? By and large, radical underspecification (and Kiparsky's position is squarely in this camp) has left this an open question, but it points in two directions for the eventual answer. The first way to explain the choice of unmarked values is to appeal to universal principles, such as the observation that the unmarked value for the feature Voice is + with no context specified, while the unmarked value for the same feature on obstruents is –. Such observations have served in the first place as phonological universals, and may now serve in the breach as universal default feature markedness principles. The second way, which is much more important for our purposes, is to look at the relative complexity of the information packed into the rule component and the lexical component of the grammar.

Let us recall that from the traditional generative point of view, a phonological grammar is divided into two major components: a set of rules, broadly construed, and a lexicon. The lexicon contains (among other things) the underlying phonological representation of all of the words of the language. The traditional generative concern has been to select the least complex grammar consistent with the data of the language. However, we – linguists – must constantly bear in mind that there is typically a trade-off between the complexity of the rule component, on the one hand, and the lexicon, on the other, in the sense that the same set of data can be treated in several different ways. Some will show greater complexity in the rule component and less complexity in the lexicon, and others greater complexity in the lexicon and less complexity in the rule component. Let us briefly review how this can arise, and what the consequences are for markedness and markedness reversal.

Imagine that we found a language much like English, in which there was a category of words relevant to the phonology (let us call the category "Proper-Nouns," for purely expository purposes; in a real case, it might be nouns, prepositions, or what have you) in which far more words began with the voiced alveopalatal affricate *ǰ* than with its voiceless counterpart *č*. In our example, this would mean that the language contained more ProperNouns like *John, Jim, Jerry, James*, and *Geoff* than it did like *Chuck* or *Charles*. While on general phonological grounds as we noted just above, *č* is unmarked for the feature Voice (it is a voiceless obstruent, after all), the fact is that there are more *ǰ*s in this particular morphophonological environment. In traditional generative terms (and this conception is unambiguously embraced by radical underspecification theory), the measure of complexity of a representation is just the set of actual marks required to specify the underlying representation, and up until now, it has served us well to mark "+" on the feature Voice when we encountered a *ǰ* or any other voiced obstruent, leaving the "–" off when we encountered a voiceless obstruent. But in this particular context – word-initially in ProperNouns – this economy serves us badly; we would be better off putting down a – on the feature Voice at the beginning of *Chuck* and *Charles*, and leaving the voiced *j̆s* unmarked. In order to achieve this economy *in the lexicon*, however, we must set down a rule in the rule component of the form:

$$(1) \quad \begin{bmatrix} \text{uVoice} \\ \text{+Strident} \\ \text{+Delayed Release} \end{bmatrix} \rightarrow [\text{+Voice}]/\# \quad \begin{bmatrix} \text{+Coronal} \\ \rule{1cm}{0.4pt} \end{bmatrix}_{\text{ProperNoun}}$$

and this rule will, of course, cost the rule component something. Thus we find a trade-off between rules and representations, and we (or the grammar) will choose to reverse the markedness of a feature just in case there is a good enough trade-off involved – for that is what we have just done; we have said that the markedness relationship flipped about in a particular morphophonological context (ProperNoun-initially). When is the trade-off *good enough*? Even phonologists committed to this perspective have not the slightest idea; perhaps one must count up the number of formal symbols in the new rule that must be financed (in the case above, the rule seems to cost about 11 units, counting (i) u (ii) Voice (iii) + (iv) strident (v) + (vi) Delayed Release (vii) + (viii) Voice, (ix) ProperNoun (x) +, and (xi) coronal). How many features must we be able to save in the lexicon to pay off the price of the rule? Perhaps eleven; perhaps one hundred eleven. We do not know.

Kiparsky's contention is that what we call *lexical diffusion* consists, first of all, of a dynamic in which the rule component pushes each phonological rule in the direction of generalizing the context in which it applies. If generalizing the context consists of leaving off formal symbols in the rule, then this makes the rule simpler and less costly; but if the language is to generate the same output after "simplifying" – i.e., generalizing – one of its rules, then it must add additional specifications to a new set of lexical items. Which lexical items? – those that satisfy the generalized form of the rule but that did not satisfy the rule in its earlier form. That is, around the *core* set of words to which Rule 1 applies, there is what we might call a *penumbra* of words that do not satisfy Rule 1, but would satisfy it if Rule 1 were generalized to Rule 2, according to which the markedness reversal holds not only for affricates but for fricatives as well.

$$(2) \quad \begin{bmatrix} \text{uVoice} \\ \text{+Strident} \end{bmatrix} \rightarrow [\text{+Voice}]/\# \quad \begin{bmatrix} \text{+Coronal} \\ \rule{1cm}{0.4pt} \end{bmatrix}_{\text{ProperNoun}}$$

In the earlier stage, when Rule 1 was present, the initial consonant in words like *John* was unmarked for Voice, while the initial consonant in *Shane* and *Sam* was unmarked for Voice and the initial consonant in *Zachary* was marked for Voice. However, if Rule 1 generalizes (simplifying the rule component) to become Rule 2, words like both *Shane* and *Zachary* will now move into the core of the rule, and the marking on their initial consonants will be reversed (*Shane*'s is now marked, and *Zachary*'s is unmarked). This does indeed sound like a move that will buy simplicity for the rule component, but it will cost the lexicon dearly in terms of markings on the feature Voice. Although this is not remarked upon, it is crucial to an account such as Kiparsky's that such an extension (cheap for the rule component, costly for the lexicon) will actually occur, and not infrequently. Once it has occurred, though, the lexicon is not only free to change, it is encouraged to do so, by the economics of markedness, and all of the words that were in the penumbra of the older Rule 1 will now be pushed toward dropping their newfound Voice markings; they will drop their new markings, and become unmarked with respect to the new, generalized Rule 2 (and hence will become voiced consonants word-initially). As they do this on a lexical element by lexical element basis, we will observe the change, and we will call it the lexical diffusion of the rule of ProperNoun-initial voicing.

Paul Kiparsky makes a strong case that this is a reasonable understanding of the process of linguistic change known as lexical diffusion. Looked at more closely as an account of underspecification, however, it seems to me that in certain respects the argument is too weak, while in others it is too strong, though the insight at the center regarding the relationship of synchronic phonological theory and our understanding of diachronic processes remains attractive and even compelling.

The insight at the center is that lexical diffusion is a set of leap-frogging simplifications, first in the rule component, and then in the lexicon, each driven by the urge toward total simplification of the grammar. The sense in which the argument is too weak is that this view in no way supports the view of radical underspecification employed in the description given above. That is, radical underspecification insists that in the underlying representations, even among the phonologically contrastive features of the language, there will be far less than fifty percent of the features in the underlying representations actually specified, because in any given environment, one feature value will always be the unmarked value, and that value will not be explicitly filled in underlyingly, but rather will become filled in during the derivation. Radical underspecification lends itself very naturally to the hyperformal understanding of "naturalness" according to which a representation is more natural or simple (or preferred, or less marked) if it has fewer formal symbols.

Radical underspecification theory assumes the presence of a formal device (let us call it D) which determines for each position, and for each lexical entry, which feature specifications may, and thus must (for that is the logic of underspecificationism), be left unspecified. Intuitively speaking, D determines (given the phonological rules of the language and univeral default rules) which feature specification(s) may be left out of a given underlying representation and still return the correct surface form. Radical underspecification theory uses *D*'s computation to leave those feature specifications out of the underlying representation. Once they are left out, they cannot and do not add anything to the total complexity of the word's lexical entry.

Once we make explicit what is going on, though, it should be obvious that radical underspecification – the requirement to leave these redundant features unspecified in underlying representation – is by no means the only way of getting the result that we were looking for above. The result that we need is that the more features there are underlyingly that are "unmarked" – that is, the result of patterns of expectation – the "simpler" the representation is underlyingly. But this can be achieved with device *D* and *no* theory of underspecification. That is, given a fully specified underlying representation, let device *D* be run, and let it paint *blue* all of the feature values that are unmarked values in their context; now we may define the complexity of that underlying representation as the sum total of all the markings that device *D* did not paint blue. It would thus be an error, I believe, to think that fundamental concerns with simplicity commit one (or even lead one) to underspecification.

But there is also, as I suggested, a sense in which Kiparsky's argument is too strong, a sense in which if the argument were valid as it stands, then it would equally support conclusions that are palpably false. The problem is this: Kiparsky's contention is that there is pressure (due to the drive for simplification of the grammar as a whole) to shift lexical features from their marked to their unmarked values, regardless of the feature.

But if the pressure to shift from marked to unmarked values in the cases which Kiparsky explores (the *just barely contrastive* sorts of cases, as I have labeled them) derives in essence from the drive to simplify grammars by simplifying representations, there are no grounds for distinguishing among the types of features that will feel this pressure, and the theory will then predict that all features will equally feel the pressure to conform, to take on the unmarked value. But this is never found in the case of what I called above *fully contrastive* features, and imagining what would happen if it were makes this point clear. Take, for example, the difference in English between the pairs of obstruents *d* and *t*, and *g* and *k*. The voiced obstruents bear, we may agree, the marked value of the feature Voice, while the voiceless ones bear the unmarked value. If there were pressure on the feature Voice to take on the unmarked value, then *dog* [dɔg] would be in danger of shifting lexically to *talk* [tɔk], with *dawk* or *tawg* as possible intermediate stages in this shift. But this prediction is not borne out by the facts: plainly, for a healthy center of our lexicon, there is no evidence of pressure of any sort at all to change one segment to another, despite the fact that radical underspecification theory, used as a tool to account for lexical diffusion and change, *treats fully contrastive pairs of segments in the same way as barely contrastive pairs of sounds.*

The conclusion that we must draw from this, it seems to me, is that we have not yet reached a satisfactory understanding of the nature of the binary contrasts that are found throughout phonology. Neither marking all contrasts as +/– nor marking all contrasts as +/Ø is sufficient; we need some more refined means for linking the notion of specification. The pressure to shift may well exist for contrasts of one or more of the categories we discussed above, but the pressure is not found in *all* of the categories. We need to find, at a minimum, a way to recognize that some markedness distinctions carry with them the impetus to eliminate the marked value: for example, in the case of the not-yet-integrated semi-contrasts, we do expect the marked feature value to give way to the unmarked feature value. But this is not the case in fully contrastive pairs of segments (like the *t*/*d* of English). We must determine how the line is drawn (if there is a clearcut line to be drawn) between these cases, and we must find a way that the two cases (or the several cases) can be dealt with without wrongly assimilating the one case to the other.

A careful study of a language will often raise some questions as to just which phonological differences are contrastive, in various parts of the vocabulary. I touched on this briefly just above, suggesting that there is a cline to be found between differences that are allophonic and those that are full-fledged distinctions in a language, but other kinds of divergence can be found, as Junko Itô and Armin Mester observe in chapter 29. They point out that a four-way distinction between Yamato, Sino-Japanese, mimetic, and foreign forms is observationally motivated; the question then arises as to how these differences are to be organized in the phonology. Itô and Mester argue convincingly that if some "peripheral" parts of the Japanese vocabulary should be thought of as being subject to weaker constraints than those parts lying at its "core", the difference "has nothing to do with 'early' vs. 'late' in the derivation: the periphery is just as underlying as the core." The burden is on phonological theory, then, to shift the style of analysis to allow us to separate properly the influences of distinct constraints and phonotactics in a nonderivational fashion so that we can account for the range of differences found in different parts of the vocabulary of a single language.

There is a central and important question that draws together underspecification theory and the nature of rule application and which comes up several times in the course of the chapters that follow, most notably in the chapters on vowel harmony, underspecification, and historical change; this question is whether rules can apply in a feature-changing fashion directly, or whether what appears to be a feature-changing process is composed first of feature-delinking followed by a feature-filling process. As van der Hulst and van de Weijer note, there is considerable controversy as to whether the range of known vowel harmony (and nasal harmony, we might add, too; see note 21) systems requires feature-changing analyses. The development of theories in this area is at a point where it is no longer profitable, as it might once have been, to determine that the best theory, a priori, is one which allows the most tightly constrained class of languages, for as much progress has been achieved in recent years by enriching the formalism as has been achieved by constraining it, as I observed above in connection with metrical theory.[21]

4   Theories and Languages

Not all of the chapters in this book fit neatly into the three by three schema presented at the beginning of this chapter. The study of tone languages, for example, has been extremely fruitful for the development of recent phonological theory, but it is the clarity and the complexity of the tonal systems rather than anything peculiar to them that has made their study so important. The chapters by David Odden on African tone languages (12) and Moira Yip on Asian tone languages (13) cover two of the best-studied areas of tonal systems, though regrettably other areas of the world with important tonal systems such as Meso-America and Southeast Asia are not discussed here.

Theories of syllable and skeletal structure have profited enormously from the study of Semitic languages and of Afro-Asiatic languages more generally. In their surveys of Chadic (chap. 26), Ethiopian (chap. 27), and of Semitic languages (chap. 30), Paul Newman, Grover Hudson, and Robert Hoberman, respectively, present the aspects of the phonology of these languages that are most significant to current work in phonological theory. Australian languages have played an equally important role in the development of metrical theory, and Nicholas Evans in chapter 25 provides a detailed account not only of the metrical structure of Australian languages, but of other aspects of their phonology which have broad consequences for phonological theory. Bernard Tranel, in his analytic overview of liaison and latent consonants in French (chap. 28), offers an up-to-date account of an important area of research for theories of skeletal positions and prosodic categories.

The study of signed languages, such as American Sign Language, promises to have a profound effect on phonological theory, and perhaps ultimately on our understanding of what a human language is. The possibilities that emerge from a linguistic system not constrained by the resources of the vocal tract exploit capacities that had until recently been hidden from linguists' view, and the broadened vista that we have today may in retrospect be as significant for the development of linguistics as was the impact on the Western tradition of the study of non-Indo-European languages. In chapter 20, Diane Brentari discusses some of the salient phonological properties of American Sign Language, itself only one of a large number of signed languages of the world, but for the moment the best studied from a linguistic point of view.

5   Conclusion

In the chapters that follow, the reader will have the opportunity to read thirty-one accounts of the ways in which current phonological theory treats the central phonological problems faced by linguists today. We have seen enormous progress over the past several decades, and it is my hope, and expectation, that this rate of progress will continue in the years to come.

NOTES

1　I would point out that these questions change very slowly in time as well, but will not discuss that issue here.

2　This briefest of summaries leaves out entirely two important subjects: how hypotheses and theories are evaluated (that is, what counts as justification for claims in a given theory), and how phonological theory is linked to other theories, both within linguistics (syntax, phonetics, morphology, etc.) and without (neurobiology, perhaps theories of lexical access, of speech production and perception, though much of the second group is arguably better viewed as being part of linguistics, not external to it). My remarks in the text above should be thought of as limited to matters *internal* to phonological theory, though there is discussion of subjects external to phonology in a number of the following chapters (chapter 2 by K. P. Mohanan and chapter 9 by John McCarthy and Alan Prince on the relationship of morphology and phonology, chapter 15 by Sharon Inkelas and Draga Zec and chapter 16 by Elisabeth Selkirk on phonology and syntax, and chapters 22 on language acquisition, 23 on language games, and 24 on experimental phonology by Marlys Macken, Bruce Bagemihl, and John Ohala, respectively). It is truer today than ever before that the studies bridging components and methodologies are critical for the

testing and refinement of phonological theory.

3　The rise in sonority between b and n is not great enough, while the rise in sonority from b to l is. See chapter 6 by Juliette Blevins below; for a different view, with an explicitly computed notion of sonority, see Goldsmith (1993a) and Goldsmith and Larson (1992).

4　English and Arabic are often-cited examples of languages in which we find longer strings of consonants word-finally than are found syllable-finally. English allows for certain strings of three consonants, as in *Pabst* or *midst*, while at most two consonants can appear at the end of a syllable word-internally, as in the first syllable of *vintner* or *Thornley*. Modern Standard Arabic permits no more than one consonant in the coda of a word-internal syllable, but two consonants are permitted word-finally.

5　On this, see, for example, Bosch (1991).

6　Itô (1986, 1989), and Goldsmith (1990).

7　See Goldsmith (1993a) for an extended discussion of this, and further references. The treatment of rule ordering plays an essential role in this discussion; see chapter 19, by Gregory Iverson, in this volume.

8　Borowsky (1986) presents an analysis of English syllable structure from this point of view; Wiltshire (1992) argues for an alternative, nonderivational analysis.

9　I should perhaps state the point a

bit more carefully. From a classical generative point of view, the basic elements that are used jointly to formulate rules are quite simple as well (names of features, feature values, etc.). The claim implicit in classical generative phonology is that these items in the vocabulary of rule formulation will coalesce into rules in a more or less random fashion; there are no preferred ways for the items to group together among all the conceivable ways that are syntactically well-formed, that is, obey the basic principles of the syntax of phonological rules (e.g., there is an arrow that points to the right, a slash further yet to the right that marks the beginning of the statement of the environment, only one dash marking the environment, etc.). If there were specific ways in which the elements of phonological rules preferred to come together, then counting up the total number of formal symbols would not be an adequate measure of the complexity of a rule. But that *is* what we find: some simple rule formulations arise frequently ("delink the first association line of a doubly-linked autosegment") while others do not occur at all frequently ("add an association line to an element that is doubly associated"). It follows that an evaluation metric for the rule component that does no more than count formal symbols in the rules is not adequate.

10 E.g., those working in government phonology (see Kaye 1990, and other papers cited there).

11 As opposed to using these generalizations to rule on what was a possible underlying form, as was done in natural generative phonology, for example (see Hooper 1979, and references cited there).

12 A widely discussed case of a process which applies in order to repair ill-formed syllable structure is epenthesis; see, for example, Itô's (1989) discussion of this. The case of rules that do not apply when their output would violate a phonotactic is discussed, for example, in McCarthy (1986b) and Yip (1988a). A typical example of this sort is the case of a vowel deletion which fails to apply if the output of the rule is two successive, identical segments, a violation of the Obligatory Contour Principle (on the OCP, see chapter 12 by David Odden). Yip makes the observation – a crucial one, in this writer's opinion – that the OCP (functioning as a measure of well-formedness condition like any other such measure) is "not an absolute rule *trigger*" (if a language has no rule to improve an OCP violation, then there's nothing to be done about it), "but it is an absolute rule *blocker*" (Yip 1988a, p. 75), for the phonology always has the option of *not* applying a rule that it contains, so to speak. In all cases, a violation of the OCP is a worse-formed structure than an otherwise parallel structure that does not violate the OCP, and phonological rules applying in a harmonic fashion (see below in the text) will only apply to improve the well-formedness of a representation.

13 And elsewhere; see Goldsmith (1993b), as well as Goldsmith (1990, chap. 6), Brentari (1990b), Bosch (1991), Wiltshire (1992). The principle of harmonic application has been summarized by the phrase, "Always change, but only for the better."

14 LaCharité and Paradis (1993) is an introductory paper in an issue of the *Canadian Journal of Linguistics* (Paradis and LaCharité 1993)

devoted to constraint-based theories on multilinear phonology, where the term "constraint" is equivalent to phonotactic.

15 I do not mean to be defending this position, but simply to point out that this has served as a background working principle for a good deal of the work in current phonological theory.

16 Or at least those in a cyclic stratum, and not a noncyclic stratum. Proposals have been made that would mark strata or even rules as noncyclic, freeing them from the operative constraints on the application of cyclic rules. See Jennifer Cole's discussion in chapter 3, as well as chapter 11, by Morris Halle and William Idsardi, and also chapter 32, by James Harris.

17 More than half, because for any given feature we will expect that a good deal less than 50 percent of its occurrences in underlying forms will be unspecified. It is obvious that the percentage of occurrences of a given feature will be less than 50 percent, since if it were greater, we could simplify the grammar by making the unmarked value the other value. Further recognition of markedness reversals, as discussed in the text, for example, will ensure that the number of occurrences of a feature that bear a specification are considerably less than 50 percent.

18 In this discussion, I focus on the issue of contrast between phones that exist in a language; but a similar question can arise with respect to the question of what the permitted segments are in the lexicon of a language. This is closely connected to the discussion above, in the sense that some existant phones in a language (say, the flap [D] in English) are taken *not* to be in the inventory of the English lexicon, because they are integrated into English phonology outside of the English lexicon, and among the "post-lexical" (nonlexical) phonological rules. But the status of segments is often unclear, in much the way in which the status of contrasts is unclear, as the hierarchy in the text below illustrates. We know that certain sounds are not part of the inventory of a given language; English has no clicks, and Ndebele does. English has no nasalized vowels, and French does. English has a velar nasal, and French does not. Or does it? Sampson (1992) reviews the case for considering the velar nasal as a segment of contemporary French (see Walker 1975 and Walter 1983 on this as well) and argues (1) that the range of cases in which ŋ appears in French words – generally borrowings from English originally – is such that it cannot be ignored in the analysis of contemporary French; (2) that there is no simple case to be made that the ŋ is the phonetic result of some combination of uncontroversial French segments in some particular context – say, /ng/ in word-final position; and (3) that it would be an error to accept that angma has a status in the phonology of French according it a freedom of distribution anything like that of the clear cases of consonants in the language. Sampson suggests that the emergence of ŋ, along with other overt nasal consonants in French (not English!) words such as *lunch, cross-country*, etc., is best understood as forming a significant subgroup in the French lexicon. In this fashion, he suggests, rather than trying to incorporate obviously aberrant pronunciations into an otherwise homogeneous phonology, one could

take into account an otherwise irregular phonological existence.

19 See Kiparsky's contribution, chapter 21, to this volume. The facts cited here reflect this author's (JG) New York dialect.

20 Proper names are notorious for stretching the boundaries of permissible sound combinations, and in this case, too, we find contrasts like *Schneider/Snider* which do not seem to faze English speakers, or to be subject to any kind of nativization.

21 See Noske 1993 on feature changing and three-valued features. In the domain of post-lexical rules, it appears to me to be established that there must be both rules that apply in a structure-changing fashion and, in other languages, rules that apply only in a structure-building (i.e., feature-filling) fashion. One example of each is given in chapter 1 of Goldsmith (1990): the former is illustrated there by San Miguel El Grande Mixtecan and the latter by Sukuma.

2   The Organization of the Grammar

K. P. MOHANAN

0   Introduction

The central issue I wish to explore in this article is the nature of the relation between subsystems of grammar, in this instance the subsystems of phonology and morphology.[1] This issue has close links with two other issues: (1) the classification and formal expression of regularities in representations in terms of systems of rules/constraints, and (2) the levels and content of representations.

The first question on the issue of the relation between subsystems is: do phonology and morphology interact? One can identify two answers to this question in the literature. The first is that they do not interact: regularities of sound patterning sensitive to morphology are part of morphophonology, not phonology. This was the position held, for instance, in neo-Bloomfieldian classical phonemics. A variant of this claim is that phonological regularities must be classified into two types on the basis of interaction with morphology: the phonological rules/constraints that interact with morphology form a separate subsystem independent of the phonological rules/constraints that do not interact with morphology. An example is the distinction between rules and processes in natural phonology (Stampe 1972), which correspond in classical phonemics to morphophonological and phonological rules respectively. The second answer, in contrast, is given by classical generative phonology (Chomsky and Halle 1968) and its descendents lexical phonology (Pesetsky 1979; Kiparsky 1982, 1985; K. P. Mohanan 1982, 1986; Pulleyblank 1983, 1986a; Booij and Rubach 1984), nonlexical prosodic phonology (Selkirk 1980; Aronoff and Sridhar 1983; Sproat 1986), prosodic lexical phonology (Inkelas 1989), harmonic phonology (Goldsmith 1989, 1993a; Wiltshire 1992), and so on; they reject the classification of rules/constraints into morphophonological and phonological subsystems, postulating a single phonological subsystem of rules/constraints, and claiming that phonology does interact with morphology. I will show that there is sufficient evidence to hold the latter position.

If phonological patterns can be sensitive to morphological information, how is this information made available to phonology? That is, how do the two subsystems interact? There are two broad classes of answers, those that appeal to entities of representations, and those that appeal to sequential modularity. Classical generative phonology appeals to tree structure representations with labels such as N and NP. In addition, morphological information about affixation versus compounding, different kinds of affixation, and the like, are expressed representationally in terms of juncture symbols such as +, #, and ##. This information is represented in prosodic phonology by labels such as phonological root, stem, and word. In these theories, the domains of phonological rules/constraints are specified in terms of representational units. In contrast, lexical phonology factors out this information into sequentially ordered modules, allowing the domains of phonological rules/constraints to be specified in terms of the modules. Prosodic lexical phonology employs both representations as well as sequential modularity. As it turns out, there exist configurations of facts that are analyzable in terms of sequential modularity but not representations, and others that are analyzable in terms of representations but not sequential modularity. How this dilemma can be resolved is an open question.

Another central preoccupation in phonological theory relevant to the question of the phonology-morphology interaction involves the need for a level of phonological representation that is most readily accessible for speech production, recognition, acquisition, and speaker judgements. This was perhaps the intuition underlying the level of phonemic representation in classical phonemics. The theory of generative phonology proposed by Chomsky and Halle in *The Sound Pattern of English* (1968, henceforth *SPE*) made a radical departure from classical phonemics by not including this level of representation. This led to a serious dissatisfaction with *SPE* phonology and a series of rebellions against it. The late seventies and early eighties witnessed a return to a preoccupation with levels of representation, particularly in the form of lexical phonology, which offered a new conception of the phonology-morphology interaction (Siegel 1974; Pesetsky 1979; K. P. Mohanan 1982; Kiparsky 1982; Pulleyblank 1986a). The main contribution of lexical phonology to the question of levels of representation was the idea that even though phonological rules/constraints themselves do not fall into two types, the interaction between phonology and morphology leads to a level of phonological representation that is distinct from underlying and phonetic representations. The last two decades have seen various versions of lexical phonology propounded, as well as many critiques and alternatives (Rubach 1984; Sproat 1985, 1986; Hargus 1985; Kaisse and Shaw 1985; Borowsky 1986; Halle and Vergnaud 1987; Fabb 1988; T. Mohanan 1989; Inkelas 1989; Goldsmith 1990; Wiltshire 1992; to mention a few). It appears to me that even though we may have to reject many of the assumptions of lexical phonology, including its sequential conception of grammar, we will need to retain the idea of an intermediate level of representation, as is done in some versions of phonological theory that reject sequentiality (Lakoff 1993; Goldsmith 1989, 1993a).

The issue of the phonology-morphology interaction is also closely involved with the formal statement of regularites of distribution and alternation, that is, the nature of the rule/constraint system. Classical generative phonology is deeply entrenched in the metaphor of grammar as a production system that gives rise to a conception of grammar in which modules as well as principles are sequential. In this conception, a principle is typically stated as a rule, that is, a procedure that takes an input and yields an output. The same input-output relation holds for levels of representation as well: a module with its set of principles takes a level of representation as the input, and yields another level of representation as the output. Between two levels of representation defined by the grammar are intermediate stages in the derivation which have no theoretical status in the overall model.

This sequential conception in phonology is currently being challenged by a growing body of work that views grammatical principles not as procedures, but as well-formedness statements analogous to the laws of physics. Unlike an instruction in a computer program, the laws of gravity and magnetism do not take an input and yield an output. They are simply statements of certain relations holding on a set of constructs. Kisseberth (1970) and Sommerstein (1974) are often cited as being influential in triggering the use of various types of well-formedness statements to build a nonsequential conception of phonology in works such as Singh (1984), Karttunnen (1989), Lakoff (1989), Goldsmith (1989), K. P. Mohanan (1989, 1992), Bird (1990), Coleman (1991), Scobie (1991), Smolenksy and Prince (1993), and Goldsmith, ed. (1993b). The elimination of input-output relations between levels of representation also results in the elimination of intermediate stages in a derivation that connects two levels. In such a conception, levels of representation are simultaneously present in a multidimensional space, as in Halle and Vergnaud's (1980) ringbound notebook metaphor. As a consequence, a principle of the grammar can state a relation holding between two entities internal to a given level of representation, or between two levels of representation. The sequentiality of *SPE* and lexical phonology has no place in this emerging declarative conception of grammatical principles, modules of the grammar, and levels of representation.[2]

In this article, I will explore the basic issues and hypotheses alluded to above, provide a critical evaluation, and attempt to outline what I consider to be the unresolved problems. The questions that I will address are:

- What is the relation between phonology and morphology?
- How is morphological information made available to phonology?
- How do controversies on rule/constraint types, levels of representation, and sequentiality affect our view of the phonology-morphology interaction?

I must warn the reader that it is not my purpose here to introduce the reader to current theories of phonology or to defend any of them. My purpose is rather to identify and explore a set of issues on the organization of grammar which have come to revolve around various debates on classical phonemics and morphophonemics, classical generative phonology, lexical phonology, and subsequent work. In doing so, my primary focus will be the concepts that are often obscured by debates on formalisms. The reader who is looking for a summary of or introduction to the latest formalisms in phonology may, I am afraid, be disappointed.[3]

1 Preliminaries

1.1 *Three Pointers from* SPE

The three themes that will connect the pieces in this article are:

1 Dependence on morphology and syntax: There is a correlation between the structures motivated by syntax and morphology on the one hand, and by phonology on the other.
2 Nonconvergence: There is a mismatch between the structures motivated by morphology and syntax, and the structures needed for phonology.
3 Construction types: Phonology requires additional information about different kinds of morphological "construction types" such as affixation and compounding, different kinds of affixation, and so on.

As with most issues in current phonology, insights on these three issues can be found in *SPE*. Therefore, it is useful to see how *SPE* dealt with them.

The place that *SPE* assigns to phonology within the overall organization of grammar is given in (1):

(1)

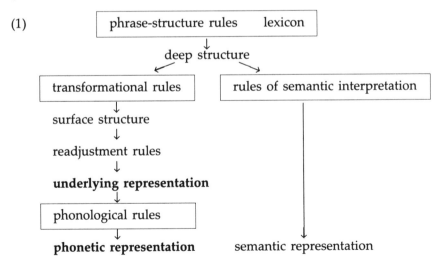

That surface structures are an (indirect) input to the phonological component shows that *SPE* recognized the correlation between morphosyntactic patterns and phonological patterns. That these surface structures are modified by readjustment rules shows that *SPE* recognized the mismatch between morphosyntax and phonology. That these readjustment rules introduced juncture symbols like + and # shows that *SPE* recognized the need to refer to information about construction types not provided by the morphosyntax.

To illustrate, the surface structure representation of the English phrase *John's sister's husband's stupidities* is something like (2a). The readjustment rules convert (2a) into the underlying representation in (2b):

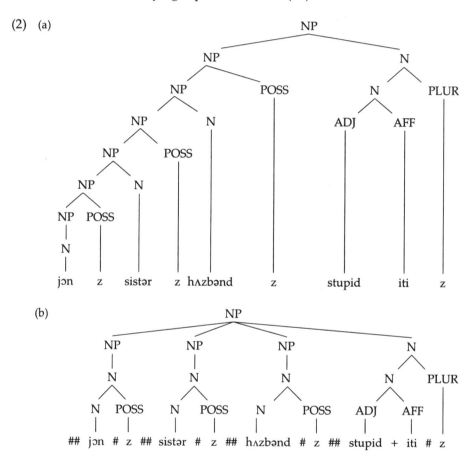

(2) (a)

(b)

As can be seen from the underlying representation in (2b), *SPE* assumes a close interaction between phonological and nonphonological systems. First, it allows phonological rules to access information about (readjusted) syntactic constituency, grammatical categories, and grammatical features. However, the tree structures that encode this information are not identical in (2a) and (2b). The readjustment rules applying to (2a) flatten the tree structure to the one required for correct stress placement.[4]

In addition to the readjustment of constituency relations, readjustment rules also introduce juncture symbols such as +, #, and ##, which encode information about the morphological construction types crucially needed for both segmental and suprasegmental phonology. For example, the difference between class 1 derivation (e.g., *-ity*) on the one hand, and class 2 derivation (*-ing*) and inflection (*-es*) on the other, is represented in terms of boundary symbols like + and # (e.g., stupid+iti#z). Unlike the information about constituency and grammatical categories, the information about construction types is expressed in terms of diacritic symbols which do not have any universal crosslinguistic substance.[5]

Thus, the use of readjustment rules in *SPE* indicates the recognition that the structure that is relevant for the application of phonological principles is governed by, but not identical to, that of pure morphosyntactic representation. This recognition was explictly voiced in *SPE*:

> we have two concepts of surface structure: input to the phonological component, and output of the syntactic component. It is an empirical question whether these two concepts coincide. In fact, *they do coincide to a very significant degree, but there are also certain discrepancies.* These discrepancies . . . indicate that the grammar must contain certain rules converting the surface structures generated by the syntactic component into a form appropriate for use by the phonological component. In particular, if a linguistic expression reaches a certain level of complexity, it will be divided into successive parts that we will call "phonological phrases," each of which is a maximal domain for phonological processes. [Italics mine: KPM] (P. 9)

We will pursue the three themes of phonology-morphology interaction pointed out by *SPE* in the rest of this article.

1.2 Strategies for Accessing Wordhood

Accessing morphological information involves distinguishing between words and units larger than words, and identifying information internal to words. Let us begin by exploring different ways of accessing the notion WORD. This construct is relevant for phonology for at least three well-known reasons: some phonological patterns crucially hold only *within words*, some hold only at the *edge* (beginning or end) of a word, and some are governed by information about *word-internal structure* for their application. An example of the first type is homorganic nasal assimilation in Malayalam, which is obligatory within a word, and optional across words (K. P. Mohanan 1993). An example of the second type is the flapping of *t* followed by a lateral in American English: in this environment, flapping takes place if *t* is word final (e.g., *The ca[D] licked the butter*) but not if it is word internal (e.g., **ha[D]less, *bu[D]ler*). An example of the third type is the gemination of obstruents in Malayalam, which applies at the junction between two stems in a subcompound where the second stem is Dravidian (K. P. Mohanan 1986).

Strategies for capturing the notion word can be divided into two broad classes, one in terms of representational labels within a single level of representation, and the other in terms of different levels of representation. The structure of the phrase *beautiful painters* in terms of representational labels is:

(3)

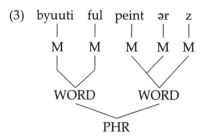

The labels PHR, WORD, and M stand for phrase, word, and morpheme respectively. Given such a representation, a principle that holds within a word but not across words can be specified as having WORD as its domain. In addition to the use of the symbol ## to indicate external word boundary, *SPE* makes use of this strategy to specify the domain of phonological rules in terms of syntactic constituency relations and lexical category labels such as N, ADJ, and V, as opposed to phrasal category labels like NP and VP. This approach is also found in prosodic phonology, where representational labels like P-WORD and P-PHRASE correspond to wordhood and phrasehood relevant for the purposes of phonology.

The structure of the same phrase in terms of different levels of representation is:

(4)

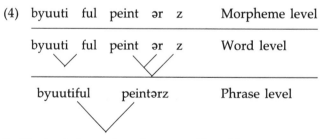

In (4), the information about wordhood is present not as labels on nodes, but as a unit along a distinct level of representation. Given such a representation, a principle that holds within words but not across words can be specified as holding at the word level.

Imposing sequentiality to the three levels of representation in (4) yields the fundamental premises of lexical phonology:

(5)   (a)   The grammar consists of two modules, the lexical and the post-lexical.
      (b)   The lexical module precedes the post-lexical module.

(c) The domain of phonological principles can be specified as the lexical module, or the post-lexical module, or both.

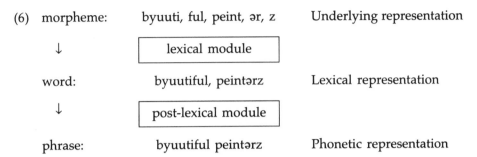

(6) morpheme: byuuti, ful, peint, ər, z Underlying representation

    ↓   lexical module

word: byuutiful, peintərz Lexical representation

    ↓   post-lexical module

phrase: byuutiful peintərz Phonetic representation

The input-output metaphor in (6) has dominated generative grammar since its inception. If we abandon this input-output metaphor of procudure, and interpret (4) as parallel or simultaneous levels of representation, we have the conception of the organization of grammar in cognitive phonology (Lakoff 1993) and harmonic phonology (Goldsmith 1989, 1993a).

As pointed out in the introductory section, a large number of proposals in the recent literature have suggested that we abandon the sequentiality of rule application in phonological theory in favor of general laws for linguistic representations analagous to the laws of gravitation or subatomic phenemona. In a conception of linguistic organization that rejects sequentiality of rule application, the idea of sequentiality of levels of representation is an anomaly, if not a logical contradiction. This would require abandoning assumption (5b) above, while retaining (5a) and (5c), the "precede" of (5b) being replaced by the part-whole relation between words and phrases. We will come back to this issue at a later point.

In sum, there is reasonable consensus that principles of phonological organization must be able to access information about wordhood. This information can be made available to phonology either in terms of node lables on a tree structure, or in terms of different levels/dimensions of representation that factor out different aspects of structure. The second choice leads to the further choice of assuming either that these levels of representation are sequentially ordered in terms of the input-output relation, or that they are simultaneously present as parallel levels.

2 The Internal Structure of Words

There are few phonologists who would dispute the claim that principles of phonological organization need access to the notion WORD. Even classical phonemicists who believed in the strict autonomy of phonology allowed statements about the distribution of allophones to refer to notions like word final and word initial. However, word-internal structure is a different matter. Are principles of phonology allowed to refer to morphological structure? The last few decades have seen a number of debates on this question, where phonologists have tended to be divided into two camps.

2.1   Morphophonology

The question of the sensitivity of phonology to word-internal structure comes up in the description of both distribution and alternation. But it is most clearly manifested in the treatment of alternation. Let us begin with prototypical patterns of alternation in English which are acknowledged to belong to phonology proper in all approaches to phonology, as they make no reference to morphological information:

(7)   (a)   rapid ['ræpid]   rapidity [rə'pʰiditi]
       (b)   Pat is a wise man.   Pat is wise.
                      [wai.z]   [wai.z̦]

In (7a), there is an alternation between aspirated and unaspirated stops; in (7b), there is an alternation between fully voiced and devoiced obstruents. The statement of these patterns does not require any reference to morphological structure:

(8)   (a)   Voiceless stops are aspirated at the beginning of a stressed syllable.[6]
       (b)   Obstruents are devoiced when adjacent to a pause.[7]

The crucial constructs required in (8), namely, distinctive features, stress, syllable, and pause, are part of phonological information. In contrast, the *t/s* alternation in (9a) and the *s/z* alternation in (9b) crucially require reference to morphological information:

(9)   (a)   resident   residency
                  [rezident]   [rezidensi]
       (b)   house (n)   house (v)
                  [haus]   [hauz]

If we intend to capture these alternations in phonology, we need to make statements that are equivalent to (10a) and (10b), crucially appealing to morphological constructs such as stem and affix:

(10)   (a)   Underlying stem-final **t** is **s** before **i** in class 1 affixation in [+Latinate] forms.

(b) Underlying stem-final s of the verb is z in a noun in a special class of morphemes.

The patterns in (8a, b) are purely phonological, while those in (10a, b) are morphophonological.[8] At the center of debates on phonological theory has been the treatment of morphophonological patterns. Bloomfieldian phonemics separates phonology and morphophonology, while *SPE* makes no distinction between the two. A large number of phonological theories since *SPE*, such as natural phonology, natural generative phonology, upside-down phonology, lexical phonology, generative phonotactics, and so on have been attempts to express the distinction between phonological and morphophonological phenomena.

Before we proceed, it is important to separate the distinction between phonological and morphophonological patterns from the distinction between allophonic and phonemic patterns. Consider the following examples of voiced/voiceless alternation in English:

(11) (a)   (b)   (c)

      twelve   twelfth   dogs   cats   Bill's away.   Pat's away.

      [twelv]   [twelfθ]   [dögz]   [kæts]   [bilz]   [pæts]

While the alternations in (7a) and (7b) are clearly allophonic in the sense that the alternating units are not contrastive in the language, the alternation in (11) is clearly phonemic, because in English, *f* and *s* contrast with *v* and *z* respectively. Until recently, both within classical phonemics and generative phonology, these alternations were considered morphophonemic (e.g., Anderson 1974; K. P. Mohanan 1982). As more recent studies have shown, however, the best way of stating the pattern in (11) is in terms of syllable structure, rather than morphological structure:

(12) Syllable-internally, adjacent obstruents agree in voice.[9]

If we accept (12), the phenomenon in (11) is an example of phonemic alternation that is not sensitive to morphology. Other examples of this type include optional external sandhi phenomena such as the *s/š* alternation in *horse* [hɔrs]/*horseshoe* [hɔrššuu]. This shows that the distinction between purely phonological and morphophonological does not coincide with the distinction between allophonic and phonemic:

(13)

	Phonological	Morphophonological
Phonemic	(11)	(9)
Allophonic	(7)	?

2.2   The Classification of Principles

As is well known, phonology in classical phonemics meant purely phonological allophonic patterns. Morphophonemic patterns belonged to a separate
component of the grammar, sandwiched between phonology and morphology. The status of purely phonological phonemic patterns was somewhat
uncertain. *SPE* eliminated this distinction, allowing phonological principles to
freely access morphological information:

(14)   (a)   Classical phonemics   (b)   *SPE*

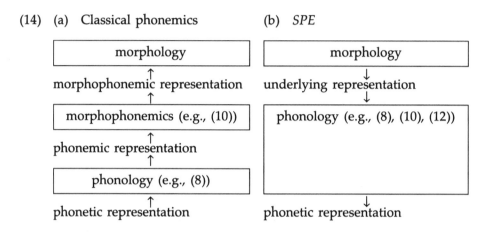

2.3   Sequential Modularity

Phonologists have always had a strong intuition that patterns such as in (9)
are significantly different from patterns such as in (7). This involves the
distiction between morphophonemic and phonemic. They have also recognized that the phonemic representation of classical phonemics tried to express
a level of representation that reflected a language user's conscious access to
certain structural elements of speech, including the number of "sounds," and
their sameness and distinctness. This involves the distinction between phonemic and allophonic.

   These two issues have often been conflated in discussions, including those
within lexical phonology. Since *SPE* had erased the lines that demarcated
these distinctions, the intuitions led to a series of proposals that were counter
to *SPE*. The questions that these proposals have tried to come to grips with
are: Where does morphophonology belong? How do we express the "contrast"
that reflects the language user's consciousness? Most of the proposals tried
to answer these questions by designing different classificatory systems for
phonological rules (for instance, rules versus processes, automatic versus
nonautomatic alternations). In the early eighties, lexical phonology proposed

a different solution by separating the statement of the principles from the domains in which the principles hold, and deriving the differences in the effects of phonological principles from differences in domains:

(15)   Lexical phonology

underlying representation

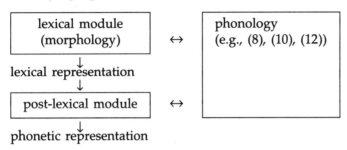

The conception of the organization of phonology in (15) makes it possible for a phonological principle to have both morphophonemic and purely phono-logical effects. A telling example is that of the place assimilation of nasals in Malayalam which has been argued to hold in both the lexical (mor-phophonemic) and post-lexical (purely phonological) modules. Malayalam has an inventory of seven nasals which are contrastive on the surface: bilabial, dental, alveolar, alveopalatal, retroflex, palatal, and velar. Mohanan and Mohanan (1984) demonstrate that the otherwise idiosyncratic distributional restrictions on these nasals can be accounted for by assuming an underlying inventory of three nasals, namely, bilabial, alveolar, and retroflex. The rules that yield the right results within this account are independently motivated:

(16)   (a)   A nasal assimilates in place to the following plosive.
       (b)   A voiced plosive becomes nasal when preceded by a nasal, option-
             ally in [–Dravidian] and obligatorily in [+Dravidian] words.

(16a) is a purely phonological rule in that it does not require morphological information. Furthermore, it applies across words: /madʰuɾam/ "sweet" and /taɾu/ "give (imp.)" → [madʰuɾantaɾu] "give (me) sweets!". (16b) is morpho-phonemic as it requires information about morphological subclassification ([±Dravidian]). Furthermore, it does not apply across words or across the stems of a compound. For (16a) and (16b) to correctly predict the distribu-tional restrictions in a procedural account, it is necessary to assume that (16a) feeds (16b), assimilating the place of the nasal to the following plosive, and then assimilating the manner of the plosive to the preceding nasal (e.g., /paɳɖi/ → paɳɖi → [paɳɳi] "pig"). In a declarative account, this would amount to saying that (16a) and (16b) hold simultaneously on the mapping between morphophonemic and phonemic representations. Either way, the main point is that (16a) should be recognized as holding between the underlying and phonemic levels as well as between phonemic and phonetic levels. This option is available to (15), but not to (14a). Nor is it available to other theories such as natural phonology and natural generative phonology, which draw a dividing line between two kinds of phonological principles rather than between two domains in which the principles take effect. Thus, it is important to realize that, as Anderson (1981) points out, a phonological principle that does not refer to morphological information in its formulation may nevertheless interact with morphophonemic principles in such a way that it creates the effect of a morphophonemic pattern.

Close cooperation between morphophonemic and purely phonological principles is also found in the phenomenon of voicing assimilation illustrated in (11). The general principle proposed for these alternations was that syllable-internally, obstruents agree in voice (12). When we put together the underlying representation of the stems /twelv/ and /kæt/ with the underlying representations of the affixes, namely, /θ/ and /z/, the result *twelvθ* and *kætz* violates (12). The ill-formedness can be repaired by changing these forms to either *twelvð* and *kædz*, or to *twelfθ* and *kæts*. Why does English choose the latter option, and not the former?

One way of avoiding this question is to revise (12) as (12′), stipulating that the winner in the conflict is [–voice].

(12′)   Syllable internally, an obstruent is [–voice] when adjacent to a [–voice].

This was the solution explored in K. P. Mohanan (1991). This formulation, though descriptively adequate, is less desirable on explanatory grounds. Observe that (12) is a universal principle that holds in (almost) all languages. In contrast, (12′) is formulated in such a way that what is common to voicing assimilation in English, and say, in Hebrew, is not reflected in the formulation. In English, [–voice] spreads to [+voice] both left to right and right to left; in Hebrew both [+voice] and [–voice] spread, but only from right-to-left. The way they are formulated, (12) holds for both English and Hebrew, but (12′) holds only for English.

The explanation, I suggest, lies in an independent principle:

(17)   Adjacent obstruents within a syllable are voiceless.
       (Absolute morpheme-internally, weak across morphemes).

Principle (17) allows monomorphemic syllables like [ækt], [lift] and [risk], but disallows syllables like *[zbin], *[rizg] and *[lizb], which cannot be bimorphemic. It allows syllables like [bægd] and [livd], but only when the cluster is formed by the addition of an independent morpheme. These facts can be interpreted as follows. Constraint (17) holds stongly within morphemes and weakly across morphemes. (17) is not strong enough to repair concatenations like *bæg+d* and *liv+d* and make the clusters voiceless. However, it exerts a force in the choice between [+voice] and [–voice] in *twelvθ* and *kætz*, yielding *fθ* and *ts*, rather than *vð* and *dz*.[10] (12) requires that the coda be changed. Given that *vθ* and *tz* are deemed to be undesirable by (17), the coda is repaired to *fθ* and *ts*.

If this line of explanation is accepted, then we must accept that (17) holds strongly in the morphophonemic domain (within morphemes, in the lexical module) and weakly elsewhere. The actual voicing assimilation in (11), which is a purely phonological alternation, is a combined result of (12) and (17). Hence the separation in (14a) is not a viable alternative.

2.4 Nonsequential Modularity

Lexical phonology incorporates the traditional sequential (i.e., derivational) conception of the organization of grammar in two senses. Firstly, the modules of the grammar and the consequent levels of representation are viewed in terms of the input-output relation, where each module or level of representation is seen as preceding or following another. Second, the output of one principle constitutes the input to another. The logical connection between two levels of representation is stated as a number of ordered steps in a derivation. The order in such a derivation is crucial, unlike in a logical or mathematical derivation where the order of application is irrelevant. As stated earlier, a large number of phonologists have started abandoning the sequential conception of linguistic derivation, and it stands to reason that these phonologists also reject the sequential conception of modularity and hence that of levels of representation. If we abandon the sequentiality in underlying, lexical, and phonetic representations, and hold that these three types of information are represented along parallel dimensions of structure, we have the organization of grammar in cognitive phonology and harmonic phonology:

(18) Harmonic/Cognitive phonology
            M-level   (corresponds to underlying level)
            W-level   (corresponds to lexical level)
            P-level   (corresponds to phonetic level)

From the discussion of the underlying, word, and phrase levels in Goldsmith (1990, p. 231), I conclude that harmonic phonology draws the line between two domains of phonology as in (15), rather than between two kinds of principles as in (13a). Factoring away the procedural implication in (15), what is common to (15) and (18) is the idea of three levels of representation, in contrast to (14b).

3   Morphology versus Morphologically Sensitive Phonology

3.1   *Are all Nonautomatic Sound Patterns Part of Morphology?*

In a series of articles, Singh (1984, in press) and Ford and Singh (1983, 1985) have put forward a view of the organization of phonology that departs from *SPE* in a more extreme form than lexical phonology, or even classical phonemics. According to this view, called generative phonotactics, alternations such as in (9a, b) should be handled not as part of phonology, but as part of the word formation rules in morphology. The formal statements that account for (9a) and (9b) are given as (19a) and (19b) respectively:[11]

(19)   (a)   Word formation rule A
$$[Xt]_{CONCR} \leftrightarrow [Xsi]_{ABSTR}$$
    (b)   Word formation rule B
$$[Xs]_{NOUN} \leftrightarrow [Xz]_{VERB}$$

This position denies a theoretical status to the construct morpheme, either in phonology or in morphology. Thus, affixation is the morphological operation of attaching a phonological string to a word to form a new word, not that of the attachement of an affix. As part of the morphological operation, the stem may undergo phonological changes as well.

Given the availability of the formal device in (19), generative phonotactics makes the extreme claim that no phonological principles can refer to morphological structure.[12] In this view, all phonological patterns that are sensitive to morphological information are part of morphology, rather than pure phonology or morphophonology.

(20)   Generative phonotactics

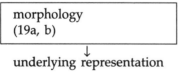

In other words, there is no morphophonology in this view. If this claim is correct, then the question of phonological rules accessing information about morphological structure is a misguided one. Therefore it is necessary to respond to this claim before we proceed further.

It so happens that if we are willing to tolerate a certain degree of duplication, the formal device of correspondence statements illustrated in (20) can be extended to cover most examples of segmental alternation triggered by affixation, particularly those which have been at the heart of *SPE* phonology such as trisyllabic shortening, velar softening, and spirantization. There exist, however, many phonological patterns which cannot be dealt with in terms of correspondence relations between words. We have already seen one of them, namely, (17), which makes crucial reference to the construct morpheme. As pointed out earlier, the contrast between well-formed coinages like [nisp] and [nisk] and ill-formed coinages like *[nizb] and *[nizg] require the assumption that (17) holds strongly within a morpheme. Consider the additional principles (21a–c) that govern syllable structure in English, and (21d), a morpheme-internal regularity in Malayalam:

(21) (a) Morpheme-internally in English, a coda can have at most three consonants.

   (b) In English, a consonantal segment can be syllabic only at the end of a morpheme / stem.

   (c) Morpheme-internally in English, dental fricatives cannot occur after an obstruent in a coda.

   (d) In Malayalam, a single dental nasal followed by a vowel can only occur morpheme-initially; in this environment, an alveolar nasal cannot occur.

Principle (21a) allows the four-consonant coda in bimorphemic words like *texts*, but does not allow a monomorphemic [beksts] (e.g., *Four bextses* [bekstsiz]). (21b) allows a syllabic lateral in bimorphemic *fickleness* [fiklnəs], but disallows it in *[klnep]. (21c) allows syllables like *fifth* [fifθ] and *depth* [depθ] only if they are bimorphemic. All these principles are nonautomatic in that they crucially refer to the morphological construct morpheme. Principle (21d) allows morpheme-initial [n̪] in [n̪ayanam] "eye" and [sun̪ayani] "person with beautiful eyes", but disallows forms like *[nayala] and monomorphemic *[pun̪ala]. None of the facts accounted for by these principles can be accounted for in terms of correspondence conditions (19). Hence the extreme claim that phonological principles are not sensitive to word-internal structure is untenable.[13]

Turning to patterns of alternation, we note that unlike the typical segmental morphophonemic alternations, many facts of word stress in English are not expressible in terms of the formalism in (19). Take, for example, the effect of suffixes like *-al*, *-ous*, and *-ant*. The productive generalization is that in words with these suffixes, stress falls on the penultimate syllable if it is heavy, and, if not, on the antepenultimate syllable.[14] Thus, stress shifts from the first syllable in *'parent* to the penultimate syllable in *pa'rental* because the penult is heavy, but from the first syllable in *'medicine* to the antepenultimate syllable in *me'dicinal* because the penult is light. The reader will find a massive number of additional examples of this kind in *SPE*.

Now, as is well known, only class 1 suffixes in English (*-ous, -ant, -al, -ity, -ive, -ion, -ic*, etc.) are capable of shifting the primary stress of the stem to some other syllable; class 2 suffixes (*-ness, -less, -hood, -dom, -ful*, etc.) do not change stress. Thus, the addition of the class 2 affix *-less* to *parent* and *medicine* has no effect on stress: *'parentless, 'medicineless*. Clearly, stress placement in English is sensitive to the morphological distinction between class 1 and class 2 affixes. It is also sensitive to the phonological distinction between light and heavy syllables. I see no way of combining the two into a morphological principle in terms of the formalism illustrated in (19).

Similar conclusions are to be drawn from patterns of alternation which do not involve affixation. Take, for example, the exceptionless patterns of stress and word melody assignment in subcompounds and co-compounds in Malayalam. Subcompounds have a single primary stress and word melody per compound, while co-compounds have a primary stress and word melody for each stem in the compound (K. P. Mohanan 1986). I see no way of expressing this generalization as a purely morphological rule, rather than as a phonological rule sensitive to morphology. We conclude, therefore, that the conventional wisdom of allowing phonological rules to access word-internal structure must indeed be retained.

3.2   *Are all Sound Patterns Part of Phonology?*

A word of caution is appropriate at this point. That there exist morphologically sensitive phonological principles does not entail that all relations between morphology and phonology should be stated as morphologically senstive phonological rules. This point is particularly important in the context of the debate between affixal morphology and nonaffixal morphology.

As far as I can see, the central hypothesis that separates the two approaches to morphology is the following:

(22)   The only permissible morphological operation is that of combining affixes and stems.

Affixal morphology (Lieber 1980; Marantz 1982; Kiparsky 1983; and so on) subscribes to (22). Thus, alternations such as ablaut, spirantization, or deletion cannot be morphological operations, and hence must necessarily be treated as part of morphologically senstive phonology. In contrast, nonaffixal morphology (Matthews 1974; Anderson 1992; Zwicky 1988) rejects (22).

The interpretation of the claim in (22) depends upon the interpretation of the term "affix." I would like to suggest that a great deal of unnecessary controversy can be eliminated if we (1) separate three levels of description, namely, features, morphemes, and formatives, and (2) define affix as a type of formative (T. Mohanan, 1993). The three-level terminology is as follows:

Features: entities like [PAST], [PERFECTIVE], [PASSIVE] and [PLU-RAL] which are part of a universal inventory
Morphemes: abstract language-particular morphological units; e.g., the English morphemes {SIT}, {GO}, {TABLE}, {ED}, and {EN}
Formatives: phonological strings which act as morphological units; e.g., the English formatives /sit/, /gou/, /d/, /n/, and /z/

The three levels of abstraction are illustrated by the following examples:

(23)

	(a) *kissed*	(b) *wrote*	(c) *kissed*	(d) *written*	(e) *written*	(f) *went*
Feature	KISS PAST	WRITE PAST	KISS PASS	WRITE PASS	WRITE PERF	GO PAST
Morpheme	KISS ED	WRITE ED	KISS EN	WRITE EN	WRITE EN	GO ED
Formative	kis d	rout	kis d	writ n	writ n	went

Why do we need to separate the three concepts? The morphological information relevant for syntax and semantics is encoded in features. The additional morphological information relevant for phonology is encoded in formatives. Within the three-level view illustrated in (23), morphemes mediate between features and formatives, providing the anchor for allomorphy. For example, the syntactico-semantic features [PERFECTIVE] and [PASSIVE] have the same morphemic realization in English. Thus, the allomorphic realization of the perfective form of the verb in *John has written/burnt/mailed the letter* is identical to the allomorphic realization of the passive form of the verb in *The letter was written/burnt/mailed by John*. In order to express this unity of allomorphy, it is useful to represent these forms as {WRITE, EN}, {BURN, EN} and {MAIL, EN}. These representations will be distinct from the past tense forms *wrote*, *burnt*, and *mailed* which will be represented as {WRITE, ED}, {BURN, ED}, and {MAIL, ED}. The mediation is schematized in (24):

(24)   Feature   Morpheme   Allomorphy

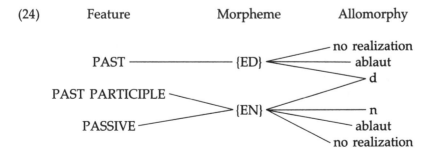

The compositionality of words in terms of their feature composition is accepted within both affixal and nonaffixal approaches. I also assume that, within nonaffixal morphology, it would be legitimate to make statements such as: "The perfective forms *sung* and *mailed* consist of {SING, EN} and {MAIL, EN} respectively; {SING, EN} is realized as /sʌng/, while {MAIL, EN} is realized as /meil/+/d/." Hence the debate between the affixal and nonaffixal approaches is not located at what I have called the level of morphemes.

I also assume that, within nonaffixal morphology, statements such as the following would not be legitimate: "{SING, EN} is realized as /sʌng/+/ø/, while {MAIL, EN} is realized as /meil/+/d/." We must conclude, therefore, the debate is located at the level of formatives. If so, the interpretation of (22) is: "the only permissible morphological operation is that of combining formatives." Under this interpretation, (22) forces the use of zero formatives in (25A). A theory that rejects (22) is free to have the representations in (25B):

(25)		A		B	
	spoke	*cut*	*spoke*	*cut*	
Feature	speak past	cut past	speak past	cut past	
Morpheme	speak ed	cut ed	speak ed	cut ed	
Formative	spiik ø	kʌt ø	spouk	kʌt	

(25A), which incorporates (22), makes the claim that past tense forms like *spoke* and *cut* have two formatives each. In contrast, (25B), which rejects (22), views these forms as noncompositional at the level of formatives, though they are compositional at the level of morphemes and features.

If we accept (25A), the vowel alternation in *speak/spoke* will be formulated as a phonological principle sensitive to morphology (26a). If we accept (25B), it will be formulated as an allomorphic rule that states a relation between morphemes and formatives (26b):

(26) (a) *ii* is changed to *ou* in a verb formative when followed by a zero formative that marks {ED}.

   (b) *ii* is changed to *ou* as a marker of {ED}.

In the preceding section, I showed that phonological theory must allow principles of phonological organization to access morphological information. However, that some of the morphologically conditioned patterns of phonological distribution and alternation must be stated as principles of phonological organization does not entail that all morphologically conditioned patterns of speech must be viewed as phonological. It is true that (21a–d) must be viewed as principles of phonological organization, but nothing that I have said in support of the conception common to (15) and (18) forces a choice between

(26a) and (26b). Within the theory of lexical phonology, for example, Kiparsky (1982) chooses the strategy illustrated in (26a), assuming affixal morphology, while K. P. Mohanan (1982) chooses (26b), rejecting affixal morphology.

In sum, I take it that there is persuasive evidence to show that a subset of phonological patterns of distribution and alternation are conditioned by the morphological structure of words. I also take it that we must separate morphophonology from the rest of phonology. The two options available for this purpose are to distinguish between (1) two types of principles, or (2) two domains for the application of principles. Lexical phonology makes the latter choice, as do most current theories of phonology (e.g., lexical prosodic phonology, nonlexical prosodic phonology). Whether or not all alternations of pronunciation should be dealt with in phonology, or whether we should allow morphology to take care of those alternations which are governed solely by morphological information, is an issue that is not settled yet.

4   Construction Types

In the late seventies and early eighties, a number of studies argued that the use of boundary symbols is both too rich and too impoverished as a formal device for the representation of phonologically relevant morphological construction types (Rotenberg 1978; Pesetsky 1979; Selkirk 1980a; Strauss 1982; K. P. Mohanan 1982). As an alternative to the use of boundary symbols, the critics proposed two broad strategies. One was to encode the construction type in terms of labeled trees, as illustrated in (3). This was essentially the move made in Rotenberg (1978), Selkirk (1980), Strauss (1982), Aronoff and Sridhar (1983), and Sproat (1985). The other was to encode the information in terms of sequential modularity, following the path of (6) and (15). This was the move in Siegel (1974), Pesetsky (1979), Kiparsky (1982), K. P. Mohanan (1982), and Pulleyblank (1986a). Various combinations of the two approaches are found in Rubach (1984), Halle and Vergnaud (1987), and Inkelas (1989).

Let me illustrate these two approaches with the treatment of gemination in Malayalam compounds. In addition to the familiar type of compound in which one of the two stems is a head and the other is a modifier (subcompounds), Malayalam also has a compound construction in which a number of stems can be strung together, each of which is a head (co-compound). These two constructions are illustrated in (27b) and (27d) respectively.

(27) (a) (i) kaaṭə "forest" (ii) maṟam "tree"
       (b)   kaaṭṭəmaṟam "forest tree"   (subcompound)
       (c) (i) aaṭə "goat" (ii) maaṭə "cow"
       (d)   aaṭəmaaṭəkaḷə "goats and cows"   (co-compound)

The stem-final /ṭ/ in (27b) undergoes gemination, but does not in (27d).[15] The generalization illustrated here is that stem-final gemination holds in subcompounds, but not in co-compounds. Now, the phrase structure for (27b) and (27d) look the same:

(28)   (a)   (b)

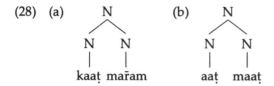

kaaṭ maṟam   aaṭ maaṭ

In order to account for the phonological distinction between the two types of compounds, therefore, one needs some other device. The strategy employed in lexical phonology is to assign the two types of compounding to two different lexical submodules, and define the domain of stem-final gemination in terms of these submodules:

(29)   (a)   The lexical module contains submodules α and β.
       (b)   (i)   Two nouns A and B can be put together to make a compound noun in which the head is the second one.

                     Domain: lexical submodule α.

             (ii)   Two or more nouns A, B, . . . can be put together to make a compound which means A and B and . . .

                     Domain: lexical submodule β.

       (c)   At the end of a form, before another, an obstruent is geminated.

                     Domain: submodule α.

Within the derivational conception of lexical phonology, the statements in (29a–c) yield the following results:

(30)   Underlying: kaaṭ   maṟam   aaṭ   maaṭ

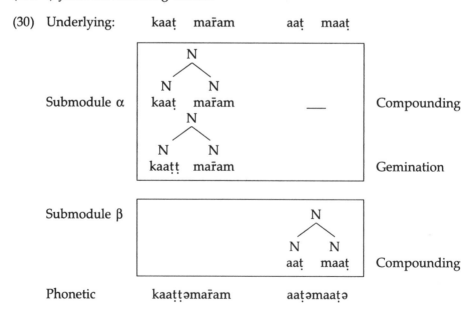

Phonetic   kaattəmaṟam   aatəmaatə

The conception underlying the derivation in (30) is that of building larger units from smaller units, allowing rules/constraints to take effect in the course of the building. Readers who are familiar with various theories in syntax will see that this is essentially the same as the conception in Montague grammar, and the device of generalized transformations in minimalist theory (Chomsky 1992). In addition, this part-whole relation is also viewed as involving a sequential ordering of modules.

The statements in (29) can be implemented in a representational approach, instead of a sequential approach, by making distinctions in representations in terms of appropriately labeled nodes and defining the domains of phonological principles in terms of these nodes. Suppose we use the representation in (31) instead of (28):

(31) (a)   (b)

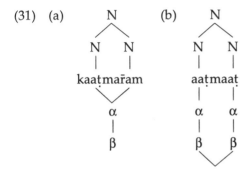

The statement of gemination can now be as given in (32):

(32) (a) There are two lexical constructions α and β.
      (b) (i)   Two nouns A and B can be put together to make an α.
                 Semantic interpretation: the second constitutent is the head.
           (ii) Two or more nouns A, B, ... can be put together to make a β.
                 Semantic interpretation: A and B and ...
      (c) At the end of a form, before another, an obstruent is geminated.
           Domain: α.

The strategy in (32) is used in Selkirk (1980), Aronoff and Sridhar (1983), Rubach (1984), Sproat (1985), and Inkelas (1989). Sproat, for example, refers to the α in (32) as phonological stem (P-STEM) and the β as phonological word (P-WORD). Inkelas employs the labels α and β as diacritics.

It must be observed that there are two fundamental differences between the approaches in Sproat's prosodic nonlexical phonology and Inkelas's prosodic lexical phonology. In the former, a phonological rule can have access to the information in either the syntactic tree on top or the prosodic tree at the bottom in (31). As far as phonology is concerned, in other words, the two sets of structures are "co-present." In the latter approach, only the prosodic tree is visible for phonological rules, not the syntactic tree. This restriction is an extension of the indirect mapping hypothesis in post-lexical prosodic phonology (Selkirk 1984; Nespor and Vogel 1986). At the conceptual level, this is like *SPE*, where phonological rules can access only the readjusted syntactic structure: (2b) is visible to phonology, not (2a).

Another difference between the two approaches is that while the former relies purely on syntactic and prosodic representations, the latter relies on prosodic representations and sequentiality. Thus, the analyses in prosodic lexical phonology crucially depend upon the successive building and erasing of prosodic trees in different lexical strata, with phonological rules applying cyclically between building and erasing.

5   Distributional Asymmetries of Construction Types

This section deals with a phenomenon in morphology rather than phonology. However, it has a place in our discussion because of its interaction with phonology. Both sequential modularity ((30)) and labeled trees ((31)) have been employed in dealing with a problem that one may call the *distrubutional asymmetry* of morphological constructions. Take, for example, the relative ordering of the causative and passive affixes in Japanese and Malayalam. Japanese allows both V-CAUSE-PASS and V-PASS-CAUSE, with corresponding differences in their syntactic behaviour. Malayalam allows only V-CAUSE-PASS, blocking a potential syntactic option.

The asymmetry in the relative ordering of the causative and passive in Malayalam applies to individual morphemes. What is of interest to us are the asymmetries in morphological construction types, rather than in individual morphemes. The most frequently cited example of such an asymmetry of construction types in morphology is that of class 1 and class 2 affixes in English. It is well known that the affixation of class 1 suffixes such as *-ity, -ion, -ic, -al, -ous, -ee, -aire, -ify , -ate,* and *-ion* can change the stress of the stem, while the affixation of class 2 suffixes such as *-ness, -less, -ful, -dom, -ed,* and *-ing* cannot do so. In terms of sequential modularity, this contrast can be expressed by assuming that stress assignment takes effect in the module in which class 1 affixes are attached. Now, it was pointed out by Siegel (1974) that while class 2 affixes can be attached to stems containing either class 1 affixes or class 2 affixes, and class 1 affixes can be attached to stems containing class 2 affixes, class 1 affixes cannot be attached to stems containing class 2 affixes. For example, the class 1 suffix *-ity* and the class 2 suffix *-ness,* can be productively attached to adjectives to derive nouns. However, only the latter can be attached to an adjective containing a class 2 affix, not the former: *paylessness* but **paylessity.* Siegel's Level Ordering Hypothesis accounts for this distributional asymmetry in morphology, and its correlation with the facts of stress, by proposing the following organization in terms of sequential modularity:

(33) (a) Class 1 affixes are attached at module α.
     (b) Class 2 affixes are attached at module β.
     (c) Module 2 precedes module β.
     (d) Domain for stress assignment: module α.

What is crucial for the account of the asymmetry is the relative ordering of the two modules in (33c). If, instead of sequential modularity, we resort to representational modularity, we can capture the morphological asymmetry using (34c):

(34) (a) Class 1 affixes are attached to α, and they yield α.
     (b) Class 2 affixes are attached to β, and they yield β.
     (c) A β contains α, but an α may not contain β.
     (d) Domain for stress assignment: α.

In various analyses in lexical phonology, the α and β of (34) are referred to as level/stratum 1 and level/stratum 2 respectively. Selkirk refers to the α and β of (34) as root and stem respectively, while Sproat calls them stem and word.[16]

Abstracting away the difference between sequential and parallel modularity, what is common to (33) and (34) are the claims that

  1 there is a clustering of phonological patterns which motivate the distinction between two classes of affixes for the purposes of phonology;
  2 there is a clustering of morphological asymmetries which motivate the distinction between two classes of affixes for the purposes of morphology;
  3 there is a correspondence between the phonologically motivated classification and the morphologically motivated classification.

Now, the first claim is not without problems. There exist affixes like *-ist* which exhibit a fluctuating behavior with respect to phonological patterns (e.g., *columnist* can be either [kɔləmnist] or [kɔləmist]). Furthermore, the convergence of phonological patterns on the dividing line between class 1 and class 2 affixes is not perfect (e.g., not all class 1 suffixes that begin with /i/ trigger velar softening). Despite these problems, the claim about the need for two classes of affixes for phonological purposes appears to be generally accepted.[17]

In contrast, various studies have pointed out far more serious problems with the morphological asymmetry claim. One is that of "bracketing paradoxes," which give evidence for assuming that a class 1 suffix is attached to a stem that contains a class 2 prefix, as in *ungrammaticality* (Strauss 1982;

Kiparsky 1982c; Sproat 1985).[18] A second is the existence of morphological restrictions which need to be stated directly in terms of individual affixes. If there is a mechanism to state such restrictions, we do not need an additional mechanism of affix classification (Fabb 1988). A third problem is the existence of instances such as *governmental* where what must be regarded as a class 2 suffix is followed by a class 1 suffix (Goldsmith 1990).

One may take these three problems facing the morphological asymmetry claim as counterevidence that requires us to abandon the claim. Alternatively, one may treat them as serious problems of detail that require a solution, while retaining the asymmetry claim as capturing a pattern that is still broadly correct.

6   The Nonconvergence of Morphology and Phonology

The discussion in the previous section suggests that convergences in phonology, in morphology, and across phonology and morphology, are hardly perfect. In this section, I discuss some more significant instances of nonconvergence. These fall into two types. First, a distinction required by morphological asymmetry is not required by phonology. Second, a distinction required by phonology is not required by morphological asymmetry.

6.1   *Multiple Domains and the Loop*

6.1.1   *The Phenomena*

As an instance of the first problem of nonconvergence, consider the need to allow the same phonological rule to hold both within the morphophonemic module and the purely phonological module, corresponding to the lexical module and post-lexical module in lexical phonology. An example of this pattern is that of the place assimilation of nasals in Malayalam (16a) pointed out in section 2.3. (16a) needs to be part of the morphophonemic-phonemic mapping because its effect is relevant for the morphophonemic alternation between voiced plosives and nasals (16b), but it also holds across words. We may represent the situation diagrammatically as follows:

(35)   Nonconvergence type 1: Phonological Patterns with Multiple domains

morphology-syntax	phonology
construction A	construction A
construction B	construction B

The phenomenon analyzed in K. P. Mohanan (1982, 1986) in terms of the loop presents the converse situation. In order to clarify the nature of what we are dealing with, I would like to separate the phenomenon of the loop from the formal device of the loop. The phenomenon is best illustrated by the morphological and phonological facts of subcompounding and co-compounding in Malayalam. As we saw in section 4, subcompounds and co-compounds behave differently for the purposes of stem-final gemination, which applies at the junction between two stems of a subcompound, but not those of a co-compound (27). This distinction also holds for stem-initial gemination:

(36) (a) (i) meeša "table" (ii) petti "box" (iii) -kal "plural suffix"
    (b) meešappettikalə "table-boxes" (= boxes made out of tables)
                                                          (subcompound)
    (c) meešapettikalə "tables and boxes" (co-compound)

Yet another phonological difference between the two constructions is that each stem in a co-compound receives its own primary stress and word melody, but the subcompound receives a single primary stress and word melody (the primary stressed syllables are underlined):[19]

(37)   Subcompound   Co-compound
   (a) (i) kaattəmařam (= (27b)) (ii) aatəmaatəkalə (= (27d))
           "forest tree"   "goats and cows"
   (b) (i) meešappettikalə (= (36b)) (ii) meešapettikalə (= (36c))
           "table-boxes"   "tables and boxes"

It is clear that the two constructions are phonologically distinct. Yet, unlike what happens with class 1 and class 2 affixation in English, there is no morphological asymmetry between the two kinds of compounds: a co-compound can have a subcompound as one of its stems, and a subcompound can have a co-compound as one of its stems (K. P. Mohanan 1986). This situation can be diagrammatically represented as follows:

(38) Nonconvergence type 2: The Phenomenon of the Loop

morphology-syntax	phonology
construction A	construction A
construction B	construction B

The formal device of the loop, proposed in Mohanan (1982) as a way of capturing the loop phenomenon, is intended to make a distinction between the two constructions in terms of sequential modularity: one module precedes the other, and yet allows the output of the second module to be input to the first:

(39)   (a)   Organization of the Lexicon

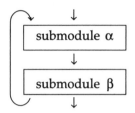

(b) Morphology
   (i)   subcompounding   (Domain: submodule α)
   (ii)   co-compounding   (Domain: submodule β)
(c) Phonology
   (i)   Stem-initial gemination   (Domain: submodule α)
          When preceded by a vowel-final stem, an obstruent is geminated.
   (ii)   Stem-final gemination: (Domain: submodule α)
          When followed by a stem, ṭ and r are geminated.
   (iii) Stress: (Domain: submodule α)
          Primary stress on the second syllable if the second syllable
          has a long vowel; if not primary stress on the first.
   (iv)   Word melody: (Domain: submodule α)
          The stressed syllable has a low tone; the final syllable has a
          high tone.

Given the looped organization in (39a), the domain specifications in terms of
the two modules in (39b) make the right predictions for gemination, stress,
and word melody. The derivation in (40) provides an illustration of how the
four-stratum organization of the Malayalam lexicon works (Mohanan 1986):[20]

(40)   Stratum 1
       [meeša], [peṭṭi], [kaḷ]   [meeša], [peṭṭi], [kaḷ]

Stratum 2 (= α in (39))		
[meeša], [peṭṭi], [kaḷ]	[meeša], [peṭṭi], [kaḷ]	
[[meeša][peṭṭi]]	——	Compounding
[[meeša][ppeṭṭi]]	——	Gemination
[meešappeṭṭi]	[meeša], [peṭṭi]	Stress, melody
[meešappeṭṭi]	——	BEC[21]

Stratum 3 (= β in (39))		
[meešappeṭṭi] [kaḷ]	[meeša], [peṭṭi], [kaḷ]	
——	[[meeša][peṭṭi]]	compounding
——	[meešapeṭṭi]	BEC

Stratum 4

[meešappeṭṭi], [kaḷ]	[meešapeṭṭi], [kaḷ]	
[[meešappeṭṭi][kaḷ]	[[meešapeṭṭi][kaḷ]]	Affixation
[meešappeṭṭikaḷ]	[meešapeṭṭikaḷ]	BEC

. . .   . . .

[meešappeṭṭikaḷə]	[meešapeṭṭikaḷə]	Phonetic

6.1.2 *Evidence for the Phenomenon of the Loop*

The four-stratum hypothesis for Malayalam forces the formal device of the loop. This formal device appears to have gained disapproval in many quarters, and the hypothesis itself has evoked a great deal of negative reaction in the phonology community (e.g., Sproat 1985; Christdas 1988; Inkelas 1989). It may therefore be useful to clarify what the analysis has successfully done, which its alternatives have failed to do. First, as pointed out in K. P. Mohanan (1986, pp. 120–2), it provides a solution for an ordering paradox (or its equivalent in non-rule-ordering frameworks). The paradox is that in subcompounds, the rules of vowel sandhi and vowel lengthening must apply prior to stress and melody assignment, while in co-compounds they have to apply after stress and word melody. The gist of the relevant phenomenon is as follows. When a vowel-final stem is followed by a vowel-initial stem in a subcompound or co-compound, the two vowels merge into a single long vowel (Vowel Sandhi). When a vowel ending stem is followed by a consonant initial stem in a subcompound or cocompound, the vowel is lengthened (Vowel Lengthening). As for stress, primary stress is assigned to the second syllable if the first syllable has a short vowel and the second syllable has a long one; if not, the primary stress is assigned to the first syllable. The primary stressed syllable gets a low tone as part of its word melody, while the last syllable gets a high tone. Now consider the following data which shows the interaction of vowel lengthening and stress:

(41) (a) (i) waḍʰu "bride"   (ii) grəham "house"
        (b) waḍʰuugrəham   "wife's house"

In the examples in (41a), the vowels in the second syllable are short, and hence primary stress falls on the first syllable in both words. In (41b), the vowel in the second syllable is long, and hence primary stress falls on the second syllable. We must therefore assume that stress assignment takes place after vowel lengthening.

Now consider the interaction between the three rules in co-compounds:

(42) (a) (i) warˈan "bridegroom"   (ii) -maar   (plural)
        (b) waḍʰuuwarˈanmaar   "bride and bridegroom"

Since the first syllable in (42b) receives primary stress despite the second vowel being long, we must assume that stress is assigned before the vowel gets lengthened. The same paradox appears with respect to vowel sandhi. The four-stratum hypothesis explains these paradoxes by specifying the domain of vowel sandhi and vowel lengthening as strata 2 and 3, and ordering stress and word melody after vowel lengthening and vowel sandhi. The subcompounding in (41) takes place at stratum 2, where vowel lengthening precedes stress and word melody. The individual stems that are put together to form a co-compound are assigned stress and word melody in stratum 2, before they are compounded. As a result, co-compounding takes place after stress and word melody, and vowel lengthening takes place after compounding. As far as I know, these facts have not been counteranalyzed in the literature that rejects the four-stratum analysis of Malayalam (e.g., Sproat 1986; Inkelas 1989; Wiltshire 1992).

The second piece of evidence that favors (39) involves the combination of segmental and suprasegmental facts in the interaction between subcompounding and co-compounding. As pointed out above, one of the stems of a subcompound can itself be a co-compound, as illustrated in (43):

(43) (a) (i) <u>mee</u>ša "table"   (ii) ka<u>saa</u>la "chair"   (iii) <u>pe</u>ṭṭi "box"
      (b) <u>mee</u>ška<u>saa</u>la<u>ppe</u>ṭṭikaḷ "boxes made from tables and chairs"
      (c) <u>mee</u>ša<u>pe</u>ṭṭi<u>kka</u>saalakaḷ "chairs made from tables and boxes"

The structure of (43b) is given in (44) as an illustration:

(44)

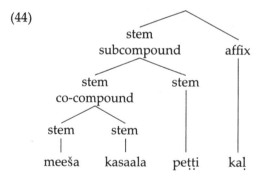

As predicted by (39ci), stem-initial gemination does not appear at the junction in the co-compound, but it does at the junction in the subcompound. What is interesting is that the second stem of the subcompound carries its own primary stress and word melody. This follows from the model in (39a) if we assume that the default principles of building suprasegmental structure (syllable, stress, word melody) do not disturb the prior assignment of structure, but assign it to the stretch that does not carry suprasegmental information (K. P. Mohanan 1986). In (43b), the substructure [[meeša][kasaala]] is assigned stress and word melody in its first pass through submodule 3. It then loops to submodule 2, to derive the structure [[meešakasaala][petṭi]], where stem-initial gemination takes place. In its second pass through submodule 3, the form [meešakasaalappetṭi] has stress and word melody in the stretch *meeša-kasaala* but not in *petṭi*. Hence the latter stretch receives stress and word melody.

6.1.3 The Loop in the Representational Formalism

We are dealing with two distinct issues here. One is the need to recognize two kinds of nonconvergence between morphology and phonology: two construc-tions which need to be kept separate for morphological purposes may need to be unified for the purposes of phonology (nonconvergence type 1), and, conversely, two constructions which need to be kept separate for phonological purposes may need to be unified for the purposes of morphology (noncon-vergence type 2). The other is the issue of the formal device that permits this nonconvergence. The loop is precisely such a device. I would like to point out that this device is equivalent to a recursive rule in a phrase structure grammar. Consider the rules in (45):

(45)   (a) $\beta \rightarrow \beta\ \beta$
      (b) $\alpha \rightarrow \alpha\ \alpha$
      (c) $\beta \rightarrow \alpha$
      (d) $\alpha \rightarrow \beta\ \beta$

If we interpret α and β as subcompounds and co-compounds, these rules correctly generate the recursive structures illustrated in (46):

(46)   (a)   co-compound   (b)   subcompound

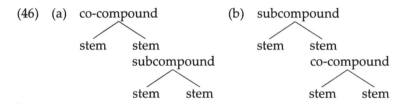

The use of representations that resemble (46) has been proposed as an alter-native to the formal device of the loop. Note that rule (45d) is the representa-tional counterpart of the loop in sequential modularity.

(47)

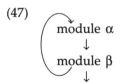

I fail to see how the looping in (47) is more unconstrained than the recursion in (45d). As pointed out earlier, no analysis can escape from the phenomenon of the loop in (38). As for the formal devices, whether the phenomenon of the loop should be captured in terms of representations as in (45d) or in terms of sequential modularity as in (47) is a secondary issue of detail.

Another representational alternative to (39) is that of prosodic phonology in Sproat (1985) and Inkelas (1989). In this approach, prosodic nodes carry the information necessary to distinguish between the phonology of subcompounding and co-compounding. Thus, the structures that correspond to (46a) and (46b) are represented as (48a) and (48b) respectively:

(48)   (a)   (b)

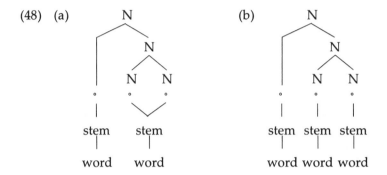

The compound in (43b) will have the structure in (48b). The domain of stress and word melody in the prosodic approach are specified in terms of the domain (P-)WORD. This correctly predicts that (46a) will have two primary stresses and two word melodies, while (46b) will have three each. However, the difficulty arises when it comes to principles such as gemination, which hold between the stems of a subcompound but not a co-compound. The representations in (48) incorrectly predict that there cannot be any gemination between the two stems of the subcompound in (46b). In addition, they also fail to explain the phenomenon that we identified earlier as an ordering paradox between the principles of stress and word melody on the one hand, and vowel lengthening and vowel sandhi on the other. In the light of these observations, we must conclude that while the representations in (46a, b) are legitimate as specifications of the domains of the principles of phonological organization, those in (48a, b) are not. These phenomena pose precisely the same challenges to the alternative analysis of the Malayalam facts in terms of harmonic phonology in Wiltshire (1992), though problems of space do not permit me to go into the details.

Recall that the problem we have been dealing with is that of the non-convergence of morphologically motivated and phonologically motivated construction types, where a construction type would mean such things as class 1 and class 2 affixation in English, or subcompounding and co-compounding in Malayalam. The phenomena that we have examined so far can be correctly described in terms of the sequential modularity of lexical phonology, but not in terms of the proposed representational alternatives in non–lexical phonology or prosodic lexical phonology. Needless to say, that the alternatives to sequential modularity have not been successful in accounting for these phenomena should not be taken to mean that there are no nonsequential accounts. I am hopeful that such an account can be found, but I have no intelligent suggestions to make at present. As we shall see in the following section, the apparent advantage of lexical phonology in accounting for the rule ordering paradox and the facts of gemination in subcompounds containing co-compounds is challenged by the picture that emerges when we consider the facts of verbal compounding in Malayalam.

6.2   A More Complex Nonconvergence: Verbal Compounding in Malayalam

The crucial phenomena relevant for the analysis of subcompounds and co-compounds in Malayalam are stress, word melody, stem-initial gemination, stem-final gemination, nasal deletion, onset fusion, sonorant degemination, vowel sandhi and vowel lengthening. We have already seen how subcompounds and co-compounds exhibit differences in stress, word melody, and the two types of gemination. T. Mohanan (1989) shows that they are different with respect to sonorant degemination and onset fusion. Despite these differences, the two types of compounds are also similar in that they both undergo nasal deletion, vowel sandhi, and vowel lengthening (K. P. Mohanan 1986).

In addition to these two types of compounds, Malayalam also has verbal compounds, as illustrated in (49c).

(49)   (a)   (i) maṟam "tree"   (ii) kuṭiṟa "horse"   (iii) kayar- "climb"
      (b)   maṟakkuṭiṟa "wooden horse" (subcompound)
      (c)   maṟaŋkayari "tree climber"   (verbal compound)

In a subcompound, the first stem is a modifier (= adjunct) of the second stem; in a verbal compound, the first stem is a complement of the second stem. In a co-compound, every stem is a head.

As far as stress and word melody are concerned, verbal compounds and subcompounds are identical. Both types of constructions carry a single primary stress and word melody. On the basis of this behavior, K. P. Mohanan (1986) incorrectly concluded that subcompounds and verbal compounds are concatenated in the same lexical stratum, namely, stratum 2. In an interesting unpublished paper, Yatabe (1991) shows that verbal compounds behave differently from subcompounds with respect to gemination, onset fusion, and sonorant degemination. They are different from both subcompounds and co-compounds with respect to nasal deletion, vowel sandhi, and vowel lengthening. The example in (49c) illustrates that verbal compounds do not undergo nasal deletion, unlike subcompounds. The following examples illustrate the absence of gemination in verbal compounds:[22]

(50) (a) (i) kaatə "forest"   (ii) aana "elephant"   (iii) ootum "will run"
    (b) kaattaana "wild elephant"
    (c) kaatooti "jungle roamer"

The phonologically motivated classifications of the three types of constructions are given in (51):

(51)   Phenomena   Classification

(a) Stress; word melody   Verbal compounds and subcompounds
                                    Co-compounds

(b) Nasal deletion; vowel   Verbal compounds
      sandhi, vowel   Subcompounds and co-compounds
      lengthening

(c) Gemination; onset fusion, Verbal compounds and co-compounds
      sonorant degemination   Subcompounds

Given this situation, one may think of assigning verbal compounding to an independent stratum, and ordering it before subcompounding as in (52a), after co-compounding as in (52b), or in between, as in (52c):

(52) (a) verbal compounding   (b) subcompounding
             ↓   ↓
      subcompounding   co-compounding
             ↓   ↓
      co-compounding   verbal compounding

    (c) subcompounding
             ↓
      verbal compounding
             ↓
      co-compounding

There are two problems with this solution. First, since the three types of compounds are inputs to one another (i.e., any one of them can contain the others), the organization, whether (52a), (52b), or (52c), will have to allow loops that connect nonadjacent strata, a situation that has so far been disallowed in lexical phonology. Second, even if we loop nonadjacent strata, none of these solutions will yield an analysis that correctly captures the situation in (51). Verbal compounds carry a single primary stress and word melody: the solution in (52b) will incorrectly predict that each stem in a verbal compound will have its own primary stress and word melody. Since onset fusion and sonorant degemination do not hold in verbal compounds, the ordering in (52a) will yield incorrect results. The solution in (52c) will not be able to account for nasal deletion, vowel sandhi, and vowel lengthening, which apply in subcompounds and co-compounds, but not in verbal compounds. Thus, no possible ordering of the modules will yield the correct predictions. This dilemma is equally true for the alternative strategies in Sproat, Inkelas, and Wiltshire. It appears, then, that none of the theories discussed above, lexical phonology, prosodic lexical phonology, non-lexical prosodic phonology, and harmonic phonology, entirely succeeds in describing the facts of the three types of compounding.

In an attempt to provide an account, Yatabe suggests that phonological principles have direct access to the morphosyntactic construction types. Details of formalism aside, Yatabe's analysis requires that we recognise the structure of the three types of compound as follows:

(53) (a) Verbal compound: complement, head
     (b) Subcompound: modifier, head
     (c) Co-compound: head, head, . . .

The domains of phonological principles are stated directly in terms of these construction types, rather than in terms of sequential submodules, prosodic nodes, or a combination.

In addition to being descriptively adequate, Yatabe's analysis has the advantage that the morphological constructs employed in the specification of phonological domains ((53a–c)) are imbued with universal substance. For example, on the basis of parallel contrasts between subcompounds and co-compounds in Japanese and English, Yatabe claims that there is a general universal tendency for verbal compounds to undergo fewer phonological principles than subcompounds. Unlike the previous proposals in the phonology-morphology interaction, the proposal in (53) lends itself to the pursuit of universal statements of this kind.

Most proposals for the interaction between morphology and phonology since *SPE* have suffered from the weakness that they employ diacritic devices to refer to construction types. Thus, *SPE* employs diacritics like + and #, while lexical phonology employs diacritics like stratum 1 and stratum 2. Proposals for constructs like phonological stem (versus phonological word) have also remained nothing more than disguised diacritical markings, in spite of the sense of security induced by the terminology. The diacritic status of prosodic categories is transparent in prosodic lexical phonology, where the terminology of α and β replaces that of P-STEMS and P-WORDS. I would like to submit that the distrust of the four-stratum analysis of Malayalam and English has its basis in the intuitive distrust of the unconstrained use of diacritics that carry no universal substance.

As I see it, what is valuable about Sproat's alternative is the use of phonological word as a construct for the statement of the domains of phonological principles. His hypothesis that each conjunct in a coordinate construction must contain at least one phonological word is a way of imbuing the notion of phonological word with substance. As Sproat himself acknowledges, this substance is absent in the proposal to use phonological stem on a par with phonological word. Yatabe escapes the use of diacritics by referring directly to construction types involving different relations of head, modifier, and complement ((53)). We observed earlier that phonologcal principles need to refer to the nondiacritic constructs morpheme and word. Let us hope that other phonologically motivated differences in construction types, such as that between class 1 and class 2 affixation in English, will also prove to be universally grounded.

It must be pointed out that if we accept Yatabe's proposal, we are forced to acknowledge that word-internal phonology must refer directly to word-internal syntax, contra the claims made in prosodic lexical phonology. We have already seen that phonological principles must have access to the unit morpheme. If the crucial contrast between verbal compounds and sub-compounds is the syntactic relation of modifier versus complement, and the effects of this relation are repeatedly found across languages, then lexical-prosodic approaches to the morphology-phonology interface cannot provide a satisfactory account of the contrast. Whether or not what is true of the relation between word-internal syntax and phonology is also true of phrasal syntax and phonology remains to be seen. If it is, it would challenge the claims of prosodic phonology as well.

To summarize, the use of prosodic representations has not yet been able to provide successful analyses of certain phenomena (rule ordering paradoxes, interaction between two types of compounds) which do have an account within the sequential modularity of lexical phonology. This is not to recommend lexical phonology, but simply to point out the problems which need to be solved in future work. Evidence also seems to suggest that phonological principles need to have access to the following kinds of information on morphological construction types: morpheme, word, affix versus stem, two types of affixes, head, modifier, and complement. The question that arises is: if we develop a formalism that allows such direct reference, independently of sequential modularity or prosodic trees, do we still need sequential modularity or prosodic trees? I leave this question open.

7   Lexical Phonology, Rule Systems, and Representations

The topic of this chapter is the organization of the grammar. It is not the formal properties of the rules/constraints that capture the patterns of distribution and alternation in phonology, or the formal representation of phonological information. However, a number of claims about the behavior of rule-constraint systems and representations crucially depend upon the modular organization of grammar. Therefore, let me now briefly review some of these claims.

7.1   Rule-Constraint Systems

The division of grammar in lexical phonology into lexical and post-lexical modules has given rise to the following claims about the application of phonological rules, most of which have been challenged:

(54)   (a)   Only lexical rule applications may refer to word-internal structure.
     (b)   Only post-lexical rule applications may apply across words.
     (c)   Only lexical rule applications may be cyclic.
     (d)   Lexical rule applications are structure preserving.
     (e)   Only lexical rule applications may have lexical exceptions.
     (f)   Lexical rule applications must precede post-lexical rule applications.

Claims (54a) and (54b) are in a sense criterial for deciding whether a rule application is lexical or not. However, given the general consensus that noncategorical gradient phenomena are a characteristic of phonetic implementation, not lexical rule application, we can derive from (54a) the prediction that morphologically sensitive patterns cannot be gradient. Sproat and Fujumura (1993) and Sproat (1993) argue that this prediction is incorrect, since both the gradient rhyme lengthening and the velarization of /l/ in English distinguish between the concatenation of words in a phrase and the concatenation of stems within a compound word, and both of these from other junctures and absence of junctures. As far as I can see, these facts can equally well be accounted for by appealing, in the post-lexical module, to the distinctions between (1) single words and phrases, and (2) phonological words as units composed of phonological feet. Both these distinctions are available in the post-lexical module. Hence, even though I acknowledge the possibility of (54a) turning out to be false, I do not see any persuasive evidence for abandoning it at the present.

The current status of (54c) is unclear, given that research within lexical phonology itself has challenged it. For example, Rubach (1984), Booij and Rubach (1984), and Kiparsky (1985) assume that the last stratum in the lexicon is or can be noncyclic; Halle and Mohanan (1985) assume that each stratum, including the first, can be specified as being cyclic or noncyclic. As pointed out in Kaisse and Shaw (1985), there are also examples of cyclic application in post-lexical phonology. Liu (1980) argues that the rule in Mandarin that changes tone 3 to tone 2 when followed by a 3 must apply cyclically across words. Dresher (1983) makes a similar argument for cyclic post-lexical rules. I refer the reader to chapter 3, this volume, for a detailed discussion of cyclicity.

Often tied up with cyclicity is the issue of the Strict Cycle Condition (SCC). As Cole (chapter 3, this volume) points out, SCC has two parts. One is the formal need to prevent rules from "reaching" back in order to preserve rule ordering in cyclic domains. I will not deal with the problem of reaching back in this chapter, because it strikes me as a purely formal issue that arises out of certain kinds of formal mechanics. I agree with Cole's judgement that there is no empirical support for this constraint. The other part of SCC is the Derived Environment Condition (DEC), which asserts (1) that certain kinds of rules apply only in derived environments, where "derived" means derived either through morphemic composition or through the application of a phonological rule, and (2) that the domains which exhibit DEC are cyclic domains. The classic example of this effect is the nonapplication of trisyllabic shortening in monomorphemic forms like *nightingale* in English. We have various versions of DEC, the weakest of them being that a structure-changing rule cannot apply in underived environments in nonfinal strata in the lexicon.[23] As pointed out in K. P. Mohanan (1986), even this weak formulation is untenable as shown by the facts of nasal spreading in Malayalam (principle (16b)). This rule applies to monomorphemic forms in stratum 1, changing underlying forms like /paṇḍi/ to [paṇṇi] "pig". Since the place-assimilation rule that applies before nasal spreading applies only if the trigger is [−son, −cont], the post-nasal voiced plosive that becomes nasal must be underlyingly specified as [−son, −cont].[24] Since the specification changes to [+son] as a result of nasal spreading, we must take it as a structure-changing rule. Thus, nasal spreading is a structure-changing rule that applies to underived forms in stratum 1.

It appears to me that the various attempts at formulating a principle of DEC have run into problems because we are pursuing a nonissue. If we decide to formulate trisyllabic shortening as a phonological rule, examples like *nightingale* can simply be treated as lexical exceptions. Independently of DEC effects, we must stipulate examples like *obese* and *scene* as lexical exceptions to shortening, as the derived forms *obesity* and *scenic* do not undergo the rule. Observe that if the rule did apply to *nightingale*, deriving the surface form [nitiŋgeil], there would be no evidence for postulating an underlying long vowel in the first syllable.

Let us consider the exceptions to obstruent voicing assimilation in English. Even though voicing agreement is a robust phenomenon in English, there are lexical exceptions to it in both derived environments (e.g., *midst* [midst]) and underived environments (e.g., *svelt* [svelt]). What special advantage do we gain by claiming that the nonapplication of voicing agreement in underived environments is due to a special principle, and that even the post-lexical application of voicing agreement is subject to this condition, rather than saying that the rule/constraint has lexical exceptions?

How can anyone produce counterevidence to the claim that trisyllabic shortening and voicing agreement cannot apply in underived environments? Suppose there is a dialect of English in which *svelt* is pronounced as [sfelt], and *nightingale* is pronounced as [nitingeil]. Would this constitute evidence for assuming that the underlying representations of the two words are /svelt/ and /naitingeil/, and that these underived forms undergo voicing agreement and shortening? Certainly not. If such phonetic forms were indeed observed, they would be analyzed as having the underlying forms /sfelt/ and /nitingeil/, as there is no evidence to assume a more abstract underlying form. Thus, the absence of examples in which trisyllabic shortening applies in underived environments is simply the result of Occam's Razor which requires us not to posultate underlying representations that are more abstract than necessary. The illusion of the need for a linguistic principle of DEC, then, is the result of the combination of (1) lexical exceptionality, and (2) patterns of alternation that are not motivated by distribution.

Let us turn to (54d). At the conceptual level, structure preservation is the *phenomenon* of the preservation of distributional regularities in the patterns of alternation. As pointed out in Goldsmith (1990) and K. P. Mohanan (1991), distributional regularities are repeatedly found to inhibit an otherwise regular alternation (i.e., block the application of rule) or motivate an alternation or a particular part of it (i.e., trigger rules, or repair the output of rules). The traditional formulation of the Structure Preservation Constraint (SPC) elevates the blocking effect into a universal constraint, and turns out to be either false or empirically vacuous.

The intuition that SPC tries to express is that certain patterns of alternation, which we would expect otherwise to hold in certain forms, are blocked because they would violate some other independent principle of the grammar. For example, Kiparsky (1985) argues that place assimilation in Catalan allows the lexical spreading of backness to an underlying /n/ from a following velar plosive, but the similar spreading of dentality from a following dental plosive does not occur, since [+distributed] is disallowed in underlying representations, and hence no lexical rule can introduce it.

As pointed out by Spencer (1991), the idea (though not the terminology) of structure preservation in phonology-morphology was first proposed in Aronoff (1976, p. 98). Aronoff defines an allomorphic rule as one which "effects a phonological change, but which only applies to certain morphemes in the immediate environment of certain other morphemes . . ." Such rules "cannot introduce segments which are not otherwise motivated as underlying phonological segments of the language." Kiparsky (1985) says:

> "In English . . . , voicing is distinctive for obstruents but not for sonorants. We express this by a marking condition which prohibits voicing from being marked on sonorants in the lexicon:
>
> (16) $\quad *\begin{bmatrix} \alpha \text{ voiced} \\ + \text{ son} \end{bmatrix}$
>
> A language in which voicing is entirely non-distinctive would have the marking condition
>
> (17) $\quad * [\alpha \text{ voiced}]$
>
> By STRUCTURE PRESERVATION I mean that marking conditions such as (16), (17) must be applicable not only to underived lexical representations but also to derived lexical representations, including the output of word-level rules."

Kaisse and Shaw (1985) interpret this as a statement that prohibits phonological rules in the lexicon from creating segments that are not part of the underlying inventory.[25] The analysis of the seven points of articulation among the nasals in Malayalam in terms of three underlying nasals (Mohanan and Mohanan 1984) is a clear counterexample to this claim. Take, for example, the complementary distribution of alveolar and dental nasals in the language. The dental nasal occurs only (1) at the beginning of a morpheme, (2) when followed by a dental stop, or (3) when adjacent to another dental nasal. In these environements the alveolar nasal cannot occur. These facts follow from the analysis that assumes that dental nasals are not part of the underlying inventory. The dental geminate is derived through assimilation from /nd̪/ through (16a) and (16b); the morpheme-initial dental nasal is derived from /n/ by a rule that makes alveolar nasals dental at the beginning of a morpheme ((21d)). Both these rules create the structure [+nasal, +coronal, +anterior, +distributed], in spite of the fact that [distributed] is not a feature that is contrastive underlyingly in the language. For similar examples of the violation in German and Welsh, see Hall (1989) and Sproat (1985).

Thus, as a universal principle of interaction between rules and constraints, SPC need not be obeyed even in the first stratum of a grammar. Conversely, we see the effects of structure preservation in the post-lexical module as well (K. P. Mohanan 1991). What this means is that structure preservation is not related to the division of the grammar into the lexical and post-lexical modules. It is not a principle of the grammar, but a recurrent phenomenon of the preservation of distributional patterns in alternation (T. Mohanan 1989; Goldsmith 1990; K. P. Mohanan 1991).

Perhaps it would be instructive to ask what the intuition of Structure Preservation would correspond to in a grammar that does not subscribe to the sequential conception of rule applications and levels of representation. Suppose a grammar has three parallel levels of representation as in (6). In such a grammar, principles of phonological organization can hold within any of the three levels, or across two or more levels. In such a situation, what is analyzed as SPC will be the effect of a principle that holds within a level winning over a principle that holds within another level, or across two levels. If a condition holds on both the morpheme and word levels, no pattern of alternation that is valid between the morpheme and word levels would violate it. This would correspond to the attested effects of SPC within the lexical module. On the other hand, if a condition holds on the morpheme level, but not on the word level, we will see violations of SPC such as those observed in Malayalam.

I would like to suggest that the only universal claim that we can make about the appearance of nonunderlying contrasts is the one that Aronoff made about allomorphic patterns. Suppose we define an allomorphic alternation as one that is conditioned *purely* by the properties of particular morphemes, i.e., an alternation that is not triggered by phonological content or morphophonological structure. By this definition, the voicing alternation in the English pair *berieve/bereft* will not be allomorphic because its trigger includes phonological content (the voiceless /t/), and the morphologically conditioned [n]/[ṇ] alternation in Malayalam mentioned above will not be allomorphic because it is conditioned by morphological structure, not by individual morphemes. In contrast, the vowel alternation in *sit/sat* will be an example of allomorphy. Such an allomorphic alternation will be a relation between two different formatives of a morpheme in the sense discussed in section 3.2. If so, an allomorphic alternation will be expressed as a relation between two different underlying forms, while a phonological alternation will be expressed as a relation between an underlying form and its phonetic form. If a segment is not part of the underlying inventory, it cannot appear in either of the two underlying forms related through an allomorphic pattern. Aronoff's generalization follows from this view of allomorphy. For example, we predict that there will be no language in which a morphological feature such as a plural or past tense is phonologically realized solely as, say, a front rounded vowel, or a nasalized vowel, where front rounded vowels and nasalized vowels are not underlying segments.

Finally, we turn to the claim of post-lexical rule applications not having lexical exceptions (54e). This claim is challenged by examples like the post-lexical voicing assimilation in English which has exceptions like *midst* [midst] and *svelt* [svelt]. Even a pervasive phenomenon such as the place assimilation of nasals in Malayalam, which applies both lexically and post-lexically, fails to apply post-lexically in the form [anpə] "kindness" (K. P. Mohanan 1986). Therefore, what (54e) states is not an absolute condition, but a recurrent tendency for lexical patterns to have more lexical exceptions than post-lexical patterns.

In sum, we conclude that most of the claims in (54) on the interaction between rule-constraint systems and modules of the grammar are questionable. Particularly dubious are the claims of cyclic application of rules, strict cyclicity, structure preservation, and lexical exceptionality. I have suggested that strict cyclicity is an illusion created by the lexical exceptionality of the patterns of phonological alternation that are not motivated by distribution, that structure preservation is simply an observed effect of the conflict between two contradictory principles of phonology, and that the claim of post-lexical rules having no exceptions as an absolute universal is simply false.

7.2 *Representations*

In recent years, most discussions of the modular organization of phonology, particularly those in lexical phonology, have involved a representational issue, that of underspecification. The fundamental claim of underspecification theories is that it is desirable to omit certain kinds of information from underlying representations. One of the central questions that theories of underspecification have tried to grapple with has been the recurrent asymmetries of phonological content (Archangeli 1984; K. P. Mohanan 1991; and Steriade, chapter 4, this volume): Why do certain feature values spread, while their complements do not? Why do segments with certain feature values undergo phonological change, while others resist the change? Why do certain feature values block spreading, while others are transparent? Is there a correlation among these different kinds of asymmetries?[26] Is there any correlation between the asymmetric effects of spreading, blocking, and resistence on the one hand, and contrastive and noncontrastive information on the other?

I have argued elsewhere that while the pursuit of these issues has led to a deepened understanding of phonological patterns in natural languages, the mechanics of underspecified representations, structure-building rules, and structure-changing rules have actually obscured the patterns rather than illuminated them (K. P. Mohanan 1991). For example, it has been argued that asymmetries in the content of features argued for in underspecification theories have also been found in language acquisition, processing, and phonetic implementation (e.g., Stemberger 1991, 1992; Keating 1988). This has been taken as evidence for the formalism of underspecification. However, that there is a systematic asymmetry between coronals and noncoronals in language acquisition, language production, and the like, does not necessarily show that the asymmetry is to be formally expressed as specified versus unspecified information.

As in other issues in phonology, I expect that the current trend toward abandoning the sequential input-output conception of phonological derivation will have a profound effect on underspecification theories. This issue is anticipated in recent works such as Archangeli and Pulleyblank (in press). However, the potential problems of combining underspecification with a nonsequential conception remain unexplored. The conclusions will emerge more clearly only when the specifics of nonsequential analyses have been fully articulated.

8   Summary

To summarize, the central problem that we have been concerned with in this chapter has been the relation between phonology and other aspects of the organization of language. In dealing with issues in this domain, we have found it useful to separate the issue of modularity from the issue of sequentiality. Thus, one can subscribe to the hypothesis that phonological theory needs to separate the module of word-internal structure from the module of structure across words, without necessarily assuming that the former module precedes the latter in a procedural sense. In a nonsequential conception, the modules and the levels of representation that are associated with them are "co-present," as structures along a multidimensional space, where information from different "levels" or dimensions of organization is simultaneously accessible to principles of the grammar.

Most recent approaches to syntax have converged on the need for different types of information being co-present. In the *Aspects*-type syntax (Chomsky 1965), for example, information about theta roles was available only at the level of deep structure. Information about grammatical functions was available only at a later stage in the derivation where information about theta roles was no longer available. *SPE* phonology inherited this conception of information distributed along various stages in a derivation, and subsequently passed it on to lexical phonology. With the advent of trace theory, the role of particular stages in a derivation became irrelevant, move alpha being simply a way of thinking about relating one level of representation to another. Furthermore, traces also allow all information to be simultaneously present. Thus, unlike the kinds of representations in generative semantics, a single tree structure in the minimalist descendents of government-binding theory can contain information about theta roles, grammatical functions, quantifier scope, and topichood (Chomsky 1992).

This conception of co-present information is present in phonology in Halle and Vergnaud's (1980) metaphor of the ring-bound note book. In addition to co-presence, this conception also opened up the possibility of distributing different types of information along different dimensions of structure. This move towards co-presence of information and multidimensionality of structure has led to the convergence of a number of proposals that abandon the input-output metaphor in generative grammar. These proposals state principles of the grammar not as rules, but as laws that state relations between entities within or across different co-present levels or dimensions of representation. In various stages of development and detail, this approach can be found in Chomsky (1981), Hale (1983), and K. P. Mohanan (1983), who suggest that lexical and configurational structures are a pair of parallel structures; Zubizaretta (1987), who makes a similar proposal for virtual and actual structures; Marantz (1984), who suggests that all levels of representation are "linked"; Sadock (1985, 1991) who proposes that morphological and syntactic structures are parallel-linked dimensions of structure; T. Mohanan (1990, in press) who proposes a multidimensional view of the representation that includes the dimensions of semantic structure, argument structure, grammatical function structure, and grammatical category structure.

This conception of simultaneous modularity conflicts with the earlier conception of sequential modularity in lexical phonology and prosodic lexical phonology. Those who subscribe to a multidimensional view of linguistic organization in syntax and phonology are therefore faced with the challenge of identifying the crucial insights expressed in terms of the mechanics of sequential modularity and sequential rule application, and exploring how they can be incorporated into a conception where different levels of representation are co-present.

Restricting the scope of this chapter to the role of morphological information in phonology, I suggested in the preceding sections that the information required by phonology is that of part-whole relations, categories, and morphological construction types. The construction types that I have demonstrated to be relevant for phonology include the following types of information: morpheme (formatives, features), word, stem, affix, type of affixation, head, modifier, and complement. Many phenomena that I reviewed above can be handled either in terms of sequential or simultaneous/representational modularity.

However, there are phenomena for which we only have a sequential analysis at present (e.g., ordering paradox and interaction between two types of compounding). Conversely, there also exist phenomena that can be analyzed only by making direct reference to morphological construction types, challenging alternative analyses within lexical or prosodic phonology. This conflict between competing conclusions will have to be resolved by future research.

Prosodic phonology and prosodic lexical phonology make two claims about phonological organization. First, phonological principles are sensitive to prosodic structures. Second, even though prosodic structures are sensitive to morphological and syntactic information, phonological principles are not directly sensitive to morphology and syntax. The evidence I reviewed above suggests that phonological principles need to refer directly to morphosyntactic constructs such as the morpheme (formative, feature), head, complement, and modifier. These findings challenge the second hypothesis in prosodic (lexical) phonology.

Evidence also points to the conclusion that even though it is necessary to distinguish between different levels of representation and different modules of organization, it is not possible to have any classification of formal principles that correspond to the levels of representation and modules. The same principle can hold in different modules of organization, yielding somewhat different results.

I have suggested that there is a possibility that the submodularity within the lexical module in lexical phonology will have to be replaced by phonological rules having direct access to morphological construction types (with or without word internal prosodic units). Whether or not lexical and post-lexical modularity should also be abandoned is an independent question. My guess at this point is that it will be impossible to state the relation between underlying and phonetic representations without an intermediate level that corresponds to lexical representations. Abstracting away from the sequentiality of lexical phonology, it is possible that the underlying, lexical, and phonetic levels will correspond to the morpheme-, word-, and phrase- levels of representation respectively. It may take another couple of decades for the dust to settle.

NOTES

1   I have very little to say in this article about the relation between phonology and syntax; I leave this issue to the articles dealing with the phonology-syntax interface in this volume (chaps. 15 and 16).

2   I use the term "principles" so as to be neutral between the different ways in which phonological regularities are formulated, e.g., in terms of "rules" versus "constraints." I will use the term "phonological patterns" to refer to both distribution and alternation.

"Distribution" is the relation between a unit and the environment in which it occurs: the statement "[h] cannot occur at the end of a word in English" identifies a pattern of distribution. "Alternation" refers to the relation between two corresponding units in two related forms: the statement "The nucleus [ai] in *divine* corresponds to the nucleus [i] in *divinity*" identifies a pattern of alternation. It is important to distinguish the classification of patterns of distribution and alternation from the classification of formal devices that capture the patterns into rules and constraints. Either rules or constraints can be used for the statement of both distribution and alternation.

3   This article is the result of a personal struggle to make sense of a number of debates involving the phonology-morphology interaction that have occurred over the last few decades. In presenting a sketch of one's conception of the state of the art, there is always the danger of a skewed perspective, colored by one's own research and preoccupations. I have tried my best to eliminate autobiography, but total objectivity is impossible when presenting an overall assessment.

4   The flat pseudo-syntactic tree in (2b) resembles the structures in current theories of prosodic structure.

5   The information about stems and affixes is represented in the *SPE* theory and subsequent work in terms of brackets. Thus, [[x][y]] denotes compounding, while [[x]y] denotes affixation. This bracket notation has no corresponding translation in the tree notation. See the objections to this notation raised in Halle and Mohanan (1985).

6   Here and in what follows, I formulate phonological principles in ordinary prose rather than in formal notation, because the use of prose statements helps me focus the discussion on the issues of the morphology-phonology interface, without getting sidetracked into debates on the formal devices for the statement of phonological regularities. Another reason is the faint hope that ten years from now, when the formalism for the statement of rules/constraints has changed radically, students and colleagues will still find the discussion useful and accessible.

7   I use the term "devoiced" to refer to an underlying voiced consonant which exhibits very little or no vocal cord vibrations, but still acts like a voiced consonant in its lenis (rather than fortis) articulation and its ability to lengthen the preceding vowel. The symbol of the voiced consonant with the circle at the bottom can represent such a consonant even if the devoicing is complete, i.e., if there is no vocal cord vibration.

8   By morphophonological pattern, I mean a phonological regularity that requires morphological information.

9   In addition to accounting for the alternation in (11), (12) also accounts for the ill-formedness of syllables like *[lisb], *[lizb], *[lifd], *[livt], *[sbin] and *[zbin], in contrast to the well-formedness of syllables like [lisp], [lift], and [spin].

10   This situation can be conceptualized more clearly through the following metaphor (K. P. Mohanan 1993). A magnetic field has a stronger hold on a piece of iron closer to its center than one farther away. When close, a magnet can make a piece of iron on a table jump towards it, but

when farther away, its effect is not visible. A weak magnetic field (e.g., (17)) may nevertheless influence the path of a piece of iron which is set in motion by some other field (e.g., (12)).

11 In these formulations, X refers to variables, and the double arrow to a correspondence relation between two words in the lexicon. These authors refer to rules like (19) as Word Formation Strategies in their model of projection morphology.

12 The claim is that all examples of "non-automatic" alternation are part of morphology, not phonology. For Sommerstein (1974), an alternation is automatic if it "occurs in every morpheme of a given general phonological form in a given phonemic environment," otherwise it is nonautomatic (1974, p. 45). This means that an alternation is "non-automatic" if (1) it has lexical exceptions, or (2) requires morphological information for its application. Under criterion (1), the alternation in (11a–c) is nonautomatic, and hence not part of phonology, as it has lexical exceptions in words like *midst* [midst] and *svelt* [svelt]. Since Singh considers (11a–c) clearly to be part of phonology, I will not consider (1) to be a defining feature of nonautomaticity.

13 In addition to showing that the claim in (19) is untenable, these examples also show that the claim that there are no morpheme structure constraints is false (e.g., Kiparsky 1982). See Christdas (1988) and T. Mohanan (1989) for additional evidence.

14 For readers who are not familiar with metrical theories of stress: a light syllable is an open syllable (i.e., without a coda) with a short vowel. A syllable with a coda, a long vowel, or a diphthong is a heavy syllable.

15 The [ə] in these forms is epenthetic.

16 Both (33) and (34) express the asymmetry by classifying morphological constructions into two types. Fabb (1988) has argued against this, on the grounds that one needs independent statements on the co-occurrence of individual affixes. See Sproat (1985) for a response to this position, and also for instances of violation of (33c) and (34c).

17 See, however, the discussion in Goldsmith (1990) for objections.

18 In *ungrammaticality*, the hypothesis that *un-* must be attached to adjectives, not nouns, dictates the bracketing [[ungrammatical][ity]], while the hypothesis that *-ity* cannot be attached to a stem countaining a class 2 prefix dictates the bracketing [[un][grammaticality]]. Another type of bracketing paradox involves the mismatch between semantically motivated and morphologically motivated constituency. Thus, in the English word *unhappier*, the semantically motivated constituency is [[unhappy][er]], while the morphologically motivated constituency is [[un][happier]]. Neither of these two types of paradoxes are relevant for the issue of the interaction between phonology and morphology.

19 Stress in Malayalam is discussed in detail in K. P. Mohanan (1986).

20 Assuming that all lexical strata are universally required to be cyclic, K. P. Mohanan (1982) was forced to assume that stress and word melody assignment take effect in the co-compounding stratum, thereby making incorrect predictions of the kind pointed out in Sproat (1985, 1986). The

formulation given in (39) is taken from K. P. Mohanan (1986), which assumes that all lexical strata in Malayalam are non-cyclic, and that all mophological operations within a stratum precede all the phonological operations within that stratum.

21 Bracket Erasure Convention (BEC) has the effect of erasing the internal brackets of one submodule when the form exits the module.

22 For more extensive data, see Yatabe (1991).

23 See Cole (chapter 3, this volume) for discussion.

24 See Mohanan and Mohanan (1984) and K. P. Mohanan (1986) for details.

25 See Sproat (1985) for the problems of arriving at this interpretation in a theory that combines structure preservation with radical underspecification.

26 The asymmetries mentioned above are not restricted to phonological features. For example, a segment in the coda is typically "weaker" than one in the onset, in the sense that the former undergoes assimilation, neutralization, and deletion more readily. Similarly, word-final segments are weaker than word-initial segments. As far as I know, underspecification theories do not have a unified account of these asymmetries.

3 The Cycle in Phonology

JENNIFER COLE

0 Introduction

The principle of cyclic rule application is taken as a fundamental property in much current theoretical work in phonology, with far-reaching effects on the behavior of phonological rules and rule systems.[1] Cyclicity is invoked to explain many characteristics of rule application, such as:

- the failure of rule application in nonderived, monomorphemic environments;
- the application of a rule to a morphological constituent which is a substring of the word;
- rule ordering paradoxes – apparent violations of the strict linear ordering hypothesis, which requires all phonological rules to apply in a sequence, with each rule applying only once.

Cyclicity was at the core of some of the earliest work in generative phonology, playing an important role in the analysis of English stress in the landmark work of Chomsky and Halle (1968, hereafter *SPE*).[2] Laying out the crucial role of morphological structure in constraining phonological rule application, cyclicity in early generative theory paved the way for the future development of the influential theory of lexical phonology (Mohanan 1986; Kiparsky 1982c, 1985a; inter alia). Current research on the syntax-phonology interface can be seen as further extending our understanding of the nature of domains which constitute complex phonological expressions (Nespor and Vogel 1986; Inkelas and Zec 1990; Kisseberth 1992). From the perspective of current work, it appears an irrefutable truth that phonological rules can be classified and constrained according to the type of structured domain in which they apply.

The principle of cyclic rule application provides a mechanism for identifying phonological rule domains (though as discussed in section 4.4, it offers at best a partial account), but its scope extends beyond the matter of domains, to include questions concerning the abstractness of phonological representation, the use of diacritics to constrain rule application, and the proper application of certain classes of rules, among others. To appreciate the multifaceted set of constraints invoked by the principle of cyclicity, we begin by considering the history and development of the Strict Cycle Condition.

1 SPE

The principle of cyclic rule application is defined in *SPE* as a component of the theory of rule ordering (p. 20). It is argued there that phonological rules appear within a grammar in a strict partial order; for two rules R_1 and R_2, either R_1 precedes R_2, R_2 precedes R_1, or the two rules are unordered (in which case either ordering will produce the correct results).[3] Phonology takes as its input a string with its labeled morphological bracketing. The ordered sequence of rules, $R_1, \ldots, R_n$, applies first to the innermost constituent of a morphologically complex word, the maximal string that contains no brackets, with each rule applying only once. The final rule in the rule sequence, R_n, is a special rule that erases the innermost brackets, as in (1).

(1)   Rule R_n applying on cycle 1: ... $[_2X \, [_1Y]_1Z]_2 \ldots \rightarrow \ldots [_2XYZ]_2 \ldots$

After the inner brackets are erased, the derivation continues with another round of application of the rules $R_1, \ldots, R_n$ applying on the next cycle, which is as before the maximal string that contains no brackets ($[XYZ]$, in our example above). The result of this convention is that each cyclic rule has a chance to apply exactly once on each cycle in the derivation of a word, with the total number of applications for any rule bounded by the maximal depth of the morphological structure.

Evidence for cyclic rule application in the analysis of English stress is adduced in the contrasting pattern of nonprimary stress in the pair of words *còmpĕnsátion, còndènsátion*. In the latter form, stress assigned on the inner cycle *condénse* carries over in the form of a secondary stress on the outer cycle. In contrast, *còmpĕnsátion* has no comparable inner cycle **compénse*, and hence derives no secondary stress on the second syllable on the outer cycle. Instead, the stress rules assign a secondary stress on the first syllable of *còmpensátion*. These two words are in other respects nearly identical in phonological form. The *SPE* analysis of stress derives the different stress patterns of the two words from their differing morphological structures by allowing stress assignment to apply on each morphologically defined cycle.[4]

2   The Strict Cycle Condition (SCC)

In his 1976 thesis on Catalan phonology, Mascaró introduces an important reformulation of the principle of cyclic rule application. Drawing from Chomsky's (1965) proposal of the Strict Cycle Condition (SCC) for syntax, and the extension of that principle into phonology by Kean (1974), Mascaró proposes a set of constraints governing the proper application of cyclic rules. A simplified version of Mascaró's SCC (from Kiparsky 1982a, p. 41) is presented in (2).

(2)   Strict Cycle Condition
   1   Cyclic rules apply only to derived representations.
   2   *Definition*: A representation φ is *derived* w.r.t. rule R in cycle j iff φ meets the structural analysis of R by virtue of a combination of morphemes introduced in cycle j or the application of a phonological rule in cycle j.

The SCC has two principal empirical effects: (1) it prevents a cyclic rule R applying on cycle *j* from reaching back inside an earlier cycle *i* to apply to a string contained wholly within cycle *i* (hereafter referred to as the Reaching Back Constraint); (2) it prevents R from applying to a string contained within a single morpheme (the "derived environment" constraint), except under very special conditions. The cyclic rule R can apply to a monomorphemic string only if that string has been altered by the prior application of another phonological rule. In the literature on lexical phonology (discussed below in section 3), it is assumed that all the cyclic phonological rules precede all the noncyclic rules (those rules not subject to the SCC); the noncyclic rules apply in a single pass to the complete string. Therefore, the only kind of rule that could precede the cyclic rule R would be another cyclic rule, which would itself be subject to the SCC.[5] The effect of the SCC is that cyclic rules typically apply across a morpheme boundary and are prohibited from applying within a morpheme. In fact, the most common argument presented for the cyclic application of a phonological rule is its failure to apply within roots or other monomorphemic environments.

We will consider both parts of the SCC in turn, beginning with the claim that cyclic rules do not reach back inside previous cycles. Consider a language with the cyclic rules in (3), applying in the counterfeeding order $a < b$. These rules applying on a single cycle will map the strings $AD \rightarrow BD$ and $CE \rightarrow DE$. The SCC prevents the two-cycle derivation in (4) mapping $ACE \rightarrow BDE$, where the rule (3a) applies on cycle 2 to a string which is not by any criterion derived on cycle 2. Given the SCC, (3a) would be blocked on cycle 2, or any subsequent cycle.[6]

(3)   (a) $A \rightarrow B / \_\_\_\_D$
      (b) $C \rightarrow D / \_\_\_\_E$

(4)   [ACE]   *cycle 1*
        n/a   (3a)
        [ADE]   (3b)
  [X ADE Y]   *cycle 2*
  [X BDE Y]   (3a)   *SCC violation
        n/a   (3b)

Without the SCC, the counterfeeding or counterbleeding ordering of cyclic rules would be undermined in words with multiple derivational cycles, and so a principle limiting the domain of application of cyclic rules would seem necessary. And yet a review of the literature on cyclic phonology reveals very few arguments which make an explicit appeal to the Reaching Back Constraint of the SCC.[7]

2.1 *The Alternation Condition*

We turn now to consider the motivation for the "derived environment" constraint on cyclic rule application. In his formulation of the SCC, Mascaró builds on a condition proposed by Kiparsky (1968–1973) governing the proper application of neutralization rules. Kiparsky claims that rules that apply without exception (automatically), with the effect of neutralizing a phonemic distinction, must not be allowed to apply to all occurrences of a morpheme. This condition is termed the *Alternation Condition,* and is the precurser to the SCC, as it prohibits analyses in which neutralization rules apply wholly within morphemes, in nonderived environments.

Kiparsky proposes the Alternation Condition as a way of constraining the abstractness of phonological analysis. He raises several strong arguments against the use of diacritics, or the diacritic use of phonological features, as a means of expressing exceptionality in forms that fail to undergo a phonological rule whose structural description is otherwise satisfied. The *SPE* analysis of English Trisyllabic Shortening and early treatments of vowel harmony in Hungarian and Finnish are used to illustrate the objectionable use of diacritics in phonological analysis.

(5) Trisyllabic Shortening
     $V \rightarrow [-\text{long}] / \underline{\quad} C_0 V_i C_0 V_j$, where V_i is not stressed

The *SPE* analysis of English involves a rule of Trisyllabic Shortening (5), which is responsible for the shortening (and subsequent laxing) of stem vowels when certain suffixes are added. It applies to shorten the long stem vowels in *divinity, opacity, tabulate, derivative,* but is somehow blocked from shortening vowels in monomorphemic words like *ivory, nightingale, Omaha.* How is Trisyllabic Shortening to be blocked in monomorphemic words? The SPE analysis involves setting up abstract underlying representations so that these forms no longer satisfy the structural description of Trisyllabic

Shortening; *nightingale* derives from underlying /nixtVngael/, with *ix* → *i* → *ay* by independent rules, and *ivory* is analyzed as bisyllabic /ivory/, with a final glide which vocalizes after Trisyllabic Shortening has applied. In some cases, the underlying representations receive no independent support beyond blocking Trisyllabic Shortening, and hence Kiparsky argues that they involve the diacritic use of phonological features to mark rule exceptionality.

Kiparsky (1982b) notes another problem with Trisyllabic Shortening – many words with invariant short vowels in the environment for Trisyllabic Shortening have ambiguous derivations. Words like *alibi, sycamore, camera, Pamela* can be represented with an underlying short vowel *or* with a long vowel that takes a "free ride," undergoing Trisyllabic Shortening. He observes that "absolute neutralization [as opposed to contextual neutralization—JC] is a consequence of setting up underlying distinctions for the sole purpose of classifying segments into those that do and those that do not meet the structural description of a rule (p. 128)." In this example, the analysis of Trisyllabic Shortening involves neutralization rules such as *ix* → *i* → *ay*, and glide vocalization (*y* → *i*).

The analysis of transparent vowels in Hungarian vowel harmony presents another example where neutralization is necessitated by positing abstract underlying representations.[8] In this system of back harmony, suffix vowels assimilate in backness to root vowels. A class of exceptions to this regular process involves roots with the "transparent" vowels /i, e/. A certain subset of such roots unexpectedly condition back suffix vowels. These pseudo–back vowel roots can be accounted for by positing the abstract back vowels /I, E/, which function regularly in harmony by conditioning back suffix vowels, and are later neutralized by a rule which attributes the feature [–back] to all unrounded non-low vowels.

Kiparsky argues on the basis of sound change that absolute neutralization does not occur in phonological systems. There are no known cases of analogical reversal of absolute neutralization, as there are for contextual neutralization. In order to constrain the use of abstract underlying representations, and the concomitant use of rules of absolute neutralization, Kiparsky formulates the Alternation Condition, as in (6).

(6)   The Alternation Condition
      Obligatory neutralization rules cannot apply to all occurrences of a
      morpheme.

The Alternation Condition constrains underlying representation in several ways. It requires the lexical representation of a nonalternating form to be identical to its surface form (with low-level, automatic phonetic processes factored out); it requires a single underlying representation for distinct morphemes which are always identical in surface form; and it requires morphemes which are always distinct in surface form to have distinct underlying phonological representations. For the analysis of Trisyllabic Shortening, it disallows the abstract underlying representations set up in *SPE* to block the application of the rule in forms like *nightingale*. Kiparsky suggests that the exceptionality of such forms can be achieved through the judicious use of rule features, such as [–Trisyllabic Shortening]. For the Hungarian vowel harmony example, the abstract analysis sketched above is ruled out since it necessitates a rule of absolute neutralization for deriving /i, e/ from /I, E/. An alternative analysis, consistent with the Alternation Condition, requires that all roots with nonalternating neutral vowels bear the same vowels in underlying form. The rule of Vowel Harmony is formulated to take an underlying back suffix vowel and convert it into a front vowel after a front vowel root. Roots with neutral vowels that trigger back suffix vowels are marked as exceptions to Vowel Harmony, and the back suffix vowels that follow are just the underlying suffix vowels.

In a subsequent development the Alternation Condition is modified, resulting in the Revised Alternation Condition (7), which introduces the notion of a "derived environment" as the constraining factor in the application of neutralization rules (Kiparsky 1973b). The Revised Alternation Condition constrains the abstractness of underlying representation by limiting neutralization rules to apply only in environments derived by morphological concatenation and other morphological or phonological processes. Thus, the Revised Alternation Condition blocks Trisyllabic Shortening from applying in the nonderived forms *nightingale, ivory*, as well as ruling out abstract underlying representations containing long vowels in forms like *Pamela, Omaha*. It provides a straightforward way of capturing the generalization that *all* nonderived words fail to undergo Trisyllabic Shortening, without systematically marking such forms as exceptional.[9]

(7) Revised Alternation Condition (RAC):
     Obligatory neutralization rules apply only in derived environments.

Kiparsky (1973b) discusses two rules in support of the Revised Alternation Condition: the Sanskrit rule of *s*-retroflexion (Ruki), and the Finnish rule of Spirantization. The Sanskrit Ruki rule accounts for a regular process by which *s* becomes ṣ following one of the class of Ruki triggers, /r, u, i,/ and velars. Ruki applies regularly across morpheme boundaries (8a), and fails to apply in monomorphemic strings (8b). However, Ruki does apply morpheme-internally when its environment is created by morpho-phonological processes (ablaut, reduplication) affecting root vowels (8c).

(8) (a) 2 sg. /-si/   bi-bhar-ṣi   "you carry"
         aorist /-s/   a-bhaːr-ṣ-am   "I carried"
         future /-sya/   bak-sya-ti   "he will say"
         desid. /-sa/   ni-niːṣa-ti   "he wants to lead"
     (b) kisalaya   "sprout"
         barsa   "tip"
         kusuma   "flower"

(c)   śaːs   "instruct"
        /śas-ta/ → śiṣ-ṭa   "taught"

        vas   "shine"
        /va-vas-us/ → uːṣ-us   "shone"

        ghas   "eat"
        /ja-ghas-anti/ → jakṣati   "they eat"

The Revised Alternation Condition permits Ruki in the morphologically derived forms (8a) as well as the phonologically derived forms (8c), and blocks Ruki in the nonderived environments of (8b). Similarly, in Finnish, the Spirantization rule ($t \rightarrow s$/ ____ i) applies across a morpheme boundary (9a), and in environments derived by Raising ($e \rightarrow i$/ ____ #) (9b), but not in nonderived monomorphemic environments (9c).[10]

(9)   (a)   halut-a   "want"
             halus-i   "wanted"
        (b)   vete-nä   "water" (ess.)
             vesi   "water" (nom.)
        (c)   tila   "place"

It is worthwhile to note that in the two decades of research since the proposal of the Revised Alternation Condition, many examples have been cited in which rules apply only across a morpheme boundary, yet there have been no additional examples in which a derived environment can be created morpheme-internally by the prior application of a phonological rule. The absence of further examples calls into question Kiparsky's definition of "derived environment." If cyclic rules were restricted to *morphologically* derived environments alone, it would be possible to reformulate the SCC as a condition requiring the positive specification of morphological structure, in which case cyclic rules would be those which are lexically governed.

2.2   The SCC in Catalan

We have seen that two independent lines of research resulted in two distinct constraints in phonological theory: (1) the Revised Alternation Condition provides a constraint on the application of neutralization rules that limits the abstractness of phonological analysis, and links underlying representation more closely with surface form in the case of nonalternating morphemes; and (2) Chomsky's condition on cyclic rule application, extended to phonology, prevents cyclic rules from reaching back. Mascaró's (1976) proposal is to merge these two constraints by identifying the class of neutralization rules with the class of cyclic rules. He recognizes that the Revised Alternation Condition's constraint on derived environments has a close connection to the Reaching Back Constraint argued to be required by cyclic rule application. By collapsing neutralizing and cyclic rules into a single class, he can derive the effects of both constraints from a single condition on rule application. Mascaró argues for this position with the analysis of a complex range of phenomena in Catalan phonology. Of the rules he proposes for Catalan, "six are neutralizing and obligatory, and can apply either cyclically or noncyclically . . . The other eight obligatory and neutralizing rules have to be cyclic . . . The remaining rules are optional or non-neutralizing. Neither can [they] be cyclic [*sic*]" (pp. 17–18).

What kind of evidence does Mascaró present for the cyclicity of eight obligatory and neutralizing rules? The most convincing type of argument would involve a rule which must apply on each cycle, does not apply to nonderived (monomorphemic) strings, and for which there is clear evidence of the Reaching Back Constraint. Although Mascaró presents five arguments for the cyclicity of eight phonological rules, no single argument demonstrates the cluster of properties noted above. Cole (1992b) reviews Mascaró's cyclic analyses of Catalan and shows that each argument for cyclicity breaks down under reanalysis of the data. It is argued there that the only rules that may require cyclic application are the metrical rules which assign stress.

In several instances, dropping Mascaró's assumption that stress is underlying in Catalan in favor of a metrical analysis of stress assignment (along the lines of Harris's 1983, 1991 analysis of Spanish) radically alters the nature of the rules which interact with stress. The resulting system no longer provides the rule interactions and rule-ordering paradoxes that lead Mascaró to posit cyclic rule application. Similar results obtain when Mascaró's analysis of obstruent contraction and deletion is replaced with one which incorporates more recent insights into the nature of affricates. The updated rule system is entirely different and does not present the problems that lead Mascaró to propose a cyclic analysis. In other cases, the phonological rules posited by Mascaró are said to be cyclic since they are subject to domain restrictions, such as applying in lexical and phrasal domains, or in word and compound domains. In current phonological theory, there are mechanisms other than cyclicity to establish rule domains, and since the rules in question do not need the cyclic constraints prohibiting "reaching back" or applying in nonderived environments, they do not provide support for the SCC. Cole (1992b) considers these and other factors of Mascaró's cyclic analyses, ultimately rejecting the claim that Catalan provides important empirical support for the SCC. The alternative analyses for the phenomena motivating Mascaró's proposals do not refute the SCC; they merely fall outside of its scope. The only rule which may plausibly have a cyclic application is stress assignment, and there is no evidence that stress assignment in Catalan is affected by the SCC.

In light of these findings, the Catalan data cannot be taken as providing decisive support for the SCC. We must now consider what empirical evidence does constitute support for the SCC. As Kiparsky notes, "the SCC is essential for *any* cyclic phonology, irrespective of those cases [of rules blocked in nonderived representations—JC], in order to permit counterfeeding order among cyclic rules." (1985a, p. 88). Thus, given that cyclic rule application is required for *any* analysis (e.g., English stress), and given that rules may be extrinsically ordered, some principle must prevent cyclic rule application from undermining the ordering of rules within the grammar. It is relevant to note at this point that extrinsic rule ordering itself seems to play less of a role in phonological analysis than it did a decade or two ago, reflecting the general trend to look for explanations in the nature of phonological representation and the constraints that govern it, rather than in the principles of rule organization that dominated much of the early work in generative phonology. We further investigate the empirical basis for the principles of cyclic rule application in sections 5–7, where we review cyclic analyses of a range of phonological phenomena, including stress, syllable structure, and some segmental processes. But before turning to empirical evidence, we complete this historical overview by considering the role of the cycle in the theory of lexical phonology.

3   Lexical Phonology

Lexical phonology is a word-based theory of morphology in which morphology and phonology interact in a component of morphophonological derivation called the lexicon. Its origins lie in Siegel's 1974 proposals for interleaving phonology and morphology, as well as Pesetsky's (1979) cyclic analysis of Russian phonology and Strauss's (1982) work on lexicalist phonology. The theory of lexical phonology is worked out in the 1982 dissertation by K. P. Mohanan (revised in Mohanan 1986), and in the contemporaneous paper "Lexical Morphology and Phonology" of Kiparsky (1982a). A revision of the theory is presented in Kiparsky (1985a).[11] Lexical phonology is based on the idea that some phonological rules apply cyclically, and presents a framework in which the basic principles and constraints of cyclic rule application derive from the model of morphology-phonology interaction.

Kiparsky (1982a) raises three questions that follow from the theory of cyclic phonology, as formulated in Mascaró (1976):

1   Why should there be two types of phonological rules, cyclic and noncyclic?
2   Why should the definition of proper cyclic application have the particular and very complex form it has?
3   What is the *inherent* connection between cyclicity, a property of rule ordering, and the restriction to derived environments? (P. 44)

He argues against Mascaró's proposal to identify the class of cyclic rules with the class of obligatory neutralizing rules, on the basis of several counterexamples. First, Kiparsky notes the existence of cyclic rules which are not neutralizing, and which must apply in nonderived environments, in apparent violation of the SCC. One such example involves the English rules of stress assignment. Kiparsky (1979) and Hayes (1981) present arguments for the cyclic application of the English word stress rules, in addition to the arguments presented in *SPE* (noted above, see also discussion in section 6.1). Yet stress applies on the root cycle, a morphologically nonderived environment. Furthermore, there is no evidence that any other phonological rules precede stress, rules which might create a phonologically derived environment.[12] Thus, in English the stress rules apply in violation of the derived environment constraint of the SCC.

Harris (1983) presents an analysis of Spanish phonology in which he argues that syllabification is cyclic. Syllabification is (universally) obligatory, but not neutralizing, since syllable structure is presumed to be unmarked in underlying representation. In other words, the rules that build syllable structure do not create output that is distinct from other lexical items on the basis of a *lexically* (i.e., phonemically) distinct feature. Harris argues for the cyclicity of syllabification on the basis of its interaction with the rules of Lateral and Nasal Depalatalization. The depalatalization rules are responsible for the alternations ñ → n and λ → *l* in a syllable rhyme, as seen in the forms in (10) (the palatal lateral is represented by orthographic *ll*).

(10) bello   "beautiful"   beldad   "beauty"
      doncella   "lass"   doncel   "lad"
      reñir   "to quarrel"   rencilla   "quarrel"(n.)
      desdeñar   "to disdain"   desdén   "disdain"(n.)

The rules of Lateral and Nasal Depalatalization follow syllabification, since they refer to syllable constituency (the rhyme) in their structural descriptions. Lateral Depalatalization is argued to be a cyclic rule, on the basis of forms like *donce[ll]es* "lads". As shown in (11), on the first cycle, syllabification applies, followed by Lateral Depalatalization, and on the second cycle syllabification applies again, this time placing the derived [l] in onset position. A noncyclic application of Lateral Depalatalization would be bled by syllabification on the second cycle (or with postcyclic syllabification), since the palatal [λ] would be in a syllable onset.

(11) *1st cycle*: [donceλ] → [don.ceλ.] → [don.cel.]
                              syll.   depal.
      2nd cycle: [doncel es] → [don.ce.les.]
                              syll.

The evidence for cyclic Nasal Depalatalization involves a similar example, in which a morpheme-final ñ depalatalizes, even though it is in onset position in the surface form, *desde[n]es* from underlying /desdeñ-es/ "disdains" (n. pl.).

Both Depalatalization rules apply cyclically, but do not themselves violate the SCC, since in each case they apply to the output of syllabification, which Harris claims creates a derived environment for Depalatalization. The analysis requires that syllabification apply cyclically; yet, its application on the root cycle in *donce[l]es* and *desde[n]es* is in clear violation of the derived environment constraint of the SCC.[13]

Kiparsky cites a rule of English phonology as another counterexample to the claim that all obligatory neutralizing rules respect the SCC.

(12)   Velar softening (Kiparsky 1982c, p. 40):

$$k \rightarrow s / \underline{\hspace{1cm}} \begin{bmatrix} - \text{ back} \\ - \text{ low} \end{bmatrix}$$

The rule of Velar Softening (12) is responsible for the *k ~ s* alternation in forms like *electric ~ electricity* and *critic ~ criticize*. Following the analysis of *SPE*, Kiparsky (1982a, p. 40) argues that the same rule applies in the derivation of *conceive, proceed, recite* from underlying /kAn-kiv/, /pro-kid/, and /ri-kayt/, respectively. The two arguments in support of this fairly abstract analysis focus on the exceptional behavior of a very restricted class of bound morphemes in English, and thus lack generalization. If one wants to maintain the *SPE* account, then Velar Softening stands as a neutralizing rule which applies in a nonderived environment, within the stems /kiv, kid, kayt/, in apparent violation of the SCC.[14]

From these four examples – English stress, Spanish syllabification and Aspiration, and English Velar Softening – we may conclude that (1) not all cyclic rules are neutralizing; (2) not all obligatory neutralizing rules apply on each cycle; and (3) not all obligatory, neutralizing rules are subject to the constraints imposed by the SCC.

To resolve these difficulties with Mascaró's analysis of cyclic rules, lexical phonology proposes a reinterpretation of cyclicity. In lexical phonology, morphology and phonology are interleaved in the process of word formation; phonological rules apply to the immediate output of each morphological process (affixation or compounding). For example, the derivation of *illegality* from /iN-legal-ity/ contains three cycles of morphology and phonology, as seen in (13).[15]

(13)   [legal]   *1st cycle*
       [légal]   stress
       [iN [legal]]   *2nd cycle*
       [il [legal]]   assimilation
       [il [légal]]   stress
       [[illegal] ity]   *3rd cycle*
       [[illegál] ity]   stress

In this model, cyclicity does not have to be stipulated; it results automatically from the interleaving of morphological and phonological processes. The details of the theory address the questions of which (if not all) morphological processes are *cyclic*, in that their output is subject to immediate phonological derivation, and which phonological rules apply *lexically*, in the process of word formation. The cyclic phonological rules then are those that apply lexically (in the process of word formation) to the output of the cyclic morphology. The criteria for determining lexical rules and cyclic morphology have changed with the evolution of the theory of lexical phonology. Kiparsky (1982a) claims that all word-formation processes are cyclic, and therefore all lexical phonological rules are intrinsically cyclic. This claim has been greatly revised in later work, as we discuss below.

3.1   Deriving the SCC

The cyclic application of phonological rules to morphological subconstituents of the word derives from the model of how morphology and phonology interact. However, lexical phonology derives not only the notion of cyclic domains, but also the constraints on the proper application of cyclic rules, formerly encoded in the SCC. Kiparsky (1982a, p. 46) argues that every lexical entry constitutes a phonological rule – an identity mapping, $\alpha \rightarrow \alpha$, for every lexical entry $/\alpha/$. The identity rule competes for application with every other phonological rule in the lexical component of the grammar. Thus, in the phonology of English there is an identity rule for *nightingale*, /niːtVngæːl/ → /niːtVngæːl/, which competes against an application of Trisyllabic Shortening producing /niːtVngæːl/ → /nitVngæːl/. The input to both rules is the same, but only one can apply since their outputs are distinct (in this case, mutually exclusive). Kiparsky argues that since both rules belong to the lexical component, they are subject to the Elsewhere Condition, a principle of rule ordering that imposes a disjunctive ordering on two rules whose structural descriptions are overlapping, and whose output is distinct.[16] The Elsewhere Condition states that only the more specific of the two rules will apply. Thus, a lexical identity rule will always take precedence over a lexical phonological rule applying to the same lexical entry, since the identity rule is the most specific (contains the most detailed structural description) of all phonological rules. Given (1) the Elsewhere Condition; (2) lexical identity rules for every lexical entry; and (3) phonological rules assigned to the lexical component, lexical phonology can derive the constraint of the SCC that prevents cyclic (now lexical) rules from applying to underived monomorphemic strings.

In addition to the lexical entries that correspond to root morphemes such as *nightingale*, lexical phonology also maintains that the output of every layer of derivation constitutes a lexical entry. This means that there will be lexical entries for nonderived forms like *topic*, as well as for derived forms like *topical* and *topicality*. Cyclic rules are blocked from "reaching back" by the presence of these derived lexical entries.

To summarize, we have seen that cyclicity in phonology derives from the architecture of morphology-phonology interaction in the lexical phonology model, and the constraints of the SCC derive from the Elsewhere Condition, together with the assumption that lexical entries constitute lexical identity rules. Within this model, rules which apply across word boundaries are outside the scope of lexical derivation. These *post-lexical* rules are not within the lexical component of the grammar. The output of the post-lexical rules do not derive lexical identity rules, and therefore the post-lexical rules are not blocked by the Elsewhere Condition from applying in nonderived environments. So, in lexical phonology only lexical rules apply cyclically, with each step of morphological derivation, and the post-lexical rules apply noncyclically. Similarly, only lexical rules are subject to disjunctive ordering by the Elsewhere Condition, deriving the effects of the SCC, and post-lexical rules apply in an unrestricted ("across-the-board") fashion. This analysis predicts that there is no cyclic iteration of phonological rules at the phrasal level, since the model has no way of deriving cyclic rule application outside of the lexical component. Any attempt to derive an account of post-lexical cyclicity similar to the analysis of lexical cyclicity would involve the bizarre claim that words are inserted into phrase structure one at a time, with phonological rules applying to the output of each step of insertion.

3.2   *Structure-building Rules and the SCC*

Earlier in this section we reviewed four counterexamples from English and Spanish to Mascaró's proposal that cyclic rules are the obligatory, neutralizing rules. In lexical phonology, the cyclic rules are the lexical rules, and there is nothing that requires lexical rules to be neutralizing or obligatory. However, all cyclic rules are subject to the Derived Environment Constraint, now resulting from the Elsewhere Condition. Yet, we have seen that stress assignment in English and syllabification in Spanish must apply cyclically and must apply in the nonderived environment of the root cycle. Kiparsky (1982c, p. 47) argues that rules that assign metrical structure (stress and syllable structure) derive output which are not *distinct* from their input, because they do not bear contradictory feature specifications, or contradictory metrical structure. These *structure-building* rules therefore are not subject to disjunctive ordering with lexical identity rules by the Elsewhere Condition. The Elsewhere Condition applies only in the case of two rules whose input is identical, and whose output is distinct. So, structure-building rules are never blocked by the Elsewhere Condition, and may apply on any lexical cycle. The question arises whether a structure-building rule applying on the root cycle qualifies as creating a derived environment for the further application of *structure-changing* lexical rules. Kiparsky claims that "cyclically derived phonological properties can trigger subsequent rules on the same cycle. Thereby, even feature-changing rules can apply on the first cycle if they are fed by cyclic rules" (Kiparsky 1982c).

In section 4.1, we examine several arguments against the claim that the SCC is derivable from the Elsewhere Condition. In later work, Kiparsky (1985a,

p. 91) rejects this notion, maintaining that only lexical rules that produce *distinct* output create phonologically derived strings. The stricter interpretation of derived environment requires a reanalysis of Spanish Depalatalization, since as it stands, Harris's analysis of Spanish involves the cyclic application of Depalatalization on the root cycle, fed only by cyclic syllabification.[17] Kiparsky suggests instead that Depalatalization applies to palatal /ñ, λ/ in coda position at the word-level. Word-level rules are noncyclic lexical rules applying at the last lexical level of the phonology, not subject to the SCC (discussed further in section 4.2). The word-level Depalatalization rule must be ordered before syllabification, which applies in both the cyclic and noncyclic levels. Under this analysis, the derivation of *doncella* "lass" and *donceles* "lads" proceeds as in (14) (cf., (11)). Note that the noncyclic rules apply after the plural suffix *es* has been added. The plural suffix is not part of Level 1 morphology, which is the cyclic level, and thus does not derive an environment for the application of cyclic rules. Noncyclic lexical rules apply after all noncyclic lexical affixation.

(14) *Cycle 1*:   donceλ   donceλas
      Syllabification   don.ceλ.   don.ce.λas

      Noncyclic: don.ceλ.-es   don.ce.λas
      Depalatalization   don.cel.-es   n/a
      Syllabification   don.ce.les   don.ce.λas

4   Challenges to the Theory of Cyclic Phonology

The formulation of lexical phonology in Mohanan (1986) and Kiparsky (1982a) stands as the strongest, most restrictive formulation. But several claims central to the strong version of lexical phonology are challenged in subsequent work. In this section we consider arguments against the following claims concerning the formal status of cyclicity in the strong version of lexical phonology:

1   The SCC is derived from the Elsewhere Condition.
2   All lexical rules are cyclic.
3   The derived environment constraint applies to all and only cyclic rules.
4   Cyclicity derives from the interleaving of phonology and morphology.

4.1   *Another Look at Deriving the SCC*

Mohanan and Mohanan (1984) argue against the claim that the SCC can be derived from the Elsewhere Condition. In their analysis of Malayalam, they maintain that a single rule can apply in both the lexical and post-lexical components. Therefore, there are not two disjoint sets of phonological rules contained in the lexical and post-lexical modules, but rather a single set of ordered rules, each of which is assigned to some lexical and/or post-lexical domain. In this interpretation, there is no principled explanation for why only lexical rule application should be subject to disjunctive ordering by the Elsewhere Condition. Yet, if the Elsewhere Condition applies uniformly to all phonological rules, then it will have the undesired result that post-lexical rules will be subject to the derived environment constraint. If a post-lexical phonological rule tries to apply to a form which is identical to a lexical entry (either a root form, or a morphologically derived form), and if the post-lexical rule creates a distinct output (is not a structure-building rule), it will be blocked by the Elsewhere Condition, just as lexical rules are.

In a revision to lexical phonology, Kiparsky (1985a) abandons the argument that the SCC is derivable, resorting to an independent stipulation of the SCC in Universal Grammar. This move enables him to formulate analyses of Catalan Nasal Assimilation, Russian consonant voicing, Vata ATR Harmony and Guaraní Nasal Harmony in which a rule applies in both the lexical and post-lexical stages of derivation, subject to the SCC only in its lexical application.

Iverson and Wheeler (1988) also argue against deriving the SCC from the Elsewhere Condition. They argue that beyond the dubious status of Lexical Identity Rules, there is virtually no evidence of phonological rules which require disjunctive application (pp. 331–332). The only possible case involves the English rules which build metrical structure, argued to apply disjunctively in *SPE*. But Kiparsky (1982a, p. 52) presents a reinterpretation of those stress rules which eliminates the need for their disjunctive application.

Iverson and Wheeler maintain that *pace* lexical phonology, the Elsewhere Condition is not required to account for phonological blocking in nonderived environments. Instead, they argue that the Revised Alternation Condition is the appropriate condition to account for phonological blocking, and is independently required even in a theory that has the SCC, in order to prevent abstract analyses involving "free rides." As it stands, the SCC does not prevent potentially neutralizing *noncyclic* rules from applying in nonderived environments. In principle it is not possible to prevent the kind of neutralization that was the focus of the early debate on abstractness – neutralization that is explicitly ruled out by the Revised Alternation Condition. Yet, as Iverson and Wheeler note, including the Revised Alternation Condition in phonological theory makes the SCC wholly unnecessary, at least in its capacity to enforce the derived environment constraint. The only duty left for the SCC is to preserve counterfeeding or counterbleeding order among cyclic rules (the Reaching Back Constraint).[18]

4.2   Noncyclic Lexical Rules

In the strong formulation, lexical phonology maintains that all lexical phonological rules are subject to the SCC. However, this claim is challenged by

Mohanan and Mohanan (1984) and Halle and Mohanan (1985), who argue that there are certain structure-changing lexical rules in English and Malayalam that must apply in the lexicon, yet which violate the SCC by applying in nonderived environments. We have already seen one example in the application of Velar Softening to forms like *receive* from underlying /ri-kiːv/. Another example is the English rule of *n*-Deletion, discussed by Halle and Mohanan, that deletes the syllable-final *n* in a nonderived environment in *damn, hymn,* but does not delete the *n* before Level 1 suffixes, as in *dam[n]ation, hym[n]al.* Thus, *n*-Deletion is a structure-changing rule (as all rules of deletion are) applying in a nonderived environment. If these were all of the facts, we might formulate a post-lexical rule to delete the syllable-final *n*; but there is evidence that the rule in question cannot be post-lexical. Notice that the rule applies in words with inflectional suffixes, such as *damning,* even though at the post-lexical level, the *n* should have been resyllabified into the onset of the following syllable, cf. *dam.na.tion.* Halle and Mohanan propose that *n*-Deletion is in fact a lexical rule, applying at Level 2, before the inflectional suffixes are added. They argue that all Level 2 lexical rules apply noncyclically, exempt from the SCC. For Halle and Mohanan, cyclicity is a property of an individual level, rather than a general property of all lexical rules. Level 1 is argued to be a cyclic level, so all Level 1 phonological rules, like stress assignment and certain lengthening and shortening rules affecting vowels, apply cyclically. Other noncyclic Level 2 rules in English include *g*-Deletion, which applies in a nonderived environment in *long* as well as in *longing* and Velar Softening.[19]

In addition to the work cited above, Booij and Rubach (1987) argue for a set of lexical, noncyclic rules (termed "post-cyclic") in their analysis of Polish phonology. As discussed in section 7.2, the cyclic analysis of Polish *yer* vowels involves a rule of *yer*-Deletion, which deletes any *yer* which is not followed by a *yer* in the next syllable. *Yer*-Deletion feeds Noncontinuant Depalatalization, a rule which is shown not to apply across word boundaries. Therefore, both *yer*-Deletion and Noncontinuant Depalatalization are lexical rules. Yet Booij and Rubach (1987) demonstrate that the cyclic application of *yer*-Deletion cannot derive the output; it would delete nearly every *yer*. The status of cyclic and noncyclic rules in Polish *yer* phonology is discussed in more detail in section 7.2. Further evidence for noncyclic lexical rules is presented by Rubach (1990) in his analysis of German syllabification, reviewed below in section 7.3.

4.3   Cyclicity and the Derived Environment Constraint

The view that only cyclic, lexical rules are subject to the Derived Environment Constraint is brought into question by certain facts from Finnish (Kiparsky 1968–73) and Ondarroan Basque (Hualde 1989). Consider first the Finnish case. As mentioned in section 2.1, Finnish has a rule raising *e* → *i* word-finally.

Raising feeds the rule of Spirantization, $(t \rightarrow s / \underline{\quad} i)$, as seen in the surface form *vesi* "water" (nom.) from underlying *vete*. The Spirantization rule is restricted to apply only in derived environments, as evidenced by monomorphemic forms like *tila* "place", which maintain /t/ preceding /i/. Thus, by the criteria of lexical phonology, Spirantization is a cyclic lexical rule, subject to the SCC. Raising, on the other hand, cannot be a cyclic rule. In the first place, it applies to monomorphemic strings, as in *vesi*. Moreover, even if it did apply cyclically, it would incorrectly apply on the root cycle in every derivation of a form with a root final /e/, such as /vete-nä/, "water" (ess.) deriving *vetinä instead of vetenä.

In lexical phonology, rules that are sensitive to the presence of word boundaries must take place after all affixation, at the word level – the noncyclic level of lexical phonology. The problem here is that the noncyclic word-level rule of Raising must feed the cyclic rule of Spirantization, and yet by hypothesis, the noncyclic word level rules follow all cyclic lexical rules. One solution would be to reject the claim that Spirantization is a cyclic lexical rule. But doing so leaves no explanation for the existence of lexical exceptions to Spirantization. Another solution, discussed by Kenstowicz (1993), is to allow Raising to apply in the cyclic component, but only in the presence of a word boundary. This is possible if we stipulate that word boundaries are inserted as the final step in the lexical derivation, and further, that such insertion suffices to create a derived environment. Under such an analysis, Raising could apply on the cycle created by insertion of the word boundary. Raising would never apply on the root cycle, since at that point the string-final boundary is still a morpheme boundary, which is not sufficient to trigger Raising. While this boundary analysis technically works, it violates the spirit of lexical phonology, which is to eliminate the explicit reference to and manipulation of boundary symbols in the phonology.

A similar problem arises in the analysis of Vowel Assimilation in Ondarroan Basque, as discussed by Hualde (1989). Vowel Assimilation raises $a \rightarrow e$ following an /i/ in the preceding syllable, and applies only at the word boundary, as in *laɣune* "friend", (abs. sg.) from underlying /lagun-a/. As a word-boundary rule, Vowel Assimilation would be ordered in the noncyclic lexical component. Yet, Hualde presents clear evidence that Vowel Assimilation applies only in morphologically derived environments, as seen by monomorphemic forms such as *eliša* "church". Thus, Vowel Assimilation is a noncyclic rule which nonetheless is constrained by the Derived Environment Constraint. Hualde concludes that the Derived Environment Constraint is not an exclusive property of cyclic rules, and suggests that cyclic application and the Derived Environment Constraint constitute independent characteristics of rule application. As with Finnish, the Basque case could be resolved under the assumption that word boundaries are inserted at the end of lexical derivation and create a derived environment for the application of cyclic rules. Then, Vowel Assimilation could be maintained as a cyclic rule, with the SCC accounting for its restriction to apply in derived environments.

4.4 *Bracketing Paradoxes*

The claim in lexical phonology that cyclicity follows from the interleaving of morphology and phonology has as a corollary that the constituency of phonological cycles is determined by morphological constituency. In other words, if phonological rules apply to the output of (a subset of) morphological processes, then the strings that are the input to phonological rules should always constitute well-formed morphological constituents. Unfortunately, the situation appears to be more complicated than this simple prediction affords. Specifically, there are well-documented cases in which a phonological rule applies to a substring containing the morphemes [A B], a part of a larger string ABC, even if the corresponding morphological constituent structure [A [B C]] does not identify [A B] as a well-formed constituent. Such cases are referred to in the literature as "bracketing paradoxes."

Bracketing paradoxes have long been the subject of heated debate in generative phonology. As early as 1974, Siegel discusses the constituency of the form *ungrammaticality*, which has become a classic example of a bracketing paradox in English. Given that *un-* attaches to adjectives but not to nouns, it must attach to the stem before the suffix *-ity* transforms the base adjective into a nominal. The morphological structure must therefore be [[un [grammatical]$_{adj.}$]$_{adj.}$ ity]$_n$. However, this structure is at odds with the structure motivated by phonological considerations. The suffix *-ity* belongs to the "Class 1" affixes, which trigger a stress shift and a host of phonological rules such as Trisyllabic Shortening.[20] The prefix belongs to the "Class 2" affixes, which characteristically do not affect stress and do not trigger the other "Class 1" rules. Siegel observes that Class 1 affixes typically do not attach to Class 2 affixes, a constraint which she explains by ordering Class 1 affixation prior to Class 2 affixation. Thus, on phonological grounds, the constituency of *ungrammaticality* should be [un [[grammatical] ity]$_1$]$_2$, with the Class 1 suffix contained in the inner constituent.

In lexical phonology, the Class 1 affixes are assigned to the cyclic lexical level (or stratum), while Class 2 affixes are assigned to the noncyclic stratum. Each stratum is characterized by different sets of morphological processes, and the cyclic phonological rules are assigned to the cyclic lexical stratum alone. Siegel's ordering principle is encoded in the Stratum Ordering Hypothesis, which maintains that morphological and phonological derivation passes sequentially through the ordered strata. Thus, forms like *ungrammaticality* present ordering paradoxes for lexical phonology as well. As discussed below, the crux of the problem is not in identifying cyclic rules and Class 1 affixes with a single lexical stratum of morpho-phonology, but in maintaining that all cyclic lexical domains occur internal to noncyclic lexical domains.

Bracketing paradoxes are not a special property of English, and examples similar to the English one discussed above have been identified in Russian (Pesetsky 1979), Warlpiri (Nash 1980), Chamorro (Chung 1983), and Indonesian (Cohn 1989). In each case, a problem arises because the cyclic domains of the phonology are not strictly internal to other noncyclic domains, thus creating a mismatch between the morphological and phonological constituency, under the assumptions of stratum ordering. The challenge for lexical phonology is how to derive the necessary phonological constituent while maintaining that phonological and morphological derivation are interleaved. One class of solutions recommends that phonological constituents (cycles) be derived from morphological structure through the optional application of a restructuring operation. Kiparsky (1983), Pesetsky (1985), and Sproat (1985) all present analyses which propose restructuring to account for bracketing paradoxes, although they differ in other details. Thus, the two structures [A [B C]] and [[A B] C] are related by an operation akin to associative rebracketing.

A second approach is taken by Halle and Kenstowicz (1991), who reject the framework of lexical phonology, maintaining that phonology and morphology belong to separate components of the grammar.[21] They claim that the Class 1/ Class 2 distinction is formally encoded by the property of cyclicity, which characterizes both affixes and phonological rules. Cyclic affixes are those which define domains for the application of cyclic phonological rules, whereas noncyclic affixation creates morphological constituents which do not define a domain for cyclic phonological rules. For English, Class 1 affixes like *-ity* are cyclic, and Class 2 affixes like *un-* are not. This proposal does not assert any necessary ordering relationship between the two types of affixes, allowing cyclic and noncyclic affixes to be intermingled.[22] Thus, the phonological component does not need to restructure the morphological form. In the analysis of a form like *ungrammaticality*, the two cyclic domains are "interrupted" by a noncyclic domain which has no affect on the phonological derivation: $[[un[grammatical]_c]_{nc} ity]_c$, where c and nc mark "cyclic" and "noncyclic" constituents, respectively. Halle and Kenstowicz argue that only their analysis can account for ordering paradoxes which involve two suffixes, rather than a prefix and a suffix, as presented by forms like *patentability* . As with *ungrammaticality*, this example has a Class 2 noncyclic affix *-able* internal to the Class 1 cyclic affix *-ity*. However, unlike the previous example, no amount of rebracketing is going to result in a structure in which all cyclic affixes are internal to all noncyclic affixes, without altering the linear order of the affixes. In their analysis, this example goes through the phonology with its morphological structure intact, $[[[patent]_c able]_{nc} ity]_c$.

Halle and Kenstowicz resolve the debate over the analysis of bracketing paradoxes with an analysis in which there is no bracketing paradox at all. It applies not only to the English examples, but also to the case of Russian *yer*-Lowering and Warlpiri. It is of interest to note that their solution would not easily extend to examples of an ordering paradox that involves two cyclic affixes, such as [A [B C]] vs. [[A B] C], where both A and B define cyclic domains for the application of a phonological rule. Klamath appears to be such an example, since in at least some examples phonological structure requires [prefix [root suffix]], while the morphology suggests [[prefix root] suffix]. In the cyclic analyses of Klamath, the cyclic rules must apply in both the prefix and suffix domains.[23] Perhaps a more serious challenge to the Halle and Kenstowicz proposal concerns the existence of "cyclic" domains that are not in any sense derivable from morphological constituent structure by associative restructuring. Cole and Coleman (1992) discuss several such cases which involve, for example, phonological domains such as [Prefixes][Stem], when the morphological constituent structure gives [prefix [prefix [. . . [Stem] . . .]]]. Kisseberth (1992) presents similar examples in his discussion of domains for High tone spread in Xitsonga.

5 Summary: The Theoretical Status of the SCC

In the preceding sections, we have traced the evolution of the principle of cyclic rule application, including the notion of the cyclic domain, the Derived Environment Constraint, and the Reaching Back Constraint. We have seen that some phonological rules apply to constituents, termed *cyclic domains*, which are internal to the word. Cyclic domains are not always isomorphic to morphological constituents, and thus cannot derive from the interleaving of morphology and phonology.

The Derived Environment Constraint, which is responsible for limiting the abstractness of phonological analysis, is supported by the existence of phonological rules which apply only in derived environments. The precise formulation of the Derived Environment Constraint is not clear however, if it must prevent the morpheme internal application of neutralization rules such as Velar Softening that would give rise to unmotivated abstract derivations of, e.g., *city* from underlying /kity/, while still allowing the morpheme internal application in morphologically derived forms such as *receive, proceed*.

In most discussions of cyclic phonology, the rules which are subject to the Derived Environment Constraint are equated with the cyclic rules. However, the Derived Environment Constraint, or a similar domain restriction, is needed for some rules which apply only at word boundaries, as seen in Basque and Finnish. If word-level rules are necessarily noncyclic, then the Derived Environment Constraint must be extended to apply to a subclass of noncyclic rules as well as the cyclic rules. In addition, there are some lexical rules – rules that apply within but not across words – which violate the Derived Environment Constraint, suggesting that not all lexical rules are cyclic.

Finally, structure-building rules such as metrical structure assignment for stress and syllabification are not subject to the Derived Environment Constraint, typically applying in derived and nonderived environments alike.

The second effect of the SCC is termed the *Reaching Back Constraint*; it is required to preserve rule ordering in cyclic derivations. There is no clear empirical support for this constraint.

Based on these findings, it is not clear that the two dimensions of cyclicity – the cyclic domain and the Derived Environment Constraint – are related at all. The arguments concerning the Derived Environment Constraint, abstractness, and domain restrictions for the most part do not overlap with the arguments for the existence of word-internal domains in which some phonological rules apply. This conclusion is even more strongly suggested by recent research on the syntax-phonology interface, which points to the existence of phrase-level domains as an extension of the cyclic domain beyond the lexical level (Inkelas and Zec 1990).

In the sections that follow, we will consider the cyclic analyses of stress systems, syllable related processes, and rule ordering paradoxes that have appeared in the literature of the past two decades. The goal is not only to present an overview of some classic examples of cyclic phonology, but also to examine which aspects of cyclicity arise in the various applications under consideration.

6   Stress Systems

Stress systems provided the basis for the earliest discussions of cyclicity in generative phonology. The stress systems of languages like English, Arabic, and Chamorro also constitute some of the most transparent evidence for cyclic rule application, and thus serve as an excellent place to begin an overview of the empirical evidence for cyclic phonology.

6.1   *English and Chamorro*

SPE argues for the cyclicity of English stress based in part on the contrasting pattern of nonprimary stress in the pair of words *còmpĕnsátion* and *còndènsátion*. The main stress of *condénse* carries over in the form of a secondary stress on the second syllable in the derived form *còndènsátion*, but the stress pattern of the base *cómpĕnsàte* does not produce a second syllable stress in the derived form *còmpĕnsátion*. Halle and Vergnaud (1987a) point to difficulties with the *SPE* analysis in light of two kinds of exceptions. First, words like *àffirmátion*, *cònfirmátion*, *cònsultátion* fail to show a secondary stress on the syllable which is assigned stress in the base forms: *affírm, confírm, consúlt*. Second, nonderived forms like *ìncantátion, òstentátion*, have a pretonic secondary stress which is analogous to the secondary stress in *còndènsátion*, and yet the secondary stress is clearly not derived in such examples.

Halle and Kenstowicz (1991) account for the pattern of secondary stress with the noncyclic Alternator rule, which parses the pretonic string of syllables from left-to-right into binary feet. This rule stresses every other syllable starting with the initial syllable (but avoids placing stress on the syllable immediately preceding the main stress). In some specially marked lexical items, the secondary stress rule is quantity-sensitive – it will always stress a heavy syllable. This explains the secondary stress on the second syllable of *còndènsátion*, *incàntátion*. Words like *còmpĕnsátion* are not marked for the heavy syllable rule, and therefore do not show stress on the second syllable.

Despite the failure of the original argument, it can still be argued that English stress assignment is cyclic. Hammond (1989) presents important new evidence that an inner cycle main stress can surface as a secondary stress in a derived word. He contrasts the pattern of secondary stress on strings of pretonic syllables in derived and nonderived words, demonstrating that the principles which place secondary stress in the nonderived words can be overridden by the presence of an inner cycle stress in derived words. For example, nonderived *Wìnnepesáukee* stresses the first syllable of the pretonic string *LLL*, while the derived form *orìginálity* has stress on the second syllable of a similar pretonic string *LLL*. Hammond argues that the secondary stress of *orìginálity* must be attributed to the main stress of the inner cycle *oríginal*. Hammond's argument is similar to the original argument for cyclic stress in *SPE*; however, while the secondary stress on *còndènsátion* may be attributed to a special noncyclic rule stressing heavy syllables, many of Hammond's examples involve contrasting stress patterns on light syllables. To account for these data, Hammond proposes that inner cycle stresses are preserved in the form of accents that carry over onto subsequent cycles.[24] The preserved inner cycle stress can prevent a light syllable from later undergoing a destressing rule which applies to other light syllables.

The conclusion to be drawn from the evolving analysis of English stress is that the rules assigning secondary stress to a string of pretonic syllables must take into account inner cycle stresses. There is no stress algorithm that could correctly place secondary stress on the basis of the outermost stress domain alone, as seen by the contrast in *Wìnnepesáukee* and *orìginálity*.

A parallel argument for cyclic stress assignment comes from the analysis of Chamorro. Chung (1983) argues that the distribution of secondary stress in morphologically derived words requires cyclic stress assignment. Stress is regularly assigned to the penult, or antepenult in words with a final extrametrical syllable (15a), and shifts rightward under suffixation (15b).

(15) (a) kítan   "cross-eyed"   aságwa   "spouse"
          púgwaʔ   "betel nut"   inéksaʔ   "cooked rice"
          inéŋŋuluʔ   "peeping"   dáŋkulu   "big"
      (b) nána   "mother"   nanáhu   "my mother"
          gúmaʔ   "house"   gumáʔmu   "your (sg.) house"
          dáŋkulu   "big"   daŋkulónña   "bigger"

The forms in (16) show that the stress assigned on the inner cycle is realized as a secondary stress. The placement of these secondary stresses could not be achieved by any general parsing of the pretonic syllables on the outer cycle, since their position varies depending on the number of syllables and the presence of a final extrametrical syllable in the inner cycle.

(16) (a) swéddu   "salary"   (b) swèddunmámi "our (excl.) salary"
        inéŋŋulu? "peeping"   inèŋŋulu?níha "his peeping"

Halle and Vergnaud (1987a) analyze these facts by assigning stress on every cycle, and copying over each inner cycle stress as secondary stress, subject to Stress Clash avoidance, which disallows a secondary stress immediately preceding a primary stress: *gúma?*, *gumá?-mu*, **gùmá?-mu*.

In considering the role of the cycle in accounting for the stress patterns of Chamorro and English, it is useful to distinguish two aspects of cyclic rule application. First, cyclic rules are subject to the SCC, which enforces both the Reaching Back Constraint and the Derived Environment Constraint. Cyclic analyses of stress assignment in English and Chamorro maintain that the parsing of stress feet is unaffected by structure assigned on previous cycles. The entire string is parsed, including those elements which are wholly contained on an inner cycle. Clearly for these analyses, cyclic stress assignment is not governed by the prohibition on "reaching back." As for the Derived Environment Constraint, stress rules clearly do apply on the root cycle and in nonderived words. The fact that stress rules are structure building provides a plausible explanation for their apparent violation of these two constraints, as discussed above in section 3.2.

The second aspect of cyclic rule application concerns cyclic domains. Cyclic rules may apply in domains which are substrings of the entire word, where the domains correspond to morphological constituents, and the derivation of an inner cycle domain *precedes* the derivation of an outer cycle domain. In other words, cyclic derivation is sequential, proceeding from the innermost to the outermost cycle. The sequential analysis of cyclic domains sets the stage for potential feeding and bleeding effects between each successive stage in the cyclic derivation. Moreover, in the (revised) lexical phonology view of cyclicity, cyclic derivation precedes the application of lexical, noncyclic (= post-cyclic) rules, giving rise to further opportunities for feeding and bleeding interaction between cyclic and noncyclic rules. The analyses of stress in English and Chamorro reviewed here provide clear evidence for the notion of a cyclic domain; however, since cyclic stress is calculated from scratch on each cycle, they do not support the need for a sequential derivation of cyclic domains. As for the ordering of cyclic and noncyclic derivation, there is evidence from the secondary stress systems of both languages that all the cyclic stresses play a role in constraining a subsequent, noncyclic rule of secondary stress assignment, supporting the view that cyclic derivation precedes noncyclic derivation.

In Chamorro, in addition to the secondary stresses that derive from inner cycle stress, there is a rule assigning secondary stress to alternating syllables from left to right, as in the monomorphemic word *pùtamunéda* "wallet". The Alternator rule is also subject to the condition on Stress Clash, accounting for the absence of secondary stress on the third syllable of *pùtamunéda*. Note that an inner cycle stress has the same affect as the outer cycle main stress in preventing the preceding syllable from bearing a secondary stress by the

Alternator stress rule. Thus, in *inèŋŋuluʔ-níha*, the secondary stress on the second syllable, derived from the inner cycle *inéŋŋuluʔ*, blocks the assignment of additional secondary stresses on the first syllable. The Alternator rule for English proposed by Halle and Kenstowicz is also sensitive to the presence of inner cycle stresses, as noted above.

To account for the bleeding relation between the cyclic and noncyclic stress rules in English and Chamorro, the analyses reviewed here assume a derivation in which cyclic rules precede the noncyclic lexical rules. They also assume that the cyclic derivation is sequential, although without direct empirical support. Cole (1992a) explores analyses of English and Chamorro in a nonderivational, constraint-based approach to phonology. Allowing the stress-assigning rules to apply simultaneously within each cyclic stress domain, blind to the stress assigned in any other domain, is shown to overgenerate stress. The overgeneration can be resolved in a number of ways. For instance, independent stress rules can simultaneously mark a syllable as a stressed position and an unstressed position, in which case a ranking defined over the set of phonological rules (or principles) determines which rule wins.[25] Alternatively, in a dynamic, network-based model such as that proposed by Goldsmith (1992a, in press), stress assigned to individual syllables exerts a negative stress influence on adjacent syllables, with the final stress values reflecting the harmonic balance achieved by the system as it attempts to optimize each principle of stress assignment.

In any nonderivational approach to cyclic stress in English and Chamorro, there must be some way of encoding the fact that the stress assigned on the outermost cyclic domain is dominant, and the only cyclic stress which is realized as primary. This is trivial for English, in which each successive cycle causes stress to shift to the right; it suffices to promote the rightmost stress in a string of cyclic stresses to primary, leaving the rest as secondary. The situation is more complex in Chamorro. Whereas cyclic suffixes cause stress to shift to the right (15b), cyclic prefixes cause stress to shift to the left: *bátku* "ship", *míbàtku* "abounding in ships", and *mìbatkónña* "more abounding in ships". Cole (1992a) observes that a directional account of stress shift will not suffice for Chamorro; both the traditional and the nonderivational cyclic accounts of stress must stipulate that the prefix cycle derives stress on the prefix (perhaps by a special stress accent on the prefix itself), and that the stress derived on the outermost cycle is designated as primary.

Goldsmith (1990) presents a different sort of argument for cyclic stress in English. He observes a prohibition on the attachment of Level 2 suffixes when suffixation would derive a stress clash across the # juncture. This constraint explains the absence of forms such as **cartóon#ístic, *escáp#ístic, *alárm#ístic* (cf., *fátal#ístic, régal#ístic*) as well as **fáll#íze, *magazíne#íze* (cf., *wínter#íze, jóurnal#íze*). Under Goldsmith's account, it is crucial that stress be assigned to the stem to which the Level 2 suffix attaches. Note also that these data provide counterevidence to the strict level-ordering hypothesis: the Level 1 suffix *-ic* attaches outside the Level 2 suffix -*ist*.[26] Thus, in the derivation of fátal#íst + ic stress must be allowed to apply cyclically to the stem [fátal] prior to Level 2 suffixation, and again on the subsequent cyclic domain [fatalístic].

6.2   Spanish Stress

English and Chamorro present rather transparent evidence for cyclic stress assignment; the inner cycle stress may surface as a secondary stress, which is nonetheless distinct from the secondary stress assigned by the Alternator rule. Spanish presents less direct, but equally compelling evidence for the assignment of stress within a cyclic domain that comprises an internal morphological constituent of the word. Harris (1969) argues for cyclic stress assignment on the basis of the interaction between stress and the rule of Diphthongization.[27] Certain roots contain a mid vowel which surfaces as a diphthong under stress, as in (17).

(17)   cont-á-ba   "he counted"   c[ué]nt-a   "he counts"
       neg-á-ba   "he denied"   n[ié]g-a   "he denies"
       pens-ámos   "we think"   p[ié]ns-o   "I think"
       solt-ámos   "we release"   s[ué]lt-o   "I release"

In addition to the forms with stressed diphthongs, some words surface with diphthongs which are not stressed. Contrast the forms in (18b) with (18a) and (18c).

(18)   (a)   b[ué]n-o   "good"   m[ié]l   "honey"
      (b)   b[ue]n-ísimo   "very good"   m[ie]l-ecíta "honey" (dim.)
      (c)   b[o]n-dád   "goodness"   m[e]l-óso   "like honey"

The analysis of these data proposed in Halle, Harris, and Vergnaud (1991) is summarized here. The forms in (18a) show the regular diphthongization under stress seen in (17). The (18c) forms are accounted for under the assumptions that the suffixes /-dad/, /-oso/ define cyclic domains, and stress is assigned from scratch on each cycle, i.e., inner cycle stresses are not carried over to subsequent cycles. When the cyclic suffixes /-dad/, /-oso/ are added, stress assignment stresses the suffix vowel and not the root vowel. A noncyclic rule of Diphthongization is formulated, affecting only those non-low vowels which are stressed in the input to noncyclic derivation, i.e., stressed on the outermost cycle. Halle, Harris, and Vergnaud (1991) suggest that the difference between (18b) and (18c) has to do with the cyclic status of the suffixes. They propose that the suffixes in (18b) are noncyclic, which means that on the outermost cyclic domain the underlying non-low root vowels are stressed, yielding *bón*, *mél*. However, the stress rules are allowed to apply again in the noncyclic stratum, where stress is assigned to the suffix vowels, yielding *bónísimo, mélecíta.*[28] Only the rightmost stress in a word is realized, which is accomplished by a special process of conflation that has the effect of deleting all but the rightmost primary stress in a word.[29] Noncyclic Dipthongization is crucially ordered before the conflation process eliminates the stress on the root vowel.

The analysis of stress and diphthongization reviewed here relies crucially on the identification of a cyclic domain internal to the word. Although the formalism employed in this analysis gives rise to word structures with multiple, nested cyclic domains, only the stress assigned to the outermost domain can trigger Diphthongization. These data do not provide evidence for the sequential derivation of cyclic domains; in fact, all of the surface forms can be derived with cyclic stress assignment in the final cyclic domain alone. The analysis also requires a distinction between cyclic and noncyclic stress assignment, with the rule of Diphthongization ordered in between. Thus, as we saw for English and Chamorro, the cyclic derivation precedes the noncyclic derivation, with cyclic stress feeding noncyclic Diphthongization in Spanish.[30]

6.3 *Palestinian Arabic*

Palestinian Arabic provides evidence for word-internal cyclic stress domains that is entirely parallel to the Spanish data seen above. As noted by Brame (1974), in the first discussion of cyclic stress to follow *SPE*, the application of a syncope rule deleting unstressed vowels is sensitive to the presence of stress assigned on a cyclic domain, even when the cyclic stress fails to be realized on the surface. The syncope rule in question deletes an unstressed high vowel in a nonfinal open syllable, as seen in the paradigm in (19).

(19) (a) fíhim   "he understood"
     (b) fíhm-u   "they understood"
     (c) fhím-ti   "you (sg.f.em.) understood"
     (d) fhím-na   "we understood"

A consonant-initial subject suffix causes stress to shift rightward onto a heavy penult, as in (19c, d), from underlying *fihim-CV*. A vowel initial suffix does not create a heavy penult, and stress is assigned to the antepenult (19b). Taking stress shift to be a property of cyclic affixes, Halle and Kenstowicz (1991) propose that the subject suffixes are cyclic. The derivation of the forms in (19b, c) involves two cyclic domains (e.g., [[fihim] na]), but only the outermost cyclic stress is preserved.

Brame notes an interesting difference in the application of syncope in words with subject markers and words with object markers. For example, the 1pl. suffix *-na* is used both as a subject suffix and an object clitic, as in underlying *fihim+na* "we understood" and *fihim#na* "he understood us". Yet only the subject suffix induces syncope, giving rise to *fhímna*, as opposed to the form with the object clitic, *fihímna*, where syncope fails to apply. Note that stress shifts rightward with both the subject suffix and the object clitic. Halle and Kenstowicz present the following analysis. The subject suffixes are cyclic, and therefore trigger the cyclic application of the stress rules. The object clitics are noncyclic; when they attach to a stem the resulting constituent is a noncyclic phonological domain. Stress applies in the cyclic as well as the noncyclic phonology, and so after cliticization of the object suffixes, stress will shift to the right, as it does with the subject suffixes. Syncope applies noncyclically, but before the noncyclic assignment of stress. It deletes a high vowel that is unstressed as it enters the noncyclic derivation. In other words, Syncope deletes a high vowel which is not stressed by the cyclic stress rules applying on the outermost cycle. The form *fihim+na*, with a cyclic subject suffix, emerges from the cyclic derivation as *[fihím na]*. The noncyclic Syncope rule then deletes the initial vowel, yielding *fhímna*. In contrast, *fihim#na*, with a noncyclic object clitic, emerges from the cyclic derivation as *[fíhim]*. Addition of the clitic produces *[[fíhim] na]*. Syncope cannot apply to the first vowel, since it still bears the cyclic stress. Noncyclic stress assignment then applies, yielding *[[fíhím] na]*. As in the analysis of Spanish, all but the rightmost stress is deleted by the process of conflation, resulting in the correct surface form, *fihímna*.

As with Spanish, the contrast between object and subject markers in the application of syncope is achieved by distinguishing cyclic and noncyclic stress assignment, and by recognizing a cyclic domain which is internal to the word. Again, only the outermost cycle is relevant for determining the placement of surface stress, and only the outermost cyclic stress is seen to have the effect of protecting a high vowel from undergoing syncope. As with Chamorro, English, and Spanish, the cyclic analysis of the Palestinian data requires that cyclic derivation precede noncyclic derivation; in this case cyclic stress assignment may bleed noncyclic Syncope.

6.4   Vedic Sanskrit

Cyclicity has been invoked to account for the stress systems in a variety of languages with lexical stress, such as Vedic Sanskrit, Russian, and Lithuanian. These are languages in which stress "accent" is a contrastive feature within classes of morphemes. Accented morphemes are strong (or dominant) and attract stress, while unaccented morphemes are weak (or recessive) and typically receive stress only in strings which contain no strong morphemes. Below we sketch the cyclic analysis of the dominant/recessive contrast in Vedic Sanskrit proposed by Halle and Mohanan (1985).[31]

Morphemes in Vedic are divided into four categories by the features Dominant/Recessive and Accented/Unaccented (Halle and Mohanan 1985; Halle and Vergnaud 1987a). Dominant suffixes neutralize the lexical accent on any preceding morpheme, including the stem. Recessive suffixes do not affect the accentual properties of the stem. Both Dominant and Recessive suffixes may themselves bear lexical accent. The surface stress patterns are given in (20).

Dominant suffixes are marked *D*, Recessive suffixes are *R*, and lexical accent is marked with an asterisk.

(20)   Stress patterns in words with Dominant suffixes
      underlying: SDD*   SD*D   Ś*DD*   Ś*DD   SD*D   SDDR
      surface: SDD́   SDD́   SDD́   ŚDD   ŚDD   ŚDDR

The patterns in (20) can be summarized as follows: in the [Stem D ... D] domain, the rightmost vowel is stressed if it is accented. (Note that the *D* suffixes are always internal to the *R* suffixes.) If the final vowel is not accented, the (leftmost vowel of the) stem is stressed. Stress is assigned to a *R* suffix in the [Stem ... R] domain only if there is no accented Stem or *D* suffix present, as shown in (21).

(21)   underlying: SRR   SRR*   SR*R   S*RR
      surface: ŚRR   SRŔ   SŔR   ŚRR

Halle and Mohanan argue that the *D* suffixes are cyclic. Within a cyclic domain, the leftmost accented element is stressed. Since a new metrical grid is constructed on each cyclic domain, disregarding any accent and metrical structure on inner cyclic domains, only the accent of the outermost *D* will be stressed. If the outermost *D* is not accented, the stress is placed by default on the leftmost vowel of the stem. In contrast, the *R* suffixes are not cyclic, and do not delete accent from the prior cyclic domain. The stress rule applies again in the noncyclic derivation, assigning stress to the leftmost accented element. It follows that an accented *R* suffix will get stressed only when it is the leftmost accented element, i.e., when there is no *D* suffix or accented stem preceding.[32]

The essential property of the Vedic Sanskrit stress system is that stress must be assigned within the domain defined by the last *D* suffix: [S ... D], as noted in Cole (1990). In the cyclic analysis sketched above, every *D* suffix defines a domain for stress assignment, although in fact it is only the outermost cyclic stress that surfaces. Thus, as we saw in the cases of Spanish and Arabic above, it is essential that stress apply in a "cyclic" domain which is internal to the word, and which is defined in terms of morphological structure. Outside of this domain, stress may apply again, in the larger noncyclic domain. In Spanish and Arabic, the noncyclic application of stress has the effect of eliminating the stress assigned to the cyclic domain (via conflation of metrical structure), although traces of the cyclic stress remain elsewhere in the phonology. On the other hand, in Vedic Sanskrit the stress assigned in the noncyclic domain is in essence eliminated in favor of the cyclic stress (again, by conflation).

6.5   Diyari

As we noted in the discussion of Vedic Sanskrit, stress assignment can be sensitive to accentual properties of individual morphemes. Morphology also plays a role in the stress system of Diyari (Austin 1981), though in a manner different from that of Vedic Sanskrit. Diyari is argued by Poser (1989) to require cyclic stress assignment. The facts are quite simply described: stress is placed on odd numbered syllables counting from the left (reflecting a binary, left-headed foot parsed left-to-right), with the exclusion that an odd-numbered final syllable is not stressed (reflecting a defooting of degenerate feet). The leftmost stress in a word is primary. The peculiar aspect of the system is that each morpheme must count as an independent stress domain. Some examples are seen in (22).

(22) ŋándawàlka+tàda   "to close"+pass.
      púluru+ni+máta   "mud"+loc.+ident.
      yákalka+yìrpa+màli+na   "ask"+ben.+recip.+part.

Poser (1989) rejects the possibility that the morpheme is indeed the stress domain in Diyari, noting that in "all known theories of rule application . . . non-root morphemes are not permitted to serve as domains of rule application" (p. 120). He also argues that it is not possible to view every morpheme in Diyari as an independent root or word, since the suffix morphemes do not independently meet either lexical or phonological requirements for word status; many of the suffixes are bound morphemes, and do not independently satisfy phonotactic conditions on syllable structure that hold of words (e.g., they have initial consonant clusters that are not well-formed syllable onsets). Thus, he concludes that stress must be assigned on every cycle, but with the property that it does not alter the metrical structure assigned on any internal cycle. Poser's analysis of cyclic stress is directly opposed to the Halle and Vergnaud (1987a) analysis, in which cyclic stress erases all inner cycle metrical structure.[33] Halle and Vergnaud discuss Diyari, and in light of their treatment of cyclic stress, are forced to accept the morpheme as the stress domain in their analysis.[34]

The issue of cyclicity in the analysis of Diyari stress is addressed again by Idsardi (1992), who presents an extension of the Halle and Vergnaud theory of the metrical grid (see chap. 11). Idsardi allows metrical rules to introduce the boundary symbols that define stress feet, which are later incorporated into the metrical parse of a string. In the case of Diyari, Idsardi proposes that each morpheme projects a left boundary at its left edge onto the metrical grid. These boundaries then serve as the basis for the noncyclic rule of constituent construction, which matches each left boundary with a right boundary to construct a bounded foot. Idsardi gives the derivation in (23).

(23) Project   (x x x   (x x   (x x   (x
      Lex. Edges: yakalka- yirpa-   mali-   na
      Construct   (x x) x   (x x)   (x x)   (x
      Feet: yakalka- yirpa-   mali-   na

Mark	x	x	x	x
Heads:	(x x) x	(x x)	(x x)	(x
	yakalka-	yirpa-	mali-	na

Although the final morpheme projects a left metrical boundary, that boundary does not initiate a foot, since there are not enough syllables following to create a full binary foot. Unmatched, extra boundaries are later deleted, which has the effect of "defooting" all degenerate feet.

By introducing foot boundaries directly on the basis of morphological structure, Idsardi is able to derive all the surface forms without cyclic stress assignment. The projected boundaries allow feet to be constructed without necessarily parsing an entire string, or even a cyclic substring of the word. In the cyclic analysis, the only way to construct a metrical foot is to parse a string, which for Diyari entails parsing each morpheme individually.

Idsardi's analysis relies on the direct manipulation of boundary symbols, a device that is rejected in much post-SPE work (c.f., Siegel 1974). However, the desired effects of aligning a morpheme boundary with a stress foot boundary can be attained without direct reference to boundary symbols, through the mechanism of a constraint which aligns morphological and prosodic constituents, as discussed in McCarthy and Prince (1993b).

6.6 *Interior Salish*

Idsardi's proposal to allow morphemes to project boundaries onto the metrical grid provides an elegant solution to another class of lexical stress systems, which like Vedic Sanskrit, have been argued to require cyclic stress assignment.

Idsardi (1991, 1992) discusses the stress systems of several Interior Salish languages. Like Vedic Sanskrit, they manifest a contrast between dominant ("strong") and recessive ("weak") morphemes. However, the Interior Salish systems are somewhat simpler, in that all dominant morphemes appear to fall into a single class; they uniformly attract stress, behaving like the *accented* dominant suffixes of Vedic Sanskrit. Czaykowska-Higgins (1993) discusses in detail the stress system of Moses-Columbian Salish, noting the similarity between that system and Vedic Sanskrit. She provides a cyclic analysis of Moses-Columbian which parallels the cyclic analysis of Vedic, with one important difference – recessive and dominant suffixes are freely interspersed. Nonetheless, the generalization remains that stress is assigned to the rightmost dominant (= cyclic) suffix. Idsardi shows that it is possible to capture the dominant/recessive distinction in Moses-Columbian, as well as in other Interior Salish languages, under the proposal that dominant morphemes project metrical boundaries, without requiring that stress assignment apply in cyclic domains.

Idsardi's analyses of Interior Salish languages show that the property of stress shift under affixation can be accounted for in a principled metrical theory that allows direct insertion of foot boundaries. Thus, it can no longer be considered valid to equate stress shift with cyclic affixation. However, this does not imply that all cases of stress shift can be reduced to morphologically governed rules inserting metrical boundaries. In particular, the analysis of Vedic Sanskrit within Idsardi's framework would still seem to require that the rules of metrical constituent construction apply within the (outermost) cyclic domain [S . . . D] prior to applying in the larger domain [S . . . (D) . . . R]. Idsardi's approach allows for a simplification of the apparent stress-deleting property of the *D* suffixes within the cyclic domain in Vedic Sanskrit, but it does not entirely eliminate the need to identify such a domain.

6.7 *Summary*

The stress systems of English, Chamorro, Spanish, and Palestinian all demonstrate the need to identify word-internal domains for the application of stress rules. In English and Chamorro, the structure of cyclic domains is recursive, with evidence that stress is assigned on each nested domain. In Spanish and Palestinian, however, there is evidence only for stress assignment on the outermost cyclic domain. Important to the analysis of all four systems, the cyclic application of stress assignment can restrict the application of rules applying in the noncyclic domain, suggesting a sequenced derivation in which cyclic derivation precedes noncyclic derivation.

Domain restrictions are one indication of cyclic rules. Other signs of a cyclic rule are the restriction to apply only in a derived environment and the prohibition on "reaching back" to affect material contained on an inner cycle, both the result of the SCC. The stress systems considered here do not appear to be subject to either of the SCC constraints.

From the discussion of Diyari and the lexical stress/accent systems, it is clear that cyclicity cannot be deduced on the basis of stress shift or morphological domains alone. In particular, allowing lexically specified metrical boundaries to define stress feet eliminates the need for cyclic stress assignment in Diyari and Interior Salish languages. This approach raises the interesting possibility of defining cyclic domains on the basis of lexically specified domain boundaries, such as has been suggested in Kisseberth's (1992) analysis of Xitsonga tone.

7 Syllable-related Processes

In this section I review evidence from English, Polish, and German for the cyclic application of syllable-related processes.

7.1 *English: Level 1 Phonology*

There is a class of rules of English phonology which apply in a morphologically restricted domain; they apply to stems derived by Level 1 affixation, but fail to apply to Level 2 stems. Largely on this basis, rules such as Trisyllabic Shortening, Closed Syllable Shortening, *m*-Deletion, and *g*-Deletion have been said to apply cyclically, in Level 1 of the lexical phonology. In this section I briefly review the behavior of several rules with domain restrictions, concluding that while the domain restriction is necessary, there is no other strong evidence of cyclic rule application.

Kiparsky (1982a) argues for the cyclic application of the Trisyllabic and Closed Syllable Shortening rules on the basis of two observations: (1) they are triggered by Level 1 suffixes and not by Level 2 suffixes (*provŏc-ative* vs. *hȳphen-ate*, *clĕanse* vs. *clēanly*); (2) they do not apply morpheme-internally (*Ŏberon*, *stēvedore*). The Level 1 restriction renders the shortening rules cyclic only because Level 1 is argued to be the (only) cyclic level of the lexical phonology; stress assignment, which is independently argued to be cyclic, applies in each Level 1 domain. In contrast, no known cyclic rules like stress assignment apply in Level 2 domains, which leads to the claim that Level 2 is uniformly noncyclic. The existence of nonderived lexical exceptions to shortening follows from cyclicity, since individual morphemes would not constitute a derived environment in which the shortening rules, subject to the SCC, could apply.

Myers (1987) proposes a reanalysis of the shortening facts in which Trisyllabic Shortening and Closed Syllable Shortening both result from a general constraint on syllable structure that prohibits long vowels from occurring in closed syllables in roots and stems with Level 1 affixes.[35] Shortening occurs because the syllabification rules can license only a single V-position (or mora) of an underlying long vowel when it occurs in a closed syllable. The unlicensed V-position is later stray-erased. To account for the failure of shortening with Level 2 suffixes, Myers proposes a domain restriction that limits the licensing condition on long vowels to bare roots and stems derived from Level 1 suffixation. For Myers, the domain restriction does not follow from cyclicity.

Myers argues that the restriction on the licensing of long vowels reflects a fundamental generalization about English roots; like Kiparsky, he notes that most monomorphemic words do in fact conform to the vowel length patterns predicted by the shortening rules.[36] In Myers's analysis, vowel "shortening" (which is now properly stray erasure of an unlicensed vowel position) is not restricted to derived environments, although he acknowledges that there are a moderate number of exceptional morphemes in which long vowels do occur in closed syllables. As Sainz (1992) notes in her critical review of cyclicity in English phonology, the list of exceptions to shortening include "a large number of proper names of foreign origin, rare or archaic words, and unassimilated loan words: just the sort of words one expects to be exceptional" (p. 182).[37] Thus, rather than treat forms like *Oberon* and *stevedore* as regular forms which reflect the derived environment restriction on a cyclic shortening rule, Myers chooses to treat them as exceptional. The only remnant of cyclicity in his analysis lies in the domain restriction of the syllable licensing constraint on long vowels. Simply put, while shortening is restricted to certain morphological domains, it does not exhibit any of the effects of the SCC, such as the Derived Environment or Reaching Back Constraints.

Domain restriction is a property of another class of so-called cyclic Level 1 rules of English involving syllable structure. As discussed by Borowsky (1986), the rules deleting a stem-final nasal in *damn* (cf., *damnation*) and *g* in *sign* (cf., *signature*) can be reformulated as the effects of stray erasure on unsyllabified segments, if bare roots and Level 1 stems count as domains for syllabification. Syllabification of *sign* or *damn* cannot incorporate the stem-final consonant cluster into the rhyme without violating the Sonority Sequencing Constraint. The examples differ in which of the two consonants in the cluster gets incorporated into syllable structure. Addition of a Level 1 vowel-initial suffix takes the second consonant of each cluster as the onset of the suffixal syllable (*sig.na.ture, dam.na.tion*). As with shortening, Level 2 vowel-initial suffixes do not have the same effect, and "deletion" still applies (*si(g)ning, dam(n)ing*). The behavior of Level 2 suffixes is accounted for if there is an inner suffixation domain, with stray deletion applying on that inner domain prior to syllabification on the outer "Level 2" domain. Like the shortening rules, the deletion rules show no evidence of being constrained by the SCC, and thus behave cyclically only in their domain restriction.

7.2   *Polish*

There are two independent lines of argument for the cyclic application of certain rules of Polish phonology. One concerns the treatment of the abstract *yer* vowels, and the other concerns a class of rules which apply only in derived environments. The latter type of argument is presented in Rubach and Booij (1990) in their discussion of Polish syllable structure. They argue for the cyclicity of certain phonological rules (syllabification, Comparative Allomorphy, Iotation) on the grounds that they are ordered before other rules (Coronal Palatalization, *j*-Deletion), which apply only in derived environments. The latter rules are argued to be cyclic, since the Derived Environment Constraint applies only to cyclic rules.[38] Under all versions of cyclic or lexical phonology, the cyclic rules apply in one block prior to the application of the noncyclic rules. Therefore, any rule which precedes a known cyclic rule must itself be cyclic. Rubach and Booij offer no evidence for the cyclicity of the earlier rules beyond their ordering with respect to Coronal Palatalization and *j*-Deletion. This argument for cyclicity is therefore rather indirect, resting entirely on the soundness of equating the Derived Environment Constraint with cyclic rule application, and on the necessity of ordering all rules subject to the Derived Environment Constraint in a single block.[39]

The behavior of yer vowels provides evidence for phonological rules applying in morphologically defined domains, as we have seen above in the analysis of several English syllable-dependent processes. Like the English examples, the analysis of Polish yers does not require either of the two constraints imposed by the SCC (the Derived Environment Constraint and the Reaching Back Constraint).

A fundamental characteristic of Polish, and one it shares with other Slavic languages such as Russian (Lightner 1965; Pesetsky 1979; Farina 1991) and Slovak (Kenstowicz and Rubach 1987), is the occurrence of vowels which alternate with Ø in certain environments, e.g., *pi[e]s* "dog" (nom.) vs. *ps-a* "dog" (gen. sg.), and *m[e]ch* "moss" (nom.) vs. *mx-u* "moss" (gen. sg.). Traditionally, the vowels underlying this type of alternation are analyzed as abstract high lax vowels /ĭ, ў/, which are either deleted or neutralized with their mid vowel counterparts by a rule called Lower. Lower applies to a *yer* only when it is followed by another yer in the next syllable, and all yers not subject to Lower are subsequently deleted. In the examples above, Lower applies to the stem *yer* in the nominative forms because of the presence of a yer in the nominative suffix /-ĭ/:/pĭs-ĭ/ → [p'es] and /mĭx-ĭ/ → [mex]. The genitive singular suffix contains no yers to trigger lowering of the stem yers, which subsequently delete.[40]

Rubach (1981) has suggested that the cyclic application of Lower accounts for the failure of Lower to apply in some prefixed forms.[41] For example, the adjective *bezdenny* "bottomless" is derived from underlying /bezĭ-dĭn-ĭnĭ/ with three yer vowels (*bezĭ-* "without", *dĭn* "bottom", *-ĭn* adj.). If yer Lower were to apply to the entire string, it should lower all but the last yer, resulting in **bezedenni*. In order to prevent the first yer from undergoing lower, the cyclic analysis derives the unprefixed form *denny* first: /dĭn-ĭnĭ/ → /den-ĭnĭ/. Lower gets another chance to apply on the next cycle, when the prefix is attached, but since there is no longer a yer in the syllable following the prefix yer, it cannot undergo lowering. Instead, the noncyclic, lexical rule of *yer*-Deletion applies to delete the remaining yers: /bezĭ-den-ĭnĭ/ → [bezdennĭ].

An important note regarding the cyclic analysis is that it presents a bracketing paradox; the cyclic phonological structure requires the prefix to attach to a suffixed stem [prefix [root suffixes]], while the morphological structure requires the prefix to attach directly to the root, as in [[prefix root] suffixes]. Assuming that the appropriate cyclic structure can be derived (perhaps through a restructuring rule), this analysis is one of the few cases where the cyclicity of a rule is evident in the feeding, or in this case bleeding relation between successive cyclic applications of the rule. It is essential for the analysis sketched above that the lowering of the first stem vowel takes place *before* the application of Lower on the prefix cycle. Cyclicity in this analysis goes beyond simply defining domains in which a rule must apply, but determines the sequential order of multiple applications of the cyclic rule.

Szpyra (1992), citing Nykiel-Herbert (1984), notes several problems with the cyclic analysis of Polish Lower. In particular, Lower fails to apply to some prefix *yers*, even though they are followed in the next syllable by a nonlowered *yer*. Consider for example, the cyclic analysis of *bezpłciowy* "sexless" from underlying /bezĭ-płĭć-oў-ĭ/. Lower will not apply on the suffixed stem /płĭć-oў-ĭ/, which contains only a single yer. Lower will apply on the prefix cycle, yielding /beze-płĭć-oў-ĭ/. Postcyclic *yer*-Deletion will delete the remaining stem yer, which yields the incorrect surface form *[bezepłćovɨ]. Clearly, Lower must be blocked on the prefix cycle to derive the correct surface form.

Szpyra argues that the nonapplication of Lower on the prefix cycle is the unmarked case, characterizing a large number of regular forms in several different morphological paradigms, such as the denominal adjective *bezdenny* "bottomless". Her solution is to place the prefixes and the suffixed stem into two distinct prosodic domains. Lower applies within each prosodic domain, but does not apply across domains. For example, bezpłciowy "sexless" is parsed into two domains [bezɨ] [płĭć-ov̆-ɨ], each containing a single yer which does not meet the structural description of Lower. Szpyra cites about thirty verb forms in which Lower exceptionally does apply to a prefix yer, triggered by a yer in the following stem vowel. All but one of these examples are seen to involve CYC roots (Y = yer). Szypra's suggests that with CYC stems the prefix is parsed as part of the stem+suffix prosodic domain.

To summarize, there is evidence in Polish for a domain restriction on certain phonological rules. In the case of Lower, the necessary domains are not taken directly from morphological constituent structure, and there are no interactions between rules applying in different prosodic domains. Specifically, in Szpyra's prosodic reanalysis there is no requirement that Lower apply in one domain prior to its application in another domain; there is no cyclic feeding or bleeding. Beyond the analysis of yers, Rubach and Booij argue that certain other rules are subject to the Derived Environment Constraint, and do not generally apply morpheme-internally. However, these so-called cyclic rules are not seen to be restricted to the morphological domains that characterize the cyclic analysis of yers. Consequently, the arguments for cyclic domains and the arguments for rules governed by the Derived Environment Constraint are entirely independent.

7.3   *German Syllabification*

Rubach (1990) presents an analysis of German Devoicing which provides strong evidence for the cyclic application of syllabification. He notes the controversy between analyses in which Devoicing applies syllable-finally and those in which it applies morpheme-finally. At the heart of the matter is the contrast between pairs of words such as those in (24).

(24)   Voiced obstruent   Voiceless obstruent
      Handlung "act"   handlich   "handy"
      Ordnung "order"   Bildnis   "portrait"
      Radler   "bicyclist"   glaublich   "believable"

In these examples, the same or similar consonant clusters (*ndl, rdn, ldn, dl, bl*) give rise to Devoicing in only some cases, although in most of the examples the underlying medial voiced obstruent is arguably in a syllable coda position in the surface form: *han[t].lich, Or[d].nung, Bil[t].nis, Ra[d].ler, glau[p].lich.*[42] Rubach demonstrates that in all of the cases where Devoicing fails to apply to a consonant which is syllable final in surface form, the voiced consonant is followed by a morpheme-final sonorant, e.g., /handl-ung/, /ordn-ung/. In contrast, in the examples where Devoicing does apply to a voiced consonant preceding a sonorant, the sonorant is not morpheme final, e.g., /hand-lich/, /bilt-nis/.

Rubach argues that a syllable-final rule of Devoicing can be maintained under the assumptions that (1) syllabification applies cyclically, (2) final sonorants are syllabic, giving rise to [CS̩] (S̩ = syllabic sonorant) syllables at the right edge of a cyclic domain, and (3) syllabic sonorants are not resyllabified as onsets of following vowel-initial suffixes during the cyclic phonology, and only desyllabify in the post-cyclic phonology subject to many restrictions. He offers the following derivations for *Han[d]lung, han[t]lich,* and *Hän[d]e* "hands".

(25) *Cycle 1*

handl	hand	händ	
han.dl.	hand.	händ.	syllabification

Cycle 2

han.dl.-ung	hand.-lich	händ.-e	
han.dl.ung.	hand.lich.	hän.de.	syllabification

Post-cyclic

—	hant.lich.	—	Devoicing

In the derivations above, post-cyclic Devoicing applies only to those voiced obstruents which are syllable final at the end of the cyclic phonology. Note that in some cases, a syllabic sonorant loses its syllabicity and resyllabifies as the onset of the following vowel-initial syllable, as in *Ra[d].ler* (also *zylin.[d]risch* "cylindrical" from /zylindr-isch/). The lexically restricted sonorant desyllabification rule does not apply in *Han[d]lung.*[43]

Rubach's analysis of the German data goes beyond a stipulation that a phonological rule applies in a morphologically defined domain. In German, syllabification must apply in *every* nested cyclic domain.[44] Thus, whereas syllabification must apply on the root cycle in the derivation of *Handlung,* it must also apply on the first suffixal cycle in *Radler.* If this is an instance of cyclicity as a domain restriction, then the domain must be recursively defined in such a way that it gives rise to nested domains like [[[root] suffix] suffix]. Furthermore, the syllabification of an inner domain can affect the syllabification of an outer domain. For instance, in the derivation in (25), syllabification on Cycle 1 yields *Han.dl.,* with a syllabic sonorant. On Cycle 2 the syllabic sonorant cannot be resyllabified as the onset of the following vowel-initial syllable,

Han.dl.ung. Thus, under Rubach's analysis derivation on Cycle 1 must precede derivation on Cycle 2.

In addition to Rubach's analysis of German Devoicing, recursive cyclic domains are also apparent in the analyses of cyclic epenthesis in Hungarian (Jensen and Stong-Jensen 1989), and Selayarese (Mithun and Basri 1986, cited in Goldsmith 1991a).

7.4   *Summary*

In this section we have seen evidence from English, Polish, and German that syllabification and rules that refer to syllable structure may apply in morphologically defined domains smaller than the word. In the case of German, the cyclic syllabification rules apply in recursive cyclic domains, and may bleed the post-cyclic application of Devoicing. Further, unrelated to the arguments for word-internal cyclic domains, there is evidence from Polish that some rules which are dependent on syllable structure are subject to the Derived Environment Constraint.

8   Rule-ordering Paradoxes

In this final section, we briefly consider the role of cyclic derivation in the resolution of rule ordering paradoxes.

A tenet of generative phonology, as put forth in *SPE*, is that phonological rules are ordered consistently throughout the grammar. This claim prohibits grammars in which two rules, A and B, are ordered A < B in some derivations, but B < A in other derivations. Rule ordering paradoxes arise when a phonological system violates the condition on consistent rule ordering by requiring A < B for some derivations and B < A for others. Yet apparent inconsistencies in rule ordering can arise in cyclic derivations when, given two ordered rules A < B , B applies on cycle n and A applies on cycle $n + 1$. In such a situation it is even possible that A feeds B in the application of the rules on a single cycle, while B feeds A in a two-cycle derivation. A theory with both rule ordering and cyclic rule application predicts that rule ordering "paradoxes" will occur in the cyclic phonology, even though very few such cases have actually been argued for in the literature.

Klamath (Kisseberth 1971) stands as the classic example of a paradoxical rule system, while Icelandic (Kiparsky 1985b) and stress in two Arabic dialects (Irshied and Kenstowicz 1984) have also been claimed to present rule ordering paradoxes.[45] Cole 1993 reexamines the Klamath and Icelandic data, and argues that the rule ordering paradoxes are resolved when deletion rules are given a metrical interpretation and syllabification is viewed as a persistent process that may respond to metrical parsing by reducing weak syllables.[46] The reanalysis is presented in the framework of dynamic phonology, in which the rules building metrical and syllable structures interact.[47] Whereas in classical generative phonology rule interaction is modeled with rule ordering, in the dynamic model each structure-building process applies only once, but may have varied results depending on the constraints imposed by other structure-building processes (e.g., stress or syllable parsing). The surface form represents the optimization of all the metrical structures taken together.[48]

In those cases examined by Cole (1993), ordering paradoxes are resolved by eliminating rule ordering in favor of dynamic rule interaction (or alternately, persistent rule application). The reanalysis challenges the role of rule ordering in phonological theory, and does not rely on cyclic rule application to derive problematic rule interaction. Given the rarity, or nonexistence, of genuine rule ordering paradoxes, the dynamic or nonderivational approach which eschews rule ordering merits serious consideration. Within such a theory, it is possible to maintain the notion of the cyclic domain, critical for the analysis of some of the stress and syllable processes discussed above, without predicting widespread, unattested rule interaction.

9 Conclusion

Putting together the conclusions concerning the theoretical status of cyclic rules with the conclusions concerning their empirical evidence, the following observations can be made. First, evidence from syllable and stress systems points clearly to the need to identify word-internal "cyclic" domains for the application of rules constructing syllable and stress constituents. In some cases, the cyclic domains are recursive. The cyclic rules are at times seen to interact with the noncyclic rules, either feeding or bleeding the rules applying in the larger word- or phrase-level domain. Moreover, in some systems with recursive cyclic domains for syllabification, the analysis of an outer cycle must respect the structure derived on an earlier cycle.

Second, a theory with both cyclic rule application and rule ordering requires the Reaching Back Constraint of the SCC, as noted by Kiparsky (1985a), to prevent cyclic derivations from undermining counter-feeding and counter-bleeding rule ordering. Yet, given a reanalysis of the Catalan facts, there is no clear evidence of the Reaching Back Constraint in any individual phonological system. Moreover, cyclic rule application and rule ordering together predict the existence of systems with superficially inconsistent rule ordering (rule ordering paradoxes), a prediction for which no clear empirical support has been found. Since cyclicity, in the sense of word-internal domains, has strong empirical support, these findings raise questions about the correctness of rule ordering as the appropriate mechanism for modeling rule interaction.

Third, some phonological rules are subject to the Derived Environment Constraint – they do not apply in monomorphemic environments. Since Mascaró

(1976), this property has been identified with cyclic rule application. Yet the rules which demonstrate Derived Environment Constraint effects are not necessarily, or even typically, those rules which are argued to apply in word-internal "cyclic" domains. The relationship between the Derived Environment Constraint and cyclic domain restrictions was established by Mascaró as a simplifying measure. As noted above, a cyclic theory requires the Reaching Back Constraint to preserve rule ordering in cyclic derivations. The similarity between the Reaching Back Constraint and the independently needed Derived Environment Constraint led to their generalization in the form of the SCC, with the result that only cyclic rules are subject to the Derived Environment Constraint. Since it is at best rare to have evidence for both cyclic domains and the Derived Environment Constraint in the analysis of a single rule, it is reasonable to reconsider the connection between the two.

From this discussion, we can conclude that a theory of phonology that can account for the phenomena attributed to cyclicity must include (1) a subtheory of domains which can construct domains on the basis of morphological structure, though not necessarily isomorphic to that structure, within which certain phonological rules may apply; (2) a condition like the Derived Environment Constraint (perhaps nothing more than the Revised Alternation Condition), which restricts certain rules from applying in monomorphemic environments;[49] and (3) a mechanism for modeling the interaction that can occur between rules applying in cyclic domains and those applying in the larger domains defined by word and phrase structure. While rule ordering is the solution offered by standard generative phonology, other possibilities are suggested in dynamic models of phonological processing.

NOTES

1 For helpful discussion and comments I thank John Coleman, John Goldsmith, José Ignacio Hualde, Charles Kisseberth and John McCarthy.

2 Chomsky and Halle cite Chomsky, Halle, and Lukoff (1956) as the first reference to the transformational cycle in the analysis of English stress.

3 A strict partial order is any relation which is (i) transitive, (ii) irreflexive, and (iii) asymmetric. The order is partial, and not total, since it is not the case that each rule must be ordered with respect to

every other rule in the grammar. In the present case the relation is "applies before."

4 But see the discussion of English stress in section 6.1 for the reanalysis of these data proposed by Halle and Vergnaud (1987a), who rely on independent arguments for the cyclicity of English stress.

5 Kiparsky (1982a) suggests that a certain class of cyclic rules, namely those that build structure but do not change existing structure in the phonological representation, are allowed to apply to nonderived

strings, and may create a derived environment for the future application of subsequent cyclic rules applying on the same cycle. See the discussion in section 3.2.

6 Arguments for the Reaching Back Constraint must rely exclusively on *lexical* rules, which apply word-internally. As discussed in section 3.1, *post-lexical* rules, applying in the phrasal domain, are not subject to the SCC. This restriction alone eliminates one of Mascaró's arguments for the Reaching Back Constraint, in which the rule of Glide Formation is said to be blocked by the SCC from applying in an environment that spans a word boundary.

7 As discussed in section 2.2, Mascaró's arguments are subject to reanalysis, none of which require the Reaching Back Constraint. The Reaching Back Constraint is also invoked in the cyclic analysis of Klamath phonology presented in Kean (1974). Kean argues that the rule of Sonorant Cluster Epenthesis is blocked by the SCC under the Reaching Back exclusion. Her analysis predates recent advances in syllable theory, which have led to alternative accounts of syllable structure and epenthesis in Klamath (Clements and Keyser 1983; Levin 1985; ter Mors 1984). While the cyclic nature of Klamath phonology continues to be debated, the particular details of Kean's analysis of the SCC blocking Sonorant Cluster Epenthesis would not be maintained under the current view of syllable theory. See the discussion of Klamath in section 8.

8 Kiparsky also notes similar facts in Finnish and Mongolian.

9 Myers (1987) presents a reanalysis of Trisyllabic Shortening, discussed in section 7.1 below. He claims that,

contra Kiparsky, all roots and Level 1 derived stems are subject to vowel shortening, which results from the stray erasure of vowel positions not licensed by the well-formedness constraints on syllable structure. Myers acknowledges the existence of exceptions to Trisyllabic Shortening, both derived and non-derived, which must presumably be simply listed in the lexicon.

10 The rule of vowel Raising is also a neutralizing rule (*e* and *i* are distinct phonemes), but is not blocked by the RAC in (9b) because the environment is derived. The rule refers to a word boundary, which is not part of the underlying representation of the morpheme /vete/, but results from the morphological process of word formation. Similarly, the English rule of *y* → *i* used in the derivation of *ivory* (discussed above in relation to Trisyllabic Shortening) applies word-finally and is therefore not blocked by the Revised Alternation Condition. Finnish is discussed further in section 4.3.

11 An excellent introduction to lexical phonology is found in Kaisse and Shaw (1985).

12 Momentarily disregarding the rules of syllabification.

13 Harris cites the Spanish rule of Aspiration (*s* → *h* in rhyme position) as an example of a neutralizing rule which must not apply cyclically. However, Goldsmith (personal communication) observes that for the majority of speakers, this rule is not neutralizing, since *h* is not part of the underlying consonant inventory, and contrasts with [x] (orthographic *j*) and [ç] (orthographic *g(i)*, *g(e)*).

14 Maintaining the correctness of Kiparsky's analysis of the Velar

Softening data, Hammond (1991) focuses his explanation of these data on a morphological WYSIWYG principle governing the formulation of underlying representations. The reader is referred to Hammond's work for further details.

15   The prefix must be attached to the base [legal]$_{adj}$, and not [legality]$_n$], because *i*N- attaches only to adjectives.

16   There is a subtle but important distinction between Kiparsky's view of lexical rules that exist only within the lexical component, and Mohanan's (1986) view that rules exist outside the morphological component, but are specified to apply within some lexical (or post-lexical) domain. This distinction is relevant to the argument that the SCC is derivable from the Elsewhere Condition (see discussion below).

17   In addition to the Spanish case, cyclic syllabification is argued to create a derived environment for the further application of cyclic rules in Clements and Keyser's (1983) analysis of Klamath. This ceases to be a problem in the analysis proposed in Cole (1993), where it is argued that the cyclic "rules" of insertion and deletion are really the effects of constraints on syllabification, and therefore part of syllabification itself.

18   Iverson and Wheeler (1988) allude to a general principle for determining rule ordering which might resolve certain cases of cyclic "counter-" orderings. They also suggest that further exploiting the notion of domain specification for phonological rules might avoid the possibility of cyclic rules violating the Reaching Back Constraint. No examples or further discussion are provided.

19   Although some domain restriction is still required, at least in the case of Velar Softening, if we care to rule out the kind of abstract analysis noted by Iverson and Wheeler (1988), discussed in section 4.1.

20   For further discussion of the Class 1/Class 2 distinction, see Siegel (1974), Allen (1978), Mohanan (1986), Kiparsky (1982a), and Sproat (1985).

21   See also Halle and Vergnaud (1987b) for a similar proposal.

22   Halle and Kenstowicz follow Fabb (1988) in rejecting the relevance of level ordering in determining distributional restrictions of affixation.

23   In the reanalysis of Klamath mentioned in section 8, only the prefix domains are cyclic, but restructuring is still required in the phonology to derive the nested cyclic domains [prefix [prefix [prefix root suffix]]].

24   Halle and Kenstowicz (1991) accept Hammond's findings, and propose that cyclic stress is copied onto the metrical grid on which noncyclic secondary stress is assigned.

25   Kager (1989) presents a nonderivational cyclic analysis which allows the simultaneous analysis of all cyclic stresses, with a different approach to the overgeneration problem.

26   Goldsmith distinguishes the Level 2 suffixation of *-ist* and *-ize*, which is fully productive and has predictable semantics, from the Level 1 suffixation of *-ist*, *-ize* on both phonological and semantic grounds.

27   See also Harris (1983, 1989), Halle and Vergnaud (1987a), and Halle, Harris, and Vergnaud (1991) for further discussion of cyclic stress in Spanish. The examples shown here are taken from the latter two sources.

28 Following Halle and Kenstowicz (1991), this analysis assumes that the crucial difference between cyclic and noncyclic stress assignment is that the cyclic rule always constructs a new metrical grid over the entire domain, erasing any metrical structure assigned on earlier cycles, whereas the noncyclic rule leaves intact the metrical structure of the final cycle, and constructs metrical structure only over material not metrified on the final cycle, such as extrametrical material, or material added by noncyclic affixation/cliticization processes.

29 Conflation is a process which deletes a layer of structure from the metrical grid, resulting in the elimination of nonprimary stresses (Halle and Vergnaud 1987a; Halle 1990; Halle and Kenstowicz 1991).

30 A nonprocedural interpretation of the interaction between stress and Diphthongization is possible, if a distinction is made between the cyclic and noncyclic stress feet. Only the vowel in the cyclic stress foot will undergo diphthongization, while only the vowel in the noncyclically assigned stress foot realizes surface stress. In the derivation of a form like *miél*, with no noncyclic affixes, the two stress feet would be identical.

31 The material in this section is adapted from Cole (1990).

32 In *SRR* forms where the *S* is not accented, it is crucial for the analysis sketched here that there be no cycle of stress assignment in the domain [S]. If there were, the *S* would be assigned stress by the default clause, as the leftmost element in the domain, with the result that in the noncyclic derivation the unaccented stem would always surface with word stress. Recall that in this case it is the leftmost *R* that receives word stress. Halle and Mohanan claim that the SCC blocks stress from applying in the nonderived [S] domain. Unlike in English, stress assignment is not a purely structure-building operation in Vedic, since morphemes may bear contrastive stress accent.

33 See also Halle and Kenstowicz (1991).

34 In discussing Poser's analysis, Goldsmith (1991a) notes that the phonological cycle required in Diyari does not correlate with the phonological word, since not all cyclic domains will qualify as minimal words. Thus, Poser's analysis requires a more lenient definition of the cycle than that proposed in the word-based approach of lexical phonology (Kiparsky 1982a). The same is obviously true of the Halle and Vergnaud analysis.

35 For the cases of Trisyllabic Shortening, his analysis involves a rule of resyllabification, in which a V.CV string is resyllabified as V́C.V, reflecting a tendency to make stressed syllables heavy. For a critique of the resyllabification process, see Halle and Vergnaud (1987a).

36 A large class of apparent exceptions includes lexical items such as *paint*, in which a long vowel is followed by a cluster of coronal consonants. Myers suggests that a string of coronals can be extrasyllabic at the edge of a morpheme, thus rendering the final syllable open; however, this explanation does not extend to examples like *mountain*, in which the coronal sequence is not word final, as discussed by Goldsmith (1990).

37 Sainz raises questions about the Level 1 restriction on vowel shortening. She notes that "long vowels consistently shorten before coronal clusters involving stratum 1 suffixes only when the cluster is derived by the addition of either the inflectional suffixes *-t*/*-d* ... or the noun-forming suffix *-th* (e.g., heal/health ...)." (p. 184). Citing Ross, she notes the possibility that shortening is "a lexically conditioned rule which applies to the presuffixal vowel in certain words prior to the assignment of stress" (ibid.). Since domains, such as "Level 1," are in any case defined in terms of the morphemes contained within them, the question really boils down to one of how many "lexical" domains there are. Is the Level 1 domain for stress rules defined by the same set of affixes which define the domains for vowel shortening, or for the deletion rules to be discussed below? Are all lexical domains nonoverlapping, and part of a large set of properly nested domains? We leave these issues unresolved.

38 But see the discussion of the Derived Environment Constraint and word-level rules in section 4.3.

39 Szpyra (1989) challenges the cyclic analysis of Coronal Palatization, presenting data which demonstrate that the rule appears to apply in certain nonderived environments, while it exceptionally fails to apply in other derived environments. She argues that the domain restriction of Coronal Palatization does not follow from the SCC, but might involve more direct reference to morphological structure.

40 More recent analyses (Kenstowicz and Rubach 1987; Szpyra 1992) distinguish yers from other vowels on the basis of their prosodic status

(such as their specification for a vowel skeletal position), rather than ascribing an abstract [−tense] feature to the yers. The yer ∼ ∅ alternation then results from general conditions on syllabification. While these proposals involve different rules to account for yer Lowering, the question of cyclic domains and cyclicity remains.

41 This discussion summarizes Szpyra (1989, pp. 203–224).

42 Rubach notes that the intuitions of native speakers with regard to the syllabification of certain clusters are not clear, but in general, the contrast between those clusters which give rise to Devoicing and those which do not is not derivable from the surface syllabification.

43 Given the lexical restrictions on Sonorant Desyllabification, it must be considered a lexical noncyclic rule, as opposed to a post-lexical noncyclic rule, although Rubach does not discuss this issue.

44 In all of the examples, the cyclic domain is a well-formed morphological constituent.

45 The Arabic system is reanalyzed without problematic rule interaction in Cole (1990).

46 See Myers 1991 for discussion of persistent rules.

47 In a similar fashion, interactive processes building syllable and metrical structures play an important role in the treatment of Latin vowel quantity alternations presented in Mester (in press).

48 Optimization in harmonic phonology is proposed in work by Alan Prince and Paul Smolensky, as cited by Archangeli and Pulleyblank (in press) and Mester (in press); see also Prince (1990). A related dynamic approach to phonology is

proposed in Goldsmith (1991b). Rule interaction can also be modeled nonderivationally in terms of conflict resolution strategies as in Cole (1992a), or encoded in the architecture of the phonology-to-phonetics mapping, as in Lakoff (1993) and Wheeler and Touretzky (1993).

49 Arguments for a morphologically-based Derived Environment Constraint are given by Hammond (1991), on the basis of considerations of morphological acquisition.

4 Underspecification and Markedness

DONCA STERIADE

0 Introduction

Not all segments are specified for all features at all times. Theories of underspecification have been proposed which aim to explain the circumstances under which segments might lack feature values, in underlying or derived representations. This chapter surveys the hypotheses about underspecification that have defined the terms of current research.

0.1 *The Basic Assumptions*

Within the generative phonological tradition initiated by Halle (1959) and Chomsky and Halle (1968), two starting assumptions are generally made:

(1) Lexical Minimality: underlying representations must reduce to some minimum the phonological information used to distinguish lexical items.[1]

(2) Full Specification: the output of the phonological component must contain fully (or at least maximally) specified feature matrices.[2]

One of the functions of the phonological component is then to supply the nondistinctive information missing from the underlying forms. Lexical Minimality requires that the maximal amount of phonological features be left out of the lexical entries, whereas Full Specification dictates that they be present in the input to phonetic interpretation. One way to extract dispensable information from lexical entries is to rely on syntagmatic processes – rules like *Palatalize velar before front vowel* or *Nasalize vocoid after nasal* – which allow us to leave unspecified contextually determined properties like the palatality of velars or vocoid nasality. But syntagmatic processes – the P rules of Stanley

(1967) – cannot be used to rid segments of constant, nonalternating yet predictable features, such as the voicing of sonorants or the continuancy of vowels. This function is then standardly reserved for context-free operations called redundancy rules, which insert the feature values originally left out of lexical entries. The redundancy rules perform functions such as *Mark vowel as [+continuant]* or *Voice sonorant* and thus allow us to eliminate these features too from underlying structures. The study of redundancy rules has been in recent years at the core of research on underspecification. That this class of rules must exist follows, as indicated, from the assumptions of Lexical Minimality and Full Specification. In this sense then, the hypotheses in (1)–(2) are the essence of contemporary theories of underspecification.

It is widely believed that one can observe the effect underspecification has on the phonology of a language by studying the interactions between the P rules and the system of redundancy rules. Why are these interactions revealing? If all redundancy rules precede all P rules, as argued by Stanley (1967), the P rules will apply to fully specified segments and it will be practically impossible to find empirical arguments for or against any individual redundancy rule. The only reason to practice underspecification, in that case, will be to uphold one's belief in Lexical Minimality. Most phonologists would agree, however, that the idea of underspecification can be empirically supported. For instance, in arguing to include *Voice sonorants* in the redundancy rule list, one cites phonological processes that ignore the phonetic voicing of sonorants. Russian, for instance, has a voicing assimilation triggered by voiced obstruents but not by sonorants (cf. Kiparsky 1985). The fact that sonorants are inactive in this process would be explained by letting the Russian voicing assimilation apply before the redundancy rule *Voice sonorants* takes effect. Prior to this redundancy rule, the sonorants are, in accordance with Lexical Minimality, lacking any [voice] values. A schematic derivation illustrating this scenario appears below.

(3) *Voice sonorants* in a language where sonorants do not act as [+voice] segments

THE ORDERED GRAMMATICAL STATEMENTS	THEIR CONSEQUENCES FOR SONORANTS
(i) Underlying representations: according to (1)	sonorants lack [+voice]
(ii) Assimilation: x → [+voice]/ ____ [+voice]	fails to apply before sonorants
(iii) Redundancy rule: [+sonorant] → [+voice]	sonorants become voiced

Much of the evidence considered in the underspecification literature is of the type sketched in (3) and has been analyzed in the past in terms of three-step derivations comparable to the one above. Cross-linguistic differences in the effect similar rules have on segments have been attributed to the possibility of switching steps (ii) and (iii) in (3). For instance we may compare Russian with English, where the voicing assimilation targeting inflectional suffixes like -*s* and -*t* is induced by voiced obstruents and sonorants alike (cf. *bug[z]* and *call[z]* with *chick[s]*). English could be analyzed, without sacrificing Lexical Minimality, by letting step (iii) *Voice sonorants* precede step (ii). By shifting the rule order, we maintain that sonorants lack underlying [voice] values, regardless of phonological patterning.

Because of its reliance on Lexical Minimality and Full Specification, most of the literature on underspecification consists of sequential analyses like (3) which, taken together, read like an advertisement for sequential rule application, rule ordering and, more generally, for a derivational as against a declarative approach to phonology.[3] Even authors who claim that the ordering between phonological rules and redundancy rules is *not* extrinsic – cf. Archangeli (1984), Archangeli and Pulleyblank (1986) – are led to justify the hypothesis of underspecification by formulating derivational analyses in the style of (3). Although the question of derivational vs. declarative phonology cannot be considered directly here, we do have to ask whether the phenomena attributed to underspecification must be analyzed derivationally, by distinguishing an earlier, less-specified stage of the derivation from a more fully specified, later stage. This will turn out to be the key issue.

0.2   The Writer's Prejudices

The present chapter has been influenced by the early work on underspecification of Richard Stanley (1967), as well as by Mohanan (1991) and the more recent literature on declarative and harmonic phonology. Stanley's article on redundancy rules was in part a reaction against what I would like to call "opportunistic uses" of underspecification. Some grammatical statements are made simpler if they are assumed to hold of incompletely specified representations: the assimilation rule in (3ii), for instance, might be written as $x \rightarrow$ [+*voice*]/ ___ [+*voice*, –*sonorant*] but it is opportune to simplify this statement by omitting [–sonorant]. We can do so if we rely on the incompletely specified lexical entries assumed in (3i). Stanley thought that the invocation of language-specific convenience is a bad reason to practice underspecification. One hopes, with Stanley, that any discrepancies in feature specification between lexical and surface structure follow from general principles, not descriptive convenience. Lexical Minimality is such a principle but it seems, as we shall see, indefensible insofar as it can be made precise. The search for other principles from which more interesting varieties of underspecification follow has also proved, in my view, fruitless. Sections 2.3.1–2.3.2 develop these points. What remains to be done is to provide plausible alternatives for all analyses relying on derivational scenarios like (3). I cannot undertake here a complete re-evaluation of the evidence, but an initial attempt is made at the end of section 2 and in section 3. In any event, the reader will need to bear in mind, in reading what follows, where my sympathies lie.

0.3 *Trivial and Nontrivial Underspecification*

I limit the scope of this survey by considering only the evidence for nontrivial
– or temporary – underspecification. We will notice repeatedly that there
exists abundant evidence for permanent – trivial or inherent – underspecification.[4] Some segments do not carry specifications for certain features, either
underlyingly or at any subsequent derivational stage. Thus plain coronals are
trivially, inherently, and permanently lacking in specifications for the features
[labial] or [tongue root]. Similarly, if [nasal] is a privative feature, oral segments will permanently lack [nasal] values. The extent of their underspecification for [nasal] is settled once and for all when we decide that [nasal] has
only one value; having done so, we do not have to wonder when or how oral
segments become specified as [–nasal]. Although there are important issues
involved in the study of permanent underspecification, they have to do more
with the relation between phonology and phonetics than with the question
that I consider central to this survey: assessing the validity of derivational
scenarios like (3), which invoke *temporary* underspecification. Consequently, I
focus here on the evidence for lexical representations from which some *surface-
present* feature has been left out.

0.4 *Outline*

The survey begins by outlining the situations in which features can be said
to be predictable, in a syntagmatic or segment-internal context (section 1). I
review next theories of underspecification that share the assumptions of Lexical Minimality and Full Specification (section 2) . In the course of the review
we will observe that neither Lexical Minimality nor Full Specification can
be defended when a closer look is taken at what these ideas entail for the
organization of the phonology and for the nature of phonetic representations. The last sections (2.3.3.5 and 3) sketch an alternative, nonderivational
view of phonological underspecification.

1 The Facts of Underspecification: Predictability and Inertness

The features of segments are frequently predictable. Sometimes a predictable
feature value fails to manifest its presence in a phonological process where
it might otherwise be expected to act. In such cases, the practice has been to
declare it unspecified and set up derivations similar to (3).[5] I review in this section several classes of feature predictability that can thus be linked to the hypothesis of underspecification. The varieties of redundancy rules corresponding

to these types of predictability were first formulated by Halle (1959) as *Segment Structure* and *Sequence Structure* rules.

1.1 Sources of Predictability: Markedness and Neutralization

1.1.1 Feature Co-occurrence and Context-sensitive Markedness

Feature co-occurrence conditions are formulated (since Halle 1959) to express restrictions on the possible feature combinations within a segment. For instance, the absence of distinctively voiceless sonorants in English may be expressed as a rule (the *Voice sonorants* process mentioned above) or as a filter *[+sonorant, −voice].[6] The consequence of adopting either one is that some feature values become predictable: if, for instance, *[+sonorant, −voice] is part of the grammar, it follows that sonorants are predictably specified as [+voice]. From such facts, Lexical Minimality derives underspecification: in this case, sonorants lacking [voice].

The vast majority of feature cooccurrence statements have some cross-linguistic validity, in the sense that they characterize the unmarked combination of articulatory gestures for the relevant segmental class. Thus, a statement like *Sonorants are voiced* is justified not only internally to English but also cross-linguistically, as a markedness statement: it characterizes the normal state of the glottis in the sonorants of all languages. The assumption is frequently made (e.g., Archangeli 1984, 1988; Kiparsky 1985; Calabrese 1987; Archangeli and Pulleyblank 1992) that cross-linguistically valid feature co-occurrence conditions are part of Universal Grammar and do not contribute to the complexity of individual linguistic systems. If so, any language learner can be relied upon to know that *Sonorants are voiced*, in advance of exposure to data, and to draw from this principle the conclusion that the voicing of sonorants need not be lexically encoded. One of the tasks of markedness theory is to document the validity of such universal statements of feature co-occurrence and seek an explanation for their universal status. We return to the issue of markedness in section 2.3.3.[7]

It must be noted, however, that any co-occurrence condition engaging two features will derive two distinct and sometimes incompatible patterns of underspecification. For instance, *[+sonorant, −voice] renders predictable not only the voicing of sonorants but also the sonority of voiceless segments. Must we then leave the [−sonorant] value of *p, t, k* out of the underlying representations? There seems to be little evidence for such a move and we need to ask why, especially as there exists substantial evidence for leaving the sonorants unspecified for [voice] (Kiparsky 1985; Ito and Mester 1986). In a different case, that of the [round] / [back] relation in triangular vowel inventories like {a, e, i, o, u}, we observe that either [round] can be left out of underlying representations or [back], since a statement like *[αback, −αround] allows us to derive the values of one feature from those of the other: but we cannot eliminate both. We must therefore, in accordance with Lexical Minimality, choose one feature as basic and derive the other. But the filter does not establish an asymmetry between the features involved in it: the values of back and round are mutually predictable, not arranged in some obvious pattern of ordered dependency. The choice of either [round] or [back] as the underlying value is not dictated by the co-occurrence condition itself and thus remains arbitrary. It appears that any grammar that fully complies with Lexical Minimality has to contain a number of arbitrary decisions of this sort.[8]

1.1.2   Context-free Markedness

Cross-linguistic asymmetries can be observed not only in the distribution of feature combinations but also in that of individual feature values. For instance, nasal segments have, in the vast majority of cases, a more limited distribution than corresponding oral ones; any aspirated or glottalized segment is more limited in occurrence than its nonaspirated, nonglottalized counterpart. Observations of this sort are also the province of markedness theory. A possible connection they have to underspecification has been formulated by Chomsky and Halle (1968, chap. 9), Kiparsky (1981, 1985, 1988), and assumed by others: Universal Grammar provides every feature with a marked and an unmarked value. The unmarked value of any feature corresponds to the normal, neutral state of the relevant articulator. For [nasal] the unmarked value is [–nasal], for [spread glottis] it is [–spread glottis] and so forth. Only one value for any given feature need be present underlyingly. Since features are assumed to be strictly binary, the other value can always be predicted by a context-free rule that mirrors the relevant markedness statement. Thus, corresponding to the statement that *Segments are normally oral*, we can have the universal rule [ ] → [–nasal]. The intention is to let this rule, like other redundancy rules, insert [–nasal] only in segments lacking a [nasal] value. A lexical contrast between *b* and *m* can then be represented as follows:

(4)   A context-free redundancy rule: *[ ] → [-nasal]*
        underlying: b   vs.   m
                                        [+nasal]
        surface: b   vs.   m
                        [–nasal]   [+nasal]

The use of markedness-based context-free redundancy rules of this sort appears to express the derivational transition between an underlying system in which all features are privative and a surface system in which all features are binary.[9] We may question the justification for this class of redundancy rules in two ways. First, we may ask whether the asymmetric distribution between the marked and the unmarked value justifies eliminating the unmarked value from underlying structure. Is underlying privativity the faithful representation of markedness facts? Second and more important is the need to question the assumption of surface binarity: should the unmarked value be represented at all on the surface? The second issue will be addressed below, in section 2.3.3. We can anticipate here the conclusion that the facts of context-free markedness do not in fact motivate any *universal* redundancy rules of the type in (4).

1.1.3   Syntagmatic Predictability of Features: Positional Neutralization[10]

A third variety of feature predictability involves not the markedness of segment-internal feature combinations or individual feature values, but the neutralization of featural contrasts in certain positions. This case has received little attention since Trubetzkoy (1939); and its particulars will be documented more carefully in section 3.

Segments identifiable as marked may, if allowed at all in a given language, be restricted to certain salient positions within the word: the syllable peak (rather than the margin), the onset (rather than the coda), the stem (rather than the affix), the stressed syllable, or the edges of the word. Maidu (Shipley 1956) allows laryngeally-specified consonants (ejectives or implosives) only in the syllable onset. Guaraní (Kiparsky 1985 and references there) allows underlying nasal vowels, but only in stressed syllables. Ancient Greek allowed aspirated vowels word-initially but not elsewhere. Copala Trique, an Otomanguean language, allows a wide range of segmental distinctions to surface only in the last syllable, which may be the one carrying stress: lenis/fortis contrasts, tonal distinctions, the laryngeals ʔ and h, and nasalized vowels occur only in the final syllable (Hollenbach 1977). Chumash (Applegate 1971) stem vowels are drawn from a crowded inventory which contains {a, e, o, i, ɨ, u}; affixal vowels, however, are underlyingly limited to the peripheral set {a, i, u}. In languages like Bashkir (Poppe 1962) and Vogul (Kálmán 1965), round vowels are restricted to initial position in both underlying and derived representations.

In all these cases, the absence of a contrast renders predictable whatever phonetic value the relevant feature might take on in the position of neutralization. Thus Bashkir and Vogul non-initial vowels are predictably unrounded; Guaraní stressless vowels are predictably oral; Chumash affixal vowels are predictably peripheral. The predictable value frequently coincides with the one normally identified as "universally unmarked," although in cases like Chumash such identification is difficult to implement. We retain, however, the need for grammatical statements which express the impossibility of a featural contrast in a given position. Such statements may take the form of filters, as in (5) (an example of which is Ito's (1986) Coda Condition) or of positive licensing conditions, as in (6) (cf. Goldsmith 1990, p. 123ff.).

(5)   Positional neutralization: filter version
       *αF in x where x is defined prosodically or morphologically.

(6) Positional neutralization: licensing version
αF must be licensed in x̄, where x̄ is defined prosodically or morphologically.

The presence of statements like (5) or (6) in a grammar induces predictability: no value for F is necessary in x, the unlicensed position, since only one value is allowed. If we adopt Lexical Minimality, underspecification follows as well: no value for F is possible in x. We return to the formalization of conditions like (5)–(6) in section 3, where their consequences for underspecification are explored in detail.

1.2 Varieties of Phonological Inertness

The purpose of the preceding sections was to inventory the circumstances under which a feature value might be predictable and hence, *potentially* unspecified. (I stress *potentially* because underspecification does not directly follow from predictability. It follows only if we subscribe to some further principle such as Lexical Minimality.) How do we determine, then, independently of the merits of Lexical Minimality, that a predictable feature is *actually* unspecified? How is the existence of underspecification diagnosed by phonologists? In what follows I will try to make explicit the reasoning that might lead to the adoption of underspecification.

Phonologists determine the presence of underspecified representations by observing facts which appear to contradict three basic expectations: that rules will apply locally, with maximal generality, and that lexically specified features will change only in response to clearly defined considerations of well-formedness. Consider first the hypothesis of local rule application:

(7) Locality: Phonological rules apply between elements adjacent on some tier.

Assimilations and dissimilations are expected, according to this statement, to involve prosodic positions, anchoring nodes, or terminal features that are adjacent. The formulation of Locality given above is deliberately vague, since phonologists disagree on the analysis of several apparently nonlocal phenomena.[11] Opinions converge, however, on the only aspect of Locality that is relevant to our concerns: no phonological rule is expected to "skip" specified features on the tier involved in assimilation or dissimilation. The operations diagrammed below are considered impossible, because they violate all proposed versions of Locality:

(8) Where skipping is impossible
Assimilation: *Spread [αF]*   Dissimilation: $[\alpha F] \rightarrow [-\alpha F]/\_\_[\alpha F]$
$[\alpha F]$ $[\beta F]$ $[\alpha F]$ $[\beta F]$ $[\alpha F] \rightarrow [-\alpha F]$

There exist, however, processes which do have the appearance of these prohibited operations. Such cases have been analyzed in the past by distinguishing an earlier unspecified stage (shown below) where the operation of the rules shown can be viewed as local, and a later stage, during which some intervening segment acquires, through redundancy rules, the [β F] value.

(9) Underspecified structures behind an apparently non-local rule application
      Assimilation: *Spread [αF]*   Dissimilation: *[αF] → [−αF]/ _ _ [αF]*
      [αF]   [αF]   [αF] → **[−αF]**

An illustration of (9) is the Russian rule of voicing assimilation mentioned earlier. It is not only the case that Russian sonorants fail to trigger voicing (*ot melodii* "from the melody" not **od melodii*) but also that Russian consonantal sonorants may intervene between the obstruent triggering voicing assimilation and the obstruent undergoing it: *iz Mtsenska* "from Mtsensk" becomes *is Mtsenska*, while *ot mzdy* "from the bribe" becomes *od mzdy*. The derivation in (10) reconciles these facts with our belief in Locality:

(10)

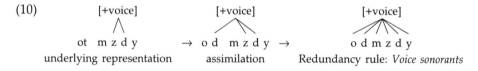

      [+voice]   [+voice]   [+voice]

      ot m z d y   → o d m z d y →   o d m z d y
      underlying representation   assimilation   Redundancy rule: *Voice sonorants*

Consider next the hypothesis of generality in rule application: all other things being equal, one expects that rules which spread, dissimilate, or are otherwise conditioned by [αF] will apply to all segments possessing [αF].

(11) Generality: If some process manipulates [αF], then all segments possessing [αF] will participate in it.

There are many phenomena which appear to contradict this expectation. Most, if not all, could be understood as stemming from underspecification. An example has already been provided in the analysis of Russian voicing: voiced sonorants do not trigger the rule (recall *ot melodii* and *is Mtsenska*) because they lack any [voice] value when the rule applies (Kiparsky 1985). A distinct example is that of Lamba height assimilation. This process, widespread among Bantu languages, turns a high suffixal vowel into a mid one when preceded by a mid vowel. The spreading feature appears to be [−high]. But low vowels – which are necessarily [−high], since they cannot be otherwise – do not trigger this rule. The facts, as recorded in Kenstowicz and Kisseberth (1977, p. 72), appear below:

(12) <u>Past</u> <u>Neuter</u>   <u>Applied</u> <u>Gloss</u>
      tul-a   tul-ika   tul-ila   "dig"

fis-a	fiš-ika	fiš-ila	"hide"
kos-a	kos-eka	kos-ela	"be strong"
sek-a	sek-eka	sek-ela	"laugh at"
pat-a	pat-ika	pat-ila	"scold"

An analysis of this data which appeals to underspecification in order to preserve Generality has been proposed in Steriade (1987b): low vowels cannot be [+high] for obvious articulatory reasons. Therefore their [high] values are predictable. Since predictable, they are unspecified: they have no height value to spread. In contrast, non-low vowels – *i, u, e, o* – have distinctive height values: no feature-co-occurence statement can predict whether a non-low vowel will turn out as [+high] or [–high]. In particular, mid vowels must be specified as [–high], which is the spreading feature in this case. Two three-step derivations illustrating this analysis appear below. Although this is immaterial to the argument, I ignore the [+high] values which high vowels might posess.

(13) (a) [–high] spreads from mid vowels

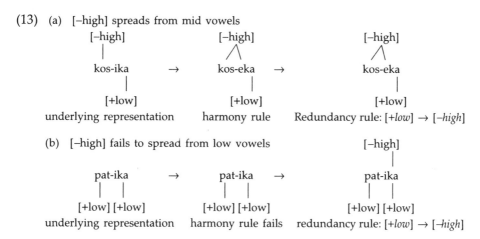

(b) [–high] fails to spread from low vowels

A final assumption from which one may draw conclusions about underspecification is the idea of invariance. As mentioned earlier, there is considerable consensus that assimilation affects mostly segments lacking values for the spreading feature. The failure of specified segments to assimilate could be attributed to Invariance:[12]

(14) Invariance: Lexically specified features prefer to remain unchanged.

I state (14) as a preference, since Invariance is not upheld at all costs: dissimilation processes like that in (9) switch or delete a feature value under the compulsion of more urgent constraints, such as the Obligatory Contour Principle.[13] Where segments are observed to undergo assimilation, this fact is made compatible with Invariance by assuming underspecification. Most such cases will be discussed in section 3, where we will conclude that the facts do not necessarily lead to the conclusion that assimilation targets are underspecified.

2   Derivational Theories of Underspecification: "Radical" or "Contrastive"?

We have reviewed so far the forms of reasoning that lead phonologists to postulate underspecified representations. Considered next are a number of ideas about the nature and ordering of redundancy rules that have been explored during the last decade. All theories articulated so far can be generally referred to as *derivational*, since they all rely on the possibility of ordering redundancy rules before or after P rules. The effect of underspecification can be determined, according to these theories, only when the rule order is settled. The first two underspecification systems to be reviewed have been known as radical underspecification.[14] The term "radical" refers perhaps to the fact that these theories uphold Lexical Minimality, by eliminating from underlying representations both feature values predictable from co-occurrence conditions and those predictable from context-free markedness statements. A distinct line of thinking, contrastive or restricted underspecification, limits the degree of underspecification in lexical forms by eliminating only feature values predictable on the basis of feature co-occurrence.

2.1   Radical Underspecification within Lexical Phonology: Kiparsky (1981, 1985)

At the source of all current work on underspecification lie Paul Kiparsky's ideas on lexical phonology and their applications to the principles of Locality and Invariance identified earlier. It is Kiparsky who first pointed out (in Kiparsky 1981) that apparent violations of Locality can be interpreted as stemming from the possibility of skipping segments which are predictably specified for a relevant feature. The connection between underspecification and Invariance was also made there. In a later study (1985), Kiparsky presents the hypothesis that the operation of different kinds of redundancy rules is tied to specific derivational levels. In a nutshell, the claim is that nondistinctive values (those predictable by the co-occurrence filters discussed in sec. 1.1.1) will occur only postlexically. We examine now the specifics of the model incorporating this idea.

Kiparsky assumes, following Chomsky and Halle (1968), a theory of markedness which provides a universal list of marked feature combinations and marked feature values.[15] Corresponding to the marked combinations there are filters similar to the *[+sonorant, −voice] condition discussed earlier. It is implied that, although universal, the filters are violable; a segment inventory will then be defined by the set of filters violated.[16] Corresponding to the marked feature values there are redundancy rule applications, such as [ ] → [−nasal], which insert unmarked specifications. Underlying representations obey Lexical Minimality: they lack features insertable by redundancy rules.

The distinguishing aspect of Kiparsky's proposal is the principle of Structure Preservation. It dictates that lexical rule applications, those taking place within the lexical rather than postlexical component of the phonology, will not have outputs violating the filters obeyed in the underlying representations of the language. A possible formulation is (15):

(15)   Structure Preservation: No lexical rule application will generate structures prohibited underlyingly.

P rules as well as redundancy rules are subject to Structure Preservation. The result aimed at is that of obtaining a limited degree of underspecification in the lexical component, by barring the lexical application of the redundancy rules linked to feature co-occurrence conditions. To understand how the system works, consider again the case of Russian voicing. There are two relevant markedness facts in this case. One is the fact that [–voice] is the unmarked value in obstruents; the other is the filter prohibiting [–voice] in sonorants. This filter is formulated as (16) by Kiparsky; it states that *no value* for [voice] is well formed in sonorants. This filter is accompanied by a unique redundancy rule, (17):

(16) $*\begin{bmatrix} \alpha \text{ voice} \\ + \text{ son} \end{bmatrix}$

(17)   [α sonorant] → [α voice]

The consequence of combining (16) with Structure Preservation is that no lexical rule applications will insert either [+voice] or [–voice] in sonorants. Thus (17) will be unable to mark sonorants as [+voice] within the lexical component. It may however apply to obstruents, marking them [–voice], since no value for voicing is prohibited in obstruents. Postlexically, (17) will apply to sonorants as well. The resulting system predicts the following generalizations:

(18)   (a)   No lexical rule application will encounter – or generate – a [voice] value in sonorants.
        (b)   Obstruents will emerge fully specified, [+voice] or [–voice], from the lexical component.
        (c)   Sonorants will be specified for [voice] at some point in the postlexical component.

Are the facts of Russian consistent with these predictions? This is not entirely clear. As noted earlier, the sonorants do not undergo, trigger or block voicing assimilation. Now, Kiparsky claims that voicing assimilation applies both lexically and postlexically in Russian: the sonorants, however, fail to trigger, block or undergo the rule in *either* component. This is not exactly what (18) predicts: (18c) leads us to expect that the voicing of sonorants will manifest itself postlexically. The facts can be made to fit the model only if an additional ordering condition is imposed: in every component, the voicing redundancy rule (17) follows the rule of voicing assimilation. The derivation in (19), modified below, illustrates the postlexical order.[17]

(19)

[+voice]	[+voice]	[+voice]

ot m z d y →   o d m z d y →   o d m z d y

output of lexical component   postlexical assimilation   (17): [α sonorant] → [α voice]

Given that the order between Assimilation and (17) must be stipulated, we should ask what empirical considerations support the assumptions in (15)–(16). Could we handle all the Russian facts by simply ordering Assimilation before (17), without appeal to (16) and Structure Preservation? The answer is not clear and the issue cannot be pursued here.[18] The major point to emerge, however, is that Structure Preservation contributes minimally, if at all, to the account of the Russian facts. The main element in the analysis is the extrinsic ordering between assimilation and redundancy rules.[19]

Similar analyses are applied in the 1985 article to a number of other phenomena in which underspecification appears to play a role. We will briefly consider here the analysis of Catalan consonantal place features, based on the original account of Mascaró (1976). The significant fact of Catalan is the contrast between alveolar coronals and all other consonants in triggering and undergoing place assimilation. The contrast is illustrated below: only the alveolars undergo place assimilation; and only the nonalveolars trigger it. Some details of the paradigm are omitted here.

(20)

Underlying alveolar in coda		Underlying labial in coda		Other codas	
son amics	"they are friends"	som amics	"we are friends"	tiŋ pa	"I have bread"
som pocs	"they are few"	som pocs	"we are few"	aŋ feliç	"happy year"
son dos	"they are two"	som dos	"we are two"		
soŋ grans	"they are big"	som grans	"we are big"		

The first task is to explain the difference between the alveolar point of articulation and the others. The explanation proposed by Kiparsky is that a marking condition, (21) below, prohibits the lexical appearance of [+coronal]. From this filter, we deduce a corresponding redundancy rule, (22):

(21)   *[+coronal]

(22)   [   ] → [+coronal]

The consequence of (21) is that the coronals are placeless in underlying representations, as well as throughout the lexical component. Structure Preservation ensures that (22) will apply only postlexically. The intention is to let the place assimilation take effect before (22). If so, we can explain both facts illustrated by (20). Only coronals undergo the assimilation rule because only they are place-unspecified: the principle of Invariance (14) applies here. Coronals fail to trigger the rule for the same reason. We note, however, that the Catalan analysis too relies on an ordering relation unrelated to Structure Preservation, or any other principle: within the postlexical component, (22) must *follow* place assimilation. The opposite order would also be consistent with Kiparsky's theory, but does not generate the data. If the alveolars became specified *before* the postlexical place assimilation, there would be no representational difference between them and the other Catalan consonants. Here too, the actual contribution of Structure Preservation is hard to pinpoint;[20] the bulk of the paradigm is handled by old-fashioned rule ordering.

There are, then, two elements in the analyses of the 1985 study: a feature co-occurrence condition (e.g., (21) or (16)) and an ordering statement which places a redundancy rule *after* some assimilation rule. We have suggested that the ordering itself cannot be derived from higher principles and, although central to each analysis, remains unconnected to Structure Preservation. We examine next the form taken by Kiparsky's feature co-occurence conditions, which are used to predict lexical underspecification. The discussion of this point owes much to Mohanan (1991).

The initial attractiveness of filters like (16) is that some statement is needed, independently of the issue of underspecification, to characterize the Russian segment inventory: any description of Russian must note the absence of voiceless sonorants. Filter (16) is presented as recording this fact. In fact, however, it does not: (16) prohibits not only [+sonorant, −voice] – the combination that is provably absent from underlying structure – but also [+sonorant, +voice], a combination that is, naïvely speaking, well formed even if nondistinctive. In the discussion of feature co-occurrence (section 1.1.1), we noted that a filter like *[+sonorant, −voice] renders predictable, and hence underspecifiable, the [+voice] value in sonorants. Kiparsky, however, is trying to derive a stronger result: the aim is not only to eliminate [+voice] from the underlying representation of sonorants but also to keep it out of the sonorants for the entire lexical component. Whether or not this is the right idea, it clearly cannot be implemented by using the well motivated filter *[+sonorant, −voice]: this filter will not prevent the redundancy rule in (17) from generating voiced sonorants in the lexicon. The hypothesis of lexical underspecification can be implemented only by adopting the extended filter (16), *[+sonorant, α voice]. In this extended form, however, the filter is motivated only by the drive to generate an underspecified lexical component, not by independent considerations. To put it plainly, the argument for lexical underspecification in Russian based on (16) is circular. This becomes fully obvious when we consider Kiparsky's observation that the sonorants are subject postlexically to [−voice] spreading (from a preceding obstruent, as in i[s m̥ts]enska "from Mcensk") but that they undergo this rule *gradiently*. Kiparsky suggests that gradient application is a possible symptom of postlexical rules. Note, however, that the application of the voicing redundancy rule (17) to sonorants is equally a postlexical process, on Kiparsky's analysis, in virtue of Structure Preservation: yet the [+voice] value normally appearing in the Russian sonorants is anything but gradient. The right conclusion to draw from this is that gradient applications mark only violations of a lexical filter, and the right lexical filter is the well-motivated *[+sonorant, −voice] not *[+sonorant, α voice].

A different criticism must be leveled at (21), the filter barring [+coronal] from the lexical component of Catalan. A statement of markedness might have to note the fact that alveolars are more common than other consonantal points of articulation: (21) appears to derive its force from this consideration. But (21), i.e., *[+coronal], does not express any observable property of Catalan consonants, nor any clearly defined markedness fact: coronals are neither impossible in Catalan nor undesirable universally. If the intended general principle is to rule out unmarked values from the lexical component, not just underlying representations, then this principle conflicts with Kiparsky's analysis of Russian, where [−voice] obstruents appear lexically, and with his analysis of Guaraní, where stressed oral vowels are lexically represented as [−nasal]. (On Guaraní, see below section 3.) Once again, we observe that the filter from which lexical underspecification is meant to follow is only supported by the need to uphold lexical underspecification in individual analyses.[21]

Aside from this criticism of the specifics, we must note that Kiparsky is seeking to address *the* essential question in the theory of derivational underspecification: that of predicting the degree of segmental specification at a given derivational level and hence of limiting the interactions between phonological rules and redundancy rules. The intuition expressed in the 1985 study is that of an orderly progression from maximally underspecified lexical entries to fully specified surface structures.[22] This progression comes in two major blocks of redundancy rule applications. First are inserted the feature values corresponding to context-free markedness preferences (such as *[−voice] is unmarked in obstruents*) and then, only postlexically, come the feature values corresponding to filters (such as *only [+voice] is possible in sonorants*). We will see in the next sections that later hypotheses about underspecification represent divergent developments of Kiparsky's views.

2.2   Radical Underspecification Outside of Lexical Phonology: Archangeli (1984, 1988)

2.2.1   Ordering Redundancy Rules and Phonological Rules: The Redundancy Rule Ordering Constraint (RROC)

The project of predicting the interactions between redundancy rules and phonological rules has been continued by Archangeli (1984, 1988), Pulleyblank (1986, 1988a, 1988b) and Archangeli and Pulleyblank (1986, 1989), within the general framework defined by Lexical Minimality. These writers seek to strenghten Kiparsky's proposals by disallowing any extrinsic rule ordering between phonological rules and redundancy rules. According to Archangeli and Pulleyblank, all ordering matters between these two types of rules are settled by one principle, the Redundancy Rule Ordering Constraint (RROC). The intended effect of the Redundancy Rule Ordering Constraint is to apply all redundancy rules inserting [αF] before any phonological rule mentioning [αF].

(23)   The Redundancy Rule Ordering Constraint (RROC) (Abaglo and Archangeli 1989, p. 474)
A redundancy rule inserting [α F] is assigned to the same component as the first rule referring to [αF].

The formulation in (23) assumes that, within any component of the phonology, the applicable redundancy rules apply as anywhere rules: that is, they precede all phonological rules and continue to apply wherever new eligible inputs are created. To understand the functioning of the Redundancy Rule Ordering Constraint in a grammar, we consider an example from Yoruba provided by Archangeli and Pulleyblank (1989). In this language, the feature [−ATR] spreads leftward from a low vowel *a*, which is noncontrastively specified as [−ATR], as well as from the mid [−ATR] vowels ε and ɔ, whose tongue root position is distinctive. The phonemic vowel system of Yoruba is {a, ε, ɔ, e, o, i, u}. There are excellent reasons, outlined by Archangeli and Pulleyblank (1989, pp. 184–187), to believe that the harmony system of Yoruba is asymmetric: the vowels {a, ε, ɔ} are triggers, while {e, o} are undergoers and {i, u} neutral segments. One reflex of this is the fact that [−ATR] spreads leftward across compound boundaries, while [+ATR] does not (data from Archangeli and Pulleyblank 1989, pp. 189–190; tones omitted):

(24)   ogbo "old" + εni "person" → ɔgbεni "sir"
ogũ "twenty" + εta "three" → ɔgɔta "sixty"
ɔkɔ "husband" + olobĩrĩ "married man" → ɔkɔlobĩrĩ "married man"

This pattern is interpreted as indicating that only [−ATR] values, the dominant ones here, exist in underlying representations. Lexical Minimality requires us to eliminate the [−ATR] feature of *a*, because it can be predicted from the feature co-occurrence *[+low, +ATR]. A further principle, discussed below, dictates that the inert [+ATR] values of {e, o, i, u} be inserted by the context-free redundancy rule [ ] → [+ATR]. This generates the underlying array of height/ATR values given below. I represent them accompanied by the corresponding redundancy rules (from Pulleyblank 1988a, p. 238).

(25)

	a	ε	ɔ	e	o	i	u		
ATR		−	−					(i)	[+low] → [−ATR]
low	+							(ii)	[ ] → [+ATR]
high		−	−	−	−			(iii)	[ ] → [+high]
								(iv)	[+low] → [−high]

Within this system, we must assume that [–ATR] spreads *after* the redundancy rule in (i) – since the non-contrastively retracted *a* does trigger [–ATR] harmony – but *before* the redundancy rule in (ii) – since the [+ATR] vowels undergo and fail to trigger harmony. (A tacit appeal to the principles of Generality and Invariance is being made here.) The Redundancy Rule Ordering Constraint predicts exactly this desired order, if we assume further that harmony belongs to the lexical component of the phonology. In virtue of the RROC, [–ATR] harmony and redundancy rule (i) must belong to the same component. Moreover, we know that, within a given component, redundancy rules are the first to apply. These assumptions derive the order *(i) ≪ [–ATR] harmony*. The low vowel *a* will now be able to propagate [–ATR]. In addition, we assume that no Yoruba lexical rule mentions [+ATR], and the RROC will therefore fail to place rule (ii) within the lexical component. Its application must be assumed to come postlexically. It thus follows that the order must be *[–ATR] harmony ≪ (ii)*: the high and mid tense vowels {i, u, e, o} will correctly lack any [ATR] values when [–ATR] harmony applies. The sequence of rule applications appears below, along with the principles motivating each ordering statement:

(26)

	Order	Motivating principles
lexical stratum	[+low] → [–ATR]	RROC: [–ATR] mentioned in lexicon.
	[–ATR] harmony	P rules follow first application of redundancy rules in any given stratum.
postlexical stratum	[ ] → [+ATR]	RROC: [+ATR] not mentioned lexically.

But the Redundancy Rule Ordering Constraint, while successful in Yoruba, is inconsistent with the Russian voicing facts. When we compare assimilated forms such as *od mzdy* (from / ot mzdy/) to unassimilated *ot melodii* (*od melodii) we must conclude (a) that [+voice] spreads postlexically and (b) that it spreads only from obstruents, with the sonorants behaving as voice-neutral. The RROC will predict that any P rule mentioning either [+voice] or [α voice] will be sufficient to trigger the prior application of the redundancy rule specifying the sonorants as voiced; but this means that the sonorants will become voiced *before* voicing assimilation, and thus able to trigger and block the rule. In a different context, Archangeli (1988, p. 199) suggests that problems of this general class may be resolved by appeal to Structure Preservation. Perhaps Structure Preservation takes precedence over the RROC in prohibiting the insertion of the nondistinctive [+voice] value in sonorants. Russian voicing is not the example considered by Archangeli, but we can use it to illustrate the pitfalls of this proposal. First, the Russian sonorants must be voice-unspecified *postlexically*, as indicated by the comparison between the two phrases *ot melodii* and *od* *mzdy*. Structure Preservation is surely not responsible for this. Second, if Structure Preservation applies to block the insertion of noncontrastive values in Russian, then it should have the same effect in the case of Yoruba ATR: the predictably retracted *a* should be unable to trigger [−ATR] harmony, at least within the Yoruba lexical component. This is not the case. No account based on the RROC can be combined with the hypothesis of Structure Preservation to derive both the Russian and the Yoruba patterns of underspecification.

2.2.2 Markedness Reversals

A second theme of the underspecification model developed by Archangeli is the idea of parametrizing markedness. Recall that the analysis of Yoruba ATR harmony requires reference to [−ATR] as the active value. In other systems [+ATR] must be assumed to be active;[23] these include the ATR harmonies of Akan (Clements 1978), Igbo (Ringen 1979), and others. The version of markedness theory espoused by Kiparsky (1985) provides for one and the same value in every feature being designated as universally marked. This marked value is the only one allowed underlyingly, in all languages, but the problem is that we need this value to be [−ATR] in Yoruba and [+ATR] in Akan. To resolve such conflicts, Archangeli (1984, 1988, pp. 193–196) proposes to consider the marked status of certain feature values as reflecting preferences, not invariant facts of Universal Grammar (UG). We may think of these preferences as the optimal, but not unique, values of universal parameters. Thus UG is said to prefer [+high], [−low], [−back], [−ATR] values in vowels. This means that, *in the normal case*, the opposite values ([−high], [+low], [+back], [+ATR]) will be marked and, hence, candidates for underlying specifications. The resulting system is merely the null hypothesis, not the only possibility entertained by a language learner, and so language specific facts may override the null hypothesis and lead to an alternative analysis of the data. In particular, evidence that a feature value such as the [−ATR] of Yoruba is phonologically active may be taken as sufficient grounds to set up an underlying inventory of values which reverses some universal preference. The UG markedness system will be able to manifest itself only in the absence of clear-cut data overriding it. The descriptive system resulting from this idea of parametrized markedness is flexible enough to handle a great deal of cross-linguistic variation in the behavior of features like [ATR]. The analyses of individual languages are, in principle, learnable, since the UG preferences act as guidelines to the language learner whenever the system of underlying values remains indeterminate.

My view of this is that parametrization is clearly involved in the Yoruba and Akan [ATR] systems; however, it is far from obvious that what is being parametrized is markedness. In the case of [ATR], we simply have no cross-linguistic basis on which to claim that one or another value is marked: [ATR] displays a cross-linguistic distribution that does not involve the sort of context-free implicational relations upon which claims of markedness are normally based. We say that laryngealized sounds are marked because their presence in a system always implies that of the corresponding non-laryngealized ones. The presence of either [+ATR] or [−ATR] vowels does not imply cross-linguistically the presence of the other value: only certain combinations between ATR and height values can be said to be marked. And, if [+ATR] by itself is no more or less marked than [−ATR], then this is hardly the feature on which to base claims about markedness variation. Indeed, we can note that features like [nasal], for which implicational statements of the form *[αF] implies [−αF]* can be formulated, are *never* involved in markedness reversals. [ATR] simply does not belong in this set. Understanding what is cross-linguistically invariant in matters of segmental markedness, what is not, and why is the critical issue here; we return to it in section 2.3.3.3, where the theory of markedness is more fully explored.

2.2.3   Null Segments

The link between underspecification and markedness reversals is also explored by Archangeli (1984, 1988) and Pulleyblank (1988a) in their discussion of *null segments*. These are segments carrying full surface specifications but behaving phonologically as if they lack many or most feature values. The typical null segment is the epenthetic vowel. By definition, this is not an underlying segment: under any reasonable account of vocalic epenthesis, the element first introduced by epenthesis into the string is a segmentally empty place-holder (Itô 1989). Only later rules specify the quality of the inserted nucleus. What are these rules? Archangeli (1984) points out that the unmarked assumption should be that these are independently needed mechanisms: the redundancy rules of the language. Yokuts (Newman 1949; Archangeli 1984) illustrates this connection between epenthesis and redundancy rules. Its underlying vowel system is {a, o, i, u}, analyzed in (27) in accordance with Archangeli's (1984) remarks:

(27)

	a	o	i	u		
high	−		−		[ ] → [−round]	[+round] → [+back]
round		+		+	[ ] → [+high]	[+low] → [+back]
					[−high, −round] → [+low]	[ ] → [−back]

In Yokuts, a vowel is inserted before an otherwise unsyllabifiable consonant (28i); this vowel is then subjected to the lexically applicable redundancy rule (28ii), after which Rounding Harmony applies between vowels of equal height (28iii). The remaining redundancy rules apply postlexically (28iv). The distinction between lexical and postlexical redundancy rules is dictated by the RROC: the lexical rule of harmony mentions [α high] (it spreads [round] only between [α high] vowels) and thus triggers the lexical application of [ ] → [+high]. All other vocalic redundancy rules are left to apply postlexically.

(28)   UR

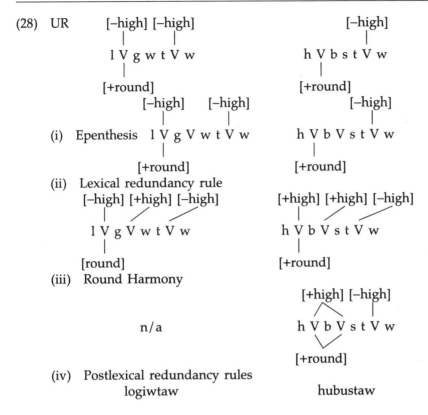

(i)   Epenthesis

(ii)   Lexical redundancy rule

(iii)   Round Harmony

n/a

(iv)   Postlexical redundancy rules
          logiwtaw   hubustaw

What evidence, other then the descriptive coherence of the system, do we have that this is the right analysis of Yokuts epenthesis? The evidence, as I see it, is that the epenthetic vowel is an undergoer, not a trigger of harmony; it is not a trigger because it lacks the harmonically active [+round] value. It lacks it because [+round] cannot be supplied by redundancy rules; it is a marked value. Beyond Yokuts, the hypothesis that redundancy rules are entirely responsible for the segmental makeup of epenthetic vowels makes the frequently correct prediction that these segments will be phonologically inert; they will never carry more specifications than other vowels and, frequently, they will carry fewer. They are typically non-triggers and undergoers, as in the Yokuts case.

Once we appreciate the attractions of this analysis of null segments, we can observe that it commits one to the hypothesis of markedness reversals, for it is clearly the case that languages with essentially identical inventories select different qualities for their epenthetic segments. A relevant comparison is that between Yokuts and Mohawk. The vocalic system of Mohawk contains {a, e, o, i, u} along with a unique nasalized vowel ʌ̃, which could perhaps be viewed as altogether lacking an oral articulatory target. Like Yokuts, Mohawk epenthesizes a vowel in clusters that cannot be properly syllabified, but the vowel epenthesized is *e*, not *i*. It is possible to analyze Mohawk *e* as underlyingly featureless, but that can only be done if we assume that Mohawk lists [+high], not [−high], as a marked value. The resulting system appears below:

(29)

	a	e	o	i	u
high				+	+
round			+		+
low	+				

[ ] → [−round]   [+round] → [+back]
[ ] → [−high]   [+low] → [+back]
[ ] → [−low]   [ ] → [−back]

Pulleyblank's (1988a) discussion of Yoruba *i*, another possible null segment, clarifies an essential aspect of the analysis: the null segment need not be epenthetic. It can be underlyingly present as a placeless vowel, a (mostly) bare root node. What the typical null segment is claimed to lack invariably are the place features; they are missing because they can be inserted by redundancy rules. Given Lexical Minimality and the possibility of postulating a redundancy rule of the form [ ] → [αF] for every underlying [−αF], the theory of radical underspecification predicts that every language will possess a placeless vowel and perhaps an underlyingly placeless consonant, whether or not the language has epenthesis rules. Before looking into the evidence bearing on this point, we should however analyze more closely the logic of these predictions and the mechanisms they require.

The first point in need of examination is the principle in virtue of which place features can be left out of the underlying structure of null segments. Consider Yokuts again and its null vowel *i*. In this language there exist underlying *i*'s as well as epenthetic ones. What distinguishes an underlying placeless vowel from the utter absence of a segment? The answer, according to Pulleyblank (1988), is the root node. What justifies the existence of an underlying root node to which no place features are associated? The underlying presence of some stricture feature, say [+sonorant] or [−consonantal]. We come now to the critical question: why is this stricture specification present underlyingly? Clearly, it too could be inserted by a redundancy rule: [ ] → [+sonorant]. Moreover, both [+sonorant] and [−consonantal] values are predictable. Thus [+sonorant] follows, in the case of *i*, from [−consonantal]: there are no obstruent vocoids. The value [−consonantal] can be predicted from either the absence of a supralaryngeal component, as in the case of *h* and *ʔ*, or from typically vocalic place specifications such as [+round], [+high], [+low]: there are no consonants bearing such features in Yokuts. Markedness does not tell us whether to predict place from stricture or stricture from place; if anything, the fact that we cannot determine the stricture degree of a constriction unless we know where it is made suggests that we should try to predict stricture from place, not vice versa. In any case, the language learner needs to find some good reason *not* to eliminate [+sonorant] and signal the existence of the underlying segment *i* by using some other feature, say [+high]. I submit that no such independent argument can be found. Pulleyblank, who touches on this issue in the course of analyzing Yoruba *i* as a null segment, suggests that Yoruba refers to [+sonorant] in one of its morpheme structure conditions. Therefore the need for underlying [+sonorant] is guaranteed, and every other insertable feature must be eliminated. But this answer, not persuasive in its details, is limited to Yoruba; it does not extend to languages lacking the relevant morpheme structure condition. The consequence is that the choice between marking an underlying null segment by using a stricture feature like [+sonorant] or by using a place feature like [+high] remains arbitrary.[24] No credible principle will lead us to the desired conclusion.

2.2.4 Placeless Segments and Phonetic Underspecification

The second point to consider is the functioning of the redundancy rules needed to provide the surface values of a null segment. Assume that Yokuts *i* starts out as a [+sonorant] root node. To be realized as [+high, –back, –round, –low], this segment has to be subjected to the application of some context-free redundancy rules. The rules were given in (27). We sketch below two steps of the filling-in process:

(30) [ ] → [+high]:   root $_{[+son]}$ . . . Place . . . [+high]
      [ ] → [–back]:   root $_{[+son]}$ —— Place ＿＿ [+high]
                                            ` ` . . . [–back]

Within the analysis proposed by Pulleyblank and Archangeli, it is critical that at least some of the redundancy rules involved in specifying null segments be context-free, for there are, by hypothesis, no input place features in a null segment that could condition the redundancy rules. It is this very assumption of context-free redundancy rules that turns out to be unworkable. The source of the difficulty are the segments, found in practically every language, which *start out and remain fully or partially placeless* on the surface: the laryngeal consonants *h* and *ʔ*, the schwa-like vowels, the central vowels lacking both [round] and [back] values, the segments displaying surface fluctuation in their exact constriction site (cf. the discussion of Gooniyandi below). We may call these segments *permanently* placeless and compare them to the null segments, which are believed to be only temporarily placeless. The supposedly cost-free, universal redundancy rules of the form [ ] → [+high], [ ] → [–back], [ ] → [+anterior] have inexplicably failed to affect the permanently placeless segments.

Let us consider one specific instance of this problem. We know that the laryngeal consonants *h* and *ʔ* are phonologically placeless (Steriade 1987a; McCarthy 1988; Pulleyblank 1988b); they must be represented as root nodes, possessing a laryngeal branch but no supralaryngeal node or values. We also know that they are phonetically placeless; they lack oral articulatory targets

(Keating 1988). We have established, then, that they never undergo any redundancy rules specifying place. The question then is what aspect of the structure of *h* tells context-free redundancy rules like those in (30) *not* to apply to it? How is *h* relevantly different from *i*? Is it the fact that *h* possesses a laryngeal feature? That suggestion makes the unlikely prediction that the inventory of aspirated or laryngealized vowels – in languages like Zapotec (Jones and Knudson 1977; Lyman and Lyman 1977) or Acoma (Miller 1965) – will somehow differ from that of modal vowels, in that the presence of aspiration will block the redundancy rules from applying to an aspirated V. In fact, however, the inventories of modal and laryngeally specified vowels are identical. Perhaps then *h* fails to undergo the vocalic redundancy rules because *h* is a consonant. But its status as a consonant refers to its possible syllabic position, not to its feature values: syllabicity should be irrelevant to the application of redundancy rules. We know, in any case, that vowels too can be permanently placeless: this is the case of schwa, which phonologists have analyzed as featureless (cf. Jakobson 1938, p. 129; S. Anderson 1982). As in the case of *h*, we can show that schwa remains featureless into the phonetic component; the discussion provided by Browman and Goldstein (1992) and their commentators indicates that English schwa either lacks a specified articulatory target or possesses a target corresponding to a vocalic neutral position "the mean tongue tract-variable position for all the full vowels" (Browman and Goldstein 1992, p. 56). Why have the universal context-free redundancy rules [ ] → [+high], [ ] → [−back], etc., failed to apply to schwa?[25]

There are several ways to look at the problem just identified. One is to characterize it as a technical issue: we must then find ways of reformulating the relevant redundancy rules in such a way as to allow certain segments to emerge as placeless from the phonological component. I doubt that a meaningful solution will be found along these lines. Another way is to abandon the hypothesis of Full Specification ((2) above) and, with it, the idea that context-free redundancy rules are needed in order to generate fully specified representations. If context-free redundancy rules are eliminated, the only feature-filling mechanisms will be of the context-sensitive category, e.g., [+back] → [+round]. They will therefore be applicable only if the segment contains some place feature to begin with; and consequently, genuinely placeless segments like *h* will be left placeless. This solution leads directly to the model of Contrastive Underspecification discussed below. The third possibility is to view the difficulty raised by context-free redundancy rules as an indication that no workable theory of redundancy rules can be formulated. This is, for different reasons, Mohanan's (1991) conclusion. We will see that the bulk of the evidence supports it. For the moment, though, we return to our discussion of Radical Underspecification to address a distinct issue: leaving aside matters of principle and technique, we should ask whether the available evidence supports the hypothesis of *temporarily* placeless segments. (I emphasize here *temporarily*, since that is the only category of placeless segment that supports the existence of context-free redundancy rules.) The next section takes up this question.

2.2.5   The Evidence for Temporarily Placeless Segments: Epenthesis and Asymmetry Effects

There are two sorts of arguments for postulating derivations like (30), in which a placeless segment acquires feature values through the application of context-free redundancy rules. One has been mentioned above: the scenario in (30) gives us a satisfying account of epenthesis, in that it uses only independently motivated mechanisms to specify the quality of inserted vowels. If we give up on context-free redundancy rules, epenthetic vowels like Yokuts *i* will have to emerge from the application of language-particular specification rules. The obvious concern here is that such specification rules are ad hoc mechanisms, revealing nothing about markedness or the functioning of individual sound systems. The other argument for context-free redundancy rules was developed at some length by Pulleyblank (1988b) and summarized by Archangeli (1988, p. 200) as *the asymmetry effect*: a variety of rules reveal that one and only one segment in a language is a selective undergoer of assimilation, a non-trigger of other processes, and a generally inert element in the system. This segment must then be underlyingly present but null: context-free redundancy rules will be needed to give it surface features.

We consider the asymmetry effect first. A distinction must be made at the outset between arguments establishing that an *underlying* segment of the language behaves as an all-around inert element and arguments showing that an *epenthetic* segment is inert. Abaglo and Archangeli (1989) demonstrate, for instance, that Gengbe *e* is inserted in a variety of circumstances, to satisfy minimal word constraints or provide a proper syllabification to underlying consonants. This *e* is also asymmetrically targeted by assimilation rules. The asymmetry effect in this case could well be due to the fact that the relevant instances of *e* contain no segment whatsoever, not to the presence of an underlying null segment. Details of Abaglo and Archangeli's derivations of Gengbe *e* (1989, p. 474) indicate quite clearly that the inert *e* starts out as a bare mora, not as a bare root node: it fails to undergo redundancy rules at the same time as other vowels of the language, presumably because there is no segment there to receive the redundant values. This case of asymmetry then boils down to the observation that epenthetic segments are not present underlyingly. We cannot dispute this fact, but the extent to which it provides an argument for context-free redundancy rules can only be determined when we look at other properties of epenthesis. A very different situation is that of Yoruba *i*, analyzed in detail by Pulleyblank (1988b). This segment *is* present underlyingly. Pulleyblank shows that its distribution is unpredictable and that it possesses a root node capable of spreading onto adjacent positions. It is then highly significant that there exist rules in Yoruba which single out this *i* as inert. The most revealing one is a phrasal-level regressive assimilation, triggered by all vowels but not by *i* (Pulleyblank 1988b, p. 238). Some examples of this optional process appear below:

(31)   V₁ # V₂ (V₂ ≠ i)   V₁ # i
       owó adé ~ owá adé "Ade's money"   ará ìlú (*arí ìlú) "townsman"
       owó ɛmu ~ owẽ ɛmu "wine money"   ɛrù igi (*ɛrì igi) "bundle of wood"
       ilé ayɔ̀ ~ ilá ayɔ̀ "Ayo's house"

Pulleyblank formulates the regressive assimilation as spreading the place node of the second vowel: if *i* has no place node, it cannot trigger the rule and the pattern in (31) is explained. The facts, however, are somewhat more complex. The only word-initial high vowel allowed in Standard Yoruba is *i*. The other high vowel, *u*, cannot occur initially. Thus we cannot tell whether the failure to trigger Regressive Assimilation characterizes all high vowels, or just *i*. According to A. Akinlabi (personal communication, 1992) the evidence of *u*-initial loanwords and dialectal forms suggests that *all* high vowels are non-triggers. This cannot be explained by claiming that both *i* and *u* are placeless. In addition, Akinlabi (1993) documents a lexical process in Yoruba whose application is triggered by high vowels: *r* deletes when next to *i* or *u*. This phenomenon calls for a reference to [+high] values in the lexical component of Yoruba, a fact which remains at odds with Pulleyblank's contention that only postlexical redundancy rules insert [+high].

Consider now the argument for context-free redundancy rules based on epenthesis. Clearly, the optimal outcome would be for epenthetic segments to be filled-in by processes needed elsewhere in the language. The question is whether this hypothesis can be worked into coherent accounts of individual systems. Several observations make this an unlikely prospect. First, there exist languages with *two* epenthetic vowels, both lexically derived: Hindi inserts *i* before *s*-obstruent clusters, and schwa between other C sequences (Mahajan 1993), while Hungarian inserts *a* before certain nominal suffixes generating disallowed CCC clusters and *o* into most other instances of CCC (Vago 1980, p. 53). Both these vowels cannot be due to the application of the same redundancy rules. Second, there exist languages where a null vowel – identifiable as such by the fact that it is a selective target of assimilation – contrasts with a non-null vowel of *identical* surface quality. Thus Hualde (1991) shows that Basque possesses a bare mora, which selectively undergoes a close-range assimilation from an adjacent vowel. Where no adjacent vowel exists, this slot is realized as *e*. Basque also possesses an underlyingly specified *e*, which does not pattern as a null vowel in assimilation. As Hualde points out, we need here a specification rule of the form *empty* μ → *[e]*, not a set of context-free redundancy rules from which all *e*'s would emerge as null segments. A very similar argument was formulated by Hume (1992, pp. 273–274) for Maltese Arabic: one morpheme class contains vowels that are selective undergoers of assimilation. Where assimilation is inapplicable, these vowels surface as *i*. But not all Maltese *i*'s are selective undergoers; most are not. We cannot therefore analyze the null vowel of Maltese as undergoing general rules of the form [ ] → [+high], [ ] → [−back], and we cannot attribute the insertion of *i* to the fact that [+high] and [−back] are absent across the board from the underlying representations of the language. Here, too, we need a specification rule that cannot be equated with an redundancy rule.

A different issue is raised by languages like Tiberian Hebrew, where epenthetic and reduced vowels receive a range of distinct surface values, depending on where in the string they occur. The data has been analyzed by Rappaport (1981), who notes that epenthetic vowels are realized as *e* in closed final syllables (/melk/ → [melek] "king"), as *i* in initial closed syllables (/k sbii/ → [kisbii]), and as schwa elsewhere (e.g., intermediate *mVlaakiim* → [məlaakiim], or underlying /b šalom/ → [bəšalom]). It is impossible to claim that the independently needed redundancy rules of Hebrew – whatever they may be – are responsible for the [+high] quality of inserted *i* in [kisbii] *and* for the [–high] of the *e* in *melek*. An added twist is that most Hebrew epenthetic and reduced vowels surface as schwa, the only plausible analysis of which is that it is placeless. There are no context-free redundancy rules operating here; there are only specification processes associating the features of *i* or *e* to certain empty nuclei.

If we conclude, then, that the quality of epenthetic segments should not be attributed to redundancy rules, we must explain several of the observations that made Archangeli's underspecification theory initially attractive. One point is that epenthetic vowels are typically targets of assimilation. The other is that when inserted vowels have a definite quality, they are generally drawn from the set {i, e, ɨ}: certain feature values (like [+round] or [+low]) and certain feature combinations (like [+round, –back] or [+low, –back]) are normally absent from the composition of an epenthetic vowel. This fact is clearly related to the markedness of these values. How then can we explain the fact that specification rules do not normally insert segments with the quality of u, ü, œ, ɑ or æ?

A possible line of investigation starts by observing that epenthetic vowels originate as schwa-sounding releases or transitions from one consonantal gesture onto the next. Many languages stop at this stage and leave the inserted vowel placeless, or subject to coarticulatory specification from neighboring sounds. In languages where a definite quality is eventually associated to the inserted segment, this quality could result from an attempt to identify the schwa-sound with a vowel quality that is phonemically present in the language. This is an instance of what Kiparsky (1968a, 1988) has dubbed "imperfect learning": the language learner comes to expects all vowels to be drawn from a certain fixed inventory and is therefore led to mistakenly identify schwa as being a deviant instance of some other vowel. If so, the crucial question will be, what underlying vowel does this schwa sound most like? It is here that considerations akin to markedness play a role: schwa is the vocalic neutral position and will therefore be identified with sounds that are in one respect or another closest to the neutral position. The absence of rounding, of front-rounding, or of a low jaw position (i.e., [+low]) can be straightforwardly explained in this way: these articulations involve a significant departure from the neutral position. We may finally speculate that the frequent choice of a high vowel – typically *i* or *ɨ* – indicates a preference for the vowels that are phonetically shortest, perhaps because schwa itself starts out as a brief transition between consonantal gestures.

Whether or not this alternative interpretation of epenthetic vowels can be successfully developed, we should note that any connection between markedness theory and the quality of an inserted segment remains precarious in the context of Archangeli's version of Radical Underspecification. The reader will recall that one of the essential aspects of that model is that markedness facts are reversible. Thus, even though [–round] is the normally unmarked value, language-specific circumstances may require underlying reference to [–round] and hence a redundancy rule inserting [+round]. To the extent then that markedness plays a constant role in selecting the quality of epenthetic vowels, the theory cannot characterize this fact, for it cannot exclude the possibility that a language learner will find some reason to postulate a redundancy rule system from which *œ* or *a* will emerge as the null vowel.

2.3   *Contrastive Underspecification*

One intuition that underlies Kiparsky's views on lexical underspecification is that redundancy rules based on context-free markedness principles, such as *[–voice] is the unmarked value of [voice]*, will be able to apply lexically. Only the feature values subject to *co-occurrence filters*, such as [voice] in **[–voice, +sonorant]*, will be uninsertable lexically. The prediction, then, is that postlexical rules will encounter segments that are fully specified for some feature F, provided that F is not subject to a co-occurrence filter within that segment class, i.e., provided that F is distinctive. Thus Russian obstruents will emerge from the lexicon fully specified for voicing, but sonorants, not being distinctively voiced, will have no lexical values for [voice]. The theory of Contrastive Underspecification originates as an attempt to verify this prediction of Kiparsky's model, in somewhat weakened form. The survey of underspecification cases presented in Steriade (1987b) was undertaken initially in order to observe whether (32) holds generally:

(32)   Priority for distinctive values: At every level of phonological analysis at which we find a feature F specified in a segment for which F is *not* contrastive, we will also find *both* values of F present in segments for which it *is* contrastive. However, the converse does not necessarily hold: we may find feature F behaving as a bivalent feature at a level at which feature F is not specified in segments where it is not contrastive.

As noted, (32) is simply a weaker version of the prediction made by Kiparsky's model, weaker because it does not mention anything about the boundary between the lexical and postlexical components. The survey results turned out to be largely compatible with (32): no credible cases were encountered in which a distinctive F value was absent at a derivational stage where nondistinctive values for F were already present. Concretely, no cases were found (at least in 1987) in which, for instance, [+voice] values would have to be present in sonorants but [−voice] would be absent in obstruents.

A striking fact emerged from that survey that was, however, inconsistent with Kiparsky's views. It was the surprising scarcity of cases illustrating distinctive underspecification, i.e., the possibility that unmarked but distinctive F values might be missing underlyingly. This observation led to the hypothesis that distinctive F values, whether marked or unmarked, are always specified underlyingly. The clearest formulation of this position is Calabrese's (1988), paraphrased below:

(33)　The Hypothesis of Contrastive Underspecification:
　　(a)　Feature values predictable on the basis of universal co-occurrence
　　　　conditions can be omitted from underlying representations.
　　(b)　No other features may be underspecified.

The statement in (33) requires that both contrastive[26] values of a binary feature be present underlyingly. Thus, if [voice] is binary, obstruents must be specified as [+voice] and [−voice] respectively in underlying structure; only sonorants can be left unspecified for voice, since they alone are governed by a co-occurrence filter, *[+sonorant, −voice]. More generally, (33) bars underspecification of any feature F, binary or not, unless in segments where some *[(α)F, βG] condition can be validated, and F's values are predictable from G's. As we shall see in 2.3.2, (33) cannot be viewed as dictating the elimination of *all* feature values predictable from co-occurrence filters; it only indicates where we may find underspecification, not where we must.

In reviewing the evidence for (33), we must consider two types of arguments: those that establish (33b) by showing that underspecification is not found in certain cases, and those that establish (33a), by showing that feature co-occurrence conditions lead to underspecification. I emphasize again that our interest here is in the instances of temporary or nontrivial underspecification predicted by (33a). It can be anticipated now that these will be hard to come by. Trivial cases will turn out to be abundant.

The most significant aspect of Contrastive Underspecification is its rejection of Lexical Minimality. That principle is clearly being violated if we specify underlying voiceless obstruents as [−voice], instead of leaving them blank and using a redundancy rule such as [ ] → [−voice]. We must consider therefore first (section 2.3.1) the arguments for weakening or eliminating Lexical Minimality. A further point to be discussed is the necessary connection between Contrastive Underspecification and some theory of privative features: many potential counterexamples to the hypothesis in (33) were analyzed (by Mester and Itô 1989 and Steriade 1987b) as involving permanently privative rather than binary features. Privative features generate systems of lexical contrast that will appear to contradict (33): whether such evidence actually falsifies

(33) depends on the prospects for a coherent theory of privativity. A sketch of such a theory is presented in section 2.3.3, but its existence turns out to eliminate most of the evidence originally presented as supporting (33). Our general conclusion on Contrastive Underspecification will be that the work done in that framework was useful insofar as it shows why Lexical Minimality must be abandoned, but that the evidence for (33) as a principle inducing under-specification remains minimal.

2.3.1   The Evidence against Lexical Minimality

We consider now the evidence backing up the second half of (33): under-specification is not found in a large number of cases, where it could have served the purposes of Lexical Minimality.

At the outset a correction must be made in (33), without which the claim of restricted underspecification will appear to be patently false. In Steriade's and Calabrese's formulations, no account was taken of the instances of positional neutralization mentioned earlier (section 1.1.3), from which a great deal of underspecification appears to follow. Thus, for instance, [+ATR] is not licensed in Akan affixes (Clements 1978; Kiparsky 1985): the result is that the affix vowels are predictably [−ATR] in the absence of harmony. Harmony may be said to proceed from root to affix precisely because the affixes have predict-able, hence underspecified, values for this feature: underspecification follows from predictability on the assumptions outlined earlier. Because the Akan affixal underspecification for [ATR] does not fall under the provision of (33a), Contrastive Underspecification appears to wrongly exclude it. This, I would suggest, was more in the nature of an oversight than an intended result; (33) can be corrected to allow all varieties of underspecification rooted in context-sensitive constraints. A revision apears below:

(34)   The Hypothesis of Contrastive Underspecification: revised
    (a)   Feature values predictable on the basis of universal co-occurrence conditions or on the basis of positional neutralization statements can be omitted from underlying representations.
    (b)   No other features may be underspecified.

Having thus extended the scope of Contrastive Underspecification, we note that the study of positional neutralization reveals several interesting difficul-ties for the principle of Lexical Minimality. What we observe is that redun-dancy rules of the form [ ] → [coronal], [+anterior] are *not* being used to eliminate the point of articulation features of alveolar coronals from underly-ing representations, despite the fact that such redundancy rules would vastly simplify the underlying consonantal inventory and individual lexical entries. Plain alveolars appear to be place-specified, at least as [coronal], frequently as [coronal, +anterior]. Place underspecification in the coronal class is encoun-tered, but only in the cases of features subject to positional neutralization.

In an important study of aboriginal Australian coronal systems, Hamilton (1993) points out that many Australian languages do not allow their full inventory of coronal features to surface in initial position. Thus Gaagudju, a language where apical consonants may be distinctively alveolar or retroflex, neutralizes this anteriority contrast in initial position: all initial apicals are, in the general case, alveolar. However, when an initial apical is followed within the word by a retroflex consonant, it surfaces as retroflex too:

(35) (a) naːwu 3rd sg. masc. pronoun
      (b) deːɳmi → deːɳmi "again, as well'
      (c) niːɲja "just"

The full range of facts considered by Hamilton suggests that certain place distinctions are perceptible, in these aboriginal languages, only postvocalically, perhaps because the transitions from a preceding vowel carry clues indispensible to the nature of the articulation. We could record such facts in the form of a licensing condition. Thus Gaagudju apicals license [−anterior] only postvocalically. In initial position, therefore, the apicals are predictably [+anterior]: they must be alveolars, since the other value for [anterior] is unlicensed in the absence of a preceding vowel. It is these apicals with predictable anteriority that are being targetted for anterior assimilation; the word-medial anterior apicals, whose anteriority is distinctive, do not undergo assimilation. One may interpret this fact, in accordance with the principle of Invariance, as indicating that the distinctive word-medial apical anterior segments (d, n) are fully specified as [−laminal, +anterior]: they do not undergo anteriority harmony *because* they are fully specified. The initial apicals are predictably [+anterior] and hence unspecified for anteriority; because unspecified, they can undergo assimilation. This analysis explains why assimilation targets precisely the site of positional neutralization. It entails, however, that no general redundancy rule of the form [ ] → [coronal, −laminal, +anterior] has been employed in Gaagudju. Apico-alveolars may well be unmarked, but they are not underlyingly placeless. This contradicts Lexical Minimality, in the form in which this principle has been invoked as the fundation of Radical Underspecification.

Even more revealing is the case of Gooniyandi, also analyzed by Hamilton (1993). Here initial apicals are realized with free variation betwen an anterior and a nonanterior (retroflex) constriction site, while in other positions Gooniyandi has a lexical contrast between alveolar and retroflex apicals. Like Gaagudju, Gooniyandi displays assimilation between an initial apical and a following one. In such cases, the articulation of the initial apical is invariably alveolar or retroflex, depending on the point of articulation of the following apical:

(36) (a) duwu or ɖuwu "cave"
      (b) ɖiɽipindi (no diripindi variant) "he entered"
      (c) dili (no ɖili variant) "flame, light"
      (d) laɳgiya or ɭaɳgiya "midday"

It appears that in Gooniyandi neither [anterior] value is licensed initially. In this case, the phonological representation of the initial apicals lacks any value for anteriority and the phonetic component inherits structures that it is free to interpret variably. Harmony targets the initial apicals precisely because they lack [anterior] values. We have then two distinct ways to identify [anterior] unspecified apicals in Gooniyandi: they are subject to [anterior] harmony and, when harmony is inapplicable, they lack constant values for [anterior]. By these criteria, the medial apico-alveolars of Gooniyandi, e.g., *d* in *ḍiṛipindi* "he entered", emerge as fully specified [coronal, −laminal, +anterior]; they are non-targets of assimilation and they do not fluctuate in their anteriority values. Once again, the data contradict Lexical Minimality. They demonstrate that a perfectly coherent, markedness-based redundancy rule ([coronal, −laminal] → [+anterior]) has not been used to simplify lexical representations, for, if such a redundancy rule had been used, the medial apicals would have been underspecified too. Only *contextually* predictable features are omitted.[27]

Comparable arguments against Lexical Minimality are provided by many systems of vocalic harmony. One example, drawn from work by McCarthy (1979) and Flemming (1993), illustrates the entire class. Tigre has a series of long vowels {aː, eː, iː, oː, uː} and a series of short ones {ə, ɐ}. The short vowels contrast in relative height, but not in localization; both ə and ɐ are central. It is these short central vowels, and only they, that undergo a harmony spreading [−back] and [+back]. To express the connection between harmony and the underlying lack of backness distinctions in the short series, we may want to write a feature-filling harmony which spreads palatality from {i, e} and velarity from {u, o} onto the vowels unspecified for [back]. (An additional filter will be needed to prohibit the co-occurrence of [low] with [α back] in underlying or derived representations, since the central vowel *aː* does not undergo harmony.) Notice then that long vowels possess both backness values, since ə, ɐ are fronted before *iː, eː* and backed before *oː, uː,* whereas *aː* and ə, ɐ possess neither. Lexical Minimality is violated here by the failure to eliminate one or the other of the two backness/rounding values from the lexicon. (This would have been feasible in this system of vocalic contrasts; among the long vowels, the system could have been based on the feature values [+low], [+high], and [+round] or [+low], [+high], and [−back]. Among the short vowels, only a height contrast would be needed.) We may also view this case, like that of Gooniyandi above, as an argument against the assumption of Full Specification (2): where harmony is inapplicable, the central vowels fail to acquire *any* [back] specification.[28] This observation points to the same conclusion as the previous ones: there are no context-free redundancy rules of the form [   ] → [αback]. For the long non-low vowels of Tigre, such redundancy rules are unnecessary, since both backness values of {i, e, o, u} are phonologically active. For the Tigre central vowels *a, ə, ɐ,* such redundancy rules would be positively harmful, since they will prevent the central vowels from ever surfacing as central.

A very similar argument involving the palatality and velarity of Barra Gaelic consonants has been formulated by Clements (1986b). In Barra Gaelic, too, one must assume that a three-way distinction between palatalized, velarized, and plain consonants exists underlyingly and persists into the surface representations. Here too we discover lexical entries that are less than minimally specified; here too we must assume that context-free redundancy rules like [ ] → [αback] are inoperative.[29]

2.3.2 An Excursus on Liquid Underspecification and Liquid Transparency

Mester and Itô (1989) had formulated an argument against Lexical Minimality that is very similar to those reviewed in the preceding section. The argument is based on the observation that the *r* of Japanese, whose coronality is predictable from its liquid status, functions as placeless, in contrast to the obstruent coronals. Mester and Itô suggest that obstruents like *t* are not placeless because their place features are distinctive, unlike those of *r*. Their overall conclusion is that, even when a coherent analysis could be built on the context-free redundancy rules mandated by Lexical Minimality – e.g., [ ] → [coronal] – such redundancy rules are not found to be in use.[30]

Mester and Itô (1989) discuss the phonology of Japanese mimetics and the behavior of palatality within this lexical class. Mimetics are characterized by a morpheme-level feature of palatalization which associates to the rightmost coronal consonant within the mimetic word (37ii). If the mimetic lacks a coronal, palatality associates to the initial consonant, including the arguably placeless *h* (37iii). Palatality does not associate to the liquid *r*, even when this sound is properly placed to receive it (37iv). It should be noted, however, that *r*-initial mimetics are not encountered.

(37) (i) Japanese consonant inventory: {p, t, k, b, d, g, s, z, m, n, r, h, y, w}

    (ii) potya-potya (*pyota-pyota) "dripping in large quantities"
           kasya-kasya (*kyasa-kyasa) "noisy rustling of dry object"
           dosya-dosya (*dyosa-dyosa) "in large amounts"
    (iii) pyoko-pyoko (*pokyo-pokyo) "jumping around imprudently"
           hyoko-hyoko (*hokyo-hokyo) "lightly, nimbly"
    (iv) nyoro-nyoro (*noryo-noryo) "slow wriggly movement"
           hyoro-hyoro (*horyo-horyo) "looking thin and weak"

The analysis of mimetic palatality proposed by Mester and Itô goes as follows: Palatality is a floating feature which seeks a coronal anchor, starting from the right edge of the stem. When it finds none (37iii–iv), it defaults on any consonant, seeking association in unmarked left-to-right fashion. The coronal liquid *r* is not chosen as an anchor for palatality in forms like *nyoro-nyoro* because *r* is place-unspecified; its place features may be assigned by a redundancy rule of the form [+cont, +cons, +son] → [coronal]. This placeless liquid is contrasted with the coronal stops and fricatives {t, d, s, z}, which must be assumed to carry at least [coronal] values. Mester and Itô point out (p. 276) that one cannot recast the analysis in terms of saying that the palatality feature seeks a coronal qua placeless consonant. If that were so, there would be no reason to skip *r* in (37iv). It appears then that Japanese invokes only one means to derive place-underspecified representations: place features are omitted only when they are predictable from stricture values.

Two unanswered questions remain, however. Japanese has only one variety of fricatives; the sibilants {s, z} do not contrast with fricatives at other points of articulation. The same logic that predicts the place-underspecified status of *r*, might be expected to give us placeless sibilants, since a redundancy rule such as [+cont, −son] → [coronal] can be formulated on the basis of the co-occurence condition *[+cont, −son, labial or dorsal] and is consistent with the markedness facts involving the preferred point of articulation in fricatives. Yet forms like *kasya-kasya* establish clearly that the sibilants are fully-specified coronals. It appears then that Japanese does not exploit systematically the strategy of eliminating place features predictable from stricture specifications. This observation leads us to conclude that no general principle predicting underspecification emerges from − or is consistent with − Mester and Itô's analysis.

Behind the question just raised lurks a more serious difficulty. Although *s* is frequently the only fricative of a language, it never patterns as placeless. There are, for instance, no V-to-V assimilation rules that can skip *s*, but not other consonants. A variety of such rules, in which some subset of coronal sonorants pattern as transparent, has been documented by Kaun (1993a), who reanalyzes evidence first provided by Paradis and Prunet (1989), and by Parkinson (1993). The typical list of consonants transparent in V-to-V assimilations is *r*, *l* and occasionally *n*. The latter can be viewed in such cases as a nasalized flap, the nasal counterpart of *r*. Obstruents, whether or not possessing a distinctive point of articulation at their level of stricture, are never transparent. This observation suggests that the syndrome of liquid placelessness identified by Mester and Itô has no connection to issues of distinctiveness: the liquid is transparent not because its place features are predictable from its stricture, but for different reasons, which remain still unclear.

I illustrate this point − which will soon become significant in a different context − with the example of Cochabamba Quechua (Wallace 1988; McEachern 1993), where high vowels lower to mid before a uvular (38i), or before a cluster of a liquid + uvular (38ii). Before other C + uvular clusters, including those where C is an alveolar obstruent, the high vowels remain unaffected (38iii). The only apparent exception is that of (orthographic) *nq* clusters, which should be analyzed as homorganic sequences [Nq] (38iv). Vowels are lowered in this context, but this case can be assimilated to that involving high vowels strictly adjacent to a uvular. A distinct process lowers a high vowel immediately after a uvular (*qu* → *qo*): this process allows no segment to intervene between the factors of the rule.

(38) (i)   pisi-qa   → pise-qa   "little" (topic)
    (ii)   riku-rqa   → rikorqa   "he/she saw it"
        chilquy   → chelqoy   "to strip bark"
    (iii) riku-sqa   → rikusqa   "he/she had seen it"
    (iv)   riku-nqa   → rikoɴqa   "he/she will see it"

The regressive assimilation shown above could be viewed as the spreading of the Retracted Tongue Root specification from *q* onto a preceding vowel, subject to the condition that *q* and the vowel should have adjacent place nodes. A placeless segment may therefore intervene. If this is the right analysis, the transparent consonants are *r* and *l*, not coronal obstruents like *s*. This conclusion is reminiscent of Mester and Itô's analysis of the Japanese data, but with the disturbing twist that two distinct liquids must count as placeless. More significantly we observe that, exactly as in Japanese, *s* – whose point of articulation is equally nondistinctive in Quechua – does not behave as transparent.

We must draw from this case several related conclusions. First, the phenomenon of liquid transparency cannot be attributed to any form of temporary underspecification: it is highly implausible that Quechua *r* and *l* are placeless simultaneously. This conclusion is strengthened by Parkinson's (1993) results, according to which all coronal sonorants of Rwaili Arabic {r, l, n} are transparent in V-to-V assimilations. Second, we infer from the Japanese and Quechua data, as well as from Kaun's (1993a) survey results, that no matter how nondistinctive its point of articulation may be in a given language, *s* is never placeless: there are no redundancy rules of the form [−son, +cont] → [coronal, +anterior]. This is another way of recording the failure of Lexical Minimality, but, in this case, the problem identified casts doubt on Contrastive Underspecification itself, since the unattested redundancy rules are in fact consistent with (33).

2.3.3 Which Features are Privative?

We return now to the discussion of Lexical Minimality begun in section 2.3.1. If this principle is under attack, we must consider once again the evidence suggesting that binary features have only one value, the marked one, represented underlyingly. The omission of the unmarked value of [ATR], [voice], [round], etc., had been attributed by Kiparsky, Archangeli, Pulleyblank, and others to the requirements of Lexical Minimality. Once we abandon that principle, the analyses illustrating it must be reconsidered. The overall conclusion emerging from this review is that in most cases where it is justified to omit a feature value from underlying structure there is also considerable evidence that the value is permanently missing; the feature is privative.

2.3.3.1 Privative [round]

Consider first the behavior of [round], a feature whose unmarked value is [−round]. Unrounded vowels are, in all well-understood cases, non-triggers of

Round Harmony. In one case at least, that of Khalkha Mongolian, distinctively unrounded vowels are also non-blockers: they allow Round Harmony to proceed across them. The relevant facts, discussed in this context by Steriade (1987a), are summarized below: Mongolian spreads [+round] from an initial [−high] vowel onto a following [−high] vowel (39i). The high front vowel *i* − in any numbers or lengths − may intervene between the target and the trigger of harmony (39ii); the round high vowels *u* and *ü* may not (39iii).

(39)　(i)　Mongolian vowels: {a, e, o, ö, i, u, ü}
　　　(ii)　sons-ogd-ox "to be heard", örg-ögd-öx "to be raised" (cf. nee-gd-ex "to be opened")
　　　(iii)　oril-ox "to weep", oril-ogd-ox "to be wept" (*oril-ax)
　　　(iv)　boogd-uul-ax "to hinder" (*boogd-uul-ox)

The difference between neutral *i* and blockers *u*, *ü*, is clearly due to the fact that the latter possess the spreading feature [+round]. Since *i* does not block harmony, Locality requires us to assume that *i* does not possess [−round]:

(40)　(i)　Transparent i　　(ii)　Opaque u
　　　　　[+round]　　　　　　　[+round] [+round]
　　　　　　　⌒⟍　　　　　　　　　│　　　　│
　　　　o r i l - o x　　　　　boːgd - uːl - ax

The problem arises when we note that the [−round] value of *i* is distinctive in Mongolian: *i* contrasts with the rounded front *ü*. Why then would *i* fail to be specified as [−round]?

A possible answer is that [−round] does not exist: the feature is universally and permanently privative. The chief predictions of this approach are that [−round] will never give rise to assimilation or dissimilation. We *can* refer to the absence of an autosegment − and unrounded vowels will a form natural class on the basis of the absence of [round] − but absence cannot spread and repeated absence does not violate the OCP and cannot lead to dissimilation. These predictions are largely correct.[31] It should be emphasized that, if the facts are correctly characterized as above, [round] must be privative regardless of the fate of Contrastive or Radical Underspecification; nothing else will explain the absence of assimilatory or dissimilatory [−round] effects. Let's grant, then, that [round] is privative. The speculation suggested by this is that all cases requiring underlying absence of a distinctive F value involve features that are in fact single-valued. We review briefly the relevant cases, with the aim to provide a general characterization of the features that may pattern as privative.

2.3.3.2　*Privative [nasal], [spread] and [constricted]*
The features of nasality, aspiration, and glottalization form a class by themselves, in that all assimilatory and dissimilatory processes involving them refer

to [+nasal], [+spread], [+constricted], never to the opposite values. To my knowledge, no explicit case for the binarity of aspiration and glottalization has been – or could be – made. The case against [–spread] and [–constricted glottis] as phonological values was presented by Lombardi (1991) and Steriade (1992). Nasality represents a slightly different case, as there exist processes possessing the appearance of local [–nasal] assimilation. Local postoralization (ma → m^{b}a) and preoralization (am → a^{b}m) have been discussed in terms of spreading orality (S. Anderson 1976; Kiparsky 1985). These phenomena, as well as other possible lines of argument for a [–nasal] value, have been reanalyzed as consistent with the idea that nasality is privative (Steriade 1993a, 1993b; Trigo 1993). There is virtually no evidence left suggesting that orality is represented phonologically, in any language.[32] The conclusion that nasality, aspiration, and glottalization are privative features helps explain, in the present context, frequent asymmetries in the patterning of nasal vs. oral sounds, or aspirated/ glottalized vs. plain consonants. Thus aspiration and glottalization are subject to frequent dissimilatory constraints, of which Grassmann's Law (Collinge 1985) is the best known: only one aspirated stop is allowed within a given root, in Indo-European, Sanskrit, and Greek. If aspiration is a binary feature, the hypothesis of Contrastive Underspecification (33) dictates that distinctively nonaspirated segments will be underlyingly marked [–spread]. Thus, in a consonant inventory like that of Sanskrit, where {p, t, k} contrasts with {ph, th, kh}, the unaspirated series will be marked [–spread]. Any reasonable extension of the principle of Generality (11) will lead us to expect then that the dissimilating feature may be [–spread] in addition to [+spread]. If it is, then roots like /p . . . k/ or /t . . . k/ will be disallowed, since they would contain two [–spread] values. But, as noted, unaspirated unglottalized stops are never disallowed from co-occurring with each other, in any domain. It is only the assumption that aspiration is a privative feature that allows us to analyze Grassmann's Law and comparable phenomena in ways compatible with (33); the plain series {p, t, k} possesses no feature value for either aspiration or glottalization, at any derivational stage. What is distinctive in this case is the permanent *absence* of laryngeal features, not the presence of a minus-value.

2.3.3.3 *Equipollent Features: ATR and [back]*

The behavior of ATR, [high] and [back] is significantly different from that of the features reviewed so far. There exist good examples of processes engaging either value of these features. If, for instance, [–ATR] is needed for Yoruba harmony (Archangeli and Pulleyblank 1989), [+ATR] is needed for Vata and Akan (Kiparsky 1985), and both [–ATR] and [+ATR] are required for Kalenjin (Ringen 1989), then it is impossible to claim that ATR is permanently and universally a privative feature with a cross-linguistically constant phonetic implementation. We might suggest that ATR's privativity is language specific,[33] but this hypothesis leads to a notational variant of the claim that the feature is binary but possesses reversible markedness (Archangeli 1988 and

Pulleyblank 1992). Let us accept then that the tongue root feature is equipollent. The problem here is, as pointed out by Archangeli and Pulleyblank (1989), that ATR gives rise to dominant/recessive harmony patterns, that are best analyzed in terms of saying that only one ATR value is present in a given system. We reviewed earlier the case of Yoruba ATR harmony, in connection with the discussion of the RROC. The Yoruba vowel system is {a, ɛ, ɔ, e, o, i, u} and it appears that only the [−ATR] values are active. Only [−ATR] triggers harmony (cf. (24) above) and only one distinctive [−ATR] value is allowed underlyingly within a root; the mid vowels ɛ, ɔ may co-occur within a root only as the result of [−ATR] harmony. All these observations suggest strongly that the recessive value [+ATR] is absent, at least in the underlying representations of Yoruba. The problem for Contrastive Underspecification is that this value is absent in {e, o}, the *distinctively* [+ATR] vowels. As discussed above, one proposed resolution of this difficulty has been to parametrize markedness, to assume that languages are free to choose which ATR value to count as marked, and thus, which ATR value to allow in underlying representations. Several problems with this line of thinking were pointed out earlier, in the discussion of Radical Underspecification. A distinct question may be raised now, after we have identified a class of genuinely privative features: if the choice between (underlyingly) privative [+ATR] and privative [−ATR] is determined on a language-specific basis, why is the choice between privative [−nasal] and privative [+nasal] not determined in comparable ways? If markedness is reversible in ATR, why is it cross-linguistically constant in [nasal], [round], etc.?

The answer I propose is that equipollent features like ATR correspond in fact to two distinct privative features defined as two opposing gestures on the same or related articulatory dimensions (see the parallel discussion in chap. 14, this volume). There are several ways to implement this idea, which can be enumerated here, but not explored. One possibility is that the privative [−ATR] of languages like Yoruba (whose vowel inventories contain {i, u, e, o, ɛ, ɔ, a}) should be identified as [+low] instead, as suggested by Goldsmith (1985) à propos of Yaka, by Goad (1992) and by Casali (1993). [ATR] is hardly needed in languages with limited vowel inventories, such as Yaka and Yoruba, where [low] is sufficient to distinguish {a, ɛ, ɔ} from {i, u}. Moreover, Yoruba-like systems never give rise to [+ATR] harmony rules, according to Casali, a surprising fact in the context of a markedness reversal theory. Casali also observes that nine-vowel systems (i.e., {i, ɪ, u, ʊ, e, ɛ, o, ə, a}), where the distinctive presence of ATR is undeniable, do not display harmony types in which [−ATR] is the active value. This too is unexpected on Archangeli and Pulleyblank's theory of parametrized markedness, but follows from Goad's and Casali's hypothesis: the set {i, u} does not differ from {ɪ, ʊ} in terms of [low], but in terms of advancement, and therefore ATR must be phonologically active in such languages. An alternative possibility, appropriate for languages like Azerbaijani Aramaic (Hoberman 1988), is that what Archangeli and Pulleyblank might call dominant [−ATR] in such systems is in fact [Retracted Tongue Root] (or [Constricted Pharynx]), a feature with distinct articulatory properties from both the [low] of Yoruba and the privative [+ATR] of Igbo or Akan. The feature active in Aramaic harmony involves active tongue root retraction relative to the neutral position, while the privative [+ATR] of languages like Igbo or Akan would involve active tongue root protraction.[34] The parameter distinguishing Yoruba from Aramaic and Igbo would then involve choice of distinctive features rather than choice of marked value. An analysis along these lines makes a number of different predictions from that proposed by Archangeli and Pulleyblank, quite aside from its very distinct implications for the theory of markedness. Most important is the prediction that the articulatory correlates of so-called [−ATR] vowels should differ, depending on whether [−ATR] is the dominant or recessive value in harmony: the dominant [−ATR] (i.e., [low]) of languages like Yoruba should involve no active tongue root retraction, whereas that of Aramaic should.[35] Further, the dominant [+ATR] of Igbo is predicted to be phonetically distinct from the recessive [+ATR] (i.e., [−low]) of Yoruba. The latter should be phonetically equivalent to the recessive [−ATR] of Igbo, whereas the former should involve active advancement of the tongue root. A different prediction is that [RTR], [ATR] and/or [low] may coexist in a language. In the case of [ATR] and [RTR], this prediction may be confirmed in Kalenjin (Hall et al. 1974; Ringen 1989) and Chilcotin (Goad 1991).

Like [ATR], the feature [back] displays no clear markedness difference between its two poles, front and back. No implicational data supports the notion that one value of [back] is, taken in isolation, more or less marked than the other. The phonological behavior of [back] is also ambiguous: some [back] harmonies, such as that of Finnish (Kiparsky 1981; Steriade 1987b) are best analyzed in terms of privative [+back] while others, such as Chamorro (Chung 1983), clearly involve [−back] as the active value. It is conceivable that both palatality (i.e., [−back]) and velarity (i.e., [+back]) represent independent privative features, which may co-occur (as in Russian, cf. Keating 1985 and 1988, and Barra Gaelic, cf. Clements 1986b), but need not. One positive consequence of such a view is that phonetically central vowels (i.e., [ä], [ə], [ɨ], [ʉ]) could be analyzed more plausibly as segments lacking either palatality or velarity. Choi's (1992) acoustic analysis of the Marshallese central vowels strongly supports this interpretation.

Space does not permit a review of the privative or equipollent behaviors of other features, in particular the tonal features, as well as nontonal [high], [voice], and [anterior]. The goal of this section was not so much to provide an inventory of the features patterning like ATR as it was to support the idea that each articulatory dimension should be studied independently in determining whether it corresponds to one or several privative features. Conclusions about privativity, markedness, and, hence, underspecification based on the study of [nasal] or [round] are not directly applicable to features like ATR. Our discussion led to a proposal from which *all* features emerge as privative. In this respect, we come to partially agree with writers like van der Hulst and Smith (1985), Schane (1984, 1987), Kaye, Lowenstamm, and Vergnaud (1985),

Anderson, Ewen, and Staun (1985), Goldsmith (1985), Rice and Avery (1989), and Rice (1990), who have proposed inventories of single-valued features.[36] We have seen, however, that a uniformly privative theory requires a considerable expansion in the feature inventory; the question that should arise now is how to constrain this expansion. This issue is discussed further below.

To summarize, then, we have proposed that seemingly equipollent features like tongue root position and backness are in fact sets of two or more privative features defined on the same or perceptually related articulatory dimensions. A language may choose to utilize just one of the features drawn from a given set: Akan chooses ATR, not RTR, whereas Yoruba chooses [low] not RTR or ATR. The features proposed are universally privative, and no appeal to reversible markedness is being made in their treatment. The recessive segments, in any given harmony system involving such features, are recessive because they permanently lack the relevant values.

2.3.3.4   *A conjecture about the neutral position, markedness and feature privativity* [37]

If [ATR] represents two distinct privative features of advancement and retraction, why is it then that nasality cannot be split into privative [raise velum] and privative [lower velum]? Why is rounding not the sum of two privative features, [purse lips] and [spread lips]? Why, in other words, is it that only certain articulatory parameters can be split into two privative features while others appear better suited for analysis in terms of a single privative feature? This is a fundamental question which should arise quite independently of the debate over the parametrization of markedness.

A possible answer to it is to be sought in Chomsky and Halle's (1968, p. 300) notion of *neutral position*, the speech-specific rest position of articulatory organs.[38] Certain articulatory dimensions, such as the vertical movement of the soft palate, may have a built-in asymmetry between their two extremes: one pole represents the rest position of the relevant organ, relative to which the other pole must count as a deviation. Such articulatory parameters will give rise to the standard analysis in terms of privative features. These features are privative because only one deviation is possible, along the relevant dimension, from the neutral position, or, alternatively, only one deviation has significant enough acoustic consequences.[39] Other dimensions, which perhaps include the horizontal movement of the tongue root, may have distinct and salient acoustic consequences regardless of the direction of displacement. Both advancement and retraction of the tongue root may, for instance, be analyzed as displacements relative to the neutral position of this organ. This interpretation of the facts allows the distinction between marked and unmarked feature values to be encoded directly into the representations. Context-free markedness in a sound reflects the fact that the sound involves a gesture that deviates from the neutral position. Corresponding to this articulatory deviation there is a linguistic mark, i.e., a feature specification. Absence of deviation along some dimension results in absence of a specification for the corresponding feature. Sounds which are unmarked, in the articulatory sense defined, are thus phonologically unspecified. This proposal encodes directly only one aspect of segmental markedness, the articulatory effort involved in a deviation from the neutral position. Other sources of markedness – other properties that make a sound phonetically nonoptimal – appear to have either no consequences at all for its representation or may have different consequences from the ones discussed here.

Our speculation about the role of the neutral position in defining markedness and the range of possible feature values acknowledges the fact that different features have different markedness properties; nasality and tongue root position pattern differently and should not be used interchangeably in discussions of markedness. I suggested that differences in the markedness properties of different features should be linked to inherent asymmetries between the perceptual consequences of different articulatory gestures.

2.3.3.5 The impact of a privative feature system in theories of underspecification
The preceding sections led to the conclusion that the hypothesis of Contrastive Underspecification (33) can be maintained in the context of a feature system in which most, perhaps all, features are privative. Since many of the arguments originally presented as supporting (33) were cast in a framework where most features are binary, we must consider what is left of that evidence. This is necessary not only in order to assess the correctness of (33), but also to answer a core question of any underspecification theory: how extensive is the evidence that features present on the surface may be underlyingly missing? This question comes up as soon as we realize that a privative feature framework eliminates the need for most forms of nontrivial underspecification. Sonorants, for instance, are presented (in analyses such as Kiparsky 1985) as nontrivially underspecified for [voice]; they are claimed to lack underlying voice values, because such values are predictable, but they acquire them on the surface.[40] It is the existence of this residual class of nontrivial instances of underspecification that is at issue, for if such cases vanish as well, we will have to conclude that (33a) is false as stated, since it implies that some nontrivial underspecification is possible and attested.

The candidate analyses requiring nontrivial underspecification fall into two categories: those that make crucial use of binary features and those that are unaffected by the transition from a binary to a privative feature system. We briefly consider both.

(1) [Lateral] In the first class falls the case of lateral underspecification presented in Steriade (1987b) and amplified by Cohn (1993). In Latin, sequences of *l* . . . *l* dissimilate to *l* . . . *r*, presumably a reaction against the OCP violation involved in the [+lateral] . . . [+lateral] sequence. The only nonlateral whose intervention blocks this process is *r*. Thus *milit-aːlis* becomes *milit-aːris* "soldierly" but *floːr-aːlis* remains unchanged. This suggests that the *l* . . . *r* . . . *l* sequence of *floːr-aːlis* contains the feature values [+lateral] . . . [−lateral] . . .

[+lateral] and thus no OCP violation. The idea then is that the liquids *l* and *r* are distinctively specified for laterality, since they differ only in that feature, whereas the nonliquids are redundantly nonlateral, hence subject to underspecification. This conclusion is compatible with Cohn's (1992a) findings for Sundanese, where it is the [−lateral] sequences /r . . . r/ that induce dissimilation. (Both analyses, it will be noted, violate Generality, since both assume that only one value of [lateral] generates OCP violations: *r . . . r* is well-formed in Latin and *l . . . l* is well-formed in Sundanese.)

The force of this argument for nontrivial underspecification resides exclusively, as Kenstowicz (1993) has noted, in the belief that nonliquid coronals like *t* acquire surface [−lateral] values. If they do not, for whatever reason, there are no grounds for distinguishing between an underspecified stage where the *t* in *militːaris* lacks a [−lateral] value and a surface stage, where it possesses one. There is in fact no reason to assume that [−lateral] is ever assigned to nonliquids like *t*. As for what distinguishes *r* from *l*, binary laterality is only one possibility. We could, alternatively, say that *r* is a retroflex rhotic (marked [retroflex] or [rhotic]) unmarked for [lateral]. Sundanese then dissimilates sequences of [retroflex] values, Latin dissimilates sequences of [lateral]. Kenstowicz suggests that the blocking effect of *r* in *floːr-aːlis* could be attributed to the fact that the dissimilated */floːr-aːris/ violates the OCP too, this time on the [retroflex] tier.[41] There is empirical evidence that an analysis along the lines suggested by Kenstowicz must be the right approach to lateral disharmony. Crowhurst and Hewitt (1993) cite a Yidiny lateral dissimilation similar to Latin (*l → r /* . . . _____ *l*) which is blocked in *r . . . l . . . l* strings, that is when a rhotic *precedes* the *l . . . l* string to which dissimilation might apply. It is clear that the blocking effect of the rhotic here could not be analyzed in terms of locality: the *r* does not come in between the potential factors of the rule and does not prevent them from being adjacent on their tier. Rather, the rhotic blocks the rule because dissimilation will turn *r . . . l . . . l* into *r . . . r . . . l*, a string violating the OCP on the retroflex tier.

(2) [Anterior] or [laminal]   The case of [anterior] as a feature subject to nontrivial underspecification has been repeatedly discussed: the feature is taken to be binary in Steriade (1987b), where the Chumash sibilant harmony of the form s . . . š → š . . . š and š . . . s → s . . . s is analyzed. The nontrivially underspecified segment in such cases is *t*, the anterior coronal stop, which fails to trigger, undergo, or block the sibilant assimilation. The suggestion here too is to treat *t* as predictably [+anterior]. The Chumash consonant system does not oppose a [+anterior] nonsibilant to a [−anterior] one, and thus *t*'s anteriority can be considered nondistinctive. A phonetician might look at this case in very different terms, however: š-type fricatives differ from s-type fricatives in terms of the shape (slit-like vs. groove-like) and length of the constriction (Brosnahan and Malmberg 1970, p. 103). Stops contrast with each other in terms of the active and passive articulators involved in the constriction, not in terms of the shape and length of the constriction. Thus, one might well treat such cases as

involving featural distinctions that are permanently unavailable in stops, not instances of nontrivial underspecification. The other possibility, suggested to me by P. Ladefoged, is that the feature involved in Chumash and Chumash-like sibilant harmonies is laminality, a feature that is typically subject to phonetic (i.e., trivial) underspecification in the nonsibilant stops of languages, like English, French, or Chumash, where only one nonsibilant coronal stop exists. Dart (1990) demonstrates that in the absence of a *t:ţ* distinction, the unique coronal stop of English and French is free to fluctuate between apicality and laminality. In contrast, the sibilants *s* and *š*, which contrast, assume fixed values for this feature. We may speculate that the same holds for Chumash. If so, *t* fails to participate in harmony because it *permanently* lacks a value for [laminal]. Such phenomena argue then against Full Specification, not for (33).[42]

The issue of distinctiveness is, however, not irrelevant in the analysis of such cases. The permanent underspecification of *t* for [laminal] stems precisely from the absence of phonological contrast. But we see that what follows from the lack of contrast is not the temporary variety of underspecification that leads to the construction of derivational theories, but the permanent variety.

(3) [Voice] The example of voicing in sonorants has been used, here and elsewhere, as typical of the reasoning which leads to derivational approaches to underspecification. As noted at the beginning of this chapter, sonorants act, depending on the language, as fully specified [+voice] or as unspecified. The voice-unspecified sonorants of Russian (Kiparsky 1985) fail to trigger or block voicing assimilation; those of Japanese (Itô and Mester 1986) fail to trigger or block a voicing dissimilation. There is no doubt that, on the surface, the "unspecified" sonorants of Russian and Japanese are realized with a vibrating glottis, and in that sense, they are clearly voiced. But it is improbable that the sonorants share with the voiced obstruents all relevant articulatory adjustments that lead to vocal cord vibration. In producing voiced obstruents, the supralaryngeal cavity may have to be actively expanded, either by continuous larynx lowering or by tongue root advancement or by both strategies.[43] That such adjustments are not phonologically irrelevant has been shown in extensive detail by Trigo (1991); tongue root advancement in the production of the voiced stops of Madurese (Trigo 1991) and certain Akan dialects (Stewart 1967, cited in Casali 1993b) results in predictably ATR vowels. Such voiced obstruents must be specified, therefore, as both voiced in the sense of [vibrating vocal cords] and voiced in the sense of being pharyngeally expanded qua [ATR]. We may conjecture, then, that voiced obstruents share in permanent exclusivity some active process of pharyngeal expansion, which, according to the remarks on markedness sketched above, would have to correspond to a phonological feature. It may well be then that what propagates in Russian and dissimilates in Japanese is this element of pharyngeal expansion, a feature which sonorants will never acquire. Underspecification would therefore be permanent in such cases as well. On the other hand, in languages like English, where sonorants and voiced obstruents pattern alike in voicing assimilation,

the propagating feature would have to be the distinct element identified here as [vibrating vocal cords].[44] Our position is then that voiced (non-flap) obstruents are always specified as both [pharyngeally expanded] and [vibrating vocal cords]. Sonorants are permanently specified for the latter, permanently unspecified for the former.

(4) [High]   We must return now to the pattern of Bantu vocalic assimilation discussed earlier. Recall that mid vowels propagate [−high] onto suffixal high vowels, whereas the phonetically non-high *a* does not. The facts are repeated below:

(41)

Past	Neuter	Applied	Gloss
tul-a	tul-ika	tul-ila	"dig"
fis-a	fiš-ika	fiš-ila	"hide"
kos-a	kos-eka	kos-ela	"be strong"
sek-a	sek-eka	sek-ela	"laugh at"
pat-a	pat-ika	pat-ila	"scold"

Two related issues arise here. One is the binarity of [high], whose plus-value is the only one to spread in Romance (Calabrese 1988; Vago 1988; Flemming 1993) and Menomini (Cole and Trigo 1989). Only [+high] represents a signifi-cant deviation from the neutral position, hence we would expect only [+high] to be active. The facts of Bantu are problematic in that [−high] is clearly active here. Second, if [−high] was phonologically available, the existence of the Bantu pattern would appear to support (33), in the sense of showing that a surface-present feature, the [−high] of *a*, is phonologically inert.

I believe that the problems identified here stem from our poor understand-ing of markedness. The key observation in this case is that mid vowels are underlyingly disallowed in Bantu suffixes, as well as most Bantu prefixes (Guthrie 1970); affixes have the reduced vowel inventory {a, i, u}. To under-stand what spreads in Bantu we must understand, even in preliminary terms, what motivates the limitation of affix vowels to this particular set {a, i, u}. The same preference for this maximally dispersed set of vowels is displayed by Chumash affixes (Applegate 1971) and by many instances of vowel reduction (Mascaró 1976; Calabrese 1988; Kamprath 1989). The high vowels may be preferred in such cases because they are maximally distinct from each other, and from the third vowel a of the triangle.[45] Articulatorily speaking, however, they are nonoptimal when compared to the non-high vowels, since they in-volve a greater deviation from the rest position of the tongue body. Con-versely, the articulatorily optimal mid vowels have the perceptual disadvantage of poorer discriminability. The point that emerges from these remarks is that there are several dimensions of phonetic optimality which may well conflict with each other; the perceptually optimal vowel may not be the articulato-rily optimal one. To fully account for the Bantu data considered here we must assume that both articulatory and perceptual nonoptimal qualities of a sound are encoded as distinct phonological features. In the case of height, the articulatory mark encoding a deviation from the neutral position is [high], the feature giving rise to assimilations in Romance and Menomini. The perceptual mark, encoding say nonoptimal discriminability, may be provisionally referred to as [nonperipheral], a property shared by mid vowels and high central ones. We may say then that the Bantu pattern of harmony shown in (41) involves spreading the marked property [nonperipheral] from root to suffixes.[46] The low vowel *a* is peripheral, hence it is expected not to participate in this process. Here too it turns out that no appeal need be made to nontrivial underspecification.

The reader might object, at this point, that we have succeeded in avoiding several cases of nontrivial underspecification, at the considerable cost of introducing new features. Note, however, that the descriptive problems addressed here had not received solutions in any other feature system or theoretical framework. The Bantu problem cannot be solved if we simply decide to accept [–high] and spread it from root to affix; such a solution does not explain the connection between the Bantu harmony and the facts of markedness reviewed above. Nor will it explain why the low *a* always fails to spread its [–high] value: several Bantu dialects (reviewed in Goad 1992) have the harmony shown in (41) and *a* is active in none of them. This is not what we would expect if our account will consist of simply ordering the [–high] assimilation relative to the redundancy rule [+low] → [–high]. Why aren't there languages where the redundancy rule comes *before* [–high] assimilation? The existence of a [nonperipheral] class of vowels is further supported by the facts of Chumash, where the set {e, o, ɨ} is allowed in roots but excluded from affixes. Chumash affixes, like Bantu ones, can only be drawn from the system {a, i, u} in underlying representation. It is clear that Chumash does not simply exclude [–high] from its affixes, since that would not account for the restricted status of ɨ. Rather, both Chumash and Bantu limit the occurrence of the least discriminable members of their vowel inventory {e, o, ɨ} to the most salient positions, that is, the root syllables. We continue the discussion of these issues in section 3.

2.3.4 Conclusion on Contrastive Underspecification

There are two sides to Contrastive Underspecification. On the one hand, it presents, as Radical Underspecification does, a derivational view of feature specification, sharing the belief that features present on the surface might be missing underlyingly. On the other hand, Contrastive Underspecification limits the cases of potential underspecification to features that are predictable in a syntagmatic context or in virtue of co-occurrence filters. In this second sense, in which Contrastive Underspecification departs from Lexical Minimality, there is some support for this view which was reviewed in section 2.3.1. We have observed, however, that most other proposed instances of nontrivial underspecification consistent with (33) can be reanalyzed. There are no truly convincing examples of a three-step scenario like (3), where we must start with contrastively underspecified representations, then apply a P rule, and then let the redundancy rules take effect. In most cases, the evidence mistakenly interpreted as support for (33) yields to a better understanding of the feature involved in the process and reveals that underspecification is trivial and permanent. In other instances – such as the case of liquid transparency – we had to admit that no reasonable account exists at present, and therefore that no theoretical conclusions can be drawn.

Looking again at the list of potential examples of temporary underspecification reviewed, we note that the only solid ones are those discussed in section 2.3.1, all of which involve underspecification induced by positional neutralization. Thus Gaagudju apicals are underspecified for [anterior] word-initially, because no contrast is allowed in that position betweeen [+anterior] and [−anterior] apicals. Is a derivational approach necessary in this case at least? Must we start by leaving [anterior] unspecified in initial coronals, then apply [anterior] harmony, and then let a default redundancy rule apply which inserts, if harmony fails, [+anterior] in the position of neutralization? We see next that more interesting options exist.

3   A Nonderivational Approach to Positional Neutralization: Harmony Without Temporary Underspecification

I consider now in more detail the ways of formalizing positional neutralization in a grammar and its consequences for underspecification. The issue turns out to have wide ramifications and can only be sketched here. Throughout the discussion we must bear in mind the fact that the feature complexes disallowed from the positions of neutralization are generaly marked: they are the same elements that many languages bar absolutely. Any statement of positional neutralization must reflect this. A second preliminary remark is that some yet-to-be-formulated theory of prominent positions is assumed here. They include prosodically defined positions such as the mora (i.e., the syllabic peak), the stressed syllable, and the onset. They also include morphologically defined positions, such as the root or the content word, or the edge – typically the beginning – of the word. What determines membership in this class of prominent positions is still unclear. Many instances of positional neutralization discussed below refer to contexts that are prominent on more than one count: nasality, for instance, is allowed to associate underlyingly to Guaraní continuants only if they are moraic (i.e., vowels) as well as stressed. How to understand such cumulative effects is also unclear.

3.1   Direct and Indirect Licensing

Consider first the case of Greek aspirated vowels, which are allowed only word-initially. We identify the relevant feature combination as [+spread (glottis),

+sonorant]. In languages that prohibit it absolutely, a filter such as *[+spread, +sonorant] obtains. We unpack the contents of this filter as follows, using licensing language inspired by Goldsmith (1990).

(42)   A [+spread] autosegment must be licensed, in every associated segment, by the presence of [−sonorant] in that segment.

This requires that every segment associated to the [+spread] feature possess the value [−sonorant]. Greek may be said to obey (42), with the diference that one class of prominent positions is also permitted to license aspiration: the word-initial vowel. The appropriate statement is (43), a version of (42) to which an escape clause, italicized below, has been added:

(43)   [+spread] must be licensed, in every associated segment, by the presence of [−sonorant]; *or by an association to a word-initial mora.*

Consider now the distribution of nasalized continuants. Most languages prohibit such segments (cf. Cohn 1993 and references there). The corresponding statement is (44):

(44)   [+nasal] must be licensed, in every associated segment, by the presence of [−continuant].

Many languages allow nasal vowels, but no other nasalized continuants. This suggests (45):

(45)   [+nasal] must be licensed, in every associated segment, by the presence of [−continuant]; *or by association to a mora.*

In Copala Trique, nasal vowels – but no other continuants – are allowed to occur, but only in the stressed syllable (Hollenbach 1977). Trique obeys a modified version of (45), (46):

(46)   [+nasal] must be licensed, in every associated segment, by the presence of [−continuant]; or by asociation to a mora, *in a stressed syllable.*

Next comes the case of Guaraní, the language where nasal vowels are allowed underlyingly under stress, whereas voiced noncontinuant nasals occur regardless of stress. Guaraní is exactly like Trique, with the difference that it also possesses nasal harmony: nasality spreads from the original segment that licenses it to all other segments of the stress foot. The consequence of harmony is the occurrence of strings like pĩřĩ "to shiver" or řõ^mbogwatá "I made you walk" – represented autosegmentally below – where [nasal] is licensed in one of its associated positions, though not in all. Association of [nasal] to the licensed position is indicated below with a bold line. The vowel of the stressed syllable is designated as μ´.

(47)   Guaraní pĩrĩ: [+nasal]   r̃õ^mbogwatá: [+nasal]

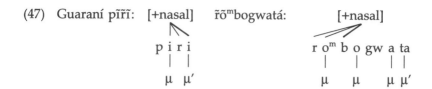

This case has been analyzed (Kiparsky 1985) in terms of an initial stage of the grammar where the equivalent of (46) is upheld, and a later one, where it is violated. The structures in (47) would then illustrate the later stage. We note however that the basic facts can also be dealt with statically: Guaraní might differ from Trique in allowing a given [+nasal] value to be licensed by at least one associated segment, *not necessarily by all*. If so, we would write (48) as the positional neutralization statement valid in Guaraní. The italics identify the difference between Trique and Guaraní.

(48)   [+nasal] must be licensed *in at least one associated segment* by the presence of [−continuant], or by asociation to a mora, in a stressed syllable.

This statement permits the [+nasal] values in (47) to be viewed as licit, since they do possess an association to a segment – the stressed í or the m – where they are licensed.[47] We may refer to conditions like (46) as requiring *direct licensing*, and to (48) as permitting *indirect licensing* (Goldsmith's conception of licensing corresponds to what we call indirect licensing). The association of [nasal] to the Guaraní stressless continuants is indirectly licensed by the fact that the same [+nasal] autosegment possesses an association to a stressed vowel or to a noncontinuant.[48]

Morphological categories may also be involved in direct, as well as indirect licensing. Thus Mazahua Otomí (Spotts 1953, p. 254) has a category of affixes (called stem formatives by Spotts) which consist of one or more consonants followed by a non-epenthetic vowel of schwa-like quality. The full vowels of Mazahua – a, ʌ, ə, ɔ, e, o, i, u, oral or nasal – may not occur in the stem formative morphemes, except in virtue of root-controlled harmony:

(49)   khù-ʔu "sister of a man"   ɲi-ʔi "head"
       kẫ-sʔã "to be on top of"   sʌ́-tʔʌ "arrive here"   tê-sʔe "climb a tree"

Simplifying somewhat, we may state that the category of stem formatives identified by Spotts is coextensive with the derivational affixes of Mazahua. In this case, the licensing statement will be the one below:

(50)   [αF] , where F is any vowel feature, must be licensed, in at least one associated segment, by a root or inflectional morpheme.

Interestingly enough, the rounded vowels of Mazahua do not induce harmony across the nonlaryngeal consonants: *khù-ʔu* "sister of a man" is a special case, encountered only when *h* and *ʔ* come between the stem-formative schwa and the root vowel. Aside from this case, there are no rounded vowels in the stem formatives: a rounded stem vowel is followed by ə in the stem formative.

(51) tʔo-šə "nest"   tʔɔ-šə "while"
     ngu-mə "house"   tʔõ-rə̃ "firewood"

We may attribute the absence of round-triggered harmony to the existence of a separate, stronger, licensing condition that governs [round]:

(52) [+round] must be licensed, in every associated segment, by membership in a root or inflectional morpheme.

(52) states that every segment possessing [round] must belong to some nonderivational morpheme. And this bars it from the stem formatives, even in the case where it is harmonically linked to the root.[49]

A similar situation is encountered in Chumash, the language where roots may contain peripheral vowels {a, i, u} as well as central ones {e, o, ɨ} (Applegate 1971). Affixes, however, may contain only peripheral vowels. Chumash too has affixal harmony: prefix *a* assimilate to a non-high vowel in the root; and prefix *u* assimilates to root *ɨ*.

(53) aqpala-woyoc → oqpolo-woyoc "to wear down crookedly" (woyoc "to be crooked")
     qal-wala-tepet → qel-wele-tepet "to roll up and tie bundle" (tepet "to roll")
     yul-cʼɨ → yɨcɨ "to be sharp of heat (= to be hot)" (cʼɨ "to be sharp")

We are here in the presence of a system which licenses marked (nonperipheral) vowel qualities only in the root morphemes. Indirect licensing is permitted, as in Mazahua.

(54) Nonperipheral vowels must be licensed, in at least one associated segment, by membership in the root morpheme.

Proto-Bantu appears to display an exactly identical restriction (Guthrie 1970): the vowel system in roots includes {i, u, ɪ, ʊ, e, o, a}, whereas affixes are drawn from the peripheral set {i, u, a}, with only a few prefixes belonging to the high lax category {ɪ, ʊ}. No affixes contain mid vowels. Indirect licensing is permitted, as in Chumash; the suffixal vowels are subject to a height harmony whereby *i, u* become *e, o* by assimilation to a preceding mid vowel.[50] The specifics of this process were discussed in section 2.3.3.5(4) above.

An interesting comparison between direct and indirect licensing is occasioned by the analysis of [round]. Several Altaic languages – Vogul (Kálmán 1965), Bashkir (Poppe 1962), and Ostyak (Trubetzkoy 1939) – allow round vowels only in the initial syllable of the word. These languages require the direct licensing statement in (55):

(55)   [+round] must be licensed, in every associated segment, by membership in the initial syllable.

This states that [+round] may be linked only to segments belonging to an initial syllable. It thus rules out both disharmonic strings like *iCu* and harmonic ones like *uCu*.

Better known, and probably more widespread, are languages where [+round] is said to originate only in the initial syllable, but where it is able to spread beyond its directly licensed position. This is the case of Yokuts (Newman 1949), a language where only the first vowel may be distinctively round. Yokuts harmony spreads the feature further into the word, from [α high] to [α high] vowel. Kuroda (1967, p. 43) describes the distribution of [round] in Yokuts as follows: "if the first vowel of the word is non-round, all the other vowels in the word are non-round; if the first vowel is round the round vowels follow until a vowel with an opposite value for diffuseness [i.e., height, D.S.] is reached, after which all vowels in the word are non-round." This indicates that [+round] may occur initially, as well as in contexts where it can be attributed to harmony, but nowhere else. Indirect licensing is clearly at work here.

(56)   [+round] must be licensed, in at least some associated segment, by membership in the initial syllable.

The effects of (56) can be inspected below: [+round] is directly licensed in (57a), indirectly so in (57b). It is unlicensed and, hence, ill-formed, in (57c).

(57)   (a)   gophin   (b)   ʔopottow   *(c)   paxattow (unattested)
               \   ＼／ |

        [+round]   [+round]   [+round]

Root controlled harmony systems, such as that of Akan (Clements 1978) are very similar to Yokuts. In Akan, the active [+ATR] value is licensed in the root. It may be indirectly licensed, and this generates the effects of harmony.

There are obvious extensions of the idea of indirect licensing to the cases of local assimilation in which onsets spread place or laryngeal features onto adjacent coda consonants. These cases have been dealt with in terms comparable to those proposed here by Itô (1986) and Lombardi (1991).[51] Thus, a coda obstruent may not possess an independent [voice] value in languages like Russian, German, Polish, or Catalan (Mascaró 1976 and Lombardi 1991). In a subset of these languages, onsets spread [+voice] onto preceding codas. Such cases fall under the statements in (58); the difference between languages like Russian, where there is onset-to-coda assimilation and languages like German, where there is not, concerns only the possibility of indirect licensing.

(58)   Licensing [+voice] in German (a) and Russian (b)
    (a)   [+voice] must be licensed, in all associated segments, by the pres-
        ence of [+sonorant]; or by membership in the onset.
    (b)   [+voice] must be licensed, in at least some associated segments, by
        the presence of [+sonorant]; or by membership in the onset.[52]

The same approach handles the cases of place feature licensing in coda
consonants that were discussed earlier in Steriade 1982 and Itô 1986: languages in which codas must be homorganic to following onset consonants. In
such cases, we would say that consonantal point of articulation features are
directly licensed in the onset, indirectly so in the coda. A statement like (59)
will handle the relevant facts of languages like Japanese or Diola Fogny:

(59)   [aF], where F is a consonantal point of articulation feature must be
    licensed, *in at least one associated segment*, by membership in the onset.

Languages where no supraglotally articulated codas are allowed (e.g., Western Popoloca, described by Williams and Pike 1973), but only *ʔ* or *h*, impose
a stricter condition of direct licensing:

(60)   [αF], where F is a consonantal point of articulation feature must be
    licensed, *in all associated segments*, by membership in the onset.

One further comment on the connection between indirect licensing and
assimilation. Indirect licensing conditions are necessary for the existence of
multiply linked structures such as (47) and (57), but they are not sufficient to
predict the occurrence of assimilation. To fully characterize individual cases of
assimilation one must define further conditions – having to do with the locality of the rule, its bounding domain, etc. – which were left out of the picture
here, because they are not related to our argument.

3.2   Significance of Indirect Licensing Conditions for the Theory of Underspecification

It is important to emphasize, in connection with the licensing conditions just
studied, a point made, I believe, by Itô: the homorganicity conditions governing coda consonants are frequently static, in the sense that they may obtain
only morpheme-internally or may not be supported by synchronic alternations. There are frequently no reasonable grounds for a derivational analysis
in which an earlier, place-unspecified coda becomes a later, place-specified
segment, through assimilation to an onset. It is significant then that our indirect licensing approach, like Itô's earlier analysis, is static; it does not distinguish
between an initial stage where place features are allowed only in the onset and
a later stage where they are allowed in the coda too. The distinction we draw

between the place features of coda and onset segments is only that between directly and indirectly licensed positions, not that between derivational stages. This is worth mentioning, because the very same device of indirect licensing, upon which we base a static analysis of coda conditions, was shown to apply equally well to phenomena such as Guaraní continuant nasalization or Yokuts rounding harmony. These rules had in the past received only derivational treatments based upon the distinction between early and late stages. The reader will recall, for instance, that Guaraní was analyzed by Kiparsky (1985) as involving a first stage where nasality is allowed only on stressed vowels and stops (our directly licensed nasal segments) and a later stage, where it is permitted on all continuants. Yokuts and similar systems had also been analyzed derivationally (by Steriade 1979 and Archangeli 1984) in terms of an initial stage where [+round] is well formed only in initial syllables and a later stage where it is permitted across the board.[53] We have suggested that the obviously static phenomena – such as the prohibition of independent place features in coda – and the less obviously static ones – such as the prohibition of independent nasality on Guaraní stressless continuants – should receive the same sort of treatment, one based on indirect licensing conditions. The static analysis presented here brings out the property shared by this entire class of phenomena, the fact that some features may surface only when licensed by an associated slot.

This conclusion has a direct consequence for the hypothesis of underspecification. One of the reasons for postulating segments that are underlyingly unspecified for some feature F, is that these segments, and only they, are targeted by assimilation rules that spread F. Specified segments, it is widely believed, do not undergo assimilation. But the largest class of unspecified segments subject to "later" assimilation for the unspecified feature is precisely the class of segments identified here as containing features subject to indirect licensing. Our analysis of indirect licensing phenomena did not appeal to underspecification. We found no reason to distinguish a first stage, where some segments lack values for F, from a second stage, where they acquire F values.

The reader may wonder whether a distinction between an initial stage and a later one must not also be built into our indirect licensing account in the case of morphemes that do not contain a proper licenser for some feature *within their underlying representations*. For instance, Yokuts suffixes do not contain a proper licenser for the feature [+round] internally to their lexical entries; only an association to the initial syllable licenses [+round] in Yokuts, and the suffixes are necessarily non-initial. Only after the suffixes have been attached to a stem possessing a licensed [+round] value can they acquire a proper association to that feature. The question then is what we declare the underlying [round] value of these suffixal vowels to be. And the only answer that appears to make sense is that they have no value for [round] at all: [+round] is impossible, [−round] is idle and probably nonexistent. My proposal here would be that [round] values in the suffixes of Yokuts, and comparable cases elsewhere, are not underlyingly underspecified. Rather, they are *unlearnable*, whether or not they are specified. They are unlearnable because they will never be in a position to manifest their existence.

That this suggestion is on the right track is indicated by the rare case of a class of morphemes which can occur in both direct and indirect licensing positions. These are the morphemes *nal* "at" and *töl* "from" of Hungarian, which can be used both as stems and as suffixes (cf. Vago 1976, p. 244ff.). In Hungarian only a stem, and in native stems only an initial syllable, can license [back] values. As stems, *nal* and *töl* display unpredictable [back] values which determine harmony onto suffixal morphemes: *nal-am* "at me" versus *töl-em* "from me". As suffixes, these morphemes cannot license their underlying [back] features and thus become subject to harmony: *ház-nal* "at the house", *ház-tol* "from the house"; *kép-nel* "at the picture", *kép-töl* "from the picture". The [back] value of these morphemes happens to be learnable only because they can also occur as stems. Any account of Hungarian harmony (e.g., Ringen 1988a) that rests on the idea that vowels must be *underlyingly* unspecified in order to undergo vowel harmony will necessarily have to leave the behavior of these morphemes unexplained.

4 Conclusions

At the beginning of this survey, I divided the circumstances in which a feature value might be predictable, and hence unspecified, into three classes: features predictable from co-occurrence conditions, feature values identified as unmarked by a context-free statement, and features subject to positional neutralization.

The first category yields no clear cases of nontrivial underspecification.[54] Let us return to the original example of sonorant voicing, a feature apparently predictable from the co-occurrence condition *[+sonorant, −voice]. Perhaps sonorants act as [0 voice] in Russian because their voicing is predictable, but an equally good explanation for the facts is that the feature involved in the Russian process is inherently a feature characterizing obstruents alone. Pursuing this second approach has two important benefits. First, it allows us to provide a one-step account of the Russian assimilation facts – and other similar paradigms – without proliferating derivational stages. All we need to state is that onset obstruents propagate onto coda obstruents the feature of pharyngeal expansion that makes vocal cord vibration possible. On this account, we need not distinguish what sonorants look like underlyingly and on the surface, and we need not invent ordering principles that will predict when they are allowed to acquire their surface [+voice] value. The second benefit of abandoning the hypothesis that predictability rooted in co-occurrence filters yields temporary underspecification is this: we need not wonder any longer why certain patterns of predictability never lead to underspecification. Why, for instance, does the predictable coronality of Japanese or Quechua *s* not lead to temporary placelessness? This is a question that does not arise once we admit that nothing follows from a feature's predictable status.

The second category of potential underspecification is that rooted in context-free markedness. I illustrate this case with the example of nasality. The unmarked state of speech sounds is to be oral. If that means that they are specified [−nasal], we might have to ask ourselves whether a redundancy rule like [   ] → [−nasal] is appropriate, and when. But, as it turns out, where context-free statements of markedness are justified, the corresponding features are best viewed as privative. Underspecification in such cases is genuine, but permanent. No redundancy rules are needed. The reader is reminded that this conclusion spares us the considerable difficulties encountered by context-free redundancy rules (these were reviewed in sections 2.2.4–2.2.5). I do not debate the existence of specification rules, rules which provide features for epenthetic vowels in specific contexts, but it seems impossible to equate these with redundancy rules affecting all the segments of a language.

We expected to encounter a third variety of underspecification in the study of positional neutralization. Neutralization means predictability and predictability may lead to temporary underspecification. But here too, we saw that it is at least possible to view the facts in purely declarative terms, without distinguishing between the underspecified lexical representations and the fully specified surface structures. Given the simplicity of the declarative analyses presented, I feel that the burden of proof belongs in this case with the defenders of a derivational approach to positional neutralization. The simplest assumption is that no cases of temporary underspecification are to be found here either.

The evidence, although not always clear, does not appear to support the hypothesis of nontrivial underspecification. We may recall now the principles that led phonologists to this hypothesis, Lexical Minimality and Full Specification. These are ideas that presuppose a derivationally organized phonological component. Neither seems likely to survive.

NOTES

This chapter originated as lecture notes written in 1991 for a UCLA seminar on underspecification theory. The contribution of the seminar participants is gratefully ackowledged. Special thanks to Abby Kaun, Jongho Jun, and Edward Flemming, all of UCLA, and to Andrea Calabrese, Morris Halle, Phil Hamilton, and Keren Rice, whose own research on related topics has clarified my thoughts on many of the issues addressed here. Dani Byrd and Ian Maddieson provided extremely useful comments and references for the sections dealing with markedness. Finally, I am grateful to Elan Dresher for reminding me that, if underspecified representations exist, that ought to follow from something.

1   Other formulations of Lexical

Minimality appear in Archangeli (1984, 1988).

2 This principle is explicitly discussed by Kenstowicz (1993).

3 See Goldsmith (1992), Prince and Smolensky (1993), Scobbie (1992), and references there.

4 The terms, and the distinction made by them, appear in Steriade (1987b) and Archangeli (1988).

5 Although the history of derivational underspecification cannot be retold here, we should mention works like Halle (1959), Ringen (1975), Clements (1977), and Kiparsky (1981) where this practice was first explicitly defended and where efforts were made to support the assumption of underspecification with empirical evidence. Trubetzkoy (1939) is also sometimes cited in this connection (cf. Clements 1987 and Archangeli 1988). He did not, however, subscribe to the version of *derivational* underspecification we discuss in the text. Trubetzkoy formulated criteria to determine which features are phonologically irrelevant in a system, but he was assuming mono-stratal grammars in the context of which it is impossible to believe that irrelevant features are specified at some late stage.

6 See Calabrese (1988) for a defense of the filter-based formulation; see also Myers (1991) for an alternative. Further discussion of this issue appears in Mohanan (1991).

7 Although the connection between markedness and underspecification is seldom made explicit, one gathers that universally valid co-occurrence statements are considered more plausible sources of underspecification than the parochial co-occurrence statements holding within one language only. Thus Calabrese (1987, p. 290ff.) cites the case of the Russian affricates *ts*,

tš, which are predictably voiceless, unlike the other Russian obstruents, because they happen to lack voiced counterparts. Although predictably voiceless, these affricates do not pattern as unspecified for [voice], unlike the predictably voiced sonorants. Calabrese suggests that the fully specified behavior of Russian *ts* and *tš* should be attributed to the fact that no universal statement bars voiced coronal affricates. In contrast, a universal statement – formulated by Calabrese as the *[+sonorant, −voice] – renders the voicing of sonorants predictable. Calabrese's proposal leaves one to wonder why language-specific feature co-occurrence conditions – like the one involved in Russian *ts* – are ignored in determining how much phonological information to leave unspecified.

8 This problem was first noted by Stanley (1967), who invokes it to motivate in part his rejection of underspecification. Attempts have been made at resolving this difficulty while accepting some version of underspecification (Christdas 1988; Steriade 1987b) but both proposals violate Lexical Minimality and offer no alternative principles as the basis of underspecification patterns. Goldsmith (1990, p. 244) also notes the problem of arbitrariness and appears to suggest, in line with proposals by Archangeli (1984, 1988), that the particulars of a phonological system will always help determine which feature to leave out of the underlying forms. On this line of reasoning, see Calabrese (1988, chap. 2).

9 This point is made by van der Hulst and Smith (1985) and Goldsmith (1990, p. 245).

10   This section and its continuation (section 3) were written in answer to questions raised by Edward Flemming, who is hereby thanked.

11   Odden (1993) provides a useful review of the issue. See also Archangeli and Pulleyblank (1987), Steriade (1987a), and Myers (1987).

12   This notion, which turns out to be considerably richer, is explored under the general name of Faithfulness by Prince and Smolensky (1993).

13   The notion that some constraints are more important than others is explored at length by Prince and Smolensky (1993).

14   The term is due to Mester and Itô (1989).

15   Unlike Chomsky and Halle, however, Kiparsky appears to assume that some markedness difference between values can be observed for every feature. Thus the marked value for [back] is assumed to be [+back] (1981); and the marked value for [ATR] is assumed to be [+ATR] (1981, 1985). The 1981 MS suggests that the markedness difference between feature values should be interpreted in privative terms: only the marked value exists, at all derivational stages. This suggestion seems to have been abandoned in the 1985 article; it did, however, reemerge in the more recent work of other phonologists, notably van der Hulst and Smith (1985 and later). We discuss it in section 2.3.3.

16   I cannot find specific statements to this effect in Kiparsky's papers, but the analyses presented all appear to rely on this assumption. This aspect of the theory of markedness was made fully explicit by Calabrese (1988). Calabrese adds the hypothesis that filters are organized in a partial ranking such that the violation of a low-ranked filter in a language entails the violation of a more highly ranked filter.

17   It is worth noting that the ordering of assimilation before (17) cannot be attributed to a general principle (such as the Elsewhere Condition: Kiparsky 1973a). In other languages, such as English, the redundant voicing of sonorants does trigger voicing assimilation.

18   If voicing assimilation must apply lexically as well as postlexically, then we need either (15)–(16) or alternative mechanisms in order to insure that sonorants will not become voiced in time to trigger the postlexical voicing assimilation. But no clear arguments establish the need for a *lexical* application of voicing assimilation. If so all we need is the stipulation about rule ordering coupled with the assumption that voicing assimilation applies postlexically both within and across word boundaries.

19   Further facts about the typology of voicing assimilation suggest that the connection to Structure Preservation should be downplayed in any case. Thus voicing spreads from sonorants in languages like English (Mascaró 1987), Yakut (Kenstowicz 1993), Greek and Latin (Steriade 1982), and many others. These cases involve word-internal assimilations that fail to apply in the phrasal contexts where postlexical processes are expected to act. These are then lexical rules applying *after* (17); only the need for extrinsic ordering appears to survive this comparison.

20   See Kaun (1993a) for a careful discussion of this case. Kaun demonstrates that the Catalan coronals must in fact be fully specified already within the lexical

component and that the asymmetry between alveolars and other consonants is unrelated to underspecification.

21 A distinct source of difficulty for Kiparsky's model involves the predictions of Structure Preservation. Although (15) expresses a widespread tendency to uphold within lexical derivations the set of filters obeyed underlyingly, the facts uncovered so far suggest that lexical rule applications are not invariably structure preserving. There is extensive discussion of this point in Calabrese (1988).

22 Goldsmith's (1990, p. 243ff.) presentation of underspecification within lexical phonology makes this point very clear.

23 Cf. also Abaglo and Archangeli (1989).

24 Archangeli (1988) appears to suggest, following Christdas (1988), that certain features are always fully specified. Stricture features are among the fully specified set. If so, [sonorant] will always be present in an underlying segment, and all other features could be left out. But this is a departure from Lexical Minimality – since we are specifying more features than we absolutely must – and we need to understand what motivates it. It is not sufficient to say that there are no markedness considerations on the basis of which to write a redundancy rule like [ ] → [α sonorant]. The model advocated by Archangeli and Pulleyblank is committed to override markedness, whenever this suits Lexical Minimality; otherwise the very hypothesis of markedness reversal would be unintelligible.

25 Levin (1987) has proposed that, at a certain point in the derivation, roughly at the onset of the postlexical phonology, redundancy rules cease to apply. Levin suggests that the difference between epenthetic vowels and "excrescent" vowels – predictable brief vowels lacking a definite quality – follows from the fact that the latter are generated *after* the last redundancy rules have stopped applying. Pulleyblank's (1988a) analysis of Yoruba *i* as a null segment is incompatible with this suggestion. Yoruba *i* must be placeless, according to Pulleyblank, well into the postlexical component, which means that it undergoes the redundancy rules at a point where Levin's theory predicts no redundancy rule application. In any case, the proposal that late-inserted segments fail to undergo redundancy rules is irrelevant to the discussion in the text, since the permanently placeless segments we discuss are either underlying (as in the case of most *h*'s and French schwa) or are derived lexically (English schwa).

26 The terms *contrastive* and *distinctive* are used interchangeably here.

27 Hamilton's analyses of Gooniyandi and Gaagudju diverge considerably from those presented here. An entirely different approach to these patterns is discussed in section 3, when we take up again the subject of positional neutralization.

28 Kaun (1993b) and Casali (1993b) have discovered numerous phonological patterns comparable with that of Tigre, in that a three-way underlying contrast between front, central, and back/rounded vowels gives rise to harmony rules that affect only the central vowels: *uCɨ* → *uCu*, but *uCi* remains *uCi*. In the cases considered by Casali and Kaun, only the feature [round] spreads, but it is clearly the case

that front vowels *i* and *e* are specified as [–back], since they do not undergo rounding harmony. It is their palatality that blocks the application of rounding: in the relevant languages (S. Paiute, Chemehuevi, Miwok, and Nawuri), front rounded vowels are disallowed. The harmony undergoers are phonetically central, rather than back unrounded, and this fact represents a violation of principle of Full Specification entirely comparable to that found in Tigre. On the phonetic side, Choi (1992) has presented extensive acoustic evidence for the surface lack of [back] articulatory targets in the central vowels of Marshallese.

29   Further arguments of this type are reviewed in Steriade (1987b).

30   A very different conclusion is presented in Paradis and Prunet (1991) and the volume in which it is found, a collection of studies based almost entirely on the assumption that alveolar coronals are underlyingly placeless. A critical review of most arguments for coronal placelessness presented there has appeared in Kaun (1993a), who demonstrates that they are invalid as formulated. See also McCarthy and Taub (1992).

31   Ringen (1988a) assumes that [–round] spreads in Hungarian. The appearance of [–round] harmony in Hungarian stems from alternations like *bab-hoz*, *hold-hoz*, *tüz-höz* versus *hit-hez*, *fej-hez* (discussed in extensive detail by Kornai 1987). It appears that suffixes like -*hoz* are basically round and undergo derounding when preceded by the unrouded front vowels. The obvious alternative to derounding is to claim that the vowel in -*hoz* is invariable as to height – a mid vowel which must stay mid – but

carries no specifications for backness and rounding. This vowel will surface as *o* when preceded by *a*, because it undergoes backness harmony. Any mid back vowel must be rounded in Hungarian: there is no ʌ. In this case, therefore, the [+round] value is due to the vowel's backness and to the fact that it must stay mid. In the other cases (*hold-hoz*, *tüz-höz* versus *hit-hez*, *fej-hez*) rounding and/or backness come from harmony. There is no need for assimilatory derounding here, or elsewhere. The Yaka facts described by Goldsmith (1985) as supporting [–round] spreading are similar to those of Lamba cited in (12) above. The phenomenon is discussed below in section 2.3.3.5(4); the assimilatory effect of [–round] is by no means obvious. I am not aware of other candidates for [–round] harmony. No disharmony effect known to me mentions [–round].

32   There exists, however, evidence – carefully assembled by Cohn (1990) – that oral segments may possess specified articulatory targets for a raised velum position. Cohn asserts, on the basis of this evidence, that [–nasal] values are needed. But the connection between phonological features and articulatory targets is far from obvious, as Keating (1990) points out. While we must conclude from the absence of a target that the corresponding feature value is also missing, presence of a phonetic target can be interpreted in ways consistent with phonological underspecification.

33   One may interpret Clements (1988) and Calabrese (1988) as invoking this general possibility. Language specific privativity was also suggested by Goldsmith (1987) for [round] and, more lamely, by

Steriade (1987b) for [voice] and [back]. The case of [voice] has since been dealt with by Mester and Itô (1989) and by Lombardi (1991).

34 This is in effect the view, defended by Czaikowska-Higgins (1987), Halle (1989), and Goad (1991). [ATR] and [R(etracted) TR] represent two distinct privative features, rather than two values of the same feature.

35 Languages like Ateso (Trigo 1991) and Akan-Twi (Painter 1973; Pike 1967) support this interpretation in that they display a phonologically active [+ATR] feature and have [–ATR] vowels articulated with the tongue root in neutral rather than retracted position. In other languages with ATR harmony, such as Igbo (Trigo 1991), all articulatory elements involved in the ATR distinction assume polar values rather than extreme vs. neutral. We may atribute this type of phonetic realization to a language-specific enhancement strategy: the phonologically recessive value [–ATR] is realized with active retraction in order to maintain a clearer distinction from the active [+ATR] value. In yet other languages, such as Anum (Painter 1971), the [–ATR] vowels are realized with active retraction, while the [+ATR] set is realized with the tongue root in neutral position. For such cases, however, there are no phonological arguments establishing that [+ATR] is phonologically active. The facts reported by Painter are consistent with the interpretation that Anum has a harmony based on [Retracted Tongue Root]. The hypothesis advanced here – that the activity of the tongue root is reflected by two independent and privative features [ATR] and [RTR] – finds an

interesting parallel in Maddieson and Ladefoged's (1985) analysis of "tense/lax" distinctions in some Lolo-Burmese languages spoken in China. Maddieson and Ladefoged show that for these languages the relevant distinctions involve two sorts of contrasts: lax (breathy) phonation vs. modal phonation and tense (laryngealized) phonation vs. modal phonation.

36 Pulleyblank (1992) mentions the following consideration as an argument against replacing one binary feature like ATR with two privative features of retraction and advancement. The two values of one feature F may not cooccur within a segment as a matter of logic: one entity cannot be simultaneously assigned to two opposite categories, such as [+ATR] and [–ATR]. But two distinct privative features should be able to freely cooccur: therefore we must find some alternative way to explain why segments cannot be simultaneously specified as ATR and RTR. This difficulty disappears when we note that many feature specifications are mutually incompatible, mostly for reasons of articulatory mechanics: one clear example is that of aspiration and glottalization, distinct features on any account, which never reside within the same segment.

37 The following discussion appears in abbreviated form in Steriade (1993b).

38 My colleagues in the UCLA Phonetics Laboratory inform me that little, if any, experimental evidence bears on Chomsky and Halle's claim (1968, p. 300) that "just prior to speaking the subject positions his vocal tract in a certain characteristic manner" which differs "from the configuration of the vocal

tract during quiet breathing," i.e., on the claim that the neutral position is a directly observable articulatory state. This does not invalidate however the usefulness of this notion. It is possible that the speaker may conceptualize his articulatory activity by reference to an abstract neutral position. It remains, of course, to understand why this reference point, whether directly observable or not, is chosen. I should note that phoneticians make extensive use of the assumption that some neutral position can be identified, for at least certain articulatory parameters; for instance, Lindblom's (1986) or Maddieson's (MS) discussion of articulatory effort presupposes some notion of rest or modal position.

39 In the case of [round], the neutral position is clearly intermediate between spreading and pursing the lips, however it may be the case that only pursing has, independently of any other articulatory gesture, a sufficiently salient acoustic effect.

40 The distinction between trivial and non-trivial underspecification is made in Steriade (1987b) and further discussed, under the name of inherent underspecification, by Archangeli (1988).

41 To complete the analysis suggested by Kenstowicz we would have to say, in the terms of Prince and Smolensky's (1993) Optimality Theory, that Latin ranks more highly the OCP as it applies to [lateral] than that applying to [rhotic]: lateral sequences dissimilate, whereas rhotic sequences do not. The full constraint sequence required for Latin under such an analysis is Parse [rhotic] >> OCP [rhotic] >> OCP [lateral] >> Parse [lateral]. The rhotic OCP effects are visible in Latin only when we determine whether or not to apply the [lateral] dissimilation. The idea to consider Parse as a separate function for each feature derives from work by Kirchner (1993).

42 Kaun (1993a) discusses other analyses, primarily Shaw's (1991) account of Tahltan sibilant harmony, from which *t* emerges as place-unspecified. Kaun demonstrates that it is not possible to maintain such an analysis consistently and that the only necessary assumption is that *t* is unspecified for anteriority. It is still unclear, given the lack of phonetic information on the articulation of Tahltan coronals, how these facts can, on Shaw's or Kaun's analysis, be made consistent with the suggestions made in the text.

43 See Westbury (1979) and Trigo (1991) for a review of this issue.

44 Rice and Avery (1989) as well as Piggott (1992) have recognized that voicing in sonorants is a phonologically different phenomenon from obstruent voicing. They represent the two features as, respectively, Sonorant Voicing (SV: a class node dominating [nasal], [lateral], and other sonorancy inducing-features) and [voice]. This proposal, whose spirit is close to that presented in the text, has the drawback that it requires implausible adjustments for the cases in which sonorants and voiced obstruents pattern together. Rice and Avery propose to attribute to the voiced obstruents of languages like English an SV node, despite the fact that these segments are genuine obstruents and lack any of the SV dependents that would justify postulating this class node in the first place. I do

not question their observation that obstruents with reduced closures – flaps – are necessarily voiced, in virtue of their manner of articulation. But the nonflapped voiced obstruents of English do not fall in this class.

45 Stevens (1972, p. 56) appears to suggest that the three vowels {a, i, u} have quantal properties: each is characterized by acoustic attributes that remain stable over a range of distinct articulatory configurations. Stevens's data unfortunately does not include a comparison between the peripheral vowels {a, i, u} and nonperipheral ones. A distinct hypothesis about what makes {a, i, u} optimal is Lindblom's (1986) notion of maximal perceptual distance alluded to in the text.

46 See Suomi (1983) and Kaun (1993b) on reasons why it might be advantageous to extend through harmony the temporal span of vowels with relatively poor discriminability.

47 The complete account of Guaraní must mention the fact that voicing is also involved in the licensing of nasality. An additional statement must express the fact that [+nasal] must be licensed *in every segment* by the presence of [+voice]. This condition must be satisfied over and above the condition discussed in the text: voiceless segments do not become nasal through harmony.

48 Languages such as Sundanese (Cohn 1990) where [nasal] originates in a stop and spreads only onto vowels, without creating nasalized nonvocalic continuants, can also be handled rather naturally by combining a direct and an indirect licensing condition: [nasal] must be licensed, in at least some associated segment, by [−continuant] and, in all associated segments, by [−continuant] or by μ. This condition will block spreading onto nonsyllabic continuants. The Sundanese case may also indicate that equating the notion vowel with a moraic position may not be quite right, although it is irrelevant for our purposes. Sundanese *h*, which can be analyzed as an aspirated, nonmoraic vowel, also undergoes nasalization.

49 The fact that rounded vowels are allowed to occur in the stem formative when it crosses a laryngeal suggests strongly that the general case of harmony in stem formatives involves separate spreading of individual features (as argued by Sagey 1986, for Barra Gaelic); whereas the case of translaryngeal harmony exemplified by *khù-ʔu* involves spreading of the entire vocalic segment *onto* the laryngeal consonant and beyond it. Thus in *khù-ʔu* we are dealing with a single *u*, and [round] in this *u* is licensed, because *u* is a root segment.

50 Thanks to Tom Hinnebusch for his help in verifying this generalization.

51 One difference between our approach and that of Itô (1986) stems from the latter's reliance on the Linking Constraint (Hayes 1986). Itô assumes that place features are ill-formed in the coda consonant, even in the case where they are licensed by association to a following onset. Her analysis relies on the idea that such violations are undetectable, in virtue of the fact that they involve multiply linked features. There are technical problems with this assumption. If the Linking Constraint could have the effect of concealing filter violations, it should be possible to spread nasality onto voiceless sounds in Guaraní (cf. n. 48) or

rounding onto stem formatives in Mazahua. The licensing approach presented in the text makes no such assumption; the feature governed by a statement of indirect licensing must be licensed in some position, in which case it is well-formed wherever else it may be associated.

52   This formulation may have to be adjusted if voicing in obstruents involves two distinct aspects, as suggested above, the presence of vocal cord vibrations and the process of pharyngeal expansion.

53   More recent treatments of Yokuts-like harmony systems (e.g., Archangeli and Pulleyblank 1993) distinguish an initial stage where [+round] is floating, a second stage where it associates to the initial syllable, and a third stage where it spreads onto the remaining syllables. Although an improvement over earlier treatments, this kind of analysis is also based on the proliferation of derivational steps which remain unnecessary.

54   This is not to say that there are no unclear cases left unsolved, but simply that the best understood examples of temporary underspecification turn out to involve altogether different principles. I have left unsettled the account of liquid transparency cases discussed in 2.3.2, beyond suggesting that Mester and Itô's account of it should be rejected. I have also not attempted to analyze here the much disputed cases of Hungarian and Finnish vowel harmony (cf. Vago 1976; Kiparsky 1981; Goldsmith 1985; Steriade 1987b; Ringen 1988a; and many others), because they raise a large number of issues that remain unsolved. Finally, I have not even attempted to touch on the question of tonal underspecification, relying in this case on Clements's (1988) suggestion that prosodically functioning features may have distinct behaviors that differ from those of features whose normal span is one segment.

Note added in proofs: Since writing this chapter, I have read Michael Broe's 1983 dissertation from the University of Edinburgh, which contains an extensive critique of the central idea of underspecification theory – that predictable feature values are under-lyingly absent – and an alternative proposal for representing dependencies among feature values.

5 Skeletal Positions and Moras

ELLEN BROSELOW

0 Introduction

Perhaps the major development in post–*Sound Patterns of English* generative phonology has been the emergence of a framework in which various aspects of phonological representation (similar to those called, in other frameworks, prosodies [Firth 1957] or long components [Harris 1944]) are factored out of individual segments and placed on independent tiers. Among the various tiers that have been proposed is a *skeletal tier* or *timing tier*, which, in its original incarnation, served a number of different functions: to mark off segments, to represent segment length, and to describe the shape of grammatical formatives. The elements on this tier were conceived of, in most theories, as part of lexical representation, serving as the units on which higher prosodic structure was built. More recently, however, the task of enumerating segments has largely been taken over by *root nodes*, which serve, in a theory that allows intrasegmental hierarchical structure, as anchors for the distinctive features which define a segment. Morphological templates, on the other hand, have been described in terms of higher prosodic units, including *moras*, which serve as indicators of syllable weight. And segment length has been described as a function of mapping either to two root nodes or to two prosodic nodes.

The overlap between the functions of the skeletal, root, and moraic tiers leaves the precise nature of the structure mediating between syllable nodes, on the one hand, and feature specifications, on the other, as one of the major questions in phonological theory. That question is the topic of this chapter. The organization of the chapter is roughly historical, beginning in section 1 with a review of the sorts of arguments that have been proposed for a skeletal tier, the content and functions of this tier (in 1.4), and the extent to which these functions have been subsumed by the root node and by higher prosodic units, including the mora (in 1.5). Section 2 examines the evidence both for and against a moraic tier: 2.1 reviews various proposals for the assignment of moraic structure, 2.2 presents arguments for the moraic tier rather than the skeletal tier, as well as problem cases, and 2.3 considers the relationship of moras and syllables.

1   Arguments for a Skeletal Tier

A skeletal tier provides a representation of the length and arrangement of segments in a word, independent of particular articulatory gestures. Early arguments for this level of representation draw explicit parallels between phenomena described by means of a skeletal tier and what at the time appeared to be more obviously autosegmental phenomena (see Goldsmith 1976a, 1990). Thus, autosegmental analyses of long segments and affricates in terms of many-to-one mappings are analogous to similar analyses of tone spreading and contour tones; the postulation of prosodic shape as a morphological entity recalls the role of stable tone melodies as independent morphological units; and arguments for empty skeletal slots parallel arguments for floating tones.

1.1   *Many-to-one Mappings*

Affricates, prenasalized stops, clicks, and other complex segments involve more than one place or manner of articulation, but frequently share the distributional properties of single segments. Conversely, long vowels and geminate consonants, which commonly involve a single gestural component, may behave as equivalent to sequences of two discrete gestural units for various processes. The lack of isomorphism between segmental and gestural structure can be represented by many-to-one mappings between the skeletal tier and what I will call the *featural* or gestural tiers (also called the *melodic, segmental,* or *articulatory* tiers). Thus, for example, a possible two-tiered representation of an affricate t^s is as in (1a), with two sets of articulatory specifications mapped to a single skeletal position. A geminate *tt*, in contrast, can be represented as in (1b), with a single set of articulatory features mapped to two skeletal positions:

(1)   (a)   Affricate t^s (b)   Geminate tt
      Skeletal tier

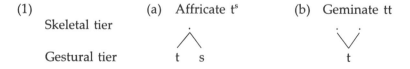

      Gestural tier   t   s   t

Leaving aside for the moment the content of these tiers, the representation in (1a) is intended to indicate that the affricate patterns with clearly mono-segmental units: for example, Japanese t^s is the only sequence of obstruent gestures to occur in syllable onset and the only such sequence not to trigger epenthesis in borrowed words, as in *furuutsu* "fruits". Similarly, prenasalized stops may occur in syllable onsets, in violation of sonority sequencing generalizations, and in languages where bisegmental onsets are ruled out (see the Bakwiri example below). The representations in (1) open the possibility that affricates and geminates may pattern with single segments for some phonological processes, with segment sequences for others. While the evidence for the dual patterning of affricates is somewhat ambiguous (see section 1.5.2 for discussion), this sort of behavior is well established for geminates and long vowels: typically, long segments add to syllable weight, but tend to resist separation by rules of epenthesis, and fail to undergo rules whose structural descriptions are met by only one portion of the geminate structure – properties termed, respectively, *integrity* and *inalterability* by Kenstowicz and Pyle (see chapter 8, this volume). A representation of long segments as in (1b) ensures that rules that scan the skeletal tier will see these segments as two units, while rules that operate exclusively on the gestural tiers will see them as single elements. The integrity and inalterability of geminates can be made to follow from general conditions on the interpretation of linked structures by phonological rules (ibid.).

An example of the usefulness of the separation of length from gesture comes from Bakwiri, a Bantu language, whose speakers play a language game in which the segmental material of two syllables within a word is transposed (Hombert 1986, and also chapter 23, this volume):

(2) Bakwiri

	Normal form	Language game form	
(a)	mɔkɔ	kɔmɔ	"plantain"
(b)	kóndì	ndíkò	"rice"
(c)	lùùngá	ŋgàálú	"stomach"
(d)	zééyá	yáázé	"burn"

As (2c, d) illustrate, length is preserved in its original position despite the reversal of segmental material (as in other languages; see Conklin 1959, McCarthy 1982). As McCarthy (1982) points out, positing independent skeletal and articulatory tiers makes this sort of phenomenon easy to account for: the skeletal tier is left intact, while the elements on the articulatory tier(s) are transposed:

(3)

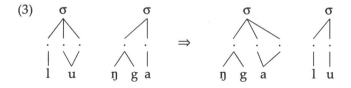

Tone also maintains its original position, suggesting that tonal melodies are anchored to the skeletal rather than to the gestural tiers. It is significant as well that after transposition, both components of the prenasalized stop are still mapped to a single skeletal slot, forcing the transposed *a* to spread to fill the second and third slots of the initial syllable.

The language game suggests the need for another type of many-to-one mapping. Certain Bakwiri forms are peculiar in failing to undergo reversal. These nonreversing forms all contain a non-low vowel followed by a homorganic glide, as in (4a) – although, as (4b) shows, some phonetically similar forms do reverse:

(4)   Language form   Game form
   (a) mbówà   mbówà   "village"
   (b) lówá   wáló   "excrement"

Hombert (1986) argues that forms like (4b) have an underlying medial glide, while in (4a) the glide is inserted to break the hiatus between two vowels. A framework allowing multiple linkings can represent the contrast between (4a) and (4b) as follows, with the vowel of the (a) form linked to positions in both syllables:

(5) (a)

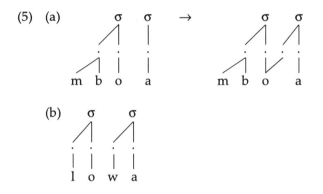

The derivation in (5a) shows the vowel features spreading to provide an onset for the second syllable. A new skeletal slot has been added to the post–vowel spreading representation of (5a); this is necessitated by the assumption that all gestural features are supported by a skeletal slot. On this account, the language game reversal of the featural material linked to the first and second syllables is stymied when faced with the *o* of (5a), which shares simultaneous membership in both syllables. While the doubly-linked vowel is not a long segment in the usual sense, it is similar to long vowels and geminates in being linked to two positions: in this case, the nucleus of the first syllable and the onset of the second (where it is interpreted as a glide). As a doubly-linked segment, the *ow* sequence should exhibit the characteristic integrity of conventional geminates.[1]

1.1.1 Contrasts in Mapping

The two-tiered representation of segment structure and length allows the possibility that languages may contrast in their mapping between gestural and skeletal tiers. The *ts* sequence in English *fruits*, for example, is presumably analyzed as two independent consonants, unlike the corresponding sequence in Japanese *furuutsu*. Such contrasts in mapping have been argued to play a role within the same language; for example, Clements and Keyser (1983) argue that Polish *czy* "whether" and *trzy* "three" (both phonetically *tši*) are distinguished only by the mapping of the initial sequence *tš* to one versus two skeletal slots. The two-tiered representation of length also in principle allows a similar one-to-one versus one-to-many contrast in geminates:

(6) (a)  (b)

However, unlike the mapping of two gestural units to separate skeletal slots proposed for Polish bisegmental *tš*, the mapping in (6b) involves two identical gestural units. McCarthy (1981) has proposed that this sort of representation is ruled out by universal constraints; if the Obligatory Contour Principle (OCP), originally formulated as a constraint prohibiting adjacent identical tones, is extended to prohibit adjacent identical elements on the gestural tier, representations like (6b) will be impossible,[2] assuming that the tiers on which the *t* gestures are specified occupy the same plane. McCarthy does propose, for independent reasons, that each morpheme occupies its own plane, which allows a representation for heteromorphemic *t + t* as in (7), in which the tiers specified for *t* are arranged on separate planes:

(7) Gestural tier(s), morpheme$_\alpha$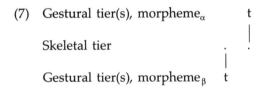

Skeletal tier

Gestural tier(s), morpheme$_\beta$

Identical segments rendered adjacent by morpheme concatenation (often called *fake* or *apparent* geminates), being immune to the OCP, presumably have the one-to-one structure illustrated in (7), while "true" (morpheme-internal) geminates have the structure of (6a). Thus, universal constraints impose contrasting representations of tauto- and heteromorphemic geminates. This contrast leads us to expect differences in behavior, an expectation that is confirmed by the generalization that the properties of integrity and inalterability typically hold only of tautomorphemic geminates (chapter 8, this volume; and Guerssel 1977; Hayes 1986; Schein and Steriade 1986).[3]

The segregation of separate morphemes onto separate planes raises the possibility of so-called long-distance geminates – a single gestural unit mapped to two skeletal positions that are nonadjacent on the surface. Convincing arguments for such structures have been offered in conjunction with arguments for the role of the skeletal tier as an independent morphological unit.

1.2   Skeletal Shape as a Morphological Element

The work that was most influential in establishing the independence of a skeletal tier was McCarthy's (1981) analysis of Arabic morphology. McCarthy argued that the Semitic root and pattern system of morphology, in which consonantal sequences appear in a number of related words of various shapes, could be best described as the mapping of consonantal roots to skeletal templates, each template defining the appropriate shape for a particular morphological category. Thus, for example, the same root appears in a number of stems sharing a semantic field:

(8) (a)   katab   "write" (perfective)
    (b)   kattab   "teach/cause to write" (perfective)
    (c)   kaatib   "writing"

Morphological categories are marked by particular shapes and vocalisms, as revealed by comparison of corresponding forms with a different root:

(9) (a)   ħamal   "carry" (perfective)
    (b)   ħammal   "make carry" (perfective)
    (c)   ħaamil   "carrying"

In McCarthy's analysis, consonantal roots, vowel melodies, and skeletal templates are all considered separate morphemes. Consonants and vowels are linked by rules of association to the skeletal template, which serves as a core anchoring the other segments and establishing the linear order of segments on discrete planes. In the face of contrasts like *kattab* versus *kaatib*, McCarthy proposed that each template position be specified as either C or V, with consonantal gestures linking only to C slots and vowel gestures to V slots. We can illustrate this approach by considering two forms that differ only in the number of their skeletal slots:

(10)   (a)   katab   (b)   kattab
Vocalic tier   a   a

Skeletal tier   CVCVC   CVCCVC

Consonant root tier   k   t   b   k   t   b

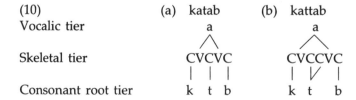

The mechanisms for mapping between tiers were argued to be the same as those employed in tonal mappings. The unmarked case involves left-to-right association. The rightmost element is spread when the number of slots on the skeletal tier exceeds the number of segments available for association – although language-specific rules may produce other spreading patterns, as in (10b).[4]

Perhaps the most convincing evidence for some form of templatic tier in morphology is the lengths to which languages go to realize skeletal template positions. While articulatory material may be lost under association (in Arabic, the final consonant of the borrowed word *majnaṭiiš* "magnetic" is lost when the root is mapped to the four-consonant CVCCVC template, yielding *majnaṭ* "to magnetize" [McCarthy 1981]),[5] languages tend to ensure that skeletal slots are filled, even in the face of limited articulatory resources (see the Template Satisfaction Condition of McCarthy and Prince 1986). The spread of segmental material to fill adjacent empty positions is illustrated in (10b) *kattab*, where spread creates a geminate consonant. The segregation of vowels and consonants on different tiers implies that gestural material may spread to nonadjacent positions as well, without crossing association lines. Such long-distance spreading is motivated by the need to fill out the template; thus, McCarthy (1981) argues, Arabic stems like *samam* "poison" (perfective) are actually derived by mapping a biconsonantal root *sm* to the CVCVC template that produces katab (10a), with association of the second consonant to two template positions. The arguments for long-distance geminates are compelling. First, Arabic otherwise forbids two consonants within a root with identical place of articulation, so if the root were *smm* (in violation of the OCP), the constraint would have to allow homorganic root consonants only if they are identical in all features, but not in other cases. Second, identical consonants are found only in the two final positions (Arabic has no verbs of the type **sasam*), as expected if biconsonantal roots are mapped to skeleta from left to right. Third, the Ethiopian Semitic language Chaha provides a dramatic demonstration of the segmental unity of two identical root consonants, as McCarthy (1983) demonstrates. In this language, the feminine marker on CVCVC imperative verbs is realized as palatalization of the stem-final consonants:

(11) Chaha

	Masculine	Feminine	
(a)	nəmæd	nəmæd^y	"love"
(b)	nəqət	nəqət^y	"kick"
(c)	wətæq	wətæq^y	"fall"
(d)	bætət	bæt^{y}ət^y	"be wide"
(e)	nəqəq	nəq^{y}əq^y	"take apart"

As (11d, e) illustrate, when the last two consonants are identical, both are palatalized, precisely as expected if the identical consonants represent the reflex of a single articulatory unit mapped to two skeletal slots.

Spreading is, furthermore, not the only tactic used to realize template shape.

For example, the Ethiopian Semitic language Amharic chooses the option of inserting a default segment, rather than spreading an existing segment, illustrated by the appearance of *t* in the final slot of certain templates (Broselow 1984). The Californian language Sierra Miwok, in which the basic roots mapped to templates include both consonants and vowels, provides both a default consonant, ?, and a default vowel which varies between high and mid central, here represented as ə (Broadbent 1964; Smith 1984). Again, appearance of the default segments is motivated by the necessity for realizing the full skeletal template:

(12)   Sierra Miwok (from Smith 1984, no glosses)

	Root	Derived (CVCVC)	Derived (CVCVVC)
(a)	polaat	polat	polaat
(b)	peeki	peki?	pekii?
(c)	tiil	tilə?	tiləə?

   While the initial arguments for skeleta as morphological entities were made from the root-and-pattern system of Semitic, the use of morphological skeleta was quickly extended both to non-Semitic languages (Archangeli 1983; McCarthy 1982; Halle and Vergnaud 1980, among others) and to other morphological phenomena, most notably reduplication. Since the allomorphs of reduplication have in common only their shape, taking their gestural color from the bases to which they are attached, reduplication can be analyzed as affixation of a skeleton to a stem, with the gestural material of the stem then copied and associated to the affixed skeleton (Marantz 1982). We will return to this phenomenon when considering the specification of the skeletal tier and the replacement of a skeletal tier by higher prosodic structure.

1.3   *Empty Skeletal Slots*

Root-and-pattern morphology and reduplication make use of empty slots to characterize morpheme shape; another possible function of empty slots is to serve as placeholders within lexical items. Thus, certain morphemes have been argued to contain, in addition to slots specified for both skeletal and gestural information, skeletal slots which are underlyingly empty, or which become empty in the course of the derivation through deletion of gestural material.[6] These empty slots may themselves remain unfilled, their presence serving only to block or trigger phonological rules, or they may be realized through spreading of neighboring segments. An example of the first sort of analysis is the familiar case of French *h-aspiré*. This involves words which, although phonetically vowel-initial, pattern with consonant-initial forms in triggering deletion of a preceding consonant in a liaison environment (*lez ami* "the friends" versus *le aš* "the axes") and in preventing deletion of a preceding vowel (*lami* "the friend", but *la aš* "the ax"). Clements and Keyser (1983) propose that a word like *aš* has in its underlying representation the skeleton CVC, with gestural material associated only with the second and third slots. Examples like the French case, in which the underlying empty slot is never filled in surface representation, are rare. Much more common are cases in which an empty slot is filled at some point in the derivation. This may be an underlyingly empty slot; in Tiberian Hebrew, for example, the definite determiner can be analyzed as containing a final empty skeletal slot, which generally triggers gemination of the consonant following it, though when this consonant is one of those that cannot geminate (such as ʔ), the vowel of the determiner lengthens instead (see Prince 1975 and Lowenstamm and Kaye 1986 for fuller discussion):

(13)   Noun   Det + Noun
   (a) bayit   habbayit   "house"
   (b) ʔiiš   haaʔiiš   "man"

Perhaps the most familiar sort of empty slot, however, is that created when a segment is deleted in the course of the derivation. In the well-known phenomenon of *compensatory lengthening*, deleted segments appear to leave a "trace" which is filled by spread of another segment. For example, Ingria (1980) cites the case of Ancient Greek /*es+mi*/ "I am" which is realized, after deletion of the *s*, as *eemi* in one dialect, *emmi* in another (see Wetzels and Sezer 1986 for numerous examples). A likely candidate for the remaining trace is the skeletal slot. But in both the Tiberian Hebrew and the Greek cases, the empty position may be filled by either a consonant or a vowel, which raises the question of precisely how skeletal slots should be defined.

1.4   Content of the Skeletal Tier: C/V Slots versus X Slots

McCarthy's (1979, 1981) characterization of skeletal slots as specifications for the feature [syllabic] was adopted in numerous analyses (with the occasional modification; for example, Yip's (1982) analysis of a Chinese secret language requires specification of some slots as glides). However, as use of the skeletal tier was extended to various phenomena, it soon became clear that the identification of skeletal slots with major class features was too restrictive. As the Tiberian Hebrew and Greek lengthening cases illustrate, certain slots seem not to discriminate between vowels and consonants as potential suppliers of articulatory material. This is particularly noticeable in compensatory lengthening, which frequently consists of deletion of a consonant followed by lengthening of a vowel. Furthermore, the same interchangeability of vowels and consonants can be found in templatic morphology. One much-discussed case in which a reduplicative affix can be realized by either vocalic or consonantal material comes from Mokilese (Levin 1983, 1985a):

(14) (a) wadek   *wad*wadek   "read"
     (b) poki   *pok*poki   "beat"
     (c) pa   *paa*pa   "weave"
     (d) andip   *and*andip   "spit"

In (14a, b) the prefix is CVC, and in (14c), where no second consonant is available, the prefix is CVV, where the third position is filled by spreading of the vowel. A similar pattern is found in Palauan (Finer 1986–87), with the interesting difference that the affix may be filled by a sequence of two different vowels rather than a single long vowel.[7] The flexibility in filling skeletal slots in Mokilese, however, goes beyond that in Palauan; as (14d) illustrates, the prefix has the shape VCC. Thus the forms in (14) can be described as a copy of the first three segments of the stem, regardless of syllabicity. To handle cases like these, Levin (1985a, p. 29) proposes removing major class specifications from skeletal slots, with each "intrinsically featureless" slot representing "a single timing unit." On this view, timing slots are not meant to represent some actual durational value, since average durations vary widely according to such factors as segment position and articulation type; timing slots encode the durational difference between long and short segments, but otherwise serve largely as segment enumerators. Slots on the timing tier are represented formally by an X, so the Mokilese reduplicative prefix illustrated in (14) would consist of three X slots.

Reduplication does not, however, generally involve simply copying a specified number of segments from a base, as expected if reduplicative affixes simply specify a fixed number of positions. As Moravcsik (1978) points out in her survey of reduplication, a reduplication process that copies the first CV(C) of consonant-initial stems will normally copy just the first V(C) of vowel-initial stems:

(15) Agta Plural Reduplication
      (a) takki   *tak*takki   "leg"
      (b) uffu   *uf*uffu   "thigh"

Thus, where the C/V specification of skeletal slots was too specific, specification in terms of X slots alone is too general. Levin accounts for facts like these by reincorporating some syllabicity information into the template. The Agta prefix, for example, can be defined as consisting of three X slots, the second of which is specified as a syllable nucleus. As in C/V-based analyses, association from gestural tier to timing tier proceeds from left to right, and from gestures to timing slots. Therefore, an initial copied vowel will map to the nucleus slot, leaving the first slot blank:

(16)

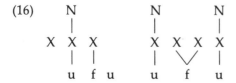

In Levin's system, then, the skeletal tier contains only nonredundant informa-tion about syllabicity; predictable information is derived by syllabification rules. However, additional information concerning the syllabic structure of the template affix may also be required. For example, while the Mokilese prefix always fills three timing slots, these slots are not necessarily filled by copies of the first three segments of the base:

(17) Mokilese
    (a) diar   *dii*diar   "find"
    (b) alu   *all*alu   "walk"

In (17a, b), reduplication involves lengthening of the second copied segment, rather than simple one-to-one association (which would yield *diadiar*, *alualu*). Since both base forms in (17) have two vowels among their first three segments, and since in Mokilese each vowel must be a discrete syllable nucleus, these facts can be accounted for by imposing an additional restriction on the Mokilese XXX prefix: it must constitute a single syllable (Levin 1985, p. 36). However, the notion that a templatic morpheme like the Mokilese prefix may be defined in terms of its syllable structure invites a very different conception of templatic morphology than the purely skeletal representation, an alternative to which we shall now turn.

1.5   *Alternatives to the Skeletal Tier*

1.5.1 *Prosodic Templates*

Once an affix is defined as a syllable, much of the information encoded in the skeletal tier (maximum number of segments, syllabicity of segments in various positions) is redundant, following from the syllable structure constraints of the language – inviting the conclusion that the skeletal tier may not be needed. One of the arguments offered in McCarthy and Prince's influential manuscript "Prosodic Morphology" (1986) for a syllabic rather than a skeletal representation of morphological templates concerns the reduplication pattern in Ilokano, in which the reduplicative affix may have the shape CVC, CCVC, CV, VC, as in (18).

(18) Ilokano
    (a) ag-*bas*basa
    (b) ag-*trab*trabaho
    (c) ag-*da*dait
    (d) ag-*ada*dal

McCarthy and Prince argue that the template to which the copied gestural material is mapped is defined simply as a syllable. The material that survives under copying is the maximum that a single syllable of the language can support. Thus, initial *tr* survives in (18b) because *tr* is a possible onset of the language, a generalization that would be obscured by merely providing another optional C or X slot in the template. The failure to copy the second vowel in (18c) also follows from the definition of the template as a syllable, since vowel sequences in this language, as in Mokilese, are bisyllabic. However, where in the analysis of Mokilese discussed above the template was defined as a sequence of slots as well as a single syllable, here syllable shape constitutes the sole definition of the template.

This approach can be extended to Mokilese as well. The generally trisegmental nature of the prefix is accounted for not by defining the prefix as both XXX and a single syllable, but rather by specifying this prefix as a heavy syllable.[8] The CVC/CVV alternation in prefix shape (illustrated by (14b) *pokpoki* and (14c) *paapa*) is motivated by this requirement. Forms like (14d) *andandip* and (17b) *allalu* are derived by associating as much of the copied material as possible to the reduplicative prefix. Since a syllable may be closed by no more than one consonant, only the first vowel and consonant of *andip* and *alu* will be copied, yielding **an-andip, *al-alu*. The realization of the *d* and lengthening of the *l*, which in Levin's analysis resulted from the presence of a third timing slot in the prefix, is in McCarthy and Prince's analysis the effect of an independent rule that spreads a consonant to the onset position of a following vowel-initial syllable under certain morphological conditions:

(19)   (a)   σ   +   σ   σ   →   (b)   σ   +   σ   σ

          a   lu   a   lu   a   l   a   lu

     (copying, association)   (onset spreading)

Under the assumptions of this analysis, one should not expect to find a language identical to Mokilese in all relevant respects except that the reduplication of forms of words like *alu* yields forms like *aalalu*, where no onset filling analysis of vowel spread is available. Cases like this, where reduplication appears simply to copy a fixed number of segments, regardless of their prosodic properties, are hard to find. If alternative analyses of the sort suggested by McCarthy and Prince can be maintained for such cases, the motivation for an X-slot analysis of reduplication is seriously undermined.[9]

In fact, Prince's (1975) and Lowenstamm and Kaye's (1986) analyses of Tiberian Hebrew lengthening and Ingria's (1980) and Prince's (1984) analyses of compensatory lengthening in Latin and Greek also treat lengthening as an effect of mapping to terminal positions of a syllable, rather than as mapping to skeletal slots. But it was not until the circulation of McCarthy and Prince's (1986) manuscript that the analysis of shape-based phenomena in terms of prosodic structure was identified as a research program. In the prosodic morphology framework, the units of templatic morphology are defined not as slots on a skeletal or timing tier, but rather as units of prosodic structure which include, in addition to syllables, constituents both above the syllable (metrical feet) and below the syllable (moras). In section 2, we consider various arguments that higher prosodic structure may assume many of the functions originally assigned to the skeletal tier: encoding segment length and ambisyllabicity; providing a rationale for lengthening phenomena; making possible a direct representation of morpheme shape. Before considering the alternatives for representing morpheme shape and segment length, I return to one additional function originally delegated to the skeletal tier.

1.5.2   Root Nodes as Segment Delineators

The skeletal tier makes possible a monosegmental representation of elements with different and sometimes contrasting articulations. For example, the representation of the affricate t^s in (1a) shows two full sets of articulatory features, one defining t and the other s, mapped to a single skeletal slot. On this view, each set of features is an independent gestural unit on some level, and hence, once detached from the skeleton, an affricate should be indistinguishable from a bisegmental stop-fricative sequence. However, these units have not been shown to exhibit the same sort of independence evidenced by true single segments. For example, while segments may be reordered in language games that sever the connection between skeletal and gestural tiers, the separate portions of affricates or prenasalized stops have never been shown to reorder under similar conditions. Furthermore, phonological rules tend to treat the contrasting specifications within these segments as unordered (as Lombardi 1990 demonstrates for affricates and Sagey 1986 for clicks and other complex segments). And, as discussed in connection with Arabic morphology, while mapping of a single articulatory complex to multiple skeletal slots is quite common, the reverse is rare or unattested; neither, to my knowledge, have cases been found where the portions of an affricate split to associate to two different skeletal positions. These facts suggest that articulatorily complex segments have a connection below the skeletal level. The model of segment-internal structure generally referred to as *feature geometry* (see chapter 7, this volume) provides a means of representing articulatorily complex segments that does not rely on a skeleton. The guiding assumption is that features within a segment are arranged hierarchically, and are ultimately dependent on a single node, called a *root node*. A segment such as t^s would, on this account, consist of a single root node dominating a single specification for place but two specifications for continuancy. The root node in some accounts is simply an anchor for the features defining a segment, though McCarthy (1988) has proposed that the root node consists of the class features [consonantal, sonorant].[10] On either account, the root node appears to have usurped the function of the skeleton in describing complex segments. I return to the question of whether segment length and segment complexity are best described at the same level of representation in section 2.1.3, in the context of a closer look at content of the moraic tier.

2   Moras

The notion of mora, or weight unit, is a traditional one, recognized in virtually every school of linguistics. The concept arose from study of languages in which two adjacent segments in syllable rhyme may carry different pitches (for discussion of the phenomenon in Japanese, see McCawley 1968), or in which the position of stress, accent, or tone depends on an opposition between light (CV) syllables and heavy (CVV or CVC) syllables (see Newman 1972 for a valuable survey of languages making this distinction). Trubetzkoy ([1939] Baltaxe trans., 1969, p. 174) characterizes certain languages as mora counting:

> Classical Latin may be cited as a generally known example, where the accent ... always occurred on the penultimate "mora" before the last syllable, that is, either on the penultimate syllable, if the latter was long, or on the antepenultimate, if the penultimate was short. A syllable with a final consonant was considered long. A long vowel was thus comparable to two short vowels or to a "short vowel + consonant."

Mora count thus encodes both the opposition between heavy (bimoraic) and light (monomoraic) syllables, and the equivalence of various types of heavy syllables.

While many early generative accounts referred informally to moras, it was not until the 1980s that the mora was proposed as an explicit level of representation, and its use extended to account for many of the phenomena formerly described by means of the skeletal or timing tiers. Recent proponents of a moraic tier include Hyman (1985), who derives moras from units on a timing tier, Hock (1986), who suggests supplementing the skeletal tier with an autosegmental mora tier, and McCarthy and Prince (1986) and Hayes (1989), who advocate wholesale replacement of the skeletal tier by the mora tier. The arguments for the mora tier come from various domains; their essence is that shape-dependent processes can be seen as depending on syllable weight rather than on number of segments, and that the units necessary for the description of syllable weight are the same units motivated for the analysis of phenomena like stress, tone, and accent. Before considering these arguments in detail, I begin with an overview of various proposals for the representation of moraic structure.

2.1   *Moraic Structure*

For languages that treat all types of heavy syllables as equivalent, we can assume that each unit in the syllable rhyme – that is, the first vowel and all following material – contributes a mora. Since syllable onsets seem not to contribute to syllable weight (but see Everett and Everett 1984), they are assumed to have no moraic value. Thus, all syllables describable as C_0VV or C_0VC are equivalent in terms of their mora count. One possible representation of the weight of various syllable types is shown in (20), with μ representing a mora:

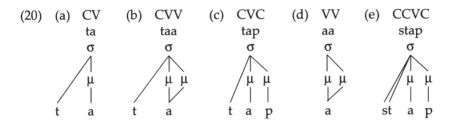

(20) (a) CV   (b) CVV   (c) CVC   (d) VV   (e) CCVC
           ta   taa   tap   aa   stap

The weightlessness of onset units is represented in (20) by direct adjunction of onset segments to the syllable node, though the adjunction of onsets directly to the first mora is equally plausible (see sec. 2.1.2).

2.1.1 Structure of the Rhyme

All versions of moraic theory incorporate some possibility for variation in the moraic structure of syllable rhymes. Hayes (1989), for example, proposes that vowels are underlyingly associated with moras (short vowels with one mora, long vowels with two), while consonants generally receive their moraic value by language-specific rules: in a language where CVC and CVV are equivalent in weight (such as English, Latin, or Arabic), a rule Hayes calls *Weight-by-Position* assigns a mora to each consonant in coda position. Weight-by-Position is language-specific, failing to apply in languages that recognize only syllables with long vowels as heavy, treating CV and CVC syllables as equivalent; examples include Mongolian, Huasteco, and Lardil. Such languages simply adjoin the coda consonant either directly to the syllable node, or to the mora dominating the nuclear vowel, as shown below:

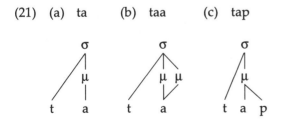

(21) (a) ta   (b) taa   (c) tap

From this it follows that no language will treat CVV syllables as light but CVC syllables as heavy, since only syllables of the latter type can be represented as either mono- or bimoraic.

Languages may also identify only particular consonants as undergoing

Weight-by-Position (see for example Hyman 1985). Zec (1988) argues that the choice of which consonants may be mora-bearing is constrained by sonority – consonants that may bear a mora are more sonorous than those which cannot. In Lithuanian and Kwakwala, for example, short-vowel syllables closed by a sonorant consonant behave as heavy, while those closed by an obstruent do not; therefore, only coda sonorants are assigned weight. The nonuniversality of Weight-by-Position provides an important part of the justification for a moraic representation, since if the set of mora-bearing segments were identical with the set of syllable rhyme segments in all languages, moraic structure would be simply derivable from syllable structure.

Hayes (1992) argues that languages may also contrast heavy and light CVC syllables that are segmentally identical (see also Kager 1989). The evidence comes from Cahuilla, in which stress patterns suggest that only CVV syllables are heavy. In a form like *welnet* "mean one", the *el* sequence is therefore dominated by a single mora. The morphological process of intensification lengthens a consonant, giving *wellnet* "very mean one". Hayes analyzes this process as addition of a mora to which the *l* of *welnet* is then associated, producing a bimoraic initial syllable. Evidence for the monomoraic/bimoraic contrast comes from the distribution of secondary stress. Syllables following CVV normally receive secondary stress in Cahuilla, and such stress is found on the second syllable of the intensive form *wellnet*.

Another possible contrast involves long vowel versus vowel-homorganic glide, found in Central Alaskan Yupik (Hayes 1989, following Woodbury 1987). If vowels and glides are featurally identical, differing only in that vowels are underlyingly moraic, this contrast should not be possible in a language that assigns weight to coda consonants, as Yupik apparently does. Both Hyman (1985) and Hayes (1989) propose therefore that in at least some languages, vowels and glides differ in their underlying specification for the feature [consonantal].

2.1.2   Structure of the Onset

In the representation shown in (20), only rhyme units are dominated by moras. This structure (assumed in McCarthy and Prince 1986 and Hayes 1986) encodes the traditional division of a syllable into onset (here, segments adjoined to the syllable node) and rhyme (segments adjoined to moras). The various arguments amassed for this constituency (see Fudge 1987) are therefore consistent with this structure. An alternative representation has also been proposed in which each segment is dominated by a mora (that is, a unit on the next level of the Prosodic Hierarchy), in accord with the Strict Layer Hypothesis of Selkirk 1984. Hyman (1985), for example, assumes that each segment is underlyingly associated with a mora but that the universal Onset Creation Rule removes the mora from a prevocalic consonant and associates it to the following mora, yielding the structures in (22):

(22) (a) CV   (b) CVV

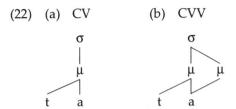

The adjunction of onsets to moras forms a constituent consisting of onset plus first vocalic position. Evidence for this constituent is hard to come by, though Katada (1990) discusses a Japanese language game which supports it (see also chapter 23, this volume, note 4). In this game, the final CV of a word is used to begin a new word; *tubame* "swallow" is followed by *medaka* "killifish", and so forth. A word ending in a long vowel must be followed by a word beginning with (the second mora of) that vowel: *budoo* "grapes" may be followed by *origami* "folding paper", but not by *doobutu* "animal". And a word ending in a nasal ends the game, since the nasal constitutes the word-final mora, and moraic nasals may not.occur word-initially. A few additional arguments have been offered on both sides of the onset adjunction question. Ito (1989) uses the structure in which onsets adjoin to moras to predict the occurrence of epenthesis, which in her analysis groups together a fixed number of moras; however, Broselow (1992) argues for the adjunction-to-syllable analysis on the basis of many of the same facts, using the contrast between syllable-dominated consonants and mora-dominated consonants to predict the site of the epenthetic vowel. Buckley (1992) analyzes certain gestural sequences in Kashaya, which pattern in some respects with single segments, as two gestural units lexically associated to a single mora. Since these sequences occur in onset position, the analysis requires that onset segments be dominated by moras. This analysis brings the mora full circle from its function as encoder of syllable weight to encoder of segmenthood, blurring the distinction between moraic and skeletal tiers.

2.1.3   *Representation of Segment Length*

Segment length is represented in a skeletal framework as mapping of a single set of features to two skeletal positions. In a moraic framework, long vowels have generally been represented as features mapped to two moras. A framework in which onsets are dominated by moras makes available a similar representation for long consonants. However, since geminate consonants typically serve both as coda to one syllable and onset to a following syllable, the bimoraic representation of consonant length is not generally available in a framework that assumes direct linking of onsets to syllable nodes, with no intervening mora. In such a framework, heterosyllabic long consonants can be represented by means of mapping a set of consonant features to two prosodic positions: mora (for the coda portion of the segment) and syllable node (for the onset portion). McCarthy and Prince (1986) and Hayes (1989) propose that geminates and single consonants contrast in that only the former are associated to a mora underlyingly. Since moraic consonants are possible only in syllable rhyme, and since prevocalic consonants must always form an onset with a following vowel, underlyingly moraic consonants in prevocalic position will end up linked to two prosodic positions, as in (23b):[11]

(23) (a) ata   (b) atta

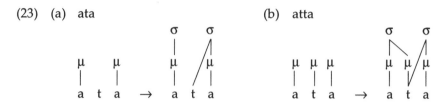

Thus, geminates may be represented as moraic single segments, in contrast to accounts in which length is indicated as two positions on the tier defining segmenthood, whether the skeletal tier or, as proposed in Selkirk (1990), the root tier. Monosegmental and two-root structures make significantly different predictions concerning the distribution, behavior, and weight of long segments.

Selkirk (1990) argues for a representation of geminates as a single set of place features mapped to two root nodes. Her major argument involves phonological rules that alter one portion of a geminate, in apparent violation of the principle of geminate integrity. One example comes from Northern Icelandic, in which geminates can split into two different consonants; geminate aspirated stops are transformed to a sequence consisting of *h* plus a single unaspirated stop (*pp^h* → *hp*). Selkirk points out that the single-segment analysis of geminates makes this fission difficult to describe; furthermore, it offers no explanation for the parallels between geminates and true consonant clusters (for example, the sequence *lp^h* becomes voiceless *l* followed by unaspirated *p*). She proposes that geminate integrity is actually a function of a constraint requiring (roughly) that the heads of multiply-linked features be identical. If geminates are analyzed as consisting of a single set of place features linked to two root nodes, the Icelandic rule, which simply delinks certain features from these root nodes, would not violate this constraint.

Selkirk also discusses the distributional predictions of the monosegmental versus two-root analyses. In the absence of exceptional licensing conditions at the periphery of morphological units, the moraic single segment analysis predicts that geminates should not occur in exclusively syllable-initial or syllable-final positions. Selkirk agrees that geminates are rare in these positions, but points out that the banning of tautosyllabic geminates may be ascribed to the independently motivated constraints on sonority sequencing within syllables; the same constraints that rule out a sequence of stops, for example, could rule out a sequence of two root nodes specified as stops, even when these are linked to the same place node.

Tranel (1991) investigates the predictions of the moraic analysis of geminates with respect to syllable weight. He points out that moraic representations predict that no language should treat syllables closed by the first part of a geminate consonant (CVGm) as light, since the first half of a geminate must, under the single-segment analysis, be moraic. Thus, a language that lacks the Weight-by-Position rule should contrast syllables closed by true single consonants (CVC), which must be light, with necessarily heavy CVGm syllables. Tranel argues that in fact a number of languages (he cites Selkup, Tübatulabal, and Malayalam; see Blevins 1991 for additional examples) treat both CVGm and CVC syllables as light for stress assignment, although these languages do have a weight contrast: CVV syllables are heavy. Furthermore, he argues, no language appears to treat only CVGm syllables as heavy. This pattern accords with the two-segment analysis of length: the first portion of the geminate is equivalent, for the purposes of Weight-by-Position, to any other coda consonant – but is inconsistent with the single moraic segment analysis.

If, as Tranel argues, CVGm and CVC syllables invariably have the same weight in any given language, various approaches might be taken to build this into moraic theory. Tranel discusses the suggestion of Hayes that Weight-by-Position be viewed as a wellformedness constraint rather than a rule, allowing moraic consonants in some languages but forbidding them in others; this constraint would then delete the moras associated with geminates once they were linked to coda position.[12] One might also interpret the negative setting of Weight-by-Position as forbidding moraic consonants at any level, including lexical representations. In this case, geminates could be represented as lexically adjoined to a preceding vowel mora, as in (24b):

(24) (a) ata   (b) atta   (c) atka

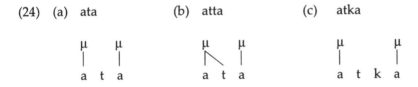

Onset formation rules would link the intervocalic *t* in both (24a, b) to the onset of the second syllable, yielding a single consonant/geminate contrast without a corresponding weight contrast. The *t* in (24c) would be adjoined to the preceding mora by regular coda formation rules. Of course, these approaches all presuppose a monosegmental analysis; Tranel's generalization that CVGm and CVC syllables always bear the same weight would follow from the two-root analysis of geminates.

2.2 Arguments for the Mora

Where skeletal tiers assign a slot to each segment, a moraic tier provides slots (that is, moras) only for segments in weight-bearing positions. Thus, given moraic representations, onsets should be irrelevant for template shape and lengthening phenomena, and empty slots of the sort considered in section 1.3 should all occur in rhyme rather than onset position (*onset/rhyme asymmetry*, section 2.2.1). Furthermore, we expect to find processes that count moras, rather than segments, and for these processes, a heavy (bimoraic) syllable should be equivalent to a sequence of two light (monomoraic) syllables (*mora counting*, section 2.2.2). And finally, a particular language's determination of which segment types can be moraic should show up in all domains in which the mora is relevant (I will call this *moraic consistency*, section 2.2.3). For example, a language that treats CVV and CVC syllables as equivalent for the purposes of stress and accent should display the same equivalence in the satisfaction of morphological templates. This potential to make predictions across different domains is both the most interesting and the most problematic aspect of moraic theory. In the following sections I examine these principles against the evidence from various domains.

2.2.1   *Onset/Rhyme Asymmetries*

2.2.1.1   *In Templatic Morphology*

The reduplicative patterns discussed in section 1.5 illustrate various onset/rhyme asymmetries. The optionality of initial consonants exemplified by Agta forms (15) *taktakki* and *ufuffu*, in which the reduplicative prefix takes the form (C)VC, makes sense once the affix is conceived of in terms of syllable weight: rhyme (moraic) positions must be filled, but the onset (the initial consonant position) is optional. The same optionality is not typical of mora-bearing positions, as illustrated by languages like Mokilese where, if no second consonant is available to give content to the final mora, the vowel is spread (as in (14b, c) *pokpoki, paapa*). Once the affix is conceived of as a syllable, the freedom in filling its third position with either a vowel or a consonant is not surprising, since it is possible for both vowels and consonants to be moraic. We would not, however, expect the same interchangeability of consonant and vowel in the initial position of a three-position affix like the Mokilese one, since this position is reserved for the onset. Since there is nothing in a timing-tier analysis to rule out such interchangeability, the moraic analysis is more restrictive. There is evidence that points the other way, such as the Mokilese VCC allomorph (illustrated in (17) *allalu*), much of which is susceptible of an alternative analysis such as the one discussed in section 1.5. The Arabic contrast (8b, c) *kattab/kaatab* is also a problem for both X-slot and moraic accounts, but there is good reason to assume that for most Arabic templates, vocalism is prespecified (Broselow, in press). Thus, templatic morphology seems generally to support the asymmetry of onsets and rhymes.

2.2.1.2   *In Compensatory Lengthening*

In skeletal accounts of compensatory lengthening, deleted material leaves a skeletal slot which is then filled by spread of remaining gestural material.[13]

However, Hayes (1989) has argued that while deletion of segments from a syllable rhyme often triggers lengthening of a neighboring segment, deletion of an onset segment rarely does. For example, deletion of word-initial or intervocalic *w* in East Ionic dialects of Greek, as in **woikos > oikos* "house", **newos > neos* "new" (Hayes 1989; Steriade 1982; Wetzels 1986), results in neither lengthening nor in the appearance of a glide, as one would expect if vowel features were spread to an onset position: spread of *e* or *o* to the empty *w* position in *newos*, for example, should yield *nejos* or *newos*, respectively (see the Bakwiri case, discussed in section 1.1 above). There is one environment, however, in which a *w* deleted from onset position does trigger lengthening, illustrated by **odwos > oodos* "threshold". But this is just the case in which deletion creates the syllable structure VC.V, which is highly marked and frequently subject to resyllabification, deriving V.CV. If, as Hayes argues, deletion of onset *w* triggers movement of the *d* out of the rhyme and into the onset, this leaves an empty rhyme position (25b), which then triggers lengthening (25c):[14]

(25)   (a)   (b)   (c)

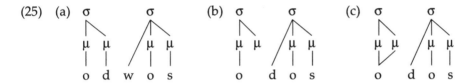

Hayes suggests that this pattern of compensatory lengthening triggered by deletion (or movement) from rhyme but not onset is what would be expected if the relevant unit for compensatory lengthening is the mora, rather than the skeletal slot. Even if X-slot theory were modified to include a prohibition against filling onset slots, this asymmetry would presumably not follow from any aspect of the representation itself, as it does when compensatory lengthening is identified as spreading to an empty mora. Much of Hayes's (1989) paper is devoted to arguments that, even with such prohibitions, it would not be possible to restrict the X-slot theory to derive all and only the attested types of compensatory lengthening. It should be observed that a theory such as that of Hyman (1985), in which all segments have underlying weight units, would have to account for the fact that only certain weight units trigger compensatory lengthening.

Hayes (1989) discusses two counterexamples to the moraic account of compensatory lengthening. These include compensatory lengthening triggered by onset deletion in Onondaga (Michelson 1986) and in Samothraki Greek (Newton 1972), both of which involve a change from CrV to CVV. Since CrV sequences are notably subject to reorganization (see Dorsey's Law in Winnebago [Steriade 1990]), Hayes's analysis of these as involving some intermediate stage in which *r* occupied a moraic position seems plausible.

2.2.1.3   Status of Empty Slots in Onset Position
Moraic theory embodies the prediction that underlyingly empty slots should not be found in onset position. A survey of the literature turns up very few such cases. One is French *h-aspiré*, mentioned in section 1.3. Other languages for which empty onset slots in stems have been posited are Onondaga (Michelson 1986) and Seri (Marlett and Stemberger 1983). Interestingly, all these cases involve empty C slots in the initial (never internal) position of a stem, as well as slots that are left unfilled in at least some environments. Such empty slots have often been justified by a contrast with earlier "abstract" analyses which required arbitrary choice of some underlying consonant which was never realized on the surface. However, Dresher (1985) argues that from the standpoint of learnability, an analysis positing empty slots that remain unfilled has no advantage over the positing of some abstract segment. If this position can be maintained, then these cases need not pose a serious problem for moraic theory.[15]

Affixes may also involve empty slots, and one case in which an empty slot in onset position has been posited involves imperfective verbs in Alabama. Verbs with open antepenultimate syllables form their imperfectives by lengthening the onset consonant of the penultimate syllable and adding a high tone to the preceding syllable. Verbs with closed antepenults lengthen the penultimate vowel, which receives a high tone (data from Hardy and Montler 1988 and from Montler, personal communication):

(26)   Alabama

	Perfective	Imperfective	Gloss
(a)	balaaka	bállaaka	"lie down"
(b)	hocifa	hóccifa	"name"
(c)	campoli	campóoli	"taste good"
(d)	ibakpila	ibakpíila	"turn upside down"

Hardy and Montler (1988) posit as the imperfective affix an empty X-slot, linked to a high tone, which is inserted in the onset of the penultimate syllable. In (26a, b) this additional slot causes the original onset to move backward to the antepenult (*ba-lXaa-ka* → *bal-Xaa-ka*). The inserted slot is then filled by spread of the preceding consonant, and since tone cannot dock on consonants, the tone moves back to the preceding syllable. In (26c, d), where the preceding syllable is already closed, the X slot (and the tone) remain in the penult, and the X slot is filled by vowel spread. If correct, this analysis argues for X slots rather than moras, which presumably cannot be added in onset position. However, since the additional prosodic position always does surface in syllable rhyme position, it seems reasonable to describe this process as insertion of a mora rather than an onset slot. The problem with this account is then to describe why the mora is added sometimes to the antepenultimate and sometimes to the penultimate syllable – the latter only when the antepenult is either

heavy or absent. Lombardi and McCarthy (1991) offer a number of arguments
that the mora is added to the final foot of the word: the final syllable is
extraprosodic, and since feet are iambic (requiring their lefthand syllable to be
light), the final foot includes the antepenultimate only if that syllable is light.
One advantage of this analysis is that the mora in question is inserted into the
same syllable in which it surfaces (penultimate or antepenult syllables), with
no movement required of the high tone from one syllable to another, as in the
X-slot analysis.

2.2.2   Mora Counting

At the level of the mora, CVCV is equivalent to a single heavy syllable (an
equivalence that can be expressed only indirectly in a skeletal theory). For
example, the formation of rustic girls' names in Japanese involves prefixing *o*
to the portion of the name containing the first two moras (Mester 1990):

(27)   Full name   Truncated name
    (a)   Yuuko   o-Yuu
    (b)   Ranko   o-Ran
    (c)   Yukiko   o-Yuki

McCarthy and Prince's (1990a) analysis of Arabic broken plurals involves a
similar truncation. The same equivalence of two-mora sequences may show
up in augmentation processes as well. For example, the Italian *radoppiamento*
sintattico normally makes a syllable heavy in certain syntactic contexts by
geminating the following consonant (*le gru selvatiche* 'the wild cranes' with [s:],
but *selvatiche* with a simple consonant in other contexts). Repetti (1989) argues
that the addition of a word-final light syllable in the development of certain
dialects (Medieval Tuscan *può* > *puone* "s/he can") represents another realization of the same process.

Constraints on minimal word shape provide another illustration of mora
counting. In many Arabic dialects, monosyllabic words must be superheavy
(either CVVC or CVCC). Words consisting of a single heavy or light syllable
are not allowed, though words consisting of two light syllables are (Cairene
sana "year"). Assuming that final consonants are extrametrical, this pattern
can be analyzed as a requirement that words contain at least two moras.[16]
Imperative verbs take the basic shape CCVC, which is subminimal. This is
repaired in many Levantine dialects by lengthening the stem vowel: *sʔaal*
"ask, masculine singular" (the basic short vowel emerges when the imperative
takes a vocalic suffix: *sʔali* "ask, feminine singular"). In Iraqi Arabic, the two-
mora constraint is obeyed by inserting a vowel to the left of the stem: *drus* →
idrus "study". Thus both dialects enforce the two-mora minimum, one by adding a syllable and one by lengthening the monosyllabic stem. The minimal word
in these dialects also constitutes the minimal domain of stress assignment

(Broselow 1982), illustrating the consistency of moraic requirements across domains; see McCarthy and Prince 1986 for detailed discussions of the relationship between stress and minimality constraints.

Compensatory lengthening provides another area in which bimoraic sequences, whether disyllabic or monosyllabic, may be expected to count as equivalent. Hayes (1989) analyzes the Old English change of *talə* to *taal* "tale" as spread of the first syllable's vowel to fill the mora freed by deletion of the second vowel.[17] The reverse change is found in the pronunciation of English words by native speakers of Korean, who typically insert a vowel after a syllable containing a tense vowel:

(28)   English   Korean
  (a) bit   bit
  (b) beat   bitɨ

Park (1992) analyzes this as mora conservation, claiming that vowel length contrasts have been lost in modern colloquial Korean, and that Korean speakers therefore resort to insertion of a syllable to maintain the mono- versus bimoraic distinction of the English forms.

Yet another process related to mora counting is the common shortening of vowels in closed syllables. For example, in Cairene Arabic, vowels shorten before any following consonant within the syllable rhyme: compare *kitaab* "book", where the word-final consonant is extraprosodic, and *kitabha* "her book", where the *b*, because no longer peripheral, loses its extraprosodic status and must be incorporated into the preceding syllable. This shortening can be analyzed as an effect of an upper limit of two moras per syllable (McCarthy & Prince 1990b); the vowel must shorten in order to accommodate a moraic consonant within the same syllable. Since stress, morphology, and minimality constraints all converge on the conclusion that coda consonants bear weight in Arabic, this case provides a convincing example of moraic consistency, a topic we turn to now.

2.2.3   Moraic Consistency

The principle of moraic consistency makes explicit predictions concerning the connection between various areas of the grammar, including stress, accent, templatic morphology, minimality constraints, compensatory lengthening, and vowel shortening. In its strongest form, it leads us to expect that a configuration that has a particular weight for some aspect of grammar should have that weight for all aspects of the grammar. A number of languages – for example, Cairene Arabic, in which the evidence from stress, minimality, morphology, and vowel shortening discussed above converge to support the moraicity of coda consonants – support this strong form of moraic consistency. Some of the most interesting cases involve languages in which only certain segment types can be moraic. For example, Zec (1988) argues on the basis of evidence from several domains that Lithuanian sonorant consonants, but not obstruents, are moraic in coda position. First, rising tone accents, analyzed as linkage of a high tone on the second mora of a syllable, are found on syllables with long vowels, or with short vowels followed by sonorant consonants, but never on short-vowel syllables closed by obstruents (see also Kenstowicz 1971; Kiparsky and Halle 1977; Hyman 1985). Second, differences between sonorant consonants and obstruents emerge in such areas of morphology as the formation of infinitive verbs:

(29)   Present   Infinitive   Gloss
    (a) tupia   tuupti   "perch"
    (b) drebia   dreebti   "splash"
    (c) karia   karti   "hang"
    (d) kauja   kauti   "beat"

The lengthening of the vowels in (29a, b) can be analyzed as mapping of infinitive stems to a bimoraic template; the sonorant-final stems in (29c, d), on the other hand, already satisfy the bimoraic requirement without lengthening.[18] And third, long vowels shorten when followed by a sonorant within the syllable, but not before an obstruent (Osthoff's Law).

   However, not all the evidence from Lithuanian points to the moraicity of sonorants as opposed to obstruents. As Steriade (1991) observes, Lithuanian imposes a minimality constraint on monosyllabic roots: CV roots are not found, though roots of the form CVV or CVC are permitted. Minimality is apparently indifferent to the sonority of a final consonant (*lip* "rise, climb" is one root). The root constraints might conceivably be the remnant of some earlier stage of the language at which weight was indifferent to consonant type. This is not, however, an isolated instance of inconsistency in moraic value. Similar facts are found in Greek (Steriade 1991), Tübatulabal (Crowhurst 1991), and a number of other languages (see Hayes 1992 and Blevins 1991). The next section reviews responses to the failures of moraic consistency.

2.2.3.1   Failures of Moraic Consistency

A number of devices have been used to account for moraic inconsistencies, including rule ordering, formation of complex moras, multileveled representations in which a segment may be moraic on one level, nonmoraic on another, and the exemption of certain processes from a strict reliance on mora count.

   In Archangeli's (1991) analysis of Yawelmani, Weight-by-Position is conceived of as a phonological rule whose application can be delayed until fairly late in a derivation. Archangeli provides convincing arguments that in Yawelmani, mapping of a CVC root to a morphological template consisting of a bimoraic syllable results in lengthening of the root vowel. This indicates that the coda consonant does not count as moraic, since it does not fill the second mora position of the template. However, long vowels shorten in closed syllables – the sort of shortening generally associated with a bimoraic limit on syllables. Archangeli's solution to this paradox orders Weight-by-Position, which assigns a mora to a coda consonant, *after* roots are mapped to templates, but *before* the rule of vowel shortening, which trims syllables down to two moras. Thus, consonants are incorporated into codas at one stage, but do not receive weight until a later stage: Weight-by-Position is not (as might plausibly be assumed) an automatic consequence of incorporating a consonant into the syllable coda.

A situation that is in some sense the converse of the Yawelmani case occurs in several Arabic dialects. As discussed above, Cairene Arabic permits CVVC syllables phrase-finally but not internally, a pattern that can be attributed to a bimoraic limit on syllables plus extrametricality of phrase-final consonants. However, several dialects do permit word-internal CVVC syllables, even though coda consonants otherwise count as heavy for stress, morphology, and minimality constraints in these dialects. Syllables of the form CVVC arise only from syllabification of a consonant that has lost its extrametrical status through suffixation, or has lost the vowel of its own syllable through syncope (compare Sudanese *kitaabha* "her book" and Cairene *kitabha* < *kitaab + ha* "her book"); since CVVC syllables do not occur underlyingly, it seems unlikely that these dialects simply tolerate bimoraic syllables. Broselow (1992) and Broselow, Huffman, Chen, and Hsieh (in press) argue that VVC sequences are actually bimoraic (an analysis supported by evidence from Arabic poetics and durational data), resulting from a rule of Adjunction-to-Mora which links the consonant to the second mora of the long vowel. Adjunction-to-Mora is restricted to derived environments (and to particular levels of the grammar, which vary across dialects). Cairene Arabic either lacks Adjunction-to-Mora at the relevant levels, or has an additional rule delinking a vowel from the second mora in the following structure:

(30)   μ   μ

    V   C

An alternative to delinking might involve a difference in the phonetic interpretation of structures like (30) in Cairene versus Sudanese; these dialects would differ in the timing of the vowel and consonant gestures linked to a single mora.[19]

An alternative to these derivational accounts of moraic paradoxes, suggested by Hayes (1991), provides different but simultaneous levels of representation for the same structure. Hayes proposes a moraic grid, where the number of grid marks associated with a segment is directly correlated with its sonority:

(31)   (a) ta   (b) taa   (c) tap
             μ   μμ   μ
             μ   μμ   μμ
             a   a   ap

Processes that treat coda consonants as moraic would refer to the lowest level on the sonority grid, while those that count only vowels would refer to the next level. Presumably, a third level of representation is needed for languages like Lithuanian, in which various processes treat sonorant consonants but not obstruents as weight-bearing.

This dual representation is reminiscent of (and possibly equivalent to) the sort of distinction made in a nonmoraic theory between the subsyllabic constituents nucleus and rhyme. In the nucleus versus rhyme approach, the two rhyme positions in (31b) would be contained within the nucleus, while in (31c) the rhyme would consist of the single-position vocalic nucleus plus the non-nuclear consonant. Steriade (1991) compares the efficacy of the moraic versus subsyllabic constituency approaches in accounting for various facts in Greek and other languages, and concludes that moraic theory, properly constrained, is more restrictive than the nucleus/rhyme approach. Among her proposals to restrict moraic theory is one which accommodates only specific types of moraic paradoxes. She claims that most of the attested moraic paradoxes involve syllable types which are light for the purposes of stress assignment, but heavy for morphological templates and minimality constraints (except for templates and constraints stated in terms of feet, since feet are the the the units of stress assignment). She argues, therefore, that CVC syllables are always bimoraic – that is, that all languages have Weight-by-Position – but that a language may restrict the set of possible stress-bearing (and/or tone-bearing) segments to those above a particular sonority threshold. Rather than employing dual representations or rule ordering to account for moraic paradoxes, this proposal simply gives up the notion that stress rules are sensitive only to the number and arrangement of moras.

One potential objection to this approach involves languages like Yawelmani, Lithuanian, or Kwakwala in which templatic morphology also gives special status to a set of higher-sonority elements. In Zec's (1988) framework, the lower-sonority elements simply cannot be mora-bearing. Though Steriade assumes that no segment is obligatorily nonmoraic, she does distinguish unconditionally moraic segments (those which always project a mora) from conditionally moraic ones (those that are moraic only in appropriate positions – essentially, those where Weight-by-Position is applicable). Templatic mapping therefore needs somehow to distinguish conditionally and unconditionally moraic segments, in order to ensure that only the former may be used to satisfy the moraic requirements of templates. Since this approach does not predict moraic consistency between stress and other moraically-based processes, different mechanisms are needed to account for why a language like Kwakwala allows sonorants but not obstruents to count both for stress assignment and for the satisfaction of morphological templates.

Clearly, moraic paradoxes pose a serious challenge to moraic theory, as evidenced by the range of devices proposed to handle them. One hopes that a better understanding of the universal principles governing the structure of prosodic units and the functioning of rules in a grammar will allow this theory to account for failures of moraic consistency without losing its predictive power. Work on such constraints is just beginning.

2.3   *Mora-Syllable Relationships*

Two additional questions in moraic theory concern constraints on the number of moras within a syllable, and constraints on the relationship between moras and higher units of prosodic structure.

Both McCarthy and Prince (1986) and Steriade (1991) suggest that syllables should be limited universally to an upper bound of two moras. Most cases of apparently heavier syllable types (such as CVVC) can be analyzed either as bimoraic (as in the Arabic dialects discussed above) or as comprising a bimoraic syllable plus extrametrical element. However, Hayes (1989) argues that trimoraic syllables must be allowed, if only as a marked option. The evidence involves first, three-way contrasts among syllable types: for example, in Hindi, CVVC and CVCC syllables, even word-internally, are treated as equivalent to a bimoraic syllable followed by a monomoraic syllable, while in Estonian, vowels can be short, long, or overlong. The second sort of evidence involves compensatory lengthening in trisegmental syllable rhymes: Old English *θaŋxta* > *θaaxta* "thought". If *ŋ* shares a mora with either of its flanking segments, its deletion should not trigger lengthening, since its mora would still be occupied; therefore, the syllable must be trimoraic. Since fairly few cases motivating trimoraic syllables have been amassed (but see also van der Hulst 1984), the necessity for giving up a universal constraint on maximal number of moras per syllable is still unresolved. A related question is whether syllables must contain at least one mora, a proposition disputed by Hyman (1985). Hyman argues that patterns like the one found in Chuvash, in which stress falls on the last full vowel of a word, but skips either of the two "reduced" vowels, can be best described by representing reduced vowels as moraless (see Odden 1986b for discussion).

While the preceding discussion has focused on moras as constituents of syllables, the assumption that a mora is always dominated by a syllable is by no means generally accepted. Hyman (1985) argues that in Gokana, for example, all those areas generally used to motivate syllables – distributional constraints, the environments of phonological rules, and the composition of higher-order units such as feet – can be accounted for by the use of moraic and morphological structure; thus for this language, at least, syllables are simply redundant. Zec (1988) and Bagemihl (1991) argue that the mora can serve as a prosodic licenser, protecting segments from stray erasure, a role generally reserved for the syllable. Bagemihl's argument involves reduplication in Bella Coola, a language that permits long sequences of obstruents within words. One type of reduplication copies the first obstruent-sonorant sequence found in the word:

(32) (a) qpsta   qps*t*ata   "to taste" (iterative)
     (b) tqn̦k   tq*n*qn̦k   "be under" (underwear)
     (c) st'qʷlus   st'*qʷ!*qʷlus   "black bear snare" (diminutive)

Bagemihl analyzes this as prefixation of a core syllable (CV) template to the first syllable of the word, where syllables consist maximally of CCVVC, and where the initial consonant sequence must consist of an obstruent followed by a sonorant. Left-to-right mapping to the syllable template puts the sonorant consonant in syllable nucleus position in (32c). The obstruents skipped over in reduplication (for example, the sequence *qps* in (32a)) are dominated not by syllable nodes, but solely by moras. Allowing some segments to be licensed by moras rather than syllables increases the power of a grammar, since it permits virtually any sequence of segments to be a possible word; however, Bella Coola may in fact warrant this sort of freedom. On the other hand, the assumptions (a) that these obstruents are indeed contained within syllables (as many Salishanists have traditionally done) but (b) that reduplication seeks out the first syllable with a rising sonority profile may provide the basis of an alternative account.

3 Conclusion

This paper has reviewed the devices used in generative phonology to represent segmenthood, length, morphological template shape, and syllable weight. Two families of proposals were compared: those involving a skeletal or timing tier, which provides a slot for each segment, and those employing a moraic tier, which provides slots only for segments bearing weight, supplemented by a root tier, which anchors the features defining a segment. The moraic definition of length and morphological shape was argued to be at least potentially more restrictive than the skeletal representation, since it distinguishes weight-bearing segments from those which cannot bear weight (for example, segments in onset position). However, problems such as apparent inconsistencies in syllable weight found in various languages have led to some weakening of moraic theory. The development of a theory that is powerful enough to accommodate the facts but constrained enough to make interesting predictions is the task of future research in this area.

NOTES

1   Hombert's account of these facts does not rely on double linking, but rather on the assumption that (4a) is underlyingly monosyllabic. However, the data reveal an apparent contrast between

monosyllabic vowel sequences, as in *lìòβá* "door" (game form *βààlíó*) and vowel sequences like those in (4a), which undergo glide formation.

2　But see Odden (1986b) and Broselow (1984), among others, for arguments that such representations do occur.

3　Compare this approach with, for example, the Adjacency Identity Constraint of Guerssel (1977), a constraint which prohibits certain sorts of rules from applying to identical sequences. This constraint must explicitly distinguish tautomorphemic from heteromorphemic geminates. The different treatments of geminate integrity and alterability in the linear and nonlinear frameworks provide a nice example of the shift in focus from rules to representations in the development of generative phonology.

4　But see Yip (1988) and Hoberman (1988) for alternative analyses of this pattern.

5　Archangeli (1991) argues for an alternative treatment of segments that do not fit into the morphological template; in Yawelmani, such segments are simply syllabified, triggering epenthesis where necessary.

6　As Goldsmith (1990) points out, the inverse case – a unit on the gestural tier that is not associated with any skeletal slot – does not seem to occur, at least in stems.

7　Although the CVV affixes surface as CV, Finer shows that this is a consequence of a general process of vowel reduction, and that the quality of the surface vowel cannot be predicted unless both vowels are copied.

8　McCarthy and Prince suggest that the prefix may be definable simply as a syllable, with an independently motivated rule of boundary

lengthening adding a mora between prefix and stem; Levin 1985a argues against this position, however.

9　I have ignored the problem of the transfer of length from base to reduplicative affix which occurs in Mokilese as well as a number of other languages; see Clements (1985b), Steriade (1988b), and McCarthy and Prince (1986, 1988, 1990a) for various approaches to this problem.

10　This proposal brings the root tier closer to the C/V skeletal tier of McCarthy's earlier proposal. Interestingly, the earlier proposal was made in the context of a framework that assumed fully specified distinctive features. More recent work in feature geometry frequently assumes either privative features or radical underspecification of features. If both [consonantal] and [sonorant] can be unspecified in underlying representations, the possibility of null root nodes arises.

11　Note that in a moraic framework the vowel-glide sequence in the Bakwiri form (5a) *mbowa*, from /*mboa*/, would have a structure similar to a geminate consonant, since the *o*, linked to its own mora, is spread to the onset of the following syllable.

12　As Tranel points out, this approach is at least potentially inconsistent with an analysis that allows Weight-by-Position to be ordered among phonological rules, as does Archangeli's (1991) analysis of Yawelmani discussed in section 2.2.3.1. If Weight-by-Position can be turned on or off at some point in the derivation, we should expect to find stages in which CVGm can contrast with CVC syllables.

13　Compensatory lengthening has attracted considerable attention in nonlinear phonology (see Wetzels and Sezer 1986). Hock (1986) argues against the exclusively phonetic account of CL propounded by de Chene and Anderson (1979).

14 But see, for example, Rice (1989) for arguments that this sort of resyllabification is generally prohibited.

15 An interesting case for comparison involves the postulation of an underlying pharyngeal fricative in Maltese (Brame 1972). As in French, the postulated segment, though never realized on the surface, has a number of phonological effects. In contrast to the French case, however, the Maltese segment patterns not just with consonants in general but with a specific articulatory class of consonants (the gutturals), requiring that the consonant be specified with gestural material as well as a skeletal slot.

16 CVV monosyllables, however, do not occur. Final long vowels are generally banned in dialect forms; exceptions include final clitics, for which there is some evidence for assuming *h* following the vowel (see Broselow 1976; McCarthy 1979).

17 This analysis requires some auxiliary assumptions to ensure that the final *l* in *taal* does not associate to the mora stranded by vowel deletion. Hayes argues that the rule filling empty moras via spreading from the left applies before stranded segments are incorporated into syllables. The *l* then associates to the second mora of the syllable, rendering *taal* bimoraic.

18 This analysis differs slightly from that of Zec (1988), which posits a rule of mora insertion in infinitives; the inserted mora remains unrealized in an already bimoraic syllable.

19 A similar approach might be extended to Yawelmani.

Archangeli's major argument that coda consonants must be mapped to stem templates early in the derivation (although they do not fulfill weight requirements of templates and therefore are argued not to receive weight until later) involves so-called "ghost consonants," which surface only under certain prosodic conditions. Thus, in the suffix *(h)atin*, the ghost *h* appears after a stem ending in one but not two consonants: *cawhatin* (←*caw* + *hatin*) but *hognatin* (←*hogn* + *hatin*). In these forms, Archangeli claims, the ghost consonant appears only when there is no other free consonant available to serve as onset for *a*. It is therefore necessary that the *w* in *caw* + *hatin* be mapped to the stem template to distinguish this case from *hogn* + *hatin*, in which *n* remains free even after the stem template is maximally satisfied. To sketch one possible alternative in which consonants are not mapped to coda position until later, one could assume that only the minimal material necessary to satisfy the stem template is mapped to that template (giving [*ca*]$_\sigma$ *whatin* versus [*ho*]$_\sigma$ *gnhatin*). A principle of optimal syllabification in the spirit of harmonic phonology (Goldsmith 1993a; Prince and Smolensky 1991b, 1993) might then ensure that ghost consonants are included in syllables only if their inclusion does not increase the number of syllables in the word. Since both possible syllabifications of CVC stems are equivalent in number of syllables (*cawhatin* versus **cawatin*), the ghost consonant is included. But in CVCC roots, inclusion of the ghost consonant cannot be accomplished without increasing the number of syllables (*hognatin* versus **hoginhatin*).

6 The Syllable in Phonological Theory

JULIETTE BLEVINS

0 Introduction

The role of the syllable in phonological theory has become more significant with each passing decade.[1] All major approaches to phonology, from the early Prague School through the London prosodicists and the American structuralists to modern generative approaches including autosegmental and metrical phonology, have recognized the syllable as a fundamental unit in phonological analysis.[2]

My goal in this chapter is to illustrate the important role played by the syllable in phonological theory. I first address the importance of recognizing the syllable as a phonological constituent (section 1). I then discuss how such constituents serve to organize segments in terms of sonority (section 2). In section 3, I present arguments bearing on the nature of syllable-internal structure, including the role of sonority and syllable weight in establishing constituency. This discussion is followed in section 4 by an overview of parametric variation in syllable types of the world's languages. In section 5, I consider the status of syllabification with respect to the phonological derivation – specifically, the question of how, and at what derivational point, syllable structure is assigned to strings, and respects in which certain phonological rules can be viewed as part of the syllabification process. Finally, in section 6, I take up several problems in current syllable theory, including the nature of coda constraints, questionable syllabifications, and mismatches between phonological and phonetic syllables.

Evidence for the syllable is plentiful, although much of it is dispersed among analyses from different schools and eras, and couched in disparate theoretical frameworks. My aim here will be to bring together a range of arguments and to extract from them the essence which any adequate phonological theory must capture.

What are syllables? Just as the feet of metrical theory supply rhythmic organization to phonological strings, syllables can be viewed as the structural units providing melodic organization to such strings. This melodic organization is based for the most part on the inherent sonority of phonological segments, where the sonority of a sound is roughly defined as its loudness relative to other sounds produced with the same input energy (i.e., with the same length, stress, pitch, velocity of airflow, muscular tension, etc.).[3] Hence, melodic organization of a phonological string into syllables will result in a characteristic sonority profile: segments will be organized into rising and falling sonority sequences, with each sonority peak defining a unique syllable. The syllable then is the phonological unit which organizes segmental melodies in terms of sonority; syllabic segments are equivalent to sonority peaks within these organizational units.

1 The Syllable as Phonological Constituent

While phonologists from a wide range of theoretical perspectives agree that the syllable plays an important role as a prosodic constituent, agreement is by no means universal concerning the precise nature of the syllable, nor for that matter the very existence of this constituent in phonology. In this section I will offer a range of arguments, both old and new, with the aim of providing a strong case for the importance of the syllable in phonology and a general foundation for the discussion to follow.

Arguments for constituency are traditionally based on the observation that a particular generalization, or group of generalizations, can be more succinctly stated in terms of the given constituents than without them. For instance, arguments for the familiar syntactic constituents NounPhrase and VerbPhrase are rooted in the position that distributional constraints and extraction phenomena are best stated in terms of such constituents. In this section I present four arguments of this sort for the syllable as a phonological constituent.

1.1 Syllable as Domain

The first argument for the syllable as a phonological constituent derives from the fact that there are phonological processes and/or constraints which take the syllable as their domain of application. Such rules and constraints are sensitive to a domain that is larger than the segment, smaller than the word, and contains exactly one sonority peak.[4]

One example of a process involving entire syllables is pharyngealization in Arabic and Berber dialects (Ali-Ani 1970; Ghazeli 1977; Saib 1978; Broselow 1979; Elmedlaoui 1985; Hoberman 1987). In these languages, the presence of an underlyingly pharyngealized or emphatic consonant gives rise to domains of pharyngealized segments which are larger than the individual segment, and often smaller than the entire word. In Cairene Arabic the smallest domain for pharyngealization is CV; this is also the minimal syllable type in this language. Broselow (1979) argues that the appropriate way to characterize pharyngealization alternations in Cairene is with reference to the syllable: pharyngealization spreads to all tautosyllabic segments, and its domain is thus the syllable.

Other phonological properties which take the syllable as their domain are stress and tone. At the phonetic level, stress and tone, like pharyngealization, are typically realized on multisegmental strings (Firth 1948; Pike 1962; Beckman 1986).

At the phonological level, there are many languages in which placement of predictable stress or tone requires "skipping" C_0VC_0 sequences.[5] Such principles of stress assignment support the existence of syllables in that the candidates for stress assignment that are skipped over are always complete syllables. Furthermore, stress and tone languages fall into two general classes with respect to general assignment algorithms: those in which mappings of stress and tone differ for *heavy* and *light* syllables, and those in which such weight is irrelevant. In the first case, the mora, or weight unit, might be viewed as the stress/tone-bearing unit; in the second case, it seems necessary to recognize the syllable as the stress/tone-bearing unit. However, even in languages which show weight-sensitivity to stress assignment, recognition of syllables is necessary. Hayes (1991) observes that in all true stress languages, the syllable appears to be the stress-bearing unit, that is, there is no contrast between tautosyllabic v́v and vv́. In order to account for this, Hayes adopts a universal constraint which prohibits a single metrical foot from splitting syllables.[6] Without access to the construct "syllable", it is difficult to imagine how such a constraint would be formulated.

Another phenomenon which argues for the existence of the syllable as a phonological constituent derives from the presence of a contrast between so-called "ballistic" and "controlled" syllables in Otomanguean Amuzgo and Chinantecan languages (Robbins 1961; Merrifield 1963; Bauernschmidt 1965; Westley 1971; Foris 1973; Rensch 1978). In these languages, ballistic syllables have some or all of the following properties: aspiration (including fortis initial Cs, voiceless nuclear Vs, final voiceless sonorants, and syllable-final aspiration); rapid crescendo to peak intensity, with sudden decrescendo; accentuation of vowel length (long vowels are longer, and short vowels are shorter); tonal variants (higher level tones, upglides and downglides); tongue root retraction. Nonballistic syllables are unaspirated, show even rise and falls of intensity, have normal vowel length contrasts, do not show tonal gliding, and have no tongue-root retraction. The group of properties distinguishing ballistic syllables all take domains larger than a single segment. Of particular relevance is the fact that aspiration is spread across the maximal $C_0V(V)C_0$ span, and that the distinct intensity patterns are also mapped over this domain. Treating ballisticity as anything other than a feature of the syllable leaves the range of properties noted and their multisegmental domains unexplained.[7] In sum, phonological properties with the syllable as their domain include pharyngealization, stress, tone, and ballisticity.[8]

1.2 Syllable Edge as Locus

Another argument for the syllable as phonological constituent is the existence of phonological rules that apply at syllable edges. In all languages, syllable edges correspond with word/utterance edges, so that without reference to the syllable, many such rules must be formulated to apply in the schematic environments / _____ {#, C} or / {#, C} _____. Such rules are problematic for the simple reason that boundary symbols and consonants do not form a natural class.[9] As a result, such rules are best interpreted as defining syllable-final and syllable-initial environments respectively. Aspiration is often associated with syllable boundaries. For instance, in English (Kahn 1976) and Kunjen (Sommer 1981), syllable-initial obstruents are aspirated, while in Sierra Popoluca (Elson 1947) and Yucatec Mayan (Straight 1976), syllable-final obstruents are aspirated.

1.3 Syllables as Target Structures

In addition to rules which take the syllable as their domain of application, and those which affect segments at syllable edges, syllables can function as targets of language games (see chapter 23, this volume) or as prosodic targets in morphological processes (see chapter 9, this volume). Numerous language games have been described with reference to the syllable. For instance, White (1955) describes a language game in Luvale where /-ti/ is suffixed to each syllable of the word. Laycock's (1972) survey of language games (or "ludlings") notes at least twenty cases where the syllable is the target of affixation, truncation, substitution, or movement.

In addition to ludlings, syllables are also the prosodic targets of morphological processes like reduplication. Within the theory of prosodic morphology and phonology as developed by McCarthy and Prince (see chapter 9, this volume), reduplication involves affixation of a bare prosodic template to a base, where the segmental properties of the template are determined by those of the base. Four syllable types are recognized in prosodic morphology: (1) (maximal) syllable; (2) light (i.e., monomoraic) syllable; (3) heavy (i.e., bimoraic) syllable; and (4) core (i.e., CV) syllable. Only by the introduction of syllable templates can the invariant properties of such affixes and their restricted types cross-linguistically be captured.

1.4 Native Intuitions

In a number of languages, native speakers have clear intuitions regarding the number of syllables in a word or utterance, and in some of these, generally clear intuitions as to where syllable breaks occur. Many descriptive grammars contain references to native speakers' awareness of syllable breaks. For instance, in Schütz's (1985, p. 537) comprehensive grammar of Fijian, he notes that "native speakers seem to recognize the syllable as a unit: covertly in their occasional use of syllabic oral spelling; and overtly in their marking syllable divisions in some material for language teachers."[10] If phonology is in part the study of the mental representations of sound structure, then such intuitions support the view of the syllable as a plausible phonological constituent.[11]

Having shown how some languages require reference to syllabic constituents, the strongest theory (that is, the easiest theory to disprove) will posit syllables as substantive linguistic universals.[12] This is the theory I will adopt in the remainder of this chapter. In addition, I will assume that the syllable has a fixed position in the universal prosodic hierarchy as pictured in (1) below.[13]

(1)   Universal Prosodic Hierarchy

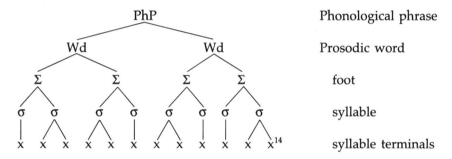

PhP	Phonological phrase
Wd	Prosodic word
Σ	foot
σ	syllable
x[14]	syllable terminals

2   Sonority

The relationship between syllables and sonority is one that has been recognized for a century or more. Jespersen (1904) points out that in each utterance, there are as many syllables as there are clear peaks of sonority, and Sievers (1881) observes that in general, between any member of a syllable and the syllable peak, only sounds of higher sonority are permitted. These and related observations are generally referred to as the Sonority Sequencing Generalization (or Sonority Sequencing Principle) a version of which is given in (2).[15]

(2)   Sonority Sequencing Generalization (SSG)[16]
      Between any member of a syllable and the syllable peak, a sonority rise or plateau must occur.

While most phonologists agree that some version of the SSG is to be integrated into phonological theory, a range of questions arise concerning its status and implementation. Is the Sonority Sequencing Generalization an absolute condition on representations, or simply a preference condition expressing universal markedness values? On what basis is segmental sonority determined? Is sonority ranking universal or language specific?

There appear to be a fair number of exceptions to the Sonority Sequencing Generalization as presented in (2). As stated, it proposes that the presence of a prevocalic C_1C_2 ($C_1 \neq C_2$) sequence within the syllable implies the absence of a postvocalic C_1C_2 sequence and vice versa. However, in English, syllable-initial /sp st sk/ occur, and postvocalic tautosyllabic /sp st sk/ are also found, and English is far from unique in this regard.[17] Such cross-linguistic facts have lead many researchers to adopt the Sonority Sequencing Generalization as a preference condition, a determinant of syllable markedness, or as a constraint on initial syllabification, which can later be violated by language-particular rules and/or constraints.[18]

Another question concerns how sonority is defined and on what measure it is based. A phonetic basis for sonority has been widely contested, though measurements based on acoustic intensity are often taken as a starting point for estimating the perceptual saliency or loudness of a particular sound. Based on such measurements, Ladefoged (1982, p. 222) presents the following partial sonority ranking for English: a > æ > ɛ > ɪ > u > i > l > n > m > z > v > s > š > d > t > k.

This particular scale conforms to most universal and language-particular phonological sonority scales proposed in the literature. Such scales come in a variety of types, with the major parameters of differentiation being feature-based vs. nonfeature based, binary vs. scalar, relative vs. absolute, and fine-grained vs. not-so-fine-grained. Distinctive feature-based models, first advocated by Basbøll (1977), have the distinct advantage of categorizing segments on the same basis as other phonological rules and constraints. Using distinctive features, I summarize in (3) the sonority relations which, to my knowledge, have not been counter-exemplified in the phonological and/or phonetic literature.[19]

(3) A working universal sonority scale
     For each node, the left branch is more sonorous than the right branch, and sonority relations for a given feature are only defined with respect to segments with the feature specification of the mother node.

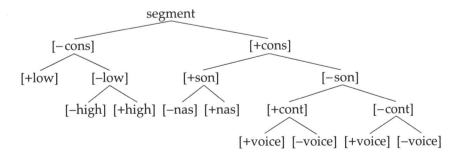

The sonority scale in (3) is organized in terms of binary relationships, with the left branch more sonorous than the right branch. The relationships in this tree are intended to be absolute; thus, for example, we will find *no* language where non-low vowels are more sonorous than low vowels. The fine-grainedness of the scale is determined by available evidence; as far as I know, for instance, there are no languages which display clear sonority rankings for place of articulation features within the class of [+consonantal] segments.[20]

3 Syllable-internal Structure

We turn now to the question of syllable-internal structure, and the relation of syllable-internal structure to syllable weight. Many proposals have been made concerning the internal structure of syllables. Some current views are listed in (4).[21]

(4) Models of syllable-internal structure
  (a) Flat structure (i.e., no subconstituents but the segments themselves) (Anderson 1969; Kahn 1976; Clements and Keyser 1983).
  (b) Moraic approaches: $\sigma \rightarrow C_0\mu(\mu)$ C_0 (Hyman 1985; McCarthy and Prince 1986; Hayes 1989).
  (c) Binary branching with Body: $\sigma \rightarrow$ Body Coda; Body $\rightarrow$ Onset Nucleus (McCarthy 1979; Vennemann 1984).
  (d) Ternary branching: $\sigma \rightarrow$ Onset Nucleus Coda (Hockett 1955; Haugen 1956; Davis 1985).
  (e) Binary branching with Rime: $\sigma \rightarrow$ Onset Rime; Rime $\rightarrow$ Nucleus Coda; (traditional Chinese scholars as represented, for instance, in the Song dynasty rhyme tables (děngyùntú), and discussed at length in Chao 1941 and Karlgren 1954; Pike and Pike 1947; Kurylowicz 1948; Fudge 1969; Halle and Vergnaud 1978; Selkirk 1982).

Evidence for subsyllabic constituency falls into the same categories already used in justifying the syllable as a constituent. Particular emphasis is usually on sonority-based, feature-based, and position-based phonotactic constraints, as these provide the strongest evidence for multisegmental domains within the syllable. Here the principle has been invoked that the presence of co-occurrence restrictions between two segment positions within a syllable is evidence that the two positions form a constituent. In this section, I present evidence in favor of the model in (4e), where the maximal syllable-internal structure is as shown in (5).

(5) Syllable-internal structure (English word *dream*)

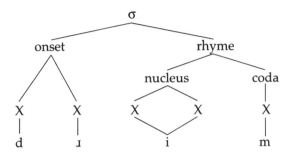

I will present first what I believe is the strongest evidence for this model, and then demonstrate that other approaches (4a–d) cannot adequately account for such facts, at least not without substantial revision.

As outlined in section 2, there have been various proposals concerning how sonority values should be integrated into syllable theory. Most proposals attempt to account for the Sonority Sequencing Generalization (to the extent that it is valid) by ranking phones on a sonority scale like that suggested by Ladefoged (1982) for English. Using such scales, two aspects of sonority sequencing favor the division of syllable into onset, nucleus, and coda subdomains. First, while initial and final C clusters in $\#\#C_0V_1C_0\#\#$ may show a rigid internal adherence to sonority scales, the sonority value of prevocalic and postvocalic Cs is not determined in relation to the sonority value of adjacent Vs. Second, for many languages, the sonority sequencing constraints holding among prevocalic C-sequences are not simply the mirror image of those which constrain postvocalic C-sequences.

Both of these points can be illustrated with reference to English. In English, all word-initial C-clusters, excluding those composed of /s/ + obstruent, conform to the Sonority Sequencing Generalization: /pr br tr dr kr gr fr vr sr pl bl kl gl fl vl sl šl tw dw kw gw sw šw/. However, there is no case in which the sonority value of the second member of these clusters is determined by the following vowel: /swuːn/ and /swan/ are both well-formed despite the fact that the sonority values of /w, u/ are much closer than those of /w, a/. In addition, while all the initial clusters above are well-formed in reverse order as postvocalic sequences, additional postvocalic clusters occur, including: /rl rm rn lm ln nd mp ŋk/. But despite the fact that all of these clusters obey the Sonority Sequencing Generalization, none of them constitute well-formed syllable-initial clusters when their order is reversed: *lrV . . . , *mrV . . . , *nrV . . . , *mlV . . . , etc. Hence, any attempt to formalize the constraints on relative sonority of segments within the English syllable must (1) recognize that sonority scales are relevant within prevocalic and postvocalic clusters, but not across CV or VC; and (2) distinguish minimal sonority distances for initial and final clusters, as segments closer in sonority value are tolerated post-vocalically. Evidence for sonority sequencing constraints within a language can then be extended to become evidence for a division of the syllable into three distinct domains: onset, nucleus, and coda. As such evidence is consistent with the models in (4c, d, e) above, further arguments focus on the necessity of a rhyme constituent which is decomposed into nucleus and coda subconstituents.

The most robust evidence for the rhyme constituent is based on phenomena sensitive to syllable *weight*. In many languages, syllables are divided into heavy and light, where heavy syllables are those which attract stress or allow two (as opposed to one) tones. In all but a very few cases, syllable weight is defined without reference to the prevocalic portion of the syllable.[22] Further, as shown in (6), in languages that show a three-way weight distinction, the heaviest syllables are those which have the most sonorous rhymes. (Recall here that, all else being equal, long segments are more sonorous than short segments.)

(6) Cross-linguistic definitions of syllable weight[23]

	Light	Heavy	Heaviest	
Type 1	C_0V		$C_0VX\ldots$	Sierra Miwok, Hausa, etc.
Type 2	C_0VC_0		$C_0VV\ldots$	Huasteco, Hawaiian, etc.
Type 3	C_0V	C_0VC_1	$C_0VV\ldots$	Klamath, Yupik
	C_0V	C_0VC_1	$C_0V\{V, R\}\ldots$	Creek

In such languages as Sierra Miwok, both C_0VC and C_0VV syllables attract stress, while in Hausa, both of these syllable types count as heavy for the purposes of phonological and morphological processes. In Huasteco, stress falls on the last syllable in the word containing a long vowel, otherwise on the first syllable, with C_0VC syllables skipped; in Hawaiian all C_0VV syllables are stressed, but this language has no closed syllables. In Klamath, stress also falls on the last long vowel of the word; but in the absence of a long vowel, stress falls on the penult if it is closed, otherwise on the antepenult. In Yupik, syllables with long vowels attract stress, as do word-initial closed syllables. Finally, in Creek, where a pitch accent system is in evidence, contour tones are found only on VV and VR sequences; however, predictable pitch accents in Creek are placed in accordance with quantity-sensitive binary feet which treat both CVV and CVC syllables as heavy.

The three language types in (6) appear to exhaust the range of syllable-weight distinctions that do not involve segments preceding the nuclear vowel. The fact that languages have at most a three-way weight distinction and variable definitions of heavy and light will then follow from the definitions of these categories in terms of the syllable subconstituents nucleus and rhyme, as shown in (7):

(7)   Structural definitions of syllable weight[24]

	Light	Heavy	Heaviest
	Light	Heavy	Heaviest
Type 1	nonbranching rhyme		branching rhyme
Type 2	nonbranching nucleus		branching nucleus
Type 3	nonbranching rhyme	branching rhyme	branching nucleus

The syllable-internal structure posited in (4c, d) above must resort to conjunctive statements to account for the cross-linguistic weight classes in (7). For instance, the definition of "heavy" for type 1 within the body/coda approach would be as follows: heavy syllables are those which are branching and/or those with branching nuclei. Moraic approaches (4b) which lack syllable-internal constituency have problems handling languages with three-way weight contrasts. In order to remedy such problems, Hayes (1991) has introduced various elaborations of moraic theory including context-sensitive weight-by-position rules, a distinction between strong and weak moras, and a prosodic grid on which extra-moraic sonority distinctions can be represented. While it would take us somewhat afield to argue the point in detail here, Hayes's emmendations can be interpreted as demonstrating that a moraic theory which eschews syllable-internal structure is forced to weaken itself to a point where the possibilities for defining distinct syllable weights are greater than those delineated by the model of annotated syllable structure summarized in (7).[25]

Other arguments for constituency focus on feature distribution and substitution classes within the syllable. Pike and Pike (1947) argue that the immediate constituents of Mazateco syllables are onsets ("margins") and nuclei. (As all syllables in Mazateco are open, there is no distinction possible between nucleus and rhyme in this language.) This division is based on the distribution of tone and nasalization; contrastive tone and nasalization are features of the nucleus, and are not realized on prevocalic glides, which are members of the onset.[26] Hockett (1947) illustrates how the traditional view of the Chinese syllable accounts for systematic restrictions on sound sequences. Only consonantal elements occur as initials (onsets), only glides appear as medials (rhyme-initial elements), only vowels occur in the nucleus, and terminals (codas) are restricted on a language-specific basis. Fudge (1969, 1987) also uses distributional evidence to support a view of the English syllable similar to that shown in (5).[27] For instance, the fact that only lax/short vowels are found before /-mp/ and /-ŋk/ is taken as an indication that nucleus and coda are more closely related than onset and nucleus are.

In other languages, evidence for the rhyme also takes the form of restrictions on the number of rhyme-internal segments: for instance, in Yokuts (Newman 1944), Afar (Bliese 1981), and Hausa (Newman 1972), no more than two segments can appear in the rhyme, with derived CVVC syllables surfacing as CVC; and in Turkish (Clements and Keyser 1983) and Spanish (Harris 1983) no more than three elements can occur within the syllable rhyme.[28] Such restrictions are difficult to formulate without reference to the rhyme itself.

Additional arguments for the rhyme as phonological constituent come from language games. In addition to ludlings which affix/replace/move entire syllables, there are also numerous examples in Laycock (1972) where the syllable rhyme is the rule focus. In English "oppen-gloppen" the sentence "you are mad" is rendered as [y-op-u op-aɹ m-op-æd].[29]

Arguments for the onset as a constituent are hard to come by. Other than the fact that sonority sequencing constraints can be shown to hold within this domain, there are few indications that the onset is anything but what is left when the rhyme is taken away.[30] Likewise, other than sonority constraints, there are few convincing demonstrations of coda sequences defining an identifiable constituent. Given the lack of positive evidence for onset and coda constituents, the original model in (5) is modified to that shown in (8) below:

(8) Syllable-internal structure (based on positive evidence)

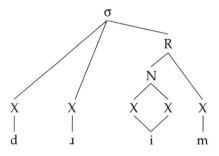

Within this model, sonority constraints holding within pre-vocalic and post-vocalic clusters can still be defined with reference to syllable structure: onset elements are those dominated immediately by σ, and coda elements are those dominated immediately by R.

4 An Overview of Syllable Typology

In this section, I shall present a brief overview of syllable typology. The purpose of this is to demonstrate the extent to which syllable types vary cross-linguistically, and to highlight cross-linguistic generalizations. Any theory of the syllable must be able to account for the wide range of syllable types that we find, and for aspects of syllable structure which remain constant across languages.[31] Variation among syllable types in the world's languages is considerable.

Table 6.1 Cross-linguistic variation in syllable types*

	V	CV	CVC	VC	CCV	CCVC	CVCC	VCC	CCVCC	CVCCC
Hua	no	yes	no	no	no	no	no	no	no	no
Cayuvava	yes	yes	no	no	no	no	no	no	no	no
Cairene	no	yes	yes	no	no	no	no	no	no	no
Mazateco	yes	yes	no	no	yes	no	no	no	no	no
Mokilese	yes	yes	yes	yes	no	no	no	no	no	no
Sedang	no	yes	yes	no	yes	yes	no	no	no	no
Klamath	no	yes	yes	no	no	no	yes	no	no	yes
Spanish	yes	yes	yes	yes	yes	yes	no	no	no	no
Finnish	yes	yes	yes	yes	no	no	yes	yes	no	no
Totonac	no	yes	yes	no	yes	yes	yes	no	yes	yes
English	yes	yes	yes	yes	yes	yes	yes	yes	yes	yes

* For language sources, see table 6.3. Note that V is used in this chart as a cover term for any nuclear sequence, i.e., both for short vowels, long vowels, and vowel sequences.

Some languages, like Hua, have only one syllable type: CV. Other languages, like English, have more than ten basic syllable shapes.[32] Despite the range of variation, certain generalizations are apparent. First, all languages have CV syllables.[33] Second, all languages exhibit the following property: if clusters of *n* Cs are possible syllable-initially, then clusters of *n*–1 Cs are also possible syllable-initially, and if clusters of *n* Cs are possible syllable-finally, then clusters of *n*–1 Cs are also possible finally.[34] In addition, if a language does not allow syllables consisting solely of V, then it does not allow any V-initial syllables. Table 6.2 illustrates the extent to which languages can vary in terms of tautosyllabic sequences of syllabic (or nuclear) elements.

Table 6.2 Parametric variation in nuclear [-cons] sequences*

Language	V	V:	V::	V:::	V_1V_2	$V_1V_2V_3$	$V_1V_2V_3V_4$
Cayuvava	yes	no	no	no	no	no	no
Yokuts	yes	yes	no	no	no	no	no
El Paraíso Mixe	yes	yes	yes	no	no	no	no
Spanish	yes	no	no	no	yes	no	no
Witoto	yes	no	no	no	yes	yes	no
Finnish	yes	yes	no	no	yes	no	no
Estonian	yes	yes	yes	no	yes	yes	no

* Language sources include: Cayuvava (Key 1961); Yokuts (Newman 1944); El Paraíso Mixe (Van Haistma and Van Haistma 1976); Spanish (Harris 1983); Witoto (Minor 1956); Finnish (Keyser and Kiparsky 1984); Estonian (Prince 1980).

Again, certain generalizations are apparent. Most notably, if a language allows tautosyllabic sequences of *n* Vs, then it also allows sequences of *n* − 1 Vs. No language appears to allow sequences of more than three Vs within a single syllable, and no language has more than a three-way contrast in vowel length. Though not apparent from this schematic table, within the nucleus domain, the SSG holds without fail.

In order to capture some of these generalizations, languages can be described in terms of a small set of binary-valued parameters which are defined over sub-syllabic domains onset (= Cs immediately dominated by the syllable node), nucleus, and coda (= Cs immediately dominated by the rhyme node).

In Table 6.3, logical combinations of five binary-valued parameters are shown along with representative languages. The Complex Nucleus parameter specifies whether or not complex nuclei are well-formed (yes) or not (no).[35] In languages without complex nuclei, VV strings will constitute disyllabic sequences. The Obligatory Onset parameter determines whether an onset is obligatory (yes) or not (no). Languages like Totonac for which the setting is yes have no V-initial syllables. The Complex Onset parameter determines whether more than one segment is allowed in the onset (yes) or not (no). The Coda parameter is an indicator of whether (yes) or not (no) a language has closed syllables, while the parameter Complex Coda (CC) allows more than one segment within the coda (yes), or only one (no). In addition to these five parameters which result in a set of well-formed syllable types, some languages allow exceptional syllable types at the edge of the syllabification domain. For instance, in Klamath, word-initial syllables may begin with CC-clusters, but CC-initial syllables are not found word-internally. Such exceptionality is included in this chart under Edge Effect, with sub-settings I(nitial)/F(inal)), for the sake of completeness. While settings for the first three parameters are independent, settings for Coda and Complex Coda are dependent: if the setting for Coda is "no," then the setting for Complex Coda is also "no". The resulting full matrix is 24 by 5, where each of the 24 rows defines a possible parameter setting for some natural language.

The parameter settings described above not only account for the generalizations noted above, but are also meant to encode markedness values, where "no" is the unmarked value and "yes" is the marked value. The unmarked case is that onsets are not obligatory; there are no complex onsets; there are no codas, and there are no systematic differences between word-internal and word-edge syllables. While it would take us somewhat afield to present a detailed justification of the syllable markedness values encoded here, the following observations are taken to be highly suggestive of such a ranking. (1) In the early stages of language development (early babbling), children appear to produce syllables in which onsets are not obligatory, there are no complex onsets, there are no codas and there are no systematic differences between word-internal and word-edge syllables (Vihman et. al. 1985). (2) In second language acquisition, speakers have little difficulty in shifting from a "yes" value to a "no" value for a given parameter, but do show difficulty in switching

Table 6.3 Parametric variation in syllable type*

	Complex Nucleus	*Oblig. Onset*	*Complex Onset*	*Coda*	*Complex Coda*	*Edge Effect*
Totonac	yes	yes	yes	yes	yes	yes/F
Klamath	yes	yes	no	yes	yes	yes/I
English	yes	no	yes	yes	yes	yes/F
Nisqually	no	yes	yes	yes	yes	yes/F
Gilyak	no	no	yes	yes	yes	yes/F
Finnish	yes	no	no	yes	yes	no
Tunica	no	yes	no	yes	yes	no
Tamazight Berber	no	no	no	yes	yes	yes/F
Sedang	yes	yes	yes	yes	no	yes/I
Cairene	yes	yes	no	yes	no	yes/F
Spanish	yes	no	yes	yes	no	yes/F
Dakota	no	yes	yes	yes	no	yes/F
Italian	no	no	yes	yes	no	yes/IF
Mokilese	yes	no	no	yes	no	yes/F
Thargari	no	yes	no	yes	no	no
Cuna	no	no	no	yes	no	no
Arabela	yes	yes	yes	no	no	no
Siona**	yes	yes	no	no	no	no
Pirahã**	yes	no	yes	no	no	no
Piro**	no	yes	yes	no	no	yes/I
Mazateco	no	no	yes	no	no	no
Fijian	yes	no	no	no	no	no
Hua**	no	yes	no	no	no	no
Cayuvava	no	no	no	no	no	no

* Language sources include: Totonac (MacKay 1991); Klamath (Barker 1963, 1964); Nisqually (Hoard 1978); Gilyak (Austerlitz 1956; Jakobson 1957); Finnish (Keyser and Kiparsky 1984; Prince 1984); Tunica (Haas 1946); Tamazight Berber (Saib 1978; Chung 1991); Sedang (Smith 1979); Cairene (Broselow 1979); Spanish (Harris 1983); Dakota (Shaw 1989); Italian (Basbøll 1974); Mokilese (Harrison 1976); Thargari (Klokeid 1969); Cuna (Sherzer 1970, 1975); Arabela (Rich 1963); Siona (Wheeler and Wheeler 1962); Pirahã (Everett and Everett 1984); Piro (Matteson 1965); Mazateco (Pike and Pike 1947); Fijian (Schütz 1985); Hua (Haiman, 1980); Cayuvava (Key 1961).

**Aspects of syllabification in these languages are questionable. The above classification requires that (i) complex nuclei in Siona include V_1V_2 and V?; (ii) voiceless stops in Pirahã be treated as tautosyllabic geminate onsets; (iii) all long vowels in Piro be derived from lengthening of V_1 in compensation of C_1-loss in ... $V.C_1C_2V$ ... strings; (iv) that V? and V both constitute simple nuclei in Hua, where V? is a short glottalized vowel.

Table 6.4 Parametric variation in syllabic segments*

Language	Sonority						
	A	I	R	L	N	S	T
Kabardian	yes	no	no	no	no	no	no
Hawai'ian	yes	yes	—	—	no	—	no
Sanskrit	yes	(yes)	(yes)	no	no	no	no
Lendu	yes	(yes)	(yes)	(yes)	no	no	no
English	yes	(yes)	(yes)	(yes)	(yes)	no	no
Central Carrier	yes	(yes)	—	—	(yes)	(yes)	no
Imdlawn Tashlhiyt Berber	yes	(yes)	(yes)	(yes)	(yes)	(yes)	(yes)

* Where A is [–high, –cons]; I is [+high, –cons]; R, L, N are rhotic, lateral, and nasal sonorants respectively; S is a [+cont] obstruent; and T is a [–cont] obstruent. "Yes" indicates that this segment type is an obligatory syllable nucleus in the language in question; (yes) indicates that the segment type is an optional syllable nucleus; "no" indicates that the segment type is an impossible syllable nucleus; — indicates that such segments are not found in the language in question.

  Language sources include: Kabardian (Kuipers 1960); Hawai'ian (Pukui and Elbert 1986); Sanskrit (Whitney 1889); Lendu (Tucker 1940); Central Carrier (Walker 1979); Imdlawn Tashlhiyt Berber (Dell and Elmedlaoui 1985; Elmedlaoui 1985).

from a "no" value to a "yes" value (Anderson 1987). (3) All languages have CV syllables. (4) Perhaps most important, there are a variety of phonological processes which take marked syllable types to unmarked types (rules of epenthesis and segment deletion), but there are few if any rules which consistently result in obligatory codas, obligatory complex onsets, or obligatory complex codas.

In addition to the parameters shown in table 6.3, for each language a set of obligatory, possible, and impossible nuclei must by specified. Table 6.4 shows the range of syllabic segments cross-linguistically, where the horizontal axis is arranged from most sonorous segments on the left to least sonorous segments on the right.

From table 6.4 we see that there is a definite relationship between the sonority value of a segment and its potential as a syllable nucleus. Three concrete generalizations emerge: (1) all languages have syllables containing non-high vocalic nuclei; (2) if a language allows a syllabic segment with sonority value *x*, then all segments with sonority values greater than *x* (i.e., more sonorous segments) are also potential syllabic nuclei; (3) within a language, optional nuclei are never more sonorous than obligatory nuclei.[36]

Parameters like those instantiated in table 6.3 coupled with the Sonority Sequencing Generalization and the three generalizations above go a long way toward defining the range of syllable types cross-linguistically.

5 Syllables and Syllabification

Having established the existence of phonological syllables, and aspects of their internal structure, we turn to the question of where syllables come from. Are they present in the lexicon, or are they somehow generated in the course of the phonological derivation? Three observations suggest that in the general case, syllable structure is not present in underlying representations: (1) minimal pairs distinguished by syllabification alone are rare, and are nonexistant in many languages; (2) segments in many languages exhibit syllabicity alternations which can be viewed as the simple result of derived syllabification; (3) individual morphemes often fail to conform to the possible syllable types of a given language, making lexical syllabification infelicitous.

With reference to the first point, consider the English near minimal pair [ʔáy.da] "Ida" vs. [ʔa.íy.da] "Aïda". In the general case, heteromorphemic /ai/ sequences are syllabified as complex nuclei: [ai] "I", [wai] "why", [ʔail] or [áil̩] "aisle", etc. For this general case then, we can formulate a syllabification rule which will result in tautosyllabic /ai/ sequences. For exceptional forms like [ʔa.íy.da] we can assume that minimal structure is specified in the lexicon. In this case, it is sufficient to mark /i/ as a syllable nucleus in the UR: /a[i]$_N$da/; this pre-specified syllable structure will bleed the regular rule assigning unsyllabified /ai/ sequences to a single nuclei.

Syllabicity alternations have been examined in numerous languages, and for the most part appear to be predictable and nondistinctive. Studies supporting the view of such alternations as the simple output of regular syllabification schemas include: Steriade (1982) for Latin and Ancient Greek; Noske (1982) for French; Sagey (1984) for Kinyarwanda; Steriade (1984) for Rumanian; Dell and Elmedlaoui (1985) for Imdlawn Tashlhiyt Berber; Guerssel (1986) for Ait Seghrouchen Berber; and Levin (1985) for Klamath.[37]

Perhaps the most striking analysis of this kind is that of Imdlawn Tashlhiyt Berber presented by Dell and Elmedlaoui (1985). In this language, all segments have syllabic and nonsyllabic allophones, with the exception of /a/ which surfaces consistently as a vowel. Syllabicity is predictable and nondistinctive (except for a set of morphemes containing high vocoids which are consistently [–syllablic]). As a result, Dell and Elmedlaoui start with unsyllabified underlying representaitons and propose a simple syllabification algorithm which predicts the syllabicity of segments based on their position and relative sonority within the string. Dell and Elmedlaoui adopt the following sonority scale for Imdlawn Tashlhiyt Berber: a> i,u > liquid > nasal > voiced fricative > voiceless fricative > voiced stop > voiceless stop. Their syllabification algorithm involves three steps: (1) Core syllabification: scanning from left to right in the string, associate a core syllable (i.e., a simple CV syllable constituent) to any sequence (Y) Z, where Y can be any segment not yet syllabified, and Z is a segment of type T, where T is a variable to be replaced by a set of feature specifications, in descending order, starting with the most sonorous elements on the sonority scale; (2) Coda rule: incorporate a single coda consonant; (3) Complex onset, complex coda: build complex onsets and/or codas where necessary.[38]

If syllable structure is generally absent in underlying representations, how does it arise? As noted above, syllabification algorithms have been proposed for a variety of languages. Perhaps the most basic division between these algorithms is that distinguishing rule-based approaches like that of Steriade (1982), and template-matching approaches such as that implemented by Itô (1986). *Template-matching algorithms* for syllabification scan the segmental string in a fixed, language-particular direction (left to right, right to left), assigning successive segments to positions in a syllable template, always mapping to as many positions inside a given syllable template as possible. *Rule-based algorithms* posit an ordered set of structure-building rules which have similar status to that of other phonological rules: such rules may or may not apply directionally and do not require that syllable structure be maximalized in any sense from the start. While the two approaches overlap in many respects, two aspects of syllabification are most simply handled in rule-based syllabification algorithms: (1) in some languages rules of syllabification have been argued to apply in an ordered fashion to potential syllable nuclei, from most sonorous to least sonorous; (2) in some languages, there is evidence that structure-building rules of syllabification must be intrinsically ordered.

Both of these points are illustrated by the brief sketch of Dell and Elmedlaoui's analysis of Imdlawn Tashlhiyt Berber just presented. First, core syllabification applies in an ordered fashion from most sonorous to least sonorous potential nuclei; second, core syllabification precedes the formation of codas and complex onsets and codas. Another language where such ordering relationships have been argued for is Klamath (Clements and Keyser 1983; Levin 1985), where the maximal syllable is [CVVCCC]. In Klamath, on the basis of glide/vowel alternations, it has been argued that (1) non-high vowels are syllabified prior to high vowels, and (2) the first rule of syllabification creates [CVX] syllables, where this rule crucially feeds epenthesis. The analyses of Imdlawn Tashlhiyt Berber and of Klamath then present an immediate challenge for templatic models in which syllables are first maximalized, since such maximalization would bleed the necessary first-stage CV-/CVX rules, respectively, and derive ill-formed surface strings.[39]

While there might not be overt evidence for directional syllabification in all languages, those with vowel/glide alternations often provide evidence for directionality in the form of attested vs. unattested glide-vowel strings. For instance, in Lenakel (Lynch 1974) the distribution of high vowels and glides is complementary: high Vs [i, u] are found in C____C, C____#, and #____C environments, while glides [y, w] are found elsewhere, i.e., ____V, V____. Note the syllabicity alternations of the morpheme /-i-/ "first person" in the following verb forms: /i-ak-ol/ yágɔl "I do it"; /t-i-ak-ol/ tyágɔl "I will do it"; /i-n-ol/ ínɔl "I have done it". The maximal syllable in Lenakel is [CVC].[40] In sequences of two or more high segments, the first is always syllabified as a glide: /iik/ yík (*iyk) "you, sg."; /uus/ wús (*uws) "man, fellow"; /uikar/ wígar (*uygar) "seed"; /kiukiu/ kyúgyu (*kiwgiw) "to shake the body"; /uiuou/ wíwɔw (*uywɔw) "boil". Whether a rule-based or templatic approach is taken, the algorithm must apply directionally: in a rule-based approach, nucleus-placement must apply from right-to-left for high segments;[41] in a templatic approach, the template must be mapped from left-to-right to ensure glide-vowel as opposed to vowel-glide sequences.[42] In a case like this, the separation of template mapping into separate nucleus- and onset-building steps in the rule-based approach results in different directionality requirements: mapping to CV as a single step must be left to right; V mapping, with a subsequent onset formation is right to left. If directional syllabification has implications for other aspects of the phonology, then the distinct predictions of these two approaches could be tested against such phenomena. In fact, Itô (1989) has claimed that the directionality of syllabification predicts the position of epenthetic vowels in languages which have vowel epenthesis. Before evaluating this prosodic treatment of epenthesis, a short excursus on cross-linguistic strategies for dealing with stray segments is in order.

Underlying and intermediate phonological representations often do not constitute sequences of well-formed syllables within a given language. Where such violations occur at the edge of the syllabification domain, they are often tolerated on the surface, and aberrant strings result. For example, in Klamath, C_1C_2 sequences occur word-intially, though VCCCV strings are consistently syllabified as VCC.CV, attesting to the ill-formedness of complex onsets in this language. In Cairene Arabic, C_1C_2 sequences are found word-finally, though triconsonantal sequences are not found intervocalically (Broselow 1979, to appear). Here, VCCV strings are consistently syllabified as VC.CV, attesting to the ill-formedness of complex codas. In such cases, it has been useful to adopt the notion of extrametricality introduced by Liberman and Prince (1977:293) and developed by Hayes (1980) for metrical stress theory: *extrametrical* (or *extraprosodic*, or *extrasyllabic*) elements are (1) limited to the edge of the stress and syllabification domain, respectively, (2) invisible to the rules of constituent construction, and (3) are adjoined to existing metrical structure late in the derivation. Where the word is the domain of syllabification, then Klamath licenses extraprosodic segments initially, and Cairene Arabic licenses extra-prosodic segments finally. Rules of syllabification do not "see" such segments, and proceed accordingly; only late in the derivation are such segments adjoined to adjacent syllables.[43]

In other languages, segments which cannot be incorporated into well-formed syllables are deleted. This process, when affecting consonants, is commonly referred to as *Stray Erasure*. When affecting vowels, rules of closed syllable shortening may result. In either case, the general process can be stated as in (9):

(9) Stray Erasure: Unsyllabified segments are deleted.[44]

Stray Erasure has been claimed to account for consonant deletion in a number of languages, including Attic Greek (Steriade 1982), Diola Fogny (Steriade

1982), English (Borowsky 1986), French (Levin 1986), Icelandic (Itô 1986), Korean (Kim and Shibatani 1976), Lardil (Wilkinson 1988), and Turkish (Clements and Keyser 1983). In English, stem C/ø alternations as in *damn/damnation* and *hymn/hymnal* can be accounted for by recognizing that *mn* is an ill-formed coda sequence in English, and hence, the pre-surface representation of /dæmn/ is /dæm.n'/ where C' represents an unsyllabified C which is deleted by stray erasure, resulting in [dæm].[45]

Stray Erasure can also be viewed as the process involved in rules of closed syllable shortening in many languages. Rules of closed syllable shortening typically take [CVVC] to surface [CVC]$_\sigma$ by deletion or shortening of a nuclear vowel. Languages exhibiting regular closed syllable shortening include Afar (Bliese 1981), Hausa (Newman 1972), Kashaya (Buckley 1991), and Yokuts (Newman 1944; Noske 1984). In such languages maximal [CVX]$_\sigma$ syllables are typical: when a . . . $V_1V_2C_1\{C_2, \#\}$ . . . string is syllabified, the syllable headed by V_1 takes C_1 (over V_2) as a post-nuclear element. For instance, in Afar, vowel shortening and glide loss both follow from constructing [CVX] syllables with priority of C over V in the post-nuclear position: /koo/ [koo] "you, acc." vs. /koo-t/ [kot] "by you"; /rakuub/ [rakub] "camel, sg." vs. /rakuub-a/ [rakuuba] "camels"; /oys-oome/ [oysoome] "I caused to spoil" vs. /oys-s-oome/ [ossoome] "I caused to spoil for my benefit".[46]

Short of deleting a stray segment altogether, a segment may be altered by a feature-changing process, in conformity with language-specific syllable structure constraints. This type of process is most common with coda consonants, as such consonants are subject to featural restrictions in many languages (see section 6.1). For instance, in Korean, the feature [+continuant] is not licensed on obstruents within the coda. As a result, /s s' čʰ č č'/ all are realized as [t'] in the syllable coda (Kim-Renaud 1977): /os/ [ot'] "clothes", /os-kwa/ [ot'k'wa] "clothes and", /os-ɨn/ [osɨn] "as for the clothes"; /k'očʰ/ [k'ot'] "flower", /k'očʰ-kwa/ [k'ot'k'wa] "flower and", /k'očʰ-i/ [k'očʰi] "flower, subj.".[47]

Having briefly reviewed these methods of dealing with underlying and intermediate phonological representations which do not constitute sequences of well-formed syllables within a given language, I turn to perhaps the most well-established and well-studied mode of dealing with stray consonants, vowel epenthesis.[48] Prosodic treatments of vowel epenthesis are suggested in work of Firth (1948), Vennemann (1972), Giegerich (1981), Noske (1984), and Itô (1989), among others. The basic insight of these approaches is that epenthesis is a strategy for saving otherwise unsyllabifiable strings. Whereas rule-based syllabification algorithms build well-formed syllables, and subsequently invoke rules of V-epenthesis triggered by unsyllabified syllable terminals, templatic approaches such as that proposed by Noske (1984) and Itô (1989) view epenthesis as an integral part of the syllabification process.

As noted above, Itô (1988) has claimed that the site of epenthetic vowels is a direct function of the directionality of syllabification: in languages with left-to-right syllabification, stray consonants will surface as syllable onsets, while right-to-left syllabification will incorporate stray Cs as coda segments. Itô (1988) illustrates such an approach with a near-minimal dialect pair: Cairene Arabic vs. Iraqi Arabic. In both languages, the maximal syllable (abstracting away from the effects of extraprosodicity) is [CVX]$_σ$. However, in Cairene, underlying / ... VCCCV ... / surfaces as [... VCCiCV ...], whereas in Iraqi, underlying / ... VCCCV ... / surfaces as [... VCiCCV ...]. In both languages / ... VCCCCV ... / strings surface as [... VCCiCCV ...]. Itô accounts for these facts by mapping [CVX]$_σ$ from left-to-right in Cairene, and from right-to-left in Iraqi. While this approach handles the epenthesis facts from these two Arabic dialects in an elegant and straightforward way, it meets with problems in other languages.[49]

One of these languages is Lenakel, discussed with respect to glide/vowel distribution above. Recall that, based on the distribution of syllabic segments, the prosodic and rule-based approaches are led to different directionality specifications: left-to-right and right-to-left respectively. The template-matching approach then predicts that epenthesis rules in Lenakel, as in Cairene, should result in stray segments syllabified as onsets, as opposed to codas. While this is true for initial (10a) and medial (10b) clusters, it is not the case for final CC clusters (10c), where a word-final C is syllabified as a coda.[50]

(10) Lenakel epenthesis (Lynch 1974)
(a) /t-n-ak-ol/   tinágɔl   "you (sg.) will do it"
     /t-r-ep-ol/   tirébɔl   "he will then do it"
     /n-n-ol/   nínɔl   "you (sg.) have done it"
     /r-n-ol/   rínɔl   "he has done it"
(b) /kam-n-m̃an-n/   kàmnim̃ánin   "for her brother"
     /əs-ət-pn-aan/   əsidbənán   "don't go up there"
     /k-ar-(ə)pkom/   karbɔ́gɔm   "they are heavy"[51]
(c) /əpk-əpk/   əbgɔ́bəkʰ   "to be pregnant"
     /apn-apn/   abnábən   "free"
     /ark-ark/   argárikʰ   "to growl"
     /r-əm-əŋn/   rimə́ŋən   "he was afraid"
     /n-əm-əpk/   nimə́bəkʰ   "you (sg.) took it"

While one might view such facts as calling for a slight emmendation to prosodic theories of epenthesis, facts from Chukchi (Bogoraz 1922; Kenstowicz 1979) support the view of epenthesis as independent of directional syllabification. In Chukchi, syllables are maximally [CVC], and onsets are not obligatory. The monomorphemic forms in (11a) are immediately problematic for template-mapping approaches, as unsyllabified /CCC/ should surface as [vCCvC] under right-to-left syllabification, and as [CvCCv] under left-to-right syllabification (where v indicates an epenthetic vowel).[52] The forms in (11b) highlight the preferential treatment of word-initial stray Cs as onsets, while the forms in (11c) show that treatment of / ... VCCCV ... / sequences in Chukchi depends on the position of the morpheme boundary: / ... CC-C ... / surfaces as [... CCvC ...] while / ... C-CC ... / surfaces as [... CvCC ...].

(11)   Chukchi epenthesis
    (a) /pnl/   pɨnɨl   "news"
          /kkl/   kukɨl   "one-eyed man"
    (b) /tke-rkin/   tɨkerkin   "thou smellest of"
          /mk-icin/   mukicin   "more numerous"
    (c) / ... C-CC ... /   ... CvCC ...

/mit-tmu-gɨt/	mitɨtmugɨt	"we killed thee"
/nalvul-chɨn/	nalvulɨchɨn	"the herd"
/n-np-qin/	nɨnpɨqin	"the old one"
/n-plu-qin/	nupluqin	"small one"

          / ... CC-C ... /   ... CCvC ...

/timk-leut/	tɨmkɨleut	"hummockhead"
/itc-pilintin/	itcɨpɨlintɨn	"precious metal"
/itc-wil/	itcuwil	"precious ware"
/iwl-walat/	iwluwalat	"long knives"
/tumg-tum/	tumgɨtum	"companion"
/pilh-pil/	pilhɨpil	"famine"

Such facts, coupled with those from Lenakel suggest that (1) rules of epenthesis preferentially take word-initial stray segments as onsets (despite the existence of onsetless syllables within a language); (2) rules of epenthesis preferentially take word-final stray segments as codas; (3) rules of epenthesis can be sensitive to morphological structure. In sum, epenthesis sites cannot be predicted by directional syllabification alone in all languages.[53]

The final issue to address in this section is at what point in the derivation syllabification takes place. A closely related question involves determining the morphological or phonological domains (stem, word, etc.) within which proper syllabification is required. In some languages, there is evidence of early cyclic syllabification. Because the prosodic hierarchy in example (1) requires that syllabification feed stress assignment, evidence of cyclic stress provides evidence for cyclic syllabification. For instance, in Palestinian Arabic (Brame 1974), where stress assignment is sensitive to syllable weight and stress is assigned cyclically, syllabification must also be cyclic.

In many languages there is no evidence for a domain of syllabification smaller than the word. For instance, in Yupik (Krauss 1985), word stress and related phonological processes provide no evidence for syllabification within a domain smaller than the word. This can also be the case in languages in which the phonological word is not the stress domain. For instance, in Yokuts (Newman, 1944; Archangeli, 1984), where stress falls on the penultimate syllable within the phonological phrase, rules of closed syllable shortening and epenthesis apply within the phonological word, providing evidence of word-level syllabification.

In still other languages, word-level syllabification is followed by later syllabification or resyllabification at the level of the phonological phrase. For instance, in Cairene Arabic, word-level syllabification is necessary for proper assignment of word-stress, but syncope, epenthesis, and spread of phrayngealization across word boundaries provides evidence for later (re-)syllabification at the level of the phonological phrase (Broselow, to appear).

In sum, rules of syllabification parallel other phonological rules in taking as their smallest domain the individual morpheme, and as their largest domain, the phonological phrase. In some languages there is evidence for cyclic syllabification, while in others the earliest evidence for syllabification is at the word level.

6   Problems in Syllable Theory

While there is a great deal of consensus on issues relating to syllable constituency, syllable typology, sonority and syllabification, other aspects of syllable structure are still debated within the phonological literature. In this section, I touch on four topics which could easily constitute whole chapters in themselves: coda constraints and their proper formulation (6.1), the syllabification of VCV strings (6.2), ambisyllabicity (6.3), and mismatches between phonological and phonetic syllables (6.4).

6.1   Coda Constraints

In addition to phonotactic constraints within the syllable which follow from sonority and syllabification, many languages have additional constraints on the featural content of segments in particular syllable-internal positions. While single member onsets appear to be unrestricted cross-linguistically,[54] many languages with single member codas allow only a small class of segments to occupy coda position. For instance, in Axininca Campa (Payne 1981), the only element which occupies coda position is /N/, an unspecified nasal segment which shares the place features of a following obstruent.

Many recent proposals have been made regarding the status of such coda constraints. Itô (1986) posits both negative and positive feature-based coda constraints which are purely phonological, and which are stated in such a way as to exempt full or partial geminates. Clements (1990) takes a more concrete view and suggests that in some cases, coda constraints instantiate the cross-linguistic preference for a sonority profile which "rises maximally towards the peak and falls minimally towards the end" (p. 301).

While there are many languagues in which the segments appearing in coda position are highly limited, it is not easy to determine in many cases whether such distributional facts reflect synchronic phonological constraints. For instance, in the Beijing dialect of Chinese, the only coda Cs are /n ŋ ɹ/. The native phonology of Chinese provides little evidence as to whether other consonants are actually prohibited from the coda position, or whether the gaps in question are accidental. In this case, examination of loan-word phonology is revealing: Beijing speakers produce ní-kè-sŏŋ, ní-kè-xùn or ní-kè-sūn for "Nixon", and ᵛjū-lī-yè or jū-lī-yè-de for "Juliette." Such forms seem to indicate that absence of obstruent-final syllables is not accidental. However, in other languages, loan-word phonology reveals that coda possibilities are more extensive than evidenced by the native vocabulary. For instance, in Italian, where the maximal syllable is CCVC, nongeminate coda consonants appear to be restricted to sonorants.[55] Based on this, Itô (1986, p. 38) proposes a coda condition that bars obstruents from the coda unless they are geminate. However, in loan words, obstruent codas of all sorts apoear both medially and finally: kakto, kaktus "cactus"; koftiko "Coptic"; kamčatka "Kamchatka"; fiat "Fiat"; vat "watt"; kopek "copeck"; etc. Given such facts, the gaps in the native vocabulary become suspect: are these representative of systematic constraints against nongeminate obstruent codas, or is the absence of such codas accidental? As with other aspects of syllable structure, distributional constraints comprise only one limited form of evidence. Wherever possible, coda constraints should be supported by positive evidence from native and loan phonology in the form of Stray Erasure, extraprosodicity, feature-changing rules, or epenthesis triggered by arguably illicit coda segments. Only in such cases is there positive evidence of the systematic nature of gaps in the coda inventory.

Itô's coda conditions for Japanese, Italian, and other languages are stated so as to exempt full or partial geminates by invoking Hayes's (1986) Linking Constraint, which requires that all association lines be interpreted exhaustively. For instance, the constraint in (12) is proposed for Japanese, where the only well-formed codas are nasals and the first C of a geminate structure (kappa "legendary being" is well-formed, but *kapka is not):

(12) Japanese coda constraint   * C]
                                        |
                                      [-nas]

As stated, (12) will only apply to singly linked instances of the feature [−nasal], exempting all geminates.[56] This theoretical innovation takes as its basis the observations of Prince (1984), that in many languages what are CVC syllables in skeletal terms, are really CV syllables melodically, as the melody of the coda segment is linked, or borrowed from a following heterosyllabic segment (see chapter 8 for additional discussion).

Chung (1991) points out that in Tamazight Berber, with maximal CVCC syllables, any single coda consonant is possible, but the only well-formed coda clusters are geminates: annli "brain" (*anlli); áaddratt "ear of corn" (*áadrratt); etc. While the parallelism between a "geminate-only" constraint for C_1C_2 in VC_1C_2V (for Japanese, Italian, etc.) and in $VC_1C_2C_3V$ (for Berber) is striking, Chung (1991) demonstrates that the constraint in Berber cannot be treated by invoking a version of the Linking Constraint; instead the geminate-only condition on complex codas in the language should be derived from positing a positive constraint like that shown in (13).

(13) Tamazight Berber Complex Coda Constraint

$$\frac{\text{IF} \qquad \text{C} \quad \text{C]}_R \text{]}_\sigma}{\text{THEN} \qquad \text{o}}$$

The existence of languages which require explicit reference to geminate structures in the statement of coda constraints leads one to question whether syllable structure constraints in Japanese might not be best represented by two distinct statements, as shown in (14):

(14) Japanese coda constraints (revised)[57]

(a) $$\frac{\text{IF} \qquad \text{C]}_\sigma}{\text{THEN} \qquad \text{[+nas]}}$$ OR   (b) $$\frac{\text{IF} \qquad \text{C]}_\sigma}{\text{THEN} \qquad \text{o}}$$

There are good reasons to adopt the disjunction of coda constraints in (14). In referring positively to geminate structures, it highlights what I believe is the ultimate nonexplanation for the patterning of geminates seen above: geminate structures are often the only ones found in consonant clusters because place assimilation and total assimilation between C_1 and C_2 are common sound changes in the context $VC_1C_2 \ldots$, with straightforward acoustic-auditory explanations (Ohala 1990). That is, the fact that many languages exhibit only assimilated clusters is a fact about the pervasive nature of assimilation rules, and not a fact about preferred syllable types or coda types.[58]

The existence of languages like Japanese also weakens Clements (1990) view that coda constraints instantiate the cross-linguistic preference for a sonority profile which "rises maximally towards the peak and falls minimally towards the end" (p. 301). Given the possibility of geminate obstruents in the coda, Clements is forced to admit that "intersyllabic articulations involving a single place specification are simpler than those involving two (or more) place specifications. This principle must clearly take precedence over the sonority principles stated earlier (p. 321)." This reference to "intersyllabic articulations", like Itô's invocation of the Linking Constraint, also fails to relate the Berber facts to those in Japanese, Italian, etc. By adopting disjunctions like those in (14), the sonority profile suggested by Clements and the synchronic reflexes of well-understood sound change are independently instantiated.

In sum, while the nature of coda constraints is ultimately an empirical question, data amassed to this point suggests that within a single language such constraints can be representative both of preferred sonority profiles and of the idiosyncratic residue of historical sound change.

6.2 *Syllabification of / ... VCV ... / Sequences*

Let us now turn to a second problem in the realm of syllabification. It has been claimed by many researchers that a / ... VCV ... / string is universally syllabified as / ... V.CV ... /. In rule-based approaches, this generalization is known as the *CV-rule* or the *Maximal Onset Principle*, and has been claimed to hold only of initial syllabification where it follows from the ordering of onset formation (and under some approaches, onset maximization) before coda formation. In template-based approaches like that of Itô (1986), the constraint is stated independently, and is taken to hold at all levels of the phonology.

Several languages have been described in which even the weak form of this generalization is violated. Kunjen,[59] an Australian Aboriginal language of the Cape York Penninsula, is described by Sommer (1969, 1970, 1981) as having only vowel-initial syllables: the maximal syllable in Kunjen is claimed to be [VCCCC].[60] Sommer (1981) bases this on the fact that all Oykangand words are vowel-initial and consonant final:[61] [og ařŋg aŋguñang eŋkoṛiy uwal ay iŋun] "I gave (some) water to the young child in the shade". However, he is aware of the nonprobative nature of such facts: "Distributional criteria are admittedly successful in the syllabification of *some* languages ... so the above criteria should not be altogether disregarded" (p. 233). A stronger argument for his syllabification of all / ... VCV ... / sequences as / ... VC.V ... / comes from partial reduplication, which marks the progressive or continuative aspect on verbs, and superlative/transcendent properties on adjectives and nouns. Some representative examples are given in (15).

(15) Oykangand partial reduplication (Sommer 1981)

Stem	Reduplicate	
/edeṛ/	edeḍeṛ	"rain", "heavy rain"
/igu/	igigun	"go", "keeps going"
/algal/	algalgal	"straight", "straight as a ramrod"
/elbmben/	elbmbelbmben	"red"

In Oykangand, it appears that the prosodic template prefixed in reduplication is simply σ, and that template satisfaction results in maximization of this template. Forms like *elbmbelbmben* "red" then suggest that [elbmb] is a possible syllable in Oykangand. While such facts are suggestive, template satisfaction does not bear on the syllabification of the reduplicative base: /σ+elbm.ben/ with the σ prefix realized as [elbmb]$_σ$ and subsequent resyllabification to elbm.belbm.ben is also possible. The real question then appears to be whether the maximal syllable in Kunjen is [CVCCCC] or [VCCCC].

Some evidence of syllable onsets in Kunjen does appear to exist. First, stress is realized both on vowels and on preceding consonants which are noticably fortis.[62] As the stress-bearing unit cross-linguistically is the syllable, prevocalic Cs would appear to constitute syllable onsets. Another piece of evidence for onsets is the distribution of aspiration. Aspirated plosives occur only in pre-vocalic position. If aspiration in Oykangand were viewed as a syllable-edge rule, it would support the existence of onsets, since the pre-vocalic context would be equivalent to syllable-initial position under V.CV syllabification.[63] Finally, the peculiarities of a rule of utterance-initial reduction suggest the existence of onsets in Kunjen. The rule in question is formulated by Sommer (1981, p. 240) as in (16), with representative examples provided.

(16) Oykangand Reduction
$VC_0 \rightarrow \varnothing \ / \ [\#\#\_\_\_\_C \dots]_{PhP}$

Unreduced	Reduced	Gloss	Deleted string
igigun	gigun	"keeps going"	[i]
ididař	didař	"kept eating"	[i]
amamaŋ	mamaŋ	"mother" (voc.)	[a]
eweweŋg	weweŋg	"evening"	[e]
uŋgul	gul	"there"	[uŋ]
elbmbelbmben	belbmben	"red"	[elbm]

Sommer's claim that reduction is a late phonetic rule is inconsistent with the fact that it is restricted to certain lexical items (an estimated twelve in the entire language.) In addition, the deleted string $[VC_0]$ preceding C ... is equivalent to the first syllable of the word only if some version of the CV-rule is at work. Despite surface phonotactics, then, C-initial syllables appear to exist in Oykangand: the syllable is the stress-bearing unit, resulting in fortis onset consonants within stressed syllables; syllable-initial voiceless stops are aspirated; and finally, a lexically determined reduction rule deletes the first syllable of a word, leaving the second C-initial syllable in phrase-initial position.

Another language in which it has been suggested that the initial syllabification of VCV is not V.CV but rather VC.V is the Barra dialect of Gaelic as described by Borgstrøm (1937, 1940) and analysed by Clements (1986).[64] Based on auditory observations and deliberate speech of native speakers ([fan. ak] "crow") in which syllables are separated, Borgstrøm (1940, p. 55) concludes: "When a single consonant stands between two vowels the syllable division takes place as follows: (1) After a long vowel the consonant belongs to the second syllable, e.g., mo:-ran 'much'; (2) after a short vowel the consonant normally belongs to the first syllable, e.g., bɔd-ɔx 'old man', ar-an 'bread', fal-u 'empty' ..." Given this much, the CV-rule can be maintained in its weak version: all VCV strings are initially syllabified as V.CV, with resyllabification taking place if the preceding vowel is short.[65] This resyllabification must precede epenthesis in Barra, which takes underlying /...VRC.../ to /...VRvC.../, with the sonorant syllabified as the onset of the syllable headed by the epenthetic vowel despite the presence of a preceding short vowel.[66] While this alternative account of Barra involves an abstract step of V.CV syllabification, with subsequent resyllabification to VC.V, stress-conditioned resyllabification rules which result in "heavier" syllables are not uncommon (see below). What does seem clear from this and other instances of resyllabification discussed below, is that VC.V syllabification is possible in derived environments, that is, as the output of context-sensitive resyllabification rules.

6.3 *Ambisyllabicity*

Related to VCV syllabification is the question of ambisyllabicity. Ambisyllabic representations are those in which a single segment is affiliated with more than one syllable. Kahn (1976) and Clements and Keyser (1983) argue for such representations in analyses of English and Efik respectively. Kahn (1976) argues that ambisyllabicity is useful in English in capturing the distribution of consonantal allophones. He claims that aspirated allophones of /p, t, k/ are exclusively syllable-initial, while flapped variants are just those consonants which are ambisyllabic.[67] Kahn's ambisyllabic segments are represented in (17a).

Borowsky (1986), following Hoard (1971), Stampe (1972), and others, argues that English flapping, as well as *h*-deletion, *y*-deletion, and palatalization, are the result of a stress-conditioned resyllabification rule. The rule of resyllabification is shown in (17b), which in English applies within the foot.

(17)   Ambisyllabicity vs. Resyllabification

 (a) Ambisyllabicity   (b) Resyllabification

The output of (17b) violates the claimed universal V.CV syllabification discussed above. To the extent that such analyses are accurate, they provide further evidence against a universal condition requiring that all / . . . CV . . . / sequences be tautosyllabic.

Extending syllable theory to incorporate ambisyllabicity allows for systems in which a minimal three-way phonological distinction in intervocalic consonants is possible: these segments may belong exclusively to the second syllable (typical output of the CV-rule); exclusively to the first syllable (17b); or to both syllables (17a). However, as argued convincingly by Borowsky (1986) for English and by Fruchter (1988) for Efik, ambisyllabic representations are unnecessary when rules of resyllabification are invoked. One is led to conclude that until such minimal three-way phonological contrasts are demonstrated, a theory without access to ambisyllabic representations is to be preferred on grounds of restrictiveness.[68]

6.4 *Mismatches*

Finally, let us address the problem of mismatches between phonological representations and phonetic representations. Phonological representations provide input to the phonetic interpretive component. As argued above, such representations include syllable structure, structure which organizes segments on the basis of relative sonority. However, due to the fact that undershoot is typical in the realization of phonetic targets, mismatches between phonological sonority peaks and phonetic sonority peaks are not uncommon. It is only with a clear view of the interaction between phonological syllables and phonetic rules that such mismatches are rendered nonproblematic.

For instance, many languages contain unstressed reduced vowels at the phonological level which are deleted optionally or in fast speech between adjacent identical consonants.[69] As a result, a phonological sonority peak is missing in the phonetic representation. McCarthy (1986) discusses such rules in Odawa, Modern Hebrew, English, and Japanese, and notes that the output strings of such apparent deletion rules are not subject to phonological principles (e.g., the Obligatory Contour Principle), nor to language-specific phonological rules (e.g., degemination in Modern Hebrew and English). For instance, English [fɔɹməˑmɪnʔt] can be realized as [fɔɹmmɪnʔt]. These properties, he suggests, follow naturally on the view that vowel loss in such instances is part of the phonetic interpretive component: the phonological representation remains unchanged with the loss of the vowel resulting from undershoot of the phonetic target (unobstructed oral vocal tract) associated with vowels.[70]

An inverse situation exists in languages where, due to lenition processes or enhancement of vowel-consonant transitions, there are more sonority peaks in the phonetics than there are syllables in the phonology. A case like this is found in English, where phonetic realizations of /l/ within the syllable rhyme are often undershot: /tayl/ "tile" [tʰayɨ], /hiyl/ "heel" [hiyɨ], etc.[71] A more extreme example of such a phenomenon is found in Maxakalí, a language of Southeastern Brazil, described by Gudschinsky, Popovich, and Popovich (1970). The maximal phonological syllable in Maxakalí is [CVC], but such syllables have phonetic realizations which range from [CVv] to [CVcvC]. Monosyllabic /tat/ "to carry" can be realized as [taɣət], while one realization of the disyllabic /pap.tɨc/ "drunk", [paə̆ptɨɣiɨ̥], has at least four phonetic sonority peaks. It appears that the phonetic interpretive component in Maxacalí has regular lengthening of V-C transitions, where such transitions can involve slight vowel-final constriction (the [ɣ] in the above transcriptions), followed by open transition as the oral articulators move toward their consonantal targets. In addition, there is drastic undershoot in the realization of consonants: according to Gudschinsky, Popovich, and Popovich (1970, p. 82) the basic consonantal allophone is "a fully syllabic vocoid, with little or no consonantal closure, in syllable coda before a homorganic consonant." For instance, /kep.pa/ "in front of" surfaces as [kæə̆pa], where /p/ is realized as a mid central rounded vowel. In sum, by viewing phonological representations as the input to interpretive phonetic rules, the mismatch between phonetic sonority peaks and phonological syllables is expected. Articulatory undershoot of vowel targets can eliminate phonological sonority peaks from the phonetic representation, while articulatory undershoot of consonantal targets and elongation of vowel-consonant transitions can result in phonetic sonority peaks which are not present in the phonological representation.

7 Conclusion

I hope to have conveyed in this chapter the important role of the syllable in phonological theory, and the extent to which there is basic agreement in the field on the role of syllables in organizing sonority, triggering epenthesis and Stray Erasure, and providing a closed class of available templates for prosodic morphological processes. At the same time, it should be clear that sonority scales, models of syllable-internal structure, and syllabification algorithms are almost as numerous as the researchers working on these topics. With this in mind, I have tried to summarize what I see as the strongest arguments for and against specific proposals in these domains. Finally, I have presented an overview of several potential problem areas in syllable theory, with the hope that such a survey will serve to stimulate further study of these important issues.

NOTES

1 I am most grateful to Nick Clements, Andrew Garrett, Morris Halle, Bruce Hayes, John McCarthy, Scott Myers, Donca Steriade, and participants in a 1991 seminar on the syllable at the University of Texas at Austin for useful discussion and commentary on syllable-related topics.

2 See Anderson (1985) for a clear exposition of the syllable as viewed by Trubetzkoy, Hjelmslev, Firth, and others. One might argue that generative phonology, as developed in Chomsky and Halle in *The Sound Pattern of English* (1968), here after *SPE*, did not recognize the fundamental role of the syllable. While this is true in theory, it is not altogether accurate in terms of execution. The use of the symbol V, a [+vocalic] segment, in countless phonological rules in *SPE*, with

subsequent recognition that this natural class might be more appropriately referred to as [+syllabic] "which would characterize all segments constituting a syllabic peak" (p. 354), can be viewed as acknowledgement of the syllable's important role in phonological theory.

3 See section 2 for further discussion of sonority. Sonority is defined here in terms of a perceptual measure, loudness, not in terms of the acoustic property of intensity. Though these will often coincide, there are cases where they do not. For instance, a vowel with a fundamental frequency of 500 hertz will be judged by the human ear as louder than an otherwise identical vowel of the same intensity at 5,000 hertz. Here and elsewhere, the

human ear imposes a sonority ranking which is not present in the acoustic signal.

4 Within the London School of prosodic analysis, such phonological processes/constraints are often referred to as "syllable prosodies." For instance, Henderson (1949) recognizes tone, stress, palatalization, and labialization as syllable prosodies in Thai.

5 Problems inherent in writing stress rules without access to syllable structure are quite serious in languages in which stress rules are quantity sensitive. For instance, in *SPE*, it is necessary to distinguish different types of consonant clusters for the purpose of assigning stress in English: following lax vowels, weak clusters include obstruent + {r, w, y, l}. The fact that weak clusters correspond with possible word- (and therefore syllable-) initial clusters is merely a coincidence within a theory which does not recognize the syllable as a constituent.

6 An early version of this principle of syllable integrity is found in Prince (1975).

7 Another property which might take the syllable as its domain is that of "register" in the Mon-Khmer languages. Distinct registers can involve distinctions in voice quality, tones, and vowel quality. See Gregerson and Smith (1973), Gregerson (1976) and Smith (1979) for diachronic and synchronic accounts of register distinctions in some of these languages.

8 Surprisingly, there are few if any feature co-occurence constraints which appear to take the syllable as their domain. Constraints on aspiration in Sanskrit hold within the morphological stem; likewise, proposed constraints on the feature [+constricted glottis] in Mayan languages within the root; in Chinese languages, labial constraints have been claimed to hold within the syllable, however, this can also be viewed as a morpheme structure constraint as the syllable is equivalent to a morpheme. In sum, while syllable-internal feature co-occurence constraints could provide potential evidence for the syllable as a phonological constituent, there are few convincing cases of such constraints.

9 In languages which allow tautosyllabic consonant clusters, like English, either of these rules would be more complex, since specific features would need to be mentioned for the conditioning C. For instance, glottalization of obstruents in English occurs word-finally, and before obstruents, but not before sonorants /l, w, y/, i.e., syllable-finally.

See Kahn (1976: 20–27) for a clear and convincing presentation of the problems inherent in rules collapsing {C, #}.

10 Syllabic oral spelling in Fijian is the case where a word is sounded syllable by syllable instead of phoneme by phoneme. So the form /vinaka/ [vi.na.ka] "good" can be orally spelled [vii naa kaa] rather than by phoneme [vaa ii naa aa kaa aa]. Note that the minimal word in Fijian is bimoraic, so that lengthening occurs when monomoriac syllables are transformed into fullblown words.

11 The evolution of syllabic writing systems has also been used to motivate the syllable as a phonological constituent. However, Poser's (1992) survey of writing systems shows that fewer truly syllable-based writing systems exist than was thought, weakening

somewhat this line of argumentation.

12   Though some languages will rarely require reference to such constituents in the phonology. See for instance Hyman's (1985) discussion of Gokana, where phonological rules focus on the mora, not the syllable. While Hyman takes the position that Gokana does not have syllables, he provides no positive evidence against syllables. Rather, he simply notes the lack of evidence for their existence. In sum, though a language may lack positive phonological evidence for syllables, this is not inconsistent with the claim that syllables exist in all languages.

13   Some model of a prosodic hierarchy is assumed in almost all modern phonological frameworks, though labels and intrinsic content of the various levels is inconsistent. Labels are immaterial here; what is important is the view that syllables organize segments, and themselves are organized into higher-level rhythmic units (feet), which in turn are gathered into stress-culminative domains (words), and so on.

14   The syllable terminals represented here are unlabeled timing slots, of the sort argued for in Levin (1983, 1985). Subsyllabic constituency is omitted. Questions of syllable-internal structure and syllable weight are addressed in section 3 of this chapter, and in chapters 5 and 10 of this volume.

15   See Clements (1990) for an extensive and original discussion of the role of sonority within syllable theory. Clements', model makes crucial use of demisyllables, onset+nucleus, and nucleus+coda constituents. As Clements's coverage is detailed and thorough, I limit myself in this

section to presenting only the outlines of a theory of sonority.

16   This version of the Sonority Sequencing Generalization explicitly tolerates sonority plateaus. Evidence in favor of such plateaus is found in languages with syllable-initial geminates (Trukese, Ulithian, Gilbertese) and those with syllable-final geminates (Berber, Estonian, Ponapean, Saipan Carolinian).

17   Such clusters are not limited to the word edge, and so cannot be handled by some version of extraprosodicity: [hɪ.spǽ.nɪk] "Hispanic", [wǽsps] "wasps", [príyst.li] "Priestly", etc.

18   For a detailed discussion, see Clements (1990). In many languages, apparent violations of the Sonority Sequencing Generalization can be shown to involve extraprosodic elements at the edge of the syllabification domain. See section 5 for further discussion of extraprosodicity.

19   This scale is a less fine-grained version of a scale presented in Levin (1985), and draws on work of Jesperson (1904), Hankamer and Aissen (1974), Basebøll (1977), Steriade (1982), and Selkirk (1984), among others.

20   Steriade (1982) and Levin (1985) make use of place features in language-specific sonority scales for Ancient Greek and Klamath, respectively. However, in both cases alternative analyses are available. Length and pitch are also omitted from this scale, since both properties are represented autosegmentally. However, data on stress systems strongly suggests that long segments are more sonorous than short segments, and that elements bearing high tone are more sonorous than those not bearing high tone, all else being

equal. For instance, stress in Klamath falls on the last long vowel of a word while stress in Fore (Nicholson and Nicholson 1962) falls on the first H-toned syllable of the word. See Hayes (1991) for further discussion of these and similar cases.

21 Omitted here are those who explicitly do not recognize the syllable as a constituent in some language, including Bloch (1958), Higurashi (1983) and Hyman (1985). In these approaches, the maximal constituents below the level of the foot are moras, with associated consonants. Also omitted is the model proposed by Togeby (1951) in which Syllable → Nucleus (Margins), Margins → (Onset) (Coda), and a movement transformation is required. See Fudge (1987) for a concise summary of these models and arguments for (4e).

22 Apparent exceptions include Pirahã and Eastern Popoluca.

23 The weight categories defined here abstract away from edge effects resulting from extraprosodicity (see section 5). This discussion of syllable weight is based in large part on Blevins (1990). See there for detailed discussion of syllable weight distinctions necessary in Hausa, Klamath, and Creek. Data sources for the languages in (6) include: Broadbent (1964) on Southern Sierra Miwok; Newman (1972) on Hausa; Larsen and Pike (1949) on Huasteco; Schütz (1980) on Hawaiian; Barker (1963, 1964) on Klamath; Krauss (1985) on Yupik; and Haas (1977) on Creek.

24 The absence of languages where $C_0[V]_N C$ is heavy but $C_0[VV]_N$ is light reflects the generalization that heavy syllables are more sonorous than light syllables. Given syllable-internal sonority profiles, a branching nucleus will always be more sonorous than (or equally as sonorous as) a nonbranching nucleus + coda sequence, resulting in the above stated generalization.

25 The view that feature specifications should be introduced in distinguishing mora types from one another has also been advocated by Steriade (1990), and using a prosodic grid representation, by Hayes (1991). Both emmendations to moraic theory result in overgeneration of weight classes for stress, and ignore the problems posed by nonmoraic geminates in languages as diverse as Creek, Klamath, and Yupik. Similar points are made in Tranel (1991a). An alternative strategy would be to argue that the distinction betwen heaviest and heavy is one between underlying weight and weight-by-position. The problem here is that both Klamath and Creek contain underlying geminate consonants which have the same weight value as other consonant clusters. Within moraic models where length and weight are collapsed, geminates are underlyingly moraic. Hence, syllables closed by geminates are expected to function as a natural class with those containing long vowels, which is not the case.

If moras or weight units are found to be necessary in addition to annotated syllable structure, then they can be defined as shown below:

(a) $X \rightarrow [X]_\mu / [\cdots \underline{\quad} \cdots]_{Nucleus}$
     Universal

(b) $X \rightarrow [X]_\mu /]_{Nucleus} \underline{\quad} \cdots]_{Rhyme}$
     Language-specific

In most languages, syllable weight is determined by properties of the syllable rhyme, without regard for the syllable onset. However, there is at least one language, and possibly more, where syllable onsets do contribute to syllable weight. Pirahã, as described by Everett and Everett (1984), has a five-way weight distinction, CVV > GVV > VV > CV > GV, where C is voiceless and phonetically long, and G is voiced and phonetically short. Stress in Pirahã falls on the rightmost syllable of the heaviest syllable type within the last three syllables of the word. Presence of an onset as well as consonant length plays a role, contributing to overall syllable length, and hence to overall syllable sonority. In order to capture such weight distinctions, the rules below are tentatively added to those above:

(c) $X \rightarrow [X]_\mu / s \ [\_X \ [\ldots]_{Rhyme}]$
        Language-specific
(d) $X \rightarrow [X]_\mu / s \ [\_[\ldots]_{Rhyme}]$
        Language-specific

Rule (d) could also be stated with reference to syllable structure: branching syllable nodes are heavier (i.e., more sonorous) than nonbranching syllable nodes, all else being equal.

The additional weight distinctions defined by rule (c) have been claimed to exist in Trukese where Churchyard (1991) has argued that syllable-initial geminates function as weight-units, and might also be used to account for the stress system of Eastern Popoloca (Kalstrom and Pike 1968) where syllables with long vowels or long onset consonants are stressed.

Any account of syllable weight must recognize that nuclear elements in the syllable contribute the most to syllable weight (i.e., are the most sonorous), while nonnuclear onset consonants

determine secondary weight classes within the major division of syllables with branching vs. nonbranching nuclei. This follows straightforwardly from the sonority sequencing principles discussed in section 2: there is a one-to-one relationship between a syllable nucleus and a sonority peak, so that viewing syllable weight as a division of syllable sonority classes results automatically in the expectation that syllables with long sonority peaks will be more sonorous than those with short sonority peaks.

26 Pike and Pike (1947) also argue for principal vs. subordinate Cs within the onset and for principal vs. subordinate Vs within the nucleus. Subordinate Cs are defined based on their secondary articulation with respect to the primary articulations of the other members of the cluster. Most of these clusters are suspect, as they include laryngeals, or nasal-stop sequences. In each case the laryngeal can be viewed either as a feature of the onset consonant, or as a feature of the following vowel, while the nasal-stop clusters can be analysed as prenasalized stops. This leaves /sk št šk šn/ as the only true CC clusters in the language. Subordinate Vs are defined by relative sonority, and it is observed that V, VV, and VVV nuclei all have the same duration, leading one to suspect that VVV clusters are simple vowels with onglides and offglides. It is somewhat ironic then that this early work on syllable-internal constituency examines a language in which the maximal syllable type appears to be {s, š} CV.

27 In addition Fudge (1969) posits a final "termination" node which can dominate the English coronals /t d

s z θ/. A discussion of exceptional segments at word edges is deferred to section 5.

28 Again, leaving aside considerations of extraprosodicity. See below.

29 Perhaps what is most striking about the ludling corpus is that there are so few examples of the "body" as target (i.e., onset + nucleus string, cf. (4c)): one Finnish word game where the first $C_0 V$ sequence of words is interchanged is reported by Campbell (1980), and the same sort of ludling is found in Hanunoo (Conklin 1959, p. 631, type A). The rarity of such processes compared to the predominance of rhyme-manipulation in ludlings is highly suggestive of immediate syllable constituents onset and rhyme.

30 Davis (1990) argues that evidence for the onset is present in Italian. However, his arguments all revolve around the appropriate representation for two classes of syllable-initial clusters: class A which includes /bl br pl pr fl fr dr tr kl kr gl gr pn kn/ and class B which includes /sp sb st sd sf sv sk sg sl sm sn ft pt mn gn / and the single Cs /š ñ ts dz/. Davis's claim is that class A are well-formed onsets, whereas class B involves single onsets, with initial consonants immediately dominated by the syllable node. However, an alternative analysis of the facts discussed would be to analyse the class A clusters as syllabified, with initial Cs of type B clusters remaining unsyllabified until later in the derivation. Under such an analysis, no reference to "onset" is necessary.

31 There has been much recent work on the syllable in signed languages, especially ASL (see Wilbur (1985), Padden and Perlmutter (1987), Perlmutter (1989), and also chapter 20, this volume). In this chapter I deal exclusively with data from spoken languages, as the majority of phonological theories have been based on spoken language data, and as there is still a great deal of debate as to whether or not signed languages have syllables. However, it should be stressed that one of the strongest arguments for the syllable as an abstract phonological entity would be the demonstration that syllables exist in signed languages. Such a demonstration would make it clear that the syllable is an abstract unit of prosodic organization independent of acoustic and articulatory properties of the vocal apparatus.

32 Table 6.1 abstracts away from the simple/complex nucleus distinction. Also, the syllable profiles in table 6.1 are not exhaustive for English or Totonac, which also have CCVCCC syllables.

33 See section 6 where a potential counterexample, Kunjen, is discussed.

34 Note that this statement is restricted to clusters, i.e., sequences of more than one C. Not all languages with CV . . . syllables also have V-initial syllables. See Greenberg (1978) for further generalizations regarding tautosyllabic consonant clusters.

35 For languages with complex nuclei, a further specification of one (unmarked) versus two (marked) additional elements is necessary.

36 See Bell (1978) for other generalizations concerning syllabic consonants. Some of these are suspect, as the representations on which they are based are sometimes not purely phonological. See section 6 for remarks on phonology/phonetics mismatches.

37 Other studies where syllabicity is viewed as a derived relational

property rather than an inherent segmental property include Grammont (1933), Rischel (1962), Kiparsky (1981), Selkirk (1982), Archangeli (1984), and Kaye and Lowenstamm (1984). These works, however, do not explicitly deal with the difficulties inherent in predicting glide / vowel alternations cross-linguistically.

38 See the discussion of this system in chapter 1 as well.

39 A further difference in these two approaches is their treatment of epenthesis. Within the templatic approach, epenthesis is syllabification. In rule-based approaches, rules of epenthesis can be interspersed with structure-building rules of syllabification. This difference is discussed with reference to stray segments below.

40 Except for the effects of extraprosodicity. CG clusters are possible word-initially, and GC clusters are possible word-finally.

41 An alternative is to collapse nucleus-placement and the onset rule into a single CV-rule, as was used for Imdlawn Tashlhiyt Berber. Left-to-right application of such a rule is possible, provided that the string is scanned *two segments at a time*. Sagey (1984) proposes an algorithm of this sort.

42 It appears to be the case, however, that all templatic approaches require an automatic restructuring to ensure that if a sequence arises with a coda preceding an onsetless syllable, the coda becomes restructured as the onset to the following syllable; thus /uiuou/ will first be syllabified as *wiw-ow*, which in turn is restructured to *wi-wow*.

43 Interestingly, in both of these languages, there are additional reasons to believe that the consonants in question are not initially part of the phonological syllable. For Klamath, attested word-initial clusters do not appear to be constrained by any version of the SSG, as they include sonorant-obstruent clusters (wqʰ wq' wq wk' wkʰ wk wpʰ wp' wp wtʰ wt' wt wčʰ wč' wč ws nqʰ nq' nq nkʰ nk' nk mpʰ mp mp' ntʰ nt' nt nčʰ nč' nč ms lq' lq lk' lp ltʰ lt' lt lč') as well as obstruent-sonorant clusters (qʰm q'm qʰn qn qʰl q'l ql qʰw q'w qw qʰy q'y q? kʰm k'm km kʰn k'n kʰl k'l kʰw k'w kʰy k? pʰn p'n pʰl pl pw py p? tʰm tm tn tʰl tl t'l tʰw t'w tw tʰy ty č'm č'n čʰl č'l čl čʰw č'w čʰy sm sm' sn sn' sl sl' sw sw' sy s?), obstruent-obstruent clusters (tpʰ tp kp' kpʰ kp qp' spʰ qp sp' sp ptʰ pt' qčʰ qč' tk ts čk ks ktʰ kt' qtʰ kt qt' stʰ qt st' st pčʰ pč' kčʰ sč kč' sčʰ sč' ps pkʰ sk tkʰ pk' skʰ tk' tq' pq sk' sq' tq pqʰ sq tqʰ sqʰ pq') and sonorant-sonorant clusters (wn wl̥ wl' wl wy' wy wh lm' lm lw l? mn). Rather than weaken the theory of syllable structure to allow blatant sonority violations, word-initial segments which cannot be syllabified are extraprosodic. (Within the Klamath rhyme, sonorants must precede obstruents.)

For Cairene Arabic, stress rules point to a rule of final consonant extrametricality: where non-final CVV and CVC syllables are heavy, in word final position CVC is light, and CVV, CVVC, and CVCC are heavy. As suggested by Hayes (1980), a rule of word-final consonant extrametricality in Cairene (c) results in homogeneous classes of heavy and light syllables:

	(a) Non-final	(b) Final
Light	CV	CV,
		CVC
Heavy	CVC,	CVV,
	CVV	CVVC,
		CVCC

(c) C → <C>/_##

Light	CV, CV<C>
Heavy	CVC, CVV
	CVC<C>, CVV<C>

The determination of syllable weight in Cairene then offers independent confirmation of the extraprosodic status of word-final consonants.

44 See Steriade (1982), Borowsky (1986), Itô (1986), and Bagemihl (1991) for detailed discussion of how and when stray erasure applies in various languages.

45 Consonant deletion under Stray Erasure is not limited to cluster environments. Borowsky (1986) assumes the h/ø alternation in English (cf. [víyəkl̩] "vehicle" vs. [vɪhík^yʊl̩] "vehicular") under Stray Erasure. In this case, the post-stress C is resyllabified into the preceding syllable, but /h/ is not a well-formed English coda, and so is deleted by Stray Erasure.

46 However, at least in Afar, Kashaya, and Yokuts, there are exceptions to closed syllable shortening. If closed syllable shortening is viewed as part of the syllabification process, as suggested here, then exceptional forms can be accounted for by lexically marked syllable structure. Hence, a form like /siib-na/ [siibna] "we uproot" in Afar has a root /s[iːb]$_{Rhyme}$/ which bleeds the regular rules of syllabification, resulting in an exceptional CVVC surface syllable.

It has been suggested that the preference for C over V in filling the post-nuclear position under closed syllable shortening is the result of a melody conservation principle whereby rules of stray erasure hesitate to delete segments whose melodies cannot be recovered. However, as shown by the Afar case, where $V_1V_2 C \rightarrow V_1 C$, vowels are lost even when their melodies cannot be recovered. A structural statement of this preference then might be more accurate: all else being equal, nuclear elements are stray erased before non-nuclear elements, or alternatively, non-nuclear elements are given priority in CVX syllabification.

47 It appears that different types of syllable structure violations are handled by different general strategies: segments which do not fit into the maximal syllabic template of a language are labeled extraprosodic, stray erased or syllabified by epenthesis (see below), whereas segments which violate featural restrictions on a position within the syllable template either are subject to feature-changing processes like those above, or are deleted.

48 Consonant/glide epenthesis also occurs in many languages. However, such epenthesis does not serve to "save" stray (i.e., unsyllabified) segments; rather, consonant epenthesis typically supplies an onset C to a V-initial syllable. For instance, in Axininca Campa (Payne 1981), an epenthetic [t] is inserted between vowels across morpheme boundaries: /i-n-koma-i/ [iŋkomati] "he will paddle" vs. /i-n-č^hik-i/ [iňč^hiki] "he will cut." Onsets are not obligatory in Axininca

Campa, as shown by these vowel-initial words, but onsets are required in non-word-initial syllables.

49   See also chapter 5 of this volume and Broselow (to appear), where arguments against a prosodic-directional account of parametric variation in epenthesis sites in Arabic dialects are presented, along with an original analysis of epenthesis/syncope facts which are claimed to follow from the definition of possible syllables in the different dialects.

50   See Lynch (1974) for justification and further exemplification of epenthesis in Lenakel. The epenthetic vowel is [+high] when preceded by a coronal; elsewhere it surfaces as schwa.

51   The vowel in parentheses is deleted by a morphologically governed rule which deletes an initial vowel in verb stems when preceded by the plural subject markers, /ar/, /ai/. This rule precedes epenthesis.

52   The epenthetic vowel in Chukchee is [ɨ]; this vowel surfaces as [u] when flanked by two velars, or by a labial and a velar, or when adjacent to [w].

53   Within a rule-based approach to syllabification, Chukchi epenthesis can be handled with cyclic syllabification. Following the creation of CVC syllables, the following cycle-final epenthesis rule would apply:

$$\emptyset \rightarrow [X]_N / X\_X'$$

This epenthesis rule requires that a segment (syllabified or unsyllabified) precede the stray segment, and hence will never result in word-initial or word-final epenthetic vowels. Whether syllabification is cyclic or not, it is

clear that a simple directional template-based model cannot correctly predict epenthesis sites in this language.

54   There are languages in which certain segments are not allowed in word-or utterance-initial position. This is a common constraint on flaps: for instance, in Pitta-Pitta (Dixon 1980), a language of Northwest Central Queensland, flaps /D/ and /r/ are found only in intervocalic position. However, if flaps are viewed as segments involving articulatory undershoot, conditioned by preceding and following vowels, or if, as proposed by Banner Inouye (1989) their phonological representations actually require featural linkage to preceding vowels, then there is a phonetic and phonological explanation for such restrictions. Other cases which might constitute onset constraints are cases where laryngeal features appear associated with vowels. For instance, in Awa (McKaughan 1973), a Papuan language of the Eastern Highlands, only nasals and glottal stop are possible codas, but glottal stop is never found word-initially (though it is found intervocalically.) The constraint here appears to be that the feature [+constricted glottis] must be segmentally linked to a preceding vowel; in word-initial position it cannot be, and so is ill-formed. Such a constraint, like that involving flaps, is independent of syllable structure.

55   Word-internally in Italian, /s/ appears to be a well-formed coda as well, but Itô suggests treating this in a special fashion, since /s/ does not appear word-finally within the native vocabulary. The problem with including /s/ in a general coda condition by barring [-son,

-cont] segments, is that this improperly also allows /f, š/ as nongeminate word-internal codas. As suggested by loan word phonology, the dilemma as to how to appropriately limit coda consonants disappears if certain gaps are treated as accidental.

56 Itô (1986, p. 32) suggests that the formulation of such coda constraints is "a clear advantage for a theory with conditions on syllable representations over a theory with conditions on syllable building rules." However, there is nothing which prevents rule-based approaches to syllabification from also making use of coda constraints like that in (12). As I see it, the issue of rule-based versus template-based syllabification hinges on whether or not syllables are maximalized in the first step of syllabification. Within rule-based and templatic models, featural constraints on positions within the syllable can either be incorporated into the syllabification algorithm, or stated separately. In some cases, separate statements seem necessary. For instance, in Klamath (Blevins 1993b) glottal stop is not a licit coda. However, should a glottal stop end up in post-vocalic position within the syllable, it is deleted, with compensatory lengthening of the preceding vowel. If compensatory lengthening is viewed as a syllable-sensitive process (Hayes 1989), then the glottal stop must be syllabified prior to its deletion, in order to give rise to compensatory lengthening. However, incorporating the constraint against glottal stop in the coda into the syllable template itself will bar such syllabification, with anomalous compensatory lengthening. It

appears then that this constraint in Klamath takes effect subsequent to syllabification, and is not part of the syllabification algorithm.

57 While (14b) violates the notion of Locality suggested in Itô's work, it does not violate the notion of locality in which a rule or constraint operating on skeletally adjacent segments is considered local.

58 A case which would further strengthen this position would be a language with maximal [CCV] syllables, where the only complex onsets are geminates. Churchyard (1991) has analyzed Trukese in just this way, and a similar analysis also seems possible for Pirahĩ as described by Everett and Everett (1984).

59 Kunjen is a dialect group composed of Oykangand, Olgol, Okunjan, and Kawarrangg.

60 Hence, Kunjen, as described by Sommer is also a counterexample to Jakobson and Halle's (1956) claim that CV syllables are found in all languages. See Dixon (1970a), Darden (1971), and chapter 25 of this volume for further discussion of the Kunjen facts. Similar arguments have been made by Breen (1991) for Arandic.

61 Reduction of vowels in utterance-initial position can lead to utterance-initial CVC sequences. See below.

62 Consonants are also stronger following stressed vowels, but in the example provided by Sommer (1981, p. 235), the C is a coda consonant, and so is also tautosyllabic with the stressed vowel.

63 Sommer's analysis is inconsistent with a rule of syllable-final aspiration, since this would also predict word/utterance-final

aspiration of voiceless stops, which does not occur.

64   Clements (1986) provides convincing arguments that syllabification in Barra is predictable and nondistinctive based on the existence of a synchronic rule of vowel epenthesis. We assume his analysis of epenthesis in the text. Bosch (1988, 1991), drawing on additional fieldwork and working within the prosodic licensing approach advocated by Goldsmith (1990), proposes a radical alternative which allows one to maintain the "Onset-first Principle." She claims that the post-vocalic C in Barra / ... VC.V ... / is technically the onset of the syllable, as its featural distribution is relatively free, while C_2 in / ... VC$_1$.C$_2$ V/ is actually the coda of the second syllable, as its featural content is linked to that of C_1.

65   I am unaware of any facts bearing on syllable weight in Barra. However, if weight-sensitive processes were identified, the two-step syllabification suggested here could be empirically evaluated.

66   See Clements (1986) for a detailed account of the epenthesis rule.

67   Though Kahn restricts his discussion of flapping to /t/, Hoard (1971) highlights the fact that "lax" varieties of all consonantal phonemes in English are found in the same environments. Hoard's rule of tensing does not require reference to ambisyllabicity, but his syllabifications are suspect: /kangrɛs/ [kʰaŋgr.əs] "congress", etc.

68   This does not exclude "phonetic" ambisyllabicity. Phonetic boundaries between syllables, just like phonetic boundaries between segments, might be difficult to define. Such blurred syllable boundaries at the phonetic level could explain the difficulty many speakers have in identifying syllabic affiliation of intervocalic consonants (cf. Kohler 1966). However, phonetic output cannot serve as the input to phonological rules. Hence, the prediction of this approach is that there will be no phonological rules and/or constraints which require a three-way contrast in syllabification of intervocalic Cs.

69   The vowel target then is simply specified as an open transition interpolated between two consonants. If the consonantal targets are distinct, the vowel will have transitional qualities. If the consonants surrounding the vowel are identical, interpolation will result in a zero-transition, and a phonetically long consonant will surface.

70   This is quite clear in the case of Japanese (Beckman and Shoji 1984), where vowel quality is recoverable from the spectrum of the preceding consonant. It is not unlikely that such phonetic cues are present in other languages with similar phenomena.

71   In some dialects, e.g., Southern American English, such words have been phonologically reanalysed as disyllabic. Here, we are limiting discussion to dialects where / ... VGl ... / is a possible tautosyllabic sequence.

7 The Internal Organization of Speech Sounds

G. N. CLEMENTS AND ELIZABETH V. HUME

0 Introduction

In recent years it has become widely accepted that the basic units of phonological representation are not segments but *features*, the members of a small set of elementary categories which combine in various ways to form the speech sounds of human languages. While features are normally construed as psychological entities, they are defined in terms of specific patterns of acoustic and articulatory realization which provide the crucial link between the cognitive representation of speech and its physical manifestation.

The wide acceptance of feature theory results from the fact that it offers straightforward explanations for many potentially unrelated observations. For example, since features are universal, feature theory explains the fact that all languages draw on a similar, small set of speech properties in constructing their phonological systems. Since features are typically binary or one-valued, it also explains the fact that speech sounds are perceived and stored in memory in a predominantly categorial fashion. Moreover, since phonological rules apply to feature representations, it accounts for the observation that phonological rules typically involve "natural classes" of sounds, that is, classes that can be uniquely defined in terms of a single conjunction of features. It also offers explanations for many generalizations in the domains of language acquisition, language disorders, and historical change, among others. Feature theory has emerged as one of the major results of linguistic science in this century, and has provided strong confirmation for the view that languages do not vary without limit, but reflect a single general pattern which is rooted in the physical and cognitive capacities of the human species.[1]

But while much research has been devoted to the questions, What are the features, and how are they defined?, it is only recently that linguists have begun to address a third and equally important question, How are features organized in phonological representations? Earlier theoreticians tended to think of phonemes as unstructured sets of features, or "feature bundles" in Bloomfield's well-known characterization. In accordance with this view, later work in the Jakobsonian and generative traditions treated segments as feature columns with no internal structure. In this approach, phonological sequences were typically characterized as two-dimensional feature matrices, as we illustrate below for the word *sun*:

(1)

	s	ʌ	n
syllabic	−	+	−
voice	−	+	+
nasal	−	−	+
coronal	+	−	+

etc.

In this view, a phoneme (or phonemic unit) is simply a column of features. Since phonemes follow each other in strict succession, such models can be regarded as *linear*.

The matrix formalism has strong arguments in its favor: it is conceptually simple, it is mathematically tractable, and it imposes powerful constraints on the way features can be organized in representations. In spite of its advantages, however, it has become apparent that this model (as well as other models in which phonemes are viewed as strictly sequential feature bundles) has two important inadequacies.

First, in such models all features defining a phoneme stand in a bijective (one-to-one) relation; thus, each feature value characterizes just one phoneme, and each phoneme is characterized by just one value from each category. It follows as a strict prediction that features cannot extend over domains greater or lesser than a single phoneme. However, there is considerable evidence that this prediction is incorrect. Simple and dramatic examples demonstrating "nonlinear" – i.e., nonbijective – relations among features can be drawn from tone languages. For example, in some tone languages, two or more tones may "crowd" onto a single syllable, forming contour tones (i.e., rising and falling tones). In many tone languages, single tones "stretch" or extend over several syllables, and in some, tones "float" in the sense that they are not associated with any particular tone-bearing unit in the representation. Tones are also found to constitute independent "tone melodies" in abstraction from the consonant and vowel sequences on which they are realized. (For discussion of these and other properties, see, e.g., Pike 1948, Welmers 1962, Goldsmith 1976, and Pulleyblank 1986.)

It was earlier thought that nonlinear relations among features of this sort are restricted to a small set of prosodic or suprasegmental speech properties, including tone, stress, and intonation. However, it has been convincingly demonstrated that segmental properties, too, show comparable behavior, if on a more limited scale. For example, in many languages the feature [nasal] may take up only part of a segment, giving rise to pre- and post-nasalized stops such as [ⁿd] and [dⁿ]; and in some languages it regularly spreads across more than one segment or syllable, establishing domains of nasal harmony (see, e.g., Bendor-Samuel 1970; Lunt 1973; Anderson 1976). Similarly, in languages with vowel harmony, features such as [back], [round] and [ATR] (advanced tongue root) have the ability to extend across many syllables at a time (see, e.g., Welmers and Harris 1942; Carnochan 1970; Vago 1980). Other segmental features also show nonlinear properties, as we shall see in the later discussion.

Problems such as these offered a direct challenge to linear theories of phonological representation, and led to the development of alternative, non-linear frameworks.[2] The earliest of these were the theory of long components developed by Harris (1944) (see also Hockett 1942, 1947 for a similar approach) and the theory of prosodic analysis developed by J. R. Firth and his collaborators after World War II (see, e.g., Firth 1948, the Philological Society 1957, and Palmer 1970). A more recent and still evolving approach is the theory of dependency phonology developed by J. Anderson, C. Ewen, and their associates (for a general overview and fuller discussion, see Anderson and Ewen 1987 and also chap. 17, this volume).

Perhaps the most influential of these frameworks at the present time – and the one we will be primarily concerned with here – is an approach emanating from the theory of autosegmental phonology developed in the 1970s and early 1980s. In autosegmental phonology, as first presented by Goldsmith (1976, 1979a, 1979b), features that are observed to extend over domains greater or lesser than the single segment are extracted from feature matrices and placed on separate "channels" or tiers of their own. Thus tones, for example, are represented on a separate tier from vowel and consonant segments, where they are able to function in a partly autonomous fashion. Elements on the same tier are sequentially ordered, while elements on different tiers are unordered and related to each other by means of association lines which establish patterns of alignment and overlap. Since associations between tones and tone-bearing units are not necessarily one-to-one, we may find other types of linking, as shown below (H = high tone, L = low tone, and V = any tone-bearing unit, such as a vowel or syllable):

(2) (a) V   (b) V   (c) V   V   (d) V

     | /\   \/ |

     L   H   L   H   H   L

Only (2a) involves a one-to-one relation between tones and tone-bearing units of the sort admitted in linear theories. (2b) shows a vowel linked to two tones, constituting a falling tone, (2c) displays two vowels sharing a single tone, and (2d) illustrates a floating tone. Multitiered representations of this type can be extended to other features showing complex patterns of alignment, such as nasality and harmonically-operating vowel features (Goldsmith 1979a; Clements 1980; Clements and Sezer 1982).

A second problem inherent in a matrix-based approach is its implicit claim that feature bundles have no internal structure. Each feature is equally related to any other, and no features are grouped into larger sets, corresponding to traditional phonetic classes such as "place" or "manner" of articulation. This claim is an intrinsic consequence of the way the representational system is designed.[3] Some linguists, however, have proposed to classify phonological features into taxonomic categories. While they have not usually assigned any status to such categories in phonological representations themselves, they have sometimes suggested that they may have a cognitive status of some sort. Thus, while Jakobson and Halle (1956) group segmental features into "sonority" and "tonality" features on strictly acoustic grounds, they suggest that these classes form two independent "axes" in language acquisition. Chomsky and Halle (1968) classify features into several taxonomic classes (major class features, cavity features, etc.), but suggest that "ultimately the features themselves will be seen to be organized in a hierarchical structure which may resemble the structure we have imposed on them for purely expository reasons" (1968, p. 300). The most extensive earlier proposal for grouping features together into larger classes, perhaps, is that of Trubetzkoy (1939), whose "related classes" of features are defined on both phonetic and phonological principles. To take an example, the features of voicing and aspiration fall into a single related class on phonetic grounds, as they are both realized in terms of laryngeal activity, independently of the oral place of articulation. But these features also function together phonologically, in the sense that they frequently undergo neutralization as a unit (see further discussion in section 2.3), or exhibit tight patterns of mutual implication. Trubetzkoy assigns such classes of features to separate "planes" of structure, and relates their independent cognitive (psychological) status to their phonetic and functional relatedness, stating that "the projection of distinctive oppositions (and thus also of correlations) sometimes onto the same and sometimes onto different planes is the psychological consequence of just those kin relationships between the correlation marks on which the classification of correlations into related classes is made" (p. 85). These pregnant suggestions did not undergo immediate development in the Jakobsonian or generative traditions, as we have seen. However, Trubetzkoy's conception can be viewed as an important precursor of the model which we examine in greater detail below.

There is, indeed, a considerable amount of evidence that features are grouped into higher-level functional units, constituting what might be called "natural classes" of features in something very like Trubetzkoy's notion of "related classes." For example, in contemporary English, /t/ is often glottalized to [t'] in syllable-final position. In some contexts, glottalized [t'] loses its oral occlusion altogether, yielding the glottal stop that we observe in common pronunciations of words like mitten [mɪʔn]. In certain Spanish dialects, the nonlaryngeal features of /s/ are lost in syllable coda position, leaving only aspiration behind: *mismo* [miʰmo] "same". In cases like these, which have been discussed by Lass 1976, Thráinsson 1978, and Goldsmith 1979b, the oral tract features of a segment are lost as a class, while laryngeal features such as glottalization and aspiration remain behind. Similarly, in many languages all place features function together as a unit. In English, the nasal segment of the prefixes *syn-* and *con-* typically assimilates in place of articulation to the following consonant, where it is realized as labial [m] before labials (*sympathy, compassion*), alveolar [n] before alveolars (*syntax, condescend*), velar [ŋ] before velars (*synchronize, congress*), and so forth. In such processes, all features defining place of articulation function as a unit, suggesting that they have a special status in the representation (Goldsmith 1981; Steriade 1982; Mohanan 1983). To describe processes such as this, traditional linear theory requires a rule mentioning all the features designating place of articulation, i.e., [coronal], [anterior], [distributed], [back], etc. But such a rule is no more highly valued than one that involves any arbitrarily-selected set of features, including those that never function together in phonological rules.

In response to this problem, a general model of feature organization has been proposed in which features that regularly function together as a unit in phonological rules are grouped into *constituents* (Clements 1985; Sagey 1986; see also Hayes 1986a for a related approach). In this approach, segments are represented in terms of hierarchically-organized node configurations whose terminal nodes are feature values, and whose intermediate nodes represent constituents. Instead of placing features in matrices, this model arrays them in the manner of a Calder mobile, as shown below:

(3)

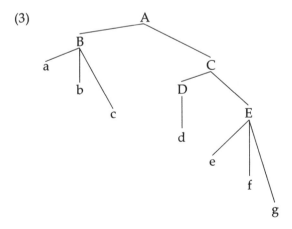

Unlike the tree diagrams familiar in syntactic theory, terminal elements (here, feature values) are unordered and placed on separate tiers, as we suggest in the diagram by placing them on separate lines. This organization makes it possible to express feature overlap, as in standard autosegmental phonology. All branches emanate from a *root node* (*A*), which corresponds to the speech sound itself. Lower-level *class nodes* (*B, C, D, E*) designate functional feature groupings, which include the laryngeal node, the place node, and others to be discussed below.

In this model, association lines have a double function. They serve first to encode patterns of temporal alignment and coordination among elements in phonological representations, as in autosegmental phonology (cf. (2)). The importance of this function will be seen later in the discussion of contour segments (section 1.3), length (section 1.4), and multilinked nodes (section 2.1), for example. In addition, as shown in (3), they group elements into constituents, which function as single units in phonological rules. The immediate constituents of such a grouping are sister nodes, and both are daughters, or dependents, of the higher constituent node; in (3), for example, *D* and *E* are sisters, and daughters (or dependents) of *C*. Notice also that if *D* is (universally) a daughter of *C*, the presence of *D* in a representation will necessarily entail the presence of *C*, a relationship that will take on some importance in the later discussion.

This approach to feature organization makes it possible to impose strong constraints on the form and functioning of phonological rules. In particular, we assume the following principle:

(4)   Phonological rules perform single operations only.

This principle predicts, for example, that a phonological rule might affect the set of features *d, e, f,* and *g* in (3) by performing a single operation on constituent *C*; however, no rule can affect nodes *c, d,* and *e* alone in a single operation, since they do not form a constituent. In general, a theory incorporating this principle claims that *only feature sets which form constituents may function together in phonological rules*. Since the set of features that form constituents is a very small proportion of all the logical possibilities, this claim represents a strong empirical hypothesis regarding the class of possible phonological rules.

One further principle is required in order to maintain this claim in its most general form. We state it as follows:

(5)   Feature organization is universally determined.

According to this principle, the manner in which feature values are assigned to tiers and grouped into larger constituents does not vary from language to language. Obviously, if feature organization could freely vary, the theory would make no crosslinguistic predictions. However, there is much reason to believe that feature organization is universal, since the same feature groupings recur in language after language.[4]

We further assume that principle (5) projects the same feature organization at all levels of derivation, from underlying to surface structure. This means that phonological rules cannot have the effect of creating novel types of feature organization. Rules that would produce ill-formed structures are often assumed to be subjected to further conventions which have the effect of preserving the wellformedness of the representation (e.g., node interpolation, Sagey 1986). Thus, the feature hierarchy operates as a template defining wellformedness across derivations. Further principles constraining the form and organization of phonological rules will be discussed as we proceed.

We may now give a preliminary answer to the question, How are features organized?

(6) (a) Feature values are arrayed on separate tiers, where they may enter into nonlinear (nonbijective) relations with one another;
   (b) Features are at the same time organized into hierarchical arrays, in which each constituent may function as a single unit in phonological rules.

A model having these general properties has been called a "feature geometry."[5] On these assumptions, the empirical task of feature theory is that of determining which nodes to recognize, and how these nodes are organized.

1   Simple, Complex, and Contour Segments

We now develop a theory of feature organization in more detail. We first take up the question of gross segmental structure, focusing on the characterization of simple, complex and contour segments. Here and elsewhere, our discussion of particular examples will be necessarily brief and incomplete, and the reader is urged to consult our sources for fuller discussion.

1.1   *Articulator-based Feature Theory*

Central to the current development of feature theory is the idea that speech is produced using several independently functioning articulators. These articulators – comprising the lips, the tongue front, the tongue body, the tongue root, the soft palate, and the larynx – may define a single, primary constriction in the vocal tract, or may combine to produce several constrictions at the same time. Since the articulators play a fundamental role in the organization of segment structure, it has been proposed that they should be represented by nodes of their own in phonological representations, arrayed on separate tiers (Sagey 1986; Halle 1988). Among these nodes, *labial, coronal,* and *dorsal* are defined in terms of oral tract articulations, as stated below (Sagey 1986, p. 274):

(7) Labial: involving the lips as an active articulator
    Coronal: involving the tongue front as an active articulator
    Dorsal: involving the tongue body as an active articulator

The articulator features are also called "place" features, because they link under the place constituent in the feature hierarchy.[6]

Unlike most other features, [labial], [coronal], and [dorsal] are treated as privative (one-valued), rather than binary. This is because phonological rules do not appear to operate on the negative values of these categories. For example, while many rules involve labial assimilation, there are few if any rules of nonlabial assimilation, turning, e.g., [p] to [t] in the context of a nonlabial sound ([t, č, k], etc.), or rules of nonlabial dissimilation, changing, e.g., nonlabial [t] to labial [p] next to a nonlabial. These observations follow directly from the assumption that articulator features are one-valued: if [–labial] has no existence in the theory, then of course no rule can carry out an operation on [–labial] sounds.[7]

Other features are either *articulator-bound*, in the sense that they depend on a specific articulator for their execution, or *articulator-free*, in the sense that they are not restricted to a specific articulator. Articulator-bound features, when present, further prescribe the specific nature of the constriction formed by a given articulator. Such features are located under the appropriate articulator node. Thus, for example, the articulator-bound features [anterior] and [distributed] are linked under the coronal node, where they distinguish anterior from posterior coronals and apical from laminal coronals, respectively. We illustrate these distinctions with a system of minimal contrasts found in many Australian languages (Dixon 1980; his digraphs represent simple sounds in all cases):

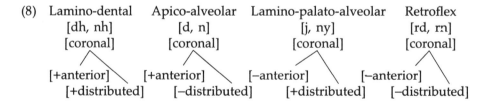

(8) Lamino-dental   Apico-alveolar   Lamino-palato-alveolar   Retroflex
     [dh, nh]   [d, n]   [j, ny]   [rd, rn]
     [coronal]   [coronal]   [coronal]   [coronal]

     [+anterior]   [+anterior]   [–anterior]   [–anterior]
     [+distributed] [–distributed]   [+distributed]   [–distributed]

The placement of the features [anterior] and [distributed] directly under the coronal node is motivated by several observations. First, these features are relevant only for coronal sounds. Thus no noncoronal sounds are minimally distinguished by these features, nor do these features define natural classes including noncoronal sounds (Steriade 1986; Sagey 1986); these observations follow directly from the treatment of [anterior] and [distributed] as dependents of the [coronal] node, since the presence of either feature in a segment entails the presence of [coronal]. Second, this analysis correctly predicts that if one segment assimilates to another in coronality, it necessarily assimilates [anterior] and [distributed] at the same time. This prediction is supported by rules of coronal assimilation in languages as diverse as English (Clements 1985), Sanskrit (Schein and Steriade 1986), Basque (Hualde 1988b), and Tahltan (Shaw 1991).

Articulator-free features designate the degree of stricture of a sound, independent of the specific articulator involved, and so are sometimes called *stricture* features. For example, [+continuant] sounds are those that permit continuous airflow through the center of the oral tract, regardless of where the major stricture is located. The features [±sonorant], [±approximant], and [±consonantal] also lack a designated articulator. Most writers place the articulator-free features higher in the hierarchy than articulator features; we will examine evidence supporting this view below.

1.2   Simple and Complex Segments

If features can be considered the atoms of phonological representation, feature complexes constituting segments may be considered the *molecules*. We now consider molecular structure in more detail. Drawing on terminology introduced by Sagey, we can distinguish between simple, complex, and contour segments. A *simple* segment consists of a root node characterized by at most one oral articulator feature. For example, the sound [p] is simple since it is uniquely [labial].

A *complex* segment is a root node characterized by at least two different oral articulator features, representing a segment with two or more simultaneous oral tract constrictions. This analysis receives striking support from Halle's observation (1983) that we can find doubly articulated complex segments involving all possible pairs of oral articulators, as defined by the articulator features *labial, coronal,* and *dorsal.* For example, the labio-coronal stop [tp] of Yeletnye is formed by simultaneous closure of the lips and tongue front (Maddieson and Ladefoged 1988), the labiovelar stop [kp] of Yoruba by simultaneous closure of the lips and tongue body (Ladefoged 1968), and the alveolar click [!] of South African Bantu and Khoisan languages by simultaneous closure of the tongue front and tongue body (Ladefoged and Traill 1984). Representations of several simple and complex segments are given below, showing relevant structure only. (Recall that nodes on different tiers are unordered with respect to each other. We disregard the distinction between major and minor articulations, to be discussed in section 3.5.)

(9)

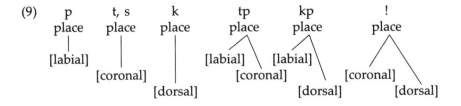

It will be appreciated that Halle's original observation follows directly from the articulator-based model on the assumption that complex segments are formed by the free combination of oral articulator features: since there are only three of these, we should find exactly the three combinations illustrated above.

1.3   *Contour segments*

Parallel to the treatment of contour tones, depicted in (2b) above, multitiered feature representations allow the direct expression of *contour segments*, that is, segments containing sequences (or "contours") of different features. The classical motivation for recognizing contour segments is the existence of phonological "edge effects," according to which a given segment behaves as though it bears the feature [+F] with regard to segments on one side and [–F] with regard to those on the other (Anderson 1976). Commonly proposed candidates for such segment types include affricates and prenasalized stops.

There are currently two main views on how such segments can be characterized, as suggested by the following figure, representing prenasalized stops (irrelevant structure has been omitted):

(10)   (a)   One-root analysis   (b)   Two-root analysis

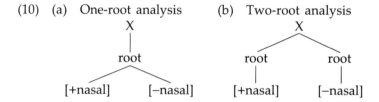

In the one-root analysis (10a), contour segments are characterized by a sequence of features linked to a single higher node (Sagey 1986); in this view, a prenasalized stop such as [ⁿd] is represented as a single root node characterized by the sequence [+nasal] [–nasal],[8] and an affricate such as [ts] is represented as a root node characterized by the sequence [–continuant] [+continuant]. This analysis assumes that only terminal features, not class nodes, may be sequenced in a given segment. Notice, however, that even with this constraint, a large number of theoretically possible but nonoccurring, complex segments are predicted, bearing such sequences as [+voice] [–voice] or [–distributed] [+distributed].

In the two-root analysis (10b), contour segments consist of two root nodes sequenced under a single skeletal position. In this view, a prenasalized stop can be represented as a sequence of two root nodes, characterized as [+nasal] and [–nasal] respectively (Clements 1987; Piggott 1988; Rosenthall 1988). This analysis assumes a constraint that universally forbids branching structure under the root node, which can be stated as follows:

(11) The No Branching Constraint:
Configurations of the form

are ill-formed, where A is any class node (including the root node), A
immediately dominates B and C, and B and C are on the same tier.

This statement is based on a proposal by Clements (1989b), generalizing a
more specific version proposed by Piggott (1988).[9] Even with this constraint,
however, further principles are required to express the fact that not every
sequence of root nodes constitutes a possible contour segment (for suggestions, see Rosenthall 1988).

In an important study of nasal spreading phenomena, Steriade (1991) presents
extensive evidence in favor of a two-root analysis of pre- and post-nasalized
stops, while taking an important step toward constraining the class of potential
contour segments. Steriade proposes that contour segments (including released
stops, in her analysis) should be analyzed as sequences of what she terms
"aperture nodes." She recognizes three kinds of aperture nodes, defined
phonetically as follows:

(12) A_0 = total absence of oral airflow (as in oral and nasal stops)
A_f = degree of oral aperture sufficient to produce a turbulent airstream
(as in fricatives and the second phase of affricates)
A_{max} = degree of oral aperture insufficient to produce a turbulent airflow
(as in oral sonorants and the release phase of stops)

Steriade suggests that such "aperture nodes" can be incorporated into the
phonological feature model as root nodes characterized by the appropriate
feature values. Inspiring ourselves freely on this proposal, we suggest the
following root-node interpretation (others are possible): [10]

(13) A_0 = a root node characterized as [−continuant, −approximant]
A_f = a root node characterized as [+continuant, −sonorant]
A_{max} = a root node characterized as [+continuant, +sonorant]

This model allows only two types of segment-internal sequences: $A_0 A_f$, defining segments with a stop phase followed by fricative release (i.e., affricates),
and $A_0 A_{max}$, defining segments with a stop phase followed by abrupt maximal
release (all other released stops).

Given these assumptions, and continuing to use the shorthand notation in
(13), we may represent oral (released) stops, affricates, prenasalized stops, and
prenasalized affricates, respectively, by the partial configurations shown in
(14) (only relevant structure is shown; we place the feature [nasal] above the
root nodes for convenience):

(14)

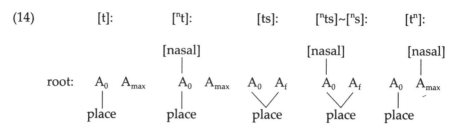

The first two figures show plain and prenasalized stops, respectively. The prenasalized stop [^{n}t] differs from its oral counterpart [t] only in having the feature [nasal] attached to its noncontinuant root node A_0; it is thus formally analyzed as nasal closure followed by (maximal) oral release. The third figure shows an oral affricate, analyzed as a noncontinuant root node A_0 followed by a (homorganic) fricative release A_f.

The fourth figure provides a single representation for the prenasalized segments often transcribed as [^{n}ts] and [^{n}s]. The latter, usually described as a prenasalized fricative, is here represented just like the former, as an affricate with [nasal] closure. This analysis assumes that the articulatory difference between [^{n}s] and [^{n}ts] is always nondistinctive, being determined by language-particular principles of phonetic implementation. The last segment type shown in (14), the postnasalized stop [t^n], can quite naturally be characterized as a [t] with maximal [nasal] release. Ordinary nasal stops such as [n] (not shown here) differ from it only in that [nasal] is associated with both the closure and release nodes.

In Steriade's proposal, true contour segments are restricted to the class of stops and affricates, as shown above. Other major classes, such as fricatives, liquids, and vocoids, have only a single root node, and thus cannot be phonologically pre- or post-nasalized.[11] Steriade's system, then, is a highly constrained one which restricts contour segments to just a few, well-attested types; it remains to be seen whether other complex segment types sometimes proposed in the literature, such as short diphthongs, should be added to the inventory.

Affricates are less well understood than prenasalized stops. While "edge effects" have been convincingly demonstrated for pre- and post-nasalized stops, they are much less evident for affricates. Indeed, in some languages, such as Basque, Turkish, and Yucatec Mayan, affricates show "anti-edge effects," behaving as stops with respect to following segments and/or as fricatives with respect to preceding segments. The formal analysis of affricates remains an unresolved question at the present time (see Hualde 1988a, Lombardi 1990, and Steriade 1991 for several different proposals).

1.4 Length

Speech sounds may be long or short. Phonological length (or quantity) can be defined as *bipositionality* on the tier representing phonological quantity, whether this is taken as the CV- or X- skeleton in the sense of McCarthy (1981, 1985),

Clements and Keyser (1983), Prince (1984), and others, or the weight unit tier in the sense of Hyman (1985).[12] In all these approaches, a long consonant or vowel is represented as a root node linked to two units of quantity, as shown in (15):

(15)   Short: Long:

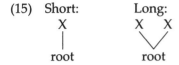

A surprising result of this analysis is that we no longer have a uniform way of reconstructing the traditional notion "segment". Thus a complex segment such as [ts] consists of one node on the quantity tier and two on the root tier, while a long consonant such as [tː] consists of two nodes on the quantity tier and one on the root tier. On which tier is segmenthood defined? Neither choice seems fully appropriate. The apparent paradox may simply reflect the fact that we are dealing with different kinds of segmentations on each tier. It might be more useful to distinguish between "melodic segments" defined on the root tier and "metric segments" defined on the skeleton; in this way an affricate would consist of two melodic segments linked to one metric segment, and so forth.

2   Phonological Processes

A classical problem in phonological theory is that of determining the class of elementary phonological processes which map underlying representations into surface representations. Standard generative phonology provided a rich vocabulary for stating phonological rules, but as Chomsky and Halle themselves pointed out (1968, chap. 9), it did not provide an intrinsic way of distinguishing plausible, crosslinguistically attested rules from highly improbable ones (for further discussion of this point, see, e.g., Clements 1976, Goldsmith 1981, and McCarthy 1988). In reaction to this problem, the theory of natural phonology developed a set of criteria for distinguishing between "natural processes" and "learned rules" (Stampe, 1980), but did not provide a formal basis for the distinction.

In this section we take up this issue from the perspective of hierarchical feature representation. We show that a small number of elementary rule types and organizational principles project to a large class of "natural" rule types, while excluding rare or unattested ones.

2.1   *Assimilation*

Perhaps the most widely recurrent type of phonological rule is *assimilation*. Standard generative phonology characterized assimilation in terms of feature copying, according to which one segment copies feature specifications from a neighboring segment. In the present model, in contrast, assimilation rules are characterized as the association (or "spreading") of a feature or node F of segment A to a neighboring segment B, as shown below (dashed lines indicate association lines added by rule.):

(16)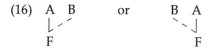

This approach represents the phonological counterpart of the articulatory model of assimilation assumed by the French phonologist Grammont, who writes (1933, p. 185): "*L'assimilation* consiste dans l'extension d'un ou de plusieurs mouvements articulatoires au delà de leur domaine originaire. Ces mouvements articulatoires sont propres au phonème agissant; le phonème agi, en se les appropriant aussi, devient plus semblable à l'autre." In this view, an assimilation involves one or more articulatory movements extending their domain from an affecting segment (*phonème agissant*), or trigger, to an affected segment (*phonème agi*), or target. There is considerable phonological support for such a view, as we shall see in section 2.1.2.

2.1.1   Assimilation Types

As a basis for the discussion, it will be useful to distinguish various assimilation types. One distinction depends on the nature of the affected segment. If the rule spreads only feature(s) that are not already specified in the target, it applies in a *feature-filling* mode. This common pattern can be regarded as the unmarked (or default) mode of assimilation. If the rule applies to segments already specified for the spreading feature(s), replacing their original values, the rule applies in a *feature-changing* mode.

We can also distinguish different types of assimilation according to the identity of the spreading node. If the root node spreads, the affected segment will acquire all the features of the trigger. In the feature-changing mode, this result, often called *complete* or *total assimilation*, gives the effect of deletion with compensatory lengthening. For example, in a well-known sound change in the Lesbian and Thessalian dialects of Ancient Greek, [s] assimilates to a preceding or following sonorant, perhaps passing through an intermediate [h] (Steriade 1982; Wetzels 1986; Rialland 1993):

(17)   *gʷolsā   >   bollā   "council"
       *awsōs   >   awwōs   "dawn"
       *esmi   >   emmi   "I am"
       *naswos   >   nawwos   "temple"

These assimilations illustrate both cases of schema (16), where F = the root node:

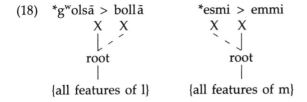

(18) *gʷolsā > bollā   *esmi > emmi

The spreading root node replaces the root node of [s], which is deleted by convention.

If a lower-level class node spreads, the target acquires several, but not all of the features of the trigger (*partial* or *incomplete* assimilation). We have already mentioned an example from English, involving the assimilation of place features in the prefixes *syn-* and *con-*. Similar rules occur in many languages, and have the general form shown in (19):

(19)   root root   or   root   root

        place   place

Finally, in *single-feature* assimilation, only a terminal feature spreads. Common types include vowel harmony, voicing assimilation, and nasal assimilation. Many examples have been presented from the earliest literature in nonlinear phonology onward (see, e.g., representative papers in van der Hulst and Smith 1982, and Aronoff and Oehrle 1984).

Assimilation rules provide a powerful criterion for answering the question, How are features organized?, since any feature or feature set that assimilates as a unit must constitute a node on an independent tier of its own. We now consider an important empirical prediction of the spreading model of assimilation.

2.1.2 Multilinked Nodes

In the spreading model of assimilation, an assimilation rule always gives rise to multilinked nodes in its output. Notice, for example, that in the output of a total assimilation rule a single root node is linked to two skeletal positions, as shown in (18). It will be recalled that this type of representation is identical to the one proposed earlier for underlying long segments (section 1.4). The spreading model of assimilation predicts, therefore, that geminates derived by assimilation rules should be formally indistinguishable from underlying geminates with regard to later stages of a phonological derivation.

This prediction appears to be correct. Hayes (1986b) shows that geminates created from dissimilar segments by assimilation rules share special properties with underlying (i.e., monomorphemic) geminates, which are not displayed by sequences of identical consonants occurring at the boundary between different morphemes or words. One of these is *geminate inseparability*, according to which "true" geminates (i.e., those exhibiting multilinked structure) cannot be separated by epenthetic vowels. This property can be illustrated by rules of epenthesis and assimilation in Palestinian Arabic, as first described by Abu-Salim (1980). In words containing clusters of three or more consonant positions, an epenthetic vowel [i] is inserted before the final two: (C)CCC → (C)C[i]CC. This rule is illustrated in (20a). The rule does not apply if the leftmost two positions correspond to a monomorphemic geminate, as shown in (20b). Epenthesis also applies within clusters separated by word boundaries (20c), even if the flanking consonants are identical (20d). (20e) illustrates epenthesis between the definite article /l-/ and a following cluster. By an independent rule, /l-/ totally assimilates to a following coronal consonant, giving surface geminates as in [š-šams] "the sun" from underlying /l-šams/. Geminates created by this rule cannot be separated by epenthesis; instead, contrary to the regular pattern, the epenthetic vowel is inserted to their left (20f).

(20) (a) ʔak[i]l-kum   "your food" /ʔakl-kum/
           ʔib[i]n-ha   "her son" /ʔibn-ha/
      (b) sitt-na   "our grandmother" (*sit[i]t-na)
           ʔimm-na   "our mother" (*ʔim[i]m-na)
      (c) ʔakl [i] mniih   "a good food"
           walad [i] kbiir   "a big boy"
      (d) samak [i] kbiir   "a big fish"
      (e) l-walad l[i]-kbiir   "the big boy" /l-kbiir/
      (f) l-walad [i] z-zɣiir "the small boy" (* z[i]-zɣiir])

In this paradigm, the inseparable geminates are just those that are monomorphemic (20b), or heteromorphemic and created by assimilation (20f).

This pattern can be explained on the assumption that "true" geminates, whether underlying or created by assimilation, have the multilinked structure shown in (21a), while "accidental" geminates created by concatenation across boundaries have separate root nodes, as shown in (21b). The failure of epenthesis to apply in true geminates can be explained by the fact that the insertion of an epenthetic vowel into the linked structure would create a violation of the constraint against crossed association lines (discussed in section 2.5), as shown in (21c):[13]

(21) (a) C   C   (b) C   C   (c) *C   V   C
           \ / | | \ ╳ /
           root   root root   root root

Not only total, but partial assimilation gives rise to multilinked nodes, as was shown in (19). Partially assimilated clusters should therefore show inseparability effects just as full geminates do. This prediction is also well supported by the evidence. For example, in Kolami, clusters that have undergone place assimilation are impervious to a later rule of epenthesis that would otherwise be expected to break them up (see Steriade 1982, after Emenau 1955). Thus, epenthesis normally inserts a copy of the stem vowel between the first two members of a CCC cluster, as shown by the first column in (22a). However, it fails to apply in homorganic clusters created by place assimilation, as shown in (22b).

(22)			past	present	UR (root)
	(a)	"break"	kinik-tan	kink-atun	/kink/
		"make to get up"	suulup-tan	suulp-atun	/suulp/
		"sweep"	ayak-tan	ayk-atun	/ayk/
	(b)	"boil over"	poŋk-tan	poŋg-atun	/poŋg/
		"bury"	min(t)-tan	mind-atun	/mind/

This behavior may be explained by attributing a multilinked place node to the assimilated clusters; as in the case of geminates, epenthesis would create an ill-formed structure.[14] Similar effects have been cited from Tamazight Berber (Steriade 1982), Sierra Popoluca (Clements 1985), and Barra Isle Gaelic (Clements 1986), among other languages.

The multiple linking of partially assimilated clusters can be demonstrated in other ways as well. For example, partly assimilated clusters show the same sort of inalterability effects that are found in true geminates, according to which certain types of rules that ordinarily affect the feature content of single segments fail to apply to otherwise eligible segments with linked structure; see Hayes (1986a, 1986b) and Schein and Steriade (1986) for discussion and examples from a variety of languages. Again, phonological rules are frequently restricted to apply only to members of partially assimilated homorganic clusters; such rules can be simply formulated by making direct reference to the linked place nodes (see Kiparsky 1985, Clements 1985, and Hume 1991 for examples from Catalan, Sierra Popoluca, and Korean, respectively). Another argument for linked structure can be cited from the many languages which restrict intervocalic consonant clusters to geminate consonants (if present in the language) and homorganic clusters; in such cases we may say that intervocalic clusters may only have one place node (Prince 1984, p. 243). In sum, there are many independent types of evidence supporting the spreading theory of assimilation, which taken together provide a strong source of support for nonlinear feature representation as outlined above.

2.2 Dissimilation and the OCP

We now consider dissimilation, the process by which one segment systematically fails to bear a feature present in a neighboring (or nearby) segment. Dissimilation rules are also common across languages, and should receive a simple formal expression in the theory.

Traditionally, dissimilation has been stated in terms of feature-changing rules of the type [X] → [–F] / ____ [+F]. However, this approach cannot be adopted in the present framework, since many features that commonly undergo dissimilation ([coronal], [labial], [dorsal], etc.) are one-valued. Instead, dissimilation can be expressed as an effect of delinking, according to which a feature or node is delinked from a segment; the orphaned node is then deleted through a general convention. A later rule may insert the opposite (typically, default) value. (See Odden 1987, McCarthy 1988, and Yip 1988 for examples and discussion.)

While dissimilation can be formally expressed as delinking, we must still explain why delinking so commonly has a dissimilatory function. A rather elegant answer comes from the Obligatory Contour Principle (OCP), originally proposed in work on tone languages to account for the fact that sequences of identical adjacent tones, such as HH, are widely avoided in both underlying and derived representations (Leben 1973). In later work, McCarthy extended this principle to the segmental phonology to explain why so many languages avoid sequences of identical (or partly identical) segments (McCarthy 1986). He stated this principle in its most general form as follows (McCarthy 1988):

(23)   Obligatory Contour Principle (OCP):
       Adjacent identical elements are prohibited.

By this statement, the OCP applies to any two identical features or nodes which are adjacent on a given tier. Its empirical content is threefold: it may prohibit underlying representations which violate it, it may "drive" or motivate rules which suppress violations of it, and it may block rules that would otherwise create violations of it (see McCarthy 1981, 1986, 1988; Mester 1986; Odden 1988; Yip 1988, 1989; Clements 1990b, 1993, for examples and discussion). A direct consequence of the OCP is that dissimilatory delinking should be a preferred process type across languages, since it has the effect of eliminating OCP violations.

We will illustrate the OCP with a well-known example from Classical Arabic (Greenberg 1950; McCarthy, in press). In this language, consonantal roots are subject to strict constraints. First, within such roots, no two consonants can be identical. Thus hypothetical roots such as /bbC/, /Cbb/ and /bCb/ are ill-formed, where C is any consonant.[15] Furthermore, roots containing homorganic consonants strongly tend to be excluded; thus hypothetical roots like /bmC/, /Cbm/, and /bCm/, with two labial consonants, are totally absent (see McCarthy, in press, for qualifications and fuller discussion).

Consider now how these constraints can be accounted for by the OCP. The constraint against identical adjacent consonants follows directly from statement (23), applied at the root tier. The constraint against homorganic consonants also follows from (23), applied in this case to articulator features. Consider the following (partial) representation of the ill-formed root */dbt/, with homorganic initial and final consonants:

(24)

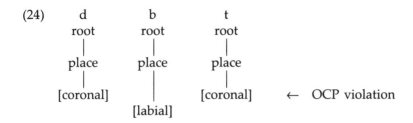

The illformedness of this representation is due to the violation of the OCP on the [coronal] tier, as shown by the arrow. Crucially, the two occurrences of [coronal] are adjacent on their tier, even though the segments they charact-erize, /d/ and /t/, are nonadjacent on the root tier. This is because the inter-vening consonant, /b/, is characterized by a [labial] node, which, lying on a tier of its own, is unordered with respect to [coronal]. This result crucially presupposes that articulator features are arrayed on separate tiers, as pro-posed earlier.

Thus in Arabic, and in many other languages, the OCP generates a per-vasive pattern of dissimilation involving identical and homorganic conso-nants. In many languages, OCP violations are resolved in other ways as well, such as the merger or assimilation of adjacent identical nodes (Mester 1986), the blocking of syncope rules that would otherwise create OCP violations (McCarthy 1986), and the insertion of epenthetic segments, as in the English plural formation rule which inserts a vowel between two coronal sibilants in words like *taxes, brushes* (Yip 1988). This evidence, taken cumulatively, sug-gests that dissimilation is just one of several stratagems for reducing or elimi-nating OCP violations at all levels of representation. Like assimilation, dissimilation (and other delinking rules) provide a criterion for feature organi-zation: any delinked node must occur on a tier of its own.

2.3. Neutralization

Another common process type is neutralization, which eliminates contrasts between two or more phonological features in certain contexts (Trubetzkoy 1939). We are concerned here with neutralization rules which are neither as-similations nor dissimilations. Common examples include rules of debuccali-zation (Clements 1985; McCarthy 1988; Trigo 1988) which eliminate contrasts among oral tract features; rules of devoicing, deaspiration, and/or deglottali-zation, which eliminate contrasts among laryngeal features (Lombardi 1991); and rules of vowel height reduction which reduce or eliminate contrasts in height or [ATR] (Clements 1991). Neutralization at the level of the root node eliminates all segmental contrasts, as in the reduction of all unstressed vowels to a neutral vowel (as in English), or of certain consonants to a "default" element such as [ʔ] (as in Toba Batak, see Hayes 1986a). Typically, neutralization rules eliminate marked values in favor of unmarked values.

Like dissimilation, simple neutralization can be characterized in terms of node delinking. We illustrate with a particularly interesting example from Korean. In this language, the three-way phonemic contrast among plain voiceless, aspirated, and "tense" (or glottalized) obstruents is neutralized to a plain voiceless unreleased stop in final position and preconsonantally (i.e., in the syllable coda). In addition, the coronal obstruents / t tʰ t' č čʰ č' s s' / and (at least for some speakers) /h/ are neutralized to [t] in the same contexts. In faster or more casual speech styles, however, the coronals may totally assimilate to a following stop under conditions which appear to vary among speakers. The two styles are illustrated by the following examples (Martin 1951; Cho 1990; Kim 1990):[16]

(25)   /-e/ "in"   /-kwa/ "and"
                        slower   faster
/patʰ/   patʰ-e   pat-k'wa   or   pak-k'wa   "field"
/os/   os-e   ot-k'wa   or   ok-k'wa   "clothes"
/čəč/   čəč-e   čət-k'wa   or   čək-k'wa   "mother's milk"
/k'očʰ/   k'očʰ-e   k'ot-k'wa or   k'ok-k'wa "flower"

Notice that the neutralization rule illustrated in the slower speech styles applies to the features [anterior] and [continuant] which, in the feature organization of Sagey (1986), for example, are widely separated: [anterior] is dominated by [coronal], whereas [continuant] is immediately dominated by the root node. To achieve this effect in terms of a single operation in accordance with principle (4), the rule must delink the root node of the coronal obstruent.[17] The resulting empty skeletal position is assigned the features of unreleased [t], the unmarked consonant, by default. The following derivation of the slower speech forms illustrates the analysis of neutralization; note that parenthesized nodes are automatically interpolated to preserve wellformedness (Sagey 1986). (Irrelevant structure is omitted.)

(26)   Delinking   Automatic deletion   Default insertion

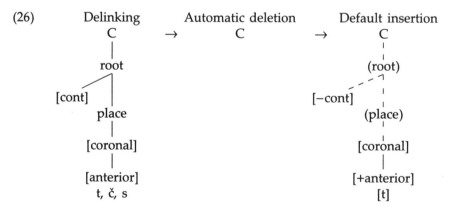

In faster speech, the default rule is preempted by a rule spreading the root node of the second consonant onto the skeletal position of the first.

Neutralization rules provide a further criterion for feature organization: since only single nodes may undergo delinking, any features that delink as a group must constitute a single node on an independent tier of its own.

2.4 *Other Elementary Rule Types*

The elementary rule types required for the processes described above are linking, delinking, and default insertion. A further process, deletion, can usually be decomposed into delinking followed by automatic deletion. This brief list is probably not complete. Feature-changing rules, affecting values of features such as [sonorant], [consonantal], and [continuant], are most likely required to express processes of strengthening and weakening, and nondefault feature insertion rules are sometimes needed to express the introduction of marked feature values. Other possible rule types include fusion (or merger), proposed to account for various types of feature coalescence processes (Mester 1986; Schane 1987; de Haas 1988), and fission, designed to account for diphthongization and other types of "breaking" phenomena (Clements 1989b). Among these various rule types, however, those which reorganize patterns of association among existing nodes (spreading, delinking) appear to represent the least marked case.

To summarize, the feature theory presented here assumes a small set of elementary rule types which carry out single operations on feature representations. It adopts the strong hypothesis that all genuine phonological rules fall into one of these elementary types. This result takes us a step closer to the elusive goal of characterizing the class of "natural" rules in formal terms.

2.5 *Transparency and Opacity*

Another classical issue in phonological theory is that of delimiting the domain within which rules may apply. It has long been known that rules may affect not only adjacent segments, but also segments that occur at some distance from each other. For example, rules of vowel harmony and assimilation typically apply from vowel to vowel, regardless of intervening consonants (see Clements and Sezer 1982, McCarthy 1984, van der Hulst 1985, and Archangeli and Pulleyblank 1989 for representative examples and analyses). Similarly, and more dramatically, many languages allow long-distance assimilations in which one consonant affects another across any number of intervening consonants at other places of articulation; languages that have been studied include Chumash (Poser 1982), Sanskrit (Schein and Steriade 1986), and Tahtlan (Shaw 1991). Dissimilatory rules, too, often operate at a distance (Itô and Mester 1986; McConvell 1988). Nevertheless, if we set aside the special case of languages with nonconcatenative morphologies (McCarthy 1981, 1985, 1989a), we find that there are important limits on how far a rule can "reach" across intervening material to affect a distant segment. In particular, it appears that assimilation rules cannot reach across "opaque" segments – segments that are already characterized by the spreading node or feature (Clements 1980; Clements and Sezer 1982; Steriade 1987a).

These limits follow, at least in part, from structural properties of the representations themselves. Of particular importance is the prohibition on crossed association lines (Goldsmith 1976), which we state in its most general form as follows:

(27)   No-Crossing Constraint (NCC)
       Association lines linking two elements on tier j to two elements on tier k may not cross.

This constraint applies as shown below, allowing representations like (28a), but ruling out those like (28b):

(28)   (a)   Tier j: P   Q   (b)   Tier j: P   Q

       Tier k: R   S   Tier k: R   S

The NCC applies not only to underlying, but also to derived representations, where it serves as an absolute constraint blocking any rule application which would produce a violation of it. Consequently, it will prevent an assimilation rule from spreading a feature [F] across a segment already specified for [F], accounting for opacity effects of the sort described above. (An example will be given in the next section.)

3   Toward a Formal Model of Feature Organization

We now consider the model of feature organization in more detail. We assume a metatheoretical principle that features have minimal hierarchical organization in the absence of evidence to the contrary. We next consider what evidence to the contrary might consist of.

3.1   *Evidence for Feature Organization*

We have already examined several types of evidence for feature organization. The most important of these is the operation of phonological rules. Thus, if a phonological rule can be shown to perform an operation (spreading, delinking, etc.) on a given set of features to the exclusion of others, we assume that the set forms a constituent in the feature hierarchy.

Two features *x* and *y* can be grouped into constituents in four ways, as shown below:

(29)   x dominates y   y dominates x   x and y are   x and y form one
                                                   sisters   node

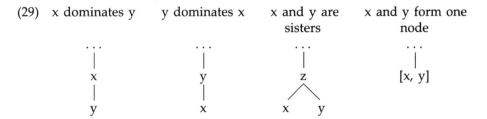

If an operation on *x* always affects *y*, but not vice versa, the first configuration is motivated. If an operation on *y* always affects *x*, but not vice versa, the second is required. If *x* and *y* can be affected independently of each other, they are each independently linked to a higher node *z*, as shown in the third figure. Finally, if an operation on one always affects the other, they form a single node, as shown at the right.

Another criterion for feature organization is the presence of OCP-driven co-occurrence restrictions. As the previous discussion has shown, any feature or set of features targeted by such constraints must form an independent node in the representation.

A further criterion, but one which must be used with caution, is node implication. If a node *x* is always linked under *y* in the universal feature organization, the presence of (nonfloating) *x* implies the presence of *y*. For example, since [anterior] is universally linked under the [coronal] node, we predict that all [±anterior] segments are coronal. Note, however, that not all implicational relations among nodes can be expressed in this way. For example, although all [+consonantal] segments must have a place node, the place node must be lower in the hierarchy, since place can spread independently of [consonantal] (Halle 1989; and see section 3.3.2 below). Similarly, for reasons that have nothing to do with node organization as presently conceived, all [−consonantal] segments are [−lateral] and [+sonorant], all [−continuant] obstruents are [−nasal], and all [+low, −back] vowels are [−rounded]. Thus while it is possible to capture some implicational relations directly in terms of the dependency relation, others must apparently be expressed in terms of explicit wellformedness conditions.

One further criterion for feature organization consists of transparency and opacity effects, as discussed in section 2.5. To see how these effects bear upon feature organization, let us consider the phenomenon of *laryngeal transparency* as discussed by Steriade (1987b). In a number of languages, including Acoma, Nez Perce, Arbore, and Yokuts, vowels assimilate in all features to adjacent vowels, but not to nonadjacent vowels. Exceptionally, laryngeal glides [h, ʔ] are transparent to this assimilation; thus in Arbore, assimilation crosses the laryngeal in examples like /(ma) beh-o/ "he is not going out" → [. . . boho]. This behavior can be explained on the assumption that laryngeal glides, unlike true consonants and vowels, have no distinctive oral tract features. In this view, [h] is only characterized by the laryngeal feature [+spread glottis] (Clements 1985), acquiring its oral tract phonetic characteristics from its phonetic context (Keating 1988). The transparency of laryngeal glides and the opacity of true consonants follows from the structure of their respective representations, as shown below (irrelevant details omitted):

(30) (a) VV   (b) VhV   (c) VCV

   V V   V h V   *V C V

  root root   root root root root root root

  place place   place   place place place place

In (30a), the place node of the first vowel spreads to the root node of the following vowel, triggering the delinking of its original place node (indicated by the ≠). Spreading may also take place in (30b), since the intervening [h] has no place node to block the spreading. In (30c), however, vowel-to-vowel spreading cannot take place without introducing crossed lines, in violation of the No-Crossing Constraint (27). The transparency of [h] is therefore fully predictable from the fact that it is not characterized by place features.[18]

 With this background, let us consider feature organization in more detail.

3.2 *The Root Node*

The root node, dominating all features, expresses the coherence of the "melodic" segment as a phonological unit. There is considerable evidence in favor of a root node, which we touched on briefly in section 2. We have seen, for example, that processes of total assimilation in languages such as Ancient Greek can be expressed as the spreading of the root node from one skeletal position to another. Without the root node, such processes would have to be expressed as the spreading of several lower-level nodes at once, contrary to principle (4).

 We have also seen that the different phonological behavior of short segments, contour segments, and geminate segments can be insightfully accounted for in terms of different patterns of linkage between root nodes and skeletal positions. Other evidence for the root node can be drawn from segment-level metathesis, segmental deletion, rules mapping segments to morphological template positions, and OCP effects on the root node (as just discussed in Arabic), as well as from the fact that single segments commonly constitute entire morphological formatives in their own right, while subparts of segments rarely do. All of these phenomena would be difficult to express without the root node.

 Schein and Steriade (1986) and McCarthy (1988) propose to assign a special status to the root node by allowing it to bear the major class features, which we take to be [sonorant], [approximant], and [vocoid] (the terminological converse of [consonantal]). The unity of these features derives from their role in defining the major sonority classes, obstruent, nasal, liquid, and vocoid. Given these features, sonority rank is a simple function of positive feature values (Clements 1990a).

(31)

	[sonorant]	[approximant]	[vocoid]	sonority rank
obstruent	−	−	−	0
nasal	+	−	−	1
liquid	+	+	−	2
vocoid	+	+	+	3

The assignment of the sonority features directly to the root node predicts that they can never spread or delink as a class independently of the root node as a whole. This prediction seems largely correct, though see Kaisse (1992) for proposed cases of [consonantal] ([vocoid]) spreading. Assuming it is generally true, we have the following representation of the root node:

(32)
$$
\begin{bmatrix}
\text{sonorant} \\
\text{approximant} \\
\text{vocoid}
\end{bmatrix}
$$

Christdas (1988) and Clements (1990a) propose that sonority features are present and fully specified in underlying representation, at least to the extent necessary to "drive" the process of core syllabification and account for root structure constraints.[19]

Piggott (1987) proposes that [nasal] attaches under the root node on a tier of its own. In Sagey's model (1986), [nasal] links to the root through an intervening soft palate node, representing its articulator.

3.3 The Feature Organization of Consonants

3.3.1 The Laryngeal Node

Primary motivation for a laryngeal node comes from the fact that laryngeal features may spread and delink not only individually, but as a unit. For example, in Proto-Indo-Iranian, voicing and aspiration spread bidirectionally as a unit from voiced aspirates to adjacent obstruents (Schindler 1976). In the Shapsug dialect of West Circassian, the distinction among voiceless aspirated, plain voiced, and glottalic (ejective) stops and fricatives is lost in preconsonantal position, the surface phonation of the cluster as a whole being determined by its final member (Smeets 1984). Similarly, in Korean, as noted in section 2.3, the three-way lexical contrast among plain, aspirated, and "tense" (glottalized) obstruents is neutralized to a plain unreleased type in syllable coda position.

To express these facts, we assign the laryngeal features to separate tiers and group them under a laryngeal node, which links in turn to the root node:

(33)

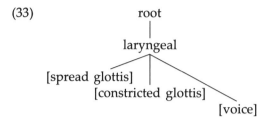

It may be preferable to characterize voicing by the features [stiff vocal cords] and [slack vocal cords] (Halle and Stevens 1971). Bao (1990) suggests that [stiff] and [slack] may form one constituent under the laryngeal node, and [spread] and [constricted] another.

3.3.2   The Place Node

In rules of place assimilation, the oral tract place features [labial], [coronal], and [dorsal] and their dependents spread as a single unit, independently of stricture features such as [continuant], [vocoid], and [sonorant]. We may capture this fact by grouping them under a single place node, as illustrated in (34).

(34)

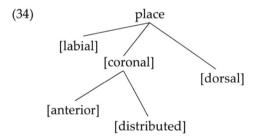

Nasals commonly assimilate to the place of articulation of following stops. Although it is rarer to find nasal assimilation before fricatives and approximants, a number of cases of this type have been reported. In Chukchi, underlying /ŋ/ assimilates to the place of articulation of following consonants, including fricatives, liquids, and glides (Bogoras 1922; Krause 1980; Odden 1987; *v* is a bilabial continuant):[20]

(35)   təŋ-əɬʔ-ən   "good" /tEŋ -/
       tam-pera-k   "to look good"
       tam-vairgin   "good being"
       tam-waɣərɣ-ən   "good life"
       tan-tˢai   "good tea"

ten-leut	"good head"
tan-ran	"good house"
ten-yəɬqət-ək	"to sleep well"

In each case, the nasal assimilates to the place, but not the stricture of the following consonant. Similar examples of place assimilating independently from stricture features can be cited from Yoruba (Ward 1952), Catalan (Kiparsky 1985), and the Yongding dialect of Chinese (Dell 1993), among many others.

Besides spreading, the place node can be delinked, accounting for debuccalization processes such as t > ʔ and s > h (McCarthy 1988). Note that debuccalized sounds are always realized as [−consonantal] ([+vocoid]) glides. This fact follows directly from the standard definition of [+consonantal] ([−vocoid]) segments as sounds produced with a radical obstruction in the midsaggital region of the vocal tract (Chomsky and Halle 1968). Sounds without oral place features can have no such obstruction, and so are necessarily nonconsonantal.

It will be noted that on this analysis, if the place node of a nasal is delinked, the feature [+nasal], which links to the root node, should remain behind. This prediction receives some support from patterns of sound change in Malay dialects observed by Trigo (1988, 1991). The evolution of final stops, fricatives, and nasals in two dialects is summarized below:

(36) (a) p, t, k > ʔ
    (b) s, f, h > h
    (c) m, n, ŋ > N (a placeless nasal glide)

The first two sets of changes (a, b) represent standard examples of debuccalization. We might suppose that the glottal features of [ʔ] and [h] were present redundantly in stops and fricatives, respectively, at the point when delinking took place, accounting for their presence in the debuccalized forms. Crucially, set (c) shows that when a nasal is debuccalized, [+nasal] is left behind. This gives direct evidence that the place node is delinked, since if the root node were delinked instead, [+nasal] should have been delinked with it. The simplest account of these phenomena (though not necessarily the historically correct one) is that the place node was deleted in all cases. Laryngeal features and [+nasal] are not affected, and the resulting segment is shifted to a [+vocoid] glide due to its lack of a place node.

3.3.3 The Oral Cavity Node

In some presentations of feature geometry, the place node links directly to the root node. However, recent work has brought to light evidence in favor of an *oral cavity* node intervening between the place node and the root node, dominating place and [±continuant] nodes. This constituent corresponds to the articulatory notion "oral cavity constriction," and characterizes it as a functional unit in the phonology.

We illustrate this node with the process of intrusive stop formation (ISF) found in many varieties of English (Clements 1987). By this process, words like *dense* and (for some speakers) *false* acquire a brief, intrusive [t] at the point of transition from the nasal or lateral to the following fricative, making them sound similar to *dents* and *faults*. The intrusive element always has the same place of articulation as the consonant on its left, as we see in further examples like *warmth* [... mᵖθ] and *length* [... ŋᵏθ]. Phonetic studies show that the intrusive stop is shorter by a small but significant margin than the underlying stop found in words like *dents* and *faults* (Fourakis and Port 1986).

Traditional accounts have sometimes viewed ISF as involving an anticipation of the orality of the fricative on the preceding nasal; however, such accounts do not explain why this process may also apply after laterals. A unified account of ISF is possible if we view it as involving a lag of the oral cavity constriction of the nasal or lateral into the following fricative. In pronouncing a word like *warmth*, for example, speakers prolong the labial occlusion of the [m] into the [θ], producing a "hybrid" segment having the labial closure of the [m] but all other features of the [θ], in other words, a [p]. This process can be formalized as a rule spreading the oral cavity node rightward onto the root node of the fricative. We illustrate its effect below:

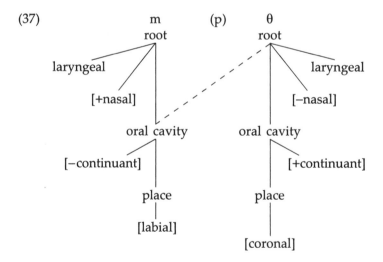

(37)

In the derived representation, [θ] bears two oral cavity nodes in succession, the labial stop node of the [m] followed by the coronal continuant node of the [θ]. Thus the two oral cavity nodes form a "contour" across the [θ], in just the same way that two tones may form a contour across a single vowel in the case of rising and falling tones (see (2b) above). In this analysis, the intrusive stop [p] is not a full segment in its own right, but results from the partial overlap of the oral cavity node of [m] with the other features of [θ]. The fact that the intrusive stop is significantly shorter in duration than an underlying stop can be explained in terms of the fact that it constitutes part of a contour segment.[21]

It will be noted that the derived segment [ᵖθ] has the internal structure of an affricate under the root node, in that it consists of a stop [p] followed by a fricative [θ]. Recall, however, that the No Branching Constraint (11) prohibits such branching structure under the root. In line with our earlier discussion, we assume that (37) is automatically converted into a structure with two root nodes by the appropriate repair convention.[22]

For alternative proposals which bundle [continuant] into a single constituent with the place features, equally consistent with the analysis of intrusive stop formation proposed here (though differing in other empirical predictions), see Selkirk 1990 and Padgett 1991.

3.3.4 The Pharyngeal (or Guttural) Node

In many languages, we find that glottal, pharyngeal, and uvular sounds define a natural class, often referred to as "gutturals." For example, in Classical Arabic many rules and constraints are defined on the [+approximant] subclass of these sounds consisting of the laryngeals [h ʔ], the pharyngeals [ħ ʕ], and the uvular continuants [χ ʁ] (Hayward and Hayward 1989; McCarthy 1989b, in press); thus with very few exceptions, no roots may contain two sounds of this group. The class of "guttural" sounds can be characterized by the feature [guttural] (Hayward and Hayward) or [pharyngeal] (McCarthy).

While this feature is now established beyond reasonable doubt, its exact status and relation to other features is still uncertain. McCarthy points out that it cannot be an articulator feature on a par with [labial], [coronal], etc., since it cannot be defined in terms of the movement of any single articulator. Rather, what the sounds of this class have in common is that they are articulated in a continuous region of the vocal tract, extending approximately from the upper pharynx to the larynx, inclusively.

There are currently two main theories of how the feature [guttural] (or [pharyngeal]) is to be integrated into the feature hierarchy. McCarthy suggests that [pharyngeal] links under the place constituent together with the oral tract place features [labial], [coronal], and [dorsal]. A potential problem for such an analysis is the phenomenon of "guttural transparency," according to which guttural sounds, and no others, may be transparent to rules spreading vowel place features. In Tigre, for example, the underlying /ə/ of the prefix /tə-/ assimilates to the following [a] across the guttural [ʕ] in words like ta-ʕārafa "he visited", but does not assimilate across the uvular [q] in words like tə-qābala "he met", since [q], though a guttural sound, is [dorsal] as well as [pharyngeal]. To accommodate such facts, McCarthy proposes to group the oral place features into a single "oral" constituent which forms a sister to [pharyngeal]. This conception is illustrated in (38a), after McCarthy (in press).

(38)   (a)   McCarthy (in press)   (b)   Halle (1989, 1992)

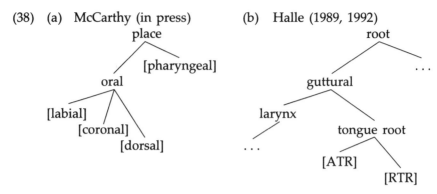

The Tigre rule may be expressed as the spreading of the oral node from the root vowel to the prefix vowel; spreading will be blocked by the No-Crossing Constraint (27) just in case the intervening consonant bears any oral feature such as [dorsal].

An alternative view, illustrated in (38b), is proposed by Halle (1989, 1992). Halle argues that since the guttural sounds are not defined by the activity of any single articulator, they should not be assigned an articulator node on a par with [labial], [coronal], and [dorsal]. Instead, he proposes to group the gutturals under a higher-level "guttural" node, which groups the laryngeal articulator ("larynx") and its dependent features on the one hand, and the tongue root articulator and its dependent features [ATR] (Advanced Tongue Root) and [RTR] (Retracted Tongue Root) on the other. In this model, the Tigre assimilation rule can be expressed as ordinary spreading of the place node, and the oral node is not needed.[23]

While both of these conceptions are consistent with the guttural transparency phenomenon, they make substantially different predictions in other respects. Given that laryngeal features are sufficient to characterize the laryngeals [h ʔ], McCarthy's model does not straightforwardly predict that these segments pattern with the gutturals, unless, following McCarthy, we allow them to bear the redundant specification [pharyngeal]. Halle's model predicts that obstruents with distinctive laryngeal features such as [+voiced] or [+spread glottis] can potentially pattern with the gutturals by virtue of their guttural node. Perhaps the central difference, however, regards their claims concerning possible spreading and delinking rules. McCarthy's model predicts that we should find rules spreading or delinking [pharyngeal] together with the oral tract place features, while Halle's predicts rules that spread or delink laryngeal and tongue root features as a unit. To date, no fully conclusive evidence has been brought to bear on these predictions.

3.4   *The Feature Organization of Vocoids*

We now consider the feature organization of vocoids, that is, vowels and glides. A long-standing issue in phonological theory has been the extent to which consonants and vocoids are classified by the same set of features. While most linguists agree that they share such features as [sonorant], [nasal], and [voiced], at least at the level at which nondistinctive feature values are specified, there has been much less agreement regarding the extent to which features of place of articulation and stricture are shared. The articulator-based framework of feature representation, as described above, has made it possible to offer a more integrated approach to this problem. In this section we first outline two approaches inspired by this general framework, and then consider some of the differences between them.

3.4.1   An Articulator-based Model

In the earlier of these approaches, Sagey (1986) retains the SPE features [high], [low], [back], and [round]. She integrates them within the articulator-based framework by treating them as articulator-bound features, linked under the appropriate articulator node. Thus [back], [high], and [low], as features executed by the tongue body, are linked under the dorsal node, and [round], as a feature executed by the lips, is assigned to the labial node, as shown below:

(39)

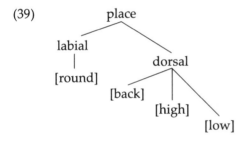

In this model, all consonants and vocoids formed in the oral tract are characterized in terms of an appropriate selection from the set of articulator nodes and their dependents, although coronal, reserved for retroflex vowels, is usually nondistinctive in vocoids. One of the central predictions of this model is that the set [back], [high], and [low], as features of the dorsal node, has a privileged status among subsets of vowel features, in that it alone can function as a single phonological unit.

3.4.2   A Constriction-based Model

A second approach, emanating from work by Clements (1989a, 1991, 1993), Herzallah (1990), and Hume (1992), proposes to unify the description of consonants and vocoids in a somewhat different way. This model is based on the preliminary observation that any segment produced in the oral tract has a characteristic *constriction*, defined by two principal parameters, constriction degree and constriction location. Since vocal tract constrictions determine the shape of the acoustic signal and thus contribute directly to the way in which speech is perceived, they can be regarded as constituting the effective goal of articulatory activity.

Given their centrality in speech communication, it would not be surprising to find that constrictions play a direct role in phonological representation itself. This is the view adopted by the model under discussion, which proposes to represent constrictions by a separate node of their own in the feature hierarchy. The parameters of constriction degree and location are also represented as separate nodes, which link under the constriction node. This type of organization was already proposed for consonants above, in which the constriction itself is represented by the oral cavity node, constriction degree by the [±continuant] node, and constriction location by the place node; this conception is summarized in (40a). A parallel structure can be assigned to vocoids, as shown in (40b). In this figure, the constriction of a vocoid is represented by its vocalic node, its constriction degree by an aperture node, and its constriction location by a place node. As in the case of consonantal constrictions, these nodes have no intrinsic content, and receive their interpetation by virtue of the feature values they dominate. In these figures, place nodes of consonants and vocoids, which occur on different tiers, are designated as "C-place" and "V-place," respectively.

(40)   (a)   Consonants   (b)   Vocoids

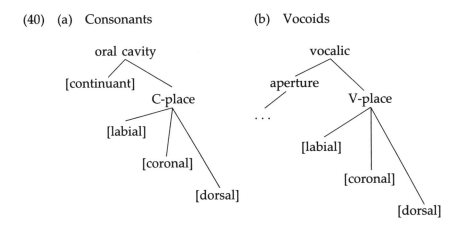

The aperture node dominates vowel height features, represented by the ellipsis, which are discussed further in section 3.4.5 below.

A further innovation of this model is that the features [labial], [coronal], and [dorsal], occurring under the V-place node in vocoids, are sufficient, by themselves, to distinguish place of articulation in vowels, and replace the traditional features [back] and [round]. In order to fulfill this new and expanded role in the theory, they must be redefined in terms of constrictions rather than articulator movements as such. This can be done as follows, to a first approximation (compare the definitions given earlier in (7)):[24]

(41) Labial: involving a constriction formed by the lower lip
     Coronal: involving a constriction formed by the front of the tongue
     Dorsal: involving a constriction formed by the back of the tongue
              (= the dorsum, cf. Ladefoged 1982, p. 281)

These statements, valid for consonants and vocoids alike, define constriction location in terms of the active articulator involved. Since all segments with oral tract constrictions are formed by the lips or the tongue body, all are characterized by at least one of these three features. As far as vocoids are concerned, rounded vocoids are [labial] by these definitions, front vocoids are [coronal], and back vocoids are [dorsal]. Central vocoids satisfy none of the definitions in (41), and are thus treated as phonologically placeless. These features appear sufficient to characterize all phonologically relevant properties of constriction location in vocoids, and make the features [back] and [round] superfluous (Clements 1989b, 1991b, 1993).

A constriction-based model incorporating the definitions in (41) makes a number of different predictions from Sagey's model regarding the phonological behavior of vocoids. First, the constriction-based model predicts that front vowels can form a natural class with coronal consonants, and back vowels with dorsal consonants, while Sagey's model predicts that all vowels form a natural class with dorsal consonants and no others. Second, the constriction-based model predicts that the aperture features, the V-place features, or the aperture and V-place features together can function as single units in phonological rules, while Sagey's model predicts that only the dorsal features [high, back, low] can do so. Third, the constriction-based model predicts that dorsal consonants (or at least "plain" dorsals with no secondary articulation, see below) will be transparent to rules spreading any two or more vowel features, while Sagey's model predicts that dorsal consonants are opaque to such rules, which must spread the dorsal node. Fourth, the constriction-based model predicts that not only dorsals but *all* ("plain") consonants will be transparent to rules spreading lip rounding together with one or more vowel features, while Sagey's model predicts that all intervening (supralaryngeal) consonants will be opaque to such rules, which must spread the place node. We examine these predictions in turn.

3.4.3 Natural Classes of Consonants and Vowels

The constriction-based model predicts that we should find a natural class corresponding to each of the oral tract place features, as shown below:

(42) [labial]:   labial consonants; rounded or labialized vocoids
     [coronal]: coronal consonants; front vocoids
     [dorsal]:   dorsal consonants; back vocoids

Each of these classes is, in fact, well documented in the literature. Of these, the first is the least controversial, since it has been recognized and discussed since the early studies of Reighard (1972) and Campbell (1974); see Selkirk (1988), Capo (1989), and Clements (1990b, 1993) for further examples. As both of the models under consideration account for this class, we will consider here only the other two.

The interaction of coronal consonants and front vowels is covered by the surveys in Clements 1976, 1990b, 1993; Pulleyblank 1989; Hume 1992; Blust 1992; and references therein. For example, in many languages, velar and/or labial consonants become coronal, and anterior coronals become posterior, before front vowels. This process, sometimes termed palatalization, may be better termed *coronalization* since the resulting sound, though coronal, is not necessarily either palatal or palatalized (Mester and Itô 1989, who attribute the term to Morris Halle and Alan Prince). While the appearance of coronal consonants in the context of front vowels has sometimes been treated in terms of automatic linking conventions or similarly arbitrary mechanisms, it can be viewed as a straightforward case of assimilation if front vowels are treated as [coronal] themselves; see the references above as well as Broselow and Niyondagara 1989; Mester and Itô 1989; and Lahiri and Evers 1991 for further discussion. We take a closer look at coronalization (and palatalization) rules in section 4.

In parallel fashion, vowels are fronted next to coronal consonants in a number of languages. The triggering consonant may be, but is not necessarily palatal. In Maltese Arabic, for example, the vowel of the imperfective prefix is always predictable. It is generally realized as a copy of the stem vowel, as shown in the second column of (43a) (the perfective stem is given to the left for comparison). However, when the following consonant is a coronal obstruent, the prefix vowel is systematically realized as the high front vowel [i], as shown in (43b).

(43)   perfective   imperfective
     (a) kotor   yo-ktor   "abound"
          rifed   yi-rfed   "support"   /rifid/
          ʔasam   ya-ʔsam   "break"
          ħebel   ye-ħbel   "rave"
     (b) ʃorob   yi-ʃrob   "drink"
          dalam   yi-dlam   "grow dark"
          žabar   yi-žbor   "collect"
          seħet   yi-sħet   "curse"

Hume (1992) points out that the pattern in (43b) cannot plausibly be attributed to default rules, and argues that it results from the spreading of [coronal] from the consonant to the vowel.

Co-occurrence constraints also reveal the special relation of front vowels and coronal consonants. In Cantonese, for example, among other patterns, if the onset and coda of a given syllable are both coronal, any non-low vowel must be one of the front vowels [i e ü ö] (Cheng 1989). Thus, while the words [tit] "iron", [tüt] "to take off", and [tön] "a shield" are well-formed, words like *[tut], *[tsot], *[sut] are excluded. Here, then, a vowel flanked by two [coronal] consonants assimilates their coronality.

Korean has a particularly interesting dissimilatory constraint, with further implications for feature organization. In underlying representations, coronal obstruents do not occur with front glides in word-initial syllables, nor do front glides occur with high front vowels; thus, syllables containing such sequences as *ty, *sy, *cy, *yi are systematically excluded (Clements 1990b, 1993, after Martin 1951). This pattern can be understood as an OCP-driven constraint against occurrences of [coronal] in successive segments, meeting the conditions just stated. This analysis is supported by parallel OCP-driven constraints involving labiality (*pw, *mw, *wu, etc.). In Korean, then, it appears that the OCP applies "cross-categorially" to rule out sequences of consonants and vocoids having identical occurrences of the features [coronal] and [labial]. Note, however, that the OCP as stated in (23) only applies to nodes which are adjacent, and hence located on the same tier. To extend the OCP to Korean (and similar cases in other languages), Hume (1992) proposes that each articulator feature of a given category should be assigned to the same tier whether it characterizes a consonant or a vocoid.[25] This proposal assigns the following structure to sequences like /ty/.

(44)

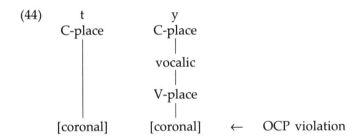

Since both instances of [coronal] lie on the same tier, they trigger the OCP as stated in (23).

There is also considerable evidence that back (but not front) vocoids and dorsal consonants form a natural class, defined by [dorsal]. For example, in the Khoisan languages of southern Africa, only back vowels may occur after velar and uvular consonants, including clicks (Traill 1985). Assuming that all clicks have a [dorsal] component (Sagey 1986; Bradlow 1992), we may view this as a syllable structure constraint spreading [dorsal] from the consonant to the vowel. We find a dissimilatory process at work in the historical development of French, where velar and labial consonants were deleted in intervocalic position when flanked on either side by one of the rounded (i.e., labiovelar) vowels [u o]; examples of velar deletion include Lat. *fagu* > *fau* (MFr. *fou*) "crazy", Lat. *ruga* > *rue* "street" (Clements 1990b, 1993, after Bourciez and Bourciez 1967). We may regard this deletion process as OCP-driven on the assumption that velars and back rounded vowels share the feature [dorsal]; were front vowels dorsal they should have triggered the deletion, too. Further examples of back vowel/velar consonant interaction are discussed in Clements (1990b, 1993), Herzallah (1990), Blust (1992), and Dell (1993).[26]

In sum, phonological rules offer considerable evidence for the natural classes of labial, coronal, and dorsal consonants and vocoids as stated in (42). This result supports a unified account of place in consonants and vowels, in which [labial], [coronal], and [dorsal] do double duty for consonants and vocoids, allowing the standard features [back] and [round] to be eliminated. (For other recent proposals to unify the feature characterization of consonants and vowels within comparable frameworks, see Pulleyblank 1989 and Gorecka 1989.) Let us now examine the internal structure of vocoids in more detail.

3.4.4   *The V-place Node*

In the constriction-based model, as we have seen, vocalic constrictions are defined in terms of the parameters of location (place) and degree (aperture). As Odden (1991) particularly has pointed out (though from a somewhat different perspective), there is considerable phonological evidence for a division of vowel features into these two general categories.

As far as place is concerned, Odden offers evidence from several languages that the features of backness and roundness, i.e., our [labial], [coronal], and [dorsal], function as a single unit. For example, Eastern Cheremis has the vowel set /i ü u e ö o a/, in which both backness and rounding are distinctive, as well as a neutral vowel /ə/. Word-final /e/ assimilates in backness and roundness, but not height, to the first preceding non-neutral vowel if it is labial; thus /e/ surfaces as [o] after [u, o] and [ö] after [ü, ö]. Examples are given in (45).

(45)   kit-še   "his hand"
       ergə-že   "his boy"
       šužar-že   "his sister"
       surt-šo   "his house"
       üp-šö   "his hair"
       boz-šo   "his wagon"
       šör-žö   "its milk"

There is good reason not to analyze vowel assimilation as two separate rules, one spreading backness and another roundness, since, as Odden points out, both rules would apply under exactly the same conditions and have exactly the same set of exceptions. The patterning of backness and roundness together to the exclusion of vowel height argues that these features form a single constituent, which we take to be the vocalic place (or V-place) node (Odden's node labels are somewhat different).

In the spirit of Odden's analysis, we assume that the rule of vowel assimilation spreads the V-place node of a [labial] vowel rightward onto a final mid vowel unspecified for a place node, i.e., in the unmarked, feature-filling mode, as shown in (46). If the spreading place node has a dependent [coronal] feature as in the case of [ü ö], this feature will spread as well. Since the aperture node is not linked under V-place, it is not affected. (Note that intervening consonants are not specified for vocalic and V-place nodes, and so will not block the rule.)

(46)

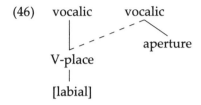

Other examples are cited from a variety of languages (see Odden for further discussion and references). As Odden remarks, this type of assimilation cannot be accounted for within Sagey's model, in which the spreading features do not form a single constituent of their own.

3.4.5 The Aperture Node

Consider next constriction degree. Hyman (1988), Clements (1989b, 1991) and Odden (1991) have presented evidence from several languages that vowel height features may spread as a single unit, supporting the aperture (or vowel height) node proposed above. Here we consider a further illustration from Brazilian Portuguese, discussed by Quicoli (1990) and Wetzels (1993).

Brazilian Portuguese vowels form a four-height system, /i u e o ɛ ɔ a/. Underlying mid stem vowels undergo an interesting pattern of alternation in stressed prevocalic position, as is shown by a comparison between 2nd and 1st person forms of the present indicative. (The structure of these examples is: stem + theme vowel + person/number ending.)

(47) 2nd person: 1st person:
      mɔr-a-s   [mɔ́ras]   "you reside"   mɔr-a-o   [mɔ́ro]   "I reside"
      mɔv-e-s   [mɔ́ves]   "you move"   mɔv-e-o   [móvo]   "I move"
      sɛrv-i-s [sɛ́rves] "you serve"   sɛrv-i-o [sírvo] "I serve"

In the 1st person forms, the mid stem vowels assimilate to the height of the following non-low "theme" vowel, becoming upper mid before [-e] and high before [-i]; the theme vowel is concomitantly deleted. No assimilation takes place in the 2nd person forms. This pattern is regular across the verb conjugation.

In his analysis of these forms, Wetzels proposes that theme vowels are deleted in hiatus before another vowel. However, by a "stability" effect similar to that found in many tone languages, their aperture node relinks to the stem vowel, replacing its original node. This analysis is illustrated below, where "(V)" represents the skeletal position of the deleted theme vowel. (As the stem consonant is not specified for vocalic and aperture nodes, it does not block the rule.)

(48)

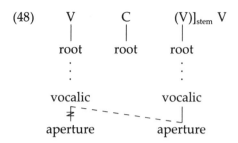

Unlinked nodes under the deleted vowel slot are subsequently deleted. As Wetzels points out, this rule (and many similar rules of height assimilation discussed in the literature) cannot be expressed as a unitary process if the aperture features are not grouped into a single unit, in the general framework assumed here.

We have not so far discussed the vowel height features as such. Traditionally, generative phonologists have used the binary features [high] and [low] to distinguish among high, mid, and low vowels, and have added a further feature such as [tense] or [ATR] to express a fourth height if necessary. These features are assumed in the geometries proposed by Sagey (1986), Hyman (1988), and Odden (1991), among others, and continue to represent the main trend in the field. However, vowel height has received a good deal of attention in recent years, and several alternative systems have been proposed. We discuss two here, both of which model vowel height in terms of aperture rather than tongue body height, consistent with the general assumptions of a constriction-based framework.

In one, vowel height (together with other vowel features) is treated as a privative feature called a particle or component, usually represented *a*, interpreted as vocal tract aperture (Schane 1984; Rennison 1986; Anderson and Ewen 1987). If it stands alone, this feature designates the low vowel [a], and if it is combined with other features, it designates vowels with some degree of openness (for example, when combined with the palatal component *i* it designates a relatively open palatal vowel such as [e] or [ɛ]). This model directly expresses the fact that when [a] coalesces with [i], the result is usually a nonhigh vowel such as [e]; this follows from the fact that [e] is just the combination of the particles *a* and *i*. A problem, however, results from its failure to provide a feature or particle corresponding to [+high] or [−low]: it is unable to express assimilatory vowel raising in terms of autosegmental spreading. Yet assimilatory raising is common across languages, and exhibits characteristics quite parallel to assimilatory lowering (see, e.g., Clements 1991; Kaze 1991).

A second alternative to the standard system, proposed by Clements (1989b, 1991), proposes a single feature [±open]. Unlike the particle *a*, [open] is a binary feature, either value of which may spread. To express various degrees of vowel height, the feature [open] is arrayed on several rank-ordered tiers. On the highest-ranked tier, [open] assigns vowels to one of two primary height registers, [−open] (relatively high) and [+open] (relatively low). Any height register can be subdivided by further assignments of [open] on the next lower-ranked tier. For example, the familiar three-height system /i u e o a/ can be represented as shown below (redundant feature values included), where the higher of the two primary registers, designated by the [–open] specifications on tier 1, is subdivided into higher and lower secondary registers on tier 2:

(49)

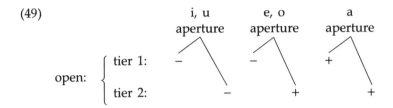

Natural classes are defined in terms of feature values on each tier. Thus low vowels are those which are [+open] on tier 1, high vowels are [–open] on tier 2, and so forth. In this system, assimilatory raising is stated as the spread of [–open] to [+open] on a designated tier. If no tier is specified, raising applies across all tiers, producing (if the rule is structure-preserving) the effect of stepwise or scalar raising.

One advantage of both of these approaches is that they allow us to eliminate the use of [ATR] as an ersatz vowel height feature, i.e., one motivated only by the need to describe a fourth height; this is because systems with four or more vowel heights can be analyzed in terms of additional *a*-particles or [open] tiers. Such analyses are strongly motivated in languages like Kimatuumbi in which "[ATR]" spreads with other features of vowel height (Odden 1991), since if [ATR] were really involved, one would expect it to spread with place features, not height features.[27]

3.4.6 The Vocalic Node

Let us now consider the status of the vocalic constriction node itself, which we called *vocalic* in (40).[28] By grouping all place and aperture features of vocoids under the vocalic node, we predict that all these features should be able to spread freely across intervening consonants, even if they are specified for place features of their own. This is because consonants (at least those with no secondary articulations; see below) have no vocalic node that would block them.

There is considerable evidence that this prediction is correct. An example can be cited from the Servigliano dialect of Italian, as described by Camilli (1929).[29] The vowel system of Servigliano is /i u e o ɛ ɔ a/, which is reduced to [i u e o a] in unstressed positions. The following examples illustrate a regular pattern of alternation involving post-tonic stem vowels (note that all final vowels in these examples are suffixes):

(50) birikɔ́kan-a "apricot tree"   birikókun-u "apricot"
      pɛ́tten-e   "comb"   pɛ́ttin-i   "combs"
      álam-a   "soul"   álem-e   "souls"
      prédok-o   "I preach"   prédik-i   "you preach"
      stómmuk-u   "stomach"   stómmik-i   "stomachs"

Strikingly, the final stem vowel is identical to the suffix vowel in all cases. Related forms such as predik-á "to preach", with stem vowel [i], and stomme-k-ósa "nauseating" (fem. sg.), with stem vowel [e], show that this vowel may have a different, unpredictable form in pretonic position, and must thus be specified for at least some features in underlying representation. It appears then, that we must postulate a total vowel assimilation rule which spreads the features of the suffix vowel to a post-tonic stem vowel. Crucial to the point at issue, all consonants are transparent, whatever their places and manners of articulation.

Let us consider how this rule can be expressed in terms of the feature hierarchy. Since the vocalic node plays a role similar (if not identical) to that of Sagey's dorsal node in the analysis of vocoids, we assume that it is linked to the same position, that is, under the place (i.e., C-place) node. The rule then applies as follows:

(51)

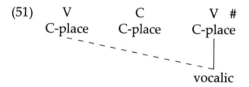

The Sageyian model cannot express the alternations in (50) straightforwardly, since the spreading of more than one vowel feature at a time can only be expressed as the spreading of the dorsal node, or a higher node (see (39)). This model predicts that velar consonants, which are [dorsal], should be opaque, but as the last examples show, this prediction is incorrect.[30]

Other ways of linking the vocalic node are equally consistent with the evidence from total vowel assimilation rules; for example, it could be linked directly to the root node.[31] However, the linkage given above is supported by further evidence, which we discuss in the following sections.

3.5 Major and Minor Articulations

A further source of evidence for feature organization comes from the study of so-called secondary articulations. Phoneticians define a secondary articulation as "an articulation with a lesser degree of closure occurring at the same time as another (primary) articulation" (Ladefoged 1982, p. 210), and usually reserve the term for inherent, as opposed to contextually-determined, articulations. The four most commonly-occurring types are *labialization*, typically realized as the addition of lip-rounding to the primary articulation; *palataliza-tion*, typically involving the raising and fronting of the tongue body in the direction of the hard palate; *velarization*, tyically realized as tongue backing; and *pharyngealization*, involving the retraction of the tongue root. Following the arguments in Chomsky and Halle (1968), it is widely accepted that secon-dary articulations involve the same features as the articulatorily similar vow-els; thus palatalization involves (some or all of) the features of [i], labialization the features of [u], and so forth.

The definition given above is not adequate as a phonological definition, since it is based on phonetic criteria. For this reason, Sagey proposes to rede-fine primary and secondary articulations in terms of a purely phonological distinction between major and minor articulations (1986, 1989). She observes that in most types of complex consonants, only one degree of closure is dis-tinctive; the other is fully predictable, and its degree of closure need not be specified in the representation. The articulator whose stricture is predictable is termed the *minor* articulator, and the other the *major* articulator. For example, in languages with secondary labialization, the degree of labial stricture in a segment is always predictable from its other features, and so labialization constitutes the minor articulation. The stricture of the other, primary articu-lation may be distinctive, as in languages that contrast a labialized velar stop [kʷ] and fricative [xʷ], and this articulation is accordingly the major one.

This definition is a purely phonological one, and does not, unlike the pho-netic definition, entail that a minor articulation has a wider degree of closure than a major one. Indeed, this is not necessarily the case. In Ubykh, for exam-ple, the minor articulation of labialization is realized as lip rounding in velars (e.g., [kʷ]) but as simultaneous closure in alveolars (e.g., [tᵖ]) (Comrie 1981). Anderson (1976) adduces evidence that the labiovelar stops [kp gb] found in many African languages consist of one primary and one secondary compo-nent, a distinction which can be reinterpreted in terms of major and minor articulations in Sagey's sense. Clicks, involving two simultaneous closures, can be analyzed into a major dorsal and minor coronal (or labial) articulation (Sagey 1986, 1989). However, when two simultaneous constrictions actually differ in degree of closure, the (phonological) major articulation always appears to coincide with the (phonetic) primary articulation, and the minor articu-lation with the secondary articulation.[32]

Sagey's proposal places the study of multiple articulations on a solid pho-nological footing, and has been widely accepted. Given the distinction be-tween major and minor articulators, however, several fundamental questions emerge: How are major and minor articulators organized in feature represen-tations? How is the major articulator distinguished from the minor articulator?

3.5.1 The Organization of Multiple Articulations

As before, we will consider two alternative models. In Sagey's model (1986), all oral articulator features, major and minor, link directly to the place node as sisters. Thus in complex segments, major and minor articulator features are not formally distinguished in terms of node organization as such. To distinguish them, a device called a "pointer" is introduced, which links the root node (and the stricture features it dominates) to the major articulator feature. This conception is illustrated below, where we give the representation of a palatalized coronal consonant such as [n']. Notice that palatalization is characterized in terms of a [–back] dorsal node, just as is a front vowel.

(52)   [n']

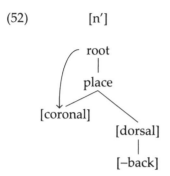

This model predicts that if the place node spreads, both the major and minor articulator features should spread with it.

Data from Irish confirm this prediction. In Irish, according to Ní Chiosáin (1991), a nasal consonant optionally assimilates to the place of articulation of a following consonant. Just in case this assimilation takes place, the nasal adopts the secondary articulation of the following consonant, becoming palatalized before a palatalized consonant and plain before a plain consonant (see (53)). In other words, when the major articulator features spread, the minor articulator features spread too.

(53)   k'aːn g'ar   →   k'aːŋ'g'aːr   "a short one"
       gan x'il   →   gaŋ'x'iːl   "with no sense"
       kiːraːn b'eg   →   kiːraːm' b'eg   "a small moor"
       nə k'iːn' + ɣuːwə →   nə k'iːŋ ɣuːwə "the black ones"

We may explain this pattern on the assumption that major and minor articulation features both link under the place node, consistently with (52).

However, Ní Chiosáin notes further data that raise a problem for the Sageyian model. Before a velar consonant, the nasal may assimilate only the major dorsal articulation, as shown in (54), illustrating a palatalized nasal before a plain velar:

(54)   nə k'iːn' + xorkrə →   nə k'iːŋ' xorkrə   "the purple ones"

Indeed, this realization is the preferred one.[33] It motivates a further rule of dorsal assimilation, also optional, which spreads the dorsal node alone. However, this result is unexpected in the Sageyian model. If the palatalized coronal [n'] assimilates to the dorsality of a (nonpalatalized) velar sound, it will acquire a second dorsal node, while losing its coronality:

(55)

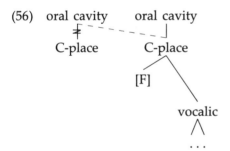

But since a single segment may not be doubly specified for dorsality, we expect the nasal's original dorsal node, representing palatalization, to be automatically delinked, to preserve well-formedness.[34]

Let us now consider how complex segments can be represented in the constriction-based model. The commonest secondary articulation types – labialization, palatalization, velarization, and pharyngealization – can be very naturally characterized as minor articulations involving the features [labial], [coronal], [dorsal], [pharyngeal], respectively, supplemented by appropriate vowel height features as necessary (Clements 1990b, 1993; Herzallah 1990; Hume 1990, 1992). If we assume that these features (or at least the first three; see section 3.3.4 for a discussion of [pharyngeal]) are members of the vocalic constituent, linked under the C-place node, then the spreading of the latter in rules of place assimilation will automatically entail the spreading of minor articulations. We represent this analysis in (56) ([F] = any major articulator feature):

(56)   oral cavity   oral cavity

C-place   C-place

[F]

vocalic

. . .

As Ní Chiosáin points out, this type of constituent structure is supported by the Irish data. First, it allows us to express the spreading of all C-place features as a unit, accounting for the data in (53); if the features of minor articulation were linked to a higher node, such as the oral cavity or root node, they would not be affected by place assimilation.[35] In addition, it allows the independent spreading of a single major articulator feature [F], directly accounting for Irish examples like (54). Note, in particular, that the spreading of the velar's [dorsal] node to the C-place node of the nasal will not trigger the delinking of the nasal's vocalic node, since the combination of a major [dorsal] node and a minor [coronal] node under the vocalic node is well-formed, and indeed constitutes the canonic representation of a palatalized velar:

(57)

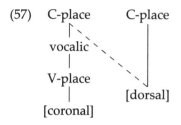

The two models also differ in the means they use to distinguish major and minor articulator features. In the Sageyian model, as we have seen, this distinction is not made by node organization and requires the pointer. Aside from this function, the pointer plays no role in the theory. In the constriction-based model, major and minor articulator features are distinguished by node organization alone, since the major feature is always the superior node in the hierarchy. The major articulation in any complex consonant is interpreted with the values of the stricture features [continuant, approximant, sonorant] present in the higher structure, and the minor articulation is assigned its noncontrastive degree of closure by independent phonetic rules and principles. In this theory, the pointer is not necessary.[36]

3.5.2   The Node Structure of Vocoids

Given this account of minor articulations, we may return to an earlier question concerning the internal structure of vocoids. We have seen that the vocalic node characterizes the functional unity of vocalic features, and expresses minor articulations in consonants. In the latter, as we have seen, the vocalic node links crucially under the C-place node.

There is reason to believe that the same structure holds in vocoids. It is a striking crosslinguistic generalization that consonantal place features do not appear to be able to spread as a unit from one consonant to another across vowels (Clements 1990b, 1993).[37] For example, although we commonly find rules in which a nasal assimilates to an adjacent consonant in all its place features, we never find rules in which a nasal assimilates to all place features of a consonant *across a vowel*. Thus while rules having the effect of (58a) are common, rules like (58b) appear to be unattested:

(58)   (a)   N   C   (b)   N   V   C

                 place   place

This fact cannot, apparently, be explained in terms of any general prohibition against the spreading of place features to a nonadjacent consonant, since single articulator features are not constrained in this way. For example, many languages have rules of coronal assimilation in which the coronal node spreads from consonant to consonant across vowels and certain consonants.[38] The rule of n-retroflexion in Sanskrit is instructive (Whitney 1889). By this rule, the first /n/ following retroflex [ṣ] or [r] is retroflexed to [ṇ], provided no coronal consonant intervenes, and a sonorant or vowel follows (Schein and Steriade 1986, after Whitney 1889). Consider, for instance, the base form /brahman-/ "brahman", from which a number of inflected forms are derived. We find, for example, that [ṇ] is assimilated to [r] in the locative singular [brahman-i], though not in the vocative singular [brahman], where no sonorant or vowel follows. Following the analysis of Schein and Steriade (1986), the rule in question spreads the coronal node of the [r] rightward across the intervening vocoids and noncoronal consonants to the following [n]; since the coronal node dominates the features of retroflexion, these features travel with it. Thus, Sanskrit shows that single articulator features, such as [coronal], may spread across vowels and consonants alike.[39]

Both of these patterns follow directly from the structure of the model. The assimilation of all consonantal place features as a unit can only be expressed as the spreading of the C-place node. If vowels also bear a C-place node, the C-place node of consonants cannot spread across them without violating the NCC (27), as shown below:

(59)   Spreading is blocked by the NCC:

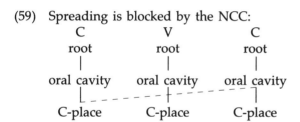

(For the same reason, a consonant's oral cavity or root node cannot spread across a vowel.) In contrast, vowels are not opaque to the spread of a *single* articulator feature. For example, a front (i.e., [coronal]) vowel does not block the spreading of [coronal] in Sanskrit, since the front vowel's [coronal] node links to the V-place tier, while the consonant's [coronal] node links to the C-place tier, by our assumptions. (Recall that the NCC (27) applies only to association lines linking elements on the *same* tiers.)[40]

3.6   Are Articulator Features Binary in Vocoids?

At this point, an obvious question arises: Since the articulator features [labial], [coronal], and [dorsal] are one-valued in consonants, shouldn't they be treated as one-valued in vowels as well? But wouldn't such treatment be empirically wrong, given that standard feature theory treats [round] and [back] as binary?

As it turns out, however, the evidence in favor of the binary nature of [round] and [back] is far from overwhelming. Already, Steriade (1987a) has noted that it is difficult to find genuine cases in which [–round] spreads. Although both values of [back] appear to spread, in the constriction-based framework rules spreading [–back] can be reinterpreted as rules spreading [coronal], and rules spreading [+back] as rules spreading [dorsal]. The real problem cases for a fully one-valued interpretation of articulator features in vocoids involve rules which have traditionally been defined on [α back]. These are of two main types: (i) assimilatory rules in which both values of [back] must spread, and (ii) dissimilatory rules which assign some vowel the value [–α back] in the presence of an adjacent [α back] vowel. We briefly review one example of each type below.

In the system of palatal vowel harmony in Turkish, as described by Clements and Sezer (1982), harmonic suffixes acquire the value [αback] from the first preceding vowel. Most consonants are transparent to harmony, as shown in (60a). However, the underlying palatalized consonants /ḷ ṛ ḵ/ and the back velar /K/ are opaque, blocking harmony from the preceding vowel and instituting new harmony domains of their own, as shown in (60b, c).

(60)　(a)　Regular vowel harmony (nom. sg./acc. sg.)
　　　　　ip　　　　ip-i　　　"rope"
　　　　　kïz　　　kïz-ï　　"girl"
　　　　　ek　　　　ek-i　　　"joint"
　　　　　tak　　　tak-ï　　"arch"
　　　(b)　Opaque [–back] consonants /ḷ ṛ ḵ /
　　　　　suaḷ　　　suāḷ-i　　"question"
　　　　　harf　　　harf-i　　"letter"
　　　　　/idrak̠/　idrak̠-i　"perception"
　　　(c)　Opaque [+back] consonant /K/
　　　　　tasdiK　　tasdiK-ï　"confirmation"

In Clements and Sezer's analysis, opaque consonants are assigned the phonetically appropriate value of [±back] as a feature of secondary articulation. Since all instances of [±back] occur on the same tier, the opacity of the consonants in (60b, c) follows from the No-Crossing Constraint (27).

To interpret these data in terms of one-valued features [coronal] and [dorsal], we must find a way of spreading these features to the exclusion of all others, while accounting for the opacity effects. Consider a possible analysis along the following lines. Let us assume that Turkish vowels fall into two classes, palatal and velar, defined as [coronal] and [dorsal] respectively. Let us further suppose, following a suggestion by Browman and Goldstein (1989), that these two features form a single constituent, termed *lingual* in view of the fact that both involve the tongue. On these assumptions, vowel harmony can be expressed as the spreading of the lingual node. The palatalized consonants /ḷ ṛ ḵ/ are now underlyingly specified for the feature [coronal], and /K/ for [dorsal], both of which constitute minor articulations under the vocalic node. Since these features link to the lingual node, which lies on the same tier in consonants and vowels, they will block the propagation of the lingual node from the preceding vowel, and will themselves spread onto the suffix vowel /I/, as follows:

(61)

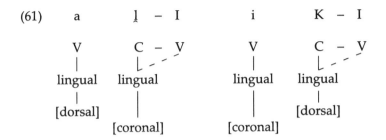

This analysis predicts that consonants specified for [coronal] or [dorsal] as secondary articulations will always block the spreading of the lingual node.[41]

An example of the apparent binary nature of [back] of the second type can be drawn from Ainu, as discussed by Itô (1984). In this language, whose vowels are /i u e o a/, vocalic suffixes are added to CVC roots to form CVC+V stems. After many stems, the suffix vowel is simply a copy of the root vowel. However, after a lexically marked set of roots, it is realized as the high vowel [i] or [u] which has the opposite value of [back] from the root vowel. Examples include *ket-u* "to rub" and *pok-i* "to lower".

We may account for this pattern without recourse to a binary feature [±back] on the assumption that an OCP-driven constraint applies to stems, disallowing two adjacent identical lingual nodes. (This analysis presupposes that the lingual node may not be multilinked.) Since by principles of contrastive feature specification, every non-low vowel must have at least one lingual feature, the only way the suffix vowel can be realized consistently with the OCP is by selecting the alternative lingual feature from the root vowel. Thus it must be [dorsal] if the root vowel is [coronal], and [coronal] if it is [dorsal].

There is some evidence that the lingual node may be needed in the description of consonants as well as vocoids. Note that the class of lingual consonants is coextensive, in the buccal cavity, with the class of nonlabial consonants. Thus rules that appear to require reference to the class of [−labial] sounds can be reformulated as rules defined on lingual sounds. Examples are not hard to find. In Mandarin Chinese, for instance, lingual obstruents (velar, uvular, retroflex, and dental, except for the dental nonstridents [t tʰ]) are replaced by laminal palato-alveolars before the high front vowels [i ü], while labials occur freely in this position (Clements 1976). In Slovak, [æ] is backed to [a] after lingual, but not labial consonants (see note 43). Thus there is at least suggestive evidence that the lingual node may be needed for consonants as well as vowels. In sum, if this somewhat speculative analysis is on the right tract, it would appear unnecessary to retain binary place features in vocoids.

3.7   Summary and Discussion

We summarize the discussion up to this point in the form of figure (62), illustrating some of the better-established class nodes and their form of organization in consonants and vocoids (as noted above, consonants with secondary articulations include a vocalic node under the C-place node, not illustrated here):

(62)   (a)   Consonants: (b)   Vocoids:

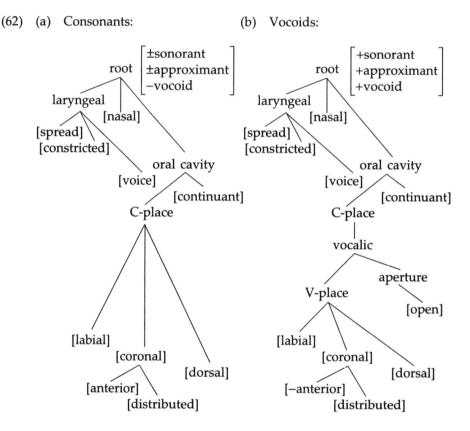

Any particular segment is represented with an appropriate selection of these features (among perhaps others) in its fully specified form. For instance, [k] has a dorsal node under the place node, but labial and coronal nodes are absent. A labiovelar consonant such as the Yoruba [kp] has both labial and dorsal nodes. Some features, such as [−voice], [+cont], and [−anterior], are universally noncontrastive in vocoids. Any speech sound can be represented in this general form. Following the universality principle (5) discussed above, we suggest that this mode of organization holds for all segment types in all languages.

A few further comments are in order. First, (62) differs from the earliest proposals in not including a supralaryngeal node. McCarthy (1988) has shown that alternative explanations are available for most of the phenomena (especially those involving debuccalization) that were originally cited in its favor. However, Dell (1993) offers new arguments for this node based on assimilation rules in two East Asian languages. In a Chinese dialect spoken in the Yongding prefecture, Fujian province, syllable-initial /h/ assimilates all supralaryngeal features from a following syllabic nasal, retaining only its aspiration. Thus the form /hm̩/ is realized as [Mm̩], /hn̩/ as [Nn̩], and /hŋ̩/ as [Nŋ̩] (upper-case letters designate voiceless aspirates). Here, apparently, the supralaryngeal node of the nasal spreads onto /h/, whose inherent laryngeal features are preserved. In Yi (a Tibeto-Burman language), in certain syllables whose onset is a (voiced or voiceless) sonorant and whose peak is a high vowel, the supralaryngeal features of the onset consonant spread onto the peak: thus, /Mɨ/ is realized as [Mm̩], /Lɨ/ as [Ll̩], etc. Again, an analysis in terms of supralaryngeal node spreading readily suggests itself; Dell shows that a number of alternative analyses can be rejected. As examples of this sort are still rare, we have not included the supralaryngeal node in (62), but further cases would support its reconsideration.

Second, the discussion so far has not touched on two features whose affiliation is still unclear, [lateral] and [strident]. In the case of [lateral], the two competing hypotheses are attachment under the coronal node or the root node. The major argument for coronal attachment comes from the node implication criterion, as discussed in section 3.1; if we attach [lateral] under the coronal node, we directly account for the fact that all segments bearing it are phonologically [coronal], without the need for further stipulation.[42] However, there are at least four problems for this view: (a) when a nasal assimilates in place to a lateral sound, it normally does not become lateral (see the Chukchi form *ten-leut* in (35) as well as similar forms in, e.g., Catalan and Yoruba, though Levin (1987) also cites several exceptions to this generalization); (b) when a lateral assimilates in place to a nonlateral, it normally retains its laterality (e.g., Spanish, Tamil); (c) when the oral cavity node spreads from [l] to [s] in intrusive stop formation (e.g., *false* [. . . lᵗs]), the resulting intrusive stop is central, not lateral (see section 3.3.3); (d) lateral obstruents may be fully transparent to rules of long-distance assimilation involving coronal obstruents (for the case of Tahltan, see Shaw 1991). These facts strongly argue that [lateral] occurs above place in the feature hierarchy. If so, it may be that [lateral] sounds are universally coronal just by virtue of the way this feature is defined.

Traditionally, [strident] has been used to distinguish the "noisy" fricatives and affricates (labiodentals, sibilants, uvulars) from the "mellow" ones (bilabials, dentals, palatals, velars); see, e.g., Chomsky and Halle (1968). More recently some linguists have suggested that this feature, like [lateral], should be restricted to coronal sounds; if this proposal is correct, it reopens the question of how bilabial and labiodental fricatives can be distinguished in languages like Ewe, in which they form minimal contrasts. Since place assimilation does not usually affect stridency, we maintain the conservative position that [strident] links under the root node, while hoping that future work will clarify the status of this feature.

4   The Expression of Assimilation Rules

We are now in a position to take up the formulation of rules of place assimilation between consonants and vocoids in more detail. Consider, as an example, the rule of palatalization and coronalization in Acadian French, which causes the velar consonants /k g/ to shift to palatalized velars [kʲ gʲ] or palato-alveolar affricates [tʃ dʒ] before front vowels. This rule is optional, the choice between the various realizations being determined in part by sociolinguistic considerations (see Hume 1992, after the descriptions by Lucci (1972) and Flikeid (1988)).

(63)   /kø/   kø   ~   kʲø   ~   tʃø   "tail"
       /gɛte/   gɛte ~   gʲɛte ~   dʒɛte "to watch for"

The rule must be phonological rather than phonetic, since it has lexical exceptions such as [pike] "to sting" and [mokø] "teasing", which are always pronounced with a plain velar consonant. Furthermore, as Hume notes, it feeds other phonological rules.

The palatalized variants [kʲ gʲ] must result from the spreading of the [coronal] feature of the front vowel onto the velar. Specifically, since the velar becomes a palatalized velar, not a coronal, [coronal] must link under its V-place node as a minor articulation. Thus the rule must spread [coronal] from the V-place node of the vowel onto the consonant, with interpolation of new V-place and vocalic nodes as is required to preserve well-formedness. Thus it applies as follows:

(64)

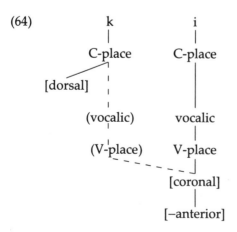

The fact that palatalization and coronalization have the same set of exceptions suggests that coronalization applies only to forms which have first been palatalized. Words like [pike] "to sting" are marked as exceptions to palatalization, and therefore cannot be coronalized. In this analysis, if palatalization applies to a form, its minor [coronal] articulation may optionally be reassigned major articulator status by a process of *promotion* (Clements 1989a), according to which a consonant's minor articulation is delinked and copied under its C-place node, where it replaces its original major articulation. If the minor [coronal] articulation already bears a redundant [−anterior] specification in the palatalized form, it accompanies the [coronal] node when it is copied, creating a nonanterior coronal, such as the palato-alveolar sounds [tʃ dʒ].

In many other languages, however, there is no direct evidence for an intermediate palatalized stage in the coronalization process. For example, in Slovak the velars /k g x ɣ/ are realized as [tʃ dʒ ʃ ʒ] respectively, when followed by a front vocoid, /i e æ j/, e.g., [vnuk] "grandson", /vnúk+ik/ [vnutʃik] (dim.), /vnúk+æ/ [vnútʃa][43] (dim.). Unlike in Acadian French, velars are never palatalized in Slovak (Rubach, forthcoming). To account for such cases, Hume (1992) characterizes coronalization as an elementary rule type in which the [coronal] feature of front vocoids spreads directly to the C-place node of the velar, replacing its original [dorsal] feature (presumably, again, as the unmarked mode of application). In this analysis, coronalization is expressed as follows:

(65)

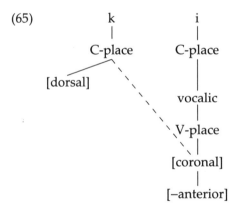

The expression of coronalization as an elementary rule type is not possible in a framework in which front vowels are characterized as [dorsal, −back] (Sagey 1986). In such a framework it is inexplicable that the assimilation of a velar ([dorsal]) consonant to a front ([dorsal]) vowel should give rise to a [coronal] consonant. To account for this change, one could, of course, posit some sort of restructuring convention having the effect of trading in the [dorsal] node for a [coronal] one in the context of the feature [−back]. This type of approach is not without problems, however, as is noted by Broselow and Niyondagara (1989), Lahiri and Evers (1991), and Hume (1992). For example, the relationship between [coronal] and [−back] is an arbitrary one. No formal property of the theory predicts that a velar consonant should become [coronal] in the context of a [−back] vowel, as opposed to, e.g., a [+back], or a [+rounded] one. Most important, perhaps, is that such an analysis requires a restructuring rule to account for a common process such as coronalization. Restructuring rules are powerful and highly arbitrary devices. By incorporating them into the theory, we seriously weaken one of our fundamental goals, which is to seek a formalism capable of expressing common processes in terms of simple descriptive parameters.

Consonant-to-vowel assimilation receives an equally simple account in the constriction-based model. We illustrate with an example from Maltese Arabic (Hume 1992). As discussed earlier (see (43)), the vowel of the imperfective prefix is always realized as [i] before a stem-initial coronal obstruent. Assuming that the prefix vowel is underlyingly unspecified, this realization can be accounted for by a feature-filling rule according to which the [coronal] node of the consonant spreads leftward to the the vowel, as in (66) (showing interpolated node structure). Vowel height is later assigned by an independently-motivated default rule.[44]

(66)

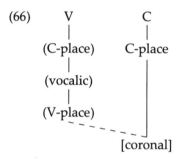

4.1   The No-Crossing Constraint Revisited

Before leaving the discussion of assimilation, we must consider a further interesting property of the constriction-based model. As we have just seen, this model allows the oral articulator features to link to different tiers: C-place and V-place. As a result, it potentially allows configurations of the following type:

(67)

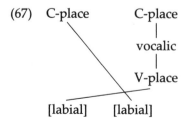

Although the lines linking the two instances of [labial] to higher nodes (C-place and V-place) "cross," they do not violate the NCC (27), since the higher nodes are not on the same tier. Without some further constraint, then, such configurations are theoretically possible.

However, at present we know of no clear-cut evidence showing that configurations like (67) should be excluded. Indeed, Hume (1992) points out that they may be required in the constriction-based model, at least in the immediate output of rules. Consider, as an example, labial harmony in Turkish. In this system, the labiality of a stem vowel spreads to a high suffix vowel, even across labial consonants. Thus, the form /mum-I/ "candle" (acc. sg.) is realized as [mum-u]. Labial harmony applies as follows:

(68)

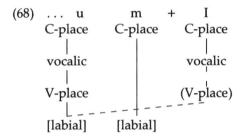

The rightmost segments in this figure present an instance of (67).

Apparently, then, line-crossing must be allowed whenever it does not create violations of the NCC (27). Whether further constraints are required at a later level of description to exclude configurations of this type (for example, to satisfy the requirements of some particular model of phonetic interpretation) is an open question (see Hume 1992 for related discussion). A full examination of this issue, while interesting, would go beyond the scope of the present study.

5 The Phonetic Interpretation of the Feature Hierarchy

In the preceding sections we have reviewed phonological evidence motivating the feature hierarchy. The later discussion has introduced the idea that the basic organizing principle of the feature hierarchy is the *vocal tract constriction*. This view is based on two main considerations. First, articulator features, such as [labial], [coronal], and [dorsal], appear best defined in terms of the constrictions formed by the articulators, rather than using the vaguer notion of "articulator involvement." Second, the phonological evidence shows that constrictions are represented by specific nodes in the feature heirarchy (oral cavity, vocalic), themselves defined in terms of dependent nodes representing the constriction's location (C- and V-place) and degree (continuance, aperture). We have suggested that this view allows for a new and more adequate treatment of such phenomena as vowel-consonant relations, the internal structure of vowels, and the representation of major and minor articulations.

It would be appropriate to offer some tentative remarks on the possible phonetic interpretation of this model, addressing such questions as, To what extent does feature organization reflect aspects of vocal tract structure? and Why should features be grouped together in terms of constrictions, as opposed to some other organizing principle? In fact, a constriction-based approach receives support from a variety of sources, including acoustic and articulatory theories of speech production, and for this reason, offers a plausible link between abstract phonological structure and phonetic intepretation.

The constriction-based model postulates that segment structure is organized in terms of oral tract constrictions which can combine with independent velic, pharyngeal, and laryngeal constrictions. Quite strikingly, this organization parallels the structure of the vocal tract, in that independently functioning articulations are assigned to independent tiers of the representation, and interdependent articulations are grouped together into constituents. This result, reached independently of phonetic considerations, provides a strong motivation for the model in the physical constraints on phonetic production. Yet at the same time, feature organization is not entirely reducible to physical or physiological considerations. In particular, we have seen evidence from common processes such as assimilation that oral tract constrictions are comprised of two types: consonantal and vocalic, with the latter embedded under the former. Even when produced simultaneously in consonants with minor articulations, these two types of constriction must be assigned to different tiers, and clearly this fact must reflect considerations other than strictly physiological ones. We suggest that this representational difference reflects a fundamental difference in the cognitive status assigned to vocoids and consonants as part of the competence of all speakers. The difference between consonants and vocoids is not merely a matter of their specification for [±vocoid], but involves a fundamental difference in their feature organization.

We must stress, furthermore, that this separation does not lead us to return to a "two-mouth" representation of segments in which consonants and vowels are defined by entirely different descriptive parameters, as in some traditional approaches (see Ladefoged and Halle 1988 for a critique). On the contrary, our characterization of consonants and vowels is a unified one in the sense that largely the same set of features is used for both, with the organization of consonants and vowels uniformally oriented around the constriction as the basic unit.

That segment structure is indeed constriction-based is suggested by a variety of further observations. Consider, first the fact that most features can be defined directly in terms of the parameters of constriction location and degree. Thus, the place features (the articulator features and their dependents) define constriction location, and the articulator-free features define constriction degree.

Note that if the basic unit of organization were articulator "involvement," as assumed in earlier work, we might expect to find features which characterize specific qualities of the articulator's movement (e.g., stiffness, velocity) rather than those relating to constriction shape and location. Insofar as dynamic features of this sort appear to be unmotivated phonologically, we derive further support for a constriction-based model of organization.

Other results in feature theory point in the same direction. As we have seen, McCarthy's studies of pharyngeal consonants (1989b, in press) also suggest that a strictly articulator-based approach to feature organization may be inadequate. This is because the natural class of [pharyngeal] consonants cannot be defined by the movement of any single articulator, but involve a constriction produced anywhere in the region between the oropharynx and the larynx.[45] Furthermore, Steriade's aperture theory, as we have seen, is based on constriction degree, ranging from full oral closure to maximum aperture. All these indicators suggest quite strongly that we are on the right track in viewing feature organization as constriction-based.

But at this point we may ask the question, Why should this be so? That the internal structure of segments is hierarchically-organized is not itself very surprising, given that linguistic structure is hierarchical at all other levels of representation (e.g., syntactic, semantic, morphological). What is less obvious is why phonological features should be organized in terms of the vocal tract constrictions they designate, instead of some other principle. In the remainder of this section we review recent research in speech production theory, which provides further support for the constriction-based organization of features.

Constrictions form the basis of many acoustically-based theories of speech production. These include, in particular, the source-filter theory as presented most completely in the work of Fant 1960 (see also Müller 1848, Chiba and Kajiyama 1941, and Stevens and House 1955), and the quantal theory of speech developed primarily by Stevens (1972, 1989). Fant showed that formant frequencies are determined by the shape of the supralaryngeal vocal tract, which acts as an acoustic filter. In the source-filter theory, the vocal tract is modeled as a tube closed at one end. Within the tube, constrictions typically form pairs of coupled resonators, such that the natural frequencies of any pair are approximately equal to the natural frequencies of the individual resonators, with some perturbation from these values resulting from the acoustic coupling between them.

Developing this model, Stevens finds that when a constriction is appropriately placed, the natural frequencies of the system are relatively insensitive to small modifications in its location; in other words, there are preferred regions within which moderate displacements of the constriction produce negligible effects in the signal. These regions form an important basis for establishing the acoustic and auditory correlates of distinctive features. As far as vowel production is concerned, Stevens (1972, p. 56) concludes that "vowels fall naturally into discrete categories instead of being identifiable as points on a continuum"; these categories, as well as those proposed by Wood (1982), are generally consistent with those that we have defined in terms of [labial], [coronal], [dorsal], and [pharyngeal]. In their further development of this approach, Mrayati, Carré and Guérin (1988) propose that the vocal tract can be divided into eight "distinctive regions" of nonequal length, defined by zero-crossings of the neutral tube sensitivity functions of the first three formants; these regions represent articulatory configurations that produce maximally stable and distinct acoustic targets in Stevens's sense, and again appear to be well correlated to the tongue and lip constriction locations defined by [labial], [coronal], [dorsal], [pharyngeal], and their dependent features.

Articulatory models of speech production also treat constrictions as central. In particular, the task-dynamic model of speech proposed by Browman and Goldstein (e.g., 1989, 1992) is based on the notion of gestures, defined as abstract characterizations of articulator movements whose "task," according to these writers, is the formation of specific vocal tract constrictions. The parallel between their model and feature-based phonological models is striking, and extends to rather subtle details, as they have themselves noted (Browman and Goldstein 1989). This is not to say that there are no important differences between the two models (see Clements 1992), but these differences are not irreconcilable in principle, and should not blind us to the significant parallels between the two approaches.

We see, then, that the notion "constriction" is central to many current theories of speech production, both acoustic and articulatory. It is therefore not surprising that phonological representations may be organized in terms of constrictions as well.

6   Conclusion

This study has attempted to summarize, and as far as possible to synthesize, some of the many recent contributions to the study of segment-internal structure. We have found considerable evidence for a hierarchical, multitiered model of feature organization along the lines presented above. Primary evidence for this model has been drawn from studies of phonological processes and segmental interactions in many languages. This evidence turns out to be surprisingly consistent from one language to another.

We have also seen that feature organization may reflect functional aspects of vocal tract organization in which independent (or partly independent) articulators, determining vocal tract constrictions, are assigned to independent, interacting tiers. In this sense, the model receives additional confirmation from an entirely independent source. While many interesting and important questions remain open and in need of further study, only some of which can be discussed in a general overview of this sort, a hierarchical approach to feature organization promises both to allow a substantially constrained account of phonological organization at the most abstract level, satisfying the requirements of formal linguistic theory, and to offer a bridge between phonological structure and phonetic interpretation which might be profitably explored in future work.

NOTES

We gratefully acknowledge the helpful comments of Chris Barker, François Dell, John Goldsmith, John Kingston, and David Odden on an earlier version of this paper. This work was supported in part by a research grant to the second author from the Social Sciences and Humanities Research Council of Canada.

1 For general discussion of features, see, e.g., Trubetzkoy (1939), Jakobson and Halle (1956), Chomsky and Halle (1968), Jakobson and Waugh (1979), Keating (1987), and Halle (1991).

2 The term "nonlinear" was first used in something like its current sense, to our knowledge, by Harris (1941), who distinguished between "successive (linear) phonemes" and "nonsuccessive" or "non-linear" phonemes such as stress. This term continued to be used by Harris, and especially Hockett, in some of their later writings, although it did not gain general currency as a designation for a general class of phonological theories until more recently.

3 It is also implicit in the IPA's graphic organization of consonant and vowel symbols into columns and rows with no further organization; see Ladefoged (1989) for criticism and an alternative proposal.

4 For suggestions that feature organization may be subject to a very limited degree of parameterization, see Mester (1986) and Cho (1990), among others.

5 Previous presentations of feature geometry have modeled phonological representations as sets of lines and planes (Clements 1985; Sagey 1986); however, planar structure is not crucial to the theory, and the following presentation adopts a purely two-dimensional approach.

6 If we prefer to consider that all phonological features are binary, the term "articulator node" (Sagey 1986) may be more appropriate; note, however, that whatever we choose to call them, *labial, coronal,* and *dorsal* have specific phonetic correlates just as other features do.

7 Rules applying in the context of nonlabial sounds have occasionally been cited in the literature. We suggest that these cases, where genuine, might be stated in terms of a node [lingual], to be discussed below. For a discussion of rules apparently referring to the class of noncoronal ("grave") sounds, see Christdas (1988), Yip (1989).

8 More accurately, in Sagey's model [±nasal] is immediately dominated by the soft palate node, which links to the root node.

9 According to Piggott's constraint, any node may immediately dominate at most one value of a given feature. This constraint, unlike (11), allows nodes to dominate sequences of nodes on a lower tier as long as they are not features.

10   We include [−approximant] in the definition of A₀ to exclude laterals, which are frequently analyzed as [−continuant] sounds.

11   Note that such segments cannot be described by linking a sequence like [+nasal] [−nasal] directly to their single root node, since this configuration is prohibited by the No-Branching Constraint.

12   The representation of length in terms of a moraic model such as that of Hayes (1989), in which long vowels occupy two positions and long consonants just one, is less straightforward; see Tranel (1991) and Sloan (1991) for discussion.

13   This explanation may be problematical, given much evidence that epenthetic vowels consist of empty skeletal slots whose content is filled in by later rules (see, e.g., Clements 1986; Archangeli 1988); the insertion of an empty slot would not itself give rise to crossing association lines. Alternatively, we might assume that in some languages only multilinked clusters (i.e., true geminates) are syllabified in the syllable coda, and that unsyllabifiable consonants trigger epenthesis; this would predict the same pattern. The important point for the purposes of the present discussion is that geminates created by assimilation show exactly the same properties as monomorphemic (and *ex hypothesis*, bipositional) geminates. See also chapter 8, this volume.

14   See note 13 for an alternative explanation. Note that in Kolami, place assimilation applies only before underlyingly voiced stops.

15   McCarthy convincingly argues that stems such as [samam] "poison" are derived from an underlying biliteral root /sm/ (McCarthy 1981, 1986).

16   Cho (1990, p. 94) notes that place assimilation is an optional rule which can be suppressed depending on the style and the rate of speech. Kim (1990) reports only the slow speech forms, and Martin (1951) only the fast speech forms.

17   Alternatively, it may delink the oral cavity node (see section 3.3.3 below), though not the place node, which does not dominate [continuant]. In a different analysis, Iverson and Kim (1987) delink *all* terminal features in the syllable coda, accounting for coronal and laryngeal neutralization at the same time. This very elegant rule, if correct, would require a relaxation of constraint (4).

18   See Kiparsky (1985) and Archangeli and Pulleyblank (1989) for discussion of a locality effect derived from marking conventions, according to which segments marked in the grammar as unable to bear a certain feature may neither receive this feature nor allow it to pass across them in the course of spreading.

19   Some linguists have suggested that the sonority degree of a given segment is determined not by features, but by node structure itself: roughly, the more class nodes in the structure, the greater (Rice 1992) or lesser (Dogil 1993) its sonority.

20   These forms, taken from Bogoras and Odden, exhibit the effects of vowel harmony. According to Bogoras (p. 653), [y] may also harden to [d] after /ŋ/.

21   Other analyses of ISF have been proposed. Davis (1989) proposes to treat ISF in terms of two independent rules of [−cont] spread and place spread. Note, however, that since ISF is optional, this analysis predicts that each rule should be able to apply

independently of the other in the same dialect, and that some dialects may have one rule and not the other. These predictions appear to be incorrect, since according to the literature on this subject, if ISF applies at all in a given dialect, it applies in toto. Iverson (1989) proposes to analyze ISF as the leftward spreading of [–sonorant]. However, as pointed out above, [sonorant] is not otherwise known to spread independently of other features, and for this reason is usually represented as part of a feature matrix on the root node, as shown in (32).

22 For example, the Node Fission Convention proposed by Clements (1989b), which has the effect of splitting a single branching node into two nonbranching homologues.

23 (38b) reflects Halle's current terminology, in which "guttural" and "larynx" replace the earlier terms "laryngeal" and "glottis," respectively.

24 "Front" in (41b) refers to the upper surface of the front of the tongue including the tip, the blade, and the forward part of the body of the tongue, which typically articulates under the hard palate. For the phonetic basis of this definition, see Hume (1992). Note that while the definitions in (41) apply to consonants and vocoids alike, consonants and vocoids typically implement them in somewhat different ways, consistently with their different articulatory requirements. Thus, [labial] consonants require a relatively narrow (and not necessarily protruded) lip constriction in order to acquire the radical vocal tract obstruction which, as noted earlier, is definitional of consonants, while [labial] vocoids require a relatively

wide and protruded constriction in order to create a supplementary resonating cavity not sufficiently obstructed to produce consonantal frication. While these two types of lip configurations are somewhat different, both involve a labial constriction in the sense of (41a), and thus conform to the definition of [labial] sounds. Analogous remarks hold for [coronal] and [dorsal].

25 Alternatively, we could place [coronal], [labial], etc., on different tiers in consonants and vocoids, and extend our definition of "adjacency" in such a way that features on different tiers also count as adjacent if they are linked to adjacent root nodes (Selkirk 1988). All else being equal, however, we would prefer the simpler definition. Notice that the OCP applies less frequently to consonant + vocoid sequences such as *ty* than it does to consonant + consonant sequences (though see Clements 1990b, 1993 and Hume 1992 for further examples of "cross-category" dissimilations). This fact can be regarded as a special instance of the more general principle (noted by McCarthy, in press) that the OCP tends to apply in preference to sounds that share major class features.

26 The Sageyian model can express back vowel/velar consonant interactions by assuming that [+back] is redundantly present in (back) velars and uvulars. However, this assumption predicts that velars and uvulars should be opaque to the spreading of [±back] in vowel harmony and assimilation, which is not the case. A striking, if atypical example of a rule in which both front and back vocoids pattern with velars is the "ruki" rule of Sanskrit,

in which /r u k i/ cause a following [s] to become retroflex (Whitney 1889). If [i] were [dorsal], as in Sagey's model, and retroflex sounds bear secondary dorsalization, all these sounds could be regarded as [dorsal]. However, it is mysterious why [s] should become retroflex in this context; if we were to spread Sagey's dorsal node rightward, [s] should palatalize to [sʲ] after [i], and velarize to [x] after [k].

27   In vowel systems like that of Akan, in which [ATR] has been proposed as the basis of tongue-root based vowel harmony, it may be possible to replace [ATR] with [pharyngeal] or [radical]. Thus, there is increasing reason to believe that [ATR] can be dispensed with altogether.

28   The vocalic node was first proposed in unpublished work by Archangeli and Pulleyblank, who called it the S-place (i.e., secondary place) node.

29   Our discussion here is indebted to unpublished work by Nibert (1991), which first brought these phenomena to our attention.

30   To address problems of this sort, Steriade (1987b) suggested that velar consonants should be characterized by a new "velar" node, with [dorsal] reserved for vowels. This proposal correctly treats velar consonants as transparent to dorsal spreading, but raises other problems. For one, the velar node is an anomaly in articulator theory, since it does not designate an independent articulator. Moreover, as Mester and Itô point out (1989), this proposal makes it difficult to express the fact that velar consonants typically form a natural class with back vowels, not front vowels, as discussed above.

31   Or to the skeleton. Observe, however, that Servigliano does not satisfy the criteria proposed by McCarthy (1989a) for languages with template-based morphologies, in which vowels and consonants lie on entirely separate planes meeting at the skeleton. If we allowed such full segregation of vowels and consonants in all languages, we would predict, incorrectly, that rules of total consonant spreading across vowels, found in such template-morphology languages as Arabic and Hausa, would occur freely in languages with concatenative and fusional morphologies.

32   See Maddieson (1990) for discussion (and rejection) of a proposed exception to this generalization in Shona. Note also that Sagey's definition allows for the possibility of segments with two major articulations. She exploits this possibility in her analysis of the surface contrast between [pʷ] and [kpʷ] in Nupe, treating the latter but not the former as having two major articulations, [dorsal] and [labial]. If this contrast can be reanalyzed in other terms, as seems possible (for instance, we might suppose that [pʷ] does not have a [dorsal] component), then crucial cases of double major articulations, in Sagey's sense, appear to be rare and perhaps nonexistant, and a maximally constrained phonological theory would exclude them in principle, by appropriate constraints on representations.

33   Ní Chiosáin's description implies that either rule may apply in such examples; the choice of rule is not predictable from other phonological factors.

34   Instead, the second dorsal node must be delinked from the nasal, after triggering the loss of the

coronal node; but no general principle predicts this delinking.

35 We cannot assume that the oral cavity (or root) node spreads, since [continuant] does not spread, as shown by our examples.

36 Like Sagey's model, the constriction-based model makes no formal claims regarding the phonetic degree of stricture of a minor articulation. It thus allows for the possibility of languages, like those discussed above, in which a minor articulation has the same degree of closure (or narrower) closure than a simultaneous major articulation. See Hume (1992) for further discussion of this point. Further evidence for the linking of minor articulations as a sister rather than daughter of the major articulation node can be cited from opacity patterns in Chilcotin (Clements 1990b, 1993). See also Goodman (1991) for comparison with the dependency-based model of Selkirk (1988), in which minor articulations are treated as daughters of major articulations.

37 It is not inconsistent to link vowels under the C-place node, since this node has no phonetic content. We may consider the C- and V-place nodes as in fact the same category of place, the terminological distinction between them being merely conventional.

38 The spreading of single C-place features (major articulations) to nonadjacent consonants appears to be restricted to [coronal], and in all known cases of [coronal] spreading, the target must also be [coronal]. We speculate that a more general constraint is at work, restricting long-distance C-place spreading to cases in which an OCP violation is involved. In effect, since spreading of [labial] onto [labial] or [dorsal]

onto [dorsal] would be vacuous, since these features do not usually have dependents, such a constraint would limit long-distance spreading just to the observed cases. Such cases would then be motivated in a manner similar to rules of long-distance dissimilation which, as was discussed in section 2.2, are also OCP-driven.

39 As David Odden points out to us, if [n] can be regarded as [−distributed], an alternative analysis is possible in which only the coronal dependent feature [−anterior] spreads. For other, less controversial examples of long-distance coronal node spreading, see Poser (1982), Hualde (1988b), and Shaw (1991).

40 A further prediction of this model is that a vowel's vocalic node may not spread across a consonant bearing a minor articulation. This prediction is supported by the rule of vowel copy in Barra Isle Gaelic (Clements 1986) in which the epenthetic vowel is realized as a full copy of the preceding vowel across a palatalized or velarized consonant, except that the vowel is always front if the consonant is palatalized and back if it is nonpalatalized. In addition, the epenthetic vowel is always unrounded, even though rounding is distinctive. To account for these facts, we must assume that the vowel copy rule does not spread the vocalic node of the preceding full vowel, but that it spreads the aperture node of the vowel and the V-place node of the consonant separately. If the vocalic node were not linked to the C-place node in vowels, we would expect the vocalic node of the vowel to be able to spread, since it would not violate the No-Crossing Constraint,

incorrectly resulting in complete vowel copy.

41   Other examples of the spreading of both values of vocalic place features have been cited in Gaelic (Clements 1986) and Chilcotin (Clements 1993, p. 139), and can be treated in a similar way. Note that a further prediction of this approach is that languages may have harmony rules spreading just the [dorsal] or [coronal] node, instead of the lingual node. In such cases, it should be possible for [dorsal] to spread across [coronal] vowels, and vice versa.

42   While phonetic lateral velars have been reported in a number of languages, there is no evidence that any of these sounds are both [dorsal] and [+lateral] at the phonological level; see Levin (1987) for careful discussion of this issue.

43   The low front vowel /æ/ is backed to [a] by an independent rule after nonlabial consonants. Thus, the diminutive suffix that surfaces as [a] in vnútʃ + a is the same suffix occurring in chláp + æ "man" (dim.).

44   In this analysis, the major articulator feature [coronal] of the consonant links under the V-place node of the vowel, creating the unmarked vowel structure. We assume this is the normal mode of operation. Given our previous analysis of V-to-C place assimilation, however, it is natural to ask whether there are also two types of C-to-V spreading: one in which the consonant's major articulator feature links under the vowel's V-place node, as above, and another in which it links directly under the vowel's C-place node. These two analyses make subtly different predictions, as discussed by Hume (1992); we leave the question open here.

45   This conclusion does not of course follow from the alternative proposed by Halle (1989, 1992), in which [pharyngeal] is not an articulator feature but a class node, renamed "guttural."

8 Phonological Quantity and Multiple Association

DAVID PERLMUTTER

0 Phonological Quantity: From a Feature to Multiple Association

Languages that have contrasts between short and long vowels and, in some cases, between single and geminate consonants, are said to have contrasts in phonological quantity. Luganda, for example, exhibits both types of contrast, e.g., *wela* "refuse" versus *weela* "rest" and *yiga* "learn" versus *yigga* "hunt" (Tucker 1962), where length is transcribed by double letters. The framework of Chomsky and Halle (1968) had relatively little to say about quantity, assuming it could be handled by means of a feature such as [+Long].

In his work on Arabic verb morphology, McCarthy (1979a, 1981a) took an important step, separating not only consonant sequences (verb stems) from vowel sequences as different morphemes on separate tiers, but also the pattern of vocalic and consonantal positions as a separate morpheme on a separate tier. Since Arabic uses quantity to distinguish morphologically distinct forms of a verb (e.g., *katab* vs. *kaatab* vs. *kattab*), McCarthy represented contrasts in quantity as contrasts in the number of V or C slots with which a melodic unit is associated:

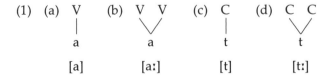

This analysis autosegmentalizes segmenthood, separating it from melodic features onto a "skeletal tier" or "skeleton," much as autosegmentalization of tone separated tonal features from melodic features of individual segments. Since linking of a single melodic unit to more than one C or V slot ("multiple

association" or "multiple linking") is realized as length, the skeleton is sometimes called the "timing tier."

Arguments for this autosegmental analysis of quantity must eliminate two
alternatives: a feature analysis of quantity and the representation of quantity
as a sequence of two identical melodic units. For example, in arguing for
multiple association of long vowels in Finnish, Prince (1984) shows an environment in which single vowels are deleted and long vowels are shortened.
Multiple association yields the correct result if a skeletal V slot is deleted (with
concomitant deletion of associated melodic material not linked to any other
slot). Having two slots for long vowels is crucial to capturing the generalization. Analogously, a rule simplifying clusters deletes a consonant before a sequence of two Cs and before geminates. Multiple association of geminates
allows the environment to be stated as preceding a sequence of two C slots.
These phenomena argue against an analysis of quantity as a single melodic
unit with the feature [+Long], but they could be handled if long vowels and
geminates were represented as sequences. That alternative is eliminated by
restrictions on consonant clusters. Geminates are systematically allowed to
end clusters where other sequences of two obstruents are not. To distinguish
sonorants from obstruents, these constraints must refer to features of melodic
units. Multiple association provides the right representation to capture the fact
that geminates count as single consonants with respect to these cluster constraints. Prince also argues that geminates do not behave like clusters with
respect to consonant gradation, which crucially refers to melodic features. The
generalization is clear: phenomena that count the number of segments "see"
long vowels and geminates as sequences of two segments, while phenomena
that look at their feature content "see" only one. This is precisely what the
representations in (1) provide.

Another type of argument for multiple association appeals to the fact that
devices familiar from the autosegmental analysis of tone can account for phonological quantity once segmental slots are placed on a separate tier from
melodic features. One such device is autosegmental spreading, used to account
for compensatory lengthening in a CV framework (Ingria 1980; Wetzels and
Sezer 1986). For example, in Luganda (Clements 1986a), concatenation of the
plural prefix *ba-* with the stem *ezi* "sweeper" yields *beezi*. The problem is how
to make lengthening of the stem vowel a consequence of deletion of the prefix
vowel. Multiple association does this:

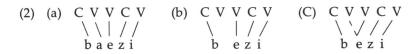

Deletion of the *a* leaves an empty V slot that associates with the neighboring
vowel by autosegmental spreading, familiar from the spreading of tone. Since
multiple association is realized as length, this analysis correctly makes lengthening of the *e* depend on deletion of the preceding vowel.

Evidence for multiple association naturally gave rise to the question of why representations should have this form. Here, too, appeal was made to a device used for tone: the Obligatory Contour Principle or OCP (see chap. 12, this volume), which rules out identical adjacent autosegments on the same tier. Since a sequence of two identical melodic units violates the OCP, long vowels and geminates must be represented with only one. Multiple association is then the only available representation that accounts for the ways they behave like sequences of segments. The evidence that rules referring to feature content "see" only one melodic unit in these cases (as in Finnish) supports this use of the OCP.

Arguments for the representation of quantity as multiple association to segmental slots figured prominently among the arguments for a CV skeleton, which included both one-many and many-one skeleton-melody associations, morphological templates like those of McCarthy (1979a, 1981a), and "empty" skeletal slots unassociated with melodic content (Clements and Keyser 1983).

1   The Special Behavior of Geminates: Integrity and Inalterability

With multiple association, attention again focused on why certain rules do not apply to geminates in the ways the representation would lead one to expect (Kenstowicz and Pyle 1973; Guerssel 1977, 1978). Geminates are said to exhibit *integrity* where epenthesis rules fail to split them up, and *inalterability* where rules fail to apply to them. Since multiple association represents geminates with only one melodic unit, the representation explains why a feature-changing rule cannot change only "half" of a geminate: application of the rule would affect the features associated with both segmental slots, resulting in a change in both "halves" of the geminate. What remains to be explained is why certain rules fail to apply to geminates at all. These are cases of inalterability.

Recent years have seen several attempts to explain the behavior of geminates. The pioneering studies of Hayes (1986b) and Schein and Steriade (1986) focus on the double association lines in geminates' representations, requiring that they both be explicitly mentioned in the rule in order for the rule to apply.[1] This approach has been criticized by Scobbie (1993) and Inkelas and Cho (1993). Scobbie attributes inalterability to the ill-formedness of a rule's output rather than to the way the rule matches against input. Inkelas and Cho argue that rules respecting inalterability are structure-filling rather than structure-changing, and that inalterability effects are also found with nongeminates. Both studies argue against constraints aimed specifically at the properties of representations with multiple association.

The special behavior of geminates has been harnessed to highlight the power of representations in achieving explanation. A key distinction is that between "true geminates," represented with multiple association, as in (3a), and "apparent geminates" (or "fake geminates"), which, though phonetically indistinguishable from them, are represented as two separate melodic units linked to separate C slots in the skeleton, as in (3b):

(3)   (a)   C   C   (b)   C   C

            k   k   k

If the OCP is a condition on lexical representations, there can be no morpheme-internal apparent geminates. Apparent geminates are necessarily hetero-morphemic, their existence indicating that (at least in some cases) the OCP does not rule out identical adjacent melodic units across morpheme boundaries.[2] Further, wherever geminates arise through autosegmental spreading (as in compensatory lengthening and total assimilation), a doubly linked geminate representation (a true geminate) results. These assumptions, then, assign multiply linked representations to tautomorphemic geminates and those that arise through spreading. Such true geminates contrast dramatically with apparent geminates in Tigrinya (Schein 1981; Kenstowicz 1982; Schein and Steriade 1986).

   The key Tigrinya rule spirantizes stops that are preceded by a vowel, even across morpheme boundaries (e.g., *gäzaxa* < *gäza* + *ka* "your house"). True geminates fail to undergo spirantization, regardless of whether they are tautomorphemic (*fäkkärä* "boast (3d sg. masc. perf.)", derived by total assimilation (*yəqqayädu* < *y* + *t* + *qayädu* "attach [imperf.]"), or by spreading of stem melodic material to an empty C slot in a suffix (*yəbarəkko* < *yəbarək* + Co "bless [3d sg. masc. jussive]"). The suffix in the last example is analyzed with an empty C slot because it characteristically causes gemination of a stem-final consonant, accomplished through spreading. These true geminates all exhibit inalterability in failing to spirantize. They contrast with the apparent geminates resulting from suffixation of *-ka* (with a specified *k*), which undergo spirantization (e.g., *baräxka* < *baräk* + *ka* "you blessed"). Given inalterability of multiply associated geminates, the contrast between the three types of true geminates (which do not spirantize) and the apparent geminates (which do) strongly supports the elements of the theory that dictate multiple association for the former.

2   The Prosodic Theory of Phonological Quantity

The theory discussed so far represents phonological quantity as the association of more than one C or V slot in the skeleton with a single melodic unit. Because it makes reference to segmental slots but not to higher prosodic structure, I call this the segmental theory of quantity.[3] Recent research has led to the elaboration of two main types of prosodic theories of quantity. One associates melodic units with segmental slots, replacing C and V slots with generalized X slots and relying on a richer theory of syllable structure that includes a nucleus node, generally representing "heavy" syllables (cf. below) as having a branching rhyme or nucleus node (Hayes 1980; Prince 1983; S. Anderson 1984; Levin 1985a; Lowenstamm and Kaye 1986; Kenstowicz and Rubach 1987; and others). The other associates melodic units with mora nodes in prosodic representations (Hyman 1985; Hayes 1989a; McCarthy and Prince 1986, 1990a, 1993; and others). Space limitations prevent discussing the former or differences between them here.[4] The important point of agreement is that an understanding of quantity requires consideration of prosodic structure above the segmental level.

The CV theory of quantity leaves some important questions unanswered. What is the relative quantity of long vowels and geminate consonants? Are other strings of segments quantitatively equivalent to either of these? Is there a common unit of measure of quantity in terms of which relative quantity can be stated? Some light is shed on these questions by the distinction many languages make between "light" and "heavy" syllables (Newman 1972; Hyman 1985; Hayes 1994), perspicuous in "quantity-sensitive" stress systems, where heavy syllables tend to attract stress.[5] Heavy syllables can be of two types: (1) syllables with a long vowel or diphthong, and (2) closed syllables, or syllables closed with certain consonants. Language-particular restrictions determine which syllables of these types are heavy. Syllables closed with a geminate fall under (2). This raises the question of what (1) and (2) have in common that makes both heavy, and how this is to be represented formally – a question on which recent studies have shed light.

Poser (1990) shows that the class of stems to which *-čan* can be suffixed in Japanese hypocoristics cannot be characterized in terms of the number of segmental slots or melodic units. From the name *hanako*, for example, three hypocoristics can be formed:

(4) (a) haa-čan (Suffix *-čan* is preceded by 2 melodic units, 3 segmental slots)
     (b) hač-čan (Suffix *-čan* is preceded by 2 melodic units, 3 segmental slots)
     (c) hana-čan (Suffix *-čan* is preceded by 4 melodic units, 4 segmental slots)
     (d) *ha-čan

For satisfying hypocoristic requirements, a syllable with a long vowel is equivalent to one closed with a geminate consonant, and both are equivalent to a sequence of two light (open, short-voweled) syllables. There is a common unit of measure – the mora: a light syllable has one, and a syllable with a long vowel or closed with a geminate has two. The forms in (4) are thus:

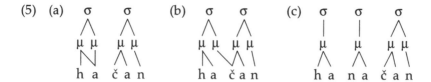

A vowel linked to two moras is long; a consonant that is moraic in one syllable and also the onset of the next is realized as a geminate. A hypocoristic stem in Japanese must consist of two moras. A long vowel or a geminate consonant contributes a second mora to the syllable, which is consequently heavy. Japanese hypocoristics bear on quantitative equivalence: with the mora as unit of measure, quantity in vowels and consonants is equivalent, for each adds a mora to the syllable, making it bimoraic. Further, a syllable with either vocalic or consonantal quantity is quantitatively equivalent to a sequence of two light syllables.

Hock (1986) and Hayes (1989a) use compensatory lengthening to argue for moraic representations. As has long been recognized, lengthening of a vowel can result not only from deletion of another vowel, but also from deletion of a consonant. Similarly, consonant gemination can result from deletion of a vowel. Hayes exploits the autosegmental analysis of quantity, but with multiple association to moras rather than to segmental slots. Deletion of a vowel or consonant leaves an empty mora node, whose association with another melodic unit results in quantity:[6]

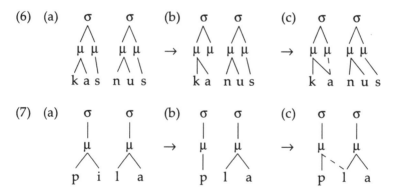

In (6), from Latin, where coda consonants are moraic and closed syllables are consequently heavy (bimoraic), deletion of the coda *s* results in association of *a* with the stranded mora, yielding *kaːnus*. In (7), attested in several African languages and as a fast speech rule in French, deletion of *i* results in linking of the following *l* with the stranded mora, yielding *plla*, in which the geminate is nucleus of the first syllable. Such cases are another source of evidence that what makes a vowel long is also what makes a consonant a geminate: association to an additional mora.

These cases do not require moraic representations, however; they can be handled by the theory with generalized X slots. Hayes' principal argument that compensatory lengthening is association to a stranded mora is based on the asymmetry between moraic and nonmoraic consonants. Deletion of an onset consonant does not cause vowel lengthening because onset consonants are not moraic. Deletion of a coda consonant can cause vowel lengthening, but only in languages where closed syllables are heavy, indicating that the coda consonant is dominated by a mora. The analysis further predicts that in languages where only certain coda consonants are moraic, only deletion of *moraic* coda consonants can cause compensatory lengthening. The general claim is that moraic structure, like tonal autosegments in tone languages, is stable under deletion of melodic material, which leaves the mora count intact. Association of the mora stranded by deletion with another melodic unit results in phonological quantity on that segment: compensatory lengthening. Phonological quantity thus cannot be understood in terms of segmental slots alone. Moraic structure, left intact under segmental deletion, shows up as quantity on individual segments with which an additional mora is linked.

Compensatory lengthening and the examples in (4) point in the same direction. First, they bring out the equivalence of different manifestations of phonological quantity and show that it can be captured in terms of the mora. Second, both are cases of *prosodically motivated quantity*: quantity appears in (4) and (5) to satisfy a bimoraic prosodic template, and in (6) and (7) because preexisting moraic structure is preserved and reassociated. Such phenomena make clear that phonological quantity is an aspect of prosodic (rather than segmental) structure.[7]

Co-occurrence restrictions between long vowels and geminate consonants show that quantity is intimately linked to syllable weight. Japanese is typical in that a long vowel can be preceded by a geminate consonant (e.g., *gakkoo* "school") but not followed by one (*gaakko* is impossible). A theory that looks only at segmental slots and not at higher prosodic structure does not see the key to an explanation: these words are syllabified as *gak.koo* and **gaak.ko*. It fails to capture the generalization that a long vowel cannot be the nucleus of a closed syllable. The syllable is thus the domain in which the co-occurrence restrictions can be explained. The explanation rests on the fact that Japanese exhibits a binary opposition between light (monomoraic) and heavy (bimoraic) syllables. Since a long vowel is bimoraic and a coda consonant contributes another mora to the syllable, a closed syllable with a long vowel (such as the first syllable of **gaak.ko*) would be trimoraic. By positing a bimoraic upper bound on syllables in Japanese morphemes,[8] the prosodic theory explains why a long vowel cannot be followed by a geminate consonant. It also explains two other facts: (1) why a long vowel cannot occur in other closed syllables, e.g., alongside *hon* "book", **hoon* is impossible;[9] and (2) why Japanese does not manifest three-way length contrasts, e.g., alongside *kite* "come!", *kiite* "listen!", and *kitte* "stamp", **kiiite* and **kittte* are impossible.[10] These aspects of the distribution of quantity are explained under the hypothesis that the syllable weight opposition is binary.

A prosodic theory of quantity that links melodic units to moras rather than segmental slots automatically explains geminate integrity. Under the segmental theory, it is necessary to prevent epenthesis rules from inserting another segmental slot between the two segmental slots used to represent quantity. With moras rather than segmental slots in the skeleton, a geminate consonant is linked to a mora in the previous syllable and serves as onset of the next, as in (5b). A geminate is not represented with two segmental slots, so there is no way anything could be inserted in its "middle." By the same token, as under the segmental theory, there is no way a rule could alter only "half" of a doubly linked geminate. However, it is still necessary to explain the cases where phonological rules fail to apply to geminates at all. Essentially the same range of explanations is available as under the segmental theory, mutatis mutandis.

An apparent anomaly of geminates' distribution lies in the fact that in many languages, certain consonants cannot close a syllable, but if they are geminates they can. In Japanese, for example, a syllable cannot be closed with an obstruent, but a geminate obstruent (e.g., *kitte*) is allowed. The same holds in Hausa. Recent proposals attribute geminates' ability to close a syllable under these conditions to the fact that they are both coda of one syllable and onset of the next. Itô (1989) proposes a filter that rules out codas with Place features, to which Hayes' (1986) Linking Constraint makes geminates immune because they are doubly linked. Under Yip's (1989) proposal, geminate codas are immune to coda constraints that ban Place features because they have no Place features of their own, "borrowing" them from the following onset. Goldsmith (1989, 1990) proposes an explanation in terms of autosegmental licensing, the idea that all features of a segment must be licensed by either the syllable node or the coda node under which they occur. The restrictions on coda consonants are interpreted in terms of the coda's restricted ability to license features. To explain geminate obstruents' ability to close a syllable, Goldsmith appeals to the fact that they are both coda of one syllable and onset of the next. An obstruent in Japanese or Hausa is licensed as onset of the next syllable, hence it need not be licensed as coda; its (unlicensed) appearance as coda is parasitic on its licensed appearance as onset.

Using the framework of harmonic phonology (Goldsmith 1993a), Goldsmith (1989, 1990) further exploits autosegmental licensing to explain geminates' integrity and inalterability. The key harmonic assumption is that phonological rules apply only in order to increase representations' wellformedness with respect to a set of word-level phonotactics. On this view, rules that weaken coda consonants do so in order to eliminate features that cannot be licensed by the coda, so that a wellformed representation results. A representation with a geminate obstruent closing a syllable is well-formed because the obstruent is licensed as onset of the next syllable. Since rules apply only to increase representations' well-formedness with respect to a phonotactic, they need not apply to geminates. Hence they do not. In this way, Goldsmith's proposal links geminates' integrity and inalterability to their ability to appear in positions where the corresponding nongeminate consonants cannot.

3   Conclusions: Phonological Quantity, Syllable Weight, and the Mora

The past fifteen years' research has significantly advanced the understanding of phonological quantity. Quantity has autosegmental properties reminiscent of the stability and spreading of tone in tone languages. This is captured by autosegmental representations that put quantity on a separate tier from melodic material. Such representations also account for the ways segments with quantity behave like a single melodic unit and for the contrast between true and apparent geminates in languages such as Tigrinya.

What does the tier with which melodic units are associated consist of? The study of quantity provides evidence that melodic units are associated with moras in prosodic representations: the unit of measure of quantity is the mora, in terms of which it is possible to state quantitative equivalences and differences between vowels and consonants, and between "long segments" and other strings of segments. Association with moras also accounts for the stability and spreading of quantity, for moras are stable and spread under deletion of melodic material; association of melodic material to a stranded mora results in quantity (compensatory lengthening). The relation between deletion and lengthening is indirect, mediated by moraic structure. Deletion causes compensatory lengthening because it results in a stranded mora. Association of a segment with an additional mora results in quantity.

What, then, is the mora? The glossary in Bright (1992) defines it as a unit of length, and the recent phonological literature generally calls it a unit of both length and weight. The mora, however, is not a unit of length in the simple sense that each mora in a phonological representation represents an equal timing unit. If that were so, a moraic nongeminate consonant and a short vowel would have the same duration, and a long vowel would have exactly twice the duration of these. Nongeminate coda consonants would also be significantly longer in languages where closed syllables are heavy than in those where they are not. Sequences of nongeminate coda consonants in such languages would be no longer than a single coda consonant, since the mora count would be the same. In this sense it is misleading to think of moras as constituting a "timing tier."

Quantity is predictable, however, from representations in which melodic units are linked to moras:

(8)   (a)   A vowel dominated by two moras is realized as a long vowel.
      (b)   A consonant dominated by two moras is realized as a geminate.

With representations like those in (5), the right results are obtained. (8) is essentially a cross-linguistic summation of language-particular phonetic rules that specify the duration of long vowels and geminate consonants in individual languages. Syllables with a long vowel and those closed with a geminate can be quantitatively equivalent without having the same duration. The mora is not a unit of length, but a unit of measure from which quantity is predictable.

What, then, does the mora measure? There is evidence that the mora is a unit of weight, and that the quantitative equivalences discussed above are consequently equivalences of syllable weight. The key fact bearing on this question concerns the distribution of segments with quantity in phonological strings. We have seen that a long vowel cannot be followed by a geminate consonant in languages such as Japanese, and that this can be explained in terms of the binarity of the syllable weight opposition in those languages, which imposes a bimoraic upper limit on the syllable. Syllable weight is thus the concept that explains co-occurrence restrictions among segments with quantity. The maximum number of moras per syllable is that needed to express a language's contrasts in syllable weight, although a larger number of segments are capable, a priori, of expressing quantity. This is evidence that the mora is a unit of weight.

Another piece of evidence that the mora is a unit of weight comes from the cross-linguistic generalization that phonological quantity is found only in languages that distinguish between light and heavy syllables (Hayes 1989a). If the mora is a unit of weight, only such languages can have structures that (8) will interpret as long vowels or as geminate consonants. The recent literature has thus been correct in characterizing the mora as a unit of weight, but incorrect in characterizing it as a unit of length. Weight is interpreted as quantity under the conditions specified in (8). "Phonological quantity" turns out to be a cover term for oppositions whose locus lies in contrasting associations of melodic material with units of weight (moras) in prosodic structure.

NOTES

* I am indebted to Juliette Blevins, Philip Le Sourd, and Moira Yip for comments on a draft of this chapter, and to Matthew Gordon for helpful discussion. Errors and inadequacies are mine alone.

1 This is also the approach of Goldsmith's (1990, p. 39) Conjunctivity Condition. One difference between Hayes's condition and the others is that the latter focus only on the association lines in the *target* of a rule, allowing a multiply associated autosegment to be the trigger.

2 Only if they are on the same tier would the domain of the OCP be at issue. The OCP has given rise to a number of issues that cannot be broached here. Among them: (1) Is the OCP a universal principle, a cross-linguistic tendency, or a cover term for a number of language-particular rules? (2) Is its domain lexical and hence morpheme-internal, or is it broader? (3) Does it merely rule out certain representations as ill-formed, or does it "actively" convert identical adjacent same-tier autosegments to

multiply linked autosegments? (2) interacts crucially with the Morphemic Tier Hypothesis (McCarthy 1979a, 1981a, 1982b, 1986b), which in crucial cases places distinct morphemes on separate tiers, where they are immune to potential cross-morphemic OCP effects. See McCarthy (1986b), Odden (1988), Yip (1988a), Goldsmith (1990, pp. 309–318), and Odden, chapter 12, this volume, for discussion.

3 This is really an abstraction for expository purposes since the CV skeleton has always been integrated into a theory of the syllable (Clements and Keyser 1983).

4 See Broselow, chapter 5 and Blevins, chapter 6, this volume, and the references cited there. Space limitations also prevent discussion here of the use of multiple association for the representation of biliteral roots in Semitic languages with so-called "long-distance geminates" (McCarthy 1981a, 1982b, 1986b) (see Hoberman, chapter 30, this volume).

5 See Kager, chapter 10, this volume, and the references cited there.

6 Onset consonants have been placed under the vowel nucleus's mora node here to conform with the Strict Layer Hypothesis of Selkirk (1984b).

7 The prosodic theory must be able to represent underlying contrasts in quantity. One proposal is that of Hayes (1989a), who represents short vowels with one mora, long vowels with two, and geminate consonants with an underlying mora.

8 Poser (1984b) shows that the handful of exceptions arise only across morpheme boundaries.

9 A handful of loan words (e.g., *toronboon* "trombone") are the only exceptions.

10 It is tempting to posit that the bimoraic upper limit is universal, and to make it follow from a putative principle of prosodic theory: the branching of prosodic constituents is *maximally binary* (see Kager, chapter 10, and McCarthy and Prince, chapter 9, this volume, and references cited there). Since syllable nodes dominate mora nodes in prosodic structure and no other node type can intervene (cf. the Strict Layer Hypothesis of Selkirk 1984b), there can be at most two moras per syllable. However, putative cases of trimoraic syllables militate against such an explanation (cf. Hayes (1989a, pp. 293–297) and the references cited there).

9 Prosodic Morphology

JOHN J. McCARTHY AND
ALAN S. PRINCE

0 Introduction

Prosodic morphology (McCarthy and Prince 1986 et seq.) is a theory of how morphological and phonological determinants of linguistic form interact with one another in a grammatical system. More specifically, it is a theory of how prosodic structure impinges on templatic and circumscriptional morphology, such as reduplication and infixation. There are three essential claims:

(1) Principles of Prosodic Morphology
   (a) Prosodic Morphology Hypothesis
      Templates are defined in terms of the authentic units of prosody: mora (μ), syllable (σ), foot (F), prosodic word (PrWd).
   (b) Template Satisfaction Condition
      Satisfaction of templatic constraints is obligatory and is determined by the principles of prosody, both universal and language-specific.
   (c) Prosodic Circumscription
      The domain to which morphological operations apply may be circumscribed by prosodic criteria as well as by the more familiar morphological ones.

In short, the theory of prosodic morphology says that templates and circumscription must be formulated in terms of the vocabulary of prosody and must respect the well-formedness requirements of prosody. Earlier proposals for including prosody in templatic morphology include McCarthy (1979), Nash (1980, p. 139), Marantz (1982), Yip (1982, 1983), Levin (1983), Broselow and McCarthy (1983), Archangeli (1983, 1984), McCarthy (1984a, 1984b), and Lowenstamm and Kaye (1986). Prosodic morphology extends this approach to the claim that *only* prosody may play this role, and that the role includes circumscription as well.

Reduplicative and root-and-pattern morphology are typical cases where the principles of prosodic morphology emerge with full vigor. In reduplicative and root-and-pattern morphology, grammatical distinctions are expressed by imposing a fixed phonological shape on varying segmental material. For example, the Ilokano reduplicative plural in (2) specifies a prefix whose canonical shape is constant – a heavy syllable – but whose segmental content depends on the base to which it is attached:

(2) Ilokano Reduplication (McCarthy and Prince 1986, 1991b; Hayes and Abad 1989)

kaldíŋ	"goat"	kal-kaldíŋ	"goats"
púsa	"cat"	pus-púsa	"cats"
kláse	"class"	klas-kláse	"classes"
jyánitor	"janitor"	jyan-jyánitor	"janitors"
ró?ot	"litter"	ro:-ró?ot	"litter" (pl.)
trák	"truck"	tra:-trák	"trucks"

In the root-and-pattern morphological system of Arabic, the productive plural and diminutive are expressed by imposing a fixed light-heavy syllable sequence (an iambic foot) on the singular noun base. As shown in (3), this canonical shape holds only of the initial boldface sequence, as a consequence of prosodic circumscription (see sec. 4 below).

(3) Arabic Productive Plural and Diminutive

Singular	Plural	Diminutive	Gloss
ħukm	/ħakaam/	**ħukaym**	"judgment"
ʕinab	/ʕanaab/	**ʕunayb**	"grape"
jaziir + at	**jazaa?ir**	**juzayyir**	"island"
šaaɣil	**šawaaɣil**	**šuwayɣil**	"engrossing"
jaamuus	**jawaamiis**	**juwaymiis**	"buffalo"
jundub	**janaadib**	**junaydib**	"locust"
sulṭaan	**salaaṭiin**	**sulayṭiin**	"sultan"

As in Ilokano, the Arabic categories "plural" and "diminutive" are expressed by an invariant shape or canonical form, rather than by invariant segmental material.

The morphemes or formatives that yield these fixed shapes are called *templates*, and the Prosodic Morphology Hypothesis regulates their form in a fundamental way. Under the Prosodic Morphology Hypothesis, templates can impose prosodic conditions, but not ordinary phonological ones – for example, they can require that the plural affix be a heavy syllable, but not that it have the shape vCv, because vCv is not a prosodically-definable unit (C and v are informal abbreviations for consonant and vowel, respectively, not to be confused with the C and V skeletal units discussed in section 5 below). The Template

Satisfaction Condition requires that a template be exactly matched in the output, within independently necessary limits on what constitutes a syllable, foot, or other prosodic constituent. Prosodic Circumscription of Domains is a distinct notion from templates, but related; its prosodic character demands that phenomena like the locus of infixation also be characterized in terms of prosodic constituents.

The goal here is to lay out and illustrate the fundamental tenets and empirical results of prosodic morphology theory. We begin (sec. 1) by describing the assumptions about prosody in which prosodic morphology is embedded, with particular focus on the important subtheory of word minimality. We turn then to the two principal types of templatic phenomena, in which the template functions as the stem or base of a form (sec. 2) and in which the template functions as an affix, leading to reduplication (sec. 3). Prosodic circumscription is the topic of section 4, and the results of sections 1 through 4 are then called on to construct a set of arguments in support of the Prosodic Morphology Hypothesis and the Template Satisfaction Condition (sec. 5). The chapter concludes (section 6) with an overview of some recent results emerging from the integration of prosodic morphology into optimality theory (Prince and Smolensky 1993; McCarthy and Prince 1993).

1   Prosodic Theory within Prosodic Morphology

The Prosodic Morphology Hypothesis requires that templatic restrictions be defined in terms of prosodic units. The Prosodic Hierarchy in (4), evolved from that of Selkirk (1980a, 1980b), specifies what those units are:

(4)   Prosodic Hierarchy

The units of prosody are the mora, μ, the syllable, σ, the metrical foot, F, and the prosodic word, PrWd. The mora is the familiar unit of syllable weight (Prince 1980; van der Hulst 1984; Hyman 1985; McCarthy and Prince 1986; Zec 1988; Hayes 1989; Itô 1989; etc.). The most common syllable weight typology is given in (5), where Cv syllables like *pa* are light and Cvv or CvC syllables like *paa* or *pat* are heavy.

(5) Syllables in Moraic Theory – Modal Weight Typology

Light   Heavy

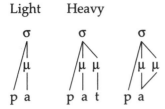

This equivalence between two types of heavy or bimoraic syllables can be seen in morphological phenomena like the Ilokano plural (2) and in phonological ones like stress, closed syllable shortening, compensatory lengthening, and versification.

Metrical feet are constrained both syllabically and moraically. The inventory laid out in (6) below is proposed in McCarthy and Prince (1986) and Hayes (1987) to account for Hayes's (1985) typological findings. (Subsequent work along the same lines includes Hayes (1991), Kager (1989, 1992a, 1992b, 1993), Prince (1991), Mester (1993), and others.) We write *L* for light syllable, *H* for heavy syllable:

(6) Foot Types

Iambic	Trochaic	Syllabic
LH	H, LL	σσ
LL, H		

Conspicuously absent from the typology are degenerate feet, consisting of just a single light syllable, though they may play a marked role in stress assignment (Kager 1989; Hayes 1991; but see Kiparsky 1992). The following general condition on foot form is responsible for the nonexistence (or markedness) of degenerate feet (Prince 1980; McCarthy and Prince 1986, 1991a, 1993, sec. 4; Hayes 1991):

(7) Foot Binarity
    Feet are binary under syllabic or moraic analysis.

Under strict Foot Binarity, single, therefore unfootable light syllables will occur, especially at edges. Unfooted syllables are immediately dominated by PrWd, rather than by F, in a "loose" interpretation of the Prosodic Hierarchy (see sec. 3 below, and Itô and Mester 1992; McCarthy and Prince 1993, sec. A.2).

The Prosodic Hierarchy and Foot Binarity, taken together, derive the notion "Minimal Word" (Prince 1980; Broselow 1982; McCarthy and Prince 1986, 1990a, 1991a, 1991b). According to the Prosodic Hierarchy, any instance of the category prosodic word must contain at least one foot (F). By Foot Binarity, every foot must be bimoraic or disyllabic. By transitivity, then, a prosodic word must contain at least two moras or syllables. In *quantity-sensitive* languages, which distinguish syllable weight, the minimal word is bimoraic; in *quantity-insensitive* languages, all syllables are presumptively monomoraic, and so the minimal word is disyllabic.

This notion of word minimality turns out to have broad cross-linguistic applicability; see among others McCarthy and Prince (1986, 1991a, 1991b, 1993); Cho (1992); Cole (1990); Crowhurst (1991b, 1992a); Dunlap (1991); Golston (1991); Hayes (1991); Itô (1991); Itô and Hankamer (1989); Itô, Kitagawa, and Mester (1992); Itô and Mester (1992); McDonough (1990); Mester (1990, to appear); Myers (1987); Orgun and Inkelas (1992); Piggott (1992); Spring (1990a, 1990b); Tateishi (1989); Weeda (1992); and Yip (1991). One particularly striking case of a word minimality effect occurs in the Australian language Lardil; it was first analyzed in these terms by Wilkinson (1988) based on work by Hale (1973) and Klokeid (1976); Kirchner (1992) and Prince and Smolensky (1991b, 1993) offer further analysis. In Lardil, Cvv(C) syllables are heavy or bimoraic, while Cv(C) syllables are light, so Lardil prosody is quantity-sensitive. The entailed bimoraic minimum is responsible for the following alternations, which involve both augmentation and truncation phenomena:

(8) Lardil

		Underlying	Nominative	Accusative	
(a)	Bimoraic base				
		/wiṭe/	wiṭe	wiṭe-n	"inside"
		/peer/	peer	peer-in	"ti-tree species"
(b)	Monomoraic base				
		/wik/	wika	wik-in	"shade"
		/ter/	tera	ter-in	"thigh"
(c)	Long bases				
		/mayara/	mayar	mayara-n	"rainbow"
		/kantukantu/	kantukan	kantukantu-n	"red"

Bimoraic roots remain unchanged in the nominative (8a). But monomoraic, hence subminimal roots are augmented to two moras (8b), guaranteeing licit PrWd status. Final vowels are deleted in the nominative with consequent loss of whatever consonants are thereby rendered unsyllabifiable, shown in (8c). Final vowels are, however, preserved in stems like *wiṭe*, which could not be made any shorter and still fulfill the minimality requirement. In Lardil, constraints on PrWd well-formedness therefore both promote augmentation and inhibit truncation. Optimality Theory (see sec. 6 below) provides the analytical tools needed to make sense of such complex interactions; a complete analysis is presented in Prince and Smolensky 1991b, 1993.

This succinct conception of prosodic word minimality, as devolving from just Foot Binarity and the Prosodic Hierarchy, has a number of correlative properties (McCarthy and Prince 1991a, 1991b):

- *Economy.* There is no "Minimal Word Constraint" in any language. Rather, observed word minimality restrictions are the result of the combination of two requirements, the Prosodic Hierarchy and Foot Binarity, that themselves never mention the notion "minimal word".

- *Role of quantity.* The nature of the smallest prosodic word in any language is fully determined by its prosody, disyllabic if quantity-insensitive, bimoraic if quantity-sensitive. (But cf. Piggott 1992; Itô and Mester 1992.)
- *No iambic minimum.* Though LH is a type of foot (the iamb), no language can demand a LH minimal word (cf. Spring 1990b, p. 79n.). Even in a language with iambic prosody, the minimal prosodic word will be the *minimal* iamb, which is simply any iamb that satisfies Foot Binarity.
- *Enforcement.* Because prosodic word minimality follows from Foot Binarity, enforcement of minimality will be by the same means as enforcement of other prosodic well-formedness requirements. Thus, just as syllabic well-formedness requirements may lead to epenthesis or block syncope, so too prosodic word minimality may lead to augmentation or block truncation.

Departures from these correlations will only be possible in cases where the underlying constraints are also violated. For instance, if there can be languages with no feet at all or with free distribution of unit feet, then such languages should not show effects of word minimality.[1]

Thus, the theory of prosodic word minimality is a very simple one, with broad universal consequences. There is, though, one important language-specific aspect to it, the level at which the minimality requirement is imposed. In Lardil, for example, the minimality restriction is visibly enforced at the level of the stem or morphological word, since the root may be subminimal. Languages differ in this respect; in other Australian languages, Dyirbal (Dixon 1972), Warlpiri (Nash 1980, p. 67f.), or Yidiɲ (Dixon 1977, p. 35; Hayes 1982), even bare roots are minimally disyllabic, and in Boumaa Fijian (Dixon 1988), with quantity-sensitive prosody, roots are minimally bimoraic. This parameter of interlinguistic variation is expressed by differing values of MCat in the following schema (McCarthy and Prince 1991a, 1991b, 1993, sec. 7):

(9) MCat = PrWd
where MCat ≡ Root, Stem, Lexical Word, etc.

In Lardil, MCat is Stem or Lexical Word, while in the other languages mentioned, it is Root. Imposition of this schema demands that the morphological constituent MCat correspond to a PrWd, which leads to the attendant observed word minimality restrictions. The difference is in whether the minimality restriction holds of bare roots, as a kind of morpheme structure constraint, or only of the surface, thereby typically leading to alternations of the Lardil type.

There are several correlative properties of the MCat = PrWd schema, important in prosodic word minimality theory and elsewhere:

- *Upward inheritance.* Once the MCat = PrWd requirement has been imposed, all superordinate MCats must also contain PrWd. Thus, if MCat = Root, as in Dyirbal and the other languages mentioned, there can be no minimality-related alternations, since Stem and Lexical Word, because they contain Root, will also contain PrWd, at least.

- *Fineness of grain.* Finer lexical distinctions of MCat can lead to differences between, e.g., nouns and verbs in the level at which word minimality is imposed.
- *Function word escape.* MCat is typically restricted to the lexical vocabulary, so nonlexical items are usually not PrWds. Hence, they are frequently exceptions to word minimality regularities.
- MCat = PCat. By generalizing the schema to *any* morphological category and *any* prosodic category, we obtain an abstract specification of what a template is – the requirement that the exponent of some morphological unit be a prosodic unit of a particular type. This idea is pursued in McCarthy and Prince (1993, sec. 4 and sec. 7), where it is interpreted within a general theory of constraints on the *alignment* of grammatical and prosodic categories.

The schema MCat = PrWd, then, provides the interface between the phonological theory of word minimality, based on the Prosodic Hierarchy and Foot Binarity, and the morphology and lexicon of a language.

Though word minimality restrictions have no independent status in the phonology, the minimal prosodic word (MinWd) is an important category-of-analysis in templatic and circumscriptional morphology. For instance, in the Australian language Diyari (Austin 1981; McCarthy and Prince 1986; Poser 1989), the minimal prosodic word is the template in prefixing reduplication:

(10)   Diyari MinWd Reduplication

Singular	Plural	
wila	wila-wila	"woman"
ŋankanti	ŋanka-ŋankanti	"catfish"
t̪ilparku	t̪ilpa-t̪ilparku	"bird species"

The underscored reduplicated string in Diyari is exactly two syllables long, in conformity with the quantity-insensitive prosody of the language. Like any prosodic word of Diyari, the reduplicative morpheme must be vowel-final. This explains why the last two examples are not *ŋankan-ŋankanti* and *t̪ilpar-t̪ilparku*, which would have been expected since they more completely copy the base (sec. 3). In essence, Diyari reduplication consists of compounding a minimal word with a full one.

In Yidiɲ (Dixon 1977; Nash 1979, 1980), the minimal word is the base to which total reduplication applies (McCarthy and Prince 1990a):

(11)   Yidiɲ MinWd Circumscriptional Reduplication

Singular	Plural	
.mu.la.ri.	mula-mulari	"initiated man"
.t̪u.kar.pa.	t̪ukar-t̪ukarpa-n	"unsettled mind"
.kin.tal.pa.	kintal-kintalpa	"lizard species"
.ka.la.ᵐpa.ɽa.	kala-kalaᵐpaɽa	"March fly"

In Yidiɲ, the disyllabic minimal prosodic word *within* the noun stem is targeted and copied completely. The syllabification of the stem determines whether the prosodic word so obtained is V-final, like *mula* from *mulari*, or C-final, like *kintal* from *kintalpa*. Further details are provided below, in section 4.

2 The Template as Base

The templatic target may be imposed on an entire stem, word, or other morphological base. It is useful to distinguish among three formally distinct types of base/template relation. One is truncation, found especially in the morphology of nicknames and hypocoristics, and exemplified below with Japanese and Yup'ik Eskimo. Another is root-and-pattern morphology, in which entire paradigms or morphological classes are organized along templatic lines. This is exemplified below with the shapes of the canonical noun stem in Arabic. The most complex cases where the template functions as a base compose template-mapping with prosodic circumscription. This is illustrated below (sec. 4) with the Arabic broken plural and diminutive, though other cases in the literature include the Choctaw *y*-grade (Lombardi and McCarthy 1991; Ulrich 1992; Hung 1992) and the Cupeño habilitative (Hill 1970; McCarthy 1984a; McCarthy and Prince 1990a; Crowhurst, to appear).

An extremely common mode of nickname or hypocoristic formation, broadly attested in the world's languages, is the result of mapping a name onto a minimal word template, bimoraic or disyllabic, depending in the usual way on the prosody of the language. This type of prosodic morphology was first identified by McCarthy and Prince (1986, 1990a), with subsequent developments including Weeda's (1992) exhaustive survey and studies of individual languages including Arabic (McCarthy and Prince 1990b), Swedish (Morris 1989), French (Plénat 1984; Steriade 1988), Spanish (de Reuse n.d.; Crowhurst 1992a), Nootka (Stonham 1990), and Japanese. (Other species of truncation, involving circumscription rather than template-mapping, are discussed in sec. 4 below.)

Truncation in Japanese has been most extensively investigated in these terms, starting with Poser (1984, 1990) and continuing with Tateishi (1989), Itô (1991), Mester (1990), Itô and Mester (1992), and Perlmutter (1992). The formation of the hypocoristics in (12) is typical:

(12) Hypocoristics in Japanese (Poser 1984, 1990)

Name	Hypocoristic
ti	tii-tyan
syuusuke	syuu-tyan
yoosuke	yoo-tyan
taizoo	tai-tyan
kinsuke	kin-tyan
midori	mii-tyan ~ mit-tyan ~ mido-tyan
wasaburoo	waa-tyan ~ wasa-tyan ~ sabu-tyan ~ wasaburo-tyan

As usual in systems of nickname formation, personal preferences may influence the form, and idiosyncrasies of segment-to-template mapping may be found (e.g., *sabu-tyan*). With complete consistency, though, the hypocoristic stem consists of an even number of moras, usually two, and it is realized in all the ways that an even number of moras can be, within the syllable canons of Japanese.

Though prominential stress is not found in Japanese, there is considerable evidence that it has a system of trochaic feet (Poser 1990) and that the minimal word is, as expected, bimoraic (Itô 1991). Thus, the template for the hypocoristic can be characterized fully prosodically as F$^+$ (one or more feet) or MinWd$^+$, the latter perhaps to be analyzed as a kind of MinWd-compound. The segments making up a name are mapped onto some expansion of this template, usually from left to right, to obtain the hypocoristic form.

In Central Alaskan Yupik Eskimo (Woodbury 1985; McCarthy and Prince 1986, 1990a), the template for the "proximal vocative" nicknaming system is, exactly like Japanese, F or MinWd. This is despite the fact that there are vast differences in the surface shape of the nicknames, because of independent differences in the prosody of the two languages:

(13) Proximal Vocatives in Central Alaskan Yupik Eskimo (Woodbury 1985)

Name	Proximal Vocative
Aŋukaɣnaq	Aŋ ~ Aŋuk
Nupiɣak	Nup ~ Nupix ~ Nupik
Cupəɬːaq	Cup ~ Cupəɬ
Kalixtuq	Kaɬ ~ Kalik
Qətunɣaq	Qət ~ Qətun

As in Japanese, there are individual preferences and idiosyncrasies of form, but the supervening regularity is that the hypocoristic template is a foot, iambic in Yup'ik and corresponding to the minimal word of the language.[2]

In some languages, the template-as-stem is much more firmly entrenched in the grammatical system, and it may be the fundamental organizing principle of the morphology. This is notoriously true in Arabic and other Afro-Asiatic languages (McCarthy 1979, 1981, 1984a, 1984b, 1989, 1993; Bat-El 1989, 1992; Dell and Elmedlaoui 1992; Hayward 1988; Hoberman 1988; Inkelas 1990; Lowenstamm and Kaye 1986; McCarthy and Prince 1986, 1990a, 1990b, 1991b; Moore 1989; Prince 1991; Yip 1988), but also in the Penutian languages Sierra Miwok (Freeland 1951; Broadbent 1964; Bullock 1990; Crowhurst 1991b, 1992b; Goldsmith 1990; Lamontagne 1989; Sloan 1991; Smith and Hermans 1982; Smith 1985, 1986), Yokuts (Newman 1944; Archangeli 1983, 1984, 1991; Steriade 1986; Prince 1987, 1991), and Takelma (Sapir 1922; Goodman 1988; Lee 1991), and to a lesser extent in Chinese (Yip 1991) and Salish (Montler 1989; Stonham 1990).[3]

These phenomena are all richly articulated, so it is not possible here to do more than sketch an approach to one of them, the canonical nouns of Standard

Arabic, abstracted from McCarthy and Prince (1990b), Prince (1991), and McCarthy (1993). Canonical nouns are integrated into the morphological system, based on their ability to form broken plurals (see (3) and sec. 4) and other criteria. The vast majority of nouns in the language are canonical, but many (such as recent loans like *tilifuun* "telephone") are not. The basic data appear in (14), which provides a classification by Cv-pattern of all the canonical noun stems of Arabic. The percentages given in (14) were obtained by counting all of the canonical noun stems occurring in the first half of the large Wehr (1971) dictionary (N ≈ 2400).

(14) The Canonical Noun Patterns

(a) H	(b) LL	(c) LH	(d) HL	(e) HH
CvCC	CvCvC	CvCvvC	CvvCvC	CvvCvvC
baħr	badal	waziir	kaatib	jaamuus
33%	7%	21%	12%	2%

(f) HL	(g) HH
CvCCvC	CvCCvvC
xanjar	jumhuur
14%	11%

Glosses: "sea", "substitute", "minister", "writer", "buffalo", "dagger", "multitude"

All patterns are well represented except for CvvCvvC (14e), which is probably an historical innovation in Arabic.

The classification of nouns in (14) according to the syllable-weight patterns (H, L) assumes final consonant extraprosodicity, which is independently motivated in Arabic. Analysis of these patterns of weight leads to two principal prosodic conditions on canonical noun stems (NStem):

(15) Prosodic Conditions on Canonicity of NStem

(a) Minimally bimoraic   (b) Maximally disyllabic
     NStem = PrWd   NStem ≤ σσ

Because the morphological category NStem is equated with the prosodic category PrWd, a NStem must contain a foot, under the Prosodic Hierarchy, and so it is minimally bimoraic, under Foot Binarity (7). That is, the minimal canonical noun stem of Arabic is a single heavy syllable (14a) or a sequence of two light syllables (14b). Furthermore, no canonical noun stem is longer than two syllables (14b–g). The maximality condition is a natural one under considerations of locality, which impose an upper limit of two on rules that count (McCarthy and Prince 1986 and sec. 5 below), but it can perhaps be given an even more direct prosodic interpretation in terms of conditions on branching (Itô and Mester 1992) or through an additional foot type, the generalized trochee of Prince (1983), Hayes (1991), and Kager (1992a, 1992b). Indeed, the generalized trochee combines the properties of (6); like the canonical noun stem of Arabic, it is minimally bimoraic, maximally disyllabic.

Within the limits set by these conditions, the bimoraic lower bound and the disyllabic upper bound, every combination of heavy and light syllables is actually attested.[4] This result shows that prosody supplies the right kind of vocabulary for describing the fundamental regularities of the system, and thus it confirms the Prosodic Morphology Hypothesis in a general way. But even more prosodic structure emerges when we look beyond the superficial properties of the system.

Specifically, all licit *templates* in the Arabic noun consist of feet or sequences of feet. In particular, this entails that there are no anti-iambic or HL noun templates in the morphological system of Arabic. The evidence of this is that the anti-iambic noun patterns like *kaatib* and *xanjar* have a very restricted role in Arabic morphology, even though such nouns are quite common. Anti-iambic nouns are derived not by mapping to a template but by other resources of prosodic morphology, to be described below. The remaining noun patterns – H, LL, LH, and HH – are actually templatic, and so they are broadly distributed in the lexicon of Arabic and used independently by the morphology.

The noun patterns H, LL, and LH are also all quantity-sensitive feet; in fact, they are all expansions of the iamb (sec. 1). The remaining authentic template HH is a sequence of two (iambic) feet; in fact, it is the only sequence of feet that meets the disyllabic upper bound on canonical nouns in (15b). In contrast, the anti-iamb HL does not have a foot-level analysis; at best it consists of a monosyllabic foot (H) plus an unfootable light syllable. The Iamb Rule (16) formalizes these observations about the difference between templatic and nontemplatic noun patterns:

(16)   Iamb Rule
       NStem *template* $\rightarrow F_I^+$

The Iamb Rule requires that the template of a noun stem consist of a whole number of iambic feet. The actual noun stem templates – H, LL, LH, and HH – are each analyzeable in this way, subject to the overall disyllabic upper bound in (15b).

McCarthy and Prince (1990b) and McCarthy (1993) review a number of arguments for the special, nontemplatic status of HL noun stems. Two are recapitulated here. The first, which is due to Fleisch (1968), involves an asymmetry between the anti-iambic noun stems and their apparent mirror images, the true iambic ones. All the nouns occurring in the first half of the Wehr dictionary were collected and grouped according to their vowel quality, a good indicator of their inherent diversity in a language like Arabic, where vowel quality is often used to distinguish morphological categories. The results appear in (17):

(17) CvvCvC vs. CvCvvC Noun Stems

HL		LH	
CaaCiC	263	CaCiiC	265
CaaCaC	7	CiCaaC	106
CaaCuC	1	CaCaaC	37
		CaCuuC	29
		CuCaaC	25
		CiCiiC	1
Total	271	Total	463

It is immediately apparent that the anti-iambic pattern is massively skewed to one vowel pattern, but the iambic one is not. Iambic nouns are more common and occur with more vocalic patterns in a more even distribution than anti-iambic ones. Nearly all anti-iambic nouns are vocalized like *kaatib*, with *aa* in the first syllable and *i* in the second. The reason is that they have just a single morphological function in Arabic, as participles of the basic or "Measure I" form of the verb. Specifically, a participle like *kaatib* "writing, scribe" is derived from a Measure I verb like *katab* "wrote". Since almost all anti-iambic nouns in Arabic are participles of Measure I, anti-iambs are found only with the characteristic *aa-i* vocalism of this participle. In contrast, true iambic nouns like those on the right in (17) have a variety of morphological functions, and some are basic lexical items, with no special morphological function at all. Therefore they occur with a variety of vocalizations.

A parallel argument can be made for anti-iambs like *xanjar*, this one based on the asymmetry between HL and HH nouns with a doubled root consonant (e.g., *sukkar* "sugar" vs. *jabbaar* "giant"). The data are in (18):

(18) CvCCvC vs. CvCCvvC Noun Stems With Doubling

HL		HH	
CvC_iC_ivC	8	CvC_iC_ivvC	109
$CvCC_ivC_i$	0	$CvCC_ivvC_i$	14
Total	8	Total	123

It is clear that there is a very strong bias in favor of the HH pattern in nouns with a doubled root consonant, either with the common medial doubling (*jabbaar*) or the rarer final doubling (*jilbaab* "a type of garment"). HL nouns of this type are rare and exceptional in other respects, such as plural formation. Remarkably, this asymmetry is limited to nouns with a doubled root consonant. Anti-iambic quadriliteral nouns like *xanjar*, without doubling, are actually slightly more common than HH nouns like *jumhuur*, though both are well represented in the lexicon.

If anti-iambic nouns are not templatic, what are they? The two types of anti-iambic nouns, *kaatib* and *xanjar*, have nontemplatic sources that correspond to their limited roles in the language.

According to the evidence presented in (17), anti-iambic nouns like *kaatib* are almost entirely restricted to active participles of Measure I verbs. Thus, there must be a direct morphological relation between the anti-iambic noun *kaatib* "writing, scribe" and the corresponding verb form *katab* "wrote". Plausibly, this morphological relationship is affixational in character: the noun *kaatib* is derived from the corresponding verb *katab* by left-adjoining a mora to the initial syllable[5] (and supplying a new vowel melody, as is quite typical in Arabic morphology). Hence there is no anti-iambic template underlying the noun *kaatib*, because the source of this noun is complex, involving affixation to the verb stem *katab*.

The other class of anti-iambs is the set of CvCCvC nouns like *xanjar*. The fundamental observation about this pattern, documented in (18), is that it is restricted to true quadriliterals, nouns with four (different) root consonants. Nouns of this type are essentially never found with a geminated or doubled root consonant. The explanation is that these nouns are *a-templatic*. In other words, the lexical specification of a noun like *xanjar* consists of just its four root consonants, without any templatic constraint on form. This does not mean that its form is free; on the contrary, the canons of Arabic syllable structure – obligatory onset and no tautosyllabic consonant clusters – limit the ways in which four consonants can be organized into a phonotactically well-formed word. The constraints on canonical nouns in (15) and note 4 limit the options still further, by imposing a disyllabic upper bound and requiring that any consonant cluster be medial. The actual surface form of CvCCvC nouns like *xanjar* is uniquely determined by these conditions. It is simply the result of organizing four consonants into a stem according to the constraints on Arabic syllable structure and noun canonicity. There is no template, nor is there any need for one. This analysis obviously provides an immediate explanation for why nouns of this type are limited to true quadriliterals: a triliteral root cannot force the CvCCvC shape without calling on an otherwise prohibited anti-iambic template.

A-templatic prosodic morphology, proposed in various forms by Archangeli (1991), Bat-El (1989, p. 40f.), and McCarthy and Prince (1990b, p. 31f.), is nothing more than the absence of a template in a morphological category; then the segmental melodemes simply organize themselves according to their lexical specifications or whatever principles of phonological well-formedness, such as epenthesis or Stray Erasure, obtain in that language.

The most striking cases of a-templatic prosodic morphology are those where it accounts for departures from *shape-invariance* – the fixed canonical form that holds within a morphological class in templatic morphology. In the Ethiopian Semitic language Chaha (19), a morphological category called the jussive is formed by imposing a CCəC or CəCC structure on the verbal root:

(19)   Chaha Jussive (Leslau 1964)

	Root	Jussive Verb	
(a)	gfr	yägfər	"release"
	k'βr	yäk'βər	"plant"
	ft'm	yäft'əm	"block'
	nks	yänkəs	"bite"
(b)	srt	yäsərt	"cauterize"
	trx	yätərx	"make incision"
	gmt'	yägəmt'	"chew off"

The choice between the two surface shapes of the Chaha jussive – *yägfər* vs. *yäsərt* – depends on the relative sonority of the last two root consonants.[6] That is to say, the schwa is inserted by a phonological rule of epenthesis, sensitive to local sonority relations in a familiar way. Because the location of the schwa in the jussive is straightforwardly predictable on purely phonological grounds, it should not be encoded in the template. This observation led McCarthy (1982a) and Hayward (1988) to conclude that the actual template of the Chaha jussive is a vowelless CCC skeleton, obviously problematic for the Prosodic Morphology Hypothesis.

But really a vowelless CCC template is the same as no template at all, since it says only that the underlying representation of the jussive consists of bare root consonants (with the agreement prefix). This is precisely what is meant by a-templatic prosodic morphology – without a template, the root consonants are organized prosodically by phonological rules of syllabification and epenthesis. An actual template is appropriate for morphological formations with a fixed, unpredictable canonical shape; where the shape is variable and phonologically predictable, as in the Chaha jussive, then no template is necessary or even possible.

Archangeli (1991) shows that the system of stem formation in Yawelmani Yokuts is partially templatic, partially a-templatic. The examples in (20) are given in their phonologically justified underlying representations, abstracting away from the results of epenthesis, closed syllable shortening, and other rules.

(20)   Yawelmani Yokuts Stems

Root size	(a)	(b)	(c)
Biliteral "devour"	CvC c'um	CvvC c'uum	CvCvv c'umuu
Triliteral "walk"	CvCC hiwt	CvvCC hiiwt	CvCvvC hiwiit
Longer (nouns only)	CvCCC t'on'ṭm "transvestites"		CvCvvCCC yaw'iilmn "Yawelmani"

Consider first columns (20b) and (20c). The stems in these columns are based on a heavy syllable template and a LH iambic foot template, respectively. These templates, like all templates, express the invariance structure of the stems – that which is constant throughout all the stems in a column. Roots are associated to these templates from left to right, leaving a residue of one or more a-templatic consonants. These remaining consonants have no templatically-specified role, so they are organized prosodically by the regular, well-studied rules of syllabification and epenthesis in this language. Only the initial substring of the stem has a fixed canonical shape specified by the template, while the final consonant sequence is a-templatic.

Column (20a) is analyzed by Archangeli (1991) with a light syllable template, but Prince (1991) argues that in this case the entire stem is a-templatic, like the Chaha jussive (19). The CvC^+ canonical pattern of (20a) requires no template at all; it is simply the result of imposing a minimal prosodic organization on the single vowel and two or more consonants that make up a Yokuts root. Elimination of the light syllable as a stem-template in Yokuts yields a worthwhile theoretical result: the true stem-templates of Yokuts, the heavy syllable and the iambic foot, are both types of minimal words, so Stem = MinWd (cf. (9)). This then accords with the special role of the minimal word as a stem-template or stem substitute in root-and-pattern morphology (12, 13, 15a), reduplication (10, 23), and prosodic circumscription (41).

A-templatic prosodic morphology may initially seem completely antithetical to the enterprise; after all, isn't the present theory of prosodic morphology a theory of *templates*? It is indeed, at least in part, but phenomenologically it is a theory of shape-invariance. Where shape-invariance does not hold, as is patently true in Chaha and Yawelmani, then there can be no template consistent with the Prosodic Morphology Hypothesis and the Template Satisfaction Condition. In these cases, and even more clearly in the Axininca Campa example analyzed in McCarthy and Prince (1993, sec. 5, sec. 7), the invariance structure is not templatic, but emerges out of other prosodic constraints of the language.

3   The Template as Affix

A template that is affixed to a base will lead to copying or reduplication of the segments of that base, which then satisfy the template. This is reduplication. There are three fundamental issues in the theory of reduplication: the form of the templatic affix; the satisfaction of the templatic affix; and the interaction between reduplication and the phonology. We will not address the last issue here, but see Carrier (1979), Carrier-Duncan (1984), Kiparsky (1986), Marantz (1982), Mester (1986), Munro and Benson (1973), Odden and Odden (1985), Uhrbach (1987), and Wilbur (1974).

The literature on reduplication within prosodic morphology theory and its predecessors is now vast, including at least the following: Marantz 1982;

McCarthy and Prince 1986, 1988, 1991b, 1993; Archangeli 1991; Aronoff 1976, 1988; Aronoff et al. 1987; Bagemihl 1991; Bao 1990; Bates and Carlson 1992; Bell 1983; Black 1991; Broselow 1983; Broselow and McCarthy 1983; Chiang 1992; Clements 1985; Cole 1991; Crowhurst 1991a, 1991b; Davis 1988, 1990; Everett and Seki 1985; Finer 1985; French 1988; Goodman 1993; Hayes 1982; Hayes and Abad 1989; Hewitt and Prince 1989; Hill and Zepeda 1992; Janda and Joseph 1986; Kim 1984; Kiparsky 1986; Kroeger 1989a, 1989b; Lee and Davis 1993; Levelt 1990; Levergood 1987; Levin 1983, 1985, 1989; McCarthy 1979, 1982b; McNally 1990; Mutaka and Hyman 1990; Nash 1979, 1980; Nivens 1992; Noske 1991; Plénat 1984; Poser 1982, 1989; Prince 1987, 1991; Schlindwein 1988, 1991; Shaw 1980, 1987, 1992; Sietsema 1988; Sloan 1988; Smith 1985, 1986; Spring 1990a, 1990c, 1992; Steriade 1988; Stonham 1990; Weeda 1987; Williams 1984, 1991; Yin 1989; Yip 1982, 1991, 1992. Obviously, we cannot review even a fraction of this here; rather, our goal, as in the previous section, is to highlight some of the main results that have emerged within prosodic morphology.

On the face of it, the idea that reduplication involves affixing a template may seem surprising, since one might expect reduplicative operations to say something like "copy the first syllable," as illustrated in (21). Moravcsik (1978) and Marantz (1982) observe that syllable-copying, in this sense, does not occur:

(21) "Copy First Syllable," Hypothetically
ta.ka   →   ta-ta.ka
tra.pa   →   tra-tra.pa
tak.pa   →   tak-tak.pa

Rather, monosyllabic prefixal reduplication always specifies a *templatic target*, following one of the patterns in (22), both from Ilokano (Hayes and Abad 1989):

(22) Monosyllabic Prefixal Reduplication: Real Cases
(a) σ_μ – e.g., Ilokano *si* + σ_μ "covered/filled with"
                  bu.neŋ   →   si-bu-bu.neŋ   "carrying a buneng"
                  jya.ket   →   si-jya-jya.ket   "wearing a jacket
                  pan.di.liŋ   →   si-pa-pan.diliŋ   "wearing a skirt"
(b) $\sigma_{\mu\mu}$ – e.g., Ilokano plural
                  pu.sa   →   pus-pu.sa   "cats"
                  jya.nitor   →   jyan-jya.nitor   "janitors"
                  kal.diŋ   →   kal-kal.diŋ   "goats"

Whether the initial syllable of the base is closed or open has no effect on the affix; rather, the prosodic shape of the affix remains constant throughout a particular morphological category. Thus, it is the morphology – via the template – and not the syllabification of the base that is the determinant of the outcome. Reduplication specifies a templatic target, not a constituent to be copied.

Cross-linguistically, the observed possibilities for reduplicative templates are rather limited, once they are properly classified in prosodic terms. The smallest template is the light syllable, seen in (22a) above and other cases. Another common reduplicative template consists of some species of minimal word, such as a heavy syllable in Ilokano (2, 22b), a disyllabic sequence in Diyari (10), or a bimoraic sequence in Manam (23):

(23)   Suffixing Reduplication in Manam (Lichtenberk 1983; McCarthy and Prince 1986, 1991b)

salaga	salaga<u>laga</u>	"long"
moita	moit<u>aita</u>	"knife"
ʔarai	ʔar<u>airai</u>	"ginger species"
laʔo	la<u>ʔolaʔo</u>	"go"
malaboŋ	malabom<u>boŋ</u>	"flying fox"
ʔulan	ʔulan<u>laŋ</u>	"desire"

Many cases can be reduced to these two reduplicative templates: the light or monomoraic template, necessarily monosyllabic of course, and the heavy or bimoraic template, sometimes specified as monosyllabic too, and equivalent to MinWd. This is precisely what we would expect under the Prosodic Morphology Hypothesis, since light versus heavy is a fundamental prosodic dichotomy.

A third type of templatic reduplicative formation does not involve an *affixal* template at all: this is quantitatively complementary reduplication, light with heavy bases and heavy with light bases. McCarthy and Prince (1986, 1991b) identify two cases of this, the Sanskrit aorist and the Ponapean verb (on which also see Rehg and Sohl 1981; Goodman 1993). Hill and Zepeda (1992) provide a third, from Tohono O'odham (Papago). The Ponapean examples in (24) are typical:

(24)   Quantitative Complementarity in Ponapean Reduplication
(a)   Heavy base, Light prefix

<u>du</u>-duup	"dive"
duup	
mand	<u>ma</u>-mand	"tame"
laud	<u>la</u>-laud	"big, old"
kens	<u>ke</u>-kens	"ulcerate"

(b)   Light base, Heavy prefix

pa	<u>paa</u>-pa	"weave"
pap	<u>pam</u>-pap	"swim"
lal	<u>lal</u>-lal	"make a sound"
par	<u>par</u>-a-par	"cut"

In Ponapean, based on independent word-minimality criteria, final consonants are extrametrical. Therefore a base like *pap* is light, while bases like *duup* and *mand* are heavy. With monosyllabic bases like these, there is perfect complementarity between the weight of the base and the weight of the prefix.

(With polysyllabic bases, a more complex pattern emerges; see Rehg and Sohl 1981; McCarthy and Prince 1986, 1991b.)

The explanation for quantitative complementarity is that the template is an output target imposed on the entire stem, prefix plus base, rather than on just the prefix. That is, quantitatively complementary reduplication has more in common formally with root-and-pattern morphology (sec. 2) than with templatic affixation. To see what the template is, assume an analysis of the reduplicant (the copied string) plus base into trochaic feet, as in (25):

(25)　(a)　du-[duu]$_F$ ⟨p⟩　　(b)　[paa]$_F$-pa

Descriptively, Ponapean reduplicated monosyllables contain one and only one foot, but they also contain an unfooted syllable, either as affix (25a) or base (25b). This structure is the *loose minimal word* (cf. discussion of (7) above and McCarthy and Prince 1991a, 1991b; Itô, Kitagawa, and Mester 1992), a prosodic word that contains one foot but not two, with additional unfooted (and unfootable) material present at an edge. Therefore the prefixal syllable is maximal, subject to the overall templatic target that the stem be a MinWd, loosely parsed.

This brief typological survey suggests that all reduplicative templates can perhaps be reduced to a set of expressions involving the category MinWd, as follows (McCarthy and Prince 1991b):

- The heavy template – a bimoraic foot or a heavy syllable $\sigma_{\mu\mu}$ – is exactly equal to the category MinWd (sometimes with further specification of monosyllabism). In languages without weight contrasts, like Diyari, all syllables are presumptively monomoraic, so the MinWd template is expressed by disyllabism. The MinWd template, as an affix on a form which is itself a prosodic word, can be thought of as a kind of PrWd compound. This is a type of *external morphology*, applying an affix outside the prosodic word.
- The light syllable template is < MinWd – i.e., less than a minimal prosodic word, and so prosodically dependent on the base, as a kind of *internal morphology*. In languages without weight contrasts, < MinWd specifies a monosyllabic template, since the minimal word is disyllabic.
- The template in systems with quantitative complementarity like Ponapean is also MinWd, but loosely parsed. This too is internal morphology, but in the specific sense that the template functions as an output condition on the entire base plus affix, rather than on the affix itself.

These are obviously broad generalizations, subject to further empirical testing and refinement. Nonetheless, like the Iamb Rule (16) of Arabic, they offer a way in which the Prosodic Morphology Hypothesis might be further sharpened in specifying the role of prosodic categories in templatic morphology.

Whatever the form of the template, the mapping of melody to template is governed by the Template Satisfaction Condition, just as in root-and-pattern morphology (sec. 2). But the reduplicative situation is somewhat more complex, involving several constraints dictating the relation between the base (abbreviated below as B) and the reduplicant (abbreviated R). We take the fundamental copying constraints to be Contiguity, Anchoring, and Maximality, which restate principles in McCarthy and Prince (1986). These constraints are developed at length, within optimality theory, in McCarthy and Prince (1993, sec. 5).

(26)   Contiguity[7]
       R corresponds to a contiguous substring of B.

This is a formulation of the "no-skipping" requirement of McCarthy and Prince (1986, p. 10).[8]
    A second constraint places a further structural restriction on the B-R relation:

(27)   Anchoring[9]
       In R + B, the initial element in R is identical to the initial element in B.
       In B + R, the final element in R is identical to the final element in B.

The reduplicant R and the base B must share an edge element, initial in prefixing reduplication, final in suffixing reduplication (McCarthy and Prince 1986, p. 94).[10]
    The third constraint governs the extent of match between B and R:

(28)   Maximality
       R is maximal.

Under the Template Satisfaction Condition, Maximality asserts that R is as big as it can be and yet not exceed the template.[11]
    All of these constraints have correlates and predecessors in autosegmental theory. Contiguity harkens back to the principle of one-to-one association in Clements and Ford (1979), McCarthy (1979, 1981), and Marantz (1982). Anchoring echoes the directionality of association in Clements and Ford (1979) and McCarthy (1979, 1981), and more directly Marantz's (1982) dictum that melody-to-template association proceeds from left to right in prefixes, from right to left in suffixes (cf. Yip 1988; Hoberman 1988). Finally, Maximality is a remote descendant of the "Well-formedness Condition" of Goldsmith (1976), with its prohibition on unassociated melodemes.
    Consider how these constraints will apply to an example like Ilokano heavy syllable reduplication (2). Assume that they must evaluate a set of candidate reduplicants (as in Optimality Theory – Prince and Smolensky 1993 and below, sec. 6) for the base *jyánitor*. As the following table shows, all candidates other

than *jyan-* violate at least one of the reduplicative constraints or the Template Satisfaction Condition:

(29) Failed Candidate Reduplicants for $\sigma_{\mu\mu}$ + *jyánitor*

Violate TSC	Violate Contiguity	Violate Anchoring	Violate Maximality
jya-	jan-	yan-	jyaː
jyani-	jyat-	nit-	jiː
. . .	jyor-	tor-	. . .
	. . .	. . .	

The procedure or operation by which the copy is made is irrelevant; the point is that the constraints must evaluate the relation between reduplicant and base according to these constraints, which essentially require a special kind of identity. This conception of reduplication is developed and exemplified in McCarthy and Prince (1993, sec. 5, sec. 7).

In (29), the Template Satisfaction Condition demands that the templatic requirements of Ilokano be matched exactly, excluding candidate reduplicants like **jya-* (too small) or **jyani-* (too big). The Template Satisfaction Condition also requires that language-particular prosodic constraints be obeyed in templates, and this can be observed with forms like **roː-ró?ot*. Ilokano bars glottal stop from syllable-final position (Hayes and Abad 1989), overriding Maximality, which would otherwise require **ro?-ró?ot*. Here, an absolute phonotactic requirement of the language blocks Maximality, but it seems clear that prosodic markedness conditions may have the same effect, as proposed in Steriade (1988) and McCarthy and Prince (1993, sec. 7).

Besides universal and language-particular prosodic constraints, three other factors are known to impinge on template satisfaction, particularly in reduplicative systems. One is the prosodic structure of the base. In the phenomenon of *quantitative transfer* (Levin 1983; Clements 1985; Hammond 1988; McCarthy and Prince 1988; Steriade 1988; Selkirk 1988), base vowel length is copied in the reduplicant, showing that the base and reduplicant cannot always be regarded as strings of segments, since the segmental level alone does not encode quantitative oppositions. An example of this is heavy-syllable reduplicative prefixation in Mokilese:

(30) Mokilese Heavy σ Prefix (Harrison 1976; Levin 1983, 1985, 1989; McCarthy and Prince 1986, 1988, 1991b)
(a) CvC . . . stems

pɔdok	pɔd-pɔdok	"plant"
mʷiŋe	mʷiŋ-mʷiŋe	"eat"
kasɔ	kas-kasɔ	"throw"
wadek	wad-wadek	"read"
pilɔd	pil-pilɔd	"pick breadfruit"

(b) Cvː . . . stems

kookɔ	<u>koo</u>-kookɔ	"grind coconut"
sɔɔrɔk	<u>sɔɔ</u>-sɔɔrɔk	"tear"
čaak	<u>čaa</u>-čaak	"bend"

Various mechanisms of transfer have been proposed and possible cases of transfer of prosodic characteristics other than length have been identified. Facts like these indicate that the copying constraints Contiguity, Anchoring, and Maximality evaluate at least some aspects of the prosodic structure of the base and reduplicant together with their segmental structure. But it remains to be seen how to obtain this result in, e.g., Mokilese without also predicting the impossible syllable-copying situation illustrated in (21).

Second, because the base also has a morphological analysis of its own, there can be competition between respecting the prosodic requirements imposed by the templatic affix and the inherent morphological analysis of the base. Cases of this sort have been discussed by Aronoff (1988), Carrier-Duncan (1984), Marantz (1987), McCarthy and Prince (1993), Mutaka and Hyman (1990), Odden and Odden (1985), Silverman (1991), Spring (1990a, 1990c), and Uhrbach (1987). For example, according to Mutaka and Hyman (1990), the Kinande noun reduplicates as in (31). (The augment, a prefix *e-* or *o-*, has been suppressed in these examples, since it does not participate in reduplication.)

(31)   Kinande Noun Reduplication

    (a) ku-gulu-<u>gulu</u>   "real leg"
    (b) mú-twe-<u>mú-twe</u>   "real head"
    (c) mw-aná-<u>mw-ana</u>   "real child"
    (d) m-bulí-<u>m-buli</u>   "real sheep"
    (e) n-dwa-<u>n-dwa-n-dwa</u> "real wedding"
    (f) swa-<u>swa-swa</u>   "real cabbage"
    (g) tu-gotseri-No Reduplication "sleepiness/*real sleepiness"

Example (31a) shows that the root reduplicates exactly if disyllabic, while (31b) shows that a classifier prefix is reduplicated if the root is monosyllabic. Examples (31c–f) show reduplication of a complete onset cluster *mw, mb, ndw,* and *sw*. Examples (31e, f) also evidence one of the peculiarities of Kinande: when the classifier + root collocation is monosyllabic like *ndwa* or *swa*, there is double reduplication to achieve template satisfaction. Example (31g) displays the other peculiarity: trisyllabic or longer roots cannot undergo reduplicative morphology at all.

The fundamental observation is that the reduplicant in the Kinande noun is always exactly disyllabic, corresponding to a MinWd template. In the case of polysyllabic roots, exact disyllabicity is enforced by suspending reduplication altogether. Mutaka and Hyman's (1990, p. 83) explanation for this is that Kinande reduplication is subject to a Morpheme Integrity Constraint, which bars incomplete reduplication of a morpheme. A form like *tu-gotseri-<u>gotseri</u>*

violates the Template Satisfaction Condition, since the template is disyllabic, while a form like *tu-gotseri-tseri* violates the Morpheme Integrity Constraint, since only part of the root is copied. The result is complete failure of the reduplicative morphology, an outcome also sometimes seen in prosodic delimitation (sec. 4). In other languages, morphological integrity has other effects, such as barring reduplication of nonroot material (McCarthy and Prince 1993, sec. 5).

Finally, since the earliest treatments of templatic and reduplicative morphology (McCarthy 1979; Marantz 1982), a special melody / template relation called *prespecification* has been recognized. In prespecification, invariant prior linking of a melodic element to a templatic position overrides or supplants productive, rule-governed linking of a melodic element to the same position. For example, Marantz analyzes the C*i* reduplication of Yoruba (*lo, li-lo* "to go/going") with a CV prefixal template whose V is prelinked to the invariant *i*.

There is considerable evidence, discussed in McCarthy and Prince (1986, 1990a), that the phenomenon of melodic invariance in reduplicative affixes cannot be reduced to prespecification. This evidence comes in part from so-called echo words, a type of total word reduplication in which some systematic change is effected in one copy. Echo word formation seems to be nearly universal; it is found in English (*table-shmable*) or, with more instructive results, in the Dravidian language Kolami:

(32)   Kolami Echo-Word Formation (Emeneau 1955)

pal	pal-gil	"tooth"
kota	kota-gita	"bring it!"
iir	iir-giir	"water"
maasur	maasur-giisur	"men"
saa	saa-gii	"go (cont. ger.)"

Descriptively, the entire word is reduplicated with the initial Cv(v) of the second copy fixed at *gi*. The sequence *gi* appears even when the original is vowel-initial, and the vowel *i* occupies both moras of an original long vowel.

This widespread phenomenon is incompatible with templatic prespecification. For one thing, there is no template to prespecify. The copying constraints alone, especially Maximality, are sufficient to ensure complete identity (modulo *gi*) between base and reduplicant, so any template would be completely supererogatory (McCarthy and Prince 1986, p. 105; McCarthy and Prince 1988, 1990a, 1993, sec. 5). Thus, Maximality alone, without a template, is responsible for total reduplication, here and elsewhere.

Suppose, though, that a suffixal template were provided, gratuitously. This template would have to be PrWd, which matches any word, regardless of its size. To what, then, would the melodic invariant *gi* be prelinked in the reduplicative affix, as prelinking theory requires? The grammar does not enumerate the terminal elements of PrWd – it cannot, since PrWd has unboundedly many terminal elements – yet it is exactly to those terminal elements that the melodic invariant *gi* would have to be prelinked. Needless to say, this problem exists independently of the choice of terminal elements: syllables, moras, onsets, nuclei, or segments all are unboundedly many in PrWd. Moreover, even if it were somehow possible to enumerate the terminal elements of PrWd, it would then be necessary to fix long *ii* in the initial syllable of the template, to obtain *maasur-giisur*. But this wrongly predicts long *ii* in all cases, yielding **kota-giita*.

Instead of melodic prespecification, what we are witnessing here is the same kind of melody-to-template mapping seen in root-and-pattern morphology, as proposed by McCarthy (1979, p. 319) and McCarthy and Prince (1986, 1990a).[12] The melody *gi* has an autonomous status as a purely melodic entity with its own autosegmental plane, just like *ktb* or *a-i* in the Arabic verbal system; the difference is that *ktb* and *a-i* are mapped to empty templatic slots in a "feature-filling" fashion, whereas the melody *gi* is applied in a "feature-changing" manner, *overwriting* the original melodic material of the base.

The echo morphology of Kolami, then, consists of exact reduplication in perfect obedience to Maximality, plus the melodic echo morpheme *gi*, along with the information that this melody links to the second member of the compound. The base itself supplies the array of prosodic positions that the melody anchors to, in a further type of a-templatic prosodic morphology (see sec. 2). Coming in on its own plane, with free access to the prosodic positions of the base, the melodic morpheme associates in the usual left-to-right fashion, delinking the base phonemes as it goes. As with feature-filling association in Arabic, the vocalic melodeme must link to both vocalic moras in a heavy syllable, so that we obtain *maasur–giisur* rather than **maasur-giasur*.[13] From this interpretation of melody-to-template mapping, which is inevitable in the context of recent rule typology, melodic invariance follows without prespecification. Within the theory of Prosodic Morphology, there is the further prediction that prosodically null positions like the onset may be supplied by melodic overwriting, so that *iir-giir* is possible, while prosodically genuine positions – like a long vowel or a moraic coda consonant – cannot be an invariant part of echo formation. Only templates, not melodies, can supply invariant prosody. Thus, we predict the nonexistence of an echo-word system that takes arbitrarily long input and that specifies both the quality and the quantity of some segment in the output (e.g., an echo-word system with *kota* → *kota-giita* and *koota* → *koota-giita* or one with *kota* → *kota-gita* and *koota* → *koota-gita*). So far as we know, this prediction is borne out.

4   Prosodic Circumscription

There is one remaining aspect of prosodic morphology theory to discuss: prosodic circumscription. Typically, a morphological operation like affixation is applied to a base specified as a grammatical category like root, stem, or word. The result is ordinary prefixation or suffixation. Under prosodic circumscription, though, a morphological operation is applied to a base that is a prosodically-delimited substring within the grammatical category. The result is often some sort of infix, though there are many applications of prosodic circumscription extending beyond infixation.

Ulwa, a language of the Atlantic coast of Nicaragua, presents a remarkably clear case of infixation by prosodic circumscription. Ulwa is analyzed by Hale and Lacayo Blanco (1989), though Bromberger and Halle (1988) first brought this example to our attention. The possessive in Ulwa is marked by a set of infixes located after the stressed syllable of the noun:

(33) Ulwa Possessive

súːlu	"dog"	súːkinalu	"our (excl.) dog"
súːkilu	"my dog"	súːnilu	"our (incl.) dog"
súːmalu	"thy dog"	súːmanalu	"your dog"
súːkalu	"his/her dog"	súːkanalu	"their dog"

Stress is iambic, assigned from left to right (though there is optional retraction of stress from a final syllable); that is, stress falls on the initial syllable if it is heavy, otherwise the peninitial syllable. Hence, the possessive infixes follow the first syllable if heavy, otherwise the second syllable:

(34) Location of Ulwa Infixes (noun + "his")
    (a) after initial syllable

bás	bás-ka	"hair"
kíː	kíː-ka	"stone"
súːlu	súː-ka-lu	"dog"
ásna	ás-ka-na	"clothes"

    (b) after peninitial syllable

saná	saná-ka	"deer"
amák	amák-ka	"bee"
sapáː	sapáː-ka	"forehead"
siwának	siwá-ka-nak	"root"
kulúluk	kulú-ka-luk	"woodpecker"
anáːlaːka	anáː-ka-laːka	"chin"
arákbus	arák-ka-bus	"gun"
karásmak	karás-ka-mak	"knee"

The fundamental idea in prosodic circumscription theory is that the Ulwa infixes *-ka, -ki, -ma,* . . . are actually suffixes, but suffixes on the prosodically circumscribed initial foot within the Ulwa noun stem.

The analysis of Ulwa and the overall theory of circumscription on which it is based are presented in McCarthy and Prince (1990a), though some aspects of the theory recall earlier proposals (Broselow and McCarthy 1983; McCarthy and Prince 1986). Central to prosodic circumscription is a parsing function $\phi(C, E)$ which returns the designated prosodic constituent C that sits at the edge E of the base B. The function ϕ induces a factoring on the base B, dividing it into two parts: one is the *kernel* B:ϕ, the part that satisfies the constraint (C, E); the other is the *residue* B/ϕ, the complement of the kernel within B.[14] Assuming an operator "*" that gives the relation holding between the two factors (normally left- or right-concatenation), the following identity holds:

(35)   factoring of B by ϕ
       B = B:ϕ * B/ϕ

In *positive* prosodic circumscription, of which Ulwa is an example, the B:ϕ factor, the specified prosodic constituent, serves as the base for the morphological operation. Let O(X) be a morphological (or phonological) operation defined on a base X. We define O:ϕ – the same operation, but conditioned by positive circumscription of (C, E) – in the following way:

(36)   Operation Applying under Positive Prosodic Circumscription
       O:ϕ(B) = O(B:ϕ) * B/ϕ

That is, to apply O to B under positive prosodic circumscription is to apply O to B:ϕ, concatenating the result with B/ϕ in the same way ("*") that the kernel B:ϕ concatenates with the residue B/ϕ in the base B. In this way, the operation O:ϕ inherits everything that linguistic theory tells us about O, except its domain of application.

In Ulwa specifically, the factor returned by ϕ is a foot at the left edge, so we characterize the Ulwa possessive as O:ϕ(F, Left), where O is the morphological operation "Suffix POSS". For example, the factoring of *karásmak* "knee" is as follows:

(37)   Factoring of Ulwa Nouns
       O:ϕ(karasmak) = O(karasmak:ϕ) * karasmak/ϕ
                        = O(karas) * mak
                        = karas-ka * mak
                        = karaskamak

The initial iambic foot, rather than the whole noun, functions as the base for suffixation of the possessive morpheme. Of course, with words consisting of a single iambic foot, like *bas* or *ki:*, the infixes are authentic suffixes, but with longer words they are infixed.

Positive prosodic circumscription is especially common with reduplicative affixes, perhaps because a reduplicative infix more robustly withstands the historical pressures of analogy. In Samoan (38), prefixing reduplication applies to the foot within the word, rather than to the word itself.

(38) Samoan Plural Reduplication (Marsack 1962; Broselow and McCarthy 1983; McCarthy and Prince 1990a, 1993, sec. 7; Levelt 1990)

táa	tataa	"strike"
nófo	nonofo	"sit"
alófa	alolofa	"love"
ʔalága	ʔalalaga	"shout"
fanáu	fananau	"be born, give birth"
manáʔo	mananaʔo	"desire"

Feet in Samoan are trochaic, located on the last two moras. The function φ(F, Right) circumscribes the base to which light syllable reduplication – in our terms, prefixation of σ_μ – applies.

In the examples discussed thus far, positive prosodic circumscription leads to infixation. But prosodic circumscription is not merely a theory of infixation; it has other consequences in a surprisingly large variety of domains.

Recall from section 3 (21) the fundamental observation that reduplication is not syllable copying: that is, reduplication is never sensitive to the difference between *tak* in *taki* and *tak* in *takti*. But in the Australian language Yidiɲ (Dixon 1977; Nash 1979, 1980; Marantz 1982; McCarthy and Prince 1990a), reduplication of a disyllabic sequence does seem to be sensitive to precisely this distinction:

(39) Yidiɲ Plural Reduplication

Singular	Plural	
mula.ri	mula-mula.ri	"initiated man"
tʲukar.pa	tʲukar-tʲukar.pa-n	"unsettled mind"
kintal.pa	kintal-kintal.pa	"lizard species"
kala.mpaɽa	kala-kala.mpaɽa	"March fly"

For present purposes, *mula-mulari* and *tʲukar-tʲukarpa-n* are a near-minimal pair, in which the syllabic affiliation of *r* in the base determines whether it also appears in the reduplicant. This phenomenon, which is quite puzzling within the context of reduplicative theory in general, has a natural interpretation in terms of prosodic circumscription. Yidiɲ reduplicates nothing more or less than the first foot, which always includes exactly the first two syllables in this language. Thus, the foot within the word, φ(F, Left), is prosodically circumscribed and subject to total reduplication. It is prosodic circumscription, rather than the reduplication mechanism itself, that accounts for the sensitivity of Yidiɲ reduplication to the syllabic affiliation of consonants in the base.

Positive prosodic circumscription is also applicable to certain types of truncation phenomena (Mester 1990; Martin 1989; Lombardi and McCarthy 1991; Weeda 1992; Hill and Zepeda 1992). In the formation of a certain class of nicknames in Japanese, called "rustic girls' names" by Poser (1990), all and only the initial bimoraic foot is retained:

(40)   Japanese Rustic Girls' Nicknames
     Name   Nickname
     Yuu-ko   o-Yuu
     Ran-ko   o-Ran
     Yuki-ko   o-Yuki
     Kinue   o-Kinu
     Midori   o-Mido

Bimoraic Cvv, CvN, and CvCv are all possible nicknames, exactly matching the first two moras of the original name. Mester (1990) proposes that the nickname is simply the kernel of prosodic circumscription ϕ(F, Left), with the residue discarded.[15]

A consistent observation about all the examples of positive prosodic circumscription we have discussed, and indeed about all of the examples we know, is that the circumscribed category is a foot. This is such a consistent finding that it demands some sort of account. A first step in that direction is to recall that the category foot is, because of the Prosodic Hierarchy, fully synonymous with MinWd. The observation, recast in this light, is stated in (41) as the Minimality Hypothesis:

(41)   Minimality Hypothesis
     In positive prosodic circumscription O:ϕ(C, E), C = MinWd.

A consequence of the Minimality Hypothesis is that morphological operations, even those subject to positive prosodic circumscription, will always apply to word-like entities, either to an actual word itself or to a prosodically-delimited minimal word within some larger word. Thus, the prosodic base, as a stem-substitute, must itself meet the MinWd requirement that holds of stems in general (see secs. 1–3). Moreover, the Minimality Hypothesis ensures that a prosodically circumscribed operation will always act like an uncircumscribed one over some central class of the vocabulary – the words that are minimal. (That is, ϕ(MinWd, Edge) will always be an identity operation on some substantial subset of the words of a language.) This restriction has obvious benefits for learnability: the morphological operation can be acquired in its simplest form from the minimal words and then extended by the application of prosodic circumscription to the supraminimal ones.

Another property common to all of the examples discussed thus far is that the foot (= MinWd) targeted by positive prosodic circumscription is already present in the form prior to circumscription. That is, prosodic circumscription picks out a preexisting foot and submits it to the morphological operation, leaving material outside that foot in the residue of circumscription. This is quite obviously true of Ulwa, Samoan, and Chamorro, essential to the analysis of Yidiɲ, and arguably the case even for Japanese, which offers no direct prominential evidence of foot structure.

This characteristic of prosodic circumscription is a very natural one, but it is nonetheless worth stating as a separate principle:

(42) Law of Parsing
Prosodic circumscription minimally restructures the input, subject to the conditions imposed by the constituent C and edge E.

In the cases of prosodic circumscription discussed above, the Law of Parsing is obeyed almost trivially: prosodic circumscription calls for a foot (= MinWd) at some edge, and the foot already present at that edge is returned by the parse, in full conformity with (42). In other words, prosodic circumscription simply picks out a constituent of the desired type from the input form. But there are various imaginable conditions when prosodic circumscription will be called on to parse out a constituent from the input, so some restructuring, albeit minimal, will be required. This will be the case whenever there is no constituent of the desired type at the desired edge – for instance, when parsing out a foot prior to stress assignment, or parsing out a foot at the left edge when feet are assigned at the right.

The principal cases in which prosodic circumscription parses out a new constituent in conformity with the Law of Parsing are the Arabic broken plural and diminutive (McCarthy 1983; Hammond 1988; McCarthy and Prince 1988, 1990a) and the Choctaw *y*-grade (Nicklas 1974, 1975; Ulrich 1986, 1992; Lombardi and McCarthy 1991; Hung 1992; cf. Montler and Hardy 1988, 1991). These examples are both quite complex, so they cannot be reviewed fully here. We will briefly sketch one of them, Arabic, focusing our attention on the circumscriptional aspects of the system.

In Arabic, the productive plural and diminutive are expressed by imposing a LH iambic foot on the singular noun base. Because singular nouns come in diverse shapes, this iambic template is imposed on only a portion of the noun. The circumscribed domain is underscored in the singular; the corresponding iambic template in the plural and diminutive is in boldface:

(43) Arabic Productive Plural and Diminutive

Singular	Plural	Diminutive	
ħukm	/ħakaam/	ħukaym	"judgment"
ʕinab	/ʕanaab/	ʕunayb	"grape"
jaziir+at	/jazaawir/	/juzaywir/	"island"
šaaɣil	šawaaɣil	šuwayɣil	"engrossing"
jaamuus	jawaamiis	juwaymiis	"buffalo"
jundub	janaadib	junaydib	"locust"
sulṭaan	salaaṭiin	sulayṭiin	"sultan"

The boldface portion of the plural and diminutive is the part of the stem expressed by the LH iambic template. The portion of the plural and diminutive in plain type is outside the template; it varies systematically among plurals and diminutives depending on the canonical pattern of the corresponding singular. The underscored portion of the singular is the part whose consonants are mapped onto the iambic template. The portion of the singular in plain type is carried over unaltered to the corresponding plural and diminutive, except for changes in vowel quality (which are determined by independent principles) and the insertion of the onset-filling consonant *w* in /jazaawir/ (surface *jazaaʔir*) and /juzaywir/ (surface *juzayyir*).

The interpretation of these observations in terms of positive prosodic circumscription is now fairly straightforward. The underscored portion is the positively circumscribed domain, a moraic trochee, the MinWd of Arabic. This string, the kernel of prosodic circumscription, is mapped onto a LH iambic template, which realizes the plural and diminutive morphology. The residue of circumscription, which varies in size depending on the singular, is simply attached unchanged to the templatic portion. In addition, vowel quality is imposed on the templatic and nontemplatic portions by further rules.

Thus, the morphological operation O involves mapping to an iambic template, and the circumscriptional function is ϕ(MinWd, Left). Since the Arabic stress rule applies right to left, and since in any case there is no reason to assume that stress has already been assigned when plurals and diminutives are formed, the function ϕ must parse out a moraic trochee from the singular noun, rather than pick out a pre-existing foot as in Ulwa or Samoan. In cases like *ħukm, šaaɣil, jaamuus, jundub,* and *sulṭaan,* ϕ simply returns the initial heavy syllable without restructuring the base at all, in conformity with the Law of Parsing (42). In *ʕinab,* the final consonant is extrametrical, so the intrametrical portion consists of a sequence of two light syllables, also matching the required moraic trochee without restructuring. But in iambic words like *jaziir,* restructuring of the input by ϕ is necessary to circumscribe a moraic trochee. The restructuring is *minimal* in that the parsed *jazi * ir* respects the moraic analysis of the input but not its syllabic analysis. That is, given the nature of the Prosodic Hierarchy, a minimal restructuring is one that preserves the hierarchy from the bottom up. Indeed, since the mora is the smallest prosodic unit that can be called by a constituent C, this guarantees that the parse will always respect the moraic analysis of the input, as of course it does in *jazi * ir.*

In positive prosodic circumscription, as we have seen, the kernel of the ϕ-parse is submitted to the morphological operation O. *Negative* prosodic circumscription is fully symmetrical: the residue of the parse is submitted to the morphological operation. Retaining the notation used above, we define O/ϕ(B) – the application of O to the base B minus some edge constituent – as follows:

(44)   Operation Applying Under Negative Prosodic Circumscription
        O/ϕ (B) = B:ϕ * O(B/ϕ)

This is essentially extrametricality. To apply O to B under extrametricality is just to apply O to B/ϕ, concatenating the result with B:ϕ in the same way that the residue B/ϕ concatenates with the kernel B:ϕ in the original base B.

Various examples of negative prosodic circumscription are discussed by McCarthy and Prince (1990a, 1991b), Crowhurst (to appear), Lee and Davis (1993), Lombardi and McCarthy (1991), McCarthy (1993), and Urbanczyk (1992).

Dakota provides a case of this sort (Boas and Deloria 1941; Moravcsik 1977; Shaw 1980; McCarthy and Prince 1993; sec. 7). In Dakota, the agreement system consists of a set of perhaps twenty affixes that are prefixed to monosyllabic verb roots and some polysyllabic ones, but infixed into other polysyllabic verb roots. The roots taking infixes are apparently a lexically specified subclass, though historically they may have been morphologically composite. The locus of infixation falls after the initial syllable, which is always open in Dakota:[16]

(45) Infixation of -*wa*- "I" in Dakota

pa–wa–xta	"I tie up"	ma–wa–ni	"I walk"
ma–wa–nų	"I steal"	c'a–wa–pa	"I stab"
ʔi–ma–ktomi	"I am Iktomi"	na–wa–pca	"I swallow it"
na–wa–tʰaka	"I lock the door"	la–ma–kʰota	"I am a Lakota"

The Dakota agreement markers are nominally prefixes, and in fact they are literally prefixes with verb roots that are not in the infixing subclass. Thus, the morphological operation is "Prefix AGR." The locus of infixation, after the first syllable, is defined by $O/\phi(\sigma, \text{Right})$:

(46) Dakota Infixation

$$O/\phi \ (\text{ʔiktomi}) = \text{ʔiktomi:}\phi * O(\text{ʔiktomi}/\phi)$$
$$= \text{ʔi} * O(\text{ktomi})$$
$$= \text{ʔi} * \text{wa-ktomi}$$
$$= \text{ʔiwaktomi}$$

It is the root minus its initial syllable, rather than the root as a whole, that serves as the base for prefixation of -*wa*- and the other AGR morphemes.

Negative prosodic circumscription may also involve some restructuring of the input, in conformity with the Law of Parsing. One simple case is exemplified by the Choctaw passive infix *l* in (47).

(47) Choctaw Passive (Nicklas 1974, p. 32; Ulrich 1986, p. 136; Urbanczyk 1992)

Active	Passive	Gloss
abani	albani	"to barbeque"
apisa	/alpisa/ ałpisa	"to set a date"
hokči	/holkči/ holokči	"to plant"
takči	/talkči/ talakči	"to tie"

This infix appears after the initial Cv sequence of the base, where it accommodates to the phonotactic requirements of the language via an independently motivated rule of epenthesis. Formally, *l* infixation is actually prefixation under negative prosodic circumscription of an initial light syllable σ_μ, requiring

Law-of-Parsing mediated restructuring of an initial heavy σ (Urbanczyk 1992). The morphological rule, restricted in this way, is expressed by O/ɸ(σ$_μ$, Left), where O = "Prefix".

Like infixation by positive prosodic circumscription, infixation by negative prosodic circumscription can be reduplicative as well. For example, reduplicative infixation in Mangarayi (Merlan 1982, pp. 213–236; McCarthy and Prince 1986, 1991b, 1993, sec. 7; Davis 1988, pp. 319–322) prefixes a σ template to a Base consisting of the word minus its initial consonant:

(48)   Mangarayi Plural Reduplication

Singular	Plural	
baraŋali	b-<u>ar</u>-araŋali	"father-in-law"
gabuji	g-<u>ab</u>-abuji	"old person"
yirag	y-<u>ir</u>-irag	"father"
jimgan	j-<u>img</u>-imgan	"knowledgeable person"
gambuṛa	g-<u>amb</u>-ambuṛa	"classificatory MB/ZC"
muyg–ji	m-<u>uyg̱</u>-uyg-ji	"having a dog"

This phenomenon may be analyzed as O/ɸ(C, Left), where O = "Prefix σ" – that is, negative circumscription of an initial consonant.[17] In this way, the Base to which σ is prefixed and which it copies is the word minus its initial consonant:

(49)   Negative Prosodic Circumscription in Mangarayi Plural

$$O/ɸ \text{ (jimgan)} = \text{jimgan:}ɸ * O(\text{jimgan}/ɸ)$$
$$= \text{j} * O(\text{imgan})$$
$$= \text{j} * \underline{\text{img}}\text{-imgan}$$
$$= \underline{\text{jimg}}\text{imgan}$$

An interesting feature of the Mangarayi case is that part of the reduplicated string (the consonant *g*) is syllabified as the onset of a base syllable rather than as a coda of the reduplicative affix σ. This property, which is found in a number of reduplicative systems, is discussed in McCarthy and Prince (1986, 1993, sec. 7).

Another quite common type of infixing reduplication seems to require negative circumscription of an initial onsetless syllable. One example of this phenomenon comes from the Austronesian language Timugon Murut. Timugon Murut copies the first Cv sequence of the word, disregarding the first syllable of vowel-initial words:

(50)   Timugon Murut Reduplicative (Prentice 1971; McCarthy and Prince 1991b, 1993, sec. 7)

bulud	<u>bu</u>-bulud	"hill/ridge"
limo	<u>li</u>-limo	"five/about five"
ulampoy	u-<u>la</u>-lampoy	no gloss
abalan	a-<u>ba</u>-balan	"bathes/often bathes"
ompodon	om-<u>po</u>-podon	"flatter/always flatter"

With considerable enrichment of the theory of prosodic constituents that can be specified in negative circumscription, it is in principle possible to give an account of this pattern of infixing reduplication. But remarkably this locus is found *only* with reduplicative infixes, never with ordinary infixes. The theory of circumscription, which does not distinguish between reduplicative and ordinary infixes, cannot account for this asymmetry. As we will see in section 6, a very different account of the Murut reduplicative can be given, one that refers directly to the inherent defectiveness of onsetless syllables.

Positive and negative prosodic circumscription cover roughly similar empirical ground, so we should ask whether both are truly necessary. It turns out that they are, based on arguments ranging from the narrowly parochial to the broadly universal. Consider first the logical possibility of replacing one mode of circumscription with the other simply by complementing the parsed-out prosodic constituent C and the edge E. For instance, this would mean replacing the Ulwa schema O:ϕ(F, Left) with O/ϕ(X, Right), where X stands for some constituent at the right edge to which Ulwa *ka* may be prefixed. The problem is that X is phonologically incoherent, ranging from the null string (for *bas*) to one or more syllables (*karasmak, anaːlaːka*). Because words come in different sizes, it is not possible to reverse the edge at which the infix is anchored.

Consider next the simple alternative of replacing positive prosodic circumscription in Ulwa with negative circumscription: O/ϕ(F, Left), O = "**Prefix** *ka, ki, ma,* etc.". That is, *ka* would be a prefix on the residue of negative circumscription rather than a suffix on the parsed-out foot. Ulwa-internal considerations show that this alternative is inferior: in about 10 percent of the nouns collected by Hale and Lacayo Blanco (1989), *ka* is an actual suffix on a word that is longer than a single iambic foot: *gobament-ka* "government", *abana-ka* "dance", *bassirih-ka* "falcon", *ispiriŋ-ka* "elbow". (Of these, about two-thirds have doublets where *ka* is infixed as expected: *bas-ka-sirih, is-ka-piriŋ*.) So *ka* is a formal suffix, as the positive prosodic circumscription account requires.

Finally, the cases of infixing reduplication provide an unambiguous diagnostic for the distinction between positive and negative prosodic circumscription. In Samoan, for example, the locus of copying and the identity of the copied string are both determined in the same way, by reference to the foot. Samoan, then, is analyzed by positive prosodic circumscription, since the base of reduplication and the locus of reduplication are the same. But in Mangarayi, the locus of infixation – after the first consonant – and the base of reduplication – everything except the first consonant – are exactly complementary. Thus, infixation in Mangarayi is via negative prosodic circumscription, since the base of reduplication is the complement of the string that defines the locus of the infix.

Positive and negative circumscription are closely related, essentially symmetrical mechanisms for defining the base of a morphological operation within a larger word. More loosely connected to the theory of circumscription is the theory of prosodic delimitation, which accounts for the common situation where minimal and supraminimal bases are subject to different morphological operations.[18] For example, in Dyirbal (Dixon 1972; McCarthy and Prince 1990a), disyllabic and longer bases take different allomorphs of the ergative suffix, while in Axininca Campa (Payne 1981; Spring 1990a, 1990b; McCarthy and Prince 1993, sec. 6), bimoraic and longer bases take different allomorphs of the "possessed" suffix:

(51)   Dyirbal Ergative

Noun	Ergative	
yaɽa	yaɽa-ŋgu	"man"
yamani	yamani-gu	"rainbow"
balagara	balagara-gu	"they"

(52)   Axininca Campa

Noun	Possessed (no-/n- "my")	
mii	no-mii-ni	"otter"
sima	no-sima-ni	"fish"
itʰo	n-itʰo-ni	"swallow"
cʰimii	no-cʰimii-ti	"ant"
sampaa	no-sampaa-ti	"balsa"
maini	no-maini-ti	"bear"
manaanawo	no-manaanawo-ti	"turtle"

In Dyirbal, the generalization is that the ergative suffix takes the allomorph -*ŋgu* with disyllabic bases, which are minimal in Dyirbal, and the allomorph -*gu* with longer bases. In Axininca Campa, the possessed suffix is -*ni* with minimal, bimoraic bases and -*ti* with longer ones. A minimality criterion partitions the lexicon into two sets, and suffixal allomorphy is determined by this partitioning. The suffix alternations in both languages are truly allomorphic, since they do not reflect any systematic phonological pattern.

Prosodic delimitation, like positive prosodic circumscription, calls on ϕ(MinWd), but it puts the result to different use. Specifically, prosodic delimitation partitions the lexicon into those bases where B:ϕ, the ϕ-circumscribed kernel of B, is identical to B, and those where B:ϕ is less than B (that is, where B/ϕ, the residue, is non-null). The clearest formalization of this is to regard suffixation of -*ŋgu*/-*ni* to minimal bases as the special, prosodically delimited case, and suffixation of -*gu*/-*ti* as a default, applicable whenever the special case has failed to apply.

The set of minimal bases can be determined using the parsing function ϕ. When applied to the morphological Base B_M, ϕ must return a prosodic Base B that is identical to the morphological Base. This special sense of ϕ, designated ϕ', is a partial function defined as in (53):

(53)   Definition of Partial Function ϕ'
$\phi'(B_M) = B$ if $B_M = \phi(B_M)$
          else, undefined.

The prosodically restricted operation O:φ′ depends on the success of the function φ′, and O:φ′ is therefore undefined when φ′ is. An operation applying under φ′ applies only to words that exactly satisfy the prosodic criterion φ′, always a (type of) MinWd.

The Dyirbal ergative, for example, consists of two morphological operations. One is "Suffix -ŋ*gu*," restricted prosodically by φ′(MinWd). The other is prosodically unrestricted "Suffix -gu", whose scope is limited only by the Elsewhere Condition. If φ′ returns a value, in accordance with (53), then -ŋ*gu* is suffixed, since the target form is a monopod. But if φ′ returns no value at all, then "Suffix -ŋ*gu*" cannot apply, and the default suffix -*gu* is provided instead. In general, a default operation needn't be specified; in other languages (McCarthy and Prince 1990a, 1993, sec. 7), the responses to blocking of the prosodically delimited morphological operation are quite diverse, ranging from complete failure (in Korean particle attachment [Cho 1992]) to zero affixation (in the Maori imperative [Hohepa 1967]) to syntactic periphrasis (in the English comparative). Such matters are outside the purview of prosodic circumscription theory and perhaps of linguistic theory more generally, to the extent that they reflect functional rather than formal factors.

In conclusion, we have seen that three types of prosodic circumscription can be subsumed under the parsing function φ, which applies to define a prosodically delimited base within some morphological base. There are alternative ways of characterizing a prosodic base without φ, and one is explored at length in McCarthy and Prince (1993, sec. 7) (also see below, sec. 6). Nonetheless, it seems clear that the notion of the prosodic base, common to all types of circumscription, must play a role in any analysis of infixation and the other types of phenomena discussed here.

5   The Prosodic Character of Templates and Circumscription

The discussion thus far has included a number of analyses that rely, often implicitly, on the fundamentally *prosodic* character of templatic and circumscriptional morphology, as embodied in the Prosodic Morphology Hypothesis, the Template Satisfaction Condition, and Prosodic Circumscription of Domains (sec. 0). The goal now is to make this reliance explicit – that is, to lay out an alternative to these principles and to show why that alternative is inferior.

Together, the Prosodic Morphology Hypothesis and the Template Satisfaction Condition demand that templates be defined in the grammar and realized in the derivation in terms of the categories and principles of prosody, as provided by the independently required theory of the syllable, the foot, and the prosodic word. Likewise, Prosodic Circumscription of Domains limits circumscriptional and delimitative morphology to reference to prosodic units. A related claim is that only the categories of prosody, together with the featural decomposition of segments, are authentically essential to phonological representation. More generally, then, this theory is a claim about reference to structural information in phonology as well as morphology, though naturally the focus here is on the latter.

In this respect, Prosodic Morphology theory is in sharp contrast to segmentalist theories of template form, such as those in McCarthy (1979, 1981), Marantz (1982), Levin (1983, 1985), and Lowenstamm and Kaye (1986).[19] In segmentalist approaches, templates are composed of segment-sized slots, either C and V, if margin versus nucleus roles are to be distinguished directly, or X if they are not. The segmental positions are essential elements of the pure segmentalist template, though they may be annotated with prosodic structure (such as syllable, onset, nucleus, or rhyme nodes) as required.

Basic findings in prosody place strong conditions of adequacy on template theory. It is worth examining the chief interactions, since they establish the general constraints within which template theory must work, and they permit clear differentiation of prosodic morphology from segmentalism.

Consider first the role of *counting* in grammar. What elements may be counted? It is a commonplace of phonology that rules count moras, syllables, or feet, but never segments. Word-minimality effects, discussed in section 1, are typical in this respect. Since the theory of word minimality derives from Foot Binarity, observed word minima always reckon the same units as feet do: two moras (e.g., Lardil (8)) or two syllables (e.g., Dyirbal (51)). Similarly, the partitioning of the lexicon by word size in prosodic delimitation, discussed in section 4, also follows foot theory in relying on a count of two moras (e.g., Axininca Campa (52)) or two syllables (e.g., Dyirbal (51)). In templatic morphology proper, counting of prosodic units may be observed in the minimal bimoraicity and maximal disyllabicity of the Arabic canonical noun (15) or the bimoraic and disyllabic foot templates of Manam (23) and Diyari (10).

In contrast, no language process is known to depend on the raw number of *segments* in a form: a robust finding, given the frequency and pervasiveness of counting restrictions. A bisegmental minimal word or a bisegmental delimitation of the lexicon in allomorphy are impossible. Thus, it should come as no suprise that templatic morphology cannot count segments either. If a reduplicative prefix template could be XXX – three segments, unadorned with prosodic structure – the following impossible type of system should be common:

(54)   Pure Segmentalism in Reduplication

Input	Output
XXX-badupi	<u>bad</u>-badupi
XXX-bladupi	<u>bla</u>-bladupi
XXX-adupi	<u>adu</u>-adupi

The system is prosodically incoherent, hence impossible under the Prosodic Morphology Hypothesis and indeed completely unattested. What is prosodically incoherent here is the segmental equation of monomoraic *bla* with bimoraic *bad* or *adu*, or of monosyllabic *bla* and *bad* with disyllabic *adu*. Obviously, XXX is equally impossible as a template in truncation or a root-and-pattern morphological system, for the same reason. Of course, pure segmentalism can be annotated with prosodic structure, thus avoiding some of the untoward effects in (54); for instance, a template [XXX]$_\sigma$ would much improve the result. But the point is not to make segmentalism look like prosodic morphology. Rather, if there were any truth to segmentalism, then segments should stand on their own, exactly as in (54). Yet this is unknown.

How long may a count run? General considerations of locality, now the common currency in all areas of linguistic thought, suggest that the answer is "up to two": a rule may fix on one specified element and examine a structurally adjacent element and no other. For example, the End Rule of Prince (1983) focuses on one edge of a domain and selects the element adjacent to that edge for some specified operation; Foot Binarity (7) demands that a foot contain at least two elements, presumably the head and one other; the licit types of stress-feet (6) are all maximally binary. Similar cases can easily be multiplied.

As we have seen, analyses within prosodic morphology respect the binarity of counting. Word-minimality effects derive from Foot Binarity, so observed word minima are always two of something, either moras or syllables. The criteria for partitioning the lexicon in prosodic delimitation (51, 52) follow the same binary limit, as does the upper bound on the Arabic canonical noun (15b). Templates consist of at most two prosodic units, such as the bimoraic and disyllabic reduplicative templates in Manam (23) and Diyari (10).

In contrast, segmentalist theories must count segments, and must count many of them. Consider the template required to characterize the maximal expansion of the canonical noun in Arabic, disyllabic in prosodic terms:

(55) Maximal Arabic Canonical Noun Template (Segmental Version)

   (a) CV Theory   (b) X Theory (N=nucleus of σ)

   CVXCVVC   XXXXXXX

By this, seven segments must be counted in order to characterize what in prosodic terms is two syllables.

General findings about prosody lead to another distinct form of argument in support of prosodic morphology. Prosodic theory must distinguish between optional and obligatory elements at all levels of structure. A syllable must contain a nucleus and, in many languages, an onset; a foot must contain at least two moras or syllables, thanks to Foot Binarity (7); a prosodic word must contain at least one foot, because of the Prosodic Hierarchy (4). In contrast, many elements of prosodic structure are entirely optional. Thus, syllables in some languages may have multisegmental onsets, but no languages require this. Likewise, codas are optional, never obligatory, elements of syllables in some languages (though syllable weight, realized by a coda or vowel length, may be demanded in some contexts). The theory of feet (6) recognizes a variety of options, mono- versus disyllabism in the quantitative trochee, and H versus LL versus LH in the iamb. Though a prosodic word must contain one foot, it may contain more, since normally there is no upper bound on its size.

This characterization of what is optional and what is obligatory, which comes from prosodic theory, plays an essential role in prosodic morphology, as various analyses above reveal. In Japanese (12) or Manam (23), for example, the surface expressions of the template are quite diverse, ranging from disyllabic sequences like *mido* to monosyllables like *mii* or *mit-*. The constant of shape uniting all of these expressions is the quantitative trochee, and the various forms enjoy all of the optionality of the quantitative trochee in prosodic theory. In Ilokano (2, 22b), the realizations of the template are almost as diverse, including *kal-*, *klas-*, and *roː-*. Here, the constant of shape is the heavy syllable template, so whether the onset is simple or complex, and whether there is a coda or a long vowel, are entirely inconsequential.

In segmentalism, though, optionality of elements is a complex and weighty matter, requiring an elaborated theory for the realization or deletion of segmental slots in templates. Following Marantz (1982), segmental theories spell out the template as the longest observed realization (or even the union of the observed realizations, if distinct from the longest); when an insufficiency of melody leaves template slots empty, they are discarded. Thus, segmentalism must analyze the Ilokano prefix as CCVX or equivalent, explicitly counting out the maximal monosyllable. As example (7) illustrates, segmentalism is typically faced with an excess of underlying slots:

(56)   Excess Slots in Segmental Analysis

    (a) CCVX + . . .   (b) CCVX + . . .   (c) CCVX + . . .

        kaldiŋ   klase   roʔot

There are well-known ways in which unfilled slots influence phonology and morphology (Selkirk 1981; Clements and Keyser 1983; Lowenstamm and Kaye 1986). It is a remarkable fact that empty templatic slots have never been convincingly detected outside their endo-theoretic role in melody association.[20] In prosodic morphology, constrained by the Template Satisfaction Condition, they do not exist.

In essence, segmentalism must hold that all template elements are optional until they are filled by melodic material. It is thus in principle incapable of specifying, in the representation, that certain elements are obligatory, a common situation. In the Ilokano CCVX template, though the onset C slot is optional, the final X slot is obligatory, even at the expense of lengthening a vowel that is short in the base form (56c). This is even more dramatically true in Ponapean reduplication (24b), where the base *pa*, which contains but a single mora, must reduplicate as <u>paa</u>-pa to satisfy the bimoraic template. The additional conditions follow immediately from the syllabic characterization, since complex onsets are of course optional and heavy syllables must have a postnuclear element. Nothing in the segmental theory guarantees this result.

The optional/obligatory distinction presents equally serious problems for segmentalism in a case like Japanese (12), which is analyzed prosodically with a trochaic template. In segmental terms, any one of the expressions in (57) is a licit hypocoristic.

(57) Japanese Hypocoristics, Segmentally
     VV   VCV
     CVV   CVCV
     VC
     CVC

The tack of taking the longest expansion as basic would, of course, give CVCV as the template,[21] and indeed all observed forms can be derived from it by deleting excess templatic elements. But so can V, CV, and even Ø, all impossible in Japanese hypocoristic formation (Poser 1990). If all templatic slots are optional, as indeed they must be if the diversity in (57) is to be obtained from a CVCV template, then, short of bald stipulation, it is impossible to demand that any truly licit expression of the template contain at least two Vs or VC.

One final observation seals the case against excess elements in templates. It is a stable empirical finding that templates imitate – up to extrametricality – the prosodic structure of the language at hand. The Ilokano template is not CCVCC; correlatively, the syllabification of the language disallows coda clusters. Segmental theory, however, cannot derive this result. Since excess or stray elements are erased, they are free to occur, and indeed must occur in other circumstances. Were they present, even fleetingly, they could perturb melody association in easily discoverable ways. Thus, left-to-right association of *kaldiŋ* to this template would yield /kald-kaldiŋ/. Applying the phonology to this form and deleting the first consonant of the unsyllabifiable triconsonantal cluster, *kad-kaldiŋ* is obtained. This is not merely wrong in Ilokano but wrong universally; by exploiting a hole in segmental theory, we have obtained the impossible reduplicative pattern C(C)VC$_0$, where C$_0$ is the onset of the second syllable of the base, skipping over the coda of the first syllable, if any.

Within prosodic morphology, the actual shape-invariant underlying a templatic formation is identified in prosodic terms, and so it is possible to assume a natural condition on template interpretation like the Template Satisfaction Condition. This solves all three of the problems stemming from segmental approaches to shape specification:

1   Under the Template Satisfaction Condition, no excess templatic material is ever present in the representation, giving the easiest and least stipulative explanation for its unresponsiveness to phonological probing: nonexistence.

2   Patterns of obligatoriness and optionality will follow in general from independent characterization of the prosodic units, both universally and language-specifically. (This is merely an extension of reasoning well-established in phonology, where such optionality-stipulating notations as "(α)" and α_0 have faded in the face of accurate representation of prosody.)

3   The fact that the templates are bounded by a language's prosody follows from their being built from that prosody.

A third form of argument for prosodic morphology, essentially independent of the previous two, rests on the problem of redundancy or recapitulation in segmentalist theories. Without even calling on sophisticated analysis, it becomes clear when languages with moderately complex prosody are examined that prosodic categories must be admitted into template theory. "CVC" seems a plausible enough prefix when proposed for Agta (Healey 1960; Marantz 1982); but when the next language over (e.g., Ilokano) shows "CCVC," correlated with the appearance of 2-consonant onsets, it becomes harder to avoid the correct generalization. The Classical Arabic templates appear relatively simple (though, as noted above, spelled segmentally they violate counting norms); turn to Modern Hebrew, with a rich range of syllable-initial clusters to include, and the stipulative character of segmental spell-out becomes apparent (Doron 1981; McCarthy 1984a; cf. Bat-El 1989, 1992). There is, then, an obvious and direct correlation between the form of the templates in a language and the organization of that language's prosody as a whole. That correlation follows immediately from the Prosodic Morphology Hypothesis and the Template Satisfaction Condition; with those two principles, the situation could not be otherwise. Yet it is hard to see how segmentalism could even stipulate, much less explain, this remarkable coincidence; that templates routinely recapitulate the prosodic requirements of the language as a whole must remain an inexplicable redundancy in segmental approaches.

The arguments from optionality and recapitulation can be combined into a final argument-form, in this case drawn from the prosodic delimitation phenomenon in Axininca Campa (52). In that language, bimoraic bases take the "possessed" suffix -*ni*; longer bases take the suffix -*ti*. Consider the problem of specifying the *ni*-taking bases in purely segmental terms. The possible bimoraic word-shapes of Axininca Campa include VV (not actually attested), CVV, VCV, CVCV, VCCV, and CVCCV, all of which require -*ni*. Putting these together, we obtain the following schema for the subcategorization of the -*ni* allomorph:

(58)   Axininca Campa *ni* Subcategorization, Segmentally
       -*ni* / (C)V(C)CV____

This schema precisely recapitulates all that is optional or obligatory in a bimoraic sequence in Axininca Campa. Two vowels are obligatory, because only vowels project moras in this language. For the same reason, a medial coda is optional. Initial onsets are optional but medial ones are obligatory, exactly as in the prosody of the language as a whole (see McCarthy and Prince 1993, sec. 4 for an explanation). Obviously, the forest of stipulations in (58) has hidden the tree of explanation: the base of *-ni* is a bimoraic foot, whose optional and obligatory elements are determined fully by the prosody of the language as a whole.

6 Prosodic Morphology within Optimality Theory

Thus far, we have described some of the more familiar results of prosodic morphology – what could be called the standard theory. More recent developments, which are the subject of McCarthy and Prince (1993), focus principally on how the theory can be conceived of as a system of constraint interaction. Here we will illustrate briefly how the theory has evolved in this work.

Throughout prosodic morphology, as elsewhere in contemporary phonological research, constraints on well-formedness play an important role. Nevertheless, our use of constraints up to this point has not been placed within the context of an actual theory of constraint application and violation. Our goal in this section is to explore some of the consequences for prosodic morphology of the conception of the role and functioning of constraints embodied in *optimality theory* (Prince and Smolensky 1991a, 1991b, 1992, 1993). In optimality theory, the output representation is selected by a set of well-formedness constraints that are ranked in a hierarchy of relevance, so that a lower-ranked constraint may be violated in order to satisfy a higher-ranked one. These characteristics of ranking and violability of constraints are what distinguishes optimality theory from other approaches to constraint satisfaction.

Optimality theory, as conceived by Prince and Smolensky, has four basic tenets:

1   *Violability*. Constraints are *violable*; but violation is minimal.
2   *Ranking*. Constraints are *ranked* on a language-particular basis; the notion of minimal violation (or best-satisfaction) is defined in terms of this ranking.
3   *Inclusiveness*. The candidate analyses, which are evaluated by the constraint hierarchy, are admitted by very general considerations of structural well-formedness; there are no specific rules or repair strategies with specific structural descriptions or structural changes or with connections to specific constraints.

> 4   *Parallelism.* Best-satisfaction of the constraint hierarchy is computed over the whole hierarchy and the whole candidate set.

Optimality theory rejects the notion that a *constraint* is a phonotactic truth at some level of description. New possibilities for explanation are opened up, as new kinds of conditions on structure are recognized as legitimate constraints, usable as principles of grammar.

The satisfaction of a system of ranked well-formedness constraints is the core analytic concept in optimality theory. Except for ties, the candidate that passes the highest ranked constraint is the output form. A tie occurs either when more than one candidate passes the highest ranked constraint or when all candidates fail the highest ranked constraint. In case of ties, all surviving candidates are tested recursively against the rest of the hierarchy. Once a victor emerges, the remaining, lower-ranked constraints are irrelevant; whether the sole surviving candidate obeys them or not does not affect its grammaticality.

The following example illustrates schematically how satisfaction of a constraint hierarchy proceeds. Assume a grammar consisting of two constraints, A and B. Like any grammar, this one functions to pair underlying forms with surface forms: (in_1, out), (in_2, out), and so on. Suppose we have a certain underlying form $/in_k/$ which gives rise to a candidate set $\{k\text{-}cand_1, k\text{-}cand_2\}$, and that $k\text{-}cand_1$ is the actual output form.

If both A and B agree in their evaluation of the candidate set, then there is nothing to say. The optimal candidate – the output associated with $/in_k/$ – is just the one that meets both constraints, as in standard approaches to constraint satisfaction. If A and B *disagree*, however, we have a constraint conflict, represented by the following tableau:

(59)   Constraint tableau, $A \gg B$, $/in_k/$

Candidates	A	B
☞ k-cand₁		*
k-cand₂	* !	

Here candidate $k\text{-}cand_1$ meets A but fails B; while $k\text{-}cand_2$ meets B but fails A. Because $k\text{-}cand_1$ is, by assumption, the actual output form, we say that constraint A *dominates* constraint B $(A \gg B)$, in the sense that, when A and B disagree on a candidate-pair, the decision between them is made by A alone. This tableau observes certain notational conventions: constraints are written in their domination order, violations are marked by "*", and crucial violations are also called out by "!". Shading emphasizes the *irrelevance* of the constraint to the fate of the candidate. A loser's cells are shaded after a crucial violation; the winner's, when there are no more competitors. As a reminder of their special status, constraints regarded as part of an optimality-theoretic hierarchy are in small capitals.

This perspective illuminates a number of problems in circumscriptional and templatic morphology, discussed at length in McCarthy and Prince (1993). Here we shall outline an Optimality-Theoretic approach to three such problems: the locus of *-um-* infixation in Tagalog and other Austronesian languages (following Prince and Smolensky 1991b, 1993); the problem of reduplicative infixation after an initial onsetless syllable in Timugon Murut, signalled above in (50); and the effect of a prosodic well-formedness constraint on reduplication in Axininca Campa.

The first example of prosodic morphology within optimality theory comes from the locus of infixation of the Tagalog morpheme *-um-*. This infix falls before the first vowel of a word:

(60) Tagalog *-um-* Infixation
     Root   -um-
     /alis/   /um-alis/   "leave"
     sulat   s-um-ulat   "write"
     gradwet   gr-um-adwet   "graduate" (French 1988)

Though McCarthy and Prince (1990a) analyze Tagalog *-um-* infixation circumscriptionally (essentially like Mangarayi (48)), this account now seems truly unsatisfactory.

Descriptively, *gr-um-adwet* is problematic. Without an Onset constituent, it is impossible to characterize the circumscribed domain either positively or negatively, since neither pre-infixal *gr* nor post-infixal *adwet* is a prosodic constituent (cf. Anderson 1992). Worse yet, the circumscriptional analysis can only stipulate, and not explain, why words with initial clusters, all of them relatively recent loans, consistently behave like *gr-um-adwet* and never like **g-um-radwet* in Tagalog and other Austronesian languages. If Onset is admitted as a constituent, circumscription theory must offer a free choice between the various options for which unit is to be circumscribed (single consonant versus whole Onset). But there is no choice: it is never just the initial consonant, but always the maximal initial cluster.[22]

A further problem of principle is that specifying the locus of the infix by circumscription cannot explain why it is just exactly a *vC*-shaped affix that falls in prenuclear position. A prenuclear, postconsonantal locus for a /vC/ affix makes eminent sense phonotactically, since it supports an unmarked . . . CvCv . . . syllable structure, as Anderson (1972) and Cohn (1992) point out. But neither they nor the circumscriptional account make this fundamental observation follow from the analysis. Indeed, circumscription theory is designed to allow for complete independence between the shape of an affix and its mode of placement.

Clearly, then, *um*-infixation in Tagalog should not be analyzed by prosodic circumscription. Nonetheless, the locus of the infix is prosodically defined, since it responds to the prosodic well-formedness condition requiring open syllables. Prince and Smolensky (1991b, 1992, 1993) use optimality theory to determine the locus of *-um-* by the interaction of the constraints No-Coda and Leftmostness:

(61)   Tagalog Constraints
　　　(a)　No-Coda[23]
　　　　　Syllables are open.
　　　(b)　Leftmostness
　　　　　A prefix is located at the left edge of a word.

No-Coda is the constraint corresponding to the familiar markedness observation (Jakobson 1962, p. 526; Clements and Keyser 1983, p. 29). Violations of Leftmostness are reckoned in terms of the distance of any prefix φ from the designated edge, where each individual phonological element (segment, say) that intervenes between φ and the edge counts as a distinct violation. This means that Leftmostness will function as a gradient constraint, judging the nearness of φ to the edge of the domain. The morpheme *-um-* is a prefix, hence subject to Leftmostness. The constraint No-Coda is also visibly in force, selecting open syllables over closed ones.

In the current context, what is of interest is the relation between these two constraints. They are in direct conflict, as the following tableau shows:

(62)   Tagalog *gr-um-adwet*

Candidates	No-Coda	Leftmostness
um.grad.wet	* !	
gum.rad.wet	* !	g
☞　gru.mad.wet		gr
grad.wu.met		gradw !

Some forms (e.g., *um-gradwet*) may violate No-Coda in more than one location – for clarity, the tableau only records violations of No-Coda involving the prefix *-um-*, since only those will differ crucially among candidates. Violations of Leftmostness are shown by the string of segments separating the formal prefix *-um-* from the left edge of the word.

The prefixed form **um-gradwet* and the post-C infixed form **g-um-radwet* respect Leftmostness more than the actual output *grumadwet* does, but they violate the constraint No-Coda – this then is a constraint conflict. Since the actual output obeys No-Coda at the expense of a Leftmostness violation, the constraints are ranked No-Coda ≫ Leftmostness.

The account of Tagalog infixation in (61, 62) answers all the objections against a circumscriptional analysis. Because it relies on the prosodic well-formedness constraint No-Coda, rather than prosodic circumscription, it does not have the liability of demanding that either *gr* or *adwet* be identifiable as a prosodic constituent. And because **g-um-radwet* violates No-Coda just as **um-gradwet* does, this analysis explains why the infix must follow the entire onset in recent loans like *gradwet*. Finally, because the locus of *-um-* is determined directly by the phonology, via No-Coda, the optimality-theoretic analysis provides a complete formal account of the observation that prenuclear *-um-* "makes sense phonotactically."

This perspective is confirmed by the optimality theory approach to the Timugon Murut type of reduplicative infixation (50), in which initial onsetless syllables are skipped over (McCarthy and Prince 1993, sec. 7). This pattern is found in a remarkably wide variety of languages. Descriptively, a light syllable (σ_μ) template is infixed after an initial onsetless syllable, otherwise it is prefixed.

Though it might be possible to construct a circumscriptional analysis of facts like these (see sec. 4 and McCarthy and Prince 1991b), the result is again profoundly unsatisfactory. For one thing, negative circumscription – extrametricality – of initial onsetless syllables requires identifying such syllables as a particular type of prosodic constituent, thus enriching the theory of prosodic categories. Furthermore, it seems likely that the other arguments in the literature for the extrametricality of such syllables are not correct (McCarthy and Prince 1993, sec. 6, sec. 7). But these technical matters pale beside a far more serious empirical problem: a circumscriptional analysis cannot explain why, in all known cases (and there are many), it is always a *reduplicative* infix that skips over the initial onsetless syllable. Since the theory of prosodic circumscription completely divorces the morphological operation (in this case, prefixation of σ_μ) from the specification of the prosodic base (in this case, the residue of onsetless syllable extrametricality), by its very nature it cannot account for any dependencies between them. Indeed, this is precisely the same reason that prosodic circumscription cannot relate the vC shape of Tagalog *-um-* to its prenuclear locus.

But prosodic morphology within optimality theory provides a compelling noncircumscriptional account of infixation in Timugon Murut and similar cases. The key fact is that simple prefixation runs into problems with Onset that infixation successfully avoids. Onset is simply the well-known constraint prohibiting vowel-initial syllables Itô (1989):

(63) Onset
      $*[_\sigma V$

Reduplicating #vCv as *#v̱-.vCv is manifestly less harmonic, syllable-wise, than reduplicating it as #v-C̱v-Cv, because *#v̱-.vCv duplicates an ONSET violation. Edgemostness of the affix suffers, just as in Tagalog.

The tableaux (64, 65) show how the correct result devolves from this ranking, assuming a set of candidates where the reduplicant exactly matches the light-syllable template:

(64) Timugon Murut σ_μ – Reduplication. C-initial Words.

Candidates	ONSET	LEFTMOSTNESS
☞ bu̱.bu.lud		
bu.lu̱.lud		bu !

Both candidates obey ONSET, so they are referred to LEFTMOSTNESS, which selects *bu̱-bulud*, whose prefix is perfectly prefixal.

(65) Timugon Murut σ_μ – Reduplication. C-initial Words.

Candidates	ONSET	LEFTMOSTNESS
u̱.u.lam.poy	* ! *	
☞ u.la̱.lam.poy	*	u

But in (65) there is a crucial ONSET violation in *u̱-ulampoy* that is absent in *u-la̱-lampoy*. Since ONSET is ranked higher, it alone determines the outcome, though LEFTMOSTNESS would give the opposite result.

To our knowledge, only *reduplicative* infixes are found in this particular locus, never ordinary segmental infixes. The proposal here explains why, sharply distinguishing it from the account based on negative prosodic circumscription outlined in section 4. The core of the explanation is apparent: copying the initial onsetless syllable of *ulampoy* duplicates the ONSET violation. No comparable pressure exists for contentful infixes, regardless of their shape, since they of course cannot duplicate a violation of ONSET. This result submits to formal proof, as shown in McCarthy and Prince (1993, sec. 7).

As in Tagalog, phonotactic well-formedness, rather than prosodic circumscription, is responsible for infixation. Considered in this way, the Timugon Murut constraint system is not merely *analogous to* but actually *identical* to Tagalog's. In both cases, a constraint on prosodic well-formedness – ONSET in Timugon Murut, NO-CODA in Tagalog – dominates a constraint on morphological well-formedness – LEFTMOSTNESS, which characterizes the proper locus of a class of morphological entities, the prefixes. The only difference between the two cases is in which prosodic constraint does the work, a fact that follows from the different lexical substance of the relevant morphemes, and merits no grammatical mention whatsoever.

The third example of an application of optimality theory in prosodic morphology is the complex pattern of reduplication in Axininca Campa, an Arawakan language of Peru (Payne 1981; Spring 1990a, 1990c, 1992; Black 1991; McCarthy and Prince 1993). Here we will focus on one small aspect of the system, drawn from the complete treatment in McCarthy and Prince (1993, sec. 5).

The normal pattern in Axininca Campa is total root reduplication (66a), but under certain circumstances, depending on the phonology of the root itself, more or less than the whole root may be reduplicated. In particular, when the root is vowel-initial (66b), its initial syllable is not reduplicated. To avoid dealing with further constraint interactions, we focus our attention here only on long (i.e., minimally bimoraic), unprefixed roots:

(66)　Reduplication of Long Unprefixed Roots in Axininca Campa
　　　(a)　Consonant-initial Roots
　　　　　/kawosi/　　　kawosi-<u>kawosi</u>　　　"bathe"
　　　　　/koma/　　　　koma-<u>koma</u>　　　　"paddle"
　　　　　/kintʰa/　　　kintʰa-<u>kintʰa</u>　　　"tell"
　　　　　/tʰaaŋki/　　　tʰaaŋki-<u>tʰaaŋki</u>　　"hurry"
　　　(b)　Vowel-initial Roots
　　　　　/osampi/　　　osampi-<u>sampi</u>　　　"ask"
　　　　　/osaŋkina/　　osaŋkina-<u>saŋkina</u>　　"write"

Axininca Campa reduplication is clearly suffixing, as we have shown by underscoring the reduplicant, since the partial copy can be found in suffixal position (66b). The normal mode is total root reduplication, but this is subverted when the root is onsetless.

The constraint responsible for total reduplication of long consonant-initial roots like those cited in (66a) is Maximality (MAX), introduced in section 3. In total reduplication, there is no templatic requirement to be met (McCarthy and Prince 1986, 1988), so MAX is the sole determining factor. For the form *kawosi*, MAX imposes a ranking on candidate reduplicants in which *kawosi* itself stands at the top, ahead of all others, including especially *wosi*, and (ranked below it) *si*, both of which meet the other reduplicative constraints ANCHORING and CONTIGUITY, as well as the prosodic requirements of the language. The optimal candidate is therefore *kawosi*, which is obviously identical to the input. Unfettered MAX will always yield total reduplication – maximal identity between base and reduplicant.

The reason for the failure of maximal identity in (66b) is not far to seek. Any candidate reduplicant which exactly copied a base shaped /v . . . v/ would have to display an impossible hiatus at the base-reduplicant frontier: . . .

v-v ..., as in *osampi-osampi*. Thus ONSET ≫ MAX, compelling less-than-full copying but satisfying ONSET. The following tableau shows this for the root /osampi/.

(67) /osampi–redup./

Candidates	ONSET	MAX
osampi.osampi	** !	
☞ osampi.sampi	*	*

Other logical possibilities, such as epenthesis at the base-reduplicant juncture, are barred by further constraints that dominate MAX (see McCarthy and Prince 1993, sec. 5). The point here is that the reduplicant needn't violate ONSET, and indeed it doesn't, at the price of a mere MAX violation. Failure on low-ranking MAX – that is, partial reduplication – is irrelevant, since the ONSET comparison decides the contest.

The property common to the Tagalog, Timugon Murut, and Axininca Campa examples is that a prosodic constraint (like No-CODA or ONSET) is ranked above a morphological one (like LEFTMOSTNESS or MAX). This ranking produces a pattern in which an essentially morphological phenomenon is determined in part by phonological conditions. Indeed, just this sort of interaction can be shown to lie at the core of all of prosodic morphology (McCarthy and Prince 1993, sec. 7).

NOTES

McCarthy's research was supported by a fellowship from the John Simon Guggenheim Memorial Foundation and a Faculty Research Grant from the University of Massachusetts. Prince's was supported by Rutgers University and the Rutgers Center for Cognitive Science.

1 Other sources of violations of word-minimality regularities are lexical exceptionality, the Strict Cycle (Itô 1991; cf. Orgun and Inkelas 1992), and post-lexical, non–structure-preserving phonology (McCarthy and Prince 1991a, 1991b).

2 The variation between mono- and disyllabism seen in Japanese and Yup'ik nicknames is a possible, but not a necessary concomitant of the prosodic nature of templates. For example, the Arabic broken plural template (sec. 4) is the canonical or maximal iamb LH. McCarthy and Prince (1991a, 1991b) develop a pair of features for specifying a particular foot species, like LH, within a genus, like iambic. The features are minimal/maximal in the moraic dimension and minimal/maximal in the syllabic dimension.

Unspecified values for these features allow variation, as in Japanese and Yup'ik.

3 Not all of these studies assume the theory of prosodic morphology, of course.

4 There are two additional conditions on canonicity of noun stems in Arabic that are not our focus here, though they are dealt with in McCarthy and Prince (1990b):

   (i)   Final Consonantality
       All stems (noun and verb) are consonant-final.

   (ii) Cluster Rule
       All and only monosyllables end in consonant clusters.

5 Cf. Lombardi and McCarthy (1991), Samek-Lodovici (1992, 1993).

6 Unexpectedly, the jussives of biliteral roots follow the pattern of *yäskək* "place a peg in the ground". This is perhaps related to the fact that Chaha nouns never have final geminates (see Leslau [1950, p. 15] on *qurər* for *qurr* "basket").

7 To proceed somewhat more exactly, we might identify a correspondence function f between R and B, which must meet three conditions:

   (i)   Totality. $f(r)$ exists for all r in R.

   (ii) Element Copy. $f(r) = b \rightarrow [r] = [b]$, for r in R, b in B.

   (iii) Element Contiguity. $\widehat{r_i r_j} \rightarrow \widehat{f(r_i) f(r_j)}$

Totality says that everything in the reduplicant has a correspondent in the base. Element Copy says that the correspondent of an element is phonologically identical to it; the Reduplicant consists of material "copied" from the Base. Element Contiguity says that neighbors in R correspond to neighbors in B. The constraint we have called Contiguity then demands the existence of such an f: R $\rightarrow$ B.

8 Violations of Contiguity are found most prominently in Sanskrit, in a phenomenon of onset simplification that pervades the system (McCarthy and Prince 1986, Steriade 1988). Apparently, complex onsets are never found in Sanskrit affixes, though they occur in roots, suggesting a generalization over all affixes, not just reduplicative ones.

9 As stated, this is nothing more than a forced association between prefixing and initial-substring copying, suffixing and final-substring copying. A more interesting characterization is possible if we define "prefix" as a leftmost substring, "suffix" as a rightmost substring (as in Prince and Smolensky 1991a). Then we can say that R and $f(R)$ must, in their respective domains – {B, R}, {B} – both be prefixes, or both be suffixes. Prefixality/suffixality is a property, like various others, on which R and $f(R)$ must agree.

10 Apparent counterexamples to Anchoring are discussed in Marantz (1982), McCarthy and Prince (1986), and Weeda (1987).

11 Within optimality theory, where constraints may be violated, but violation is minimal, Maximality can be formulated simply as R = B (McCarthy and Prince 1993, sec. 5).

12 For further applications of melodic overwriting theory, see Steriade (1988), Bao (1990), and Yip (1992).

13 This presents some interesting complications, discussed by Katz (1991) and Urbanczyk (1992).

14 Some aspects of this approach to formalizing the theory of prosodic specification are influenced by Hoeksema's notion of a "head operation" (Hoeksema 1985). Compare also the developments in Aronoff (1988).

15   A similar case is presented by the formation of various auxiliary languages in Buin, of Papua New Guinea (Laycock 1969; Tateishi 1989; McCarthy and Prince 1991b). Other applications of prosodic circumscription to auxiliary or secret languages are proposed by Hammond (1993). Other work on secret languages, broadly related to the overall prosodic morphology program, includes Bagemihl (1988a, 1988b, 1989), Bao (1990), Chiang (1992), Duryea (1991), Hammond (1990), Itô, Kitagawa, and Mester (1992), Tateishi (1989), McCarthy (1982b, 1984b, 1991), Plénat (1985), Vago (1985), Yin (1989), Yip (1982), and many of the contributions to Plénat (1991). (Bagemihl 1988a and Plénat 1991 also include comprehensive bibliographies.)

16   The examples in (45) are cited directly from Moravcsik (1977) and they preserve the dialectal and transcriptional idiosyncrasies of her sources.

17   Circumscription of "consonant," in cases like Mangarayi, looks like a prima facie counterexample to the claim that only *prosodic* constituents are circumscribed. Thus, this phenomenon is analyzed very differently in more recent work; see McCarthy and Prince (1993, sec. 7) and the discussion of Tagalog below, section 6.

18   Prosodic delimitation is distinct from the "morphemic circumscription" of Hammond (1991b). It is, however, not unrelated to the prosodic subcategorization of Inkelas (1989); see McCarthy and Prince (1993, sec. 4, sec. 7) for further discussion.

19   Though Lowenstamm and Kaye (1986) require that templates be prosodic, they also specify the terminal positions of templates as segmental slots.

20   The one argument in the literature which crucially relies on unfilled template slots is Everett and Seki (1985); this case is analyzed differently in McCarthy and Prince (1986, 1993, sec. 7).

21   Strictly speaking, (CVCV)$^+$ is required, since Japanese has 4-mora hypocoristics as well as 2-mora ones. But of course this notation simply sneaks in the foot constituent without calling it that. Thus, we have here yet another argument against segmentalism.

22   The Austroasiatic languages of Southeast Asia, such as Temiar and Kammu, seem to counterexemplify this claim. The counterexample disappears, however, once the "sesquisyllabic" syllable structure of these languages is properly understood – see, inter alia Huffman (1972), Dell (1985), Sloan (1988), McCarthy and Prince (1991b), and cf. Anderson (1992).

23   It might be objected that Tagalog *has* closed syllables, and so No-Coda could not be active in the language. But in Optimality Theory, the presence of closed syllables in output forms of the language merely indicates that No-Coda is dominated, hence violated, not that it is entirely *hors de combat* – as indeed it is not. In Tagalog, No-Coda is dominated by the faithfulness constraints Parse and Fill (see Prince and Smolensky 1993) so input /vCCv/ is parsed faithfully as [vC.Cv] in the output.

10 The Metrical Theory of Word Stress

RENÉ KAGER

0 Introduction

0.1 Remarks on the Nature of Stress

The study of word stress addresses the location of prominent syllables within words, as well as the rhythmic, positional, quantitative, and morphological factors that govern patterns of syllable prominence. Although the mental reality of prominence is undisputed, an unambiguous phonetic correlate has not yet been discovered. Prominent syllables are potentially capable of bearing pitch movements with a strong perceptual load. They also tend to be of longer duration, as well as of higher intensity, but both of the latter factors are usually subordinated to pitch. On the other hand, the use of pitch is by no means an exclusive property of stress systems, as it is widespread in tonal and pitch accent systems. However, stress is different from both tone and pitch accent in several ways.

Firstly, stress is culminative, that is, in stress languages (with few exceptions) every (content) word has at least one stressed syllable. Second, stress is hierarchical, since a prominence hierarchy may occur among multiple stresses. Third, stress is delimitative in systems where it marks word edges. Fourth, stress is rhythmic in systems where stressed and stressless syllables alternate, and where clashes (adjacent stresses) are avoided. Naturally, stress does not assimilate to adjacent syllables, as this would produce clashes. Fifth, stress contrasts tend to be enhanced segmentally: stressed syllables may be strengthened by vowel lengthening or by gemination, while stressless syllables may be weakened by vowel reduction.

Traditionally, word stress systems have been categorized along various dimensions. One distinction is between fixed systems, where the location of stress is predictable (that is, rule-governed), and free systems, where it is unpredictable (that is, distinctive). A second distinction is that between systems where stress is governed purely by phonological factors such as distance from word edges, rhythmic factors, and syllable weight, and systems where it is governed by morphological factors, such as the distinction between roots and suffixes. A third distinction is that between bounded systems, where stresses fall within limited distances from each other and from word edges, and unbounded systems, where no constraints on interstress distance hold.

We outline below developments in the metrical theory of word stress over the past decade. On the empirical side, this implies a narrowing to those aspects of word stress that have been most closely studied for their theoretical relevance, and some inevitable neglect of other aspects.

0.2   The Origins of Metrical Theory

Metrical theory arose during the late seventies as part of nonlinear phonology, the research program of which autosegmental phonology is the other main branch. Founded by Liberman (1975), and elaborated on by Liberman and Prince (1977) and Halle and Vergnaud (1978), metrical theory shared with its autosegmental counterpart the goal of developing alternatives to the nonlocal devices of linear theory, such as rule variables and abbreviatory conventions. To that end, hierarchical representations were defined, on which processes involving nonadjacent elements could be formalized as local operations. From the beginning, word stress has been the central empirical domain of metrical phonology, although the theory has also been applied to nonstress phenomena such as vowel harmony and syllable structure.

0.2.1   The Metrical Tree

A central idea of metrical theory is to capture the hierarchical nature of stress in a representation of its own, outside the segmental matrix that includes other features. In the metrical tree, stress is represented as a hierarchy of binary branching structures, each of which is labeled *strong-weak* (*sw*) or *weak-strong* (*ws*). Consider the metrical tree of the word *Alabama*, in (1).

(1)   word

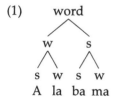

Stress, as represented in the metrical tree, is a *relational* property: a node is strong only by virtue of the fact that it is the sister of a weak node. Thus in (1), the first syllable is stronger than the second, while the third is stronger than the fourth. The superior nodes are themselves in a weak-strong relationship, which represents the relative prominence of the first and third syllables.

0.2.2 Metrical Grids

While the metrical tree displays the relative prominence of nodes, it fails to represent rhythmic alternation between strong and weak syllables, as well as clash, a situation which occurs when adjacent syllables are stressed. Liberman (1975) introduced the metrical grid as a representation of rhythmic structure. The grid corresponding to the tree in (1) is (2):

(2)
```
           *
    *      *
    *  *   *  *
    A  la  ba ma
```
    Alabama

The height of the grid columns represents the degree of prominence. Thus in (2) the third syllable is the most prominent, the initial one is less prominent by one degree, while the second and fourth are the least prominent. The grid perspicuously depicts the rhythmic alternation of strong and weak syllables. Early metrical theory derived the grid from the tree by a mapping rule, which imposes a prominence relation between syllables dominated by pairs of sister nodes.

0.2.3 Prosodic Categories and the Foot

Purely relational trees without feet, as in (1), fail to represent *non*relational stress contrasts that may actually be found in trees of identical shape. Such a contrast occurs between the final syllables of pairs such as *cóntèst* vs. *témpest*, whose strong-weak trees are indistinguishable. Thus, purely relational trees do not provide a uniform representation of stressed syllables. For this purpose, Liberman and Prince (1977) retained a segmental stress feature. Aiming at a fully metrical theory, Halle and Vergnaud (1978) and Selkirk (1980) introduced the foot as a categorial label into trees. Each foot has a unique head (its strong, or only syllable), and optional weak syllables. This introduction allowed the elimination of segmental stress features, since the distribution of stressed syllables coincides with that of *heads* of feet. Consider the enriched trees in (3):

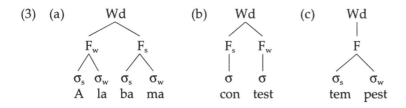

The foot is included in a hierarchy of prosodic categories ranging upward from the syllable (σ), the foot (F), the prosodic word (Wd), to still higher categories (see chapters 15 and 16, this volume). The hierarchy is closed, in that every category of level n must be dominated by some category of level $n+1$. An exhaustivity condition requires every syllable to be included in metrical structure. Since the word *Wd* dominates at least one foot *F*, every word must have a stressed syllable (culminativity).

Independent evidence for feet was found in their function as a domain for segmental rules. Selkirk (1980) observed that some consonantal allophones in English are conditioned by feet; for example, aspirated alveolar stops occur foot-initially, their flapped allophones foot-medially (cf. tʰówDəl, tʰowtʰælIDi). Nespor and Vogel (1986) adduce a large number of cases from other languages.

1   Classical Metrical Theory

Metrical theory was given a substantial body of principles in Hayes (1980), elaborating on earlier versions of parametric stress theory such as Prince (1976), Halle and Vergnaud (1978), and McCarthy (1979), and on typological work by Hyman (1977) and Odden (1979). Hayes broadened the scope of metrical theory to include a large number of typologically widely varying systems, while shifting the focus of the theory to a small number of parameters. In this parametric approach, grammars fall apart into a *core* and a *periphery*. Core grammars consist of a set of rule specifications, defined by values of parameters that are provided by Universal Grammar. Limiting the number of parameters constrains the expressive power of the theory, which is desirable from the perspective that grammars can be learned.[1] Stress systems turned out to be a highly successful testing ground for the parametric approach.[2]

1.1   Basic Parameters of Word Stress

Parameters govern the shape of metrical feet, the way in which feet are assigned, as well as metrical structure above the feet. We start our review with foot-shape parameters.

1.1.1   Boundedness

A major distinction can be drawn between systems in which stresses fall within limited distances both from each other and from word edges, and systems where the distribution of stresses is not restricted in this way. The relevant parameter of *boundedness* has two values: bounded and unbounded. Bounded feet contain no more than *two syllables*, while unbounded feet are not subject to any restrictions on size. We illustrate this with head-initial feet, in (4).

(4) (a) Bounded feet   (b) Unbounded feet

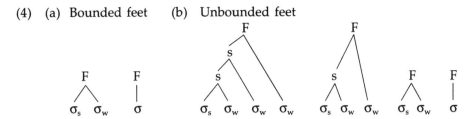

Feet are always uniformly right-branching or left-branching. Foot construction is constrained by a universal Maximal Foot Construction Principle, which ensures that the largest possible foot must be constructed. Monosyllabic expansions, or degenerate feet, are motivated both by culminativity and by exhaustivity. By culminativity, every content word must contain one stressed syllable, hence one foot. A monosyllable cannot fulfill this requirement unless its single syllable forms a degenerate foot. By exhaustivity, all syllables of a word must be organized into feet. Words whose syllables cannot all be parsed in maximal feet (such as words with an odd number of syllables which are parsed into bounded feet) require the help of degenerate feet to parse the remaining syllables. See section 1.2 below.

1.1.2 Foot Dominance

The second foot-shape parameter, *foot dominance*, determines the side of the foot where the head is located. It achieves this indirectly, through the notions dominant and recessive node. In left-dominant feet, all left nodes are dominant and right nodes recessive, while the reverse situation holds in right-dominant feet. Universally, recessive nodes may not branch, so that left-dominant feet must be left-branching, and right-dominant feet right-branching. The unmarked foot-labeling principle marks all dominant nodes as strong, as in (5), but we will see below the justification for keeping the dominant/recessive distinction separate from the strong/weak distinction.

(5) (a)   F   (b)   F

In informal terminology, which we will occasionally use in following sections, bounded left-dominant feet are called *trochees*, and bounded right-headed feet are called *iambs*.

1.1.3 Quantity-sensitivity

The third foot shape parameter, *quantity-sensitivity*, governs the distribution of light and heavy syllables in terminal nodes of feet. In quantity-*insensitive* feet, no restrictions hold, so that all syllables are treated as light (or equally heavy). In quantity-*sensitive* feet, heavy syllables may not occur in recessive positions, and are stressed. Quantity-*determined* (or Obligatory Branching) feet are quantity-sensitive, with the extra requirement that dominant terminal nodes must dominate heavy syllables. The three types are shown below with left-dominant, bounded feet in which dominant nodes are strong. We indicate heavy syllables as H, and light syllables as L in (6). Where either H or L is indicated, the template indicated refers specifically to patterns possessing the requisite H or L; when a simple σ is indicated, the template is appropriate for either an H or L syllable, with the more specific template taking precedence over the more general, in this informal presentation.

(6) (a) Q-insensitive   (b) Q-sensitive   (c) Q-determined

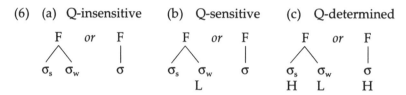

We made reference above to an unmarked labeling convention. Here we observe the marked convention, according to which dominant nodes are marked as strong *iff* they dominate a branching node (heavy syllables count as branching, as we will see shortly). This produces one more quantity-sensitive foot, the *Labeling Based on Branching* (LBOB) foot. Its left-dominant version is in (7).[3]

(7)   F   or   F   or   F

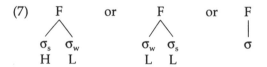

In the geometrical spirit of early metrical theory, Hayes proposes that syllable weight is tied essentially to whether certain syllable-internal constituents do or do not branch. The constituents in question are the *rhyme* and the *nucleus*.[4] Foot construction inspects branchingness on one of two projections. On the rhyme projection (8), both long-voweled and closed syllables are heavy, as opposed to open short-voweled syllables. On the nucleus projection (9), long-voweled syllables are heavy as opposed to all others.

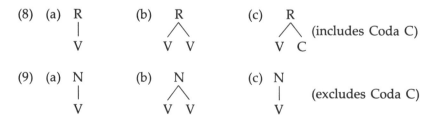

1.1.4 Directionality and Iterativity

Next we consider the parameters of foot construction. One parameter of *directionality* determines the direction in which foot construction scans the stress domain: starting at the right edge (right-to-left), or at the left edge (left-to-right). As a rule of thumb, construction starts at the word edge where the stress pattern is invariant, while at the other edge it systematically varies with the number of syllables in the word. By a second parameter of *iterativity*, feet are constructed iteratively or noniteratively. In noniterative systems, words have a single foot at the edge. *Bidirectional* systems result from noniterative foot assignment at one edge, and iterative foot assignment starting at the opposite side.

1.1.5 Word Tree Dominance: Branching and Labeling

Finally, let us turn to the parameters of the *word tree*, the supra-foot structure governing prominence hierarchies among stresses. The word tree branches uniformly, and its labeling is derived indirectly, much as at foot-level. The *dominance* parameter has two values: *left*-dominant and *right*-dominant. Again, the unmarked convention labels dominant nodes strong, placing main stress on a peripheral foot (10a, b). The marked rule labels dominant nodes strong if and only if they branch, so that nonbranching dominant feet are weak (10c, d). This is illustrated with right-dominant word trees in (10).

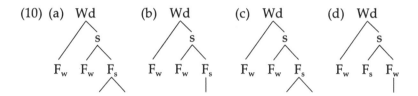

Word-level labeling may refer to the internal structure of feet, but never to that of syllables. More generally, the *Metrical Locality* principle (Hammond 1982) states that rules may refer only to elements at the same or adjacent layers of metrical structure.

1.2 Exemplification of Bounded Systems

1.2.1 Quantity-insensitive Bounded Systems

Four quantity-insensitive bounded patterns arise by varying the parameters of dominance and directionality, as in (11).

(11)   (a)   L-dominant,
left to right
(b)   L-dominant,
right to left

(c)   R-dominant,
left to right
(d)   R-dominant,
right to left

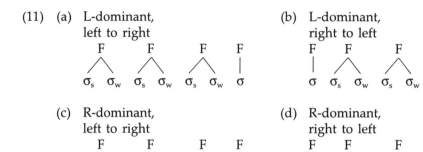

Hungarian (Kerek 1971) exemplifies (11a). Main stress is initial and secondary stresses fall on all odd-numbered syllables. A left-dominant word tree produces initial main stress, as in (12).

(12)   (a)   bóldog   "happy"
(b)   bóldogsà:g   "happiness"
(c)   bóldogtàlan   "unhappy"
(d)   bóldogtàlansà:g   "unhappiness"
(e)   légešlègmegèngestèlhetètlenèbbeknèk
"to the most irreconcilable ones"

Warao (Osborn 1966) exemplifies (11b). Main stress is on the penultimate syllable, and secondary stresses on even-numbered syllables counting backward from the main stress:

(13)   (a)   yà.pu.rù.ki.tà.ne.há.se   "verily to climb"
(b)   e.nà.ho.rò.a.hà.ku.tá.i   "one who caused him to eat"

The word tree is right-dominant. Words such as (13b) require an additional rule to delete initial degenerate feet in weak positions (such *destressing* rules are discussed in section 1.5).
The pattern of (11c) is attested in Araucanian (Echeverría and Contreras 1965), where main stress is on the second syllable, and secondary stresses on following even-numbered syllables. The word tree is left-dominant, and weak degenerate feet are deleted, as in Warao. See (14).

(14)   (a)   e.lú.a.è.new   "he will give me"
(b)   ki.mú.fa.lù.wu.lày   "he pretended not to know"

The pattern of (11d) occurs in Weri (Boxwell and Boxwell 1966). Main stress is on the final syllable, and secondaries are on preceding odd-numbered syllables counting from the word end. The word tree is right-dominant. See (15).

(15)   (a)   ʊlʊ̀amɪ́t   "mist"
       (b)   àkʊnètepáĭ   "times"

Piro (Matteson 1965) is a *bidirectional* system. Main stress is on the penult, and secondary stresses are on odd-numbered syllables counting from the word begining. Quantity-insensitive trochees are assigned noniteratively at the right edge, and then iteratively from left to right:

(16)

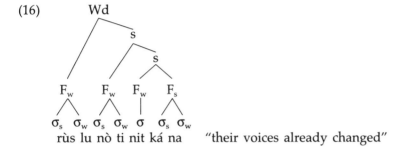

rùs lu nò ti nit ká na   "their voices already changed"

The word tree is right-dominant, and the weak degenerate foot preceding the main stress foot is eliminated.

In all systems discussed so far, main stress falls at the edge where foot construction starts. Hammond (1985) states this in his Directionality Dominance Hypothesis, according to which the first application of foot assignment uniquely determines word tree dominance.[5] The Directionality Dominance Hypothesis seems to be falsified by Creek (Hayes 1981) and Cairene Arabic (McCarthy 1979), where rightward foot construction combines with a right-dominant word tree. Hammond, observing that both systems lack overt secondary stresses, suggests that main stress and secondary stresses are on distinct parallel metrical planes, a situation which renders them immune to the Directionality Dominance Hypothesis. However, overt secondary stresses running towards the main stress do occur in systems such as Wargamay (Dixon 1981) and Cayuga (Foster 1982), which seems to reduce the Directional Dominance Hypothesis to a statement regarding frequency, rather than a firm metrical universal.

1.2.2   Quantity-sensitive Bounded Systems (Uniform Labeling)

Four types of quantity-sensitive bounded systems result from Dominance and directionality:

(17)   (a)   L-dominant,   (b)   L-dominant,
             left to right   right to left

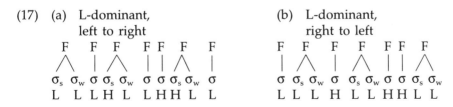

(c)   R-dominant,
left to right

(d)   R-dominant,
right to left

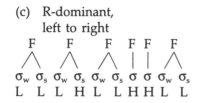

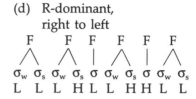

Central Siberian Yupik (Jacobson 1985) has rightward iambs (the final syllable is never stressed, see section 1.4 on extrametricality) (see 18a), while Tübatulabal (Voegelin 1935) has leftward iambs (see 18b).

(18)   (a)   (b)

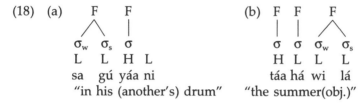

sa gú yáa ni   táa há wi lá
"in his (another's) drum"   "the summer(obj.)"

Both languages seem to lack prominence distinctions between stresses, which is accounted for by not assigning a word tree. Iterative quantity-sensitive trochaic systems are extremely rare, an observation to which we will return in section 5.1. A noniterative example is Latin, as we see in section 1.4.1.

1.2.3   Bounded Labeling-Based-on-Branching Feet

In Cairene Arabic (McCarthy 1979), main stress is (a) on final *superheavy* syllables (CVVC, CVCC), else (b) on heavy penults (CVV, CVC), or else (c) on the rightmost nonfinal odd-numbered light syllable counting from the nearest preceding heavy syllable or the intial syllable; see (19).

(19)   (a)   sakakíin "knives"   (e)   muxtálifa "different (fem. sg.)"
       (b)   ʕamálti "you (fem. sg.) did"   (f)   šajarátuhu "his tree"
       (c)   martába "mattress"   (g)   šajaratahúmaa "their (dual)
       (d)   búxala "misers"   tree (nom.)"

McCarthy analyzes superheavy syllables into a heavy syllable plus a degenerate syllable which is the final consonant. The absence of final stress is analyzed by making final syllables invisible to the stress rules (by extrametricality, see section 1.4 below). Word stress is located by assigning right-dominant Labeling-Based-on-Branching feet from left to right, and building a right-dominant word tree, as in (20).

(20)   (a)   Wd   (b)   Wd

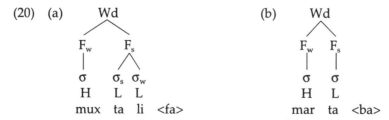

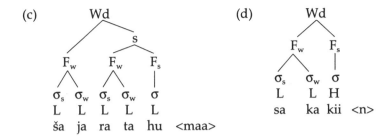

1.2.4   Obligatory Branching (OB) Feet

Yapese (Jensen 1977) has final stress except in words whose final vowel is short and whose penultimate vowel is long. A bounded left-dominant Obligatory Branching (OB) foot at the right edge of the word produces this pattern. In (21c) we have a word that has no heavy syllables, and thus no OB foot can be constructed; as a result, a right-dominant word tree is constructed directly over syllables; see (21).

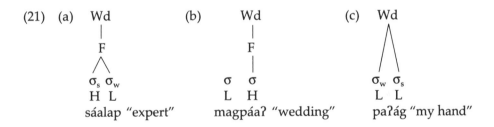

The mirror-image pattern of Yapese occurs in Malayalam (Mohanan 1986).

1.3   Exemplification of Unbounded Systems

There are three basic types of unbounded systems, default-to-opposite, default-to-same and peripheral-plus-heavies.

Default-to-opposite systems stress a heavy syllable closest to an edge, else (in words without heavy syllables) the syllable at the opposite edge. They occur in two mirror-image variants: Eastern Cheremis (Sebeok and Ingemann 1961) stresses the rightmost heavy, else the initial syllable, while Komi Jazva (Kiparsky 1973a) stresses the leftmost heavy, else the final syllable. Prince (1976) introduced an analysis based on unbounded quantity-sensitive feet, which are left-dominant when stress defaults initially, and right-dominant when it defaults finally. Word tree dominance is of opposite parity to that of feet in such a language; see (22), which represents the analysis of Eastern Cheremis.

(22)   (a)

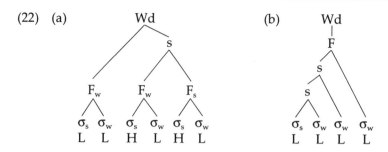

(b)

Default-to-same systems stress a heavy syllable closest to an edge, else the syllable at the same edge. Again, two mirror-image variants occur. Aguacatec Mayan (McArthur and McArthur 1956) stresses the rightmost heavy syllable, else the final syllable, Khalka Mongolian (Street 1963) the leftmost heavy syllable, else the initial syllable. Halle and Vergnaud (1978) employ unbounded Obligatory Branching feet. In words that have no heavy syllables, and hence no feet, the word tree is constructed directly over syllables. Word tree dominance matches the default side, as in (23), which represents the analysis of Aguacatec Mayan.

(23)   (a)

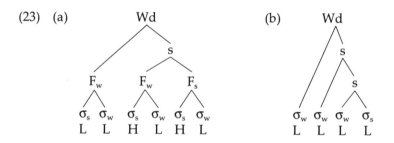

(b)

Peripheral-plus-heavies systems stress a peripheral syllable and all heavy syllables. The mirror-image variants are initial main stress plus heavies (Papago, see Saxton 1963), and final main stress and heavies (Western Greenlandic Eskimo, see Schultz-Lorentzen 1945). Here, the dominance of feet and word trees match, as shown in (24), which represents the analysis of Papago.

(24)   (a)

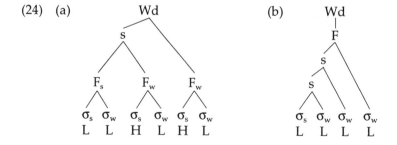

(b)

1.4 Extrametricality

The concept of *extrametricality*, introduced by Liberman and Prince (1977), became a cornerstone of metrical theory in Hayes (1981). Extrametrical elements are not analyzed by the metrical stress rules, neither regarding its structural descriptions nor its structural change; informally speaking, rules may be said to be "blind" to extrametrical elements, and those extrametrical elements may be said to be "invisible" to the rules. Extrametricality is restricted to peripheral elements, and has three types of motivation: (a) at word edges, it avoids foot types that are otherwise rare or not found; (b) it functions to analyze stresslessness of peripheral syllables, and (c) it marks exceptions to the stress rules.

1.4.1 Motivating Extrametricality

Extrametricality helps to constrain foot typology in bounded systems that stress the third syllable from the edge. Cross-linguistically, *ternary* feet are relatively rare in nonperipheral positions (but see sections 4.2.3 and 5.4), and extrametricality theoretically eliminates them in favor of *binary* feet.

In Latin, stress is antepenultimate if the penult is light (*réficit*), else penultimate (*reféːcit, reféctus, fácit*). The pattern is generated by making final syllables extrametrical and by assigning a quantity-sensitive trochee at the right edge. We indicate extrametricality by angled brackets:

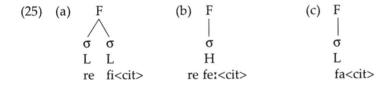

Hayes claims that extrametricality allows the elimination of ternary feet in languages like Latin and English, universally restricting the class of bounded feet to binary feet.[6]

Extrametricality's second function can be illustrated with Hopi (Jeanne 1982). Hopi has second syllable stress (manifested as high tone) in words whose initial syllable is light, and initial stress otherwise. But disyllabic words have initial stress regardless of the weight of the initial syllable:

(26) (a) ʔácvewa "chair"   (b) qötósompi "headband"
     (c) táávo "cottontail" (d) kóho   "wood"

Both quantity-sensitive trochees and iambs fail to produce this pattern. However, final syllable extrametricality leads to a simple analysis with a quantity-sensitive iamb at the left edge, as in (27); this illustrates how final extrametricality may affect foot construction at the opposite edge.

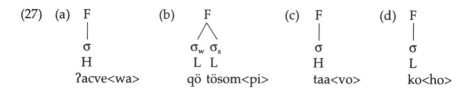

(27)   (a) F   (b)   F   (c) F   (d) F

σ   σ_w σ_s   σ   σ
H   L L   H   L
ʔacve<wa>   qö tösom<pi>   taa<vo>   ko<ho>

Finally, extrametricality as an exception-marking device can be illustrated with Polish (Franks 1985), where main stress is penultimate except for a small number of words, such as *uniwérsytet* "university", which have antepenultimate stress. Interestingly, the addition of a suffix leads to regular penultimate stress, as in *uniwersytét+u*. This is explained by the assumption that extrametricality markings are lost automatically in nonperipheral positions, as illustrated in (28b):

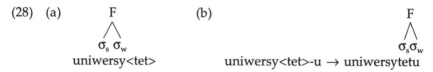

(28)   (a)   F   (b)   F

σ_s σ_w   σ_s σ_w
uniwersy<tet>   uniwersy<tet>-u → uniwersytetu

Segment extrametricality is motivated by systems that have different criteria for syllable weight in final and nonfinal positions. In Estonian (Prince 1980) nonfinal CVV and CVC syllables are heavy. But in final position, only CVV(C) and CVCC are heavy. By consonant extrametricality, CV<C> is formally nonbranching, hence light, but CVC<C> is still formally branching.

1.4.2   Constraining Extrametricality

Extrametricality is subject to the following constraints (Hayes 1981): (a) Only phonological or morphological constituents, such as the segment, syllable, suffix, etc., can be extrametrical. (b) A Peripherality Condition requires extrametrical elements to be at the edge of the stress domain. Harris (1983) deviates from this in his analysis of Spanish, where the stem is the domain of segment extrametricality, but the word is the stress domain. Archangeli (1986) solves a similar problem in Yawelmani by transferring extrametricality from the stem, in which it is lexically marked, to the stress domain. (c) The *right* edge is the unmarked (and perhaps only) edge where extrametricality may occur. (d) Nonperipheral extrametricality is automatically erased (as in 28b). Kiparsky (1985) argues that extrametricality can be persistent even when temporarily suppressed by nonperipherality, and is lost only at the end of the lexicon.[7] Inkelas (1989) construes extrametricality as a mismatch between morphological and prosodic structures of words in the lexicon, as in (29).

(29)   [Pame]_P la   prosodic structure
       [Pamela]_M   morphological structure

She argues that peripherality, nonexhaustivity, and postlexical erasure of extrametricality are consequences of this domains approach. (e) Finally, extrametricality is blocked when it would affect the entire domain (e.g., a monosyllable), which guarantees culminativity.

1.5   Destressing and Stray Syllable Adjunction

In section 1.2, we discussed systems that required a rule to eliminate excessive stresses produced by foot construction. Destressing is implemented as foot deletion in foot-based theory. Consider again Piro, where weak degenerate feet are deleted, as in (30).

(30)

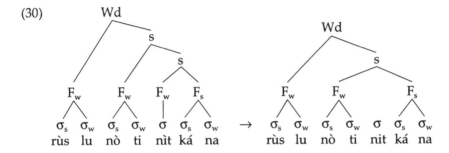

The output of destressing in (30) violates the prosodic exhaustivity requirement. Metrical theory assumes that repair is automatic, in the form of a universal convention of Stray Syllable Adjunction. Hayes suggests that Stray Syllable Adjunction is structure-preserving: the dominance of derived feet matches the system's parametric value, when possible. In (30) this makes the stray syllable adjoin leftward under the preceding foot. Where this is impossible, stray syllables are adjoined directly under the word tree.

Foot deletion renders the surface pattern stress opaque with respect to foot assignment rules. Familiar considerations of learnability thus necessitate constraints on destressing rules, an example of which is Hayes's condition that destressing may not affect the main stress foot.

2   Grid Theory

Tree theory came under attack when Prince (1983) and Selkirk (1984) introduced a pure grid theory. They showed that rhythmic notions such as *alternation* and *clash* are best represented in grids. They also argued that metrical theory is simplified by eliminating constituency altogether, since parametric theory can be stated equally well in terms of pure grids.

2.1   The Autonomous Metrical Grid

The grid is a hierarchical representation of stress and rhythm, and in its purest form eliminates reference to the notion of constituency. It consists of a sequence of columns of grid marks, whose height represents *prominence levels*, while horizontal distance between marks represent *rhythmic structure*. All syllables are represented by a mark at the lowest layer, stressed syllables by a mark on the next layer up, while distinctions between main and secondary stresses are represented on still higher layers. Grid layers roughly correspond to the categorial levels (σ, F, Wd) of tree notation, as indicated vertically alongside the grid in (31).

(31)　　　*　　　　　　Wd
　　　　*　*　*　*　F
　　　*　*　*　*　*　*　*　σ

Let us now focus on some formal properties of grid notation: (1) The grid represents stress as a hierarchical rather than a relational property. (2) Grid structure is subject to a constraint that forms the analogue of the closed prosodic hierarchy in tree theory:

(32)　*Continuous Column Constraint* (after Hayes 1994)
　　　A grid containing a column with a mark on layer $n + 1$ and no mark on layer n is ill-formed. Phonological rules are blocked when they would create such a configuration.

(3) Culminativity is not a formal consequence of the grid, whereas it follows from the prosodic hierarchy in tree theory. Deriving culminativity in grid theory would require an ad hoc principle to the effect that every grid has at least one Foot layer mark, and another to the effect that the highest layer consists of only one mark. (4) Rhythmic notions are defined in grids quite adequately: *clash* as the adjacency of two marks on layer n without an intervening mark on layer n–1 (as in 33a); *lapse* as a sequence of marks on layer n, none of which has a corresponding mark on layer n+1 (as in 33b); *alternation* as a sequence of marks without clash or lapse (as in 33c). (5) The grid allows for straightforward implementation of the delimitative aspects of word stress. By definition, End Rules affect peripheral marks, and so does extrametricality.

(33)　(a)　*　*　　　(b)　　　　　　(c)　*　　*　　*
　　　　　*　*　　　　　*　*　*　　　　*　*　*　*　*　*

　　　　　Clash　　　　　*Lapse*　　　　*Alternation*

The autonomous grid requires parametric construction principles, which, as van der Hulst (1984) shows, fully match up to those of tree theory in descriptive capacities.

2.2 Parameters of Grid Theory

2.2.1 Quantity-sensitivity

Prince (1983) introduces a mora-based approach to quantity-sensitivity (on the mora, see chapter 5, this volume). The moraic representation he proposes consists also of marks organized in rows. In the grid, a light syllable is represented with one mark at the mora layer, a heavy syllable with two (this is referred to as *bipositional* representation). The characteristic sonority decline between the moras of heavy syllables, interpreted as falling prominence, is projected on the Foot layer by a rule called *Quantity-sensitivity* (QS):

(34)   (a) 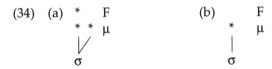   (b)

Thus grid theory marks heavy syllables as *inherently* stressed. In contrast, tree theory marks heavy syllables as stressed only if they are heads of feet, and unfooted heavy syllables are stressless.

2.2.2 Perfect Grid

The best illustration of the rhythm-based nature of grid-only theory is its treatment of iterative bounded systems by the rule of Perfect Grid. Perfect Grid (PG) provides the rhythmic basis of such systems by adding a Foot layer mark on top of every other syllable layer mark:

(35)
```
                            PG    *   *   *   *   *       F
* * * * * * * * *           →     * * * * * * * * *       σ
```

Perfect Grid is governed by two parameters. *Directionality* fixes its starting point at the left or right edge. A *starting* parameter makes Perfect Grid start either with a rhythmic *peak*, or with a rhythmic *trough*. This generates the four basic quantity-insensitive systems of section 1.2.1, as illustrated in (36).

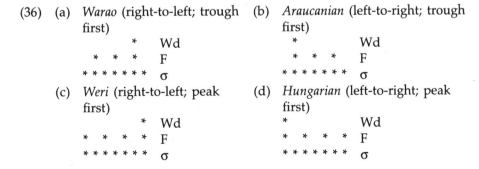

(36)   (a) *Warao* (right-to-left; trough first)   (b) *Araucanian* (left-to-right; trough first)

       (c) *Weri* (right-to-left; peak first)   (d) *Hungarian* (left-to-right; peak first)

Starting with a trough at the right edge, or with a peak at the left edge, produces "trochaic" rhythm (36a, d). Starting with a trough at the left edge, or with a peak at the right edge, produces "iambic" rhythm (36b, c). Thus Perfect Grid makes a notion such as *trochaic* stress rule undefinable, since the starting edge has to be taken into account. By the strictly alternating clash-avoiding nature of Perfect Grid, no additional rules are needed to eliminate analogues of degenerate feet in clashing positions. Compare (36a) to (11b), and (36b) to (11c).

Since Perfect Grid only fills out portions of the grid that have been left blank by the rule Quantity-sensitivity, quantity and rhythm become separate notions. In contrast, tree theory integrates both into the concept of *Foot*.

2.2.3   End Rules

End Rules place a mark on top of a mark that is peripheral on the next layer down. A particular instance of End Rule must be specified for which row of the grid it applies to; we may say it is "parameterized" in that respect. When applying to the Foot layer, or row, End Rule produces edge stresses, but its common function is to assign main stress at Word layer by promoting a Foot layer mark to word prominence. *Dominance* specifies whether to select the rightmost (ER(F)), or leftmost (ER(I)) landing site, which is to say, whether the leftmost or the rightmost stress has the greatest prominence in the word; see (37).

End Rules are constrained by the Continous Column Constraint. Thus, for a mark to be inserted at a layer, a landing site has to be present in the form of a mark at the next layer down.

(37)   (a)   ER(F;Wd)   *   Wd   (b)   ER(I;Wd)   *   Wd
             *   *   *   *   F   *   *   *   *   F
             * * * *   →   * * * *   * * * *   →   * * * *

2.2.4   Unbounded Systems

The analysis of unbounded systems is based on two devices: Quantity Sensitivity (QS) and the End Rule (ER). *Default-to-opposite* systems require an End Rule at Foot layer, and another at Word layer at the opposite edge. The "rightmost heavy, else initial" type is defined by the rule set QS, ER(I;F), ER(F;Wd):

(38)   (a)   *   (b)   *   ER(F;Wd)
             *   *   *   *   ER(I;F)
             * * ** * * ** *   * * * * * * * *
             L L H L L H L   L L L L L L L

For *Default-to-same* systems, tree theory constructs the word tree over syllables without intervening feet in the default case (see section 1.3.2). Analogously, in grid theory, the End Rule defaults one layer down if no proper Foot layer landing site is found, as in (39).

(39) (a)
```
            *
            *           *
    *   *   **  *   *   **  *
    L   L   H   L   L   H   L
```
(b)
```
    *
    *   *   *   *   *   *   *
    L   L   L   L   L   L   L
```
ER(I;Wd)

Peripheral-plus-heavies systems require End Rules at Foot and Word layers, at identical edges, as in (40).

(40) (a)
```
    *
    *   *           *
    *   *   **  *   *   **  *
    L   L   H   L   L   H   L
```
(b)
```
    *
    *
    *   *   *   *   *   *   *
    L   L   L   L   L   L   L
```
ER(I;Wd)
ER (I;F)

2.3   Operations on Grids

Grid theory shows its rhythm-based nature in its formalization of destressing and rhythmic stress shifts. Such processes become simple operations (deletions, insertions, movements) of grid marks, triggered by illformed grid configurations such as clash or lapse. We will review these operations here.

2.3.1   Delete x

Destressing rules can be written in a simple format: *Delete x*. Three advantages come from this. (a) This is a local operation, requiring no deletion of a prosodic category, nor stray adjunction. (b) The triggering clash is directly represented. A dominance parameter specifies whether to delete the first or the second of two clashing grid marks, as in (41). (c) The integrity of the main stress needs no stipulation, because the Continuous Column Constraint blocks deletion of a grid mark supporting another on the next layer up.

(41) (a)
```
    *   *               *
    *   *    →      *   *
```
(b)
```
    *   *               *
    *   *    →      *   *
```

2.3.2   Insert x

The second type of adjustment is the insertion of a grid mark to resolve a lapse. *Insert x* is parametrized for dominance in much the same way as *Delete x*, yielding two basic types, those in (42a) and (b).

(42) (a)
```
            *
    *   *    →      *   *
```
(b)
```
                    *
    *   *    →      *   *
```

Insert x typically applies peripherally to produce a "rhythmic antipole." Selkirk (1984) observes that rhythmically conditioned *Insert x* preserves culminativity, i.e., the relative prominence of main stress. She proposes a convention to the effect that insertion of a mark on the highest layer is automatically accompanied by a corresponding rise of the culminative peak:

(43)

```
                                *
        *          *    *           *       *
   *  *    *       *  *   *         *   *    *
   * * *  * * *    * * *  * * *     * * *   * * *
              →
   Apalachicola    Apalachicola   (not Apalachicola)
```

2.3.3   *Move x*

Move x involves a (leftward or rightward) shift of a mark to resolve a clash, as in (44).

```
(44)  (a)    *           *      (b)  *           *
           * *         *   *         * *        *   *
           * * *   →   * * *         * * *  →   * * *
```

By the Continuous Column Constraint, *Move x* cannot affect the strongest of two beats (45a), and requires a proper landing site on the next layer down (45b).

```
(45)  (a)   *            *       (b)  * *        *   *
          * *          *   *          * *        * *
          * * *   →    * * *          * * *  →   * * *
```

Prince and Selkirk suggest that *Move x* may be decomposed into *Delete x* and *Insert x*. *Delete x* resolves the clash, while *Insert x* assigns the rhythmic "antipole."

3   Early Bracketed Grid Theory

Evidence for feet in studies of prosodic morphology and foot-governed stress shifts have renewed interest in the question of whether rhythmic structure in phonology involves consituent structure. The advantages of the grid sketched above encouraged not a return to metrical trees, but rather a metrical grid with constituency markers added to it. The representations that arose were characterized by flat, *n*-ary constituency and direct representation of rhythmic structure.

3.1 New Arguments for Constituency

3.1.1 Stress Shifts by Deletion of Stressed Vowels

Significant arguments for metrical constituency were advanced based on the behavior of stress shifts accompanying deletions of stressed vowels. Al-Mozainy, Bley-Vroman, and McCarthy (1985) found that syncope in Bedouin Hijazi Arabic leads to migrations of stress whose direction depends on the shape of the metrical tree. In Bedouin Hajazi Arabic, stress is on superheavy final syllables (46a); if there is no superheavy final syllable, it falls on a heavy penult (46b); if there is no heavy penult, it falls on the antepenult (46c).

(46) (a) maktúub "written"   (b) maktúufah "tied" (fem. sg.)
      (c) máalana "our property"

   The analysis is essentially the same as for Latin (see section 1.4.1), while final superheavy syllables are analyzed as in Cairene Arabic (see section 1.2.3). Final syllables are extrametrical, and a quantity-sensitive trochee is constructed at the right edge. A rule of Low Vowel Deletion deletes short /a/ in an open syllable if the following syllable is also open and contains short /a/. This rule produces alternations such as *sáḥab* "he pulled", *saḥábna* "we pulled", versus *shábat* "she pulled". A particular interaction between stress and Low Vowel Deletion is revealed by alternations such as *ʔínkisaṛ* "he got broken" vs. *ʔinksáṛat* "she got broken" (> /ʔinkasaṛat/). Stress assignment cannot follow Low Vowel Deletion, since this would produce *ʔínksaṛat. The surface opacity is explained by ordering stress before Low Vowel Deletion, if it is assumed that a deletion of the vowel in the head of a foot results in a rightward migration of stress within the foot:

(47)

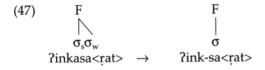

   This analysis has two interesting implications, both of which have been confirmed by studies of similar phenomena in other languages, including Tiberian Hebrew (Prince 1975), various Arabic dialects (Kenstowicz 1983; Hayes 1994), Russian (Halle and Vergnaud 1987), and Sanskrit (Halle and Vergnaud 1987). First, the deletion of a stressed vowel does not result in the deletion of the stress, but rather into its migration to an adjacent vowel. Thus, stress seems to display a *stability* effect that hitherto had been observed only in autosegmental phenomena such as tone and length. Second, the *direction* of the stress shift is predictable from the dominance of the foot whose head is deleted: stress shifts rightward in trochees, leftward in iambs. More generally, within the foot, the stress shifts to the nonhead syllable. Stability follows from the integrity of constituency, and the assumption that every constituent must have a head.

3.1.2 *Prosodic Morphology and Phrasal Rhythmic Adjustments*

McCarthy and Prince (1986) demonstrate that many languages have morphological operations (infixation, reduplication, etc.) that refer to prosodic units such as the syllable and the foot. Minimal word conditions also refer to feet. See chapter 9, for extensive discussion. Another domain of evidence for metrical constituency is in stress shifts and other rhythmic adjustments at the phrasal level. Chapters 15 and 16 discuss phrasal phonology in more detail.

3.2 *The Arboreal Grid*

The arboreal tree notation of Hammond (1984) has ancestors in Leben (1982), Lerdahl and Jackendoff (1983), as well as work in dependency phonology. These proposals shared a flat, *n-ary* constituent structure, and a direct representation of constituent heads and nonheads. The strict relationality of early tree notation, with its binary branching and strong-weak labeling, were weakened within tree theory by the nonrelational notion of *head of a prosodic category*. Moreover, Prince (1983) demonstrated how tree geometry could be bypassed by pure grid mechanisms to locate heavy syllables and peripheral elements. Hammond (1984) added to this by detecting inadequacies in the classical tree with respect to the representation of rhythm.

Hammond (1984) modified the classical tree by vertically aligning heads with their mother constituent nodes, so that a grid-like hierarchical configuration of heads arises. Compare the standard tree of *Apalachicola* (48a) to that in Hammond's notation (48b), where circles represent heads of constituents:

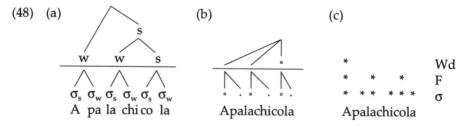

Containing all information present in grids, the notation is equally adequate as a representation of rhythmic structure (compare 48b and 48c). Hammond builds a major argument for arboreal grids on the fact that they allow for an adequate format of destressing rules. He hypothesizes that universally, stress clash is the obligatory trigger for destressing rules:

(49) Clash Resolution Hypothesis (CRH)
All destressing rules must apply so as to eliminate adjacent heads of feet.

In the arboreal grid, clash is very directly represented as the adjacency of two heads of subtrees. Consequently, rules of destressing can be stated as deletion of a head of a foot (with the automatic removal of the foot). (50a) illustrates prestress destressing, (50b) poststress destressing (both outputs are subject to further stray syllable adjunction):

(50) (a)   (b)

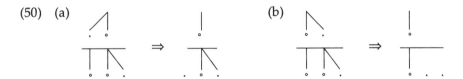

Thus arboreal grids rationalize restrictions on foot-branching in Hayesian defooting rules.

3.3 Improving tree theory: Prince (1985)

Prince (1985) argues that the boundedness parameter can be eliminated from tree theory, as unbounded feet are derivable by independently needed means. Unbounded feet serve to locate heavy syllables, and to mark domain edges, as he had already suggested in Prince (1983). Tree theory already provides machinery for both purposes: heavy syllables can be located by bounded Obligatory Branching feet, while edges are marked by peripheral noniterative bounded feet. For example, "Rightmost heavy, else initial" systems can be reanalyzed by bounded Obligatory Branching feet, and a noniterative trochee at the left edge. A right-dominant bounded word tree is constructed at the right word edge:

(51) (a)   Wd   (b) Wd

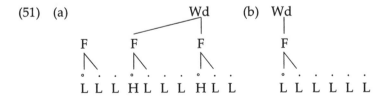

The exhaustivity requirement makes primitive bounded feet expand into derived unbounded feet by Stray Syllable Adjunction. Elimination of primitive unbounded feet is supported by the observation that they are hard to motivate as prosodic constituents by familiar diagnostics such as stress shifts, foot-domain rules, and prosodic morphology (Prince 1983; Kager 1989).

The second major contribution of Prince (1985) is collapsing foot construction and destressing rules. Let us see how this is achieved. First, Prince spells out a principle of foot assignment tacitly assumed in earlier work. Iterative rules produce "back-to-back" parsings (52a), and never apply to syllables that have already been footed on previous iterations (52b).

(52) (a) F   F F   (b) F   F F
           $\diagdown$ $\diagdown$ $\diagdown$ $\diagdown$ $\mid$ $\diagdown$
           σ σ σ σ → σ σ σ σ   σ σ σ σ → σ σ σ σ

This is formulated in the Free Element Condition (53).

(53) Free Element Condition
      Rules of primary metrical analysis apply only to Free Elements – those
      that do not stand in the metrical relationship being established; i.e., they
      are "feature-filling" only.

The Free Element Condition constitutes a diagnostic of rules that build metrical structure. It excludes destressing rules from this class, as they do not respect previously assigned structure. Under the hypothesis that the Free Element Condition explicates the difference between foot assignment and destressing rules, the rule types may be collapsed in every other respect. This can be formally achieved by merging the parts of destressing (deletion of the foot and a subsequent application of Stray Adjunction) into one format, foot *reassignment*: $[\sigma]_F[\sigma]_F \rightarrow [\sigma\ \sigma]_F$. Destressing rules are then structure-*changing* applications of foot assignment. This hypothesis correctly predicts that foot shape parameters extend to destressing rules. *Foot dominance* determines which of the two syllables survives as the head of the new foot. *Quantity-sensitivity* may restrict the weight of syllables to be destressed (in some cases, heavy syllables are immune in English, cf. *banána* vs. *bàndánna*, while in others, they are not: *dəpártment* vs. *dèpàrtméntal*).

4   The Halle and Vergnaud Theory

Halle and Vergnaud (1987), proposed a different approach to metrical theory, based on a bracketed grid notation. The theory strongly emphasizes formal properties of constituency.

4.1   *The Representation of Stress*

In Halle and Vergnaud's bracketed grid notation, stress is represented as a grid enriched by bracketing to indicate stress constituents. A hierarchy of layers is assumed, in which they are labeled as line 0, 1, and so forth. By bracketing, adjacent marks on the same line are organized into constituents, whose unique head is vertically aligned with a mark at the next-higher line:

(54)   *   line 2
         (*   *   *)   line 1
         (* *) (* *) (* *)   line 0
         Apa lachi cola

Line 0 represents the place markers of stress-bearing units, which may be either syllables or rhyme elements (moras, under some interpretatons). Brackets on line 0 match the foot boundaries of tree theory. Line 1 contains the heads of line 0 constituents, which may be organized into constituents that correspond to the higher level prosodic categories of tree theory, such as the word tree. Line 2 contains the heads of line 1 constituents, and so forth.

The bracketed grid notation shares with Hammond's arboreal grid simultaneous representation of prominence, rhythm, and constituency. However, bracketed grid notation has the additional option of representing constituency without prominence, and prominence without constituency, applications of which we will see below.[8] A related difference is that bracketed grids allow the formulation of rules that move, delete, or insert grid marks, as in pure grid theory, as well as operations on brackets.

4.2 Parameters and Conditions

4.2.1 Constituent Construction

Three major parameters of constituent construction are *Boundedness* (bounded, unbounded), *Headedness* (left-headed, right-headed), and *Directionality* (left-to-right, right-to-left). For Hungarian (cf. 12), bounded left-headed constituents are constructed on line 0, whose heads are located on line 1. On line 1, an unbounded left-headed constituent is constructed whose head is located on line 2:

(55)   *   line 2
         (*   *   *   *)   line 1
         (* *) (* *) (* *) (*)   line 0

In Halle and Vergnaud's terminology, the rule set that constructs bounded constituents on line 0 and locates their heads on line 1 is the *Alternator*, similar to Perfect Grid, discussed above. It must be iterative by the *Exhaustivity Condition*, requiring all line 0 elements to be in a constituent, and which they construe as a condition on foot construction, i.e., on rule application. Thus Halle and Vergnaud reject the *iterativity* parameter.

4.2.2   *Quantity-sensitivity and Premarked Brackets*

Halle and Vergnaud's approach to quantity-sensitivity follows Prince (1983): a rule pre-assigns a grid mark on line 1 (an "accent") to all heavy syllables.[9] The Faithfulness Condition guarantees that heavy syllables are parsed as heads of line 0 constituents:

(56)   Faithfulness Condition (HV, pp. 15–16)
       The output metrical structure respects the distribution of heads (accented elements), in the sense that each head is associated with constituent boundaries in the output structure and that these are located at the appropriate positions in the sequence. [...]

   In (57), an accent blocks construction of a left-headed foot over the first and second syllable (under rightward application).

(57)
```
                      QS    *                    *  *     *         line 1
      * * * * *        →    * * * * *      →    (*) (*  *) (*  *)    line 0
      L H L L L             L H L L L            L  H  L  L  L
```

Decomposition of quantity-sensitivity and rhythm unifies all bounded feet construction by a single rule, the Alternator. We will see advantages of this in section 4.3 on bidirectionality.
   Another way in which heavy syllables can be marked off is by preassigning a bracket at line 0, a mechanism introduced in Halle (1990). This device may be employed in systems where stress-bearing units are rhyme segments (moras), as in Cairene Arabic (see section 1.2.3). A preassigned left bracket "[" before a heavy syllable blocks the construction of a line 0 constituent over the first and second moras in (58):

(58)
```
                                             *   *    *   *
    * ** * * *      →    * [** * * *    →   (*) [**) (* *) (*)
    L H L L L            L H L L L           L  H   LL   L
```

   If rhyme segments (moras) can be stress-bearing units, it is predicted that foot boundaries may occur inside heavy syllables. Halle and Vergnaud argue that this is the case in systems such as Winnebago. In words starting with a sequence of light syllables, stress is on the third syllable, while in words starting with a heavy syllable, stress is on the second syllable. The third mora is stressed by initial mora extrametricality, and an initial right-headed bounded foot, as in (59).

(59)   (a)
```
                            *        (b)                           *
     <*>  *  *   →   <*> (*  *)          <*>* *  *   →   <*> (*  *)
      L   L  L        L   L  L            H   L        H    L
```

4.2.3 Ternarity

Hayes (1980) and Levin (1988a) draw attention to the stress pattern of Cayuvava (Key 1961), where stresses are on the antepenultimate syllable and on every third syllable preceding it. For such ternary systems, Halle and Vergnaud introduce a parameter (+/− Head-Terminal). If the parameter is set negatively, one nonhead element is allowed between a foot bracket and the head. The result is a ternary, head-medial, *amphibrach*. The Cayuvava pattern is generated by marking final syllables extrametrical and a leftward application of bounded [−HT] feet:

(60)
```
                            *       *       *            line 1
* * * * * * * * * *  →  (* * *) (* * *) (* * *) <*>      line 0
```

4.3 Line Conflation and Bidirectionality

In the analysis of most unbounded systems, one stress is realized phonetically, while the other "stresses" are merely potential. Halle and Vergnaud eliminate the latter by *Line Conflation*. When two lines are conflated, a constituent on the lower line is preserved only if its head is also the head of a constituent on the next higher line. Consider conflation of lines 0 and 1:

(61)
```
                      *                             *       line 2
(*         *         *)       (                    *)       line 1
(*  *  *) (*  *  *) (*  *)      *  *  *  *  *  *  * (*  *)   line 0
 L  L  L  H  L  L  L  H  L      L  L  L  H  L  L  L  H  L
```

Line Conflation also functions to analyze *bidirectionality*. Rejecting the iterativity parameter, HV reanalyze bidirectional systems by means of two iterative rules of opposing directionality. Main stress is generated by one iterative pass, the output of which is subject to Line Conflation. A second iterative pass from the opposite edge generates secondary stresses as in (62).[10]

(62)
```
        *                  *                  *            line 2
(*  *      *)        (       *)        (*  *  *)           line 1
(*) (* *) (* *)  →    * * * (* *)  →  (* *) (*) (* *)      line 0
```

Finally, Halle and Vergnaud use Line Conflation for systems such as English, that have a quantity-sensitive main stress rule and a quantity-insensitive secondary stress rule. The rules can be identified if the Alternator applies in two strata. In the *cyclic* stratum, where the Alternator is preceded by Quantity Sensitivity, Line Conflation eliminates all stresses but the primary. The *noncyclic* Alternator assigns secondary stress quantity-insensitively, since Quantity Sensitivity is not in the noncyclic stratum.

4.4   Cyclicity and Stress Erasure

Halle and Vergnaud develop a theory of cyclic stress which can be appreciated by reviewing their analysis of Vedic, based on generalizations proposed by Kiparsky in an unpublished manuscript. In Vedic, vowels in stems and suffixes can bear lexical stress diacritics, which we will call accents. The location of the word stress is determined by the Basic Accentuation Principle: "Stress the leftmost accented vowel or, in the absence of accented vowels, the leftmost vowel." The Basic Accentuation Principle is apparently restricted to words that are composed of a stem and a set of suffixes which we will refer to as *recessive* suffixes. Words with one or more suffixes not chosen from the set of recessive suffixes (which we may therefore call *dominant*) follow a different mode: stress falls on the last dominant suffix in the word if it is accented, else on the initial syllable, even if the stem is accented. Two aspects need explanation. First, the contrast between accented and unaccented stems is neutralized before dominant suffixes (accented *-iṇ* takes stress in *rath+íṇ+e* "charioteer" (dat. sg.), with an accented stem *rath*, as well as in *mitr+íṇ+e* "befriended" (dat. sg.), with an unaccented stem *mitr*). Second, accented recessive suffixes that follow a dominant suffix are ignored.

Following a proposal by Halle and Mohanan (1985), HV assume that dominant suffixes are *cyclic*, and trigger the rules of the cyclic stratum, while recessive suffixes are *noncyclic*. Noncyclic affixes are represented on the same metrical plane as the stem, but each cyclic affix induces a new metrical plane. Below, we show the addition of a cyclic suffix m_2 to a stem m_1. Stem and suffix each have their metrical planes P_1, P_2. The suffixal plane P_2 is automatically expanded with a copy of the content of previous planes (here P_1):

(63)

The stress rules of the cyclic stratum apply to each of the planes P_1, P_2. Halle and Vergnaud propose that information about stress recorded on the stem plane is not carried over in the plane-copying;[11] see (64).

(64)   **Stress Erasure Convention (SEC, HV, p. 83)**
The input to rules of cyclic strata information about stress generated on previous passes through the cyclic rules is carried over only if the affixed constituent is itself a domain for the cyclic stress rules. If the affixed constituent is not a domain for the cyclic rules, information about stresses assigned on previous passes is erased.

Let us see how the Vedic stress data are analyzed under this proposal. The Basic Accentuation Principle can be formalized by a rule set which essentially functions as the analysis of default-to-same systems (see section 1.3). In the noncyclic stratum this rule set accounts for words with only recessive suffixes. The same rule set is applied in the cyclic stratum to words containing dominant cyclic suffixes. Here, stress erasure neutralizes any contrasts between accented and unaccented stems before dominant suffixes. When the last dominant suffix is accented, it ends up as the only accent surviving erasure, and it attracts word stress. When the last dominant suffix is unaccented no accents survive at all, and stress defaults to the initial syllable; see (65).

(65) (a)   Accented stem plus accented dominant suffix

```
*                    Plane copy,              Stress
 *  *                stress erasure           rules
 σ σ + σ        →      σ σ + σ    →    σ σ + σ
      *                * *    *         * *    *
      *                       *                *
                                              *
```

(b)   Accented stem plus unaccented dominant suffix

```
*                    Plane copy,              Stress
 *  *                stress erasure           rules
 σ σ + σ        →      σ σ + σ    →    σ σ + σ
      *                * *    *         * *    *
                                       *
                                       *
```

Addition of an accented recessive affix has no effect on the stress pattern of the base, as it is adjoined onto the same plane. The cyclic stress rules guarantee one accent on the base plane to the left of the recessive accent, so that the noncyclic stress rules (i.e., the Basic Accentuation Principle) ignore the latter.

4.5   *Integrity of Metrical Structure*

Integrity of metrical structure (that is, the tendency for rules not to change metrical structure once assigned in a derivation) is a main source of motivation of constituency. Here, we will review Steriade's (1988) argument for integrity from enclitic stress in Latin. (See for nonenclitic stress section 1.4.1). Upon addition of an enclitic element such as *-que* "and", stress shifts to the syllable immediately before the enclitic:

(66) (a)   líːmina   "thresholds"   liːminá#que   "and thresholds"
     (b)   múːsa   "the muse"   muːsá#que   "and the muse"

The patterns of the enclitic forms do not match the basic generalization on stress, which is that stress is antepenultimate (instead of penultimate) when the penult is light. The opacity of stress is explained if the stress rules reapply to enclitic forms while respecting the metrical structure of the base (cf. the Free Element Condition discussed in section 3.3). Nonperipheral base-final syllables lose their extrametricality:

(67) (a)   *   *   *   *   *
               (*   *).   (* *) (*)   (*) (* *)
               líːmina<que>   →   liːminá<que>   *not* *liːmína<que>
      (b)   *   *   *   *
               (*).   (*) (*)   (*   *)
               múːsa<que>   →   muːsá<que>   *not* *múːsa<que>

A right-headed line 1 constituent promotes final feet. This analysis demonstrates the integrity of constituency in two ways. First, stress rules, when reapplying, cannot construct a foot over syllables that are already part of a foot (cf. 67a). Second, stress rules, when reapplying, fail to expand existing feet by incorporation of free elements (cf. 67b). Steriade employs a stronger version of Prince's Free Element Condition, one that extends to foot reassignment.

5   Asymmetric Rhythmic Theory

Hayes (1985, 1987, 1994), McCarthy and Prince (1986), and Prince (1990) develop a theory based on an *asymmetric* inventory of foot templates. It is motivated by the typology of iterative bounded systems, as well as by processes that change syllable quantity in foot-governed contexts. Another field of motivation, prosodic morphology, is discussed in chapter 9 this volume.

5.1   *The Iambic-Trochaic Rhythmic Law and the asymmetric foot inventory*

At the root of asymmetric rhythmic theory is an observation about the correlation between quantity-sensitivity and rhythm in iterative systems. Hayes (1985) proposes a significant asymmetry between iambic and trochaic styles of alternation. Iterative iambic systems display quantity-sensitivity almost without exception, and use feet whose members are of *uneven* duration. In contrast, iterative trochaic systems strongly tend towards durational *evenness* of the members of feet.[12] Hayes (1987, 1994) reflects this asymmetry in his asymmetric foot inventory:

(68) (a) Syllabic trochee: Form (* .)
                                  σ σ
      (b) Moraic trochee: Form (* .) or (*)
                                  L L   H
      (c) Iamb: Form (. *) if possible; else form (. *) or (*)
                                  L H   L L   H

Trochees are durationally balanced, and contain two elements of identical duration, either syllables or moras. Iambs are durationally unbalanced, and contain a light syllable plus a heavy syllable in their maximal (canonical) expansion. This foot inventory is slightly less parametric than that of Hayes (1981), since quantity-sensitivity and dominance no longer combine freely to yield four foot types. A comparison of the feet in (68) to those of Hayes (1981) shows us that the syllabic trochee closely corresponds to the quantity-insensitive left-dominant foot, and the iamb to the quantity-sensitive right-dominant foot. There is one important difference, however, since degenerate feet are no longer automatically constructed when no larger foot can be formed. That is, in many systems the syllabic trochee lacks a monosyllabic expansion, while mora-based feet (the moraic trochee and the iamb) lack monomoraic expansions.[13] We will address degenerate feet in section 5.2.

Continuing the comparison with the foot inventory of Hayes (1981), we see that the bounded quantity-insensitive right-dominant foot has disappeared. This is motivated by the typological rarity of quantity-insensitive iambic styles of alternation (see Weri and Araucanian in section 1.2.1, and the reanalysis in section 5.1.3). Finally, the quantity-sensitive left-dominant foot has been replaced by the bimoraic trochee, which embodies the ancient law of equivalence between one long syllable and two short ones. This foot no longer includes an uneven expansion of a heavy plus a light syllable [H L]$_F$, which seems to be unattested in iterative systems. Let us now exemplify the asymmetric foot inventory.[14]

5.1.1 Syllabic Trochees

The syllabic trochee produces the following patterns in its rightward and leftward modes:

(69) (a) Syllabic trochees   (b) Syllabic trochees
           (left-to-right)   (right-to-left)
           (* .) (* .) (* .) (* .) .   . (* .) (* .) (* .) (* .)
           σ σ σ σ σ σ σ σ σ   σ σ σ σ σ σ σ σ σ

Warao (see section 1.2.1) exemplifies (69b). In contrast to the approach described earlier, no defooting of degenerate feet is required. Pintupi (Hansen and Hansen 1969) exemplifies (69a):

(70) (a) púliŋkàlatʲu   "we (sat) on the hill"
      (b) tʲámulìmpatʲùŋku   "our relation"

In the earlier theory, this pattern would be generated by syllable extra-metricality. Section 5.2 addresses the apparent complication of secondary stresses at edges in rightward trochaic systems such as Hungarian. Most syllabic trochee systems, such as Warao and Pintupi, have no underlying quantitative distinctions. Piro constitutes a truly quantity-insensitive system, in which underlying weight distinctions are completely ignored by trochaic feet.

5.1.2   Moraic Trochees

The moraic trochee produces the patterns of (71):

(71)   (a)   Moraic trochees   (b)   Moraic trochees
             (left-to-right)   (right-to-left)
             (* .) (*) (* .) . (*) (* .)   (* .) (*) . (* .) (*) (* .)
             L L H L L L L H L L   L L H L L L   H L L

The *rightward* pattern is attested in Cairene Arabic. It had been captured in classical theory by Labeling-Based-on-Branching (LBOB) feet (see section 1.2.3). Since LBOB feet are not motivated outside the cases that the moraic trochee now serves to analyze, they can be eliminated from the theory. *Leftward* moraic trochees occur in Wargamay (Dixon 1981) and in some other systems. In the earlier theory, this pattern would require *uneven* quantity-sensitive trochees, with an irrelevant difference of bracketing: a string of a heavy syllable plus a light syllable is parsed by uneven trochees as a single foot $(H L)_F$, while moraic trochees parses it as a heavy foot followed by a stray syllable $(H)_F L$. The case for uneven trochees is weakened further by Hayes's (1985) observation that their rightward mode is unattested (this would parse a heavy syllable followed by light syllables as $(H L)_F (L L)_F$). Hayes claims that, consequently, the uneven trochee can be completely eliminated. However, evidence for the uneven trochee is presented by Myers (1987) and Kager (1989) for English, Jacobs (1990) for Latin, and Dresher and Lahiri (1991) for Germanic.

5.1.3   Iambs

The iamb produces patterns such as those below:

(72)   (a)   Iambs (left-to-right)   (b)   Iambs (right-to-left)
             (. *) (. *) (*) (. *) .   (. *) . (. *) . (. *)
             L H L L H L L L   L H L L H L L L

Absence of degenerate feet is motivated by the stress patterns of final syllables in systems with rightward iambs, which form the great majority of iambic systems. The few leftward iambic systems (such as Tübatulabal [Voegelin 1935], 18b) apparently require degenerate feet. Kager (1989), however, shows that these can be reanalyzed by moraic trochees.

Most iambic systems have underlying quantitative contrasts, and are what we might call truly quantity-sensitive. However, iambic rhythms also occur in a few systems lacking weight distinctions, such as Weri. Hayes argues that such systems are formally within the scope of the iambic expansion (L L)$_F$, even though they lack the uneven expansion (L H)$_F$. Moreover, some of these systems establish unevenness at the *surface* by rhythmic lengthening (see section 5.3).

5.2 Degenerate Feet

Degenerate feet are often discriminated against by metrical rules and conditions in several ways. (a) Many languages impose minimal word conditions requiring words to contain minimally one bimoraic or bisyllabic foot. (b) Degenerate feet tend not to qualify as proper foot templates in *prosodic morphology* (cf. chapter 9 this volume). (c) Degenerate feet in weak positions often lose their foot status at the surface by *destressing* (see section 1.5). (d) Degenerate feet are "repaired" by various strategies such as lengthening and reparsing (cf. Kager 1989, 1993, Prince 1990, Hayes 1994, Mester to appear).

Although metrical theory has always recognized the marked status of degenerate feet, they were motivated on both theoretical and empirical grounds. (a) *Exhaustivity*, the theoretical requirement that all syllables be parsed as part of a foot, dictates that a degenerate foot be produced automatically when no larger foot is possible. (b) *Edge beats* with secondary stress in iterative systems are generated automatically by degenerate feet. (d) Degenerate feet may trigger rules, in particular destressing rules, at intermediate stages in the course of the derivation. (4) *Culminativity* requires degenerate feet in languages that do not impose minimal word conditions.

With respect to exhaustivity, Hayes (1994) takes the position that foot construction is maximally exhaustive within the limits of what constitute well-formed feet in a particular system, and exhaustivity becomes a "soft" constraint whose satisfaction is weighed against other constraints. The favorable consequences of eliminating degenerate feet for the typology of alternating systems, as reviewed above, support this. Nonexhaustive foot parsing finds another application in Hayes's theory of ternarity; see section 5.4. Hayes claims that *phonological* evidence for weak edge beats is meager, and that their phonetic or perceptual status may derive from sources other than stress, both durational (prepausal lengthening) and intonational (boundary tones). For example, weak degenerate feet in Icelandic (Árnason 1985) show a different phonological behavior than binary feet, since they are ignored by the rule of compound stress assignment. Finally, in view of the fact that degenerate feet bear main stress, Hayes (1991) proposes to restrict the occurrence of degenerate feet on a parametric basis, as in (73).

(73) Degenerate foot parameter:
    Parsing may form degenerate feet under the following conditions:
    (a) *Strong prohibition*: absolutely disallowed.
    (b) *Weak prohibition*: allowed only in strong position; i.e., when dominated by a higher grid mark.

The weak prohibition may be circumvented by the proposal of Kager (1989) to generate strong degenerate feet by means of a default option of the End Rule, as suggested by Prince (1983) for unbounded systems. Where no proper Foot layer landing site can be found, the End Rule assigns default word stress to the next layer down, i.e., the syllable layer.

5.3   *Templatic Structure and Quantitative Rules*

As a consequence of templatic foot structure, feet are defined independently of the rules that assign them. Thus foot templates may be referred to transderivationally by both stress and nonstress rules, a phenomenon called *metrical coherence* (Dresher and Lahiri 1991). A templatic view of foot structure echoes similar results in the theory of syllabification (Itô 1986), which invites a general templatic prosodic theory.

Metrical coherence provides the second main source of motivation for the asymmetric foot typology. It manifests itself in processes which conspire toward the iambic-trochaic rhythmic law by altering the quantity of syllables. Hayes (1985) observes that iambic systems tend to aspire towards durational unevenness, and have rules such as rhythmic vowel lengthening, consonant gemination, vowel reduction, and vowel deletion, all of which increase the durational constrasts between syllables. This makes sense from the viewpoint that foot templates actively impose their quantitative requirements through phonological rules. Consider Hixkaryana (Derbyshire 1979; Hayes 1994), where iambs are assigned from left to right with final extrametricality. Bimoraic iambs of the form $[L\ L]_F$ are expanded into canonical iambs $[L\ H]_F$ by rhythmic iambic lengthening: *(tóh)(kurʲéː)(honáː)(hašaː)<ka>* "finally to Tohkurye".

In contrast, syllabic trochee systems generally lack rules that introduce durational unevenness. Moraic trochee systems, which by definition have underlying quantitative contrasts, are predicted to display processes that increase durational evenness within the foot. Prince (1990) argues that English instantiates the prediction by vowel shortening to match the moraic trochee foot template. The addition of suffixes such as *-ic* and *-ity* to a stem with a long vowel induces a shortening of the latter, as can be seen in alternations such as *cóːne* ~ *cónic*. As Myers (1987b) shows, the suffixes that trigger shortening are nonextrametrical Level-1 suffixes, whose addition produces a disyllabic trochee over the final heavy stem syllable and the suffix. Prince construes shortening as a process that modifies an *uneven* trochee $(H\ L)_F$ into a rhythmically balanced *even* bimoraic trochee $(L\ L)_F$, cf. $(koːn)_F$ → $(kɔnɪk)_F$. Observe that the uneven trochee, which forms the domain of trochaic shortening, must be allowed as a possible foot under this analysis. Prince suggests a markedness theory of foot well-formedness, according to which the uneven trochee is a legal, but marked expansion of the ideally bimoraic trochee.

5.4 Ternarity and Persistent Footing

Hayes (1994) proposes a theory of ternary systems which does not postulate ternary feet, but rather derives ternarity by a marked foot assignment mode. In the unmarked case, systems employ the unmarked Strong Local Parsing mode (74a), which assigns feet adjacently, producing binary rhythm. Ternary systems draw from the universal asymmetric foot inventory, but follow a Weak Local Parsing mode (74b), which skips a syllable after each foot that has been established. The extra unbracketed syllables between feet produce ternary rhythm:

(74) (a) (* .) (* .) (* .) (* .) .   (b) (* .) .   (* .) .   (* .)
          σ σ   σ σ   σ σ   σ σ σ   σ σ σ   σ σ   σ   σ σ

In systems based on the iamb or the moraic trochee, one mora may be skipped, in systems based on the syllabic trochee, one syllable (the *Minimal Prosodic Distance*).

Weak Local Parsing is another source of nonexhaustive foot parsing in Hayes's theory. It may even produce sequences of two unbracketed syllables when after skipping, one syllable remains at the end of the domain, which cannot be footed, because of the ban on degenerate feet. Such sequences are dealt with on a language-specific basis. They are tolerated in Cayuvava (75a), which has leftward construction of syllabic trochees under final extrametricality. Alternatively, foot construction is reapplied to the unbracketed sequence. This option of persistent footing is exemplified by Chugach Yupik (Leer 1985) (75b), which has rightward iambs:

(75) (a)   . . (* .) . (* .)
          σ σ σ σ σ σ σ <σ>

     (b) (. *) . (. *) . .   →   (. *) . (. *) (. *)
          L L L L L L L   L L L L L L L

6 Conclusion

After a decade of theoretical work on metrical systems, a consensus has emerged on a number of points. First, stress requires hierarchical representation in order to capture culminativity and prominence differences between stresses. Second, the rhythmic nature of stress is most adequately represented by the grid. Third, the grid is enriched by metrical constituency in order to capture stress shifts, requirements of prosodic morphology, and template-governed phenomena such as quantitative asymmetries. Researchers still seem to differ in opinion about the symmetrical nature of the foot inventory, the status of degenerate feet, exhaustivity, and the issue of what may constitute stress-bearing units.

NOTES

This research was partially supported by the Linguistic Research Foundation, which is funded by the Netherlands organization for scientific research, NWO, grant no. 300–171–023. For valuable comments on earlier versions of this paper, I wish to thank John Goldsmith, Harry van der Hulst, and Wim Zonneveld.

1   The learnability of stress systems is studied from a parametric viewpoint by Dresher and Kaye (1990) and Hammond (1990).

2   Other applications are dialectal variation (Kenstowicz 1983) and diacronic phonology (Wheeler 1980).

3   Hammond (1986) argues for a foot type that restricts its dominant nodes (to heavy syllables), without restricting its recessive nodes. He proposes that this *Revised Obligatory Branching* foot should replace the Obligatory Branching foot. The complex arguments for Revised Obligatory Branching feet will not be reviewed here.

4   Onsets fail to contribute to weight, or only hardly ever do, though the reader may see Everett and Everett (1984) on Pirahâ, and Davis (1988) on Western Aranda, Madimadi, Italian, and English.

5   Van der Hulst (1984) proposes a more radical *Main Stress First* theory: Main stress is assigned first, and secondary stresses run from the main stress, or the opposite edge.

6   Nonbinary bounded feet have been proposed by Prince (1980) for Estonian, Levin (1988a) for Cayuvava, Woodbury (1987) for Yupik, and Dresher and Lahiri (1991) for Germanic. See also sections 4.2.1 and 5.4 on ternarity.

7   For a discussion of interactions between metrical structure and lexical phonology, see Kiparsky (1982a, 1985) and chapters 2 and 3, this volume.

8   Hammond (1987) claims that this power is not crucially needed.

9   There is thus no inherent connection between internal syllable structure and prosodic prominence, a link whose absence has been noticed.

10 HV's analysis of bidirectionality is disputed by Levin (1988b). For an answer, see Halle (1990).

11 See for discussion of the SEC, Harris (1989) and Halle, Harris, and Vergnaud (1991).

12 Hayes cites experimental evidence from Woodrow (1951), who found that rhythmically alternating stimuli with durational prominence marking were perceived as iambic, and those with intensity marking were perceived as trochaic.

13 Here we follow Hayes (1994), who eliminates the degenerate stressless feet of Hayes (1987).

14 Recently, the asymmetric foot inventory has been challenged by proposals that advocate a symmetric foot inventory, and derive the rhythmic asymmetry by independent means, cf. Jacobs (1990), Hammond (1990), Kager (1993).

11 General Properties of Stress and Metrical Structure

MORRIS HALLE AND WILLIAM IDSARDI

0 Introduction

The fundamental insight into stress systems remains that expressed by Mark Liberman in his 1975 dissertation. Liberman suggested that stress is not a simple phonetic feature, as had been assumed by most linguists and phoneticians, but rather that it is a phonetic means for marking various kinds of groupings of linguistic elements. Typical examples of the kinds of groupings Liberman had in mind are given in (1).

(1) (a) auto/bio/graphic
       ono/mato/poeia
       super/cali/fragi/listic/expi/alo/docious
   (b) their new Lincoln Continental/was made in California
       none of his books/made it to the top of the list

It is not difficult to see that in each of the groups or constituents there is one element that is more prominent than the rest. It is the left-most elements in (1a) and the right-most elements in (1b). We shall use the term "head" to designate the element in the constituent to which prominence is assigned.

In addition, the examples in (1a) differ from those in (1b) with regard to the elements that are being grouped. Syllables are grouped in (1a) and words in (1b). This difference is also reflected in the units that are made to stand out phonetically: it is the head of the syllable in (1a), whereas in (1b) it is the head of the syllable bearing main stress in the word.

In what follows we describe and illustrate a new algorithm – that of Idsardi (1992)[1] – which seems to us to assign stress contours to words and phrases in a manner that might plausibly be attributed to speakers and learners of a language. Our primary purpose here is to show how the framework deals with concrete stress patterns. Hence, most of the examples that we review below have been previously discussed in the literature, most notably in Hayes (1980, 1991), Prince (1983), and Halle and Vergnaud (1987). A defense of the framework and comparisons with some alternatives can be found in Idsardi (1992, 1993).

The simple facts exemplified in (1) suggest that a formal account of stress phenomena will require at least the following three devices: a device for designating the elements in the sequence that are capable of bearing stress; a means for delimiting the groupings of the elements; and a marker to distinguish in each grouping or constituent the prominent head-element from the rest. The remainder of this section will introduce mechanisms that build appropriate representations of stress. These mechanisms – parameterized rules and constraints – constitute our theory of stress assignment.

We propose to satisfy these requirements by representing the stressable elements in a phoneme string as a sequence of abstract marks. These marks will constitute a line that we label line 0. We illustrate this in (2).

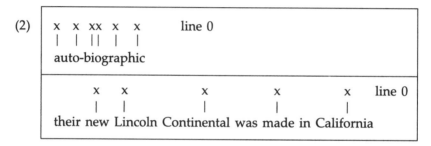

An immediate consequence of this decision is the creation of two parallel sequences of elements: a sequence of phonemes and a sequence of abstract marks. Two parallel lines constitute a plane, and we shall call the plane defined by the parallel sequences of phonemes and abstract marks the metrical plane.

In order to delimit the different groupings we shall employ ordinary parentheses and these will be placed by different rules, to be discussed presently, among the x's that make up the line, as illustrated in (3).[2]

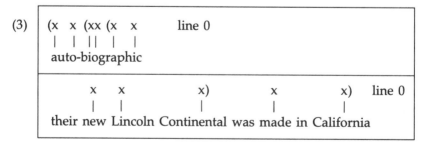

In each of the metrical constituents thus generated a special rule will designate the right- or left-most element as the head of the constituent. We mark the head of each constituent by projecting and linking the element to a new element on the next higher line of the grid, as shown in (4).

(4)
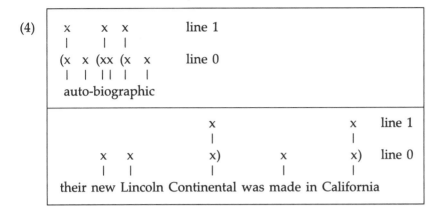

The x's in line 1 are naturally interpreted as signalling an enhanced degree of prominence. We notice that in the two examples in (4) not all elements with enhanced prominence are of equal prominence. One of these elements bears the maximal prominence in the string. This is the right-most element in both of our examples. To capture this formally we construct a constituent on line 1 and mark its right-most element as the head. In conformity with the procedure followed above we project and link the head elements onto the next line, shown in (5).

(5)
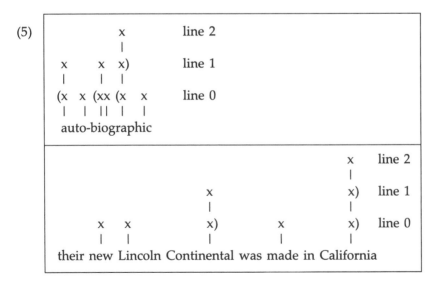

The arrays of x's and parentheses constructed in this manner are called metrical grids and they contain the information about the grouping of elements into constituents, about the headedness of the constituents, and about the different degrees of prominence of the elements in the string. In constructing the grids we have employed only two formal mechanisms: the placement of grid marks and the placement of parentheses. Note in particular that we locate the heads of constituents by placing a mark on a line in the grid, that is, by the same formal mechanism that marks elements in the phoneme sequence as stress-bearing.

1   Projection, Edge Marking, and Head Location

To provide some practical experience with the devices just presented we will consider how they might be used to account for the stress pattern of words in the Koya language (Tyler 1969; Hayes 1980), described in (6), where the stress-bearing elements are the syllable heads.

(6)   Stress falls on the head of every closed or long syllable as well as on the head of the initial syllable. Main stress is on the initial syllable.

According to (6) a typical Koya word will have the stress pattern shown in (7).[3]

(7)   2 x
      1 x   x   x
      0 x x x x x x x x x x x

In the following abstract examples, C stands for a consonant, V for a vowel and X for a post-vocalic element which contributes to syllable weight. An abstract word – a string of phonemes organized into syllables – compatible with (7) will therefore appear as in (8) where the square brackets represent syllable constituents.

(8)   [CV] [CV] [CV] [CVX] [CV] [CV] [CVX] [CV] [CV] [CV] [CV]

To capture the effects of syllable structure on stress there must be an interface between the metrical grid and strings of phonemes such as the string in (8). The mechanism implementing this interface is called *projection*. Projection adds an element to the grid and links it to the element which is projected. Since words are sequences of phonemes organized into syllables, the projection mechanism involves both phonemes and syllables, in particular, syllable boundaries.

As already noted, not all phonemes are capable of bearing stress. We reflect this fact in the formalism by projecting onto the metrical plane only phonemes that can bear stress. In most languages the stress-bearing phonemes are the phonemes that are heads of syllables, and therefore in these languages it is syllable heads that are projected onto the metrical plane as its first line – line 0. We implement this by means of (9).

(9) *Line 0 mark projection*
     Project a line 0 element for each *syllable head.*

In Koya only the head of a syllable is capable of bearing stress. Elements within syllables other than heads can be stress-bearing in some languages. In such languages such elements will also be projected onto line 0 by a suitably extended version of (9).

In many languages, including Koya, syllable boundaries play a role in the computation of the stress contour of words. Since only elements that appear on the metrical plane can be involved in the computation of stress we need a means for projecting syllable boundaries onto the metrical grid. This is accomplished with the Syllable Boundary Projection parameter, (10).

(10) *Syllable Boundary Projection parameter*

     Project the $\left\{\begin{array}{l}\text{left}\\\text{right}\end{array}\right\}$ boundary of *certain syllables* onto line 0.

The projection of syllable boundaries governed by (10) is independent of the projection of grid marks governed by (9). Therefore, though all languages with stress invoke some form of (9), some languages fail to invoke any form of (10). Notice, therefore, that it is not the case that every parameter has a setting in every language. In these languages differences in syllable structure have no effect on stress. Languages differ in what kind of syllables trigger (10), but the effect of (10) on line 0 is always the same: it projects syllable boundaries onto line 0, inserting parentheses among the grid marks in the appropriate places. Languages also choose which of the two syllable boundaries to project; some project the right boundary, others project the left boundary. Likewise, as noted above, some languages use a variation of (9) to project more than one grid mark for some syllables. Again, the effect on the grid side of the interface is the same – the presence of extra metrical elements.

Thus, to account for the stress on heavy syllables in Koya we will project the left boundary of syllables that are either closed or contain long vowels, that is, we set (10) as in (11).

(11) Project the *left* boundary of [. . . VX] syllables onto line 0.

This setting for Syllable Boundary Projection will contribute a left parenthesis to the left of each x linked to the head of a heavy syllable, as shown in (12).

(12)   x   x   x (x   x   x (x   x   x   x   x line 0
       | | | | | | | | | | |
      [CV] [CV] [CV] [CVX] [CV] [CV] [CVX] [CV] [CV] [CV] [CV]

To mark the head element in each metrical constituent, we introduce the Head Location Parameter, (13).

(13) *Head Location parameter*

Project the $\begin{Bmatrix} \text{left} \\ \text{right} \end{Bmatrix}$-most element of each constituent onto the next line of the grid.

The Head Location parameter is the grid-internal interface between layers of the grid. Recall that projection is our interface mechanism; to build further layers of the grid, we must again project certain elements. The Head Location parameter is the only grid-internal interface and thus each constituent is restricted to a single projected element. Koya sets Head:L as the interface between lines 0 and 1, giving (14).

(14)   x   x   line 1
       x   x   x (x   x   x (x   x   x   x   x line 0
       | | | | | | | | | | |
      [CV] [CV] [CV] [CVX] [CV] [CV] [CVX] [CV] [CV] [CV] [CV]

As a comparison with (7) shows, the constructed grid in (14) correctly reproduces all the secondary stresses in the abstract Koya word, but fails to reproduce the initial main stress in the word. To achieve the initial stress we need a means for adding a left parenthesis before the left-most element. Universal Grammar provides the Edge-Marking Parameter, given in (15), which will place a parenthesis at one edge of a sequence of marks.

(15) *Edge-Marking parameter*

Place a $\begin{Bmatrix} \text{left} \\ \text{right} \end{Bmatrix}$ parenthesis to the $\begin{Bmatrix} \text{left} \\ \text{right} \end{Bmatrix}$ of the $\begin{Bmatrix} \text{left} \\ \text{right} \end{Bmatrix}$-most element in the string.

For line 0, Koya sets Edge:LLL, that is, it places a *left* boundary to the *left* of the *left*-most element. The grid in (16) is the result after the application of the line 0 parameters and the universal principles: Projection, Edge-marking, and Head Location.

(16)   x   x   x   line 1
      (x   x   x (x   x   x (x   x   x   x   x line 0
       | | | | | | | | | | |
      [CV] [CV] [CV] [CVX] [CV] [CV] [CVX] [CV] [CV] [CV] [CV]

To obtain initial main stress we need to apply Edge Marking and Head Location to line 1. In Koya the line 1 settings are Edge:LLL, and Head:L, giving (17).

```
(17)    x                                                      line 2
        (x              x                   x                  line 1
        (x    x    x ( x       x    x ( x       x    x    x    x  line 0
        |    |    |    |       |    |    |       |    |    |    |
       [CV] [CV] [CV] [CVX] [CV] [CV] [CVX] [CV] [CV] [CV] [CV]
```

We summarize the action of the Koya parameters in (18). To reduce the clutter in the diagrams, we will adopt the typographical convention that H stands for a heavy syllable in the language (one subject to (10)), and L stands for a light syllable in the language (one not subject to (10)).

(18) Line 0   Project:L

```
x x x (x x x (x x x x x    line 0
L L L H L L H  L L L L
```

Edge:LLL

```
(x x x (x x x (x x x x x    line 0
L L L H L L H L L L L
```

Head:L

```
x     x     x              line 1
(x x x (x x x (x x x x x    line 0
L L L H L L H L L L L
```

Line 1   Edge:LLL

```
(x     x     x             line 1
(x x x (x x x (x x x x x    line 0
L L L H L L H L L L L
```

Head:L

```
x                          line 2
(x     x     x             line 1
(x x x (x x x (x x x x x    line 0
L L L H L L H L L L L
```

A given set of stress patterns can be consistent with more than one parameter setting. So, we should ask at this point, Could Koya be right-headed on line 0? That is, could we obtain the skeleton grid (7) by means of right-headed constituents. Indeed, we could. This would, of course, require changes in the other parameters. In particular, Koya would have to project the right boundary of heavy syllables instead of the left one. Likewise, the Edge parameter would have to be set to put a *right* parenthesis to the *right* of the *left*-most mark on line 0, to ensure that the initial element gets stress. The derivation for this alternative is shown in (19).

(19) Line 0   Project:R

x x x x) x x x) x x x x	line 0
L L L H L L H L L L L	

Edge:RRL

x) x x x) x x x) x x x x	line 0
L L L H L L H L L L L	

Head:R

x x x	line 1
x) x x x) x x x) x x x x	line 0
L L L H L L H L L L L	

Line 1   Edge:LLL

(x x x	line 1
x) x x x) x x x) x x x x	line 0
L L L H L L H L L L L	

Head:L

x	line 2
(x x x	line 1
x) x x x) x x x) x x x x	line 0
L L L H L L H L L L L	

For the facts of Koya stress, both systems will work. So which one does the speaker actually have? In her review of Halle & Vergnaud (1987), Blevins (1992) points out that many other kinds of evidence could bear on this issue. Various morphological processes such as reduplication could give evidence for foot structure. Likewise, phonological processes other than stress can be sensitive to metrical structure, and can affect metrical structure. For example, assume that we found out that some vowels were deleted. If a vowel in a stressed syllable happened to be deleted what would happen to its stress? The two sets of parameter settings differ in their predictions of where the stress would migrate. As we see in (20), left-headed feet would predict rightward shift, right-headed feet leftward shift.

(20)

	Head:L			Head:R		
Project	x	(x	x	x	x)	x
	. . . V	. . . V	. . . V	. . . V	. . . V	. . . V
Deletion	x	(	x	x	)	x
	. . . V	. . .	. . . V	. . . V	. . .	. . . V
Head			x	x		
	x	(	x	x	)	x
	. . . V	. . .	. . . V	. . . V	. . .	. . . V

But what if no such evidence is available? Notice that all parameter settings involve the choice between *left* and *right*. When all parameters are set to the same value, we shall say that the settings are *homogeneous*. Other settings will be referred to as *heterogeneous*. It appears that there is a universal preference for homogeneous parameter settings of the type found in (18) over heterogeneous settings such as those in (19).[4] Thus, in the absence of other evidence, we claim that Koya speakers have the homogeneous parameter settings of (18). Though homogeneous languages seem to be more common than heterogeneous ones, languages are not restricted to being homogeneous. Winnebago (discussed below) is one example of a heterogeneous language. In Winnebago the left boundaries of certain syllables are projected, but the heads of line 0 metrical consistuents are located on the right.

Since we have hypothesized that bracketed grids consist of two kinds of elements – grid marks and parentheses – our theory so far counts as valid any sequence of marks and parentheses. Although this does not pose any immediate empirical problems because we have such a limited set of mechanisms for inserting marks and parentheses, this is still not an ideal state of affairs. Specifically, we want to eliminate the possibility of distinctions based on the number of parentheses beside a grid mark. It is plausible that Universal Grammar disallows certain configurations of marks and brackets. The vacuous constituents ((,)), and ( ) are obvious candidates for universal prohibition. Should such vacuous constituents arise during a derivation, the situation will be remedied by deleting the bracket defining the vacuous constituent. There are also metrical configurations which are banned in particular languages, but allowed in others. These language-particular disfavored configurations will be treated in a similar fashion, discussed in detail below.

2   Case Studies in Edge Marking

A host of stress patterns can be elegantly accounted for with different settings of the Edge parameter. Consider the stress patterns in the three languages in (21): Koya, Selkup (Kuznecova, Xelimskij, and Gruškina 1980; Halle and Clements 1983) and Khalkha Mongolian (Street 1963; Hayes 1980). Each of these languages has some words which have initial stress.

(21)   Koya   Primary stress on the initial vowel.
Secondary stresses on long vowels and vowels in closed syllables.

Selkup   Stress on the right-most long vowel, otherwise on the initial vowel.

Khalkha   Stress on the left-most long vowel, otherwise on the initial vowel.

Recall the parameter settings for Koya, repeated in (22).

(22) Line 0   Project:L   Edge:LLL   Head:L
      Line 1   Edge:LLL   Head:L

In (23) we see the application of the Koya parameters to two abstract words, one containing only light syllables, the other including two heavy syllables.

(23) Line 0   Project:L

x x x x x	x(x x x (x x
L L L L L	L H L L H L

      Edge:LLL

(x x x x x	(x(x x x (x x
L L L L L	L H L L H L

      Head:L

x	x x x
(x x x x x	(x(x x x (x x
L L L L L	L H L L H L

      Line 1   Edge:LLL

(x	(x x x
(x x x x x	(x(x x x (x x
L L L L L	L H L L H L

      Head:L

x	x
(x	(x x x
(x x x x x	(x(x x x (x x
L L L L L	L H L L H L

To capture the Selkup facts we propose the parameter settings in (24).

(24) Line 0   Project:L   Edge:LLL   Head:L
      Line 1   Edge:RRR   Head:R

Thus, Selkup and Koya have the same line 0 parameters, but differ in the line 1 parameters. In (25) we show the Selkup derivations for the same two kinds of words.

(25)

Line 0	Project:L	x x x x x L L L L L	x(x x x (x x L HL L H L
	Edge:LLL	(x x x x x L L L L L	(x(x x x (x x L HL L H L
	Head:L	x (x x x x x L L L L L	x x x (x(x x x (x x L HL L H L
Line 1	Edge:RRR	x) (x x x x x L L L L L	x x x) (x(x x x (x x L HL L H L
	Head:R	x x) (x x x x x L L L L L	x x x x) (x(x x x (x x L HL L H L

As shown in (25), the settings in (24) locate main stress on the right-most long vowel, but in words without long vowels, stress is located on the first syllable. In addition to main stress, however, the parameter settings in (24) also generate subsidiary stresses, which, according to our sources, are not present in the speech of Selkup speakers. We shall therefore postulate that unlike Koya, Selkup is subject to a special rule of Conflation which eliminates all but the main stress in the word.[5]

Khalkha stresses the first heavy syllable, or, when there are no heavy syllables, the first syllable. Thus Khalkha, like Selkup, must end up eliminating secondary stresses through Conflation. In fact, Khalkha must be the line 1 mirror image of Selkup, placing word stress on the first constituent. However, if the Edge Marking parameter were set to LLL on line 0 this combination would produce uniform initial stress. But we know that the presence of heavy syllables in a word disallows the initial syllable from heading a line 0 constituent. We can achieve this by setting the line 0 Edge parameter to RRR, giving Khalkha the parameter settings in (26).

(26)

Line 0	Project:L	Edge:RRR	Head:L
Line 1		Edge:LLL	Head:L

By placing a *right* parenthesis to the *right* of the *right*-most element we will get initial stress in words consisting solely of light syllables. However, in words with at least one heavy syllable, the insertion of a right parenthesis at the end of the word will be vacuous, as it will not define a constituent separate from the constituent defined by the right-most heavy syllable. This will prevent the placement of stress on the initial syllable, as illustrated by the derivations in (27).

(27)

Line 0	Project:L	x x x x x L L L L L	x(x x x (x x L H L L H L
	Edge:RRR	x x x x x) L L L L L	x(x x x (x x) L H L L H L
	Head:L	x x x x x x) L L L L L	x x x(x x x (x x) L H L L H L
Line 1	Edge:LLL	(x x x x x x) L L L L L	(x x x(x x x (x x) L H L L H L
	Head:L	x (x x x x x x) L L L L L	x (x x x(x x x (x x) L H L L H L

Khalkha thus differs from Koya in the setting of the Edge parameter on line 0. In words without heavy syllables, this difference has no effect. Either setting yields the same stress contour. In words with heavy syllables, Khalkha will leave the initial string of light syllables unmetrified, but, as shown in (28), in Koya the initial string of light syllables will form a constituent and therefore the initial syllable will receive stress.

(28)

Koya	Khalkha
x (x x x (x (x x x (x x L H L L H L	x x x x (x x x (x x) L H L L H L

Recall that Koya and Khalkha differ in one other respect. The secondary stresses remain in Koya words, but are eliminated in Khalkha by Conflation.

3 Lexical Stress and Syllable Boundary Projection

It has long been known that there are languages where stress is an idiosyncratic property of individual morphemes. A typical example of this is provided by the distinctions in the stress patterns in the nominal inflection of the so-called a-stem nouns in modern Russian, illustrated in (29).

(29)

	cow	head
nominative singular	koróv-a	golov-á
accusative singular	koróv-u	gólov-u

As was noted first by Kiparsky and Halle (1977), when a word has one or more inherently accented morphemes, stress surfaces on the left-most accented vowel. Otherwise, stress falls on the initial syllable. A comparison of this description with that of Khalkha stress in (21) will readily reveal that these are identical except that in Russian inherently (= idiosyncratically) accented vowels behave like the long vowels in Khalkha. We recall that in Khalkha the left boundary of any syllable with a long vowel was projected onto line 0 by the Syllable Boundary Projection parameter. If we now assume that in Russian the Syllable Boundary Projection parameter is triggered not by a phonetically manifested property of the syllable, but rather by an idiosyncratic property of a morpheme, then we can use the parameter settings, (26), that we used for Khalkha to compute the stress in the Russian words in (29).[6] We illustrate this with the derivations in (30).

(30) Line 0	Project:L	x(x (x korov-a	x(x x korov-u	x x (x golov-a	x x x golov-u
	Edge:RRR	x(x (x) korov-a	x(x x) korov-u	x x (x) golov-a	x x x) golov-u
	Head:L	x x x(x (x) korov-a	x x(x x) korov-u	x x x (x) golov-a	x x x x) golov-u
Line 1	Edge:LLL	(x x x(x (x) korov-a	(x x(x x) korov-u	(x x x (x) golov-a	(x x x x) golov-u
	Head:L	x (x x x(x (x) korov-a	x (x x(x x) korov-u	x (x x x (x) golov-a	x (x x x x) golov-u

The morphemes, *korov* and *-a*, are lexically marked to trigger Syllable Boundary Projection on one of their syllables. This is the meaning of inherent accent in the present theory. As in Khalkha and Selkup, Conflation also applies to words in Russian, eliminating all but the main stress.

Kiparsky and Halle (1977) argued that the same stress principles found in Russian applied in Lithuanian and in Sanskrit, and that therefore the stress system of the Indo-European protolanguage must have been based on the same principles. This means that Indo-European stress had the parameter settings of (26), with the special proviso that Syllable Boundary Projection was triggered in lexically marked syllables.

Turkish is another language with morphologically and lexically determined stress. Discussions of Turkish stress can be found in Sezer (1983), Poser (1984), Kaisse (1985), Halle and Vergnaud (1987), Barker (1989), Halle and Kenstowicz (1991), and van der Hulst and van de Weijer (1991). In (31) we quote Poser's description of the basic facts of Turkish stress.

(31)   In Turkish stress generally falls on the last syllable of the word [cf. 32a] . . . Exceptions are of two kinds. First, there are a number of words with inherent stress on some nonfinal syllable [32b]. In this case, stress does not shift when suffixes are added . . . [Second,] there are a number of suffixes that never bear stress [32c].

Examples are given in (32); (32a) is a normal stem, (32b) is a stem with fixed non-final stress, and (32c) illustrates the prestressing suffix *-dur*.

(32)   (a)   adám   "man"   adam-lár   "men"
                adam-lar-á   "to the men"
        (b)   mása   "table"   mása-lar   "tables"
                mása-lar-a   "to the tables"
        (c)   yorgún   "tired"   yorgun-lár "tired" (pl.)
                yorgún-dur-lar "they are tired"

We will now translate the analysis of Halle and Kenstowicz (1991) into the present framework. To do this, we assume that Turkish has the stress parameters shown in (33).

(33)   Line 0   Edge:LLL   Head:R
        Line 1   Edge:LLL   Head:L

For unexceptional words, such as the paradigm for *adam* (32a), final stresses will be correctly generated, as shown in (34).

(34) Line 0   Project:L

x x	x	
adam-lar		

Edge:LLL

(x x	x	
adam-lar		

Head:R

	x	
(x x	x	
adam-lar		

Line 1   Edge:LLL

	(x	
(x x	x	
adam-lar		

Head:L

	x	
	(x	
(x x	x	
adam-lar		

The formal problem that arises at this point is how to represent the morphemes that generate the exceptional patterns in (32b, c). We note that these are of two kinds. The stem morpheme, *masa* in (32b) takes stress on the penultimate syllable whereas the exceptional suffix morpheme *-dur* of (32c) places stress on the immediately preceding syllable. We can achieve this by postulating that the Syllable Boundary Projection parameter can be triggered by individual morphemes. Specifically, we shall assume that Turkish contains a set of morphemes that trigger a left Boundary Projection on their final syllable. Under this assumption, we get the derivations in (35), correctly placing main stress in these words.

(35) Line 0   Project:L

x(x x	x x (x x
masa-lar	yorgun-dur-lar

Edge:LLL

(x(x x	(x x (x x
masa-lar	yorgun-dur-lar

Head:R

x x	x x
(x(x x	(x x (x x
masa-lar	yorgun-dur-lar

Line 1 Edge:LLL	(x x (x(x x masa-lar	(x x (x x (x x yorgun-dur-lar
Head:L	x (x x (x(x x masa-lar	x (x x (x x (x x yorgun-dur-lar

Turkish words, like those in Selkup, Khalkha, and Russian, are subject to Conflation, which eliminates secondary stresses.[7] Thus, the lexically governed application of Syllable Boundary Projection in Turkish interacts with the general stress parameters of Turkish to derive the stress contours of the exceptional words.

4   Iterative Constituent Construction

Languages are not limited to placing stresses only on elements near an edge or on elements with special properties. Languages also can construct a train of constituents over the sequence of metrical elements. In all known cases these constituents are either binary or ternary. We shall have nothing to say here about ternary constituents other than to note that they are attested in a few languages such as Cayuvava and the Chugach dialect of Yupik Eskimo. We have listed three well-known stress patterns in (36): Warao (Osborn 1966), Weri (Boxwell and Boxwell 1966), and Maranungku (Tyron 1970). We shall discuss each of these in turn.

(36)   Warao   Stress falls on even-numbered syllables counting from the
                          end of the word. Main stress is on the penultimate syllable.
          Weri   Stress falls on all odd-numbered syllables counting from
                          the end of the word. Main stress is on the last syllable.
          Maranungku   Stress falls on all odd-numbered syllables counting from
                          the beginning of the word. Main stress is on the initial
                          syllable.

Languages achieve such binary stress patterns by setting the Iterative Constituent Construction parameter, (37).

(37)   *Iterative Constituent Construction parameter*
          Insert a $\left\{\begin{array}{l}\text{left}\\\text{right}\end{array}\right\}$ boundary for each pair of elements.

Iterative Constituent Construction (ICC) constructs constituents by scanning across the form, placing the "far" parenthesis. That is, going left to right, ICC inserts right parentheses; going right to left, ICC inserts left parentheses.[8] We hypothesize that Iterative Constituent Construction is one of a small number of directional rules provided by Universal Grammar.[9] Following the suggestion of Howard (1972) on the directional application of rules, the ICC rules have no "look-ahead." Putting these ideas together thus means that (37) actually governs the application of the two rules in (38).

(38)   ICC:L   = $\emptyset \rightarrow (\ / \underline{\quad} \ x \ x$ (right to left)
       ICC:R   = $\emptyset \rightarrow) \ / \ x \ x \underline{\quad}$ (left to right)

Each of the two rules in (38) will generate a series of binary constituents when applied to a sequence of elements. We assume – in contrast to Halle and Vergnaud – that the ICC rules do not have the option of generating constituents with less than two elements. As a result, in a string with an odd number of syllables the application of a binary ICC rule will leave the furthest element unmetrified. An immediate consequence of this fact is that the ICC can never apply to monosyllabic words. However, in some languages with binary constituents monosyllabic words do bear stress. This fact calls for an explanation. The explanation in the present theory is quite simple: these languages require the setting of the Edge Marking parameter.[10]

Warao places stress on all even-numbered syllables starting from the end of the word, as shown by the examples in (39).

(39)   yàpurùkitàneháse   "verily to climb"
       yiwàranáe   "he finished it"

Clearly constituents of two elements are being created from right to left. So the parameters settings for Warao are those in (40).

(40)   Line 0   Edge:RRR   ICC:L   Head:L
       Line 1   Edge:RRR   Head:R

The settings in (40) applied to the words in (39) yield the derivations in (41).

(41) Line 0 Edge:RRR	x x x x x x x x) yapurukitanehase	x x x xx) yiwaranae
ICC:L	(x x(x x(x x (x x) yapurukitanehase	x (x x (xx) yiwaranae
Head:L	x x x x (x x(x x(x x (x x) yapurukitanehase	x x x (x x (xx) yiwaranae

Line 1   Edge:RRR

x x x x)	x x)
(x x(x x(x x (x x)	x (x x (xx)
yapurukitanehase	yiwaranae

Head:R

x	x
x x x x)	x x)
(x x(x x(x x (x x)	x (x x (xx)
yapurukitanehase	yiwaranae

As is evident from the descriptions in (36), Maranungku must assign binary constituents left to right, and Weri must assign them right to left. The line 0 parameter settings for Maranungku and Weri are given in (42).

(42)   Maranungku   Edge:RRR   ICC:R   Head:L
       Weri   Edge:LLL   ICC:L   Head:R

Derivations for two words of Maranungku, one odd and one even, are shown in (43).

(43)

	Odd	Even
Edge:RRR	x x x x x)	x x x x x x)
	langkarateti	welepenemanta
ICC:R	x x)x x)x)	x x)x x) x x)
	langkarateti	welepenemanta
Head:L	x x x	x x x
	x x)x x)x)	x x)x x) x x)
	langkarateti	welepenemanta
	"prawn"	"kind of duck"

And derivations for two similar Weri words are given in (44).

(44)

	Odd	Even
Edge:LLL	(x x x x x akunetepal	(x xx x uluamit
ICC:L	(x (x x(x x akunetepal	(x x(x x ulu amit
Head:R	x x x (x (x x(x x akunetepal	x x x (x x(x x ulu amit
	"times"	"mist"

Notice that the two different parameter settings in (43) produce the same stress contours for words with an odd number of syllables, just as Koya, Selkup, and Khalkha have different parameter settings, but all produce initial stress in words with only light syllables. Furthermore, it is again possible for other parameter settings to achieve the same patterns for both even and odd words. For example, the Weri stress patterns can also be generated with the line 0 parameter settings given in (45).

(45)   Edge:LLR   ICC:L   Head:L

The settings in (45) yield the derivations in (46).

(46) Edge:LLR

Edge:LLR	x x xx (x akunetepal	x x x (x ulu amit
ICC:L	(x x (x x(x akunetepal	x(x x (x ulu amit
Head:L	x x x (x x (x x(x akunetepal	x x x(x x (x ulu amit

Parameter homogeneity will not decide between the settings in (42) and (45). Each of these two possibilities for Weri stress contains one R specification. However, there are differences in the metrical structure assigned to the Weri words. The structure for *uluamit* shown in (44) has two-element constituents exclusively. In contrast, the structure for *uluamit* shown in (46) has a constituent with two elements, a constituent with one element, and one unmetrified element. Thus, the metrical structures assigned to Weri even words by (42) are more homogeneous than those assigned by (45). It has also been suggested (see Hayes 1991, for example) that unary constituents and unmetrified elements are disfavored in constructing metrical constituents. For these reasons, we conjecture that the settings in (42) are preferred over those in (45).

5   Avoidance Constraints

The stress patterns of Garawa are similar to those of Warao, but not identical. According to Furby (1974), stress falls on even-numbered syllables counting from the end of the word, and on the first syllable, but never on the second. Main stress is on the first syllable. Examples are given in (47).

(47)   wátjimpàŋu   "armpit"
       nářiŋinmùkunjìnamìřa   "at your own many"

If we modify the Warao settings by adding Edge:LLL we will ensure that the first syllable is stressed. So the first approximation to the Garawa parameters is the parameter settings shown in (48).

(48)   Line 0   Edge:LLL   ICC:L   Head:L
       Line 1   Edge:LLL   Head:L

The settings in (46) yield stresses on all even-numbered syllables counting right to left and also on the first syllable. However, something must still be added to prevent stress from occurring on the second syllable. We can accomplish this by preventing the creation of certain grid configurations. Specifically, we want to prevent orphans – constituents with only one element – from being created. The constraint in (49) specifies the metrical configuration that Garawa does not tolerate.

(49)   Avoid (x(

Avoid (x(prevents what is called "stress clash." If Garawa did not have this constraint, sometimes two adjacent syllables would both be heads of line 0 constituents, and thus would both be stressed. Some languages, including Garawa, do not tolerate such a situation. Other languages, for example Tubatulabal (Hayes 1980), do allow adjacent stressed syllables. The addition of Avoidance Constraints provides us with sufficient tools to correctly locate Garawa stress; the derivations are given in (50).

(50)

Line 0	Edge:LLL	(x x x x x x x x x nařiŋinmukunjinamiřa	(x x x x watjimpaŋu
	ICC:L	(x x x (x x (x x (x x nařiŋinmukunjinamiřa (x (avoided	(x x (x x watjimpaŋu
	Head:L	x x x x (x x x (x x (x x (x x nařiŋinmukunjinamiřa	x x (x x (x x watjimpaŋu
Line 1	Edge:LLL	(x x x x (x x x (x x (x x (x x nařiŋinmukunjinamiřa	(x x (x x (x x watjimpaŋu
	Head:L	x (x x x x (x x x (x x (x x (x x nařiŋinmukunjinamiřa	x (x x (x x (x x watjimpaŋu

Thus, the effect of Avoid (x(is to give words with an odd number of syllables a constituent with three elements at the left edge.

The blocking of the application of a rule in this fashion is the same as the "active" formulation of the OCP of McCarthy (1986), quoted in (51), in which the OCP *prevents* the application of rules which would produce unacceptable configurations.

(51)   ... the OCP operates not only in a passive way, on the lexical listing of morphemes, but also actively in the course of the phonological derivation. Its function in the derivation, I claim, is not that sporadically assumed in the tonal literature (a process that fuses adjacent identical tones into a single one), but rather is more typical of other principles of grammar, accounting for a hitherto unnoticed constraint, called antigemination, which prohibits syncope rules from creating clusters of identical consonants.

We adopt this view of constraints: that they prevent the creation of disfavored structures. However our Avoidance Constraints are different from McCarthy's formulation of the OCP in one respect: some Avoidance Constraints are active only in particular languages. Thus, the constraints act as output conditions on the rules. The rules are the only means of creating metrical structures, and the function of the constraints is to limit the application of these rules. As such, the Avoidance Constaints cannot be violated. Thus, a child acquiring a language must learn which rules are operative in the language and which constraints are utilized.

This analysis of clash avoidance must be contrasted with clash resolution accounts. In Halle and Vergnaud (1987), the full metrical constituency was constructed, and at the end disfavored configurations were eliminated by the application of a rule. Under such a view, the origin of the constituent structure plays no role in the resolution of clash. Parentheses are parentheses, no matter what parameter licensed their occurence. With Avoidance Constraints, the function of the derivation is extremely important. Since disfavored configurations are not allowed to arise, the origin of each parenthesis is very much at issue. Simply put, parentheses that get placed first preclude the introduction of later parentheses that would result in a disfavored configuration. As a result, in avoiding a configuration such as (x(, the presence of a parenthesis will prevent the introduction of a parenthesis both to the left and to the right. By contrast, in a rule-based account like that of Halle and Vergnaud (1987), clash is always resolved in a particular direction.

Latin exemplifies a common stress pattern in which main stress is restricted to the last three syllables of the word. Stress is assigned to the penultimate syllable if it is heavy, otherwise to the antepenultimate. We propose the parameters in (52) for Latin.

(52) Line 0   Project: L   Edge: RLR   ICC:L   Head: L
      Line 1   Edge: RRR   Head: R
      Conflation

In Latin final syllables are not stressed, even when they are heavy. That means that they must not be subject to Project:L. To capture this fact we propose that Latin avoids creating final orphans; that is, Latin has the constraint Avoid (x#. In Garawa certain applications of ICC rules were blocked in avoiding orphans, while in Latin, certain applications of Syllable Boundary Projection are blocked in avoiding orphans. Derivations for two Latin words are shown in (53).

(53) Line 0 Project:L

| x x x x | x x (x x | (x# avoided |
| reprimitur | reprimuntur | |

Edge:RLR

| x x x)x | x x (x)x |
| reprimitur | reprimuntur |

ICC:L

| x (x x)x | (x x (x)x |
| reprimitur | reprimuntur |

Head:L

x	x x
x (x x)x	(x x (x)x
reprimitur	reprimuntur

Line 1 Edge:RRR	x) x (x x)x reprimitur	x x) (x x (x)x reprimuntur
Head:R	x x) x (x x)x reprimitur	x x x) (x x (x)x reprimuntur

Notice that as a consequence of the fact that the Iterative Constituent Construction cannot construct constituents with less than two marks, the last element is systematically precluded from being part of a constituent because of the effect of the Edge parameter. Since the last mark will effectively be "frozen out," it acts as if it is not there. Previous metrical theories had to invoke a special device of extrametricality to skip these elements. We are able to capture the extrametricality effect as a specific manifestion of the general Edge Marking.

There is a problem with the parameters in (52), however. This system incorrectly predicts that monosyllabic words should not be stressed, as shown in (54).

(54) Line 0   Project:L | x
mu:s | (x# avoided

         Edge:RLR |) x
mu:s |

         ICC:L

         Head:L

   Line 1   Edge:RRR

         Head:R

Mester (1991) notes that Latin has a minimal word constraint (see McCarthy and Prince 1986): #CV# words are systematically excluded in Latin. Thus all Latin monosyllabic words must consist of a heavy syllable. Then all that is required is to exempt monosyllabic words from the constraint against final orphans. This can be accomplished by embellishing Avoid (x# to Avoid x(x#, making specific reference to two grid marks. Because all monosyllabic words consist of a heavy syllable, Syllable Boundary Projection will apply to them, as shown by the derivation in (55).

(55) Line 0   Project:L

x
muːs

x(x# avoided

Edge:RLR

ICC:L

Head:L

x
(x
muːs

Line 1   Edge:RRR

x)
(x
muːs

Head:R

x
x)
(x
muːs

This account of Latin stress is also compatible with the accounts of Latin enclitic stress in Steriade (1988) and Halle and Kenstowicz (1991). When enclitics are added to a word, stress shifts onto the last syllable of the host word regardless of the length of the host or the clitic, as shown in (56).

(56) (a) líːmina   "thresholds"   liːminá#que   "and the thresholds"
      (b) úbi   "where"   ubí#libet   "wherever"
      (c) quáː   "which"   quáː#propter   "because of which"

Words with bisyllabic enclitics (56b, c) have antepenultimate stress, as do words without enclitics. However, the enclitic stress is not attracted to a heavy penultimate syllable, as shown by (56c). Words such as (56a) show an unexpected pattern of penultimate stress. Steriade's insight into this unexpected pattern was to apply metrification rules both before and after cliticization, with the second round of metrification respecting the constituent structure built during the first.

We can translate the analyses of Steriade (1988) and Halle and Kenstowicz (1991) into the present theory. We will assume, following Halle and Vergnaud (1987), that phonological rules are assigned to two distinct blocks. The first of these is the cyclic block, and the second is the noncyclic block. The morphemes that make up a word are each labeled for the feature [± cyclic]. Only morphological constituents whose heads are [+ cyclic] are subject to the rules in the cyclic block. After the cyclic rules have applied to the largest [+ cyclic] constituent in the word, the entire word is subjected to the rules of the noncyclic block. We assume that in Latin the line 0 parameters are part of both the cyclic and the noncyclic block, with the exception of Syllable Boundary Projection, which applies only in the cyclic block.[11] Sincle the enclitics are all noncyclic affixes, this correctly captures the fact that syllable quantity is not relevant in the calculation of enclitic stress. Words without enclitics will nevertheless still be subject to all of the metrical parameters, and the two applications of Edge Marking in such words is equivalent to a single application. Derivations for words with bisyllabic enclitics are shown in (57).

(57)					
Cyclic	Line 0	Project:L	x x ubi	xx eaː	x(x# avoided
		Edge:RLR	x) x ubi	x) x e aː	
		ICC:L			
		Head:L	x x)x ubi	x x) x e aː	
Noncyclic	Line 0	Edge:RLR	x x) x x)x ubi#libet	x x) x x) x e aː#propter	
		ICC:L	x x) (x x)x ub i#libet	x x) (x x) x e aː#propter	
		Head:L	x x x) (x x)x ub i#libet	x x x) (x x) x e aː#propter	
	Line 1	Edge:RRR	x x) x) (x x)x ub i#libet	x x) x) (x x) x e aː#propter	
		Head:R	x x x) x) (x x)x ub i#libet	x x x) x) (x x) x e aː#propter	

The procedure also correctly yields penultimate stress in words with mono-syllabic enclitics, as shown in (58).

(58) Cyclic

Line 0	Project:L	x x x li : mina	(x x mu : sa	x(x# avoided
	Edge:RLR	x x) x li : mina	(x)x mu : sa	
	ICC:L	(x x) x li : mina	(x)x mu : sa	
	Head:L	x (x x) x li : mina	x (x)x mu : sa	

Noncyclic

Line 0	Edge:RLR	x (x x)x)x li : mina#que	x (x)x)x mu : sa#que
	ICC:L		
	Head:L	x x (x x)x)x li : mina#que	x x (x)x)x mu : sa#que
Line 1	Edge:RRR	x x) (x x)x)x li : mina#que	x x) (x)x)x mu : sa#que
	Head:R	x x x) (x x)x)x li : mina#que	x x x) (x)x)x mu : sa#que

Finally, this analysis correctly predicts the position of stress in the enclitic forms with monosyllabic stems, as shown in (59).

(59) Cyclic	Line 0	Project:L	(x qua:	x(x# avoided
		Edge:RLR		
		ICC:L		
		Head:L	x (x qua:	
Noncyclic	Line 0	Edge:RLR	x (x x)x qua:#propter	
		ICC:L		
		Head:L		
	Line 1	Edge:RRR	x) (x x)x qua:#propter	
		Head:R	x x) (x x)x qua:#propter	

Notice that the structure built by the cyclic rules for monosyllabic hosts differs from that for polysyllabic ones. A monosyllabic host gains a metrical constituent that is open at the right edge. A polysyllabic host instead gains a metrical constituent that is closed at the right edge (and also a following grid element). Thus, the metrical constituent in a monosyllabic host can accomodate new material that is added to the right edge, in particular, enclitic elements.[12] Additional material cannot be incorporated in this way into the final metrical constituent of a polysyllabic host. This behavior is subtly different from that predicted by the Free Element Condidition of Prince (1985). The analyses of Steriade (1988) and Halle and Kenstowicz (1991) both restrict the enclitic metrification to free elements – elements not belonging to metrical constituents – and thus incorrectly predict stress on the first syllable of a bisyllabic enclitic following a monosyllabic host: *qua:#própter*. In the present theory, a single parenthesis suffices to define a constituent, thus it is possible for constituents to be "open-ended." Such representations were not possible in

previous metrical theories, where all constituents had both a left parenthesis and a right parenthesis, leading to incorrect predictions regarding free
elements.

6   Winnebago

The accentual system of Winnebago has been very important in the development of metrical theory. Metrical analyses of Winnebago have been presented by Hale and White Eagle (1980), Halle and Vergnaud (1987), Miner
(1989), and Hayes (1991). In particular, Winnebago was the source of the
Domino Condition of Halle and Vergnaud (1987). The present theory allows
for a simpler characterization of the Winnebago stress system, which renders
the Domino Condition unnecessary. The source of the complications in
Winnebago stress is the rule known as Dorsey's Law, informally stated in (60),
which inserts an echo vowel between a consonant and a sonorant in the onset
of a syllable.

(60) $\emptyset \rightarrow V_i / C$——$RV_i$

Halle and Vergnaud (1987) note that rules adding new stressable elements
(such as Dorsey's Law) could take place either before or after metrical constituent assignment. If such rules apply before metrification, then the epenthetic
vowels will bear stress if they appear in an appropriate location in the string.
If the epenthesis follows metrical constituent construction, then no epenthetic
vowel should ever bear stress. Winnebago words, however, seem to act both
ways: epenthetic vowels can sometimes bear stress, but at other times they
seem to be completely ignored.

Hale and White Eagle (1980) observe that in words (with light syllables)
not subject to Dorsey's Law, stress is assigned to every odd mora except the
first one. Winnebago is a language where all vowels can bear stress, not
just syllable heads, and therefore all vowels are projected. To get stress on
every odd mora except the first one, we will employ the parameter settings
in (61).

(61)   Line 0   Edge:LRL   ICC:R   Head:R
       Line 1   Edge:LLL   Head:L

Derivations for two words not subject to Dorsey's Law are given in (62).

(62) Line 0 Edge:LRL

x(x x x na ana?a	x (x x xx ha akitujik

ICC:R

x(x x)x na ana?a	x(x x)xx) ha akitujik

Head:R

x x(x x)x na ana?a	x x x(x x)xx) ha akitujik

Line 1 Head:L

(x x(x x)x na ana?a	(x x x(x x)xx) ha akitujik

Head:L

x (x x(x x)x na ana?a	x (x x x(x x)xx) ha akitujik

"you weigh"	"I pull it taut"

From this point on we will ignore the line 1 parameters. Hayes (1991) points out that syllables with long vowels or diphthongs behave differently depending on their position in the word. Those in initial position behave as described so far, those in noninitial position attract stress. In order to capture this fact we will analyze these as Halle (1990) analyzes Cairene Arabic and Chugach Alutiiq – in addition to projecting two marks, long vowels and diphthongs will also receive a left bracket. In order to correctly characterize initial cases, we will also include the constraint Avoid #(, which prevents left parentheses from being projected in initial syllables.[13]

Some words with epenthetic vowels (capitalized in the following examples) seem to ignore the epenthesized vowels in stress assignment, as shown in (63).

(63) hoshAwazhá   "you are ill"

In other words the epenthetic vowels bear stress, as in (64).

(64) maashÁrach   "you promise"

And in still other words the epenthetic vowels do not bear stress, but do count in determining pairs, as in (65).

(65) xOrojíke   "hollow"

Under the Halle and Vergnaud (1987) analysis there are two places an epenthesized vowel in a Winnebago word can occur: between two elements belonging to the same constituent or between two elements belonging to different constituents. As noted by Hale and White Eagle (1980), when the echo vowel occurs between two elements belonging to different constituents, it has no effect. When it occurs between two elements in the same constituent, the effect is to re-metrify all subsequent elements. It is this fact that the Domino Condidition, (66), was designed to capture.

(66) The introduction of an additional position inside a bounded constituent destroys the constituent and all constituents to its right if the Constistuent Construction rule applied left to right, and all constituents to its left if the Constituent Construction rule applied from right to left. Constituent structure is reimposed on the affected substring by a subsequent re-application of the Constituent Construction rule. (Halle and Vergnaud 1987)

Notice that in a left to right system the structure to the right is deleted, and that in a right to left system the structure to the left is deleted. This ensures that the effect of the Domino Condition is to restart the metrical count from the location of the epenthesis in a constituent. That is, new positions inserted inside existing constituents act like heavy syllables in restarting the metrical count. Obviously, it is preferable to have a theory that captures these facts without such a special stipulation. We believe that the theory sketched above accomplishes this. The invariant effect is that the echo vowels must coincide with a metrical constituent boundary. Thus, the appearance of an epenthetic vowel correlates with stress two syllables later. If a constituent boundary would have been placed there anyway, then it will appear as though stress is assigned before Dorsey's Law. If a boundary would not have been placed there, the apparent effect of Dorsey's Law is to provide a constituent boundary.

To capture the stress effect of these epenthetic vowels we will also project a left parenthesis for CRV syllables – those syllables that will be subject to Dorsey's Law. Thus, Dorsey's Law syllables behave like long vowels in projecting a left parentheses. To begin with, however, they project only a single grid mark. Another grid mark will be supplied by the operation of Dorsey's Law. The new grid mark is added to the left (outside) of the left parenthesis. Thus, the net effect of Projection and Dorsey's Law is to provide Dorsey's Law sequences with the metrical pattern x(x. Since line 0 constituents are right-headed, Dorsey's Law syllables have a post-accenting effect. After Dorsey's Law has applied, the rest of the metrical parameters will apply. Derivations for three such words are shown in (67).[14]

(67) Project:L

	x x x xrojike	x x (x x x hirakrohoni	x x (x x x x hirakrohonira
DL	x xxx xOrojike	x x x(x x x hirakOrohoni	x x x (x x x x hirakOrohonira
Edge:LRL		x(x x(x x x hirakOrohoni	x(x x (x x x x hirakOrohonira
ICC:R	x (xx)x xOrojike	x(x x)(x x)x hirakO rohoni	x(x x) (x x)x x) hirakO rohonira
Head:R	x x (xx)x xOrojike	x x x(x x)(x x)x hirakO rohoni	x x x x(x x) (x x)x x) hirakO rohonira
	"hollow"	"you do not dress"	"the fact that you do not dress"

As Miner (1989) notes, there is one case where epenthetic vowels do not always correlate with a following stress: when the Dorsey's Law syllable is final in the word, as shown by the words in (68).

(68) hojisÁna "recently" boopÉres "to sober up" kerepÁna "unit of ten"

To account for such words we will constrain Syllable Boundary Projection as we did in Latin, with Avoid (x#. This prevents final Dorsey's Law syllables from projecting parentheses and forming orphans, and yields the derivations in (69).

(69) Project:L

	xx x hojisna	xx x boopres	(x x krepna
DL	xx x x hojisAna	x x x x bo opEres	x(x x x kErepAna
Edge:LRL	x(x x x hojisAna	x (x x x bo opEres	
ICC:R	x(x x) x hojisAna	x (x x)x bo opEres	x(x x) x kErepAna
Head:R	x x(x x) x hojisAna	x x (x x)x bo opEres	x x(x x) x kErepAna
	"recently"	"to sober up"	"unit of ten"

Notice, however, that the ICC does pick up a final pair formed from a Dorsey's Law syllable when the preceding material coincides with the end of a constituent, as shown in (70).

(70)   Project:L

	x x x (x x x harakishrujikshna
DL	x x x x (x x x x harakishUrujikshAna
Edge:LRL	x(x x x (x x x x harakishUrujikshAna
ICC:R	x(x x) x (x x) x x) harakishUrujikshAna
Head:R	x x x x(x x) x (x x) x x) harakishUrujikshAna
	"you pull taut"

The derivation in (70) also illustrates a case where Dorsey's Law would have inserted a vowel between constituents in the Halle and Vergnaud (1987) analysis. Because the ICC cannot create constituents with only one element, the epenthetic vowel remains unmetrified, yielding a surface stress lapse of two syllables.

Of special interest are the cases where main stress falls on the fourth surface vowel of form, such as the examples in (71).

(71)   hikOrohó   "to prepare"   wakIripÁras   "flat bug"
       wakIripÓropÓro   "spherical bug"

Notice that the last two examples have final Dorsey's Law syllables, which will not project parentheses because of Avoid (x#. Thus far our account of Winnebago predicts that stress will occur on the second syllable of such forms, because of Edge Marking, as shown in (72).

(72) Project:L

x (x x
hikroho

DL

x x (x x
hikOroho

Edge:LRL

x (x (x x
hikOroho

ICC:R

x (x (x x)
hikOroho

Head:R

x   x
x (x (x x)
*hikOroho
"to prepare"

There are two possible ways to address this problem: order Dorsey's Law after Edge Marking, or prevent Edge Marking from applying in these forms. However, reordering Dorsey's Law and Edge Marking will not work with other words, as the derivation in (73) demonstrates.

(73) Project:L

x   x
hip res

Edge:LRL

DL

x x x
hipEres

ICC:R

x x)x
hipEres

Head:R

x
x x)x
*hipEres
"to know"

Rather, the correct derivation has Dorsey's Law preceding Edge Marking, as shown in (74).

(74) Project:L

x x
hipres

DL

x x x
hipEres

Edge:LRL

x (x x
hipEres

ICC:R

x (x x)
hipEres

Head:R

x
x (x x)
hipEres

| "to know" |

Therefore, we need to prevent Edge Marking from applying to these forms. The same constraint as in Garawa, Avoid (x(will accomplish this. Recall that Winnebago has a constraint against final orphans, Avoid (x#. That is, Winnebago has a general constraint against orphans, incorporating both Avoid (x(, as in Garawa, and Avoid (x#, as in Latin.[15] However, this system is still not sufficient, as the ICC can also create a constituent from the initial pair of marks, again yielding stress on the second syllable, as shown in (75).

(75) Project:L

x (x x
hikroho

DL

x x (x x
hikOroho

Edge:LRL

ICC:R

x x) (x x)
hikO roho

Head:R

x   x
x x) (x x)
*hikO roho

| "to prepare" |

The correct constraint to add is somewhat surprising – Avoid)(. This constraint will prevent the ICC from creating constituents that abut projected parentheses. Thus, Winnebago has the constraints Avoid #(, (x#, (x(and)(. After adding this constraint, we get the derivations in (76).

(76) Project:L	x (x x hikroho	x (x x wakripras	x (x x x wakripropro
DL	x x(x x hikOroho	x x(x x x wakIripAras	x x(x x x x x wakIripOropOro
Edge:LRL			
ICCC:R	x x(x x) hikOroho	x x(x x) x wakIripAras	x x(x x) x x) x wakIripOropOro
Head:R	x x x(x x) hikOroho	x x x(x x) x wakIripAras	x x x x(x x) x x) x wakIripOropOro
	"to prepare"	"flat bug"	"spherical bug"

The ICC is prevented from creating a constituent out of the initial pair of elements by Avoid)(. Because the initial pair of elements does not form a constituent, the main stress falls on the fourth mora of the word. Futhermore, Avoid)(also predicts the location of stress in more complicated forms, correctly modeling the curious three-syllable lapses observed by Hale (1985), as shown in (77).

(77) Project:L	x x x x (x x hirat'at'ashnakshna
DL	x x x x x (x x x hirat'at'ashAnaksAhna
Edge:LRL	x(x x x x (x x x hirat'at'ashAnaksAhna
ICC:R	x(x x) x x (x x) x hirat'at'ashAnaksAhna
Head:R	x x x(x x) x x (x x) x hirat'at'ashAnaksAhna
	"you are talking"

This form exhibits an interior lapse of three syllables, as the preceding cases exhibited in initial position. Miner (1989) and Hayes (1991) also cite further cases of lapses, involving long vowels, as shown in (78).

(78) Project:L

x x x x x(xx x x	x x(xx x x(xx x x
waGiGigishgapuizhere	hizhakiichashgunianaga

DL

Edge:LRL

x (x x x x(xx x x	
waGiGigishgapuizhere	

ICC:R

x (x x)x x(xx) x x)	x x(xx) x x(xx)x x)
waGiGigishgapuizhere	hizhakiichashgunianaga

Head:R

x x x	x x x
x (x x)x x(xx) x x)	x x(xx) x x(xx)x x)
waGiGigishgapuizhere	hizhakiichashgunianaga

"baseball player"	"nine and"

Perhaps somewhat anticlimactically, this analysis also correctly predicts the stress placement in monosyllables subject to Dorsey's Law, as shown in (79).

(79) Project:L

x
kre

DL

x x
kEre

Edge:LRL

ICC:R

x x)
kEre

Head:R

x
x x)
kEre

"to leave returning"

The analysis of Winnebago presented above has several important characteristics which we want to emphasize. By allowing boundaries to be projected it is possible to account for the effect of Dorsey's Law syllables on the stress patterns of Winnebago words without resorting to mechanisms such as the Domino Condition of Halle and Vergnaud (1987). Winnebago also employs both Avoid (x# and Avoid (x(, showing that languages can have very general prohibitions against orphans. Perhaps most interestingly, Winnebago shows that the parameters for Syllable Boundary Projection and Head Location do not need to be homogeneous. By projecting left parentheses for CRV syllables while line 0 constituents are right headed we achieve the post-stressing effect of syllables subject to Dorsey's Law.

7   Summary

The discrete calculus presented above formally captures Liberman's insight that stress in language is a reflection of the groupings that speakers impose on sequences of linguistic elements. Once these groupings have been established, greater prominence is supplied to certain elements in the group than to the others. The prominence is thus a by-product of the grouping of the elements into constituents.

We suggested that for purposes of notating these groupings Universal Grammar provides a special plane on which the metrical grid is constructed. The grid consists of a number of parallel lines composed of marks and parentheses. The various parameter settings then interact with universal and language particular constraints to produce the stress systems found in different languages. Thus, metrical constituents are not composed of sequences of phonemes, or (as in Kager 1992) moras or syllables. Rather metrical constituents group projections of particular units in the phoneme sequences, specifically, those that are capable of bearing stress. In this way, the framework captures the fact that not all elements in the sequence have a bearing on stress assignment. In particular there are languages in which certain syllable heads (usually schwa) are metrically inert while behaving as normal syllable heads in every other respect. Thus, we deny the hypothesis that units of prosody are strictly layered in a hierarchy (McCarthy and Prince 1986; Selkirk 1986). In particular, stress and syllable structure are represented on different planes.

For the purposes of constructing metrical grids, the theoretical framework proposed here has available only two mechanisms. One of these generates a line on the metrical grid by the Projection of marks and boundaries from the next lower line. The other mechanism constructs constituents by the placement of appropriate boundaries. The functioning of these two mechanisms is constrained by universal restrictions so that only a narrow range of options is available for the placement of boundaries and marks. Because of the parameterized nature of the framework, the addition of parameters to the set utilized in characterizing a body of data causes a geometric increase in the number of patterns characterized. Since learners of such a characterization need to look only for cues to set the individual parameters (Dresher and Kaye 1990; Dresher to appear), they need to make only a relatively small number of decisions to be able to generate a large number of distinct stress patterns. This explains the well-known fact that speakers of different languages master their stress patterns with great facility and speed.

The most significant innovation of the present theory is in the representations of bracketed grids. By eliminating superfluous parentheses, we change the meaning of the parentheses themselves. A single parenthesis is now sufficient to define a metrical constituent. This has the important consequence that metrical constituents can be open-ended. This, in turn, means that constituency can be modified while still respecting the already assigned structure in the sense of Halle (1990). The addition of new elements can augment constituents and the (re)application of parameter settings can subdivide constituents. Operations that must destroy previously built structure in tree theory can be formulated in the present theory so that they only add structure. Thus this theory gives a whole new meaning to constituent structure and Free Elements.

We also deviate from previous metrical theories by not requiring exhaustive parsing of the sequence of elements, that is we do not require that every element belong to some constituent, thus also denying the fundamental basis of Prosodic Licensing (Itô 1989; see also Bagemihl 1991).

Another innovation of the present theory is the Edge Marking Parameter, which, among other things, captures the effects ascribed to Extrametricality and the End Rule in Prince (1983). This simple device solves a number of puzzles in generative stress theory. For example, as we showed in our discussion of the stress patterns of Koya, Selkup, and Khalkha, these very different patterns are elegantly characterized by different settings of the Edge Marking parameter. This represents an advance over previous theories since they were able to characterize the stress pattern of languages like Khalkha only with the help of special ad hoc devices. This is important because Khalkha-type stress patterns show up in languages the world over. Salish languages, certain Northwest Caucasian languages, and Indo-European languages such as Russian, Lithuanian, and Sanskrit all show this kind of stress pattern.

In constructing iterative constituents we deviated from the procedure in Halle and Vergnaud (1987) and restricted this operation to construct only full constituents, agreeing in this respect with Hayes (1991). However, the theory of binary constituent construction through the operation of the ICC is to be contrasted with Hayes (1991) and other recent work in stress theory, which claim that binary constituents are universal, and that there is a taxonomy of foot types. In such theories each foot type encodes both constituency and prominence simultaneously, so that parsing a word into feet assigns prominence at the same time. In our framework the foot is not a theoretical primitive. Rather, metrical boundaries are placed among the stress-bearing elements.

In this way the sequence of stress-bearing elements is subdivided into constituents of various kinds, including iambs and trochees, although iambs and trochees have no privileged status. In fact, the ICC, like Syllable Boundary Projection and Edge Marking can be present or absent in a language's parameter settings. If there is a setting for the ICC, then a sequence of constituents is generated. If there is no setting for ICC then the constituents that arise are only those defined by either Syllable Boundary Projection or Edge Marking. This also means that there are no parameters that directly control the size of the metrical constituents, as the parameters of [±Bounded] and [±Head Terminal] did in Halle and Vergnaud (1987). Unbounded constituents result from the absence of the application of the ICC.

For example, the projection of elements onto the higher lines in the grid is limited to the operation of the Head Location parameter. The framework therefore lacks the capability of increasing an element's prominence directly. As a consequence, any element with increased prominence must always be first or last within its constituent. Furthermore, in the present theory constituent construction precedes the assignment of heads. By separating the construction of constituents from the marking of heads we predict that the constituents of a word will all have the same headedness. For instance, words parsed into a combination of trochees and iambs are forbidden within this framework. Likewise, we also predict that syllables which project boundaries will not necessarily receive more prominence. The post-accenting effect of Dorsey's Law syllables in Winnebago is an example of just such a system.

Finally, the new representations and rules are subject to various constraints on well-formedness – the Avoidance Constraints. These constraints act in concert with the application of specific parameterized rules of element and parenthesis insertion to yield a derivation. This means that parentheses that are inserted by earlier parameters have priority over those inserted by later parameters. Taken together, these innovations in representations, rules and constraints yield a novel and more accurate conception of the meaning of metrical structure and operations.

NOTES

We would like to acknowledge the help of many people in clarifying the material presented here: Steve Anderson, Elan Dresher, San Duanmu, Jim Harris, Michael Kenstowicz, Jay Keyser, Charles Kisseberth, John McCarthy, Eric Ristad, Donca Steriade, Loren Trigo, Jean-Roger Vergnaud, Irene Vogel, and the students in our classes.

This material is partially based upon work supported under a National Science Foundation Graduate Fellowship held by William Idsardi while a student at MIT.

1   We will introduce some departures from Idsardi (1992), which we will indicate in footnotes.
2   We depart from previous work in

bracketed grid theory (Halle & Vergnaud (1987), Hayes (1991), etc.) in proposing that a single parenthesis serves to define a metrical constituent. Thus, where the former representation of a three element constituent is (xxx), the present theory can also have (xxx or xxx), depending on other factors within the language.

3   In (7) and subsequent examples the links between elements on different lines of the grid have been suppressed.

4   Notice that settings which employ only one kind of parenthesis will be more homogeneous than those employing both. Other kinds of preferences could also play a role, such as dispreferences for unmetrified elements and orphans. See below for one method of encoding such dispreferences.

5   See Halle & Kenstowicz (1991) and Idsardi (1992) for formulations of Conflation.

6   In Idsardi (1992), idiosyncratic stress is analyzed as morphologically triggered applications of Edge Marking. We have chosen in this paper to outline how morphologically triggered Syllable Boundary Projection can be used to the same ends. At the present time there seems to be insufficient evidence for a definitive conclusion as to which theory of lexical stress is preferable, or if both views are required. For discussion see Idsardi (1992).

7   See van der Hulst and van de Weijer (1991) for a discussion of cases of final secondary stress in Turkish words.

8   In Idsardi (1992) Iterative Constituent Construction settings are described from the starting element. We have chosen to describe them here in terms of the

parenthesis inserted. By doing this we gain a better match between observed iterative stress systems and the principle of homogeneity preference discussed above.

9   The syllabification rules also seem to be directional, for some arguments to this effect see Sloan (1991).

10   See also the analysis of Latin, below for a related point.

11   We have chosen here to maximize the similarity between the line 0 parameters in the cyclic and noncyclic blocks. Note that other allocations of line 0 parameters to the two blocks will yield the same results. Edge Marking must apply in both blocks, and Syllable Boundary Projection must apply only in the cyclic block. Head Location must apply in the noncyclic block. Finally, ICC must apply in at least one of the blocks.

12   Notice that subsequent application of other rules can, in effect, steal elements from constituents, for example, ICC:L applied to (xxx + x yields (xx(x + x.

13   Miner (1989) notes that there are separate principles of accent placement on long vowels and diphthongs following the initial metrical calculations. He also notes that similar proposals can be found in Vance (1987) for Japanese and Steriade (1988) for Greek. Hayes (1991) gives an analysis in terms of the sonority hierarchy, with the more sonorous mora receiving the accent. This can be handled in the present theory by deleting the second line 0 mark of a long vowel or diphthong with nonrising sonority.

14   The derivations for the second and third words will change slightly with the addition of Avoid)(, discussed below. This change will

not affect the stress patterns in these words.

15   Since Avoid (x(is operative in Winnebago, in a sequence of Dorsey's Law syllables not all syllables will be able to project a boundary. Instead, an alternating pattern of projected left brackets will be created, going from left to right. This effect is exactly the same as the alternating heavy syllable stresses of Wolof, discussed in Idsardi (1992), and it indicates that Projection is also a directional rule.

12   Tone: African Languages

DAVID ODDEN

0   Introduction

The study of tone in African languages has played a significant role in the development of nonlinear phonology, since the independence of tone and other "segmental" features is most easily demonstrated in the domain of tone, and many African languages have rich systems of morphophonemic tonal alternations. Autosegmental phonology, as presented in Goldsmith (1976a), was motivated primarily by investigation of tonal problems in African languages, and as Yip, in chapter 13 of this volume observes, African languages have received most of the attention in theoretical studies of tone. While it is true that African tone systems are better understood today than they were twenty years ago, it is also true that the vast majority of the more than one thousand languages spoken in Africa are tonal, and are for all intents and purposes undescribed. Much work therefore remains to be done in understanding tone as it is represented in Africa.

1   The Autosegmental Analysis of Tone

Drawing on earlier suprasegmental research in tone (Leben 1973; Williams 1976), Goldsmith (1976a) sets forth the theory of autosegmental phonology. The thesis advanced there is that certain feature groups, such as tone versus segmental features, define independent levels of representation (autosegments), and that there is not a one-to-one relationship between the number of tones and the number of segments in a string.

One of the classical problems of tonology which autosegmental phonology resolves is the representation of contour tones. It is widely recognized that

falling tones are functionally equivalent to the tone sequence HL, and rising
tones to LH. This is apparent when considering the possible (assimilatory)
rules that create contour tones. Rules like (1) are common.

(1) (a) L → Rise /_____ $\left\{ \begin{matrix} H \\ Fall \end{matrix} \right\}$

    (b) H → Fall /_____ $\left\{ \begin{matrix} L \\ Rise \end{matrix} \right\}$

    (c) L → Fall/ $\left\{ \begin{matrix} H \\ Rise \end{matrix} \right\}$ _____

    (d) H → Rise / $\left\{ \begin{matrix} L \\ Fall \end{matrix} \right\}$ _____

Other imaginable changes like those in (2) are unattested.

(2) (a) L → Rise/_____ $\left\{ \begin{matrix} L \\ Rise \end{matrix} \right\}$

    (b) H → Rise/_____ $\left\{ \begin{matrix} L \\ Fall \end{matrix} \right\}$

This fact, whose explanation eluded linear phonology, is solved in autosegmental phonology, where contour tones are multiple tones linked to one
vowel. The well-attested processes expand the domain of a tone to a neighboring vowel.

(3)   V   V

      |- - - - - -⅃\

     L   H (L) (= 1a)

    V   V

   /⅃- - -⌐|

  (H) L   H (= 1d)

The unattested processes, on the other hand, cannot be described in this way.
    There are occasional challenges to the view that contour tones are sequences
of level tones. An argument for primitive contour tones in Wobe (Kru: Côte
d'Ivoire) is presented by Bearth and Link (1980). The evidence from Wobe is
difficult to evaluate; see Singler (1984) and Paradis (1984) for alternative
analyses. Grebo (Kru: Liberia), discussed in Newman (1986a), is clearer,
though open to reinterpretation. In Grebo, there are four level tones, noted
by 1, 2, 3, 4, with 1 indicating the highest and 4 the lowest. Contour tones
are indicated as sequences of these four (e.g., 21 for a tone rising from 2 to
1). A 21 contour does not act like a combination of a 2 plus a 1 tone. For

instance, the pronoun *na-* "my" has a 2 before a noun with a 1 tone, and has a 1 tone before nouns with a 2 tone or lower. Before a 2̱1 tone, *na* has a 2 tone as it does before a 1 tone – in other words, 2̱1 does not act like it begins with a 2 tone.

(4) (a) na² to¹   "my store"
     (b) na¹ tu²   "my stick"
     (c) na² ta²̱¹   "my salt"

As a second illustration of the difference between simple 2 tone and the 2-tone component of a 2̱1 contour, a 2 tone downsteps to 3 after a 4 tone, so ɔ² *yi²̱¹kla⁴fo²* becomes ɔ² *yi²̱¹kla⁴fo³* "She didn't wait for Kla", but the 2̱1 contour of ɔ² *yi²̱¹kla⁴nyɛ²̱¹* "she doesn't hate Kla" does not downstep. Examples like these, and other problems discussed by Newman, show that rising tones do not act like a combination of level tones, and do act like single tones. The historical cause of the peculiar behavior of 2̱1 and 3̱2 is that they arise from level 1 and 3 tones; synchronically, level 1 and 3 tones do exist in Grebo (*to¹* "store", *mɔ³* "you" (sg.)).

A second classical puzzle of tonology which is solved by autosegmental phonology is *tone preservation*, also known as *stability*. In many languages, when a vowel deletes, the tones which it bore are not deleted. Goldsmith (1976a), drawing on Lovins (1971), illustrates this with the now-classic example of Lomongo (Bantu: Zaire), where phrase-level rules delete (consonants and) vowels, but tones borne by the deleted vowels are preserved and surface on the surviving vowel of the sequence.

(5) (a) bálóngó   băkáé   →   bàlóngăkáé   "his book"
     (b) bɔ̌mɔ̌   bòmtámbá   →   bɔ̌mɔ̌támbá   "another tree"

Given the independence of the tonal and segmental tiers, deletion of a vowel does not entail deletion of tones linked to the vowel.

(6) balong (o)   (b) a k a e
     | | | |
     L H   H   L   H   H H

The H formerly borne by *o* survives, and by general convention is automatically docked on the following vowel.

Further evidence for autosegmental theory is that it allows abstraction of tonal patterns which are comprehensible only when viewed independently of the syllables and segments bearing the melody. Leben (1973) argues for a suprasegmental representation of tone in Mende (Mande: Mali, Senegal) based on restrictions on tone patterns: there are (supposedly) five tonal classes of nouns.

(7)	(a)	L	kpà	bèlè	kpàkàlì
	(b)	H	kɔ́	pélé	háwámá
	(c)	LH	mbǎ	fàndé	ndàvúlá
	(d)	HL	mbû	ngílà	félàmà
	(e)	LHL	mbã̌	nyàhâ	nìkílì

The tone melodies may be abstracted away from the syllables which bear them phonetically, mapping tones to vowels from left to right, creating contour tones only at the end of the word when no toneless vowels remain. This separation of tone pattern and segmental content explains a number of facts: (a) the left-to-right mapping of tone to vowels only creates contour tones at the end of the word. (b) The analysis predicts that, since there are no tone melodies *HHL or *HLH, there could be no words like *páwû or *lákátà (illustrating *HHL) or *mbálǎ or *máninká (illustrating *HLH) – the characterization of possible tone patterns holds irrespective of the number of syllables in the word.

While the tone patterns illustrated in (7) are the most common, Dwyer (1978) and Leben (1978) note that other patterns exist.

(8)	(a)	HHL	hókpô	"navel"	kpɔ́ngbɔ́nì	"palsy"
	(b)	HLH	tá'tó	"start"	yámbùwú	"tree (species)"
	(c)	HLHL	gó'niê	"cat"	njégùlû	"tarantula"
	(d)	LLH			làsìmɔ́	"amulet"

Furthermore, contrary to the prediction of the left-to-right mapping theory, contour tones can appear in word-medial position, e.g., *klàáki* "clerk". Such word-medial contour tones are controversial; *klǎkì* "clerk" could be transcribed as *klàáki*. There is apparently no phonological evidence that decides whether these vowels are long, although it is apparent that they have greater phonetic duration than level-toned syllables.

A fourth problem for the treatment of tone which an autosegmental treatment resolves is floating tones, that is, tones which are independent of vowels. Certain phenomena in (Aŋlo) Ewe (Kwa: Togo, Ghana) illustrate floating tones (Clements 1978; see also Clements and Ford 1979 and 1981 for floating tones in Kikuyu). Postulating floating H tones for certain words solves various analytic puzzles, even though the floating tone is not directly manifested. For example, word-final M tone in Ewe generally becomes L tone, which then spreads leftward to preceding M tones. By these rules, /ētō/ becomes [ètò] "buffalo". However, some words do not lower final M, e.g., [ētō] "mortar". Failure of lowering is explained by positing that *eto* ends with H not associated to a vowel, i.e., is underlyingly /ētō´/. M cannot lower, since it is not word final.

Floating H explains other problems. The locative postposition *me* generally has L (*ètó mè* "in a mountain", *ètò mè* "in a buffalo"), but has a falling tone after nouns with floating H such as *ētō* (*ētō mê* "in a mortar"). Finally, there is a rule of Raising (see section 2.2) changing M to R (Raised H), which changes HMH to HRH. This applies to /ētó mēgbé/ and gives *ētó mégbé* (which, because of other rules, surfaces as [ètő mégbé] "behind a mountain"). The phonological effect of floating H can be seen here: /ētő˘ mēgbé/ becomes [ētō mégbé] "behind a mortar".

Across-the-board tone changes give more evidence for the model. In Shona (Bantu: Zimbabwe, Mozambique), the first H tone of a noun is lowered after a (morphological) class of H-toned "associative" prefixes (Odden 1980).

(9)	(a) mbwá	"dog"	né-mbwa	"with dog"
	(b) hóvé	"fish"	né-hove	"with fish"
	(c) mbúndúdzí	"army worm"	né-mbundudzi	"with army worm"
	(d) hákáta	"diviner's bones"	né-hakata	"with diviner's bones"
	(e) bénzíbvunzá	"inquisitive fool"	né-benzibvunzá	"with an inquisitive fool"

The fact that the rule lowers an unbounded sequence of stem-initial H tones is explained if these words have one H, linked to a sequence of vowels.

(10)   mbwa   hove   mbundudzi   benzibvunza

The rule affects the initial H of the stem, which is phonetically transmitted to a number of vowels. The reason why the word-final H in *bénzíbvunzá* does not lower, but the H of the first two syllables does, is that the first two syllables have one H tone which they share, and the final syllable has its own H.

2 Tonal Geometry

There are two central questions about the geometry of tones: (a) where do tones link in phonological representations, and (b) what features define tones?

2.1 *The Tone-bearing Unit*

One of the fundamental problems in understanding tone is determining what the *tone-bearing unit (TBU)* is. Goldsmith (1976a) speaks of the vowel as the TBU, but the preface to that work suggests that it would be better to treat the syllable as the tone-bearing unit. The view that tones link to a higher prosodic unit is echoed in Clements and Ford (1979): "There has been some ambiguity in previous uses of the term tone-bearing unit. It is maintained here that tones are not directly associated with vowels or other segments, but rather with higher-level units ('tone-bearing units') such as the syllable or syllable-final (rhyme), in which vowels typically function as peaks of prominence (p. 181, n. 3)."

In terms of feature geometry (see chapter 7 this volume), the question of what the TBU is becomes, what do tones link to? There is good evidence that tones link to the mora (on the mora, see chapter 5 this volume). In certain Bantu languages (Odden 1989a), verbs stems are assigned an H in various positions, depending on the tense-aspect of the verb. In Kikuria (Bantu: Kenya, Tanzania), every stem has an H, which appears on one of the first four moras of the stem;[1] which mora takes the H is determined by tense-aspect. H is assigned to the fourth mora in the perfective; a syllable with a long vowel is functionally equivalent to two syllables with short vowels.

(11)   (a)   n-[tɛrɛk-eré   "I have cooked"
      (b)   n-[ga-tɛrɛk-ére   "I have cooked them"
      (c)   n-[karaang-ére   "I have fried"
      (d)   n-[ga-karaáng-ére   "I have fried them"
      (e)   m-[beebeét-ére   "I have sieved"
      (f)   m-[ba-beebéét-éeye   "I have sieved for them"

H is assigned to the third mora in the subjunctive.

(12)   (a)   n-[tɛrɛk-ɛ́   "I should cook"
      (b)   n-[ga-tɛrɛ́k-ɛ   "I should cook them"
      (c)   n-[karaáng-ɛ   "I should fry"
      (d)   n-[ga-karááng-ɛ   "I should fry them"
      (e)   m-[beebéét-ɛ   "I should sieve"
      (f)   m-[ba-beébéeter-ɛ   "I should sieve for them"

The second mora receives the H in the recent past.

(13)   (a)   nnaaga-[tɛrékére   "I just cooked"
      (b)   nnaaga-[karáángére   "I just fried"
      (c)   nnaaga-[beébéetere   "I just sieved"

Finally, in the remote past, the H is assigned to the first mora.

(14)   (a)   nnaa-[tɛréka   "I cooked"
      (b)   nnaa-[káráanga   "I fried"
      (c)   nnaa-[béébéeta   "I sieved"

Regardless of how one counts, what is counted are vowel moras, not segments and not syllables. Stated in terms of a mora count, H is simply assigned to the fourth mora in the perfective, but there is no consistent locus of tone assignment if one counts either syllables or segments.

(15)   Segment   Syllable
    (a)   n-[tɛrɛk-eré   8   4
    (b)   n-[karaang-ére   7   3
    (c)   n-[ga-karaáng-ére   6   3
    (d)   m-[beebeét-ére   4   2
    (e)   m-[ba-beebéét-éeye   6   3

Another possibility is that the syllable is the TBU, a suggestion made for Kikuyu (Bantu: Kenya) in Clements (1984). As pointed out by Hyman (1988a), there is an overgeneration problem in permitting the mora to be the TBU, in that one could have a language with many types of contour-toned syllables. A bimoraic contour-toned syllable could be represented in five ways.

(16)

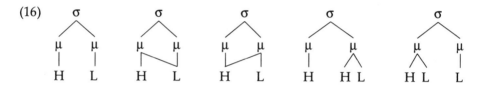

Yet no language has more than one kind of contour tone. Linking tones to syllables, not to moras within the syllable, solves this problem.

(17)

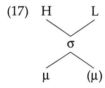

In the syllabic tone theory, all that can be said is that the whole syllable has a falling tone. In the syllabic TBU theory, there simply is no way phonologically to manipulate the realization of tones relative to the moras of a syllable.[2]

The Chimaraba dialect of Makonde (Bantu: Tanzania, Mozambique) provides evidence for the syllable as the TBU, in the form of rules which refer to the toneless status of syllables. There is a rule that spreads H rightward to the following syllable, provided that the recipient syllable is followed by a toneless syllable (Odden, 1990b).

(18) (a) /vanachítelekelaána/ → vanachítélekelána   "they will cook it for
                                                           each other"
     (b) /vanachítelekeéla/   → vanachítélekeéla   "they will cook it for"
     (c) /vanachíteleéka/   → vanachíteleéka   "they will cook it"

Failure of H spreading in the last example is explained because the syllable *te* is followed by a syllable with a H tone. But the mora which follows *te* is itself toneless—the blocking H tone stands on the second mora of the syllable.

Clements (1984) gives evidence for the syllable as the TBU in Kikuyu, noting that bisyllabic noun stems within a tone class have the same surface tone patterns whether the stem vowel is long or short (HL nouns do not directly manifest the L, which surfaces as a downstep; see Clements and Ford 1979, 1981).

(19) (a) LH   mo-ɣatĕ   "bread"
                    ke-roomĭ   "cheetah"
      (b) HL   mo-ɣɛká   "bed"
                    mo-raatá   "friend"

Despite the advantages outlined above which the syllable-as-TBU theory enjoys, there are two problems: (a) It is not clear how languages such as Kikuria which count moras are handled in the syllable-based theory. (b) The syllable theory has no way to represent contour tones when one tone of a contour is phonologically unspecified (see section 5). In Makonde, long syllables display a contrast between rising and falling tones. As discussed in Odden (1990b), L toned moras are represented phonologically with no tone, and surface L tone is assigned by a late rule of default tone assignment. The moraic theory easily represents the contrast between *chikáapu* "basket" and *vamaáka* "cats".

(20) (a)   (b)

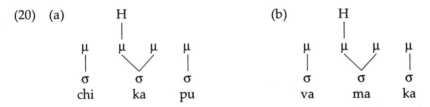

Since there *are* no L tones in the (early) phonology of Makonde, if tones link to syllables, there is no way to represent this contrast.

Another possibility, suggested in Clark (1990), is that tone features are under the Laryngeal node, and therefore are segmental features. This view runs into many problems, especially that of counting moras in a language like Kikuria, and it is hard to see how tone preservation resulting from vowel deletion would be handled, since by making tone a segmental feature, there is no reason for it and it alone to be preserved when all other features of the vowel delete. However, the laryngeal tone theory draws some support from the fact that tone interacts with laryngeal features in synchronic phonologies. The phonetically expected interaction is for voiceless obstruents to "act like" they have H tone, and for voiced obstruents to "act like" they have L tone. This may be manifested in a number of ways. Spreading of H in Bade (Chadic: Nigeria) is blocked by voiced obstruents (Schuh 1978a).

(21) (a) nə́n kàtáw   →   nə́n ká'táw   "I returned"
     (b) nə́n làwáw   →   nə́n lá'wáw   "I ran"
     (c) nə́n gàfáw   →   nə́n gàfáw   "I caught"

In Nupe (Kwa: Nigeria), L spreading is blocked by voiceless obstruents (George 1970).

(22) (a) /èbé/   →   èbě   "pumpkin"
     (b) /èlé/   →   èlě   "past"
     (c) /èfú/   →   èfú   "honey"

If a complete identification of tonal and phonatory features were made, in such a way that the feature for voicing *is* the feature for L tone and the feature for voicelessness is the feature for H tone, then such effects could be explained in terms of the ban against crossing association lines.

(23)   e b e   e f u

       L ⌐ ⌐   ⌐⌐⌐

       L   H   L H H

Phonological tone-consonant interactions are actually rare; there are many languages where the phonatory features of consonants are transparent to tone spreading, and only a few where they are not. In Digo (Bantu: Kenya, Tanzania; Kisseberth 1984) and in the Nguni languages (Bantu: South Africa; Khumalo 1987) where interactions between tone and consonant type are found, early rules treat voiced and voiceless consonants alike, making them transparent to tone rules. It is only later in the grammar that voiced obstruents influence tone, blocking rightward spreading of H in Digo (*anafúrukǔtâ* → *anafúrúkútâ* "(s)he is moving about restlessly" but *akasúrubǐkâ* → *akasúrúbǐkâ* "(s)he has thatched with"), and causing insertion of L in Zulu (*ízihlâlo* → *izǐhlâlo* "seats").

Certain peculiar cases remain unexplained. As noted in section 3, verb stems in Kanakuru (Chadic: Nigeria) beginning with a voiced obstruent have the tone pattern HL (*bómbə́lè* "to scrape"), and those beginning with a voiceless obstruent have LH (*tə̀kə̀lé* "to trick"). Stems beginning with sonorants take either LH or HL (*lùkùré* "to disperse", *lápə̀rè* "to hold down"). While there is a correlation between tone and phonation, it is not the expected one: voiced obstruents should be followed by L, not H, and voiceless obstruents should be followed by H not L. In Ewe (Stahlke 1971; Clements and Halle 1983) the noun prefix has M tone if the stem begins with a sonorant (*ā-ɲígbá* "floor"), but has L tone if the stem begins with an obstruent, voiced or voiceless (*à-gbádzé* "reed sieve", *à-šíké* "tail"). At this point, the most that one can say is that there are a number of good candidates for the TBU, and further work is required to give a definitive answer to this question.

2.2 Tone Features

The theory of tone features is faced with two problems. The first is stating what the features are for distinctive pitch levels. The second, unique to tone among phonological phenomena, is downstep and upstep.

Yip (1980b) postulates two features, a register feature [upper] and a tone feature [High] which allows the following tonal representations.

(24)

	Raised H	H	Mid	Low
Upper	+	+	−	−
High	+	−	+	−

This model predicts that there could be partial tonal assimilation, where tonal register assimilates without making the tones identical. Viewing tone height as a continuous function, such rules would appear to "skip over" a phonetically intermediate tone. Ewe has a rule raising M to R when flanked by H tones.

(25) a. /ākplɔ̄ mēgbé/ → ākplɔ̄ mēgbé "behind a spear"
      b. /ētɔ́ mēgbé/ → ētɔ̄ mɛ́gbé "behind a mortar"
      c. /ēkpé mēgbé/ → ekpɛ́ mɛ́gbé "behind a stone"

This spreads the register feature [+upper] from the surrounding [+upper, –high] H tones to the [–upper, +high] M and deletes the existing [–upper] designation, giving not H tone but R tone.

(26)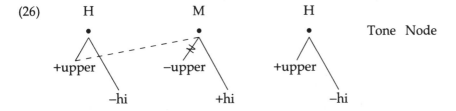

One problem with this model is that it does not allow more than four tone levels. But languages with five levels do exist: Hollenbach (1984) mentions Copala Trique, Ticuna, Ivory Coast Dan, and Kporo as examples. The greatest number of tone levels in any language is found in Chori (Plateau: Nigeria), with six surface levels. Dihoff (1976) points out that dictionary entries require only three underlying tones, namely level 1 (the highest), 4, and 6 (the lowest). Most cases of tone 2 come from a rule turning a 4 tone into 2 before 1. Tones 3 and 5 can be derived from underlying contour tones, where 1̲6 → 3 and 2̲6 → 5. These systems could be handled by an enrichment of the Yip model, adding a third feature to give distinctions between primary register, secondary register, and tone feature. It would then be possible for a language to distinguish eight levels of tone, though the extreme rarity, if not downright absence, of such systems could be attributed to perceptual problems with maintaining such a rich surface tone system.

Describing downstep and downdrift is more challenging. Downstep and downdrift canonically describe lowering of pitch range at the transition from L to H tones (Welmers 1959). The following Shona example is composed of alternating L and H tones, but the pitch level of the L syllables or of the H syllables is not identical. This is due to downdrift, whereby pitch level is lowered at every transition from L to H. Pitch lowering can progress to the point that a H tone relatively late in the utterance has a lower pitch than an earlier L.

(27)   zvavákadána   bhúku

Pitch lowering can be contrastive (and is then termed downstep), as in Kenyang (Mamfe Bantu: Cameroon), where the site of pitch lowering is notated with ¡.

(28)   é'béy 'mé'mwét   "it hurts me"

Upstep (pitch raising) also exists. In Kimatuumbi (Bantu: Tanzania), adjacent H tones are separated by upstep (notated with ⁱ).

(29)   baatʄ'lyá ⁱkʄⁱndyé "they ate the birds"

Earlier literature on downdrift postulated rules performing arithmetic manipulations. In Peters (1973), initial L has the value [3pitch], initial H has [1pitch], and all other vowels have [0pitch]. H toned vowels are given the value [−2pitch] after L, and L toned vowels are given the value [+3pitch] after H; subsequently every vowel is given a pitch value equal to the sum of its own pitch value and that of the preceding syllable.

(30)

L	H	L	H	L	H	
3	0	0	0	0	0	Initialization
3	−2	+3	−2	+3	−2	Contextual adjustment
3	1	4	2	5	3	Surface pitch value

Clements (1979) points out many problems with this approach. The most cogent, from a contemporary perspective, is that it gives phonologies the power to do integer arithmetic, a level of descriptive power which is unwarranted.

Clements (1981b) proposes a hierarchical account of lexical tone and phrasal pitch readjustments. In this theory, tone levels are represented as tonal matrices containing multiple rows of *h*, *l*, and Ø.[3] Specifying a tone in the first row with *h* or *l* indicates that the tone is in the upper or lower register respectively; *h* or *l* in the second row indicates the higher or lower tone within that register. Such a two-row system allows four levels of tone.

(31) Raised High   High   Mid   Low
　　　h   h   l   l
　　　h   l   h   l

This is similar to Yip (1980b). By extending the representation in a fashion analogous to metrical trees, the formalism gives a representation for downstep and upstep. The Shona example (27) would be treated as follows. Every *h* after *l* begins a new tonal foot, which includes the maximum string of tones not already in a tonal foot. Any remaining tones are gathered into a foot, and feet are grouped into a right-branching tree labeled [h, l].

(32)

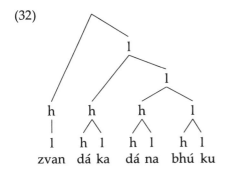

Starting at the top, tones dominated by *h* on the left branch (the L of *zva*) are produced in a higher register than those dominated by *l* (the remaining tones). Within that right branch, tones dominated by *h* (*ndáka*) have a higher pitch register than those dominated by *l* (the remaining tones); this interpretation procedes to the bottom of the tree, with any tones dominated by *h* being in a higher register than those dominated by a sister *l*.

Reversing the direction of the tree and the labeling gives upstep: each *h* forms a tonal foot, and a left-branching tree labeled [l, h] is built.

(33)

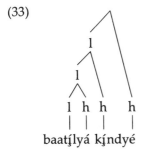

Downstep is handled quite naturally in this framework, at least in the majority of cases where it arises because of a floating or linked L tone between H tones. Tree construction operates entirely on the tonal string, where a floating *l* serves as the trigger for tonal foot construction just as linked *l*'s do in (32). Not all phonemic pitch lowering occurs because of floating L tones. In Kishambaa (Bantu: Tanzania; Odden 1982b), Supyire (Gur: Mali; Carlson 1983) and Temne (West Atlantic: Sierra Leone; Nemer and Mountford 1984), any time two H tones are concatenated, a downstep emerges between the H's. The following example from Kishambaa can be accounted for by generalizing the rule for building tonal feet. Each *h* begins a tonal foot, without the requirement for a preceding *l*.

(34)

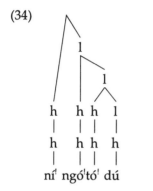

nímí ngóʼtóʼ dú   "It's just a sheep"

3   Wellformedness and the Association Conventions

Autosegmental phonology has put great emphasis on questions of representations. The fundamental principle in Goldsmith (1976a) governing tone-vowel linkages is the Wellformedness Condition in (35).

(35)   All vowels are associated with at least one tone;
        All tones are associated with at least one vowel.
        Association lines do not cross.

Violation of this condition is repaired in the simplest way possible: insertion or deletion of association lines is simpler than insertion or deletion of auto-segments. Multiple ways of satisfying the Wellformedness Condition exist, so it is taken to be preferable to link a tone to a vowel which does not already bear a tone, and it is preferred to link an unassociated tone with a vowel. The theory does not include a universal algorithm for attaining a well-formed state. However, in the vast majority of cases, there is only one simplest way to satisfy the Wellformedness Condition. If there are more vowels than tones in a string, the tones and vowels are linked one-to-one from left to right,[4] until the tonal string is exhausted (given the preference to not reassociate an element already associated). When the last tone is linked to a vowel, that tone spreads to the remaining vowels, since now there is no possibility of satisfying the Wellformedness Condition without reassociating the already associated final tone.

(36)   one-to-one   spreading of
        mapping   associated tone

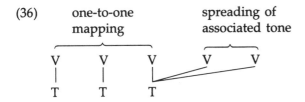

Clements and Ford (1979) propose three explicit association conventions. The first exhaustively matches free tones and free vowels in a one-to-one fashion after an existing tone-vowel link.

(37)   V V_k V_{k+1} ··· V_{k+n}
        | | | |
        | | | |
       T ... T_i T_{i+1} ··· T_{i+n}

The second links a free tone to the maximal sequence of free vowels providing the tone is neither proceded nor followed by a free tone.

(38)   V   V   V $\begin{pmatrix} V \\ | \\ T \end{pmatrix}$

           T

The third spreads a linked tone to the maximal sequence of free vowels (given a choice, not a tone linked to an accented TBU, and preferably a tone from the left).

(39)   (−*)

       V V_Q
        |
       T

Besides providing an explicit characterization of how the Wellformedness Condition is satisfied, these conventions have empirical differences from Goldsmith's approach.

First, floating tones are not required to automatically dock to a neighboring vowel which already bears a tone. This is motivated in the analysis of Kikuyu downstep, which they argue is a floating L that remains floating throughout the phonology. From this it follows that creating a contour tone comes about by a language-specific rule docking a floating tone to a syllable already bearing a tone.

Second, the one-to-one mapping of tones to vowels is implemented by the first convention (37), which requires that there already be a vowel-tone association. Therefore, one-to-one mapping must be preceded by a language-specific rule, the Initial Tone Association Rule, which associates some tone with some vowel. Generally, the first tone associates with the first vowel, but in Kikuyu, the first tone associates with the second vowel. It is claimed that the conventions come into effect immediately after application of the Initial Tone Association Rule.[6]

Finally, the conventions resolve an ambiguity in Goldsmith's approach. In a structure such as (40), either tone could spread to the free vowel, given that both tones are already associated (and therefore the preference to not spread associated material has no effect). The Clements and Ford conventions state that the tone on the left will spread.

(40)   V   V   V
       | |
       T   T

Although Clements and Ford reject the assumption that floating tones automatically link to vowels already bearing a tone, such a convention was at the heart of the autosegmental analysis of tone preservation. Clements and Ford offer an alternative convention which reassociates *floated* tones without incorrectly requiring that all floating tones dock to a vowel. In Lomongo the first of two vowels deletes, and tones thereby freed shift to the following vowel (so *balóngo bǎkáé* → *balóng´ǎkáé* → *balóng ãkáé*), but in Ewe, the second of two vowels deletes and the resulting floating tones shift to the preceding vowel (*mēkpɔ́ ètú* → *mēkpɔ́ `tú* → *mēkpɔ̂ tú*). To account for such patterns of tone preservation, Clements and Ford propose that "given two related levels (tiers) L_j, L_k, a segment of level L_j that is 'set afloat' due to a process affecting the segment of level L_k with which it was associated, reassociates to the segment of L_k that conditioned the deletion." (1979, p. 207, n. 18).

Halle and Vergnaud (1982) further restrict the Wellformedness Condition, proposing that automatic spreading only applies to free tones, simultaneously linking a floating tone to all available toneless vowels. Pulleyblank (1986a) argues that the Association Conventions should be further restricted to one-to-one left-to-right linkage of free tones and free vowels. All forms of automatic spreading are rejected, and where spreading exists, it results from language-specific rule. The argument for rejecting automatic spreading of tones to free vowels is that there are languages such as Tiv (Bantoid: Nigeria) which allow linked tones before toneless vowels throughout the phonology.

The underlying representation of the General Past tense 'yévèsè "fled" is as follows.

(41)   yevese
              |
     L   H

By (39), the H tone should spread to all vowels, giving *'yévésé. But since there is no rule in Tiv which spreads H here, and by hypothesis there is no universal convention spreading tones, we do not derive the incorrect form.[7]
There is evidence that even one-to-one docking of free tones to free vowels is not universal, since there are languages with words having free vowels and floating tones persisting into the phrasal phonology. Such cases arise in Kikuria (Odden 1987c) and Chiyao (Bantu: East Africa). In Chiyao, every verb stem is assigned a floating H, which is mapped either to the first or to the second stem vowel, as determined by the tense-aspect of the verb (see section 2.1 for a similar system in Kikuria). In the far past negative, the H is linked to the second stem vowel (that H may spread to the following nonfinal syllable). If there is no second stem vowel, the H just floats, and the stem surfaces as toneless.

(42) (a)   nganina-[ga-lyá   "I didn't eat them"
      (b)   nganiin-[deléka   "I didn't cook"
      (c)   nganiim-[bilíkána   "I didn't hear"
      (d)   nganiin-[dya   "I didn't eat"

There is evidence that this floating H is present postlexically. There is a rule in Chiyao assigning H to the first vowel of any word preceded by a toneless stem.

(43) (a)   mandaanda   "eggs"
      (b)   a-[suume mándaanda   "he should buy eggs"
      (c)   cháá-[teleche mándaanda "he will cook eggs"
      (d)   a-[telééche mandaanda   "he cooked eggs"
      (e)   aka-[téléche mandaanda   "he should go cook eggs"

We saw that in the far past negative (42), the H is linked to the second stem vowel, and if there is only a single vowel in the stem, there is no H on the surface. The phrasal insertion of H after a toneless stem gives us a way of detecting the floating stem H tone. In (44) we see that the floating H of monomoraic stems blocks phrasal assignment of H.

(44) nganaa-[ng'wa mandaanda   "he didn't drink the eggs"
              H

This suggests that one-to-one docking of free tones and vowels is also governed by language-specific rules. Mende-style floating tone melodies, which depend on one-to-one linking of tones to vowels, are rare and even the celebrated Mende case can be reanalyzed with tones all lexically prelinked.[8]

Some languages have been claimed to employ right-to-left linking of tones and vowels, rather than left-to-right linking. Newman (1986b) proposes this for Hausa, based on the fact that certain suffixes seem to expand their tone to the left, not the right, as left-to-right mapping would predict. Illustrating the LLH pattern of the suffix *-aCCee* mapped right-to-left, we find *dàf-áffée* "cooked" and *gàagàr-árrée* "unmanageable". However, Leben (1985) reanalyses these suffixes as having a floating L tone preceding a lexically linked H on the initial vowel.

(45)   gaagar arree
         |
       L H

Hausa, then, does not seem to make a case for right-to-left linking.

Kanakuru (Newman 1974) provides better evidence for right-to-left linking. Stems either have the tone pattern HL or LH subject to the condition that if the stem begins with a voiced stop the stem selects the pattern HL, and if the initial is voiceless, the pattern LH is selected. Stems with an initial vowel or sonorant unpredictably select either HL or LH.

(46)   (a)   ˋtúi   "to eat"   ˋwái   "to get"
       (b)   ˊbùi   "to shoot"   ˊyài   "to arrive at"
       (c)   tùké   "to hide"   wùpé   "to sell"
       (d)   gárè   "to leave"   lákè   "to untie"
       (e)   tàkàlé   "to trick"   lùkúré   "to disperse"
       (f)   bómbálè   "to scrape"   lápárè   "to hold down"

In monosyllabic verbs, the stem is preceded by the first tone of the pattern: floating L is realized as a downstep (mán ˋtúa → mán ˈtúa "we ate it"), and floating H docks to the word creating a falling tone, or else docks to the preceding word (nà´ gài → ná gài ~ nà gâi "I entered it"). In trisyllabic words, the first two syllables always bear the first tone of the melody, and the last vowel alone bears the final tone of the melody. In short, the distribution of tones in Kanakuru is the mirror image of Mende. This falls out from assuming that Kanakuru selects the marked option of right-to-left mapping.

(47)   (a)   tui   (b)   tuke   (c)   təkəle
                 | | | \/ |
               L H   L H   L H

4   The Obligatory Contour Principle

One of the most controversial principles relating to representations in phonology, a principle later called the Obligatory Contour Principle (OCP) is assumed in Leben (1973, 1978) and is formulated in Goldsmith (1976a) as "at the melodic level of the grammar, any two adjacent tonemes must be distinct. Thus HHL is not a possible melodic pattern; it automatically simplifies to HL."

The OCP is at the heart of Leben's explanation for the (supposed) lack of words in Mende with the tone patterns CV́CV̂ or CV̀CV̌ (see section 1), which would have the underlying tone melodies HHL and LLH. The OCP prohibits HH and LL, so words with the patterns CV́CV̂ and CV̀CV̌ would not exist.

Actually, the tone patterns CV́CV̂ and CV̀CV̌ do exist in Mende, as pointed out in Dwyer (1978), Leben (1978), Conteh et al. (1983), and Singler (1985), for example *hókpô* "navel" and (in some analyses) *fàndě* (which becomes *fàndé* "cotton" by an independent rule). Different conclusions can be drawn from these examples: Leben (1978) argues for lexical prelinkage of the first tone of the melody to the last vowel for such words; the melodies still obey the OCP. Conteh et al. and Singler conclude that these words have the melodies LLH and HHL, violating the OCP. Mende has no phonological processes which can be called on to arbitrate this dispute, so it is not certain what the correct representation of such words is.

Odden (1986a) surveys a number of cases relevant to the OCP, showing that a blanket prohibition against adjacent identical tones is untenable. In Shona, the OCP holds of underlying representations, but not of derived representations. In section 1 it was seen that there is a rule lowering the first H of a stem (which may be linked to a number of vowels) after "associative" prefixes, whereby /né-mbúndúdzí/ becomes *né-mbundudzi* "with army worms". All nouns beginning with a string of H tones lower the entire initial string of H's: we do not find nouns such as hypothetical **hwáhwáhwá* which lower only the H's of the first, or first two, syllables of the stem, giving **né-hwahwáhwá* or **né-hwahwahwá*. In short, representations such as (48a), which obeys the OCP, are allowed, but ones such as (48b) and (48c), which violate the OCP, are not.

(48)   (a)   mbundundzi   (b)   *hwahwahwa   (c)   hwahwahwa

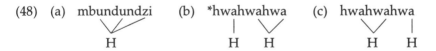

While we do not find multiple adjacent H's within morphemes, we do find them across morphemes. An associative prefix may precede an associative prefix (which has an underlying H tone), resulting in multiple H tones. The examples in (49) show that the Lowering rule iterates from left to right through the string of H's. If a prefix has a H tone, it lowers the following H, which may be the H of another prefix; if the prefix has a L tone (because its underlying H has been lowered), then the prefix does not lower the following H.

(49)   né-e-hóvé   "with of fish"
       sé-ne-é-hove   "like with of fish"

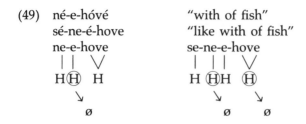

Were the OCP an active derivational constraint in Shona, such representations would be impossible – we would expect the multiple H tone autosegments to fuse into a single H associated with a multitude of vowels. Instead, it serves as a filter defining well-formed underlying lexical entries.

In some languages, such as Kishambaa, the OCP does not even hold for underlying representations. It was seen in section 2.2 that adjacent H's in Kishambaa are separated by a downstep. For instance, we find that /ní kúi/ surfaces as *ní¹ kúi* "it is a dog", and /a-ngé-lyá/ surfaces as *angé¹lyá* "he should eat". However, we do not find downstep between every two syllables with H tones. One place where adjacent H's persist not separated by downstep is in the output of H tone spreading, whereby /ní kughoshoa/ becomes *ní kúghóshóa* "it is to do". The lack of downsteps between these H tones is expected, since in reality, there is a single H, linked to multiple vowels.

(50)   ni kughoshoa
           \|/
            H

The significance of Kishambaa for the OCP is that there is a contrast within stems between a multiply-attached H tone (obeying the OCP) which surfaces as CV́CV́ and a sequence of H's (violating the OCP) which surfaces as CV́¹CV́.

(51)   (a)   nyóká   "snake"   (b)   ngó¹tó   "sheep"
                 \/ | |
                  H   H H

In other languages, such as Kipare (Bantu: Tanzania), there is an active tone-fusing version of the OCP which combines adjacent H's arising even at the phrasal level into one multiply-linked H. A prepausal sequence of H's becomes L after a floating L (otherwise realized as a downstep).

(52)   /vá¹ná vékíjílá nkhúkú ndórí nkhúndú jángú/
       [vána vekijila nkhuku ndori nkhundu jangu]
       "while the children eat those little red chickens of mine"
       [vá¹ná vékíjílá nkhúkú ndórí nkhúndú jángú θáno]
       "while the children eat those five little red chickens of mine"

We can explain the across-the-board lowering of multiple H's by postulating that there is one H in such cases.

(53)

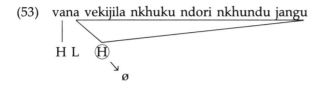

Underlyingly, however, there are multiple H's: each word (*nkhúkú* "chickens", *nkhúndú* "red" and *ndórí* "little") contributes an H, and in some words (*vé-kí-lá* "while they eat", *já-ngú* "my"), each morpheme contributes an H. The situation in Kipare, while similar to Shona in illustrating multiply-attached tones, is different since we find across-the-board lowering of H's standing in different morphemes or even different words. The explanation for this is that a phrase-level rule in Kipare fuses multiple adjacent H tones. Such a rule can be seen as a way of satisfying the OCP in a derivation; Shona does not exploit this option.

An OCP based explanation for other tonal phenomena may be considered. A common rule in Bantu languages, Meeussen's Rule (Goldsmith 1984a), deletes H after H. An example will be considered from the Chimahuta dialect of Makonde. In the future tense, the penultimate syllable has a H tone. If the verb is inflected for 3rd person subject, the initial stem syllable also has H.

(54) (a) tuna-[chi-kaláánga   "we will fry it"
       (b) vana-[chí-kaláánga   "they will fry it"
       (c) nna-[telééka   "I will cook"

When the stem-initial and penultimate H's are on adjacent syllables, for example /vanatéleéka/, the second H tone deletes, giving the surface form *vanatéleeka* "they will cook". This is consistent with the OCP, since the input contains two adjacent H's and thus violates the OCP. Not all languages have such H tone deletion rules, and even languages which exhibit some OCP symptoms (e.g., Karanga Shona, with its Associative Lowering rule and morpheme-internal version of the OCP) may still leave sequences of H tones undisturbed, for example *nda-ká-tórá* "I took", where the H of the prefix *ka* stands before the H of the verb root *tórá* without causing lowering of any tones. Interestingly, in the Zezuru dialect, there is lowering of the verbal H, so we get *ndakátora*. And in Arusa (Nilotic: Tanzania; Levergood 1989) there is long-distance phrase-final lowering of H if a H precedes, no matter how far apart the H's stand.

(55) (a) /en-ker sida-y/ → ènkér sìdày   "good ewe"

(b) /ol-orika sida-y/ → òlórìkà sìdày   "good chair"

```
    |      \/
    H      H
```

We have the same dissimilative deletion of H after H which looks like an OCP effect, though the H's are not on adjacent TBU's. A similar long-distance dissimilative effect is found in versions of Meeussen's Rule in some Bantu languages, so for example Kimatuumbi has a rule deleting final H in phrase-medial verbs when a H stands somewhere in the stem; thus /paníjn-tyátya-kjkjyé ñụýmba/ becomes *paníjn-tyátyakjkjye ñụýmba* "when I plastered a house for him". Kihunde (Bantu: Zaire) has a similar rule deleting word-final H when the second stem vowel has H tone – in both cases, the target H and the triggering H to the left may be nonadjacent. But again, long-distance versions of Meeussen's Rule are the exception rather than the rule.

Another phenomenon which may be related to the OCP is blockage of rules that spread or assign H, in case the target syllable is adjacent to a H tone. This can be seen in Karanga Shona, which has a phrase-level rule spreading H from one word into the next word, provided that the initial vowel of the second word is not itself followed by a H toned syllable. In other words, H spreading maintains a buffer syllable between H's, as dictated by the OCP.

(56) (a) ákapá chirongo   →   ákapá chírongo   "he gave a pot"
     (b) ákapá mapadzá   →   ákapá mápadzá   "he gave hoes"
     (c) ákapá murúmé   →   ákapá murúmé   "he gave a man"

This could be explained in terms of the OCP; spreading in the last case would have made H tones stand on adjacent syllables. However, there are just as many languages which allow spreading with no OCP blockage. For example, there are H spreading rules in Kikuria that turn underlying /oko-beebeeta/ first into *okobéébeéta*, then into the phonetic form *okobéébééta* "to sieve": if OCP blockage of spreading were universal, we would expect *okobéébeéta. Spreading or assignment of H in violation of the OCP also occurs in Kihunde (Goldsmith 1986), Kikongo (Bantu: Zaire), Kimatuumbi, and Bukusu (Bantu: Kenya), to name a few examples.

The strongest possible version of the OCP at this point is that there may be a dispreference for adjacent identical tones; languages are free to express this dispreference by constraining lexical representations, by adding rules of tone fusion or tone deletion, or by putting conditions on tone spreading rules. Ultimately, languages retain the option of doing nothing about OCP violations.

5   Underspecification

There has been a significant sentiment in the study of Bantu tone that H and L tones do not have equal status in the grammar. Meeussen (1954), Stevick

(1969), Carter (1971, 1972), Odden (1981), and many others subsequently have proposed in different ways that the contrast is not between two equal members of a two-way opposition, but between a tone – H tone – and lack of tone. L is assigned at some point in the phonology to any vowel which is toneless. This notion is echoed in Pulleyblank (1986a), who grounds this viewpoint in a general theory of feature underspecification and defaults (see chapter 4, this volume).

Pulleyblank proposes two default tone specification rules. One assigns [–upper] to vowels not having a specification for the register feature, and the other assigns [+raised] (=Yip's [+High]) to vowels lacking specification for [raised]. In the context of the underspecification theory adopted there, only [+upper] and [–raised] can be specified in lexical entries; in a four-tone language, underlying representations would be as in (57).

(57) Raised H   High   Mid   Low
      [+upper] $\begin{bmatrix} +\text{upper} \\ -\text{raised} \end{bmatrix}$ [–raised]

In this system (as well as in a three-tone system), M has a special status – it lacks tonal specifications. In a two-tone system, the feature [raised] is superfluous, so the contrast between H and L is expressed as the contrast between H(= [+upper]) and L(= Ø, by default, [–upper]), so in a two-tone system L has properties like those of M in three- and four-tone languages.[9]

Four arguments support tonal underspecification and default rules. First, in a three-tone language, neutralization of tonal contrasts by tone deletion will be to M. An example of this can be seen in Nama (Khoisan: South Africa; Hagman 1977). Reduplication of the root in the causative has the tonal effect that the tones of the second copy of the root all become M.

(58) (a) !óm̄   "difficult"   !óm̄!ōm̄   "make difficult"
      (b) pùrú   "wonder"   pùrúpūrū   "cause to wonder"

This can be explained by letting reduplication copy the segmental tier, but not the tonal tier. The copy is unspecified for tone, so its vowels receive M by applying the default rules for tone.

Margi (Chadic: Nigeria; Hoffman 1963) points to further motivation for context-free rules assigning tone feature values to toneless vowels. Verb roots and suffixes in this language fall into three tonal groups: H, L and "changing."[10] Changing roots and suffixes are simply toneless, and assimilate the tone of the neighboring morpheme.

(59)   H suffix
      H root   tá + bá → tábá   "cook all"
      L root   ndàl + bá → ndàlbá   "throw out"
      Toneless root   ɗəl + bá → ɗə́lbá   "buy"

	L suffix	
H root	ná + ɗà → náɗà	"give me"
L root	hə̀ì + ɗà → hə̀rɗà	"bring me"
Toneless root	skə + ɗà → skə̀ɗà	"wait for me"
	Toneless suffix	
H root	tá + na → táná	"cook and put aside"
L root	ndàl + na → ndàlnà	"throw away"

These patterns follow from postulating that the underlyingly toneless "changing" morphemes undergo a rule spreading tone from one vowel to a neighboring toneless vowel. But once we grant that there can be toneless morphemes, there is no guarantee that a toneless morpheme such as *ɗəl* will always be joined with a morpheme having an underlying tone. Systematically, toneless roots combined with toneless suffixes result in words with all L tones, so /ɗəl+na/ surfaces as *ɗə̀lnà* "to sell". The existence of default rules for tone assignment serves as a guarantee that such words will be pronounceable.

An argument for default rules assigning M tone to toneless vowels, and for treating M as the lack of tonal specification underlyingly, derives from the phonologically asymmetrical status of M in Yoruba (Kwa: Nigeria). Although there are rightward spreading rules creating contour tones out of H and L tones, M tones can never be the first or second member of a contour tone.

(60)	(a)	ó pò̩	→	ó pô̩	"it is plentiful"
	(b)	ò̩ré̩	→	ò̩rě̩	"friendship"
	(c)	ò̩bē̩	↛	*ò̩bè̩	"knife"
	(d)	ōjú	↛	*ōjǔ	"eye"

If M is phonologically the lack of tone specification, then it follows that one cannot create a contour tone composed of some tone plus nothing, hence the lack of contours involving M tone is explained.[11]

The final and most powerful argument for leaving some tones unspecified is the phonological transparency of L in a number of languages (under the assumption that L and H are characterized by the same feature(s) and are on the same tier). As noted in section 4, Arusa has a rule lowering a prepausal H tone preceded by a H tone anywhere in the phrase. The H tones may be separated by syllables which have surface L tones. In the following examples, a sequence of H tones within a word is represented as a single H tone linked to multiple vowels, hence the across-the-board lowering of what seem to be multiple H tones.

(61)	(a)	/ènkér sídáy/	→	ènkér sìdày	"good ewe"
	(b)	/òl-órìkà sídáy/	→	òlórìkà sìdày	"good chair"

If the L toned syllables of *òlórìkà* have L tones when Lowering applies, then the L standing between the two H's in the last example should block lowering. A further interesting point about the specification of L tones in Arusa is that the L component of a falling tone (which is contrastive in Arusa) is *not* underspecified. For example, if the phrase-final word ends in a falling tone, lowering does not apply (*ènkér kùrêt* "cowardly ewe"). Second, if the preceding H is part of a falling tone, there is no lowering (*òl-kìlâŋéjúk* "new garment"). In precisely these two cases, L cannot be assigned by a default rule, since a contour-toned syllable would already bear a H tone, and would therefore be ineligible to undergo a tonal default rule. Hence L is not unspecified when it is part of a contour tone.

6 Accent

The notion that "tone languages" are distinct from "accent languages" is a rather old one. Trubetzkoy (1969, p. 184) states that "distinctive oppositions of tone register must not be confused with the so-called musical accent." In the preautosegmental period, as exemplified by McCawley (1970, 1978) and Hyman (1978a, 1978b), attempts were made to formalize the difference between tone and accent, drawing initially on Japanese, Tonga (Bantu: Zambia) and Luganda (Bantu: Uganda). Accent is treated as a distinctive feature, which in McCawley (1968) is directly translated into pitch integers. Hyman (1981) similarly translates accents in Somali (Cushitic: East Africa) directly into pitch integers, bypassing tones entirely.

It has been a matter of controversy whether there is a legitimate distinction between tone and accent languages, and if there is such a distinction, what the criteria are for treating a language tonally versus accentually – in fact, there are languages which have been analyzed as tonal and accentual by the same authors. In the earlier typological studies of Hyman and McCawley, it was noted that languages tend to exhibit different properties, depending on whether they are accentual or tonal. A sharp dichotomy between tone and accent emerged relatively early in the history of this study, based largely on McCawley's contrasts between Chinese and Japanese. The most widely accepted differences between tone and accent were the following.

Tone	Accent
For a language with n tones, the number of contrasting tonal patterns in words with k syllables approaches k^n: each syllable has its own tone, with no regard for the tone of other syllables of the word.	The number of contrasts in words with k syllables approaches $k+1$: at most one syllable (perhaps no syllable) in the morpheme is identified as bearing an accent.
Phonological rules are triggered by tones of an immediately adjacent syllable.	Phonological rules may apply over great distances.

Rules are assimilatory or dissimilatory (as discussed in Hyman and Schuh 1974).	Rules are primarily insertion, deletion, and movement of accents.

But as noted in later works, especially McCawley (1978), languages are not wholly tonal or wholly accentual. Rather, certain earlier stages of a derivation are accentual, and later stages are tonal.

The "autosegmental accent" theory is set forth for Tonga in Goldsmith (1976a) and worked out in more detail in Goldsmith (1984b). In this framework, accent (notated with a star) is not an intrinsic phonetic property, and therefore is not represented as a distinctive feature. Rather, accent is a formal structural object which governs the autosegmental derivation. Vowels may be unaccented, or have an accent.[12] An accent language defines a particular tone melody, one tone of which is starred. One copy of this tone melody is inserted for each accent, and accented vowels and accented tones are linked (one-to-one, left-to-right), whereupon the normal association conventions apply.

The view that tones and segments are underlyingly separated was pursued in early autosegmental phonology to the point that in Goldsmith (1976a) there are no lexical linkings between tones and vowels.[13] In many cases where tone-vowel linkages cannot be predicted, the unpredictable linkage is encoded by accenting the relevant vowel, so that the Wellformedness Condition will link the starred tone and vowel. For example, under Goldsmith's analysis of Tonga, words have the melody HL, where L is associated with a lexically specified vowel of the stem (and all vowels thereafter), and H is associated with preceding vowels.

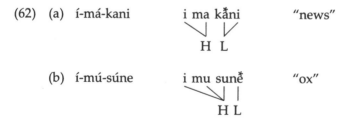

(62)   (a)   í-má-kani   i ma kǎni   "news"

      (b)   í-mú-súne   i mu suně   "ox"

In this account, rather than shifting, inserting, or deleting tones, one shifts, inserts, or deletes accents; since presence of accent usually entails presence of H tone, these manipulations result indirectly in changes in tone. For instance, certain stems (*i-ma-tongo* "ruins") are underlyingly unaccented – on the surface they lack H tone. Since surface L (and H) tones arise only when an accentually-driven tone melody is inserted, there is no apparent source for the surface L tones. An accent is therefore assigned by rule to the word-initial vowel, allowing the tonal sequence HL to be inserted (giving i̇-ma-tongo – however there being no contour-toned vowels in Tonga, this surfaces as *i-ma-tongo*, with all low toned vowels.).

Another operation, accent deletion (Meeussen's Rule; see section 4), deletes an accent after an accent. Underlying /bǎ-la-bǎ-bǒna/ surfaces as *balábabona* "they see them". Inserting one copy of the tone melody for each accent, mapping L to the accented vowel and linking H to vowels by the WFC, we would expect **balá' bábona* (derived from *bâlábábona* by a rule deleting the first H in verbs and by decontouring rules of the language).[14]

(63)

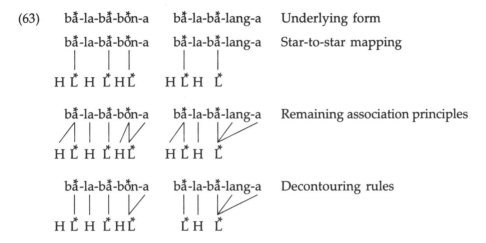

The surface form is analogous to *balábalanga* "they look at them" which derives from /bǎ-la-bǎ-langa/. Yet the two stems are accentually distinct: *lang* is unaccented (cf. *balalanga* "they look" from /ba-la-langa/) and *bon* is accented (cf. *balábona* "they see" from /bǎ-la-bǒna/). This surface neutralization in tone pattern is explained by Meeussen's Rule, which deletes an accent after an accent.

(64) $\overset{*}{V} \rightarrow \overset{\circ}{V} / \overset{*}{V}C \circ$ ____

By this rule expected /bǎ-la-bǎ-bǒna/ becomes /bǎ-la-bǎ-bona/ prior to insertion of the HL tonal melody: inserting two copies of the tone melody and mapping L tones to the accented vowels, we arrive at the surface form.

Accentual analyses are proposed for Somali (Hyman 1981; Banti 1988), Oromo (Cushitic: Ethiopia, Kenya; Banti 1987), Ci-Ruri (Bantu: Tanzania; Massamba 1982, 1984; Goldsmith 1982), Haya (Bantu: Tanzania; Hyman and Byarushengo 1980), Luganda (Hyman 1982a), and Kimatuumbi (Odden 1982b, 1985). The last two languages provided what seemed to be compelling evidence for accents independent of tones, since these languages taken together make a four-way contrast between accented and unaccented H, and accented and unaccented L.

In Luganda, the accentual melody is HL, and the H links to the accented syllable. The H tone of a noun object associates with unaccented vowels of the preceding verb (save for the unaccented initial vowel of *abálá ébíkópo*, which bears an obligatory boundary L).

(65) (a) /a-bal-a/   abala   "he counts"
     (b) /e-bi-kǒpo/   ebikópo   "cups"
     (c) /abala e-bi-kǒpo/   abálá ébíkópo   "he counts cups"
     (d) /a-bǎ-tǎ-lǐ-lǎb-il-a abátalilabílílá ábápákasi "they who will not
         a-ba-pǎkasi/   look after porters"

H spreads to unaccented syllables, but it does not spread to accented syllables (the final example), even though the accented syllables have L tone.

It is claimed that in Kimatuumbi (Odden 1982a, 1985) nouns may accent a single syllable. This syllable receives a H tone and all others receive L. In this account, all underlying H tones are accents, and all derived H tones are inserted as tones, not accents. Thus, /ngalibǎ/ becomes ngalibá "circumciser" and /kị-pǐingili/ becomes kịpíingili. A tone shift rule, Nominal Retraction refers to "unaccented H," which should show the autonomy of tone and accent. By a general rule, a H is assigned to the second vowel of a prepausal unaccented word, so prepausal /lụ-bagalo/ becomes lu-bágalo "lath" and /m-bagalo/ becomes m-bagálo "laths". Nominal Retraction shifts word-final H of CVCV noun stems to the stem-initial syllable, as long as the final syllable is unaccented. This means that a shiftable H is assigned by secondary tone rules, and is not an underlying (hence accented) H. Unaccented nouns of the type CVCV unexpectedly manifest their prepausal H on the initial vowel of the word, so /ñama/ surfaces as ñáma "meat", not *ñamá. But final accented H does not shift: /mbakǎ/ becomes mbaká "cat", not *mbáka.[15] Hence the retraction rule only targets unaccented H's, as distinct from accented H's.

The validity of "autosegmental accent" is questioned in Hyman (1982b), Pulleyblank (1984) and (1986), and Hyman and Byarushengo (1984). Rather than specifying a vowel with an accent, one could link the vowel to its tone in underlying representations. The argument against accent is its excess power, in comparison to lexical prelinking of tones. In an accentual system, it would be possible for the tonal melody of one morpheme to link to an accented vowel of another morpheme. In a prelinked-tone system (i.e., where "accented" vowels are lexically prelinked to their tones), this is an impossibility. Such "cross-morpheme prelinking" appears to be unattested.[16] Second, rules in an accent system can refer to tones, accents, or tones and accents. Rules in a strictly tonal grammar can only refer to tones, so are more constrained. Finally, there is no parallelism between accents and tone melodies in the segmental domain; we do not find "continuant melodies" centering around "accented consonants."

Pulleyblank points out that the argument for accent based on limited distribution of tone is not compelling.[17] First, it is arbitrary to attribute a limit of one locus of pitch contrast per morpheme to accent but not tone. Such limitations, though not common, are known from segmental phonology (e.g., Japanese only allows one specification [+voice]; see Itô and Mester 1986) but such facts have not generally caused segmental phonology to be treated accentually.[18] The accentual accounts of Kimatuumbi and Haya actually overgenerate, in the sense that in Kimatuumbi one would expect four syllable stems to have five surface tone patterns (any syllables could have accent, or the stem could be unaccented), but in fact there are only three tone patterns. The accentual analysis must still stipulate restrictions on the location of accent. Finally, while a restriction of one main stress per word falls out of the formal properties of a metrical word tree, autosegmental accent does not have those properties, so there is no theoretical basis for the supposed one-per-morpheme restriction.

Pulleyblank reanalyzes Goldsmith's accentual account of Tonga. Earlier accentual analyses have been reanalyzed (by the authors of the original accentual analyses), namely Haya (Hyman and Byarushengo 1984), Luganda (Hyman 1982b) and Kimatuumbi (Odden 1989a). It is shown there that the accented L and unaccented H phenomena of Luganda and Kimatuumbi can be handled without recourse to accents independent of tones.

More recently, a number of "accentual" analyses of tone in Bantu languages have been set forth. These analyses differ from the earlier analyses, in that accent is construed as metrical prominence. The earliest analysis within that framework is an analysis of Kimatuumbi in Pulleyblank (1983b). Subsequent analyses within the metrical accent approach include Goldsmith (1987a, 1987b, 1992b), Goldsmith, Peterson and Drogo (1989), Peterson (1989), and Downing (1990) for Nguni; Kenstowicz (1987) and Kisseberth (1991) for Chizigua (Bantu: Tanzania), Cassimjee and Kisseberth (1989) for Shingazidja (Bantu: Comoros); Sietsema (1989) for Kimatuumbi, Ciruri, Digo, and Sukuma (Bantu: Tanzania), and Bickmore (1989) for Runyambo (Bantu: Tanzania). In this approach, formal analogies between metrical systems and tone are sought: these include long-distance operation, binary groupings, and quantity sensitivity.

The fundamental question which arises in these recent discussions of (metrical) accent and tone is why H is attracted to certain positions. For example, in Chizigua (Kisseberth 1991), the rightmost H in a word is assigned to the penultimate syllable, no matter where the H arose.

(66) (a) /ku-lómbez-a/ → ku-lombéza   "to request"
   (b) /ku-lómbez-ez-a/ → ku-lombez-éz-a   "to request for"
   (c) /ku-lómbez-ez-an-a/ → ku-lombez-ez-án-a   "to request for each other"
   (d) /n-a-wá-tohol-a/ → n-a-wa-tohóla   "I am loosening them"

What makes the shift to penult suspicious is that the penultimate syllable is a common position for metrical stress, inviting the inference that H is attracted to a metrically prominent syllable. Spreading of H to the antepenultimate syllable is found in the Nguni languages (Goldsmith, Peterson and Drogo 1989; Downing 1990), by which underlying /ú-ku-namathelisa/ becomes *úkúnámáthélisa* (and in Zulu, *ukunamathélisa* by a later rule of tone delinking). Again, antepenultimate position is a known target for stress assignment.

Van der Hulst and Smith (1988) observe that in some languages, tones are attracted to accented syllables (Eastern Norwegian, Copala Trique), and H toned syllables receive accent (Fasu; see Hyman 1978b). This correlation is recognized in the Tone-Accent Attraction Condition (Goldsmith 1987b, 1992b):

> A tone-to-grid structure is well-formed if and only if there is no tone-bearing syllable which has a lower level of accent than a toneless syllable. [Thus, if a syllable S has a tone, all syllables with a greater level of accent than S must also bear tone.]

Accounting for tone spreading in a principled way is even more important when one considers the descriptive apparatus which seems to be required using strictly tonal devices. Spread of H to the antepenultimate syllable in the Nguni languages would necessitate a rule such as the following.

(67)   H

$\uparrow$ $\diagdown$

σ σ σ σ

This rule would iterate through the word, reapplying as long as there are at least two vowels following the syllable taking the H. The operation terminates at the antepenult (*úkúnámáthélisa*), since there are no longer the requisite number of syllables after that point.

A widely held desideratum in phonological theory – indeed much of the motivation for nonlinear phonology and one of the outstanding problems of linear phonology – is that rules should be "local." Though there are many unresolved problems in the locality issue, it is generally agreed that a local rule formulation would only allow specification of one element to the right and/or left of the focus. Formulations such as (67) are patently nonlocal.

In the analyses of Nguni in Goldsmith, Peterson, and Drogo (1989), Peterson (1989), and Downing (1990), the antepenultimate syllable is made metrically prominent by rendering the final syllable extrametrical, and constructing a left-headed binary foot at the end of the word. The Zulu form /ú-ku-namathelisa/ is accented as /ú-ku-namathělisa/. Subsequently the H tone spreads to the accented syllable (because of the Tone-Accent Attraction Condition) giving /ú-kúnámáthělisa/, and after deleting all but the last branch of a multi-attached H, we arrive at *ukunamathélisa* "to make stick".[19]

A second – and, though less well documented, potentially more compelling argument – for interaction between tone and metrical structure comes from tone alternations where one must parse syllables or moras into groups of two to get the correct forms. Note that the only mechanism for grouping prosodic elements into binary units is metrical structure. One way in which binary grouping might be detected would be to find a language where H is assigned to every other syllable. Pulleyblank (1983b) makes the claim that Kimatuumbi acts in this way: starting leftward from the lexically specified accent, binary tone feet are formed on the mora, and H tone is assigned to the head of each foot. Starting from /ka-lу̯-tebeelě̌/ binary right-headed feet are built, giving/ ka-lу̯̌-tebě̌elě̌/, which is interpreted tonally as *ka-lу̯́-tebéelé* "little amaranthus".[20]

As it turns out, "binary alternating H" is the wrong characterization of Kimatuumbi. Odden (1985) shows that the penultimate H of *ka-lу̯́-tebéelé* is the "accented" H (underlying H), so this word is underlyingly /ka-lу̯-tebeele/. The final H derives by a rule assigning H to the last vowel of a word with penultimate H, and the initial H comes from a rule assigning H to a syllable after a noun class prefix (subject to the condition that assignment of H cannot bring two H tones together). Inspection of sufficiently long stems shows that there is no tendency to binary alternating H's, cf. *ma-sі́pі̯taálі̯* "hospitals", *ma-bwánaankу̯bwá* "bosses".

Sietsema (1989) claims that binary feet are required in Sukuma to account for the shift of H two syllables to the right, whereby /ku-tónol-anij-a/ surfaces as *kutonolánija*. Again we encounter the problem of locality; H cannot shift two syllables to the right without running afoul of various theoretical strictures. In Sietsema's analysis, binary feet are built starting with the underlying H, giving (ku)(tóno)(lani)(ja); H then spreads from the head of one foot to the head of the following foot, giving (ku)(tónó)(láni)(ja). This is followed by a delinking rule (exactly like that required for Zulu), giving the surface form. However, Sietsema's analysis requires a number of devices whose theoretical status is suspect (phrase-internal extrametricality and improperly bracketed metrical constituents); Roberts (1991) shows that the apparent tone shift by two syllables arises from two quite independent processes, each of which spreads H tone to the immediately following syllable. So, /kutónolanija/ spreads H once lexically giving /kutónólanija/, and then because of a later postlexical spreading rule becomes /kutónólánija/ (then *kutonolánija*).

A final phenomenon which suggests a connection with metrical structure, quantity sensitivity, has been noted (Goldsmith 1987b, 1992b): H tones resist being moved off of heavy syllables, and may move from light syllables to heavy syllables. This is another case of tone-accent attraction: heavy syllables tend to be accented and vice versa, and H toned syllables tend to be accented and vice versa. Work in this area of tone and metrical structure is less well developed, but attraction of H to heavy syllables is well attested, appearing in a number of languages such as Yao, Kimatuumbi, and Chichewa (Bantu: Malawi).

NOTES

I would like to thank Jill Beckman, John Goldsmith, Beth Hume, and Larry Hyman for helpful comments on an earlier draft of this paper. Data used here derive either from the cited source, or from my own field notes on the language. Tone transcriptions will follow the convention that Raised H tone is transcribed with a double acute accent, H tone with an acute accent, M tone with a macron, and L tone with a grave; or, following the conventions of the original sources for Chori and Grebo, raised numbers are used, with 1 indicating the highest pitch. Following the practice of Bantu linguistics, L toned vowels in Bantu languages are generally transcribed with no accent, rather than with a grave.

1   In addition, a number of separate tone rules primarily sensitive to vowel length will spread the stem H rightward by as many as three moras.

2   It is an open question whether phonetic implementation provides finer control over the timing of pitch changes: it might be that in some languages pitch changes are timed relatively early in the syllable, and in other languages they are timed relatively late. Such control would only be phonetic, never phonological.

There is a way around the excessive-power objection to moraic linkage of tones, which is to allow only the final mora to bear multiple tones. Possible representations of contour tones would be:

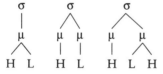

Or, following Hyman (1988a), multiple linking of tones to moras could be restricted to the first mora of the syllable.

3   There is no substantial difference between representing the tonal elements with *h* and *l* on the one hand, or with [+H] and [−H] on the other.

4   The left-to-right application of linking is observed almost universally – though see the discussion of Hausa and Kanakuru below. The theory does not contain any provisions which would explain this.

5   The Q-subscript notation expands to an infinite set of subrules applied conjunctively, similar to the star-parenthesis notation of linear phonology.

6   Odden (1984) argues that the Wellformedness Condition must not take effect until after application of the last rule referring to free vowels. Since the Wellformedness Condition would map some tone to any free vowel, no toneless vowels could persist in the grammar, and therefore rules which refer to toneless vowels could not exist, unless the Wellformedness Condition is suspended until after such rules.

7   The final two syllables take L tone phonetically, due to a rule assigning L to any toneless syllable – see section 5.

8   The convention – or rule – which maps tones to vowel one-to-one either left-to-right or right-to-left might appear to require that vowels and tones be underlyingly unassociated. But there is a different way to interpret this convention, namely as a static filter on well-formed underlying representations, rather than as a derivational instruction to link floating tones with free vowels.

9   However, Clark (1990) argues that the default tone in the two-tone language Igbo is not L but rather H.

10 A fourth class, the "rising" class, has the tone pattern LH. These are not relevant here.

11 The theory does not claim that languages cannot have contours involving M tones. The three-tone language Lulubo allows all possible

two-tone contours including those with M, viz., t̪ɔ̀mbɛ̌ "it is Tombe", ʔā́ "in the stomach", ízí̄ "his wife" (Andersen 1987). In such cases the default rules have applied to supply features for the M tone before creating the relevant contours. Another possibility would be that in such a language, all tonal features are specified underlyingly, in which case we would not find any phonological asymmetries.

12 Vowels may also have preaccent or postaccent: preaccent is realized as accent on the previous vowel, and postaccent is realized as accent on the following vowel.

13 In Clements (1981b) and Leben (1978), underlying representations do contain links between autosegments and the segmental core.

14 Goldsmith's analysis is carried out in the context of a framework where all tones link to some vowel, hence the necessity of creating the initial falling and medial rising tones.

15 Besides resisting the retraction rule, a host of other tone rules discussed in Odden (1985) can be used to determine that this word has a final accent; for example, it retains its final H tone phrase-medially (*mbaká ywaángu* "my cat") whereas unaccented final H's phrase-medially are lost (*n'oombé* "cow", *n'ombe ywaángu* "my cow").

16 To be sure, a tone in one morpheme can link to a vowel of another morpheme – such tone shifts happen in Nguni languages – but the target vowel is always in a constant location, such as the penultimate or stem-initial syllable. What the prelinked tone theory could not handle would be a language where the melody shifts to a lexically unpredictable location in a different morpheme.

17 In fact, Goldsmith (1984b) rejects "one-per-morpheme" as being criterial for accent, and his analysis of Tonga has noun stems with multiple accents.

18 An important exception is that Guarani, which allows a single nasal specification, is treated accentually in Goldsmith (1976a).

19 Nguni languages also have phonetic stress on the penultimate syllable. It is not clear how the antepenultimate tonal accent is to be reconciled with penultimate stress accent – perhaps there are multiple planes of metrical organization, or perhaps the antepenultimate accent is shifted to the penult after tone attraction.

20 Sietsema (1989) provides an alternative metrical formalism which expresses the same generalizations as Pulleyblank's analysis.

13 Tone in East Asian Languages

MOIRA YIP

0 Introduction

Theoretical phonologists have devoted more attention to African tone languages than to East Asian ones, probably because phonologists thrive on alternations, and the morphological characteristics of East Asian languages make alternations (segmental or tonal) relatively rare. Given this, one might ask what we can learn about tone from East Asian languages that we cannot learn from African languages. One striking observation about East Asian languages is the richness of their tonal inventory. Where African languages typically contrast two, perhaps three level tones (see chap. 12, this volume), East Asian languages, particularly Chinese languages, frequently contrast four levels and several rising or falling (i.e., contour) tones. They are thus fertile territory for exploring the distinctive features of tone – what they are, how they relate to segmental features, and how they are organized in the feature geometry. The first and longest section of this chapter is devoted to this question.

A second way in which East Asian languages may be helpful is in illuminating our understanding of what may be the tone-bearing unit (TBU) in language. Some Chinese languages appear to use the mora, so that only long syllables may bear two tones, which surface as contours. However, I will adopt the view that the lack of contour tones on short syllables is a phonetic effect, and any syllable may phonologically bear any tone. It then follows that the TBU is the syllable, not the mora. I will then discuss the metrical foot, which typically limits tones to one per foot (Mandarin); this raises the issue of the relationship between tone and stress, which can coexist in Chinese. Finally I discuss the prosodic word and the phonological phrase (Shanghai).

A third area of investigation addresses the types of tone sandhi rules that we find. What form do the rules themselves take (assimilation, dissimilation, rules conditioned by phrasal position, etc.)? The remaining issues will receive only brief mentions for reasons of space. One observation that needs an explanation is the apparent absence of downstep in East Asian languages.

Another cluster of issues arises over how to define the domains within which sandhi rules apply.

In a summary like this, each of these issues receives only a cursory treatment; it should be clear that there are many questions awaiting further research. I give more attention to Chinese languages than other East Asian language families as an unavoidable consequence of the fact that I am more comfortable making generalizations about Chinese than I am about such other East Asian tone languages as those of Tibeto-Burman, Miao-Yao, Tai, and Austroasiatic (Vietnamese). I draw heavily on the work of previous researchers, especially that of Matthew Chen, Bao Zhi-ming, and Duanmu San, without whose insights this chapter could not have been written. Since this article is for the general phonologist, rather than the specialist in Chinese, I have largely limited the references to English-language sources, even though these are often secondary works using data from Chinese-language field studies. Specialist readers may pursue the original sources for themselves.

1   Tonal Features

1.1   Six Proposals for Tonal features

A satisfactory feature system for tone must meet the familiar criteria of characterizing all and only the contrasts of natural language, the appropriate natural classes, and allowing for a natural statement of phonological rules and historical change. In looking at East Asian tone systems the main issues are these:

(1)   (a)   How many different levels must be represented?
       (b)   Are contour tones single units or sequences of level tones?
       (c)   What is the relationship between tonal features and other features, especially laryngeal features?

These issues are discussed in great detail by many researchers, most notably Anderson (1978), Yip (1980, 1989), Pulleyblank (1986), Hyman (1986, 1989), Snider (1990), Bao (1990), Duanmu (1990a), and references cited therein. The features I will use are Register, a binary feature referred to in Yip (1980) as [+/ −upper], but which I will here call upper case H/L for convenience, and Pitch (following the usage of Duanmu 1990a), also a binary feature, denoted here by lower case h/l. Two binary features can produce four combinations, giving four level tones. Hyman and Duanmu differ from the other authors cited above in that they allow for a three-way contrast in both register and pitch. The resulting nine levels are not attested in any language, so I continue to restrict the system to a four-way contrast. The languages that have been described as having five level tones (notably Black Miao (Chang 1953), see Duanmu for a good summary) may require revision of this assumption, but so little is known about the phonological behavior of these tone systems that some of the "level" tones may turn out to be phonologically contours.

Contour tones (rising or falling tones) are sequences of Pitch values, with a single Register value. For example, [H, lh] is a high rising tone, whereas [L, hl] is a low falling tone. We therefore get the following eight-tone inventory:

(2) H, h   L, h
     H, l   L, l
     H, hl   L, hl
     H, lh   L, lh

This system is found almost perfectly in Cantonese; the digits are the Chao "tone letter" system, in which 5 denotes high pitch and 1 low pitch, used by all workers on Chinese tone; a single digit is used to denote an obstruent-final (i.e., short) syllable.

(3) H, h   55 si "poem"   L, h   22   si "affair"
     H, l   33 si "try"   L, l   —
     H, hl 53 si "silk"   L, hl 21¹ si "time"
     H, lh 35 si "cause"   L, lh 24   si "city"

Morphemes are almost exclusively monosyllabic in Chinese, and with rare exceptions each lexical morpheme has one of the lexical tones. In some dialects some suffixes may be toneless.

Since the work of Clements (1985), Sagey (1986), and others on segmental feature geometry (see chap. 7, this volume), the arrangement of the tonal features has been an object of inquiry. A variety of different models have been proposed, each making slightly different predictions. One of the fundamental ideas of feature geometry theory is that groups of features that spread together are grouped together under a single node. I will use spreading as the diagnostic for constituency in the feature geometry, and survey the extant proposals for tonal features, and the evidence. The major proposals of which I am aware are given below; I will not discuss earlier proposals such as Wang (1967) or Woo (1969) because their conversion into autosegmental terms is not obvious. I have grouped the proposals by the structural relationship between the Register and Pitch features (independence, sisterhood, and dominance) and standardized the terminology across proposals as much as possible. Proposals differ in what they take to be the tone-bearing unit (TBU), and these differences are retained here. I show a high rising tone, [35], in each system:[2]

(4) (a) Independence (Yip 1980b)

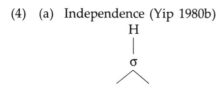

(b) Sister-hood (Bao 1990b; Duanmu 1990a; Clements 1989a; Hyman 1989b; Snider 1990b) Clements, Snider:[3]

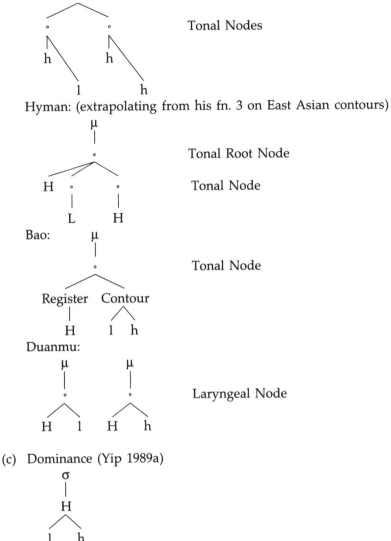

TBU

Tonal Nodes

Hyman: (extrapolating from his fn. 3 on East Asian contours)

Tonal Root Node

Tonal Node

Bao:

Tonal Node

Duanmu:

Laryngeal Node

(c) Dominance (Yip 1989a)

These theories make the following predictions. (Note that all theories allow terminals to spread):

(5)
	Whole Tone	Spreading Register only	Contour as a whole, w/out register
Yip 1980b		x	
Clements		x	
Hyman	x	x	
Yip 1989a	x		
Bao	x	x	x
Duanmu		x	

I will briefly review the evidence for each type of spreading. I will start with contour spreading as a whole, but without register.

1.2　*Contour Spreading*

Bao's is the only model which allows for spreading contour without register. It seems, however, that the cases he offers as instances of such spreading are not entirely convincing, and I will conclude that in the absence of more clear-cut cases a more restrictive model is to be preferred.

Bao (1990b, p. 96ff.) offers Zhenjiang and Wenzhou as cases of spreading just a contour node. Zhenjiang (Jiangsu province, Zhang 1985) is analyzed by Bao as spreading the property of being level (i.e., the contour node) from a final syllable back onto a penultimate syllable. Data from Zhenjiang are given below; these changes apply to the penultimate syllable of domains of two to three syllables long. Zhang tells us that the initial syllable in three-syllabled cases is always level, with /55,5/ staying unchanged and all others becoming 33.

(6)

$\sigma_1 \backslash \sigma_2$	42	31	35	55	5
42				33	
31		35			
35				22	
55		55			
5		5			

The leveling is found for falling tones not just before level tones, but before the rising 35 tone as well. This throws doubt on Bao's analysis, which would have to treat these cases separately. The general character of the system appears to involve greater neutralization and leveling the further from the end of the word the syllable lies. Antepenultimate syllables are all level, penultimate syllables are level or rising, and only final syllables may fall. I thus conclude that Zhenjiang is not a clear case of contour spreading.

Another reason for finding Zhenjiang less than wholly convincing is that spreading of levelness will never be as convincing as spreading of a rise or a fall, since one cannot distinguish spreading of the contour node from spreading of the subordinate tone. Wenzhou (Zhengzhang 1964) is more interesting since Bao claims that /hl/ spreads as a unit, but without register. Underlining indicates glottalization. Bisyllabic compounds composed of (1) 45, 34, or 22 before falling 42, 31, or (2) 42, 323, or 212 before falling 42 surface as falling-falling [42–21]. Bao analyzes this as the spread of the /hl/ contour from the final syllable backwards. There are empirical problems with the analysis, however, when extended to the larger data set in Bao's appendix. Bao predicts that all phrases ending in an underlying /hl/ should show this spread, but they do not. For example, all tones except 45, 34, and 22 before 31 surface as 22–2, level throughout both syllables. Conversely, we find falling syllables before the underlyingly level /22/, and even before the underlying rise, 34. I should also note that Duanmu (p. 147) argues against Bao's analysis on several other grounds, and points out that in the 42–21 pattern the [21] may be phonologically level, and indeed has a [42–1] alternant.

In order to understand what is going on, we again need to look at the complete tonal system of Wenzhou. Wenzhou is a Wu dialect, and it has eight contrasting tones on monosyllables. On longer phrases there are still only eight possible patterns, determined by the underlying tone of the last, and sometimes also the penultimate, syllable. On spans of three, four, or five syllables, it is clear that if the last two syllables are one of the sequences analyzed by Bao as spreading a /hl/ contour to give 42–21, the pattern of the whole phrase is a consistent exception to the general pattern of Wenzhou. The data is given below. The letter *t* stands for tones whose value depends on the underlying tones of the final two syllables in a non-obvious way. The phrases of interest here are those in the lefthand column; note that it is not only the final syllables themselves that are different, but the *preceding* span as well.

(7)　　　　　Final two syllables 42–21 in [σσ] cases　All other phrases
　　σσσ　　　　42–21–21 / 21–42–21　　　　　　　43–t-t
　　σσσσ　　42–21–31–21　　　　　　　　34–43–t-t / 2–4–t-t
　　σσσσσ　42–21–31–21–21　　　　　　2–4–43–t-t

Bao and Duanmu both note that stress plays a role in Wenzhou sandhi, since 42–21 phrases have initial stress, and there is a 21–42 variant with final stress. In longer spans there is an alternating tonal pattern, with a 31 breaking the string of 21s. These patterns may in fact be the result of imposing alternating stress on a toneless span, with no tone sandhi involved at all. In this view, 42–21–31–21–21 is simply the phonetic instantiation of a stress grid:

(8)　x
　　　x　　x
　　　x x x x x　→　42 21 31 21 21

As to why the tone deletes in these particular circumstances, I have no answer at present, but I conclude that Wenzhou is also not a clear case of spreading contour alone.

Since neither of the putative cases of contour node spreading seems to hold up under closer scrutiny, I conclude for now that our tonal model should not admit this possibility, and opt for one of the more restrictive models. I now turn to whole tone spreading.

1.3   Whole Tone Spreading

Hyman, Yip (1989) and Bao allow spreading of a complete tone. Bao offers two examples of whole tone spreading, Changzhi and Danyang. In Changzhi (Shanxi province; Bao 1990, using data from Hou 1983) we have the following pattern upon attachment of the suffixes /ti/ or /tə?/ to a base:

(9)   suaŋ^{213} suaŋ^{213} ti^{213} "sour"
      xuaŋ^{24} xuaŋ^{24} ti^{24} "yellow"
      yaŋ^{535} yaŋ^{535} ti^{535} "soft"
      laŋ^{53} laŋ^{53} ti^{53} "rotten"

Bao analyzes this as whole tone spreading, but Duanmu (p. 145) suggests that Changzhi reduplicates the tone rather than spreading it. However, Hou's data shows quite clearly that Bao is right, and this must be whole tone spreading. The evidence comes from overt reduplication, which shows quite different tonal patterns, with sandhi rules that dissimilate one or another of the reduplicated tones.

(10)   /213/   saŋ^{213} saŋ^{35} "fan"
       /53/   tuŋ^{35} tuŋ^{53} "move"?
       /535/   ts'ɔ^{535} ts'ɔ^{35} "fry"
       /24/   tɕ'iəu^{24} tɕ'iəu^{53} "ask for, beg"

Although the reduplication is obscured by the subsequent sandhi rules, note that neither syllable has a fixed tone, showing that tonal reduplication must have taken place. If (10) is the result of tonal reduplication, the data in (9) must be something else, and spreading is the obvious candidate. I conclude that Changzhi shows true spreading of an entire tone.

The last case to be discussed here is Danyang, where one phrasal tone pattern is 42–42–42– ... 24, roughly conditioned by an initial /24/ tone. Using data from Lü (1980), Chen (1986), Chan (1988), Yip (1989), and Bao have proposed analyses that in one way or another involve spreading of the entire contour tone, usually accompanied by a sandhi rule that changes 24 to 42 before another 24, although details vary. There is some question, however, as to whether this is spreading of any kind. Duanmu argues that the 42–42–42 ... 24 pattern is derived from a sequence of underlying /24/ tones, /24–24–24 ... 24/, followed by the sandhi rule that changes 24 → 42 / _____ 24, and no spreading is involved. Wang Hong-jun (1991) shows clearly that this is not the case, and that some of these patterns do not have underlying /24/ throughout. What determines the phrasal pattern is the tone of the first syllable alone, provided its historical origins are taken into account (specifically, it is phrases that begin with a Ze, a literary style syllable, and we must assume that just as English still distinguishes between the Greco-Latin and the native vocabulary, or Malayalam between Dravidian and Sanskrit vocabulary, Danyang distinguishes Ping and Ze, and literary and colloquial). It would seem, then, that Danyang can be maintained as a case of a complete contour tone spreading as a unit, although it is not as clear-cut as the Changzhi example. The only two models which allow this, without also allowing contour node spreading without Register, are those of Hyman (1989) and Yip (1989). They differ in whether they allow independent Register spreading, a matter to which I now turn.

1.4 Register Spreading

Bao gives two cases that he analyzes as spreading just Register. In Wuyi, a Wu dialect, two-syllable nominal compounds with the first syllable /24/, high rising, and the second syllable either /24, 213, 53, or 31/, surface with the second syllable high falling, [53]. Data from Bao (p. 209), citing Fu (1984).

(11)	/24–24/	t'ie koŋ	[24–53]		"Heavenly Lord"
	/24–213/	hua ɸioŋ	[24–53]	[hua ʔoŋ]	"a fruit"
	/24–31/	sa vuo	[24–53]	[sa fuo]	"raw meal"

Bao and Duanmu both analyze this as spreading of H Register, since the rising contour does not appear to spread too. However, since the final syllable is always falling, it is not possible to tell whether (1) the whole tone with its contour, or (2) just the Register, has been spread, since neutralization to falling on the final syllable (possibly by addition of a final low tone) is needed in both accounts.[4] Since the previous section demonstrated the need for whole tone spreading, and the Wuyi data can be dealt with by this means, Wuyi cannot be used to establish the need for Register spreading.

The other case offered as Register spreading is Pingyao (Hou 1980). Schematic Pingyao facts are given in (12), with the sequences of most interest in boldface:

(12)

σ_1	13	35	53
13	13–13	31–35	**35–423**
35	**13–13**	31–35	35–423
53	53–13	53–35	35–423

$$13 \rightarrow 35 \: / \: \underline{} \: 53$$
$$35 \rightarrow 13 \: / \: \underline{} \: 13$$

For Bao, rising tones receive Register from the following syllable, so that in the first column the /35/ initial syllables acquire L Register from the following /13/, and in the third column /13/ becomes /35/ before the H Register /53/. In the second column, an earlier metathesis rule changes the first syllable /lh/ to /hl/, so Register spread never applies. Chen (1991) gives an alternative analysis of Pingyao in which Register does not spread, but is neutralized under the influence of the Pitch features of the following tone, so that for rising tones Register becomes H before hl (column 3), and L before lh (column 1). He retains Bao's metathesis rule. A somewhat similar connection between pitch and Register features has been observed in Hausa, by Inkelas, Leben and Cobler (1987), although I know of no other cases in Chinese. Pingyao remains the most convincing case of Register spread I have encountered, but its restricted nature (only rising tones are targets, and it is bled by a metathesis rule) and the alternative offered by Chen's analysis makes it less than totally convincing.[5] I conclude that in our present state of knowledge the only kinds of spreading for which we have strong motivation are spreading of terminal features, and spreading of the entire tone, and we should adopt the most restrictive model compatible with these types of spreading. The only model in (5) with these properties is one where Register dominates the pitch features, and there is no special contour node, as in Yip (1989), and for now I will use this as my working model.

1.5   Tonal and Laryngeal Features

A brief note is needed here on a major topic: the relationship of tonal and other laryngeal features. The earliest attempt to characterize a set of features that would relate tone, voicing, aspiration, and glottalization was that of Halle and Stevens (1971). Both Bao and Duanmu take the strong position that identifies Register and obstruent voicing as one and the same thing. Bao allows a two-way distinction, using the feature [+/− stiff vocal cords]. Duanmu adopts the same idea, but uses the pair of features [stiff vocal cords] and [slack vocal cords] for a three-way distinction. Putting the details aside, if we equate Register and voicing, and incorporate this insight into the working model of Yip (1989) arrived at in the previous sections, the result is shown in (13). (13a) shows the purely tonal model; (13b) substitutes a Register node, variously realized as H/L tonal register or [voice], for the plain H Register, and a Pitch node, realized as h/l Pitch, for the simple h/l Pitch features. This Pitch node appears twice, to allow for contour tones. The Glottal Aperture node dominates the features Constricted Glottis (c.g.) and Spread Glottis (s.g.). I will not discuss the issue of whether the Laryngeal node associates directly to the syllable, as shown here, or via the segmental Root node.

(13) (a) Yip (1989)

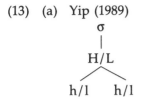

(b) Incorporating this into a laryngeal feature model:

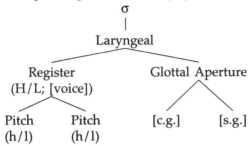

Duanmu makes two claims: first, languages with too many tonal levels to deal with by the Pitch distinction alone, and that thus use contrastive Register, will always show voice quality distinctions alongside pitch distinctions. This claim is probably too strong. Cantonese, for example, which makes a rich use of Register, as shown in (3) above, is not reported to have voice quality distinctions between the Registers.

The second consequence is that spreading of Register or the whole tone should, ceteris paribus, interact with the voicing of intervening obstruents. Obstruents should block the spreading of incompatible Register values, or assimilate in voicing to the spreading value. The potential blocking effect means that any spreading involving Register will be rare, as Duanmu points out. The rarity of whole tone spreading (the only way Register can spread in the view of this paper) is striking. In Wuyi, where high registered tones spread, the spreading is indeed accompanied by onset devoicing, as shown by the data from (11), repeated here:

(14) /24–24/   t'ie koŋ   [24–53]   "Heavenly Lord"
      /24–213/   hua ɦioŋ   [24–53]   [hua ʔoŋ]   "a fruit"
      /24–31/   sa vuo   [24–53]   [sa fuo]   "raw meal"

In Changzhi, on the other hand, whole tone spreading does not have any effect on obstruent voicing, even when a low register tone spreads across a voiceless obstruent, as in [suaŋ²¹³ ti²¹³] "sour". Since Changzhi (unlike Wuyi) has no voiced obstruents, this may perhaps be attributed to structure preservation.

The intimate connection between tone and laryngeal features is very clear when one looks at the historical development of tone (see Kingston and Solnit

1988 for a detailed study). In some dialects today this clear connection can still be seen. The Wujiang dialect (Ye 1983), brought to my attention by Ting Pang-Hsin, has twelve tones, which would seem to exceed the limits of the system. Arranged according to laryngeal qualities of the onset, and taking the short (Ru sheng) tones as variants of the level tones, however, they are reducible to the more manageable three:

(15)

	h	hl	hlh
Voiceless plain, including fricatives, onsetless, and /h/.	55/5	51	412
Voiceless aspirated	33/3	42	312
Voiced, obstruent, and sonorant, including	13/2	31	212

Following Duanmu, and equating voice with low register, the voiced series in (15) will be L Register, and the others H. The difference between the plain and aspirated sets will be in [+/− spread glottis], so only six tones will contrast underlyingly (where voicing and low register are one and the same feature). Why aspiration should have a lowering effect is unclear, and for detailed discussion of this point I refer the reader to Kingston and Solnit's paper.

The two most noticeable interactions between laryngeal features and tone are the effects of voiced obstruent onsets, touched on above, and the effects of glottal codas, and I will discuss each in turn. Voiced obstruent onsets usually lower pitch, as in Wujiang (above), Shanghai, or Tibetan. Tibeto-Burman languages offer fertile ground for the tone-larynx connection. In these languages there is an interaction between onset voicing, voice quality on the nuclear vowel, and tone. Consider Eastern Tamang as described by Weidert (1987, p. 260ff.). There are four "tones," two of which are associated with clear phonation and two with breathy phonation. Voiced obstruents and breathy phonation go together, as do voiceless obstruents (plain or aspirated) and clear phonation. The two breathy tones are lower in pitch than the two clear tones. Within a single phonation type, the tones are distinguished by level or shape:

(16)   Voiceless obstruent onsets: Clear phonation: H (or HL)
                                                        M
       Voiced obstruents: Breathy phonation: LM
                                                        L

Since the four "tones" are contrastive in sonorant-inital syllables, they can be taken as phonemic and obstruent voicing as derived. If we follow Bao and Duanmu in identifying low register with obstruent voicing, this is a straightforward assimilation rule, spreading low register/obstruent voice leftwards. Such cases make clear the need for the feature geometry to capture the close relationship between tonal and laryngeal features. Tibetan shows interesting neutralizations in compounding that lead us to the same conclusion.

See Yip (1990) and Meredith (1990) for two different recent accounts of the Tibetan facts. Within Chinese the Wu dialects show similar phenomena; see Bao (1990) and Duanmu (1990a), and references cited therein. Also Duanmu (1990b) on Shanghai.

The full picture of the tonal-laryngeal relationship is undoubtedly more complex than I have implied so far. Burmese (Bradley 1981) has a three-way contrast in phonation type and pitch between plain (clear) (L), breathy (M/ HM) and creaky (HL). The tones are my interpretion of Bradley's description. Although Burmese is a Tibeto-Burman language, this system of voice quality distinctions is typical of that found in Mon-Khmer languages. Exactly how to translate this into tonal and laryngeal features is quite unclear, and I leave this for further research. See Duanmu (1990a, p. 125ff.) for one approach.

An interesting problem arises if we take the model to which we have been led by the East Asian data, and apply it to African languages. Typically H and L tones spread freely across long spans of syllables, across any kind of consonant (depressor consonants aside). For example, Luganda (Hyman, Katamba, and Walusimbi 1987) has a HL pattern on accented words, and the H span may encompass voiced stops, the low portion may encompass voiceless stops.[6] If Duanmu is right about identifying voice and register, the spreading in African languages, which does not usually interact with voicing, must be Pitch, not Register, and yet in my model Pitch is dependent on Register, and can thus only be specified if Register is first specified. But if the language only distinguishes two surface tones, surely only Pitch *or* Register is being used distinctively, not both. The only resolution to this impasse that occurs to me is that the dependency relations between Register and Pitch might differ between Chinese and African languages, along the lines discussed by Mester 1986 and Selkirk 1988 for vowel and consonant features).

The second widespread laryngeal-tonal connection is the effect of glottal codas and unreleased (perhaps glottalized) stop codas. These typically shorten the syllable, and often permit only level tones on the preceding vowel. Cantonese, for example, contrasts seven tones on vowel- and nasal-final syllables, but allows only the three level tones on obstruent-final syllables. A particularly interesting case of interaction between glottal stops and tone is reported in Weidert (1987, p. 420). Boro is a Tibeto-Burman language with no tone contrasts on monosyllables. In bisyllables, however, a tonal contrast is observed on the second syllable; the acute accent marks high pitch, and unaccented vowels are mid.

(17) dɣisaʔ   "rivulet"   daosá?   "chicken"
      bajiʔ   "fifty"   dojí?   "sixty"

It turns out that this pitch difference is predictable from the presence or ab-sence of a final glottal stop in the underlying form of the first morpheme. The glottal stop is lost in compounding, but surfaces as high tone on the following syllable.

(18) dɣi   "water"   dɣisaʔ   "rivulet"
      daoʔ   "fowl"   daosáʔ   "chicken"
      ba   "five"   bajiʔ   "fifty"
      doʔ   "six"   dojíʔ   "sixty"
      jiʔ   "ten"

No current theory of tonal features can explain the details of this process, but it serves to illustrate the intimate relationship between the various tonal and laryngeal features.

2   The Tone-bearing Unit

2.1   *Obstruent-Final Syllables*

In some African languages (e.g., Luganda, Clements 1986), contour tones appear only on long vowels or closed syllables. This suggests that the TBU is the mora, and tone association is strictly one-to-one (though see chap. 12, this volume). In Chinese languages we observe a related but interestingly different situation. Sonorant-final syllables (vowel or nasal final) may bear any tone, but if a language has obstruent-final (i.e., unreleased plain voiceless stops) syllables, they may bear only a subset of tones, usually level tones. These syllables are shorter than the sonorant-final syllables (see Kao 1971). These facts can be explained given the following assumptions:

(19) Contour tones have two tonal root nodes.
      The mora is the TBU.
      Only sonorant codas can be moraic.
      There is open-syllable lengthening.

The obstruent codas will be nonmoraic, and thus not TBUs, so such syllables will have only one TBU and hence only one (level) tone. Duanmu (1990a) takes a rather different approach. He argues that all Chinese syllables are bimoraic, so that even obstruent codas are TBUs.[7] The failure of contours to surface on these syllables is seen as phonetic: on an unreleased stop no tone can be realized, even though it is phonologically present. He shows that in Shanghai and Taiwanese (pp. 137–138) these tones may surface if the stop coda is deleted.

What both these analyses share is the assumption that contour tones are made up of two tonal root nodes, contra the model argued for in section 1. It is worth considering whether the lack of contour tones on stop-final syllables can possibly be explained if they are in fact one tonal Root Node, as argued for above. In fact, there is a straightforward way to understand these facts: I shall adopt Duanmu's view that phonetic realization is the reason that contour tones fail to surface on unreleased stop-final syllables, even though they may be phonologically present.[8] This move allows us to maintain the model in which contour tones are units (and thus explain why they can spread as a unit, as in Changzhi), while understanding their restricted distribution. This suggestion also removes the motivation for taking the mora to be the TBU in Chinese. If contour tones are single tonal nodes, and the syllable is the TBU, then all the facts follow. In fact, if the mora is the TBU, a contour tone could be associated to each mora, giving highly complex tones such as rise-rise, which are not found, so it is not only possible but essential that the syllable be the TBU in Chinese.[9]

2.2 *Distribution of Contour Tones in East Asian Languages*

I would like to address the striking contrast between the distribution of contour tones in Chinese (where they are found on any syllable) and African languages (where they are found only at margins). There are three possible explanations for the typological difference. The first is that of Yip (1989), where I argue that in African languages underlying tones are all level, and contour tones are always the result of associating two tonal Root Nodes to one TBU, a configuration usually only possible at domain edges. In East Asian languages, by contrast, underlying tones include contours under a single Root Node, and these can associate to any single TBU just as a level tone can. This explanation best fits the feature model espoused here.

The second possible explanation is offered by Duanmu (1990a), for whom the facts follow from his assumption that only bimoraic syllables may bear contour tones, plus the claim that in Chinese *all* syllables are bimoraic, whereas in most African languages syllables are usually monomoraic, except when word-final lengthening provides an additional mora for a final contour tone.[10]

The last possible explanation is morphological. The best-studied group of African languages, the Bantu languages, has a rich affixing morphology producing long polysyllabic words, and roots do not usually surface without affixes. Roots and affixes may have tones or be toneless, and tone association takes place at the stem level, where stem consists of a root plus a number of suffixes (see Myers 1987 and Hewitt and Prince 1989 for details). Chinese languages, as is well-known, have little in the way of affixes. Each lexical morpheme is a single syllable with its own tone, and can usually surface unadorned, although a prolific use of compounding means that most words are in fact bisyllabic or longer. If tone association is assumed to take place at the stem level as in Bantu, then in Chinese this means that each syllable will undergo tone association as a separate domain, (the few suffixes, all toneless, will be adjoined to the stem later). As a consequence each syllable will be the end of a domain for tone association in Chinese, and thus can bear a contour tone, whereas in Bantu only the last syllable of the relevant domain can bear a contour.

2.3   *Foot and Phonological Word*

Before closing this discussion of tone-bearing units, let's look briefly at the behavior of tones in units larger than the syllable. In some dialects the stress foot plays a clear role in tonal phenomena. First, toneless syllables typically cannot bear stress, and adjoin to the preceding toned and stressed syllable to form a foot. Mandarin, Taiwanese, and many other dialects show this behavior. It is almost as if the foot is the TBU in such languages, and the tone surfaces on the head of the foot, i.e., the stressed syllable.

Second, the foot may be the domain of tone sandhi rules. Shih (1985) and Chen (1990) have argued that this is the case for the third-tone sandhi rule in Mandarin, but it is not entirely clear that "foot" is the right characterization of the prosodic unit involved, since this "foot" groups together two fully-toned syllables of roughly equal prominence, and cannot be identified with the other Mandarin foot created by grouping together one toned and stressed syllable with one or more toneless stressless syllables. Since in stress theory a foot means a grouping of one prominent syllable and one (or more, perhaps) less prominent syllable, I prefer to reserve the term for the units containing only one toned syllable. In that case the domain of third-tone sandhi must be larger, perhaps the prosodic word.

Leaving this open, another set of cases occurs in which the prosodic word more obviously plays a role. Selkirk (1986), Chen (1987), and Selkirk and Shen (1990) build prosodic words and phrases from syntactic information, and these then define tone sandhi domains in Amoy and Shanghai. In Amoy (Southern Min), which is sometimes reported to have final stress, nonfinal syllables change into specific sandhi tones. In Shanghai (Wu), which has initial stress, noninitial syllables lose their tones altogether, and the tone of the initial syllable controls the tone of the whole domain. Extending the notion of TBU still further, one could speculate that this is an example of the phonological phrase as TBU. In any case, there is a clear connection between the inability of toneless syllables to bear stress in Mandarin, and the inability of stressless syllables to bear tone in Shanghai. Taking a wider view, these are in turn related to the known tendency of prominent syllables to attract tone in Bantu languages.[11] Meredith (1990) argues that in Mandarin stress is assigned on the basis of tone, with the high and high falling tones tending to attract stress, and the low tone tending to reject it. However, native speakers tend to reject the idea that there is any detectable stress in such words, and data collected in the phonetics lab at the Academy of Social Sciences in Beijing found no consistent judgements on the relative stress of fully toned syllables (Wang Hong-jun, p.c.).

3 Types of Sandhi

The types of tone sandhi found in Chinese are by and large familiar enough, at least in the clearly understood cases. There is a fundamental division between tone changes caused by a specific tonal environment, such as assimilation and dissimilation, and tone changes caused by purely positional factors, such as special phrase-final variants, or spreading over a phrasal domain.

As one would expect, among the first type we find both assimilation and dissimilation. Assimilation is common, as in Gao'an (Bao 1990a, p. 111). High tones /55/ [H,h] become falling before any /1/ tone, 33 [H,l] or 11 [L,l]. This is the result of the /1/ spreading leftward onto the preceding syllable:

(20) TBU   TBU

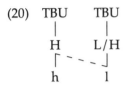

Dissimilation is also found, as in Tianjin. Data are from Chen (1985), the analysis is that of Yip (1989). Tianjin has four tones: 21, 45, 213, 53. When two tones are juxtaposed the following changes take place. All other sequences are unchanged.

(21) Tones: 21 [L,l]   213 [L,lh]   45 [H,h]   53 [H,hl]
      21 21   → 213 21   l.l   → lh.l
      213 213 → 45 213   lh.lh → h.lh
      53 53   → 21 53   hl.hl → l.hl
      53 21   → 45 21   hl.l → h.l

This is clearly dissimilatory, presumably OCP triggered, and, crucially, treats contours as units, as expected in our working model. Register plays no role here, and I assume that the accompanying register changes are secondary; that is, when 53 [H,hl] becomes 21 [L,l], it is the tones that dissimilate, and the Register change follows because in Tianjin all [l] tones are predictably [L].

Among the positional type of sandhi, the Wu dialects, like Shanghai, spread the tone of the first syllable over a phrasal domain (data from Xu, Tang, and Qian 1981–83). Here the tone of the first syllable spreads over the first two syllables.

(22) Tone of first syllable   Tone of polysllabic domain
      53   55 33 33 ... 33 31
      24   33 55 33 ... 33 31
      13   22 55 33 ... 33 31

This pattern is easier to explain if contour tones have two tonal Root Nodes, and each then associates to one syllable of the longer domain. If contours are single Root Nodes, as proposed above, this sandhi may require some kind of splitting operation, obscuring its naturalness. Perhaps Shanghai has developed an African-style system, in which there are no underlying unitary contours.

Less well understood is the system common in the Min dialects, such as Taiwanese. Known as the Min tone circle, this was first discussed in a generative framework by Wang (1967). Each tone has two variants, one found in phrase-final position and one elsewhere. The details are given below:

(23)   Phrase-finally   55   35   53   11   33   2   4
       Elsewhere   33   33   55   53   11   4/53 2/11

Attempts to write a single simple rule relating these two sets have largely failed; even though the analyses worked mechanically (notably Wang 1967; see also Yip 1980 for an unconvincing account), they failed to throw light on the phenomenon. Traditional scholars have viewed this as a case of paradigmatic replacement, but within generative phonology this is unappealing. Two recent attempts (Tsay 1990 and Truckenbrodt 1991) look at the data from the point of view of underspecification theory, and although each has some problems they come closer to a solution than anything else I have seen.

4   Additional Issues

Inevitably in a short article of this type there are areas that cannot be addressed; I mention a few here. Note that whether or not some topic has been covered in any detail or left till this section has less to do with the importance of the topic than with whether it seemed possible to do the issues justice in so brief an article.

One interesting question is why African languages often have downstep, and East Asian languages apparently do not. Downstep is a process whereby a low tone (which may or may not surface) causes lowering of a following high tone. One possibility is that the tonal geometry of the two language areas differs in such a way that two tones are adjacent in African languages but not in Asian languages. Specifically, suppose African languages have Pitch directly associated to the TBU, with Register either absent, or dependent on Pitch. This is shown in (24a). In Chinese-type languages, shown in (24b), Pitch features are lower in the feature tree, and an appropriate definition of locality might then block downstep effects in (b) type cases.

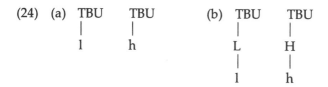

A major topic of current research on tone deals with how the domains within which tone sandhi rules apply can provide clues to the higher level prosodic structure of the string. Chen (1987, 1990), Selkirk and Shen (1990), Shih (1985), and others have investigated this complex issue. Some recent results are summarized in Chen (1990).

5   Conclusion

I have tried to show that the study of East Asian languages can tell us much about tone. On the assumption that distinctive features are part of Universal Grammar, the features required for Chinese must be those used by all tone languages, although of course, as with segmental features, no language will necessarily use all features distinctively. Given underspecification theory, nondistinctive features may then be unspecified underlyingly, and possibly even in the output of the phonology. Indeed, despite the assumptions of most researchers on Chinese tone, it is entirely possible that many syllables may leave the phonology still toneless, and have their pitch filled in by the phonetic component, as has been argued so convincingly for Japanese by Pierrehumbert and Beckman (1988). I leave this and a myriad other matters for future research.

NOTES

1   This tone may be phonologically level, [L,l], and the fall may be simply phonetic.

2   A further difference lies in how many register values are available per syllable: two for Clements and Duanmu, one for everyone else. A single register value restricts the possible contours to two of a single shape, which appears to be correct. See Duanmu (1990a) for a dissenting view.

3   For Clements and Hyman (see below), H=h and L=l. They use a single feature with different geometry rather than two features.

4   Reduplication is unlikely to be involved here, since Wuyi is a Wu dialect, and such dialects typically show rightward spreading in compounds.

5   Yip (1980b, p. 170) proposes a Register spreading rule in Fuzhou, but the analysis is complex, and other explanations can be envisaged.

6   I am assuming a tonal analysis of Luganda accent. Similar examples may be readily found in other languages.

7   Duanmu does not actually use the mora. He takes all syllables to have three X-slots, one of which is for the onset, and two for the rhyme. I have translated his two rhymal X-slots into two moras.

8   Some support for this phonetic explanation comes from its apparently gradient nature. There

are a few dialects in which contour tones do surface on stopped syllables, such as Pingyao and Wenzhou, and the contours tend to be gentle (54 instead of 53, 23 instead of 24, for example), as if there were an incomplete attempt to realize them on the shorter syllable. See also the F_0 tracings of one of the stopped tones in Shanghai in Zee and Maddieson (1979), which shows a slight rise. It is clear that *derived* contours can indeed surface on stopped syllables, such as the Cantonese "changed tone" formed by addition of a high tone, but Duanmu points out that these are probably lengthened, and thus would be bimoraic under his account.

9   One interesting possibility is that Register and Pitch have different TBUs. Register might have the syllable as its TBU, while Pitch has the mora. This idea has been suggested to me independently by Strang Burton and Mei-chih Laura Chan.

10   McCarthy and Prince (1986, 1990a) have argued for the existence of the Minimal Word, and suggest that it is always either bimoraic or bisyllabic. Since any syllable can be a word in Chinese, this would entail that the syllable is bimoraic, in line with Duanmu's (1990a) claim.

11   See, for example, Clements and Goldsmith (1984); Goldsmith (1982, 1987a, 1988b, 1992b); Sietsema (1989); Hyman (1978b, 1981, 1982a, 1982b); Odden (1982a, 1985).

14 Vowel Harmony

HARRY VAN DER HULST AND JEROEN VAN DE WEIJER

0 Introduction

0.1 Goals

This chapter contains a discussion of the phenomenon of *vowel harmony* (henceforth VH). We start with a few straightforward examples and an introduction to some of the relevant terminology (sec. 0.2). Three issues will receive special attention throughout this chapter, viz., the domain of vowel harmony, the nature of the (vowel) features that participate in vowel harmony, and the fact that vowel harmony involves a relation between nonadjacent segments. These issues are introduced in section 1.

Section 2 presents an overview of harmony types in general. We do not offer extensive or detailed analyses of particular systems, nor do we attempt to develop a comprehensive theory which accounts for all aspects of vowel harmony. Our goal is both more modest and more appropriate in the context of this volume: we indicate which issues continue to come up in the theoretical analysis of this phenomenon and we discuss some of the prevailing answers to the questions these issues raise. In some cases, however, we do suggest how a particular approach could be further developed. In section 3 we discuss some cases in which consonants interfere with vowel harmony. Finally, section 4 presents some conclusions and suggestions for future research.[1]

0.2 Straightforward Examples

To set the stage for the discussion in the next sections, let us examine briefly one typical example of vowel harmony, the case of Tangale, a Chadic language spoken in Nigeria, described in Jungraithmayr (1971) and Kidda (1985). Tangale has nine vowel phonemes, which Jungraithmayr presents in the following chart:

(1)   front   back
    high   i   u   close
            ɪ   ʊ   open
    mid   e   o   close
            ɛ   ɔ   open
    low   a   open

The vowels of Tangale can be divided into two subsets, which Jungraithmayr labels *close* and *open* vowels: the close ones are /i u e o/, and the open ones are /ɪ ʊ ɛ ɔ a/.[2] These subsets are called *harmonic sets*.

The phenomenon of vowel harmony consists of the fact that, adopting the nomenclature of the chart in (1), non-low vowels in a word must be either all close or all open. The first word in (2) is one of the rare examples that we found of a polysyllabic stem. Tangale predominantly has monosyllabic stems, however, so vowel harmony is mainly visible in the fact that all affixes containing a vowel have two allomorphs, one with a close vowel and one with an open vowel.[3] The choice between these allomorphs depends on the stem to which the affix is attached: when added to a stem with a close vowel, the vowel in the affix is also close, and when added to a stem with an open vowel, the vowel in the affix is also open. Intervening consonants have no effect. This is shown in (2):

(2)   ŋʊldɛdɛ   "dog"
      seb-u   "look" (imp.)
      kɛn-ʊ   "enter" (imp.)
      tug-o   "pounding"
      wʊd-ɔ   "farming"

Stems in Tangale are invariant: they control the harmonic set to which the vowels of a word belong and the affixes act like chameleons. We refer to this type of vowel harmony as *stem-controlled*. It is also possible for affixes (in addition to stems) to control the harmony. Examples of such systems, which are called *dominant*, will be discussed in section 2.1.2.[4]

Data such as those from Tangale suffice to illustrate the basic character of vowel harmony in a stem-controlled system. The addition of more affixes does not change the picture: all vowels are subject to harmony. In principle, this is true for prefixes as well as suffixes.

Let us now examine the behavior of the low vowel in Tangale. As shown in (1), there is no distinction between an open and a close low vowel. The open low vowel does not have a harmonic counterpart. The (potential) distinction is neutralised, and vis-à-vis the close-open distinction /a/ is therefore a *neutral* vowel. Still, we are justified in classifying the low vowel in Tangale as open, because stems with this vowel select suffixes with vowels from the open set:

(3) ʔn kas-kɔ   "I have cut"
     ʔa-nɔ   "my belly"
     war-ʊ   "go" (imp.)

The low vowel may also appear in affixes and, as we expect, these affixes do not have two allomorphs: they contain the vowel /a/, whether they appear after a stem with an open or with a close vowel:

(4) top-a   "start" (nom.)
     tɔp-a   "answer" (nom.)
     peer-na   "compelled"[5]
     pɛd-na   "untied"
     la-pido   "tree" (dim.)
     la-ŋʊldɛdɛ   "dog" (dim.)

The first, third, and fifth example in (4) show that neutral vowels may lead to *disharmony*, namely when the stem contains a vowel of the close set. We might now ask what happens when a second suffix is added to such disharmonic words as in (4). Will the suffix vowel agree with the stem vowel (/o/) and be close, or will it agree with the suffix vowel (/a/) and be open? This situation is presented schematically in (5):

(5) [[C V C]ₛ /a/] V]

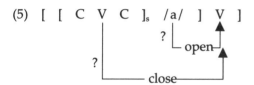

In harmony systems of the Tangale type, it turns out that the suffix vowel agrees with the immediately preceding /a/, and not with the stem vowel:

(6) (a) ped-na-n-gɔ   "untied me"
          peer-na-n-gɔ   "compelled me"
          d'ob-na-g-gʊ   "called you" (pl.)
          d'ib-na-m-gʊ   "cooked for us"
     (b) kulag-dɔ   "her frying pan"

Tangale does have some polysyllabic stems (cf. (2)) and in a few of these the low vowel combines with a preceding close vowel. The last example, (6b), shows that in such stems, which are called *mixed*, the /a/ imposes its openness on the suffix vowel. We may say, then, that in general the neutral low vowel imposes its value on vowels in following syllables.

It has been claimed, however, that this may vary from language to language and indeed there are cases in which suffix vowels agree with the vowel which precedes a neutral vowel; it seems as if in such cases the neutral vowel is completely ignored. The latter type of vowels are referred to as *transparent*, as opposed to the low vowel in Tangale which is called *opaque*. Transparent neutral vowels occur in the vowel harmony system of Finnish.

Finnish has the following vowel inventory (see, e.g., L. Anderson 1975, 1980):

(7)   front   back
     non-round   round   non-round   round
         i   ü   u   high
         e   ö   o   mid
         æ   a   low

Each vowel may be short or long.

Finnish vowel harmony is based on the front-back opposition, and is an example of a *palatal harmony* system. Vowels within a word must either be all front or all back. (This statement ignores a number of subtleties that we will deal with later.) Note that /i/ and /e/ have no back counterparts; hence these vowels are neutral.

Some examples (taken from Ringen 1975; Kiparsky 1981) are given in (8) (phonetic /æ/ corresponds to orthographic ä):

(8)   Front words   Back words
      väkkärä   "pinwheel"   makkara   "sausage"
      pöytä   "table"   pouta   "fine weather"
      käyrä   "curve"   kaura   "oats"
      tyhmä   "stupid"   tuhma   "naughty"

As expected, suffixes show front and back alternants depending on the quality of the stem vowel(s) (Finnish has no prefixes):

(9)   tyhmä-stä   "stupid" (ill.)   tuhma-sta   "naughty" (ill.)

Consider now the behavior of the two neutral vowels /i/ and /e/. In (10) we give examples of mixed stems, in which these neutral vowels cooccur with either front or back stem vowels:

(10) Front words   Back words
      värttinä "spinning wheel"   palttina "linen cloth"
      isä   "father"   iso   "big"
      kesy   "tame"   verho   "curtain"

If the neutral vowel is preceded by a back vowel and occurs in the stem-final syllable, the suffix alternant is back, which shows that neutral vowels in Finnish are *transparent*:

(11) tuoli-lla   "on the chair"

Thus, neutral vowels may behave in two ways. Tangale /a/ is opaque. A preceding close vowel does not impose its closeness on a vowel which follows /a/. Such a following vowel will therefore agree with /a/ in being open. Below we will see that we can interpret this in two ways: we may say that /a/ spreads its openness to a following vowel, or we may say that opaque vowels (or neutral vowels in general) do not spread their value, and vowels following an opaque vowel show up with a default value, which in Tangale happens also to be the value of the neutral vowel /a/. The situation in Finnish is different, however. A vowel following /i/ or /e/ takes on the value of the vowel that precedes the neutral vowel. If a front vowel precedes the neutral /i/ or /e/, suffixes show up with front vowels:

(12) Front words
       värttinä-llä-ni-hän   "with spinning wheel, as you know"
       lyö-dä-kse-ni-kö   "for me to hit"

       Back words
       palttina-lla-ni-han   "with linen cloth, as you know"
       lyo-da-kse-ni-ko   "for me to create"

As in the case of Tangale /a/, the neutral vowels /i/ and /e/ in Finnish behave the same whether they are part of the stem or of a suffix (as the examples in (12) demonstrate). One interpretation is that, as before, the neutral vowels do not spread their value, and that vowels that follow the neutral vowels do not receive the default value, but the value of the preceding vowels. On this account, Tangale /a/ differs from Finnish /i/ and /e/ as a result of a parameter setting: whereas /a/ is specified as opaque, /i/ and /e/ are specified as transparent, the choice being a language-specific one.

Perhaps, however, the behavior of neutral vowels as either transparent or opaque can be predicted from general principles, rather than be stipulated on a case-by-case basis. In a given harmonic system, neutral vowels may have the active value of the harmonic feature, i.e., the value that spreads, or the passive value, i.e., the value that is assigned by default rule (see sec. 1.2.1 for a further clarification of these terms). Van der Hulst and Smith (1986) argue that in the former case the invariant vowels act as transparent, and that in the latter case they act opaquely, regardless of whether these vowels appear in a stem or an affix. Assuming that in Tangale [ATR] is the active value, the prediction is made that the low vowel is opaque since it is incompatible with this value. In Finnish [front] spreads, which is a value that both /i/ and /e/ can obviously bear. There are problematic cases for this approach as well: for a detailed discussion of these, see van der Hulst (1988a, 1988b).[6]

A further topic of considerable interest is the fact that most vowel harmony systems allow *disharmonicity* even where neutral vowels are not involved. First, polysyllabic stems may contain non-neutral vowels from opposite harmonic sets, and second, certain affixes may fail to harmonize with the stem even though they do not contain a neutral vowel. Such morphemes are referred to as disharmonic stems and disharmonic affixes, respectively. Often, but not always, disharmonicity results from unassimilated loan stems or loan suffixes.

We will illustrate disharmonicity with examples from Hungarian, which, like its relative Finnish, has palatal harmony. The dative suffix, for instance, has two variants: one with the front vowel /e/ and one with its back counterpart /a/ (pronounced [ɔ]). Consider the behavior of this suffix after the following disharmonic roots:

(13)   sofőːr-nek   "driver" (dat.)
       büroː-nak   "bureau" (dat.)

It would appear that the *last* vowel of the disharmonic root determines the quality of the suffix vowel, i.e., the backness of /o/ does not spread across the front vowel /őː/ and the frontness of /üː/ does not spread across back /o/. Put differently, /ő/ and /oː/ behave opaquely.[7] We return to the representation of disharmonic roots below.

Vago (1980a) lists a number of invariant suffixes in Hungarian. Consider the following suffixes from Hungarian (we use standard spelling except for the vowels):

(14)   -kor, -us, -u, -koː, -a

The suffixes in (14) have only non-neutral vowels (which all turn out to be *back*). If another suffix with a vowel that could harmonize is added, this vowel is back, even if the stem vowel is front. Examples are given in (15):[8]

(15)   Diminutive name   Instrumental
       Évus (Éva+us)   Évus-nak
       Gittus (Margit+us)   Gittus-nak
       Petyus (Péter+us)   Petyus-nak
       Rékus (Réka+us)   Rékus-nak
       Terus (Teréz+us)   Terus-nak
       Tündüs (Tünde+us)   Tündüs-nek[9]

The combination of a front-vowel stem and a disharmonic back suffix behaves identically to a simple disharmonic stem such as *büro*: the vowel immediately preceding the suffix determines the harmony.

To summarize, disharmonicity on the phonetic surface may have two distinct sources. Neutral vowels are invariant on phonological grounds. They may occur with vowels from the opposite set. As such they form "harmonic islands" (if they are transparent) or initiate a new "harmonic span" (if they are opaque). Disharmonicity may also have a *lexical*, i.e., idiosyncratic basis. This is the case with disharmonic stems and disharmonic affixes. In all cases monomorphemic and polymorphemic sequences behave the same way.

Even though we will discuss cases which differ in several ways from Tangale, Finnish, and Hungarian, the prototypical situation is that all vowels (regardless of their number) within a particular domain, usually said to be the (prosodic) word, agree with each other for one of their properties; interruptions of this pattern are due to neutral vowels or lexical exceptions.

1   Three Crucial Issues

1.1   *The Harmonic Domain*

Vowel harmony requirements are usually claimed to hold within the "word." The relevant notion of word is not necessarily that of the (complete) grammatical word, however. One case which frequently shows a mismatch between grammatical word and harmony domain is that of *compounds*, which, although single words grammatically, usually constitute as many harmonic spans as they have stems.[10] The phonological independence of compound constituents is relevant in a variety of phenomena, involving both stress and segmental processes, and in these cases members of compounds are said to form separate prosodic words.

This is in fact also the principal reason for postulating that the typical domain of vowel harmony is the *prosodic* word, rather than defining the domain in morphosyntactic terms. In this section we raise some questions with respect to the domain issue. There are two main arguments that suggest that characterizing the domain as the prosodic word is not completely satisfactory.

First, processes which make reference to higher-level prosodic categories such as the prosodic word are usually fully automatic, and often allophonic and "optional" (i.e., post-cyclic and perhaps even post-lexical). Vowel harmony is typically rather different in this respect, since it often has exceptions and is usually neutralizing and "obligatory." This suggests that vowel harmony is somewhat anomalous among the phonological processes that refer to prosodic categories.

Second, if the harmonic domain is indeed the prosodic word, we might expect to find cases of vowel harmony which take stems as their domain including only those affixes which form one prosodic word with their base, and excluding affixes which form a prosodic word by themselves. Following Booij and Rubach (1984), we refer to the former type of affixes as *cohering* affixes. If the prosodic word is the domain for vowel harmony we expect noncohering affixes to behave like members of compounds and, furthermore, that cohering affixes added to a noncohering affix will harmonize with the latter. We illustrate both cases in (16) (c=cohering; nc=noncohering):

(16) (a)   (b)

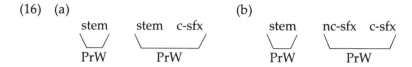

Contrary to what one might expect, analyses of vowel harmony never make reference to a distinction between cohering and noncohering affixes, so far as we are aware. Rather, if certain affixes fail to agree with the stem this is usually regarded as an idiosyncratic property of these affixes (i.e., they are lexically marked as disharmonic), and no independent evidence is supplied to show that these suffixes form independent prosodic words. In fact, in the case of vowel-initial suffixes, syllabification evidence indicates that they are not (cf. (15) above, where *Rékus* is syllabified *Ré.kus*, not *Rék.us*).

Third and perhaps most important, the existence of disharmony *within* prosodic words, we believe, invalidates the claim that prosodic words form the domain of vowel harmony. An alternative hypothesis concerning the vowel harmony domain is that vowel harmony applies with direct reference to the morphological structure, i.e., at some level in the morphological derivation, assuming a notion of level in the sense of Siegel (1974) or Kiparsky (1982). On this view of the domain issue, however, one would expect harmony systems in which all affixes on a particular level fail to harmonize, as well as affix-ordering effects, i.e., cases in which nonharmonizing affixes would be peripheral to harmonizing ones, or vice versa. We are, however, unaware of descriptions of vowel harmony systems that point clearly in this direction. Still, a positive argument in favor of the hypothesis that vowel harmony is sensitive to morphological structure in some way or other is the fact that inflectional affixes are usually more regular undergoers of harmony than derivational affixes.

A further issue concerns the question whether vowel harmony applies cyclicly or not. The two possibilities are schematized in (17):

(17)   (a) Cyclic harmony rule   (b) Post-cyclic harmony rule

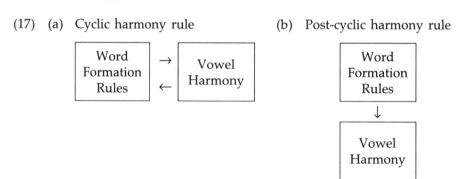

Descriptions and analyses of vowel harmony in the literature are often compatible with either option.[11]

We do not exclude the possibility that vowel harmony may take place within prosodic constituents. Foot-level vowel harmony has been reported, for example in Chamorro (see Topping 1968); it appears to apply in the foot carrying the main stress.[12] Among the vowel harmony cases discussed in the literature there may very well be cases where the domain is indeed the prosodic word.

It has also been suggested that vowel harmony may apply in domains which are even larger than the prosodic word. This involves cases where clitics harmonize with their hosts. It has been argued that the resulting prosodic unit forms a separate level called the *clitic group*. Vowel harmony, then, may also hold at this level. Whether the clitic group and the prosodic word form distinct prosodic categories has been disputed, however.[13] Still, the typical case involves a morphologization of the harmony domain, although the precise characteristics remain to be worked out.

Finally, there is no reason to exclude allophonic (non-neutralizing) and/or "optional" harmony. We are aware of two examples, namely the cases of Chukchee (see sec. 2.2 below) and Sesotho (see sec. 2.3 below). Given the considerations presented above, we expect to find such cases when harmony is post-lexical and prosodically conditioned.

1.2 Features

The phonological representation of an utterance contains a string of syllabic positions (Xs), which form the terminal nodes of a syllabic organization and the anchor point for phonological features (see chap. 5, this volume). With respect to the phonological features, two issues are of paramount importance for the analysis of vowel harmony. The first concerns the question of whether features are *binary* or *unary*, the second, the question of how features are organized among themselves. The relevance of the syllabic organization is discussed in section 1.3.

1.2.1 Binary or Unary Features

There are at least two relevant approaches to phonological primes. The first views primes as *binary features* (Jakobson, Fant, and Halle 1952; Chomsky and Halle 1968). A binary feature consists of a feature name, for example [round], and a value, + or −. Segments are specified as either [+round] or [−round]. On this view, we may define *harmony* as a state in which segments agree with respect to their value for some feature within the relevant domain.

A recent development within binary feature theory is *radical underspecification theory* (see chap. 4, this volume, and Archangeli 1984, 1988; Archangeli and Pulleyblank 1989, in press). Central to this approach is the proposal that for each feature one value is specified in the lexical representation of words, i.e., it is the value which is phonologically active.[14] The other value, on this view, is filled in by a default rule at later stages or at the end of the phonological derivation. This default value, then, becomes active late in the derivation (when "called upon" by a phonological rule) or is completely passive (when no phonological rule refers to it).[15]

It is important to realize that it may be difficult to decide which of the two values of a given feature is the active one and which is the default one on the basis of vowel harmony alone. In an exceptionless stem-controlled system, this is fundamentally impossible.[16] The default value can only be established in circumstances where it is certain that no spreading takes place. To make this clear, consider again the dative suffix in Hungarian, which alternates between -*nek* and -*nak* (see (13) and (15) above). Hence, on the assumption that vowel harmony is feature-filling, the vowel in this suffix is unspecified for front/backness and receives its value for this feature by spreading. However, the root *híd* "bridge", which has only a transparent vowel, takes a back vowel suffix:

(18) hiːd   "bridge"   hiːd-nak   "bridge" (dat.)

One interpretation is that neutral vowels cause no spreading. In that case, the behavior of roots like *híd* is evidence that the default value in Hungarian is [+back] and hence that the active, spreading value is [−back].[17]

A second approach to primes holds that segments consist of *unary components* (or *elements*), so that there is a single element [Round]. On this view, an unrounded segment lacks the element [Round] and harmony may be defined as a state in which segments agree in that they all have or all lack a particular element. We will refer to this approach as *unary component theory* (see chap. 18, this volume, and Rennison 1986; Anderson and Ewen 1987; van der Hulst 1989, 1991; Ewen and van der Hulst 1985, 1988).[18]

The unary approach can be regarded as a radical version of radical underspecification theory. Essentially, its claim is that one and the same value is active across languages and that default values are never phonologically active in any part of the phonology. With respect to vowel harmony, radical underspecification theory and unary component theory make different predictions. All other things being equal, radical underspecification theory allows [−round] to play an active role in the phonology of a given language, whereas unary component theory can under no circumstances refer to the property of not being round, or to the class of nonround segments: it is a widespread assumption that phonological rules cannot refer to the absence of the component. This means that the two approaches make different predictions with respect to the number of possible vowel harmony systems. According to radical underspecification theory, vowel harmony involving roundness may involve either [+round] or [−round] (or perhaps both). In other words, assuming the same set of features, radical underspecification theory predicts the existence of twice as many VH systems as does unary component theory. Compared to binary theories which do not adopt radical underspecification, radical underspecification theory makes at best statistical predictions, in that presumably vowel harmony systems based on the unmarked values are predicted to be more frequent.[19]

Proponents of binary feature systems have indeed argued that there are vowel harmony systems which involve [–back] and [+back], and [–ATR] and [+ATR] (as we will see below). No examples of [–round] harmony systems have been put forward. Unary systems with components like [round], [front], and [ATR] therefore must address the question how systems that are claimed to be based on [+back] and [–ATR] must be (re)analyzed. In this chapter, we will assume that the unary view is tenable. This is relatively clear for the front-back dimension and probably certain for the liprounding dimension, for which we use [front] and [round], respectively. For the tongue-root and height dimensions, however, we will make use of *two* components per dimension: [ATR]/[RTR] and [high]/[low], respectively. We view these as *pairs* of unary components.[20]

1.2.2   *Relations Among Features: Autosegmental Phonology*

We now turn to a second important aspect of subskeletal organization, namely the question of how features are organized among themselves, and how they are related to the skeletal positions. We will briefly outline the relevant aspects of the prevailing model, *autosegmental phonology* (Goldsmith 1976), bearing in mind that this model can be combined either with a binary-feature theory or with a unary-feature theory. We will draw attention to the possibilities and problems that both combinations lead to.

Central to autosegmental phonology is the claim that there is not necessarily a one-to-one relation between syllabic positions and features. Let us illustrate this point, first in the case of representations involving binary features. In addition to (19a), (19b), and (19c) are also possible phonological representations:

(19)   (a) X X X X   (b) X X X X   (c) X X X X
            | | | | \ \ / / | | /\
            [+ – + –]_f   [+   –]_f   [+ – +   –]_f

The notation introduced here is merely a typographical convenience: a series of values for the same feature *plus* the syllabic position for which they hold are enclosed within a pair of square brackets, which is labeled with the feature name. In autosegmental phonology such a structure is called a *plane*, and the sequence of values is referred to as a *tier*.

In (19a) each slot has its own specification for the feature [±f], but in (19b) the first three slots *share* the same value. In (19c) the last slot is provided with two values, the first of which is shared with the preceding segment.

Assuming that the plus value corresponds to a unary component, the equivalent of (19) in unary component theory would be:

(20)   (a)   X X X X   (b)   X X X X   (c)   X X X X

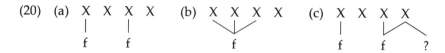

Neither the unary approach nor a binary feature model incorporating radical underspecification theory has an equivalent to (19c): one segment cannot be said to bear two "values" of a single feature, because it does not exist (in unary component theory), or because only one value is allowed lexically (radical underspecification theory). This issue, however, is not critical to vowel harmony, so we will not dwell upon this point.

Unlike the system of phonological representations proposed in Chomsky and Halle (1968), autosegmental phonology allows us to represent cases in which segments, or rather skeletal points, agree with respect to a feature value in terms of multiple association or sharing. (In unary component theory, harmonic agreement only involves sharing if the agreement involves the *presence* of a component.) This applies to cases of local assimilation, i.e., assimilation between adjacent segments, but also to non-local phenomena, involving relations between nonadjacent segments. In such an approach, vowel harmony is an example of the latter type. Harmony (within morphemes) and the harmonizing of affix vowels is expressed in terms of feature sharing. A certain domain containing segments which must agree with respect to a particular feature need only be provided with a single instance of this feature, which can then be said to associate to all possible target segments in the domain D:[21]

(21)

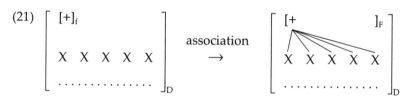

(The dots represent the other planes)

Let us refer to a feature which associates to all segments of a certain type in a domain as a *prosody* or *prosodic feature*, and to the segments to which it associates as the *anchors*.

Stems, on this view, consist of two independent, unordered pieces of information, the relation between which is predictable, namely the harmonic feature and the rest (including the anchor positions). The relation between both is established by harmony rules whose application is controlled by a set of universal association conventions.

We will assume that association takes place in two steps. First, the feature is associated to a *designated anchor position*; this could be the rightmost or leftmost vowel (or perhaps the stressed vowel). It then *spreads* to other vowels. The second step may have to be further specified for *directionality* if the designated position is not peripheral.

We have now introduced sufficient terminological background to proceed with a discussion of the third central issue of interest raised by the phenomenon of vowel harmony, viz., the issue of *locality*. This will lead us to discuss further developments in autosegmental phonology.

1.3   Locality

A question of obvious relevance in any analysis of vowel harmony is that of its *non-local* nature. Vowel harmony essentially consists of the requirement that all vowels in a certain domain must agree with respect to a certain property. If this is expressed as association of a single feature to an unspecified number of anchors, the association procedure must pick out specific types of segments (here, vowels), and the resulting configuration of multiple association will involve skipping the slots filled by consonants.

To illustrate the issue, let us for the sake of simplicity encode the distinction between vowels and consonants on the skeletal tier, so that we can use c and v instead of X (leaving aside the issue whether in actual fact there are two types of skeletal points or whether this distinction is purely expressed in terms of syllable structure, cf. Levin 1985a and chap. 5, this volume). A harmonic configuration appears in (22):

(22)
$$\left[\begin{array}{c} [+]_f \\ \diagup\diagdown \\ \text{C V C V C} \\ \cdots\cdots\cdots \end{array} \right]_D$$

It is generally agreed that non-local association must be regarded with great suspicion (Steriade 1987, and chap. 4, this volume). Analyses of vowel harmony have therefore sought to reconcile the idea that vowel harmony involves feature sharing with the assumption that all feature sharing is local in some sense or another. Clearly, if vowel harmony can be shown to conform to some sort of locality, this will not be strict locality, which we will define as locality at the skeletal level.

We will consider two approaches to this issue. The first is crucially based on a "geometrical" elaboration of autosegmental phonology, whereas the second is based on the idea that vowels occupy a privileged position in the syllabic organization.

1.3.1   The Geometrical Approach

In an influential offshoot of autosegmental phonology, features do not associate directly to skeletal positions, but rather to *class nodes* to which features of the same kind are associated (i.e., place features under a Place node, laryngeal features under a Laryngeal node, etc.). These class nodes in turn are associated to a *root node* and root nodes associate to skeletal slots. This approach is referred to as *feature geometry* (see chap. 7, this volume).

For our purposes one aspect of such a tree-like organization is important, viz., the claim that vowel features associate to a class node which consonants lack.[22] One might propose that the set of harmonic units for some harmonic feature P can quite straightforwardly be defined as the set of segments which have the class node to which P associates. In (23) below, this class node is labeled V-place (see chap. 7, this volume). Hence, as long as intervening consonants do not have a V-place node, feature sharing between vowels *is* local because their class nodes are adjacent:[23]

(23)

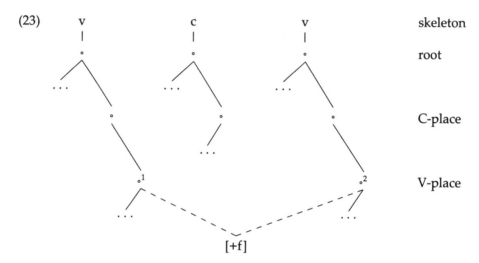

The consonant in (23) will be invisible when the feature [+f] is associated to the nodes labeled 1 and 2. Hence the multiple association pattern that arises is local. We will say that the consonant is legitimately skipped.[24]

The structure in (23) is intended to explain another fact. It has often been claimed that harmony among consonants is much rarer than vowel harmony. The structure in (23) accounts for this: since vowels have a C-place node, consonantal place features cannot spread from one consonant to another if a vowel intervenes. However, since it is not clear whether vowels *need* the C-place node, or whether a contrast could exist between vowels with and vowels without such a node, or whether there are harmony processes which affect *all* segments with a C-place node, the C-place node on vowels seems largely a diacritic device.[25]

1.3.2   *The Syllable-head Approach*

There is a different line of explanation for the asymmetry noted in the previous section, which has, however, been less well developed. This approach makes use of the idea that vowels are syllable heads. The central idea is that vowel harmony involves a relation between syllable nodes and by implication, because vowels are syllable heads, between vowels. We shall take this idea quite literally by assuming, first, that harmonic features associate to syllable nodes and then percolate to the heads of these nodes, i.e., the vocalic root nodes.

(24)

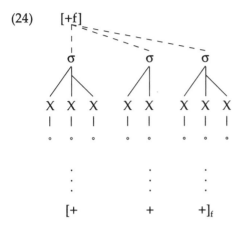

$$[+ \qquad + \qquad +]_f$$

Lexically, no relation between [+f] and syllable heads need be assumed, just as in what may be called the "standard" autosegmental approach discussed in the previous section. Moreover, if it is assumed that locality is a constraint governing *all* linguistic representations, we expect that vowel harmony involves a local relation between adjacent syllable nodes.

The syllable-head approach has the advantage of making the extra geometrical apparatus in (23) largely unnecessary, while it also explains the asymmetry between consonants and vowels in vowel harmony: consonants are *not* heads of constituents which are adjacent at any level. Hence, it may lead to the possibility of developing a more restricted conception of the segment-internal geometry. A view like this has been proposed in dependency and government-based approaches to phonology (see chap. 17, this volume, and Anderson and Ewen 1987; Kaye, Lowenstamm, and Vergnaud 1985), but as yet no systematic treatment of vowel harmony has been cast in such a theory (cf. Vergnaud 1976, Hart 1981). It would seem that a "syllable-head" theory of vowel harmony is ultimately committed to the claim that vowel harmony involves a relation which is different from assimilation processes that apply strictly locally, i.e., between adjacent skeletal slots. Vowel harmony, on this view, would not involve feature sharing below the skeleton at all.[26]

2 Types of Harmony Processes

In this section we offer a typology of vowel harmony systems. In section 0.2 we presented the basic types of harmony systems: Tangale had a vowel harmony system based on the "open-close" distinction. This has been called a "cross-height," or, in more current terminology, a tongue root harmony system. Tongue root harmony systems may be analyzed in different ways, namely by way of the feature Advanced Tongue Root [ATR], or Retracted Tongue Root [RTR], or by way of height features [high] and [low], in which case the terms aperture or height harmony seem more appropriate.[27] It is important to realize that this is partly a matter of theoretical interpretation and partly a result of the fact that different types of tongue root or aperture/height harmony are involved.

We will discuss a number of harmony types that involve either the tongue root dimension or aperture (or height). The literature reports harmony systems using all these features:

(25) (a) [ATR] harmony   (sec. 2.1)
      (b) [RTR] harmony   (sec. 2.2)
      (c) [high] harmony   (sec. 2.3)
      (d) [low] harmony   (sec. 2.4)

It has been pointed out by several researchers that the tongue root dimension is closely related to the aperture/height dimension. Advancing the tongue root almost inevitably leads to raising (and fronting) the tongue body; see Hall and Hall (1980) for a discussion of this correlation. *Aperture* is often used to refer to the same dimension as tongue height, but if we take this as referring to jaw opening it is strictly speaking independent of tongue body activity, irrespective of the question whether the latter is entirely determined by tongue root activity (as Wood 1981 seems to suggest). Nonetheless, it seems that aperture and height conspire to produce a single dimension along which a four-way distinction can maximally be made and that, independently of that dimension, a two-way distinction is produced by activity of the tongue root. In other words, aperture/height and tonge root are independent, even though certain correlations are strongly preferred.

The four-height aperture/height distinction calls for two vowel components, [high] and [low] which, then, can both be harmonic features. Both function in the representation of a single vowel system if more than two aperture degrees are made. We will discuss harmony systems that appear to involve either [low] or [high] spreading. We do not know of systems that involve spreading of both. Also, given the fact that [high] and [low] characterize a single dimension, it is not always clear which of the two is involved.

For the [ATR]/[RTR] distinction one component per language seems sufficient. Still, we believe there is evidence for two types of tongue root harmonies, i.e., those in which [ATR] is the spreading value and those in which [RTR] is. However, again, it is not always obvious which of the two is active.

The ambiguity between [high]/[low] and between [ATR]/[RTR] combined with the fact that both dimensions are closely related may lead the phonologist to hesitate between four possible analyses when confronted with a particular harmony system (i.e., those above). In fact, we believe that particular systems may be truly ambiguous, which is also suggested by the fact that historical shifts have occurred from one type to another. In sections 2.1 to 2.4 we offer a discussion of tongue root and aperture/height cases.

In section 2.6 we will deal with palatal harmony (as in Finnish and Hungarian), in section 2.7 we will deal with rounding harmony, and in section 2.8 a number of other harmony systems appear.

2.1 [ATR]

2.1.1 Root-controlled Systems

In this section we briefly discuss a number of systems which have been described as involving [ATR] or which can easily be interpreted as such. We emphasize the fact that many [ATR] systems are complicated by the various types of mergers that have taken place, creating "crazy" alternations, and by the partial reinterpretations of ambiguous aspects of such systems that have led to mixed harmony systems in which [ATR] spreading seems to co-occur with the spreading of [low], sometimes creating three-way alternations.

We focus on the African continent. [ATR] harmony may very well be an areal feature of this continent. Tongue root systems occurring elsewhere in the world, especially in Asia, more often seem to involve [RTR] spreading, although, as pointed out above, this ultimately depends on the analysis. These cases will be discussed in section 2.2.

In ATR harmony systems, segments that form harmonic pairs differ in the articulatory dimension of tongue root placement. [ATR] vowels are produced with an advanced tongue root. We will use a unary feature [ATR] to refer to vowels produced with an advanced tongue root, and [RTR] for vowels with a retracted or neutral tongue root position. An example of a harmony system based on the distinction might have the vowel system in (26):

(26) advanced tongue root   retracted tongue root
       front   back   front   back
         i   u   ɪ   ʊ
         e   o   ɛ   ɔ
                a   ɑ

Vowel harmony systems based on the ATR distinction are common among the Niger-Kordofanian and the Nilo-Saharan language families on the African continent; among the two other major African families there are some examples in the Afro-Asiatic family (Semitic and Chadic branches). In the other branches of this family (Cushitic and Semitic) there are also vowel harmony languages. For Cushitic we mention Somali (Armstrong 1934) and for Chadic we mention

Kera (Ebert 1974, 1979) and Ga'anda (Newman 1977). Harmony systems in Semitic languages are analyzed in Puech (1978). A number of Kru languages have full systems (e.g., Vata; see Kaye 1982). We are not aware of any cases in the Khoisan language family.

ATR-systems are typically *reduced*, i.e., they either lack the low [+ATR] vowel /a/ (27a) or the high [−ATR] vowels /ɪ/ and /ʊ/ (27b), or both, as in (27c) (see Williamson 1973, 1983; Lindau 1975):

(27) (a)   advanced tongue root   retracted tongue root
        front   back   front   back
         i   u   ɪ   ʊ
         e   o   ɛ   ɔ
                           ɑ

   (b)   advanced tongue root   retracted tongue root
        front   back   front   back
         i   u
         e   o   ɛ   ɔ
             a   ɑ

   (c)   advanced tongue root   retracted tongue root
        front   back   front   back
         i   u
         e   o   ɛ   ɔ
                           ɑ

The Tangale vowel harmony system has the (27a) vowel inventory. Recall that Jungraithmayr (1971) described the two sets of vowels as *close* and *open*. This used to be a common way of referring to this opposition, which was later proposed to involve the feature [ATR] (Stewart 1971; see also Halle and Stevens 1969). Before the feature [ATR] came into use, African systems were also described in terms of features referring to vowel height (open/close, high/ low), or in terms of a feature [±tense]. The latter type of analysis was inspired by the fact that the distinction between the two vowel sets, especially where the mid and high vowels are concerned, is auditorily similar to the distinction between tense and lax vowels in the Germanic languages (see also Ladefoged and Maddieson 1990: 106ff.).

The mergers which are behind the reduced systems in (27) above lead to unexpected alternation:

(28)

                            Change in height   Alternation
                            /ɑ/ → /ɛ/, /ɔ/   /a/ – /ɛ/ (a)
                                                  /a/ – /ɔ/ (b)
                            /ɪ/, /ʊ/ → /e/, /o/   /i/ – /e/ (c)
      Change in class   /u/ – /o/ (d)
                            /e/, /o/ → /ɪ/, /ʊ/   /ɪ/ – /ɛ/ (e)
                                                  /ʊ/ – /ɔ/ (f)

	No change in height		
	/ɑ/ → /ɑ/	neutralized	(g)
	/ɪ/, /ʊ/ → /i/, /u/	neutralized	(h)
	/e/, /o/ → /ɛ/, /ɔ/	neutralized	(i)
No change in class	Change in height		
	/ɑ/ → /e/, /o/	/ɑ/ – /e/	(j)
		/ɑ/ – /o/	(k)
	/ɪ/, /ʊ/ → /ɛ/, /ɔ/	/i/ – /ɛ/	(l)
		/u/ – /ɔ/	(m)

The above scheme implies a classification of the different routes into three groups. If a marked vowel (i.e., /ɪ/, /ʊ/ or /ɑ/) merges, it either falls together with a vowel within the other harmonic class, or it falls together with a vowel in its own class (necessarily of a differrent height). In the first case it falls together with its harmonic counterpart or with a vowel of a different height. In (29), we illustrate the possibilities, taking the marked vowel /ɪ/ as an example:

(29) /ɪ/ → /i/   (f)   Alternation /ɪ/ – /i/ is neutralized.
      /ɪ/ → /e/   (c)   Alternation /ɪ/ – /i/ is changed to /e/ – /i/, i.e.,
                          that ATR difference is replaced by a height difference.
      /ɪ/ → /ɛ/   (f)   Alternation /ɪ/ – /i/ is changed to /ɛ/ – /i/, i.e., a
                          height difference is added to the ATR difference.

It is easy to see that these changes have different consequences for the synchronic analysis of the vowel harmony system. In the first case we get a disharmony effect, since the /i/ which derives from */ɪ/ now co-occurs with non-ATR vowels. In the third case no disharmony results, but we do get the complication of having an extra change in height. The second case combines both the disharmony effect and the extra height change. We must also bear in mind that it may happen that vowels in stems and affixes take different routes, and that the vowel which a particular vowel merges with may vary from language to language.

A language which has a rather complicated system of this type is Ogori (Niger-Kordofanian, Niger-Congo, Kwa) (Chumbow 1982; Calabrese 1988, pp. 63–96).[28] Ogori has the following vowel system:

(30) i   u
        e   o
          ɛ   ɔ
              a

In stems mid /e o/ cannot co-occur with /ɛ ɔ/. /i u a/ occur with both. Affixes show a remarkable set of alternation patterns:

(31)   [ATR]   —
          i   ɛ
          u   ɔ
          e   a

It seems that different patterns of merger have arisen in stems and affixes in this case.

We find remarkable patterns of reduction in the Moru-Madi languages (Chari-Nile (east) (Andersen 1986a, 1986b, Dimmendaal 1983). One language, Moru, has ten vowels on the surface and appears to be the most conservative dialect. All the other languages have reduced systems. Among the mergers that have taken place, there are two which are unexpected, i.e., the loss of the mid ATR vowels /e/ and /o/ (which merge with /I/ and /U/). The mid vowels are usually more stable than both the ATR low vowel and the non-[ATR] high vowels.

2.1.2   Dominant Systems

The systems described in the previous section have usually been analyzed in terms of ATR-spreading. However, it would not be easy to prove that they could not be analyzed in terms of [RTR]. A distinction between the two possibilities could be made on theoretical grounds if the behavior of the low vowel is taken into account. If the low vowel behaves as opaque it would be a theoretical indication that [ATR] spreading is involved (see van der Hulst and Smith 1986).

This indeterminacy is not present in dominant systems, since it is not stems that determine the behavior of affixes, but a given harmonic value that takes precedence. We find a number of dominant systems in the Nilo-Saharan family, especially in the Chari-Nile (east), Nilotic branch.

We consider Turkana to be an example of a dominant system, which shows an additional interesting complication (Dimmendaal 1983; van der Hulst and Smith 1986; Noske 1987; Vago and Leder, to appear; Trigo 1991). Turkana has a nine-vowel system:

(32)   i   u
              I   ʊ
          e   o
              ɛ   ɔ
                    a

The dominant character of Turkana vowel harmony appears from the fact that there are ATR-determining suffixes. This is shown in (33):

(33) (a) ak-ɪs-ɪmʊj   INF-CAUS-eat   "to feed"
     (b) a-ɪmʊj-ɪ   1-eat-ASP   "I ate"
     (c) ak-imuj-eeni   INF-eat-HAB   "to eat regularly"

The forms in (33a) and (33b) establish that the root vowels in the stem for "eat" are underlyingly [RTR], and the habitual suffix in (c) imposes its [ATR] value on these vowels (see Vago and Leder, to appear, p. 3).

In addition, however, some suffixes appear to spread [RTR], despite the fact that the dominant value is [ATR]. If this is correct, this would contradict our claim that [ATR] and [RTR] are never active in one language.

(34) /ɛ-ibus-a-kɪn-a / [ɛɪbʊsakɪna]

The whole word is [RTR] in the presence of the last suffix /-A/.

Outside the Nilo-Saharan family we find a dominant [ATR] system in Tunen (Bantu A.44; see van der Hulst, Mous, and Smith 1986). In the next section we will consider the cases of Chukchee and Nez Perce, in which [RTR] appears to be the dominant value. We are not aware of dominant systems involving such features as [high], [low], [front], or [round].

2.2 *[RTR]*

Archangeli and Pulleyblank (1989) argue that vowel harmony in Yoruba involves leftward spreading of [RTR]. Yoruba has a seven-vowel system (ignoring nasality):

(35) /i/   /u/
      /e/   /o/
      /ɛ/   /ɔ/
          /a/

The high mid vowels (e, o) and low mid vowels (ɛ, ɔ) do not co-occur, but in addition /e/ and /o/ do not occur to the left of /a/. Furthermore, /ɛ/ and /ɔ/ can only precede high vowels if the latter are word final, i.e., the sequence in (36) is illformed:

(36) *...ɛ/ɔ - i/u - V ...

Archangeli and Pulleyblank claim that the data can be straightforwardly analyzed if [RTR] spreads from right to left. /i/ and /u/ lack [RTR] counterparts and are opaque.

It is possible to analyze the Yoruba data in terms of [low] spreading if /e/ and /o/ are analyzed as the unmarked front and round vowels:

(37) /i/   /u/   /e/   /o/   /ɛ/   /ɔ/   /a/
      [front]   [round]   [front]   [round]   [front]   [round]
      [ATR]   [ATR]   [low]   [low]   [low]

The most remarkable aspect of this representation is perhaps the fact that high mid vowels are represented as [ATR]-less high vowels. We do not believe that this characterization is objectionable. Given the fact that the full range of possible contrasts is not exploited, the phonological characterization cannot be established without taking the behavior of the vowels into consideration. The featural analysis in (37) permits a different view on the spreading process. Segments which in the analysis of Archangeli and Pulleyblank cause [RTR]-spread constitute a natural class here in being specified as [low].

The Tungusic languages (Altaic) provide another potential case for [RTR] harmony, although no detailed analyses are available to us which present a conclusive case.

Ard (1981, 1984) provides surveys of the vowel systems and harmonies found in these languages. His general claim is that the harmony is based on tongue position (plain vs. retracted) in the most conservative dialect of Even and on height in the other languages. Hayata (1980) and Hattori (1982), who speaks of the "open-close" type, make the same point (other sources on harmony systems of this sort are Comrie (1981) and Kim (1978), the latter of whom uses the term "diagonal vowel harmony" to refer to this type of harmony). By way of an example, we will briefly consider the case of Even. The language has the following vowel system:

(38)   i   (+)   u
       ɪ   (ɪ)   ʊ
       e   ə   ɵ
       a   ə̂   ɔ

There are alternations for all "higher-lower" pairs (/i/-/ɪ/, etc.); the lower series is called *hard*, the higher *soft* (this contrast is also known as masculine/feminine). The hard series is described as involving retraction. In most Tungusic languages the difference co-occurs with a distinction in back velars (uvulars) and plain velars, although front hard, retracted vowels usually fail to condition uvulars.[29]

In the generative literature, the vowel harmony system of the Tungusic language Manchu has received a great deal of attention. There has been an extensive discussion of the treatment of exceptions within the vowel harmony system of this language (Vago 1973; Odden 1978; Finer 1978), who analyze it in terms of a front-back harmony. Hayata (1980) and subsequently Ard (1984), however, argue that the harmony in this language, too, is based on relative height, just as in the other Tungusic languages: retracted versus plain, or high versus low.

Kenstowicz (1983) analyzes the harmony system of Chukchee in terms of [RTR] spreading. The same approach has been pursued for Nez Perce (Hall and Hall 1980; Anderson and Durand 1988), Coeur d'Alene (Johnson 1975; Doak 1992) and Middle Korean (Kim 1978).

Consider the VH systems of the first two languages:

(39) (a) Chukchee

high		non-high	
front	back	front	back
i	u		
			o
æ		a	

(b) Nez Perce

high			non-high	
front		back	front	back
i	ɨ	u		
e			ə	o
			a	

In (39a) /æ/ and /a/ form a harmonic pair and /i/ is unpaired, i.e., it is neutral. In (39b), the vowel /e/ is phonologically a member of the high set, whereas /o/ is the lower harmonic counterpart of /u/ and is part of the low set.

Mongolian languages have often been analyzed as having palatal harmony, but Svantesson (1985) argues that at least the eastern branch (Khalkha, Chakhar, Buriat, Bargha) have vowel harmony based on pharyngeal width. He refers to this as [ATR]-harmony. Rialland and Djamouri (1984) propose that [−ATR] is the spreading value in Khalkha Mongolian. This means that, in the terms used here, Khalkha has [RTR] harmony.

As in the case of Yoruba, these systems could also be classified as [low] harmony systems. That is, in a feature system using [low], with a somewhat broader interpretation than in Chomsky and Halle (1968) of [+low] values (i.e., including (lower) mid vowels), one might classify [RTR] harmony systems which do not involve a retracted set for high *and* mid vowels among the systems based on aperture.

2.3 *[high]*

In this section we discuss a number of harmony systems that have been described as involving the *aperture* dimension of vowels in a particular domain, more specifically involving the spreading of [high].

Consider first the case of Kinande (Clements 1991), which has seven underlying vowels. Vowels *raise* one degree before the stem vowels /i u/. Mid vowels raise to an intermediate level:

(40)

$$
\begin{array}{ll}
\begin{array}{l}
\rightarrow \text{i} \\
\;\; \text{ɪ}
\end{array} &
\begin{array}{l}
\text{u} \leftarrow \\
\text{ʊ}
\end{array} \\[1em]
\begin{array}{l}
\rightarrow [\text{e}] \\
\;\; \text{ɛ}
\end{array} &
\begin{array}{l}
[\text{o}] \leftarrow \\
\;\; \text{ɔ}
\end{array} \\[1em]
\quad \text{a} &
\end{array}
$$

The low vowel does not raise, but appears to be transparent, although Hyman (1989) points out that *long* low vowels do undergo the rule. Even though this system has been described as involving raising, the tradional feature [high] is not adequate, since the raised version of /ɛ/ and /ɔ/ is not a high vowel.

Schlindwein (1987), Hyman (1989), and Mutaka (1991) analyze this system with a rule that spreads [ATR], which is clearly a possible analysis. There are a number of systems for which an analysis in terms of [high] spreading is more strongly supported. McCarthy (1984) claims that aperture harmony in Pasiego is manifested in two ways, depending on the aperture of the stressed vowel, which is the trigger. The low vowel is transparent.

(41)   (a)   i/u   →   e/o % ... (a) ... é/ó   (lowering)
     (b)   e/o   →   i/u % ... (a) ... i/u   (raising)

Leftward raising is also triggered by a /j/ or /w/ occurring as a prenuclear vowel in a stressed syllable. The two-way nature of this harmony process has been used as an argument in favor of the binary status of the feature [high], and as an argument to analyze harmony as a feature-changing process. In the analysis of McCarthy (1984), Pasiego harmony is analyzed as a rule spreading [αhigh] bidirectionally.

Vago (1988) argues that lowering is not a rule of Pasiego, however, because there is little evidence for a rule that lowers vowels that can be shown to be underlyingly high. On the other hand, the raising aspect of the analysis is well founded. The importance of this finding is that harmony need not be analyzed as a feature-changing process. Nor do we need a binary feature [±high]. The facts are compatible with an analysis which specifies morphemes as either [high] or leaves them unspecified (see chap. 4, this volume, as well). The feature [high] links to the stressed vowel and then spreads bidirectionally to unstressed targets. The default is to leave vowels non-high. Glides are also specified as high. They spread only leftwardly because on their right there is a stressed vowel, i.e., a non-target.

An analysis of vowel harmony in the Apulian dialect of Francavilla-Fontana (Southern Italy) as involving [high] spreading is offered in Calabrese (1986) and Sluyters (1988). However, even for these cases an analysis can be maintained in which the spreading feature is [ATR] (Durand 1991), if /e/ and /o/ are regarded as the [RTR] counterparts of /i/ and /u/, respectively.

However, not all harmony systems that have been analyzed as aperture harmony systems are susceptible to a reanalysis in terms of advanced tongue root. The clearest case comes from Sesotho (Harris 1987). As in Kinande, mid vowels raise, but in Sesotho the trigger can be any high vowel, i.e., /i ɯ ʊ/.[30]

The interest of the Sesotho raising rule is that it is difficult to see how this rule could involve just [ATR] in view of the fact that all high vowels trigger it. Hence this looks like evidence for spreading an aperture feature. Again, however, the spreading feature cannot be [+high] in the traditional sense, because the raised output of the lower mid vowels do not become high themselves. An analysis based on aperture which does not use traditional features [high] and [low] is offered in Clements (1991).

2.4 *[low]*

As pointed out by Clements (1991), Bantu languages vary in having a seven- or a five-vowel (or more complex) system. A seven-vowel system is reconstructed for Proto-Bantu. Five-vowel systems have undergone a merger of the two highest series:

(42)   i   u
          ɪ   ʊ   ɪ   ʊ
          e   o   e   o
                a   a

A common pattern of height assimilation is that the first vowel of the stem determines the height of subsequent vowels in the stem and the suffixes.
   In Kikuyu, the applied suffix shows the following alternations:

(43) tiY-ɪr-a   "stop for"   ker-er-a "chop for"
      rut-ɪr-a   "work for"   ror-er-a "look at"
      rɪh-ɪr-a   "pay for someone else"
      kʊm-ɪr-a   "rebuke for"
      Yamb-ɪr-a "bark at"

In five-vowel languages, the same alternations are found. Suffixes may also show an /ʊ/-/o/ alternation, which in Kikuyu happens only after /o/, though in other languages (e.g., Kongo), it is also triggered by /e/. Clements mentions that the harmony is extended to prefixes in a few languages (Gusii, Llogoori). Round vowels are more resistent to this process, but in Kikuyu they participate if they share their roundness with the trigger.
   This lowering can be interpreted as the spread of the feature [low], which forces us to explain formally why the low vowel /a/ does not trigger the process. The low vowel is also opaque, in the sense that lowness does not propagate across it.
   The question can also be raised how the highest vowels in seven-vowel systems can be excluded as targets. A possibility that comes to mind would be to claim that the component [low] cannot spread to the highest vowels because this would lead to an incompatible combination of components (in the relevant language). For instance, if we say that the highest vowels are [ATR], we could assume that the combination [ATR, low] is excluded.

2.5   Mixed Systems

In some languages we encounter a three-way alternation as a result of [ATR] and [low] spreading, e.g., Klao (Kru) (Singler 1983) and Togo-remnant languages (Ford 1973). Van der Hulst, Mous, and Smith (1986) present an analysis of the latter group of languages, and argue that the three-way alternation is caused by a mixture of two harmonies, one presumably involving [ATR], the other [low].

Most of these languages have a seven-vowel system. In Santrokofi, for example, the following alternations occur:

(44)   affix   i   e   ɛ
             u   o   ɔ
         – – – – – – – – – – – – – – – – – –
       stem   i   u   e   o   ɛ   ɔ   a

Apparently the suffix vowels undergo [ATR]-spreading (from /i u e o/) and [low]-spreading (from /e oɔ a/).

2.6   Palatal Harmony

In palatal harmony systems, vowels which form harmonic pairs differ in relative frontness. Depending on the vowel system, the vowels which form such pairs may differ just in their value for the harmonic feature (as in (45a)), or also in their value for another feature, if this is predictable on the basis of the value of the harmonic feature (as in (45b)):

(45)   (a)

	front		back		
	non-round	round	non-round	round	
	i	ü	ɨ	u	high
	e	ö	ə	o	mid
	æ		a		low

(b)

	front		back		
	non-round	round	non-round	round	
	i			u	high
	e			o	mid
	æ		a		low

In a system such as (45b) /i/ and /u/ form a harmonic pair; however, they differ with respect to two features, and one might wish to argue that the harmonic feature could just as well be [round]. The low vowel pair /æ/: /a/, however, shows that the relevant difference between the two sets involves backness and that for non-low vowels roundness is redundant. Palatal systems in which /i/:/u/ and /e/:/o/ form pairs are rare. It is more usual that vowels which form a harmonic pair differ *only* in the harmonic feature, as in (45a). The system of (45b) is relevant for vowel harmony in Chamorro (Topping 1968; Poser 1982).

Palatal harmony also occurs in Caucasian languages: Hinalug (Dressler 1985) and Bezhta (also Caucasian, more specifically North East, belonging to the group of Daghestan languages).[31]

(46) i   ü   u
      e   ö   o
             ä   a

Harmony affects vowels and coronal consonants (but not /t/ and /l/), which alternate between a non-palatal and palatal form:

(47) I   a o u i   s z c c′
      II   ä ö ü i (e)   S Z C C′ and two emphatic laryngeals

It was pointed out above that in many harmony systems, not every vowel will have a harmonic counterpart. Recall the case of Finnish, which has the vowel system in (48):

(48)

	front		back		
	non-round	round	non-round	round	
	i	ü		u	high
	e	ö		o	mid
	æ		a		low

The front vowels /i/ and /e/ do not have a harmonic counterpart. We have referred to such vowels as *neutral*. They are typically the result of phoneme mergers in the inventory. The important question of how neutral vowels behave in harmony systems has been discussed above. A peculiarity of Finnish is that transparency has also been reported for the non-neutral vowels /ü/ and /ö/ (Campbell 1980; Demirdache 1988).

Many Turkic languages have the following system:

(49) Turkic palatal harmony:

	front		back		
	non-round	round	non-round	round	
	i	ü	ɨ	u	high
	e	ö	ə	o	non-high

Palatal systems are usually analyzed with [-back], or [front] as the active value. Some researchers, however, have argued that [+back] can also be the active value. Probably the most challenging case to a unary approach to palatality harmony is the Estonian VH system (Kiparsky 1992). Farkas and Beddor (1987) argue in favor of an active [+back] value in Hungarian.

2.7 *Labial Harmony*

In labial harmony, harmonic pairs differ in having or not having lip rounding as a distinctive feature. This involves the feature [±round]. In principle, a vowel system such as that in (50) can be divided into a set of [+round] vowels and a set of [−round] ones:

(50)   round   non-round
       front   back   front   back
        ü   u   i   ɨ   high
        ö   o   e   ə   mid
                   ɒ   a   low

Many Turkic languages have a two-height eight-vowel system, showing both palatal harmony (cf. (49) above) and labial harmony:

(51) Turkic labial harmony:
               round   non-round
       front   back   front   back
        ü   u   i   ɨ   high
        ö   o   e   a   non-high

In the Turkish system /e/ and /a/ do not function as the harmonic counterparts of /ö/ and /o/, however, so that labial harmony effectively applies to high vowels only (see also n. 6 for this type of "contextual neutralization").

Labial harmony systems may be reduced in various ways. Korn (1969) provides some information on different patterns of reduction in labial harmony in Turkic languages.

A topic of special interest concerns *parasitic harmony* (Steriade 1981; Cole and Trigo 1988; Odden 1991). There are cases in which labial harmony is restricted to words the vowels of which are all front as a result of palatal harmony. The vowel harmony system of Kirghiz (C. Johnson 1980) is a case in point. The vowel system is as in Turkish, and suffixes have either a high or a low vowel. Suffixes have four variants, as shown below:

(52) bil-di   bil-gen   bil-üü   "know"
      ber-di   ber-gen   ber-üü   "give"
      kül-dü   kül-gön   kül-üü   "laugh"
      kör-dü   kör-gön   kör-üü   "see"
      kɨl-dɨ   kɨl-gan   kɨl-uu   "do, perform"

al-dɨ	al-gan	al-uu	"take"
tut -tu	*tut-kan*	tut-uu	"hold"
bol-du	bol-gon	bol-uu	"be, become"

Unlike Turkish, Kirghiz has suffixes which are intrinsically round. A further difference is that /I/ and /A/ (which are not intrinsically round) *both* undergo labial harmony with one notable exception: /A/ is not rounded after a high back vowel: *tut-kan* instead of *tut-kon*.

Kirghiz has a labial harmony rule, then, which fails to produce /o/. This is the same as in Turkish, but in this case it cannot be attributed to the absence of /o/ in non-initial syllables, since low rounded suffixes do exist (i.e., with intrinsic rounding).[32] Why the sequence of a high followed by a non-high vowel is the most likely to have rounding harmony awaits a theoretical explanation (see Odden 1991 for discussion). Low vowels are more resistant to rounding. In a front domain, a high low sequence already shares a feature, namely [front], which facilitates the harmony. In a sequence of two low vowels, harmony is facilitated by the fact that the vowels are already identical.

Labial harmony is widespread in Uralic languages (see, e.g., Collinder 1960; Finnish, Hungarian, and Cheremis are well-known examples) and in Altaic languages (with examples from all well-known families, Turkic, Tungusic, and Mongolian). We wish to observe that in most cases labial harmony co-occurs with another type of harmony, and that the labial harmony is more restricted in these cases (see Vago 1973 for a general discussion). This was the case in the Turkic systems that we have just discussed. It also applies to the Tungusic languages, where labial harmony co-occurs with tongue root harmony and is generally restricted to the low-vowel region. An extremely limited form of labial harmony co-occurring with palatal harmony occurs in Hungarian (see, e.g., van der Hulst 1985).

In the African languages Chumburung (Snider 1990) and Igbo (Battistella 1980) labial harmony also occurs, in both cases together with ATR-harmony. Archangeli (1985) discusses one of the few cases of labial harmony where it occurs without another system of vowel harmony, namely in a number of Yokuts dialects. These cases, especially that of the Yawelmani dialect, have received a great deal of discussion in the literature.

The vowel system of Yawelmani is as follows:

(53) non-round   round
       i   u   high
      a   o   non-high

Suffixes contain a high or a low vowel which agrees in roundness with the last stem vowel *if this vowel is of the same height*. Archangeli (1985) discusses a number of formal possibilities for dealing with the dependency of harmony on height-agreement, ending up with the proposal that in the formal representation the feature [round] is dependent on the feature [high]:

(54)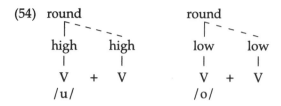

We may assume that the suffixes are not specified lexically for the feature [round]. Given such representations, the type of harmony in Yawelmani Yokuts can be seen as the result of fusing the aperture feature of adjacent vowels if these features are identical. The agreement of other properties is then a result of this fusion. In other words, harmony in Yokuts does *not* apply to labial, but to aperture features, and the process is *not* spreading, but fusion.

2.8   Summary and Remaining Issues

2.8.1   Summary

In the preceding discussion we encountered six types of vowel harmony:

(54)	labial	palatal	height/aperture		pharyngeal	
	[round]	[front]	[high]	[low]	[ATR]	[RTR]

Various close relations, both synchronic and diachronic, hold among the established harmony types. This might be explained by the way the components involved are organized intrasegmentally (Odden 1991). There are close relations between raising and ATR harmony on the one hand, and lowering and RTR harmony, on the other. In specific cases it is not entirely clear whether a system involves [high] spreading or [ATR] spreading. The same ambiguity applies to the role of the components [low] and [RTR].

Clements (1991) has claimed that there is a single set of *aperture features*, which is the locus of expression of both height and ATR differences. Clements applies his model to a number of harmony systems based on height, and suggests that we need no separate feature [±ATR] for systems which are usually dealt with in terms of this feature. Van der Hulst (1993), like Clements, argues that ATR and height involve the same phonological primitives and differentiates between the two interpretations by arguing that the [ATR] version involves the relevant component in a dependent position, while the height version involves the same component in head position. A similar proposal is made for the pair [RTR] and [low].

We do not want to go beyond highlighting the options and correlations we have just summarized. A proposal for a segment-internal organization of the vowel components is unfortunately beyond the scope of this overview of harmony systems.

2.8.2 *"Total Harmony Systems"*

In a number of languages, usually with "simple" triangular vowel systems, there is a kind of vowel harmony which involves the complete copying of a vowel, so that there are alternations between /i/, /a/, and /u/ depending on the context or specific case.

Such harmonies occur in a number of Australian languages (see chap. 25, this volume, and van der Hulst and Smith 1985). In Djingili, for example, /a/s in the stem alternate with /i/ before suffixal /i/s. This leftward "spreading" of /a/ is unbounded. An intervening /u/ blocks spreading. In Warlpiri several harmonies are found. Some suffixes have /i/ after stem /i/, and /u/ elsewhere. This progressive harmony is also unbounded. Other suffixes have /u/ after /u/ and /i/ elsewhere. Finally, there is regressive harmony producing /u/ before /u/ and /i/ elsewhere. A third example is Nyangumarta (Hoard and O'Grady 1976), where suffixes take /i/, /u/, /a/ depending on the last stem vowel. All three languages have a triangular /i a u/ vowel system.

These cases can be separated from the previously discussed cases in that the harmony does not involve a "secondary property alone," like frontness, tongue root position, and labiality. These alternations can often be analyzed by taking one vowel to be a completely unspecified vowel, e.g., the vowel /a/ in Djingili. Total harmony systems are not limited to Australian languages, however. A similar system occurs in the Dravidian language Telugu (Kiparsky 1981).

2.8.3 *Non-place Harmony*

All harmony systems discussed so far, including those in the previous section, involve vowel place properties. There are other vowel harmony cases, however, which either clearly do not involve place or could be argued to involve something different from place. We tentatively propose the following typology:

(56)   vowel harmony types

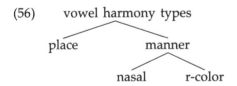

We exclude here from consideration cases of nasal "spreading" which do not only affect vowels, but rather strings of adjacent sonorant segments (see Piggott 1988 for an extensive study of these cases). The term "r-coloring" is meant to include retroflexion. Retroflex harmony is found in Yurok (see Smith et al. 1988).[33]

It is possible that some harmony systems may also involve a "register" distinction, which may very well refer to a laryngeal property. Trigo (1991) offers a discussion of register and suggests that vowel harmony in Turkana involves a tense versus lax distinction. Her proposal is that the fundamental register distinction may manifest itself through a laryngeal feature involving laryngeal lowering or raising, or a pharyngeal feature like ATR/RTR. This may imply that vowel harmonies which are interpreted as involving ATR/ RTR may be close to or misanalyzed as cases of harmony that involve a laryngeal feature.

3   Consonantal Interference

So far the discussion of locality has focused on the fact that consonants are skipped in vowel harmony. This assumes that vowel harmony takes into account all vowels while ignoring all consonants. In this section, we focus on cases of consonantal interference.

The issue of consonantal interference is a difficult one and there is not much systematic research on this topic. We will briefly indicate what kinds of interactions have been reported and refrain from a detailed theoretical discussion. The issue is obviously of great relevance, especially in the context of theories which employ the same set of features for vocalic and consonantal place properties. We discuss three types of consonantal interference: cases in which consonants with secondary articulation have an effect on vowel harmony (sec. 3.1), cases in which vowels have an effect on consonants (an effect in the opposite direction; see sec. 3.2), and cases in which consonants that do not have secondary articulation appear to influence the harmony (sec. 3.3).

3.1   Secondary Articulation

Consonants with secondary articulation can interfere with a harmony system. For example, palatalized consonants can interfere with the harmony system in a language with a palatal harmony system. A case in point is Turkish, where palatalized consonants spread their vocalic specification to suffix vowels (Clements and Sezer 1982):

(57)   infil'ak   infil'aːk'i   "explosion"
       ittifak   ittifaːk'i   "alliance"
       imsak   imsaːk'i   "fasting"
       eml'ak   eml'ak'i   "real estate"

Since palatalized velars do not occur word-finally, the palatalized character of these velars will only show up if a suffix is added.[34]

Such interference can be explained in a geometrical autosegmental phonology model by assuming that palatalized consonants have the specification [front] under a V-place node:

(58)

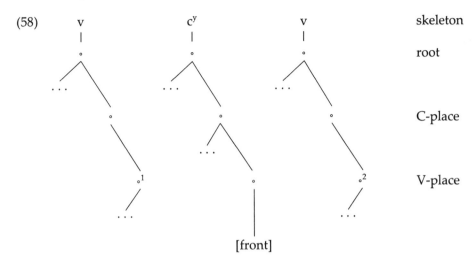

Indeed, in the geometrical approach it is predicted that consonants with secondary articulation *always* interfere with harmony.

With a syllable head approach to the vowel harmony domain, one is presumably forced to analyze this phenomenon as a secondary, local case of feature spreading, since consonants are not visible on the syllable head tier. In the syllabic approach, then, harmonic interaction between vowels and consonants with a secondary articulation must be stated locally by way of a spreading rule, and consonants are not directly involved in the harmonic relations that hold between syllable heads. The local requirement could be, for example, that vowels adjacent to a palatalized consonant become [front] by local spreading. This feature is then propagated to the syllable nodes and spreads rightward to the suffix vowel, as shown below. The syllable head approach does not *require* vowel harmony to be influenced by consonants with secondary articulation.

(59)

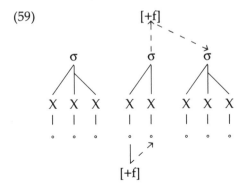

3.2   *Allophonic Variation*

In some languages with a palatal harmony system, front velars are found in words with [−back] vowels, and back velars (or uvulars) appear in words with [+back] vowels. This distinction is usually allophonic.

The harmony system of Bashkir is given in (60):

(60)	high	i	ü		u
	mid	ə	ö	ï	o
	low	ä		a	

Bashkir has palatal and labial harmony. The former affects the whole vowel system, but labial harmony is restricted in that it is only triggered by mid vowels, which also constitute the targets. A case in which non-dorsals are affected in a palatal harmony system is that of Bezhta, discussed in section 2.5.

Poppe (1962, p. 22) informs us that the consonants /g k/, in words of Turkic origin, occur only in words of front vowels: /büläk/ "gift", /igən/ "crops". The consonants /G q/ occur only in native words that contain back vowels: /ayaq/ "foot", /GwaGa/ "noise".[35] A similar alternation was mentioned in our discussion of the Tungusic languages, which are claimed to have a tongue root harmony system. The question why a similar alternation occurs in both palatal and tongue root harmony systems suggests a common denominator for both types. In this respect it is interesting to note that Svantesson (1985) makes the claim that both harmony systems are in complementary distribution in the Mongolian language family.

In a geometrical approach to locality, this can be analyzed by stating (in some way or another) that velar consonants are allowed to have a V-place node, which includes them in the class of possible targets of vowel harmony. That is, front velars would be analyzed as palatalized velars and uvulars as non-palatalized velars. Alternatively, if one could make the case that [+back] is the spreading feature, the uvulars would be the consonants which have the secondary articulation. A drawback to this is that the difference between velars and uvulars is perhaps not one that should be expressed in terms of secondary articulation. Such an approach would fail to explain why labials do not participate in a similar fashion in palatal systems and also why velars fail to participate in other types of harmonies, such as labial harmony. We should express somehow that [front] can be used to "subcategorize" dorsals and not coronals or labials (see van der Hulst 1993 for a discussion of this issue).

3.3   *Primary Place Properties*

Consonants without secondary articulation may also have an effect on vowel harmony, and it is useful to divide these into two cases: those where glides are reported to have such an effect and those where "real" consonants do.

3.3.1 Glides

In Turkish the approximant /j/ has an influence on surrounding vowels. It is claimed that to its left, /j/ (as well as palato-alveolar consonants) only allows /i/ or /ɪ/ (the choice depending on the frontness of preceding vowels), while to its right /i/ and /ɪ/ as well as /e/ and /a/ occur (the choice again depending on the harmonic property of the root). In other words, /j/ derounds and raises vowels to its left, while to the right only derounding applies (Kumbaraci 1966).

In Bashkir (Poppe 1962) /w/ is reported to interfere with labial harmony. For example, in Bashkir /w/ blocks rounding just as the high vowels do: /qorowlï/ "loaded (of a rifle)". The final /ï/ is not rounded due to the interfering /w/ (cf. Poppe 1962, p. 20). In Turkana, vowels preceding semivowels are predictably [ATR] (Dimmendaal 1983).

One might argue that these approximants are like the vowels /i/ and /u/ *as far as their feature content is concerned*, but they are not in the syllable head position and therefore are not expected to participate in the harmony. Such cases, then, raise problems for a syllable head approach and seem to indicate that segments in non-head position can directly interfere with the harmony if they are vowels as far as *content* is concerned, which is what approximants arguably are.

3.3.2 "Real" Consonants

There are several cases in which non-approximant consonants interfere with vowel harmony, either by imposing a value on neighboring vowels or by blocking the interaction between vowels.

In a number of cases, labial consonants impose their roundness on neighboring vowels. For example, in Warlpiri labial consonants require a following vowel to be /u/ (Nash 1979; van der Hulst and Smith 1985). Another well-known case is "labial attraction" in Turkish (Clements and Sezer 1982; van der Hulst and van de Weijer 1991). In the literature on vowel harmony in Turkish, special status is sometimes assigned to the pattern /a C^w u/, in which C^w is a labial consonant. The unexpected rounding of the non-initial high vowel is attributed to the preceding labial consonant. However, Clements and Sezer (1982) show that the pattern /a – u/ also frequently occurs when the consonant is non-labial (61a), while on the other hand the pattern /a C^w ɪ/ (61b) can also easily be found:

(61) (a) marul   "lettuce"   (b) sabır   "patience"
          fatura   "invoice"   kapı   "door"
          yakut   "emerald"   kamıs   "reed"

We conclude that "labial attraction" does not form part of the synchronic phonology of Turkish.

In Finnish, velar consonants may prevent frontness from spreading so that vowels following the velars end up being back. Some examples of this are given in (62), from Kiparsky (1981).

(62)   itikka   "mosquito"
       etikka   "vinegar"
       tiirikka   "lock pick"

In section 3.2 we saw that velar consonants can vary between (front) velars and uvulars, depending on the harmonic class to which the word they occur in belongs. This is reported for palatal systems. In Coeur d'Alene (Johnson 1975; Doak 1992) a class of "faucal" consonants (articulated with tongue root retraction) cause vowels to their right to lower. In many Semitic languages, lowering influences from "back consonants" (i.e., gutturals) are reported as well (cf. McCarthy 1991). Whether such cases belong in this section or in section 3.1 depends on one's analysis of back consonants such as uvulars and pharyngeals. We will not enter into this issue here.

As discussed in section 3.3.1, cases where consonants interfere with harmony are an embarrassment to the syllable head approach. It is, on the other hand, also fair to say that vowel-consonant interactions form an ill-understood area. Cases where such interaction takes place have been used to argue that features for representing place in consonants and vowels are partly the same, but precisely under what circumstances vowels harmonize with consonants is not clear, and, in any event, such harmony appears to be local in all cases, i.e., where a consonant interferes there is never evidence that a new harmonic span starts.

4   Conclusion

We have presented a brief overview of what are, in our opinion, the major types of vowel harmony systems. Vowel harmony has always been a challenging area of research for developing theories of segmental structure. There is no reason to believe that this will change in the near future.

The previous sections have also made clear that our knowledge of the structure and classification of harmony systems is still extremely limited. The phonological community will benefit from an extension of the set of well-documented cases and analyses. We hope that this overview will be an impetus for further theoretical and descriptive work.

NOTES

1   Previous cross-linguistic studies of vowel harmony appear in Greenberg (1963), Aoki (1968), Ultan (1973) and L. Anderson (1975).

General introductions appear in Vago (1980b); see especially S. Anderson's contribution to that volume (S. Anderson 1980). Influential early treatments include Stewart (1967), Clements (1976), Halle and Vergnaud (1981), and formal aspects are highlighted in Vergnaud (1980) and Tohsaku (1983).

2 No claim is made here as to which phonological feature is used to make the distinction; we will return to VH systems like that of Tangale in section 3.

3 In the literature one can find empirical, descriptive, and theoretical reasons for making a distinction between stem-internal vowel harmony and harmony between stem and affixes. A descriptive distinction is found in Clements and Sezer (1982), who claim that vowel harmony in Turkish is active in stem-affix combinations, but no longer in polysyllabic stems. In the traditional generative literature stem-internal harmony and harmony between stem and affixes was often treated by means of separate rules (viz., morpheme structure rule and P-rule; cf. Kenstowicz and Kisseberth 1977, pp. 136–145 for a discussion of such treatments).

4 Dominant VH systems have also been referred to as asymmetric, and stem-controlled systems have been referred to as symmetric. This is merely a terminological issue.

5 Kidda (1985, pp. 143, n. 4) states that -*na* is the only suffix containing the vowel /a/.

6 Neutral vowels are also called invariant. There are in fact three sources for invariance. First, vowels may be *absolutely neutral*, such as /a/ in Tangale. Second, vowels may be invariant in certain positions of the word, such as non-initial position. We refer to this as *contextual neutralization* (as in Turkish, see sec. 2.6). Finally, vowels may be invariant in particular lexical items, whether stems or affixes: these are cases of lexical (or exceptional) neutralization. Van der Hulst and Smith claim that all invariant vowels are subject to the generalization that they propose.

7 Transparency effects in disharmonic stems are also found in Finnish; see Campbell (1980), Steriade (1987).

8 We thank Krisztina Polgárdi for help with these examples.

9 This is the only exception; otherwise the suffix is invariably -*us*.

10 This is the case in Tangale; see Kidda (1985, p. 133).

11 Levergood (1984) argues that vowel harmony in Maasai is subject to cyclicity.

12 Umlaut as we find it in the early stages of Germanic languages, where the stressed vowel harmonizes with vowel endings, has also been analyzed as foot-based vowel harmony (cf. McCormick 1981; Hamans 1985). The term *metaphony* has been used for such cases (see S. Anderson 1980, p. 3 for discussion).

13 Reference has also been made to an even larger domain; this is the case of Somali (Armstrong 1934; Hall and Hall 1980).

14 Which value is filled in may furthermore depend on the phonological context. For instance, it might be claimed that in front vowels [+round] is a marked and therefore specified feature value, and in back vowels the same goes for [−round].

15 A further claim is that languages may override the universal

markedness relations and treat the unmarked value as the lexically present value. In those cases the unmarked value effectively functions as a default value. Moreover, *both* values may be active from the start, namely if both function in statements of morpheme structure conditions.

16 In dominant systems (see sec. 2.1.2), morphemes that do not change provide a clear indication what the default value is.

17 An alternative is to postulate a "floating" feature [+back]. Not all neutral vowel roots behave like *híd*, but this does not alter the point.

18 In some theories it is claimed that some features are binary, whereas others are unary. The distinction between binary and unary primes is sometimes referred to as a distinction between *equipollent* and *privative* features (cf. Goldsmith 1985, p. 254).

19 In practice, however, theories will differ from each other in other respects as well, most notably in terms of which phonological primes are adopted, and whether they incorporate structural notions such as intrasegmental feature grouping and dependency relations. As a result, it may not always be straightforward to establish how different theories differ in the predictions they make.

20 A point that complicates this discussion is that a unarist might argue that there are two unary features, [front] and [back], or [round] and [spread] to replace any binary feature. What this point reveals is that the set of features adopted in a theory should not have the status of a random list. In other words, a feature theory is only meaningful if it can be shown that the proposed set of features is

closed. See van der Hulst (1993) for a defence of the set we use here.

21 This approach is identical in spirit to the Prosodic School analysis of vowel harmony (see Firth 1948; Palmer 1970; Goldsmith 1976).

22 We discuss consonants that have a secondary articulation in section 3.1. Such consonants have a class node to which vowel features associate, and are therefore expected to interfere with vowel harmony.

23 The question whether the sets of place features for consonants and vowels are distinct or the same is separate and irrelevant here (see chap. 7, this volume). The crucial point is that vowels have a class node which consonants lack.

24 In a model that adopts underspecification, a situation may arise in which a particular vowel has no features at all in its underlying representation, in which case such a vowel will presumably also lack a V-place node. This adds a technical complication to the class-node definition of the notion harmonic unit. We must say that a unit is harmonic (with respect to some harmonic feature) if it (a) has the class node to which the harmonic feature can associate or (b) *can* have that class node in the language at stake. Somehow, then, it must be possible to recognise a vowel as being able to have a V-place node, even if it lacks all vowel features. This identification will presumably have to rely on an inspection of the syllabic position of the relevant skeletal point, which shows that the skeletal tier must be inspected even for processes that are not strictly local (also for the OCP).

25 In some versions of autosegmental phonology it has been proposed that the segmental properties of

vowels and consonants appear on entirely separate planes. This would explain why consonannts do not intervene in vowel harmony, but it would allow consonant harmony just as easily:

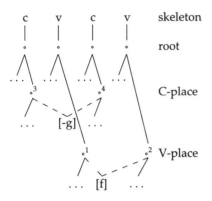

In this representation the association of [–g] to nodes 3 and 4 is also local, which it would not be if the intervening vowel had a C-place node. Another approach could be to make use of planar segregation, i.e., to arrange consonant and vowel features on independent planes. However, this kind of segregation should be restricted to the level of lexical representation.

26 The question whether there are solid cases of feature sharing between class nodes of nonadjacent consonants will not be dealt with here (see Poser 1982 and Shaw 1991 for examples). It is consistent with the above that such non-local relations will involve properties which are never distinctive for vowels, such as manner features (with the exception of [nasal]). Sibilant harmony is a case in point. Hence, it is not an ad hoc move to claim that vowels do not participate in sibilant harmony because, since there are no contrasts in sibilancy between vowels, they have no node

to which the relevant features could attach. Finally, within *declarative* approaches to phonology (e.g., Scobbie 1991), it has been claimed on formal grounds that all feature sharing must be local. Hence, in such a view, vowel harmony cannot involve local assimilation.

27 Or in terms of their binary equivalents, [+ATR]/[–ATR], [+RTR]/[–RTR] and [+high]/[–high], [+low]/[–low].

28 See Stewart (1971) on the related language Anyi-Bawuke.

29 The descriptions of Even vary somewhat. Comrie (1981) gives.

(i)

		i		u
		ɪ		ʊ
ie		e	ə	o
ɪa		a	ə̣	ɔ

i.e., he adds two diphthongs.

30 According to Clements, the vowels /e o/ are not only derived by raising but occur also underlyingly. There is a further process of raising affecting /ɪ/ and /ʊ/ in the context of /i/ and /u/. This rule does not affect underived /e/ and /o/.

31 Mongolian has also been analyzed as a kind of palatal harmony system.

32 Hungarian has a reduced system of rounding harmony, which affects suffixes with short /ɛ/. There are three types of suffixes with mid short vowels:

(a) ɛ-a   (e.g., nek/nak)
(b) ɛ-o-ö   (e.g., hez/hoz/höz)
(c) ɛ-a-o-ö   (e.g., el/ak/ok/ök)

We also find labial hamrony co-occurring with the RTR harmonies in Mongolian and Tungusic languages.

33 Tone spreading can be seen as a

form of harmony, especially when this involves tone affixes which harmonize with stems. No cases of stem-internal tonal harmony are known to us. Hence, formally speaking, stems tend to be tonally disharmonic.

34 In a dialect of Akan, palatalized consonants have an effect within a relative-height harmony system (see Boadi 1963).

35 This kind of consonant harmony is also reported for Kirghiz (Johnson 1980).

15   Syntax-phonology Interface

SHARON INKELAS AND DRAGA ZEC

0   Introduction

How are the syntactic and phonological components of the grammar organized with respect to each other? Are these components independent, or do they exert mutual influence in at least some ways? The syntax-phonology interface has a solid empirical basis, documented in a large body of literature (recent collections include *Phonology Yearbook 4* and Inkelas and Zec 1990). The primary source of evidence is provided by phonological rules that operate over syntactically defined domains, showing that constituency in one component (syntax) is relevant to the processes in another (phonology). But interactions between syntax and phonology have also been manifested in the opposite direction: constraints that are phonological in nature may be relevant to syntactic processes.

In this article, we review old arguments and present new evidence for the different facets of syntax-phonology interaction. We focus on the bidirectionality of the influence of these two components upon each other, taking this property as a basis for proposing what we believe to be the most appropriate representation for this kind of interaction across the components of the grammar. The article is organized as follows: section 1 examines the nature of phonological rule domains generally; sections 2 and 3 discuss syntactic and prosodic constraints, respectively, on phonological phrases, and section 4 evaluates the evidence that phonological phrasing requirements may also constrain syntax. Probable directions of future research in the syntax-phonology connection are presented in section 5.

1   The Nature of p-structure

Evidence for the syntax-phonology interface comes from the numerous cases of phonological rules with syntactically conditioned environments. Observe the functioning of Raddoppiamento Sintattico, a well-known phonological rule of gemination applying over syntactic domains in Italian (Nespor and Vogel 1982, 1986):

(1)   Raddoppiamento Sintattico (RS): In a sequence of two words w_1 and w_2, the initial consonant of w_2 geminates if w_1 ends in a stressed vowel, and if certain syntactic conditions are met.

A simple example is given in (2), and some of the intricate syntactic conditioning is illustrated in (3)–(5).[1] The application of Raddoppiamento Sintattico is indicated by bracketing the geminated segment; failure of RS is indicated with double slashes. All examples are taken from Nespor and Vogel 1982, p. 228, 1986, pp. 38, 170.

(2)   Parlo [bː]ene
       "He spoke well"

(3)   Devi comprare delle [mappe [di citta [vː]ecchie]$_{PP}$]$_{NP}$
       "You must buy some maps of old cities"

(4)   Devi comprare delle [mappe [di citta]$_{PP}$ // vecchie]$_{NP}$
       "You must buy some old maps of cities"

(5)   Devi comprare delle [mappe [di citta // molto vecchie]$_{PP}$]$_{NP}$
       "You must buy some maps of very old cities"

Note that Raddoppiamento Sintattico applies across certain syntactic junctures but not across others. It applies between a verb and an adverb in (2), and between a noun and an adjective in (3). It fails to apply between adjacent words that satisfy the phonological condition but are not immediate syntactic constituents, such as *citta* and *vecchie* in (4) or *citta* and *molto* in (5).
    The essential question raised by data of this type is which aspects of syntactic structure are systematically called upon in characterizing the environments of phonological processes. Each of the following features of syntactic phrase structure has been considered necessary for this purpose (and some researchers have proposed more than one of them). References are necessarily incomplete:

(6)   (a)   Phrasal rank, or bar level, as proposed in Chomsky and Halle 1968 (henceforth *SPE*) and subsequent work in the same framework (Selkirk 1972, 1974; Rotenberg 1978), as well as in later work (e.g., Selkirk 1986; Selkirk and Shen 1990)
       (b)   the head/complement relation (Nespor and Vogel 1982, 1986; Hayes 1989b)
       (c)   syntactic sisterhood (Zec and Inkelas 1990)

Certain other aspects of the syntactic constituency, such as syntactic category or the morphological specifications of terminal elements, appear to be irrelevant for the purposes of phonology and, in a sufficiently constrained theory, the phonological component should not be able to access them.

1.1 *The Characterization of Rule Domains*

One possible approach to characterizing phonological rule domains is that taken by Kaisse (1983, 1985a): phonology may access the syntactic component directly, and syntactically conditioned phonological rules are governed by known syntactic relations such as c-command and edge membership (Kaisse 1985a, p. 155). It has become a majority view among researchers in this area, however, that syntax does not provide domains for phonological rules in a direct fashion. Both the impoverished amount of syntactic information needed by the phonological module and the variety of mismatches between phonological rule domains and syntactic constituency argue for positing another level of representation (Selkirk 1978, 1980a; Nespor and Vogel 1986).[2] In the following section we focus on the justification of this additional level; we will refer to this prosodic level as p-structure and to the corresponding syntactic constituency as s-structure. P-structure mediates between the syntactic and the phonological modules, and serves as the locus of their interaction.

1.2 *Boundary Symbols*

An early version of p-structure was proposed in *SPE* and developed in subsequent work (Selkirk 1972, 1974; Rotenberg 1978). According to this view, domains of phonological rules are expressed in terms of phonological boundary symbols, generated by rules such as the following (*SPE*, p. 366):

(7) The boundary # is automatically inserted at the beginning and end of every string dominated by a major category, i.e., by one of the lexical categories "noun," "verb," "adjective," or by a category such as "sentence," "noun phrase," "verb phrase," which dominates a lexical category.

The only syntactic property relevant for this version of p-structure is phrasal rank, or bar level, which maps into boundary symbols. Boundary strength is quantitative, expressed by the number of boundary symbols present. A given phonological rule specifies only the minimal boundary strength across which it cannot apply – or, alternatively, the maximal boundary strength across which it does apply.

Under the *SPE* view, boundary symbols alone express constituency at the level of p-structure. But boundary symbols form a constituency only in the weakest sense, precluding any systematic statement of the range of possible domains for phonological processes. (For a summary of criticisms of boundary symbols, see Selkirk 1980a and Hayes 1989b). Moreover, as elements of the phonological representation, boundary symbols are subject to powerful restructuring processes in the *SPE* framework. Deleting boundary symbols has the effect of reducing boundary strength; inserting boundary symbols strengthens a boundary. The capability for adjustments of this kind diminishes even further the predictive power of the boundary symbol theory of p-structure.

1.3   *Prosodic Structure*

Far more constrained is the "prosodic" view of p-structure. Under this view, p-structure occupies a level with its own hierarchical organization and a high degree of autonomy. The constituency at p-structure is distinct from that at s-structure; though the two constituencies are related to each other, they are not isomorphic. As initially proposed by Selkirk (1978, 1980a), and further developed by Nespor and Vogel (1982, 1986) and Hayes (1989b), p-structure is composed of the specific hierarchy of prosodic constituents in (8):[3]

(8)   phonological word
      phonological phrase
      intonational phrase
      utterance

Each phonological rule applies within a selected prosodic domain, which explains why certain syntactic junctures are too strong for a rule to apply over while others are not. The former, but not the latter, correspond to the boundaries of prosodic constituents.

   As an illustration, the noun phrase from (3) is reproduced below, with both s-structure (above) and p-structure (below) represented:

(9)

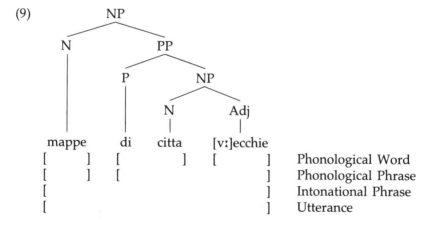

The rule of Raddoppiamento Sintattico applies within the phonological phrase, and as shown in (9), the juncture at which the rule applies in this specific case is internal in a phonological phrase.

In the next section we look at the relationship of s-structure and p-structure, focusing first on different characterizations of the phonological phrase, and then on the phonological word.

2 The Impact of s-structure on p-structure

The two smaller domains in the Prosodic Hierarchy,[4] namely the phonological word and the phonological phrase, have been studied in a variety of languages, and the results are quite encouraging. The morpho-syntactic characterizations of these two domains exhibit impressive cross-linguistic similarities; moreover, the attested range of variation appears sufficiently small to be viewed as parametric in nature (see Nespor and Vogel 1986; *Phonology Yearbook 4*; Inkelas and Zec 1990; Zec 1993). Unfortunately, this cannot be said of the larger domains. While the intonational phrase is viewed by some researchers as directly related to s-structure (Rice 1987), others, such as Selkirk (1984b) and Vogel and Kenesei (1990), question this assumption and assume a more semantic or even pragmatic role for intonational phrasing. In this overview we focus on the phonological word and phonological phrase, whose origins are uncontroversially morphosyntactic in nature.

Researchers differ as to which of the properties of s-structure are mapped into p-structure, and which are excluded from this mapping. We compare three proposals of mappings between s-structure and p-structure:[5]

(10) (a) relation-based mapping (e.g., Nespor and Vogel 1982, 1986; Hayes 1989b)
   (b) end-based mapping (e.g., Chen 1987; Selkirk 1986; Selkirk and Shen 1990)
   (c) arboreal mapping (Zec and Inkelas 1990)

2.1 Relation-based Mapping

Relation-based mapping algorithms make a crucial distinction between heads and complements of syntactic constituents. According to Nespor and Vogel (1986) and Hayes (1989b), the mappings in (11)–(13) give the range of possibilities predicted under this view. The first possibility is that the head and the complement obligatorily map into separate phonological phrases, as shown in (11).

(11)

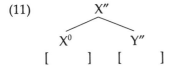

A second option is for the head and complement to map into a single phonological phrase, as shown in (12).

(12)

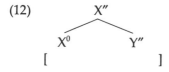

The first case is illustrated by Chi Mwi:ni (Kisseberth and Abasheikh 1974), in which a stress assignment rule makes reference to phonological phrases of the type characterized in (11) (Hayes 1989b; Nespor and Vogel 1986; Selkirk 1986). The second case is illustrated by French. One type of liaison, which operates in colloquial French, applies within phonological phrases as characterized in (12) (Nespor and Vogel 1986; Selkirk 1986; de Jong 1990b).

While these examples have involved head-initial languages, relation-based mapping is equally applicable to head-final languages, which exhibit the same range of possibilities. The only difference is that the relevant s-structure constituencies are a mirror-image of those in (11)–(13). The mirror-image of (11) is illustrated by Japanese (Poser 1984b; Nespor and Vogel 1986; Selkirk 1986), and the mirror image of (12), by Korean (Cho 1990b).

A complication for this mapping algorithm is posed by languages such as English and Hausa (Zec and Inkelas 1990) and Kinyambo (Bickmore 1990). In these languages, the complement and head phrase together whenever the complement is nonbranching (13a), and otherwise phrase separately (b):

(13)   (a)   (b)

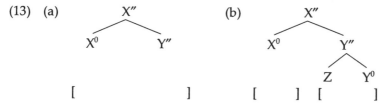

Italian presents a mixed type, instantiating either the situation in (11) or, as an option, the situation in (13). That is, a nonbranching complement in Italian may optionally compose a single phonological phrase with its head (Nespor and Vogel 1986). To describe languages of the type in (13), the relation-based mapping must thus make reference to the internal structure of complements in addition to the basic head-complement relation.

2.2   End-based Mapping

The end-based mapping of Chen (1987), Selkirk (1986), Selkirk and Shen (1990), and others, attempts to reduce the syntactic sensitivity of the mapping algorithm to a single property of syntactic phrase structure, namely phrasal rank. Mapping algorithms impose phonological phrase junctures at the designated edge (either left or right) of syntactic constituents of a selected rank.

The end-based approach differs from the relation-based approach in that the same set of parameters makes opposite predictions for head-initial and head-final languages. To see this, let us inspect the possibilities for a head-initial language, based on the selection of X", the maximal projection, as the relevant syntactic constituent. As shown in (14), the phrasing of head and complement in a head-initial language depends entirely on whether the right or left edge of X" is selected by the end-based algorithm:

(14)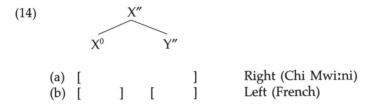

 (a) [   ]   Right (Chi Mwiːni)
 (b) [ ] [ ]   Left (French)

If the right edge is selected, the head and the complement form a single phonological phrase (a); if the left edge is selected, the head and the complement phrase separately (b). These cases (predicted by the relation-based mapping as well) are exemplified by Chi Mwiːni (Selkirk 1986) and French,[6] respectively.

 The opposite correlation between edge-selection and head-complement phrasing occurs in head-final languages. As shown in (15), selection of the right edge of X" causes the head and the complement to phrase separately, while selecting the left edge causes head and complement to form a single phonological phrase:

(15)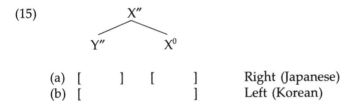

 (a) [ ] [ ]   Right (Japanese)
 (b) [   ]   Left (Korean)

Examples of the two types of phrasing predicted for head-final languages are Japanese (Poser 1984b) and Korean (Cho 1990b).

 As is the case with relation-based algorithms, branching plays no direct role in the algorithm. This creates difficulties for phrasing languages like Italian and English, in which branching complements phrase differently from nonbranching ones. As shown in (16), the end-based algorithm, sensitive only to edges, cannot in its basic form discriminate between simple (a) and complex (b) constituents.

(16)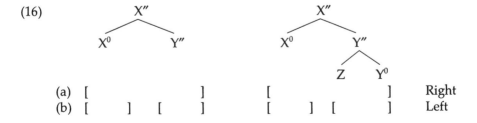

 (a) [   ] [   ] Right
 (b) [ ] [ ] [ ] [ ] Left

Languages like Italian and English, in which branchingness is relevant to phrasing, require special adaptations of the basic end-based algorithm. Cowper and Rice (1987) and Bickmore (1990) have suggested adding the parameter [+/– branching] to the algorithm. However, as [branching] is not a standard syntactic feature, this move weakens the end-based theory, one of whose main virtues is a highly constrained and principled access to syntactic information.

2.3   Arboreal Mapping

The arboreal mapping proposed in Zec and Inkelas (1990) makes sisterhood, and thus branchingness, a central property in the mapping from s-structure to p-structure. This algorithm groups syntactic sisters into phonological phrases, giving priority to immediate sisters. The effects are illustrated in (17). A non-branching complement, as in (a), cannot form a phrase by itself – as it fails to meet the sisterhood requirement – and thus phrases with its head, to which it bears a sisterhood relation. By contrast, a branching complement satisifies the sisterhood requirement by itself, forming a phonological phrase of its own. Since no nesting of phonological phrases is permitted – a standard assumption underlying most phrasing algorithms – the head is forced to phrase separately in this case.

(17)   (a)   (b)

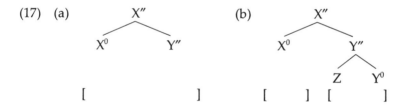

This phrasing is clearly what is needed for languages like English and Hausa. Thus, the arboreal algorithm captures naturally the sensitivity to branchingness which posed problems for both the relation-based and end-based algorithms. By the same token, however, the arboreal algorithm has difficulty handling those cases in which branchingness is not relevant for phrasing. Clearly, in order to account for languages in which complements never phrase with heads – or in which complements always phrase with heads – an arboreal algorithm will have to be made sensitive to the level at which branching is relevant.

2.3.1   Subjects

A distinctive feature of the arboreal algorithm, worth mentioning here, is its treatment of subjects. In its unadulterated form, the arboreal algorithm phrases together any two nonbranching sisters, regardless of syntactic bar level. This has the consequence that a nonbranching subject is predicted to phrase with a nonbranching verb phrase. English data support this prediction, as at least for some speakers, the Rhythm Rule (Liberman and Prince 1977) treats the phrases in (18a) and (b) identically. The Rhythm Rule, whose domain is, for many speakers, the phonological phrase (Nespor and Vogel 1986), retracts the first of two adjacent stresses onto a preceding syllable. Note that stress retraction applies to *Annemarie* in both (18a) and (b). (18a) is a simple noun phrase, which any of the algorithms we have discussed would presumably predict to form a single phonological phrase, while (b) is a whole sentence:

(18) (a) Ánnemarìe's hérd [cf. the isolation form: Ànnemaríe]
     (b) Ánnemarìe héard.
     (c) Ànnemaríe héard about it already.

Stress retraction does not occur in (18c) . This is predictable: the complexity of the verb phrase prevents the arboreal algorithm from phrasing the verb and subject together.

In contrast to the arboreal algorithm, both relation-based and end-based theories predict subjects and verb phrases to phrase separately. Under the relation-based view, subjects are not verbal complements (of the right kind) and should not phrase with verbs. End-based algorithms will also inevitably introduce a phonological phrase margin between subject and verb phrases, which belong to distinct maximal projections. In apparent support of these algorithms, a number of examples are attested in which subjects phrase separately from verb phrases (see, e.g., Hayes 1989b). However, systematic investigation of subjects, or of the effect of subject or predicate complexity on overall sentence phrasing, has yet to be undertaken.

3   Branchingness as a p-structure Property

A recurrent problem for the various syntax-phonology mapping algorithms that have been proposed is the effect of syntactic branchingness on phonological phrasing. Relation-based and end-based algorithms must add special stipulations to their basic set of parameters in order to capture the effects of branchingness, while the arboreal algorithm places undue emphasis on branchingness, at the cost of complicating the description of languages in which internal complexity is irrelevant to phrasing. One promising solution to the problems branching poses for syntax-phonology mapping may be in factoring out the property of branchingness altogether from the syntactic properties known to influence phrasing. Support for this move, which would certainly simplify the syntactic knowledge needed by phrasing algorithms, comes from evidence that the type of branchingness at issue may in fact be prosodic, rather than syntactic.

The first piece of evidence is a widely observed asymmetry in the phonological behavior of content and function words. Only a subset of morphological entities known as words – commonly those that belong to open classes such as nouns, verbs, or adjectives – acquire the status of phonological words (see, e.g., Nespor and Vogel 1986).[7] Those that belong to closed classes, and share at least some properties with grammatical formatives, are not mapped into phonological words. This distinction is in many cases isomorphic with the content/function word distinction (Selkirk 1984b, 1986; Selkirk and Shen 1990; Inkelas 1989). In English, for example, it is well-known that function words such as pronouns and prepositions do not, except in positions of contrastive emphasis, receive the same degree of word stress that content words exhibit (Selkirk 1984b). In addition to accentual asymmetries, function words are known cross-linguistically to be exempt from word-level rules and to violate morpheme structure constraints, including minimal prosodic word size.

The relevance of the function/content word asymmetry for present purposes is its effect on the status of branchingness for phonological phrasing. In English, Rhythm Rule data suggest that phonological phrase formation is sensitive not directly to the syntactic complexity of syntactic constituents, but rather to the number of phonological words present. Example (19) illustrates that a verb phrase made complex by virtue of a function word object – the pronoun in (a) – patterns phonologically with a verb phrase which is syntactically simplex (b). Both phrase phonologically with the preceding (nonbranching) subject and trigger the Rhythm Rule, unlike the verb phrases in (c) and (d) which contain more than one content word and are branching by any measure.

(19) (a) [Ánnemarìe áte it]$_\phi$
      (b) [Ánnemarìe áte]$_\phi$
      (c) [Ànnmaríe]$_\phi$ [áte]$_\phi$ [with her fingers]$_\phi$
      (d) [Ànnemaríe]$_\phi$ [ate and drank]$_\phi$

This effect strongly suggests that phonological phrasing is sensitive to complexity at the prosodic level. That is, a preferred phonological phrase is one which consists of at least two phonological words:

(20) [[ ]$_\omega$ [ ]$_\omega$]$_\phi$

An obvious parallel that comes to mind is the minimal size constraint on metrical feet, which minimally have to contain two moras (see, e.g., McCarthy and Prince 1993a):

(21) [μ μ]$_\phi$

From this perspective, the constraint (20) can be understood as a p-structure-internal requirement on phonological phrases. It is entirely independent of the mapping between s- and p-structure, which makes reference solely to syntactic properties.

4   P-structure Effects on s-structure

We have now conjectured that, in addition to syntactic constraints on s- and p-structure, languages may also impose prosodic (minimal size) constraints on p-structure. This raises the question of the interaction between these conditions. Being independent, the mechanisms may, but need not, act in tandem. Thus we expect to find at least the three types of cases in (22):

(22) (a)   Phonological phrases have to branch (constraint (20) always in effect).
    (b)   Phonological phrases preferably branch (constraint (20) is not an absolute requirement).
    (c)   Phonological phrases don't have to branch (constraint (20) is not in effect).

Type (22a) is instantiated by English, in which branchingness is strongly enforced, while type (b) characterizes Italian, in which branchingness is preferred but not an absolute requirement. French plausibly belongs to category (c). In French, the preference for branching phrases is so weak or nonexistent that it apparently never causes nonbranching complements to phrase phonologically with heads.

In all of these cases, however, the prosodic branchingness requirement is always weaker than syntactic conditions. For example, in English the requirement that phonological phrases be branching is met only when syntactically possible. If a complement is branching, then its head will phrase separately even though it is nonbranching; this type of "violation" of the branching condition is manifest.

This raises the question of whether languages ever allow the opposite "ranking" between the constraint in (20) and syntactic requirements. In fact, there do appear to be languages, or, rather, specific constructions within languages, in which prosodic requirements have greater force and can even "overrule," so to speak, the syntax. Zec and Inkelas (1990) describe two cases in which syntactic constructions are subject to phonological constraints best described in terms of prosodic branchingness.

In the first example, Serbo-Croatian topicalization is subject to the constraint that the topic must be a branching phonological phrase. Thus, topics consisting of only one phonological word are judged ungrammatical, as in (23b).

(23) (a)   [[Taj]$_\omega$ [čovek]$_\omega$]$_{NP}$ voleo-je   Mariju
            that   man   loved-AUX   Mary
            "that man loved Mary"
    (b)   *[[Petar]$_\omega$]$_{NP}$ voleo-je   Mariju
            Peter   loved-AUX   Mary
            "Peter loved Mary"

(c) [[Petar]$_\omega$ [Petrović]$_\omega$]$_{NP}$ voleo-je   Mariju
     Peter Petrovic   loved-AUX   Mary
     "Peter Petrovic loved Mary"

Proving that the constraint on topicalization is truly phonological, rather than syntactic in nature, example (23c) shows that a proper name consisting of two phonological words can serve as a syntactic topic, while a proper name consisting of only a single phonological word cannot (b). Zec and Inkelas conclude that the prosodic phrasal branchingness constraint in Serbo-Croatian is sufficiently strong to constrain topicalization.

Similarly, well-known but complicated constraints on Heavy NP Shift in English appear best characterized in prosodic terms. Zec and Inkelas observe that in grammatical Heavy NP Shift constructions, such as that in (24a), the "shifted" noun phrase contains at least two phonological phrases, while any attempt to shift an NP consisting of only a single phonological phrase is judged ungrammatical (e.g., (b)).

(24) (a) Mark showed to John   [[some letters]$_\phi$ [from Paris]$_\phi$]$_{NP}$
      (b) *Mark showed to John   [[some letters]$_\phi$]$_{NP}$

Similar effects have been observed by Swingle (1993) for Right Node Raising in English, showing that Heavy NP Shift is not an isolated example.

As Zec and Inkelas observe, the constraint in the Heavy NP construction is not on the branchingness of the phonological phrase. Rather, it appears to be imposed one level higher up in the Prosodic Hierarchy: a dislocated NP must correspond to a prosodically branching intonational phrase.

4.1   The Copresence Model and Phonology-free Syntax

The English and Serbo-Croatian data discussed by Zec and Inkelas suggest that, just as s-structure constrains p-structure, in the familiar form of syntactic constraints on phrasing algorithms, p-structure may affect s-structure as well. Based on this finding, Zec and Inkelas propose a bidirectional model of the syntax-phonology interface. Past theories of the Prosodic Hierarchy have stipulated a unidirectional, even transformational mapping from s-structure to p-structure (see, e.g., Selkirk 1986, p. 373; Vogel and Kenesei 1990); Zec and Inkelas reject this stipulation and assume that the two structures co-exist. This nonderivational "copresence" model enables each level of representation to be constrained by the other.

Though descriptively adequate to handle the observed data, this copresence model violates a well-known principle which Pullum and Zwicky (1988) have named "Phonology-Free Syntax." Intended to account for the absence of syntactic rules (e.g., movement) which refer to segment identity or other details of the phonological string, this principle prevents any access to phonological information by the syntax. In its strong form, the Phonology-Free Syntax rules out even the limited amount of bidirectional syntax-phonology interface observed by Zec and Inkelas.

However, a weaker form of the Phonology-Free Syntax Principle is still consistent with the proposed copresence model. If, as Zec and Inkelas propose, the interactions between syntax and phonology are limited to mutual, local constraints on syntactic and prosodic hierarchical configurations, then syntax will still lack access to segmental information – the undesired interaction emphasized by Pullum and Zwicky.

4.2 *How Phonology-free is Phonology-free Syntax?*

In practice, the gap between so-called unidirectional theories of the syntax-phonology interface and the bidirectional model proposed by Zec and Inkelas is not as great as it appears. The distinction is blurred by the widespread usage in unidirectional theories of output filters which reject certain syntactic constructions as prosodically ill-formed (see, e.g., Vogel and Kenesei 1990 for specific proposals along these lines to handle data discussed by Zec and Inkelas). For example, the syntax might generate both shifted and nonshifted "Heavy NP" constructions, and a phonological filter could eliminate the prosodically less felicitous of the two.

Although the use of phonological filters of this sort technically maintains the claim that syntax (as a generating component) is insensitive to phonology, it weakens the generalization that syntax (as sentence production) is phonology-free. A theory equipped with such filters still requires the copresence of syntactic and prosodic information, albeit in the phonological component, and thus shares certain basic properties with the outright bidirectional copresence model. The status of output filters will presumably be a topic of continuing debate in the theoretical literature on the syntax-phonology interface.

5 Conclusions

In addition to the issues of mapping and directionality explored above, a number of open questions, both old and new, confront theories of the syntax-phonology interface.

5.1 *Consequences of the Prosodic Hierarchy Hypothesis*

An important consequence of any theory postulating a single level of p-structure is the predicted convergence among domains of rules in any given language.

No matter how many rules exist in a system, Prosodic Hierarchy theory predicts them to utilize a maximum of four domains ("domain clustering"); moreover, those domains must enter into a hierarchical relationship (the "Strict Layer Hypothesis" (Selkirk 1984b).

In making these predictions, the Prosodic Hierarchy Theory distinguishes itself dramatically from so-called direct access theories (e.g., Kaisse 1985a; Odden 1987b, 1990a), in which each individual phonological rule may specify its own unique syntactic conditions. There is no expectation in such theories of any convergence or mutual constraining effect among rule domains.

While the predictions are clear, in practice the evidence is less so. Testing the domain-clustering hypothesis and strict-layering hypotheses has proved difficult because of the small number of (described) postlexical phonological rules applying in subutterance domains in a single language. For example, analyses of English phonological phrases typically draw solely on the Rhythm Rule; Nespor and Vogel base their conclusions about Italian on only one rule in each dialect they discuss. Analysis of several Bantu languages (McHugh 1990; Hyman 1990) has begun to unearth convincing examples of domain convergence, but has also turned up at least one apparent counterexample, in which rule domains intersect (Hyman, Katamba, and Walusimbi 1987). More data is clearly needed before any conclusion can be drawn as to the verity of the domain clustering and strict layering predictions.

One interesting application of, and likely source of further evidence for the Strict Layer Hypothesis is in the so-called "top-down" parsing of the string into prosodic domains. Both Selkirk and Shen (1990) (for Shanghai) and Condoravdi (1990) (for Modern Greek) have observed that phonological phrasing algorithms can be greatly simplified if the syntactic string is first (or simultaneously) parsed into intonational phrases. Since, according to the Strict Layer Hypothesis, each intonational phrase boundary must coincide with a phonological phrase boundary, this sort of "top-down" parsing reduces the work of the phonological phrase algorithm.

5.2   Directions of Future Research

Work on the phonology-syntax interface has emphasized certain languages or families, namely Indo-European, Bantu, Chinese, and Japanese. Much insight will surely be gained from improving the typological coverage of the data base. Particularly illuminating will be the in-depth investigation of non-configurational languages, to which many standard phrasing algorithms are not presently applicable.

Another significant area of research that should inform work on the phonology-syntax connection is the phonology-morphology connection. Preliminary work on highly agglutinating languages has suggested that words, like sentences, may also be parsed into a phonological structure distinct from their morphological structure (Cohn 1989; McDonough 1990; Myers 1992;

Halpern 1992; Inkelas forthcoming), and that, as in syntax, prosodic branchingess requirements may restrict morphological operations (Itô and Hankamer 1989; Orgun and Inkelas 1992).

Finally, it is to be hoped that further work on the phonology-syntax interface will increase the usefulness of phonological evidence in determining the syntactic structures of a language. Some work in this direction has yielded fruitful results already in Kiyaka (Kidima 1990) and Korean (Cho 1990b).

NOTES

1 See Chierchia (1982) for an analysis of the phonological aspects of this rule.

2 See, however, Odden (1987b, 1990) for arguments, based on Kimatuumbi data, against this view and in favor of a "direct syntax" model more like that proposed by Kaisse.

3 It is often assumed (see, e.g., Nespor and Vogel 1986) that the hierarchy of prosodic units extends below the word level to include the metrical constituents of foot and syllable. However, in light of many differences between metrical units and those which function as rule domains, a number of researchers have suggested that the two constituent types belong to separate hierarchies (Selkirk 1986; Zec 1988; Inkelas 1989). For present purposes we may safely ignore the lower end of the Prosodic Hierarchy, as only the constituents at and above the word level bear any relation to syntactic structure.

4 Nespor and Vogel (1986), following Hayes (1989b), include the clitic group between the phonological word and phonological phrase in the Prosodic Hierarchy. We are asuming here that the clitic group is a specific subtype of one or another of the other constituents in the hierarchy (the phonological word [Selkirk 1986] or even the phonological phrase [Inkelas 1989; Zec and Inkelas 1991]), not a distinct member of the prosodic hierarchy in its own right.

5 The term "mapping" is used here in a neutral sense, covering both a derivational relation, whereby a set of entities is replaced by virtue of mapping with another set, and a redundancy relation, whereby one set of entities is associated with another.

6 According to Selkirk (1986), this domain is characterized as a small phonological phrase derived by an end-based mapping selecting the right edge of each lexical *head* (see de Jong 1990b for a somewhat different analysis along these lines.) However, since French is head-initial, selecting the right edge of X^0 appears to give the same results as selecting the left edge of X'', the analysis we have given French here.

7 These authors technically assign phonological word status to all syntactic terminals, but exempt closed class items, including clitics, from the processes (such as phonological phrasing) to which phonological words are otherwise subject.

16 Sentence Prosody: Intonation, Stress, and Phrasing

ELISABETH SELKIRK

0 Introduction

The term sentence prosody encompasses three distinct aspects of the phonological representation of the sentence: intonation, phrasal rhythmic patterning, and prosodic phrasing. This article examines the relations between these aspects of sentence prosody as well as the relation of sentence prosody to the meaning of the sentence. Drawing on earlier work by Schmerling (1976), Gussenhoven (1984), Selkirk (1984), and Rochemont (1986) on the relation between intonation and meaning, I intend to show that the distribution of intonational pitch accents in the sentence in English directly constrains the focus structure of the sentence, which in turn constrains the range of meanings available for the sentence (section 1). I will also argue that the distribution of pitch accents places constraints on the possible rhythmic stress patterns of a sentence in English (section 2). The view of the organization of the grammar of English that emerges is one that gives the tonal representation of the sentence – its intonation – a pivotal position, crucially mediating the meaning-sentence prosody relation. In so doing it denies to the phrasal stress pattern of the sentence any such central role.[1]

1 The Grammar of Intonation

1.1 The Phonological Representation of Intonation

The term *pitch accent* has been used in the description of tone languages in which the distribution of tone within words is highly restricted. For example, in standard Japanese, the paradigm case of a "pitch accent language" (McCawley 1968), the phonological representation of a word contains at most one locus of tonal activity, a HL pitch fall. In nouns the location of that fall must be specified lexically, in verbs and adjectives it is positioned on the penult syllable. A pitch accent, then, is simply a tonal entity with a restricted distribution within a word. In her groundbreaking work on the phonology and phonetics of intonation in English, Pierrehumbert (1980) shows that the English intonational contour must be analyzed as a sequence of one or more pitch accents, an analysis earlier suggested in the work of Bolinger (1958). In English a pitch accent associates to a stress-prominent syllable in a word (typically the main word stress). Pierrehumbert shows that a variety of pitch accent types, both monotonal (H* or L*) and bitonal (e.g., H*+L), must be recognized for English. (The * marks the tone that is realized on the stressed syllable, the other tone is realized on the adjacent syllable.) This variety accounts for the comparative richness in intonative shapes that characterizes English (see Kingdon 1958; O'Connor and Arnold 1973; Palmer 1938; etc.). Following Liberman (1975), Pierrehumbert isolates a further tonal entity, the *boundary tone*, which is positioned at the edge of a phrasal constituent. The end of an English sentence is necessarily marked by a final H% or L% boundary tone (a "%" following a tone indicates that the tone associates with the final (or initial) syllable of the phrase). Beckman and Pierrehumbert (1986), building on Pierrehumbert (1980), distinguish two types of boundary tone, one associated with the edge of an intonational phrase and another with a smaller, intermediate-level phrase.

Consider the figure in (1),[2] which graphs a fundamental frequency contour, the phonetic implementation of the tonal representation of the sentence:

(1)

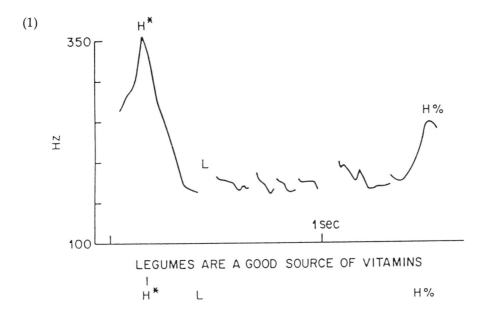

This intonational contour has a high peak at the stressed syllable of *legumes*; this is followed by a fall to a low pitch, which is maintained, plateau-like, up to the final syllable, where there is an abrupt rise in pitch to another peak. According to the Pierrehumbert (1980) theory of phonetic implementation, H and L tones in the phonological representation mark the targets of the movements in fundamental frequency. In (1) the H tone associated to the stressed syllable *le-* is a pitch accent; the H tone appearing on the sentence-final syllable is a boundary tone. As for the L tone responsible for the fall in pitch following *le-*, I will assume here that it is the second half of a bitonal pitch accent whose first element is the preceding H.[3] This utterance of *Legumes are a good source of vitamins* would be appropriate only in certain discourse contexts. The absence of pitch accent on *vitamins* indicates that the predicate noun phrase is "given" in the discourse (see sec. 1.2). The H boundary tone at the end indicates that the sentence is not a simple declarative assertion, which in English would end in a L% boundary tone. Rather, the fall-rise contour of (1) would make it appropriate as a contradiction of the assertion *Nothing in this cupboard is a good source of vitamins* (see, e.g., Ward and Hirschberg 1985).

I will argue below that the presence of a pitch accent on *legumes* implies that the word is focused (in a sense to be made precise). Different distributions of pitch accents imply different focus structures. So, in contrast to (1), the intonational contour in (2) calls for the focusing of *vitamins* and would be appropriate as a contradiction of the assertion *Legumes aren't good for anything.*

(2)

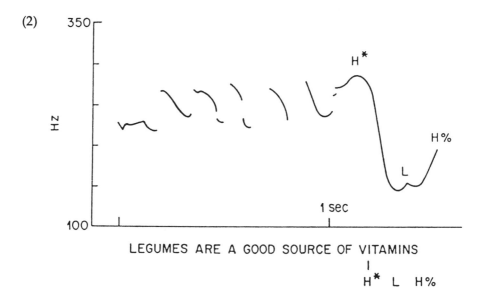

LEGUMES ARE A GOOD SOURCE OF VITAMINS

Moreover, if both *legumes* and *vitamins*, or any other combination of words in the sentence, were pitch accented, yet different focus structures and different appropriateness conditions would be defined for the utterance.

It has been shown that in Dutch (Gussenhoven 1984) and German (Selkirk 1984; Uhmann 1987; Féry 1989) pitch accents have the same relation to focus and meaning that they do in English. Pitch accents have also been shown to play a role in the phonological and phonetic characterization of intonation in the Romance languages (see Avesani 1990 on Italian and Sosa 1991 on Spanish) and appear to correlate with the focus structure of sentence as well. In so-called "pitch accent languages" like Swedish, Serbo-Croatian, or Japanese, by contrast, pitch accents have a radically different role in the grammar. In Serbo-Croatian and Japanese, accent is exploited for lexical contrast and makes no more contribution to meaning than, say, the phonological features [labial] and [voice].[4] In Swedish (see Bruce 1977) pitch accent is not an idiosyncratic property of morphemes, rather it is a redundant property, located on the first (stressed) syllable of every word in the sentence.

Boundary tones appear to be more uniformly exploited crosslinguistically. In English, and in languages as diverse as Chinese, Japanese, Serbo-Croatian, Hungarian, and Igbo, a sentence-final boundary tone may mark whether a sentence is an assertion, a contradiction, a question, etc. Medial boundary tones, such as the H% of the "continuation rise" in English, may set off topics, focus, parenthetical expressions, nonrestrictive relative clauses, and other syntactically definable classes of constituents.[5]

1.2   *Intonation and focus in English*

Consider the two different utterances in (3), homophonous except for their prosody.

(3)   (a)   TRESpassers will be prosecuted.
      (b)   Trespassers will be PROsecuted.

(Capitals indicate the presence of a H* pitch accent on a syllable.) Only the first is an appropriate answer to the question "Who will be prosecuted?". Only the second is a possible answer to "What will be done to trespassers?". A *wh*-expression focuses a constituent, and an appropriate answer to a *wh*- question must focus the same constituent. I will use the term *Focus* to designate the constituent that is conventionally referred to as "the focus of the sentence." Generative theories of the semantics of Focus from Jackendoff (1972) to Rooth (1992)[6] have assumed that in the surface structure of a sentence a Focus constituent is *F-marked*,[8] thus [[TRESpassers]$_F$ will be prosecuted] vs. [Trespassers will be [PROsecuted]$_F$] for (3a) and (3b), respectively, when uttered as answers to the *wh*- questions above. Retained in the Logical Form of the sentence (LF in the Chomskyan sense [see May 1985]), this F-marking figures crucially in the input to the semantic component. The basic function of Focus is to introduce a set of alternatives into the discourse, which are put to use in various ways in the semantics.[7] These examples show there is a relation between pitch accent and Focus in English. Given the notion of F-marking, we can understand this as a relation between pitch accent and the F-marking of syntactic constituents.

The central problem in the characterization of the prosody-focus relation is the question of what principles govern the relation between pitch accent and F-marking . Call this the problem of *focus projection*. Consider, for example, the different F-markings that are possible when the sentence *Mary bought a book about bats* is pronounced with a pitch accent on *bats*:

(4)   Mary bought a book about BATS.
    (a)   Mary bought a book about [BATS]$_F$.
                           (What did Mary buy a book about?)
    (b)   Mary bought a book [about BATS]$_F$.
                           (What kind of book did Mary buy?)
    (c)   Mary bought [a book about BATS]$_F$.
                           (What did Mary buy?)
    (d)   Mary [bought a book about BATS]$_F$.
                           (What did Mary do?)
    (e)   [Mary bought a book about BATS]$_F$.
                           (What's been happening?)

This same sentence is an appropriate answer to the set of *wh-* questions listed at the right, meaning that the same location of pitch accent is consistent with the corresponding range of F-markings. The sentence *MARy bought a book about bats*, on the other hand, is an appropriate answer to just one question, "Who bought a book about bats?", which means that only the subject noun phrase in this sentence may be F-marked:

(5)   MARy bought a book about bats.
    [MARy]$_F$ bought a book about bats.   (Who bought a book about bats?)

The earliest generative solutions to the problem of focus projection (Chomsky 1971; Jackendoff 1972) hypothesized that the location of the intonational accent within the F-marked constituent was determined by the location of the main phrase stress within that constituent. A formulation in the spirit of the Jackendoff (1972) proposal would read as follows:

(6)   Accent to Main Stress within Focus
$$[\ldots\ldots\sigma_{\text{main stress}}\ldots\ldots]_F \quad \rightarrow \quad [\ldots\ldots\sigma_{\text{main stress}}\ldots\ldots]_F$$
$$\mid$$
$$\text{pitch accent}$$

According to the Nuclear Stress Rule (NSR) of Chomsky and Halle (1968), assumed in earlier accounts, the rightmost word-level stress of a phrase would carry the main stress of the phrase, therefore *bats* would carry the main stress within any of the F-marked constituents in (4) and hence would receive an accent. This NSR-based theory also correctly predicts that an accent on *Mary* in the same sentence would only be possible if it were the subject noun phrase that was F-marked, since only in the subject noun phrase would *Mary* carry the main phrase stress. However, the examination of a broader range of cases – in English and in other languages like German and Dutch – has shown that the Nuclear Stress Rule does not predict the right location of pitch accent within a focused constituent.[8]

Gussenhoven (1984), Selkirk (1984), and Rochemont (1986) – building on initial insights in Schmerling (1976) – argue that the theory of focus projection is instead framed in terms of syntactic notions and in particular makes appeal to the *argument structure* of the sentence. As Gussenhoven (1984) and Selkirk (1984) show, an argument-structure-based account of focus projection in English can be carried over intact to Dutch and German. The theory of focus projection laid out in Gussenhoven (1984, 1991), while different in conception, covers much the same empirical ground as theory to be laid out here. The Selkirk (1984) theory of focus projection, refined in Rochemont (1986), consists of a set of principles for the *licensing* of F-marking. The Basic Focus Rule states that the assignment of a pitch accent to a word entails the F-marking of the word:

(7) Basic Focus Rule
    An accented word is F-marked.

The F-marking of higher constituents is projected from the F-marking of words through two principles, grouped under the heading of Focus Projection:

(8) Focus Projection
    (a) F-marking of the *head* of a phrase licenses the F-marking of the phrase.
    (b) F-marking of an *internal argument* of a head licenses the F-marking of the head.

This theory of focus projection hypothesizes that the F-marking of the Focus of a sentence is licensed by a chain of F-marked constituents at the bottom end of which is the word bearing the pitch accent. I propose that the Focus of a sentence (FOC) is defined as an F-marked constituent not dominated by any other F-marked constituent. Given this theory, the focus structures compatible with the utterance *Mary bought a book about BATS* will read roughly as in (9) (rather than as in (4)), where FOC marks the highest F-marked constituent.

(9) Mary bought a book about BATS.
    (a) Mary bought a book about $_{FOC}[[BATS]_F]_{FOC}$.
    (b) Mary bought a book $_{FOC}[[about]_F [[BATS]_F]_F]_{FOC}$.
    (c) Mary bought $_{FOC}[a [book]_F [[about]_F [[BATS]_F]_F]_F]_{FOC}$.
    (d) Mary $_{FOC}[[bought]_F [a [book]_F [[about]_F [[BATS]_F]_F]_F]_F]_{FOC}$.
    (e) $_{FOC}[Mary [[bought]_F [a [book]_F [[about]_F [[BATS]_F]_F]_F]_F]_F]_{FOC}$.

(For the sake of simplicity, these representations ignore functional projections like IP and DP.) The F-marking of the noun *bats* licenses the F-marking of the NP *bats*, which in turn licenses the F-marking of its head the preposition *about*. The F-marking of *about* licenses the F-marking of the prepositional phrase, and so on. The F-marking of the direct object *a book about bats* licenses the F-marking of the verb and so of the verb phrase, which via licensing of the various intervening inflectional heads (Pollock 1989), licenses F-marking of the sentence. The syntax-based theory of Focus Projection thus correctly predicts the variety of Focus representations that are possible on the basis of the presence of an accent on BATS. As for the utterance *MARy bought a book about bats*, the F-marking of the accented subject NP cannot license the F-marking of the verb, since the subject is not a sister argument to the verb here, and hence F-marking cannot be projected any further than the subject noun phrase itself. Since there is no F-marked constituent dominating *Mary* in this sentence, *Mary* qualifies as the Focus of the sentence:

(10)   MARy bought a book about bats.
       $_{FOC}$[[MARy]$_F$]$_{FOC}$ bought a book about bats.

This theory thus coincides with the "standard" phrase-stress–based theory of focus projection in its predictions about the accent-Focus relation in the utterances *Mary bought a book about BATS* and *MARy bought a book about bats*. But the two theories differ significantly in their ability to account for (i) the relation between accent and the "given-new" structure of the sentence, (ii) the lack of focus projection from accent in positions where main phrase stress would be predicted, and (iii) the projection of focus from accent in positions that current theories would not define as positions of main phrase stress.

The F-marking that is posited in the theory of focus projection proposed above has a role to play in defining the given-new articulation (the "information structure") of the sentence. It appears to be the case that F-marked constituents which are not a Focus are interpreted as new in the discourse, while a constituent without F-marking is interpreted as given. A Focus constituent, on the other hand, may be interpreted as either given or new in the discourse. For example, every constituent making up the verb phrase in (10) is interpreted as given in the discourse, while the Focus subject *Mary* may be either given or new. Compare the dual-accented sentence *MARy bought a book about BATS*, uttered in response to the question "What's been happening?", which calls for the entire sentence to be the Focus. Accented *Mary* must be interpreted as new in this discourse. This would follow from the F-marking of *Mary* since it is not itself a Focus in this context.

(11)   MARy bought a book about BATS.
       $_{FOC}$[[MARy]$_F$ [[bought]$_F$ [a [book]$_F$ [[about]$_F$ [BATS]$_F$]$_F$]$_F$]$_F$]$_{FOC}$.

(Compare (9e), also a case of sentence Focus, but where unaccented *Mary* must be assumed to be "old information" in the discourse.) Note that in (11) the nonFocus F-marking which our theory says must be a property of *about, book, bought* and the phrases they head – if sentence Focus is to be projected from *bats* – also calls for the interpretation of these constituents as "new," and that is the right result.

With this understanding of focus projection and of the given-new interpretation of nonFocus F-marking, we can also explain the phenomenon infelicitously referred to as "deaccenting," studied in Ladd (1980), Gussenhoven (1984), Selkirk (1984), Rochemont (1986), and exemplified in the utterance *MARy bought a BOOK about bats*. A sentence such as this, which lacks accent on *about bats*, would be appropriately uttered in a discourse where *(about)* bats is "given." (The presence of an accent on *about bats* would entail F-marking and therefore an interpretation as "new.") The "deaccenting" puzzle is that a higher phrase, even the sentence, may be a Focus with this utterance, despite the absence of accent on *about bats*. This projection of focus is explained by the present theory, since focus may project from a head, in this case *book*:

(12) MARy bought a BOOK about bats.
     $_{FOC}$[[[Mary]$_F$]$_F$ [[bought]$_F$ [a [BOOK]$_F$ [[about] [[bats]]]]]$_F$]$_F$]$_{FOC}$.

Indeed, the syntax-based theory of focus projection predicts that if the sentence is the Focus and if *about bats* (but not *book*) is given, then the accent must fall on *book*, since this is the only location of accent in the verb phrase that will both project F-marking to the sentence and at the same time ensure the nonFocus F-marking that the newness of the remaining constituents in the verb phrase requires. That the presence of pitch accent on *book* may indeed license sentence Focus here is shown by the fact that (12) could be uttered in a context where sentence Focus is called for. For example, *only* may associate to the Focus of an embedded sentence in a configuration such as "I only thought that $_{FOC}$[. . . . .]$_{FOC}$." Embedding (12) would give (13a). The fact that sentence (13a) may be appropriately uttered when the alternatives under consideration are entire sentences, such as in (13b)–(13d), rather than ones where nouns like *game* or *poster* substitute for *book*, shows that the accenting of *book* here may license sentence Focus.

(13) (a) I was only thinking that $_{FOC}$[MARy bought a BOOK about bats]$_{FOC}$.
      (b) I was thinking that they (bats) eat mosQUItoes.
      (c) I was thinking that we should reMOVE them from South COLLege.
      (d) I was thinking that ROBert never found the one that bit his CAT.

Embedded sentence Focus would moreover be possible with the utterance *I was only thinking that MARy had BOUGHT a book about bats*, where *a book about bats* is given in the discourse. Note, finally, that this theory allows us to understand why sentence Focus is possible through the accenting of the auxiliary *do*:

(14) $_{FOC}$[[Mary] [[DID]$_F$ [buy a book about bats]]$_F$]$_{FOC}$.

As a head of an inflectional projection (assume it is the affirmation/negation projection of Laka 1990), accented *DID* licenses sentence Focus. Employing the accented auxiliary *do* solves the problem of how to focus a sentence when everything in it is old information.

We have seen that an array of F-markings are possible internal to the Focus of a sentence. NonFocus F-marking is interpreted as "new." The correlation of given and new with the absence and presence of accent is captured by the theory of Focus Projection proposed here. By contrast, the phrase-stress–based theory of the accent-focus relation, proposed by Jackendoff (1972) (and revised by Cinque 1993), gives no recognition to the given-new articulation that is possible within the Focus phrase. It wrongly predicts that sentence Focus should be impossible in cases of "deaccenting" like (12). And it has no means of characterizing the fact that under the same Focus condition systematic contrasts in the discourse-appropriateness of utterances are possible, depending on the distribution of accents. *MARy bought a BOOK about bats; MARy bought a book about BATS; Mary bought a book about BATS;* etc., differ in their given-new articulation, but are all possible as cases of sentence Focus.

As Gussenhoven (1984) and Selkirk (1984) point out, a non-argument does not project focus. It is well known that an accented pre-head modifier does not project focus. The utterance *I saw my OLDer sister* has Focus restricted to the adjective phrase, and so sets up alternatives like *I saw my YOUNGer sister* or *I saw my MIDDle sister* which all presuppose that "I saw my x sister" is given in the discourse. Accented adjunct phrases in post-head position also fail to project focus. For example, focus does not project from an adjunct locative PP in *He smoked in the TENT*. For such a sentence to have VP or sentence Focus, there must be an accent on the verb: *He SMOKED in the TENT* (or *He SMOKED in the tent*). (Experimental work (Gussenhoven 1983) confirms this distinction.) Placement of Focus-sensitive *only* before the VP brings out the difference:

(15)   (a)   He only smoked $_\text{FOC}$[in the TENT]$_\text{FOC}$.
            *He only $_\text{FOC}$[smoked in the TENT]$_\text{FOC}$.
        (b)   He only $_\text{FOC}$[*SMOKED* in the *TENT*]$_\text{FOC}$.

The alternatives implied by the pronunciation in (15a) include *He smoked by the campfire, He smoked in the outhouse,* and other sentences where the locative PP is substituted for. (15b), on the other hand, may evoke alternatives like *He left trash on the trail, He picked the endangered toadflax,* or other such infractions of sound eco-policy. Compare the case where a post-verbal PP is an argument; here accenting of the prepositional object licenses focus on the VP:

(16)   He only $_\text{FOC}$[looked at the GARden]$_\text{FOC}$.

(16) is a possible answer to the question "What did he do?". Alternatives could be *He put the sprinkler on, He refilled the bird feeder,* and so on, showing VP Focus and hence projection of F-marking from accented *garden*.

There is a further broad range of counterexamples to the phrase-stress–based theory of focus projection, ones which are readily accounted for with a minor revision of the theory of Focus Projection given in (8). These involve projection of focus from an argument which is neither phrase-final nor sister to its head in surface structure. It is widely recognized that accent on the subject of an intransitive verb may license sentence Focus:

(17) $_{FOC}$[JOHNSON died]$_{FOC}$.
       $_{FOC}$[The SKY is falling]$_{FOC}$.
       $_{FOC}$[The SUN came out]$_{FOC}$.
       $_{FOC}$[The BABY's crying]$_{FOC}$.

These utterances are appropriate "out-of-the-blue" responses to "What's been happening?," or may be embedded in the sentence frame "I was only thinking that $_{FOC}$[. . . . .]$_{FOC}$. Note that alternative pronunciations with additional accent on the verb, e.g., *JOHNson DIED*, are equally possible, with identical F-marking possibilities. The interesting point is that the accent on the verb is not necessary. The utterance *JOHNson died* is appropriate in a context where both *Johnson* and *dying* are new in the discourse and where the sentence is the Focus.

   Current syntactic analysis understands the surface subject in the sentences in (17) to be generated within the verb phrase in deep structure (see Diesing 1992 and references therein). Only a small amendment is required for the syntax-based theory of Focus Projection to be able to account for the accent Focus relation in these cases, namely the provision that the F-marking of a constituent licenses the F-marking of its *trace*. The Focus status of the sentence *JOHNson died* is therefore licensed in virtue of the F-marking chain given in (18):

(18) $_{FOC}$[[[JOHNson]$_{F1}$]$_{F2}$ $_{VP}$[[t]$_{F3}$ [died]$_{F4}$]$_{F5}$]$_{FOC}$.

An alternative to this appeal to trace would be to assume that Focus Projection held at the level of Logical Form, where the raised subject NP would be restored to its deep structure position through reconstruction. The trace-based account is adopted here.

   The notion that focus projection from an argument to its head proceeds through the mediation of a trace allows us to explain other classic puzzles. For example, Gussenhoven (1992) observes that while accenting *clock* in (19a), a small clause structure, allows for tick to be interpreted as new information and for the entire sentence to be Focus, in (19b) accenting *clock* does not allow the accentless *tick* to be interpreted as new, and the sentence is not a Focus:

(19)   (a)   I heard a CLOCK tick.
       (b)   I forced the CLOCK to tick.

These facts follow, given the proposed amendment to Focus Projection (as they do in the Gussenhoven 1984/1991 theory). The surface syntactic representation of (19b) involves a control structure, with a PRO in the VP-internal subject position, whereas the surface representation of (19a) has a trace in that position, the subject having been moved out of the VP by NP-movement:

(20)   (a) $_{FOC}$[I heard [[a [CLOCK]$_F$]$_F$ $_{VP}$[[t]$_F$ [tick]$_F$]$_F$]$_F$]$_{FOC}$.
      (b)   [I forced [the [CLOCK]$_F$]$_{FOC}$ to $_{VP}$[PRO [tick]]]].

The absence of an F-marked argument or its trace as sister to the accentless *tick* in (20b) accounts for the lack of F-marking on *tick*, and therefore its interpretation as given and failure to project focus to higher phrases.

Two other intriguing sorts of contrast receive a similar account. Gussenhoven observes that when a sentence like *Trespassers will be prosecuted* is uttered, out of the blue, as a description of an event (as in the mouth of the town crier or a headline in the *Gazette*), it may have a pronunciation with accent only on the subject, as in (21a), or with accent on both the subject and the verb, as in (21b):

(21)   (a)   TRESpassers will be prosecuted.
      (b)   TRESpassers will be PROSecuted.

In both cases sentence Focus is possible and in neither case is *prosecuted* interpreted as given. However, when the sentence does not describe an event but rather has the status of a generic-like statement about the properties of the subject, as it would when posted as a sign on the edge of a neighbor's woods, then accent is required on the VP if it is to be interpreted as new and the sentence is to be in Focus. Diesing (1992) argues that generic sentences involve control structures, where the surface subject controls a VP-internal PRO. As Diesing points out, if we assume this analysis, it explains why projection of focus from the subject (via F-marking of verb, verb phrase, etc.) is not possible in generic sentences, and thus why such sentences require accent within the predicate if they are to qualify as cases of sentence Focus. In the case of the event reading in (21a), where the subject receives an existential interpretation ("There are trespassers who will be prosecuted"), Diesing argues that the subject is raised from a deep structure position within the VP. In this case the trace(s) left by NP-movement provide the route along which F-marking of the surface subject can ultimately license Focus of the sentence, and hence accent within the predicate is not required.

Gussenhoven (1984, 1992) notes further that the difference between an individual level and a stage-level predicate (Kratzer 1988; Diesing 1992) is reflected in the accentual properties of the sentence under sentence Focus, citing the examples in (22)

(22)   (a)   Your EYES are red.   *or*   Your EYES are RED.
      (b)   Your EYES are BLUE.   *not*   *Your EYES are blue.

A stage-level predicate like redness, when predicated of eyes, does not require accent in an utterance with sentence Focus, while an individual-level predicate like *blue*, when predicated of eyes, does. The pair in (23), discussed by Diesing (1992), have the same possibilities for sentence Focus:

(23) (a) FIREMEN are available.   *or*   FIREMEN are AVAILABLE.
       (b) FIREMEN are ALTRUISTIC. *not*   *FIREMEN are altruistic.

Altruistic is an individual-level predicate. *Available* is stage-level. Diesing posits a raising from VP-internal position (leaving a trace) for the stage-level case and a control structure, with VP-internal PRO for the individual-level case. She points out that the focus projection facts follow, assuming the Focus Projection theory.

A final puzzle which the appeal to traces in focus projection allows us to explain involves *wh-* movement. The question *Which BOOK did Helen review?* can be appropriately uttered in a discourse where *Helen* is given in the discourse, but *reviewing* is not. That *Helen* is interpreted as old follows from its lack of accent, since the subject NP could not have F-marking licensed by anything else. But the accentless verb *review* can get F-marked, through the trace of the *wh*-moved NP:

(24) [$_{FOC}$[What BOOKS]$_{FOC}$ has [[Helen]] $_{VP}$[[reviewed]$_F$ [t]$_F$]$_F$]?

This particular sort of example is one of a set of puzzles for the phrase-stress–based theory of focus projection noted by Bresnan (1971, 1972) which the present theory of focus projection solves.[9]

We are now in a position to formulate the necessary revision of our syntax-based theory of Focus Projection:[10]

(25) Focus Projection (Selkirk 1984; Rochemont 1986)
       (a) F-marking of the head of a phrase licenses the F-marking of the phrase.
       (b) F-marking of an internal argument of a head licenses the F-marking of the head.
       (c) F-marking of the antecedent of a trace left by NP- or *wh*-movement licenses the F-marking of the trace.

These three principles of Focus Projection combine with the language-particular Basic Focus Rule ("A word with a pitch accent is F-marked") to define the relation between accent and focus in intonational languages like English, Dutch, and German.

Work by Ladd (1980, 1983), Ward and Hirschberg (1985), Pierrehumbert and Hirschberg (1990), McLemore (1991), and others has sought to show that different choices of pitch accent and boundary tone in a sentence correlate with different conditions of appropriateness in a discourse. To the extent to which different choices of tonal entity – e.g., a H% versus a L% boundary tone or a H* pitch accent versus a L*+H pitch accent – entail differences in pragmatic or semantic interpretation, further support is provided for construing these tonal entities as morphemic in character, varieties of "floating" tonal particle which must occupy a position in surface structure.[11] It may turn out that only certain of the pitch accents of English license the projection of focus. Should this be the case, the Basic Focus Rule, which as currently stated makes no distinction between the different pitch accents, would have to reformulated. However, the theory of Focus Projection, which makes no appeal to accent, would be predicted to remain intact.

2   Phrase Stress

The relative prominence of a syllable within a sentence has been attributed to three different factors: (1) the presence or absence of a pitch accent on the syllable (the *accent* factor), (2) the position of the syllable within a constituent structure (the *phrasing* factor), and (3) the presence or absence of other prominent syllables in the immediate vicinity of the syllable (the *rhythm* factor). A fuller role for phrasing-based constraints on prominence than is conventionally assumed might remove motivation for the rhythmic component of a phonological theory of phrase stress.

2.1   Pitch Accents and Nuclear Stress

Informally stated, the Nuclear Stress Rule reads as follows:

(26)   Nuclear Stress Rule
       The most prominent syllable of the rightmost constituent in a phrase P
       is the most prominent syllable of P.

I assume that the constituent structure relevant to the NSR is the *prosodic structure*[12] of the sentence, and that for each constituent in a prosodic structure there is a most prominent syllable. I assume that prominence relations are represented with a *metrical grid*,[13] where each constituent-prominence is marked with an x. The NSR would predict the grid prominences in (27) for the sentence *Volunteer firemen save lives*:

(27)
```
                                                    x
                          x                         x
              x           x               x         x
    IP( MaP( (Volunteer) (firemen) )MaP MaP((save) (lives) )MaP)IP.[14]
```

But violations of the NSR are commonplace, as examples discussed in the previous section and other works cited there show. In cases like *FIREmen are available, I heard a CLOCK tick,* or *Mary wrote a BOOK about bats,* the most prominent syllable of the sentence is not the main-stressed syllable of the final word or phrase, but rather the pitch accented syllable. The generalization holds that a pitch-accented syllable is always more prominent than a syllable which lacks a pitch accent. Assuming that prominence is not merely a matter of intonation, but also of stress, this generalization reflects that the grammar of English gives place to a constraint on the relation between pitch accent and stress prominence, which Selkirk (1984) formulates as the Pitch Accent Prominence Rule:

(28)   Pitch Accent Prominence Rule (PAPR)
        A syllable associated to a pitch accent has greater stress prominence than a syllable which is not associated to a pitch accent.

The Pitch Accent Prominence Rule is understood to take precedence over the Nuclear Stress Rule. In *FIREman are available,* the NSR calls for greatest prominence on *-vail-*, while the PAPR calls for greatest prominence on FIRE-. The PAPR wins,[15] as shown in (29a). Where the NSR and the PAPR are not in conflict, however, the NSR would be predicted to be in effect. Consider the combined effect of the NSR and the PAPR in (29b), where the accented syllables of both *volunteer* and *firemen* are more prominent than *-vail-*, by virtue of the PAPR, and the NSR assures the greatest prominence of the final pitch accented syllable *Fire-*.

(29)   (a)   (b)

                                                                        x
           x   x   x
           x   x   x   x   x
           FIREmen are available.   VOLunteer   FIREmen are available.
           H*   H*   H*

Given the Pitch Accent Prominence Rule, the Nuclear Stress Rule has the status of a default principle, applicable only when "all else is equal." It will indeed be responsible for the phrasal stress pattern in (27), but only when all the words are accented (as in an all-new utterance), or when all are unaccented (because given in the discourse):

(30)   (a)   VOLunteer FIREmen SAVE LIVES.
        (b)   I already TOLD you that volunteer firemen save lives.

Any study of patterns of phrase stress clearly must control for the presence/absence of pitch accents. In what follows, assume that the stressed syllables are all pitch accented.

2.2   Rhythmic Alternation Versus Edge Prominence

Consider now the stress pattern of the right-branching and left-branching phrase structures in (31a, b):

(31) (a)

```
                                x        (b)                              x
             x                  x                    x                    x
             x      x           x                    x        x          x
        ( (hard-boiled) (eggs) )                  ( (four) (new mugs) )
    (c)  *                      x        (d)  *                          x
                    x           x                                        x
             x      x           x                    x        x          x
        ( (hard-boiled) (eggs) )                  ( (four) (new mugs) )
```

The presence of the initial prominence in (31a) and (31b) is not predicted by the NSR, which, instead, predicts the patterns in (31c) and (31d). A standard explanation for the presence of the initial secondary prominence has relied on the idea, due originally to Liberman (1975), that principles of rhythmic alternation complement, and sometimes even override, constituency-based principles like the NSR in defining the stress pattern of a sentence. The ideal arrangement of prominences, the story goes, is one in which beats alternate, one in which both *clash* and *lapse* are avoided:[16]

(32) (a) Ideal   (b) Clash   (c) Lapse

```
           x   x                 x x
        x x x x x            . . . x x . . .              . . . x x . . .
```

When the rhythmic principles Avoid Clash and Avoid Lapse are violated, as in (31c, d), it has been assumed that these violations may be repaired through operations moving or adding rhythmic prominences (= beats), resulting in rhythmically well-formed surface representations like those in (31a, b).

The claim that rhythm-based principles like Avoid Clash and Avoid Lapse are central to an explanation of the distribution of secondary prominences in examples like (31a, b) is the subject of some debate (see Bolinger 1958, 1965; Hayes 1984; Kager and Visch 1988; Gussenhoven 1991). Bolinger argues that what is at issue is a propensity for pitch accents to be placed closer to the left edge of a constituent. A tendency to "early accent," even in the absence of stress clash, is amply documented in recent work by Shattuck-Hufnagel, Ostendorff, and Ross (to appear), as well as in work by Beckman and her colleagues (Beckman et al. 1987, 1991). I want to argue that the tendency to early placement of accent is to be ascribed, in part at least, to a constraint calling for stress prominence at the left periphery of a constituent, rather than to a constraint calling directly for accent placement at the left edge. If we assume a peripheral stress prominence constraint we can indeed account for the presence of early accent in standard "inversion" cases like *fôurtèen múgs*, where the first pitch accent is left-peripheral rather than in the otherwise final position of *fourtéen*: in phrasal contexts where the phrase edge prominence constraint calls for word-initial stress prominence, the Pitch Accent Prominence Rule (PAPR) will guarantee that a pitch accent in such a word be realized on the syllable with that initial stress prominence. Yet, more than this, a phrase edge prominence constraint will also explain prominence patterns in collocations like *fôur nèw múgs*, in the case where each of the words is pitch accented. The intuition is that the phrase-initial *four* has greater prominence than *new*, a fact that cannot be explained by the distribution of pitch accents, since they are both accented in this case. Rather, *four* must have greater stress, a fact predicted by assuming the stress-based account of early accent sketched here.

Note that it is a recurrent fact about patterns of word stress that the syllables heading feet at both the right and left periphery of a word are more prominent than those in nonperipheral feet. We see this in English words with three feet, e.g., *Âppalàchicóla, chîmpànzée*. Of the two edge prominences, the Main Word Stress Rule declares that it is the rightmost one which is most prominent. This word-level patterning is arguably replicated at the phrase-level in English. *Fôur nèw múgs, Fârrah Fàwcett-Májors, côlorless grèen idéas, hârd-bòiled éggs, ôver-dòne stéak, thîrty-nìne stéps* all show peripheral prominences, with the greatest prominence of all on the right, guaranteed by the Nuclear Stress Rule. We assume, then, a role for a Phrase Edge Prominence constraint.

(33) Phrase Edge Prominence
   The most prominent syllable of an edge constituent is more prominent than that of a constituent not located at an edge.

(Both Phrase Edge Prominence and the Nuclear Stress Rule are End Rules in the sense of Prince 1983 or edge-alignment constraints in the sense of McCarthy and Prince 1993.)

In the case of *fôur nèw múgs*, (31b), Phrase Edge Prominence and the NSR complement each other. The case of (31a) is more interesting. Satisfying Phrase Edge Prominence with respect to the higher level phrase *hard-boiled eggs* entails violating the NSR within the phrase *hard-boiled*. This sort of constraint interaction, where the violation of one constraint is the consequence of the satisfaction of another, is formalized within optimality theory (Prince and Smolensky, to appear). Note further the stress pattern of the sentence in (34) (cited in Hayes 1991):

(34)

```
                                          x
              x                           x
              x              x            x
              x       x      x            x
IP(MaP((Nineteen thousand)(linguists))MaPMaP((sing))MaP)IP
```

Within the Intonational Phrase the NSR provides for greatest prominence in the sentence on *sing*. Satisfying Phrase Edge Prominence at the level of the IP has the consequence that within the lefthand Major Phrase the prominence on *nineteen* is greater than the prominence on *linguists*, in violation of the NSR within that MaP. Quite generally, satisfying Phrase Edge Prominence on a higher level phrase can be seen as responsible for the failure to respect the NSR within a lower phrase, rendering superfluous an appeal to rhythmic constraints in many cases.

A theory of early accent based on Phrase Edge Prominence provides a straightforward explanation for a classic puzzle for rhythm-based accounts of early accent – the different locations of main word stress in the medial words of near minimal pairs of the type in (35):[17]

(35)   (a)   (b)
      ((nôrthern) (Càlifórnia wínes))   ((Nôrthern Califòrnia) (wínes))
      ((nôrthern) (Jàpanese béetles))   ((Nôrthern Japanèse) (áccent))
      ((grêen) (bàmboo tábles))   ((grêen bambòo) (tábles))

In the right-branching (a) cases, main stress on the medial words has "moved" to (i.e., appears in) initial position in the embedded phrase. This locus of main word stress allows the embedded phrases to satisfy Phrase Edge Prominence. A comparable positioning of main word stress in the left-branching (b) cases is not to be expected, since it would purchase no better-formedness with respect to Phrase Edge Prominence. Viewed in purely rhythmic terms, the retention of final word stress in the medial words in the (b) cases has no explanation, since it creates a clash with main stress of the following word, just as it does in the (a) cases.

3   Intonational Phrasing

The term *intonational phrase* is usually applied to spans of the utterance which are delimited by boundary tones (cf. sec. 1.1):

(36)   H%   H%   L%
  (a)   IP(Fred,)IP IP(who's a volunteer fireman,)IP IP(teaches third grade)IP.
              H%   L%   L%
  (b)   IP(Alice,)IP IP(this is Mary,)IP IP(my sister)IP.

More than a unit with respect to which the distribution of boundary tones is defined, the intonational phrase (IP) appears to consititute a domain relevant to various aspects of the phonetic implementation of the sentence, including timing effects like constituent-final lengthening,[18] and the setting of register for the realization of tone.[19] Ladd (1986) claims that intonational phrasing is relevant to the phenomenon of "rhythmic inversion" examined in 2.2. In an example like (37a), where the subject is set off as a separate IP, there is no alteration in the locus of main stress in *hotel*, but there can be in (37b), where the subject and what follows occupy the same IP:[20]

(37) (a) ₁ₚ(The hoTEL's)ᵢₚ ₁ₚ(TERRible)ᵢₚ. [But the beach is great.]
      (b) ₁ₚ(The HOtel's TERRible)ᵢₚ.   [It's not even on the beach.]

The prediction, which seems to be correct, is that a backwards shift in stress away from the edge of a constituent that ends in a boundary tone – the mark of an IP edge – is not possible.

At present, the principles governing intonational phrasing are not well understood. Certain syntactic constructions – vocatives, appositives, parentheticals, preposed clauses, nonrestrictive relative clauses – are necessarily set off in separated IPs.[21] In other cases, like the examples in (37), there are options in phrasing. There are impossible phrasings. Compare the set of examples in (38), due to Mark Liberman:

(38) (a)   ₁ₚ(Three mathematicians in ten)ᵢₚ ₁ₚ(derive a lemma)ᵢₚ.
      (b) *₁ₚ(Three mathematicians)ᵢₚ ₁ₚ(in ten derive a lemma)ᵢₚ.
      (c)   ₁ₚ(Three mathematicians)ᵢₚ ₁ₚ(intend to rival Emma)ᵢₚ.

(38) gives one possible phrasing of the sentence *Three mathematicians in ten derive a lemma*. The phrasing in (38b), which divides the subject noun phrase and groups its second half with the verb phrase, is ungrammatical, however. The nearly homophonous (38c) is fine with that phrasing, since the break falls at the end of the subject noun phrase.

It has been suggested that the material contained within an IP must constitute a "sense unit,"[22] though this idea is difficult to implement. It has also been suggested that notions like Topic or Focus are relevant to a theory of intonational phrasing. Cross-linguistic examinations of the phonological and phonetic correlates of prosodic phrasing and of the relation of phrasing to notions like Topic and Focus have only recently begun to accumulate.[23] Together with investigations of the syntax and semantics of Topic and Focus that are "intonationally aware," they will doubtless form the basis of a fuller understanding of the relation between sentence prosody, meaning, and discourse.

NOTES

1 Jackendoff (1972), Liberman (1975), Bing (1979), Ladd (1980), Pierrehumbert (1980), Williams (1980), Culicover and Rochemont (1983), Halle and Vergnaud (1987), and Cinque (1993) are proponents of phrase-stress–based theories of the prosody-focus relation.

2   Thanks to Janet Pierrehumbert for these figures, which first appeared in Selkirk (1984).

3   The debate about whether the L tone in such a sentence is part of a bitonal pitch accent or has the status of an independent phrase accent assigned to the edge of the constituent *legumes* (see, e.g., Pierrehumbert 1980 and Ladd 1983) will be ignored here.

4   See Lehiste and Ivić (1986), Inkelas and Zec (1988) and Zec (1988) on Serbo-Croatian; see McCawley (1968), Poser (1984), and Pierrehumbert and Beckman (1988) on Japanese.

5   See, e.g., Bruce (1977) on the H tone marking Focus in Swedish; Hayes and Lahiri (1991) on focus-marking by H tone in Bengali; and Bing (1980), Ladd (1980), and Beckman and Pierrehumbert (1986) on medial boundary tones in English.

6   The list includes Williams (1980), Rooth (1985), Rochemont (1986), von Stechow (1989, 1991), and Kratzer (1991). See also Carlson (1983, 1984).

7   See Rooth (1985, 1992) for details as to how these alternatives are used in the semantics of various constructions.

8   See Bresnan (1971, 1972), Berman and Szamosi (1972), Bolinger (1972), Schmerling (1976), Ladd (1980), Gussenhoven (1984), Selkirk (1984), Rochemont (1986), and others.

   Cinque (1993) attempts to remedy the problems for a phrase-stress–based theory by modifying the theory of phrase stress. He rejects the Nuclear Stress Rule and proposes instead that main stress within a phrase is assigned to the "most deeply embedded constituent" within that phrase. The "greater prominence" he ascribes to the main phrase stress within a Focus constituent derives from the presence of a pitch accent, which in his approach, like Jackendoff's, could be assigned by the rule of Accent to Main Stress within Focus. Most of the counterexamples to Jackendoff's NSR-based theory of the prosody-focus relation stand as counterexamples to Cinque's theory of focus projection as well.

9   See Selkirk (1984) and Rochemont (1986) for further discussion of the Bresnan cases.

10   The cases examined involve traces left by NP-movement and *wh*-movement. A further case from Gussenhoven (1984, 1992) suggests that the traces left by quantified NPs do not project focus. Whereas the utterance *The PRISoners escaped* allows the interpretation of *escaped* as new information and allows for VP or sentence Focus, the utterance *EVERYbody escaped* does not. Moreover, Angelika Kratzer (p.c.) points out that in German a noun phrase that has undergone Scrambling cannot project focus.

11   These would fall into the same class as the well-known and little understood discourse particles of German, Greek, and other languages.

12   See, e.g., Selkirk (1981, 1986), Nespor and Vogel (1986), Pierrehumbert and Beckman (1988), Selkirk and Tateishi (1988, 1990), Selkirk and Shen (1990), and the chapter by Inkelas and Zec, (chap. 15, this volume).

13   See chapters 10 and 11, this volume, as well as Liberman (1975), Liberman and Prince (1977), Prince (1983), and Selkirk (1984).

14   IP = Intonational Phrase, MaP = Major Phonological Phrase.

15   This sort of constraint interaction finds a welcome formalization in the context of optimality theory (Prince and Smolensky, to appear).

16 On the role of clash and lapse avoidance in stress patterning, see Liberman and Prince (1977), Nespor and Vogel (1979, 1989), Bing (1980), Prince (1983), Selkirk (1984) and numerous others.

17 See Prince (1983), Hammond (1984), Hayes (1984), Selkirk (1984), Kager and Visch (1988), Hayes (1991), and especially Gussenhoven (1991), by whom these pairs are inspired.

18 See, e.g., Selkirk (1984), Ladd (1986), Edwards and Beckman (1988), Beckman and Edwards (1989), Price et al. (1991), and Gussenhoven and Rietveld (1992).

19 See, e.g., Ladd 1988.

20 Vogel and Kenesei (1990a) report contrasts in inversion which they say are dependent on the focus structure of the sentence. These cases probably reduce to differences in intonational phrasing such as those examined here.

21 See especially Bing (1979).

22 See Selkirk (1984) and Steedman (1991), for example.

23 See Poser (1984) and Pierrehumbert and Beckman (1988) on Japanese, Kanerva (1989, 1990) on Chichewa, Vogel and Kenesei (1990a, 1990b), and Rosenthall (1992) on Hungarian, and Vallduví (1990) on Catalan.

17 Dependency Relations in Phonology

COLIN J. EWEN

0 Introduction

The concept of dependency has been utilized in linguistic theory to characterize the claim that elements within a particular domain may be asymmetrically related. Within the syntactic domain, the introduction of dependency can be associated with the claim that the two constituents of a constitute display a head-modifier relation, rather than being simply sisters. The incorporation of the dependency relation into phonological representations, in particular those characterizing the internal structure of the segment, has been primarily associated with the theory of phonological structure referred to as *dependency phonology* (Anderson and Jones 1974, 1977; Durand 1986; Anderson and Ewen 1987; den Dikken and van der Hulst 1988; van der Hulst 1989). However, something closely approximating to the dependency relation of dependency phonology is utilized in various other approaches to phonological structure, although generally only in the suprasegmental domain, for example with respect to syllable structure. Furthermore, a number of writers have proposed introducing a segmental relation termed "dependency" into theories of representation other than that of dependency phonology. On closer inspection, though, we find that the term is typically used to denote different kinds of relation, especially with respect to segment-internal structure.

Although this contribution is primarily concerned with the role of dependency within the segment, I devote some space in section 1 to a discussion of suprasegmental structure, in particular to the relationship between dependency in the sense of dependency phonology and other kinds of relations which have been proposed. In sections 2–3, after a brief introduction to the character of dependency within the segment, I consider the way in which the relation has been developed within dependency phonology (sec. 2), and how notions of dependency have been utilized in other frameworks (sec. 3). Finally, in section 4, I consider very briefly how proposals within dependency phonology for the representation of the internal structure of the segment relate to those within feature geometry approaches to segmental structure.

1 Dependency above the Segment

The dependency relation is a binary asymmetric relation in which one element in a construction is the *governor* or *head,* and the other the *dependent* or *modifier.* The head-modifier relation was initially more familiar from syntactic work, and its interpretation as dependency is indeed first found in syntax (e.g., Hays 1964; Robinson 1970), in particular in the framework of Case and Dependency Grammar (Anderson 1971, 1977). The application of the relation to phonological sequences incorporates the claim that such sequences are headed. Thus a syllable is a construction which is headed by a syllabic segment, a foot by a stressed syllabic segment, and so on.

Such claims, which received their first formal statement in the dependency model, have now become commonplace, especially in the light of developments within metrical phonology (see chaps. 10 and 11, this volume), where the relational interpretation of strong-weak is functionally more or less identical to the dependency relation. Thus it is generally accepted that sequences are headed, and furthermore that this formal relation has a physical correlate, relative prominence.[1] Stressed syllabic segments are inherently more prominent than unstressed syllabic segments, and syllabic segments are more prominent than nonsyllabic segments (chap. 6, this volume). In addition, within the syllable, sonorant consonants are inherently more prominent than nonsonorant consonants (simply by virtue of their greater sonority), so that the dependency relation also holds between the elements of a consonant cluster.[2]

In view of these observations, it is clear that dependency phonology, like metrical and autosegmental approaches, can properly be reckoned as belonging to the general theory of phonology and phonological representation now referred to as nonlinear phonology. It is obvious, too, that the differences among the various nonlinear approaches to suprasegmental structure, at least insofar as these are crucial to the individual models, are no longer sufficiently great as to warrant, in the context of this overview, a detailed account of the formalism used in dependency phonology for the representation of phonological sequences. However, it is interesting to observe that recent notational proposals, both within syntax and phonology, adopt some of the formal conventions of dependency grammars, in the sense that an element which is head of more than one projection is characterized as a projection on a vertical line. Thus, in (1), the representation for the English word *marinade,* the line associated to the vowel /eː/ is a projection which indicates that the vowel is simultaneously head of the rhyme /eːd/, the syllable /neːd/, and the larger construction formed by the whole word (I ignore here the question of the representation of the length of the vowel):

(1)

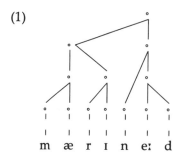

m   æ   r   ɪ   n   eː   d

As noted above, similar considerations apply to the structure of subsyllabic constructions such as the onset and the coda, in which the more sonorant consonant is the governor, as in (2a, b):

(2)   (a)   (b)

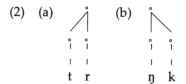

t   r   ŋ   k

Dependency phonology as such is strictly agnostic with respect to the issue of whether particular suprasegmental constructions are required in phonological representation. Thus Anderson and Ewen (1987) adopt a view of sequential structure compatible with (1) and (2); however, the particular structures proposed there are independent of the more general question of whether dependency relations are appropriate to the representation of units such as syllable, foot, or coda. The content of the claim made by dependency phonology is that any such structure is headed, and that this asymmetric relation is best represented in terms of dependency; (1) and (2) are particular interpretations of this claim.[3]

2   Dependency within the Segment

As we have seen, the relation of dependency applied to suprasegmental representations is largely equivalent to other proposals involving asymmetric relations. What distinguishes dependency phonology from other nonlinear approaches is the fact that segment-internal structure is also considered to involve headedness, and therefore that the dependency relation also plays a role within this domain. As in the case of suprasegmental structure, it is important to realize that there are various aspects of the proposals made within dependency phonology concerning the internal structure of the segment which are independent of this basic property of the theory, and which therefore can, and should, be assessed independently.

In this respect, we should observe that the set of features commonly used within dependency phonology is not, as such, crucial to the model. However, the nature of the features – in particular, the fact that they are all *unary*, i.e., single-valued – is determined by the fact that these features can interact in terms of relative prominence, as we shall see. Unary features, or *components*, as they are commonly referred to in dependency phonology, have been proposed elsewhere, especially with respect to the characterization of vowel systems (e.g., Schane 1984 and chap. 18, this volume; Goldsmith 1985; Rennison 1986), and more recently as single-valued, or monovalent, nodes in a feature geometry (e.g., Sagey 1986; Avery and Rice 1989).

2.1 Vowel Representations

The motivation for incorporating dependency in vowel representations comes from vowels in which more than one single-valued feature is present. Thus, assuming a standard set of monovalent features [front], [round], and [sonorant] (or [open]), represented in dependency phonology as |i|, |u|, and |a|, respectively, there is clearly only a limited set of representations in which two or more of the features simply co-occur, viz., |i, u|, |i, a|, |u, a|, and |i, u, a|, the representations for the vowels /y/, /e/, /o/, and /ø/, respectively (the order of the features in the representation of the vowels here is not significant). In common with other single-valued systems, such a system of representation incorporates an inherent evaluation metric: the more complex the vowel, the more features are required in its representation. This is argued to be appropriate to the extent that it reflects notation-independent interpretations of the notion of phonological complexity and also insofar it accords with the "quantal" theory of speech, in this case as applied to the vowel space (Stevens 1989).[4]

Theories which do not incorporate an asymmetric relation holding between features cannot, without introducing one or more new features or incorporating reiteration of the existing features, characterize a vowel system containing more than the seven vowels already mentioned. In particular, systems with more than one mid front vowel, say /e/ and /ɛ/, require a feature such as [tense] or [ATR] to distinguish between these two vowels. Thus a single-valued system incorporating a feature |ATR| might characterize the distinction between /e/ and /ɛ/ as |i, a, ATR| vs. |i, a|.

It can be argued that such representations are appropriate for familiar systems where ATR is the feature involved in dividing the set of vowels of a language into two distinct subsets involved in harmony processes, for example. Ewen and van der Hulst (forthcoming) suggest moreover that while some systems involve an ATR opposition, others may also be organized in terms of [tense] vs. [lax]. RP (British "Received Pronunciation") English is such a case. In the absence of other types of systems, then, it would not be immediately clear that there is any call for more complex structures involving dependency in the characterization of the vowel space.

There is, however, a third type of system, in which, it is claimed, the relationship between /i/ and /e/ is not different from that between /e/ and /ɛ/, nor from that between /ɛ/ and /a/ (assuming a system with all four of these unrounded vowels). Such systems are typically involved in apparently scalar processes such as vowel raising or lowering affecting, say, all of /i e ɛ a/ in the same way. Thus the English Great Vowel Shift is such a process, involving raising of all long vowels,[5] as is the lowering process of the Scanian dialect of Swedish, discussed by Lindau (1978). Given the correctness of the analysis of these systems as involving vowels arranged along some type of scale, it seems inappropriate to appeal to an extra feature such as |ATR| to distinguish between *individual* members of the scale (this, of course, is also the motivation for a multivalent scalar feature of vowel height of the type proposed by Ladefoged (1971)). Rather, dependency phonologists argue, in a system containing two mid vowels /e/ and /ɛ/ in which the relationship between the vowels is scalar in this sense, both vowels contain only the features |i| and |a|. They differ in the relative prominence of the two features: for /e/, |i| governs |a|; for /ɛ/, |i| is dependent on |a|. This can be represented as in (3):

(3)   i   a
      | |
      a   i

      /e/   /ɛ/

As in (1) and (2), dependency is represented on the vertical axis. As the two elements are simultaneous, they are nondistinct on the horizontal axis, so that the line linking them is vertical. Whereas the vertical line dominating the vowel /eː/ in (1) is a projection of the vowel in question, with the unlabeled nodes characterizing the various headships of the vowel, the lines in (3) link labelled "content" nodes in terms of the dependency relation.[6]

As in the suprasegmental domain, dependency in segment-internal representations is the formal characterization of relative prominence. Thus /e/ is characterized as being a vowel in which frontness is more prominent and sonority less prominent than for /ɛ/. This allows vowel height to be characterized as a scale involving relative prominence of two interacting components, in the case of unrounded vowels frontness and sonority, as in (4):

(4)   i   i   a   a
            | |
            a   i
      /i/   /e/   /ɛ/   /a/

Further advantages are claimed for the characterization of the dimension of vowel height in (4) over other univalent systems which do not utilize dependency. It is typically claimed by the proponents of univalent systems that the treatment of front rounded and mid vowels as complex is given support by their behavior in monophthongization and diphthongization processes – in Schane's (1984) terms, *fusion* and *fission*, respectively (see chap. 18, this volume). Schane suggests that such changes typically involve sequential reordering, with no alteration in the features involved, so that a change from /ai/ to /e/, for example, consists of the fusion of the two vowels into one, with realization as the mid vowel corresponding to the combination of the two features involved. Similarly, the fusion of /au/ gives /o/ and the fission of /y/ gives /iu/ (or /ju/), as we would expect, given the representations |a, u| for /o/ and |i, u| for /y/.⁷

Dependency phonology, however, makes a stronger claim, in particular with respect to monophthongization. In systems in which the dependency relation is invoked in the representation of mid vowels (e.g., those with both /e/ and /ɛ/), the claim is made that fusion will not only maintain the identity of the features involved, but also the dependency relation holding between them. Thus Anderson and Ewen (1987, p. 129) claim that the monophthongization of the Middle English diphthongs /aɪ/ and /aʊ/ to /ɛː/ and /ɔː/ in late Middle English, as illustrated in (5), shows the expected development:

(5) Early Middle English /daɪ/ > late Middle English /dɛː/   "day"
     Early Middle English /klaʊ/ > late Middle English /klɔː/   "claw"

The input to the change is a falling diphthong, in which the first element (containing only |a|) is more prominent than the second element (|i| or |u|), and therefore governs it. The dependency relation is maintained after fusion, which gives a low mid vowel rather than a high mid vowel, as shown in (6) for the front vowels involved (for illustration, I assume that the representation of the vowel is linked to some kind of segmental node):

(6)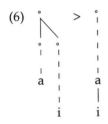

For processes involving diphthongs in which the element containing either |i| or |u| is the governor, we expect interaction with the high mid vowels, i.e., those in which |i| or |u| governs |a|, so that the dependency relations are maintained.

To the extent that they can be substantiated, these claims provide strong evidence in favor of positing a dependency relation in the representation of the mid vowels. However, as Anderson and Ewen point out, only those systems in which the dependency relation is required (because there is more than one mid vowel) provide the evidence required. In a system with only one mid vowel, no dependency relation is required, and therefore fusion will not maintain the asymmetrical relation which holds in the suprasegmental domain between the two elements of the original diphthong.

2.2   *Major Class and Manner Representations*

Dependency phonology shares with feature geometry the notion that features display grouping (see chap. 7, this volume). We have already examined one such group, the vowel features, which would be dominated by a single (class) node in the context of feature geometry. It is not immediately obvious how the formalism of dependency phonology is compatible with that of feature geometry, given the claim of dependency phonology that features do not simply co-occur, and given that appeals to "dependency" within feature geometry involve different types of relation, to which I return in section 3.[8] However, this does not affect the basic insight involved, that groups of features may operate in phonological processes as units independent of other features.

One area more than any other has proved controversial within feature geometry, namely the organization of features characterizing major class and manner (see van der Hulst and Ewen 1991 for some discussion). Which, if any, of these features should be dominated by a single class node, and what the character of that node should be, are issues of great debate, as is illustrated by the different geometries proposed by Clements (1985), Sagey (1986, 1988) and McCarthy (1988), for example. This controversy is largely due to the fact that the set of major class and manner features does not seem to meet any of the criteria proposed by McCarthy (1988) for membership of a group: they do not spread as a group, they are not implicated as a group in delinking, and they are not subject to Obligatory Contour Principle effects.

One criterion for the grouping of features which is appealed to in dependency phonology, but which has been largely ignored in feature geometry, is that a set of features which takes part in hierarchy-based processes should be considered to be part of the same group, or, in geometrical terms, to be dominated by a single node. This applies particularly to the set of features under consideration, the manner and major class features, which are involved in sonority hierarchy-based processes such as weakening and relations such as syllabification, as already noted above.

The question of whether sonority should be encoded – either directly or indirectly – in segmental representations is a familiar one, and various strategies have been adopted for allowing sonority to be read off the representations in some way. Recent proposals have involved the suggestion that sonority can be related to the amount of structure in the geometry of a segment, although without much agreement about the details. Thus Dogil (1988) argues that sonority "is inversely proportional to the number of nodes that have to be consulted on the way to the first articulator node," and suggests that the more sonorous a segment is, the less geometric structure it has. Rice (1992) proposes something similar: in her feature geometry "greater sonority involves . . . less structure." Within a government-based model of phonological representation, Harris (1990) takes the reverse standpoint: the least sonorous segments, voiceless stops, are composed of the greatest number of "elements." It is not my concern here to discuss the relative merits of these approaches, but rather to observe that there is a significant body of opinion which holds that sonority must be derivable from the representations, and also that some appeal is often made to the notion of complexity in this area.

These two points of view – that the major class and manner features form a group, and that relative sonority is relevant to the organization of phonological representations, and hence must be computable in some way – are given an interpretation in dependency phonology in terms of the same types of representations as proposed for the analysis of the vowel space. The major class or *categorial* features which have usually been proposed are the familiar [sonorant] and [consonantal], represented as |V| and |C|, respectively. (These should not be confused with the timing units of the CV tier in the Clements and Keyser (1983) approach; |V| and |C| are simply labels for unary features.) Like the vowel features, they may occur alone in the representation of a segment, or in simple combination, or related by dependency, again according to the same basic criteria: segments with governing |V| are more sonorous than otherwise identical segments with dependent |V|.

Just as different writers have put forward different proposals for feature geometries in this and other areas, so there have been various suggestions within dependency phonology for the appropriate characterization of the major class categories. The most familiar proposal is that of Anderson and Ewen (1987), the basic elements of which can be found in one of the earliest publications in the framework, Anderson and Jones (1977). Den Dikken and van der Hulst (1988) offer an alternative to this proposal, and the most recent statement is that of van der Hulst and Ewen (1991). I will not devote space here to an extensive comparison of the various proposals (see van der Hulst and Ewen 1991 for a brief discussion), but will instead consider those aspects which are common to all three, and indeed to other suggestions within dependency phonology.

Common to these approaches, then, is the claim that the major class categories are characterized by various combinations of |V| and |C|. However, although |V| is primarily associated with sonorancy, and |C| with consonantality, they also subsume the other major class and manner properties, such as continuancy, stridency and "approximation" (in terms of the feature system proposed by Clements 1987), as well as the source feature [voice]. All these features are involved in sonority-based processes, and are therefore viewed as contributing to the relative sonority and consonantality of the various segment-types. Thus the sonority of a segment at the consonantal end of the scale can be increased by various means, e.g., by the addition of voicing, or by reduction of the degree of stricture. In both cases, this involves the representation becoming more "|V|-like," either by addition of |V|, or, as we shall see, by increase in its relative prominence.

To illustrate the principles involved in the representation of the major class and manner segments, I consider here the system proposed by Anderson and Ewen (1987). As in the representation of vowels, the extremes of the sonority scale have the simplest representations. Thus, vowels as a major class are represented with |V| alone, corresponding to the fact that they constitute the maximally sonorous class, and voiceless stops, the optimal consonant class, are |C| alone. All other major classes contain combinations of the two components, with the representations of nasals, voiceless fricatives, and voiced stops all involving different relations:

(7)
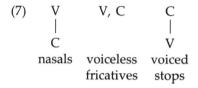

The voicing of a stop thus involves the addition of |V| in dependent position, while, in comparison with vowels, the representation of nasals shows a dependent |C|, corresponding to the oral closure. The continuancy of the fricative as opposed to the stop involves addition of |V| at the same hierarchical level; the resulting node |V, C| is the formal representation of continuancy. The association of particular configurations with particular phonetic properties leads to an interpretation of the concept of natural class, as well as to other representations of major classes, shown in (8):

(8)

V	V, C
|	|
V, C	V
liquids	voiced
	fricatives

In the context of this survey of dependency phonology it is not appropriate to consider the motivation for the individual representations. We should, however, note certain aspects of the system. In the first place, |V| may occur more than once in a representation, as in the case of voiced fricatives, which involve both voicing and continuancy. This is a property not found in the vowel representations in section 2.1.

Second, it is clear that relative sonority can be straightforwardly derived from the representations: in (8), the representation of the more sonorant category, liquids, shows a greater "preponderance" of |V| than that of the voiced fricatives. Application of this property to the analysis of phenomena such as lenition and syllable structure can be found in various publications, to which the reader is referred for discussion.[9]

Third, given that the "vowel" feature |a| and the "major class" feature |V| are both defined in terms of sonority, it has been suggested that these are in fact the same feature, occurring within different domains, in much the same way that Clements and Hume propose in chapter 7, within a feature geometry model, that the set of vocalic and consonantal place features is the same, but occur twice in the feature geometry, dominated by different class nodes.[10]

The fourth point involves the relationship between relative sonority and complexity of structure, mentioned above. We have seen that phonologists have argued that complexity of structure can be associated with degree of sonority, in such a way that more sonorous segments have less structure (Harris 1990), or the reverse (Rice 1992). Dependency phonology, as represented by Anderson and Ewen (1987), takes a different standpoint: structural complexity is associated with phonological complexity in rather traditional Jakobsonian terms, akin to concepts of markedness. Less marked segments are structurally less complex (fewer features, and/or no utilization of the dependency relation) than more marked segments. Crucially, the notion of structural complexity, as we saw above with respect to vowel representations, has its basis in factors independent of the notation; like any system based on unary features, dependency phonology claims that the features which appear in the representation of a particular segment are those which are salient to its production. As such, the claims which Rice (1992) makes, i.e., that "the model of representation proposed here provides a learning path based on increasing complexity," would also be claimed to hold of dependency phonology. This approach leads to a very different interpretation of lenition from that of Harris, who notes (1990, p. 265): "under an element-based analysis, lenition is defined quite simply as any process which involves a reduction in the complexity of a segment." Such an analysis is not available to dependency phonology, in which intervocalic (i.e., sonority-increasing) lenition can involve increase in complexity (e.g., stop becoming fricative) or decrease in complexity (fricative or liquid becoming nonsyllabic vowel).

A further characteristic of the theory is that the set of major class representations proposed in Anderson and Ewen (1987) allows the sequence of segments within onsets and rhymes to be read off from the representations themselves. The segments within these constructions do not require to be underlyingly ordered, given that the canonical ordering of segments within the syllable is determined by relative sonority (see Anderson 1987).

3   Other Interpretations of the Dependency Relation

As I have already noted, the concept of dependency was originally introduced into phonological representations within the model of dependency phonology. In recent years, however, the notion has been appealed to within other approaches, two of which I consider in the following subsections.

Let us first, however, consider rather more closely what is meant by the dependency relation of dependency phonology, with respect to segment-internal structure. It is a relation holding between two elements – features – which characterizes the relative contribution of each element to the segment. Thus, as we have seen, in a vowel in which the frontness feature governs the sonority feature, the frontness feature contributes more to the segment than one in which the reverse dependency relation holds.

Much the same can be said of the characterization of secondary articulations. Although we have not here considered the characterization of place of articulation in dependency phonology,[11] it is clear that dependency can be used to characterize the relationship between the primary articulation and the secondary articulation in, say, the velarized alveolar lateral [ɫ]. The primary (alveolar) articulation, which, by definition, is of a greater degree of stricture than the secondary (velar), contributes more to the segment, and thus the representation of the primary articulation will govern that of the secondary articulation. Again, the motivation for the dependency relation is derived from the "content" of the segment. In what follows, then, I will refer to the relation of dependency phonology as *inherent dependency*.

3.1   Structural Dependency

Other theories of phonological representation make use of the term "dependency," in particular various recent versions of feature geometry. Given the title of McCarthy (1988), "Feature geometry and dependency," we might expect the concept to play a central role in this theory. And this is indeed the case: the dependency relation of feature geometry is a relation holding between features on different tiers, and is thus referred to as feature dependency, or dependent tier ordering. Paradis and Prunet (1991, p. 5) observe that "a node or feature X immediately dominated by a node Y is said to be a dependent of node Y." Thus, as pointed out by van der Hulst (1989, p. 258), "immediately dominate" and "depend" are used as complementaries.

McCarthy (1988, p. 98) notes that "by the logic of the dependency relation, the presence of a subordinate or dependent feature entails the presence of the superordinate or dominating feature" (see also McCarthy and Taub 1992). This claim can be illustrated by reference to (9), from McCarthy (1988, p. 103):

(9)

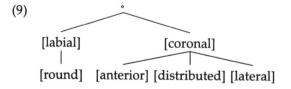

Here, [anterior] is said to be a *dependent* of [coronal], [round] a dependent of [labial], and so on. The interpretation of this dependency relation is thus that a dependent feature can only occur if the feature on which it is dependent is also present. As both [labial] and [coronal] are unary in McCarthy's approach, consonants which are neither labial nor coronal lack these features, and therefore also their dependents.

This relation is clearly of a different type from that of dependency phonology, although there too it is true to say that the presence of a dependent implies the presence of the governor (but see van der Hulst 1990 for a proposal that segments may have "empty heads" in dependency phonology). In feature geometry, we are not dealing with inherent dependency, but with what we might refer to as "dependency of occurrence" or *structural dependency*. There is no claim that the *content* of the features involved is in any way affected by the dependency relation: the dependent feature is in no sense less prominent than the "dominating" feature. Rather, the interpretation of the dependency relations represents an attempt to formalize the constraints holding on the human articulators. To that extent, it leads to a universal feature geometry.

3.2 Parametric Dependency

The notion of dependent tier ordering is sometimes given a less rigorous interpretation than in McCarthy's account. Mester (1988, p. 127), for example, notes that "dependent tier ordering means that a hierarchical organization is imposed on the set of features," as in (10). (Here and in what follows I adapt Mester's formalism so that it more closely approximates that used above.)

(10)

In (10), "individual features, while occupying separate tiers, are not entirely autonomous and are dependent on other tiers which have a more central location" (ibid.). Thus [back] is dependent on [high]. These features are binary in Mester's approach, so that the crucial notion here is that the behavior of a dependent feature may be determined by the feature immediately dominating it. Mester's arguments are primarily concerned with Obligatory Contour Principle effects, such as those involving [labial] in Ponapean, a language in which all labials within a morpheme must agree in their specification for velarization. He assumes that velarization involves the presence of a feature [back], which is dependent on [labial]. The OCP determines that there will be only a single specification for [labial] for each morpheme. As [back] is dependent on [labial], it is affected by the same constraint; that is, an OCP effect on any feature automatically carries through to its dependent, as in (11), which shows the only two possibilities involved:

(11) (a)   p u p   (b)   p a p

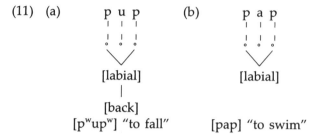

[p^{w}up^w] "to fall"   [pap] "to swim"

In (11a) the whole morpheme is velarized; in (11b) it is not.

Although the details of Mester's model differ from those of McCarthy, it is clear that we are dealing with largely the same kind of dependency here, which I have labeled structural. However, Mester goes further, by introducing the possibility of parametric tier ordering, or *parametric dependency*. His example concerns the relative ordering of the features [back] and [high] in the two languages Ngbaka and Ainu, both of which display vowel co-occurrence restrictions. In Ngbaka, vowels of the same height must agree in backness, a situation which Mester represents by the use of dependent tier ordering and the extension of the OCP to dependent features in the way described above. Thus (12) is well-formed in Ngbaka:

(12) l i k i

[+high]
|
[−back]

A morpheme with vowels which are [+high] but which differ in backness is thus correctly characterized as nonoccurring.

In Ainu, however, we find a situation in which vowels with the same value for [back] must agree in height. Thus two front vowels occurring in a morpheme must be identical (there are no front rounded vowels in Ainu). This situation can be characterized in the same way as in the Ngbaka case, but only if the dependency relation between the two features is reversed, as in (13):

(13) p i s i

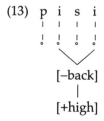

[−back]
|
[+high]

This type of parametric dependency is even further from inherent dependency than is the structural dependency more commonly found in feature geometry.

4 The Place of Dependency Phonology in Nonlinear Phonology

It will be clear from the above that this writer considers dependency phonology to fall squarely within the research program of nonlinear phonology. However, as noted above, the relationship between the formalisms of dependency phonology and feature geometry is not straightforward: the two models propose fundamentally different types of structural relation. Nevertheless, various attempts have been made to incorporate inherent dependency representations into a feature geometry, and I conclude this contribution by briefly discussing a few of these.

One approach involves the organization of the |i u a| components on tiers or "lines," reminiscent of those proposed in government phonology (Kaye, Lowenstamm, and Vergnaud et al. 1985). (14a, b) show the structures proposed by Durand (1990, p. 301) and van der Hulst (1989, p. 267), respectively:

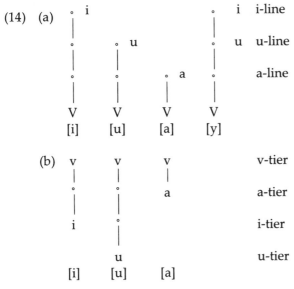

The space available here does not permit me to discuss these models. However, both proposals involve the introduction into the dependency phonology model of "structural dependency" as found in feature geometry. Durand notes that the vertical lines in (14a) "no longer indicate dependency but geometrical anchorage," while for van der Hulst the tiers are in a "dominance" relation. The reader is referred to the sources for a defense of the two different feature hierarchies proposed in (14).[12]

In a similar vein, van der Hulst and Ewen (1991) suggest that the major class and manner features |V| and |C| can be assigned a geometry incorporating structural relations other than simple dependency.

It is clear that much remains to be done in reconciling the formalisms of dependency phonology and feature geometry. Nevertheless, I hope to have shown that the differences between them are not such that dependency phonology is incompatible with other non-linear approaches, and, indeed, that interaction between the various models can lead to a better understanding of phonological structure.

NOTES

My thanks to John Anderson, Jeannette van Dalen, Paula Fikkert, Harry van der Hulst, and Ellen Kaisse for comments on previous versions of this paper. None of it is their fault, of course.

1   I ignore here the question of how prominence is to be measured.

2   The claim that sonorant consonants are inherently more prominent than nonsonorant consonants requires more detailed phonetic justification than is possible here.

3   Furthermore, factors other than relative prominence may be invoked in characterizing dependency. Anderson (1986, sec. 6), for example, proposes that the head of clusters like those in (2) should not be the consonant with the greatest inherent sonority, but rather the most "consonantal" segment, so that in (2a) /t/ would govern /r/, and in (2b) /k/ would govern /ŋ/.

4   But see Lass (1984, pp. 278–279) for the view that complexity should *not* be encoded in phonological representations, and the conclusion that the feature of dependency phonology should be replaced by the features |ɯ| ([velarity]) and |ɷ| ([labiality]/[roundness]).

5   I assume that high vowels also acted as input to the process, but that they did not undergo raising because of their height specification.

6   I ignore here the question of the precise way in which segmental representations such as those in (3) are incorporated into the suprasegmental representations in (1) and (2).

7   Here, and in what follows, I ignore the problem of the representation of length; I am merely concerned with the content of the features and segments involved.

8   See section 4 below for a brief consideration of the relation between feature geometry and dependency phonology.

9   E.g., Anderson and Ewen (1987, chap. 4).

10 In work in progress, Harry van der Hulst makes the further claim that |C| in the major class gesture can be equated with |i| in the articulatory gesture.

11 But see, e.g., Anderson and Ewen (1987, chap. 6). Smith (1988) proposes a dependency interpretation of place of articulation utilizing the components |i u a|.

12 Van der Hulst's hierarchization of the vowel features forms part of a more general approach to dependency phonology (see van der Hulst 1988, 1989), in which he incorporates the proposal that the phonetic interpretation of a particular component differs according to whether it is a head or a dependent feature. Thus |i| has a different interpretation (palatal constriction) in governing position than in dependent position (ATR). See both works for discussion.

18 Diphthongization in Particle Phonology

SANFORD A. SCHANE

0 Introduction

At the heart of particle phonology is a set of unary features: the aperture particle |a| and the tonality particles |i| and |u|. These three particles encompass the traits of openness, palatality, and labiality, respectively. The different combinations of single occurrences of the particles (including the null set) yield the eight vowels in (1).[1]

(1)	[ɨ]/[ə]	[a]	[i]	[u]	[e]	[o]	[ü]	[ö]
	—	a	i	u	a	a	i	a
					i	u	u	i
								u

The initial impetus for the theory of particle phonology stemmed from limitations of the binary distinctive features of generative phonology in expressing interrelationships between diphthongs and monophthongs. The standard notation, as presented in Chomsky and Halle (1968), did not reveal in an enlightening manner processes such as the diphthongization of [üː] to [iŭ] or the monophthongization of [aĭ] to [eː].[2]

In the earliest work on particle phonology (Schane 1984a, 1984b), diphthongization was viewed as the splitting apart (fission) of a particle complex and a realignment of the component particles into the two halves of the diphthong.

Conversely, monophthongization was the fusion of a sequence of particles into a simultaneously occurring configuration. Fission and fusion acted directly on the particles. In (2) we illustrate, for that early framework, the fission of [ü:] into [iṷ] and the fusion of [aị] into [e:].[3]

(2) (a) V V   V V   (b) V V   V V
          \\/ → | | | | → \\/
          i   i u   a i   a
          u   i
        [ü:] > [iṷ]   [aị] > [e:]

Phonological representation has become considerably richer, and we shall see that the fission/fusion that characterizes diphthongization/monophthongization no longer operates on individual particles but rather on the root nodes that dominate those particles.

In this paper, we examine the phonological structure of vowels and diphthongs and the processes of diphthongization and monophthongization. We establish the following points: (1) In phonological representation, long vowels and falling diphthongs have two timing slots; short vowels and rising diphthongs have one. Diphthongs (whether falling or rising) have two root nodes; monophthongs (whether long or short) have one. (2) Fusion, which merges two root nodes into one, is the formal mechanism that underlies monophthongizations; fission, which splits apart one root node into two, accommodates diphthongizations. (3) Two kinds of OCP constraints govern the representation of diphthongs: the two halves of a diphthong have neither separate occurrences of the same particle nor all of their particles in common. (4) The notation for representing diphthongs refers to three parameters: particles shared by both halves of a diphthong, particles unique to the first half, and particles unique to the second half. The various monophthongization and diphthongization processes will manipulate one or more of these parameters. (5) Differences in vowel height are characterized by the number of aperture particles, and one-step shifts in height by the addition or deletion of an aperture particle. (6) One half of a diphthong can change without affecting the other half. Consequently, when a diphthong has multiple aperture particles, they may behave independently.

1   The Representation of Diphthongs and Monophthongs

We adopt a multitiered representation with five distinct levels: a syllable tier, a nucleus tier, a timing tier, a root tier, and a particle tier. Example (3) depicts the representation of English *wipe* [waịp].[4]

(3)

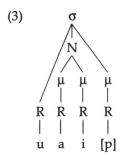

The syllable node (σ) encompasses the various constituents of a syllable: an optional onset, an obligatory nucleus, and an optional coda. The nucleus node (N) dominates the different types of nuclear material: long and short vowels, syllabic nasals and liquids, and the peak and nonpeak components of diphthongs and triphthongs. Because there is no separate rhyme node, both onset and coda consonants are linked directly to the syllable tier. This notation is able to differentiate between those glides that function as onset or coda consonants and those that are elements of diphthongs. In (3) the initial consonantal glide is attached directly to the syllable tier, whereas the diphthongal glide is connected through the intermediary of the nucleus node.[5]

The μ nodes represent syllable weight: within the nucleus, a single μ node dominates one-mora entities (i.e., short vowels and rising diphthongs such as [i̯a]), whereas two μ nodes dominate entities that count as two moras (i.e., long vowels and falling diphthongs such as [ai̯]).[6] The root node (R) organizes segmental content – that is, in the case of vowels and diphthongs it dominates the particles |a|, |i|, and |u|. Moreover, within the nucleus, the number of root nodes is what distinguishes monophthongs from diphthongs: a monophthongal vowel (whether long or short) always has a single R node, whereas each half of a diphthong must have its own R node. It is the R node that most closely embodies the notion of segment. A monophthong, even when long, intuitively is one segment; a diphthong corresponds to a sequence of two nonidentical vowels (segments) within a single nucleus. The representations of (4) depict various kinds of syllable structures.

(4)

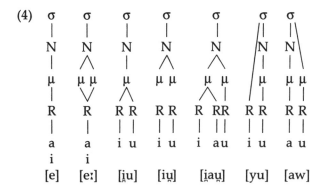

What kinds of connections are permitted between R nodes and the particles that they dominate? Within the syllable nucleus N, two contiguous R nodes may not dominate separate occurrences of the same particle. This constraint can be viewed as an OCP violation, a prohibition against sequential occurrences of the same autosegment at the melodic (particle) level.[7] For example, the diphthong [ei̯] must have the representation of (5a), where the two halves of the diphthong share the |i| particle, and not that of (5b), where each half would have its own |i| particle.[8]

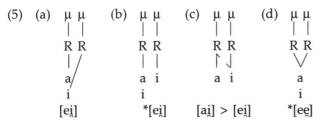

(5) (a)   (b)   (c)   (d)

The structure of (5a) finds corroboration from autosegmental spreading, the analog of assimilation. In (5c), we illustrate a partial assimilation whereby [ai̯] becomes [ei̯]. Here the |i| particle from the nonpeak element of the diphthong has spread to the root of the peak. (Spreading is indicated by the dotted line.) The resulting structure corresponds to that of (5a).

There is a second kind of OCP effect governing the representation of diphthongs. The two halves of a diphthong may not have all of their particles in common – that is, all the particles may not be doubly-linked to the two R nodes. The structure in (5d) represents this type of illegal configuration. A root node and its constituent particles constitute the formal analog of a segment. Consequently, adjacent root nodes dominating identical features would represent the same segment, and a sequential representation of R nodes would count as a violation of the OCP.[9] This representational constraint is in accord with a fundamental fact about the nature of diphthongs, what I have called *diphthongal differentiation* (Schane 1984a, 1989): The two halves of a diphthong may not be identical. That is, at least one of the halves must have a particle that it does not share with the other. This is not to deny the occurrence of phonetic sequences such as [ii̯] or [uu̯], but when such sequences are found, they function as noncontrastive variants of the corresponding long vowels [iː] and [uː]. Thus, whereas a language may have among its contrastive nuclei both [eː] and [ei̯] (viz., Early Modern English immediately after the Great Vowel Shift), no language will have a phonemic contrast between [iː] and [ii̯].[10]

The two kinds of OCP constraints find strong support in conversions of diphthongs and monophthongs. We turn now to these phenomena.

1.1 Monophthongization (Fusion)

Different diphthongs may monophthongize to the same vowel. For example, [eː] is a frequent outcome of the monophthongizations of both [ai̯] and [ei̯].

These two diphthongs and the resulting monophthong are represented in (6). The converging arrow heads around the R nodes in (6a–b) symbolize the fusion operation that will result in (6c).

(6)   (a)   μ μ   (b)   μ μ   (c)   μμ
          | | | | V
        >R R<   >R R<   R
          | | |/ |
          a i   a/   a
                        i   i
        [ai̯]   [ei̯]   [eː]

For [ai̯] there is no sharing of particles between the two halves of the diphthong, whereas for [ei̯] there is sharing of the |i| particle. What is important, of course, is that both of these diphthongs (regardless of sharing) contain only the particles |a| and |i|, and the combining of these two particles into a single segment can result only in [eː]. Because it is the number of R nodes (i.e., two vs. one) that distinguishes diphthongs from monophthongs, we can define the process of monophthongization as the fusion (or closure) of the R nodes of a diphthong, the result being their complete overlap. As a consequence of fusion, any separately occurring particle from either half of a diphthong as well as any originally shared particle will find itself under the single R node of the monophthongal vowel.

There are more dramatic cases of different diphthongs fusing to the same monophthong. In Old French [u̯e] and [eu̯] both became [ö], in Old English [eọ] changed to [ö], and in some Greek dialects [oi̯] fused to [ö]. All of these diphthongs exemplify different distributions of the particles |a|, |i|, and |u| (see (7a–d)), and the monophthong [ö] is composed of the same particles (see (7e)).

(7)   (a)   >R R<   (b)   >R R<   (c)   >R R<   (d)   >R R<   (e)   [ö]
              | | | | | | | | |
              u a   a u   i u   a i   a
              i   i   V   u   i
                                          a   u

            [u̯e]   [eu̯]   [eọ]   [oi̯]   [ö]

1.1.1   Diphthong Notation

Because any given particle may be shared by both halves of a diphthong, may belong only to the first half, or may belong only to the second half, every diphthong can be specified by an ordered set of three parameters: {s, h_1, h_2}. In this formula s stands for the particle(s) shared in the diphthong, h_1 for the particle(s) unique to the first half, and h_2 for the particle(s) unique to the second half. One or two of the parameters may be null.[11]

The formulas of (8a–b) represent the diphthongs of (6a–b). (RR signifies the two R nodes that characterize a diphthong.) Because the two halves of the diphthong [ai̯] of (6a) share no particles, the *s* parameter is null for the representation of this diphthong in (8). On the other hand, for the diphthong [ei̯] of (6b) there is sharing of the particle |i|; consequently, this particle occupies the *s* position in the representation of (8b). But because the second half of this diphthong has no unshared particle, it is the h_2 position that is null. Additional examples of the notation are found in (8c–f), which represent the diphthongs of (7a–d).

(8) (a) RR {Ø, a, i} (b) RR {i, a, Ø} (c) RR {Ø, u, ai}
         [ai̯]   [ei̯]   [u̯e]
     (d) RR {Ø, ai, u} (e) RR {a, i, u} (f) RR {Ø, au, i}
         [eu̯]   [eo̯]   [oi̯]

When a diphthong turns into a monophthong there is fusion of the R nodes and, consequently, all particles will become shared. The notation readily lends itself to a representation of the resulting monophthong. In the formulas, as shown in (9a) for [e] and (9b) for [ö], a monophthong has one R and both *h* positions can only be null.

(9) (a) R {ai, Ø, Ø}   (b) R {aiu, Ø, Ø}
          [e]   [ö]

1.1.2 *Extending the Notation: Fusion*

The notation for diphthongs will allow us to express directly fusion processes. We need only add converging arrowheads around the R nodes of the original diphthong to indicate fusion. Arrows (from particles in the *h* positions) pointing to the *s* position indicate, for the resulting monophthong, the sharing of those particles that were unique to each half of the diphthong.[12] The monophthongizations of [ai̯] to [e] and of [eo̯] to [ö] are depicted in (10). These notations function as rules that will convert the structures of (6a) and (7c) to (6c) and (7e), respectively.

(10) (a) >RR< {Ø, a, i}   (b) >RR< {a, i, u}

           [ai̯] > [e]   [eo̯] > [ö]

1.1.3 *Extending the Notation: Tonality Vowels*

It is traditional to portray vowel systems in a two-dimensional articulatory array, where the vertical dimension corresponds to tongue height, and the horizontal to tongue placement and lip configuration. Particle phonology makes a similar dichotomy. (11) shows a main division of aperture and tonality, and for the latter, a further division of palatality and labiality.

(11)

Aperture |a| Tonality |y|

Palatality |i| Labiality |u|

Front unrounded and back rounded vowels form a natural class – viz., the widespread symmetry in their distribution and in the phonological processes they undergo. It is convenient, then, that there be some way of referring, within rules, to any vowel with tonality. Following Ewen and van der Hulst (1988), we shall adopt |y| as a notational convention for either |i| or |u|. For example, the following rule of Sanskrit states that [ai̯] and [au̯] monophthongize to [eː] and [oː], respectively:[13]

(12) μμ, >RR< {Ø, a, y}

1.2 *Diphthongization (Fission)*

Fusion, as we have described it, entails that the particles that are distributed throughout the diphthong will occur intact in the resulting monophthong. It would seem that fission should be the converse operation – i.e., the fused particles of the monophthong should find themselves distributed between the two halves of the diphthong. Moreover, if fusion, as an operation, is the closure of two R nodes into one, then fission should involve the opening of a single R node into two. In the conversion of a monophthong to a diphthong, this splitting apart of the R node will indeed happen, but this operation alone would lead to an OCP violation, since the resulting R nodes would come to dominate identical particles. Because of the requirement of diphthongal differentiation, there will have to be a redistribution of the particles within each half of the diphthong. Consider, for example, the diphthongization of [üː] to [iy̯], a change that occurred in Faroese (Rischel 1968). The fission of the R node of the monophthong in (13a) yields the ill-formed intermediate structure of (13b), where both tonality particles are doubly-linked to the R nodes. This OCP violation has been resolved in (13c) by the delinking of |u| from the left R and of |i| from the right R. Note that both tonality particles end up unshared.

(13) (a) μ μ (b) μ μ (c) μ μ
          \/ | | | |
          R   R R   R R
          | \/ | |
          i   i   i u
          u   u
         [üː]   *[üy̯]   [iy̯]

Because diphthongal differentiation requires that the two halves of a diphthong not have all particles in common, shared particles will be permitted just
so long as there is also at least one unshared particle. The common change of
[eː] to [eị] illustrates this kind of partial sharing. In the diphthong of (14c), the
|a| particle has been delinked from the right R (i.e., it has become unshared),
but both halves of the diphthong continue to share the |i| particle.

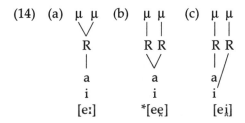

(14) (a) [eː] (b) *[eẹ] (c) [eị]

There is another means for diphthongal differentiation: all the particles from
the monophthong may remain shared in the diphthong on condition that one
of the halves acquire a particle not present in the original monophthongal
configuration. This change is *de rigueur* where the monophthong contains a
single particle, but it is not limited to this environment. The diphthongization
of [iː] to [eị], which was part of the English Great Vowel Shift, provides an
obvious example of this change, as shown in (15). The |i| particle continues
to be shared in the resulting diphthong of (15c), but to comply with diphthon-
gal differentiation, the left half has acquired an |a| particle.

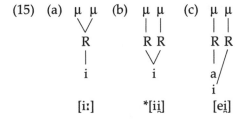

(15) (a) [iː] (b) *[iị] (c) [eị]

The addition of an aperture particle is a common way of resolving diphthongal differentiation for vowels of all heights.

1.2.1 *Extending the Notation: Fission*

The notation for diphthongization can be adapted to the representation of
fission: (1) A single R node and the particles in the *s* position denote the
original monophthong; diverging arrowheads around the R node signify its
opening into two nodes. (2) An arrow (from a particle in the *s* position) pointing to one of the *h* positions indicates, for the resulting diphthong, the unsharing
of that particle – i.e., it becomes unique to that half of the diphthong. (3) A
particle preceded by + in one of the *h* positions is added to that position of the

diphthong. The changes of [üː] to [iy̯], of [eː] to [ei̯], and of [iː] to [ei̯] are characterized in (16).[14]

(16)   (a)   μμ, <R> {iu, Ø, Ø}   (b)   μμ, <R> {ai, Ø, Ø}   (c)   μμ, <R> {i,+a, Ø,}

      [üː] > [iy̯]   [eː] > [ei̯]   [iː] > [ei̯]

1.3   Other Diphthongal Changes

Not only do monophthongs turn into diphthongs, and diphthongs fuse to monophthongs, but diphthongs change into other diphthongs. There are three avenues of change: (1) the two halves of the diphthong may become less alike (dissimilation); (2) the two halves may become more alike (assimilation); (3) the two halves may retain their degree of similarity but undergo feature exchange (i.e., corresponding to the delinking of a particle from one of the halves and its reattachment to the other).[15]

The halves of a diphthong will become less alike whenever a particle shared by both halves is delinked from one of them (i.e., unsharing) and/or one of the halves acquires a new particle. The change of [oy̯] to [ay̯] in (17a) illustrates unsharing of the |u| particle, that of [ay̯] to [ey̯] in (17b) the acquisition of an |i| particle, and that of [y̯o] to [y̯e] in (17c) unsharing of |u| and the acquisition of |i|. In the conversion of one diphthong to another, the R nodes are not affected (i.e., neither fission nor fusion has taken place). Arrows show the movement of particles (i.e., delinking and/or sharing) from the *s* and *h* positions of the original diphthong to those of the derived one.

(17)   (a)   μμ, RR {u, a, Ø}   (b)   μμ, RR {Ø, a+i, u}   (c)   μ, RR {u, Ø, a+i}
        [oy̯] > [ay̯]   [ay̯] > [ey̯]   [y̯o] > [y̯e]

The halves of a diphthong will become more alike whenever a particle *unique to one half* becomes shared or else is deleted. In the notation, a particle preceded by – in one of the *h* positions is deleted from that position of the diphthong. The change of [ai̯] to [ei̯] in (18a) illustrates the sharing of |i|, and that of [ey̯] to [iy̯] in (18b) the deletion (i.e., complete delinking) of |a|.

(18)   (a)   μμ, RR {Ø, a, i}   (b)   μμ, RR {Ø, i–a, u}

      [ai̯] > [ei̯]   [ey̯] > [iy̯]

Feature exchange involves delinking and reattachment of a particle from one half of a diphthong to the other. This process often accompanies the shift of a falling diphthong to a rising one. The change of [ey̯] to [i̯o] is an example of this kind of particle exchange. Here there have been a delinking and a reattachment of the |a| particle. In the notation, a particle has been shifted from one of the *h* positions to the other. The fusion of the μ nodes in (19) is what converts a falling diphthong of two moras into a rising diphthong that counts as one mora.[16]

(19) >μμ<, RR {∅, ia, u}
      [eu̯] > [i̯o]

1.3.1 Chain Shifts

Within the evolution of a language there may be a string of diphthongal changes. Romance and Germanic richly exemplify such chains. Vulgar Latin [eː] changed to Old French [ei̯] (diphthongization), then to Middle French [oi̯] (dissimilation), then to [u̯e] (feature exchange), and then finally to Modern French [u̯a] (assimilation). This sequence of events is depicted in (20).

(20) [eː] > [ei̯]   μμ, <R> {ia, ∅, ∅}   (fission of R; unsharing of |a|)

      [ei̯] > [oi̯]   μμ, RR {i, a+u, ∅}   (unsharing of |i|; addition of |u|)

      [oi̯] > [u̯e]   >μμ<, RR {∅, ua, i}   (fusion of μ; exchange of |a|)
      [u̯e] > [u̯a]   μ, RR {∅, u, a–i}   (deletion of |i|)

Old High German [eː] took an entirely different route. It diphthongized to [ea̯], which became [ia̯] (dissimilation), then [ie̯] (assimilation), and then Modern German [ii̯] (assimilation), which is equivalent to [iː]. These Germanic changes are shown in (21).

(21) [eː] > [ea̯]   μμ, <R> {ai, ∅, ∅}   (fission of R; unsharing of |i|)

      [ea̯] > [ia̯]   μμ, RR {a, i, ∅}   (unsharing of |a|)

      [ia̯] > [ie̯]   μμ, RR {∅, i, a}   (sharing of |i|)
      [ie̯] > [ii̯]   μμ, RR {i, ∅, −a}   (deletion of |a|; OCP violation)
      [ii̯] > [iː]   μμ, >RR< {i, ∅, ∅}   (resolution of OCP violation; fusion of R)

Note that from these notations one can easily construct the corresponding tree structures.

2   The Representation of Height

The combination of single particles (including the null set) yields the eight vowels that were shown in (1). With the exclusion of [a], this system can accommodate at most two vowel heights. In particle phonology, additional occurrences of the aperture particle specify vowels of lower height. The common seven-vowel system, for example, has the particle structure shown in (22).[17]

(22) [i]   [e]   [ɛ]   [a]   [ɔ]   [o]   [u]

i	a	a	a	a	a	u
	i	a	a	a	u	
		i		u		

The representation for [a] is a function of the other vowels in a language system and of the number of aperture particles for characterizing them. The vowel [a] will have the same number of aperture particles as the lowest tonality vowel(s). In Schane (1984a), I refer to this phenomenon as the Law of Maximum Aperture, because whenever [a] interacts with a tonality vowel, the interaction most typically involves the lowest one.[18] Moreover, the vowel [a] will have more than one aperture particle whenever there are several central vowels. For the series [ɨ ə a], there will be zero, one, and two aperture particles, respectively.[19]

2.1   *Extending the Notation: Vowel Height*

In rules, one needs to be able to refer to natural classes of vowel height. Consider the three-height system: [i e ɛ]. All three vowels as well as any pair of adjacent vowels will form a natural class. Within the notation we need a way of specifying minimum and maximum number of |a| particles. We shall use the standard device of subscript and superscript numerals, or, alternatively, of parenthesized elements. (23) illustrates these notational conventions for the natural classes derived from [i e ɛ].

(23) [i e] $\{ia_0^1\} = \{i(a)\}$
      [e ɛ] $\{ia_1\} = \{ia_1^2\} = \{ia(a)\}$
      [i e ɛ] $\{ia_0\} = \{ia_0^2\} = \{i(a)(a)\}$

Note that this notational system correctly excludes classes composed of noncontiguous vowel heights.

On occasion, one may need to refer to the absence of a particle. We shall use a superscript[0] (with no subscript) to indicate no occurrences of a particle. For example, a^0 would represent the natural class of high vowels.

2.2   *Justification for Multiple Aperture Particles*

The occurrence of multiple aperture particles has been criticized by some of the adherents of dependency phonology (see den Dikken and van der Hulst

(1988), but see also Hayes 1990 for a defense). The original justification came from multiple one-step shifts in vowel height. For example, in the Great Vowel Shift, [eː oː] shifted to [iː uː], and [ɛː ɔː] to [eː oː]. This upward one-step movement can be succinctly summarized as loss of an aperture particle from any long vowel having a tonality particle and one or two aperture particles.[20]

(24) μμ, R {y(a) – a}

I shall now adduce another argument for multiple aperture particles: They may function independently. This independence is most striking for diphthongs. As shown in (25), a diphthong, such as [eɛ], with two |a| particles, has one of them shared by both of its halves but the other is unique to only the second half.

(25) R R

     a a
     i
     [e ɛ]

Each aperture particle should be able to undergo some change independently of the other. This phenomenon, which often interacts with movement along the height scale, does indeed exist, and it provides compelling confirmation for the multiple occurrence of aperture particles. In support of this claim, we shall look at some data from Frisian and from Malmö Swedish.[21]

2.2.1 West Frisian Breaking

Standard West Frisian has nine vowels – [i e ɛ u o ɔ ü ö a] – that occur both long and short. A tenth vowel [ə] (schwa) occurs only short.[22] Because the front unrounded and back rounded vowels exhibit three heights, the particle representation for [a], in conformity with the Law of Maximum Aperture, will require two |a| particles. The schwa vowel has a root node with no particles under it. (See n. 1.)

(26)

[i]	[e]	[ɛ]	[u]	[o]	[ɔ]	[ü]	[ö]	[a]	[ə]
i	a	a	u	a	a	i	a	a	—
	i	a		u	a	u	i	a	
		i			u		u		

Now the higher and lower mid vowels of the standard dialect have two different diphthongal reflexes in the "breaking" dialects. The latter exhibit alternations between falling and rising diphthongs, as illustrated by the following pairs (de Graaf and Tiersma 1980, pp. 110, 112).

(27)   Standard Breaking

	Sg.	Pl.	Sg.	Pl.	
e(ː)	iə̯	i̯e	stiən	stienən	stone(s)
			vi̯ət	vietə	wet(ness)
ɛ(ː)	eə̯	i̯ɛ	beəm	biɛmən	tree(s)
o(ː)	uə̯	u̯o	stuəl	stuolən	stool(s)
			gu̯ət	guodlək	good(ly)
ɔ(ː)	oə̯	u̯a	doər	duarən	door(s)
			moəj	muajər	pretty/ier

In these same environments, standard West Frisian shows alternations between monophthongal long and short vowels (de Graaf and Tiersma 1980, p. 113).

(28)

Sg.	Pl.	Sg.	Pl.	
iː	i	viːf	vifkə	(small) woman
eː	e	heːx	hextə	high/height
ɛː	ɛ	bɛːt	bɛtsjə	(small) bed
aː	a	baːrx	bargən	pig(s)
üː	ü	slüːf	slüfkə	(small) envelope
öː	ʌ	gröːt	grʌtər	larg(er)
uː	u	muːs	muzən	mouse/mice
oː	o	knoːp	knopkə	(small) button
ɔː	ɔ	lɔːn	lɔnən	land(s)

Historically, all dialects had both long and short vowels. In standard Frisian, the long vowels were shortened when followed by another syllable or by a cluster of two or more consonants. In these same environments the dialects with breaking have rising diphthongs, but they exhibit falling diphthongs where standard Frisian has retained long vowels. To account for the evolution of original long vowels in the breaking dialects, van der Meer (1977) claims that the four long mid vowels became falling diphthongs whose first halves were one step higher in height than the original monophthongs. These diphthongs then changed in two different ways: in the "shortening" environments, they became rising diphthongs with high first components; otherwise, their second half changed to schwa.

(29)

Monophthong	Diphthongization	Shortening environment	Elsewhere
eː	i̯ɛ̯	i̯e	iə̯
ɛː	e̯ɛ̯	i̯ɛ	eə̯
oː	u̯o̯	u̯o	uə̯
ɔː	o̯ɔ̯	u̯ɔ > u̯a	oə̯

The notational representation for this chain of events is provided in (30).

(30) (a) μμ, R {ya(a), ∅, ∅}   (original monophthongs)

    (b) μμ, \<R\> {ya(a), ∅, ∅}   (diphthongization)

    (c) \>μμ\<, RR, {y(a), ∅, a}   (shortening environment)

    (d) μ, RR {u, ∅, aa}   (u̯ɔ > u̯a)

    (e) μμ, RR, {y(a), ∅, –a}   (elsewhere)

We see in (30a) the representation for the class of vowels that undergoes breaking – i.e., each of the four vowels possesses a tonality particle and one or two aperture particles. In the diphthongization of (30b), the first half of each diphthong must become one degree higher in height. In addition to the fission of the R node, there is an unsharing of an aperture particle (i.e., it is delinked from the first half of the diphthong); the other aperture particle, if present, continues to be shared. Here we see the first example of different behaviors manifested by aperture particles. In (30c), there is conversion of a falling diphthong to a rising. Recall that this change for diphthongs in the breaking dialects is equivalent to the shortening of monophthongs in standard Frisian. The equivalence has an identical notational representation: for both kinds of changes, there is fusion of μμ. In addition, the first half of the rising diphthong must become high (if it is not already high). A shared |a| particle, if present, must be delinked from the first half. The unshared aperture particle of the second half is unaffected. Here is another example of multiple aperture particles behaving differently. In (30d), the rising diphthong [u̯ɔ] is adjusted to [u̯a]. Its tonality particle becomes unshared. The second half of the diphthong will retain its two |a| particles, the representation for [a] in Frisian. In (30e), the second half of those falling diphthongs that did not change to rising will become [ə]. Recall that the representation of Frisian schwa has no particles. Consequently, all particles must be delinked from the second half – i.e., any shared particle(s) will become associated only with the first half of the resulting diphthong, and the aperture particle unique to the second half will be deleted. Here too aperture particles are affected differently. An originally shared aperture particle becomes unshared, and an originally unshared one gets deleted.

To illustrate the application of the rules in (30), we provide in (31) derivations for the vowel [ɔː].

(31)

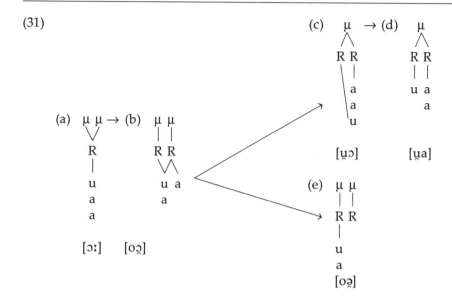

2.2.2 *Malmö Swedish Height Shift*

Diphthongizations of aperture can take one of two forms: delinking of an aperture particle or acquisition of one. Delinking causes a one-step upward shift in height, and acquisition a one-step downward shift. The first stage of diphthongization in Frisian exemplifies upward shift. As an example of downward shift, we consider the multiple diphthongizations of the Malmö dialect of Swedish.

In Malmö Swedish, all long vowels diphthongize (Bruce 1970; Lindau 1978). The first halves of the resulting diphthongs take a one-step downward shift in height, and those emanating from back rounded vowels also become front unrounded. (See (32).)

(32) /iː/ > [ei]   /üː/ > [öü]   /uː/ > [eu]
      /eː/ > [ɛe]   /ʉː/ > [öʉ]   /oː/ > [ɛo]
      /ɛː/ > [æɛ]   /öː/ > [œö]   /a/ > [æa]

The particle representations for the Malmö vowels are presented in (33).[23]

(33)

[i]	[e]	[ɛ]	[æ]	[ü]/[ʉ]	[ö]	[u]	[o]	[a]
i	a	a	a	i	i	u	u	u
	i	a	a	u	u		a	a
		i	a		a			a
			i					

Two rules are required: a rule that diphthongizes long vowels by a one-step downward shift in height in the first half of the diphthong, and a rule that makes that first half front unrounded when the original vowel was back rounded. The rules are given in (34a–b).[24]

(34) (a) μμ, <R> {α,+a, Ø}

  (b) μμ, RR {a₀i⁰u, a+i, Ø}

The diphthongization rule in (34a) adds an aperture particle to the first half of a diphthong. All original particles (tonality and/or aperture), which are represented in the rule by α, remain shared. The tonality rule in (34b) applies to the class of back rounded vowels (i.e., those with any number of aperture particles, no palatal particle, and a labial particle). The rule adds an |i| particle and delinks an |u| particle in the first half of the diphthong. The Malmö shift provides another illustration of the independence of aperture particles. Any aperture particle(s) from an original monophthong will remain intact and will continue to be shared by both halves of the derived diphthong. The added aperture particle, needed for the one-step downward shift in height, will be associated with the first half only.

3   The Diphthongization Paradox

Hayes (1990) contains a discussion of the notational problems of diphthong representation and a proposal for the expression of diphthongization processes. The "diphthongization paradox" to which Hayes alludes can be stated as follows: If monophthongs require one root node in their representations but diphthongs need two, then, in conversions between these two kinds of vocalic entities, how is this discrepency in number of root nodes to be handled? Hayes critiques three other proposals and he presents his own solution to the problem.

  Clements (1985a) supposes that long segments (i.e., those with two timing units) have two root nodes at the outset. Each featural daughter node is doubly-linked to the R nodes. Diphthongization, then, is simply the addition or delinking of one or more daughter features from either R node. Hayes finds this solution to be flawed because "it contradicts the basic principle of prosodic theory that long segments are doubly-linked single units" (Hayes 1990, p. 36). That is, long segments should have one R node.

  Steriade (1987b) suggests eliminating altogether root nodes from phonological representations and, instead, linking certain feature nodes directly to timing units. Since feature nodes, under this approach, would be doubly-linked to the two timing nodes of a long segment, for diphthongization processes, they could be individually delinked from one of the timing nodes or a new feature could be added to it. Hayes points out that the absence of root nodes would play havoc with total assimilation, which, in autosegmental treatments, has been viewed as the spreading of root nodes.[25] He argues also that Steriade's proposal would require low-level features to have direct access to the timing nodes, a maneuver that would essentially wipe out the higher-level feature nodes advocated in feature geometries.

Selkirk (1990) sets up two root nodes for long segments. For vowels, the root nodes would also bear the feature value [− cons]. Daughter nodes are permitted to be doubly-linked only when they are connected to identical root nodes, which will be the case for long vowels. Dipthongization is the relabeling of one of the root nodes – the one to become the nonpeak of the diphthong – as [+cons]. Because the root nodes are no longer identical, by general convention, there will be delinking of all features from the [+cons] root. Feature values that are to remain identical in the two halves of the diphthong will be spread from the [−cons] root back to the [+cons] root, and any feature values unique to one of the halves will be added. Hayes notes that this theory erroneously assumes that the glide elements of diphthongs are always [+cons]. The [+cons] specification may be appropriate for those glides that function as onset or coda consonants, but not for those that are in the nucleus. Moreover, the mechanism is overly cumbersome. Instead of delinking only those features that will not be shared by both halves of the diphthong, Selkirk is forced to delink all features from one of the halves, only to spread many of them back again.

Hayes (1990) claims that the diphthongization paradox arises because of ambiguity in the interpretation of association lines in autosegmental representations containing feature trees. The line between a higher-level node in a feature tree (e.g., Root) and a lower-level node (e.g., the feature [high]) indicates category membership, whereas the line between a timing unit (e.g., μ, X, or V) and the element it dominates signifies simultaneous realization in time. Hayes proposes to separate these two functions by getting rid of autosegmental tree structure. Instead, he develops a notation with labeled brackets for indicating category membership and with indices for temporal relations. Long vowels continue to have two adjacent timing units (labeled V_1 and V_2, respectively). A single root element and single feature values are coindexed to the timing units (e.g., R_{12}, $[-high]_{12}$). Diphthongization becomes the deletion of one of the indices of a feature specification and its replacement by the opposite specification (e.g., R_{12}, $[-high]_1$, $[+high]_2$).[26]

In Hayes's representation of long vowels and diphthongs there are two timing units. But how many root entities are there? Is R_{12} equivalent to one root node or to two? Perhaps this question is unfair, since it is Hayes's intention to distance his notation from a conventional tree structure, where one would have no difficulty in counting number of nodes. In any case, what is important for us to notice is that in Hayes's notation, diphthongs and long vowels have an identical specification at the root, namely R_{12}. Hence, the distinction between diphthongs and monophthongs does not reside in the specification of the root, but is to be found at a lower level of the representation, where some feature(s) will bear one or two indices, respectively. Hayes too, like Clements, Steriade, and Selkirk, ends up positing an identical root configuration (or its complete absence for Steriade) for both long vowels and diphthongs. The notion that monophthongs correspond to one segment and diphthongs to two is not an aspect of any of these representations.

The frameworks of all four of these researchers permit diphthongs to be derived only from long vowels, because of the nature of double linkages. Both Clements and Selkirk allow a long vowel to have two R nodes, one corresponding to each timing unit. It is dubious, though, that they would permit two R nodes to emanate from the single timing unit of a short vowel, which would be required in order to derive a diphthong from it. For Steriade, features can be doubly-linked to the two timing nodes of a long vowel; it is the delinking of a doubly-linked feature from one of the timing slots that converts a monophthong to a diphthong. But there is no way for features to be doubly-linked to the single timing node of a short vowel, the structure that would be needed in order for a short vowel to diphthongize. Hayes requires that multiple indices be associated with the same number of timing units. The diphthongization of a short vowel would necessitate the unlikely structure of features with two indices (so that one of them could be deleted) that are associated to a vowel with only one timing unit.

Although diphthongization, as a process, generally applies to long vowels, there are languages, such as the Romance family, that have synchronic alternations of diphthongs and short vowels. Moreover, there are "shortened" diphthongs, such as those found in some of the Scandinavian languages, which occur in the same environments as short vowels, and then there are rising diphthongs, such as [ịa] and [ụi] in Sanskrit, that count as one mora. An adequate theory of diphthongization must allow for the representation of shortened and rising diphthongs and for the possibility of deriving them from short vowels.

3.1 The Particle Answer to the Diphthongization Paradox

I claim that, in their phonological representations, shortened diphthongs and those rising ones that count as one mora, have one timing unit but two root nodes. Falling diphthongs that are not in shortening environments always count as two moras and, consequently, they have two timing units and two root nodes. In (35) we see configurations of timing and root nodes for long vowels, falling diphthongs, short vowels, and rising and shortened diphthongs.

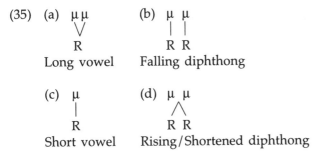

(35) (a) μ μ
           V
           R
        Long vowel

(b) μ μ
     | |
     R R
  Falling diphthong

(c) μ
     |
     R
  Short vowel

(d) μ μ
      ⋀
     R R
  Rising/Shortened diphthong

Standard autosegmental tree structure has no difficulty in representing these four types of vowels and diphthongs. The problem for autosegmental phonology has been the inability to convert a monophthongal representation to a diphthongal one and vice versa. The so-called diphthongization paradox, in reality, stems from an inadequacy of the standard operations of autosegmental phonology (i.e., insertion, deletion, spreading, delinking) for increasing or decreasing the number of root nodes in a tree without, at the same time, disrupting connections with other nodes.

The particle phonology operations of fission and fusion *can* increase and decrease the number of nodes without any other disruptions. For diphthongization, the fission or splitting apart of the R node into two R nodes retains the connections to the timing and feature (particle) tiers. The features, which were singly-linked for the monophthong, automatically will become doubly-linked in the diphthong. With all features doubly-linked (shared), the two halves of the diphthong would be identical. Hence, diphthongal differentiation has to kick in: one or more features may be delinked from one of the halves, or else a new feature value may be adjoined to one of the halves.

For monophthongization, the fusion of two R nodes into one has interesting consequences for the features dominated by those nodes. The features of the original diphthong, whether doubly-linked to both R nodes or linked to only one of them, will end up dominated by the single R node of the monophthong. Fusion is similar to the set operation of union: If R_1 dominates the particle set {ai} and R_2 {au} (where |a| is shared in the tree), then fusion yields R, which dominates the particle set {aiu}. This set theoretic union works only with unary features, and it is this property of fusion that was the original inspiration for particle phonology. Note what would happen with binary values: If R_1 dominates the feature set {+low, −back} and R_2 {+low, +back} (where [+low] is shared in the tree), the fused set R containing {+low, −back, +back} has contradictory specifications for the feature [back].[27]

The solution to the diphthongization paradox does not require that one abandon the tree structures of autosegmental representation, as Hayes was compelled to do. It does require, though, phonological operations and a featural representation that hitherto have not been standard characteristics of autosegmental phonology. The solution to the diphthongization paradox requires the recognition of fission and fusion as autosegmental operations and the utilization of unary features for segmental specification. There is, however, one aspect of diphthongization on which we are in complete agreement with Hayes. He argues that diphthongizations involving height shifts demonstrate the appropriateness of multiple occurrences of the aperture particle for characterizing vowel height differences. Only in this way is one able to account for the independence of height changes that can take place in each half of a diphthong.

4   Conclusion

Because this paper deals with diphthongization and monophthongization, the processes of fission and fusion have acted primarily on root nodes. These processes, however, turn out to be much more general. They are not restricted just to roots. Any node above the root is a candidate for fission/fusion.[28] We have already seen in (19), (20), and (31c) some instances where the timing node is affected. The fission of a μ node will convert a short vowel to a long one, or a rising diphthong to a falling; conversely, the fusion of two μ nodes will convert a long vowel to a short one, or a falling diphthong to either a rising or a shortened one (Schane 1989). The fusion and fission of μ nodes can replace the operations of deletion and insertion of a μ node, which are the only devices otherwise available in autosegmental phonology for handling vowel shortenings and noncompensatory lengthenings.

The fusion of adjacent syllable nodes (σ) and their daughter nucleus nodes (N) is a common way of dealing with vowel hiatus (Schane 1987). For example, in Sanskrit vowel sandhi, the disyllabic sequences [i]+[a] and [a]+[i] become monosyllabic [i̯a] and [e:], respectively. In (36), we illustrate these operations. In both cases, there is fusion of the σ and N nodes as well as one of the lower nodes: the μ nodes for [i]+[a], which yields a rising diphthong; and the R nodes for [a]+[i], which produces a long monophthong.

(36)

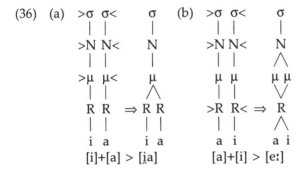

NOTES

1 Languages with [ə] and no [ɨ] have the schwa vowel as the null particle set. Within a set there is no ordering of particles. Hence, {ia} and {ai} both represent [e]. In dependency phonology (see chap. 17, this volume), which also makes use of unary vowel components, hierarchic ordering plays a role: |i| dominating |a| represents a higher mid vowel; |a| dominating |i|, a lower mid. In particle phonology, vowels of lower height have additional occurrences of the |a| particle; see section 2.

2 Because a sequence of segments was involved, processes affecting diphthongs necessitated a transformational format. For example, the monophthongization of [ai̯] to [e:] (ignoring the length of the resulting vowel) required conversion of the first element of the diphthong to [e] and deletion of the second:

$$\begin{bmatrix} V \\ +\text{low} \\ +\text{back} \\ -\text{round} \\ 1 \end{bmatrix} \begin{bmatrix} V \\ +\text{high} \\ -\text{back} \\ -\text{round} \\ 2 \end{bmatrix} \rightarrow \begin{bmatrix} 1 \\ -\text{low} \\ -\text{back} \end{bmatrix} \varnothing$$

3 In (2), V represents a vocalic timing unit: long vowels and falling diphthongs have two V slots.

4 As I am not concerned with the representation of consonants, other than the glides, I have given no feature analysis for the segment [p] in (3).

5 Language-internal criteria determine how glides will function. In English, the variant *a* (**an*) of the indefinite article before word initial [y] and [w] demonstrates the functioning of these glides as onset consonants, and morphophonemic alternations of vowels and diphthongs (e.g., *divinity:divine, profundity:profound*) establish post-vocalic glides as belonging to the nucleus. For the transcriptions enclosed within square brackets, [y] and [w] represent glides functioning as onset or coda consonants; [i̯] and [u̯], glides functioning as nonpeaks of diphthongs. This distinction between consonantal and nuclear glides is phonological; their phonetic manifestations may often be indistinguishable.

6 In many languages a coda consonant may also count as a mora (see chaps. 5 and 6, this volume).

7 Contiguous R nodes may dominate separate occurrences of a particle whenever their vowels belong to separate morphemes or are in hiatus (i.e., belong to different syllables). In such cases, each R node will be dominated by its own N node.

8 From here on, in order to economize on space, I shall omit

the syllable and nucleus nodes. All of the structures to be illustrated are dominated by one occurrrence of each of these nodes. In the representation of (5a), the vertical alignment of the particles is for ease of deciphering and has no other import. The horizontal representation below would be another way of representing [ei̯], and I shall make use of that mode on occasion.

μ μ
| |
R R
N
a i

The vertical and horizontal representations are equivalent, for both portray the sharing of the |i| particle by the two halves of the diphthong and the possession of the |a| particle by the left half only.

9 William Morris first brought to my attention the characterization of this kind of OCP violation.

10 A language may contrast [iː] and [iy]; however, the latter sequence is not a diphthong (i.e., with both elements in the nucleus), but a vowel followed by a coda consonant.

11 Two of the parameters can be null only where one of the halves is [ɨ]. Note that both h_1 and h_2 may not be null. There would then be a total sharing of all particles – i.e., a monophthong (see (9)).

12 The arrows are redundant, in actuality, for the sharing of all particles is deducible from the very nature of fusion. I have included them, though, because they are essential for the representation of fission (see sec. 1.2.1) and of other kinds of diphthongal changes (see sec. 1.3).

13 From here on, we shall indicate in the formulas the number of moras. For the Sanskrit example, this tells us that the resulting vowels are long and that they arise from falling diphthongs.

14 Recall that μμ represents a long vowel where there is one R node, and a falling diphthong after fission of that node.

15 See Donegan (1978) for a thorough treatment of these different kinds of diphthongal changes.

16 In Japanese, [eu̯] became [i̯oː] (Poser 1986, p. 181). The lengthened peak of the rising diphthong preserves the mora count of the original falling diphthong. For this change, there is no fusion of μ nodes; rather, concomitant with the particle exchange, the R node emanating from the second μ spreads back onto the first μ. The following tree structures depict [eu̯] > [i̯o] and [eu̯] > [i̯oː]. (Dotted lines represent spreading.)

(a)
```
    >μ   μ<          μ
     |   |          /\
     R   R    →    R   R
     |×,↑          |  /\
     i a u         i a u
```
[eu̯] > [i̯o]

(a)
```
    μ   μ          μ   μ
    ┌~┘            N
    R   R    →    R   R
    |×,↑          |  /\
    i a u         i a u
```
[eu̯] > [i̯oː]

17 Since vowel systems with more than four heights are rare, in general there can be at most a maximum of three aperture particles – e.g., for a system with the four front unrounded vowels [i e ɛ æ], the vowel [æ] would have three |a| particles.

18 The pairing of [a] with a particular

vowel in vowel-harmony systems illustrates the Law of Maximum Aperture. Turkish and Hungarian have two front unrounded vowels – [i] and [e], but Finnish has three – [i], [e], and [æ]. In conformity with the Law of Maximum Aperture, the representation for [a] will have one |a| particle in the former two languages, but two of them in the latter. These representations find corroboration in palatal harmony, which is the addition of an |i| particle to an underlying nonfront vowel. In Turkish and Hungarian, [a] alternates with [e]; in Finnish, with [æ]. See the discussion in Goldsmith (1987c).

19 For languages with [ə a] (but without [ɨ]), the schwa vowel will generally be without any aperture particle. See (1).

20 There is no need to indicate the null h_1 and h_2 positions when one monophthongal vowel is converted to another; *h* positions are needed for the representations of diphthongs and of conversions between diphthongs and monophthongs. In Chomsky and Halle (1968), combinations of the features [high], [low], and [tense] specify vowel height. Because three binary features are attempting to describe what is essentially a continuum, in order to express shifts in height, the notation necessitates a complex use of Greek-letter variables (see Yip 1980a).

21 Hayes (1990) analyzes similar data from Eastern Finnish, Lund Swedish, and Quebec French. In the analyses of these languages, Hayes makes use of aperture particles, and he argues that the data provide convincing evidence for multiple occurrrences of |a|. However, his mechanism for diphthongization is radically different from mine. He

proposes a notation for indexing all nodes and for percolating indices from higher nodes downward. I evaluate Hayes's framework in section 3.

22   The data on Frisian breaking are taken from de Graaf and Tiersma (1980). The vowel [ö:] has [ʌ] as its short counterpart. I have represented the short high mid vowel as [e] (instead of using their [I]).

23   The vowels [ü] and [ʉ] are both high front rounded: The rounding for the former is made with protruded lips, and that for the latter with compressed lips (Lindau 1978, p. 548). I shall not venture on what the particle distinction should be, as that determination is not relevant for the shifts treated here. Bruce (1970, p. 13) describes [a] as a back rounded vowel whose feature composition is equivalent to [ɔ].

24   In (34a), alpha stands for any set of particles.

25   In total assimilation, it is the root node of the source segment that spreads to the μ (timing) node of the target segment with concomitant detachment of all featural nodes that were linked to the target. In this way, the target will come to share all the segmental content of the host's R node.

26   For example, the conversion of [e: o:] to [ei̯ ou̯] would have these changes as part of the representation. Other features would be required, of course, for the representation of this particular diphthongization process. See Hayes (1990, p. 47) for the complete specification required for the diphthongization of [o:] to [ou̯].

27   Fusion could be made to operate with underspecified binary features on condition that default and redundant specifications are filled in only after the monophthong has been derived. However, de Haas (1988, pp. 46–47) has demonstrated that radical underspecification (Archangeli 1988a), which allows one of the vowels to be totally unspecified, may give the wrong results. For example, if [u] is specified as [+round], [a] as [−high], but [i] is unspecified, the fusion of [a] + [u] would correctly yield [o] (= [+ round, −high]), whereas that of [a] + [i] would erroneously give [a] (= [−high]). In order for [a] + [i] to yield [e] (= [−back, −high]), the vowel [i] needs to be specified minimally as [−back].

28   Fission/fusion will not apply below the root node, i.e., it will not apply to any feature node or particle.

19 Rule Ordering

GREGORY K. IVERSON

The role of phonological rules is to express generalizations about phonological structure. Rules are also ordinarily taken to represent specific derivational instructions, or steps along the path relating deep to surface representations. In this capacity, certain of the rules may affect the application of others, either increasing or decreasing the number of forms to which the others may apply.

Under the assumptions of conventional generative phonology as laid out in Chomsky and Halle (1968), the individual rules are all applied sequentially, arrayed in an extrinsically ordered, or language-specifically determined linear list. With respect to a rule A ordered before another rule B in such a list, A will bear one of three possible relations to B (terms adapted from Kiparsky 1968):

1 A *feeds* B just in case the application of A increases the number of forms to which B applies.
2 A *bleeds* B just in case the application of A decreases the number of forms to which B applies.
3 A *does not affect* B just in case A neither feeds nor bleeds B.

For example, contraction of the copula in English (e.g., *Bill is here* → *Bill's* [z] *here*) creates a syllabically stranded fricative, /z/, which cliticizes onto the preceding noun; if this noun happens to end in a voiceless segment, then the /z/ further devoices to /s/ because of the application of progressive devoicing among obstruents clustered in the syllable coda (*Jack is here* → *Jack's* [s] *here*). Contraction thus *feeds* devoicing in derivations where both rules are applicable because it is only through operation of the former that the /z/ of *is* comes to be syllabically affiliated with a voiceless segment in the preceding word, i.e., contraction precedes devoicing. Applied in the reverse sequence, devoicing before contraction, the ordering relation would be one in which contraction *counterfeeds* devoicing (assuming that once a rule is scanned for application it may not be applied again in the same derivation); in this case, the structural description of devoicing would not be met at the point it is considered for application because the vowel in *is* would not yet have been contracted, i.e., the /z/ in this word would then still be postvocalic, not part of an obstruent cluster.

Counterfeeding rule interaction is actually a kind of nonaffecting relation, since the counterfeeding rule neither increases nor decreases the number of forms to which the counterfed rule applies (contraction will take place irrespective of whether devoicing precedes or follows it in the applicational sequence). Its status is singled out from other nonaffecting rule interaction types, however, because counterfeeding represents the potential – albeit unrealized – for a dynamic, additive effect: while application of contraction after devoicing would not increase the number of forms to which devoicing applies, the reverse applicational sequence does have this (feeding) result. The effect of devoicing on contraction, by contrast, is neither additive nor subtractive no matter what order the rules are applied in, hence devoicing simply *does not affect* contraction. Strictly speaking, then, the ordering relation between any pair of sequentially applied rules A and B is compound, such that A bears one relation (possibly nonaffecting) to B, and B bears another to A.

The most common analysis of English inflections characterizes the regular noun plural affix also as /z/, phonologically identical with the contracted form of *is*. Progressive devoicing in coda clusters then distinguishes voiceless plurals such as in *shacks* [s] from voiced ones as in *pills* [z], but clusters of sibilants, as arise in the derivation of plurals like *raises* [əz](< /rez + z/) and *races* [əz](< /res + z/), are instead subject to a rule of epenthesis. Even when the cluster which epenthesis interrupts is heterogeneous with respect to voicing, as intermediate /s + z/ is in the derivation of *races*, devoicing of the suffix /z/ does not occur. The explanation from rule ordering for this nonapplication of devoicing, despite the fact that its structural description is satisfied by morpheme sequences like /res + z/, is that epenthesis is applied prior to devoicing, and hence *bleeds* it. The number of forms to which devoicing applies is accordingly decreased because of the applicational priority of epenthesis, for were epenthesis not in the grammar to begin with, all things being otherwise equal, devoicing would be able to apply even in sibilant clusters. Devoicing could also apply in these environments, however, if the order of application of the rules were reversed (to devoicing before epenthesis), or indeed if the rules were applied simultaneously. Under either of these possibilities (/res + z/ → *[resəs]), the ordering relation would be one in which epenthesis *counterbleeds* devoicing, resulting in the special kind of nonaffecting interaction in which a rule fails to realize its potential to reduce the number of forms to which another rule applies. Irrespective of whether epenthesis bleeds or counterbleeds devoicing, though, there is no (real or potential) effect on epenthesis, because devoicing is capable neither of increasing nor decreasing the number of forms which are subject to epenthesis.

Another kind of technically nonaffecting interaction between rules arises in cases in which the sets of inputs remain constant irrespective of applicational sequence, but where ordering nonetheless makes a difference in the phonetic results. For example, if there exist both a rule to stress the penultimate vowel of a word and a rule to apocopate word-final vowels in trisyllabic or longer words, neither would be capable of feeding or bleeding the other, but the order in which they are applied is still crucial. For a representation like /pine + ta/, which satisfies the structural requirements of both of these rules, the applicational precedence of stress assignment over apocope yields [pinét]; but applied in the reverse sequence, apocope before stress assignment, the rules produce [pínet]. Since both rules do apply in either of the sequences, it is not the case that the application of one is facilitated (fed) or blocked (bled) by that of the other. Following Kiparsky (1971), the form [pínet] in this example is said to be *transparent* with respect to the rules involved in its derivation, because the conditions for their application are neither violated (there is no word-final vowel present to contravene apocope) nor concealed (the vowel which is stressed appears superficially in penultimate position). The form [pinét], on the other hand, is *opaque* with respect to stress assignment since that rule calls for stress to fall on the penult, not the ultima.

Feeding and bleeding (as well as nonaffecting) rule interaction result in transparency, as just illustrated, but counterfeeding and counterbleeding interaction cause opacity in surface forms. Early work in rule applicational relationships (Kiparsky 1968; Koutsoudas, Sanders, and Noll 1974; Anderson 1974) suggested that the *natural* mode of rule interaction, presumably the one easiest learned and to which phonological change would gravitate, was that which resulted in *maximal application* of the rules, i.e., feeding and counterbleeding interaction. Under the terms of *local ordering* (Anderson 1974), in fact, the same pair of rules might interact in one way in some derivations, but in the reverse in others, particularly if the variation coincides with differences attributable to presumed naturalness in the ordering relation. For example, in its inflectional morphology, Modern Icelandic gives evidence of feeding interaction between rules of syncope and *u*-umlaut, the latter of which modifies the vowel *a* to *ö* before a *u* in the next syllable: *katil + um* (syncope) → *katl + um* (*u*-umlaut) → *kötlum* "kettle" dat. pl.; cf. *katli* dat. sg., *ketill* nom. sg. But it appears the same rules interact in a counterbleeding fashion, i.e., in the reverse applicational sequence, when that is possible in the derivational morphology: *bagg + ul + i* (*u*-umlaut) → *bögg + ul + i* (syncope) → *böggli* "package" dat. sg.; cf. *baggi* "pack".

Other work (Kenstowicz and Kisseberth 1971; Kiparsky 1971; Iverson 1974; Goldsmith 1991) leads to the conclusion that natural interaction favors the feeding and bleeding relations of transparency, with rules applying only minimally (but persistently) to remove representations which satisfy their structural descriptions. The predominently self-feeding and self-bleeding mode of application among *iterative* rules, which are capable of applying to their own outputs (Howard 1972; Kenstowicz and Kisseberth 1977), would seem to support this view, particularly if it is assumed that the principles which govern the application of individual rules are also at play in their interaction with one another. In the 1970s, considerations such as these led to the hypothesis of *universally determined rule application*, i.e., to the idea that the ordering relation between rules (and rule applications) is predictable from other aspects of the grammar, and from principles with the universal force of the "Elsewhere Condition" (Kiparsky 1973), "Proper Inclusion Precedence" (Sanders 1974), or the "Survival Constraint" (Anderson 1974). By the end of the decade, however, attention had turned more toward the increasing richness of phonological representation than to the specifics of rules and their interaction; in fact, the entire class of stress rules had been supplanted by the configurations and parameters of metrical theory, and the rise of autosegmental and metrical representation cast an entirely different light onto the conventional rules of linear phonology (cf. Goldsmith 1990 for summary elaboration and chapters 5–8 of this volume).

Today, some researchers assume that the question of rule order in phonology has essentially been answered, and that rule interactions are governed by general, though obviously still developing principles (within the context of radical underspecification theory, cf. especially Archangeli 1988, p. 185). Others maintain that at least some language-specific rule ordering stipulations may be necessary. Bromberger and Halle (1989), in particular, consider that phonology differs from the rest of grammar primarily in its requirement for *extrinsic* ordering (Chomsky 1967; but cf. Klausenburger 1990), a point which they consider to be demonstrated by instances of language change or dialect variation where differences in rule order alone might be at play. Certainly if rule applicational interactions are specific to individual grammars, then it should be expected that rule order will vary from stage to stage of a language, or from dialect to dialect, presumably in about the same magnitude as do other linguistic constructs, including the lexicon and the phoneme inventory. Such variation is in fact very difficult to establish, however; in the cases that have been suggested, alternative explanations of equal or greater generality, with order determined by principle, are easily available, and are often also necessary (Iverson 1974; Koutsoudas, Sanders, and Noll 1974). The familiar case of Canadian vowel raising, for example, which Bromberger and Halle review in this connection, has often been cited as justification for extrinsic rule ordering; but many alternatives have been offered, including one by Kiparsky and Menn (1977) involving different phonemicization, and it is not clear to begin with, following Chambers (1973), that exactly the same rules are involved in both of the dialects.

As first reported by Joos (1942), Canadian raising affects the diphthongs /ay/ and /aw/, centralizing them to [əy] and [əw] before voiceless consonants, as in *write* [rəyt] versus *ride* [rayd]. Voicing (and tapping) of /t/ also takes place intervocalically, so that /t/ merges with /d/ in *writer* and *rider*. But whether these words are homophonous depends on the applicational interaction of the voicing and raising rules. If raising takes place before (counterbleeds) voicing, then, as characterizes one variety of Canadian English, the diphthong in *writer* [rəydəʳ] will be centralized in comparison to that in *rider* [raydəʳ]. But if voicing is applied before raising, and so bleeds it by eliminating the voicelessness which raising requires, then the two words will be pronounced the same, i.e., both as [raydəʳ], which represents the pronunciation of the other dialect. As Kiparsky and Menn (1977, p. 48) observe, however, this variation can also be accounted for with the assumption of /ay/ and /əy/ as separate phonemes, with in the second dialect an additional rule (which the first one has lost) lowering /əy/ to [ay] before voiced segments. Under this interpretation, of course, the rules are not the same, and the variation between the dialects is due to a commonplace difference in the rules themselves rather than to stipulations on their mode of interaction.

The model of lexical phonology (Kiparsky 1985) offers another account of how what appear to be the same rules may apply in different orders under different conditions. On this view of the lexicon and its relation to phonology, "deeper", less productive morphological operations involved in derivation and irregular inflection affiliate with certain phonological rules at Level 1, while the "shallower," more general aspects of word formation typical of regular inflection are governed by another class of rules at Level 2. Some phonological rules apply throughout the lexicon, however, essentially whenever their structural descriptions are met. The Icelandic rules of syncope and *u*-umlaut discussed above would appear to be of this type, for they interact in the counterbleeding sequence of *u*-umlaut before syncope in the derivational morphology, which produces *böggli* from /bagg + ul + i/, but in an order reverse of this in the inflectional morphology, a feeding which produces *kötlum* from /katil + um/. Construed as cyclic, lexical rules available throughout the derivation, syncope and *u*-umlaut will apply until their structural descriptions are no longer satisfied, which yields the observed counterbleeding interaction in some derivations, feeding in others.

Even if the same phonemic inventory is assumed for the two Canadian dialects under discussion, similarly, lexical phonology provides a natural basis for distinguishing the "bleeding" dialect (*writer* = [rəydəʳ]) from the "counterbleeding" one (*writer* = [raydəʳ]). As Chambers (1973) points out, there are exceptions in the former to the raising rule (e.g., *cyclops* with [ay], not [əy]), which would imply it is lexically restricted, whereas voicing has to be a postlexical rule in order to be able to apply in multiword phrases like *fight it*. Since it is a general property of the theory that lexical rules precede postlexical rules, the bleeding of voicing by raising is predicted; in the counterbleeding dialect, by contrast, which Chambers maintains no longer exists and for which there is no evidence of exceptionality with respect to raising, both rules were presumably postlexical, free to apply, in counterbleeding fashion, whenever their structural descriptions were met.

The idea that at least some rules are *persistent*, applying throughout the grammar whenever their structural descriptions are satisfied, was first suggested by Chafe (1968), and has found new vitality in the proposals of Myers (1991), who seeks to identify such rules on the basis of their form alone, without reference to language-specific function. In other recent work, particularly Hyman (1993), it is argued that conventional ordering of rules confounds rather than facilitates the description of certain tonological phenomena, i.e., that the rules involved cannot be ordered in any sequence without significant loss of generalization. In the geometric representations of current phonological description, (see chap. 7, this volume), feature and node delinking operations, or neutralizations, are found always to feed into feature spreading rules, or assimilations, not to counterfeed them. In the theory of "harmonic phonology" (Goldsmith 1991), similarly, or in the connectionist modeling of Wheeler and Touretzky (1991), rule interactions are all determined by the nature of the grammar itself, too: these approaches exploit the "natural" sequencing provided by, on the one hand, the precedence of rules relating morphological representations to the word level, and the word level to phonetic representations (cf. also Anderson 1975), and, on the other hand, the predicted precedence of rules which determine syllabic and other prosodic structure over those which impose traditionally segmental changes (cf. also Kenstowicz and Kisseberth 1971). Details vary from model to model still, but the machinery available in present phonological theory appears to provide sufficient descriptive capacity without the stipulation of special constraints on rule ordering.

20 Sign Language Phonology: ASL

DIANE BRENTARI

After one of the Bampton lectures at Columbia in 1986, a young member of the audience approached him [Zellig Harris] and asked what he would take up if he had another lifetime before him. He mentioned poetry, especially the longer works of the 19th century poets like Browning. He mentioned music. And he mentioned sign language.

— Bruce Nevin, "A Tribute to Zellig Harris"

0   Introduction

Linguists have been drawn to the study of signed languages for about 35 years because of the challenges they pose to our theoretical tools as we attempt to deal with a natural language that uses vision rather than audition. It is important to consider what the state of our knowledge about American Sign Language (ASL) is, since signed languages also offer unique opportunities for testing ideas about the nature of language itself, ideas generally formulated exclusively from observations about spoken language. Our task as ASL phonologists is to ascertain which are the minimal units of the system, which aspects of this signal are contrastive, and how these units are constrained by the sensory systems that produce and perceive them. Of all the items on the list of differences and similarities between signed and spoken languages, the areas that present the most striking divergences occur in morphophonemics and phonology. I use the term "morphophonemics" here, because there is nothing strikingly different about the types of morphemes that ASL possesses, but the interface between morphology and phonology is indeed different, given the freedoms and constraints available to the system.

Consider, for example, the treatment of grammatical aspect in ASL. Many languages from a variety of language families express grammatical aspect of the verb using primarily concatenative morphology – for example, Navajo (Hoijer 1974), Atsugewi (Talmy 1972), West Greenlandic (Fortescue 1984), Russian (Halle 1959; Chung and Timberlake 1985), and Tamil (Fedson 1981), to name just a few. In none of these spoken languages, however, is the aspectual system expressed in the phonology primarily by means of altering the distinctive feature specification within a single segment. Even in Semitic languages, which utilize the riches of nonconcatenative morphology, the lexical roots and grammatical vocalisms alternate with one another in time; they are not layered onto the same segments. In contrast, the aspectual system in ASL is achieved by layering shapes of movement onto one another. For example, the *exhaustive* aspect (meaning "perform *x* to each of a group") is a composite of two layered movement shapes. One is that of a sweeping arc, which captures the meaning "give to a group," and the other is a repeated, straight path, which captures the meaning "perform *x* to each individual." Additional small circular paths, which taken together mean "perform *x* continuously to each member of a group" can be layered onto this form, adding the "continuative" aspect. It is not the aspectual categories themselves that are unusual in ASL, it is the rendering of these categories into phonological form that is so different from its spoken language counterparts with equally rich aspectual systems. The visual system allows for the exploitation of trajectory and shape of path in a simultaneous way that the auditory system does not. A comparable situation in a spoken language would be having three vowel qualities in a single syllable nucleus, each realizing separate morphemes. This difference between signed and spoken languages is one example of the kind of differences that have led phonologists to study how morphemic information is encoded in the morphophonemics in a signed language, and how phonological forms are organized by the grammar.

This chapter has two main parts. The first traces the kinds of questions phonologists have asked of signed languages, giving the reader a kind of minihistory of the development of the discipline. The second part will present some of the similarities and differences between signed and spoken language that have been well established through a variety of theoretical frameworks during the last three decades.

1   Historical Development of Phonological Issues in ASL

1.1   *Simultaneous and Sequential Units*

One of the most long-standing issues taken up by ASL phonologists during the last 30 years is the extent to which the underlying phonological structure of ASL is composed of sequential and simultaneous units. The first attempt by Stokoe (1960) and Stokoe, Casterling, and Croneberg (1965) to analyze lexical items into phonemes rejected the assumption imported from spoken-language phonology that sequential organization must be the most important way that signs are constructed. Stokoe proposed that we should look instead at the principal components of signs as they present lexical contrast, and he concluded that these units were simultaneously, rather than sequentially, organized. He called these components *cheremes* to distinguish them from the phonemes of speech, but the principles used for isolating one chereme from another were those of phonemic analysis. There were three types of cheremes in Stokoe's system, each of which he gave a name that was distinct from any term used in spoken-language phonology: *tab* (tabula) – one of 12 distinctive places of articulation on the body; *dez* (designator) – one of a group of 18 distinctive handshapes; and sig (signation) – one of a group of 24 distinctive aspects of movement. He established a distinct notation utilizing these categories. Stokoe Notation for the uninflected form of the sign GIVE is O_a'. The large O represents the handshape with the four fingers contacting the tip of the thumb. The subscript a indicates that the orientation of the palm is up, rather than down (Stokoe included orientation as an aspect of tabs); the ⊥ indicates that the movement is in a direction away from the body. This analytical view of the underlying representation of signs being simultaneous (i.e., with no temporal ordering included) was adopted by Klima and Bellugi: "A simple lexical sign is essentially a simultaneous occurrence of particular values (particular realizations) of each of several parameters" (1979, p. 43). While Stokoe Notation was primarily considered a phonemic method of transcription, it was implicit in the program that the transcription could be expanded to serve as a notation for phonetic transcription if it were thoroughly fleshed out and if redundant features were added.

The notion of simultaneous organization of underlying structure in ASL was argued against, and indeed displaced, during the 1980s. Newkirk (1981), Liddell (1984), Liddell and Johnson (1986, 1989) and Johnson and Liddell (1984) presented arguments for sequential underlying structure in ASL. Morphophonemically, this was demonstrated by Supalla and Newport (1978), who cited the contrast between, for example, the infinitive TO-FLY,[1] and the verb phrase FLY-THERE. TO-FLY has a continuous movement with no obligatory periods of stasis at the beginning or end of the movement. FLY-THERE has a similar trajectory and shape of movement, but must end with a period of stasis at a particular location in space. The linguistic arguments for sequential organization of underlying phonological structure in ASL are set forth in Liddell (1984), and they can be summarized as follows:

1. During a string of signing, it may look as if the hands are in constant motion, but they are not. In signs where the hands contact the body, the range in duration of period of stasis of the hands, or "hold" duration, varies considerably – from approximately 0.1 second to 2.0 seconds (measured in frames of video footage, where 1 frame = 0.033 seconds). The hands are in stasis

during roughly half the time; therefore holds must be phonologically important, in the sense that if there is equal time taken up phonetically by Movements and Holds, they must be roughly equally important in the phonological grammar.

   2   In signs like THINK (1), which contain a movement to a point of contact on the body, the movement has a purpose, so to speak, when contact is achieved. However, the movement is present regardless whether there is actual contact made with the body or not (i.e., even when it has no purpose); therefore, movements are phonologically important – presumably, movements with no physiologically based necessity must be phonologically important.

(1)   The ASL sign THINK.

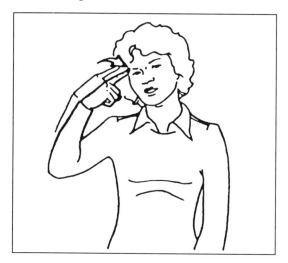

   3   Nonmanual signals are timed with respect to these periods of stasis and movement in the sign stream. In a sign like FINALLY (2), which contains an obligatory nonmanual feature, the form is ungrammatical unless the nonmanual feature is timed correctly with respect to the initial Hold and following Movement. The nonmanual component consists in a pursing of the lips, synchronized to the initial Hold of the sign, followed by the opening of the mouth, synchronized with the Movement of the sign, culminating with an open mouth during the final Hold of the sign.

   4   Compound formation in ASL had been described, in general terms, as "temporal compression" (Klima and Bellugi 1979, p. 216). By using sequential segments of holds and movements to describe this compression, we can systematically and analytically describe the process. The example THINK-MARRY "believe" (3) was one example given in Liddell (1984). Notice that, in this analysis, the first segment of THINK and the first segment of MARRY are deleted in the formation of BELIEVE.

(2) The ASL sign FINALLY. Notice that the nonmanual feature must be correctly timed with respect to the initial and final Hold. Both figures are part of the same sign.

(3) Segmental Analysis of Compound Formation (Liddell 1984) (AP = approaching movement, H = hold; hs = handshape features; or = orientation features; loc = location features; con = contact features; NMS = nonmanual signals; subscripts index individual segments in the string.)

	THINK			MARRY				BELIEVE		
	AP_1	H_1		H_2	AP_2	H_3		H_1	AP_2	H_3
hs	1	1		C	C	C		1	C	C
or	ti	ti	+	Pa	Pa	Pa	=	Ti, Pa	Pa	Pa
loc	FH	FH		c	c	c		FH	c	c
con	−	+		−	−	+		+	−	+
NMS	−	−		−	−	−		−	−	−

The following passage summarizes the guiding principle of Liddell and Johnson's research program:

> Stokoe's proposal that handshape, movement and location are phonemic in ASL is a very appealing and long-held idea. However, the entire segment, rather than these aspects of a segment, is the ASL unit which carries out the contrastive functions of a phoneme. A preliminary look at the number of possible contrastive segments in ASL suggests that the number will be considerably larger than that found in spoken languages. If this result is born out after a thorough analysis, it would represent a very interesting modality difference. (Liddell 1984)

Current work pursues both the generalizations about simultaneous structure made by Stokoe and the generalizations about sequential structure made by

Liddell and Johnson (Sandler, 1989; Brentari 1990a, 1990b, 1994; Perlmutter 1990, 1992b, 1993; Wilbur 1987, 1990).[2] First, I will discuss Sandler's *Hand Tier* phonological model (1986, 1987, 1989, 1990, 1992) to illustrate this duality between sequentiality and simultaneity in ASL in current work on segmental structure; then I will discuss major developments in work on the ASL syllable. Sandler argues for underlying representations that consist of a skeletal timing tier of the sequential units *Location* and *Movement*, comparable in some respects to consonant and vowel, respectively; these units can be, and are, sequentially ordered. Sandler's work focuses on the temporally ordered segment in sign:

> If ASL phonemes are simultaneously executed, however, a key aspect of the phonological structure of spoken words would not characterize signed words: sequentiality. The temporally segmented units of spoken-language phonology would not be available in sign. The more alike signed and spoken languages turn out to be, the more we can assume they are examples of the same types of cognitive operations, and the less we depend on metaphor to bridge the gap between the two (Sandler 1989, p. 3).

For example, like Liddell and Johnson (1989), Sandler (1989) analyzes compound formation and reduplication in ASL as segmental operations, and she also proposes that the ASL syllable could be a sequence of three segments Location-Movement-Location.

Along with this work on sequential structure employing a CV skeletal tier, Sandler addresses issues of simultaneity with the formalism of autosegmental phonology and feature geometry. Handshape and orientation features occupy a separate autosegmental tier, called *Hand Configuration*. Her reasons for analyzing handshape in this way are sound, and they are the classic reasons for setting up a separate autosegmental tier for a set of features (Goldsmith 1976a,b): (1) *stability*: handshape behaves autonomously in phonological rules, slips of the hands, etc.; (2) *many-to-one association*: handshape often contains two postures which associate to a single slot on the timing tier; (3) *morphological status*: ASL's system of classifiers is expressed predominantly through handshape. By introducing these arguments for a separate Hand Configuration tier, Sandler reemphasizes structural simultaneity by showing that employing full specifications for handshape on each segment is not only redundant, but it misses generalizations that are best specified by phonological constituents larger than the segment. An example of this can be seen in her analysis of the set(s) of fingers that are *selected* during the articulation of a sign. *Selected* fingers are those that make contact with the body and have a wider range of postures than the rest of the fingers; the other fingers are referred to as *unselected*. Sandler was the first to make formal arguments against the segmental specification for selected fingers, and to make a concrete proposal for selected fingers that had a larger domain than the segment (also see Mandel 1981 for this observation in ASL phonetics). We will return to this issue in our discussion of the syllable.

One way that simultaneity is explicitly addressed in the Hand Tier model is in its use of feature geometry. Sandler provides several analyses aiming to establish dependency relationships among ASL features. One of these analyses argues that the features expressing palm orientation are dominated by other handshape features expressing which fingers are selected to articulate the handshape – for example, whether the index finger alone or the index and middle finger are extended during execution of the sign. Sandler's evidence is primarily based on compound formation. In the initial sign of the vast majority of compounds in ASL, either orientation alone, or orientation and handshape features assimilate to those in the second sign of the compound. If handshape assimilates, so does orientation: that is, orientation alone may assimilate, but not handshape alone without orientation. This is illustrated in the compounds listed in (4) (from Sandler 1989, p. 93). They all have two forms, one containing partial assimilation (orientation alone), and one with total assimilation (handshape and orientation features).

(4) Compounds that have two alternants – one with total assimilation, and one with partial assimilation.
 MIND-DROP   "faint"
 RED-FLOW   "blood"
 THINK-HOLD   "memorize"
 FEMALE-MARRY   "wife"
 THINK-TOUCH   "obsessed"

The earliest discussion of the syllable in ASL (Kegl and Wilbur 1976; Chinchor 1978) sketched some possible parallels between signed language and spoken language syllables based on segmental structure. This work rests primarily on the notion that a syllable in ASL must have at least one movement segment, and that movements are analogous to vowels in spoken languages, but the first linguistic evidence for syllables in ASL is given in Brentari (1990b) and Perlmutter (1992b, 1993). Perlmutter uses distributional evidence from secondary movement to show that movements function as syllable peaks when not adjacent to a movement. Further, Brentari (1990b) and Perlmutter (1992b, 1993) show that the distribution of handshape changes provides a way of counting syllables in ASL.

Perlmutter (1992b, 1993) concluded that movements are indeed more sonorous than positions and that movements are analogous to vowels in spoken languages, thereby supporting the pretheoretic notion expressed in early work. In addition to these broad categories of movements and positions, there is a full sonority hierarchy in ASL, which can only be arrived at by comparing simultaneously occurring features (Brentari 1994). These matters will be discussed in more detail in the next section on the syllable and the phonological word in ASL, but I mention this work here to show that simultaneous and sequential structure have both been shown to be important for describing segments and syllables in ASL.

As we will see in the description of ASL phonological structure below, the question of analyzing ASL by means of simultaneous or sequential structures and constraints on form appears in many of the central concerns of ASL phonologists. Among them are syllabification, the relationship of the two hands in two-handed signs, and the problem of devising tests which will establish a sonority hierarchy for ASL.

2   Sketch of ASL Phonological Structure

In order to conceptualize and catalogue our current knowledge about ASL, I will group issues roughly into three categories: (1) issues concerning the syllable and the phonological word; (2) redundant features and those issues that concern constituents larger than the word; (3) issues that surround underlying representations. I have chosen this tripartite division of the issues simply as a useful organizational tool, and to avoid couching the following observations in theory-internal terms that might make the discussion less accessible.

2.1   Syllables and Words In ASL

Let us now turn to the level of the phonology responsible for constructing well-formed syllables and words. We will assume that at this level of the phonology, only distinctive features are taken into account by the phonological system. This would be true from the perspective of lexical phonology (Kiparsky 1982c, Mohanan 1986) or from that of a nonderivational, harmonic approach (Goldsmith 1990, 1993a).

2.1.1   Words in ASL.

It is here that constraints are spelled out on the two hands used in executing ASL signs. While they are physiologically independent, to a large extent the two hands are phonologically interdependent. They must, together, form a single phonological string. Although it is physically possible to do something like "talk out of both sides of your mouth" in sign, the two hands are virtually never engaged in separate messages presented simultaneously under typical conversational conditions. Some signs in ASL are specified in the lexicon as two-handed. A signer is linguistically either left-hand or right-hand *dominant*, depending on which hand typically executes one-handed signs. We will refer to this hand as *H1*, also called the *active* or *strong* hand in the literature. The other hand will be called the *H2*, also known as the *passive, base,* or *weak* hand. Battison (1978) captures some aspects of the interdependence between the two hands in two principles he calls the Symmetry Condition and the Dominance Condition, given in (5a, b).

(5) (a) The Symmetry Condition
      If both hands of a sign move independently, then both hands must be specified for the same location, the same handshape, the same movement (whether performed simultaneously or in alternation), and the specification for orientation must be either symmetrical or identical. (Battison 1978, p. 33)
     (b) The Dominance Condition
      If the hands of a two-handed sign do not share the same specification for handshapes, one hand must be passive while the active hand articulates the movement, and the specification of the passive handshape is restricted to a small set (B, A, S, C, O, 1, 5). (Battison 1978, p. 33)

The Symmetry Condition captures the idea that H2 may always copy features from H1 at no cost. The Dominance Condition expresses the relationship of the two hands when they are not identical. Some signs which obey the Symmetry Condition are given in (6a); some signs obeying the Dominance Condition are given in (6b).

(6) (a) Signs obeying the Symmetry Condition [note columnar structure]

GESTURE	SAUSAGE	SEPARATE	WORLD
VACATION	CLOTHES	DESTROY	MOCK
BEAR	AMAZED	SIGN	TRAVEL-AROUND

     (b) Signs obeying the Dominance Condition

START	HELP	PUT-DOWN	PAY-OFF
SODA-POP	ENOUGH	BACKGROUND	PASSPORT
SHOW	FULL		

The Dominance Condition also expresses the fact that only three types of handshapes are allowed on H2: the handshape where all fingers are active (that is, the "4" handshape), the handshape where only the index finger is active (that is, the "1" handshape), or one where no fingers are active (that is, the "A" or "S" handshape). These three possibilities, combined with the finger positions "open," "closed," "flat," "curved," and the thumb positions "opposed" and "unopposed" account for this set of seven handshapes that are allowed on H2.[3] These parameters are shown in (7).

(7)   Handshapes available to H2

	Selected fingers	Thumb position	Handshape position
B	"4"	opposed	open
A	none	unopposed	closed
S	none	opposed	closed
C	"4"	opposed	curved
O	"4"	opposed	flat
1	"1"	opposed	open
5	"4"	unopposed	open

These handshape features are the only distinctive features that can appear on H2 when not also appearing on H1. No other handshape, movement, or orientation features can occur independently on H2. In addition to these H2 constraints, there may be a maximum of one set of features specified for H2 per word (Brentari 1990a, p. 132); that is, there are no signs that change H2 values word-internally, independent of H1.[4] Since H1 and H2 are participating in sign production at the same time, we cannot capture the restrictions on H2 without a constraint expressed in terms of simultaneous structure. Further, this constraint must have a larger domain than the segment. While there is no space to present the alternatives here, competing proposals for the treatment of H2 and an analysis of H2 as a syllable coda are presented in Brentari and Goldsmith (1993).

The number of contrastive positions assumed by H1 – open, curved, flat, closed – is limited within a monomorphemic word (Sandler 1989, p. 72; Brentari 1990b). There is a maximum of one flat or curved handshape per monomorphemic word (Brentari 1990b). Phonological tendencies also exist concerning the area of location – that is, place of articulation. Battison (1978) and Sandler (1987) observed that there is a strong (though not exceptionless) tendency for monomorphemic words to contain a single distinctive place of articulation.

2.1.2   *The ASL syllable.*

ASL phonologists have not reached a consensus concerning the ASL syllable, so here I can only present conclusions based on converging evidence from several analyses. Clearly, the syllable does important work for ASL, but the idea of a syllable based solely on sequential elements is of limited utility in this language, given all the simultaneous morphophonological and phonological structure present. There have been three syllable templates proposed (Wilbur 1987, 1990; Perlmutter 1990, 1992b, 1993; Brentari 1990a; 1993). While differing considerably in their details, they are all centrally based on the idea that the syllable is sensitive to dynamic information along some scale of sonority (Corina 1990; Brentari 1990a, 1990c).

(8) Syllable template (Wilbur 1987, 1990)

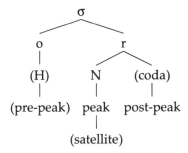

(9) Syllable template (Perlmutter 1990)

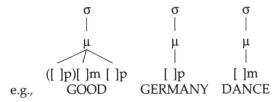

(10) Syllable template (Brentari 1990a; Brentari 1993; Brentari and Goldsmith 1993).

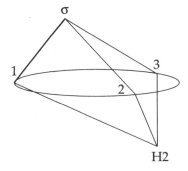

1. Movement Class Node
2. Handshape/Orientation Class Node
3. Location Class Node

e.g., DRIVE-TO

The three syllable templates are presented in (8), (9), and (10). Wilbur (1987, 1990) proposes a template with a flat structure, with an optional onset, a branching rhyme containing a three-way branching nucleus, and an optional coda. She uses this template to describe ASL reduplication of stems to form nouns. Perlmutter proposes a moraic model of ASL syllable structure, and argues for a taxonomy of three types of syllables in ASL. He uses his syllable template to explain the distribution of the three types of holds in ASL. Both Wilbur's and Perlmutter's models have strong similarities to the syllable in spoken languages in their use of sequential units in defining subsyllabic constituents. The template shown in (10) is a proposal for a nonhierarchical, simultaneous syllable template (Brentari 1990a; Brentari and Goldsmith 1993; Brentari 1993), with the syllable nucleus indicated by a bold line. This structure is used to explain the behavior of H2 in syllables and in phonological words, and the behavior of alternating movements. The class nodes for movement (1), handshape/orientation (2), and location (3) are indicated in (10) around the circle. The relationship of handshape and orientation is adopted from Sandler (1989).

Let us consider how these models deal with the questions regarding (1) what evidence there is that the signing stream consists of syllables as in spoken language; (2) whether syllables have the same internal structure as spoken language syllables; and (3) how syllables are counted in ASL.

One way that all of the three above proposals count syllable nuclei is by counting movements, but the three do not agree on what can count as a lexical movement. Perlmutter (1992b, 1993) argues that secondary movements in ASL, which are small, uncountable repetitions of a movement, handshape change, or orientation change, dock onto syllable peaks, and I have adopted this diagnostic in my work as well. Another way of counting syllables is by observing the behavior of handshape changes. Brentari (1990b) and Perlmutter (1992b, 1993) both conclude that there can be a maximum of one set of selected fingers per syllable in ASL, but there can be two positions of the hands. Perlmutter calls the former *handshape contrasts* and the latter *handshape contours*. So far, then, while all three proposals accept lexical movements for identifying syllables, only Perlmutter and Brentari use secondary movements and handshape changes to count and identify syllables. Perlmutter and I differ in the extent to which we consider ASL syllable-internal structure to be like that of spoken languages. Perlmutter argues for a syllable-internal structure very similar to that of spoken languages, based on adjacent root nodes and moras similar to that put forth in Hayes (1989a). Brentari (1990a, 1990b, 1990c, 1994) and Brentari and Goldsmith (1993) argue for a syllable-internal structure different from that found in spoken languages. We argue for a simultaneously organized syllable at the level of the phonological word on the basis of the behavior of H2 and on the finer distinctions that can be made in establishing a visual sonority hierarchy using simultaneously occurring features.

No discussion of the ASL syllable would be complete without discussing *visual sonority*. Lexical movements, handshape changes, orientation changes, and location changes can all occupy a syllable peak.[5] Blevins (1992a), Corina (1990), and Brentari (1994) have all proposed sonority hierarchies, which are given in (11). Two things should be noted about these proposals. First, there is complete agreement among them that movement is the most sonorous element. Second, Blevins's term "non-static articulator" encompasses Corina's "handshape change," "orientation change," and "location change," and my hierarchy focuses on distinguishing among handshape change, orientation change, and secondary movement. In other words, each proposal makes progressively finer distinctions (ordered a, b, c) among members of the class of "non-static articulators."

(11)   Sonority proposals
    (a)   Blevins: Path Movement > non-static articulator > static articulator > location-hold
    (b)   Corina: Movement > handshape change = orientation change > location change
    (c)   Brentari: Movement > handshape change > orientation change > secondary movement

      Perlmutter (1992b, 1993) concludes that Movements are more sonorous than Positions but this is similar to saying that vowels are more sonorous than consonants, and a very broad generalization. To make these careful distinctions among non-static articulators, a simultaneous local domain (i.e., the syllable) is necessary. Corina argues that the Sonority Sequencing Principle, which states that "between any member of a syllable and the syllable peak, only sounds of higher sonority rank are permitted" (Clements 1990; see also chap. 6 in this volume) is not adhered to in signed languages. Corina (1990) writes, "The ASL syllable does not seem to honor a principle which sequences elements within a syllable in terms of sonority, a principle which on some accounts holds for spoken languages." By observing the behavior of properties of a sign that can occupy a syllable peak under various phonological conditions, the relative sonority among these properties can be determined; that is, which property is the preferred syllable peak when a sign has two of these dynamic elements (Corina 1990; Brentari 1994). Corina observed signs that have two variants – one variant containing a handshape change and a lexical movement, and the other containing just one of these. He argued that the one deleted was the less sonorous one. In signs containing lexical movement and handshape change or orientation change, the lexical movement will be the preferred syllable peak, manifested by the fact that it is the property preserved when one of these two properties is deleted. This is shown in the two variants of the sign APPOINTMENT, given in (12a and 12b). One variant contains a lexical movement and a handshape change, while the other contains only the lexical movement.

      In Brentari (1994), I employ a linguistic test developed by Perlmutter (1992b, 1993). This test involves observing where secondary movements *dock* to determine the syllable peak in a sign. These results were born out in the test of secondary movement docking. Since Corina's work establishes that path movement is more sonorous than handshape change, I will illustrate here how secondary movement docking distinguishes the sonority value of handshape change and orientation change, showing that handshape change is more sonorous than orientation change. We see the test for secondary movement docking in the ASL pair EXCERPT and EXCERPT [habitual]. EXCERPT contains a

(12)   Two variants of the ASL sign APPOINTMENT. (12a) is articulated with a handshape change and a movement; (12b) is articulated with a movement only (i.e., without a handshape change).

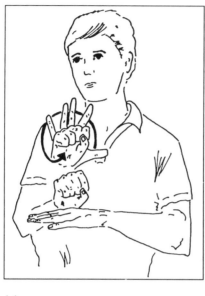   

(a)   (b)

handshape change and an orientation change; EXCERPT [habitual] contains only a handshape change. The pair EXCERPT and EXCERPT [habitual] are given in (13a and 13b).

Using a sequential syllable, we can capture generalizations about reduplicated forms and phrase-final lengthening, as well as the timing of nonmanual features with respect to segmental structure originally observed by Liddell (1984); using a simultaneous syllable, we can capture generalizations about sonority, and about the behavior of H2 in two-handed signs.

A summary of the facts we have discussed about phonological words in ASL is given in (14).

(14)   Word-Level Summary
   1. H2 can only be specified for the features [closed] and [peripheral] and may only contain selected finger constellations 1 and 4, and the closed variant of these, the fist.[6]
   2. H2 may be specified independently from H1 once per word.
   3. There is a maximum of one curved or flat handshape per phonological word.
   4. At this level the syllable is constructed on dynamic properties of the sign.
   5. The sonority hierarchy in ASL is based on the dynamic properties of signs.

(13) The ASL signs EXCERPT and EXCERPT [habitual]. EXCERPT (13a) is articulated with a handshape change and an orientation change; EXCERPT [habitual] (13b) is articulated with a handshape change only (i.e., without an orientation change).

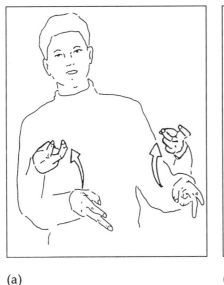

(a)   (b)

2.2 *The Phrase and Redundant Features in ASL*

It is clear that signing activity can be divided into periods of stasis and movement. In developing their framework, Liddell and Johnson (1989) use this overt "phonetic" distinction and make the units of stasis and movement the foundation of their model. They call these units *Holds* and *Movements*, respectively; a hold must be a period of stasis of at least 0.1 seconds (100 msecs). They incorporate this division into Holds and Movements into the underlying structure of their analysis. Sandler (1987, 1989) divides the static and dynamic units into *Locations* and *Movements*, with a location defined in terms of an obligatory place of articulation. The other two models (Perlmutter 1990, 1992b, 1993; and Brentari 1990a, 1990c) do not use a segmental timing tier, but phonetically Perlmutter labels bundles of features containing dynamic elements *Movement feature bundles*, and those containing static features *Position feature bundles*. Regardless of the label – or whether or not the segments must be crucially divided into two groups – there are static and dynamic aspects in the phonetic signal.

Let us first address redundant segments in the system. We have strong evidence that there are redundant holds and movements in the signed string. I will use *hold* as a generic term for static segments and *movement* as a generic term for dynamic segments. Perlmutter (1989) has presented compelling arguments for a phrase-final Mora Insertion rule ($\emptyset \rightarrow \mu /$ ____ ##) – an analysis which provides evidence for the predictability of the three ways that signs can be terminated. Perlmutter specifically addresses the role of the mora as a timing unit in ASL. Phrase-internally, signs can either have no hold (in signs where a position shares a single mora with a movement) or a short hold (in syllables composed of a single Position). Phrase-finally signs can have (1) no hold in signs consisting solely of a bidirectional movement (e.g., DANCE, AWKWARD)[7], (2) a short hold for phrase-final Positions that share a mora with an adjacent movement, or (3) a long hold in syllabic Positions in phrase-final position. Syllabic Positions are syllables constructed without a path movement, but which contain two different specifications for another feature (i.e., those that spell out handshape change or orientation change) that can constitute a well-formed syllable in ASL.

In addition to Mora Insertion, which primarily illuminates redundancies in holds, we have a Movement Insertion rule that supplies a movement between two nonidentical locations postlexically (Sandler 1989, p. 139) ($\emptyset \rightarrow M / L_1$ ____ L_2). This rule applies both word-internally and across word boundaries. In addition to these phrase-level rules, we can make a generalization about phrase-level assimilation; namely, it occurs regressively. An example of regressive assimilation of handshape cited in Liddell and Johnson (1989) occurs in the phrase ME CURIOUS, where the handshape of CURIOUS occurs on ME as well, replacing the handshape normally used in ME.

Let us now address redundant features in the system. We noted above that a signer is either left-hand or right-hand dominant. The *ipsilateral* side is the side of the signing hand, and the *contralateral* side is the other, the side opposite the signing hand. ASL has vertical and horizontal place of articulatory contrast, reflected in the distinctive feature [Vertical Place of Articulation] ([VPOA]) for the vertical dimension, and [contra] and [distal] for the horizontal dimension (Brentari 1990a). The values for [VPOA] slice the signing space into distinct horizontal areas – e.g., head (with finer distinctions within the head, such as forehead, eye), shoulder, torso, etc. The two values for [contra] divide the signing place into ipsilateral and contralateral sides of the body, and the two values for [distal] divide the signing space into a radial area approximately a forearm's length from the body and one that is further away from the body. APPLE vs. ONION, signed at the cheek and eye respectively, exhibit a vertical contrast. PITTSBURGH and LEATHER – signed on the ipsilateral and contralateral side of the body at the shoulder – exhibit horizontal contrast.

A default specification is filled in for [contra] in cases where none is specified.[8] To illustrate this, if a [Vertical Place of Articulation], such as [VPOA: cheek] is specified for the sign APPLE and no value for the [contra] feature is specified, the value is filled in as [−contra] by rule (Liddell and Johnson 1989). Signs exhibiting the redundant value [−contra] are given in (15). Another redundancy in the feature system at this level concerns the Vertical Place of

Articulation. This is a default value – namely [VPOA: torso] – filled in if no other value for VPOA is specified. Signs exhibiting a redundant Vertical Place of Articulation [VPOA: torso] are given in (16).

(15) Phonetic [–contra] redundancy
        APPLE   ONION   TOUGH   BROKE (no money)
        SHAVE   THROW   SUBSCRIBE   THINK

(16) Phonetic [VPOA: torso] redundancy
        ROCKET   CHEESE   ABOUT   SAUSAGE   WORK
        JAPAN   WHITE   LIKE   ENTHUSIASM   BACKGROUND

  A summary of the phrase level facts we have discussed in the above section is given in (17).

(17) Phrasal-level summary
        1. There is a basic division between static and dynamic segments – Holds and Movements respectively.
        2. Hold length is predictable.
        3. Epenthetic movements occur between any two nonidentical locations.
        4. Phrase-level assimilation occurs regressively.
        5. Feature redundancies include:
              a. an unspecified value for [Vertical Place of Articulation] – [torso]
              b. an unspecified value for [contra] – [–contra].

  In sum, the evidence concerning H2 and sonority points to the need for a syllable template and phonotactics that are constructed on the basis of simultaneous dynamic properties. The evidence from the distribution of phrase-final holds points to the need for a second set of constraints on the sequentially ordered units (i.e., moras, segments) in constituents which may extend beyond the phonological word. While the issue is far from settled, it appears that ASL utilizes a different syllable template at different levels of the phonology. Evidence for languages using different syllable templates at the word level and phonetic level has been found for Malayalam and Luganda (Wiltshire 1991a, 1991b). For example, Malayalam licenses a small subset of consonant features in coda position at word level and two onset positions; however, at the phonetic level codas are disallowed and license a third position.

2.3 *Underlying Representation*

Let us now turn to the most abstract level of phonological representation of ASL, where morphemes are encoded into phonological structures. Let us assume that this level adheres to principles of contrastive underspecification, since we know very little about what a universally unmarked set of features across sign languages would contain. If we use radical underspecification, all unmarked and redundant features are eliminated from underlying representations, while in contrastive underspecification only redundant features are eliminated (Archangeli 1988a).

In order to frame our next discussion, I would like to group languages of the world into four groups which highlight their morphophonemic structure, as in (18). Languages are grouped according to their preferred number of morphemes and syllables per phonological word. Group 4 is composed exclusively of signed languages.

(18)   Morphemes/syllables in natural languages
   Group 1:   monomorphemic/polysyllabic – e.g., English, French
   Group 2:   monomorphemic/monosyllabic – e.g., Chinese, Thai
   Group 3:   polymorphemic/polysyllabic – e.g., Greenlandic, Turkish
   Group 4:   polymorphemic/monosyllabic – e.g., ASL (Supalla 1982), Italian Sign Language (Corazza 1990), Swedish Sign Language (Wallin 1990), New Zealand Sign Language (Collins-Ahlgren 1990)

The groups in (18) identify general preferences for morphophonemic realization; these are not hard and fast laws, to be sure, but the words in these languages largely conform to these generalizations. The structural diversity in ASL lexical items can be expressed in the following way (this description follows analyses contained in Johnson and Liddell 1984, Perlmutter 1989, and Supalla 1982). (1) There is a very small set of polysyllabic/monomorphemic lexical items – e.g., BACKGROUND, CURRICULUM, SOCIAL WORK. To my knowledge, these are all forms etymologically related to English borrowings, expressed in fingerspelling (this is a way for ASL to spell out words using a handshape for each English letter; see Battison 1978). (2) There is a set of monomorphemic/monosyllabic signs, referred to as "frozen" signs – e.g., ADMIT, UNDERSTAND, SHIRT. (3) There is a group of stems that are referred to as "incomplete." Most of these are polymorphemic/monosyllabic; a few are polymorphemic/polysyllabic. That is, the word may contain values for additional morphological material, such as classifier, verb agreement, or aspectual morphology, e.g., GIVE (classifier, verb agreement, aspect), LOOK-AT (aspect), INVITE (verb agreement). See (19).

(19)   Structural diversity in ASL
   1.   Monomorphemic/polysyllabic forms – BACKGROUND, SOCIAL-WORK
   2.   Monomorphemic/monosyllabic forms – UNDERSTAND, ADMIT, SHIRT

3. Polymorphemic/monosyllabic forms:
    (a) Incomplete stems[9]
        3sg-GIVE-4sg ("She gave her")
        TELL-3sg ("Tell him")
        GIVE-2pl ("Give all of you")
    (b) Verbs of motion and location
        small animal- JUMP-ONTO- flat surface
        HOLE expand in size over a period of time

(4) In the portion of the lexicon known as the "verbs of motion and location" (Supalla 1982, 1985), each feature or cluster of features represents a morpheme. (20) gives an example of such a form. The features and representation used here are from Brentari (1990a; 1993).

(20) This example of an ASL verb of motion and location means "two hunched, upright beings make their way carefully forward side by side from point 'a' to point 'b.'"

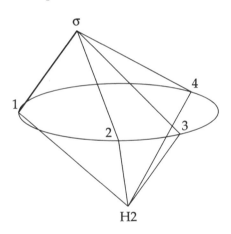

Distinctive features

1. Movement Class Node
    [tracing: straight]
2. Handshape/Orientation Class Node
    [selected fingers: 1]
    [H2: radial plane of finger]
    [-peripheral]
    [-closed]
    [prone]
3. Location Class Node
    [HPOA: proximal], [HPOA: distal]
4. Nonmanual Class Node
    [pursed lips]

Morphological identity

move forward

upright beings
side by side
stooped

facing forward

from "a" to "b"

carefully

This sort of example is by no means unusual in ASL. The formalism represents the simultaneous possibilities of the ASL syllable by simulating three-dimensional space by the circle. The nucleus is shown by a bold line – here, [tracing], which is a lexical movement feature. In this particular case, both H1 and H2 realize each of the features (they are identical); the features are associated to the class nodes indicated, although the problem of their particular organization remains unresolved. This representation shows the sheer volume of morphological information that can be captured in one syllable. Further, this type of syllable-to-morpheme structure – nine morphemes to one syllable – is surely a striking difference between spoken and signed languages, one conditioned by the differing feedback loops that the two types of languages use. Since signed languages use the visual-gestural (as opposed to the auditory-spoken), they are more likely to incorporate the task of parsing simultaneous information into their grammars.

Despite an emphasis on simultaneity in underlying structure, ordering of morphophonemic material does occur in ASL. For example, the two values for [distal] in (20). These must be ordered with respect to one another if we are to have the beings moving correctly with respect to spatial mapping (Padden 1990; Liddell 1993). In addition to this type of ordering, fingerspelling must allow ordering of [Selected Finger Constellation] features. This accounts for the ordering that occurs in the polysyllabic/monomorphemic forms cited in Perlmutter (1992b, 1993), and those noted in Supalla and Newport (1978) – i.e., the contrast in pairs such as FLY and FLY-THERE noted earlier. There are also forms where places of articulation must be ordered (GOOD, GOAT, NUN). The type of ordering discussed here (that is, the ordering of specific occurrences of features) along with the syllable templates discussed earlier, taken together provide a way of expressing contrast in ASL that need not resort to the fully specified segments of Liddell and Johnson (1989) in underlying structure.

To address the nature of distinctive features in ASL, we return to the citation above from Liddell (1984), suggesting that the number of distinctive features in ASL is considerably larger than that found in spoken languages. Descriptively, we know the regions of the body, handshapes, and movements that are contrastive, as we do for thumb position and orientation. However, providing the *distinctive feature system* these contrasts express is another matter. Liddell and Johnson's (1989) phonetic transcription makes no effort to limit itself to differences that are contrastive, with its 126 handshapes, 51 locations on the body, 27 locations in space, and 70 locations on H2. The Hand Tier model (Sandler 1989) contains 16 handshape features, 4 features for orientation, 16 for location, and 1 movement feature. While Liddell and Johnson's (1989) 299 features are extremely useful in doing transcription, further phonological analysis is necessary to determine which features are distinctive in ASL, and whether they are n-ary, binary, or privative. Brentari (1990a) has proposed a group of 20 distinctive features by reorganizing the observations of Liddell and Johnson, by eliminating redundancy where it can be ascertained, and by using 7 n-ary, 8 binary and 5 privative features.[10] There is a parallel move in spoken languages in uniting places of articulation, such as labial, dental, velar, etc., under the single feature [place of articulation] (McCarthy 1989b). If Liddell and Johnson's 299 contrasts must all be separate features, there is indeed a strong modality difference between signed and spoken languages in this regard. If we admit n-ary features to the system and the 20 distinctive features can handle the data, there is no modality difference between the number of distinctive features in spoken and signed languages, and Jakobson's observation that there are approximately 20 distinctive features in any natural language holds for signed languages as well as spoken languages, as far as initial study indicates.

If we eliminate the syllable template from underlying structure, there are several types of phonological information other than the phonological features themselves that are available at this level. I would like briefly to sketch the role that feature geometry, markedness, and sonority play in ASL's underlying representations. All three are types of phonological information that may be present in underlying representation and that could feed other aspects of the phonology. We have already seen that a sonority hierarchy plays a role in constructing syllables. Since this information must be readily available to syllable structure, and since sonority is not predictable from any phonetic measure in a definitive way, it must be present in underlying representations (see Zec 1988 for a discussion of these matters for a set of spoken languages).

Markedness has proved useful for reducing the information necessary in underlying representation of ASL. I have proposed an explicit set of criteria for markedness in handshape (Brentari 1990a); see (21).

(21)   Markedness Criteria in ASL Handshapes

		More marked	Less marked
1.	Frequency of occurrence	less frequent	more frequent
2.	Order of acquisition	acquired later	acquired earlier
3.	Allows handshape change	disallow change	allow change
4.	Contrasts in position	fewer contrasts	more contrasts[11]
5.	Classifier forms	no	yes
6.	Independent H2	no	yes

Battison (1978), Mandel (1981), McIntire (1977), and Friedman (1977) observed a range of behaviors in two groups of selected fingers: the group that contains the index finger (and optionally the thumb) [Selected Finger Constellation: 1] and the group that contains all four fingers (and optionally the thumb) [Selected Finger Constellation: 4]. These two selected finger constellations are the earliest acquired handshapes, they allow the fullest range of possibilities for handshape position and handshape change, they are the easiest to produce, and they are the most frequently occurring. These are also the two selected finger constellations that appear on H2 when H2 and H1 are nonidentical. These observations allow us to conclude that these are the least marked of all selected fingers in ASL. In two-handed signs where the two hands are nonidentical, two sets of handshape features will be realized on the surface, yet the underlying representation need not contain two completely specified handshapes in order for us to know which features associate to H1 and which associate to H2. Examples of the kinds of predictions given the markedness criteria in (18) are (1) if the specification [H2] is the only indication that the sign is two-handed, we can assume that H2 copies everything from H1 and has no independent values of its own; (2) if a selected finger constellation is other than 4 or 1 it must be assigned to H1; (3) if a feature has two ordered values on it [−closed] before [+closed], that feature must be assigned H1. In addition, Mohanan (1991) has proposed that unmarked (his *non-dominant*) feature values should tend to be (1) easy targets of assimilation, (2) the output of neutralization rules, and possibly (3) prone to elision. These characteristics are true for [Selected Finger Constellation: 1] and [Selected Finger Constellation: 4]. The facts about underlying structure we have discussed are summarized in (22).

(22)   Summary of facts about underlying structure
    1.   Morphophonemic information is sequentially ordered.
    2.   Selected finger constellations are ordered in fingerspelling and fingerspelled borrowings.
    3.   There are cases of feature ordering on a single tier for some signs.
    4.   Sonority information is specified here.
    5.   Markedness criteria can determine which features associate to H1 and which ones associate to H2.
    6.   Feature geometry is specified here.

3   Discussion

The tension described here in ASL between simultaneous and sequential structure exists in work on the phonology of spoken languages as well, but the problems have not taken the same form. For example, the idea that sequential organization of segments must be central at all levels of phonological analysis has been called into question in spoken language phonology by McCarthy (1989b), who points out that, given morphological and prosodic well-formedness constraints, the extent to which segments must be ordered in the underlying representations of each lexical item varies widely. On the one hand, English has few morphological constraints and a liberal syllable template, allowing almost all distinctive features in coda position in the coda as well as in the onset. For these reasons, English is a language that requires a great deal of sequential ordering. On the other hand, languages with morphological templates (e.g., Arabic in the extreme case, Yawelmani to a lesser degree)[12] or languages with a highly restrictive syllable template (Luganda, for example, which allows only the feature [nasal] in the coda) will need little or no underlying ordering of featural material because the morphological and/or prosodic templates can perform this work. In addition to using syllable restrictions to eliminate item-specific sequential ordering, there are other mechanisms that might function in this way. For example a dynamic feature, such as [delayed release] for affricates, actually captures the [−continuant] > [+continuant] ordering since the progression of the articulatory gesture is from completely obstructed to approximate contact, rather than the reverse. The use of dynamic features in spoken-language feature systems is not as prevalent as it is in sign, since a visual linguistic system can be very sensitive to shape and manner of articulatory movement in a way that audition can not. A dynamic feature, such as [direction of movement], in ASL can predict the initial and terminal locations.

ASL is a language that can provide us with a great deal of information about aspects of underlying structure involving underspecification and feature systems. Since simultaneity in sign is impossible to ignore, we can explore the upper limits of phonological information that the brain can process at one time. It is clear that the auditory system does not have the capability to approach the upper limit since the physiological range of possibilities, at any one moment, for articulatory movements is much narrower in the vocal tract than in the signing space. We assume that the restrictions on the physiological possibilities are taken into consideration by the grammar. The question of how many distinctive contrasts the grammar can process within a single simultaneous unit is more aptly asked of signed languages than of spoken languages.

In addition, we must construct a feature system for ASL that takes into account the radically different constraints and potentials that signed languages have, given the use of the visual system for perception and the wider range of articulators available. The articulators in sign – the arms, the hands, the body, the face – are also larger than their counterparts in spoken language – the tongue, the velum, the larynx, etc. Further, from the point of view of motor control, there are qualitative differences between the articulators used in signed and those used in spoken languages. While the tongue, the velum, and the larynx are articulators composed of soft tissue, the arms and hands contain a number of joints as well. These comparatively different properties influence the range of motion of the articulators, as well as the properties exploited for meaningful contrast. Work in this area has begun (see Lane, Boyes-Bream, and Bellugi, 1976; Mandel 1981; Corina 1990; Brentari 1990c; Ann 1991), and this task of composing a distinctive feature system for ASL will provide a test of such long-held assumptions as the preference for binary features.

While there are still many issues that are unresolved in ASL phonology, we have learned a great deal about ASL specifically, and how signed languages are organized in general. It is true that familiarity with sign language phonological studies requires an initial effort to become acquainted with the details of the phonetic system and how these relate to the phonology, the rewards make the effort worthwhile. It is not the case that signed languages present just another set of interesting language facts: signed languages can allow us to study the link between nonlinguistic cognitive processes and linguistic ones in a way that spoken languages cannot, in part because the visual system in humans is much better understood than the auditory system. Its location in the brain on the posterior parietal surface makes it more accessible for direct investigation by evoked potential studies and metabolic tracing studies. Further, the visual system of higher order nonhuman primates is much more similar to ours than is their auditory system, and because of this we can make inferences about the human visual system from studies done on the visual systems of these animals that we cannot make from similar studies done on the auditory system in nonhumans. We have been able to ascertain that lesions in Broca's area and Wernicke's area of the left hemisphere result in the same type of linguistic disruptions in both signed and spoken languages (Poizner, Klima, and Bellugi 1987). From this we can conclude that, regardless of the evolutionary roots of language, the visual system of signers can be linked to the linguistic centers of the brain in the same way as the auditory system of nonsigners. As a result of this convergence, we are able to test our phonological models in a way not available for spoken language, and we can see that work on signed languages is central for our understanding of how linguistic and nonlinguistic capacities of the brain feed into one another.

NOTES

This work was supported in part by NSF grant BNS-9000407, awarded to Howard Poizner at the Center for Molecular and Behavioral Neuroscience, Rutgers University. Special thanks to David Perlmutter, Wendy Sandler, and Caroline Wiltshire for comments on earlier drafts of this paper.

1   English glosses of ASL signs are presented in uppercase letters. Hyphenated glosses (e.g., TO-FLY) indicate that they are executed as a single word in ASL. When the words "movement" and "hold" appear with an upper case "M" and "H," they refer to Liddell and Johnson's segment classes; otherwise these terms refer to the static and non-static aspects of the sign signal.

2   Here I am only citing comprehensive proposals for the entire phonological component of ASL, during the period of time in question. There are many other works that have taken up specific problems in the phonological system of ASL.

3   Thumb position is contrastive on H1 (see Brentari 1990a, pp. 67–69; Moy 1990); these specifications are redundant on H2.

4   Naturally, if H2 is identical to H1, H2 may copy the change on H1, as in the signs in (8).

5   A handshape change involves a change in selected fingers or finger position during the articulation of a syllable (e.g., "closed" to "open" in the sign UNDERSTAND). An orientation change involves the change in orientation of the palm (e.g., "palm down" to "palm up" in COOK). Secondary movements are small, uncountable, rapidly repeated instantiations of movements, handshape changes, or orientation changes, similar to a "trilled"

manner of articulation in spoken languages.

6 [Closed] is a feature included in several feature systems to date (Boyes-Braem 1981; Sandler 1989; Liddell and Johnson 1989); [peripheral] is a feature argued for in Brentari (1990a, 1990b).

7 This is a logical extension of the analyses in Perlmutter (1990, 1992b, 1993).

8 This set of facts is more complicated than this in signs that undergo metathesis – DEAF, MEMBER, FLOWER, etc. See Brentari 1990c for further discussion.

9 Gender is not marked in ASL.

10 A change in the feature [H2] is reflected here, which must be n-ary if it is to capture the contrast in place of contact and orientation between pairs, such as WITH and WORK.

11 By "position" I mean the four contrastive handshape positions: open, closed, flat, and curved.

12 Sandler (1989) argues that ASL has morphological templates and Liddell and Johnson (1986) have proposed an analysis of "inchoative" or "unrealized-inceptive" verbal aspect using morphophonemic frames.

21 The Phonological Basis of Sound Change

PAUL KIPARSKY

Tout est psychologique dans la linguistique, y compris ce qui est mécanique et matériel.

— F. de Saussure 1910/1911

0 Sound Change

The neogrammarians portrayed sound change as an exceptionless, phonetically conditioned process rooted in the mechanism of speech production.[1] This doctrine has been criticized in two mutually incompatible ways. From one side, it has been branded a mere terminological stipulation without empirical consequences, on the grounds that apparent exceptions can always be arbitrarily assigned to the categories of analogy or borrowing.[2] More often though, the neogrammarian doctrine has been considered false on empirical grounds. The former criticism is not hard to answer (Kiparsky 1988), but the second is backed by a formidable body of evidence. Here I will try to formulate an account of sound change making use of ideas from lexical phonology, which accounts for this evidence in a way that is consistent with the neogrammarian position, if not exactly in its original formulation, then at least in its spirit.

The existence of an important class of exceptionless sound changes grounded in natural articulatory processes is not in doubt, of course. It is the claim that it is the *only* kind of sound change that is under question, and the evidence that tells against is primarily of two types. The first is that phonological processes sometimes spread through the lexicon of a language from a core environment by generalization along one or more phonological parameters, often lexical item by lexical item. Although the final outcome of such *lexical diffusion* is in principle indistinguishable from that of neogrammarian sound change, in midcourse it presents a very different picture. Moreover, when interrupted, reversed, or competing with other changes, even its outcome can be different.

Against the implicit assumptions of much of the recent literature, but in harmony with older works such as Schuchardt (1885) and Parodi (1923, p. 56), I will argue that lexical diffusion is not an exceptional type of sound change, nor a new, fourth type of linguistic change, but a well-behaved type of analogical change. Specifically, *lexical diffusion is the analogical generalization of lexical phonological rules*. In the early articles by Wang and his collaborators, it was seen as a process of phonemic redistribution spreading randomly through the vocabulary (Chen and Wang 1975; Cheng and Wang 1977). Subsequent studies of lexical diffusion have supported a more constrained view of the process. They have typically shown a systematic pattern of generalization from a categorical or near-categorical core through extension to new phonological contexts, which are then implemented in the vocabulary on a word-by-word basis. In section 1 I argue that lexical diffusion is driven by the rules of the lexical phonology, and that the mechanism is analogical in just the sense in which, for example, the regularization of *kine* to *cows* is analogical. In fact, the instances of "lexical diffusion" which Wang and his collaborators originally cited in support of their theory include at least one uncontroversial instance of analogical change, namely, the spread of retracted accent in deverbal nouns of the type *tórmènt* (from *tormént*). In most cases, of course, the analogical character of the change is less obvious because the analogy is nonproportional and implements distributional phonological regularities rather than morphological alternations. For example, the item-by-item and dialectally varying accent retraction in nonderived nouns like *mustache, garage, massage, cocaine* is an instance of nonproportional analogy, in the sense that it extends a regular stress pattern of English to new lexical items. What I contend is that genuine instances of "lexical diffusion" (those which are not due to other mechanisms such as dialect mixture) are *all* the result of analogical change. To work out this idea I will invoke some tools from recent phonological theory. In particular, radical underspecification and structure-building rules as postulated in lexical phonology will turn out to be an essential part of the story.

The second major challenge to the neogrammarian hypothesis is subtler, less often addressed, but more far-reaching in its consequences. It is the question how the putatively autonomous, mechanical nature of sound change can be reconciled with the systematicity of synchronic phonological structure. At the very origins of structural phonology lies the following puzzle: if sound changes originate through gradual articulatory shifts which operate blindly without regard for the linguistic system, as the neogrammarians claimed, why don't their combined effects over millennia yield enormous phonological inventories which resist any coherent analysis? Moreover, why does no sound change ever operate in such a way as to subvert phonological principles, such as implicational universals and constraints on phonological systems? For example, every known language has obstruent stops in its phonological inventory, at least some unmarked ones such as *p, t, k*. If sound change were truly blind, then the operation of context-free spirantization processes such as Grimm's Law to languages with minimal stop inventories should result in phonological systems which lack those stops, but such systems are unattested.

With every elaboration of phonological theory, these difficulties with the neogrammarian doctrine become more acute. Structural investigations of historical phonology have compounded the problems. At least since Jakobson (1929), evidence has been accumulating that *sound change itself*, even the exceptionless kind, is structure-dependent in an essential way. Sequences of changes can conspire over long periods, for example to establish and maintain patterns of syllable structure, and to regulate the distribution of features over certain domains. In addition to such top-down effects, recent studies of the typology of natural processes have revealed pervasive structural conditioning of a type hitherto overlooked. In particular, notions like underspecification, and the abstract status of feature specifications as distinctive, redundant, or default, are as important in historical phonology as they are synchronically. The neogrammarian reduction of sound change to articulatory shifts in speech production conflicts with the apparent structure-dependence of the very processes whose exceptionlessness it is designed to explain.

A solution to this contradiction can be found within a two-stage theory of sound change according to which the phonetic variation inherent in speech, which is blind in the neogrammarian sense, is selectively integrated into the linguistic system and passed on to successive generations of speakers through language acquisition (Kiparsky 1988). This model makes sound change simultaneously mechanical on one level (vindicating a version of the neogrammarian position), yet structure-dependent on another (vindicating Jakobson). The seemingly incompatible properties of sound change follow from its dual nature.

My paper is organized as follows. In the next section I present my argument that lexical diffusion is analogical and that its properties can be explained on the basis of underspecification in the framework of lexical phonology. I then spell out an account of sound change which reconciles exceptionlessness with structure-dependence (sec. 2). Finally in section 3 I examine assimilatory sound changes and vowel shifts from this point of view, arguing that they too combine structure-dependence with exceptionlessness in ways which support the proposed model of sound change, as well as constituting additional diachronic evidence for radical underspecification in phonological representations.

1   Lexical Diffusion

1.1   *"It walks like analogy, it talks like analogy . . ."*

If lexical diffusion is not sound change, could it be treated as a subtype of one of the other two basic categories of change? Clearly it is quite unlike lexical *borrowing*: it requires no contact with another language or dialect (i.e., it is not reducible to "dialect mixture"), it follows a systemic direction set by the language's own phonological system (it is a species of "drift"), and it involves a change in the pronunciation of existing words rather than the introduction of new ones.

On the other hand, it does behave like lexical *analogy* in every respect, as summarized in the following table.[3]

Table 21.1

	Sound change	Borrowing	Lexical analogy	Lexical diffusion
Generality	Across-the-board	Item by item	Context by context, item by item	Context by context, item by item
Gradience	Gradient	Quantal	Quantal	Quantal
Origin	Endogenous	Contact	Endogenous	Endogenous
Rate	Rapid	Rapid	Slow	Slow
Effect on:				
Rule system	New rules	No change	Rules generalized	Rules generalized
Sound/phoneme inventory	New inventory	Peripheral	No change	No change
Vocabulary	No change	New words	No change	No change

It seems to be the case that lexical diffusion always involves neutralization rules, or equivalently that lexical diffusion is structure preserving (Kiparsky 1980, p. 412). This has been taken as evidence for locating lexical diffusion in the lexical component of the phonology (Kiparsky 1988). Being a redistribution of phonemes among lexical items, it cannot produce any new sounds or alter the system of phonological contrasts. Its nongradient character follows from this assumption as well, since lexical rules must operate with discrete categorical specifications of features.

An important clue to the identity of the process is its driftlike spread through the lexicon, by which it extends a phonological process context by context, and within each new context item by item. This is of course exactly the behavior we find in many analogical changes. An example of such lexical diffusion is the shortening of English /ū/, which was extended from its core environment (1a), where it was categorical, by relaxing its context both on the left and on the right (Dickerson 1975). In its extended environments it applies in a lexically idiosyncratic manner. The essential pattern is as follows:

(1) (a) [−anterior] ___ $\begin{bmatrix} -\text{anterior} \\ -\text{coronal} \end{bmatrix}$

    cook, hook, shook, rook, brook, crook, hookah (short)

(b) ___ $\begin{bmatrix} \text{–anterior} \\ \text{–coronal} \end{bmatrix}$

took, book, nook, look, forsook, Wookie (short)
snook, snooker, stook, boogie, Sook, gadzooks, spook (variable)
bazooka (long)

(c)   [–anterior] ___

good, could, should, hood "covering", hoodwink (short)
roof, rooster, hoodlum, cooper, hoof, room, root, hoodlum, hood
"ruffian", coop, proof (variable)
brood, shoot, hoot, behoove, scoop, coon, coot, roost, groove
. . . (long)

We can provide a theoretical home for such a mechanism of change if we adopt lexical phonology and combine it with a conception of analogical change as an optimization process which eliminates idiosyncratic complexity from the system – in effect, as grammar simplification.[4] The mechanism that drives such redistribution of phonemes in the lexicon is the system of structure-building rules in the lexical phonology. The direction of the phonemic replacement is determined by the rule, and its actuation is triggered jointly by the generalization of the rule to new contexts, and by the item-by-item simplification of lexical representations in each context. When idiosyncratic feature specifications are eliminated from lexical entries, the features automatically default to the values assigned by the rule system, just as when the special form *kine* is lost from the lexicon the plural of *cow* automatically defaults to *cows*. The fact that in the lexical diffusion case there is no morphological proportion for the analogy need not cause concern, for we must recognize many other kinds of nonproportional analogy anyway.

To spell this out, we will need to look at how unspecified lexical representations combine with structure-building rules to account for distributional regularities in the lexicon. This is the topic of the next section.

1.2   The Idea behind Underspecification

The idea of underspecification is a corollary of the Jakobsonian view of distinctive features as the real ultimate components of speech. All versions of autosegmental phonology adopt it in the form of an assumption that a feature can only be associated with a specific class of segments designated as permissible bearers of it (P-bearing elements), and that such segments may be lexically unassociated with P and acquire an association to P in the course of the phonological derivation. But in phonological discussions the term "underspecification" has come to be associated with two further claims, mostly associated with lexical phonology, namely that the class of P-bearing segments may be extended in the course of derivation, and that lexical (underlying) representations are minimally specified.

How minimal is minimal? There are several alternative versions of underspecification on the market which differ in their answers to this question.[5] The most conservative position, *restricted underspecification,* is simply that redundant features are lexically unspecified. On this view, the feature of voicing in English would be specified for obstruents, where it is contrastive, but not for sonorants, which are redundantly voiced. An entirely nondistinctive feature, such as aspiration in English, would not be specified in lexical representation at all.

Radical underspecification (the version which I will assume later on) carries the asymmetry of feature specifications one step further, by allowing only one value to be specified underlyingly in any given context in lexical representations, namely, the negation of the value assigned in that context by the system of lexical rules. A feature is only specified in a lexical entry if that is necessary to defeat a rule which would assign the "wrong" value to it. The default values of a feature are assigned to segments not specified for it at a stage in the derivation which may vary language-specifically within certain bounds.

A third position, departing even further from *SPE,* and currently under exploration in several quarters, holds that the unmarked value is never introduced, so that features are in effect one-valued (privative).

Contrastive and radical underspecification both posit *redundancy rules* such as:

(2) [+ sonorant] → [+ voiced]

Radical underspecifications in addition posits *default rules,* minimally a context-free rule for each feature which assigns the unmarked value to it:

(3) [   ] → [−voiced]

The following chart summarizes the theoretical options, and exemplifies them with the values of the feature [voiced] which they respectively stipulate for voiceless obstruents, voiced obstruents, and sonorants, at the initial and final levels of representation:

(4)

		/p/	/b/	/r/
None (full specification)	Lexical: fully specified	—	+	+
	Phonetic: fully specified	—	+	+
Contrastive	Lexical: contrastive values	—	+	+
	Phonetic: fully specified	—	+	+
Radical	Lexical: minimal specifications		+	+
	Phonetic: fully specified	—	+	+
Privative	Lexical: only marked values		+	
	Phonetic: only marked values		+	

As (4) shows, fully specified representations and privative representations are homogenous throughout the phonology. Contrastive underspecification and radical underspecification both make available *two representations*, by allowing an underlying minimal structure to be augmented in the course of the derivation.

Radical underspecification moreover assumes that default values are assigned by the entire system of structure-building lexical rules. For example, in a language with a lexical rule of intervocalic voicing such as (5),[6] the lexical marking of obstruents in intervocalic position would be the reverse of what it is in other positions, with voiced consonants unmarked and voiceless ones carrying the feature specification [−voiced] to block the rule.

(5)   [   ] → [+voiced] / V ＿＿ V

At what point are default values and redundant values to be assigned? I will here assume that default feature values are filled in before the first rule that mentions a specific value of that feature.[7] Many assimilation rules do not mention a specific feature value, but simply spread the feature itself, or a class node under which that feature is lodged. Such rules can apply before the assignment of default values, yielding the characteristic pattern "assimilate, else default."

To summarize:

(6)   (a)   For each feature F, a universal default rule of the form [   ] → [αF] applies in every language.
      (b)   In each environment E in underlying representations, a feature must be either specified as [αF] or unspecified, where E is defined by the most specific applicable rule R, and R assigns [$-\alpha$F].
      (c)   Default feature values are filled in before the first rule that mentions a specific value of that feature.

(6a) guarantees that the basic choice of unmarked value of a feature is fixed language-independently, but leaves open the possibility that particular rules (universal as well as language-specific) may supersede it in special contexts. (6b) says essentially that the lexicon is minimally redundant: feature specifications are only allowed where needed to defeat rules. Subject to (6c), default feature values can be assigned either cyclically, at the word level, or post-lexically. Redundant values are normally assigned post-lexically.

An early argument for radical underspecification was that it makes it possible to extend the first level of phonological rules to account for the structure of morphemes (Kiparsky 1982), eliminating from the theory the extremely problematic "Morpheme Structure Constraints (MSC)," never satisfactorily formalized, and heir to a multitude of embarrassing problems and paradoxes. The structure of morphemes in a language can now be treated simply as derivative of the rules and conditions on its earliest level of phonological representations.[8]

The distinction between structure-changing and structure-building (feature-filling) operations is important here. Feature-changing assimilations (i.e., those which override existing feature specifications) have been shown to consist of two independent processes, delinking of the features of the target, followed by spread of a feature to it (Poser 1982; Cho 1990). The introduction of structure-building rules, which make essential use of radical underspecification, has several striking consequences. It has provided the basis for new accounts of "strict cycle" effects (Kiparsky 1993) and of inalterability (Inkelas and Cho 1993). If these prove to be correct, they will provide the strongest kind of support for underspecification. My contention here is that it is also implicated in the explanation of lexical diffusion. In the next section, we will see how this works.

1.3   *Lexical Diffusion as Analogy*

Equipped with this theory of lexical rules and representations, let us go back to the *ū*-shortening process (1) to illustrate the general idea. [ū] and [ŭ] are in the kind of semi-regular distribution that typically sets off lexical diffusion processes. The core context (1a) has almost only [ŭ] to this day. Exceptions seem to occur only in affective or facetious words of recent vintage: *googol (-plex), googly, kook*. And the context most distant from the core, not included in any of the extensions of (1a), has overwhelmingly long [ū]: *doom, stoop, boom, poop, boob, snood, loose, Moomin, loom, baboon, spoof, snooze, snoot, snoop,* etc. Even here some subregularities can be detected. There are a few shortened [ŭ]'s before coronals even if the onset is coronal or labial (*foot, stood, toots(ie), soot* versus *booth, moon, pool, tool, loose, spoon, food, mood, moose* . . . with long [ū]). Before labials, however, the exclusion of short [ŭ] is near-categorical.[9]

Let us suppose that the core regularity is reflected in the lexical phonology of English by a rule which assigns a single mora or vocalic slot to stressed /u/ between certain consonants, and two moras or vocalic slots elsewhere, provided that syllable structure allows. Suppose the original context of this rule was [−anterior] ＿＿＿ [−anterior, −coronal]. As a structure-building rule it can, however, be extended to apply in the contexts (1b) and (1c). This part of the change is a natural generalization (simplification) of the rule's environment, in principle no different from the extension of a morphological element to some new context. But because structure-building rules are defeasible by lexical information, such an extension of the shortening rule need not effect any overt change at first: the extended rule simply applies (in the synchronic grammar) to the words which always had short [ŭ] in that context, now reanalyzed as quantitatively unmarked, while words with long [ū] in those contexts are now prespecified with two moras in the lexicon to escape the effect of the generalized shortening rule. But once the rule's context is so extended, words can fall under its scope, slowly and one at a time, simply by being "regularized" through loss of the prespecified length in their underlying representations. This is the lexical diffusion part of the process.

The model for this phase of the analogical regularization is the existence of a systematic context (the core shortening environment) where length is systematically predictable, which is extended on a case-by-case basis. The normal scenario of lexical diffusion, then, is contextual rule generalization with attendant markedness reversal and subsequent item-by-item simplification of the lexicon. In principal, it could proceed until the rule is extended to all contexts and all quantitative marking is lost in the lexicon. In this example, however, the robust exclusion of short [ŭ] in the context between labials sets a barrier to further extension of the rule to those contexts. The result is the pattern of partial complementation that we find in the modern English distribution of [ŭ] and [ū].

Let us now turn to the rule which thanks to Labov's work has become the most famous case of lexical diffusion: the "æ-Tensing" of Philadelphia and several other Eastern U.S. dialects, applying in the core environment before tautosyllabic -*f*, -*s*, -*θ*, -*n*, -*m*.

First, I would like to raise a terminological point, relating to a larger issue of fact which is tricky but luckily does not have to be settled here. Although usually referred to as æ-Tensing, æ-Lengthening would be a more appropriate term because the vowel is not always tense. Phonetically, it is typically a lax long [ɛ] in the dialects I am concerned here with (see, e.g., Bailey 1985, p. 174). Phonologically, that may be a better analysis as well, because it is the same vowel as the word-finally lengthened lax [ɛ] in the truncated form of *yes* ("*yeah*"). At least in the feature system that I will be using in section 3.2 below, this is a genuine [–Tense] vowel. But since it won't make much of a difference for present purposes, I'll just follow tradition and continue to talk of "Tensing," while writing the "tensed" vowel noncommittally as *A*.

What is the status of [æ] and [A] in these dialects? Are the two phonemically distinct? Is their distribution governed by rule? It is clear that they are two distinct phonemes, in the sense that there is an irreducible lexical contrast between them in certain environments. From the viewpoint of many phonological theories, that settles the second question as well: they contrast and they do not alternate with each other, so their distribution cannot be rule-governed.

The distribution of [æ] and [A] is however far from random. In the framework proposed in Kiparsky (1982c), the regularities that govern it have a place in the lexical module of the grammar as structure-building lexical rules which assign the appropriate default specifications of tenseness to the underlying unspecified low front vowel, which we can write /*a*/. The lexicon need specify only those comparatively few instances of lax /æ/ which fall out of line. This analysis follows from the requirement (6b) that the redundancy of the lexicon must be reduced to a minimum.

The Philadelphia version of æ-Tensing (Ferguson 1975; Kiparsky 1988; Labov 1981, 1993) includes all the core environments -*f*, -*s*, -*θ*, -*n*, -*m* as well as the extension -*d*, -*l*, as discussed further below.

(7) Philadelphia lexical æ-Tensing rule:
   æ → A before tautosyllabic *f, s, θ, m, n, (d, l)*

In New York, the rule applies also more generally before voiced stops and before -š.

(8) New York lexical æ-Tensing rule:
   æ → A before tautosyllabic *f, s, θ, š, m, n, b, d, ǰ, g*

In accord with our previous discussion, (7) and (8) are structure-building rules which assign [+Tense] to *a* in regular words like (9a). The value [–Tense] is then assigned by default to *a* in regular words like (9b). The only cases of lexically specified Tenseness are exceptional words with [–Tense] in Tensing environments, such as [9c]:

(9) (a) pAss, pAth, hAm, mAn
    (b) mat, cap, passive, panic
    (c) alas, wrath

   In fact, the unpredictable cases for which lexical specification of [±Tense] is required are probably even fewer than is apparent at first blush. Consider the contrast before consonant clusters in polysyllables illustrated by the words in (10):

(10) (a) astronaut, African, plastic, master (lax *æ* OK)
    (b) After, Afterwards, Ambush, Athlete[10] (Tense A)

These data follow directly from rule (7) on standard assumptions about English syllable structure. English syllabification tends to maximize onsets, and *str-, fr-* are possible onsets, but *ft-, mb-, θl-* are not, so the relevant VC sequence has to be tautosyllabic in (10b) but tends to be heterosyllabic in (10a). Independent evidence for this syllabification is the fact that vowel reduction, restricted to unstressed open syllables, is possible before permitted onsets, as in *astronomy,* but not before other clusters, as in *athletic* (Kahn 1976).[11]
   Rule (7) must apply at level 1 in the lexical phonology of English. Five arguments for this position were given in Kiparsky (1988). We can now add two more. First, the observations in the preceding paragraph show that (7) must precede the "left capture" rule that attaches onset consonants to a preceding stressed syllable (perhaps making them ambisyllabic). But left capture can be shown to apply at level 1 (as well as at later levels), so æ-Tensing must apply at level 1 as well. The evidence that left capture applies at level 1 is the pattern of shortening seen in derived words such as (11):

(11) (a) cȳcle cȳclic cȳclicity
    (b) trībe trībal trībality

Myers (1987) has shown that the various English shortening processes, including "Trisyllabic Shortening" and the shortening before -ic as in *cycle ~ cyclic*, are special cases of a general lexical rule which shortens nuclei in closed syllables, including those which become closed through the application of "left capture" resyllabification. But the short initial syllable of *cyclicity* is clearly inherited from *cyclic*, since the conditions for shortening no longer hold in the derivative *cyclicity* (cf. *tribality*). It follows that the shortening must be cyclic. Therefore, the left capture rule that feeds shortening, as well as the æ-Tensing rule (7) that itself precedes left capture, must also be cyclic. But cyclic phonology is located at level 1.

My second new argument for the level 1 status of æ-Tensing is that it explains the variation in the past tenses of strong verbs such as *ran, swam, began*. These /æ/-vowels are regularly lax in Philadelphia, a fact accounted for by ordering æ-Tensing before the æ → A ablaut rule which introduces /æ/ in the past tense. Since ablaut is a level 1 rule, æ-Tensing, which precedes it, must also apply at level 1. The possibility of applying the rules in reverse order, still within level 1, predicts a dialect in which the vowels of these verb forms do undergo æ-Tensing. Such a dialect is in fact attested in New York, as Labov notes. In contrast, nonmajor category words such as *am, had, can* and the interjections *wham!, bam!* have lax æ in all dialects where æ-Tensing is lexical. The lack of variation in these cases is likewise predicted because nonlexical categories are not subject to the rules of lexical phonology.

With these synchronic preliminaries out of the way, let us turn to the rule's lexical diffusion. Labov shows that [+Tense] vowels have replaced (or are in the process of replacing) [–Tense] vowels in a class of words in Philadelphia, especially in the speech of children and adolescents. The innovating class of words includes: (1) words in which æ is in the proper consonantal environment of the tensing rule (7) but, contrary to what the core rule requires, in an open syllable, such as (12a), and (2) words in which æ is before *l* and *d*, voiced consonants not included among the rule's original triggers.[12] In cases like (12c), both extensions of the rule are combined.

(12) (a) plAnet, dAmage, mAnage, flAnnel
      (b) mAd, bAd, glAd, pAl
      (c) personAlity, Alley, Allegheny

There are several facts that need explaining about these developments. First, the environments into which tense *A* is being extended are not arbitrary phonologically. There is no "lexical diffusion" of *A* before voiceless stops, the class of consonants that is systematically excluded from the core tensing environment as well as from the Philadelphia and New York versions of the rule. Second, there are no reported cases of lax æ being extended into words which have regular tense *A* in accord with (7), e.g., in words like *man, ham, pass*. Third, [æ] changes not to any old vowel, but precisely to [A], the very vowel with which it is in partial complementation by (7).

If we assume that lexical diffusion is nothing more than the substitution of one phoneme for another in the lexical representations of words, we have no explanation either for the direction of the change, nor for the envelope of phonological conditions that continues to control it. Such a theory cannot distinguish the Philadelphia development from a wholly random redistribution of tense and lax *a*, nor even explain why it should involve this particular pair of vowels at all.

If we recognize that the distribution of tense and lax *a* in Philadelphia is an analogical extension of rule (7), then we are in a position to explain these facts. The phonological conditions under which tense *A* spreads through the lexicon are an extension of the rule's original context in two respects: (1) the condition requiring the triggering consonant to be tautosyllabic is dropped (here one might also explore the possibility that the tensing rule gets reordered after left capture), and (2) *l*, *d* are included among the conditioning consonants. This development conforms to the pattern of contextual generalization with item-by-item implementation of the extended environment that is typical of lexical diffusion. The scenario is similar to the one sketched out above for the shortening of /ū/. The old tensing rule, applicable before a class of tautosyllabic consonants, is generalized by some speakers to apply before certain additional consonants and the tautosyllabicity condition is dropped. Speakers who have internalized the rule in this generalized form can pronounce tense *A* in words of the type (12). But being structure-building (feature-filling), the rule applies only to vowels underspecified for the feature of tenseness, and speakers with the generalized rule can still get lax *æ* in the new contexts by specifying the vowels in question as law in their lexical representation. In the resulting variation in the speech community, the generalized rule, and the forms reflecting the unmarked lexical representations, will enjoy a selective advantage which causes them gradually to gain ground.

I conclude that *æ*-Tensing supports the claim that lexical diffusion is the analogical extension of structure-building lexical rules. We see that, on the right assumptions about the organization of phonology and about analogical change, lexical diffusion fits snugly into the neogrammarian triad, and all its by now familiar properties are accounted for. A wider moral that might be drawn from this result is that even "static" distributional regularities in the lexicon, often neglected in favor of productive alternations, can play a role both in synchronic phonology and in analogical change.

1.4   *What Features are Subject to Diffusion?*

According to the present proposal, the prerequisite for lexical diffusion is a context-sensitive structure-building lexical rule and its starting point is an existing site of neutralization or partial neutralization of the relevant feature in lexical representations. The original environment of the *æ*-Tensing rule (originally the broad *a* rule) was before tautosyllabic *f*, *s*, *θ*, *-nt*, *-ns*, as in *pass*, *path*,

laugh, aunt, dance. It became generalized to apply before the nasals *n, m* in all
the Mid-Atlantic dialects, and later before voiced stops as well (see (7) and
(8)). The cause of this generalization of the lexical æ-Tensing rule is probably
the merger with a *post-lexical* raising/tensing rule in those dialects where their
outputs coincided (Kiparsky 1971, 1988). In those dialects which either lacked
the lexical rule entirely (as in the Northern Cities), or retained it as a different
rule (as in Boston, where broad *a* was pronounced as [a]), the post-lexical æ-
tensing rule can today be observed as a separate process in several variant
forms. In the Northern Cities, it yields a continuum of tensing and raising,
with most tensing before nasals and least tensing before voiceless stops.

(13)   Tensing environments in Northern Cities dialects:

      nasals   voiced stops   fricatives   voiceless stops
      (tensest)   ←————————————————→   (laxest)

In Boston, only the environment at the top of the scale, the nasals, triggers
tensing and raising; before other consonants, the dialect retains lax æ (Labov
1993).

    The merger of the inherited lexical æ-Tensing rule with these two types of
post-lexical æ-Tensing gives the Philadelphia and New York versions of lexical
æ-Tensing, respectively. Specifically, by adding the environments of the original lexical æ-Tensing rule (-*f*, -*s*, -*θ*, -*ns*, -*nt*) and the environments of the post-
lexical æ-Tensing/Raising of the Boston type (nasals), we get exactly the
environments of the core Philadelphia rule (7). And by adding the environments of the original lexical æ-Tensing rule and the most active environments
of the post-lexical æ-Tensing/Raising of the Northern Cities type (13) (nasals,
voiced stops, and fricatives), we get very nearly the New York rule (8). Only
the failure of -*ŋ* to trigger æ-Tensing in New York remains unexplained.[13]

    Having acquired lexical status in this way, Tensing then spreads to new
lexical items, that is, it undergoes lexical diffusion. Thus, the lexical diffusion
of æ-Tensing in the Mid-Atlantic dialects is due to its lexical status in those
dialects, inherited from the lexical broad *a* rule of British English.

    Labov (1981, 1993) makes the interesting suggestion that lexical diffusion is
an intrinsic characteristic of some kinds of phonological features and neogrammarian sound change is characteristic of others. Lexical diffusion affects
"higher order classes," phonological features such as tenseness and length,
which are defined in terms of several unrelated phonetic properties, such as
duration, height, peripherality, and diphthongization. Features like front/back
and high/low, on the other hand, will not undergo lexical diffusion because
their physical realization is more direct. If lexical diffusion really does depend
on whether a feature is realized on a single physical dimension or on several,
my account of lexical diffusion as the analogical extension of structure-building lexical rules would have to be given up at least in its present form.

    One problem with Labov's idea is that æ-Lengthening, though it involves the same feature in all dialects, undergoes lexical diffusion in the Mid-Atlantic dialects and not in the Northern Cities. In response to that objection, Labov suggests that the rule operates at a "high level of abstraction" in the Mid-Atlantic dialects and at a "low level of abstraction" in the Northern Cities. But this amounts to using the term "abstraction" in two different senses. On the one hand, it is a phonetic property having to do with the degree of diversity and complexity of the feature's phonetic correlates. With respect to æ-Tensing, however, it has to be understood in a functional/structural sense, as something like the distinction between phonemic and allophonic status, or lexical and postlexical status – for that seems to be the one relevant distinction between the Mid-Atlantic and the Northern Cities versions of æ-Tensing. But there is no reason to believe that these two kinds of "abstraction" can be identified with each other. Certainly features differ in the intrinsic complexity and diversity of their phonetic realizations: stress and tenseness probably tend to have relatively complex and diverse phonetic effects, whereas fronting, lip rounding, height, and voicing probably tend to have more uniform phonetic effects. But this would appear to be true whether they are distinctive or redundant. I know of no evidence to show that the intrinsic complexity and diversity of the phonetic reflexes of a feature is correlated with its lexical/phonemic status, let alone that these two kinds of "abstractness" are the same thing.

The interpretation of lexical diffusion that I have advocated here would entail that the structural notion of abstractness is all we need, and the phonetic character of the feature should be immaterial. The generalization that only lexically distinctive features can undergo lexical diffusion, itself a rigorous consequence of LPM principles, predicts exactly the observed difference between the Mid-Atlantic dialects and the other U.S. dialects. The contrast between them shows that the same feature, assigned by one and the same rule in fact, can be subject to lexical diffusion in one dialect and not in another, depending only on whether it is lexically distinctive or redundant. In addition, it also correctly predicts the existence of lexical diffusion in such features as height and voicing, which on Labov's proposal should not be subject to it.[14]

2 The Structure-dependence of Sound Change

2.1 *Sound Change is Not Blind*

The majority of structuralists, European as well as American, thought they could account for phonological structure even while conceding to the neogrammarians that sound changes are "blind" phonetic processes. In their view, the reason languages have orderly phonological systems is that learners impose them on the phonetic data, by grouping sounds into classes and arranging them into a system of relational oppositions, and by formulating distributional regularities and patterns of alternation between them. The reason languages have phonological systems of only certain kinds would then have to be that learners are able to impose just such systems on bodies of phonetic data. But, on their scheme of things, fairly simple all-purpose acquisition procedures were assumed to underlie the organization and typology of phonological inventories, and the combinatorial regularities apprehended by learners.

It seems clear, however, that a battery of blind sound changes operating on a language should eventually produce systems whose phonemicization by the standard procedures would violate every phonological universal in the book. The linguist who most clearly saw that there is a problem here was Jakobson (1929). Emphasizing that phonological structure cannot simply be an organization imposed ex post facto on the results of blind sound change, he categorically rejected the neogrammarian doctrine in favor of a structure-governed conception modeled on the theory of orthogenesis (or nomogenesis) in evolutionary biology (a theory now thoroughly discredited, but for which Jakobson always maintained a sneaking fondness). His basic thesis is that sound changes have an inherent direction ("elles vont selon des directions déterminées") towards certain structural targets.[15]

Jakobson was in fact able to cite fairly convincing long-term tendencies in the phonological evolution of Slavic, involving the establishment of proto-Slavic CV syllable structure by a variety of processes (degemination, cluster simplification, metathesis, prothesis of consonants, coalescence of C + *y*, coalescence of V + nasal), and the rise of palatal harmony in the syllable domain through a series of reciprocal assimilations. Since it is human to read patterns into random events, it would be prudent to look at such arguments with a measure of suspicion. But the number and diversity of phonological processes collaborating to one end do make Jakobson's case persuasive. Others have since argued for similar conclusions. For example, Riad (1992), working in the framework of prosodic generative phonology, has analyzed the major sound changes in North Germanic over the past two millennia as so many stepwise resolutions of an inherent conflict between fixed accent, free quantity, and bimoraic foot structure.

Jakobson further argued that sound change respects principles of universal grammar, including *implicational universals*. The point is quite simple. How could an implicational relation between two phonological properties A and B have any universal validity if sound changes, operating blindly, were capable of changing the phonetic substrate of A and B independently of each other?

Moreover, Jakobson's implicational universals were crucially formulated in terms of *distinctive* features. But purely phonetically conditioned sound changes should not care about what is distinctive in the language (distinctiveness being, by the structuralists' assumptions, a purely structural property imposed a posteriori on the phonetic substance). So what prevents sound change from applying in such a way as to produce phonological systems that violate universals couched in terms of the notion of distinctiveness?

For some reason, Jakobson's work is rarely taken notice of in the literature on sound change, and I am not aware of any explicit attempts to refute it. Perhaps it has simply been rejected out of hand on the grounds that it begs the question by invoking a mysterious mechanism of orthogenesis which itself has no explanation, and that in addition, it throws away the only explanation we have for the regularity and exceptionlessness which are undeniably characteristics of a major class of sound changes. Nevertheless, the existence of sound changes that respect structure and are derived by it in certain ways seems well supported. How can we account for the coexisting properties of exceptionlessness and structure-dependence?

I believe that Jakobson was on the right track in looking to evolutionary biology as a paradigm for historical linguistics. We just need to reject the disreputable version of evolutionary theory that he claimed to be inspired by and replace it by the modern view of variation and selection. In the domain of sound change, the analog to natural selection is the inherently selective process of transmission that incorporates them into the linguistic system. Thus sound change is both mechanical in the neogrammarian sense, and at the same time structure-dependent, though not exactly in the way Jakobson thought.

We are now free to assume that variation at the level of speech production is conditioned purely by phonetic factors, independently of the language's phonological structure, and to use this property to derive the exceptionlessness property, just as the neogrammarians and structuralists did. The essential move is to assign a more active role to the transmission process, which allows it to intervene as a selectional mechanism in language change. Traditionally, the acquisition of phonology was thought of simply as a process of organizing the primary data of the ambient language according to some general set of principles (for example, in the case of the structuralists, by segmenting it and grouping the segments into classes by contrast and complementation, and in the case of generative grammar, by projecting the optimal grammar consistent with it on the basis of Universal Grammar). On our view, the learner in addition selectively intervenes in the data, favoring those variants which best conform to the language's system. Variants which contravene language-specific structural principles will be hard to learn, and so will have less of a chance of being incorporated into the system. Even "impossible" innovations can be admitted into the pool of phonetic variation; they will simply never make it into anyone's grammar.

The combined action of variation and selection solves another neglected problem of historical phonology. The textbook story on phonologization is that redundant features become phonemic when their conditioning environment is lost through sound change. This process (so-called secondary split) is undoubtedly an important mechanism through which new phonological oppositions enter a language. But the textbooks draw a discreet veil over the other cases, surely at least equally common, where – in what may seem to be exactly analogous situations – the redundant feature simply disappears when its triggering environment is lost.

The two types of outcome are not just distributed at random. The key generalization seems to be that phonologization will result more readily if the feature is of a type which already exists in the language. We could call this the *priming effect* and provisionally formulate it as follows:

(14)   Redundant features are likely to be phonologized if the language's phonological representations have a class node to host them.

This priming effect, a diachronic manifestation of structure-preservation is documented for several types of sound change, tonogenesis being perhaps the most interesting case. The merger of voiced and voiceless consonants normally leaves a tone/register distinction *only in languages which already possess a tone system* (Svantesson 1989). There is one special circumstance under which nontonal languages can acquire tone by loss of a voicing contrast: in certain Mon-Khmer languages, according to Svantesson, "strong areal pressure to conform to the phonological pattern of those monosyllabic tone languages that dominate the area" (ibid.). It seems, then, that when the voicing that induces redundant pitch is suppressed, the pitch will normally be phonologized only if the language, or another language with which its speakers are in contact, already has a tonal node to host it. On the neogrammarian/structuralist understanding, the priming effect remains mysterious. On our variation/ selection model, such top-down effects are exactly what is expected.

Analogous priming effects can be observed in such changes as compensatory lengthening and assimilation. De Chene and Anderson (1979) find that loss of a consonant only causes compensatory vowel lengthening when there is a preexisting length contrast in the language. So the scenario is that languages first acquire contrastive length through other means (typically by vowel coalescence); then only do they augment their inventory of long vowels by compensatory lengthening.[16] Yet loss with compensatory lengthening is a quintessentially regular, neogrammarian type of sound change (in recent work analyzed as the deletion of features associated with a slot with concomitant spread of features from a neighboring segment into the vacated slot). Similarly, total assimilation of consonant clusters resulting in geminates seem to happen primarily (perhaps only?) in languages that already have geminates (Finnish, Ancient Greek, Latin, Italian). Languages with no pre-existing geminates prefer to simplify clusters by just dropping one of the consonants (English, German, French, Modern Greek). In sum, we find a conjunction of exceptionlessness and structure-sensitivity in sound change which does not sit well with the neogrammarian/structuralist scheme. The two-level variation/ selection model of change proposed is in a position to make much better sense of it.

The two-level scheme can be related to certain proposals by phonemic theorists. It has often been argued that redundant features help to perceptually identify the distinctive features on which they structurally depend.[17] Korhonen (1969, pp. 333–335) suggests that only certain allophones, which he calls *quasi-phonemes*, have such a functional role, and that it is just these which become phonemicized when the conditioning context is lost. This amounts to a two-stage model of secondary split which (at least implicitly) recognizes the problem we have just addressed: in the first stage, some redundant features become quasi-distinctive, and in the second stage, quasi-distinctive features become distinctive when their conditioning is lost. If the conditions which trigger the first stage were specified in a way that is equivalent to (14), this proposal would be similar to the one put forward above. Korhonen's suggestion is however based on the direction of allophonic conditioning: according to him, it is allophones which precede their conditioning environment (and only they?) which become quasi-phonemicized. This is perceptually implausible, and does not agree with what is known about secondary split, including tonogenesis. Ebeling (1960) and Zinder (1979) propose entities equivalent to Korhonen's quasi-phonemes in order to account for cases where allophones spread to new contexts by morphological analogy. They do not spell out the conditions under which allophones acquire this putative quasi-distinctive status either. However, the cases they discuss fit in very well with the priming effect, since they involve features which are already distinctive in some segments of the language and redundant in others becoming distinctive in the latter as well.

2.2   The Life Cycle of Phonological Rules

Early generative work on historical phonology thought of sound change as rule addition. One of the most interesting consequences of this idea was that sound changes should be capable of nonphonetic conditioning, through the addition of morphologically conditioned rules, and through the addition of rules in places other than the end of the grammar ("rule insertion"). But of course not just any sort of nonphonetic conditioning is possible. It turned out that the only good cases of rule insertion involved the addition of rules before automatic (transparent) rules, often of a phonetic character, so that an interpretation along the lines of the above structure-preservation story seems more likely. Moreover, this approach by itself does not explain one of the most basic facts about sound change, its phonetic naturalness. Nor, in the final analysis, does it address the question of the relationship between universals and change in a principled way.

By articulating the phonological component into a set of modules with different properties, lexical phonology allows us to think of sound change in a more constrained way that is still consistent with the selection/variation model (Kiparsky 1988). Sound change can be assumed to originate through synchronic variation in the production, perception, and acquisition of language, from where it is internalized by language learners as part of their phonological system. The changes enter the system as language-specific phonetic implementation rules, which are inherently gradient and may give rise to new segments or combinations of segments. These phonetic implementation rules may in turn become reinterpreted as phonological rules, either post-lexical or lexical, as the constraints of the theory require, at which point the appropriate structural conditions are imposed on them by the principles governing that module. In the phonologized stages of their life cycle, rules tend to rise in the hierarchy of levels, with level 1 as their final resting place (Zec 1993).

In addition to articulatory variation, speech is subject to variation that originates in perception and acquisition, driven by the possibility of alternative parsing of the speech output (Ohala 1986, 1989). Sound changes that originate in this fashion clearly need not be gradient, but can proceed in abrupt discrete steps. Moreover, like all reinterpretation processes, they should be subject to inherent top-down constraints defined by the linguistic system: the "wrong" parses that generate them should spring from a plausible phonological analysis. Therefore, context-sensitive reinterpretations would be expected not to introduce new segments into the system, and context-free reinterpretations (such as British Celtic $k^w \rightarrow p$) would be expected not to introduce new features into the system; and neither should introduce exceptional phonotactic combinations.

Dissimilation provides perhaps the most convincing confirmation of this prediction. That dissimilatory sound changes have special properties of theoretical interest for the debate on levels of phonological representation was first pointed out by Schane (1971). Schane marshaled evidence in support of the claim that "if a feature is contrastive in some environments but not in others, that feature is lost when there is no contrast," and argued on this basis for reality of phonemic representations. Manaster-Ramer (1988) convincingly showed that the contrastiveness of the environment is not a factor in such cases, and rejected Schane's argument for the phoneme entirely. However, all his examples, as well as Schane's, conform to a kindred generalization which still speaks for the role of distinctiveness in sound change: *only features which are contrastive in the language are subject to dissimilation*. But in this form, the generalization is a corollary of what we have already said. The reasoning goes as follows. Dissimilation is not a natural articulatory process. Therefore, it must arise by means of perceptual reanalysis. But the reanalyzed form should be a well-formed structure of the language, hence in particular one representable in terms of its authentic phonological inventory.

The other properties of dissimilation, that it is quantal rather than gradual, and that it is often sporadic, can be derived in the same way. They likewise hold for the other so-called minor sound changes, such as metathesis. Not that minor sound changes are *necessarily* sporadic. On the contrary, they will be regular when the phonotactic constraints of the language so dictate. Dissimilation is regular where it serves to implement constraints such as Grassmann's

Law, and the same is true of metathesis (Hock 1985; Ultan 1978): e.g., the Slavic liquid metathesis is part of the phonological apparatus that implements the above-mentioned syllable structure constraints.

The respective properties of major and minor sound changes are summarized in (15):

(15)		Major changes	Minor changes
	Source in speech:	Production	Perception and acquisition
	Parameter of change:	Articulatory similarity	Acoustic similarity
	Gradiency:	Gradient	Discrete
	Effect on system:	New segments and combinations	Structure-preserving
	Regularity:	Exceptionless	Can be sporadic

Conditions on sound change can then be seen as categorical reinterpretations of the variable constraints that determine the way optional rules apply. Because of the formal constraints on possible structural conditions, obligatory rules cannot fully replicate the complex pattern of preferences generated in language use at the optional stage. Consequently, when a rule becomes obligatory, its spectrum of contextual conditions is simplified and polarized. Thus, this view of sound change explains both why structural conditions on phonological rules retain a gross form of naturalness, and why they nevertheless do not show the intricate microconditioning observed at the level of phonetic implementation.

Not only are phonological conditions on rules derived from phonetic conditions motivated by perception and production, but also the nature of conditions involving morphology, style, and even sex and class can be explained in the same way. For example, some languages of India have undergone sound changes restricted to the speech of lower castes. Such changes are a categorical reflection, under conditions where social boundaries are sharply drawn, of the generally more advanced nature of vernacular speech, due to the fact that the elite tends to stigmatize and inhibit linguistic innovations for ideological reasons (Kroch 1978).

Our conclusion so far is that the neogrammarians were right in regarding sound change as a process endogenous to language, and their exceptionlessness hypothesis is correct for changes that originate as phonetic implementation rules. They were wrong, however, in believing that sound change per se, as a mechanism of change, is structure-blind and random. The process also involves an integration of speech variants into the grammar, at which point system-conforming speech variants have a selective advantage which causes them to be preferentially adopted. In this way, the language's internal structure can channel its own evolution, giving rise to long-term tendencies of sound change.

3 Naturalness in Sound Change

The study of natural phonology offers a further argument for the structure-dependence of even neogrammarian-type exceptionless sound change, and thereby for the selection/variation view of sound change. In this section, I support this claim by showing the role that underspecification plays in the explanation of natural assimilation rules and vowel shifts – not only of the synchronic rules, but equally, and perhaps in greater measure, of the historical processes that they reflect.

3.1 *The Typology of Assimilation*

Autosegmental phonology allows assimilation to be treated as the spread of a feature or feature complex from an adjacent position. Coupled with assumptions about underspecification, feature geometry, and the locality of phonological processes, it yields a rich set of predictions about possible assimilation rules. Cho (1990) has developed a parametric theory of assimilation based on these assumptions. The following discussion draws heavily on her work, which, though formulated as a contribution to synchronic phonology, bears directly on sound change as well.

If feature-changing processes consist of feature deletion plus feature filling, we can say that assimilation is fed by weakening rules which de-specify segments for the feature in question, to which the feature can then spread by assimilation from a neighboring segment. The feature-deletion (neutralization) process which on this theory feeds apparent feature-changing assimilation can be independently detected by the default value it produces wherever there is no assimilation (complementarity between assimilation and neutralization).

If we assume that assimilation is spreading of a feature or class node, then it immediately follows that there should be no assimilations which spread only the unmarked value of a feature, since there is no stage in the derivation where only unmarked values are present in the representation. For example, there are two-way assimilations of [±voiced], as in Russian, and one-way assimilations of [+voiced], as in Ukrainian and Santee Dakota, but no one-way assimilations which spread only [–voiced]. Cho's survey confirms this striking prediction for a substantial sample of languages.[18]

(16) (a) Russian: /tak+že/ → ta[g]že "also", /bez tebja/ → be[s] tebja
                                                          "without you"
       (b) Ukrainian: /jak že/ → ja[g]že "how", /bez tebe/ → be[z] tebe
                                                          "without you"

One-way assimilation (spread of the marked feature value) as in (16b) results from ordering assimilation after the assignment of default feature values. Since two-way assimilation applies when default feature specifications have already been assigned, it must involve feature deletion at the target as a prior step, followed by spread to the vacated site. This yields the following additional predictions.

First, two-way assimilation should apply preferentially in environments where neutralization is favored. This seems to be correct: for example, the prevalence of feature neutralization in coda position explains the prevalence of assimilation in coda position (e.g., regressive assimilation in consonant clusters).

Second, in environments where neutralization applies but where no trigger of assimilation is present (for example, in absolute final position), two-way assimilation should be associated with neutralization in favor of the unmarked (default) value. This prediction is also confirmed by such typical associations as (two-way) voicing assimilation with final devoicing, or place assimilation with coda neutralization of place.[19]

Suppose we also allow assimilation to be ordered either before or after *redundant* values are assigned. This gives two subtypes of two-way assimilation: one in which only distinctive feature specifications (e.g., [±voiced] on obstruents) trigger assimilation, the other where redundant feature specifications also trigger assimilation. For voicing assimilation, the first type is represented by Warsaw Polish (as well as Russian and Serbo-Croatian), the second by Cracow Polish:

(17) (a) Warsaw Polish: ja[k] nigdy "as never"
      (b) Cracow Polish: ja[g] nigdy "as never"

The theory predicts that one-way assimilation cannot be triggered by redundant feature values (i.e., it must be of the Warsaw type, not of the Cracow type). In fact, the voicing assimilation rules of Ukrainian and Santee (e.g., (16b)) are triggered by obstruents only. It also follow that if a language has both Warsaw-type and Cracow-type assimilation, then the former must be in an earlier level. For example, Sanskrit has lexical voicing assimilation triggered by obstruents and post-lexical voicing assimilation by all voiced segments. For similar reasons, if a language has both one-way and two-way assimilation, then the former must be in an earlier level.

In combination with the formal theory of phonological rules, underspecfication provides the basis for Cho's parameterized typology of assimilation. According to this theory, every assimilation process can be characterized by specifying a small number of properties in a universal schematism:

  1 Site of spreading (single feature or a class node)
  2 Specification of target and/or trigger
  3 Locality (nature of structural adjacency between trigger and target)
  4 Relative order between spreading and default assignment
  5 Directionality of spreading
  6 Domain of spreading

This approach has a number of additional consequences of interest for both synchronic and historical phonology.

Since codas are the most common target of weakening, and adjacency the most common setting of the locality parameter, it follows that regressive assimilation from onsets to preceding codas will be the most common type of assimilation. Thus, no special substantive principle giving priority to regressive assimilation is required.

Additional consequences follow if we bring in feature geometry. Since the domain of spreading can be limited to a specific node in the feature hierarchy, it follows that assimilation between segments belonging to the same natural class is a natural process. The traditional generalization that assimilation is favored between segments which are already most similar in their feature composition (Hutcheson 1973; Lee 1975) is thus explained in a principled way. "Strength hierarchies" (proposed, e.g., by Foley 1977 to account for the direction of assimilation) also turn out to be epiphenomenal.

An element may be ineligible to spread either because it already bears an incompatible feature specification (whether as an inherent lexical property or assigned by some rule), or because some constraint blocks it from being associated with the spreading feature value. Once the spread of a feature has been so interrupted, further spread is barred by locality. Thus, "opaque" elements need not themselves be specified for the spreading feature; they must only bear the relevant class node.[20]

It seems clear from the work of Cho and others that underspecification is not only relevant for the synchronic analysis of lexical phonology, but plays a role in defining the conditioning of phonetic processes. The difference between marked, default, and redundant feature values – a basically structural difference – constitutes a major parameter along which assimilatory processes vary. We must conclude that a large and well-studied class of sound changes is *simultaneously* exceptionless and structure-dependent.

3.2   Vowel Shifts

The point of this section is similar to that of the last, though this one is offered in a more speculative vein. I argue that vowel shifts are another type of natural sound change whose explanation, on closer inspection, depends on the *structural* status of the triggering feature in the system, specifically on whether the feature is specified in the language's phonological representations or is active only at the phonetic level.

Vowel shifts fall into a few limited types. The most important generalizations about the direction of vowel shifts is that tense (or "peripheral") vowels tend to be raised, lax (nonperipheral) vowels tend to fall, and back vowels tend to be fronted (Labov 1994). How can we explain these canonical types of vowel shifts, and the direction of strengthening processes in general? The attempt to answer this question will reveal another kind of top-down effect.

One of the puzzling questions about vowel shifts is their "perseverance"

(Stockwell 1978). What accounts for their persistent recurrence in languages such as English, and their rarity in others, such as Japanese?[21] A simple argument shows that tenseness-triggered raising and laxness-triggered lowering occur only in languages which have both tense and lax vowels in their inventories at some phonological level of representation. Otherwise, we would expect languages with persistent across-the-board lowering of all vowels (if they are lax) or persistent across-the-board raising of all vowels (if they are tense). But there do not seem to be any such languages.

But why would the shift-inducing force of the feature [±Tense] depend on the existence of both feature specifications in the language's vowels? A reasonable hypothesis would be that vowel shifts are the result of a tendency to maximize perceptual distinctness. Consider first the idea that vowel shifts are the result of the enhancement of contrastive features, in this case, tenseness. This hypothesis is undermined by several facts. First, vowel shifts often cause mergers, both through raising of tense vowels (as in English *beet* and *beat*) and through lowering of lax vowels (as in Romance). If the motivation is the maximization of distinctness, why does this happen? Second, even when vowel shifts do not cause mergers, they often simply produce "musical chairs" effects, chain shifts of vowels which do nothing to enhance their distinctness (for example, the Great Vowel Shift). Third, tenseness does not by any means have to be distinctive in order to trigger vowel shifts. In English, for example, tenseness has been mostly a predictable concomitant of the basic quantitative opposition of free and checked vowels, and at some stages it has been entirely that. Yet tenseness is the feature that seems to have triggered the various phases of the Great Vowel Shift. Moreover, those vowels for which tenseness did have a distinctive function do not seem to have shifted any more than the ones for which it did not.

The alternative hypothesis which I would like to explore here is that tenseness can trigger vowel shift if it is present in the language's phonological representations – not necessarily underlyingly, but at any phonological level where it can feed the phonological rules that assign default values for the height features. Vowel shifts can then be considered as the result of suppressing marked specifications of the relevant height feature in lexical representations, resulting in the assignment of the appropriate default value of the feature in question to the vacated segment by the mechanisms discussed above. For example, loss of the feature specification [–High] from a tense vowel will automatically entail its raising by default. The reason why tenseness and laxness activate vowel shifts only if they are both present in the language's phonological representations would then be that, as the theory predicts, only those feature values which are specified in phonological representations can feed default rules, and a feature that plays no role whatever in a language's phonology will not figure in its phonological representations, but will be assigned at a purely phonetic level if at all. This would mean that an abstract distinction at yet another level, that between phonetic and phonological tenseness/laxness, would also be critical to sound change.[22]

Let us see how this approach might work for the Great Vowel Shift. Assume, fairly uncontroversially, that height is assigned by the following universal default rules:[23]

(18) (a) [–Tense] → [–High]
     (b) [   ] → [+High]
     (c) [   ] → [–Low]

In a language where tenseness plays no role, (18a) is not active, and default height is assigned only by the "elsewhere" case (18b). The canonical three-height vowel system is represented as follows:

(19)

	Distinctive value	Default values (assigned by [18b])
High vowels (i, u)	[ ]	[+High, –Low]
Mid vowels (e, o)	[–High]	[–Low]
Low vowels (æ, ɔ)	[+Low]	

To augment the system with the feature [±Tense], I'll assume the classification of vowels motivated in Kiparsky 1974:[24]

(20)

		–Back –Round	+Back –Round	+Round
+Hi, –Low	+Tense	i	ɯ	u
	–Tense	ɪ	ɨ	ʊ
–Hi, –Low	+Tense	e	ɤ	o
	–Tense	ɛ	ʌ	ɔ₁
–Hi, +Low	+Tense	æ	ɐ	ɔ₂
	–Tense	a	ɑ	ɒ

Tenseness itself is related to length by the following default rules:

(21) (a) VV → [+Tense]
     (b) V → [–Tense]

Now we are ready to lay out the vowel system of late Middle English (ME) (ca. 1400). At this stage, all front vowels were unrounded and all back vowels were rounded. So ME ā, a were low nontense *front* vowels, like the [a] of Boston *car, father* and of French *patte* (Dobson 1968, p. 545, 594). The distinction between free and checked nuclei appears to have been basically quantitative (long versus short). Tenseness was distinctive, however, in the long mid vowels (*beet* vs. *beat, boot* vs. *boat*). I will assume that *all other vowels were nontense.* The vowel specifications were accordingly as follows (default and redundant features parenthesized):

(22)

		−Back, (−Round) Long Short	+Back, (+Round) Long Short
(+Hi, −Low)	(−Tense)	ī bite ɪ bit	ū bout ʊ but
−Hi, (−Low)	+Tense	ē beet	ō boot
	(−Tense)	ɛ̄ beat ɛ bet	ɔ̄ boat ɔ pot
+Low	(−Tense)	ā bate a bat	

The default values for the features High and Low are assigned by (18). Tenseness plays no role in the assignment of vowel height. Only the default rule (21b) is active, assigning the feature specification [−Tense] to vowels not lexically marked as [+Tense].

Tenseness was neutralized in short vowels; hence [ɛ] represents both shortened [ē] (*kēp:kĕpt, mēt:mĕt*), and shortened [ɛ̄] (*drēm:drĕmt, lēp:lĕpt, clēn:clĕnliness*), and [ɔ] represents both shortened [ō] (*lose:lost, shoot:shot*) and shortened [ɔ̄] (*clothes:cloth, nose:nozzle, prōtest:prŏtestation*).

The ME diphthongs were:[25]

(23) ay   *bait*   aw   *law*
      ɔy   *boy*   ɔw   *blow*
                      ɛw   *dew*
      uy   *buoy*   ɪw   *pew*

According to the analysis of the historical records by Dobson (1968), the vowel shift took place in three stages, from our perspective consisting of two height shifts with an intervening tensing process:

(24)

Middle English	Raising (≈ 1500)	Tensing (≈ 1650)	Raising (18th c.)
ī	ei		
ū	ou		
ē	ī		
ō	ū		
ɛ̄		ē	ī
ɔ̄		ō	
ā		ǣ	ē
a		æ	

First shift: Raising. In the first stage of the vowel, shift, which Dobson dates to the 15th century, [ē] and [ō] (the only tense vowels of the system according to our assumption) were raised (unmarking of [–High] and default assignment of [+High] by (18b)), and [ī], and [ū] were diphthongized (activation of (18a)). *Second shift: Tensing.* The next phase of the Great Vowel Shift (17th century) was a general tensing of the long vowels: [ɛ̄] was tensed to [ē], [ɔ̄] was tensed to [ō], and long and short [a] were tensed to [æ]:[26]

(25)

		−Back, (−Round) Long Short		+Back, (+Round) Long Short	
(+Hi, −Low)	(+Tense)	ī beet		ū boot	
	(−Tense)		ɪ bit		ʊ but
−Hi, (−Low)	(+Tense)	ē beet		ō boat	
	(−Tense)		ɛ bet		ɔ pot
(−Hi), +Low	(+Tense)	ǣ bate	æ bat		

The tensing process can again be seen as an activation of a default rule, in this case (21a). We have now arrived at a system of long and short vowels (25) where *tenseness is entirely predictable.* Yet tenseness in this system feeds the next, third stage of vowel shift, which again raises tense vowels.

Third shift: Raising with merger. The second raising of tense vowels (18th century) again implements the default rule (18), which assigns height on the basis of tenseness. But this raising was more restricted, applying only to the long tense front vowels: [ē] was raised to [ī] (loss of [–High]), and [ǣ] was raised to [ē] (loss of [+Low]). This stage of raising differed from the first in that the resulting vowels merged with existing nuclei (the reflexes of ME /e/ and /ai/, respectively). Moreover, not all dialects underwent this change, and words such as *great, steak, break* retaining the older mid vowel in the standard language are probably from those dialects.

To sum up: the Great Vowel Shift is triggered by both distinctive and nondistinctive tenseness. Evidently it is not the distinctiveness of the feature but its phonological (as opposed to phonetic) status that counts. This supports the idea adopted in lexical phonology that the assignment of phonological default features can take place at several levels of the derivation, including in particular post-lexical phonology.

4   Conclusion

I have defended the neogrammarian hypothesis that sound change is exceptionless and subject only to phonetic conditioning against two potentially serious objections. The first objection, based on lexical diffusion, is answered by the analysis of the phenomenon as a species of nonproportional analogical change proposed and motivated in section 1. The second objection is based on top-down effects in sound change. Structural work in historical phonology in the Jakobsonian tradition supports the position that phonological organization plays a role in sound change, in particular through diachronic "conspiracies" implementing canonical syllable structure. In section 2, I discussed two other types of structure-dependency in sound change: priming effects in secondary split, and maintenance of universal constraints on phonological systems (e.g., the stability of implicational universals, and the failure of cascades of secondary splits to produce giant phonemic systems). Finally, in section 3, I discussed the role in sound change of the status of features as distinctive versus redundant, and phonological versus phonetic, drawing in part on the parametric rule typologies emerging from recent work on natural phonological processes, which make use of abstract properties of phonological representations to explain generalizations in domains where purely physical explanations have hitherto dominated. I argued that all four types of top-down effects can be reconciled with exceptionlessness by giving the transmission process an active selectional role in language change.

NOTES

1   This paper is in part the result of an exchange with Andrew Garrett and of a reading of portions of Labov 1993 in draft form, though neither Garrett nor Labov necessarily agrees with me, or with the other. I am also grateful to them both as well as to the other participants of a workshop on sound change at Stanford University in February 1993 for valuable comments on a draft of this paper.

2   Such a move is of course legitimate in so far as the exceptions can be identified in some principled way, as when "minor sound changes" such as dissimilation and metathesis are systematically set aside as being of perceptual origin.

3   I exclude here from sound change the "minor" sound changes discussed below in section 2.2. Also,

the "no-change" entries in the last line abstract away from *lexical split*, which can result from sound change by the mechanisms discussed at the end of section 2.2 (e.g., *ass/arse*), by analogy (*staff/ stave*), and, I would expect, from lexical diffusion as well.

4   However, no commitment to any particular formal evaluation measure need be made at this level. Virtually any theory which characterizes analogy as structural optimization ought to be able to get the same results.

5   See Steriade (1987), Archangeli (1988), and Mohanan (1991) for general surveys from varying points of view. For simplicity of presentation, I will illustrate the point here with segmental features. But everything I say holds equally for other phonological information

such as syllabic structure and stress (Kiparsky 1993).

6   This is not how such a rule would actually look. I give it in this old-fashioned form just for simplicity's sake.

7   For two other formulations, see Kiparsky (1982, 1985) and Archangeli (1984), Archangeli and Pulleyblank (1989). The position put forward here is in a sense intermediate between those two.

8   The elimination of MSCs invalidates the objection to underspecification by Christdas (1988), Clements (1985), Mohanan (1991), and others based on the claim that that Morpheme Structure Constraints must be able to refer to default values. The objection is in any case internally incoherent because many of the MSCs cited by these authors require reference to syllable structure assigned by phonological rules, so they couldn't possibly apply to underlying forms. All that these examples show is that level 1 phonological rules in some languages require reference to both feature values. But radical underspecification predicts exactly that because it says that default values can be assigned cyclically, a possibility independently motivated by the cyclic interaction of default and spread rules in harmony systems.

9   The affective words *oops, whoopee,* and *shtup* are the only exceptions I am aware of.

10   Labov (1993) records one token of lax *æ* in *athlete;* this could be the result of lexicalization of the trisyllabic pronunciation with anaptyctic *ə.*

11   Another apparently idiosyncratic contrast is reported by Labov in hypocoristic names, where *Frannie, Danny, Sammy* normally have tense

A and *Cassie, Cathy* normally have lax *æ.* This could be accounted for on the assumption that the former are analyzed, by speakers who have this contrast, as derived from monosyllabic bases (*Fran, Dan, Sam*), to which the rule applies regularly on the first cycle, whereas the latter are treated as unanalyzed. So even these seemingly unpredictable cases may well turn out to be rule-governed.

12   For the three *-d* words in [12b], the tensing is now obligatory for Philadelphia speakers of all ages.

13   On the other hand, this derivation of the New York pattern would also explain the relatively high rate of tensing/raising before *š* compared to other fricatives in New York, by the relatively high rate of post-lexical tensing/raising before *š* compared to other fricatives in the Northern Cities (Kiparsky 1971).

14   For example, Wanner and Cravens (1980) argue for the lexical diffusion of an intervocalic voicing rule in the Tuscan dialect of Italian.

15   As early as 1886, Kruszewski had cited Darwin on "directed evolution" in order to explain why sound changes, though originating in random articulatory fluctuations, progress in specific directions ("sich in bestimmter Richtung auf der erwähnten Linie fortbewegen").

16   The only contrary case I know of, where compensatory lengthening is reported to have created distinctive length, is Occitan (Morin 1992).

17   Jakobson, Fant, and Halle (1952, p. 8) note that redundant features may under certain conditions even substitute for the conditioning distinctive features.

18   If the devoicing in /bit+z/ → [bits] were a genuine case of assimilation, it would refute the theory. In fact, it appears to reflect a phonetically-

based constraint (as far as is known, valid in all languages) which restricts voicing to a continuous portion of the syllable that includes the nucleus (Cho 1990).

19 Place neutralization yields coronals. E.g.,: "For Fante, the pattern of nasal plus consonant may be stated as involving homorganicity with the predominant articulation if any, or otherwise [n]" (Welmers 1973, p. 65). A similar pattern of nasal place neutralization to [-n] (with or without concomitant assimilation) is found in Finnish, Greek, and Italian, and reportedly in Croatian dialects, Avar and Lakk. With debuccalization, the result is a placeless nasal (Sanskrit *anusvāra*), see Ferré (1988) and Paradis and Prunet (1991); apparent neutralization to [ŋ] is via coronal or placeless nasals.

20 The argument of Steriade (1987) that contrastive underspecification is to be preferred over radical underspecification is based entirely on the following important generalization about transparency: a feature spreads only through segments for which the feature in question is redundant, never through segments for which it is distinctive and which have the default value of the feature. But this follows from the assumption that all segments for which a feature is distinctive bear a class node for that feature, together with normal locality considerations. So, contrary to what Steriade implies, her generalization is fully consistent with radical underspecification.

21 It is true that the Okinawan dialect has undergone a kind of vowel shift (M. Matsuda, *in litt.*). However, this was apparently a raising of the *short* vowels *e*, *o* to *i*, *u*, their long counterparts remaining

unaffected. So on my assumptions, tenseness cannot have been the triggering factor of this change. Rather, I assume that it is a vowel reduction phenomenon, consisting of the neutralization of the distinctive feature [–High], with the neutralized vowels assigned default [+High] by rule (18b) below.

22 The same issue arises in the case of the feature of nasality. According to Schourup (1973) and Ruhlen (1978), whether nasal vowels are raised or lowered depends on whether nasalization is distinctive in the language or not. However, it is not impossible that the relevant distinction is really whether nasalization figures in the language's phonological representations or not.

23 I assume that default rules operate in gradient fashion at the level of phonetic implementation, in this case accounting for the general tendency for lax vowels to be articulated lower than tense vowels.

24 I have left out the front rounded vowels in this version of the chart because they play no role in the English data discussed here.

25 The diphthong [ʊy] (*buoy, boil, oil*) merged with [ɔy] (*boy, choice, noise*) in most dialects in the ME period. The other old diphthongs were eliminated as part of the vowel shift as follows. ME [ay] merged with ME [ā] and [ɛw] with [ɪw] about 1650, earlier in Northern and Eastern dialects (Dobson 1968, p. 594, 778, 798). The diphthong [aw] (*law*) was monophthongized to [ō] in the 17th century (p. 786), and [ɔw] (*blow*) was monophthongized to [ō], merging with the vowel of *boat* ca. 1600 (p. 805).

26 I am here departing from Dobson's chronology by assuming that long

and short [a] were tensed at the same time along with the other long vowels. Dobson (1968, p. 594) thinks that long [ā] was tensed earlier than short [a] was, as early as the 15th century, which would make this part of tensing part of the first shift. Adopting his account would make the first shift more complex but not alter my main point that vowel shift is an unmarking of vowels with concomitant assignment of default values to the vacated features. Since the orthoepic evidence does not seem altogether clear on this point, I have assumed that the tensing processes were concurrent, which gives the simpler schema in (24).

22 Phonological Acquisition

MARLYS A. MACKEN

0 Introduction

Over the years, Chomsky has encouraged us to ask, how is it that human beings, whose contacts with the world are brief, personal, and limited are nevertheless able to know as much as they do? How does the child come to master a complex, abstract system like language when the evidence available to the child is so sparse? This question is one of the great scientific puzzles of our time, and phonology is only one of the many disciplines that have attacked the problem, but found the answer elusive. The field is large, interdisciplinary, and relatively young. Each discipline generates its own theories, ideologies, and heated debates, but this theoretical diversity is warranted by the complexity of the puzzle, for language is indeed complex, and many descriptions are possible for each phenomenon. Language acquisition data are at times like Rorschach ink blots. Phoneticians see in a CVCV transcription (already multiply removed from the original object) evidence for articulatory primitives, gestures, or mandibular open-close frames, while phonologists look at the same ink configuration, see abstract units, and debate about syllables, moras, features, nodes, and feet. Inherent descriptive equivalence or indeterminancy is compounded because of the dual nature of a representation that is input to the two different systems of phonology and phonetics.

To the descriptive problems, one must add the complication that the child is also complex and changing at a remarkable rate. Studying the developing child presents many challenges and requires dealing with a large number of correlations that can be misinterpreted. Yet a theory of language acquisition is incomplete without a theory of cognition and learning that is compatible with what we know about the mind and human development.

Finally, one must factor in the child's world. Is a particular structure observed because language possesses that form, because the mind does, or because the world is structured that way? Language, mind, environment: these three aspects of our puzzle make "explanations" easy to come by and short-lived. The problem is compounded by the goal of separating the structure of language from the way it is used and acquired. As the mind is simultaneously both structure and process, our data conflate the two, but we must attempt the difficult, perhaps impossible, task of separating the grammar from the processor, declarative from procedural knowledge, propositional content from images. Different fields have different versions of this problem: in phonology, there is no grammaticality judgement technique to separate the underlying grammar from other levels of description or other systemic effects.

Much of the acquisition field is predictably, then, a vigorous debate over what the child knows and in what format the knowledge is represented. Does the infant who distinguishes two stimuli "know" the syllables [ba] and [da] or the segments [b], [d], or [a]? Does the child who says "wanna go" have an optional subject rule or know a particular kind of verb complement structure? How, we must ask, do these questions differ from the question of what a thermostat "knows" about temperature and raising/lowering? And does language structure exist separately from the time, acquisitional distance traveled, and situations of its use?

Unfortunately, some divisive issues, like innateness, continue to impede progress. The field is still polarized between empiricists, who tend to be phoneticians and/or general learning theorists (usually today connectionists), and rationalists, who tend to be formal phonologists or cognitive psychologists. To show that phonetics and learning are sufficient to account for phonology, the former theorists concentrate on developmental continuity from infancy through the transition to speech. In contrast, the latter theorists focus on ages two to four (and up), on the properties of phonologically more complex systems, on developmental discontinuities from earlier phonetic stages, and on nonlinearities and other evidence of reorganization in terms of abstract units or rules.[1] This polarization, the legacy of the Chomsky wars, still shackles the field, pointlessly dividing some groups of people and obscuring two indisputable points. First, phonology subsumes phonetics. Articulatory and perceptual systems play key roles in acquisition, while part of phonology is an abstract and semiformal system with objects, constraints, and principles not fully determined by phonetic content nor fully explained by phonetic theory. Second, some aspects of language are learned and some are innate. The question of how learning is accomplished in the presence of incomplete and contradictory input is still the central question to be asked, and the answer lies in part on the a priori structures that determine the speed of acquisition, constraints on variation, and the independence from limiting factors like intelligence. Empirical evidence showing the need for innate, domain-specific structure has also come from a variety of other sources, like the failure of animal language-learning and the structure and acquisition of sign languages, etc. Empirical evidence showing the significant role of learning includes individual variation and cross-language differences; research using computational modeling of acquisition phenomena provides intriguing support for some empiricist claims.

The challenge for us is to partition the domains properly between phonology and phonetics, determine the interplay between learning and innate constraints, and separate general learning from domain-specific linguistic process and structure. The multiple aspects of language acquisition are complex and indeed very apparent today, yet that variation falls within strict limits. It is the task of the theory to explain both the freedom that the variation documents and the constraints imposed by the innate structure. Though there is controversy over each point, the evidence to date shows that acquisition constraints are in the mind, not in the world, and that they are specifically linguistic, explicitly represented structures.

Granted that acquisition is a very hard problem for the scientist to study and resolve, why is it an important problem? First, studying real-time acquisition will provide the clearest answers to the central questions on language variation constraints and the interaction between innate structure and the environment. Second, language acquisition data can directly influence the theory of phonological structure. For many cognitive systems, the end state necessarily is constrained by the way in which it is acquired: earliest phonological capacities structure what we learn, thus setting boundaries for what is learned and perhaps leaving an imprint on the phonological knowledge acquired during the final stages as well; in addition, these earliest capacities remain basic to the adult phonological system and provide one of the clearest windows on the core structure of phonology.

This paper examines (1) the structure that is acquired and (2) the relationship between acquisition and theory. I shall argue that the capacity of children and adults is the same – the strong identity thesis – and that phonological principles explain variation among children and particular differences between children and adults. Thus, acquisition data can provide direct answers to certain core phonological issues, and any phonological theory that fails in principle to account for acquisition data fails as a theory of phonology. Given the focus (and length) of this chapter, much of the literature – which is overwhelmingly descriptive – is not covered here. For example, there is much sophisticated research on infant perception and the transition from babbling to speech that shows, respectively, the innate status of phonetic features (e.g., Kuhl 1987) and the infant's sensitivity within the first year to specific properties of the environmental language (e.g., Boysson-Bardies 1993). For an overview of the descriptive literature, acquisition data, stages and acquisition theories, see Ingram (1989), while Smith (1973) remains the best theoretical study of phonological acquisition. For representative research, one may see the papers in Yeni-Komshian, Kavanaugh, and Ferguson (1980) and Ferguson, Menn, and Stoel-Gammon (1992). The model of phonological acquisition presented here follows on the work of Kiparsky and Menn (1977b), Macken and Ferguson (1983), and others, notably Smith (1973). For alternative views, the reader may look to evolutionary, self-organizing theory (e.g., Lindblom 1992; MacNeilage and Davis 1993), performance theories (e.g., Stemberger 1992a), natural phonology theory (Stampe 1969; Edwards and Shriberg 1983), and Firthian phonology (Waterson 1987).

1   Nature of the Relationship

Children begin saying first words around 12 to 18 months of age. Early on, they may use long, prosodically sentential jargon or invented, idiosyncratic protowords not clearly based on words of their language, but generally, for at least this first year, the form of words in their native language is reduced, highly restricted, and somewhat variable. For the next several years, their speech continues to differ substantially from the speech of adults. Assuming that the speech of adults reflects a uniform underlying grammar, we may ask how the speech of children is related to the language of their parents. In nature, we find two contrasting developmental relations. In a relation manifesting essential continuity, the young are unskilled and simpler, yet they are fundamentally like the adults of the species in key respects; in a qualitatively different kind of developmental relation (which we might call "nonlinear"), there is a radical difference between the beginning and end states and a major discontinuity in development.

Children acquiring phonology do change over time, going through a recognizable set of stages. This progression is an indication, along with independence from the limiting effects of ability and environment and the presence of a critical period, that shows that language acquisition is a biologically controlled behavior. We are interested here in the nature of those changes: are they qualitative, in the sense that the basic structures or capacities change, or quantitative, in the sense that the information or knowledge of a specific domain changes. If the principles and objects of phonology are present at the outset of language learning, and thus instantiated at each stage and in each interim grammar constructed by the learner as in Chomsky's theory, then the developmental model is one of basic continuity. We would then look to nonqualitative factors to explain the developmental stages. If, on the other hand, some phonological principles or objects are not present at the outset, then there is no necessary relationship between a developmental stage of the child and the properties of phonological systems: the developmental model will then be one of discontinuity, and we will explain the qualitative characteristics of each stage in terms of the maturation of new linguistic skills or changes in other cognitive capacities, as presented in Piaget's theories.

Roman Jakobson's hallmark monograph (1968) provides both answers to our question about the relationship between the child's stage/grammar and the adult's. The central and unifying claim of Jakobson's theory is that the speech of children from first words on is both *simpler* in a highly principled way and the *same* as the universal structure that underlies the language of their parents. Yet he also believed that there was a categorical difference between the babbling stage of the first year of life and the true language stage that begins in the second year of life. The hypothesized discontinuity – as striking as, say, a tadpole-frog discontinuity – was predicted to be accompanied in some cases by a silent period. On the first point, Jakobson's elegant theory is correct in substance if not always in detail.

With respect to the second point, however, there is considerable evidence that there is a close connection between the specific features of babbling and of first words and that babbling and word use are not discrete stages but overlap in time as well as in substance. These facts show that there is no major discontinuity between the so-called prelinguistic babbling period and the presumably phonological stages that begin in the second year. This has been taken by many to refute Jakobson's theories concerning phonology, as if by demonstrating the absence of a discontinuity we had proved there was no phonology, a view advanced by the "it's all tadpoles/phonetics" school. The pendulum has swung back somewhat in the direction of phonology with recent research that shows that, in the last six months of the first year, children's babbling takes on segmental and prosodic characteristics of the surrounding language and that their perceptual systems attune to the specific language of their communicative environment with the loss of the ability to discriminate noncontrastive differences by eight to ten months of age. These findings undermine the anti-Jakobsonian school's argument that the absence of a discontinuity between babbling and speech (early in the second year) shows the primacy of phonetics to the phonological systems of the second year. Rather, these findings show that specific learning about the child's own language is strongly affecting the supposedly "phonetics-only" stage of babbling and discrimination in the first year. Clearly, the label "prelinguistic" is an inaccurate description of the abilities of the first year. Equally clear is that there is a complex relationship between this stage and that of the second year, just as there is in general a complex relationship between phonetics and phonology in all aspects of speech. Let us return to the question of how the stages of language learning from the second year on are related to the end state.

1.1   The Strong Identity Thesis

Jakobson argued that one universal phonological system determines the structure of synchronic languages and the supposedly "extralinguistic" domains of acquisition, sound change and disordered speech. In advancing this strong identity relationship between the child and adult phonological capacity, Jakobson is one of many phonologists who have taken the same thesis to argue various issues in phonological theory – Schleicher, Paul, Ament, Grammont, Meillet, Jespersen, Saussure, Baudouin de Courtenay, Halle, Kiparsky, Stampe, and Ohala. Like Grammont (1902, 1933), many have viewed phonological acquisition as a microcosm of diachronic sound change. Ohala and others have observed the same acoustically-motivated rules in acquisition and sound change and taken this to show that both children and adults create such sound patterns independently because they possess the same physical phonetic apparatus (e.g., Greenlee and Ohala 1980). Generative theorists argue that the parallels between acquisition and diachrony are due to the same shared phonological system and that children may be the actual source of sound change (cf. 19th and early 20th century phonologists like Paul and Saussure). For example, Stampe (1969, 1972) argued there are universal processes and that change in a language occurs when processes are not correctly limited during acquisition. (See the discussion by Paul Kiparsky in chapter 21 of this volume for a related discussion.)

In Jakobson's theory, features are the central unit of phonology: there is a small universal set of binary features that function to differentiate elements in natural language; the feature system is hierarchical and implicational; and this system constrains phonological inventories, systems, and rules. The same structural principles that determine this invariant hierarchy in phonemic systems also determine sound change and an invariant acquisition order of sound classes. The patterns of stratification, change, and acquisition derive ultimately from the principle of maximal contrast along acoustic axes of sonority and tonality: maximal contrasts are found in all languages and acquired first. Implicational relationships govern features, such that if Y occurs in a phonemic system, then X does too; and X is acquired by children before Y. The child's acquisition of feature oppositions proceeds through the universal feature hierarchy from the most general contrast to the finest, rarest contrasts. Furthermore, the relative frequency, combinatorial capacity, and assimilatory power of particular features once acquired, and the substitution patterns within each stage of the child's development are also determined by the priority relationships within the universal feature hierarchy (1968, p. 58).

To exemplify the specific proposals (since the theory is well-described in many places, e.g., Anderson 1985; Ingram 1989), we will look briefly at consonants. The stages should be (1) optimal consonant /p/ versus optimal vowel /a/, (2) /p:m/, (3) /p:t/ and (4) /m:n/, yielding the basic consonantal system /p, t, m, n/. Other predictions include that stop consonants are acquired before fricatives; front before back; voiceless unaspirated before voiced; fricatives before affricates; strident fricatives (/f, s/) before the corresponding mellow fricatives (/ɸ, θ/); in early stages, fricatives and affricates are replaced by stops of the same place, voiced by voiceless unaspirated, continuants by noncontinuants; liquids as a class are acquired late with one, usually /l/, possibly early; dentals have a natural priority after stages (1)–(4).

Data from a wide variety of languages have been shown to conform to the general Jakobsonian outline of development – for example, English (the classic study of Leopold 1947 and many others), French, Norwegian, Spanish, Greek; as well as Jakobson's source languages (then and since), Swedish, Danish, Russian, Serbo-Croatian, Polish, Czech, Bulgarian, and Zuni. Although many of the specific predictions have been shown to have exceptions in at least one child (particularly the precise order of stages (1)–(4) above), the general markedness relations – where [−voice] (voiceless and unaspirated), [−continuant], [+coronal][2] and "front" or [+anterior][3] are unmarked – hold for the great majority of children. In general, the unmarked consonants are acquired first

(1), are most frequent in the child's lexicon (2), have the fewest restrictions on their distribution (3), and serve as replacements for the corresponding marked consonants during the stage when the contrast is neutralized (4), precisely as Jakobson predicted. As generalizations about simple inventories of segments in both children (e.g., Dinnsen 1992) and in languages of the world (e.g., Maddieson 1984), Jakobson's system of implicational relationships among features is overwhelmingly valid. While there is justifiable concern over the validity of statistical "universals" as opposed to absolute universals, the significance of this achievement should not be underestimated, though it usually is today. From the earliest stages of learning the lexicon (and perhaps earlier), children are working within the same distinctive feature constraints that structure the phonological systems – inventories and segmental rules – of languages of the world.

Nevertheless, there are important problems with the specific predictions of the theory. The acquisition data do not clearly verify the notion that the underlying framework of oppositions is completely "contrastive" in the strict phonological sense (of phoneme minimal pair oppositions) or "acoustic" along Jakobson's sonority and tonality dimensions. While features play an important role, other units are equally (and in early stages more) important. Markedness relationships are more complicated than indicated, particularly in certain categories (e.g., "coronal/dental," where unmarked specifically means /t, s, n/ and later /l/ and not other members like /š, θ/; the category of glides is not included at all in the hierarchy or text; etc.) and in certain properties, like their supposedly greater assimilation power (Jakobson's fifth property of unmarked members): for [coronal] and possibly [voice], the more accurate observation (following Trubetzkoy's distinction) would be that the unmarked members are used by children in the earliest stages because they appear in neutralization contexts (cf. property (4) above) but, rather than having uniformly greater assimilatory power, they (may) undergo assimilation in later stages when both members of an opposition are represented; thus coronals serve as replacements for velars in the early stages but assimilate to velars in later stages (cf. 1968, p. 54). Other attested acquisition assimilatory relationships – like coronals to labials, labials to velars, and (less commonly) velars to labials – are not discussed by Jakobson. In contrast, the unmarked [–continuant] appears both to be used in neutralization contexts and to have greater assimilatory power throughout all stages. Finally, there are three basic types of unpredicted variation.

1.2   Variation

First, there are individual differences among children learning the same language. As we find in the study of early syntax (most children use single words during the one-word stage, yet some use large units only partially analyzed), so too in phonology: most children use feature-sized units fairly consistently but others work on larger, more global structures (typically the prosodic word, perhaps the syllable) and vary features considerably by prosodic position and context, where, e.g., the sequencing of place and manner features is linked to prosodically dominant (initial) and nondominant (medial or final) positions. Basically, any study of ten or more children acquiring the same language will be virtually a typological study of possible variations in structure and content. Yet there are no reports of normally developing children who produce forms outside the constraints of synchronic theory. Children with "phonological disorders" show delay and are sometimes highly idiosyncratic, but their rules too are phonetically and phonologically natural (see, e.g., the research and publications of Dinnsen, Edwards, Gandour, Grunwell, Kent, Leonard, Shriberg, Spencer, Stoel-Gammon). Children simply do not produce types of structures unattested in languages of the world.

The variation seen across different learners of the same language – like dialect variation – reveals the small number of particular parametric options within core grammar in a particularly clear way: since the basic system is in important respects the "same," potentially interacting variables are absent or inherently controlled and the system structure intrinsically clearer to the observing scientist. Acquisition data provide a particularly simple view of core phonology in part because there are few if any interactions with morphology.

Second, there are the consistent cross-linguistic differences (see, e.g., Pye, Ingram, and List 1987). For example, the palato-alveolar affricate is predicted by Jakobson to be acquired late, and this is the case in English. In Spanish, however, this affricate is acquired quite early, partly because it is more frequent in the corpus addressed to children by virtue of its high frequency in nicknames, diminutives, and sound-symbolic terms. Alternations between nasal and nonnasal stops is common in French acquisition but infrequent in other well studied languages. Laterals show substantial differences: [l] interacts with [j] in English (and retroflex [r] with [w]). In Spanish, [ð] (the spirant allophone of /d/, used intervocalically and in a few other contexts) frequently patterns with the liquids and is replaced by [l] and in some cases flap or trill [r]. The use of [l] for [ð] is common in the acquisition of Greek, but is extremely rare in the acquisition of English, the general replacement being [d] or [t]. In some languages, the acquisition alternation is [l] and [n] (e.g., Arabic, Yucatec Maya, and, with stage and learner variation, Spanish). In the case of [l], the acquisition differences are due to the intrinsic phonetic structure of [lateral], the phonetic properties of different [l]s in different languages and cross-linguistic phonological patterning differences – the same properties that underlie theoretical arguments about the feature geometric position of [lateral].

The third source of cross-linguistic acquisition differences comes from distributional regularities of the input. A consistent and originally surprising finding of the last ten years has been the at times close relationship between certain statistical properties of sounds and sound patterns in particular languages and the stages of children learning those languages. In Finnish, [d] – one of the easiest and earliest acquired obstruents in other languages – is acquired very late, which is very surprising; but phonologically and in the input, [d] is highly restricted in the adult language. In Spanish, the hierarchical dominance of labial in the adult language (Hooper 1976) underlies the predominance in Spanish acquisition of velar-to-labial harmony (which may be less common cross-linguistically than labial-to-velar harmony) and in the generalizations some children make.

The child's (and adult's) ability to extract distributional and statistical regularites must be accommodated in our theory by acknowledging that a phonological grammar has not only an abstract, symbolic algebraic system of the type proposed in current generative theories but also a statistical or stochastic component common to many connectionist and phonetic theories. To account for this and the other variation types, an acquisition model must recognize that the universal language acquisition device (LAD) is not so constrained as to result in invariant stages, as rigid order theories like Jakobson's would predict. Rather, the form of a possible phonology and a possible stage is universally constrained, but the learner has some freedom to work within this formal space to extract generalizations from the input. This constrained hypothesis formation or cognitive model (see Kiparsky and Menn 1977b and Macken and Ferguson 1983) incorporates the general acquisition patterns and universal structure envisioned by Jakobson and Chomsky, while recognizing the freedom the system must have to allow individual learners the creative flexibility they show in forming generalizations and inventing rules. Indeed, all rules may be invented or discovered by each learner. This degree of freedom may simply be a consequence of the freedom that the LAD must have in any case, since an interplay between learning and innate structure must take place to permit different languages to be acquired. The individual learner appears to have a similar degree of freedom to construct interim grammars. Why or how these grammars change over the stages of acquisition as the child's lexicon expands rapidly is a different though crucial question on which there is very little work.

1.3 Acquisition and Theory Results

The structure and variation in children's data fall within the same constraints found in the language of adults. This confirms the strong identity thesis that the same phonological system or grammar accounts for both synchronic language systems and diachronic and acquisitional change.[4] Thus, the theory of phonology can be applied to explain language acquisition data and data from children can, in principle, be used to change or confirm the theory. However, using acquisition evidence to modify theory or change theories has rarely been done. Menn (1980) cited three findings that she and other researchers thought were idiosyncratic phenomena in children (e.g., the prosodic word as a minimal unit), and yet each has independently found expression in later theoretical developments. The underlying unity of formally dissimilar rules effecting harmony and a CVCV canonical form could not be captured in the *SPE* framework of Smith (1973) (though recognized by Smith) – with the profound significance of their central role lost to the theory. Some of these problematic data can be handled by syllable theory (Spencer 1986) but could have been arguments for the syllable or other phonotactic structure template at the time. Similarly, early acquisition work identified lexical (phonotactic) patterns and associated constructs; what at the time seemed idiosyncratic to acquisition are, rather, instances of what are now called templates and planar segregation (Macken 1992a).

More often, acquisition data have been used to support (or disconfirm) aspects of phonological theory. Smith (1973) provides convincing arguments for the validity of segments, distinctive features, particular features (especially [coronal]), two levels of representation, realization rules, and some formal universals (especially rule ordering); and for the lack of evidence for other formal universals like particular abbreviatory devices (especially Greek letter variables) and *SPE* marking conventions. Spencer (1986) reanalyzes Smith (1973) in a nonlinear framework, showing its advantages in several areas, notably in motivating underspecification and a third level of representation, in capturing the bidirectionality of lateral harmony, and in explaining the simultaneous changes in rules (e.g., labial assimilation and cluster rules) which were simply an accident in the original framework. The experimental work in Gordon (1985) provides supporting evidence for the innate status of grammatical levels and constraints on level ordering proposed in lexical phonology (Kiparsky 1982c). Bradley's work on the relationship between phonological acquisition and reading provides experimental evidence on the structure and role of subsyllabic constituents (e.g., Bradley's review article in Ferguson, Menn, and Stoel-Gammon 1992). Using acquisition data, Stemberger (1993) confirms the transparency of glottals to spreading rules and argues for the placelessness of glottals. Dresher and Kaye (1990) use learnability-theoretic computational modeling to provide a perspective on the formal properties of stress systems. Yet the richness of acquisition data for constructing phonological theory has been drawn on only minimally.

The strong identity thesis, however, does not imply that there cannot be differences between children and adults. The thesis is that there are no qualitative differences: phonological structure, features, levels, hierarchy, and constraints are available from the outset, universal then in the way basic syntactic categories and the binding principle may similarly be present. Phonology (and language generally) is like vision in these respects, where, similarly, the infant's first mechanisms for perceiving objects remains central to perception and thought, the fundamental capacities may be enhanced but not fundamentally changed, and the study of infants and children likewise helps reveal the core visual system (e.g., Spelke 1990 and Spelke et al. in press).

The rejection of a significant, qualitative stage theory of development is problematic to some theorists because it is at odds with the dominant theory of cognitive development – a significant problem if a language acquisition theory must integrate with theories of the mind and cognitive development. A discrepancy could mean several things – for example, that language is unlike other cognitive domains or, if language is like other cognitive domains, that the strong identity thesis is wrong for language or that stage theories are wrong for cognition. Let us turn, then, to Piaget, the premier stage theorist.

1.4   Stage Theory

In contrast to Jakobson and Chomsky, Piaget focused on fundamental discontinuities throughout development. His theory is that the thinking of children is qualitatively different from that of adults, that there are four stages (discontinuities) in reasoning during development, and that the reasoning anomalies at each stage will be across-the-board in all content domains. Piaget's experiments show that children of different ages "think" differently in that they give nonadult answers to questions. These task findings are robust: if a task is given as Piaget did to children from a culture like that of Piaget's children, then the results are as described. However, cross-cultural research has revealed significant differences between cultures which appear to be related to the experience children have in a particular area. For example, children from a pottery-making culture have considerably fewer problems at very young ages with conservation of matter tasks than French children do. More broadly, research of the last 15 years has challenged the foundations of Piaget's stage theory, by showing that after simplifying Piaget's tasks, children have many of the representational capacities that Piaget believed they lacked and by providing different explanations for children's performance. For example, if three year olds are drilled on different days on hundreds of pair-wise comparisons of balls of different sizes, they can then create linear orderings and make relevant deductive, transitive inferences over new comparisons where they previously could not. For both conservation and transitivity, there are differences in experience – and perhaps memory utilization differences – between children and adults, but children have the same representational capacity as adults. In general it appears that knowledge differences account for more "cognitive" differences between children and adults than do qualitative differences in, for example, representational capacity (e.g., Carey 1985). This shift to a quantitative model places cognitive development more in accord with Jakobsonian and Chomskian language development than under the traditional Piagetian view.

2   The Nature of Developmental Change

A theory of acquisition must include a theory of change, both describing the changes that occur, and then explaining them. We have found that, despite anatomical changes in the vocal tract during the second year, the words of even young children show the same basic system of features and featural relationships that structure adult languages of the world. Jakobson's original theory explained the feature hierarchy and the acquisition order in terms of phonological organization based ultimately on perception (the principle of maximal contrast along two acoustic dimensions), but the acoustic foundation to the theory has been the target of considerable criticism. Of the several possible explanations for acquisition stages, articulatory factors are primarily cited, but the evidence is usually indirect and the arguments often theory-rather than data-driven. To explore these issues, we will look at the earliest stage, where words are either one or two syllables in length, characteristically CV(CV) or CVC structures composed from a small inventory of segments and prosodically restricted to initial stress or level tones.

Even the simplest cases present analytic and theoretical issues. The child who says [du] for *juice*, as most English-speaking children are reported to say, is drawing on the basic Jakobsonian inventory and implications relationships. But we also must ask: Does the child know her word differs from the adult form? Does she know segments (as represented in the adult's transcription)? Is her word two segments long? Why two? Why CV? Why a voiced [d]? Why is the vowel more accurate than the consonant(s)? What significance does this simplification in form and content have for adult systems? Many explanations are compatible with the surface form: the simplification can be due to random or idiosyncratic effects, context effects, memory limits, articulatory inability, perceptual confusions, phonological organization or simplification, or a perceptual miscategorization or expectancy bias in the adult observer/transcriber.

2.1 Methodological Issues

Acquisition research deals with the methodological problem by obtaining many tokens of each word spontaneously produced in different contexts (with detailed verification of form, meaning, and intent) and collecting such data for the child's complete lexicon weekly or biweekly for many months. Complete lexicon and longitudinal data are crucial. Children are acquiring systematic rules (or operating under systematic constraints), and it is systems of rules (constraints) that are changing. Acquisition data can seem chaotic when taken out of the context of a given child's system, and many of the differences between children are due to differences between types of systems. Only longitudinal data can show the complete nature of structure. All developmental stages and diachronic changes yield possible synchronic states. But any "stage" can be the observer's arbitrary cuts along the time dimension, and any cross-sectional observation may contain odd elements. Some are unassimilated or idiosyncratic elements (e.g., family conventionalized forms). But most synchronically "odd" elements are temporary residues of earlier stages, atypical only with respect to the current primary system. Given the variation, similar data must be collected from several children matched for all variables.

As to the problem of perception and bias, we as adults listen with highly phonemically (and psychophysically) categorized ears, and as observers and theoreticians we look and "see" with other types of preexisting ideas. An example is the way in which we hear the voiced stop in [du]. Cross-linguistic acoustic analyses of the speech of 18 to 24(+) month old children show they initially produce all stops in the short-lag voice-onset time (VOT) range – voiceless and unaspirated, as Jakobson predicted – and that English-learning children go through a second stage in which their short-lag stops show a significant difference in mean VOT between stops that correspond to adult voiced versus voiceless phonemes (Macken and Barton 1980). From the perspective of the adult observer, the voiceless stops in both stages fall within the perceptual boundary category of voiced phonemes /b, d, g/ for adult English speakers. This accounts for the strong tendency for English-speaking writers to (mis-)transcribe [du] and (erroneously) discuss the (context-free) "voicing" of all stops in the speech of very young children.[5] The significant difference in mean VOT shows that the voicing contrast exists in the child's underlying representation at least by stage two. While acoustic evidence is rarely available, the listener's perceptual bias problem can be dealt with in a number of ways. The problem of projecting our theories of the world onto our observations is tougher. Assuming for the moment that forms like [du] (or [tu]) are systematic and accurate realizations of their targets and representative of the child's lexicon and stage of development, we can turn to the major explanatory theories – qualitative capacity constraints, motor development, perceptual development, and phonological systematization.

2.2   Capacity

Let us consider the canonical length of words during this stage. This restriction is of particular interest, because the next stages are not similarly constrained: there are no three-syllable or four-syllable stages, etc. Do these characteristically short utterances verify the universality and core status of the CV syllable and the disyllabic foot – a conclusion that assumes that the explanation lies with innate, end-state phonological constraints? Are there other possible explanations? As for nonlinguistic capacity constraints, there is little direct evidence that bears on a possible memory or general cognitive, neurological or biological base to this restriction of lexical forms to one or two syllables.[6] But there are data on a similar string restriction in digit and letter span, arguably an analogical domain. It is well established that there are great differences between children and adults when asked to repeat strings of letters or numbers. Adults can remember and reproduce seven (plus or minus two) items, while the four year old generally can repeat only three. If this difference is due to a qualitative difference, say in memory capacity, we might expect that adults have more "slots" in short-term memory. Similarly, the two-year old child who produces [du] for *juice* or [nana] for *banana* may have fewer "slots" for lexical performance. If this difference were due to such a fundamental capacity difference, we would not expect any necessary relationship between how children and adults "lexicalize" digit spans or word strings. The fact that a two-year-old child might "lexicalize" a string "485791" as "91" would have no particular significance for adult cognition and the status of binary units. Similarly for words, forms like [du] might show the same type of string or slot constraint and be of equal nonsignficance for adult representation.

If, however, this difference in performance is due to basic differences in knowledge or experience (quantitative differences between children and adults), we would expect that because children are less familiar with numbers or words, they are less able to use their memory capacity, while adults who have much greater knowledge of numbers can use that knowledge and familiarity to increase their efficiency (where, e.g., noticing even-odd patterns or ascending-descending patterns simplifies the recall of "485791"). For digit and letter span, experimental work has been done that distinguishes these alternative explanations. If stimuli of equal familiarity are presented to adults and children, the marked developmental difference is nearly wiped out: on strings of very high frequency lexical items or equally unfamiliar nonsense items, the adult-to-child advantage goes from over 2 to 1 to only 1.3 to 1 (Chi 1976). Thus for number, letter, and word span, memory capacity does not change much over the course of development.[7]

In the case of acquisition data on word production, we have further evidence that memory or some other capacity constraint is not the explanation. Complexity of the string matchings makes this constraint questionable. For example, the full range of a given child's forms will not be explainable by either a simple left-right or right-left filter (e.g., *banana* [bana], *balloon* [bun], *juice* [du]). More importantly, the reductions correspond to constituent structure. To know that [du] for [dʒus] is a segmented, syllable-type constituent structure and not the result of recency slot mapping, we must know that the child segments the word and "recognizes" in some way the last string element [s] and that [d] corresponds to [dʒ]. Indeed, other evidence does show such knowledge. In general, children know considerably more than their production behavior would suggest. To show this brings us to the fundamental issue of the child's mental representation and the remaining major theories – production, perception and/or phonological systematization – proposed for explaining developmental change.

We can infer the structure of the internal grammar by looking at the linguistic descriptions of the child's performance – which leads usually to indeterminacy – or by examining the order in which particular structures are acquired, much as Jakobson did. A different window on the mind can be found by looking at the properties of change itself. If the characteristics of diachronic change differentiate linguistic synchronic structure, the nature of structure will become clear during change in the same way that objects in a complex visual field – objects that appear interlocked when still and perceptually fused – separate into distinct forms when one of them moves. By looking for explanations in the properties of change in this way, we can identify three basic types of rules, each associated with a hypothesis about the child's underlying lexical representation and one aspect of development (Macken 1992b).

2.3 Acoustic Constraints

For some words, we find that they are produced correctly (in certain respects) at one stage and incorrectly at a next stage. Consider the following pairs of words, where the first member of a pair shows this incorrect second stage: (a) *chalk* [tšak] T1 (Time 1), [trak] T2 (Time 2); *train* [tšen] T1, [tren] T2; (b) *bran* [bræn] T1, [brænd] T2; *hand* [hæn] T1, [hænd] T2. For this type of change, Type 1, (i) two segments *x* and *y* are neutralized as *y*, (ii) a phonological change *x'* spreads slowly through the learner's lexicon (over a period of months) (iii) word-by-word, with some consistent lexical exceptions, and (iv) appears in the correct *x* and incorrect *y* environments, resulting in errors on *y*. The simplest explanation of this kind of change is that the child's underlying representations at T1 are the same as the surface representations and, in other words, there is no actual phonological rule of neutralization operating during this stage: e.g., adult /tr/ and /tš/ are both underlyingly /tš/ for the child. Actual rules for Type 1 phenomena operate at Time 2 when the lexical representations are changed: e.g., at Time 2, a rule of [tš] → [tr] is applied piecemeal to (correctly) construct underlying representations in words like *train* but creating errors on words like *chalk*. What appears to be going on in these cases is that the child does not completely perceive the relevant adult contrast at Time 1. Thus, even after age two, some perceptual learning takes place (cf. also Ingram 1974 and Waterson 1987) – typically in words where the segmental structure is complex and the acoustic cues for the constituent segmental contrasts are difficult to perceive. Type 1 change appears to characterize a small number of the rules found between the ages of two and four.

2.4 Articulatory Constraints

Type 2 change is considerably more common than Type 1 between the ages of two and four. In this type, (1) two segments *x* and *y* are neutralized as *y*, (2) a phonological change *x'* spreads rapidly through the learner's lexicon (in a matter of days usually) (3) in all and only the correct environments (4) with no errors on *y*. Examples of Type 2 change include the acquisition of fricatives and [r] shown in the first word of the following pairs of words: (a) *bus* [bət] T1, [bəs] T2; *but* [bət] T1, [bət] T2; (b) *pretty* [bIdi] T1, [prIdi] T2; *pip* [bIp] T1, [pIp] T2; (c) *rain* [dein] T1, [rein] T2; *den* [dɛn] T1, [dɛn] T2. The across-the-board nature of these changes, in all and only the correct environments, suggest that the child's underlying representations are accurate at T1 and at T2 and what has been learned at T2 is how to say particular segments that have been perceived and represented correctly for some period of time (Smith 1973; Stampe 1969, p. 146). For example, *bus* is /bəs/ at both T1 and T2; and /s/ is changed at the surface at T2. If so, articulatory constraints account for much of the child's development. Many Type 2 rules are, however, instances of Jakobson's implicational rules (e.g., fricatives and affricates are replaced by stops of the same place of articulation). Thus, although fricatives may have to be "learned" motorically, the phonological relationship between fricatives and stops (which explains why the fricative replacement is a stop) may be based on acoustic principles of contrast within phonological systems.

Type 1 relationships at Time 1 show the existence of a perceptual filter; Type 1 rules proper at Time 2 operate between the child's underlying representation and the child's lexical (or phonemic) representation, while Type 2 rules operate between the latter and the child's surface phonetic form. In terms of properties like slow, word-by-word spread, Type 1 rules are a developmental analogue of lexical diffusion sound change; rapid across-the-board changes show Type 2 rules to be the analog of classical Neogrammarian change. This parallel suggests that substantive phonetic content of features (acoustic versus articulatory) may play a role in these two different types of historical change as well. The two rule types also resemble the distinction in lexical phonology between, respectively, lexical rules which may have exceptions and post-lexical rules which do not, and thus may be an early reflex of the grammar organization. There are other types of variation not covered by Type 1 and Type 2 rules. First, because children are unskilled, there is much phonetic variation (especially in fricatives) as children acquire adult-like control; this variation is not evidence of a slow spread of a Type 1 rule across the lexicon. Second, occasionally a word can become an isolated lexical exception and remain so for a long period of time; such words have been relexicalized or "restructured" (e.g., *take* which remained [keik] until 3 years, 1 month, and 15 days of age [abbreviated henceforth in the style 3; 1.15], long after the velar harmony rule disappeared (2; 8.4), Smith 1973). Such restructured exceptions are not necessarily evidence of a Type 1 rule change.

2.5   *Lexical Generalizations*

Type 3 rules are more complicated than either Type 1 or Type 2, in that the underlying mechanism appears to be the imposing of pure, systemic phonological organization itself. In Type 3 change, (1) two or more segments x and y (, z) are distinct, (2) then a phonological change x' spreads through the learner's lexicon in the correct environments and (3), some time later (typically, a couple of weeks), spreads rapidly and across the board to the incorrect y (, z) environment(s), (4) resulting in errors on y (, z). For example, at T1 (from 1; 6 to 1; 10), a child reduced initial stop + /r/ clusters by deleting /r/: *pretty* [pItī]; *tree* [ti], *drink* [tIŋk]; *cradle* [kedəl]. At T2 (1; 11.0), initial /tr/ and /dr/ change to [f], *tree* [fi], *drinking* [fɪŋkiŋ], etc. The coalecence of frication and rounding in [f] is probably due to the strong aspiration in this cluster in English and the labiality of English /r/. To this point, the rule is a typical Type 1 or Type 2 rule: if the former, then we would expect later some errors on true /f/-initial words when the rule is "unlearned," but no errors if a Type 2 rule. The next development however, at T3 (2; 0), is one where the rule is generalized, rapidly spreading across the board to all voiceless stop clusters, wiping out the previous contrasts at all three places of articulation: e.g., *pretty* [fItī], *tree* [fi], *cradle* [fedəl], and so on. The child here has made a generalization in terms of phonological (onset) categories and a major phonetic step backwards (or regression) at the level of correct [p, t, k] segment production.

That the generalization to /pr/ and /kr/ takes place very fast (within days) and in an across-the-board manner tells us, as with Type 2 rules, that the change is operating on underlying, well-defined categories. Thus, we can conclude that the child has distinct underlying representations for /pr/ and /kr/ initial clusters (versus initial /p/ and /k/ words). This fact, with the delay of several weeks between the origin of the [f]-rule and its subsequent spread to labial and velar clusters, tells us that all three places of articulation are underlyingly distinct and that the rule is not a Type 1 rule (cf. also harmony regressions, Macken and Ferguson 1983, p. 269). Is it an articulatorily based Type 2 rule that just happens to have been independently generated in each of the three clusters? Not likely. First, the properties of change are not completely the same as with Type 2 rules (cf. the delay). Second, although all acquisition rules are phonetically natural, the articulatory motivation for each case is not equally convincing: [f] for [tr] is phonetically natural and common among children; the phonetic case for [f] from [pr] is weaker, and this alternation is rare among children; the phonetic argument for independently deriving [f] from [kr] is even weaker, and there are no other cases in what is a very large literature of a child using [f] for only [kr]. Finally, it is extremely unlikely that three such formally similar rules would spontaneously arise independently at the same time. What these Type 3 rules show is the child actively forming generalizations over classes of segments and subsets of the lexicon, in effect constructing interim, relatively abstract, autonomous phonological rule systems. These cases show, sometimes dramatically, that a significant part of development involves cases of getting better *phonologically*, by getting worse phonetically. This kind of (individual rule) nonlinearity in development shows most clearly the phonological aspects of acquisition and demonstrates that some aspects of acquisition fall outside the explanatory range of phonetic (segment-centered) theories.

Type 3 rules generally simplify lexical representations by creating symmetry along some abstract dimension of phonological organization as in the above example and in Amahl's "acquisition" of a velar fricative which filled out a symmetric system of /bdg, mnŋ, wlγ/ (see Smith 1973, pp. 109, 179; cf. also examples cited in Macken and Ferguson 1983). These rules operate between the underlying representation and the child's lexical representation on perceptually and phonologically distinct categories, and hence may be psychologically real in a way that Type 2 rules do not seem to be. Type 3 rules appear to be discovered or invented by the child: the general pattern is (1) isolated accuracy (i.e., "progressive idioms"); (2) a period of experimentation; (3) construction of a rule; (4) overgeneralization, which causes the loss of accuracy or regression in some forms; (5) construction of a new, more general (and ultimately accurate) rule (Macken and Ferguson 1983). To take a single word as an example, *pretty*, Hildegard Leopold's first permanent word, was pronounced with near perfect phonetic accuracy for a year (a "progessive idiom") and then was systematically pronounced as [pIti] and still later in a third stage as [bIdi], a month later (Leopold 1947). The two regressions correspond to the times when rules of consonant cluster reduction and consonant voicing (respectively) appeared in her system. Both these rules show the properties of change associated with Type 2 rules and are typically assumed in the literature to be articulatorily-motivated rules; however, the first year accuracy shows that the child could literally articulate both clusters and voiceless stops – which raises a question about the underlying explanation for the rules. While Type 2 rules most likely do have a basic articulatory component and Type 3 rules are most clearly nonautomatic, organizational generalizations, it may be, as suggested by Kiparsky and Menn (1977b), that *all* actual rules are discovered or invented by the child. These three types of developmental change suggest that there are three basic aspects to acquisition – perception, articulation, and phonological generalization.

2.6   *Phonological Units*

The Jakobsonian data and examples like the generalization underlying the velar fricative in Smith (1973) show that features are integral to acquisition and can be the unit of generalization. For the types of questions raised at the beginning of this section, we can reasonably be certain that the surface [d] is distinct from the affricate /dʒ/ and that the surface omission of /s/ is likely to be a similar Type 2, articulatorily-based rule. As rules change, systematically affecting all lexical instances of, say, /d/ or /s/, we reasonably infer that the child "segments" the input and represents words in terms of a linear sequence of segment-sized or equivalent-length units. As to how early segmentation takes place prior to this stage, we only can say that from the earliest stages of word use, in most cases, children behave in accordance with the hypothesis of segmented underlying representations; and we acknowledge that, alternatively, the underlying representations may be in a nonsegmented, Gestalt format at an early point during the first stage (e.g., Waterson 1987). The format of these beginning representations cannot be decided at this point. This raises other issues and is a problem to which we return below.

The acquisition evidence strongly suggests that the CV syllable, disyllabic foot, and prosodic word are basic to the universal core of phonological systems. We can exclude general memory constraints as an explanation here. In the case of Type 3 rules, children form interim phonological generalizations over the subsets of the lexicon known at each stage. Humans are powerful pattern recognizers, and this process of rule discovery or invention (Type 3 rules and possibly Type 2 rules) is a central part of phonological acquisition. What is the purpose of creating generalizations only to discard them at the next stage? Perhaps the construction of these rules is a way to learn about and systematize the lexicon. These cross-lexicon patterns then improve memory for the sound system and increase performance accuracy similar to the way that learning about relationships between numbers increases the efficiency of memory and improves performance on tasks like digit span. Thus memory would play the same indirect role in the quantitative changes that occur in phonological development as in cognitive development (transitivity, conservation, etc.). In both, change is tied to learning knowledge about specific domains. For phonology, while the content of the specific rules changes as the subset of the lexicon known changes at different stages, the form of rules, the capacity and fundamental structure do not change over development. It is equally important to recognize that it is not the lexicon per se driving the change or rules: for the same lexical subset, different children will use/invent different rules; and children will change rules when there has been no corresponding structural change in the child's lexicon. Rules are not passive, emergent properties of the lexicon, but active, creative constructions of the user.

3 Differences Between Child and Adult Phonology – Problems for the Theory?

A corollary, though not a necessary one, of the strong-identity thesis is the view advanced by Halle (1962), and Kiparsky (e.g., 1968b, 1971, 1988), among others, that children may be one source of historical change in individual languages, either through imperfect learning (Kiparsky; cf. also Paul 1886) and/or through an alternative grammar compatible with the set of utterances learned at a particular stage (Halle). Children are a highly unlikely source of the particular rules of language change, because first and foremost, children do ultimately get it right: they learn to sound identical to their (native speaker) parents and presumably have the same underlying representations and the same or an equivalent grammar by age five or six generally (e.g., the nearly complete adult compentence at 4; 0 in Smith 1973).[8] Second, the general universality of their stages would hardly be compatible with the diversification of languages or of a particular language, and conversely, where children do differ (from other children), it is precisely the idiosyncrasy of those individual children's interim rules that limits their "adoption" by others and the potential explanatory value of such rules for typical sound changes. Third, given cross-cultural child-rearing practices, children's interim acquisition rules have absolutely no social support for transmission.[9] Finally, and of particular interest for this paper, there are certain cases where the content of acquisition rules and of sound change *is* different and, likewise, where acquisition and synchrony – the resulting states of sound change – differ. Do these differences create problems for the strong-identity thesis?

At the most specific, we can find highly unusual interim rules. Consider, for example, the rule system reported in Priestly (1977), where a child generalized a *CVjVC* template to cover most disyllabic words: *cracker* [kajak], *breadman* [bijan], *records* [rejas], etc. The form of this rule at the CV template level is typical of children who construct templatic generalizations (though the use of both left-to-right and edge-in association is not typical); however, the content of the rule, particularly the medial glide, is unique in acquisition as far as we know, and unattested in known templatic languages of the world. Classical generative theory, which distinguished formal and substantive universals, would not be concerned with the singularity of a particular rule (or statistical facts of rule distribution, see below) provided a rule was a possible rule on formal grounds, which this rule is. However, more restrictive theories that require that constraints on form and content be universal may encounter difficulty with such data (e.g., McCarthy and Prince, chapter 9 of this volume). For such theories, these cases may demonstrate that some acquisition data fall outside the domain of phonological theory; or there can be a synchronic grammar with such a constraint, and the theory must generate both the child and adult structures.

3.1　Asymmetries

More interesting are two types of asymmetries between acquisition on the one hand and diachrony/synchrony on the other: (1) phonological processes with one typical directionality in acquisition and typically the inverse in diachrony – e.g., fricatives frequently replaced by stops in acquisition versus the more common sound change where stops change to fricatives; and (2) inverse distributions – consonant harmony common in acquisition, rare in synchrony, while vowel harmony is common synchronically in languages of the world yet infrequent in acquisition (and rare in recorded histories of sound change for that matter). For both (1) and (2), the issue is not one of mutually exclusive occurrence but rather statistical asymmetry – a fact about the world that under classical generative theory would again not necessarily concern the formal theory but that may be the province of Praguean marking theory and nonlinear theories.

The (1) cases seem to stem largely from what is, I believe, one central but not previously discussed difference between acquisition and diachrony: many historical sound changes and synchronic alternations are due to contextual effects between string adjacent consonants and vowels (e.g., palatalization), while none of the primary rules of acquisition and few of the other attested rules in the first year or two (ages one to three) show interactions between consonants and vowels. To the extent that sound changes like stops to fricatives begin in and/or are limited to positions after particular vowels or strictly string-based post-vocalic/intervocalic weakening processes (e.g., Spanish spirantization of medial voiced stops), they would not occur in early acquisition. The nearest acquisition analogues are the context-sensitive, word-based or syllable-sensitive processes like devoicing in final position (voicing in initial and medial positions) and fricatives acquired first in final (or medial) position, and low-level phonetic effects like stops showing somewhat greater closure variability in medial position. A full-scale acquisition analogue of Grimm's Law is unattested (and thus the kind of case where children are clearly unlikely sources of sound change); and the typical, across-the-board acquisition pattern of fricatives to stops is only diachronically common for the interdental fricatives (e.g., Germanic). Not enough is known about the rule types of diachrony and acquisition to pursue this question much further for other rules (cf. Dressler 1974 for other suggestive examples).

3.2 *Harmony*

Though the data are incomplete also for the (2) consonant-vowel asymmetries, these are more widespread and raise interesting questions for nonlinear theories of spreading, adjacency, and locality. The basic facts to explain appear to be an early acquisition of vowels as a set, frequency of consonant harmony, infrequency of vowel harmony, the protracted stage of consonant harmony, and patterns of individual differences. Typically, vowel harmony (where documented) characterizes only the stages before age two, while consonant harmony is more widespread in a child's system and lasts well into the third year (e.g., Smith 1973).

As to the individual differences, some children are reported to have a minimal consonant inventory and extensive vowel contrasts (e.g., Braine 1974), while the reverse (many consonantal contrasts, small number of vowels) is reported for other children acquiring the same language (e.g., Velten 1943); such a difference presumably could be correlated with consonant harmony versus vowel harmony, respectively. To some extent, observer categories and/or psychophysical constraints may contribute to the reported greater diversity among vowels: consonants are highly categorically perceived, while vowels are perceived in a more continuous manner; an adult then will tend to perceive greater variation and contrast in the child's vowels and fewer differences in the consonants.

Finally, consonant harmony though common is not universal among children (e.g., Vihman 1978). Some children show basically no consonant harmony (and no melody rules), such as G reported in Stemberger (1988) and E in Moskowitz (1970). For those children who use harmony, a wide variety of place and manner harmony rules will be found. In contrast, there are children who have long distance rules but who do not or only rarely use harmony. These children show constraints of a very different kind, namely where place and manner features are linearly ordered – a "melody" grammar, as opposed to the other or "harmony" grammar: thus, for example, while coronal consonants frequently undergo harmony in the former type systems – *sopa* "soup" [popa] – melody grammars will metathesize or otherwise sequence coronal consonants to the right of a noncoronal consonant – *sopa* [pota] (Macken 1992a).

In synchronic languages, in contrast, vowel harmony is common and consonant harmony is infrequent. Furthermore, synchronic consonant harmony almost always involves coronal or laryngeal features only (e.g., Chumash sibilant harmony or Rendaku/Lyman's Law in Japanese, respectively), and place of articulation harmony is rare (reported for Eskimo Inupiaq dialects). Nonlinear theory treats assimilation as spreading between a specified element and an underspecified element (e.g., coronals), both of which are adjacent at some level of representation, as for example on an autosegmental tier or between adjacent nodes in the feature geometry. One motivation for the geometric separation of vowel features from consonant features is to capture the natural assimilation of vowels over intervening consonants and the rarity or nonexistence of noncoronal place assimilation of consonants over vowels (e.g., Archangeli and Pulleyblank in press). Such theories cannot in principle account for the naturalness of acquisition harmony rules nor any acquisition place harmony over an intervening vowel that shares the same place feature as the trigger consonant (e.g., *doggie* [gɔgi]), a violation of the no–line crossing constraint. Alternatively, treating harmony as V-to-C assmilation (to handle [gɔgi]) fails with the equally frequent velar harmony over high front vowels (e.g., *drink* [gɪŋk]). The consonant-vowel metathesis rules of melody grammars similarly violate the no–line crossing constraint in feature-geometric theories of locality. The observed differences between adult and child harmony rules, then, would place acquisition data outside the explanatory framework of the synchronic (adult) theory.

3.3 Templates

However, planar segregation provides a third approach to locality, one that permits consonants and vowels to be on separate planes under specified morphological or phonological conditions (McCarthy 1981a, 1989b). With planar segregation, acquisition harmony templates and the templatic, melody V/C metathesis representations are well-formed, if in the latter cases, the medial consonant is a default consonant: precisely as would be expected, the medial consonant in such melody templates is typically a voiceless coronal stop.[10] In addition, acquisition melody and harmony grammars fit all the McCarthy (1989b) diagnostics for phonological planar segregation: rigid consonant-consonant constraints in CVC(V) words (cf. harmony), V/C metathesis, and highly restricted prosodic structure constraints (e.g., CV syllables), as found for example in the Mayan and Oceanic languages. With planar segregation, then, the frequency of consonant harmony is related to the predominance of highly rigid, simple prosodic structure; the rarity in synchronic languages is a function of the rarity of the enabling conditions. Moreover, the same representational structure – planar segregation – provides a uniform account of what had been thought to be two unrelated acquisition facts (the harmony versus melody grammars) and shows the underlying unity between the adult and child data. In general, the consonant-consonant constraints in acquisition strongly resemble, not distant assimilation, but (1) string-adjacent assimilation rules in sound change (e.g., Pali intervocalic consonant assimilatory changes from Sanskrit) and synchronic grammars (e.g., place assimilation in Spanish nasal clusters) and (2) string adjacent consonant constraints that permit only geminates or homorganic consonant clusters in languages like Diola Fogny (Sapir 1965), those that permit place to vary in consonant clusters only if the second consonant is coronal as in languages like Attic Greek (Steriade 1982), or the less common constraints where CC sequences are ordered left-right according to point of articulation as in Georgian where C1 must be further front than C2 (Tschenkéli 1958). The apparent difference between child and adult harmony and melody rules is, rather, a function of the same constraints operating on adjacent consonants – string adjacent consonants in adult languages and consonants adjacent at a planar level of representation in child templatic harmony and melody systems (Macken 1992a).

3.4   C-V Interactions

If, then, consonants and vowels are segregated on different planes, we would expect in acquisition that there would not be assimilatory changes between vowels and consonants, which is the general case, as previously noted. There is, however, a counterexample reported sporadically for the very first stage of word use for some children acquiring English: for these children, there is a statistical tendency for coronal consonants to occur before high front vowels (e.g., Braine 1974; Fudge 1969) and possibly labials before back round vowels (e.g., MacNeilage and Davis 1993). If these representations are segmented (cf. the discussion above) and the data are not related to extraneous factors like the structure of the adult models, reduplication or the (English) diminutive, this distribution would suggest consonant-vowel interactions (C-to-V assimilation). If in addition, these children are among the children who use harmony or melody processes, then planar segregation is not the solution; it remains to be seen whether in such a case other locality mechanisms (like feature geometry or C-to-V assimilation for the harmony cases) would uniformly work.

It appears, however, that many cases of C-V co-occurrences are not due to active vowel-to-consonant assimilation rules in the child's system but are cases where the C-V distributions are a direct reflection of characteristics of the lexicon and further that some of the children who show the C-V co-occurrence restrictions do not produce active harmony or melody forms (e.g., Braine 1974; the first stage in Fudge 1969, sect. 3.1). It may, however, be that some of these cases indicate that another option available to children is the syllable as the primary organizing unit (cf. Moskowitz 1973) although there is little data that would support the centrality of syllables as a general stage. Most likely, these early representations are rather in a gestalt, nonsegmented form and nonrepresentative of those children's representations in later stages. For example, in Fudge (1969), at the second stage (sect. 3.2) when vowel harmony and velar harmony appear, the evidence for active C-V harmony (tenuous even in the first stage) is sparse at best. For the majority of English-learning children, there is little or no evidence of C-to-V assimilation, of consonant-vowel co-occurrence restrictions, or of the types of developmental progressions that would be expected if consonants and vowels were on the same representational plane or if the primary phonological unit were the syllable and children used an inventory of syllable types. In contrast, there is considerable evidence that vowels and consonants are representationally and developmentally autonomous (during the time period in question). Recent cross-linguistic research has not found C-V co-occurrences except where the child data reflects the adult language distribution (e.g., Boysson-Bardies 1993). Thus, this would be one Aristotelian case where the structure is not in the child but in the world.

While phonological theory has not settled all locality and adjacency issues and confirming evidence must come for the acquisition issues as well, current nonlinear theory provides a unifying account of the major case of differences between children and adults – the (2) type consonant-vowel asymmetries – and brings greater insight into the variation found in the acquisition literature as well, turning an apparent exception into verification of the strong-identity thesis.

4   Conclusions

For many issues concerning underlying representations and for many different phonological domains – particularly prosodic structure, tone, the interaction with morphology and syntax – much additional research is needed. But for the well-studied phonology of features, segmental rules, templates, and the prosody of the CV syllable and the foot, the evidence from children shows the same structure and variation as found in adult systems. Given the validity of the strong-identity thesis, acquisition data not only can be used to confirm and change phonological theory, but each relevant theoretical proposal must be able to incorporate acquisition data.

Ultimately, phonological theory will explain the stages, constraints on variation, and the form of rules found across all learners either as options available in universal grammar or through interactions between subdomains. Yet, as striking as the differences are between harmony and melody learners or between children who appear to construct rule systems based on quite different core units, there is no evidence at all that subsequent stages show the effects of earlier rule types. Thus, structure of language does exist separately from the particular acquisitional paths traveled. The absence of any residue of the content of particular interim grammars is a significant problem for all empiricist learning theories: stochastic learning is cumulative and where paths differ, outcomes differ. The acquisition data confirm that language is, rather, a formal problem space. It does not matter to the learner the different points of entry or the particular trajectories through this space. The outcome is the same – a shared, fully adult phonological grammar and competence by six years of age. We can look at the variation across children as a mix of "correct" rules (in the sense of being steps that can be considered, with miminal adjustments, as toward the target language) and "incorrect" rules (where no miminal, local adjustments could reorient toward the target). Given the sheer number of children in the latter category, it is not unremarkable that those children get to the end state at all. That they do so in virtually the same amount of time would approach miraculous in a stochastic, indeed in any empiricist, world.

NOTES

1 The term "discontinuity" is used in two senses in the literature. In the most common, Jakobsonian sense, the theorized discontinuity between babbling and speech is supposed to indicate a complete break between the abilities and knowledge that characterize the two stages. The term is also used to describe the nonlinearity in development seen during phonological acquisition when the acquisition of a new rule or reorganization of structures causes a temporary, surface loss of ability or other anomaly; in this case, the change is within one part of a single system and does not mean the two temporal stages show two fundamentally different systems.

2 The Jakobson term is [dental], a category that excludes the true palatals, as did [coronal] in the original features (Chomsky and Halle 1968, hereafter cited as *SPE*). For the dentals, Jakobson explicitly characterizes their corresponding marked place of articulation as the velars.

3 In general, "front" is a valid category for acquisition order and developmental and cross-linguistic inventories. This is in opposition to the general lack of evidence for the corresponding Chomsky/Halle feature [+anterior] as a natural class.

4 Most acquisition researchers agree tacitly or explicitly in the strong identity relationship but disagree among themselves what the "system" is that is shared: formal phonology (Dresher 1981; Dresher and Kaye 1990), both an abstract, formal phonology and a stochastic component (Macken 1987), only a stochastic (connectionist) system (Stemberger 1992a), only a concrete,

phonetic system (Lindblom 1992; MacNeilage and Davis 1993).

5 This same kind of problem arises in cross-linguistic typological surveys and all areas of phonology.

6 Or, similarly, of sentences to two words during the first stage of syntax acquisition.

7 This is the same kind of result noted earlier for Piagetian conservation and transitivity. Children differ from adults in quantitative knowledge and experience but, it now appears, not in basic or core capacity.

8 This age is based on the existing acquisition studies. However, little if any work has been done on languages with complex phrasal phonology (e.g., the interaction of tone and phrasal position in Chaga) or languages with highly complex, productive morphology (e.g., the many thousand possible forms of verbs in Shona); children learning such languages may take longer to reach adult competence. If there is any doubt that phonological acquisition is the learning of rules rather than the memorization of word forms, data from these children will no doubt resolve this debate resoundingly on the side of rules.

9 These arguments apply to primary phonological acquisition – the child learning her native language. This of course leaves open whether adolescents who recreate language for peer solidarity can be a source of sound change.

10 Some melody template systems metathesize labial-velar consonants (e.g., Grammont 1902).

23 Language Games and Related Areas

BRUCE BAGEMIHL

0 Introduction

Language games have had a long and uneasy relationship with phonological theory. There has been a general hesitancy to incorporate this linguistic behavior into mainstream phonological theory until fairly recently, and even now, language games are often seen as useful only to the extent that they can support a particular line of argumentation. Although it probably has multiple roots, this hesitancy stems largely from two factors intrinsic to the data themselves: (1) language game operations are superficially quite unlike ordinary language operations; and (2) language games are alternate linguistic systems which, although found in nearly every human language, have a relatively restricted sociolinguistic function, small speaker population, and uncertain acquisitional process. For these reasons, language games have been brought in to function as so-called external evidence to confirm or falsify the particular analysis of various aspects of the ordinary languages they are based upon, with little attempt to understand them as linguistic systems of their own.

Ironically, it was only with the advent of nonlinear theories of phonology that a better understanding of the true nature of language game mechanisms was gained, thereby allowing them to be taken more seriously. With the insights into phonological representation and nonconcatenative operations offered by autosegmental and prosodic models, language game operations were revealed to be systematic, principle-governed, and formally related to well-known phenomena in ordinary language such as reduplication, in spite of their surface appearances to the contrary. In other words, in terms of their formal structure, language games were shown to differ not so much *qualitatively* from ordinary language, but rather *quantitatively* in the degree to which ordinary language operations were modified or extended in the derivation of language game forms. This paved the way for insightful formalizations of the language game operations themselves. Still, the ultimate question most often asked was What do these systems tell us about the nonlinear representations, prosodic operations, etc., of their source languages? rather than, Why do these systems take the particular forms that they do, and how do they manifest the human linguistic capacity in its broadest sense? In this survey of the results of theoretical language game studies, responses to both of these (equally valid) questions will be addressed, although it will be shown that often the most significant insights have been gained by focusing on the second question.

In section 1, a brief survey of language games and their coverage in the literature will be provided. Then, the interaction of language games with linguistic theory will be explored in relation to three areas: the formalization of language game operations (section 2), the structure of nonlinear representations (section 3), and the location of language games within the larger model of the grammar (section 4). Section 5 will present some concluding remarks.

1   A Brief History of Ludling Studies

What exactly is a "language game"? Traditionally, definitions have focused on the sociolinguistic functions that such systems perform, as revealed by their myriad names in the descriptive literature: language game, secret language, argot, code language, speech disguise, play language, word games, ritual language, speech play, and so on. The problem with such categories is that they obscure the formal similarities that are usually shared by these alternate linguistic systems regardless of their function – similarities that distinguish them as a group from other systems with identical functions but vastly different forms. While it is true that such languages are typically used to disguise the identity of their speakers and/or facilitate private communication between them, or else to serve as a challenging (and fun) test of linguistic prowess, these functions are also performed by many other types of alternate language which would never be classified as "language games."

For example, the merchant's argot used among Amharic speakers (Leslau 1964) is a "speech disguise" or "secret language," but it simply involves a vocabulary (lexicon) which is distinct from the ordinary language: the phonological and morphological systems of the two languages are identical. The function of concealment may also be performed by a surrogate language (a language which uses a sound-producing mechanism other than the larynx, for example, a whistle pitch or musical instrument): an example is the whistle language of Igbo adolescents described in Carrington (1949).[1] Another form of "speech disguise" is the purely phonetic modification found in *Fensterle*, a speech form of Swiss German in which pulmonic ingressive airstream is used to conceal the identity of the speaker in courtship situations (Catford 1977). Finally, within this same functional category one could probably also include Morse code: its use as a secret language is of course well known, and it is clear that from a functional perspective this phenomenon (and even more divergent systems) would be subsumed under the same general category.

In this chapter, language games will be defined in strictly formal terms, a move which is implicit in most current work on these systems but which was first suggested in Laycock (1972) and made fully explicit only in Bagemihl (1988a, 1988b). A significant advance in the classification of alternate languages was heralded by the appearance of Laycock (1972), in which attention was shifted away form the sociolinguistic functions of "play languages" to their formal properties. Laycock recognized that most of what had previously been labeled as play languages, secret languages, etc., share a very specific type of manipulation of linguistic structure; this property transcends the particular functions of these alternate linguistic systems and can be used as the basis for a more meaningful classification of them. Laycock coined the term *ludling* to refer to such systems, and I adopt this term here.[2]

For our purposes, a ludling is defined as a language which meets the following criteria: (1) its morphological system is limited to one or more operations drawn from the following: (a) infixing/affixing, (b) templatic, (c) reversal, (d) replacement; (2) its affixes (whether fully specified or defined only in prosodic or melodic terms) are limited to one or at most a handful of lexical items; and (3) its morphology is semantically empty.

The primary unifying characteristic of ludlings is that they exhibit an alternate and impoverished morphological system superimposed on the ordinary or non-ludling language. The four broad categories listed in (1) are not mutually exclusive (for example, a given ludling may combine infixation with reversal) and each includes a number of distinct subtypes, but the examples in (1) serve to illustrate the essence of each of these categories.

(1) Ludling operations
   (a) Infixing/affixing: Tigrinya, *-gV- Infixation* (Bagemihl 1987)
      bítŝa "yellow"   >   bigitŝaga
   (b) Templatic: Amharic, *Cay(C)(C)CC Template* (McCarthy 1985)
      bet "house"   >   baytət
   (c) Reversing: Tagalog, *Golagat* (Gil 1990)
      puti "white"   >   itup
   (d) Replacement: Cuna, *i-Replacement* (Sherzer 1982)
      nuka "name"   >   niki

The first and simplest type is the infixing or affixing ludling, which involves concatenation of a ludling affix in a non-ludling word. Typically the added element is an infix unspecified for its vowel or, less commonly, its consonant, although fully specified infixes and straight prefixes/suffixes are also attested.[3] The second major type of ludling morphology is templatic, in which the melodic portion of an ordinary language word is mapped onto a word-sized ludling template specified in terms of skeletal or perhaps more appropriately, prosodic structure. Sometimes certain segments in the template are prespecified or "overwritten," and other phonological features such as nasality or voicelessness may be mapped onto the template as well. The third major category is the reversing ludling, involving many different possible types of operations such as total segment or syllable reversal, transposition (moving a peripheral constituent to the opposite end of the word), interchange (switching the first two or the last two syllables), false syllable reversal (syllable reversal with timing properties held constant), and so on. Some of these ludlings have been analyzed as forms of reduplication, for example in Yip (1982) and Bao (1990a), while Bagemihl (1989) presents a comprehensive analysis of all these types in terms of line-crossing. Finally, in replacement ludlings, all or most of the vowels in a non-ludling utterance are replaced by one or two segments in the ludling form: in the Cuna example, all vowels are replaced by *i*. Consonant replacement is also attested: in Chaga, for example, one ludling uses only the consonants *k*, *r*, and *j* (Raum 1937). These systems have not received a theoretical analysis in the literature, but it is quite likely that they are examples of the process of melodic overwriting proposed by McCarthy and Prince (1990) for the analysis of certain types of nonconcatenative morphology.[4]

Another crucial characteristic of ludlings is that their morphology (whether an affix, a template, or an inserted segment) is semantically empty (cf. McCarthy 1982, 1985; Bagemihl 1988a, 1988b): any added elements do not carry an identifiable meaning. Rather, "they signal that an exceptional register is being used to classify the speaker or hearer as belonging to a particular category of individuals . . . In particular, they cannot be considered to modify or combine with the meaning of the words they are attached to or to carry information about other words in the sentence as do meaningful affixes" (Bagemihl 1988a, pp. 37–38).

The relationship of ludlings to modern phonological theory goes back to the earliest works of generative phonology. In Chomsky and Halle (1968), Pig Latin data were used to argue for the necessity of rule ordering, while even earlier, Halle (1962) used Pig Latin to argue for the idea that language is a rule- and principle-governed grammar rather than a list of utterances. However, such use of ludling data was somewhat atypical for what we may refer to as the "first wave" of theoretical ludling studies. In early studies, ludlings were usually used as confirming evidence for aspects of the phonology of their source languages rather than for addressing (meta)theoretical questions. (Most of the time, however, ludlings were simply considered irrelevant and ignored altogether.) This sort of approach continues to this day, and the majority of ludling studies (historical to contemporary) divide almost uniformly into two categories: (1) descriptive, nontheoretical studies of individual ludling systems, and (2) ludlings used as external evidence. Examples of the first type range from early accounts with only a handful of data items, such as Hirschberg (1913) and Schlegel (1891) to recent, more detailed studies such as Demisse and Bender (1983).[5] A number of authors have also developed typologies of ludling systems within a descriptive vein, most notably Laycock (1972) and

Haas (1967); see also Davis (1985) for a more recent survey, and Seppänen (1982) for a typology of Finnish ludlings from a computational perspective.

Studies in which ludlings are used as external evidence are, by now, fairly well established in the linguistic literature. Ohala (1986), in a survey of the relative merits of different types of evidence in phonological descriptions, ranks ludling data second only to experimental evidence; cf. Campbell (1986) for a similar endorsement. Perhaps the best known example of this type of study is Sherzer (1970), in which ludling data are used to argue for certain syllable structures and other aspects of the non-ludling phonological representations. Recent works such as Campbell (1980), Cowan, Braine, and Leavitt (1985), French (1988), and Demolin (1991) continue this tradition. A new type of study has also emerged fairly recently, one in which novel word games are created to test certain aspects of language structure; see Treiman (1983), Hombert (1986), and Campbell (1986).

In the "second wave" of theoretical studies, initiated primarily by the work of McCarthy (1979, 1982), phonologists discovered that ludling operations, rather than being bizarre or random, were outstanding examples of non-concatenative morphology which lent themselves to elegant analyses under the emerging theories of nonlinear phonology/morphology. Where simple verbal descriptions of ludling operations sufficed in the first wave, explicit and rigorous formalizations now began to be offered, and ludlings were in many cases considered to have "mini-grammars" worthy of theoretical investigation in their own right. Studies such as Yip (1982) and Broselow and McCarthy (1983) continued this "second wave," paving the way for a number of theoretically informed works devoted entirely to ludlings, such as Lefkowitz (1988), Bagemihl (1988b, 1989), Bao (1990), and Plénat (1991). Also falling into this category (and combining the "external evidence" approach) are studies in which ludlings are used as evidence for certain constructs in phonological theory (rather than aspects of their non-ludling language per se); examples include Vago (1985), Bagemihl (1987), and Tateishi (1989, 1991).

2   The Formalization of Ludling Operations

One of the most significant developments in the theoretical study of ludlings has been the recognition that ludling operations involve, to a large extent, modifications or extensions of ordinary language processes and principles. This discovery allowed ludling operations to be formalized as they had never been before, for nonlinear and prosodic models at last offered an idiom that was well-suited to the type of deformations performed by ludlings. At the same time, the fact that these frameworks could countenance naturally-occurring ludling operations while also excluding unattested ludling types, was powerful support for the models being developed. This is the sort of cross-fertilization between ludling systems and phonological theory that has led to some of the most important advances in each.

The first type of ludling to receive detailed theoretical attention was the infixing/affixing ludling, whose operations were used to argue for two basic constructs in the theories of nonlinear phonology/morphology: recognition of an independent level of timing structure or *skeleton* (see chap. 5, this volume, and also McCarthy 1982; Broselow and McCarthy 1983), and the placement of separate affixes on distinct morphological planes, sometimes known as the *Morphemic Tier Hypothesis* (McCarthy 1986; Cole 1987). Both of these assumptions were crucial in early nonlinear accounts of infixing ludlings to explain their apparent "vowel copying," which was analyzed as the result of an empty vowel slot supplied by the ludling infix which received its segmental specification by spreading of the nearest non-ludling vowel. If the infixed segment occupied the same plane as the non-ludling word, spreading of a vowel from an adjacent syllable could not be achieved without crossing association lines.

The fundamental insight that ludling infixes involve an unspecified skeletal or prosodic position has remained intact with the continuing evolution in the representation of such structure through X-theory (Levin 1985a; Lowenstamm and Kaye 1986) to moraic theory (McCarthy and Prince 1986; Hayes 1989). However, ludling evidence for the Morphemic Tier Hypothesis has not remained nearly as strong, given recent developments in feature geometry. The Morphemic Tier Hypothesis is by no means unchallenged in non-ludling phonology (cf. Lieber 1987; McCarthy 1989b), and its validity is less immediately apparent for ludling systems. In particular, with a hierarchical model of feature geometry it is in principle no longer necessary to assume that ludling and non-ludling morphemes occupy separate planes: vowel features can spread across an intervening consonant without planar segregation, provided their class node is distinct from the consonant's (as in Clements's (1985) original proposal). However, for theories which distribute vowel features between two or more articulator class nodes (e.g., Sagey 1986; Steriade 1987), the Morphemic Tier Hypothesis must be assumed to account for the spreading onto ludling infixes: if [round] is dominated by the class node Labial, for example, while [low] is dominated by Dorsal, then it will not be possible to spread both features across a consonant without having to refer to each of these articulator nodes separately. On the other hand, for a theory which advocates entirely separate tiers for vowels and consonants (e.g., Clements 1990), the Morphemic Tier Hypothesis is no longer necessary, and it once again becomes an empirical issue as to whether ludling affixes do in fact occupy separate planes.

Evidence bearing on this question is difficult to find, but several cases discussed in McCarthy (1991) and Bagemihl (1988b) appear to show that in the unmarked case the Morphemic Tier Hypothesis is observed. The most compelling example concerns the fact that there is a major asymmetry in infixing ludlings: when the infix follows the non-ludling syllable, its V-slot is unspecified (eventually acquiring the preceding non-ludling vowel through spreading), but when the infix precedes the non-ludling syllable, its vowel is always prespecified. This is illustrated by a ludling in Brazilian Portuguese (Sherzer 1982):

(2)   menina > mepenipinapa   *or*   pemepenipena

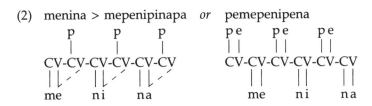

In this ludling, words can be formed in two different ways: one uses a postfix *-pV-* with unspecified vowel, the other has a prefix *-pe-*. What we do not find is the opposite case: there do not appear to be any ludlings which infix a syllable unspecified for its vowel *in front* of a non-ludling syllable. Such a result follows from the planar segregation of ludling affixes, if we assume that in the unmarked case spreading applies to root nodes: for a postfix, the non-ludling vowel can spread rightward "across" the ludling consonant on a separate plane, whereas it cannot spread leftward to a hypothetical ludling infix with an empty V slot because of the non-ludling consonant intervening on the same plane. (However, this argument would not hold under the theory proposed in Clements (1990)). Similarly, cases of ludling affixes unspecified for consonants but specified for vowels (cf. examples in Swedish and Benkulu discussed in Bagemihl 1988b and McCarthy 1991) would also argue for the Morphemic Tier Hypothesis, unless Clements's theory is assumed. For cases in Samoan and Tigrinya which seem to require ludling and non-ludling affixes on the *same* plane, see Bagemihl (1988b).

Like infixing ludlings, reversing and templatic ludlings first received theoretical attention in the context of the emerging theories of nonconcatenative morphology based on the CV-skeleton, in particular McCarthy's (1979, 1981) theory of "root-and-pattern" morphology and Marantz's (1982) theory of reduplication. Yip (1982) proposes that a particular class of Chinese reversing ludlings, the *fanqie* languages, are a startling example of prespecified reduplication/templatic morphology, in which the non-ludling phonemic melody is copied and then mapped onto a template with certain segments prespecified. Bao (1990) subsequently argued that Steriade's (1988) theory of reduplication, involving full copy of syllables followed by (in this case) replacement of certain subsyllabic constituents with fixed ludling segments, offers a better analysis. Specifically, this approach can account for the behavior of glides and the full range of tone patterns in the ludling, among other properties.

While in this instance a full-copy approach may be preferable, neither Bao's (1990) account nor Yip's (1982) account extends to the full range of reversing ludlings which are found in human language. The Chinese *fanqie* languages represent simply one type of ludling known as Sequence Exchange, to use the terminology of Bagemihl (1989); examples of additional reversal types are given in (3).

(3) (a) Exchange
  (i) *Segments*:   Tagalog: dito > doti "here" (Conklin 1956)
                 Javanese: satus > tasus "100" (Sadtano 1971)
  (ii) *Sequence*:   Hanunoo: rignuk > nugrik "tame" (Conklin 1959)
                 Thai: khab rod > khod rab "to drive"
                            (Surintramont 1973)
                 Mandarin: ma > (ma key >) mey ka (Yip 1982,
                            Bao 1990)

   (b) Total Reversal
  (i) *Segments*:   Javanese: dolanan > nanalod "play around"
                            (Sadtano 1971)
  (ii) *Syllables*: French: verite > terive "truth" (Lefkowitz 1987)
   (c) Transposition Fula: deftere > teredef "book" (Noye 1975)
   (d) Interchange   Chasu: ikumi > imiku "ten" (Raum 1937)
   (e) "False" Reversals
  (i) *Total*:   Bakwiri: zeeya > yaaze "burn" (Hombert 1973)
  (ii) *Interchange*: Sanga: mukweetu > mutuukwe (Coupez 1969)

The Chinese *fanqie* languages involve switching segments between a non-ludling word and a ludling "nonsense" word (e.g., *key* in the Mey-ka language); hence, reduplicative accounts are available for such ludlings because the segments of the nonsense word can always be construed as the prespecified information on the template (or the substituted onset/rhyme/etc.). However, sequence exchanges in many languages involve switching segments between consecutive non-ludling words, or within a single non-ludling word, and therefore cannot be analyzed as the substitution or prespecification of fixed information. Bagemihl (1989) proposes that these types of sequence exchanges as well as the full range of reversal types exemplified in (3) are derived through a combination of parameter settings which regulate the crossing of association lines. Line crossing is only available for ludling systems, and may combine with affixation of various prosodic constituents (e.g., syllables for transposition and interchange), template mapping (e.g., for total reversal), and segment spreading rules (e.g., for exchange processes). For example, a case of syllable transposition such as Fula *deftere > teredef* would result from suffixation of a maximal syllable, template satisfaction with maximum crossing of association lines, followed by movement of constituents to resolve the inconsistencies in linear ordering.[6]

True templatic ludlings (i.e., those which do not involve any reversal) have received less theoretical attention than other types. The few examples that have been considered argue for the recognition of the independence of the segmental and prosodic levels of representation, as well as operations which can take the melodic content of one word and map it onto a new skeletal/

prosodic frame. For example, McCarthy (1985, 1986) utilizes an Amharic templatic ludling to argue for the autonomy of the CV-skeleton, as well as the effect of the OCP in limiting consecutive occurrences of the same segment to a single element on the melodic tier.[7] Bagemihl (1988a) explores the theoretical implications of an Inuktitut vocal behavior known as *Katajjait* or throat games, arguing that they are a well-developed form of templatic ludling. In this system, Inuktitut and/or nonsense words are mapped onto a number of different ludling templates (which may themselves be reduplicated or triplicated); metrical structure is then constructed on top of this, governing the association of independent features regulating voicing and direction of airflow.

3   Nonlinear Representations

From their earliest treatments in the linguistic literature, ludlings have been used to argue for the psychological reality of phonological units such as the segment or phoneme. In more recent guises, ludlings provide important evidence for many aspects of nonlinear representations and prosodic categories. As we have seen, ludling data have fueled the recognition of a CV or timing tier precisely because many of their operations involve affixes which are unspecified for segmental material or involve manipulation of the melodic portion of a word independently of its timing properties. These characteristics have also been important diagnostics for some specific aspects of multi-dimensional structures, in particular the representation of long vowels and diphthongs and the autosegmental status of tone features.

Vago (1985) demonstrates that ludlings provide clear support for the nonlinear representation of long vowels, in which a single melodic element is doubly-linked to two V-slots or prosodic positions. In particular, ludlings of the "false syllable reversal" or "false interchange" types, as well as sequence exchange ludlings, reverse elements at the segmental level while leaving the skeleton or prosodic framework of the word intact (cf. the examples in (3a, e)). The Finnish sequence exchange ludling *kontti kieli* also provides evidence for recognizing a structural difference between heavy diphthongs (two segments linked to two V-slots/moras) and light diphthongs (two segments linked to one V-slot/mora):

(4)   Heavy: /veitsi/ "knife" > veitsi + kontti > koitsi ventti
      Light: /tee/ "road" > tie > tie + kontti > koo tientti

Heavy diphthongs are present underlyingly; as can be seen, only the first half of such a sequence participates in the reversal. Light diphthongs are derived from underlying long vowels, and in this case the entire diphthong behaves as a single unit in the reversal (with the replacing vowel *o* then occupying both of the original V-slots). Vago shows that this difference derives from the structural distinction between these two diphthongs. The ludling affects only the first CV sequence at the melodic level (his analysis is couched within a CV-framework); assuming that root nodes are being manipulated,[8] the difference between the two diphthongs follows from the fact that a light diphthong involves a many-to-one linking while a heavy diphthong is a one-to-one linking.

However, McCarthy (1991) examines the behavior of (derived) heavy diphthongs in English with respect to infixing ludlings and concludes that they also involve a many-to-one linking. Because such diphthongs act as single short vowels in the ludling (but are structurally long segments), we must consider these diphthongs to be a single segment (root node) linked to two prosodic positions, with branching only of the features that the two halves differ in:

(5)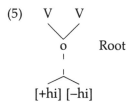

Such structures are compatible with the *kontti kieli* data only if we assume that in Finnish the ludling is manipulating units below the level of the root node.

The independence of tone from segmental features provided much of the original impetus for the development of autosegmental phonology; many of the earliest theoretical treatments of ludlings have also focused on this aspect. Hombert (1986) points out that reversing ludlings which affect segments while leaving tones intact provide strong evidence for what he refers to as the "suprasegmental" status of tones. A number of researchers have subsequently developed more detailed analyses of the relationship between tones, segments, and prosodic structure. Bagemihl (1989) develops a theory of ludling reversals in which elements can be reversed at either the segmental or the prosodic levels (through crossing of association lines); if the reversal is segmental (i.e., affects root nodes), tones are unaffected, while if reversal is prosodic, i.e., affects syllables, tones will also move. Furthermore, tone reversal is tied to the reversal of length: timing patterns are predicted to reverse whenever tone reverses, since both are achieved by manipulating elements at the prosodic level. Bao (1990) makes similar observations concerning *fanqie* languages: if segmental units are manipulated (through an operation of substitution) tones are unaffected, while if prosodic units are manipulated (e.g., various syllable subparts) then tones will be replaced as well.

In addition to enhancing our understanding of melodic-prosodic interactions, ludlings have recently offered support for the recognition and structure of strictly prosodic units such as the syllable, mora, and foot. Of course, syllable-reversing ludlings such as the examples given earlier were offered in the early generative literature as compelling evidence for recognition of the syllable as a bona fide phonological unit. More recently, the question of subsyllabic structure has come to the forefront. Originally, sequence exchange ludlings such as English Pig Latin were taken to support an onset-rhyme subdivision of the syllable, since in this ludling all word-initial pre-vocalic consonants (the putative onset) are affected: *street → eetstray*. However, Yip's (1982) templatic analysis of the similar Chinese ludlings demonstrated that prespecification on a fixed prosodic frame could account for the same type of facts without recognizing any internal syllabic constituency; this approach is echoed in McCarthy and Prince (1986) within a prosodic morphology framework. Bao (1990) advocates a return to subsyllabic constituency in the analysis of *fanqie* languages, utilizing a version of Steriade's (1988) framework where units such as onset, rhyme, nucleus, etc., can be replaced by fixed material (see chap. 6, this volume). The debate is far from resolved, however: Bagemihl (1989) shows that whatever mechanism is used for sequence exchanges with fixed material (e.g., Pig Latin, *fanqie* languages), it will not necessarily generalize to ludlings that exchange segments between or within non-ludling words. A line-crossing account, involving (iterative) segment-spreading rules, can account for all such cases without reference to an onset-rhyme division. Moreover, parallel to cases of putative rhyme manipulation (where a syllable-final VC sequence is moved, as in the Thai example in (3aii) above), we find cases where an initial CV sequence excluding any coda consonants is affected (e.g., Hanunoo in (3aii)). If we assume that ludlings can only manipulate phonological constituents, these ludlings are potentially problematic within traditional theories of syllable structure since this C_0V sequence does not form a constituent. Bagemihl (1989) analyzes these as consecutive spreading (exchange) of the prenuclear consonant(s) and vowel (since both consonant and vowel exchange are attested as independent operations; cf. (3ai)). Alternatively, in some theories which recognize the mora as a prosodic unit, the first C_0V sequence of a syllable is dominated by the same mora (see chaps. 5 and 6, this volume; see also Hyman 1985; Zec 1988), so it could be that these ludlings are accessing moras rather than segments or any other subsyllabic constituents.

The Japanese *Musician's Language* discussed in Tateishi (1989, 1991), Poser (1990), and Perlmutter (1991) provides further evidence for the mora as a subsyllabic constituent, as well as for the prosodic unit of foot. In this ludling, the largest rightmost constituent that does not exhaustively cover the word is transposed to the beginning of the word and mapped onto a bimoraic foot; the remainder of the word is also mapped onto a bimoraic foot (if only a single segment is transposed, a copy of it remains in the original syllable).

(6)	(a)	Foot	ku[suri]$_F$	"medication"	>	surikuu
			mane[zyaa]$_F$	"manager"	>	zyaamane
	(b)	Syllable	ha[ra]$_\sigma$	"stomach"	>	raahaa
	(c)	Mora	ha[i]$_\mu$	"lungs"	>	iihaa
	(d)	Segment	hi	"fire"	>	iihii

As can be seen, this ludling accesses both feet and moras in addition to syllables and segments.[9] These data have also been used to argue for right-to-left foot construction in Japanese, since in trisyllabic words left-to-right construction would incorrectly bracket together the first two syllables as a foot. This directionality is also consistent with a number of other phonological/morphological processes in Japanese such as the accentuation of noun-noun compounds and loanwords, and the gemination in intensive mimetics.[10]

4   The Organization of the Grammar

Although many descriptive and theoretical accounts of ludlings are now available, there are few definitive proposals regarding where ludling conversion is located within the larger model of the grammar. The most explicit early proposal is that of Mohanan (1982) who places the ludling component (where all ludling-specific phonology and morphology takes place) between the lexical and post-lexical components (within the framework of lexical phonology). This is based on two fundamental observations: all ludlings follow (non-ludling) morphological operations and lexical phonological rules, and all ludlings precede post-lexical phonological rules. A number of other authors have made passing statements about which level(s) of representation they consider to serve as input to the particular ludling they are examining (e.g., Yip 1982, p. 640; McCarthy 1986, p. 229; Cowan, Braine, and Leavitt 1985, p. 687; Churma 1979, p. 90). While there is no overall consensus on the location of ludlings, these authors seem to share the observation that ludling conversion may take place at some intermediate level or levels of representation within the phonology. Some authors also hypothesize that either quite shallow (surface) representations as well as fairly deep (lexical or underlying) representations may serve as input.

The most comprehensive proposal put forward is that of Bagemihl (1988b), who presents a detailed model of the ludling component based on data from more than fifty ludlings; this is schematized in (7). This model (also couched within the lexical phonology framework) preserves Mohanan's (and others') essential insight about an intermediate location for the ludling component, but posits a highly modularized internal structure to account for the cross-ludling variations. The basis of this model is a highly articulated conception of the post-lexical phonology-syntax interface, combining proposals of Selkirk (1984, 1986), Kaisse (1985a), Pulleyblank (1986a), Mohanan (1986), Rice (1990), and others, which converge in the recognition of at least five distinct post-lexical levels of representation within the non-ludling phonology.

According to this model, there are three points in the grammar where the ludling component can access the phonological representation, each corresponding to a particularly salient juncture within the grammar. The first module is located at the output of the lexicon prior to Tier Conflation,[11] the

(7)

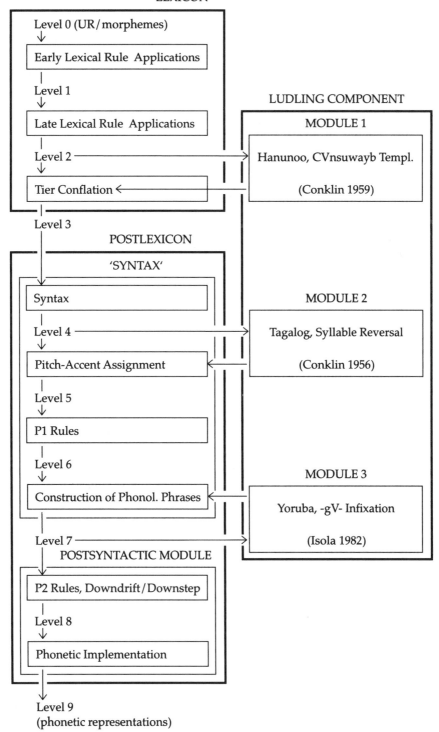

second at the output of the syntax prior to the post-lexical phonology, and the third at the division between the syntactic and postsyntactic modules of the postlexicon. Depending on which module a ludling is assigned to, it will exhibit a variety of distinctive properties which are specific to that location, summarized in (8).

(8)	Ludling Properties	Module:	1	2	3
	(a) Follow all lexical phonological/ morphological processes		+	+	+
	(b) Precede P2 post-lexical rules and phonetic implementation		+	+	+
	(c) Follow Tier/Plane Conflation		−	+	+
	(d) May violate Melodic Conservation		−	+	+
	(e) May apply between words/access sentence position		−	+	+
	(f) Precede intonation/pitch-accent assignment		+	+	−
	(g) Precede P1 post-lexical rules		+	+	−
	(h) May access post-lexical prosodic constituents		−	−	+
	(i) May violate geminate integrity, OCP		−	−	+
	(j) May ignore function words		−	−	+
	(k) Are structure-violating		−	−	+

In addition to accounting for the cluster of properties associated with each conversion location, the use of several modules within the ludling component has a number of other important consequences. For example, it predicts that a given language can have ludlings located in different modules (e.g., Tagalog *Golagat* (segment reversal) is a Module 1 ludling, while *Syllable Reversal* in the same language is a Module 3 ludling). In addition, the operations associated with a single ludling may be distributed across more than one module: for example, one Hanunoo ludling involves reduplication of non-ludling syllables (a Module 1 operation) and insertion of clitics between words and at phrase boundaries (a Module 3 operation). Finally, this model allows us to account for different dialects of the same ludling which differ in their location with respect to the operation of non-ludling rules (e.g., the dialects of the Cuna transposition ludling, *Sorsik Sunmakke*, reported in Sherzer (1970)).

5 Conclusion

As we have seen, the relationship between ludlings and phonological theory has finally developed into one that is mutually beneficial: by addressing the phenomena found in ludlings, linguistic theory has found important independent evidence as well as challenges for many of its hypotheses, and by incorporating the advances of phonological theory, ludlings have received insightful explanations for why they take the forms that they do. It is vital that this two-way interaction continue. Three things are necessary for such a continuation: (1) more primary data are required, and longitudinal studies into the acquisition of ludlings must be initiated.[12] (2) Detailed theoretical studies of individual ludlings should be pursued, as in Tateishi (1991) and Gil (1990). (3) Informed synthesis of the theoretical implications of these studies must be made, now that a broad theoretical base has been established. Finally, the rightful place of ludling data in theoretical discussions must not be forgotten: ludlings are an integral part of the human linguistic capacity and as such, an integral part of linguistic theory.

NOTES

1 For a more detailed discussion of surrogate languages, including a theoretical treatment, see Bagemihl (1988a).

2 This term was actually first introduced into the *linguistic* literature in Laycock (1969); it also appeared as the Esperanto word for "language game" in Otsikrev (1963). The origin of the coining is the Latin *ludus* "game" and *lingua* "language" (Laycock 1969, p. 14).

3 Actually, the term "infix" is something of a misnomer in this case. Often the ludling will treat each syllable of the non-ludling word as an individual (prosodic) word to which the affix is added, giving the impression of infixation; cf. McCarthy and Prince (1986), Bagemihl (1988a).

4 It follows that a linguistic behavior which has been labeled a "language game" but whose formal operations do not fit into any of these categories would not be classified as a ludling. For example, Katada (1990) describes a Japanese language game which involves turn-taking between two speakers, each of whom must say a word which begins with the same mora sequence that the previous speaker's word ended with (see the discussion of this in chap. 5, this volume). Unless it can be shown that this involves, for example, some sort of templatic operation, this language game is not a ludling.

5 For more extensive bibliographic listings, see Laycock (1972), Kirshenblatt-Gimblett (1976), Bagemihl (1988b), and Plénat (1991).

6 Tateishi (1989, 1991) examines ludlings in Japanese and Buin which involve, among other processes, transposition of a bimoraic foot; these cases would be analyzed under a line-crossing account as prefixation or suffixation of this prosodic constituent, combined with maximum crossing.

7 For another example of the use of ludling data to argue for the OCP, see Yip (1988).

8 See Bagemihl (1989) for a full

discussion of this operation. It is also possible that this ludling is manipulating the first mora in the word.

9   The recognition that this ludling can manipulate segments is due to Perlmutter (1991), who also claims that morphemes and words can be accessed (e.g., in compounds). Tateishi (1991) shows that apparent cases of morpheme reversal actually reduce to the operation of the ludling on cyclically-constructed feet, and this may be true of the apparent word-reversal examples as well.

10   One templatic process, the formation of Rustic Girls' Names, seems to require the opposite directionality; cf. Poser (1990).

11   This is assuming that Tier (or Plane) Conflation applies only once, at the end of the lexicon, as proposed by Cole (1987).

12   Two studies which begin to look at the ludling acquisitional process are Cowan (1989) and Cowan and Leavitt (1987).

24 Experimental Phonology

JOHN J. OHALA

0 Introduction: The Basis of Experimental Phonology

Experimentation in phonology and indeed in any scientific discipline has two basic elements for its philosophical foundation: the first is doubt. Doubt or scepticism that perhaps the things we believe or what others would have us believe may not correspond to the way things are. We realize that perhaps the sources of our beliefs are imperfect: the authority or impartiality of our teachers (including those who teach us through the printed word) may be flawed and our own senses may give us distorted or contaminated information about the world. Such scepticism, of course, has been the basis of many religious and philosophical systems. In these other domains the typical response to suspect beliefs is the promotion of additional, different beliefs (which may themselves be suspect!). What experimental methods propose in response to doubt – and this is the second element – is that it is possible to do something to counteract the suspected sources of error.[1] Specifically, it should be possible to anticipate them and to eliminate them or at least to limit their influence. In sum, experimentation rests on the following equation: if one believes, one may doubt; if one doubts, one can strive to resolve the doubt. Part of the lore of every scientific discipline are the possible sources of error in interpreting uncontrolled observations and the procedures, often quite ingenious, for compensating for them.

Thus, it must be emphasized that an experiment is prompted by a belief, i.e., a hypothesis or theory, which is subject to reasonable doubt. There can be no true experiments without theories; they have to be done with a purpose. And conversely, the only beliefs not subject to doubt and thus never subjected to test are religious dogmas (but see Kings 3.18, 21–40 [Douay version]). Second, an experiment consists physically of an observation under contrived or controlled circumstances, the control or contrivance being such that would eliminate or attenuate some anticipated or suspected distortion in the prior observations or events that gave rise to the belief.

Claude Bernard (1957) differentiated between nature-made experiments and man-made experiments. In nature-made experiments, nature manipulates the variables and the only contrivance on the part of man is to be in the right place at the right time to make the relevant observations. In man-made experiments, the experimenter controls the variables and makes the observations. Man-made experiments are far more efficient ways to test theories since nature often does not oblige us by presenting situations where the variables of interest – and no others – are systematically manipulated. But man-made experiments often require considerable ingenuity so that the artificiality of the conditions of observation do not themselves introduce unacceptable distortions.

There are opportunities in phonology to take advantage of nature-made experiments: speakers making novel derivations (adding the suffix *-ity* to *mundane*), speech errors, naturally-occurring defects of the speech production and perception system (e.g., aglossia or the absence of a tongue). In this chapter, however, I consider only man-made experiments because they are, potentially at least, applicable to any theoretical issue – limited only by resources and the experimenter's ingenuity.

1   Experimentation in Phonology

No claims in phonology are above doubt: the existence of the phoneme, syllable, or the feature [voice]; the reconstructed Proto-Indo-European form for Sanskrit *budh-*; that speakers know the posited rule-governed phonological link between the pair of words *repose/repository*. All of these are potential subjects for experimental study. But, experiments are expensive: in time, effort, and other resources. It is a matter of research strategy, the availability of reliable experimental methods, and the amount of personal commitment we have to one belief or another which determines which issues one chooses to address experimentally. It is also worth noting that in every discipline, even those where a tradition of experimentation is well established, like chemistry and physiology, scientists engage in nonexperimental activities such as description and classification of observations, delving into the history of ideas and methods in their discipline, offering speculations that range from the "wild and woolly" to those bolstered by extensive and rigorous arguments. No discipline "closes up shop" just because experiments are not applied to every issue. It takes time to develop an arsenal of reliable experimental methods, and even after that is achieved they may not be applied because of expense or lack of interest. Nevertheless, adequate testing of claims remains a prerequisite to understanding.

So many experimental paradigms have been proposed for testing phonological hypotheses (Ohala and Jaeger 1986; Ohala 1986; Ohala and Ohala 1987; Prideaux, Derwing, and Baker 1980; Kingston and Beckman 1990; Docherty and Ladd 1992; Diehl 1992) that it is impossible to review them all in a single chapter. I can only give representative examples from different domains in phonology.

1.1 *Experimental Assessment of the Distinctive Features of Speech*

One of the most fundamental tasks of phonology is to establish how different linguistic messages are conveyed by sound. Whether it is lexical differences or grammatical function, distinct messages must have distinct physical encodings, whether these are paradigmatic (different ciphers from a finite inventory of ciphers) and/or syntagmatic (different permutations of the ciphers). This is far from a trivial issue and certainly not one to be determined unequivocally by the unaided ear. Well-established methods exist for discovering the physical correlates of different linguistic messages in cases where they are uncertain or disputed. Although such studies are often regarded as having purely phonetic, not phonological, interest, this is a mistake: without having an "anchor" in the real world, phonology risks having its claims apply only in an imaginary universe of little interest to those outside the narrowly circumscribed world of autonomous phonology. Fortunately, such a parochial view of phonology is disappearing.

Consistent differences may be sought in the physiological or acoustic domains but the relevance of any difference found must ultimately be validated in the perceptual domain (Lehiste 1970). For example, in a series of instrumental and experimental studies, Lisker and Abramson (1964, 1967, 1970) found that in initial position (before stress), the distinction between pairs of English words like *paid* vs. *bade, tie* vs. *die, cool* vs. *ghoul,* is carried largely by the relative timing of voice onset after the stop release, that is, what is called *VOT* (for *Voice Onset Time*): the phonemes /p t k/ showed a substantial delay in VOT (modal VOT = 50–70 msec) whereas /b d g/ had a short VOT (modal VOT = 0–20 msec). Phonetically, this contrast is said to be between voiceless aspirated stops and voiceless unaspirated stops. Perceptual studies demonstrated that VOT was the dominant cue for such lexical distinctions although several secondary cues also played a role (Lisker 1986). Although this contrast among stops is commonly attributed to presence vs. absence of voice, voicing *per se* plays only a secondary role in this environment and in other positions in the word as well (Denes 1955; Raphael 1972). Lisker (1957) showed that in intervocalic position, in addition to voicing, the duration of stop closures helps to cue lexical distinctions such as *rapid* vs. *rabid,* where the voiceless stop is longer.

The stops that appear in prevocalic clusters after /s/, e.g., *spade, sty, school,* may only be voiceless unaspirated. Lotz et al. (1960) showed that to English speakers these are perceptually most similar to the stops in *bade, die,* and *ghoul,* i.e., /b d g/ (though they are not completely identical, Caisse 1981). Thus, although traditionally the prevocalic stops in *paid* and *spade* would be counted as allophones of the same phoneme /p/ in English, there is greater physical and perceptual similarity between the stops in *bade* and *spade*.

1.2   Can Phonetically Different Sounds Be Psychologically the Same?

This still leaves open the question of whether native speakers regard the voiceless unaspirated stops in *sC-* clusters to be psychologically similar to the voiceless aspirated or the voiceless unaspirated in absolute initial position. This question was investigated by Jaeger (1980, 1986) who used the so-called concept formation method to address the question of the assignment of allophones to the /k/ phoneme. Without being given any more instructions than (approximately) "assign the following words to two different categories depending on the pronunciation at their beginning," linguistically naïve subjects were first presented orally with uncontroversial examples with initial stops such as *kiss, chasm, cattle,* and *quake* designated "category," intermixed randomly with noncategory examples, *grip, gash, lime, ceiling, chest,* and *knife.* Initially subjects were given feedback on each trial, i.e., they were told whether their category assignment was correct or not. If they reached some preset criterion of performance in this training, they were then presented with words containing the stop allophone whose phoneme membership was controversial, such as *school* and *scold.* This time there was no feedback. If they put these words in the same category as *cool* and *cold* it would imply that they regarded the [k] and [kʰ] as somehow psychologically equivalent. In fact, this is what they did. (See also Ohala 1986.)

Jaeger attempted to control for bias from orthography (in case subjects visualized the spelling and let this influence their judgments): thus the words with [kʰ] were spelled with varying letters, *k, c, ch, qu,* and some of the same letters started noncategory words. Nevertheless, it is difficult to control completely for orthographic bias when using literate subjects. In fact, there is a growing body of evidence that much of what is regarded as native speakers' knowledge of the phonology of their language is very much influenced by, if not based on, their knowledge of how their language is spelled (Wang and Derwing 1986; Derwing and Nearey 1986; Read, Yun-fei, Hong-yun, and Bao-qing, 1986; Morais, Cary, Alegria and Bertelson 1979).

1.3   Experiments on Morpheme Structure Constraints

As it happens, some of the earliest linguistic and phonological experiments ever done were intended to address the issue of language change but in fact also gave evidence on the psychological processes underlying language use.

Thumb and Marbe (1901) tested the posited effect of word association on language change. Inspired by this work, Esper (1925) explored the effect of analogy on the change in phonological shape of words and morphemes. His experiment was a task where he required his subjects to learn the names of 16 objects, each having one of four different shapes and one of four different colors. (He trained them on 14 object-name associations but tested them on 16 in order to see if they could generalize what they learned.) In three different experimental conditions, each with a different group of subjects, the relationship between the names and properties of the objects differed. The names presented to subjects in group 1 were of the sort *nasliŋ, šownliŋ, nasdeg, šowndeg*, where *nas-* and *šown* coded color and *-liŋ* and *-deg* coded shape (though they were not told of their "morphemic" constituents). Since these names consisted of two phonologically legal morphemes, this group could simplify their task by learning not 16 names but 8 morphemes (if they could discover them) plus the simple rule that the color morpheme preceded the shape morpheme in each name. Group 3, a control group, were presented names that had no morphemic structure; they had no recourse but to learn 16 idiosyncratic names. As expected, group 1 learned their names much faster and more accurately than group 3. Of interest was the performance of group 2 which, like group 1, were presented with bi-morphemic names and thus could, in principle, simplify their task by learning just eight morphemes. But, unlike group 1, the morphemes were not phonologically legal for English, e.g., *nulgɛn, nuzgub, pelgɛn, pezgub* (where now *nu-* and *pe-* were color morphemes and *-lgɛn* and *-zgub* were shape morphemes, the latter two, of course, violating English morpheme structure constraints). Could the subjects in group 2 extract the hidden morphemes and perform as well as those in group 1? Apparently not: their performance was similar to (and marginally worse than) that of group 3, which had 16 idiosyncratic names to learn. Furthermore, analysis of the errors of group 2, including how they generalized what they'd learned to the two object-name associations excluded from the training session, revealed that they tried to make phonologically legal morphemes from the ill-formed ones. Esper's experiment achieved his goal of showing the force of analogy in language change, i.e., paradigm regularization, but it also demonstrates the psychological reality of morpheme structure constraints.

1.4 *Experiments on Phonological Change*

One of the earliest accomplishments of phonology was the development of a method, the comparative method, which allowed one to reconstruct the history of languages, in particular the changes over time in the phonological forms of words (Rask 1818; Grimm 1822). To oversimplify, the comparative method consists in finding an optimal single unbranching path between pairs or groups of words judged to be cognates, where the "path" consists of (a) intermediate forms between the two, one of which is the "parent form" and

(b) sound changes which operate unidirectionally and convert the parent form into the attested daughter forms. Historical phonology might seem at first to be an unlikely domain for experimentation since most of the events of interest occurred in the inaccessible past and thus cannot be manipulated by the experimenter. But if one is willing to make the unformitarian assumption,[2] that is, that whatever caused sound changes in the past is still present and causing sound changes now, then although we cannot be there when Proto-Indo-European k^w changed to Greek p, e.g., PIE *ekwos* "horse" > Gk. *hippos*, we may be able to contrive circumstances where the same or similar changes occur in front of our eyes or our microphones. In fact, the parallelism between diachronic and synchronic variation has often been remarked by researchers and sometimes has led to laboratory-based studies of sound change (Rousselot 1891; Haden 1938). One of the most fruitful areas of experimental phonology, then, involves studies on the phonetic influence on sound change or on phonological universals in general (see, e.g., Lindblom 1984; Wright 1986; Kawasaki 1986; Kawasaki-Fukumori 1992; Stevens 1989; Goldstein 1983; Ohala 1992, 1993).

One of the most common processes evident in sound change is assimilation and one of the common textbook examples of it is the case of medial heterorganic clusters assimilating in Italian: Late Latin *octo* > Italian *otto* "eight". Such assimilations are overwhelmingly of the form $-C_1C_2- > -C_2C_2-$; rarely does C_2 assimilate to the place of C_1 (and many of these cases could be reanalyzed as involving a different process; see Murray 1982). Such a change is usually attributed to *ease of articulation* or conservation of energy (a heterorganic cluster requiring more energy than a homorganic one). But if so, why is it C_1 that usually changes, not C_2? Expenditure of articulatory energy is presumably cumulative through an utterance and thus would be greater by the time C_2 was reached than C_1. Thus we might expect C_2 to assimilate to C_1, just the reverse of what is found. Such doubts lead us to entertain an alternative explanation for this process. Ohala (1990) reported the results of an experiment designed to test whether the process might better be attributed to acoustic-auditory factors. This was an experiment where the two halves of VCV utterances ([apa, ata, aka, aba, ada, aga]) where separated at the middle of the stop closure and reattached via digital splicing in order to create a variety of VCV stimuli where the stop onset and stop release had different places, e.g., first part of [apa] spliced to last half of [ata] to yield [ap-ta], but the medial closure duration was that for a singleton stop. These were presented, randomized, to listeners who were asked to identify the stop, being allowed the options of reporting it as C_1, C_2, or "other." Of the tokens where $C_1 \neq C_2$, 93 percent of the responses were C_2. A subsequent test showed that if the stop closure interval were lengthened, eventually the majority of listeners could hear the heterorganic cluster but the threshold duration for this was longer for voiceless stops than voiced stops. Presumably listeners were influenced by their awareness that singleton voiceless stops are longer than voiced stops (see above). Plausibly the place cues for C_2 dominate over those for C_1 (even when they are inconsistent) because they are acoustically and auditorily more salient (and listeners learn where to invest most of their auditory attention): both onset and offset have some formant transitions which cue place but only the offset has the very important cues contained in the stop burst. Although there is still much to be learned about the historical processes that changed *octo* to *otto*, this study at least shows that there is plausibly a major acoustic-auditory component to it; appeals to "ease of articulation" may be unnecessary. It also demonstrates the potential for an experimental approach to questions in historical phonology.

1.5   Experiments in Lexical Representation

It was mentioned in note 1 above that tests may only be made of claims which involve things that ultimately, even if indirectly, have observable consequences. As soon as a claim is associated with observable consequences, it becomes testable. Lahiri and Marslen-Wilson (1991, 1992) put underspecification theory into the empirical arena. They suggested that the lexical representations posited by phonologists "correspond, in some significant way, to the listener's mental representation of lexical forms . . . and that these representations have direct consequences for the way . . . the listener interprets the incoming acoustic-phonetic information." Lahiri (1991) argued specifically that "the surface structures derived after postlexical spreading do not play a distinctive role in perception; rather, a more abstract underspecified representation determines the interpretation of a phonetic cue."

In English, vowels are not lexically specified for the feature [nasal], and thus an oral vowel heard without a following consonant is predicted to be ambiguous as to whether it is in a CVC or a CVN word.[3] Lahiri and Marslen-Wilson tested this using a paradigm that involves gating (truncating) the ends of words in increments of 40 msec and presenting the gated fragments to English-speaking subjects in the order of most to least gated, and then asking them to guess what the word is. Although 83.4 percent of the responses to the CVC stimuli to the point where the final consonant abutted the vowel were correct (i.e., CVC), Lahiri and Marslen-Wilson interpreted the 16.6 percent CVN-responses as consistent with the vowels being unspecified for [nasal] and thus ambiguous between their coming from CVC or CVN words. Figure 24.1 shows their subjects' responses as a function of the gating point (circles).[4] Lahiri and Marslen-Wilson did not perform any statistical analyses on their data and, of course, it would have been impossible given the open response set subjects could choose from; that is, to know whether the CVN responses occurred at a rate equal to, more than, or less than chance, one would have to know how many possible responses they could have made of each word type.

Ohala and Ohala (1993) attempted a replication of Lahiri and Marslen-Wilson's experiment,[5] but restricted the subjects' responses to just one of two choices, e.g., when presented with an end-gated version of *rube* the choices specified on the answer sheet were *room* and *rube*. The results are seen in

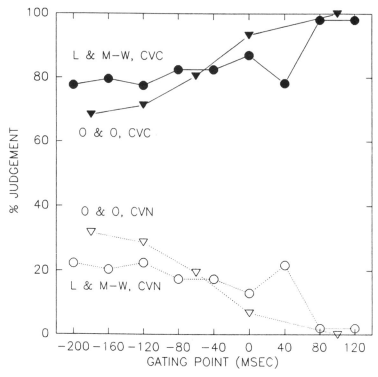

Figure 24.1   Listeners's judgements (vertical axis) of CVC syllables truncated at various points (horizontal axis, gating point in msec, where 0 = the VC boundary): Circles: results of Lahiri and Marslen-Wilson (1992); triangles: result of Ohala and Ohala (1993). Solid lines: CVC judgements; dotted line: CVN judgements. See text.

figure 24.1 as triangles superimposed on the circles representing Lahiri and Marslen-Wilson. This curve appears to be quite similar to theirs, but there is a crucial difference: a statistical analysis is possible in the Ohala and Ohala case. In fact these results show that listeners made the correct identification of the stimuli up to the point where the consonant joined the vowel 82.8 percent of the time; this is highly significant (x^2 = 92.03, 1 df, p < .001). Conversely, the same statistic shows that the subjects' choice of the incorrect CVN responses were much below chance level. Lahiri and Marslen-Wilson state that according to the notion that redundant features are specified in the lexicon and accessed by listeners when interpreting the incoming speech signal (i.e., the hypothesis contrary to underspecification theory) "listeners should *never* interpret CVCs as potential CVNs" [italics added]. But this is an unrealistic requirement. Rather than "never", the most that can be required is that they give CVN responses to gated CVC stimuli much less than would be predicted by chance; this is what Ohala and Ohala found.

2 Do Experiments Ever Settle Issues?

Leaving aside divine revelation, there are no perfect routes to the truth (if one believes truth exists) and experiments are no exception. Being performed by fallible humans, they can be fallible, too. The answer to an experiment suspected of being flawed is a better-controlled experiment which overcomes the flaw. Thus experimental phonology or experimental anything should be viewed as a spiral process: make a claim; test the claim; revise (or abandon) the claim; test the revised claim, etc. Ultimately, this continuous process should lead to a convergence of results which support a more confidently held belief.

NOTES

1 It probably goes without saying, but I'll say it anyway: that it is only reasonable to subject to experimental study those claims which matter – that is, where, if they are wrong, there are major consequences for the way people think and act – and those which are connected in some way, even if indirectly, with the observable universe. Claims that a given phenomenon may be described, labeled, or classified in a certain way are candidates for debate rather than experimentation, unless the descriptions are grounded in empirical properties. Claims that don't specify the domain of the universe to which they apply – physical, psychological, social – would be hard to test experimentally. But equally, if one cannot specify the domain in which the claim holds, how did the belief come about in the first place? A belief arises from some constellation of evidence, even if suspect; the domain from which this evidence came is the domain in which the claim is to be tested.

2 The "uniformitarian hypothesis" guided and catalyzed the development of scientific geology in the 18th century. Rather than assuming cataclysmic events, often thought to have divine origins, it was posited that for the most part constant processes like erosion, sedimentation, and land upheaval accounted for the formation of mountains, valleys, and other conspicuous features of the earth's surface.

3 Lahiri and Marslen-Wilson make asymmetrical claims about how listeners will judge CVN and CVC stimuli with the final consonants gated off. Although both syllable types are said to have vowels which are lexically unspecified for the feature nasal, only the CV(C) stimuli are claimed to be ambiguous; the CV(N) stimuli they allow will be unambiguously identifiable as CVN because of the post-lexical rule spreading [+nasal] from the N to the preceding V. This admission strikes me as undercutting the claim, quoted above, that "surface structures derived after postlexical spreading do not play a distinctive role in perception." In fact, there is no major dispute that listeners' *can* identify CVN syllables with the final

N gated off (Ali, Gallagher, Goldstein, and Daniloff 1971). The present discussion is concerned with how to interpret listeners' reaction to end-truncated CVC stimuli.

4 The caption to the Lahiri and Marslen-Wilson (1992) figure (fig. 9.4) on which figure 24.1 was based indicates that the curves show percentage of response types. However, the abscissa in this figure clearly does not correspond to percentages and in fact is labeled "mean number of responses." I have tried to make a reasonable interpretation of the data they presented, but the data in figure 24.1 could be off by 2–3 percent.

5 Lahiri and Marslen-Wilson (1991, 1992) also studied the role of vowel nasalization and other phonological phenomena in Bengali; Ohala and Ohala (1993) similarly reported a study of vowel nasalization in Hindi. I report here only the results pertaining to English.

25 Current Issues in the Phonology of Australian Languages

NICK EVANS

0 Introduction

Between the 1960s and the early 1980s Australianist phonology saw its "classical" period, in which the main structural and phonetic characteristics of segmental systems were worked out properly, a large body of high-quality descriptions was produced for the first time, and many problems of morphophonemics and historical phonology were tackled. This phase is best represented by the surveys in Capell (1967), Dixon (1980), and Yallop (1982), as well as in the phonology chapters of many classic grammars written in this period.

The last decade has seen a shift of focus toward the more complex problems of nonlinear and metrical phenomena, which were often described in grammars of the classical period[1] but which the unavailability of adequate theoretical models kept somewhat marginalized. With few exceptions, however, there has been an unproductive bifurcation between descriptive work by field-workers, and theoretical analyses by phonologists "squatting in their theoretical cocoons" (Dixon 1977a, p. xvii); as a result, the potential for fruitful interplay between phonological theory and description has only been scratched. This demarcation of tasks contrasts with the fields of syntax and typology, which have benefited enormously from over 20 years of cross-fertilization between descriptivists, theoreticians, and practitioners strung out along the path between these poles.

I am therefore writing this article with two partially disjoint sets of readers in mind. On the one hand, I wish to make theoretical phonologists aware of many phonological properties of Australian languages that are of great interest to current theories of phonology; often the relevant data is buried in publications little-known outside Australia. On the other, I wish to encourage descriptively oriented Australianists to widen their brief by paying more attention to nonlinear phenomena: a welcome effect of recent theoretical developments has been to reveal a great deal of variation under the superficial phonological uniformity of Australian languages. As a general principle, wherever the choice has arisen I have elected to include more empirical material, rather than outlining its consequences for one theory or another.

1 Genetic Overview

All the indigenous languages of Australia, including the language of the Western Torres Strait, probably form a single genetic phylum, although relations between some are extremely remote and suggestive of a great time depth. There is no evidence for genetic relationships with languages outside Australia.

Seven-eighths of Australia (see fig. 25.1) is occupied by languages of the Pama-Nyungan family, including such well-known languages as Dyirbal, Warlpiri, Diyari, Yidiny, and Ngiyambaa. The remainder is far more complex genetically, containing around 20 families, collectively known as non-Pama-Nyungan.

There is a strong correlation between genetic and typological groupings. Pama-Nyungan languages are generally dependent marking, and use only suffixes; some make additional use of auxiliary clitic complexes. Non-Pama-Nyungan languages are head marking and generally use both suffixes and prefixes; in those such as Gunwinyguan and Tiwi, which are highly polysynthetic, their complex morphologies create complex rules of stress assignment.

While there were long-standing contacts with Papuan languages across the Torres Strait, and over the last few centuries with Austronesian languages on the north and northwest coast of Australia, the phonological effects of this were not substantial. The only clearcut example is the appearance of alveolar fricatives /s/ and /z/ in the Western Torres Strait language (see sec. 2.1).

2 Phonemic Inventories

Australian languages are remarkably homogeneous in their phonemic inventories – far more than in their grammar or lexicon. Detailed surveys of their phonemic systems are in Dixon (1980), Busby (1980), and Yallop (1982); Butcher (to appear b) is a thorough instrumental study of the phonetics of Australian sound systems, which are much more variable than their phonemic homogeneity would suggest.

A typical Australian consonant phoneme inventory is that for Kayardild,[2] given in tabel 25.1. Characteristically Australian are the presence of six paired stops and nasals, that can be grouped into pairs of peripheral, apical, and laminal articulations, the lack of a voicing contrast, the lack of fricatives, the presence of two "rhotics" (/r/ and /ɹ/), and a triangular vowel system with

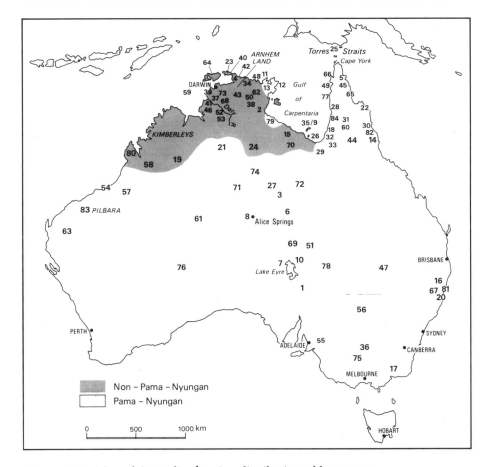

Figure 25.1 Map of Australia showing distribution of languages

Language locations, alternative names and primary sources

1 *Adnyamathanha* Schebeck (1974)
2 *Alawa* Sharpe (1972)
3 *Alyawarr* (Alyawarra) Yallop (1977)
4 *Amurdak* Handelsmann (1991)
5 *Anguthimri* Crowley (1981)
6 *Antekerepenh* (Antegerebenha) Breen (1977)
7 *Arabana* Hercus (1972)
8 *Arrernte* (Aranda) Wilkins (1989), Breen (1991)
9 *Damin* Hale (1973)
10 *Diyari* Austin (1981)
11 *Djambarrpuyngu* Wilkinson (1991)
12 *Djapu* Morphy (1983)
13 *Djinang* Waters (1980)
14 *Dyirbal* Dixon (1972)
15 *Garrwa* (Garawa) Furby (1972), Breen (to appear b)
16 *Gidabal* Geytenbeek & Geytenbeek (1971)
17 *Gippsland* Hercus (1986)
18 *Gog-Nar* Breen (1976)
19 *Gooniyandi* (Kuniyanti) McGregor (1990)
20 *Gumbaynggir* Eades (1979)
21 *Gurindji* McConvell (1988)
22 *Guugu Yimidhirr* Haviland (1979)
23 *Iwaidja* Pym & Larrimore (1979), Sayers & Pym (1977)

24   *Jingilu* (Djingili) Chadwick (1975)
25   *Kala Lagaw Ya* (Kennedy 1981), *Kala Kawaw Ya* Ford & Ober (1985) (two dialects of the Western Torres Strait language)
26   *Kayardild* Evans (in press)
27   *Kaytetye* (Kaititj, Kaytej) Koch (1980), Breen (1991)
28   *Kugu Nganhcara* Smith & Johnson (1985), MS.
29   *Kukatj* Breen (to appear)
30   *Kuku-Yalanji* (Gugu-Yalandji) Oates (1967), Patz (1982)
31   *Kunjen* Sommer (1969)
32   *Kurtjar* Black (1980)
33   *Kuthant* Black (1980)
34   *Kunparlang* Coleman (1982)
35   *Lardil* Hale (1973)
36   *Madimadi* Hercus (1986)
37   *MalakMalak* Birk (1976)
38   *Mangarayi* Merlan (1982)
39   *Maranungku* Tryon (1970)
40   *Marrgu* Evans field notes
41   *Marrithiyel* Green (1989)
42   *Mawng* (Maung) Capell & Hinch (1970)
43   *Mayali* Evans (1991)
44   *Mbabaram* Dixon (1991)
45   *Mpakwithi* Crowley (1983)
46   *Murrinhpatha* (Murinbata) Walsh (1979), Street & Mollinjin (1981)
47   *Muruwari* Oates (1988)
48   *Ndjébbana* (Djeebbana) McKay (1979, 1984), McKay & Coleman (to appear)
49   *Ntra?ɲiṭ* Hale (1976a)
50   *Ngalakan* Merlan (1983)
51   *Ngamini* Austin (1988b)

52   *Ngan'gityemerri* Reid (1990)
53   *Ngankikurungkurr* Hoddinott & Kofod (1988)
54   *Ngarla* Geytenbeek (1992)
55   *Ngarrinjerri* Johnson (1986)
56   *Ngiyambaa* Donaldson (1980)
57   *Nyangumarda* (Nyangumarta) Hoard & O'Grady (1976), Sharp 1986, Geytenbeek (1992)
58   *Nyigina* Stokes (1982)
59   *Paccamal* (Bajjamal), (Ford 1990)
60   *Olgolo* Dixon (1970b)
61   *Pintupi* Hansen & Hansen (1969)
62   *Rembarrnga* (Rembarnga) McKay (1975)
63   *Tharrgari* Klokeid (1969)
64   *Tiwi* Osborne (1974)
65   *Umpila* Harris & O'Grady (1976)
66   *Uradhi* Crowley (1983)
67   *Waalubal* Crowley (1978)
68   *Wagiman* Cook (1987)
69   *Wangkanguru* Hercus (1972)
70   *Wanyi* Breen (to appear b)
71   *Warlpiri* Nash (1986)
72   *Warluwarra* Breen (1971)
73   *Warray* Harvey (1986)
74   *Warumungu* Simpson & Heath (1982), Simpson (1992)
75   *Wergaia* Hercus (1986)
76   *Western Desert* Douglas (1964)
77   *Wik-Mungkan* Sayers (1974, 1976, 1977)
78   *Yandrruwandha* Austin (1988b)
79   *Yanyuwa* Kirton & Charlie (1979)
80   *Yawuru* Hosokawa (1991)
81   *Yaygir* Crowley (1979)
82   *Yidiny* Dixon (1977a, 1977b)
83   *Yindjibarndi* Wordick (1982)
84   *Yir-Yoront* Alpher (1973, 1991)

phonemic length. This table also illustrates the main symbols upon which I have standardized the rather variable orthographies now used for writing Australian languages.[3]

Most differences across Australian phoneme inventories comprise variations on the above theme – the apical and/or laminal series may be collapsed into one; the glottal stop or a seventh place of articulation may be added. Further lateral phonemes, or another rhotic, may be found, or fricatives, or some sort of stop contrast (fortis/lenis, short/long, etc.). Within the vowel system, length may be eliminated, or the set may be reduced to two, or enlarged to anywhere

Table 25.1   The Kayardild phoneme inventory

		CONSONANTS				
	PERIPHERAL	*APICAL*		*LAMINAL*		*PERIPHERAL*
	bilabial	*apico-alveolar*	*apico-post-alveolar (retroflex)*	*lamino-dental*	*lamino-palatal*	*dorso-velar*
stop	p	t	ʈ	t̪	c̪	k
nasal	m	n	ɳ	n̪	ɲ	ŋ
lateral		l				
trill		r				
approximant	w		ɻ		y	

VOWELS

	front	back
high	i, iː	u, uː
low		a, aː

up to 17. These variations are discussed in section 2.1 (consonants) and section 2.2 (vowels). In addition, various elements may combine into complex segments, such as prestopped nasals or prenasalized stops, and features like retroflexion or rounding may be spread or transferred; these possibilities are discussed in section 3.

2.1   Consonant Inventories

Linear positions. Traditional Australianist terminology recognizes both active and passive articulators: "apical" and "laminal" series are first characterized in terms of both their active articulators (tongue-tip and tongue-blade)[4] and their passive articulators, i.e., by the point of contact. The Australianist term "peripheral" is identical to the standard term "non-coronal."

There is an enormous amount of evidence – from phonotactics, morphophonemics, diachronic changes, and synchronic variation – for these groupings. To begin with, in many languages that collapse the apical or laminal series, the allophones are in complementary distribution – lamino-palatal and lamino-dental phones are in complementary distribution in some dialects of Western Desert, conditioned by adjacent vowels, while in Wanyi apico-alveolar and apico-postalveolar phones are in complementary distribution. Often phonemic contrasts within a series are neutralized in certain positions – most languages neutralize the alveolar/retroflex contrast word-initially,[5] and some neutralize the lamino-dental/lamino-palatal contrast word-finally.

Many morphophonemic processes pick out one or another of these classes. In Kayardild, stem-final laminals of both series become apico-alveolars in the nominative; in Mayali iterative reduplications, inserted velar nasals dissimilate to apicals between peripheral-initial syllables (sec. 8). And descriptions of several languages (e.g., Muruwari and Ngiyambaa) report interspeaker or cross-dialectal variation within one of these classes – in Ngiyambaa "Keewong speakers say *munu:ga* for 'elbow' and *mandaba:* for 'red-bellied black snake' while Trida speakers say *ŋunu:ga* and *ŋandaba:*" (Donaldson 1980, p. 18). Dixon (1970a) has argued that two-laminal series are a phonemic split from an original single-laminal system, and similar arguments have sometimes been made for the retroflex series.

A number of arguments have been made concerning the markedness relations of these six positions. Laughren (1990) proposes that, for Central Australian languages, laminals are the unmarked coronal, citing the fact that apicals become laminals in Warlpiri baby talk (Laughren 1984), and the existence of diachronic changes from initial apical to laminal in proto-Pama-Nyungan (Evans 1988), but against this it may be argued that baby-talk exploits sound-symbolism rather than markedness relations, and that diachronic and morphophonemic changes in the other direction, such as Kayardild delaminalization, are also attested. Within the apical series, she argues that the retroflex articulation is unmarked, since retroflex articulation is found in Warlpiri when the contrast is neutralized, e.g., word-initially, and in onsets after syllables beginning in /r/.

Hamilton (1989, 1992) discusses the similarity between the multivalent gradation of articulators in Australian languages and the well-known patterns of the sonority hierarchy. He proposes the articulator continuum LABIAL > DORSAL > LAMINAL > APICAL as an explanation for phonotactic patterns widespread in Australia: in a given language, syllable-final consonants will be drawn from a continuous portion from the right of the continuum, and syllable-initial consonants will be drawn from a continuous portion from the left of the hierarchy. Interestingly, this hierarchy also correlates with the commonness of fricative phonemes in Australian languages (see below), which are increasingly rare as one moves from left to right on the articulator continuum (cf. McConvell 1988, p. 162ff.).

Some languages augment the six canonical linear positions in one of two ways. Dorso-palatals /k^y/ and sometimes /ŋ^y/ appear as an areal feature in the Barkly region, southwest of the Gulf of Carpentaria, though only in Yanyuwa does this make seven linear positions, since the other languages have but a single laminal series. These dorso-palatals probably derive historically from clusters of lamino-palatal plus dorso-velar, and controversy continues about whether this is also the best synchronic analysis for some of the Barkly languages.

A second type of seventh position is found in the Arandic languages Kaytetye, Antekerepenh and Alyawarra, where apical consonants may be prepalatalized. These languages have just two major vowel phonemes, and prepalatalized consonants condition high front vowel allophones; they essentially represent a transfer of frontness from vowel to consonant phonemes.

Glottal stop phonemes have developed in two areas – Cape York, in a number of relatively closely related languages, and Arnhem Land, as an areal feature spanning the Pama-Nyungan/non-Pama-Nyungan border. The synchronic behavior and diachronic sources of /ʔ/ are quite different in the two areas. In Cape York it is a normal segmental phoneme, can occur intervocalically, and derives from /t/, /r/, /g/, /b/ or some combination thereof (Dixon 1980, p. 201). In Arnhem Land it is restricted to syllable-final position and is best analysed as an autosegment (sec. 3.6); it appears to have originated there as a *Grenzsignal* rather than from a segmental phoneme (Harvey 1991).

Laterals. Though languages in the eastern third of the continent have only a single lateral phoneme (Dixon 1980, p. 141), those in the western two-thirds may have up to four – one for each coronal articulation. Diyari, for example, has /l/, /ʟ/, /ḽ/ and /ḻ/. The set may be further augmented by prestopped laterals (sec. 3.2) or prelateralized stops (sec. 3.3).

Rhotics. Most Australian languages contrast at least an alveolar tap/trill /r/ and a retroflex continuant /ɹ/. Some have a third r-like phoneme – Warlpiri adds a retroflex tap /ɽ/, Diyari contrasts alveolar tap and trill phonemes, and Yaygir has a voiceless trill /r̥/.

The phonological validity of the term "rhotic," often used for the above class of sounds, remains a matter for debate. On the one hand, in languages such as Yidiny (Dixon 1977a, pp. 98–100) /r/ dissimilates to /l/ in the presence of /ɹ/ or /r/, i.e., either rhotic. On the other hand, Alpher (1988) and McGregor (1988) show that in many languages /r/ patterns with the laterals, and /ɹ/ with the approximants.

Approximants. Australian languages typically have a peripheral glide /w/ and a palatal glide /y/, in addition to /ɹ/. A few languages have richer systems: Yindjibarndi adds an interdental glide; Bajjamal contrasts labiovelar /w/ and bilabial /β/, at least phonetically and possibly phonemically;[6] and a number of Arandic dialects contrast rounded and unrounded velar approximants (Wilkins 1989, pp. 89–90).

Fricatives are rare, and where they exist the place of articulation is marked cross-linguistically. A sample of fricative inventories is given in table 25.2; as can be seen, labial and velar fricatives are commonest, while /s/, the commonest fricative cross-linguistically (Maddieson 1984), is confined to Kala Kawaw Ya (which shows Papuan influence) and Anguthimri, which has the richest fricative inventory. In Marrithiyel there is an incomplete contrasting triplet of long-stop, short-stop, and fricative series; for the lamino-dental, lamino-palatal, and retroflex series the contrast between short stop and fricative is neutralized.

Two-stop series. Around 40 languages have developed a contrast between twostop series. In different languages the contrast has been described as geminate/non-geminate, lenis/fortis, long/short, voiced/voiceless, tense/lax, and aspirate/non-aspirate,[7] but these terms should not be taken at face value as only in a few cases are they based on instrumental phonetic analysis or tight

Table 25.2 Sample Fricative Inventories

Peripheral		Laminal			Apical			Languages
β, φ, v	γ	ð	ʒ	ʃ/ɕ	ẓ	r	s	
	+							Tiwi; Mawng, Iwaidja, Amurdak; Kunparlang; Kuthant
+								Adnyamathanha
		+						Tharrgari
+	+							Gog-Nar
	+	(+)[a]						Marrgu
+	+	+						Kurtjar, Kunjen, Uradhi
+	+			+	+			Ngan'gityemeri
+	+			+	+			Marrithiyel
+	+	+	+	(+)[a]		+	(+)[a]	Anguthimri
							+	Kala Kawaw Ya (s, z)

[a] Parentheses indicate doubtful phonemic status because of the small size of the corpus.

phonological argumentation. In some languages, such as Warray and Mayali, long stops contrast with geminate stops, which always span a morpheme boundary – a Mayali example is *kukːu* "water" versus *kuk-kuḍuk* "Aboriginal person", lit. "body-black."

A careful instrumental survey of Arnhem Land languages by Butcher (to appear a) shows that length is the primary phonetic parameter in the Gunwinyguan and Burarran families, voicing is the primary parameter in the Daly languages Ngan'gityemeri and Murrinhpatha, while in the Yolngu subgroup short voiced stops contrast with long voiceless stops. A survey by Austin (1988a) examines languages of the Pilbara, Cape York, and south Central Australia. References to instrumental work on particular languages can be found in these two surveys.

In most languages the stop contrast is intimately linked to stress, meter and vowel length in the flanking syllables. In Warluwarra the voiced/voiceless contrast almost corresponds to a long/short vowel contrast in the preceding syllable – cf. /pantu/ "waist" and /paːndu/ "butt of tree"[8] – and in many Cape York languages the development of a voicing contrast was conditioned by vowel length in the preceding syllable.[9] In Warumungu some case suffixes have long-initial allomorphs after trimoraic stems and short-initial allomorphs after dimoraic stems. Many languages have non-phonemic lengthening of consonants between adjacent stressed syllables – in Kayardild, for example, stops are lengthened between two stressed short syllables – or to meet targets of initial heavy syllables, as in Djapu. Further advances in our understanding of this phenomenon will almost certainly depend on integrating accounts of meter, syllable weight and other manifestations of "prominence" such as the glottal stop (Hyman 1975); an attempt to do this for Djinang is in Waters (1980).

The most radical departure from the standard Australian consonant inventories is found in Damin, an auxiliary language used by second-degree Lardil initiates on Mornington Island. It augments Lardil's standard consonant inventory (which adds /ḻ/ to the Kayardild one above) with a bilabial fricative, four nasal clicks, an ingressive lateral fricative /ɬ̰/, a velar nasal made with extra pulmonic pressure, an ejective velar stop /k'/, and a velaric egressive bilabial stop /ọ/ made "not with glottalic pressure . . . but by creating pressure between the tongue and the bilabial closure" (Hale 1973, p. 443). Uniquely among the world's languages, it uses all five phonetic initiation types – the standard pulmonic egressive, pulmonic ingressive (/ɬ̰/), velaric ingressive (the nasal clicks), velaric egressive (/ọ/) and glottalic egressive (/k'/).

2.2   *Vowels*

The typical Australian language has a triangular three-vowel system with a length contrast. In some languages length is lost, sometimes conditioning new developments in the consonant system (see below). Or vowel length may develop anew, as in the Cairns rainforest area, where phonemic vowel length has developed as an areal feature, partly to compensate for the loss of syllable-final liquids and /y/, though the mechanisms by which it developed in Yidiny are quite different from those of the adjacent northern Dyirbal dialects (Dixon 1990).

As for vowel quality, some Arandic languages have reduced to a two-vowel system by transferring roundedness and frontness to adjoining consonants (see sec. 3.5), while many languages of Cape York have augmented it, largely through processes of historical ablaut, to anywhere between four (Ntraʔŋiṯ) and up to 17 (Anguthimri)[10] phonemes. Five-vowel systems are found in many non-Pama-Nyungan languages and, in the case of Gunwinyguan at least, are of considerable antiquity (Harvey to appear). Nasal vowel phonemes are surprisingly rare, being found only in Anguthimri, although some languages (e.g., Yidiny, Mayali) have nasalized allophones when word-final nasals are elided.

3   Autosegments and Complex Segments

A major source of variation in Australian phonological systems has been the spilling of articulatory gestures beyond the phonemic segment with which they were originally associated, resulting either in syllable-level prosodies or in the merging of two segments on a single consonant position. This has created a variety of types of complex segment: prenasalized stops and prestopped nasals, prestopped laterals and prelateralized stops, stops with trilled release, and labialized consonants. Many languages have also developed syllable prosodies, such as glottalized syllables in Arnhem Land languages, and retroflexion in others. While the last three decades has seen a great deal of diachronic work that is implicitly non-linear (Dixon 1980: chapter 7 provides an excellent summary); it is only in the last few years that explicitly non-linear synchronic accounts have appeared.

While autosegmental theories make a clear distinction between complex segments, where two or more elements on the same tier are associated with a single skeletal position, and autosegments, where elements from distinct tiers are associated with the same skeletal position, in practice it is not always clear which analysis is to be adopted, and we shall see that such phenomena as retroflexion may yield best to an autosegmental analysis in one language, and to a complex-segment analysis in another. I therefore treat both phenomena in this section.

3.1   *Prenasalized Stops*

The desirability of treating homorganic nasal plus stop sequences as unitary phonemes was first pointed out by Oates (1967), who noted that phonotactic statements of Kuku-Yalanji could thus be simplified. Alawa (Sharpe 1972, pp. 14–16) contrasts prenasalized stops with sequences of nasal plus stop (which may or may not be homorganic). Sharpe's arguments for a prenasalized stop series are largely phonotactic: nasal-stop sequences can occur word-initially, provided they are homorganic, and the relevant sequences would, if treated as two phonemes, be the only word- and syllable-initial clusters in the language. In addition, a homorganic nasal-stop structure (using the term here and throughout without prejudice as to its ultimate analysis) is broken up differently in slow speech, depending on whether it is a prenasalized stop or a biphonemic sequence (ibid., p. 16). Sequences spanning a morpheme boundary furnish many examples of two-phoneme sequences. The difference is shown by the words *ki.ṭa.^{n}ṭi* "circumcised boy" and *kar.kaɲ-.ṭi* "kitehawk-erg."

For many Australian languages the only evidence bearing on whether nasal stop sequences should be treated as bi- or mono-phonemic is from the phonotactics of non-initial syllables. But occasionally other phonological evidence for a complex segment analysis can be found. Nash (1979b) reanalyses Yidiny, described in Dixon (1977a, 1977b), as containing prenasalized stop phonemes, which are realized phonetically as simple stops word-initially and as nasal-stop clusters elsewhere.

In addition to phonotactic considerations (which are actually rather weak for Yidiny – they simplify the morpheme-structure conditions, and eliminate some but not all three-consonant clusters), Nash gives three further arguments. First, a complex segment analysis can explain why a homorganic nasal appears at the reduplication boundary in *paykaɪmpayka-ɪ* "feeling very sore", from the base ᵐ*payka-ɪ*, whose nasal onset is suppressed word-initially but appears in the reduplicand, as opposed to words like *punja-punja-n* "hit each other", whose root is simply *punja-n*. Second, it accounts for another characteristic of reduplications, formulated by Dixon (1977a, p. 156) as "a syllable-final nasal which is homorganic with the following stop is not reduplicated"; this contrasts with other syllable-final elements which are – cf. *kintal-kintalpa* "lizards" and *jukar-jukarpan* "have unsettled mind for a long period" but *kala-kalampaɪaː* "marchflies" and *maji-majintan* "keep walking up". On a complex-segment analysis this falls out automatically, since the nasal segment actually belongs to the following syllable. Third, the loss of nasals in the slow, syllabified pronunciations of some words (e.g., *kilpaynta*, pronounced slowly as *kilpay-ta*) can be explained as the loss of prenasalization when pauses place the complex segment in word-initial position.[11]

A recent article by McConvell (1988) has drawn attention to a problematic phenomenon, Nasal Cluster Dissimilation (NCD), in Gurindji and related languages.[12] One rule, NCD deletion, reduces true homorganic nasal stop clusters to stops after nasal stop sequences (not necessarily homorganic) in the same phonological word. In the following Gurindji examples, eliminated prenasalizations are in brackets, retained prenasalizations are underlined, and the determining sequence is in bold.

(1) (a) lutju-ŋka   (b) wiɲji-(ŋ)ka   (c) pinka-(ŋ)ka
         ridge-LOC   spring-LOC   river-LOC
         "on the ridge"   "at the spring"   "at the river"

(2) (a) ɲampa=(n)ta ɲa-ɲa   (b) waɲji=(ŋ)ku   ɲunu-ɲ-ma ?
         what-2SUBJ   see-PST   which-2IOBJ   you-DAT-TOP
         "What did you lot see?"   "Which is yours?"

NCD deletion fails to apply to nasal-stop clusters that span morpheme or word boundaries, and as such are clearly bisegmental:

(3) (a) tampaŋ   kariɲa   (b) nuŋkiyiŋ-ku
         dead   bePST   relation-DAT
         "He died."   "for a relation"

However, the segments of the determinant may span morpheme boundaries:

(4) (a) ŋaɪin-ku(ɲ)ja   (b) ɲin-ku(m)palŋ
         food-COMIT   drown-LEST
         "with meat"   "to avoid drowning"

NCD deletion may apply over an unlimited number of syllables containing only liquids and/or glides (5), but is blocked by any intervening stop or nasal (6):[13]

(5) ɲampa-wu-waḻa-yi-(n)ta   ɲa-ɲa
     what-DAT-now-1sgOBJ-2plSUBJ   see-PST
     "Why did you lot look at me?"

(6) (a) waɲji-ka-n̲ta   (b) kuya-ŋka-ma-n̲ku   pa-ni
          which-LOC-2plSUBJ   thus-LOC-TOP-2sgOBJ   hit-PAST
          "Where are you lot?"   "It was for that reason that he hit you."

A second and related type of nasal cluster dissimilation rule, NCD denasalization, applies to *any* sequence of nasal plus stop – not necessarily homorganic, and possibly spanning a morpheme or word boundary – converting the nasal to its corresponding stop. In the following examples the underlying nasal is given in parentheses after the resulting stop.

(7) ɲampa-t(n)-pula   ɲa-ɲa
     what-2SUBJ-DU   see-PST
     "What did you two see?"

(8) ɲampa-wu-waḻa-t(n)-jina   pa-ni
     what-DAT-NOW-2SUBJ-3plOBJ   hit-PST
     "Why did you hit them?"

(9) waɲji-waḻa-t(n)   ka-ɲa
     which-now-2SUBJ   bring-PST
     "Which did you bring?"

Although the long-distance dissimilations found with Nasal Cluster Dissimilation resemble OCP effects, the phenomenon has so far resisted an autosegmental treatment, since it is not clear how the nasal-stop clusters can be represented in a way that will capture the similarity between both NCD rules – deletion of the nasal with complex segments, and denasalization with diphonemic sequences – and that will motivate the correct blocking conditions. Ultimately we may need to develop new conceptual tools, such as cluster weight, to explain it; the metrical structure of Gurindji is surely also relevant but has yet to be described explicitly. Diachronic changes resulting from various sorts of nasal dissimilation, such as the loss of prenasalization following nasal-initial syllables, have been widely reported in Australian languages (Dixon 1980, pp. 216–8).

3.2 *Prestopped Nasals and Prestopped Laterals*

Prestopping of nasals and laterals is an areal feature of languages in southeastern Central Australia. Arandic languages have complete series of prestopped nasals, but no prestopped laterals; languages of the Lake Eyre region have both, though the series are not always complete, and the prestopping is often allophonic rather than phonemic. In some Arandic languages, such as Alyawarra, they are restricted to the first consonantal position in the word, and should right-reduplication or compounding place them in a later position, an ordinary nasal will be substituted – cf. Alyawarra $a^p m^w$ a "bad", $a^p m^w$-$am^w a$ "rubbishy"; *akŋima* "carry, take"; $a^y lpuɹa$ "shoulder"; $a^y lpuɹ$-*aŋima* "carry on the shoulder" (Yallop 1977, p. 18).

Accounts of prestopping as a Central Australian areal feature are in Hercus (1972), Austin, Ellis, and Hercus (1976), and Austin (1981). In Cape York, Kunjen can be analyzed as having a prestopped nasal series, or more abstractly as nasals "plus tensity," and Yir Yoront has a non-phonemic prestopped lateral: it realizes the sequence /ll/ as a prestopped lateral [^{d}l], as in /mall/ [ma^{d}l] "long-tailed white stingray". Gidabal has prestopped nasal and lateral allophones in word-final position, before other consonants, and in intervocalic position when preceded by at least two other syllables and followed by no other lateral or nasal.

Evidence for treating prestopped nasals and laterals as single phonemes, in which the prestopping is the less salient part, comes from their phonotactic, morphophonemic, and etymological sources. Phonotactically, "prestopped nasals . . . have the same distribution as nasals in Kaititj . . . and sometimes alternate with long nasals in both Kaititj and Alyawarra" (Busby 1980, p. 88). Perceptually the nasal or lateral portion is more salient. Etymologically, they develop from nasals or laterals, e.g., proto-Pama-Nyungan *kuna* "shit, guts" > Diyari /kuna/, phonetically [ˈku^{d}na], and Mparntwe Arrernte /aˈna/ (Wilkins 1989, pp. 88–9).

The commonest environment for the development of prestopped nasals and laterals is following a stressed syllable. Hercus (1972) shows that the first step in their development is for intervocalic nasals and laterals to be geminated after stressed syllables, followed by dissimilation to stop+nasal or stop+lateral sequences. However, word-initial nasals inhibited this dissimilation. The development of prestopped nasals in Kunjen is still not fully understood, but appears to be linked to complex combinations of stress and vowel length that have yet to be reconstructed satisfactorily .

3.3 Prelateralized Stops

Most languages of the Iwaidjan family have a series of complex segments that have been described as "lateral flaps" (Pym and Larrimore 1979) or "prelateralized stops" (Handelsmann 1991). In all four languages apico-alveolar and apico-postalveolar complex segments /^{l}t/ and /^{l}t/ exist; fuller investigation of these languages may reveal palatal /^{l}t̪/ as well. The complex segments contrast with simple laterals /l/ and /ɭ/, and with true clusters /lt/, /ɭt/ which span two syllables. Prelateralized stops pattern phonotactically like single phonemes. Unlike clear clusters, they can be syllable- and word-initial, as in Amurdak /ˈtaɲ/ "dingo" and /aˈta.wuʈ/ "water", and in slow syllabifications both segments are kept with the following syllable. Their duration in Amurdak is comparable to ordinary single segments and shorter than that of the corresponding clusters. In the mainland languages prelateralized stops are restricted to syllable-initial position, but in Marrgu they can also occur syllable-finally, as in /ˡʈumaˡʈ/ "ear"; in this position they are sometimes pronounced as a retroflex tap.

3.4   *Trilled-release Stops*

Apical stops with a trilled release[14] occur as an areal phenomenon in the Lake Eyre region, where it is merely allophonic in most languages except for Ngamini and Yandruwandha, although its origins as a sound change that has yet to propagate completely through the lexicon make classical phonemic analysis difficult. The historical sources of the phenomenon are surveyed in Austin (1988). In Cape York, trilled-release phonemes are found in a number of Cape York languages such as Anguthimri and Ntʳaʔɲiʈ. In Anguthimri the trilled-release series is articulated further back than the regular alveolars, though they are not retroflexed; they derive from homorganic apical nasal plus stop in intervocalic position following a labial-initial first syllable that was subsequently lost.

3.5   *Roundedness*

In the Arandic languages phonemic roundedness has been transferred from vowels to adjacent consonants. In some Arandic languages, e.g., Kaytetye, this has reduced the number of vowel phonemes to two (/a/ and /ə/), while in others such as Mparntwe Arrernte two further phonemes /i/ and /u/ play a restricted role. The locus of roundedness is not immediately clear at the phonetic level, since both consonants and vowels are rounded in a Mparntwe Arrernte word like [pʷɔʈɪrə-] /pʷəʈirə-/ "turn to stone", but a number of morphological processes show its association with the consonant.

For example, one reduplication type copies the initial (V)C(C), inserting -əlpə- between copy and stem. Applying this to /pʷəʈirə-/ gives [pʷɒlpə-pʷɔʈira] /pʷəlpəpʷəʈirə-/. Since this pattern copies only the first C in words of this type, the roundedness on the first vowel must stem from the consonant. Compare this with the same reduplicative pattern applied to [pɔːʈɪrə-] "clump, cluster". Here the rounding is due to the vowel, phonemicizing as /puʈirə-/, and it does not carry leftward with the reduplication: [pəlpə-pɔːʈɪrə-] /p-əlpə-puʈirə-/. This pattern, then, can be used to detect labialization on initial consonants.

A second reduplication pattern right-reduplicates the final (V)(C)Cə- of the stem, and insets -pə- between stem and copy. This can be used to see whether the roundedness is part of vowels. Thus the labialization of the [ɔ] in [ɪlɔɳə-] "extinguish", which fails to be copied into [ɪlɔɳə-p-əɳə-] "extinguish again and again", is seen to be associated with the preceding consonant, justifying the phonemicization /ilʷənə/.

While facts such as this justify associating labialization with the consonant, several analytical possibilities remain. Some analyses (e.g., Breen 1977; Wilkins 1989) postulate a series of labialized (or "rounded") consonants, essentially doubling the inventory of consonant phonemes. But a recent paper by Breen (1991) has argued that "[r]oundness is not associated with consonants as such, but with consonant positions in a word – which might be occupied by one or two consonants. Roundness may be manifested either on the onset side or the release side of a consonant or cluster . . ."

He further points out that roundedness tends to spread or migrate within words. Spreading is shown by the second [ʊ] in the optional pronunciation [kútʊɹə] of the word kʷətəɹə "nulla-nulla (a weapon)" and migration by the two forms ṭəᵖmʷaɹə and ṭʷəᵖmaɹə for "nail". This often makes it difficult to locate the roundness on a particular segment. These facts suggest roundness in the Arandic languages should be represented on a separate tier, associated with the C position, and able to spread to other V and C positions, or reassociate with other C positions, under certain conditions. This implies the following representations for "nulla-nulla":

(10)

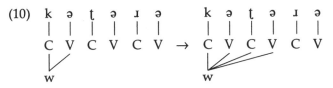

Outside Arandic, incomplete sets of labialized consonants are found in Mbabaram (Dixon 1991) which has syllable-initial labialized /dʷ/, /nʷ/, and /gʷ/, the velar deriving historically from rounded vowels in the preceding syllable (e.g., proto-Paman *guŋgaɹi "north" > Mbabaram ŋgwaɹ(ə)), and in Tiwi, which can be analyzed as having syllable-initial peripheral stops and nasals. In Tiwi labialized consonants appear to have gained their roundedness from the following vowel, rather than the preceding one as in Arandic and Mbabaram – compare kuku-ni "water" (-ni is the masculine suffix) and kukwa "water hole', yuruku-ni "long-masculine" and yurukwa "long-feminine", as well as cognates like Tiwi muŋkwa-ni "small stone axe", Lardil muŋkumuŋku "wooden axe". For none of these languages is our understanding of the phonology sufficient to decide whether rounding should be associated with consonant phonemes, or with a consonant position on the CV skeleton.

3.6 The Glottal Stop as Autosegment in Arnhem Land Languages

In many languages of Arnhem Land, /ʔ/ occupies an anomalous position in the phonemic inventory. Although it contrasts with other segmental phonemes and with zero (Mayali *yiṭuʔme* "you swim", *yiṭutme* "you pierce it"; *kun-milʔ* "forehead"; *kun-mil* "slice of yam"), and would therefore be treated as a segmental phoneme by classical structural phonemics, five features distinguish it from other phonemes:

1 In most Arnhem Land languages it is the only possible final element of three-consonant syllable codas.

2 Several languages have rules preventing successive syllables or morphemes from having glottal stops. Thus in Djapu reduplication of *liwʔ-yun* "go round" gives *liwʔ-liw-yun* instead of the expected *liwʔ-liwʔ-yun*. Such rules suggest the glottal stop should be located on an independent tier.

3 The glottal stop almost always occurs at morpheme boundaries, particularly in junctures within complex verb stems, reduplicated elements, and certain types of suffix; in the Gunwinyguan family most occurrences of glottal stop appear to have arisen as boundary markers (Harvey 1991).

4 Patterns of suffixal allomorphy in Rembarrnga, Ngalakan, and the Yolngu languages ignore the glottal stop. For example, the three allomorphs of the ergative in Djambarrpuyngu, which are conditioned by stem-final nasals, semi-vowels, and vowels, all ignore the presence of stem-final glottal stops:

(11)   N__   Semi-vowel__   V__
       ɹaŋan-ṭːu   kalay-yu   ṭarwa-y
       "paperbark-ERG"   "cousin-ERG"   "many-ERG"
       warakanʔ-ṭu   kalpawʔ-yu   maːrma-yʔ
       "animal-ERG"   "boil-ERG"   "two-ERG"

5 The ergative form *maːrmayʔ* of "two" in (11) illustrates another unusual fact about the glottal stop in Arnhem Land languages – its position disregards morpheme boundaries, passing over affixal material in such a way that it is always syllabified as the final segment of the coda. In certain conditions it may even cross two morphological boundaries, as when the dative and "prominence" suffixes are added to a stem ending in vowel plus glottal stop: *maːrma-w-ɲʔja* [2-DAT-PROM]. Similar phenomena occur in the other Yolngu languages, as well as Rembarrnga and Wagiman.

A number of linguists, such as Schebeck (n.d.) for Yolngu in general (as well as Wood 1978 on the Yolngu dialect Galpu and Morphy 1983 on Djapu), and McKay (1975) for Rembarrnga, have treated the glottal stop as a syllable prosody. However, this fails to account for the segmental-like contrasts contracted by ʔ with other phonemes, and Harvey (1991) has recently proposed that in Ngalakan, Rembarrnga, and the Yolngu languages the glottal stop should be represented on a separate plane to the other consonants as a completely unspecified segment underlyingly. In the Yolngu languages and Rembarrnga, on Harvey's analysis, it only becomes associated with a skeletal position after affixation and partial syllabification have taken place. In other languages, such as Ngalakan, in which suffix allomorphy treats stem-final ? as a consonant, the glottal stop is syllabified before affixation.

3.7 Retroflexion as Complex Segment or Autosegment

The location of retroflexion within phonological representations is by no means uniform in Australian languages. Most descriptions postulate a separate series of retroflex consonants, but even in such languages adjacent vowels may receive a clear "retroflex coloring" or on-glide; in Mpakwithi the retroflex coloring from syllable-initial /ɹ/ can pass through preceding consonants: /gwapɹa/ "is eating" is pronounced [ᵑgwaˀfɹa). While it is usually the preceding vowel so affected, in some languages such as Marrithiyel the following vowel is colored – /maʂi/ "belly" may be pronounced [maẕi] or [maẕɭi].

Two analyzes of Tiwi (Osborne 1974, p. 10; Oates 1967, pp. 36–41), and an article on Kukatj by Breen (1992), propose two-segment analyses of phonetically retroflex consonants as a sequence of /ɹ/ plus apical consonant. The Tiwi argument, which rests on phonotactics (the absence of word-initial retroflexion can be subsumed under the general ban on word-initial clusters) and certain morphological alternations, has certain problems, and a stronger argument for a cluster analysis of retroflexion is given by Breen for Kukatj.

In Kukatj, verb stems are reduplicated according to the rule $C_1VLX \rightarrow C_1LVLX$ where L is a liquid, /l/ or /r/. Examples are

(12) karpel- "be afraid" → krarpel-   yirŋk- "talk"   → yrirŋk-
      milmel- "suck"   → mlilmel-   t̪al- "copulate" → t̪lal-

Now, words containing phonetically retroflex consonants copy /r/ under reduplication (13); this can readily be explained if phonetically retroflex consonants are phonemically complex segments whose first element is r (realized as ɹ before other apical consonants, with which it then merges) and whose second element is an apical stop or nasal.

(13) [t̪aɳ-] /t̪arn-/ "stand" → [t̪raɳ-] /t̪rarn-/

While Tiwi and Kukatj provide evidence for a cluster or complex segment analysis of retroflexion, a number of facts about Mayali suggest it is best analysed as having retroflexion as an autosegment associated with the syllable:

1   Within a syllable, all apical stops and nasals agree in retroflexion: there are words like /ɖiɖ/ "moon" and /ɖoɖ/ "louse" on the one hand, and /dadguyeŋ/ "long-legged" or /nan/ "I see you" on the other, but no syllables like */diɖ/, */ɖid/, */naṇ/ or */ṇan/.[15] Note that the retroflex continuant /ɹ/ does not participate in these effects, and hence we find words like /naɹin/ "snake".

2   Agreement in retroflexion is also found over apical stops and nasals in successive open syllables: there are words like ɖaɖːa "older brother" (ː here represents fortition rather than length; fortis consonants are always syllable-initial) and ɖuɖːu "heart" (incorporated form) but none like *daɖːa or *ɖadːa.

3   Syllables may be retroflexed even when there is no apical segment, with the retroflexion manifested on the vowel in rather variable ways. For example, the word for "death adder" is pronounced [beᶦk], [bᶦek], [beᶦek] or [bek] by different speakers, or even the same speaker. Such variability is not found with regular phonemes. And it is noteworthy that literate speakers have difficulty placing the ɹ when spelling these words; the only other sound with which they have similar difficulties is the other autosegment, /ʔ/.

These three factors suggest retroflexion is an autosegment associated with the syllable, and manifested clearly on any apical stops that may be present, as well as variably on any vowel. Similar phonetic facts have been reported for Murrinhpatha.

The autosegmental representations these facts suggest are illustrated below:

(14)

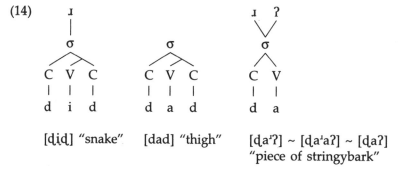

[ɖiɖ] "snake"   [dad] "thigh"   [ɖaᶦʔ] ~ [ɖaᶦaʔ] ~ [ɖaʔ]
                                  "piece of stringybark"

In articulatory terms, retroflexion involves a gesture of the tongue-tip, which is independent of the movement of the whole tongue. Since the timing of this gesture may be synchronized with the occlusion by the tongue, may immediately precede or follow it, or may be slower (i.e., at syllable pace) than that of the occlusion itself, it is not implausible that phonologically retroflexion should have the variable range of treatments that have been discussed here – as part of a unitary retroflex phoneme, as the first or second part of a complex segment, or as a syllable prosody. It is likely that the next decade will see many more subtle phonological effects reported.

4 Vowel Harmony

Vowel harmony is an areal feature of languages across the northern desert fringe, including the Ngulipartu dialect of Nyangumarda, Gooniyandi, Warlpiri, Warumungu, and Jingilu;[16] it is also found in a few other areas, such as in the inland dialect of Kuku Yalanji in Cape York.

In most Australian languages, harmony affects just /i/ and /u/ of a three-vowel system, through the spreading of frontness and roundedness respectively, and it is surely significant that the affected languages lie just to the north of the Arandic languages, which have developed roundedness autosegments (sec. 3.5). However, in Warumungu and the Ngulipartu dialect of Nyangumarta /a/ can also propagate harmony into suffixes – cf. Warumungu *murumuru-ku* "sickness-DAT", *kaṯi-ki* "man-DAT" and *ŋapa-ka* "water-DAT". In Warlpiri vowel harmony may be regressive or progressive. The former is confined to the past tense suffix *-Nu*, which propagates regressive roundedness harmony back to the beginning of the verb root – cf. *kiṯi-ṉi* "throw-NonPast", *kiṯi-kaḻa* "throw-irrealis" but *kuṯu-ṉu* "throw-Past"; preverbs are exempt, as shown by *piri-kuṯu-ṉu* "DISTR-throw-Past". Progressive harmony is more productive, being spread by any positionally appropriate high vowel (in (15a), the first vowel of the proprietive suffix; in (15b) by the final vowel of the root and then again by the enclitic *-lku* "then") across any suffix and clitic boundary; /a/ always blocks the spread of vowel harmony:

(15) (a) miniṯa-kuḻu-ḻu=lku=ṯu-lu
          cat-PROP-ERG-then-1sgO-3plS

(b) maliki-kiḻi-kira=lku=ṯu-lu
     dog-PROP-ALL-then-1sgO-3plS

[Nash 1986, p. 92, with glosses and clitic and suffix boundaries added]

The labial high consonants /p/ and /w/ block the rightward spread of vowel harmony in words like *ŋamiṉi-puɻaji* and *ŋali-wuru*; Nash (1986, p. 93) argues this is because autosegments associated with non-syllabic segments cannot be deleted.

The facts of vowel harmony in Nyangumarta are more complex. Vowel harmony is progressive, and can affect all three vowels, as with the realis suffix and first person subject clitics in (16):

(16) yiri-ṉi=ṉi   "see-REALIS-1sgNOM"
      kalku-ṉu=ṉu   "hold-REALIS-1sgNOM"
      wiḻa-ṉa=ṉa   "hit-REALIS-1sgNOM"

However, when there is a second spreading trigger to the right, the morphemes just discussed surface with an /a/ "buffer vowel":

(17)	yiri-ɳa=li	"see-REALIS-1sg.inclusive.NOM"
	kalku-ɳa=li	"hold-REALIS-1sg.inclusive.NOM"
	wiḻa-ɳa=li	"hit-REALIS-1sg.inclusive.NOM"

(18)	yiri-ɳa=ŋu	"see-REALIS-2sgDAT"
	kalku-ɳa=ŋu	"hold-REALIS-2sgDAT"
	wiḻa-ɳa=ŋu	"hit-REALIS-2sgDAT"

Sharp (1986), from whom these examples are cited, argues that the affected vowel slots here should be left unspecified; when there is only one harmony trigger its vowel features spread to them, as in (16), but when there are two triggers the buffer vowel is delinked and surfaces as the unspecified vowel /a/ (17, 18); the delinking is motivated by the Obligatory Contour Principle which would prohibit the spreading of the identical feature [+high] to adjacent skeleton positions.

There is a second set of suffixes that are immune to vowel harmony and always surface as /a/ (19). Sharp concludes from this that Nyangumarta "phonology distinguishes among four different vowels even though only three are phonetically realized," and proposes that the unchanging /a/ vowel be represented as an empty feature matrix linked to a V position, while the vowels that only surface as /a/ in buffer position should simply be represented as unspecified vowel slots.

| (19) | yiri-nama-ɳa | "see-IRR-1sgNOM" |
| | kalku-nama-ɳa | "hold-IRR-1sgNOM" |

5   Word and Syllable Structure

Australian languages tend to have a disyllabic (or at least dimoraic) minimum word, although monosyllabic structures are found in several areas including Arnhem Land, Cape York, Arandic, and Victoria.

Syllable structures tend to be simple; Kayardild is typical in having CV(L)(N), where L = liquid and N = nasal. Itô (1986) and Wilkinson (1988) show how the well-known battery of truncation-rules in the related language Lardil, first described by Hale (1973), can be motivated by rules of syllable structure and a dimoraic minimum word size.

In almost all Australian languages the maximum coda is more complex than the maximum initial; an exception is Mpakwithi which allows some clusters (basically stop plus continuant) in the onset but only a very limited set of single consonant segments syllable-finally.

A few languages of the southeast allow initial clusters of peripheral stop plus liquid, e.g., Wergaia *bra* "man", *gri* "canoe" and Gippsland *mragen* "face". The South Australian language Ngarrinjerri allows liquids after all sonants, e.g., *ŋlelin* "knowing", *mrukun* "basket", *yrottulun* "lean, poor", *wraŋgi* "bad, silly". Some languages of the northern Pilbara region, such as Ngarla and Nyangumarta (Geytenbeek 1992), elide first-syllable /i/ and /u/ just between initial /k, p, t/ and /r, w/, leading to phonetic cluster-initial words like [kwari] "now" < /kuwari/ and [pɹiri] "man" < /piɹiri/.

More complex codas are found in languages of Arnhem Land and Cape York, e.g., Mayali *nakurŋʔ* "son-in-law-VOC", Kunjen *alᵖmp* "opossum", Wik-Munkan *wolmp* "big noise", Yir-Yoront *kaɳtl* "big". In some of these languages, such as Urningangk, the most complex clusters only arise at word boundaries and can be treated as containing extrasyllabic segments. An interesting case is Kayardild, where prosodic truncation at the end of intonational phrases eliminates final /a/ (sec. 6.5). For older speakers this is a prosodic process, and final syllables underlyingly have a restricted, vowel-final structure, e.g., *ki.yarŋ.k(a)* "two". But for younger speakers, who take these truncated forms as underlying, the final syllable of a word can have a more complex structure, e.g., *ki.yarŋk*, resulting in the extrasyllabic licensing of a third coda element.

The most common additional stipulations applying to word structure but not syllable structure tend to be those requiring words to end in vowels (e.g., Warlpiri) or consonants (Kunjen), or adding vowel-initial words as a possibility (in Mayali the only V-initial syllables are word-initial) or as the canonical type (Olgolo – Dixon 1970b). But there may also be constraints on intervocalic clusters beyond those on syllabic structure. Thus although the heterosyllabic clusters *ny* and *ŋw* are allowed across a syllable boundary by the syllable-structure conditions in both Mayali and Kayardild, they only actually occur in Mayali (e.g., *apanyameŋ* "I speared them", *kaparaŋwayʔme* "the escarpment goes up"). This is due to the existence in Kayardild of an additional syllable-contact constraint stating that the coda consonant of the first syllable must be lower or equal to the onset of the second on the sonority hierarchy; morphophonemic rules eliminate many would-be violations (e.g., underlying *ŋaɳwulaʈa* "from the beach" surfaces as *ŋaɳwulaʈa*). Where the two segments are equal in sonority, the first is always to the right of the second on Hamilton's articulator hierarchy (sec. 2.1); this permits clusters like *ŋm* in the example just given, and *ʈp* in *ŋiʈpaluʈa* "to cool food", but outlaws the reverse sequences.

5.1 The VC Problem

Data from a number of Australian languages have been used to challenge claims about the universal unmarkedness of CV syllables. Sommer (1969, 1970) proposed that all syllables in Kunjen had the structure VC* and hence were counterexamples to claims that CV is a universal syllable type. He based his arguments on the segmentability of all Kunjen words into VC* units (e.g., *id.un.aɣ.al* "make a spear"), and on the easier formulability of reduplication rules in terms of VC* syllables – e.g., "copy the first VC syllable" giving *eḍ.eḍ.eɹ* "heavy rain" and *alg.alg.al* "straight as a ram-rod", "copy the second VC syllable", as in *iy.alm.alm.ey* "keeps playing", or "copy the third VC syllable" in *an.aŋ.um.um.in* "keeps peeking". (In fact, the generalization that the penultimate VC syllable is copied would be compatible with all the data except one word which Sommer admits is exceptional anyway.)

Sommer's original paper has engendered considerable controversy (see Dixon 1970b; Darden 1971; and McCarthy and Prince 1986); the restated position in Sommer (1981) is that *underlying* Kunjen syllables must have a VC* structure, while *surface* syllables[17] may have a CV structure as a result of late rules such as reduction; it is these surface CV syllables that are responsible for the effect, pointed out by Dixon (1970b), that consonants are articulated more forcefully before stressed vowels.

More recently, data from the Arandic languages has been employed by Breen (1991) to give a more convincing case for underlying VC syllables. The phonology of the Arandic languages is exceptionally complex and interesting, and they are still vigorous enough for detailed phonological analysis to be possible; the existence of a play language called "Rabbit Talk" (Turner and Breen 1984) has furnished a number of phonological insights. Excellent work by a number of linguists has gradually led to a radical and unusual view of Arandic phonological structure, but very little of this work is published, even in samizdat form.[18]

We have already seen the arguments for treating rounding in Arandic as an autosegment primarily associated with C positions. Of the two main vowels[19] /a/ and /ə/, the phonetic realization of the latter is, apart from its vocalicness, "completely determined by the consonants preceding and following it"; furthermore, /ə/ "is a realization of an underlying vowel that appears on the surface only when there is a need for something to separate consonants" (Breen, 1991). /ə/ is added in final position on some words when they are utterance-final, or a C-initial word follows; the exact conditions vary according to the dialect and age of the speaker.

With this background we can now turn to Breen's main claim, that Arrernte has an underlying VC(C) syllable structure, even though surface syllables have the structure (C)V(C). This analysis implies the initial syllabifications in (20). Note that in the initial syllabification there will be many empty V slots which will eventually be candidates for realization as /ə/; others will eventually be eliminated by joining C-only underlying syllables as onsets to the following syllable; and underlying word-final Cs are resyllabified on the surface with final ə.

(20)

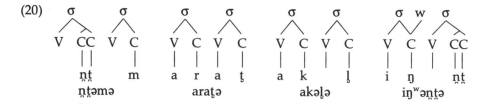

(21)

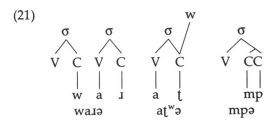

There are a number of motivations for this analysis. First, there is great variability in the number of surface syllables: "sits", for example, can be pronounced [anə́mə] (three syllables), [nə́mə] (two), [anə́m] (two), or [nəm] (one). Yet the number of underlying VC syllables stays constant at two, namely:

(22)

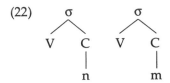

Second, speakers break up words not into CV syllables, but into word-like parts with initial /a/, /i/, or /u/, e.g., giving /uʰnaṯəṯə/ "mulga blossom" as /uʰnə, aṯəṯə/; such breaks do preserve the postulated underlying VC-syllabification.

Third, stress rules can be neatly stated in terms of underlying VC-syllables. In terms of conventional syllables, the rule needs to incorporate references to syllable onsets, giving formulations like "for words of two or more syllables, stress falls on the first syllable containing an onset": cf. /inə́mə/ "gets", /nə́mə/ "sits". But in terms of VC syllables the rule can be formulated simply as "for words of two or more VC-syllables, stress falls on the second VC-syllable."

In addition to these general considerations, a number of morphological rules can be formulated most neatly in terms of the VC model. Let us begin by considering the formation of words in the play language "Rabbit Talk"; I leave aside the treatment of monosyllables, which is exceptional under any analysis.

(23)		Normal	Rabbit Talk	Gloss
	(a)	Initial vowel slot unfilled:		
		kəɹə	ɹəkə	"meat"
		ṉt̪əmə	məṉt̪ə	"giving"
	(b)	Initial and second vowel slots filled:		
		araṯə	aṯarə	"right"
		itirəmə	irəmitə	"thinking"
	(c)	Initial vowel slot filled; second unfilled:		
		ulkəṯə	ṯulkə	"prentie (goanna)"
		itəṯəkə	ṯəkitə	"to light (a fire)"

(d) Initial vowel slot unfilled; second filled:

| waɹə | aɹəwə | "only" |
| ḻatə | atəḻə | "now" |

Under the VC analysis of underlying syllables, the rule for all four sets can be formulated elegantly: the first underlying VC syllable is simply shifted to the end of the word, as in the following examples:

(24)   Normal   Rabbit

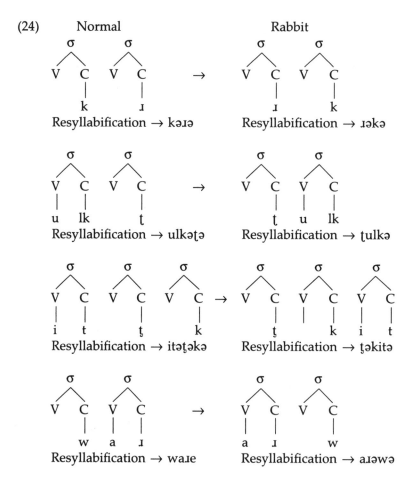

Formulating the main Rabbit Talk rule in terms of normal syllables, on the other hand, would require a number of complex and unnatural rules. Another advantage of the VC analysis is that the Rabbit Talk forms always have the same number of VC-syllables as their ordinary equivalents, whereas the number of surface CV syllables may vary – decreasing from three to two with *ulkətə*, and from four to three with *itətəkə*, but increasing from two to three with *waɹə*.

A number of "normal" rules of affixation and reduplication likewise allow more elegant formulations in terms of underlying VC-syllables. For example, the formation of nominalizations is exemplified by:

(25) a̠ɭkʷə   "eat"   a̠ɭkʷən̠a̠ɭkʷən̠ə   "food"
      aŋkə   "talk"   aŋkən̠aŋkən̠ə   "talker"
      atʷərə   "fight"   atʷərən̠ərən̠ə   "weapon"

On a conventional syllable model, the rule needs to be expressed as "suffix ən̠ to the stem and right-reduplicate the last two syllables that result, minus the onset of the first syllable." But the VC syllable model permits the neater formulation "add n̠ to the stem and right-reduplicate the last two VC syllables thus formed."

Any claim about preferred syllable structure depends on the level being discussed. In both Arrernte and Kunjen the level of surface syllabicity presents no great problems to claims for the universal status of CV as preferred syllable structure. But at the deepest level of representation the arguments for VC being the canonical syllable in Arrernte must now be considered very strong.

5.2   Syllable Constituency

Data from certain Australian languages also challenge a second oft-made universal claim about syllable structure, namely that all syllables can be broken down into an onset and a rhyme, which may then be further broken down into nucleus and coda. Davis (1985, 1988) marshals data from several Australian languages to argue instead for a flat syllable structure;[20] his main arguments for a flat syllable structure in some Australian languages rest on onset-sensitive stress assignment. Rhyme-sensitive stress assignment has, of course, been a mainstay of rhyme-based syllable analyzes given the common tendency of heavy syllables (defined in terms of a complex rhyme) to attract stress.

Davis reviews evidence from a number of Australian languages – Western Aranda, Alyawarra, and Ma̠dimạdi – in which certain onsets attract stress in a way that appears comparable to heavy rhymes. For example, in Ma̠dimạdi, words normally bear initial stress (e.g., púkumanàma "kangaroo", wálwạta "to burn") but second syllables which do not begin with a peripheral consonant attract stress (e.g., wirántu "your whiskers", ḍináɲu "(his) foot", kùyúni "a large spear").[21] Davis shows that this is best accommodated by a metrical analysis of stress if a level syllable structure is proposed; however, it must be borne in mind that Hercus's description is based on work with the last, very old speaker and contains a limited corpus. The other two languages cited by Davis are the Arandic languages Western Aranda and Alyawarra; as we saw in (5.1), Arandic languages stress the initial syllable if it begins with a consonant, and the second syllable if the first begins with a vowel. These examples lose their force, of course, if we adopt Breen's VC syllable analysis, which treats both cases as second-syllable stress.

To these examples we may add several Yolngu languages, in which stress assignment is sensitive to apical initials: in Djapu first syllables are normally stressed, but apical-initial second syllables may attract stress if heavy[22] (e.g., *puṭápṭun* "go down and cross"). In Djinang stress assignment is more complicated, depending on a prior division of the word into feet, which act as timing units. I will indicate intraword foot-boundaries with brackets. Within each foot that is longer than an open monosyllable the initial syllable is stressed, and primary stress is assigned to the first syllable of the word. A new foot will be initiated after any closed syllable (e.g., [míːl][kùl][ṭːìn][ṭìke] "covet"); after an open syllable a new foot can only be initiated if it begins with a non-apical consonant (cf. [káṭi][kàr] "track, road" and [míri][kàl] "clothes" with *wákiri* "crow" and *ṭúmiliŋ* "blunt").

As this Djinang example shows, it is simplistic to base stress assignment simply in terms of local syllable structure. If it depends indirectly on the structure of higher-order units such as feet, then the force of Davis's arguments is weakened. We must conclude that there is no knock-down stress-based argument for a level syllable structure in Australian languages, since all relevant cases are either based on a limited corpus, an underlying VC-syllable, or are epiphenomena arising from the sensitivity of phonological feet to intervocalic consonants.

A second line of argument for a syllable structure in which quantity is onset-sensitive has been proposed by Hale and Nash (1987) for the Lardil auxiliary language Damin. Unlike Lardil, Damin has initial consonant clusters such as /fŋ/ and /ṭr/, and Hale and Nash raise the possibility that the various complex unusual initiation types behave phonologically as complex segments (e.g., /ɬ/ as underlying /l/ plus /l/). They then relate this to a second difference between Lardil and Damin: where Lardil words must be at least dimoraic (i.e., disyllabic, or monosyllabic with a long vowel), Damin permits short-vowelled monosyllabic words only if they begin with a cluster or complex segment: "the minimal Damin word would be of the form CVV or CCV (but not CV). It would seem that Damin continues to satisfy the Lardil bimoraic minimal word requirement only if CCV words are considered to be bimoraic. If the CC of CCV is a single onset, then we are faced with an unusual onset-rime or onset-nucleus dependencies (sic) involving quantity." (ibid, p. 9).

6   Prosodic Domains

In this section I review phonological processes sensitive to particular levels of the hierarchy of prosodic domains proposed by Nespor and Vogel (1986): the syllable (see above), the foot, the phonological word, the clitic group, the phonological phrase, the intonational phrase, and the phonological utterance (though of course authors may not use these terms). I shall say nothing about intonation which, with a few honorable exceptions largely within the tagmemic tradition (e.g., Sharpe 1972 on Alawa; Sayers 1974, 1976 on Wik-Munkan; and Pym and Larrimore 1979 on Iwaidja; see also Ford and Ober 1985), has been seriously neglected.

6.1 The Foot

Following Nespor and Vogel, I assume that the foot exists as a phonological constituent independent of stress rules, and indeed we have already seen that in Djinang foot-construction must precede stress assignment. Feet are used in the treatment of Warlpiri phonology by Nash (1986, p. 103ff.) as a means of indirectly making morphological structure available to the stress assignment rules, and to formulate the verbal reduplication rule: the first foot of a verb is left-reduplicated. The reanalysis of Yidiny stress by Hayes (1982) uses the foot as a formal device to eliminate the need for syllable-counting rules; foot construction also precedes stress assignment in Mayali (sec. 7.2).

6.2 The Phonological Word

An interesting case in which a grammatical word can comprise two phonological words is Yidiny. Monosyllabic suffixes form part of the same word both grammatically and phonologically; for example, they feed rules which lengthen the penult, and delete final suffixal syllables of odd-syllabled words (cf. (26a) and (26b)). But suffixes of more than one syllable, though part of the same grammatical word by such criteria as fixed morpheme order and distribution across phrases, will initiate separate phonological words (delimited here by [ ]$_\omega$). These phonological words are the input to the rules of penultimate lengthening and final-syllable deletion (27a, b). Other processes responsive to phonological rather than grammatical words are the selection of case and tense allomorphs, and the assignment of stress.

(26) (a) [milpa-ŋa-l-ɲu]$_\omega$ →   milpaŋalɲu
           clever-CAUS-CONJ-PST
           "made clever"
      (b) [kumaɹi-ŋa-l-ɲu]$_\omega$ →   kumaɹiŋaːl
           red-CAUS-CONJ-PST
           "made red"

(27) (a) [milpa]$_\omega$[-taka-ɲu]$_\omega$ →   [milpa]$_\omega$[-takaː-ɲ]$_\omega$
           clever-INCH-PST
           "became clever"
      (b) [kumaɹi]$_\omega$[-taka-ɲu]$_\omega$ →   [kumaːɹi]$_\omega$[-takaː-ɲ]$_\omega$
           red-INCH-PST
           "became red"

6.3   *The Clitic Group*

Clitics in various positions are widespread in Australian languages. Complexes of pronominal enclitics, sometimes also including tense/mood marking, are found in Wackernagel's position in many languages, including Warlpiri and Ngiyambaa: they may follow either the initial word or the initial phrase. Clitics marking such functions as interrogation, focus, and restriction are also common, encliticizing to the word in their scope. More unusually, some languages (e.g., Kugu Nganhcara) have enclitics to the preverbal constituent:

(28) ṇila   pama-ŋ   ŋaʔa=la   yenta
      3sgNOM   man-ERG   fish=3sgNOM   spear
      "The man speared the fish."

It is often said that clitics are part of the same phonological word as their host – in Warlpiri, for example, clitic auxiliaries count as part of the same phonological word as their host for purposes of vowel harmony and stress assignment,[23] and in Gurindji the domain for nasal cluster deletion includes enclitics (sec. 3.1). But rules specific to the clitic phonological domain are sometimes found. In Ngiyambaa, for example, clitic pronouns behave like normal suffixes in a number of ways, participating in normal stress assignment rules within the word, and in an alternation that sees initial laminal stops realized as /ṭ/ after /i/ and /t̪/ elsewhere. But whereas normal suffixes induce a preceding homorganic nasal on stems ending in the "nasal archiphoneme" N, pronoun enclitics parallel word boundaries in failing to induce the nasal. Thus the underlying final nasal in palka:N "boomerang" (palka: in citation form) will appear before the diminutive suffix (palka:n̪-t̪ul "boomerang-DIM") but not before a clitic (palka:-ṭu "boomerang=1sgNOM").

In some languages of the Barkly region (Warumungu, Garawa) pronominal clusters may occur as clitics or may stand alone. Simpson and Withgott (1986) argue that such clusters in Warumungu cannot be accommodated in the normal, layer-ordered cycles of lexical phonology and are formed in the lexicon as flat structures, by template morphology. One piece of evidence comes from a rule that retroflexes nasals in the environment [[. . .]$_\sigma$[V____]$_\sigma$] just inside clitic clusters; this derives aṭilaɳk:a, for example, from underlying aṭilaŋk:u "1du.excl.subj → 2sg.obj" (the change in the final vowel is due to vowel harmony).

6.4   *The Phonological Phrase*

External sandhi rules within phonological phrases are not uncommon in Australia. An example is the Iwaidjan language Mawng, with four sets of external sandhi rules. One lenites initial peripheral stops of quantifying and emphatic particles after vowel-final nouns, pronouns, verbs, or adverbs (29b).

(29) (a) yinimaɲ   kirk   (b) kinima   yirk
          he.took.it   all   he.takes.it all
          "He took it all."   "He takes it all."

A second involves another set of lenitions – initial /k/ becomes /ɣ/ before
/i, e, a/ and /w/ before /u/ after vowel-final words in phrases comprising
a verb and its intransitive subject (30b), or a noun and its premodifier (31b).

(30) (a) karkpin   kapala   (b) kɛ   ɣapala
          big   boat   it.goes   boat
          "big boat"   "The boat goes."

(31) (a) marik   kupuɲ   (b) mata   wupuɲ
          not   canoe   the:CLIII   canoe
          "not a canoe"   "the canoe"

Two further processes, not illustrated here, involve the denasalization of
verb-final nasals before uninflected roots or adverbs beginning with a stop,
and the merging of like vowels across word boundaries, including like vowels
separated by a homorganic glide. Although the syntactic constituents within
which external sandhi can apply are not specified in the source, all examples
are consistent with a phonological-phrase domain of either the NP or the
"verbal group" (i.e., verb plus adverb, auxiliary, quantifier, or absolutive noun),
and this corresponds closely to the conditions on the "phonological phrase"
defined by Pym and Larrimore (1979, pp. 16–18) for the related language
Iwaidja.
    More limited examples of sandhi rules within a phonological phrase come
from Yir-Yoront, which inserts schwa to break up certain consonant clusters
between words within a phonological phrase, and Diyari, where inflected verb
stems plus a following auxiliary verb merge into a single unit in rapid speech.

6.5 *The Intonational Phrase*

In Kayardild final /a/ is deleted from the last syllable of each intonational
phrase (including, of course, the citation form). In (32) two words, each ending
in /a/, are repeated in different orders, pausing after each intonational phrase.
In rapid speech intonational phrases may span a whole clause, but as speech
is made slower they may shrink to single (syntactic) phrases, or even single
words within a phrase.

(32) [ṭirkuɹ-uŋ-ka   ṭaa-ṭ]ɪ;   [ṭaa-ṭa   ṭirkuɹ-uŋ-k]ɪ
      north-ALLAT-NOM   return-ACT   return-ACT   north-ALLAT-NOM
      "From the north (he) returned; he returned from the north."

6.6   *The Phonological Utterance*

An interesting set of sandhi rules whose domain is the phonological utterance have been described by Crowley (1980) for the Cape York dialects Atampaya, Angkamuthi and Yadhaykenu; a later publication (Crowley 1983) gives a pan-dialectal grammar under the cover name "Uradhi."

Most Atampaya words have three surface forms: one in utterance-final position (an environment which affects the citation form), one in non-final position before vowels, and one in non-final position before consonants. The effects of these environments on the word for "tree" is illustrated below, for the moment in phonetic rather than phonemic transcription.

(33)   (a)   [yukuŋ]ᵤ   (b)   [yuku   wampaŋ]ᵤ
            tree   treeNOM   float-PRES
            "tree"   "The tree is floating (on the floodwaters)."

       (c)   [yuk   anaːluŋ]ᵤ
             treeNOM   float:PRES:hither
             "The tree is coming this way (with the flood)."

Words with final -*n*, e.g., *wapun* "head" or *aŋan* "dig" either delete -*n* or add -*a* before a following consonant (34); before vowels they replace *n* with *r* (35).

(34)   [ayu   muṯ   aŋa / aŋana   nani-mun]ᵤ
        1sgERG   grubACC   dig-PST   ground-ABL
        "I dug the grubs from the ground."

(35)   [uŋkyaw   mayi-wapur   uŋyaw]ᵤ
        flying.foxERG   food-headACC   eat-PRES
        "The flying fox is eating fruit."

The full set of Atampaya sandhial alternations is as follows:

Underlying form	Utterance final	Prevocalic	Preconsonantal
-V	-Vŋ	-ø	-V
-n	-n	-r	-ø/-na
-Vn̪/-Vɲ/-Vy	-Vn̪/-Vɲ/-Vy	-ø	-V/-Vn̪a /-Vɲa /-Vya
-l	-w	-l	-w

The remaining dialects are basically similar, but with some additional alternatives – for example Yadhaykenu responds to the sequence V#V either by eliding the first vowel, or by inserting a velar nasal: cf. *yapi* "forehead" but either *yap aɽama wiɲṯuŋ* or *yapiŋ aɽama wiɲṯuŋ* "his forehead is not wrinkled".

Crowley argues that these sandhi patterns developed to resolve anomalies arising as Uradhi lost or lenited initial consonants and moved from an ancestral

CV-initial word structure to a modern (C)V-initial word structure, but retained constraints against successive vowels. The unacceptable sequences of adjacent vowels that would have arisen as Uradhi moved from an ancestral sequence like *kutakampu ŋaɲi ŋampuŋku paṯan* to a would-be modern sequence *utaɣampu aɲi ampuŋku waṯan* were avoided either by elision of the first vowel (as in Atampaya) or by inserting a consonant (as with Yadhaykenu ŋ-insertion). Other sandhial alternations can be traced to new constraints on sequences at word and utterance boundaries: against CC sequences across word boundaries (explaining the loss of *n* in the environment __#C) and against V utterance-finally (resulting in the addition of ŋ). Finally, the *l/w* alternation preserves original *l* just in the environment V__#V; it has changed to *w* in preconsonantal and prepause (including citation form) positions. The current complicated alternations are thus due to a series of interactions between loss of word-initial segments, preservation of certain sequencing constraints across word boundaries, and the introduction of new constraints across word boundaries and at utterance boundaries.

7   Stress and Metrical Structure

No Australian languages utilize tonal contrasts, and with the exception of Wik-Mungkan and Ndjébbana (McKay and Coleman to appear) they all have fixed-accent systems. In Wik-Mungkan different stress patterns distinguish segmentally identical compounds (cf. *méːʔ-pèɲṯ* [eye-hair] "to be born", *mèːʔ-péɲṯ* "eyebrow"). Sayers also claims that the future versus past tense contrast is distinguished by a contrast between secondary and no stress (cf. *ṯáṯàŋ* "I will see", *ṯáṯaŋ* "I saw"), but an alternative is to admit syllabic nasals and phonemicize these as *ṯáṯaŋ* and *ṯáṯŋ̩* respectively (Gavan Breen p.c.). Most Australian languages appear to be stress-timed, but Kugu-Nganhcara is syllable-timed.

7.1   Meter that Ignores Morphological Boundaries

Although almost all Australian languages have fixed-accent systems, there is enormous diversity in their stress patterns; data from a number of languages have already been of central importance to the development of metrical theory but much remains unexplored.[24] In general, the unmarked primary stress position is on the initial, though in some prefixing languages (e.g., Tiwi) it is on the penultimate.

Much of the cross-language variation comes from the setting of various parameters which are easily accommodated by existing metrical theories. Are feet constructed from left to right, as in Maranungku and Yidiny, or from right to left, as in Garawa? Is stress allowed on final syllables, as in Guugu-Yimidhirr, or disallowed, as in Pintupi, and more generally are there extrametrical syllables in initial position (as on one analysis of Arandic) or final position (e.g., Pintupi)? Is the word stress left-headed (as in most Pama-Nyungan languages), or right-headed as in Jingilu, which has penultimate stress, and Uradhi, which has prepenultimate stress unless there is a long vowel. Are feet quantity-sensitive, being attracted to long vowels (e.g., Waalubal) or heavy syllables more generally (Gumbaynggir)? Or does the mora form a more appropriate unit than the syllable for stress assignment, as in Gooniyandi? Are feet binary, as is the case in most Australian languages, or unbounded, as in Waalubal, which gives primary stress to the first syllable, and secondary stress to any remaining long vowel, allowing unbounded feet between any long syllables, e.g., *ɲámàːlu* "tree goanna-ERG", *wúrkulùːm* "magpie", and *páɲʈanibèː* "only covered".

To these differences we may add the possible effects of syllable- or foot-onsets on stress assignment, already discussed in 5.2, which sees certain syllable onsets attracting or spurning stress in Ma<u>d</u>imadi, Djinang, and possibly Arandic.

A particularly intricate system is that of Yidiny, which shows a complex interaction between vowel-length, syllable-count and stress: (1) syllables alternate between stressed and unstressed (e.g., *ʈámpuláɲalɲúnta*), (2) all long vowels occur in stressed syllables (e.g., *wúɲapáːʈiɲúnta*), (3) long vowels must always be separated by an odd number of syllables (e.g., *makíːriɲáːldaɲúːn*), and (4) all words with an odd number of syllables must have a long vowel in at least one even-numbered syllable. In the initial descriptions by Dixon (1977a, b) a number of rules sensitive to syllable-count were used to derive surface forms satisfying the above constraints; for example, Penultimate Lengthening lengthens the penultimate vowel of any word with an odd number of syllables, and Illicit Length Elimination shortens long vowels occurring in odd-numbered syllables of odd-syllabled words. These facts have been subjected to various reanalyses, largely motivated by the localistic need to reformulate Dixon's rules without actually counting syllables; the reader is referred to Hayes (1982), and Halle and Vergnaud (1987a) for details.

7.2   *Meter and Morphological Structure*

In many Australian languages the most natural account of stress assignment makes reference to morphological structure. For example, the basic Warlpiri pattern is for odd-numbered syllables to be stressed, with the proviso that word-final syllables must be unstressed: *mánaŋkàḻa* "spinifex plain", *wátiya* "tree". However, this basic pattern is broken when suffixes of two or more syllables initiate new domains for stress assignment; this leads to such minimal pairs as (36a, b). Successive monosyllabic suffixes may be merged as a single disyllabic foot, whose first syllable then receives stress (36c).

(36)   (a)   yápaḻa-ŋùḻu   "father's mother-ELAT"
   (b)   yápa-ḻàŋu-ḻu   "person-for.example-ERG"
   (c)   wáti-[ŋkà-ḻu]₌   "man-LOC-ERG"

Diyari stress behaves similarly, with each plurisyllabic suffix bearing an initial secondary stress (37a), but unlike in Warlpiri monosyllabic suffixes may not be merged into a foot (37b).

(37) (a) kàɳa-wáɹa-ɳúndu   man-PL-ABL
      (b) máda-la-ntu   hill-CHAR-PROPR

Although many grammars make reference to morphological structure in their formulation of stress rules, some theoreticians have sought ways of representing the stress facts without overt reference to morphology (see the treatment of Diyari and Warlpiri stress by Poser 1989); others (e.g., Halle and Vergnaud 1987a: 93) tacitly accept the role of morphological structure in conceding that "the property of being a stress domain is not necessarily coextensive with that of being a word."

Poser's approach eliminates the need for metrical rules to refer to morphological structure by making foot construction cyclical, applying after each morpheme is added; monosyllabic suffixes are assigned degenerate feet which block them from appearing in new feet and are postcyclically defooted. This works for Diyari and Warlpiri because both affixation and stress assignment go from left to right, but there are other languages, such as the polysynthetic Gunwinyguan languages, where Poser's solution will not work: the basic problem there is that stress is assigned from right to left, while the relevant affixes are added from left to right; consequently stress assignment cannot begin until all affixation has been completed.

The following examples of stress assignment in Mayali verbs will illustrate the problem, and the need to recognize morphological structure; the simplest analysis first builds feet on the basis of morphological structure, and then stresses the leftmost syllable of each foot, with the final non-degenerate foot receiving word stress; feet are the timing unit, and are of approximately equal duration. Normally each morpheme before the root is a foot, even if mono-syllabic (38a, b), but from the root rightwards things are more complex: tense suffixes are merged with the preceding morpheme (the root, or the reciprocal-forming suffix) into a single foot (38a, b, c, d). Complex stems (prepound plus root), whose elements separated in these glosses with a +, behave slightly differently; the root of complex stems merges with single monomorphemic word-final syllables to the right (38a), otherwise the complex stem forms one foot (38c). All stems are shown in bold.

(38) (a) [pàri]$_\Sigma$-{mìm]$_\Sigma$-**[bò]$_\Sigma$**+**[wó**-ni]$_\Sigma$ they-seed-water.give-past. imperfective

      (b) [pà]$_\Sigma$-[kàɲ]$_\Sigma$-[**ŋú**-neŋ]$_\Sigma$ (s)he-meat-eat-past.perfective

      (c) [pàri]$_\Sigma$-[ʈàrk]$_\Sigma$-**[màn+ka]$_\Sigma$**-[ré-ni]$_\Sigma$ they-together-fall-recip-past. imperf

      (d) [àri]$_\Sigma$-**[pù]$_\Sigma$**-[ré-ni]$_\Sigma$ we-hit-recip-past.imperf

Verbs in the irrealis behave uniquely, in requiring the formation of a final trisyllabic foot (39a) regardless of the position of the irrealis morpheme break; any remaining stem material forms its own foot (39b) even if this breaks up a morpheme (in 39b, it fractures the root *ware* "bad").

(39) (a) [àpan]$_\Sigma$-[**kárme**-niɲ]$_\Sigma$ I/them-get-irrealis
      (b) [bà]$_\Sigma$-[**wà**]$_\Sigma$[ré-m-eniɲ]$_\Sigma$ it-bad-inchoative-irrealis

Once foot-construction has been carried out, it is easy to state the stress rules. Stated informally, stress is assigned to the first syllable of each foot, and word-stress to the first syllable of the rightmost non-degenerate foot; if stress has still not been assigned once left of the root, it goes on the first syllable of the first foot left of the root, degenerate or not. The latter condition is needed to account for cases like (40), where all feet right of and including the root are degenerate and hence ineligible to bear primary stress, though they still receive secondary stress. Because of constraints on root-size this means that the primary stress will fall two, three, or four syllables to the left of the word-edge.

(40) (a) [pá]$_\Sigma$-[ŋù-ø]$_\Sigma$ (s)he:PST-eat-IMP "may (s)he eat!"
      (b) [án]$_\Sigma$-[**pò**-m]$_\Sigma$ (s)he/me-hit-past.perfective
      (c) [àn]$_\Sigma$-[máɳe]$_\Sigma$-[**pò**-m]$_\Sigma$ (s)he/me-benefactive-hit-
                                         past.perfective
      (d) [kàpani]$_\Sigma$-[kúk]$_\Sigma$-[**pù**]$_\Sigma$-[rè-n]$_\Sigma$ they.two-body-hit-reciprocal-
                                         non.past

Roots beginning with /d/ behave anomalously: following the comitative applicative *yi-*, and a small set of prefixes whose last vowel is lexically accented, e.g., *mint é* "many", such roots merge with the preceding syllable in a new foot, and change /d/ to /r/ (41a, b), but not if the stem is more than disyllabic (cf. 41c). Elsewhere these prefixes behave normally, and are their own foot with initial stress (41d, e); the accent fails to surface. As we would expect given the right-to-left construction of meter, this pattern of stress assignment is bled by the irregular stress found with the irrealis.

(41) (a) [à]$_\Sigma$-[yí-**ruɳ**ʈe-ŋ]$_\Sigma$ I/it-comitative-return-non.past
      (b) [kàpari]$_\Sigma$-[mìɳ]$_\Sigma$[té-**ri**]$_\Sigma$ they-many-stand-non.past
      (c) [kàpari-[míɳʈe-[**dúlu**+bo-m]   they-many-shoot-past.perfective
      (d) [àn]$_\Sigma$-[yì]$_\Sigma$-[**báwo**-ŋ]$_\Sigma$ (s)he/me-comitative-leave-
                                         past.perfective
      (e) [bà]$_\Sigma$-[mìɳʈe]$_\Sigma$-[**bìm**]$_\Sigma$+[**bú**-ni]$_\Sigma$ she-many-paint-past.perfective

Such complex stress patterns force a view of metrical phonology in which stress assignment follows the building of feet over the fully assembled word, a process which must be responsive to morphological boundaries and peculiarities of certain affixal elements. More complete phonological studies of other Gunwinyguan languages are likely to confirm this picture.

8 Prosodic Morphology: Reduplication

Given the essentially concatenative nature of most Australian morphological systems, the main interest of Australian languages for prosodic morphology (see chap. 9, this volume) comes from their rich possibilities of reduplication, surveyed in Dineen (1989). We have already seen examples of both left- and right-reduplication in Arandic (sections 3.5 and 5.1), left-reduplication in Yidiny (sec. 3.1), and reduplicative infixing of syllable-codas in Kukatj (sec. 3.7); in general, left-reduplication is more common.

Many languages, such as Mparntwe Arrernte, have a number of reduplication templates each with their own meaning, and at least two of these may apply to the same verb: (42a) shows "continuous inceptive" left-copying with infixed *əlpə-*, and "frequentative" right-copying with infixed *-p* together, expressing repeated inception, and (42b) the "inceptive" and "sporadic" together; the phonology and semantics of multiple reduplication need further investigation.

(42) (a) t-əlpə-taṇtə-p-aṇtə-mə
REDUP-CONT.INCEP-spear-FREQ-REDUP-non.past.progressive
"always making as if to spear, over and over again, without doing it"

(b) aŋk-əlp-aŋkə-ḷ-aŋkə-ḷiwə-mə
speak-CONT.INCEP-REDUP-FREQ-speak-FREQ-non.past.
progressive
"stuttering from time to time"

One aim of prosodic morphology is to replace characterizations of reduplication in terms of segment strings with simpler characterizations in terms of roots, morphemes, or syllable templates, and to use morphemic tiers to capture patterns that are hard to characterize in a simple linear model. Certainly, reduplicative processes in Australia are often sensitive to these structures (see for example Levin 1985 on Umpila). Reduplication involves verbal roots in Nyigina, and verbal stems (= root plus conjugation marker) in Kuku Yalanji. Verbal reduplication uses a syllable-pruned version of the inflected form in Warlpiri and Mayali (see below); Dineen points out that reduplication based on inflected forms is found only with verbs, not nouns, in Australian languages.

In many languages reduplication is sensitive to the syllabicity of the source morpheme(s). In Ngiyambaa, verbal reduplication involves the first two syllables of the stem, with pruning of the second syllable to make it light, e.g., *kaṭi-kaṭinma-ɹa* "REDUP-smash-PRES"; if the stem is a monosyllabic root, it cannot reduplicate. In Mayali, "iterative" verb reduplication takes the tense-inflected stem as input; if this has two or more syllables the first syllable and next CV are reduplicated (43a), but if the inflected stem is a monosyllable a second template is used, which has the form CVNV-, where N is realized as *n* if C is a peripheral (43b), and ŋ elsewhere (43c):

(43)	(a)	ta-ŋen	stand-NonPast	→	taŋe-ta-ŋen
		wo-ni	give-PastImperfective	→	woni-wo-ni
	(b)	ma-ŋ	get-NonPast	→	mana-ma-ŋ
		mey	get-PastPerfective	→	mene-mey
		wo-n	give-NonPast	→	wono-won
	(c)	ta-ɲ	stand-PastImperfective	→	taɲa-ta-ɲ
		yo-y	lie-PastImperfective	→	yoŋo-yo-y

Another interesting example of the interaction of syllable targets, morpheme structure and inserted morphemic material comes from the Mayali terms for ecozones, formed by reduplicating a root designating some dominant plant or landscape feature. The template for this involves a disyllabic foot, with second syllable, open except possibly for ʔ, prefixed to the root. The coda of the first occurrence of the reduplicated root must be ʔ, displacing any copied coda material. (44) illustrates how monosyllabic, disyllabic and trisyllabic roots are adapted to this template; notice that the initial CV of monosyllabic roots gets copied twice to meet the foot requirements.

(44)	kun-waṭe	"rock"	→	kun-waṭeʔ-waṭe	"rock plateau"
	an-kapo	"creek"	→	an-kapoʔ-kapo	"area with lots of creeks"
	an-yakŋara	"pandanus"	→	an-yakŋaʔ-yakŋara	"pandanus scrub"
	an-powk	"seasonal swamp"	→	an-poʔpo-powk	"alluvial plains"
	kun-kot	"paperbark tree"	→	an-koʔko-kot	"paperbark swamp"

In some languages, the reduplicated portion often fails to correspond to a natural phonological unit. We have already seen examples where the coda is absent from reduplicated monosyllabic or disyllabic prefixes, or is replaced with a final glottal stop; here it is a CV-, rather than a syllable, that is copied.[25] A number of languages (Jingilu, MalakMalak, Warumungu, Kugu-Nganhcara, Mangarayi) have a distinctive type of reduplication appearing at first glance to involve rightward copying and infixation of the rhyme of the first syllable and the onset of the second:

(45) țapanța   "young"   →   țapapanța   "young ones"
      maļuka   "old man"   →   malaļuka   "old men"
      piɳmiriɳi   "old woman"   →   piɳminmiriɳi "old women"

However, McCarthy and Prince (1986) account for the Mangarayi version of
this by rendering the initial C extramelodic and then prefixing a syllable to
which a copy of the phonemic melody is linked; this melodic copy saturates
the prefixed syllable and fills the vacant onset slot left by the detachment of
the initial melodic element from the base. An example of how their account
can be adapted to the Jingilu data is (46); note that this postulates left-copying,
and avoids the need for postulating infixation.

(46) (a)   σ   σ   σ   σ
            /Λ   /\   /\   /\
            piɳ   mi   ri   ɳi

      (b)   σ   +   σ   σ   σ   σ
                    /\   /\   /\   /\
                   (p)iɳ   mi   ri   ɳi

      (c)   σ   +   σ   σ   σ   σ
            /Λ _____ /\   /\   /\   /\
            piɳmiriɳi   (p)iɳ   mi   ri   ɳi

NOTES

I am grateful to Gavan Breen, Andy
Butcher, Carolyne Coleman, Bob Dixon,
Brian Geytenbeek, John Hajek, Robert
Handelsmann, Mark Harvey, John
Henderson, Mary Laughren, Patrick
McConvell, Bill McGregor, David Nash,
Rachel Nordlinger, Nick Reid, Janet
Sharp, Jane Simpson, and Oscar
Whitehead for their helpful discussions
of various issues in this chapter, and for
their generosity in making unpublished
work available. I would also like to take
this opportunity to thank the compilers
– Bob Dixon, Michael Walsh, Harold
Koch and Geraldine Triffitt – of the
annual bibliographies of work on
Australian languages that appear in the

Australian Journal of Linguistics, which
have been invaluable in preparing this
article; I recommend them as a means
of following recent developments in the
years that will follow the publication of
this chapter.

1 Most descriptive work has been
   based on classical phonemic, early
   generative, Firthian prosodic, or
   tagmemic models. The availability
   of models from the last two
   traditions in particular saved many
   descriptions from ignoring prosodic
   facts that could not easily be
   accommodated in the generative
   tradition and were thus at risk of
   being omitted from more theory-

bound descriptions. Notable early descriptions based on the richer phonological models offered by the tagmemic tradition are Sharpe (1972) on Alawa, Sayers (1974) on Wik-Mungkan, and Pym and Larrimore (1979) on Iwaidja. Sayers's descriptions, for example, recognize a phonological hierarchy comprising syllable, foot, word, phonological clause, and phonological sentence. A phonological description applying the Firthian notion of syllable prosody to the glottal stop in Rembarrnga is McKay (1975), while McGregor (1993) examines Gooniyandi phonology from a systemic perspective.

2   For brevity's sake I give the primary sources for all language data with the list of language locations.

3   The symbols used here have their standard IPA values, except that I use *y* for IPA *j* and *ɹ* for IPA *ɻ*.

4   Although Butcher (to appear b) shows that in some languages, e.g., Warlpiri, "retroflexes" are actually sublaminal rather than apical.

5   And Butcher (to appear b) has shown that the point of apical contact word-initially is actually intermediate between the normal contact points when the phonemes are distinct.

6   We still lack a definitive treatment of Bajjamal phonology, and the bilabial glide may be an allophone of /b/ after vowel plus liquid sequences (Andy Butcher p.c.).

7   E.g., Hosokawa (1991) discusses a possible "tense/lax" contrast in the Kimberley language Yawuru, predominantly cued by unreleased versus aspirated realization in word-final position.

8   But there is a single disyllabic exception, kaːn̪t̪a, plus a number of exceptions in longer words.

9   However, some languages, such as those of the Yolngu group, have both a contrasting stop series and contrastive vowel length.

10   Crowley's description of Anguthimri is a salvage study only and the data is too limited to give unquestioned phonemic status to all 17.

11   Consistent with this analysis is the observation by Brian Geytenbeek (p.c.) that attempts to teach literacy in Aboriginal languages by the "syllable method" often lead to learners omitting the nasal.

12   The phenomenon is found in various other languages of the northern desert fringe. McGregor (1990) describes a similar phenomenon in Gooniyandi, though here is it restricted to adjacent syllables.

13   These facts hold for the major dialect considered. In a second dialect /p/ fails to block NCD deletion, and in a third both /p/ and /k/ fail to block it (McConvell 1988, p. 161).

14   Breen (1975) analyzes these as prestopped trills.

15   The two exceptions to this involve (a) cases where an apical in one syllable changes its value for retroflexion through assimilating to another in an adjoining affixed syllable: cf. ɖoɖ 'louse' but ŋan-doɖ-maŋ 'he delouses me', and (b) underlyingly non-retroflex syllables whose initial has been retroflexed following a glottalized syllable – cf. *naŋ* "I saw you" and *woʔŋaŋ* "I looked after you". This process is as yet poorly understood, but there is some evidence that apicals after glottalized syllables are ambisyllabic, since the retroflexion colors the preceding vowel: *woʔŋaŋ* is phonetically [wɔ^ɪʔn̪aŋ].

16 Theoretical discussions are in Steriade (1979), Nash (1979a), van der Hulst and Smith (1985), Archangeli (1986), Nash (1986), and Sharp (1986).

17 The terms "underlying syllable" and "surface syllable" are my own. Sommer uses the terms "phonological" and "phonetic" syllable.

18 Two short but influential papers on Arandic phonology – Turner and Breen (1984) and Wilkins (1984) – appeared in the now-defunct *Language in Central Australia,* available from the Institute for Aboriginal Development, Alice Springs.

19 Two more vowels, /i/ and /u/, have a much more restricted distribution.

20 In a beautiful example of structurally parallel phonological and syntactic arguments in temporal décalage, this recapitulates the use of data from Dyirbal, Nunggubuyu and other Australian languages to argue against the universality of a VP constituent in syntax.

21 The diachronic operation of a similar rule followed by loss of the first vowel is likely to have led to the initial clusters in Ngarrinjerri and some Victorian languages (see sec. 5).

22 However, the discrepant status of the apical stops in Djapu (as the only ones not descending from long stops intervocalically) suggests the following hypothesis: only apicals are not ambisyllabic, so that non-apical stops all follow closed syllables. This would then allow us to formulate the stress rule in terms of first-syllable weight.

23 In fact, Warlpiri presents problems for Nespor and Vogel's prosodic hierarchy, which says that the clitic group exhaustively subsumes lower constituents, in particular the phonological word. Warlpiri vowel harmony presents problems from this view, since harmony spreads rightward into the enclitic group, but does not spread out of preverbs, reduplicated elements, or compounded nouns:

(a) piri-kuʈu-ŋu=ju-ḻu
     DISTR-throw-PST=1sgO-3plS
(b) yukiɹi-yukiɹi-ḻi
     green-green-ERG
(c) miyi-kupu-ŋu
     food-winnow-PST

If the harmony domain is used as evidence for a prosodic constituent, the first break is between the preverb, etc., and the remainder plus clitics, rather than between the clitics and the complex word, as Nespor and Vogel's theory would suggest.

24 And in fact the primary data on which discussions of MalakMalak and Maranunggu stress are based may not be accurate. In particular, it seems that these languages do in fact take morpheme boundaries into account in their stress assignment rules (Mark Harvey and Ian Green, p.c.).

25 However, the possibility that this pattern can be analyzed as an open or light syllable template warrants investigation.

26 Hausa Tonology: Complexities in an "Easy" Tone Language

PAUL NEWMAN

0 Introduction

Hausa, a Chadic language spoken in Nigeria and Niger, has long attracted the attention of phonologists because of the richness of its inflectional and derivational morphology and because of interesting problems concerning gemination and vowel length. On the other hand, compared with languages of coastal West Africa or Southeast Asia, the tonal system of Hausa appears quite simple. It has just two basic level tones: H(igh), indicated by an acute accent á(a), e.g., *jáa* "pull", and L(ow), indicated by a grave accent à(a), e.g., *wàa* "who?", plus a F(alling) tone, indicated by a circumflex *âa(a)* e.g., *sâa* "bull". (With long vowels, indicated by double letters, tone is marked on the first vowel only.) And yet, Hausa turns out to be an excellent language to illustrate essential concepts and problematic areas in the analysis of tone. This is partly because the tone system is relatively simple and easy to comprehend and partly because the surface simplicity masks a range of interesting complexities. In this chapter, I shall focus on four general tonological issues, drawing examples mostly from Hausa, but occasionally from related Chadic languages. Although the issues to be treated are all of importance to current phonological theory, my approach will be nonformalistic and, in some sense, atheoretical. That is, the attempt will be to provide analyses that fit properly with our overall knowledge of Hausa – including diachronic and dialectal information – and that also jibe comfortably with our general notions about the nature of tone derived from years of experience working on tone languages.

Let us begin with a few essential facts about Hausa segmental phonology before turning to the issues at hand. Standard Hausa has five vowels, all of which can occur short or long, namely i(i), e(e), a(a), o(o), u(u), and 32 consonants.[1] The semivowels /y/ and /w/, which occur only as syllable onsets, alternate with /i/ and /u/, respectively, in other syllable positions, e.g., *sàyí* "buy" = *sái* (optional apocopated form); *háwáa* "riding", cf. *háu* "mount". Three syllable types occur: CV, CVV (where VV can represent a long monophthong or a diphthong), and CVC. Syllables of the CV type are light; CVV and CVC syllables are heavy (see Newman 1972). CVVC syllables occur in intermediate structure, but are automatically reduced to CVC by syllable overload rules. Short /e/ and /o/, which often result from shortening in closed syllables, generally centralize to /a/ in non–word-final position.

1   Contour Tones

The general issue here is whether contours should be treated as unitary tonal elements or as a complex composed of two (or more) level tones.

1.1   *Falling Tone as High-Low Sequence*

From an early period, Hausaists such as Abraham (1941), Greenberg (1941), and Hodge and Hause (1944), have proposed that the falling tone be analyzed as a sequence of H plus L on a single syllable. This type of analysis has been posited more generally for African languages viewed typologically (see chap. 12 this volume).[2] Yip (1989, pp. 149–150), for example, describes contours in African languages as "tone clusters" which result from associating two tonal root nodes (i.e., two level tonal units with one syllable). This type of analysis also has strong formal theoretical support. Consider, for example, the statement by Goldsmith (1990, pp. 39–40): "The possibility of many-to-one associations between one tier and another opens up the possibility of treating rising and falling tones as sequences of level tones . . . associated with a single vowel . . . Among African tone languages it has been demonstrated in countless cases that these tonal patterns [falling and rising tones] are best treated as sequences of High-Low and Low-High respectively." Taking Hausa as a case in point, there is indeed ample evidence for treating F as HL on a single syllable. Consider the following factors: (a) Falling tones only occur on heavy (= 2-mora) syllables, i.e., those with two potential tone-bearing-units, whereas simple H and L tones occur on light (= short vowel) syllables as well as on heavy syllables, see (1).

(1) (a) F: yâaráa   "children"
                   mântáa   "forget"
                   shâddáa   "latrine"
     (b) H / L: bàkáa   "bow"
                   gòobé   "tomorrow"
                   wàa   "who?"
                   dà   "with"
                   sái   "until"
                   tá   "via"

(b) In phonologically shortened words, an original L tone combines with an H to produce a Fall. This can be seen in coexistent variants and frozen reduplicative forms as in (2).

(2) (a) kâr̃ = kádà "don't", làadân = làadáanìi "muezzin", dâbgíi = dáabùgíi "anteater"
     (b) bêlbéelàa "cattle egret" < *béelàbéelà, dûddúfàa "white ibis" (< *dúfàdúfà)

That F equals HL is particularly evident in paradigms that have a set H-L tone pattern, e.g., (3).

(3) (a) zân (< záanì) "I will", zâi (< záayà) "he will", cf. záakà "you (masc.) will", záatà "she will"
     (b) mîn (= mínì) "to me", mâr̃ (= másà) "to him", cf. mákà "to you", mátà "to her"

(c) The grounding of floating L tones, which are associated with certain morphemes, produces an F, e.g., (4).

(4) fítóo "come out" + -̀wáa "ing" → fítôowáa "coming out"
     gídáa "house" + -̀n "the" → gídân "the house" (Note: the vowel shortening *gídâan → gídân results from the impermissibility of overheavy syllables.)
     wàa yá káshè zóomôo? "who killed the hare?" where zóomôo < zóomóo + the question morpheme /-̀ː/, which is composed of floating length and a floating L tone.

(d) Disyllabic verbs with the tone pattern F-H fall into the same morphological class (called grade [gr.] in Hausa) as comparable H-L-H verbs, e.g., (5).

(5) shâidáa (gr. 1) "inform", cf. báyyànáa (gr. 1) "explain"
     shânyée "drink up" (gr. 4), cf. bíncìkée (gr. 4) "investigate"

(e) Words with a final F tone behave as if they had a final L in assigning tone to the stabilizer morpheme (*nee* "masculine or plural", *cee* "feminine"), whose tone is always polar to that of the preceding syllable, e.g., (6).

(6) (a) hàr̃âm née "it's religiously unlawful", mâi née "it's oil", r̀igâr̃ cée "it's the gown"
     (b) zóobèe née "it's a ring", móotàa cée "it's a car", húulúnàa née "they're caps"
     (c) r̀igáa cèe "it's a gown", kèeké(e) nèe = kèekè née "it's a bicycle", ʔílìmíi nèe = ʔílmùi née "it's knowledge"

1.2 Falling Tone as a Unit Contour

The above evidence seems at first sight incontrovertible. There are, however, other factors that point in another direction. Or, to put it differently, even if one were to agree that contour tones in Hausa are underlyingly nothing but sequences of level tones, as one approaches the surface these contours acquire a linguistic reality which sets them apart from the level tones. This reality manifests itself most prominently in the tendency to do away with contours by simplifying them to level tones.

To begin with, there is the simple fact that Hausa does not have a R(ising) tone. Hausa has many disyllabic H-L words and, as illustrated above, when, for any number of reasons, HL becomes associated with a single syllable, the HL surfaces as an F. Since L-H is also a common disyllabic pattern in Hausa, one would expect to find words where the LH has become attached to a single syllable resulting in a surface Rise. So, what has happened to the missing Rise?

It is now generally accepted by Hausaists that the absence of the R is due to a general rule, first mentioned by Parsons (1955) and presented more systematically by Leben (1971), whereby R (= LH) → H. This is illustrated in the examples in (7), in which the indication =/< means that the form on the left is dialectally or stylistically equivalent to and derived from the form on the right. (The notation [NW] marks northwest dialect forms and the hacek on vowels indicates a Rising tone.)

(7) (a) *ɗwǎi (=/< ɗòoyíi) → ɗwái "stench" [NW], *nǎu (=/< nàawá) → náu "mine" [NW]; *'yǎa (=/< dîyáa) → 'yáa "daughter", *tàusǎi (=/< tàusàyíi) → tàusái "pity"

(b) *jǎnjàmíi (< *jàmíjàmí) → jánjàmíi "horse crupper" (cf. *kánàkánà → kânkánàa "a melon")

(c) *cǎn (L-H pattern) → cán "there, far distant", cf. cân "there" (H-L pattern)

(d) *ɗǎukàa (L-H-L gr. 2 pattern) → ɗáukàa "take, lift", cf. tàimakàa "help" (typical 3-syllable L-H-L gr. 2 verb)

Further research, however, has indicated that the R → H change is not as regular as originally thought. Rather, it appears to be a conditioned rule that is sensitive to the preceding tones. If the R is preceded by L or is word initial, as in the examples above, then the rule does apply as postulated, presumably in an exceptionless manner. If, however, there is an immediately preceding H tone in the same word, i.e., one has an H-LH sequence, then the R simplifies to L, i.e., R (= LH) → L / H_____. Thus H-LH results not in H-H, as predicted by the originally formulated unconditioned rule, but in H-L, e.g.,

(8) *gáwǎi (=/< gáwàyíi) → gáwài "charcoal", not *gáwái
*kútǔr̃ (=/< kútùr̃íi) → kútùr̃ "hindquarters of donkey or horse", not *kútúr̃

*múkǎi (=/< múkà yí) → múkài "we did", not *múkái
*ʔílmǐi (=/< ʔílìmíi) → ʔílmìi "knowledge", not *ʔílmíi

Although the discovery of the correct conditioning for the elimination of the surface rise is an important advance in our understanding of the details of Hausa, it does not really affect the general point, which is that rising tones in Hausa do not occur. Viewed as a sequence of LH on a single syllable, the restriction is totally ad hoc, i.e., there is no reason why HL associated with a single syllable occurs and LH does not, rather than vice versa. Viewed as a suppression of surface rising tones, however, the gap is perfectly normal. As pointed out by Gandour and Harshman (1978), Hombert (1975), Ohala (1978), and Sundberg (1979), among others, rising tones have marked articulatory and perceptual weaknesses as compared with falling tones. As a result, there is a natural tendency for rising tones to simplify to level tones (especially high). This explains why among the languages of the world that have contour tones, rising tones appear to be less common than falling tones (Cheng 1973; Maddieson 1978).[3] In short, although we can formally represent rising tones in Hausa as LH attached to a single syllable, a rule such as R → H (under the appropriate conditions) tells us much more about the linguistic and psycholinguistic factors involved in the tone change than does an LH → H rule.

In contrast to Rising tones, which are totally absent in Hausa, Falling tones are common. Nevertheless, these, too, are subject to simplification pressures. The rules are morphologically restricted and vary from dialect to dialect, but they still illustrate an ongoing drift, the direction of which is to eliminate contour tones.[4] There are a number of different, independent manifestations of this loss that can be illustrated.

1.2.1 Maradi Contour Simplification

In the dialect of Maradi (Niger), there is an optional but favored rule which operates on F tones preceded by H, namely F → L / H____ if the F is on a monosyllabic word.[5] The result is to change an H-F (= H H̱L) sequence into a simple H-L sequence, the initial high component of the Fall being subject to absorption. The rule only affects monosyllabic words. As the numerous examples in (9) show, the rule depends strictly on the phonological environment. It does not seem to matter what part of speech the phonologically relevant words are nor how they function syntactically.

(9) sâa "bull": (a) yánàa búgùn sâa "he is beating the bull"; (b) ƙàrámín sàa "small bull"
sôo "pail": (a) yáa cíkà sôo "he filled the pail"; (b) kàawóo sòo "bring a pail"
mâi "oil": (a) gíshíríi dà mâi "salt and oil"; (b) gíshíríi kóo mài "salt or oil"

sôo "love": (a) sábòodà sôo "because of love"; (b) dón sòo "for sake of love"

jâa "pulling": (a) yánàa jâa "he is pulling"; (b) yáa zánkí jàa "he kept on pulling"

sâa "to put": (a) bàmù sâa sú bá "we didn't put them"; (b) mún sàa sú "we put them"

bâa "to give to": (a) yà bâa Súlè "he should give Sule"; (b) yáa bàa Súlè "he gave Sule"

cêe "to say": (a) sái kà cêe "as you say"; (b) káa cèe "you said"

nân "here": (a) kù tsáyàa nân "stop here"; (b) kù zóo nàn "come here"

yâu "today": (a) yáa gámàa yâu "he finished today"; (b) yáa dáawóo yàu "he returned today"

mâa (< mákà) "to you": (a) náa gáyàa mâa làabáaŕìi "I told you the news"; (b) náa ʔáikóo màa tákàŕdáa "I sent you a letter"

Recent unintegrated loanwords, e.g., *pîl* "battery", *kwâs* "course", *bîk* "ballpoint pen", (but cf. *sôo* "pail" above) do not undergo the rule. There are also a few other exceptions, such as the F tone 2nd future pronouns in (10), but these seem uncommon.

(10) (2nd future): ín sûn ... "if they will ...", wái tâa ... "it is said she probably will ...")

The rule is limited to monosyllabic words; falling tones in polysyllabic words, as in (11), are thus not affected.

(11) yáa cânyée "he ate it up", mún shâidáa "we bore witness"
      gídân "the home", ráanâi "the day"

Contour simplification similar to that in Maradi also occurs in Standard Hausa, but here it is restricted to just a few specific words, see (12).

(12) (a) kà cêe "you should say", káa cêe "you said", sún cêe "they said", but ká cèe "and you said" (where the rel-perfective pronoun ká preceding the L tone variant of the verb cèe has H tone *and* consists of a light syllable).
      (b) *kàazáŕ-nân → kàazáŕ-nàn "this hen", *àkún-cân → àkún-càn "that parrot"
      (c) cf. yáa zóo nân "he came here" (not *yáa zóo nàn)
           záa tà tàfí cân "she will go there" (not *záa tà tàfí càn)

1.2.2 Northwest Contour Simplification

A simplification with interesting dialectal variation concerns the so-called *waa*-verbal nouns (or "-ing" forms). These items, which correspond to English gerunds or progressive participles, are formed by adding a suffix -wáa to the verb. This morpheme has H on the *wáa* syllable and is preceded by a floating L tone.[6] When the verb ends in L, the floating L is absorbed and has no effect. When the verb has a final H tone, the floating L attaches thereto and produces a Fall. This is shown in the examples in (13).

(13)   káamàa "catch" / káamàawáa "catching", káràntáa "read" / káràntâawáa "reading"
         fáshèe "smash" / fáshèewáa "smashing", ƙéetàrée "cross" / ƙéetàrêewáa "crossing"
         kóomóo "return" / kóomôowáa "returning", sáyóo "buy" / sáyôowáa "buying"
         ṝúbúutóo "write" / ṝúbúutôowáa "writing", záabúṝóo "leap" / záabúṝôowáa "leaping"

In northwest dialects, however, there are various strategies to eliminate the Falling tone. With "-ing" forms corresponding to trisyllabic and quadrisyllabic (H)-H-L-H verbs, final F-H on the last two syllables simplifies to H-L, e.g., (14).

(14)   [NW] káràntáawàa "reading", lúgúlgùdáawàa "kneading", ƙéetàréewàa "crossing"

There are two possible explanations for the change. If the L of the HL Fall were to attach to the final syllable, it would produce a final Rise which would simplify to L as illustrated earlier in (8), e.g., *káràntâawáa → *káràntáawǎa → káràntáawàa*. Alternatively, the L of the HL Fall could occupy the final syllable in a "hostile manner"[7] and directly obliterate the final H, e.g., **káràntâawáa → káràntáawàa*. In either case, the contour is eliminated in favor of a sequence of level tones.

   With level H tone verbs (the so-called "ventive" grade 6 verbs ending in -*oo*) three different patterns emerge in different northwest dialects. In Ader, the F-H to H-L rule applies (15a). In Dogondoutchi, as seen in (15b), the F-H simplifies to L-H. Finally, Maradi (15c), uses both of the above strategies. With disyllabic verbs, it behaves like Dogondoutchi and simplifies F-H to L-H whereas with longer words it behaves like Ader and simplifies F-H to H-L, e.g.,

(15)   (a)   [Ader]: káawóowàa "bringing", lúgúlgúdóowàa "kneading (and bringing)"
         (b)   [Dogondoutchi]: hítòowáa "coming out", híssúwòowáa "bringing out"
         (c)   [Maradi]: sáyòowáa "buying"), kóomòowáa "returning", ṝúbúutóowàa "writing", záabúṝóowàa "leaping"

Considering the tone changes illustrated here, what ties them all together? The simple answer is, *they get rid of contours.* As Schuh (1978b, p. 242) has observed, "There is the tendency in African languages for contour tones to be simplified to level tones." The theoretical generalization that we can draw from these various processes and rules is that they argue for the linguistic reality of contours. I would suggest that whatever underlying representation tones may require, there is something special about contours. From a formal point of view, if a language has H-L and L-H sequences on the tonal tier, there is no reason why they should not equally attach to a single syllable. But they do not. Cross-linguistically – at least in African languages – rising tones seem to be much less common than falling tones (Maddieson 1978, pp. 347–348). The reasons have nothing to do with the geometry of formal representations, but follow from the lack of articulatory and perceptual parallelism between rising and falling tones. If, however, we jump to the conclusion that contour tones are unit primes, we run up against the strong theoretical arguments and mass of empirical data on African languages which show convincingly that contours *are* internally complex elements. The solution to this apparent conundrum can best be phrased in terms borrowed from the old argument about the nature of light: whereas in some respects contours are like particle combinations, our linguistic experience and linguistic intuition tell us that in others they are like waves. A proper theory of tone and tonal representation has to be able to capture the ambiguous nature of contours. This phonological ambiguity may be inconvenient for the formalist – as it is for the descriptivist – but it cannot be ignored.

2   Tone/Segment Interaction

Many Chadic languages are characterized by significant tone/segment interaction reflecting the universally widespread influence of consonants on tone (see Hyman 1973, for example). Although this phenomenon is not found in Hausa, the language does appear to have a more interesting and previously unreported example of tone influencing segments.

Synchronically, Hausa has two diphthongs, orthographically indicated as *ai* and *au*. (Historically, it also had two other diphthongs, /iu/, and /ui/, both of which have simplified in fairly recent times to /uu/ and /ii/ respectively.) The *ai* diphthong, which is the only one of the two that I shall deal with here, has two quite distinct pronunciations shown in (16).

(16)   (a)   [ɛi] [ei], even [ee]   (I shall transcribe this variant as [ei].)
         (b)   [əi] [ɔi], [ai]   (I shall transcribe this variant as [ai].)

The pronunciation differences are mentioned briefly by Cowan and Schuh (1976, p. 29) and Kraft and Kirk-Greene (1973, p. 11), and were explicitly noted much earlier by Abraham (1941, p. 2). The general assumption seems to have been that the phonetic variants were conditioned by the preceding consonants and thus could be ignored as a minor subphonemic matter. For example, after apical consonants, one normally gets [ei] whereas after glottal stop and /h/ one gets [ai], see (17).

(17) (a) láimàa = [léimàa] "umbrella", tsáikòo = [sʔéikòo] "roof frame"
      (b) ʔáikìi = [ʔáikìi] "work", háihù = [háihù] "give birth"

In other cases, however, e.g., after bilabials, the two diphthongs appear to be in contrast. Compare the two different pronunciations of orthographic *mai* "return (something)" and "oil" in the phrases in (18).

(18) (a) mai da yaji [méi dà yáajìi] "return the spices"
      (b) mai da yaji [mâi dà yáajìi] "oil and spices"

Abraham (1959, p. 131) claimed that practically speaking, one did not need to overtly mark the varying pronunciations since "the difference is purely of phonetic interest." This has implicitly been the opinion of all scholars since. But if [ei] and [ai] occur in the same environment and serve to distinguish words from one another, do we not have a phonemic contrast? The answer is that the differences between [ei] and [ai] are in fact conditioned, i.e., they are indeed allophones of the same phoneme; the conditioning factor that has been overlooked is tone. What I am reporting here is a new observation about Hausa that has never previously been suggested so far as I am aware, and thus it needs rechecking, verification, and refinement; but since it is important for understanding Hausa and has major general linguistic implications, it deserves public presentation. Basically, what we find, limiting ourselves to /ai/ preceded by a word initial labial, is that /ai/ is realized as [ei] (often even [ee]) if it has a level tone, whether H or L, and [ai] if it has a Falling tone, e.g., (19).

(19)   H   L   F
      /mai/ [méi] "return"   [mèi]   "owner of"   [mâi] "oil"
      /bai/ [béi] "give"   [bèi]   "3masc.neg."   [bâi] "back"
      /fai/ [féiféi] "record" [fèilûu] "peppermint"   [fâi] "openly"

From an a priori point of view, the conditioning of the phonetic quality of diphthongs by tone is not so strange.[8] It does, however, run up against commonly held, and empirically well supported, views about the relationship between segments and tones, which is that, "Almost all the examples of inter-action of tone and segments involve consonants" (Schuh 1978b, p. 224). Regarding tone/segment interaction, Schuh (1978b, pp. 224–225) reiterates the position expressed in Hyman and Schuh (1974): "[I]t is virtually always segments which influence tone; tone rarely, if ever, influences segments . . .

[V]irtually no clear cases of tonal influence on segments have been found, whereas the opposite case is common in all areas where tone languages are found." He argues that the putative examples of tonal influence on consonants cited, for example, by Maddieson (1974) – see, also, the early imaginative analysis by Welmers (1962) – can be rejected if "tone is understood in the normal sense of 'pitch'" (p. 224).

But tone does *not* equal pitch (much less fundamental frequency); its phonetic parameters include numerous factors such as intensity, length, phonation properties, etc., which *would* be expected to affect vowels. (We'll leave the question of consonants aside.) And, in fact, influence of tone on vowels has been noted in different language families widely spread across the continent of Africa, e.g., Dimmendaal and Breedfeld (1986) on Turkana, Nilotic; Kaye and Charette (1981) on Dida, Kru; and Schuh himself (Schuh 1978a) on a historical change in Bade/Ngizim, Chadic. Compared with these other cases, the Hausa situation is really quite simple, so simple in fact that you have to wonder why no one else observed this before. The short answer is that discoveries often look simple after they've been made. The other answer, which is of greater methodological importance, is that received knowledge of a typological or theoretical nature necessarily puts blinders and limitations on what we look at and what we see, even when it's staring us straight in the face. As all scientists know, there is no way to avoid this, but the job of the probing empiricist is to try one's best to overcome it.

3   Tonal Polarity

The notion of "tonal polarity" refers to a usually morphemic segment whose tone is invariably opposite that of a preceding or following tone. Examples of surface polarity lend themselves to two different analyses: dissimilation and "true polarity." In dissimilation, a particular specified tone is changed if certain conditions are met. For example, as shown in (20), the pre-pronoun forms of the genitive marker (*náa* "masculine and plural", *táa* "feminine"), which have underlying H tone, as evidenced by the tonally invariant pre-noun forms of the marker, change to L when attached to the H tone 1st person pronoun -*wá*, e.g.,

(20) (a) ná yáaròo née / tá yáaròo cée "it's the boy's"
      (b) náa-sà née "it's his", táa-mù cée "it's ours"
      (c) nàa-wá nèe / tàa-wá cèe "it's mine"

In the case of "true polarity," the tone of some element is always assigned as opposite to that of a neighboring tone, but there is no compelling synchronic reason to presume that the tone started underlying as some specified tone or other. Historically, one might be able to determine that the polarity started out as a dissimilation phenomenon; but synchronically, the tone appears to be underlyingly unspecified (or specified as "polar," however one wants to look at it).

3.1   Polarity in Hausa

In Hausa the most often cited case of polarity is one that has been described as such for a half century (e.g., Abraham 1941, p. 32; Parsons 1960, p. 13), namely the direct object pronoun paradigm, cf. *yáa sàyée tà* "he bought it" with *yáa káamàa tá* "he caught it", where *ta*, the 3fem. pronoun, is assumed to have polar tone. Surface exceptions to the presumed polarity rule, e.g., *yáa káȓàntáa tá* "he read it", *kàamáa tá!* "catch it!" have necessitated complex and imaginative manipulations (cf. Leben 1971) while even simple operations of the rule have presented uncomfortable ordering paradoxes. As pointed out in Newman (1979), however, polarity in this case is actually an old error that has become embedded in our thinking about the language. Instead of the presumed polarity, what one actually has is two distinct pronoun paradigms: a fused, clitic paradigm that has L (or perhaps no) tone, e.g., *yáa sàyée tà* "he bought it", *yáa gáishée mù* "he greeted us", *yáa bíi sù* "he followed them", and a less tightly bound set, which invariably has H tone regardless of the tone of the preceding syllable, e.g., *yáa káȓàntáa tá* "he read it", *yáa bíncìkée sú* "he investigated them", *kàamáa tá!* "catch it!", *yáa báayán ní* "he gave me up". For genuine polarity in Hausa one has to look elsewhere.

3.1.1   Stabilizer

In Standard Hausa, there is really only one morpheme with true polar tone. This is the so-called "stabilizer" (*nee/cee*, depending on gender) which is used in equational and identificational sentences, see (21). The tone is always opposite to that of the final tone of the preceding word. The polar nature of the stabilizer shows up clearly with words that have tonal variants.

(21)   (a)   jàakíi nèe "it's a donkey", rìigáa cèe "it's a gown", zóobèe née "it's a ring", móotàa cée "it's a car", húulúnàa née "they're caps"
       (b)   kèekè née = kèeké(e) nèe "it's a bicycle", ʔílmìi née = ʔílìmíi nèe "it's knowledge"

In other dialects, other cases of this phenomenon occur in addition to the stabilizer.

3.1.2   Guddiri Polarity

In the Guddiri dialect (Bagari 1982; Zaria 1982) polarity shows up with a couple of small morphemes: *don* "for sake of/ for purpose of", which is invariably H in Standard Hausa, and the diminutive *ɗan* (masc.) / *ʔyař* (fem.) (again invariably H in Standard Hausa), which serves to modify both nouns and verbs, see (22).

(22) (a) don "for": dòn kóowáa "for everyone", dòn Állàh "for the sake of God", dón wàa "for whom?", dón Ànnábì "for the sake of the Prophet"

 (b) ɗan (masc.) / ʔyař (fem.) "diminutive": dán ràagóo "a small ram", ʔyář kàazáa "a chick", ɗàn ƙáuyèe "a small village", ɗàn yáaròo "a small boy", yáa ɗán màarée shì "he slapped him lightly", yáa ɗàn móotsàa "he moved a little"

Schuh (1978b, p. 242) suggests that the diminutive tone is really an instance of dissimilation since the forms *dáa* "son" and *ʔyáa* "daughter" exist as independent nouns with H tone. While this may be true – although the tonal behaviour is good evidence that the diminutives are in the process of lexically separating themselves from their cognate nouns – I would contend that we are at least dealing with a case of incipient polarity and that its development into true polarity cannot be far into the future.

3.1.3 Ader Polarity

The next instance of polarity takes us back to the "-ing" marker in the Ader dialect (Caron 1987). Above, we saw the effects of various phonological processes when the morpheme *-wáa* was added to a verb. These processes could be analyzed in terms of tone spreading, tonal aggression, contour tone simplification, etc. If we now focus on the result, we find that whatever the diachronic pathway or deep synchronic derivation, *-wáa* in Ader can be described most simply as a morpheme with polar tone, see (23).

(23) káamàa / káamàawáa "catch", ɓóoyèe / ɓóoyèewáa "hide", súngùmáa / súngùmáawàa "lift heavy object", tánkàɗée / tánkàɗéewàa "winnow", káawóo / káawóowàa "bring", řúbúutóo / řúbúutóowàa "write"

In the case of the stabilizer, we don't know how it came to have polar tone. In the case of the Guddiri markers, we can see that the polarity developed from dissimilation and in the case of Ader "-ing", from contour tone simplification. Nevertheless, the evidence strongly suggests that synchronically these morphemes now have polar tones as their underlying specification.

3.2 Polarity in Chadic

Because of the importance of polarity as a tonal phenomenon and mistaken statements that have been made about it, let me illustrate its occurrence in two additional Chadic languages: Kanakuru, which belongs to the same West Chadic branch as Hausa, and Margi, a more distantly related member of the family.

3.2.1 *Kanakuru*

In Kanakuru (Newman 1974, see esp. pp. 59–62), negation in most finite tense/ aspects is indicated by a discontinuous morpheme *wo-* . . . *-u.*,[9] where the *wo-* attaches to and takes the opposite tone of a following tense-aspect pronoun and the *-u* polarizes with the final word of the sentence, to which it attaches, e.g., (24).

(24)   wò-mə́n wùrà wóròm-ú "we didn't fry beans"
   wó-nàa də́lè gám-ù "I am not pushing a ram"

The pronouns used in the continuous normally have L tone; however, when followed by *gə̀n* "with" to form "have" sentences (i.e., "he is with a car" = "he has a car"), the pronouns dissimilate to H, whereupon the negative *wo-* must polarize to L, e.g., (25).

(25)   wò-náa gə̀n áyìm-ú "I don't have money"

When attached to a vowel-initial future pronoun, *wo-* obligatorily drops the /o/, but still requires the tonal polarity. The /w/ may then optionally be dropped, leaving the tone change as the marker of the negation, e.g., (26).

(26)   *wo-ànò áy Láwàn-u → w-ánò áy Láwàn-ú (→) ánò áy Láwàn-ú "I will not help Lawan"
   *wo-àtò yír-má-u → w-átò yír-má-ù (→) átò yír-má-ù "she will not stop"

When attached to a word ending in a consonant, the final *-u* normally manifests its expected tone, i.e., H after L, and L after H. (The main exception is when the word preceding *-u* has a falling tone, in which case the sequence F-H may be realized as H-Downstepped H, e.g., *wó-nàa nái mêen ú = wó-nàa nái méen!ú* "I don't drink beer".) When attached to a word ending in a H tone vowel, the *-u* takes L tone and the final H-L combination is realized as a Fall, e.g., (27),

(27)   wò-shée dùshá-ù → wò-shée dùshâu "she didn't pound (it)"
   wó-shìi táa-má dé-ù → wó-shìi táa-má dêu "he is not going tomorrow"

Like Hausa, Kanakuru does not have Rising tones. Therefore, when *-u* is added to a vowel with L tone, the L-H sequence that should result cannot surface. As in the case of the newly discovered Rising tone simplification rule in Hausa, R in Kanakuru is realized as an L, not an H, e.g., (28)

(28)   wó-shìi néenè-u → *wó-shìi néenè-ú → wó-shìi néenèu "he is not here"
   wò-náa shìrà déenò-u → *wò-náa shìrà déenò-ú → wò-náa shìrà déenòu "I didn't steal peanuts"

3.2.2   *Margi*

In Margi (Hoffmann 1963, see esp. pp. 190–200), polarity shows up most clearly with the marker /a-/ which is used in both the present tense and the past. In the latter case the verb is also marked by a suffix *-(ə)r(ì)*.[10] The tone of this preverbal tense marker is always opposite that of the initial tone of the verb stem, see (29). For purposes of the polarity rule, the Rising tone behaves like an LH sequence.[11] (Examples are given with the subject pronouns following the verb; they can equally occur in front of the *a* + verb. The 1st and 3rd person singular pronouns have H tone; the other pronouns have polar tone.)

(29)   (a)   à-tá mà "we (two) cook", à-fə́l mà "we (two) bathe", á-wì má "we (two) run", á-və̌l mà "we (two) jump"

     (b)   à-sá-r yə́ "I erred", à-fə́l-ə́r yə́ "I danced, á-bà-r yə́ "I went out", á-və̀l-ə́r yə́ "I jumped"

In contrast to the straightforward rule of polarity presented by Hoffmann and adopted here, Pulleyblank (1983a) generates the surface forms by an abstract set of rules. He treats /a-/ as underlyingly H, which in some environments has to be considered extrametrical and thereby loses its tone. Later a rule applies whereby toneless vowels get L by default so that one ends up with the appearance of polarity. This surface result is presumed to be an accident of no phonological or morphological significance. What is at issue here is not the validity of Pulleyblank's proposal, to which I obviously have not done justice, but the assumption that an analysis such as his is theoretically/conceptually superior to one that directly employs the notion of underlying polarity.

This claim is made in a stronger, more explicit manner by Kenstowicz, Nikiema, and Ourso (1988), who provide alternative explanations for cases of presumed polarity in some Gur languages. They then go further and propose on essentially *theoretical* grounds that true polarity, i.e., tones that are specified underlyingly as polar, shouldn't exist. They suggest that polar tones in *all* languages are underlyingly H and that appearances of polarity are generally due to the presence of rules dissimilating successive high tones.

But what is the evidence for this presumed language universal? They do not cite data from a large sample of languages around the world to show that it is empirically supported, nor do they provide any cogent arguments why it should be so from a theoretical perspective. I would argue that compared with convoluted derivations involving association lines, extrametricality, and such, polarity is a very simple notion, one that is simple not just for the linguist, but also for the native speaker of a tone language. It is because polarity is such a normal tonal process that we find it occurs so often. The reason why polarity is so natural and its occurrence so expected is because tone functions prosodically and works naturally with melodic patterns. One of the insights of autosegmental phonology that current-day formalists seem to have lost sight of is the idea of tone being represented by melodies rather than atomic units. Whereas content words (especially nouns and verbs) have the body to carry distinctive tone, with short, unstressed grammatical morphemes, a specific tone, whether it be high or low, has very little saliency. What works well for short words, clitics, and affixes, is for the morpheme to join up with a substantive word to become part of a tonal melody whose preferred tune will in many cases be H-L or L-H. In some cases these toneless grammatical morphemes will acquire surface tones by tone spreading or by the assignment of a default tone, but in others the principle underlying the tonal assignment will be to produce a tonal opposition, which surely must have natural advantages in terms of production, perception, memory, and/or other psycholinguistic factors.[12] That polarity occurs frequently in different languages, in different directions, and under different conditions is exactly what one should expect. Whatever may have been the thinking that led Kenstowicz, Nikiema, and Ourso to rule out polarity, the claim runs counter to my intuition as a linguist and, I would expect, to that of most other practicing linguists who have worked on tone languages over long periods of time.

4   Ideophones and Key Raising

In this final section, I propose to take up the question of key raising, or register shift, since data from Hausa have been crucial in the development of this concept. The focus of the discussion will be on ideophones.

As has commonly been noted, the ideophone in Hausa is characterized by an extra high pitch. Moore (1968, p. 13), for example, says: "The ideophone occurring utterance finally is likely to have an extra high pitch which ignores the downward drift of the rest of the utterance . . ." Similarly, Inkelas, Leben, and Cobler (1987, p. 333) state: "Certain emphatic particles [= ideophones] are always pronounced with an extra-High tone . . ." The extremely high pitch of ideophones had also been observed by Greenberg (1941, p. 319) and before him by Prietze (1908, p. 316). This is illustrated in (30), where the ideophone is underlined.

(30)   fáríi <u>fát</u> "very white", kóořèe <u>shář</u> "very green", táa táashì <u>fářát</u> "she got up suddenly", yáa gàjí <u>túɓús</u> "he became very tired"

A problem plaguing ideophone research in most languages, including Hausa, is that the ideophones are not put in any kind of context and not related to other phenomena in the language. An exception is Inkelas, Leben, and Cobler (1987) where an attempt is made to view ideophones in a normal sentential/ intonational context. Their description has to be modified since the scope of their examples is too restricted, but at least they were asking the right questions. In order to go beyond the study of ideophones in artificial out-of-context phrases, such as in (30), I made a point of collecting a number of longer, more complex sentences which are represented in (31). These examples were collected at different times and from a number of different speakers.

(31) (a) yáaròn dà yá kùɓútà dàgà hánnún ʔyán sàndáa gàjéerée nèe <u>dúƙús</u> "the boy who escaped from the hands of the police was very short"

(b) mùtúmìn dà yá zóo ƙóofàr̃ fáadà yánàa sànyé dà hùuláa báƙáa <u>wúlík</u> "the man who came to the palace entrance was wearing a very black cap"

(c) wání tsóohóo <u>túkúf</u> yáa shígèe nân "a very old man passed by here"

(d) yáa báa nì góor̃ò ɗányée <u>shátáf</u> dà shíi "he gave me a very fresh kolanut"

(e) káayàn bà sù jíƙèe <u>shár̃áf</u> bá "the goods didn't get soaking wet"

(f) hádárìi bài háɗóo à gábàs yáa yí báƙii <u>ƙírín</u> bá "the storm didn't rise up in the east and become very black"

From sentences such as these, a number of interesting clarifications emerge. First, Inkelas, Leben, and Cobler (1987) explain the extra H on ideophones in terms of its being obligatorily linked to a register High, this register High (described as key raising by Newman and Newman 1981) also being a property of yes/no questions. They provide examples comparable to those in (32).

(32) (a) táa sàamí fárár̃ múndú ↑ wáa? "did she get a white bracelet?"
                                    (< múndúwáa)
(b) táa sàamí káráa ɗáyá ↑ ták. "she got exactly one stalk" (< ták)

Looking at a larger corpus, one quickly finds that the similarity between key raising with yes/no questions and with ideophones is an accident of the specific example they used, which just happened to have a monosyllabic ideophone. When, however, a disyllabic ideophone is used, it is clear that one cannot use the same mechanism of register shift for questions and ideophones because the resulting output is different in the two cases. The real rule is that in yes/no questions, the *last* H tone in the appropriate phrase gets raised whereas in ideophones, the raising applies to the *first*. (Of course, with a monosyllabic word the first syllable and the last happen to be the same.) Thus we get a contrast such as in (33).

(33) (a) yáa sàyí rìigáa bá ↑ ƙáa?   "Did he buy a black gown?"
(b) yáa sàyí rìigáa báƙáa ↑ wúlík.   "He bought a very black gown"
    Not (c) *yáa sàyí rìigáa báƙáa wú ↑ lík.

The obvious next question is what takes place when a yes/no question contains an ideophone? In this case, as correctly described by Inkelas and Leben (1990), the ideophone loses its extra H and the interrogative key raising dominates, see (34).

(34)   yáa sàyí rìigáa báƙáa wú ↑ lík?   "did he buy a very black gown?"

Up to now, for sake of the discussion, I have accepted the oft-stated claim that ideophones obligatorily manifest an extra high tone because of key raising (unless overridden by the interrogative key raising). This turns out to be inaccurate when one looks at a more expanded corpus. Of course if you specifically ask a native speaker to give you a phrase with an ideophone, "How do you say *very* old?" you will undoubtedly get an answer such as *tsóohóo túkúf*, with *túkúf* pronounced louder and higher than normal – but this is not required. Although all Hausa ideophones probably have a *latent* potential for what I will call expressive prominence, if the prominence is not there, then the ideophone will not have the extra H tone. For example, ideophones in negative sentences generally lack expressive prominence and thus are pronounced without the extra High, e.g., (35).

(35)   bài sàyí bàabûr̃ sáabóo fíl bá   "he didn't buy a brand new motorcycle"

Súlè dà Béllò bà sù gàjí túɓús bá   "Sule and Bello didn't become exhausted"

bài zámá tsóohóo túkúf bá   "he hasn't become very old"

Answers to questions containing ideophones often lacked key raising, i.e., with the focus having switched to the truth value of the sentence, the ideophone no longer qualified for expressive prominence, e.g., (36).

(36)   ée, káayân sún wànkú fés   "yes, the loads were washed spanking clean"

ée, náa gá ɗán tsàakóo tsígíl   "yes, I saw a wee small chick"

To highlight the contrast, the sentences in (37) allow us to compare statements with ideophones having expressive prominence, yes/no questions with obligatory key raising, and answers to questions in which the ideophone is out of focus and does not carry expressive prominence.

(37)   (a)   cíiwòn yáa hánàa tá ↑ sákát.   "the illness prevented her completely"

cíiwòn yáa hánàa tá sá ↑ kát?   "did the illness prevent her completely?"

ée, cíiwòn yáa hánàa tá sákát.   "yes, the illness prevented her completely"

(b) báɓ ín kèekè ↑ sídík yáa ɓátà.   "a very black bicycle got lost"
    báɓ ín kèekè sídík yáa ↑ ɓataa?   "did a very black bicycle get lost?"
    ée, báɓ ín kèekè sídík yáa ɓátà   "yes, a very black bicycle got lost."
(c) míyàr̃ táa yí gíshíríi ↑ fáu   "the soup is much too salty"
    míyàr̃ táa yí gíshíríi ↑ fáu?   "is the soup too salty?"
    ée, míyàr̃ táa yí gíshíríi fáu   "yes, the soup is much too salty"

Finally, in (38), we illustrate an ideophone in a question-word question. Since the focus here is presumably on the word "who?", the ideophone does not quality for expressive prominence and thus occurs with its normal tone.

(38) wàa yá báa kà ɗányée shátâf?   "who gave you a real fresh one?"
      Hàbúu nèe yá báa nì ɗányée shátáf   "Habu gave me a real fresh one"

5 Summary and Conclusions

In this chapter, I have demonstrated that if one studies a particular language in great depth, using a full array of synchronic (including dialectal) and comparative data, and if one allows oneself to draw on one's linguistic intuition and accumulated knowledge, one can come up with insights that provide a different perspective from the normally accepted analyses and generalizations. I have presented new findings and interpretations about Hausa, all of which have implications for our ideas about phonological theory and general phonological processes: (1) At some level (and this level will vary from language to language), contour tones in Hausa have a linguistic reality all their own and cannot be analyzed simply as a High-Low sequence attached to a single syllable. This is consistent with the asymmetry of Rising vs. Falling tones and the ongoing tendency to simplify contours to level tones. (2) With regard to the phonetic specification of the diphthong /ai/, tone has been shown to affect segments. (3) Tonal polarity is an inherent property of certain morphemes (generally short grammatical elements) rather than being a surface result of manipulations such as dissimilation or default assignment affecting fully specified underlying tones. (4) The key raising on ideophones is a function of "expressive prominence" and is not the same as the intonational key raising that characterizes interrogative sentences.

NOTES

This is a revised version of a paper originally presented at the 23rd Annual Conference on African Linguistics, MSU, March 1992. The research reported in the paper is part of an ongoing Hausa Reference Grammar project supported by grants from the U.S. Department of Education (P0-17A10037), the National Endowment for the Humanities (RT-21236), and the National Science Foundation (DBS-9107103).

1   In the transcriptions, c represents English *ch*, and j either the affricate *j* (as in English jury) or the fricative *zh* (as in French jour), depending on dialect. The digraph ts is an ejective sibilant, which belongs to the set of "glottalized" consonants including the implosives ɓ and ɗ and the ejective ƙ. The phoneme ʔy is a glottalized semivowel, derived historically from *ɗy < *ɗiy. Glottal stop is indicated by ʔ. The symbol r̃, which is not used in standard orthography, represents the rolled rhotic which contrasts with the retroflex flap /r/.

2   A typologically aberrant exception is Grebo, a Kru language of Liberia, whose contour tones do seem to be basic and fundamental (see Newman 1986).

3   Although Maddieson acknowledges that Falling tones probably predominate numerically over Rising tones – and he is thought to be a key authority for this generalization – a rereading of his paper shows that he actually has doubts about the significance of this view. He goes on to make the following statement, surprising for a scientifically trained, empirical phonetician: "The . . . absence of any marked prevalence of HL over LH in level tone sequences suggests that any possible articulatory . . . or perceptual . . . asymmetries favoring falling patterns do not play a major role in determining the constraints on phonological inventories of tone." But it is *precisely* these phonetic factors which account for the asymmetry between L-H/H-L sequences, on the one hand, and Rising and Falling contours on the other.

4   This drift runs counter to the strong tendency in Hausa to preserve tones when segments are deleted, which, in the case of L tones, results in the ever-constant creation of new Falling tones. Other examples of the ebb and flow of language diachrony due to conflicting tendencies are described for Hausa in Newman (1991).

5   This description embodies the results of primary research carried out by Dr. Mahamane L. Abdoulaye and myself.

6   The ꜜ*wáa* is also preceded by a floating mora which ensures that any verb-final vowel before ꜜ*wáa* is long, i.e., /ꜜwáa/ is perhaps better represented as /ꜜːwáa/.

7   The general notion of friendly and hostile tones was stimulated by a more elaborate system presented by Matthew Y. Chen at the 18th Annual Meeting of the BLS (February 1992).

8   Note that the "diphthongal" contour Falling tone is associated with the most diphthongal pronunciation of the /ai/ whereas the level tones are associated with a vowel pronunciation that is tending towards monophthongal. For the moment, I leave open the question whether this correlation is fortuitous or significant.

9   The clitic *wo-* alternates in morphosyntactically defined environments with a free marker *wói*, which doesn't concern us here. The negative subjunctive (which serves as the negative imperative) uses the same final *-u* but a different initial marker (*bò*).

10 The underlyingly toneless schwa gets its surface tone either by

copying the preceding syllable or, when attached to a monosyllabic Rising tone verb, by tone spreading.

11 Rising tones in Margi are much more common than Falling tones; this is unusual in the Chadic family.

12 Disyllabic proper names in Hausa that have tonal variants are invariably H-L or L-H (e.g., Shátù = Shàtú); there are no cases where a name can, for example, be pronounced alternatively as H-L and H-H.

27 Phonology of Ethiopian Languages

GROVER HUDSON

0 Introduction

There are about 70 Ethiopian languages (Bender et al., 1976, pp. 10–16), and most of these are spoken in a 100,000 square-mile area of the Ethiopian south-central highlands, so each language averages a territory of only some 2,000 square miles. Ethiopia is the eastern edge of the linguistic "fragmentation belt" (Dalby 1970, p. 162) which extends, only about 700 miles in width, across the breadth of Africa south of the Sahara desert. Despite the number and diversity of languages, Charles Ferguson identified Ethiopia as a "linguistic area," most languages of which "tend to share a number of features which, taken together, distinguish them from any other geographically defined group of languages in the world" (Ferguson 1976, pp. 63–64). Their rather rich inflectional systems and, in the case of the Semitic languages, their root and pattern morphologies, the presence of neighboring and closely related languages and, again in the case of the Semitic languages, a long written record, typically make possible thorough testing of synchronic phonological hypotheses against considerable evidence from internal and comparative reconstruction.

Discussion in this paper will concern the phonology of two families of Afroasiatic languages well represented in Ethiopia: Semitic and Cushitic. There are good bibliographies of the literature on these languages, very complete at the time of their publication: Leslau (1965) on the Semitic languages of Ethiopia, and Unseth (1990) on the non-Semitic languages (Cushitic, Omotic and Nilo-Saharan). The Ethiopian Semitic languages have recently been the object of considerable theoretical phonological interest, especially in the work of John McCarthy. The eight topics discussed below include cases of assimilation, metathesis, and epenthesis, including effects at a distance, followed by some aspects of morphology of relevance for phonology, root and pattern morphology, reduplication, and a language "disguise."

1   Assimilation, Epenthesis, and Metathesis in Sidamo

In the four Highland East Cushitic languages Gedeo, Hadiyya, Kambata, and Sidamo, the combination of consonant-final (lexical) stems of form CVC(C) and consonant-initial suffixes leads to syllable contacts disallowed by the phonotactic structure of the languages. Only two consonants are allowed intervocalically in the languages, and these must be a geminate "cluster," a glottal stop followed by a sonorant consonant, or a sonorant consonant followed by an obstruent. There results a "conspiracy" in which epenthesis, assimilation, and metathesis interact to provide acceptable contacts at suffix boundaries.

In Sidamo, when the verb stem ends in a cluster and the suffix begins with a consonant, an epenthetic vowel (-*i*-) separates the morphemes, as in (1), which presents the perfective paradigm of the verb *gurd*- "knot" (v. trans.).

(1)

		Singular	Plural
1		gurd-ummo	gurd-i-nummo
2		gurd-i-tto	gurd-i-tini
3 masc.		gurd-i	
	fem.	gurd-i-tu	gurd-i-tu
	pol.	gurd-i-ni	

When the stem ends in a single sonorant consonant, as in *ful*- "go out", this fully assimilates suffix-initial *n* of the 1pl. and 3sg. polite: *ful-nummo > fullummo*, *ful-ni > fulli*. When the stem ends in a single obstruent, as in *ag*- "drink", this fully assimilates suffix-initial *t* of the 3fem.sg. and 2pl.: *ag-tu > aggu, ag-tini > aggini*, and metathesizes with suffix-initial *n*, with the nasal agreeing in place of articulation with the following obstruent: *ag-nummo > a* [ŋ]*gummo* "we drank", *ag-ni > a*[ŋ]*gi* "he (pol.) drank". Rice (1992, p. 73) offers an under-specification analysis of Sidamo nasal metathesis according to which nasality is delinked from the nasal and relinked to the preceding stop. Sidamo's siblings Gedeo, Hadiyya, and Kambata have almost identical rules with different, noncognate suffixes, suggesting that the rules are independent, natural innovations in each. In Kambata, a difference is that a stem-final sonorant consonant is fully regressively assimilated by suffix-initial *n*: e.g., *ful-noommi* "we went out" → *funnoommi* (Hudson 1980).

2   Velar Spirantization in Tigrinya

In Ethiopian Semitic Tigrinya the voiceless velar stops *k* and ejective *k′* alternate with spirants *x* and *x′*, respectively, which appear in postvocalic environments. The significance of this rule for the analysis of geminates was noted by Schein

(1981) and further discussed by Kenstowicz (1982). In the Semitic languages, ideal and typical roots consist of three consonants, which form stems with different vocalization depending on grammatical environment. In (2), consider four 3masc. forms of three regular Tigrinya triconsonantal roots, whose first, second, and third consonants, respectively, are historic velar stops.

(2)	Sg. perfect	Sg. imperfect	Pl. imperfect	Sg. jussive	Gloss
	k'ətəl-ə	yɨ-x'əttɨl	yɨ-x'ətlu	yɨ-x'təl	"kill"
	nəxəs-ə	yɨ-nəkkɨs	yɨ-nəxsu	yɨ-nkəs	"bite"
	bətəx-ə	yɨ-bəttɨx	yɨ-bətku	yɨ-btəx	"cut"

The perfect stem is CəCəC and the 3masc.sg. imperfect stem is CəC:ɨC (CəC:C before epenthesis of the high central vowel ɨ), with gemination of the second consonant. The 3masc.pl. imperfect stem is CəCC (no gemination), with plural suffix - *u*, and the jussive stem is CCəC. Assuming underlying velar stops, the environment of spirantization appears to be postvocalic except that postvocalic geminate velars are unspirantized. When a sequence of velar obstruents arises in suffixation, however, the first is spirantized, e.g., bətəx-*ku* "I cut" (perfect), suggesting to Hayes (1986, p. 337) and Lowenstamm and Prunet (1986, pp. 191–193) that spirantization takes precedence over the Obligatory Contour Principle (OCP), according to which the underlying *k+k* sequence should be replaced by a geminate, which would resist spirantization.

Hayes (1986) and Schein and Steriade (1986) noted the significance of Tigrinya velar spirantization for their general accounts of geminates and geminate formation in autosegmental phonology, in which on the CV tier geminates are represented C C (see chaps. 5 and 8, this volume). Hayes's account is based on

$$
\begin{matrix} C\ C \\ \vee \\ X \end{matrix}
$$

his "Linking constraint": "Association lines in structural descriptions are interpreted as exhaustive" (p. 331). His rule of Tigrinya velar spirantization (which lacks [−voiced]; according to his evidence *g* is also affected) is shown in (3). Since the affected velar must be referred to as following a vowel, it must be referred to on the CV tier as well as on the segmental tier, thus with an association line. Since there is one association line (though nothing, in principle, requires only one), according to the Linking Constraint the velar must be nongeminate.

(3)

$$
\begin{bmatrix} -son \\ +back \end{bmatrix} \rightarrow [+cont] \: / \: \underline{\quad\quad}
\qquad
\begin{matrix} V\ \ C \\ \ \ \ | \end{matrix}
$$

   In the proposal of Schein and Steriade (1986), the failure of spirantization to affect geminates is explained by their "Uniform Applicability Condition," which requires that a condition on the rule like right adjacency must be met by every member of the set of Xs (Cs and Vs) to which the target of the rule is linked. Their rule conditions spirantization by a preceding nuclear (vowel or glide) X. "Therefore, a geminate velar, one of whose Xs cannot be postnuclear, will block the rule" (p. 728). They consider (p. 731) that the Uniform Applicability Condition and not the Linking Constraint can explain other facts, including Tigrinya vowel rounding by geminate and nongeminate [w]: *yɨwləd → yuwləd* "may he father", *yɨs'ɨwwər → yɨs'uwwər* "he is carried", apparently assuming that Hayes's Rounding Rule must be complicated by reference to both single and double association lines. But the rule for such vowel roundings would refer to vowels next to [−consonantal, +round], without referring to the CV tier, so there is no need for association lines, and both geminates and nongeminate round glides will cause rounding.

It appears that both proposals will explain a detail of Tigrinya spirantization, that it does not affect the labialized velar k^w (Leslau 1978/1988, p. 179), which would presumably be one C doubly linked on the segmental tier (similarly Amharic k^w; see sec. 4 below).

A number of complicating facts suggest that the alternation of velar stops and spirants in Tigrinya may be at least somewhat morphologized: (1) Spirantization preempts geminate formation when a stem-final velar precedes a suffix-initial velar (noted above). (2) The spirants often appear in word-initial position (Bender et al. 1976, pp. 108–109; Schein and Steriade 1986, p. 711) and occasionally in postconsonantal position, particularly suffix-initial in certain suffixes which frequently follow vowels (Leslau 1978/1988, p. 179). (3) The spirants are frequently found after glides and laryngeals as well as after vowels (Leslau, 1978/1988, p. 178). (4) The spirants are written with special characters provided in the Tigrinya syllabary, suggesting that they are not allophones with the stops as the spirantization rule would have it (though Sampson 1985, p. 108ff.) mentions cases in which writing systems may provide separate graphs for allophones). (5) The orthographic distinction makes it possible to see in texts that the spirants are often absent in postvocalic environments of words not all of which are apparently borrowings. (6) Finally, in "broken" plurals formed, historically, with gemination, the velars may be degeminated but the stop articulation remains (Palmer 1962, pp. 141–143; cf. Hebrew in which, after postvocalic spirantization of stops, degemination has produced a regular contrast of spirants and simple stops).

3   Palatalization in the Ethiopian Semitic B-type

Geʕez shows the earliest stage of a palatalization whose most advanced stage is seen in Amharic. In Geʕez, a common lexical class of roots, termed "B-type," is characterized by gemination of the second consonant of the root in the perfect stem (and, like roots of other types, also in the imperfect stem) and additionally by a front vowel after the first consonant of the root in the imperfect stem. In (4), consider comparisons of 3masc.sg. forms of B-type roots in three languages.

(4)		Perfect	Imperfect	Jussive		Root
	Geʕez	t'əyyək'ə	yɨt'eyyɨk'	yɨt'əyyɨk'	t'yk'	"examine"
	Chaha	met'ərə	yɨmet'ɨr	yəmət'ɨr	mt'r	"choose"
	Chaha	č'ənəmə	yɨč'ənɨm	yət'ənɨm	t'nm	"get dark"
	Amharic	č'əlləmə	yɨč'əllɨm	yɨč'əllɨm	č'lm	"get dark"

The facts, basically, are these: consonant gemination was lost in Chaha by a regular sound change, but the B-type vowel characteristic is extended to the perfect stems. In Chaha, roots with initial coronal obstruents have palatalization of this obstruent with corresponding centralization of the vowel; other roots preserve the front vowel. In Amharic, palatalization was extended to jussives (identical for this type to the imperfect) and all other stems of B-type roots with historical initial coronal obstruents (Leslau 1957; Hudson 1974; exceptions can generally be explained as dialect borrowings). This and the comparative evidence of other languages make it reasonably clear that Geʕez reflects earlier stages of Chaha and Amharic. (Geʕez, unknown as a spoken language since at least the 18th century, is not, however, the ancestor of the modern languages; see Hetzron 1972.)

In Amharic, as in Chaha, palatalization must also have been extended to both the perfect and imperfect stems. In Amharic, imperfects express the habitual, the present, the future, and even the past of many subordinate verbs, so the palatalization was presumably an exponent of the majority of forms of roots with initial coronal obstruents. Thus the palatalized consonant would have become the basic or lexical exponent of these roots in Amharic and so naturally extended to jussives and other forms. In Chaha, perhaps the alternation is preserved by factors such as the employment of the nonpalatalizing jussive rather than imperfect stem in the expression of the future. An interesting question is whether, even at a stage like that of Chaha, in which the front vowel characteristic is evident in nonpalatalizing verbs such as *mt'r* "choose", the alternation is phonological (conditioned by underlying *e*), or grammatical (conditioned by the category "imperfect").

Grammatically conditioned phonological alternations, of course, occur. Kenstowicz and Kisseberth (1979, pp. 223–225) discuss a case in the Ethiopian Semitic language Harari. The 2fem.sg. suffix of verbs is *-i*, which historically palatalizes stem-final dental consonants: *ti-kəfč-i* < *ti-kəft-i* "you fem. open". There is also epenthesis of *i* after word-final clusters: *ti-kəft-i* "you (masc.sg.) /she open(s)", but no palatalization by epenthetic *i*. A phonologically conditioned palatalization rule may be ordered before epenthesis. But Kenstowicz and Kisseberth argue that additional evidence favors an analysis with grammatical conditioning: as seen in (5), there is optional palatalization of non–stem-final dentals when the 2fem.sg. suffix follows. They say of palatalization that it "appears to be exploited as a sign of the 2nd sg. fem . . . and is being extended to mark the root as a whole in this particular grammatical category. If the rule were purely phonologically based, it would be difficult to account for this (phonetically unnatural extension) of the palatalization further back in the root" (p. 225).

(5) 2 masc. sg.   2 fem. sg.
    ti-sabr-i   ti-šabr-i   "break"
    ti-katb-i   ti-kačb-i   "vaccinate"
    ti-k'adm-i   ti-k'ajm-i   "precede"
    ti-sagd-i   ti-sagǰ-i   "prostrate oneself"

An interesting case of grammatical conditioning concerns gemination in the Amharic reflexive/passive imperfect stems (Hudson 1978). These stems historically took the reflexive/passive prefix *t-*, which was regressively assimilated fully by the first consonant of the root (e.g., **yi̵-t-səbbər* "it will be broken" > *yi̵-ssəbbər*, **yi̵-t-wəssəd* > *yi̵-wwəssəd* "it will be taken". Comparative and internal reconstruction makes this history clear. It seems reasonable, synchronically, to derive the stem-initial gemination by regressive assimilation, but this will not account for stems like *yi̵-ttammən* "he will be believed", *yi̵-ttaggəs* "he will be patient", which, on the Geʕez and other comparative evidence, come from *yi̵-t-ʔammən*, *yi̵-t-ʕaggəs*, with historical laryngeal and pharyngeal consonants otherwise lost in the language without effects in assimilation. On the comparative evidence, that is, these imperfect stems should have a simple rather than geminate *t*. This suggests that the assimilation was reanalyzed as grammatically conditioned gemination, which was then extended to vowel-initial stems in which there had been no assimilation.

4 Amharic Epenthesis

Epenthesis is extensive in word-formation in the Ethiopian Semitic languages, since many morphemes, both roots and affixes, consist only of consonants. In Amharic, epenthesis may be said to provide almost all occurrences of the high central vowel *i̵* (Hetzron 1964; Hayward 1986b; Hayward 1988). In (6) are shown various constructions of the imperfect stem *səbr* "break" in which, as the parenthesized presumed underlying forms show, all occurrences of *i̵* may be considered epenthetic.

(6) yi̵səbral   (y-səbr-al)   "he breaks"
    aysəbri̵m   (a-y-səbr-m)   "he does not break"
    saysəbi̵r   (s-a-y-səbr)   "when he does not break"
    si̵tsəbi̵r   (s-t-səbr)   "when she breaks"

Employing the notion "extrasyllabic consonant" and a morpheme boundary, Hayward (1988, p. 157) provides two epenthesis rules which, assuming a universal principle of geminate integrity (which blocks epenthesis within a geminate), account for all but a small minority of occasions of internal *i* in Amharic, including *akist* "aunt" (**aksit*), and *betiš* "your (fem.sg.) house" (**betš*). In the derivation of an Amharic word like *iddil* "luck" (**didil*), he attributes the absence of epenthesis, allowing prothesis to apply, to geminate integrity (chap. 6). (In fact, consonant epenthesis within geminate vowels is reported in the Ethiopian Cushitic language Arbore (Hayward 1986a, p. 72): "the second mora of a long vowel and an immediately following laryngeal are transposed when the latter is followed by an obstruent or nasal. Though optional, the process is usual," e.g., *zeehs-e* → *zehese* "I caused to melt", *kee?-te* → *ke?e-t-e* "she planted".)

Hayward (1988, p. 151) notes that the representation of the Amharic labialized consonants (*k^w*, *b^w*, etc.) as two-tiered, i.e., C, can explain the appearance of

$$\bigwedge$$
$$X \quad X$$

these as onsets, where no other clusters appear, and the interpretation of these, in epenthesis, as one segment. Hayward's analysis (1986b, pp. 317–322) also shows how, consistent with underspecification theory (chap. 4, this volume, and Archangeli 1984), epenthetic *i* may be understood as the minimal (i.e., maximally underspecified) vowel, and he notes (1988, pp. 158–162) the relevance of the sonority scale to an aspect of epenthesis in Chaha: whether a jussive stem is formed as CCiC (e.g., *yɘfk'id* "let him permit") or CiCC (*yɘk'ims* "let him taste"); the greater sonority of *d* than *k'* disallows the final cluster *k'd*. In Amharic, likewise, epenthesis is generally not necessary when the sonority of the peripheral consonant is less than that of the more nuclear consonant. Thus two obstruents may close the word-final syllable of, e.g., *yiwɘk't* "he winnows" (root *wk't*), but epenthesis must separate a stop followed by a liquid in *yigɘdil* "he kills" (root *gdl*). Generally, however, the only allowable final clusters are geminates and those of which one is a coronal obstruent, as in Chaha *yɘk'ims* and Amharic *yiwɘk't* , just noted, or *mist* "wife", so perhaps the special status of coronals in addition to sonority is relevant (see Paradis and Prunet 1991).

5   Palatalization and Labialization in the Chaha Impersonal

In the Ethiopian Semitic language Chaha, there are regular and morphologically significant rules of palatalization and labialization which interact in the formation of the impersonal stem of verbs. The impersonal is used in contexts in which other languages would employ the passive stem. Only labials and velars may be labialized, and only dental obstruents may be palatalized. A few examples of perfective impersonal stems contrasted with personal stems are seen in (7). The right-most labializable consonant is labialized, as in the first three examples, which have a labializable root-final, root-medial, and root-initial consonant, respectively. As in the fourth example, only the right-most labializable consonant, here root-medial, is labialized. There are no palatalizable consonants in the first four examples. In the fifth example there are no labializable consonants, but the right-most consonant is palatalizable. If, as in the sixth example, the stem-final is palatalizable and there are also labializable consonants, both are affected. If none of these conditions are fulfilled, as in the seventh example, the impersonal stem is identical to the personal stem.

(7)

Personal	Impersonal	Root meaning
dənəg	dənəg^w	"hit"
č'əfər	č'əf^{w}ər	"put in the mouth"
bənər	b^{w}ənər	"demolish"
bəkər	bək^{w}ər	"lack"
arəs	arəš	"build"
dəməg	dəm^{w}əǰ	"join"
nət'ər	nət'ər	"separate"

These facts may be understood according to the analysis of McCarthy (1983a), in which palatalization and labialization apply on the root tier; subject to the OCP, application of the rules is constrained by structure preservation, according to which only noncoronal consonantals may be labialized and only anterior coronal obstruents may be palatalized, and labialization takes precedence over palatalization. The rules (McCarthy 1983a, p. 180) are shown in (8).

(8)
$$\begin{bmatrix} +\text{high} \\ -\text{back} \end{bmatrix} \qquad [+\text{round}]$$
$$\begin{array}{c} | \\ [X\ \alpha]_{root} \end{array} \qquad \begin{array}{c} | \\ [Q\ \alpha\ X] \end{array} \quad \text{Condition: Q is maximal}$$

These palatalizations and labializations give evidence for the OCP when roots with repeated second consonant, so-called "122" types, are considered, e.g., Chaha "be wide" and "place a peg", the perfect stems of which are respectively *bətət* and *səkək*. In the impersonal stems of these roots, the palatalizations and labializations appear twice, on the repeated consonants: *b^{w}əčəč* and *sək^{w}ək^w*. This result is consistent with the OCP, which requires these roots to be biradical *bt* and *sk*. Palatalization and labialization take place on roots, not stems, and are spread with the association of root consonants to the stem-template, CV-tier, as shown in (9), for the palatalizations of "be wide".

(9)
$$
\text{C V C V C} \quad \rightarrow \quad \text{C V C V C} \quad \rightarrow \quad \text{C V C V C}
$$

bt   bč   bč

$$\begin{bmatrix} +\text{high} \\ -\text{back} \end{bmatrix}$$

However, expressed as biconsonantals, such 122 roots must still select the stem-forming pattern of triconsonantals, as in (9), unlike traditionally recognized "true" biconsonantal stems such as *sn* "arrive" and *fč'* "grind", which select patterns without repetition of the second consonant, i.e., perfect *sən* and *fəč'*, respectively. The impersonal stems of these "true" biconsonantals have peculiarities (e.g., impersonal perfects with w: *sənəw* and *fəč'əw*), so it might be argued that they are lexically triconsonantals with third *w*, enabling the requirements of the OCP to be honored in the 122 types. The root *w* would have to be deleted in most stems, but this might be seen as partial expression of the fact that, indeed, glides are generally absent as third root consonants in Chaha and other Ethiopian Semitic languages.

There is another complication: Chaha has undergone sound changes of geminate obstruent devoicing and degemination. This is apparent in perfective stems, which often in Ethiopian Semitic languages are characterized by gemination of the second consonant; thus cognate with Amharic *səbbərə* "he broke", Chaha has *səpərə*. Verbs of the 122 type are, however, exceptions to devoicing, though they show degemination, e.g., *nədədə* "it burned", *fəgəgə* "it died" (of cattle). By reference to the OCP and Hayes's Linking Constraint, McCarthy (1986a) provides an explanation of these exceptions: since according to the OCP these verbs are biconsonantal, before degemination the second consonant is triply linked in the perfect stem, e.g., C C C C, and a devoicing

$$
\begin{array}{cc}
| & \diagdown\!\diagup \\
n & d
\end{array}
$$

rule which refers to a doubly linked element will not, by the Linking Constraint, refer to such triply linked consonants.

Exceptional to this set of exceptions are 122 roots with a labial stop in the environment of devoicing, e.g., *čəpəbə* "close halfway". Voicing in the labial stop is not otherwise contrastive in Chaha (or, more generally, in Afroasiatic), and on this basis McCarthy (1986a) argues that these exceptions may be understood in terms of lexical phonology, the distinction of neutralizing and nonneutralizing rules, and tier conflation. This extensive argument cannot be taken up here; the interested reader may see McCarthy (1986a) and also additional arguments of McCarthy (1986b) concerning tier conflation, from Chaha's sibling language Ennemor (pp. 229–230), and for the OCP, from a case of "anti-gemination" in the Ethiopian Cushitic language Afar (pp. 220–222).

If the OCP is rejected, an alternative expression of the 122-type roots would stipulate the repetition, e.g., *b* [*t*]$_\alpha\alpha$ "be wide" and *s* [*k*]$_\alpha\alpha$ "place a peg", where the subscript α identifies the second consonant of the root and the following alpha the repetition of this. This makes apparent the traditionally recognized triradical as well as repetitive aspect of the 122 types. Such representation could also provide for spreading of palatalizations and labializations, and, with a limitation of the identity reference to contrastive, or lexical, features, and thus not to the allophonic feature [voice] in labial stops, account for the exceptionality of labials to devoicing.

6 Amharic Root-and-pattern Morphology

The Ethiopian Semitic languages have a root-and-pattern morphology much like that of Arabic, but with considerably more lexical variation of roots and associated lexical conditioning of patterns. Amharic for example, in the classification of Bender and Fulass (1978, pp. 24–25), has eleven root-types, each with its associated pattern of stem formation. In (10) are exemplified seven of the eleven types, each by one root in its perfect, imperfect, and imperative stems.

(10) | Perfect | Imperfect | Imperative | |
| --- | --- | --- | --- |
| səbbər | səbr | sibər | "break (v. trans.)" |
| fəlləg | fəllɨg | fəllɨg | "want" |
| k'ərr | k'ər | k'ir | "remain" |
| ləyy | ləyy | ləyy | "separate (v. trans.)" |
| sam | sɨm | sam | "kiss" |
| hed | hed | hid | "go" |
| mot | mot | mut | "die" |

These paradigms raise interesting questions for morphophonological theory (Broselow 1984, 1985). The eight types may be understood to derive historically from triconsonantal roots as preserved in the first two examples: *sbr* and *flg*. Stems of the second type (e.g., *flg*) are characterized by gemination of the second consonant of the root in all stems. Many verbs of the third to seventh types can be related by comparative and internal reconstruction to historical triconsonantals which have lost one consonant. Laryngeal and pharyngeal consonants were lost, leaving behind their traces in most environments as vocalizations in *a* (for the outcome of these phonemes elsewhere in Ethiopian Semitic, see Leslau 1971); *y* as second or third consonant of the root was lost leaving behind palatalization of a preceding dental and, sometimes, vocalization in *e* or *i*, and *w* in this position was lost leaving behind labialization of the preceding consonant and vocalization in *o* or *u*.

It has frequently been proposed that the generalization of triconsonantal roots be synchronically preserved by positing the historically lost consonant or its reflex, a "morphophoneme," as lexical in roots of the third to eighth types (cf. Bender and Fulass 1978; Podolsky 1980): *h* which is replaced by *a* (e.g., *shm* "kiss" < *sʕm* whose imperfect stem *sam* < *saam* < *səhm* by regular vowel coalescence and vowel lowering), *y* which conditions palatalization and is replaced by *e* or deleted (e.g., *hed* < *kəyd*), and *w*, replaced by *o* (e.g., *mot* < *məwt*). The alternative view that the sound changes have resulted in lexicalization of vowels in roots is argued by Hudson (1985).

Notice that the first two types, and the third and fourth, differ in their imperfect and imperative stems by presence and absence, respectively, of gemination of the second consonant. Thus the lexical representations of the first two might reasonably be *sbr* and *fl:g*. In the usual model of autosegmental phonology, in which the OCP prohibits repetitions in the root tier and in which length is represented by two positions on the timing (CV) tier, the lexical representation of the latter root might be C C.

$$\overset{\vee}{\underset{\text{f l g}}{}}$$

There are Amharic 122-type roots, e.g., *wdd* "like" and *kbb* "surround", whose perfect and imperfect stems are, respectively, *wəddəd, wədd* and *kəbbəb, kəbb*. As discussed above for Chaha, according to the OCP *wdd* and *kbb* are disallowed, and these roots must be lexically *wd* and *kb*. The resulting roots, although lexically biconsonantal, select triconsonantal stem-patterns or templates, and undergo spreading to achieve the repetition of the second consonant, as in (11), for the imperfect stem *wədd* of "like".

However, as in Chaha, biconsonantal lexical representation for Amharic 122

(11)

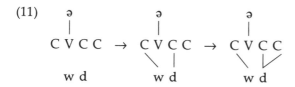

types appears to make them lexically identical to verbs of the third type in the list of (10), which select biconsonantal stems, e.g., perfect *k'ərr* (cf. first type perfect *səbbər*), imperfect *k'ər* (cf. first type *səbr*). Unlike in Chaha, no w or other unusual characteristics appear in stems of these biconsonantals. Furthermore, there are traditionally recognized 4-consonant roots, e.g., *mzgb* "register", in some of which the fourth is a repetition of the third, e.g., *dnzz* "be dull, blunted". If the latter, by the requirement of the OCP, is lexically represented as *dnz*, it merges with the type of *sbr* "break", although it must be lexically distinct in order to select a quadri-consonantal stem-pattern.

Lowenstamm (1986) argues that the gemination which characterizes the types of *flg* and *ly* in comparison with the types of *sbr* and *k'r*, respectively, can be understood as the product of a compensatory lengthening deriving from vowel centralization. He notes that in other Ethiopian Semitic languages the stems formed with gemination of the second consonant of the root are characterized by both the gemination and by a front vowel following the first consonant of the root (e.g., the verbs of (4) above), and that centralization of the vowel characteristic may be reconstructed for Amharic from internal and comparative evidence (Leslau 1957). For example, the Geʕez perfect/imperfect stems parallel to Amharic *fəlləg/fəllg* are *fəlləg/fellg*. Lowenstamm notes that if, as generally the case in Amharic, *e* is nucleus of an open syllable and *ə* nucleus of a closed syllable, centralization of *e* of hypothetical earlier Amharic stems *feləg/felg* might naturally be compensated for by consonant gemination, to close the syllable of the secondary, centralized vowel. Synchronically, then, the same feature can characterize the geminating stems without need for lexical gemination in violation of the OCP. Some additional understanding would still be required, however, for those Ethiopian Semitic languages like Geʕez (and Masqan and Gogot, mentioned by Lowenstamm (p. 162)), at least one of whose stems of this type are characterized by both the front vowel and gemination. (The history of the Ethiopian Semitic geminating stems is controversial; see Hudson 1991 for a review of the evidence that the contrast of geminating and nongeminating roots may be reconstructible for Semitic and perhaps Afroasiatic.)

Gemination appears in the perfect stem of all the Amharic verbs of the first four types as shown in (10) and in others not shown. In triconsonantals of the first two types (and in 4-consonant roots like *mzgb* "register", perfect stem *məzəggəb*), this gemination is of the next-to-last consonant of the root, so ordinary right-to-left spreading cannot accomplish it, and a special association rule is required in the formation of the stem, or a dissociation which would feed right-to-left association. Thus for the perfect of *sbr* "break", steps in the derivation might be as in (12), with dissociation as the fourth step and reassociation as the fifth.

(12)

$$
\begin{array}{ccccc}
\vartheta & \vartheta & \vartheta & \vartheta & \vartheta \\
| & \wedge & \wedge & \wedge & \wedge \\
\text{CVCCVC} \rightarrow \text{CVCCVC} \rightarrow \text{CVCCVC} \rightarrow \text{CVCCVC} \rightarrow \text{CVCCVC} \\
\text{s b r} & \text{s b r} & \text{s b r} & \text{s b r} & \text{s b r}
\end{array}
$$

Goldsmith (1990, pp. 87–90) suggests a treatment of such geminations according to which association with the third C position may be blocked – the notation he suggests for this is the parenthesis – leading to regular left-to-right associations followed by a conventional association to the left by the segment associated to the right of the parenthesized position; see (13).

(13)

$$
\begin{array}{ccc}
\vartheta & \vartheta & \vartheta \\
\text{CV(C)CVC} \rightarrow \text{CV(C)CVC} \rightarrow \text{CV(C)CVC} \\
\text{s b r} & \text{s b r} & \text{s b r}
\end{array}
$$

Hudson (1986, pp. 104–105) employs an identity sign in the expression of such a stem in Arabic – so-called form II, also with doubled second consonant: $CVC_\alpha C_\alpha VC$. This is not in violation of the OCP, which is typically interpreted to apply only on segmental or "melodic" tiers (McCarthy 1986b, p. 208).

Based on Arabic and Hebrew facts, Lowenstamm and Kaye (1986) argue that the stem-forming classes of Semitic root-and-pattern morphologies "must observe syllabic homogeneity," i.e., that syllable structure is a necessary and sufficient expression of such classes, so the CV-tier is redundant. However, Hayward (1988) shows that some stems of Ethiopian Semitic root-and-pattern morphology belie this claim. He presents cases from Amharic, Chaha, and Tigrinya in which CV-patterns of single morphological classes are syllabically heterogeneous. The Amharic minor-clause imperfect presents an additional example: the stem is CəCC when a vowel-initial suffix follows, as in *si-səbr-u* "when they break", but CəCiC when epenthesis is necessitated, as in *si-səbir* "when he breaks". Hayward's least controversial example is the Tigrinya imperfect, which in unsuffixed forms has gemination of the second root consonant (*yɨ-səbbɨr* "he breaks"), but with suffix vowels lacks gemination and epenthesis (*yɨ-səbr-u* "they break").

7   Reduplication in Chaha

One of the characteristics of the Ethiopian linguistic area identified by Ferguson was a reduplicative intensive. This formation appears, at least vestigially, in almost all the Ethiopian Cushitic and Semitic languages. In Sidamo, in which, as in the other Cushitic languages, lexical verbs are typically monosyllabic stems, the intensive is formed by repeating the stem, with regressive assimilation in the resulting syllable-contact, e.g., *kad-* "kick", *kakkad-* "kick repeatedly", *gan-* "hit", *ga* [ŋ]*gan-* "hit repeatedly, smash", *dar-* "split (wood)", *daddar-* "split repeatedly". In Amharic, a "frequentative" of triconsonantal roots is expressed by a reduplicative stem, if often with idiomatic narrowings and extensions of meanings, in which the second consonant of the root is geminated and preceded by the vowel *a*, thus (examples limited to regular triradicals to avoid complications): *sbr* "break", perfect stem *səbabbər-* "break repeatedly, smash", *kfl* "pay", perfect stem *kəfaffəl-* "divide, classify", *wrd* "descend", *wərarrəd-* "recite".

McCarthy (1983a) noted an interesting interaction of reduplication with the palatalizations and labializations of the Chaha impersonal stem formation (see the rules in (8), above). Many reduplicated biconsonantal verbal roots have a meaning of repetitive action (e.g., *nk'nk'* "shake", *sbsb* "gather"); many are semantic causatives of intransitive notions (e.g., "shake"). In stem formation of roots of this type, the palatalizations and labializations which mark the impersonal stem and which affect a stem-final dental obstruent and a rightmost labial or velar, respectively, are repeated according to the reduplicative pattern of these verbs, as in (14), which shows the personal and impersonal imperative stems of three such roots.

(14) | Personal | Impersonal | |
|---|---|---|
| bɨtəbət | bʷɨčəbʷəč | "dissolve"(v. trans.) |
| sɨbəsəb | sɨbʷəsəbʷ | "gather" (v. trans.) |
| nɨk'ənək' | nɨkʷ'ənəkʷ' | "shake" (v. trans.) |

In McCarthy's analysis (p. 184), such Chaha verbs are provided biconsonantal lexical form (bt, sb, nk') and an associated reduplicative template, $[\mu \ \mu]_\mu$, as argued for in his analyses of reduplications of other languages (McCarthy 1982b). In derivation of the impersonal stem bʷičəbʷəč, for example, palatalization and labialization directly affect the root tier, and are projected by the reduplicative template to the CV-tier as in (15). The template assures that palatalization and labialization are appropriately copied. Notice that the reduplicative template is not strictly required by the OCP, since the root pattern 1212 (e.g., *btbt*) does not properly violate the principle; however, the template analysis expresses the reduplication of the root pattern and accounts for the spread of palatalization and labialization as well.

(15)
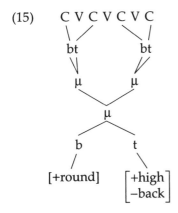

Alternative representation for these verbs would parallel that suggested in section 5 for Chaha verbs of the 122 type (e.g., *btt* as b $[t]_\alpha\alpha$); a 1212-type root like *btbt* employing such identify reference would be represented as $[bt]_\alpha\alpha$. This may seem like a notational variant of the reduplicative template as in (15). However, we saw in section 5 (and, implicitly, for Amharic in sec. 6) that such notation for the 122 types avoids the problematic merger of true biconsonantal and 122-type verbs which results when the latter, though represented as biconsonantals, must select the stem-forming patterns of triconsonantals. The identity notation also expresses the reduplicating parallelism of the 122 and 1212 types.

8   An Amharic Speech Disguise

Leslau (1964) described a number of argots of Ethiopian Semitic languages. For example, an argot used by a ceremonial group of Chaha involves vocabulary replacements (for example, words for names of wild animals), phonological modifications including reduplicative stems (e.g., *kinanna* from *kənna* "prevent", *əžažžə* from *ažžə* "see"), root augmentations (*ərebbə* from *abə* "give", *wɨraddəʔə* from *wəddəʔə* "fall down"), and augmentation plus palatalization (*šɨraddəbə* from *səddəbə* "insult", *čʼraffa* from *tʼəffa* "be destroyed") (Leslau 1964, pp. 16–22).

Teshome and Bender (1983) present an argot clearly intended as "speech disguise" by its users, young women "hosts" in Addis Ababa bars, who employ it to exchange comments with each other without being understood by clients. The argot employs a special verb formation and a particular CV-pattern for other words derived from Amharic and, occasionally, English words. In (16) some disguise words are compared with their presumed Amharic sources (Teshome and Bender 1983, pp. 343–345).

(16) Disguise word   Amharic word
     gaynən   gɨn   "but"
     k'ayldəd   k'əld   "joke (n.)"
     daygəg   dəgg   "kind (adj.)"
     kayfəf   kɨfu   "cruel"
     t'ayfəf   t'əffa   "he disappeared"
     gʷayrər   gʷaro   "area back of house"
     wayštət   wɨšət   "lie (n.)"
     saydbəb   səddəbə   "he insulted"

McCarthy (1984) discusses this speech disguise as exemplifying an unusual case of "manipulation of the CV-skeleton while the root phonemic melody remains unaltered" (p. 305), in contrast with such forms of other languages "where the CV-skeleton is ignored by the process of speech disguise." He suggests an analysis in which the CV-tier template supplied by the disguise is CV(C)(C)CVC, so that, because of the OCP, "any reference to the number of *different* consonants in a surface form is equivalent to referring to the number of consonants in the root itself" (pp. 307–308). To assure this outcome, he suggests a universal requirement that "optional skeletal slots are expanded only when some phonemic material would otherwise remain unassociated" (p. 309) or a stipulated association (formalized in McCarthy 1986b, p. 212) of the two final C-positions of the template to one element on the segmental tier.

The glottal stop is not contrastive word-initially in Amharic, but argot words derived from Amharic words with initial vowels, e.g., disguise *aymrər* "Amhara" / Amharic [ʔ]*amara*, appear to give evidence that the allophonic glottal stops are treated like other consonants in argot word formation (Teshome and Bender give the possible but less common Amharic source *amhara* for this, making the output appear irregular). McCarthy (1984, p. 311, after Bender and Fulass 1978) suggests initial *h* for such roots, however, *h* is contrastive in Amharic and appears as *h* in disguise forms (*haydəd* / *hedə* "he went").

Labials and velars in Amharic tend to be labialized before the labial (round) vowels *o* and *u* (there are also labialized velars appearing before the nonround vowels *ə* and *a*: *kʷəssələ* "he was wounded", *kʷas* "ball"). McCarthy notes that disguise forms like *gʷayrər* / *gʷaro* "area back of house" *mʷayzk'ək'* / *muzik'a* "music" argue that this labialization, like the glottal stop, must be "underlying (redundantly)" (McCarthy 1984, p. 310).

From the examples *waylgdəd* / *tə-wəlaggədə* "stagger" and *maynkək* / *mank-*

iya "spoon", in which, respectively, the consonants of the reflexive-passive prefix and instrumental suffix are absent in the disguise form, the argot word-formation rule may be said to be insensitive "to any aspect of the base word other than its root" (McCarthy 1984, p. 307). But the examples are problematic. Teshome and Bender note (p. 347) that the source of the first might lack the prefix; the Amharic verb *wələggədə* is uncommon but exists, and the adjective *wəlgadda* "staggering, drunk" is frequent. Indeed, the etymological reflexive-passive prefix *t-* of the Amharic source is retained in another argot word: *taymrər / tə-mara* "learn(ed)". As for *maynkək* "spoon", input is probably not *mank-iya* but the colloquial pronunciation of this word, *manka*. For additional discussion of this argot, see Hudson (1993).

The context for field work on the data of this section, it may be noted, is suggestive of the richness of Ethiopia as a source for phonological research.

28 Current Issues in French Phonology: Liaison and Position Theories

BERNARD TRANEL

0 Introduction

Since the inception of generative phonology some thirty years ago, the treatment of liaison has been a dominant issue in French phonological studies and a standard testing ground for theoretical proposals. The topic was initially placed on the generative agenda in the late 1960s in one of the first extensive accounts of a single language's phonology within the framework of the new theory (Schane 1968, chap. 1). In *SPE*, French liaison was singled out to motivate, in conjunction with vowel elision, the introduction of the feature [syllabic] and the use of the alpha notation (Chomsky and Halle 1968, pp. 353–355). In the 1970s, French liaison became linked to central theoretical concerns such as (local) rule ordering (e.g., Dell 1973), natural rules and exception theory (e.g., Schane 1973), the abstractness issue (e.g., Selkirk and Vergnaud 1973; Klausenburger 1974, 1978; Tranel 1974, 1981a, 1981b), and the syntax/phonology interface (e.g., Selkirk 1972, 1974; Rotenberg 1978; with subsequent work in the 1980s, e.g., Morin and Kaye 1982; Kaisse 1985; Selkirk 1986; De Jong 1988, 1990b). Throughout the 1980s and continuing into the 1990s, French liaison has found a relevant niche in discussions surrounding the development of nonlinear phonology, particularly with respect to the mediating structures assumed between phonemic melodies and syllable nodes (position theories). The focus of this chapter is on this most recent interaction between phonological theory and French liaison.

1 Background

As illustrated by the examples in (1), French words may end in two types of consonants: (a) consonants that are always pronounced (*fixed consonants*), and

(b) consonants that are pronounced only under certain circumstances, such as liaison contexts (*latent consonants*). (In the examples in (1), a word-final consonant is underlined if pronounced and crossed out if silent.)

(1)   Types of final consonants in French

(a) Fixed consonants	(b) Latent consonants	Contexts	Gloss
ne<u>t</u> avantage	peti<u>t</u> avantage	prevocalic	"clear/small advantage"
ne<u>t</u> défaut	peti~~t~~ défaut	preconsonantal	"clear/small defect"
ne<u>t</u>	peti~~t~~	prepausal	"clear/small"

The pronunciation of *petit*'s final consonant in *petit avantage*, as opposed to its absence in *petit défaut* and *petit*, illustrates the phenomenon of liaison.

In the earliest generative studies on French liaison (e.g., Dell 1970; Schane 1968; Selkirk 1972), the pronunciation of latent consonants was somewhat awkwardly viewed as a phonological nonevent, namely the consequence of the prevocalic *non*-application of an otherwise general process of final consonant deletion (Final Consonant Deletion). Fixed consonants received immunity from the effects of Final Consonant Deletion through a complex parasitic apparatus involving final protective schwas, rule ordering, and exception features.[1] Couched as they were in a linear framework, these deletion analyses of C-Ø alternations were inherently unable to encode in the representations of the two types of final consonants any *intrinsic* formal property that could explain their different behaviors with respect to Final Consonant Deletion.[2] Within the same linear framework, subsequent accounts sought to remedy this fundamental inadequacy by attributing a distinct morphological status to fixed consonants and latent consonants. For instance, while fixed consonants continued to be regarded as part of the regular phonological representations of morphemes in the lexicon, just like any other consonant, it was proposed that in the case of liaison, latent consonants ought to be viewed as connective elements *inserted* between words under certain conditions (Tranel 1981a, 1981b; see also Klausenburger 1978 and Morin and Kaye 1982 for related proposals).

An important contribution of nonlinear phonology has been to offer an approach transcending the deletion/insertion debate. The leading idea for distinguishing between fixed consonants and latent consonants in nonlinear phonology is that with respect to some higher level of prosodic structure, latent consonants are floating, whereas fixed consonants are anchored. Because fixed consonants are anchored, they are prosodically licensed, and thus phonetically realized. By contrast, as floating elements, latent consonants are not prosodically licensed, and thus not phonetically realized (the deletion effect), unless they become anchored in some fashion under certain conditions (the insertion effect). Thus, while maintaining the view of the deletion treatment that both fixed consonants and latent consonants are final consonants in the phonological representations of words, the new approach also borrows from the insertion analysis by considering liaison as a process *integrating* a consonant into a pronounced phonological string. The floating characterization of liaison consonants in nonlinear phonology has been regarded as an apt formal translation of their traditional description as latent consonants (Clements and Keyser 1983, p. 101) and as an appropriate mark of lexical structural instability leading to phonetic variability (Encrevé 1988, pp. 239–241). This case has also been cited as a paradigm example where a theoretical advance allows the resolution of a controversy within a superseded model (Clements 1983; Encrevé 1988, p. 127).

In the course of the last ten years or so, this general outlook on fixed consonants and latent consonants has received an impressive array of competing implementations, raising in the process stimulating new questions as well as reviving old issues. This chapter seeks to sort out the various proposals in terms of their theoretical and descriptive claims, focusing first on the deletion effect (section 2) and then on the insertion effect (section 3). Section 4 reviews the case of the famous *h*-aspiré words, whose failure to allow liaison despite being vowel-initial has also led to a variety of formal proposals within nonlinear phonology.

2   The Deletion Effect

The deletion effect on latent consonants is generally attributed to a lack of prosodic licensing. The basic assumption is that latent consonants, unlike fixed consonants, can be unrealized phonetically because they are floating with respect to the syllable. The issue is to identify what distinguishes latent consonants from fixed consonants to make them floating with respect to the syllable. Two conceptions of latent consonants's status have been proposed, which I will refer to as "skeletal flotation" and "syllabic flotation," indicating the level of prosodic structure with respect to which latent consonants are fundamentally floating. In sections 2.1–2, I outline the basic characteristics of these two approaches within the skeletal framework of nonlinear phonology in which they were originally elaborated, and in section 2.3, I examine how they fare within the more recent moraic framework.

2.1   *Skeletal Flotation*

Under the skeletal flotation approach, fixed consonants are anchored to skeletal slots, whereas latent consonants have no skeletal slot. The diagram in (2) depicts this view, together with the relevant predictable syllabification (σ represents whatever syllable structure is assumed above the skeleton, c and v refer to consonants and vowels).

(2) (a) Fixed consonants   (b) Latent consonants

In this system of representation, latent consonants are primarily floating with respect to the skeleton. They are also floating with respect to the syllable, but derivatively. That is, as a consequence of having no skeletal slot, latent consonants cannot be syllabified, since syllable structure is built on skeletal slots. By contrast, fixed consonants, being anchored to the skeleton, are syllabified and occupy the coda position. Under this approach, then, latent consonants are not inherent exceptions to syllabification; the reason they do not undergo coda formation is that they are skeletally slotless.

This type of structural distinction between fixed consonants and latent consonants has been independently proposed or adopted by numerous authors within otherwise distinguishable theoretical frameworks or analyses of French phonology, in particular Hyman (1985) in the context of a skeletal tier composed of moras; Durand (1986) in the context of dependency phonology; Charette (1988) and Kaye (1988) in the context of government phonology; and De Jong (1990a), Paradis and El Fenne (1992), Prunet (1986), Tranel (1990), Vergnaud (1982), and Wetzels (1987) within the context of a discussion of the skeletal tier.[3]

In general, the literature has at least implied that the structural distinction between fixed consonants and latent consonants depicted in (2) is truly basic. That is, it is typically assumed that *lexically*, fixed consonants are anchored to a skeletal slot, whereas latent consonants are skeletally slotless. But the case might be made that aside from latent consonants, skeletal slots are predictable in French, thus that melodies in this language can be assumed to project their own skeletal slot, except for latent consonants.[4] If latent consonants are viewed as melodies lexically marked as unable to project their own skeletal slot, then the ultimate difference between fixed consonants and latent consonants is diacritic rather than structural, but the diacritic marking has immediate structural consequences.

To summarize, whether a diacritic or a structural version of skeletal flotation is adopted, the essential claim of this approach is that the special behavior of latent consonants with respect to syllabification is not primary, but derives from their lack of inherent timing.

2.2 Syllabic Flotation

In a different conception of the distinction between fixed consonants and latent consonants, syllable nodes, rather than skeletal slots, are viewed as the primary elements with respect to which latent consonants are floating. By contrast with skeletal flotation, syllabic flotation thus holds that the skeleton is irrelevant to the lexical distinction between latent and fixed consonants. Indeed, proponents of this view have both types of consonants anchored to the skeleton, and as shown by the desired outcome in (3), they assume that while fixed consonants straightforwardly syllabify into coda position, latent consonants fail to do so directly.

(3)   (a)   Fixed consonants   (b)   Latent consonants

The extrasyllabicity of latent consonants displayed in (3b) has been achieved in two basic ways. The first consists in directly marking latent consonants as exceptions to syllabification (e.g., Clements and Keyser 1983; Booij 1983; De Jong 1988). See (4), where I have replaced Clements and Keyser's CV slots with x's, and where [ex] stands for their [extrasyllabic] marking.

(4)   (a)   Fixed consonants   (b)   Latent consonants

The other type of approach also invokes extrasyllabicity to characterize latent consonants, but attempts to derive the effect from special syllable-templatic restrictions on word-final rhymes, instead of imposing it lexically (e.g., Bosch 1991; Levin 1987; Piggott 1991; Plénat 1987). The basic claim here is that coda consonants are not allowed word-finally;[5] latent consonants therefore remain floating with respect to the syllable, as desired (see 3b above). The challenge for this approach shifts to the representation of fixed consonants, which must be prosodically licensed, despite the ban on word-final coda consonants. Various brute force solutions have been proposed to ensure the prosodic safety of fixed consonants. Plénat (1987) provides fixed consonants with a lexical marking (labeled [+app] in 5a below) allowing them to occupy a special appendix Chomsky-adjoined to the syllable. In a related proposal, Bosch 1991 assumes that words in French are marked for whether or not they license final consonants; latent consonants are found in words that do not and fixed consonants in words that do (see 5b, where Ω denotes the special word-final appendix licensing fixed consonants). In fashion reminiscent of linear phonology's protective schwas, Piggott (1991) posits that fixed consonants are onsets of empty-headed syllables (see 5c).[6]

(5) (a) Plénat   (b) Bosch   (c) Piggott

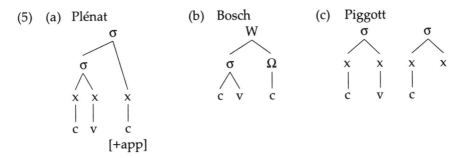

Regardless of the specific implementation, the central characteristic of the syllabic flotation approach is its *direct* identification of the distinction between fixed consonants and latent consonants to different syllabification properties. By contrast, as we saw in section 2.1, the skeletal flotation approach views the different syllabification properties of fixed consonants and latent consonants as a *consequence* of a more fundamental difference, namely the presence versus the absence of inherent timing.

2.3 *Moraic Theory and the Representation of Latent Consonants*

The proposals considered so far for the representation of latent consonants were basically couched within a vocabulary using segmental skeletal positions, rather than moraic positions (see chapter 5). But with its own various implementations, the use of a mora-based skeletal tier allows the reenactment of the skeletal and syllabic flotation approaches to latent consonants described above.

For our purposes, extant moraic models can be divided into two main categories: those that are analogous to skeletal theories and those that are not. Thus, Hyman's moraic model (1985) is not really different from a skeletal model when it comes to being able to provide a lexical structural distinction between fixed consonants and latent consonants: segments in Hyman's theory are normally expected to carry an inherent weight unit, but they may also be characterized as weightless (Hyman 1985, chap. 5). However, in other moraic models (e.g., Hayes 1989; McCarthy and Prince 1986, 1988; Zec 1988), consonants carry no inherent weight (unless they are syllabic or geminate), and the concept of skeletal flotation is therefore intrinsically ruled out, leaving only the possibility of syllabic flotation to distinguish between fixed consonants and latent consonants. In sum, the skeletal and syllabic flotation approaches discussed earlier are also relevant for the representation of fixed consonants and latent consonants in a framework using moras instead of segmental skeletal positions, although for a group of moraic models, syllabic flotation is the only available approach.

In the remainder of this section, I explore briefly the possibility of using ingredients specific to Hayes's moraic model (1989) to build a syllabic flotation treatment of latent consonants. For languages where closed syllables count as heavy, Hayes proposed that consonants acquire a mora when they syllabify into coda position (cf. his rule of *Weight by Position* [WBP]). If French coda consonants are moraic, i.e., if French has Weight by Position, then latent consonants can be viewed as exceptions to Weight by Position ([–WBP]).[7] Assuming that in languages with Weight by Position, a coda position occupied by a consonant without a mora is ill-formed, latent consonants will remain floating with respect to the syllable. This approach resembles Clements and Keyser's syllabic flotation analysis in directly preventing the syllabification of latent consonants, but it is also close to skeletal flotation in making latent consonants exceptional to moraification.

An interesting characteristic of the [–WBP] approach is that the potential for a consonant to be latent is linked to its ability to be moraic. Nonmoraic consonants could not be latent, since they are able to syllabify into well-formed nonmoraic codas. However, this interesting characteristic may be a liability rather than an asset. As Zec (1988) has shown, if a language makes a distinction between moraic and nonmoraic consonants, the moraic consonants will be more sonorous than the nonmoraic ones; for example, moraic consonants will be sonorant while nonmoraic consonants will be obstruents (as in Kwakwala). But studies by Schane (1973) and Plénat (1987) indicate that the prevailing tendency in French regarding the potential for latency in consonants is the exact reverse of Zec's universal for potential moraicity. Thus, in contrast to obstruents (the least likely consonants to be moraic), liquids (the most likely consonants to be moraic) tend to be fixed.

2.4   The Deletion Effect: Summary

Nonlinear phonology derives the deletion effect on latent consonants from lack of prosodic licensing. Lack of prosodic licensing can be obtained through skeletal flotation or syllabic flotation. Skeletal flotation provides a structural explanation for the phenomenon: latent consonants lack inherent timing, hence fail to be syllabified. Syllabic flotation encodes the extrasyllabicity of latent consonants directly, either through stipulated extrasyllabicity, or by prohibiting coda consonants word-finally and placing the burden of representation on fixed consonants.[8]

3   The Insertion Effect

This section examines the explanations that have been proposed for the integration of floating latent consonants into prosodic structure, particularly in liaison. Beside the question of latent consonants's representation, other issues intertwined here include the representation of vowel-initial words and the types of phonological principles assumed to regulate the syllabic meshing of consonant-final words with vowel-initial words. I consider the issues first within the skeletal flotation paradigm (section 3.1) and then within the syllabic flotation paradigm (section 3.2).

3.1   The Insertion Effect under Skeletal Flotation

Within a framework employing segmental skeletal positions, the syllabification of any melody demands the existence of an intermediate skeletal slot. Under skeletal flotation of latent consonants, the question is, Where does the required skeletal slot come from that will allow the insertion effect observed in liaison? Three different sources have been proposed: (1) insertion by universal convention, (2) the following vowel-initial word, and (3) insertion by language-specific rule.

The first proposal (e.g., Kaye 1988; Paradis and El Fenne 1992; Vergnaud 1982) assumes that the floating consonant anchors into the following available onset by virtue of general autosegmental principles of association, and that by universal convention, a skeletal slot is automatically inserted between the consonantal melody and the onset node. This approach to the prosodic licensing of latent consonants threatens the theoretical integrity of the segmental skeletal tier, since a skeletally slotless melody is linked directly to an onset node (the required mediating skeletal slot is added after the fact in purely cosmetic fashion). If allowed to stand, this move could be taken as an argument for Moraic Theory, which does not attribute weight to onset consonants.

The second proposal supplies the needed skeletal slot from an existing source in the phonological string, namely the following vowel-initial word. De Jong (1990a) and Prunet (1986) assume that vowel-initial words begin with an empty skeletal slot in onset position.[9] In liaison, the floating consonant will now automatically associate to this empty skeletal slot and thus be ensured of phonetic realization through prosodic licensing. Although convenient in the case of liaison, this initial empty skeletal slot gets in the way in other situations: when (already slotted) fixed consonants resyllabify into onset position in enchaînement, an extra skeletal slot must somehow be eliminated (Paradis and El Fenne 1992).[10]

These two proposals share the perspective that the phonetic realization of latent consonants in liaison directly results from the application of *universal* principles of association. They also share the view that liaison *is* syllabification, more specifically syllabification into onset position. There may be problems with both claims. In order to be valid, the first claim needs to be reconciled with the fact that liaison is subject to a number of apparent idiosyncrasies (see Tranel 1981a, 1981b) which speak against the automatic realization of prevocalic floating consonants. For example, the plural latent consonant /z/ participates in liaison in contexts where other latent consonants are basically barred from doing so (compare *un court entracte* "a short intermission" [ɛ̃kurãtrakt], *l'étudiant entra* "the student came in" [letüdyã̄atra] with no liaison, with their plural counterparts *de courts entractes* [dœkurzãtrakt], *les étudiants entrèrent* [lezetüdyã(z)ãtrɛr] with liaison).[11] Similarly, different latent consonants in otherwise identical contexts link with different degrees of frequency (compare *très attentif* "very attentive" [trɛzatãtif] with relatively frequent liaison, with *trop attentif* "too attentive" [tro(p)atãtif] with relatively rare liaison).

With respect to the second claim, that liaison is syllabification into onset position, the problem lies in the existence of liaison without enchaînement, that is, cases where latent consonants may appear in coda position as well as onset position (Encrevé 1988). The two possibilities are illustrated in (6b–c) (the periods indicate syllable divisions).

(6) J'avais un rêve. "I had a dream".
    (a) [.ža.vɛ.ɛ̃.rɛv]   (no liaison)
    (b) [.ža.vɛ.zɛ̃.rɛv]   (liaison with enchaînement)
    (c) [ža.vɛz.ɛ̃.rɛv]   (liaison without enchaînement)

If the phonetic realization of latent consonants in liaison depends on their direct placement into onset position, then the existence of liaison without enchaînement is rather mysterious. It requires an unlikely and awkward process of backward *re*syllabification undoing forward syllabification (see De Jong 1990a for such a proposal).

A different, language-specific, approach to the generation of a skeletal slot for latent consonants in liaison has been proposed by Wetzels (1987) (see also Tranel 1990). The basic idea is that in French, a floating consonant followed by a vowel is typically assigned a timing unit, thereby becoming phonetically available in the string for prosodic processing. This analysis borrows from Encrevé the important claim that two separate steps preside over the phonetic realization of latent consonants: (1) skeletal anchoring and (2) syllabification.

One advantage of this approach is that because liaison is kept distinct from syllabification, a straightforward explanation for the existence of liaison with and without enchaînement becomes possible. A floating consonant is made available for prosodic processing by first being attributed a skeletal slot. Syllabification applies next: forward syllabification into onset position (the unmarked case) will yield the more standard liaison with enchaînement seen in (6b), while backward syllabification into coda position (the marked case) will yield the more unusual liaison without enchaînement seen in (6c).

If the process of skeletal slot insertion in liaison is language-particular, it can also rather naturally be subject to specific conditions having to do with the morphological or phonetic nature of the linking consonants, thereby accounting for the idiosyncratic cases mentioned earlier (see Tranel 1981a and 1981b for transposable accounts of such data).

This language-specific approach may furthermore explain differences observed across languages. For instance, according to Archangeli (1988), in Tiwi (Australia), regular vowel-initial words do not trigger the phonetic realization of latent consonants. It may be that what separates Tiwi from French is that Tiwi lacks French's language-specific rule of skeletal slot insertion (Tranel 1988b). If the realization of latent consonants was ruled entirely by universal principles, then one would expect no divergence between French and Tiwi.[12]

One apparent drawback of the language-specific approach to skeletal slot insertion in liaison is that it does not explain why a floating consonant is realized before a vowel, but not before another consonant or at the pause. The other approaches do provide a natural phonological explanation for this fact, through the notions of available onset and automatic association. This debit on the language-specific approach ledger is the price paid for keeping liaison and syllabification distinct. It is actually not implausible to think that the prevocalic context for the realization of floating consonants is merely a historical relic that must be synchronically stipulated. It is interesting to note in this respect that, as illustrated in (7), floating consonants do get phonetically realized under conditions where no vowel follows.

(7)   (a) Masculine [pœti] vs. feminine [pœtit]   (petit/petite "small")
      (b) Indicative [sɔr] vs. subjunctive [sɔrt]   (sort/sorte "go out")
      (c) [ɥit] amis, [ɥi] cours vs. ils sont [ɥit]   (huit "eight": "eight
                                                        friends", "eight courses"
                                                        /"they are eight")

Such cases indicate that the surface emergence of latent consonants is not necessarily syllabically motivated. Thus, it may have a purely morphological raison d'être, as in (7a–b), where skeletal slots for the relevant latent consonants can be said to be generated by the feminine and subjunctive morphology, respectively (see Bosch 1991 for a similar proposal).[13] This view leaves open the possibility that the prevocalic context for the phonetic realization of latent consonants in liaison is interpreted by native speakers as a phonological stipulation, rather than a fall-out from universal grammar.

To summarize, in accounting for the insertion effect, the challenge for the skeletal flotation approach is to provide latent consonants with skeletal slots. One appears to be forced into a language-particular analysis that keeps skeletal anchoring and syllabification separate, and for which supporting evidence can be adduced from liaison without enchaînement, idiosyncratic aspects of liaison, and cross-linguistic differences in the behavior of latent consonants.

3.2   *The Insertion Effect under Syllabic Flotation*

Syllabic flotation analyses have no alternative but to conceive of the insertion effect as direct syllabification of latent consonants. This requirement creates a serious dilemma. If latent consonants's syllabification is derived from universal principles, then the approach faces the same descriptive problems affecting the skeletal flotation analyses that resort to automatic onset formation to derive the insertion effect (see section 3.1 above). If latent consonants' syllabification is derived from French-specific general principles, then it becomes difficult to explain why liaison with a floating latent consonant such as /t/ does not occur, at least as an option, before /r/-initial words (*petit rot* "small burp" [pœ.ti.ro]/*[pœ.ti.tro]; cf. *petit trot* "easy trot" [pœ.ti.tro]), since /tr/ syllable onsets are otherwise created in French, obligatorily word-internally (*métro* [me.tro]/*[met.ro]) and optionally across words (*petite roue* "small wheel" [pœ.tit.ru]/[pœ.ti.tru], the latter homophonous with *petit trou* "small hole"). Clearly, liaison does not reduce to syllabification. It therefore looks as if latent consonants' syllabification should be achieved in construction-specific fashion, for example by saying, as Booij (1983) does, that in liaison, latent consonants are syllabified into onset position before vowel-initial words. But then an important generalization is missed, since when latent consonants are phonetically realized, their syllabification does not fall outside the norms of syllable formation in French. The syllabification of latent consonants should not be derived independently of the notion of possible syllable in French, which construction-specific rules of syllabification in effect do.

Syllabic flotation's basic premise – that latent consonants are exceptions to syllabification into coda position (either directly or because of a constraint on word-final rhymes) – also creates difficulties.[14] Even if one grants backward resyllabification in order to account for liaison without enchaînement, the landing site (a coda) turns out to be an unauthorized position for the consonant. Phonetically realized latent consonants in feminine and subjunctive forms (see 7a–b above) face the same problem.[15] If the restriction on the appearance of latent consonants in coda position is somehow relaxed, perhaps in the postlexical phonology, then liaison without enchaînement, and feminine and subjunctive forms will be derivable, but at the same time the deletion effect will be incorrectly negated, since nothing will prevent floating latent consonants from generally incorporating into coda position whenever they cannot find an available onset.

To summarize, direct syllabification of latent consonants is the only option available under syllabic flotation to explain the insertion effect. The challenge for this approach is twofold: (1) to separate effectively what pertains to syllabification from what pertains to other phenomena in the realization of latent consonants and (2) to capture the permissible syllabifications for latent consonants without letting in the impermissible ones.

3.3   The Insertion Effect: Summary

Under a floating analysis of latent consonants, nonlinear phonology must derive the insertion effect through prosodic licensing. The skeletal flotation approach can provide this effect through skeletal anchoring, which involves the insertion of a skeletal slot under a variety of specifiable conditions (miscellaneous factors in the case of liaison, purely morphological factors for feminine and subjunctive formation); skeletal anchoring makes latent consonants available for syllabification. The syllabic flotation approach must resort to the direct syllabification of latent consonants and seems inherently less able to handle the range of facts explained under skeletal flotation.

4 The Case of *h*-aspiré Words

This final section is devoted to *h*-aspiré words, which are traditionally described as vowel-initial words that act as if they were consonant-initial (for example, they do not allow liaison: *petit héros* "little hero" [pœtiero]/*[pœtitero]). This small class of words has special significance in the context of the debate over the existence and formal representation of so-called ghost segments. The goal of this section is to review the types of representation that have been proposed for *h*-aspiré words (section 4.1), and in this theoretical context to give some attention to two empirical questions (section 4.2): (1) Do *h*-aspiré words behave exactly like consonant-initial words? and (2) Are they uniformly deviant with respect to a given range of phonological phenomena?

4.1 *The Representation of* h-aspiré *Words*

In keeping with the traditional description of *h*-aspiré words, most generative approaches have posited in the lexical representation of these words some initial *structural* element rendering them analogous to consonant-initial words. In many linear accounts (e.g., Dell 1970; Schane 1968; Selkirk 1972; Selkirk and Vergnaud 1973), this special element was an abstract consonant requiring deletion following the performance of its function (e.g., the triggering of latent consonant deletion).

This type of representation for *h*-aspiré words was adopted in some nonlinear studies. Thus, Hyman (1985) and Prunet (1986) viewed *h*-aspiré words as beginning in some minimal consonantal material on the melodic tier.[16] By contrast, several other authors exploited the skeletal tier's resources to the fullest by resorting to empty skeletal slots to distinguish *h*-aspiré words from regular vowel-initial words. As shown in (8a), Clements and Keyser (1983), Encrevé (1988), and Piggott (1991) essentially made *h*-aspiré words consonant-initial on the skeletal tier and vowel-initial on the melodic tier (8b gives the contrastive representation assumed for regular vowel-initial words, here *ami* "friend").

(8)   (a) *h*-aspiré words   (b)   Regular vowel-initial words

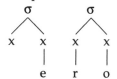

The paradox in representation (8a) is that it actually provides a free onset slot when its very purpose is to block a consonant from coming into onset position. (8a) was specifically designed for the mechanics of liaison analyses with skeletally slotted latent consonants: the initial empty skeletal slot prevents the latent consonant's skeletal slot from associating into the onset. It is not obvious what prevents the latent consonant from leaving its syllabically floating skeletal slot to anchor into the available onset slot.

Reversing representations to suit his skeletally slotless latent consonants, De Jong (1990a) proposed (9a) for *h*-aspiré words and (9b) for regular vowel-initial words (see section 3.1 above).

(9)   (a) *h*-aspiré words   (b)   Regular vowel-initial words

 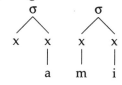

Given (9a), a preceding (skeletally slotless) latent consonant will correctly fail to syllabify into onset position because there is no skeletal slot available.

While use of a skeletal tier offers the alternative of relying on empty skeletal slots or on abstract consonantal melodies to separate *h*-aspiré words from regular vowel-initial words, moraic models where onset positions do not exist at any level (e.g., Hayes 1989) have no structural option but a melodic distinction mirroring Hyman's approach.

In an altogether different type of approach, the difference between *h*-aspiré words and regular vowel-initial words has been assumed to be *diacritic* in nature rather than structural (e.g., Gaatone 1978; Kaye and Lowenstamm 1984; Klausenburger 1977; Tranel 1981a, 1987a, 1987b; Wetzels 1987). At one extreme of the diacritic spectrum, *h*-aspiré words could be lexically marked with as many exceptions features as there are rules from which they deviate. As opposed to structural approaches, such rule-feature analyses are unable to provide a unified explanation for the behavior of *h*-aspiré words. But this inability is not a necessary characteristic of diacritic approaches, for at the other extreme is the possibility of isolating a single diacritic feature that will explain all the special properties of *h*-aspiré words. One such proposal, discussed in section 4.2 below, has been to view *h*-aspiré words as some sort of syllable island, that is, to consider that the initial vowels of *h*-aspiré words are resistant to onset formation (Tranel 1987a, 1987b, 1992; Wetzels 1987. See also Cornulier 1981; Kaye and Lowenstamm 1984; Kiparsky 1973; Morin 1974; Schane 1978a, 1978b, for related ideas).

A diacritic approach holds a number of advantages over a structural approach: (1) It clearly encodes that *h*-aspiré words are exceptional vowel-initial words, thus explaining why they tend to regularize, as evidenced by so-called errors in child language, popular speech, and spontaneous speech. (2) It does not make *h*-aspiré words consonant-initial in any way; as a consequence, it does not have to face the thorny issue of the surface fate of the abstract element posited in the structural analyses.[17] (3) It can help isolate a relatively independent characterization of *h*-aspiré words, and thus clarify the debate by disengaging it somewhat from the issues surrounding the representation of regular vowel-initial words and final consonants.

4.2 *Empirical Issues Regarding* h-*aspiré Words*

Structural approaches to the distinction between regular vowel-initial words and *h*-aspiré words are typically motivated by the belief that *h*-aspiré words, although phonetically vowel-initial, otherwise behave exactly like consonant-initial words and should therefore include in their lexical representation some sort of initial abstract consonant. However, the fact is that *h*-aspiré words do not behave exactly like consonant-initial words. As observed for instance by Cornulier (1981), Dell (1970), Tranel (1981a), Wetzels (1987), and Withgott (1982), they exhibit properties characteristic of regular vowel-initial words and they also behave like words with properties of their own.

As shown in (10), *h*-aspiré words indeed act like consonant-initial words with respect to liaison (10a) and elision (10b): neither liaison nor elision occurs before *h*-aspiré words and consonant-initial words, whereas both phenomena occur before regular vowel-initial words (e.g., *le gros étau* "the big vise" [lœgrozeto]; *l'étau* "the vise" [leto]).

(10)		*h*-aspiré words			True consonant-initial words		
	(a)	gros	"big	[groero]	gros	"big	[grotero]
		héros	hero"		terreau	compost"	
	(b)	le	"the	[lœero]	le	"the	[lœtero]
		héros	hero"		terreau	compost"	

But, as shown in (11), *h*-aspiré words are in other respects like regular vowel-initial words: (1) they phonetically begin in a vowel (11a), (2) they always ignore their initial syllable in reduplication (11b), and (3) they cannot contain a schwa in their initial syllable (11c).

(11)		*h*-aspiré words	Regular vowel-initial words	
	(a)	héros [ero]	étau [eto]	(cf. terreau [tero])

(b) Henri [riri]   Eric [riri]   (cf. Robert [roro])
(c) no initial schwa no initial schwa (cf. chemise "shirt" [š(œ)miz])

In yet other respects, illustrated in (12), *h*-aspiré words behave unlike either consonant-initial or vowel-initial words: (1) Their consonant-like behaviors are actually unstable (12a). (2) Contrary to consonant-initial words, they do not allow schwa deletion (12b). (3) They allow a preceding fixed consonant to be followed by a schwa (12c). And (4) most of them (optionally) allow a preceding fixed consonant to syllabify into their onset (enchaînement), but a few do not (12d).

(12) (a) le haricot   "the bean"   [lœariko] / [lariko]
           les haricots   "the beans"   [leariko] / [lezariko]
      (b) dans le haut   "at the top"   [dãlœo] / *[dãlo]
           (cf. dans le bas "at the bottom"   [dãl(œ)ba])
      (c) une hausse   "an increase"   [ünœos]
           (cf. une fosse   "a pit"   [ünfos])
      (d) quel hasard   [kɛl.a.zar] / [kɛ.la.zar]   (most *h*-aspiré words)
           quel héros   [kɛl.e.ro] / *[kɛ.le.ro]   (a few *h*-aspiré words)
           "what coincidence" / "what hero"

Consider these properties in the framework of the syllable-island hypothesis. The properties that *h*-aspiré words share with consonant-initial words and regular vowel-initial words can be explained fairly straightforwardly. Basically, liaison and elision are blocked (see 10) because both processes normally force a consonant into onset position (cf. *gros étau* [gro.ze.to]; *sous l'étau* "under the vise" [su.le.to]). *h*-aspiré words are otherwise like regular vowel-initial words and thus behave like them (see 11). Property (12a) follows from the very fact that *h*-aspiré words are lexically marked and thus naturally tend to regularize. Property (12b) can be explained away if the rule of schwa deletion is formalized as applying interconsonantally; it will not apply before *h*-aspiré words because these words are vowel-initial (Tranel 1981a; see Tranel 1987a, 1987b for an alternative account relying on the view that *h*-aspiré words are syllable islands). Property (12c) can be interpreted as a possible strategy for resolving the conflict caused on the one hand by the phonological pressure exerted by forward syllabification in VCV sequences and on the other hand by the syllable-island constraint characteristic of *h*-aspiré words.

A number of difficulties nevertheless remain. The data in (12d) constitute a serious problem, since they indicate that most *h*-aspiré words actually allow the syllabification of a consonant into their initial onset. The question is why fixed consonants, but not latent consonants, are allowed this apparent transgression. It would seem that the initial vowels of *h*-aspiré words must be exceptions to liaison, but not necessarily to onset formation. A rule-feature analysis may therefore be necessary after all.

Additional evidence for this possibility comes from other observations indicating that at least for some *h*-aspiré words, the three phenomena of liaison, elision, and enchaînement are apparently treated independently by certain speakers.

1   First, as illustrated in (13), Cohen (1963) observed that in his own speech, elision but not liaison took place with the word *hameçon* "fishing hook". For him, then, *hameçon* behaved like a regular vowel-initial word with respect to elision, but exceptionally with respect to liaison.

(13)   (a)   l'hameçon   "the hook"   [lamsõ]   regular elision
       (b)   mon hameçon   "my hook"   [mõamsõ]   [–liaison]

2   Conversely, as shown in (14), Durand (1986) observed that in the speech of four subjects, the word *hongrois* "Hungarian" behaved like a regular vowel-initial word with respect to liaison, but exceptionally with respect to elision.

(14)   (a)   le hongrois   "Hungarian"   [lœõgrwa]   [–elision]
       (b)   en hongrois   "in Hungarian"   [ãnõgrwa]   regular liaison

3   Similarly, as shown in (15), Durand also observed that in the speech of his parents, the word *hollandais* "Dutch" can behave like a regular vowel-initial word with respect to liaison (although not always), whereas it consistently behaves exceptionally with respect to elision.

(15)   (a)   le Hollandais   (def. sg.)   [lœɔlãdɛ]   [–elision]
       (b)   les Hollandais   (def. pl.)   [le(z)ɔlãdɛ]   ([–liaison])

4   Finally, I return to the data in (12d), repeated in (16) below. Cornulier (1981) observed that in the speech of some speakers, *h*-aspiré words could be divided into two categories with respect to enchaînement. A few words never allow such resyllabification (e.g., in his own speech *héros* "hero", *haïr* "to hate", *hideux* "hideous", *honte* "shame"), while the others do (e.g., *hasard* "chance"). This dichotomy indicates that one cannot in a blanket manner assume that *h*-aspiré words are syllable islands. What must be recognized is that a majority are optional exceptions to enchaînement, while a few are obligatory exceptions.

(16)   (a)   quel hasard   [kɛl.a.zar]/[kɛ.la.zar]   ([–enchaînement])
       (b)   quel héros   [kɛl.e.ro]/*[kɛ.le.ro]   [–enchaînement]

4.3   h-*aspiré Words: Summary*

The syllable-island hypothesis goes a long way toward providing a unified account for the behavior of *h*-aspiré words, but some data remain outside its scope. Unexplained are why most *h*-aspiré words allow syllabification with fixed consonants (but not with latent consonants), and why for at least some speakers, *h*-aspiré words do not necessarily behave uniformly with respect to the expected range of phenomena. A rule-feature analysis is able to handle these facts, but essentially by brute force. At any rate, *h*-aspiré words do not make a case for the existence of empty skeletal slots or abstract consonantal melodies.

5   Conclusion

The concept of floating consonant available in nonlinear phonology provides an attractive formal representation for French latent consonants. Deletion and insertion effects on latent consonants boil down to conditions on prosodic licensing. The efforts at implementing this basic idea have raised and revived stimulating questions about the precise nature of the phenomena (e.g., liaison) where latent consonants are phonetically realized, and they can also constructively inform the current debate on the development of theories regarding skeletal and moraic positions in nonlinear phonology.

Contrary to common claims, *h*-aspiré words do not provide evidence for the concept of empty skeletal slots or for abstract consonantal melodies. Rather, the special behavior of these vowel-initial words suggests the necessity of a diacritic account. The notion of syllable island comes tantalizingly close to yielding a unified explanation for *h*-aspiré words, but the brute force of rule features may ultimately have to be invoked.

NOTES

1   For example, *honnête* "honest", pronounced [ɔnɛt], was underlyingly /ɔnɛtə/, the fixed consonant /t/ being protected from the application of Final Consonant Deletion by the presence of the final schwa and the extrinsic ordering of final schwa deletion after Final Consonant Deletion. Lexical exceptions to Final Consonant Deletion were also posited, for instance for words such as *net*, underlyingly /nɛt/ and pronounced [nɛt], which do not end in orthographic *e*.

2   A number of other phenomena went unexplained as well, e.g., the divergent effects of fixed consonants and latent consonants on word-internal processes affecting immediately preceding vowels, e.g., Quebec French High Vowel Laxing and standard French Closed Syllable Adjustment, which are triggered by fixed consonants but not by latent consonants (see Tranel 1981a, 1981b, 1986, 1988a).

3　Proponents of government phonology depart slightly from the other authors in viewing fixed consonants as onsets of empty-headed syllables, rather than as coda consonants (see Tranel 1993 for discussion). This difference is due to government phonology's universal Coda Licensing Principle (Kaye 1990).

4　If one follows Hyman (1985) and Tranel (1987a), schwa would also behave exceptionally in this respect.

5　This statement actually simplifies Plénat's elaborate proposal. See Tranel (1993) for a more accurate description and discussion.

6　Piggott's representation for fixed consonants is identical to government phonology's (see note 3), but on language-specific rather than universal grounds, namely the need to distinguish fixed consonants from latent consonants. See Tranel (1993) for further discussion of Piggott's approach.

7　It is actually difficult to establish positively that coda consonants in French are moraic. At least fixed consonants can perhaps be argued to carry weight. The slim evidence comes from allowed patterns for abbreviated words. Typically, words may reduce to one or two syllables. There are no special constraints on the shape of the syllables in bisyllabic abbreviations (CVCV: *laboratoire* → *labo*; CVCVC: *bénéfice* → *bénef*; CVCCV: *calvados* → *calva*; CVCCVC: *formidable* → *formid*), but monosyllabic ones must normally end in at least one consonant (e.g., *mathématiques* → *mat*, *permission* → *perm*). The generalization I would tentatively propose is that these abbreviations must in some sense be heavy: a branching foot (two syllables) will naturally do, but if a single syllable is kept (forming a nonbranching – presumably light – foot), then the syllable itself must count as heavy, i.e., have a branching rhyme with at least one coda consonant. This account is only valid if coda consonants carry weight, at least word-finally.

8　Encrevé (1988) combines both skeletal and syllabic flotation for latent consonants. See Tranel (1993) for discussion.

9　This type of representation has actually been often proposed for *h*-aspiré words, the vowel-initial words that precisely do not allow liaison (see section 4.1 below).

10　In Hyman's framework (1985), a vowel-initial word also provides a weight unit for the preceding latent consonants to link to, but this weight unit is the one carried by the vowel itself, not a separate onset slot as in De Jong's (1990a) and Prunet's (1986) proposals.

11　*Court* and *étudiant* are assumed to have a final latent /t/ because of the feminine forms *courte* [kurt] and *étudiante* [etüdyãt]. For a recent challenge to this commonly held assumption, see Morin (1992).

12　See Piggott (1991) for a different analysis of both Tiwi and French, and Tranel (1993) for further discussion on the issue.

13　Note that the required presence of skeletal slots for phonetically realized latent consonants does not contradict latent consonants' skeletal diacritic marking suggested earlier in section 2.1, since these skeletal slots are generated by outside information, not projected by the consonants themselves.

14　In this respect, see Tranel (1991) for a discussion of the meaning of Clements and Keyser's (1983) [extrasyllabic] feature.

15 The [–WBP] approach suggested
    earlier in section 2.3 actually
    escapes the problem posed by
    feminine and subjunctive forms,
    inasmuch as one could claim that in
    these cases the morphology supplies
    a host mora (see end of section 3.1
    for a similar proposal involving
    skeletal positions).

16 For Hyman, this minimal
    consonantal material is simply the
    floating feature [+consonantal], as
    shown in (a) below. For Prunet,
    who follows Piggott and Singh
    (1985), it is an empty segment
    dominated by a skeletal slot and an
    onset node, as sketched in (b).

(a) Hyman   (b) Prunet

                x x x   σ   σ
                | | | /\   /\
      [+cons]   e r o   x x   x x
                                | | | |
                                [ ] e r   o

17 For example, given
    underspecification theory (chapter
    4), what sort of surface realization
    will an empty slot on the skeletal
    tier or a minimal consonantal
    specification on the melodic tier
    yield? The fact is that nothing
    should surface that is not also
    found before a regular vowel-initial
    word.

29   Japanese Phonology

JUNKO ITÔ AND R. ARMIN MESTER

0   Introduction

This article sketches some of the most important aspects of the sound pattern of Modern Japanese, focusing on segmental processes and restrictions. Even at this basic level of phonological organization, an empirically and conceptually adequate description requires explicit reference to the large-scale stratification of the Japanese lexicon into morphemes of different classes. A secondary purpose of this article is to show that a formal explication of the structure of the phonological lexicon – a complex network of partially overlapping phonological regularities of various degrees of generality – calls for significant emendation and extension of traditional views on morpheme classes and necessitates the development of a constraint-based model of lexical organization.

1   Lexical Organization

One of the best-known aspects of the Japanese lexicon is its stratified structure, corresponding in kind to the distinction in English between the Germanic and the Latinate vocabulary. In Japanese, stratification is more elaborate in that four different morpheme classes have traditionally been distinguished. *Yamato* forms constitute the native stratum,[1] corresponding to the Germanic/Anglo-Saxon vocabulary in English. Like the Latinate/Greek stratum in English, *Sino-Japanese* roots constitute the vast technical and learned vocabulary of the language. They are mostly bound forms and occur only compounded with other Sino-Japanese roots. Taking over the role of Sino-Japanese as the main source of new technical vocabulary are the ever-increasing loanwords of the *Foreign* stratum. Alongside these three strata (Yamato, Sino-Japanese, and Foreign), there is a substantial class of *Mimetic* vocabulary items.[2] The examples in (1) illustrate the four morpheme classes.

(1)

	Morpheme Class			
Gloss	Yamato	Sino-Japanese	Mimetic	Foreign
"shine"	kagayak-u	-koo-	kira-kira	šaiN
"dog"	inu	-keN-[3]	waN-waN	doggu

While the items in each row of (1) all occupy approximately the same semantic field, they are used in radically different contexts and are by no means homonymous (the same holds for English: *cow*/*beef*/*bov*ine/*buc*olic, *write*/ de*scribe*, *moon*/*lun*atic, *six*-pack/*sex*tet/*hex*agon, etc.). If such morpheme classifications were nothing more than a record of etymological history, they would have no claim to a place in a synchronic grammar.[4] However, as is familiar from the classical linguistic literature on the subject (see, e.g., Chomsky and Halle 1968, pp. 174, 373; McCawley 1968, pp. 62–75; Postal 1968, pp. 120–139; Saciuk 1969, pp. 505–512), such classifications require explicit synchronic recognition if, and as far as, they continue to play a role in the grammar. Here their role is not confined to the task of drawing lexical demarcation lines, across which morpheme combinatorics is limited or altogether prohibited (for example, Latinate suffixes attaching only to Latinate stems; Sino-Japanese roots compounding only with other Sino-Japanese roots, etc.). Morpheme classes also figure prominently in organizing the lexical domains of phonological regularities, affecting both segmental alternations and structural constraints (see, e.g., Lightner 1972, p. 433). Thus the Velar Softening alternation in English (*criti*[k]~*criti*[s]ize~*criti*[s]ism, etc., see Chomsky and Halle 1968, pp. 48, 174, 223) is restricted to the juncture between Latinate stems and Latinate suffixes, both level 1 suffixes like *-ize* and level 2 suffixes like *-ism* (see Kiparsky 1982, pp. 3–4, for this classification of [certain uses of] these suffixes, and Goldsmith 1990, pp. 261–262, for further discussion).

The native stratum of Chamorro (Chung 1983, p. 37) has no underlying mid vowels, but such segments do exist in Spanish loans. In the native stratum of German, a word-initial sibilant can be either the voiced alveolar [z] or the voiceless postalveolar [š], but not the otherwise unmarked voiceless alveolar [s] (Trubetzkoy 1939): ([z]*ee* "sea", [š]*ön* "beautiful", [š]*tuhl* "chair"; *[s]*ee, *[s]*ön, *[s]*tuhl, etc.). This restriction does not hold in a large class of loans ([s]*ex*, [s]*teak*, [s]*kandal*, etc.). In Mazateco (Fries and Pike 1949, p. 30), postnasal stops are uniformly voiced in native words (similar to Japanese, cf. (3) below), but not in Spanish loans (*siento* "one hundred"). In Mohawk (Postal 1968, p. 130), the stratum consisting of French loans shows word stress on the final syllable (instead of native penult stress), and in addition allows the labials [m,b,p], which are not permitted in native items. In Turkish (Lees 1961; Zimmer 1969), the Labial Attraction Constraint requiring high vowels to be round after tautomorphemic labial consonants (*armud* "pear", *armɨd*) holds only for native items.

In Japanese, several phonological constraints are stratum-specific and hold only for a particular morpheme class. Thus the compound voicing alternation traditionally known as *Rendaku* "sequential voicing", whereby initial consonants of second members are voiced (2a), is only found in [Yamato] items (Martin 1952, pp. 48–9; Martin 1987, pp. 26–29; McCawley 1968, pp. 86–87; Itô and Mester 1986, pp. 54–55, 66, 72). Also restricted to [Yamato] is the voicing restriction allowing only a single voiced obstruent per morpheme (*Lyman's Law*, (2b)). A property specific to the Sino-Japanese stratum is the restriction that all stems must be (underlyingly) monosyllabic ((2c), see Martin 1952, pp. 24–26; Tateishi 1989a; Itô and Mester 1993a). And the canonical shape of [Mimetic] roots is the minimal word of Japanese (2d): one bimoraic foot (see section 4 below), i.e., two moras (*kira-kira* "glittering", etc., see Hamano 1986; Mester and Itô 1989; and Poser 1990).[5]

(2) (a) Rendaku [Yamato]: Voicing on second compound member
　　　　 yu "hot water" + toofu "tofu"　　 →　 yu**d**oofu　"boiled tofu"
　　　　 de "leave"　　 + kuči "mouth" →　 de**g**uči　"exit"
　　(b) Lyman's law [Yamato]: Morphemes contain at most one voiced obstruent.
　　　　 futa "lid"　　 fuda "sign"　　 buta "pig"　　 *bu**d**a
　　　　 cf. also: onna + kotoba → onnakotoba "feminine speech" (*onna**g**otoba)
　　(c) Monosyllabism [Sino-Japanese]:　　 | root | = σ
　　(d) Foot Restriction [Mimetic]:　　　　 | root | = minwd = F (= $\mu\mu$)

Of considerably greater interest, in the context of Japanese phonology, are the three syllable-related constraints in (3), which each extends over more than a single morpheme class while still not holding over the entire lexicon.

(3)　*P　 A constraint against single [p]: Yamato and Sino-Japanese forms tolerate /p/ only in a geminated or at least partially geminated form (*kappa* "river imp", *nippoɴ* "Japan", and *kampai* "cheers", but never *kapa* or *nipoɴ*). The *P-constraint governs neither mimetics (cf. *pika-pika* "glittering") nor foreign items (cf. *peepaa* "paper").
　　*NT　 A nasal cluster voicing constraint, ruling out clusters like *nt, *mp, *ŋk: Post-nasal obstruents must be voiced in Yamato and Mimetic (*tombo* "dragonfly", *kande* "chewing", *šombori* "lonely", *unzari* "disgusted", cf. Itô, Mester, and Padgett 1993). The *NT-constraint does not hold in Sino-Japanese and Foreign (*sampo* "walk", *hantai* "opposite", *kaŋkei* "relation"; *kompyuutaa* "computer", *santakuroozu* "Santa Claus").[6]
　　*DD　 A constraint ruling out voiced obstruent geminates (*bb, *dd, *gg, *zz): Geminate obstruents must be voiceless in Yamato, Mimetic, and Sino-Japanese (*katte* "buying", *nikkori* "smiling", *šippai* "failure"). Foreign items do allow geminate voiced obstruents (*doggu* "dog", *beddo* "bed").

Notice that each of the constraints in (3) holds of more than one morpheme class, as shown schematically below in (4).

(4)   (a)   Yamato   *P   *NT   *DD
       (b)   Sino-Japanese   *P   —   *DD
       (c)   Mimetic   —   *NT   *DD
       (d)   Foreign   —   —   —

In the Yamato stratum (4a), all three constraints hold, which contrasts markedly with the Foreign stratum (4d), where none of them is observed. Sino-Japanese and Mimetic occupy an intermediate position. What we are beginning to see in this simple example are the outlines of a core-periphery organization characterizing the overall lexicon. The maximum set of lexical constraints hold in the core lexical domain, occupied by lexical items traditionally referred to as [Yamato], in the case of Japanese. As the peripheral domain is approached, many of the constraints cease to hold (are "turned off"), or are weakened in various ways.[7]

A second, and equally important, observation about (4) is that it is not in general possible to impose a total ordering on vocabulary strata, in the way lexical phonologists conceive of lexical levels as being strictly ordered, with level 1 preceding level 2, etc. To be more precise, a total ordering of the Japanese strata is not possible in a theory that conforms to the domain continuity principle, which holds that the domain of a constraint or rule must always be continuous, i.e., not interrupted by areas where the constraint or rule is not in force (see, e.g., Mohanan 1986, p. 47). In the case of (4), no total ordering of the four strata is compatible with such continuity. While in one respect (*P) Yamato should be directly followed by Sino-Japanese and not by Mimetic, another constraint (*NT) leads exactly to the opposite conclusion.

Given this kind of evidence for structural patterns within the phonological lexicon of natural languages, how can the grammar take formal account of such facts of lexical organization? It turns out that standard morpheme class features, with labels like [Germanic], [Spanish], etc., by themselves do not constitute an adequate tool for this purpose. In the case of Japanese, we would be dealing with four such features: [Yamato], [Sino-Japanese], [Mimetic], and [Foreign] (cf. McCawley 1968, pp. 62–75, for such a proposal), suggesting a total partitioning on the lexicon, as pictured in (5). What we see emerging, in this conception, are four separate sublexicons, each one obeying its own specific rules and its own specific constraints (as triggered by the relevant diacritic features: [+Yamato], [+Sino-Japanese], [+Mimetic], and [+Foreign]).

(5)   The sublexicon model:

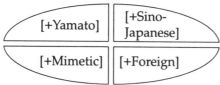

The straightforward prediction of this kind of model is that the strata/ sublexicons should each be equipped with their own independent mini-phonologies, much like the early lexical phonology model of morphological levels, where each level had its associated level-specific phonology (Kiparsky 1982), a model since abandoned in favor of an integrated and unitary phonological component governed by the Strong Domain Condition (Kiparsky 1985; Borowsky 1986; Myers 1991b; Padgett 1991), where rules and conditions can be turned off at the end of a certain level, but otherwise cannot be entirely specific to one lexical level.[8] McCawley (1968, p. 73) noted this kind of problem, pointing out that even with a partitioned lexicon the grammar itself remains single and undivided. There is a unitary phonological component of Japanese, not a separate one for each stratum. The problem with the sublexicon model is that it misses the systematic relationships among the various lexical areas visible in (4): the sometimes overlapping constraint domains, and the overall core-periphery structure.[9] Such relationships could of course be imposed from outside, by explicit stipulation, but this would miss the central point – basic design features of lexical structure should form an integral part of the model of the lexicon itself.

The sublexicon model also fails to adequately reflect the often gradual character of lexical stratification, suggesting instead a kind of homogeneity within all the subclasses that is not found in the empirical world, where, e.g., different degrees of nativization among foreign words are commonplace (see, e.g., Holden 1976 for Russian and Nessly 1971 for English). As we will show below, a stratum like Foreign in Japanese is not a homogeneous class of lexical items, all behaving alike with respect to phonological alternations and constraints, but rather covers a whole range of items at different stages of nativization, from the almost fully assimilated to the barely integrated. It might be said that glossing over such differences constitutes harmless idealization, but this is a questionable understanding of this notion. We are here not dealing with grammatically random lexical variation, but instead with lexical variation that provides a window into the inner organization of the lexical constraint system.

Some of these empirical and conceptual inadequacies of morpheme class features like [Latinate] have been pointed out, in different theoretical contexts, by Kiparsky (1968), Nessly (1971), Lightner (1972), Holden (1976), and most extensively by Saciuk (1969). Kiparsky (1968a, 19–20), recognizing the gradual-ness inherent in the notion "foreign lexical item," calls for a theory in which the feature [Foreign] is replaced by a cascade of redundancy rules of the form "[-Rule X] → [-Rule Y]," predicting, in the typical case, "a hierarchy of foreignness, with exceptions to one rule always being exceptions to another rule, but not vice versa." This important observation strikes at the heart of the sublexicon model in (5). Saciuk (1969, pp. 480–505), taking up this non-homogeneity problem, introduces the class labels [+homogeneous] and [−homogeneous] as nodes within an overall model of the lexicon as a branching tree diagram, illustrated for the case of Japanese in (6). Here the overall lexicon is divided into a nonhomogeneous ("foreign") part and a homogeneous part, the latter further subdivided into native and nonnative, and the nonnative part finally splitting into Sino-Japanese and Mimetic. The whole approach is cast within the Markedness Theory of Chomsky and Halle (1968), with [+native] and [+homogeneous] acting as the unmarked feature values.

(6)   The bifurcation model:

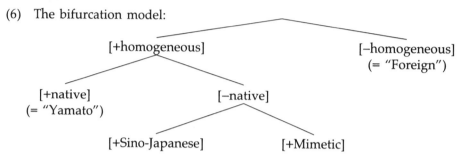

While this markedness approach in principle represents an important insight into the core-periphery structure of the lexicon (see below for further discussion), there are a number of serious problems with any attempt, along the lines in (6), to model lexical structure by a series of successive bifurcations of the lexicon by means of binary features. It seems, first, that nonhomogeneity is, at least to some degree, a property of all strata, and not only of the foreign stratum (even though the issue is most pronounced in the latter case). Second, partitioning the lexicon into two parts and calling one of the resulting sublexicons [−homogeneous] does not amount to a formal characterization (as opposed to a labeling) of nonhomogeneous behavior. Finally, a tree diagram with successive bifurcations, as in (6), has the inherent limitation that any given node can have only one mother node. This property makes it impossible to give formal expression, for example, to the fact that both Mimetic and Sino-Japanese have close, but different, affinities with Yamato (see (4)). This problem cannot be overcome by restructuring the diagram. Once one of the two, either Mimetic or Sino-Japanese, is grouped into a single constituent with Yamato, it is impossible for the other one to be grouped in a similar way. This is an unfortunate trade-off relation: expressing one generalization in the grammar means sacrificing another one. But it is incumbent upon the grammar to capture the precise patterning of *all* the various constraint domains. We are faced with a situation of partial crossclassification, which in the general case (see Chomsky 1965) cannot be captured by branching tree diagrams as in (6).

All these consideration suggest that it might be worth having a closer look at the empirically tangible patterning of (phonological) constraint domains in the lexicon. Instead of directly partitioning the lexicon with labels like "Yamato," "Sino-Japanese," etc., which each imply various phonological properties (constraints), let us begin more modestly by directly modeling the constraint domains within the lexicon, and study the resulting configurations, which we will graphically express by means of Venn diagrams serving as constraint

domain maps. Consider first the class-specific constraints in (2), whose domains
are each coextensive with a single morpheme class, as shown in (7)

(7)

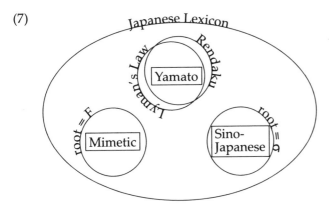

More interesting are the overlapping constraints in (3), whose domain map
appears in (8). The outermost ellipse represents the lexicon as a whole. The
two innermost ellipses represent the single-p constraint, *P, and the nasal
cluster voicing constraint, *NT, whose domains do not stand in an inclusion
relationship, but rather overlap in the core area, containing the items of the
[Yamato] class (see (4)). This central area is also the domain of Rendaku and
Lyman's Law (2a, b). The ellipse immediately surrounding the two overlapping domains represents the *DD-constraint, which includes the areas occupied
by Yamato (innermost area), Sino-Japanese (within *P) and Mimetic (within
*NT).

(8) The constraint domains model:

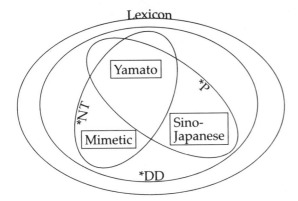

The constraint map (8) indicates that there exist lexical areas which are non-
Yamato, non–Sino-Japanese, non-Mimetic, but still obey the *DD constraint.
This is exactly as desired: such areas are occupied, e.g., by strongly assimilated
loans like *hando-bakku* "handbag" (with a devoiced geminate).

We will develop the constraint domain model in (8) by filling in more of the constraints which collectively make up the phonology of Japanese and locating their relative domains. Abstracting away from the fact noted above that the boundaries of *all* strata are to some extent in flux, we will continue to assume that Yamato, Sino-Japanese, and Mimetic exist as lexical areas ("strata") (see (8)), relatively well-defined in terms of bundles of closely coinciding constraint "isoglosses." On the other hand, the large and very heterogeneous class of Foreign items (cf. Saciuk's 1969 [–homogeneous] class) should not be considered as constituting a uniform stratum. Rather, we are simply dealing with less central areas of the lexicon, where more and more constraints are violated. Thus the overall lexicon is viewed as an abstract space, with a core and a periphery.[10] The distinction between more and less nativized items (Kiparsky 1968; Nessly 1971; Holden 1976) concerns the number of constraints that an item complies with: the less nativized an item, the more it is exempt from lexical constraints, i.e., the more it is located toward the periphery, falling outside of various constraint domains. These constraint domains are centered around an abstract core, governed by the maximum set of lexical constraints (the core is thus "unmarked," cf. Saciuk 1969). This is illustrated in (9) (where for graphical perspicuity constraint overlap is ignored).

(9)   Core-periphery structure:

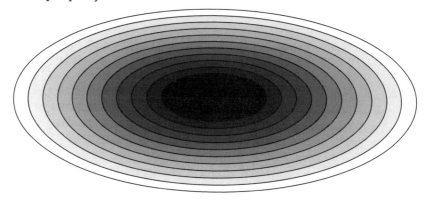

As the periphery is approached, many of the constraints cease to hold, or are weakened in systematic ways (we will encounter the latter type of situation in section 3). A plausible hypothesis is that the periphery usually does not add a new constraint, nor strengthen an existing one. Compare this with a simple bifurcation between Foreign and non-Foreign, as in (6), which does not yield any predictions as to what kinds of differences might arise. The core/periphery distinction suggests that we should not expect to find a language where, e.g., the *NT-constraint holds in the foreign loanwords but not in the native vocabulary, or a situation where the stronger version of the constraint holds in the periphery and the weaker version in the core. What the core-periphery distinction entails, then, is a notion of distance from the lexical core: as the distance increases, constraints are weakened and abolished, and the range of admissible structures increases.[11] With this conception of constraint domains, we will now illustrate the various constraints of Japanese, asking what they tell us about the design of the phonological lexicon.

2 Segment Inventory Differences and Allophonic Rules

The goal of this section is to further substantiate the distinction between the lexical core, including Yamato, Sino-Japanese, and Mimetic, and the lexical periphery. One of the most salient differences lies in the underlying segment inventories. We first focus on the bilabial fricative [f] and and the alveolar affricate [tˢ].[12] As shown in (10), these segments do not occur in the core domain except before [u].

(10)   (a)   *[fa]   *[fe]   *[fi]   *[fo]
              *[tˢa]   *[tˢe]   *[tˢi]   *[tˢo]
      (b)   [fu]:   too**fu**   "tofu"   **fu**ǰi   "Fuji"   afureru   "overflow"
              [tˢu]:   **tˢu**kue   "desk"   fu**tˢu**u   "ordinary"   ka**tˢ**-u   "win" (pres.)
                                                             cf. kat-anai "win" (neg.)

In phonemic terms, [f] and [tˢ] are allophonic variants of /h/ and /t/, and the fact that [fu] and [tˢu] are allowed goes hand in hand with the fact that *[hu] and *[tu] are excluded. Thus in the recitation of the lines of the syllabary, we find *kakikukeko* "k-column", but *tačitˢuteto* "t-column" and *haçifuheho* "h-column". We analyze these facts as resulting from the interaction of two pairs of constraints. First, there are the segmental constraints in (11) barring the labial fricative [f] and the coronal affricate [tˢ].

(11)   (a)   *F: $*\begin{bmatrix} -\text{son} \\ \text{LAB} \\ | \\ [+\text{cont}] \end{bmatrix}$ (b)   *TS: $*\begin{bmatrix} -\text{son} \\ \text{COR} \\ +\text{ant} \end{bmatrix}$
                                                                   [−cont]   [+cont]

Second, we posit the sequential constraints in (12) requiring labialization of [h] and affrication of [t] before [u] (where the broken line represents the association relation which must necessarily (indicated by □) hold in configurations fulfilling the rest of the structural description).

(12) (a) □FU:　　　　　　　　　　(b) □TSU:

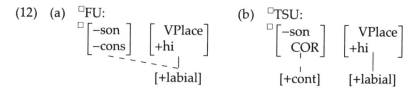

These sequential constraints disallow [h] and [t] before [u] and require [f] and [tˢ], respectively. Since each of the constraints in (12) is operative in the grammar and conflicts, as a more specific constraint, with the corresponding more general constraint in (11), it follows by the Pāṇinian theorem of optimality theory (Prince and Smolensky 1993, pp. 81–82) that (12a) must rank over (11a), and (12b) over (11b).

The decision to separate the segmental constraints (11) from the sequential constraints (12) is confirmed by the behavior of peripheral items. In the peripheral domain, [f] and [tˢ] are found before all vowels (13), indicating that the segmental constraints (11) are no longer in force.

(13)

[fa]	faito	"fight"	[tˢa]	tˢaitogaisuto	"Zeitgeist"
[fe]	fesutibaru	"festival"	[tˢe]	tˢerutozakku	"Zeltsack"
[fi]	sufiŋkusu	"Sphinx"	[tˢi]	eritˢiN	"Yeltsin"
[fo]	šifoN	"chiffon"	[tˢo]	kantˢoone	"canzone"
[fu]	furutaimu	"full-time"	[tˢu]	tˢuŋge	"Zunge"

Even though /f/ and /tˢ/ are phonemes in their own right in the lexical periphery, the sequences [hu] and [tu] are still disallowed. Where the loan source contains [hu] or [tu] (14), these sequences are rendered with labialization or affrication the resulting homonymy in cases like *fuudo* notwithstanding (or, as in the case of *hook*, a variant pronunciation lowers the vowel so as to keep the [h] quality of the consonant in the source word).

(14) (a) fuupu　　　　　　"hoop"　　　(b) tˢuaa　　"tour"
　　　　fuuzufuu　　　　"Who's Who"　　tˢuiN　　"twin"
　　　　fukku~hokku　　"hook"　　　　tˢuuraN　"two-run homer"
　　　　fuudo　　　　　　"hood/food"　　tˢuna　　"tuna"

The resulting constraint map is given in (15).

(15)

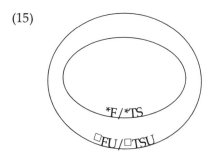

Here the inner ellipse represents the domain of the segmental *F/*TS-constraints, and the larger containing circle that of the sequential □FU/□TSU-constraints.[13]

3 Palatality Constraints and Peripheral Weakening

Traditional classification divides the Japanese CV-moras into plain and palatal moras, where the term "palatal" refers to several different phonetic correlates. For coronals, "plain/palatal" refers to a contrast in primary place of articulation (dental/alveolar vs. alveopalatal:[14] *ta* "field" vs. *ča* "tea", *saku* "fence" vs. *šaku* "wine-serving"). The palatal versions of noncoronals are complex segments with a secondary palatal articulation (*boo* "stick" vs. *bʸoo* "second", *kuukoo* "airport" vs. *kʸuukoo* "express"). Finally, the plain counterparts of palatal glide moras are onsetless syllables (*ane* "sister" vs. *yane* "roof", *umi* "sea" vs. *yumi* "arrow").

Although allowed as underlying elements, these segments have associated sequential restrictions, somewhat similar to *FU/*TSU discussed above. One such restriction is the *TI-constraint (16), which excludes nonpalatal coronal consonants followed by the high front vowel [i] (e.g., *ti, *di, *si, *zi).

(16) *TI:[15] $\quad$ *[Coronal] $\qquad \begin{bmatrix} \text{VPlace} \\ -\text{back} \end{bmatrix}$

$\qquad\qquad\qquad\qquad$ | $\qquad\qquad\qquad$ |

$\qquad\qquad\qquad$ [+anterior] $\qquad$ [+high]

(17) (a) /kat/ $\quad$ kat-oo $\quad$ kat-e $\quad$ kač-i $\quad$ "win", tentative/
$\qquad\qquad\qquad\qquad\qquad\qquad\qquad\qquad\qquad\qquad$ imperative/infinitive

$\qquad\qquad$ /hanas/ $\quad$ hanas-oo $\quad$ hanas-e $\quad$ hanaš-i $\quad$ "talk", tentative/
$\qquad\qquad\qquad\qquad\qquad\qquad\qquad\qquad\qquad\qquad$ imperative/infinitive

$\qquad$ (b) /-suru/ $\qquad\qquad\qquad$ kiN-zuru ~ kiN-ǰiru $\quad$ "forbid"

When a verbal root ends in an alveolar consonant (17a), concatenation with an [i]-initial suffix results in the sequence [ti] or [si], and the coronal obstruents are realized as palatal [č] and [š]. And the form /-zuru/, itself a postnasal alternant of the bound suffix /-suru/ "do", has a variant form [-ǰiru], with a front vowel and a palatal consonant (17b).

The *TI-constraint also applies in assimilated foreign loans. Where the source word contains the illicit [nonpalatal] + [i] sequence, the loanword avoids this sequence in one of two ways: usually by palatalizing the consonant (18) (i.e., by changing its anteriority value), but sometimes by lowering the vowel (19) (i.e., by changing its value of [high]).

(18)

SOURCE: [ti/di] → LOAN: [či/ǰi]		SOURCE: [si/zi] → LOAN: [ši/ǰi]	
team	čiimu	cinema	šinema
ticket	čiketto	dressing	doreššiŋgu
dilemma	ǰiremma	zigzag	ǰiguzagu

(19)

SOURCE: [ti/di] → LOAN: [te/de]	
spaghetti	supagettee
tissue	teššu
disco	desuko

Both (18) and (19) can be interpreted as the result of enforcing the *TI-constraint.[16] Different from □FU, which holds throughout the lexicon, *TI is not enforced in the periphery, and we encounter the sequence [ti] unchanged in recent loans (20).

(20)

SOURCE: [ti] → LOAN: [ti]		
teen(ager)	tiiN	(*čiiN)
party	paatii	(*paačii)
disc jockey	disuku-ǰokkii	(*ǰisuku-ǰokkii)
duet	dʸuetto	(*ǰuetto)

The relevant part of the constraint map is given in (21).

(21)

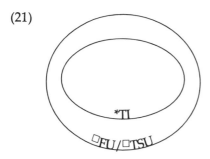

Related to the *TI-constraint, but less well known, is a set of sequential restrictions in Japanese which rules out all kinds of palatal segments preceding the mid front vowel [e] (Bloch 1950; McCawley 1968). The individual subcases are listed in (22).

(22) (a) *CE: No sequence [alveopalatal C] + [e] (*če, *še, *že, *ǰe, etc.)
     (b) *KYE: No sequence [palatalized C] + [e] (*kʸe, *pʸe, mʸe, *dʸe, etc.)
     (c) *YE: No sequence [palatal glide] + [e] (*ye)

The *ČE-constraint holds in Yamato, Sino-Japanese and Mimetic. The sequence [palatal C] + [e] does not occur underlyingly, and there are no conceivable derived cases (roots do not end in palatal obstruents; for root-final [y], see the discussion in conjunction with the *YE constraint below). Among Foreign items, we find cases of depalatalization. If the loan source contains a [palatal-C] + [e] sequence, (23), the palatal is reanalyzed as a plain coronal (i.e., as [+anterior]).

(23)

| SOURCE: [še]/[ǰe] | → | LOAN: [se]/[ze] |

shepherd (dog)   sepaado
gelatine   zeračiɴ[17]
Los Angeles   rosanzerusu
general strike   zene-suto

The *ČE-constraint can be merged with the *TI-constraint by positing a single feature implication statement, (24), governing the relative positioning of tongue blade and tongue body (see Archangeli and Pulleyblank in press for similiar tongue configuration constraints governing [ATR] and height features).

(24) ČE/*TI:[18]

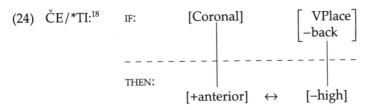

(24) yields two licit and two illicit types of combinations, e.g., with a voiceless fricative: *se*, *ši*, and **si*, **se*. The combined statement in (24) makes a strong prediction: being part of a single constraint, *TI and *ČE should have the same domain of applicability. Since [ti] is allowed in the periphery (20), [če] should also be found there, e.g., in recent loans. This is indeed the case, as (25) shows.

(25)

| SOURCE: [če/še/ǰe] | → | LOAN: [če/še/ǰe] |

chain   čeeɴ
Nietzsche   niiče
sherry   šerii
jet   ǰetto

Within the lexicon as whole, the *ČE/*TI-constraint forms a proper subdomain, as in (26), leaving a periphery ungoverned by this restriction. The constraint domain map shows the location of loans like *sepaado* "shepherd dog", which obey the *ČE/*TI-constraint, and that of unassimilated loans like *šerii* "sherry", which do not.

(26)

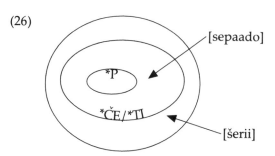

One might at this point entertain the question whether assimilated Foreign words should be considered as having joined the Yamato morpheme class. That is, should a form like *sepaado* in (26) now be considered totally "native"? Even though it fulfills the *ČE-constraint, it still lies outside of the domain of the *P-constraint, and the form clearly cannot be identified as Yamato. Thus to undergo the process of nativization does not mean that a loanword necessarily joins a native morpheme class (see Holden 1976 for similar cases in Russian). It is of course possible for a form to already obey all the constraints holding in [Yamato]. In such cases, it has the potential to be fully admitted to the morpheme class. For example, *tabako* "tobacco", an unaccented form with a single voiced obstruent, counts in all relevant respects as a native item.[19] Another more striking example is *karuta* "carta" (a sixteenth-century Portugese loan), which even undergoes the Rendaku voicing rule (2a) (normally restricted to [Yamato] items) in *hana-garuta* "flower card game" (see note 5 for similar phenomena in Malayalam). Nativization cannot be equated with the enforcement of a single constraint like *ČE/*TI – the forms in (18) and (23) are clearly non-Yamato, non-Mimetic, and non-Sino-Japanese. They cannot and should not be categorized as another morpheme class – a proliferation of terms like "Foreign," "Assimilated Foreign," "Fully Integrated Foreign," etc., is misleading and gives rise to the illusion that such labels refer to homogeneous classes (see the discussion in section 1, and Saciuk 1969).

It is also important not to entirely equate "peripheral" with "foreign." Violations of the *ČE-constraint are not restricted to recent loans, but are also found among items of native origin, as in (27).

(27)   če?   (swearword)
       šee   (exclamation used by famous cartoon figure)

Such forms are undoubtedly native, but peripheral.[20]

It is not the case that hardly any constraint holds in the outer lexical periphery – many basic constraints of Japanese are in full force (e.g., basic syllable constraints making nonhomorganic consonant clusters impossible, etc.). In fact, as we will see immediately below, the palatality restrictions *YE and *KYE are also still observed in the periphery, even though *ČE and *TI are not.

The *YE-constraint (22c) disallows the sequence [palatal glide] + [e].[21] Where such a sequence would be expected, we find the disappearance of the prevocalic /y/. With roots ending in /y/, the intransitive ending /-eru/ would result in the illformed sequence [ye] (28b), cf. (28a). In these cases we find deletion of the root-final /y/ in the output (/moy-eru/ → *mo-eru*).

(28)   Transitive   Intransitive
   (a) tob-asu   tob-eru   "fly"
        sam-asu   sam-eru   "cool down"
        hag-asu   hag-eru   "peel off/become bald"
   (b) moy-asu   mo-eru   "burn"
        tay-asu   ta-eru   "extinguish/be extinct"
        koy-asu   ko-eru   "make/become fat"

Two strategies of dealing with loan sources containing the sequence *ye* are illustrated in (29). Either the [y] is deleted, as in the core verbal paradigm above ([erit^{s}iN] for "Yeltsin"), or it vocalizes the [i] as in [i.e.meN] for "Yemen".

(29)   (a) e.ri.t^{s}iN   "Yeltsin"
        (b) i.e.meN   "Yemen"
             i.e.su.maN   "yes-man"

The crucial point here is that the *YE-constraint is never violated, even with very recent loans like [erit^{s}iN].[22]

Turning next to the *KYE-restriction (22b), it turns out that we are not dealing with an additional independent constraint, but rather with a different facet of the *YE-constraint. The *KYE-restriction excludes [palatalized C] + [e], there are no restrictions on any other vowels after palatalized consonants (e.g., b^{y}ooki "sickness", m^{y}aku "pulse", k^{y}uuri "cucumber"). This suggests a straightforward solution, given the feature-geometrical analysis of palatalized segments as containing a secondary place characterizing [y] besides a major consonantal place (cf. Clements and Hume, chapter 7 in this volume, and references cited there).

We can use this idea to make formal sense of the intuitive analysis encoded in the kana syllabaries. In these terms, [C^{y}V] = [C + yV], such that all [k^{y}a], [b^{y}o], etc., originate in /k+ya/, /b+yo/, etc. It follows that consonantal complexes containing [y] (*[kye], *[mye], *[bye], etc.) cannot occur before [e], simply because they would have to contain the illformed sequence *[ye], which is already ruled out by *YE.[23] Thus *KYE and *YE are not separate constraints, but reduce to the *YE-constraint. The *ČE-constraint, on the other hand, plays a role independent of the *YE-constraint in the grammar, and must remain formally separate. As we have seen, *ČE holds only within a portion of the lexicon, whereas *YE holds everywhere. Thus the periphery allows the sequence [če], (25), but not the sequences [ye] nor [kye]. The *YE-constraint must encompass the entire lexicon, with an inner *ČE circle, as in (30).

(30)

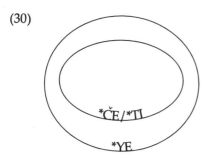

What, then, is the formal relation between *ČE and *YE? We are here dealing with a weakening of the palatality constraint towards the periphery. Different from constraints like *P and *NT, the palatality constraint does not become inoperative, but instead is reduced in force. The close relation between *ČE and *YE becomes evident with a formal statement of the *YE-constraint:

(31) *YE: $*\begin{bmatrix} \text{Coronal} \\ \text{approx} \end{bmatrix} \quad \begin{bmatrix} \text{VPlace} \\ -\text{back} \end{bmatrix}$

　　　　　　　　　|　　　　　　　　　|
　　　　　　[−anterior]　　　[+high]

(31) assumes that [y] is specified for [COR, −ant] (see Mester and Itô 1989) and that the articulator is specified for glidehood with the feature [approximant] within the "gestural" articulator complex (Browman and Goldstein 1989; Padgett 1991). *ČE (24), the stronger version of the palatality constraint disallowing all palatals before [e], is domainwise limited to the lexical core; *YE (31), the weaker version disallowing only approximants in this position, has the whole lexicon, with core and periphery, in its domain.

Just as the approximant constraint *YE is still enforced in the periphery, there is also a fricative remnant of the *TI-constraint, namely the *SI-constraint, that is still operative in the periphery. It ensures that coronal fricatives must be palatal before [i], as illustrated by the examples in (33).

(32) *SI: $*\begin{bmatrix} \text{Coronal} \\ \text{fricative} \end{bmatrix} \quad \begin{bmatrix} \text{VPlace} \\ -\text{back} \end{bmatrix}$

　　　　　　　　　|　　　　　　　　　|
　　　　　　[+anterior]　　　[+high]

(33)

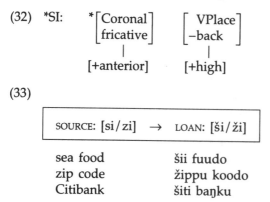

SOURCE: [si/zi]	→	LOAN: [ši/ži]

sea food	šii fuudo
zip code	žippu koodo
Citibank	šiti baŋku

As a result, a fricative coronal followed by [i] always appears as palatal, even though its stop counterpart does not. The asymmetry between stops and fricatives is most clear in the last example, *Citibank*, where [s] becomes palatal [š], but [t] remains alveolar.[24] The constraint domain model straightforwardly depicts the rather subtle patterning of the palatal sequences and their distribution in the lexicon, and the notion of "weakening" of constraints makes sense in terms of core and periphery.

The overall structure emerging in the lexical constraints model, with more and more constraints "turning off" toward the lexical periphery, is highly reminiscent of certain proposals encountered in the lexical phonology literature with respect to the notion of structure preservation, within a theoretical approach strongly committed to the notion of a sequential derivation. Thus both Kiparsky (1985, p. 135 n. 3) and Myers 1991 have argued for a derivationally articulated notion of structure preservation. Here the successive loosening of the constraints (which collectively define the "structure" to be "preserved") is identified with the "turning off" of rules during the derivation (Strong Domain Condition). It is noteworthy, then, that the lexical core/periphery distinction substantiated in this paper has nothing to do with "early" vs. "late" in the derivation: the periphery is just as underlying as the core. Since we are dealing with the same formal relations between constraints and constraint domains, a single theory should encompass both areas. This means that the lexical-phonological idea of "turning off" rules and constraints must be subsumed under a more general theory of the lexicon organized by concentric constraint domains of the kind discussed here. The lexical facts of Japanese (and no doubt of most other languages, if studied with a sufficient degree of detail, see again Saciuk 1969 for a rich collection of relevant evidence) reveal the need for a more general concept of what it means for an item or a morphological formation to obey a certain constraint ("structure preservation") and what it means for a constraint to be out of force ("turned off"). In order to capture these aspects of lexical wellformedness with an adequate degree of generality, the notion of structure preservation must be made independent of the notion of a phonological derivation proceeding in a step-by-step fashion (for arguments against the traditional "sequence-of-operations" view of phonology, see recent work in Optimality Theory, in particular Prince and Smolensky 1993, and in a more general vein, other work making use of the harmony concept in phonology (Goldsmith 1990, 1991, 1992)).

As a conclusion of this section, (34) shows an overall constraint map of the phonological lexicon of Japanese, incorporating all the constraints presented in this paper.[25]

(34)

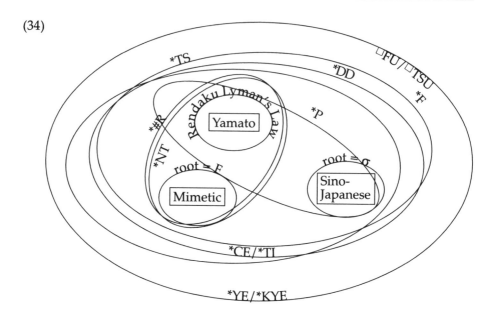

4   Concluding Remarks

Besides some brief remarks on templatic constraints (2c, d), this article has hardly touched on the prosodic aspects of Japanese. This should not be taken as minimizing the importance of the work in this area – on the contrary, we believe that the more important and influential discoveries have been made in the areas of prosodic constituency and accent, with far-reaching consequences not only for Japanese, but also for phonological theory.

Regarding the prosodic organization of Japanese, strong evidence has emerged for both the mora and the syllable as prosodic units. Influenced by the standard syllabaries whose basic unit (the *kana*) is a (C)V unit roughly coextensive with the mora, most naive phonological categorization is built on the mora and makes no use of the syllable. This reflects the fact that the mora, as a phonological unit of abstract timing, is exceptionally well established for Japanese (see, e.g., Katada 1990; Nagano-Madsen 1992; Otake et al. to appear). While invariant local phonetic cues for moras are apparently not uniformly detectable in the acoustic signal (Beckman 1982), recent work has corroborated the phonetic relevance of moras for phonetic timing at the level of the phono-logical word (Port, Dalby, and O'Dell 1987). Beginning with McCawley's (1968) characterization of Standard Japanese as a mora-counting but syllable-accenting language, numerous writers have adduced significant evidence in support of syllabic organization in addition to moraic organization (see Itô 1986, 1989; Itô and Mester to appear; Poser 1990; Kubozono 1989b; and references cited there).

A significant finding (Poser 1990) about higher-level prosody in Japanese is its organization in terms of foot structure. The fact that such higher-level organization into feet asserts itself in Japanese, a language lacking an intensity-based system of prominence ("stress," see Beckman 1986), has helped theorists overcome the illfounded limitations of a conventional understanding which sees foot structure only motivated for stress languages like English. In Japanese, the relevant evidence includes a multitude of template-based formations built on a strictly bimoraic foot, i.e., a unit realized as a single heavy syllable or as a sequence of two light syllables. As the minimal word (see chap. 9, this volume, and McCarthy and Prince 1986; Itô 1990) of Japanese, it plays a pivotal role in various types of name truncations (Poser 1990; Mester 1990), monomoraic lengthening cases, loanword clippings (Itô 1990; Itô and Mester to appear), language games (Tateishi 1989b; Itô, Kitagawa, and Mester to appear), and in a number of other areas (see Haraguchi 1992 for a collection of relevant work currently pursued in Japan).

The Japanese pitch accent system has been the subject of a number of recent analyses, building on the classical studies of Hattori (1960), Akinaga (1960), Martin (1952), and McCawley (1968). Haraguchi (1977) initiated the auto-segmental analysis of pitch accent, continued in the work of Higurashi (1983), Poser (1984b), Kubozono (1989a, 1993), and others. One of the central questions in all these approaches concerns the way in which metrical (prosodic) organization (into moras, syllables, feet, and prosodic words, etc.) interacts with tonal structure. The analysis in Pierrehumbert and Beckman (1988) makes crucial use of boundary tones (tonal elements assigned to higher levels of the prosodic hierarchy and realized in peripheral position) and of tonal underspecification, supporting the view that phonological representations of Japanese utterances remain tonally only sparsely specified up to and including the level that constitutes the input to phonetic interpretation.

Thus, Japanese has played a pivotal role in almost every area related to modern prosodic phonology, and the contributions are so numerous that an overview article like the present one cannot do justice to the relevant research. Rather than offering a cursory survey of well-known work, we have instead chosen to focus on some of the segmental and sequential constraints of the language. This allowed us to present in some detail the less well-known, but no less interesting, constraint-based organization of the phonological lexicon, which is of fundamental importance as a frame of reference for all in-depth work on Japanese phonology.

NOTES

1 Here and throughout, we follow established practice (see e.g. Saciuk 1969) in reserving the term *stratum* for subdivisions of the total vocabulary. Strata in this sense should not be confused with the affixation levels of lexical phonology, which will be referred to as *levels*, using the term introduced for this purpose in the work of Kiparsky (1982, 1985, etc.).

2 Mimetics are sound-symbolic items

that play a much more important role in the overall system than corresponding words in English. As McCawley (1968, p. 64) points out, mimetics "function syntactically as manner adverbs and may refer to just any aspect (visual, emotional, etc.) of the activity involved, rather than just its sound."

3   Cf. *koo-taku* "brilliance", *hak-koo* "white light", *keɴ-ši* "canine tooth", *kyoo-keɴ* "rabid dog". We use small capital ɴ for the placeless coda nasal of Japanese.

4   In fact, it is well-known that the synchronic classifications, as evidenced by the overt behavior of speakers, in numerous cases diverge from the true etymological origin of the items in question. Thus certain Yamato items, like *fude* "brush" or *uma* "horse", are in fact probably very early (and nowadays unrecognizable) borrowings from Chinese, mediated through Korean (see Sansom 1928, pp. 29–30), etc.

5   Japanese is by no means alone in possessing a rich and intricate system of this kind. For example, Mohanan (1986, pp. 80–83) points out that in Malayalam several phonological rules are sensitive to the distinction between Sanskrit and Dravidian lexical items. This distinction is productively applied to newly coined items (on the basis of the overall phonological "type" of the item, as defined by various lexical constraints of the kind investigated in this article for Japanese). The Sanskrit/Dravidian distinction is superimposed, as an independent classification, onto a lexical phonology itself organized into several levels of affixation. And just as there is no "Sanskrit level" or "Dravidian level" in Malayalam, there is also no "Yamato level" or "Sino-Japanese level" in Japanese.

Rather, such morpheme classifications exist and operate independent of any level distinctions (see also Inkelas and Orgun 1993).

6   A similar affiliation of a constraint with both Yamato and Mimetic, to the exclusion of the two other strata, is manifested by the *#R-constraint: Yamato and Mimetic stems never show initial [r]. On the other hand, Sino-Japanese stems (like *raku* "ease") and foreign words (like *rajio* "radio") with initial [r] are not at all uncommon. But there is some legitimate basis for doubting the synchronic validity of this constraint (thus forms like *risu* "squirrel" or *riŋgo* "apple" are usually regarded as Yamato in spite of their initial [r]).

7   It goes without saying that there are constraints that hold even in the Foreign vocabulary, e.g., basic syllable structure restrictions, as evidenced by the massive "epenthesis" occurring in loans (*kurisumasu* "Christmas", *sutoraiki* "strike", etc.). We will return to this issue below.

8   Thanks to John McCarthy, Jaye Padgett, and Alan Prince for helpful discussion on these issues.

9   Further problems arise if the binarity of morpheme class features as depicted in (5) is at all taken seriously. If every morpheme class feature [F] allows both [+F] and [−F] as values, this makes the implausible prediction that the complement of every morpheme class should automatically also constitute a "natural" morpheme class.

10 It should be noted that "core" and "periphery" do not correspond to "lexical" and "postlexical," in the sense of lexical phonology. Both core and periphery are lexical.

11 This is comparable to the derivational and level-oriented weakening of constraints known from lexical phonology, where the abstract point of reference is always the beginning of the derivation, and distance is being measured from there (see the end of section 3 and note 5 for further discussion).

12 Following standard transcriptional practice for Japanese, the symbol [u] is used for the labial unrounded [ɯ], and [f] for the bilabial fricative [ɸ].

13 The larger circle may not be coextensive with the entire lexicon. In certain highly anglicized pronunciations, younger speakers use the unaffricated coronal before [u] (*duu itto yuaserufu* "do-it-yourself", *duu-wappu* "doo-wop (music)"), which might indicate that for such speakers there is still an outermost lexical area beyond the □TSU-circle.

14 Denoted here, following standard usage, by [š, ž, č, ǰ], but realized in Japanese as "prepalatal": [ç, ʑ, etc.], in particular before front vowels (see Vance 1987 and Keating 1991).

15 If CPlace and VPlace are (partially) comprised of the same features, this statement can be simplified in various respects. Since our present goal is not the exploration of feature-geometric microstructure, we have adhered to a conservative set of features and minimal node structure (cf. McCarthy 1988, and work cited there). On the role of VPlace and feature unification issues, see Broselow and Niyondagara 1989, Clements 1991, Gnanadesikan 1993, Hume 1992, Keating 1991, Lahiri and Evers 1991, Mester and Itô 1989, Ní Chiosáin and Padgett 1993, Pulleyblank 1989, Selkirk 1993, and others.

16 The onglide [y] in a source word is treated in the same way as the vowel [i], so that SOURCE (tyu/dyu/syu] → LOAN [ču/ǰu/šu]: *čuubu* "tube", *šičuu* "stew", *čuurippu* "tulip", *ǰuusu* "deuce/juice", *šuururearisumu* "surréalisme".

17 In this form, the constraints have resulted in a kind of "palatality reversal": The source palatal [ǰ] appears as the alveolar [z] before [e], and the source alveolar [t] appears as the palatal [č] before [i].

18 In more familiar notation with traditional coefficient variables, (24) is equivalent to (i):

(i) $*\begin{bmatrix} \text{Coronal} \\ \alpha\text{anterior} \end{bmatrix} \begin{bmatrix} \text{VPlace, } -\text{back} \\ \alpha\text{high} \end{bmatrix}$

19 Unaccentedness is a hallmark of nativeness (loanwords usually receive antepenultimate accent, see McCawley 1968, 1977), and the word is written in hiragana (or kanji) and not in katakana, the usual way of rendering western loans.

20 In the same category belongs an observation about the *TI-restriction attributed by Vance (1987) to B. Bloch: The quotation marker *to-yuu*, consisting of the complementizer *to* followed by *yuu* "to say", is in casual speech often contracted to *tʸuu*, but not to the fully palatal *čuu*. Other casual speech contractions of this kind include provisional forms like *tatakeba* → *tatakʸaa* "if pro hit(s)", *hanaseba* → *hanasʸaa* "if pro talk(s)", *kateba* → *katʸaa* "if pro win(s)" (Hasegawa 1979; Martin 1975; Miyara 1980; Poser 1988; Shibatani 1990; Vance 1987).

21 The sequences *[yi] and *[wu] are ruled out for independent OCP-related reasons (McCarthy and Prince 1986; Hayes 1989). Both are universally disfavored sequences

(Maddieson and Precoda 1992). See also Komatsu (1981, pp. 21–53) for a useful discussion of the historical development of glide-initial moras.

22 This item is clearly marked as extremely peripheral since it contains the affricate [tˢ] preceding a vowel different from [u]; moreover, this alveolar sibilant remains unpalatalized in spite of the following high front vowel.

23 This is somewhat reminiscent of the on-glide analysis of the English [y] in Borowsky 1986, where the on-glide is analyzed in conjunction with the vowel [u] (building on the proposal in Chomsky and Halle 1968). In English pronunciations of Japanese place names, we find a very similar effect: The city name *Kyoto* is usually pronounced by speakers of American English with a vocalized *i* in a separate syllable [kióʊɾoʊ], but vocalization is less prone to occur for the island name *Kyushu* [kʲúːšuː], because the on-glide [y] can appear before the vowel [u] in English, but not before [o]. An interesting case is the name of the *Ryukyu* islands [riyúːkʲuː], where only the first [y] is required to vocalize (since the sequence [rʲu] is not established in English).

24 This may be in a process of flux in Japanese, since many younger speakers (who are conversant in English) incorporate the nonpalatal [si] quite often in spontaneous usage of English words in Japanese. We hypothesize that asymmetries in the influx of nonpalatalized coronals before [i] are a reflection of a general tendency of sibilants to palatalize in this environment.

25 The sequential CV-constraints that we have seen throughout this section (ᵓFU, ᵓTSU, *ČE/*TI, *YE, *SI) can be conceived of in various ways. One of the most attractive possibilities, in our view, is to think them as demisyllable constraints. A demisyllable, in the sense of Fujimura (1979, 1989), is a set of unordered feature specifications: the syllable core is divided into initial and final halves – demisyllables – each of which can contain only one specification of the place of articulation. Fujimura argues that order specification of segments is redundant within demisyllables, as minimal integral units. Whether the feature incompatibilities themselves that make up the substance of the palatality constraints can be partially or totally reduced to the Obligatory Contour Principle (a possibility explored in Itô and Mester 1991) is somewhat unclear. A slightly different line of attack would be to try to reduce the sequential CV-constraints to segmental constraints, by forcing a projection of the relevant vocalic features onto the preceding consonant. Such a feature-geometric "compression" might be carried out, for example, by positing a general principle of CV-linkage requiring all demisyllabically integrated CV-units to be vocalically linked. All of these points are in need of further investigation, a task that goes beyond the limits of this presentation (thanks to Linda Lombardi and Jaye Padgett for helpful discussion of these and other issues).

30 Current Issues in Semitic Phonology

ROBERT D. HOBERMAN

0 Introduction

A great variety of phonological properties of Semitic languages, especially Arabic and Hebrew but also Tigrinya, Amharic, and Aramaic, have been studied within modern phonological frameworks. In fact, the very first work within the generative phonological tradition (Chomsky 1951) and several works that lead up to that tradition were analyses of Semitic languages. These languages have attracted the attention of phonologists for several reasons:

- Some Semitic languages exhibit phonetic properties, especially the use of the pharynx as a main or secondary place of articulation, that are rare in the languages of the world.
- The Semitic languages are notorious for the discontinuous or non-concatenative structures that pervade their morphologies and interact in many ways with their phonologies.
- The Semitic family consists of a group of closely related languages which are fundamentally similar but nevertheless exhibit a wide variation in phonological structure; this is especially salient within the Arabic language family, where classical or standard Arabic is essentially identical to the ancestor of the many vernacular dialects, most of which are similar in their inventories of segment types and features but diverse in such properties as syllable structure.
- There is a long history of study of many of these languages, beginning with sophisticated and hotly argued debates among Arabic and Hebrew grammarians in the Middle Ages, and continuing with comprehensive grammars and dictionaries within the Western philological tradition and with excellent structuralist work including several superb structuralist grammars.[1] Consequently it has been possible to propose and test analytical hypotheses with relative ease, compared to many non-Western languages.

1   The Role of the Pharynx

The Semitic languages are famous for possessing consonants articulated in the pharyngeal and uvular region, and consonants, chiefly apicals, with a coarticulation in that region. The phonetics of this coarticulation are complex, usually described as including pharyngealization, velarization, labialization, and sometimes additional gestures. As a cover term for this varying constellation of properties the traditional term "emphatic" is useful. (Other cover terms sometimes used are "flat" and "back.") Acoustically the chief mark of emphasis is a lowering of the second formant in vowels and sonorants.[2]

Lexically, emphasis is in most cases a property of one or more consonants of a root morpheme, rather than of an affix or of a vocalic stem morpheme. Thus in Cairo Arabic [ṣaaḥib] "friend", the source of the emphasis in the first syllable is the ṣ of the root ṣḥb, rather than either the vowel morpheme ai or the prosodic template CVVCVC, as the latter two are found in the word [kaatib] "writer" with no emphasis. Phonetically, however, emphasis frequently spreads, affecting a string of adjacent segments, so that the phonetic domain of emphasis ranges from a single consonant, to one or more syllables (as in [ṣaaḥib]), to a whole word. Thus in [ṣaḥbak] "your-(masc.) friend", underlyingly ṣaaḥib + ak, the entire word is emphatic, while in [ṣaḥbik] "your-(fem.) friend" only the first syllable is affected. The chief phonological problem in the analysis of emphasis in any language is to predict the extent of the spreading.

The character of emphasis as a prosodic or "long" component in a Semitic language was first recognized by Iushmanov (1938), writing about a dialect of modern Aramaic in which emphasis most often affects an entire word. The suggestion of Charles Ferguson that emphasis in Arabic can be analyzed as a long component or prosodic feature was adopted by Harris (1942, 1944) and by Lehn (1963), who demonstrated that in Cairo Arabic emphasis is a property of syllables as a whole, and examined several alternative surface-phonemic representations, all of which are observationally adequate: (a) mark all emphatic consonants (šarrafti "you-(fem.) honored"; (b) mark all emphatic vowels (šarrafti); (c) mark all emphatic segments (šarrafti; (d) mark each emphatic syllable (.šar.rafti); he considers (c) and (d) to represent prosodic analyses. Lehn prefers representation (d) because it involves the smallest number of units with the greatest freedom of distribution and the minimum of morphophonemic alternations. Broselow (1976, pp. 32–47; 1979) was the first to write generative rules specifying the extent of spreading of emphasis in any language, and the nucleus of Broselow's analysis was translated into autosegmental terms by Van der Hulst and Smith (1982). The first extended autosegmental treatment of emphasis was by Card (1983, pp. 126–152).

In the Arabic dialects described by Broselow, Card, and Herzallah (discussed below), the spreading of emphasis in a word is strictly limited by factors which include the direction of spreading, the type of syllable, and the particular vowels and consonants involved. In some varieties of Aramaic and Arabic spoken in Kurdistan, emphasis generally spreads throughout a word.[3] Hoberman (1988) analyzes one such Aramaic dialect, proposing that the emphasis feature (represented by [+constricted pharynx] or [+CP]) in underlying forms is most often floating, i.e., unassociated with any segmental position, in which case it applies to the whole word including all affixes. In a small minority of words, such as [pešṭaṃạḷ] "towel", the feature is underlyingly linked with a particular syllable, which must contain the vowel *a*, and spreads rightward to the end of the word, including suffixes, as in [pešwạẓ-ọx] "welcoming-you". A few derivational suffixes contain prelinked emphasis: [naqškạṛ] "engraver", cf. [naqš] "engraving".[4] The facts that nonemphatic pronunciation never spreads and that no affix is immune to the spread of emphasis show that [CP] in this language must be a privative feature, not binary: the negative value [–CP] cannot appear in the underlying representation of any root, stem, or affix. The privative nature of the feature also accounts for several other properties of this language: the lack of words with three sections, plain-emphatic-plain or emphatic-plain-emphatic; the absence of any affix that remains plain in an emphatic word; the fact that emphatic words are only half as numerous in the lexicon as plain words; and that in irregular, lexically marked alternations between plain and emphatic allomorphs it is always the more basic or general (less marked) form that is plain and the derived (or more narrow, more marked) form that is emphatic: [tmanya] "eight", [ṭṃạni] "eighty"; [brata] "daughter", [bḷạnẹ] "daughters"; [idaa] "to come", imperative singular [ida], but imperative plural [ịdaṃụn].

McCarthy (1989, 1991, to appear) has presented an array of arguments demonstrating that the "guttural" consonants, i.e., the laryngeals ʔ *h*, the pharyngeals ħ ʕ, and the uvulars χ ʁ, form a natural class that functions in many processes in various Semitic languages, processes which are independent innovations in the various languages, and proposed representations for them in terms of feature geometry. He introduces the feature [pharyngeal], which characterizes not only all six gutterals but also the uvular *q* and the coronal emphatics such as ṣ ṭ, etc.[5] The following is a selection of the evidence presented by McCarthy.

(1) Well-known co-occurrence restrictions limit the consonants which may appear together in an Arabic root (Greenberg 1960); in general, two homorganic consonants do not appear together. While there are a small number of exceptions, the statistics show that the gutterals ʔ *h* ħ ʕ χ ʁ co-occur significantly less often than expected from their frequency in the language. The uvular stop *q* avoids co-occurring either with the six gutterals or with the velars,[6] but it has a closer affinity (stronger avoidance of co-occurrence) with the velars than with χ ʁ. These restrictions follow formally from the Obligatory Contour Principle (see chap. 12, this volume) in combination with a language-specific rule forbidding the feature [pharyngeal] from spreading, that is, being linked (in underlying form) with more than one root consonant.

(2) Syllable-final gutterals are avoided in Biblical (Tiberian) Hebrew and in

Beduin Arabic by the insertion of epenthetic vowels (except at the end of a stem). In the Arabic case this is known as "the *gaháwah* Syndrome" (Blanc 1970, pp. 125–127) from the word for "coffee" (from *qahwah*), a typical instance. While this applies with some morphological limitations and variably in some cases (both *áħla* and *aħála* "nicer" occur), it apparently applies equally with all the gutterals except ʔ, which does not exist in the dialect:

(1)   Plain roots   Gutteral roots
      ašrab   "I drink"   aħalam   "I dream"
                                              aʕarf   "I know"
                                              aχabar   "I know"
      yašrab   "he drinks"   yaharǰ   "he speaks"
      bnašrab   "we drink"   bnaˣazil   "we spin (thread)"

The phenomenon in Hebrew is similar, with *yaħălom* "he dreams", compared with *yiktob* "he writes".

(3)   In both Ge'ez (classical Ethiopic) and Hebrew short vowels assimilate in height (and in Hebrew in backness and roundness as well) across a gutteral. Ge'ez has two short vowels, *i* and *a*. Before a gutteral only *i* appears if the vowel after the gutteral is *i* or *ii*, and only *a* appears if the following vowel is *a*.

(2)   Sound root: yinabbir
      Gutteral roots: yaʔammin   yiliʔʔik
                         yaħanniṣ   yisiħħit
                         yaʕak'k'ib   yibiʕʕil
                         yaχabbir   yiʔiχχiz

(4)   In both Hebrew and Tigre (Raz 1983, p. 4) the gutterals ʔ h ħ ʕ never appear geminated, even in morphological environments in which other consonants are geminate. Both languages lack the velar/uvular fricatives χ and ʁ.

McCarthy's work raises but leaves unresolved several questions concerning the affinities and differences in the phonological behavior of the six gutterals, the uvular *q*, velar *k g*, and coronal emphatics such as *ṭ ṣ*, and how these differences are to be expressed in a feature-geometry framework. These questions are treated in detail by Herzallah (1990), in a work characterized by meticulous attention to acoustic and articulatory phonetics. Herzallah treated a Palestinian Arabic dialect, examining many rules involving this group of sounds and many problems of feature hierarchy and adjacency.

Herzallah, following unpublished work by George N. Clements and the proposals by McCarthy mentioned in the preceding paragraphs, adopts a framework in which a single set of features characterizes both consonants and vowels: [labial], [coronal], [dorsal], and [pharyngeal].[7] In consonants these features are dominated by the node "C-place," while the same features dominated by the node "V-place" determine both the quality of vowels and secondary articulations of consonants. The following are examples of Palestinian Arabic sounds and their underlying feature specifications (Herzallah 1990, p. 249). Derived feature specifications are in parentheses.

(3) Segments   C-place   V-place

Segments	C-place	V-place
t ṣ ḍ z ṛ	[+coronal]	[+dorsal, +pharyngeal]
k	[+dorsal]	[−dorsal]
x ġ K[8]	[dorsal, pharyngeal]	([−dorsal, −pharyngeal])
ħ ʕ	[pharyngeal, radical]	
h ʔ	[pharyngeal]	
a		[pharyngeal]

These features make it possible to express the natural classes of segments that function in the phonology of this dialect. Three such instances are summarized here:

(1)   The class of the emphatics, back velars, pharyngeals, and laryngeals, *ṭ ṣ ḍ z ṛ x ġ K ħ ʕ h ʔ*, consists of all consonants with [pharyngeal] under either the C-place or the V-place node. These trigger a rule of Feminine Vowel Assimilation, by which the feminine noun and adjective suffix −*i* is lowered to *a* ([a] or [ɑ]) by acquiring the feature [pharyngeal] from the immediately preceding consonant. Examples: [barzi] "projection", [ħilmi] "a dream", [zɑrɑɑfi] "an ostrich", [quṭni] "piece of cotton-wool", but [marġa] "loitering", [fallaaħa] "peasant woman", [zarriiʕa] "plants", [šaṭħɑ] "picnic", [baḍʕa] "type of goods", [burḥc̣] "period of time".

(2)   The class including the emphatic coronals *ṭ ṣ ḍ z ṛ* and the back velars *x ġ K* is specified as having the features [dorsal, pharyngeal] dominated by either the C-place or the V-place node. The segments of this class trigger the change from *i* to *u* in the Imperfective of Form I verbs; [yunṣub] "he sets up", [yubluġ] "he reaches", but [yiktib] "he writes".

(3)   The class of back-velar continuants, pharyngeals, and laryngeals (McCarthy's six gutterals: *x ġ ħ ʕ h ʔ*) is characterized by the feature [pharyngeal] dominated by C-place, with the additional stipulation of [approximant] to exclude *K*. This class triggers the rule of Imperfective Pharyngealization, which applies in the same morphological situation as the preceding rule, Form I Imperfectives, and those verbs to which both rules could apply must be lexically marked to take one or the other. Imperfective Pharyngealization lowers the vowel *i* to [a] or [ɑ]: [yiftaħ] "he opens", [yimraġ] "he stains", [yisʔal] "he asks".

2   Templatic Morphology

In a word containing a Semitic-style discontinuous consonantal root such as Arabic *kaatib*- "writer", the root consonants behave in some respects as though they were adjacent, despite the intervening vowels, as if they formed an abstract entity separate from the vowels. For instance, the consonantal root may be shared with other words with related meanings, and so constitute a morpheme; there are also restrictions on the segments that may co-occur in a root, restrictions that do not apply to affixal segments. Early attempts to formalize this bivalent structure took the shape of a transformational rule of interdigitation (for instance Chomsky 1951, p. 28, rule MR3, discussed in McCarthy 1981, pp. 414–416), basically of the form $C_1C_2C_3 + V_1V_2 \rightarrow C_1V_1C_2V_2C_3$. McCarthy (1979, 1981) introduced an autosegmental approach to such structures by proposing what later came to be called the Morpheme Tier Hypothesis: the segments of a morpheme lie on its own autosegmental tier, separate from the segments of other morphemes. Chomsky's interdigitation rule was replaced by the conventions of autosegmental association, which had been developed in the analysis of phonological, not morphological, processes.

The most extensive and penetrating analysis of a Semitic language in terms of templatic morphology is Heath's (1987) analysis of Moroccan Arabic. He finds that morphological processes may work through three general kinds of mechanisms (Heath 1987, p. 3):

1   The "*local-rules model*: the output is based on the input shape with one or two specific phonological operations applied to it (geminating a C, infixing a V, or the like). This model would be most attractive for ablauts in which a wide variety of input shapes is associated with a similarly wide variety of output shapes." Heath concludes that this is not a suitable model for the ablaut (internal stem changes) he is examining, though of course it is the mechanism of ordinary linear affixation.

2   The "*fixed-template model*: the input is mapped onto an output such as /CCaCC-i/ . . . consisting (in MCA [Moroccan Colloquial Arabic]) of unfilled C positions and already specified Vs . . . This model is appropriate for ablauts whose output shape is invariant although inputs of various shapes feed into it . . ."

3   The "*template-plus-projection model*: the output consists of a fixed template such as /CCiC/ at the beginning or end, plus a *projection* of variable canonical shape and length that carries over those input segments that are not involved in the mapping of the input onto the partial fixed template."

An example of the template-plus-projection model is the process of forming broken plurals, that is, noun and adjective plurals formed by changing the syllabic makeup and vocalism of the stem (Heath 1987, pp. 100–113). The output of the pluralization process is represented as a fixed template containing a projection variable:

(4)   Moroccan Arabic Nominal Plural Ablaut (Heath 1987, p. 108)
      Output Representation
      "/CCVCX*/, where V is /a/ when X* is nonnull, and is otherwise a
      lexical choice among /a u/ (rarely /i/), with /u/ as the default choice."

The process also involves several rules, specific to ablaut (broken) plurals, which determine vowel selection and manner of association.

This general approach to nonconcatenative morphology has been recast in terms of prosodic units (mora, syllable, and foot) by McCarthy and Prince (1990a, 1990b) and broadened to accommodate the analysis of many more kinds of morphological processes, especially reduplication. McCarthy and Prince's solution to the broken plural problem is essentially the same as Heath's except for their prosodic formulation.[9]

Bat-El 1989 proposes that much of the work which in other analyses has been performed by templatic morphology can be accomplished, at least for modern Hebrew (and to a more limited extent in Arabic) by rules of syllabification. Taking as input linear representations annotated to indicate consonant clustering potential, the syllabification rules accomplish the interdigitation of roots and patterns, after which the separate identity of morphemes is not required. Derivation of new words is based not on preidentified roots but on sequences of consonants extracted from existing words.

3   Association Conventions

One problem of Semitic morphology for which many solutions have been proposed has nonetheless still not gone away. Arabic verbs of Conjugation II (and similar conjugations in most Semitic languages) always have geminate middle consonants, as in *kattab-a* "he made (someone) write". Arabic roots and prosodic stem templates are regularly aligned by autosegmental association from left to right, and this direction of association and consequent spreading accounts for the large number of stems from biconsonantal roots in which the second consonant of the root morpheme appears twice, as in *radd-a* "he returned", *radad-tu* "I returned" and for other facts of Arabic morphology (McCarthy 1979, 1981). No stems appear with duplication of a root segment in the other direction: **rarad-tu*. Furthermore, just such left-to-right spreading takes place in Conjugation IX forms of triconsonantal verbs, such as *ḥmarar-tu* "I turned red". Several approaches are conceivable for distinguishing the association pattern of Conjugation II (*kattab-tu* from that of Conjugation IX (*ḥmarar-tu*). Nearly all the proposals take for granted that Conjugation II and similar structures involve some sort of ad hoc rule, lexical or grammatical marking; the main options for this approach are to incorporate the ad hoc marking into the stem template through some elaboration of the formalism (Heath 1987, pp. 69–71; Goldsmith 1990, pp. 93–98; Farwaneh 1990), or to specify these forms as undergoing a rule which repairs an inappropriate initial pattern of association (McCarthy and Prince 1990, pp. 44–48). Contrary to all these approaches it has been argued that it is Conjugation IX and similar patterns that are the exceptional cases while the far more productive type represented by Conjugation II is the normal pattern in a variety of morphological categories in several Semitic languages (Hoberman 1988). These facts fall out automatically if the fundamental principle of association is not left-to-right but edge-in (Yip 1988). In Heath's treatment of Moroccan Arabic morphology several derivational processes involve edge-in association, while other derivational processes require left-to-right or right-to-left association; the direction of association must be specified for each process.

4   Other Topics

Several other areas in the phonologies of Semitic languages have received significant attention from theoreticians in recent years, and it is impossible to do more here than to mention the most salient of recent publications.

A great deal of work has been done on the interrelated problems of syllable structure, epenthesis, and stress in various Arabic dialects and in Biblical Hebrew. On Arabic see Angoujard (1990) and Broselow (1992). Rappaport (1984) is a treatment of Biblical Hebrew stress and vowel length and reduction in terms of metrical trees and the grid.

NOTES

1   The indigenous Arabic grammatical tradition has become much more accessible in recent years. See, for example, Owens (1988).

2   Languages of the Ethiopian Semitic group have ejective stops and fricatives in place of the pharyngealization, etc., of the other Semitic languages. Thus the first consonant of Tigre s'alót "prayer" (Raz 1983, p. 10) is ejective, while the cognate consonant in Arabic ṣalaː(t) is pharyngealized. Both are traditionally called "emphatic" and indicated with an inferior dot. In contrast to the traditional usage, I

restrict both the term emphatic and the dot to the Arabic type, pharyngealization.

3   Heath (1987, pp. 295–326) describes a variety of Arabic in which the distribution of emphasis remains predominantly a matter of underlying emphatic consonants with spreading, but the system is in the process of moving toward one of emphasis harmony affecting whole words.

4   This example illustrates the fact the there is no necessary co-occurrence between uvular articulation and emphatic coarticulation: *q* can occur in plain environments and *k* can

occur in emphatic ones, where it can have an allophone [ḳ]. This fact has yet to be incorporated into a system of phonological feature (see work by McCarthy and Herzallah discussed below).

5   Thus the set of segments characterized by the feature [pharyngeal] includes much more than the pharyngeals of traditional phonetic terminology. McCarthy stresses that this feature refers not to the active articulator (which may be the vocal cords or the dorsum of the tongue) but to the general region of the articulation, which is the oropharynx as a whole.

6   Arabic *ǰ* behaves as a velar in this respect as well as in other ways.

7   Herzallah's analysis (following Clements's unpublished work) requires that some features be equipollent (or bivalent) rather than privative.

8   These sounds, corresponding to χ ʁ *q* in other varieties of Arabic, are back velar but not uvular in Herzallah's dialect. Consequently the low vowel in their vicinity is [a], not [ɑ] – in this dialect it is only the emphatic coronals that condition the back allophone [ɑ]. In this dialect, too, *k* is front velar and slightly palatalized, varying for some speakers with [č]. Not only do the back velars *x ġ K* not constitute a source for the spread of emphasis, as their cognates χ ʁ *q* do in some other dialects, but they even trigger de-emphaticization of underlying emphatics: the emphatic sounds [ṣ ð̣ r̩] do not appear to the left of a back velar in the word, so the dialect has [sabaġ] "he dyed", [ð̣aaK] "it became narrow", cf. Classical Arabic ṣabaʁa, ð̣aaqa. There is no such restriction on [ṭ].

9   McCarthy and Prince appear to have discovered the solution independently of Heath.

31 Representations and the Organization of Rules in Slavic Phonology

JERZY RUBACH

0 Introduction

The rich and complex phonologies of the Slavic languages are of particular interest for studies that deal with the structure of phonological representations and the organization of phonological rules. In this chapter, we shall pursue both of these issues, showing that representations must be nonlinear and that distinctions must be drawn between segmental melodies, skeletal slots, and syllabic structures all of which function independently of each other. With regard to the organization of rules, it is necessary to distinguish between cyclic, post-cyclic, and post-lexical rules, in a fashion predicted by the theory of lexical phonology.

In the first part of this chapter we look at several rules of Slovak and discuss the problem of how phonological structure should be represented. Marginally, we look at an example of a cyclic rule that applies in derived environments. The second part of this chapter is a study of consonant palatalization and vowel retraction rules in Polish and Russian. These two languages have virtually the same rules, yet their surface effects are different. This problem, as well as certain language-internal ordering conflicts, can be resolved in an illuminating way by drawing a distinction between post-cyclic and post-lexical rules.

1 Representations

In this section we look at some length alternations in Slovak, a language that contrasts long and short syllable nuclei both at the underlying and at the phonetic level:[1]

(1) (a) krik   "shout"   krík   "bush"
     (b) kur+a   "chicken"   kúr+a   "cure"
     (c) rad   "row"   grád   "degree"

where the accent indicates a long vowel.

Length is affected by several lengthening and shortening rules. It should be noted that Slovak rising diphthongs [ie ia uo] behave in exactly the same way as long vowels. This reflects the fact that, historically, Slovak diphthongs come from long vowels. If we now show that the parallel behavior of long vowels and diphthongs can be captured only by appealing to the skeletal and the syllabic tiers and ignoring the distinctions made at the melodic tier, then we have an argument that representations must be multitiered rather than linear as traditionally construed in the classic generative phonology of *The Sound Pattern of English* (Chomsky and Halle 1968, hereafter *SPE*) type. We begin our presentation by introducing two lengthening rules.

Consider the following alternations of short and long vowels in the class of neuter nouns:

(2) | Nom.sg. | Gen.pl. | Gloss |
|---|---|---|
| piv+o | pív | "beer" |
| put+o | pút | "chain" |
| lan+o | lán | "cable" |

Vowels lengthen in the genitive plural.[2] Schematically:

(3) Vowel Lengthening $\acute{V} \rightarrow$ [+long] / _____ C]$_{\text{gen. pl.}}$

A similar lengthening is found in several other contexts, for example, before the diminutive suffix -*ik*:

(4) znak   "sign"   znáč + ik   "sign" (dim.)
     puk   "bud"   púč + ik   "bud" (dim.)

The mid vowels /e o/ and the front low vowel /ä/ (phonetically [æ]), diphthongize in the lengthening contexts. Note: ô is the orthographic represenation of the diphthong [uo].

(5) (a) čel+o   "forehead"   čiel (gen. pl.)
        kol+o   "wheel"   kôl (gen. pl.)
        mäs+o   "meat"   mias (gen. pl.)
     (b) človek   "man"   človieč+ik (dim.)
        krok   "step"   krôč+ik (dim.)

The occurrence of the diphthongs is commonly explained by assuming that vowels first lengthen by general rules and subsequently diphthongize by a rule that is schematically stated as follows (Kenstowicz 1972; Kenstowicz and Kisseberth 1979):

(6)   Diphthongization é ó ä́   →   ie uo ia

The most important sources of motivation for Diphthongization come, on the one hand, from the fact that several independent lengthening rules (but not all) yield diphthongs from the lengthened /e o ä/ and, on the other hand, from the fact that lengthening may sometimes be undone by subsequent shortening rules (see Rubach 1993). The latter is simple if the shortening rule applies at the stage prior to Diphthongization. On a more general level, Diphthongization helps establish the parallel between long vowels and diphthongs. That such a parallel is essential is shown, for example, by the operation of the Rhythmic Law.

Standard Slovak exhibits a widespread regularity with regard to the distribution of short and long vowels. In (7) we adduce some examples from both inflectional and derivational morphology:

(7)   (a)   Neuter nouns

Nom. sg.	Nom. pl.	Dat. pl.	Loc. pl.	Gloss
lan+o	lan+á	lan+ám	lan+ách	"cable"
stád+o	stá+da	stád+am	stád+ach	"herd"
čísl+o	čísl+a	čísl+am	čísl+ach	"number"

(b)   Masculine adjectives

Nom. sg.	Gen. sg.	Dat. sg.	Gloss
mal+ý	mal+ého	mal+ému	"small"
múdr+y	múdr+eho	múdr+emu	"wise"
čír+y	čír+eho	čír+emu	"clear"

(c)   Agentive -*nik*:

hut+a	hut+ník	"steel works"
montáž	montáž+nik	"assembling"
čalún	čalún+nik	"wallpaper"

Thus, vowels shorten after long vowels:

(8)   Rhythmic Law $\acute{V} \rightarrow [-\text{long}] / \begin{bmatrix} V \\ +\text{long} \end{bmatrix} C_0 \underline{\quad}$

The situation becomes more complex when we realize that not only long vowels but also diphthongs trigger the Rhythmic Law. The examples in (9) parallel those in (7):

(9)   (a)

miest+o	miest+a	miest+am	miest+ach	"place"
hniezd+o	hniezd+a	hniezd+am	hniezd+ach	"nest"

(b)	čiern+y	čiern+eho	čiern+emu	"black"
	priam+y	priam+eho	priam+emu	"direct"
(c)	papier	papier+nik		"paper"
	požiar	požiar+nik		"fire"

Furthermore, diphthongs, exactly like long vowels, can undergo the Rhythmic Law whereby they change into short vowels. Thus, the present tense morpheme *ie* of, for instance, *strež+ie+m* "I guard" becomes *e* in *môž+e+m* [muož+e+m] "I can". Given these facts, the statement of the Rhythmic Law seems to call for very complex disjunctions, because both the input and the environment would have to be specified to include either a long vowel or a diphthong. Worse, such complex disjunctions would have to be repeated in every shortening rule, and these abound in Slovak. For example, in addition to the Rhythmic Law there is a rule that shortens vowels and diphthongs before the suffix *-ák*:

(10)	(a)	múdr+y	"wise"	mudr+ák	"sage"
	(b)	biel+y	"white"	bel+ák	"white hare"

Classic generative phonology solves the problem of how to express the parallel between diphthongs and long vowels by assuming that diphthongs do not exist at the underlying level (cf. Kenstowicz and Kisseberth 1979). Rather, they are represented by respective long vowels /é ó ǻ/. Diphthongization (6), which exists in the grammar of Slovak anyway, derives surface diphthongs in all instances wherever /é ó ǻ/ have not been shortened by one of the shortening rules. In view of this, then, the parallel behavior of long vowels and diphthongs is understandable. The derivation of our earlier examples *stád+a* "herds", *miest+a* "places" as well as *strež+ie+m* "I guard" and *môž+e+m* "I can" is now as follows. Recall that the nominative plural ending is a long *-á*:

(11)	stád+á	mést+á	strež+é+m	móž+é+m	
	stád+a	mést+a		móž+e+m	Rhythmic Law
		miest+a	strež+ie+m	muož+e+m	Diphthongization

This analysis recapitulates synchronically what has taken place historically. Diphthongization is a late rule that applies in an unrestricted manner irrespective of the source of the long vowel, whether it is derived by a lengthening rule such as (3) or whether it is underlying as in (11).

Serious problems with this *SPE* interpretation begin to appear when we look at the etymologically foreign vocabulary of Slovak. It contains literally hundreds of items with morpheme-internal long mid vowels that systematically fail to diphthongize:

(12)	režisér	"director"	šofér	"driver"	krém	"cream"	afér+a	"affair"
	mód+a	"fashion"	póz+a	"pose"	vagón	"carriage"	gól	"goal"

In the days of classic generative phonology, etymologically foreign words were left out of the analysis since it was believed that they would form a system of their own. While this assumption might be true of a certain subset of foreign vocabulary in a language, it clearly need not generalize to all etymologically foreign words. The Slovak data are a good illustration of this thesis.

On the one hand, the words in (12) are composed entirely of segments that appear in the native part of the Slovak vocabulary, and their canonical structure does not diverge from that of the native roots. Even the fact that a mid vowel remains undiphthongized does not automatically assign the words in (12) to a class of "borrowings," since some etymologically native words also surface with a long mid vowel, for example, *dcér+a* "daughter", and *-ého*, the genitive singular ending of masculine adjectives. In the *SPE* theory these would be treated as exceptions to Diphthongization. On the other hand, all other tests, both morphological and phonological, indicate that words such as those in (12) have been fully integrated into the grammatical system of Slovak.

Morphological integration is seen in the fact that these words are indistinguishable from the etymologically native words in terms of both inflectional and derivational morphology. Compare the etymologically foreign *režisér* "director" with the native *pisár* "writer":

(13)

Nom. sg.	Gen. sg.	Dat. sg.	Adj. form	Abstr. nom.	Fem. formation
režisér	režisér+a	režisér+ovi	režisér+sk+y	režisér+stv+o	režisér+k+a
pisár	pisár+a	pisár+ovi	pisár+sk+y	pisár+stv+o	pisár+k+a

Similarly, phonological tests indicate that the behavior of etymologically foreign words is identical to that of etymologically native words. For example, they trigger the Rhythmic Law. In (14a) we compare the foreign *mód+a* "fashion" with the native *lúk+a* "meadow" for their triggering effects. We adduce also the native *skaz+a* "flaw" with a short root vowel in order to show that the endings have underlying long vowels. In (15b) the native *dvor+sk+ý* "courtly" shows the underlying representation of the endings. The native *stál+y* "constant" and the foreign *šofér+sk+y* "driver" (adj.) both induce the Rhythmic Law.

(14)   (a)   Dat. pl.   Loc. pl.

         skaz+ám   skaz-ách

         lúk+am   lúk+ach

         mód+am   mód+ach

     (b)   Nom. sg.   Gen. sg.   Dat. sg.

         dvor+sk+ý   dvor+sk+ého   dvor+sk+ému

         stál+y   stál+eho   stál+emu

         šofér+sk+y   šofér+sk+eho   šofér+sk+emu

Etymologically foreign words also undergo shortening rules. Thus, for instance, there is a rule which shortens the stem vowel when an agentive suffix *-ár* is appended, as in the native *slovník* "dictionary" – *slovnik+ár*. The same rule affects the foreign *scén+a* "scene" → *scen+ár* and *betón* "concrete" → *beton+ár*.

In sum, etymologically foreign words both trigger and undergo the shortening rules. Even more striking is the fact that they undergo lengthening rules as well and if the vowel is mid, then it is also diphthongized:

(15)   Nom. sg.   Gen. pl.   gloss
   (a) fabrik+a   fabrík   "factory"
         pyžam+a   pyžám   "pyjamas"
   (b) oper+a   opier   "opera"
         bomb+a   bômb [buomp]   "bomb"

We conclude that on all counts etymologically foreign words are fully integrated into the system of Slovak, and hence constitute legitimate evidence on which to evaluate competing phonological solutions. But this creates a problem. How are we going to account for the parallel behavior of long vowels and diphthongs? Notice that the *SPE* solution – that in all instances diphthongs derive from underlying long vowels – is not open to us any more.

If morpheme-internal diphthongs in words such as *miest+o* "place" and *biel+y* "white" were to be derived from underlying /mést+o/ and /bél+í/, then they would be indistinguishable from words such as *režisér* "director" and *afér+a* "affair". That is, we would not be able to predict where Diphthongization should and where it should not apply. Consequently, we must assume that diphthongs are actually underlying in today's Slovak. Thus, *miest+o* is /miest+o/[3] while *režisér* is /režisér/ as indeed found in the surface representations. In other words, we must admit that in historical terms a restructuring of underlying representations has taken place: morpheme-internal diphthongs are now part of the underlying structure. However, given this conclusion, the parallel between long vowels and diphthongs achieved by the *SPE* analysis disappears. A new solution is available, but only in a nonlinear theory of phonological representations.

It has been recognized for some years now that phonological representations should be construed as three-dimensional (cf. chapters 1, 5, 6, 7 this volume). In addition to the melodic tier, two other tiers have been introduced: the skeletal tier and the syllabic tier. These tiers are independent of each other in the sense that there is no requirement of a one-to-one correspondence between them. Thus, for instance, a long vowel is a single melody unit but it occupies two slots in the skeleton. The opposite is also true. The so-called contour and complex segments occupy one skeletal slot but correspond to two articulatory gestures at the melodic tier (cf. chapter 7 this volume). Skeletal slots reflect the facts of phonological length and segmentation. In this theory long vowels and diphthongs have a common property: the presence of two skeletal slots. Thus, *miest+o* "place" and *krém* "cream" are represented as follows:[4]

(16)

Within the view that long vowels and diphthongs can be related at the skeleton, we would expect that differences found at the melodic tier should be irrelevant. That this is a correct expectation is shown convincingly by the behavior of long liquids.

In addition to short and long vowels as well as diphthongs, Slovak has also short and long syllabic liquids:

(17)   prst   "finger"
       vŕb+a   "willow"
       vlk   "wolf"
       tĺk   "pestle"

Relevant at this point is the observation that long liquids parallel long vowels and diphthongs in that they trigger the shortening rules. Thus, the long vowel of the dative plural ending exemplified in (14a) shortens in *vŕb+am* "willow". With this observation it is clear that reducing diphthongs to underlying long vowels cannot solve all the problems anyway since long liquids would not be included in such a statement. What then is the relevant property for triggering the shortening rules? A partial answer to this query has already been given: the presence of two slots at the skeletal tier. This includes long liquids because they have a representation that parallels long vowels: a single melodic segment linked to two X-slots. However, our analysis is not yet complete. Words such as *ú+mr+t+n+ý* "dead" with a syllabic *r* show that the Rhythmic Law counts syllable nuclei. In this instance the final *+ý* is not shortened because it is preceded by a short syllable nucleus – that of the *r*. Consequently, the presence of the long *ú+* in the prefix has no effect on the ending *+ý*.

To summarize, shortening rules apply if two conditions are fulfilled: there are two skeletal slots and the segments are syllabic. Unfortunately, even these restrictions are not sufficient. The evidence comes, on the one hand, from vowel sequences and, on the other hand, from combinations of glides and vowels.[5]

Slovak contrasts diphthongs and vowel sequences, both phonetically and phonologically. In the following examples, the former are perceived as one and the latter as two syllables (we separate them by a dot).

(18)   Diphthong   Vowel sequence
       rias+a "cassock"   mili.ard+a "milliard"
       riek+a "river"   paci.ent "patient"

The phonetic distinction between diphthongs and vowel sequences is corroborated by phonological behavior. The former do, while the latter do not, trigger the Rhythmic Law:

(19) Dat. pl.   Loc. pl.
      rias+am   rias+ach
      mili.ard+ám   mili.ard+ách

We conclude that shortening rules require that both of the skeletal slots be contained in one syllable. Under such a formulation, vowel sequences are correctly excluded. However, even this restrictive environment turns out to be too permissive, as shown by the different effects of the Rhythmic Law in (20):

(20) Nom. sg.   Dat. pl.   Loc. pl.   Gloss
      miest+o   miest+am   miest+ach   "place"
      jedl+o   jedl+am   jedl+ach   "meal"

In both instances the relevant segmental structure is the same: a gliding element followed by *e*. In both instances the two segments belong to a single syllable; yet, it is only in the case of *miest+o* that the Rhythmic Law applies. How is therefore *miest+o* different from *jedl+o*? In *miest+o* the onglide is a constituent of the syllable nucleus while in *jedl+o* it is a syllable onset.[6] (At the melodic tier they are identical.) This shows conclusively that shortening rules are sensitive to the structure of the nucleus.

To summarize briefly, it is essential to distinguish between the melody and the skeleton, since only then do we have a level of representation which is common to long vowels, diphthongs, and long liquids. Furthermore, the syllabic tier must also be recognized in order to identify correctly the type of nucleus that triggers shortening rules. We thus have an argument that represenations must be three-dimensional. With these representations we can correctly distinguish between a short vowel in (21a), a long vowel in (21b), a diphthong in (21c), a vowel sequence in (21d) and a glide-vowel combination in (21e):

(21)

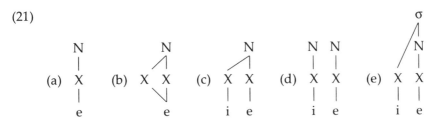

We assume that Slovak nuclei are right-headed, which is motivated by the fact that Slovak has rising rather than falling diphthongs.

Against this background we can now return to the statement of the lengthening and shortening rules. The former add while the latter delete a nuclear slot:

(22)

$$\text{Vowel Lengthening} \qquad X \rightarrow X\ X / \underline{\quad\quad} C]_{\text{gen.pl.}}$$

(23)

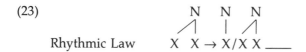

Rhythmic Law $X \ X \rightarrow X / X \ X \underline{\quad}$

Thus, quantitative operations are manipulations at the skeletal tier. Melodic representations play no role there, precisely as desired.

We now return to Diphthongization in order to determine its status in the grammar of Slovak. We demonstrated earlier that the difference between long vowels and diphthongs is contrastive and thus it is not possible to assume that all diphthongs derive from long vowels, as they did historically. However, it is still true that, as shown by the examples in (5) and (15b), most lengthening rules lead to the rise of diphthongs from lengthened /e o ä/. Thus, Diphthongization exists as a rule, but its application has been restricted to derived environments. Such rules are not at all uncommon. In the framework of lexical phonology they are regarded as cyclic and the Strict Cyclicity Constraint limits their application to derived environments. Since we know that Diphthongization used to apply to underlying long vowels, that is, in non-derived environments, the historical development lies in the fact that the rule has changed its status from noncyclic to cyclic.

We conclude this section by looking at two sample derivations. Our examples are the dative plural *afér+am* "affair" and the genitive plural *čiel* "forehead". The latter comes from *čel+o*, that is, it has a short vowel in the underlying representation.

(24)

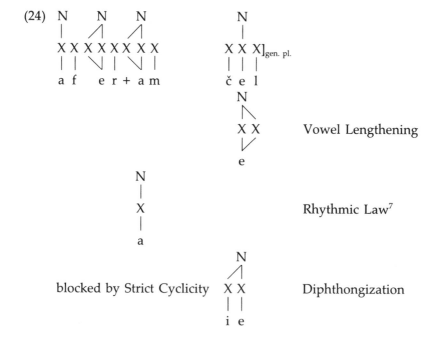

The reason that Diphthongization applies to *čiel* but not to *afér+a* is that only in the former has a feeding change with regard to Diphthongization been made in the course of the derivation: a second X slot was added by Vowel Lengthening.

2   Post-cyclic and Post-lexical Rules

In the preceding section, we considered the case of a cyclic rule. In this section, we show that it is essential to recognize a class of post-cyclic lexical rules as well (Booij and Rubach 1987). These rules are distinct from both cyclic lexical rules and post-lexical rules. They differ from cyclic lexical rules in that, first, they do not apply cyclically and, second, they are not subject to the Strict Cyclicity Constraint. The effect of these properties is that post-cyclic rules apply across the board in both derived and underived environments. A common characteristic of cyclic and post-cyclic rules is their confinement to the lexicon. Since words but not sentences are available in the lexicon, it is natural that these rules take the word as their maximal domain. In contrast, post-lexical rules exist outside the lexicon and apply to all strings, including those derived by the syntax. That is, they apply in an unconstrained fashion both inside words and across word boundaries. A further property shared by cyclic and post-cyclic lexical rules (though not by post-lexical rules) is their ability to refer to lexical information such as exceptionality features (cf. Mohanan 1982, 1986). That is, post-lexical rules cannot have exceptions.[8]

Against this background we turn now to an analysis of two rules of Polish and Russian. We show how the distinction between post-cyclic and post-lexical rules helps solve ordering conflicts in the grammar of each of these languages as well as illuminate a way in which related languages may differ. We begin with two sets of rather puzzling examples which have been selected from the class of words that are virtually identical in Polish and Russian.[9]

(25)

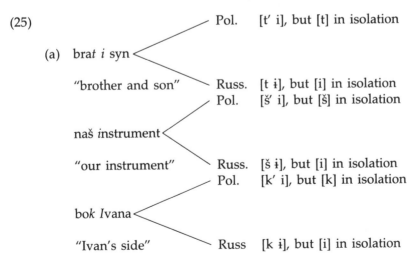

	Pol.	[t′ i], but [t] in isolation
(a) bra*t i* syn		
"brother and son"	Russ.	[t ɨ], but [i] in isolation
	Pol.	[š′ i], but [š] in isolation
na*š i*nstrument		
"our instrument"	Russ.	[š ɨ], but [i] in isolation
	Pol.	[k′ i], but [k] in isolation
bo*k I*vana		
"Ivan's side"	Russ	[k ɨ], but [i] in isolation

(b) Polish   Russian   Gloss
     ins*ty*tut [t ɨ]   ins*ti*tut [t'i]   "institute"
     *dy*rektor [d ɨ]   *di*rektor [d'i]   "director"
     eksper*y*ment [r ɨ]   eksper*i*ment [r'i] "experiment"

The data in (25a) show that Polish has a palatalization while Russian a vowel retraction rule. Schematically:

(26) (a) Surface Palatalization C → C' / ____ i
      (b) Retraction i → ɨ / nonpalatalized C ____

However, (25b) indicates that the reverse is true as well: Polish also has Retraction while Russian also has Surface Palatalization. The words in (25b) are latinate borrowings in both languages. Regardless of whether they came directly from Latin or, which is more likely, via some Western European language, one fact is clear: the source language did not have palatalized consonants or a back vowel [ɨ] since such segments simply do not exist in any of the likely source languages. Thus, palatalization and retraction are Slavic innovations. This claim is supported by the fact that a sequence of a nonpalatalized consonant followed by an [i] is phonetically impossible in both Polish and Russian. That is, either the C is palatalized or the /i/ is retracted to [ɨ]:

(27)
                ⟋ C' i by Surface Palatalization
        C i ⟨
                ⟍ C ɨ by Retraction

Since both of these options are exploited in both languages, a question arises as to which option is selected under which circumstances. Notice that Surface Palatalization and Retraction are mutually bleeding: if one applies the other one cannot apply. Before we attempt to solve this dilemma, we need to look at the details regarding the statement and the application of these rules in each language.

   Polish Surface Palatalization is exceptionless and it applies before *i* and *j*, both inside words and across word boundaries:

(28) (a) [š'] Chicago, dasz im "you will give them", dasz jej "you will give her"
           [t'] Tirana, brat idzie "my brother is going", brat je "my brother is eating"
           [r'] Riwiera "Riviere", dar inwencji "gift of invention", dar Janka "Janek's gift"
      (b) [p'] pisk "scream", kup inny "buy another', kup jogurt "buy yogurt"
           [m'] miska "bowl", prom indianski "Indian ferry", prom jedzie "the ferry is coming"

    [k'] kino "cinema", brak informacji "lack of information", brak
           jasności "lack of clarity"
    [x'] Chiny "China", zamach iracki "Iraqi coup", zamach jordanski
           "Jordanian coup" etc.

The rule is a straightforward spreading assimilation: the vowel node VOC is spread onto the place node of the preceding consonant:

(29) Surface Palatalization (Polish)

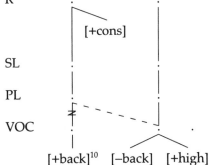

Note: R stands for root, SL for the supralaryngeal node, PL for place, and VOC for the vocalic node. In the representation of the feature hierarchy I follow Clements (1985a, 1991a).

    Unlike Surface Palatalization, Retraction is restricted to coronal consonants, that is, it never applies after labials and velars. Retraction accounts for the [i]–[ɨ] alternations that occur throughout the whole phonological system of Polish. Below we look at the verbalizing suffix *i/ɨ*. (Note: [ɨ] is spelled *y*; [ć], a prepalatal affricate, is the infinitive suffix).

(30) (a) dym   "smoke"

(30)	(a)	dym		"smoke"
		dym+i+ć		"to smoke"
		garb		"hunch"
		garb+i+ć		"to be hunch-backed"
	(b)	towarzysz		"companion"
		towarzysz+y+ć	[tovažiš+i+ć]	"accompany"
		tłumacz		"interpreter"
		tłumacz+y+ć	[twumač+i+ć]	"interpret"
	(c)	grzech		"sin"
		grzesz+y+ć	[gžeš+i+ć]	"to sin"
		tłok		"crowd"
		tłocz+y+ć	[twoč+i+ć]	"to crowd"

While the data in (30a-b) might seem ambiguous, as it is not immediately clear whether the [i] or the [ɨ] should be underlying, the data in (30c) leave little doubt that the underlying segment is /i/. This follows from the fact that the verbs show reflexes of the so-called First Velar Palatalization, a rule that is found in all Slavic languages.[11] Schematically:

(31) First Velar Palatalization k g x → č ǰ š / _____ front vowels

This rule changes velars into postalveolars, and these stops become affricates (see Rubach 1984). In fact, First Velar Palatalization spreads *coronal* rather than [−back] and hence its outputs are hard (that is, nonpalatalized) consonants. This brings up a more general problem of the phonetic contrast between hard and soft consonants.

In Polish and Russian (as well as in Byelorussian, Ukrainian, and Lusatian) there are no consonants neutral with respect to the feature [back]. Phonetically, a consonant is always either [+back] (hard), or [−back] (soft). Since some consonants need to be specified as [−back] underlyingly, it is [+back] that is assigned by default. In effect, at the stage at which Retraction applies, all consonants that are not palatalized underlyingly or have not been palatalized by an earlier rule[12] are marked as [+back]. Now Retraction can be stated as a straightforward spreading rule which applies in the environment of hard coronals:

(32) Retraction (Polish)

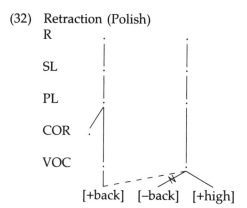

A striking fact about Russian is that the statement of the rules is, in all essential matters, the same as in Polish. There are two minor differences. First, Surface Palatalization applies not only before *i* (and *j*) but also before *e*.[13] Second, Retraction is more general as it applies not only after coronals but after all consonants including labials and velars. (Most of the examples below are from Lightner 1972.)

(33) (a) Surface Palatalization (Russian)

[b']	bomb+a	"bomb"	bomb'+e	(dat. sg.)	bomb'+i+t'	"to bomb"
[n']	žen+a	"wife"	žen'+e	(dat. sg.)	žen'+in	"wife's"
[r']	sestr+a	"sister"	sestr'+e	(dat. sg.)	sestr'+in	"sister's"

| | [g'] | nog+a | "leg" | nog'+e | (dat. sg.) | nog'+i | (nom. pl.) |
| | [x'] | mux+a | "fly" | mux'+e | (dat. sg.) | mux'+i | (nom. pl.) |

(b) Retraction

    (i) šum "noise" šum+i+t'   "make noise"

         grex "sin" greš+i+t' [š+i] "to sin"

         drug "friend" druž+i+t' [ž+i] "to be friends with"

    (ii) xleb iz peci [pi] "bread from the oven"

         dar iskustva [ri] "a gift of art"

         les i voda [si] "forest and water"

The data in (33bi) parallel those given for Polish in (30): the verbalizing suffix /i/ is realized as [i] after hard consonants.[14] That the consonant must be hard and not underlyingly palatalized is shown by examples in (33bii). If the consonant is underlyingly palatalized as in *gost'* "guest", then the following *i* does not undergo Retraction: *gost' iz Polši* [is] "guest from Poland". Needless to say, *iz* is pronounced [is] in isolation, hence all the instances of [is] must be due to Retraction.

One further comment is in order. In Russian, unlike in Polish, Surface Palatalization has exceptions. For example, borrowed words such as *teza* "thesis" *šose* "freeway", and *kafe* "cafe" do not show any trace of Surface Palatalization, but many others appear with palatalized consonants, for example, *t'ekst* "text", *t'echn'ika* "technology", etc. (Avanesov 1968). Needless to say, some words show variation. This class includes even names such as *Voltaire*: [t]~[t'] (Halle 1959, p. 73). That is, exceptions to Surface Palatalization tend to be suppressed. With regard to Retraction the situation is different; the Russian rule is entirely exceptionless while the Polish one is not (see below).

We are now in a position to consider some theoretical implications of Surface Palatalization and Retraction and to determine how Polish differs from Russian. Recall that the two rules mutually bleed each other. In the early version of lexical phonology which distinguished only between lexical and post-lexical rules, where lexical meant cyclic, this would create a serious difficulty. One thing is clear, neither of the rules in any of the languages can be cyclic. We have conclusive evidence from the assimilation of borrowings that both rules may apply morpheme-internally, thus in nonderived environments. In the early version of lexical phonology (Kiparsky 1982c), the rules would therefore have to be post-lexical. But this leads to a paradox: whichever order we assume, the output is incorrect. In (34) we investigate both logically possible orderings. We look at the Polish examples given earlier in (30b) and (28a): *towarzysz+i+ć* [tovažiš+i+ć] from underlying /tovažiš+i+ć/[15] "accompany" and *dasz im* [daš' im] "you will give them":

(34) (a) tovažiš+i+ć   daš im

              i   i   Retraction

              —   —   Surface Palatalization

                      *daš im

(b)   tovaži̮š+i+ć   daš im

ʃ′   ʃ′   Surface Palatalization

—   —   Retraction

*tovaži̮š+i+ć

Exactly the same problem arises in Russian if we try to analyze the examples given in (25). In sum, Surface Palatalization and Retraction cannot be ordered.

Our dilemma is solved easily if we recognize post-cyclic lexical rules as a legitimate class. If Polish Retraction is post-cyclic and Polish Surface Palatalization is post-lexical, then things fall into place. Retraction applies in the lexicon, hence in the domain of words. Consequently, it affects *towarzyszyć* "accompany" but not *dasz im* "you will give them". The latter is a phrase produced by the syntax, hence outside the lexicon. It thus escapes Retraction and falls within the scope of Surface Palatalization which is post-lexical.[16] Note that given the post-cyclic/post-lexical distinction, Retraction and Surface Palatalization need not be ordered with respect to each other. The former is in the post-cyclic component in the lexicon, whereas the latter is in the post-lexical component and by definition, the lexical components (cyclic and post-cyclic) precede the post-lexical component. Derivation (34) is now corrected as follows:

(35)   tovaži̮š+i+ć   *Post-cyclic*
              i̮   Retraction
— —
        tovaži̮š+i+ć   daš   im   *Post-lexical*
              —   ʃ′   Surface Palatalization

Now we return briefly to the data in (28). We look at the examples which end in coronal consonants because in principle they could be inputs to both Retraction and Surface Palatalization. (Recall that Polish Retraction applies after coronals.) As we notice, Retraction fails to apply to foreign names and they thus become inputs to Surface Palatalization, for example, *Chicago* [ʃ′i].[17] How should such words be treated? They are best viewed as exceptions to Retraction, particularly since they are unstable as a class. They tend to lose their status as exceptions and yield to Retraction. Needless to say, whether a given newly borrowed word or a foreign name is already pronounced with [i̮] or still with [i] is a matter of considerable variation. Thus, more educated and conservative speakers tend to retain the variant with [i] for a longer time, especially in careful and monitored speech. The accomodation of borrowings with regard to Retraction proceeds on a word-by-word basis. For example, *bridge* (card game) borrowed into Polish earlier in this century is now fully assimilated: *brydż* [bri̮č], where [č] is the effect of Final Devoicing. The word *reżim* "regime" is pronounced more often with [i̮] than with [i] while *rizotto* "risotto" just the opposite, more often with [i] than with [i̮], and so forth (see Rubach 1984 for details).

We conclude that Polish Retraction may have exceptions, but this is not surprising since the rule is post-cyclic and hence lexical. To carry on with the same reasoning, Russian Surface Palatalization has exceptions and consequently it must be post-cyclic. On the other hand, Russian Retraction is exceptionless and hence it can be post-lexical. We now solve an ordering conflict that would arise in the grammar of Russian, exactly as it did in the grammar of Polish (see (34)). Our examples from (25), *institut* "institute" and *brat i* "brother and", are now derived as follows:

(36) institut   Post-cyclic
         t′   Surface Palatalization
       ‒
       inst′itut brat i   Post-lexical
       —   ɨ   Retraction

If post-cyclic rules did not exist as a class (and consequently, Surface Palatalization would have to be post-lexical) there would be no way in which the rules in (36) could be ordered: either the *i* would be incorrectly retracted to [ɨ] in *institut* "institute" or the *t* would be incorrectly palatalized to [t′] in *brat i* "brother and". That Russian Surface Palatalization cannot be post-lexical is demonstrated independently by the way it applies in the environment of *e*. Note that *i* but not *e* is affected by Retraction, and hence the *e* contexts could be available to Surface Palatalization if it were post-lexical. On the other hand, if Surface Palatalization is post-cyclic, then it is predicted that the *e* that occurs across a word boundary cannot induce palatalization. This prediction is borne out. For example, the *t* of *brat* "brother" remains hard in *brat etovo čeloveka* "this man's brother".

Finally, if Surface Palatalization applies in the domain of words and precedes Retraction, it is legitimate to ask how Retraction could ever apply inside words. Would it not be preempted by Surface Palatalization in all instances? We asked the same question about Polish, but there the relation was reversed, it was Retraction that could preempt Surface Palatalization in word-internal position. In the case of Polish we simply said that we were dealing with a class of lexical exceptions. In the case of Russian this would be inappropriate. The [ɨ] in *greš+i+t′* [gr′eš+ɨ+t′] "to sin" and *druž+i+t′* [druž+ɨ+t′] "to be friends with" given earlier in (33bi) is perfectly stable and it is never pronounced as [i]. The problem is that with Surface Palatalization preceding Retraction, we derive [š′ ž′] rather than [ɨ]. We propose to solve this problem by postulating a hardening rule (Lightner 1972). Schematically:

(37) Hardening š′ ž′ → [+back]

This rule applies after Surface Palatalization and provides an environment for Retraction. While at first glance Hardening may seem quite arbitrary as a rule, it is well motivated in the grammar of Russian. The point is that not only the derived [š′ ž′] in words such as *greš+i+t′* "to sin" (from /x/, see (33b)) but also the underlying /š′ ž′/ need to be hardened in the course of the derivation. (Needless to say, underlying /š′ ž′/ also induce Retraction.) That /š ž/ need to be treated as underlyingly soft is demonstrated by their behavior with respect to a number of morphological and phonological rules of Russian. That is, they function together with underlying palatalized consonants /t′ s′ r′ . . . /.[18] Thus, Hardening is motivated independently of the problems that arise in the derivation of our examples in (33b).

3   Conclusion

To summarize, an inspection of palatalization and vowel retraction processes in Polish and Russian has unveiled a striking fact. Both languages have essentially the same rules. In both languages the rules are mutually bleeding and hence potentially cause derivational problems. These problems are solved without difficulty in a version of lexical phonology that recognizes a distinction between post-cyclic lexical and post-lexical rules. In this theory the conflicting rules are interpreted as belonging to different components: one is post-cyclic and the other post-lexical. Now not only the ordering conflict but also the very need for ordering the rules disappears altogether. The properties of post-cyclic and post-lexical rules in Polish and Russian accord well with the assumptions of lexical phonology; post-cyclic but not post-lexical rules have exceptions. A remarkable fact is that even though Polish and Russian have virtually the same rules, their status in each of these languages is different. Russian is, as it were, a mirror image of Polish. In Polish, Surface Palatalization is post-lexical, whereas in Russian it is post-cyclic. On the other hand, Polish Retraction is post-cyclic whereas Russian Retraction is post-lexical. The mysterious facts adduced at the beginning of this section in (25) now fall out from the theory in a natural fashion. In phrase phonology, assimilations are handled in Polish by Surface Palatalization and in Russian by Retraction. In word phonology, on the other hand, the same assimilations work differently: in Polish they are handled by Retraction while in Russian by Surface Palatalization. To conclude, not only does lexical phonology solve internal rule conflicts within each language separately but it also illuminates the fact that, typologically, languages may differ solely by assigning a different status to what are patently the same rules.

NOTES

This article was written while I was a visiting professor at the Ohio State University and the University of Iowa. I would like to thank both of these institutions for their sponsorship.

1   The data for this analysis are drawn from standard descriptive sources such as Dvonč (1966), D'urovič (1975), Letz (1950), Pauliny (1979), and Sabol (1989), as well as from Slovak dictionaries. Note the following transcription symbols used in Slovak, Polish, and Russian:

[c]   alveolar voiceless affricate
[č, ǰ]   postalveolar affricates
[ć]   prepalatal voiceless affricate
[š, ž]   postalveolar fricatives
[x]   velar voiceless fricative

2   This is a simplification. I have argued elsewhere that the lengthening is triggered by one of the fleeting vowels known as "yers" which functions here as the gen.pl. ending. These vowels surface phonetically only in restricted contexts (cf. Kenstowicz and Rubach 1987; Rubach 1986).

3   In fact, it is not necessary to fully specify both elements of the diphthong since the quality of the onglide can be determined from the vowel in the head position by spreading, see Rubach (1993).

4   Whether the skeleton is composed of skeletal X-slots or moras is an open question; see chapter 5, this volume, for extended discussion. In Rubach (forthcoming) I claim that only the X-slots and not the moras are appropriate for Slovak.

5   The analysis of the Slovak syllable nuclei in the remainder of this section is based on Kenstowicz and Rubach (1987).

6   Distinctions of this type have been suggested earlier for French by Kaye and Lowenstamm (1984). The authors point out that, for example, the [w] in *watt* (borrowed from English) and the [w] in *oie* [wa] "goose" behave differently with regard to liaison which applies in the latter but not in the former case.

This difference is understandable if one assumes that the [w] of *watt* is part of the onset while the [w] of *oie* is in the nucleus and hence forms a diphthong with the following vowel.

7   The relevant adjacency for the application of the Rhythmic Law is established at the level of Ns.

8   I mean the phonetically-oriented postlexical rules, the class of rules designated as P-2 in terms of Kaisse (1985).

9   The Russian words are transliterated. In (25a) Polish [š] is spelled *š* rather than *sz* to facilitate a comparison with Russian. [i] is a high back unrounded vowel. It is an underlying segment in both Polish and Russian.

10 As we explain below, Surface Palatalization applies after Retraction, hence at the stage at which all nonpalatalized consonants have been specified as [+back]. Surface Palatalization is therefore a "spreading cum delinking" rule.

11 There are also good descriptive reasons for why the assumption of underlying /i/ would be impossible: labials admit both [i] and [ɨ], thus next to *dym+i+ć* "to smoke" we have *dom+y* "houses".

12 Polish – but not Russian – has such a rule. It is Coronal Palatalization, discussed in Rubach (1984).

13 This means that the Russian Surface Palatalization is a rule spreading the feature [–back], but not [+high] because /e/ is not [+high]. The missing [+high] is added later by a redundancy rule.

14 The consonants are derived by First Velar Palatalization (31) with /g/ first changing into an affricate and then spirantizing into a fricative, as is the case in most Slavic languages.

15 Whether the [ɨ] in the root

morpheme is underlying or not is irrelevant at this point. Either assumption would produce the correct result.

16   In classic generative phonology, the desirable effect would be achieved by a clever encoding of boundaries in the structural descriptions of the rules. However, for many good reasons, boundaries have been rejected as a permissible instrument in phonological analysis (see, for example, Kiparsky 1982 and Mohanan 1986).

17   Many Poles say [č'ikago], with an affricate, but this does not affect our argument.

18   For example, Ikan'e, a rule that reduces unstressed nonhigh vowels to [i] if they are preceded by a soft consonant, applies not only to [č'is+i], from underlying /č'as+i/ "clock", but also to [ž'il'+e+t'], from underlying /žal'+e+t'/ "to regret". In the latter Hardening provides an environment for Retraction and we derive the final output [žɨl'+e+t']. The nonreduced vowels appear in the nominative singular of the nouns *čas* "time" and *žal'* "regret".

32 Projection and Edge Marking in the Computation of Stress in Spanish

JAMES W. HARRIS

0 Introduction

In the period deemed "current" in this *Handbook*, theoretically committed studies of Spanish phonology have investigated a broad spectrum of language-particular phenomena, including but not limited to[1] aspiration of /s/; cliticization; morphophonology of diminutivization; diphthongization of high and mid vowels; glide-vowel and glide-obstruent alternations; interpretation of early Spanish orthography; intonational discourse signals; liquid assimilation and vocalization; nasal assimilation, velarization, and deletion; distribution, structure, and depalatalization of palatal consonants; varieties and distribution of *r*-type segments; low-level vowel sandhi (reduction and deletion); phrasal stress; primary word stress; spirantization of voiced obstruents; syllabic effects in hypercorrection; text-to-music accommodation; voicing and continuancy assimilations of voiceless stops; vocalic height alternations; vowel and consonant epenthesis; vowel harmony/metaphony.

Because of the richness and variety of these studies of Spanish, I have found it impossible to squeeze into the space allotted a comprehensive review from which, in my opinion, a substantive and durable contribution to our understanding of some aspect of phonology can be derived. Therefore, as an alternative to scattering my shots unproductively, I have chosen to concentrate on the one topic that has all but overwhelmed the field of Spanish phonology in the last decade, namely, stress assignment. This topic has dominated the attention of investigators not only by the measure of pages of print in major publications but also in terms of concern with theoretical underpinnings.[2] It is decidedly odd that so much paper and energy have been invested in a subject which everybody thinks is easy, which children catch on to quickly (Hochberg 1988; Lee 1989), and for which Halle and Vergnaud (1987, pp. 93–95), for example, toss off an analysis in a few sentences. This disparity begs for an explanation.

Having narrowed my focus to stress assignment, I aim to do more than simply provide a critical survey of the literature. My goal is to confront certain issues that have been either ignored or treated equivocally in available analyses (including my own), and to do so within the framework of a more explicit and more restrictive metrical theory than has been employed heretofore.[3] If the endeavor is successful, it will establish a benchmark for the assessment of both present and future studies of Spanish stress.

1   Spanish Word Stress, Basic Observations[4]

It seems at first glance that the location of primary stress in Spanish words is subject to a bizarre restriction: it can fall on any one of the last five syllables, but not on the sixth (seventh, etc.) from the end. This is illustrated in (1), where periods mark syllable boundaries:

(1)   . . . 6 5 4 3 2 1   (position counting from right)
            a.na.li.**zó**   "(s)he analyzed"
            a.na.**lí**.za   "(s)he analyzes"
            a.na.**lí**.ti.co   "analytic"
            a.na.**lí**.za.me.lo   "analyze it for me"
            a.na. **lí**.ce.se.me.lo   "have it analyzed for me"
         *a.**ná**.li.ce.se.me.lo

These data are not really odd, however: the words with stress in the two most remote positions (4 and 5) are penultimately stressed verb forms followed by two or three pronominal enclitics (e.g., *se, me, lo*). It is clear that these clitics lie outside the domain of word stress assignment in Spanish, since their attachment to the right edge of a word never triggers rightward migration of stress. In this respect clitics differ crucially from ordinary suffixes, as can be seen from countless sets of words like those in (2):

(2)   (a)   Clitics
            prep**á**re   "prepare"
            prep**á**re-me   "prepare me"
            prep**á**re-me-lo   "prepare it for me"
            prep**á**re-se-me-lo   "let it be prepared for me"
      (b)   Suffixes
            pár+o   "stop"
            par+**ád**+o   "stopped"
            par+a+**dór**   "stopping place"
            par+a+dor+**cít**+o   "*id.,* dim."

The domain of Spanish word stress is thus the constituent that I will call the "M(orphological) word" (with suffixes, without clitics), as opposed to the "P(honosyntactic) word" (M word plus clitics). In Spanish M-words (henceforth, simply "words"), stress is confined without exception to a three-syllable window at the right edge. This limitation finds a deep explanation in the assumption that antepenultimate stress is the theoretical maximum leftward displacement that can be measured – as a leftheaded foot followed by an unparsed or extrametrical syllable: *si.(lá.bi.) co*–that is, if metrical theory provides no representation for the inadmissible type **sí.la.bi.co* in a right-edge-oriented system that parses binary feet.

Phonologically minimal stress contrasts like those illustrated in (3) are by no means rare in Spanish:

(3)　　　. . . 3 2 1
　　　　so.li.ci.**tó**　　"(s)he solicited"
　　　　so.li.**cí**.to　　"I solicit"
　　　　so.**lí**.ci.to　　"solicitous"
　　　　(***só**.li.ci.to)

Obviously, morphological factors and/or lexical idiosyncracy must play a role in the location of stress within the three-syllable window. In essence, the system works as follows. Stress on the penult is canonical in Spanish in the sense that it is found in about 90 percent of the lexical stock of nouns, adjectives, and adverbs and in around 75 percent of the forty-odd inflected forms of each verb stem.[5] In the remaining cases, antepenultimate stress is triggered by specifically designated morphemes. In nouns, adjectives, and adverbs, both stems and affixes can be triggers, as illustrated in (4a); in verbs only certain inflectional affixes play this role, as illustrated in (4b):[6]

(4)　　　Canonical　　　　　　　　Special triggers
　　(a)　noun/adjective/adverb
　　　　　obó+e　　　　"oboe"　　　HÉRO+e　　　"hero"
　　　　　numer+ós+o　"numerous"　numér+IC+o　"numerical"
　　(b)　verb
　　　　　llama+ré+mos　"we will call"　llamá+RA+mos　"we should call"

Final stress in vowel-final words occurs predictably, under morphological control, in two verb paradigms (5a) and in a small residue of nonverbs, mostly borrowed nouns (5b):

(5)　(a)　**pas+ó**　　"(s)he passed" (past perfective)
　　　　　pas+a+**rá**　"(s)he will pass" (future)
　　(b)　me**nú**　　"menu"
　　　　　ra**bí**　　"rabbi"

The three-syllable stress window is not available unconditionally. Segmental and prosodic restrictions shrink it to two, or in the extreme case, a single syllable, as illustrated in (6):

(6)   Two-syllable window
    (a)   penult rhyme = GV: No.**ryé**.ga   (*C$\acute{\text{V}}$.CGV.CV)[7]
    (b)   penult rhyme = VG: Ja.**máy**.ca   (*C$\acute{\text{V}}$.CVG.CV)
    (c)   penult rhyme = VC: a.**lár**.ma "alarm"   (*C$\acute{\text{V}}$.CVC.CV)
    (d)   final rhyme   = GV: ca.**rí**.cya "caress"   (*C$\acute{\text{V}}$.CV.CGV)[8]
    (e)   final rhyme   = VC: ca.**ní**.bal "canibal" (*C$\acute{\text{V}}$.CV.CVC)
    One-syllable window
    (f)   final rhyme   = VG: ca.**ráy** (interjection)   (*C$\acute{\text{V}}$.CVG)

The disallowed forms are not simply fortuitous lexical gaps. Rather, they reflect robust native judgments. For example, hypothetical nouns such as *cá.nas.ta* and *tí.nam.bo*, which violate (6c), are consistently judged to be strongly deviant.

The generalizations illustrated in (6) seem to constitute prima facie evidence that consonants and glides are syllabic weight units in Spanish, i.e., that they make "heavy" syllables: if stress assignment in Spanish were entirely "quantity insensitive", then all of (6) would be a mystery. For example, *á.la.mo* "poplar" and *cá.ma.ra* "chamber" are stressed on the antepenult while the class of words like *a.lár.ma* (6c) cannot be. It is hardly obvious what this limitation could plausibly be attributed to other than the heavy penult closed by C in all the words of the latter class. Similarly, *cá.ra* "face" is stressed on the penult while words like *ca.ráy* (6f) cannot be. Again, it is hard to plausibly attribute this limitation to anything other than the final glide of all the words in the latter set. But if both C and G contribute to syllable weight, then they do so in a puzzling and apparently inconsistent way. For example, why does VG (6f) but not VC (6e) attract stress to the final syllable? On the other hand, if rhymal C is not a weight unit, why do VC rhymes in the penult (6c) attract stress just as VG rhymes (6b) do? And why does final VG attract stress to the final syllable (6f) while final GV only limits stress to the penult (6d) as does penult VG (6b)? Finally, if G is counted as a unit in stress placement, how are some words – e.g., *lá⁴w³da²no¹* "laudanum", *terapé⁴w³ti²co¹* "therapeutic" – stressed on the *fourth* vocoid from the right word-edge – evidently outside the *three*-position window?[9]

In the face of (6), there is incontrovertible evidence that stress is assigned to some classes of Spanish words in a "quantity-insensitive" mode – i.e., to the heads of syllables without regard to their internal makeup. As illustrated by the verb form *so.li.cí.to* in (3) and countless others like *pla.tí.ca* "(s)he chats", *cir.cú.lo* "I circulate", stress is assigned without exception to the penultimate syllable in polysyllabic present tense verb forms – there is no verb like **so.lí.ci.to*, **plá.ti.ca*, **cír.cu.lo* – despite the availability of antepenultimate stress in segmentally identical *so.lí.ci.to* (adjective), *plá.ti.ca* "chat", and *cír.cu.lo* "circle" (nouns). Now, the placement of stress in numerous contrasting verb forms like those illustrated in (7a) versus (7b) confirms that it is precisely the penultimate *syllable*, not the penultimate *vocoid* or *mora* (italicized in (7)), to which stress is uniformly assigned in these cases.[10]

(7) (a) envíd*ya*   "(s)he envies"   acaríc*ya*   "(s)he caresses"
      (b) var*í*a   "(s)he varies"   vac*í*a   "(s)he empties"

In sum, we are left with an unresolved tension between quantity-sensitive (6) and quantity-insensitive (7) modes of stress assignment in Spanish.

A related tension arises in the choice of the word (the "M word", of course) versus the "stem" as the domain of stress assignment.[11] A strong argument in favor of the word as the relevant domain is that if segments outside the stem did not count, we could not give a principled explanation for the "window" facts (though, uninterestingly, we could of course stipulate them). For example, in words like [{miscelán*e*}o] "miscellaneous" (whose final *o* is an inflectional class marker) the stem could be parsed as {mis.(cé.la.)ne} to yield the inadmissible word contour *Xóσσσ (*mis.cé.la.ne.o). On the other hand, as noted in the preceeding subsection, exclusion of this contour (in favor of correct [{mis.ce.(lá.ne.)}o]) can be explained by universal metrical theory without language-particular stipulation if the whole word is included in the parse.

An independent, theory-neutral argument that also shows the necessity of parsing syllables external to the stem is provided by countless examples like [{có.me}]/[{co.mé.}mos] "(s)he eats/we eat". The rightward "shift" of stress in the stem {come} in the latter form is transparently due to addition of the inflectional suffix -*mos*. If the stress rules scanned only the stem, this constituent would have to be stressed identically – either {cóme} or {comé} – in all inflected forms. In short, it is obvious that stress rules scan the entire word.[12]

The stem, however, may appear to play some role in stress assignment. Recall window condition (6e): stress cannot appear on the antepenult if the final rhyme is *VC* (*C*$\acute{V}$*CV.CVC*). But it seems to be the final rhyme of the *stem* that matters, not rhymes of inflectional suffixes. For example, [{ca.ní.ba.l}es] (-*es* is the plural inflection), [{a.ná.li.s}is] (-*is* is an inflectional class marking suffix), [{so.li.ci.tá.}-ba.mos] (-*ba*- marks imperfective aspect, -*mos* is the first person plural verb inflection).

In short, some generalizations of stress assignment in Spanish clearly hold over the domain of the entire word while others seem to require reference to the subword stem constituent.

Summarizing, the present section has laid out the basic facts of Spanish word stress and introduced certain stress-related puzzlements. This brief sketch suffices to show that deceptively simple (though essentially correct) generalizations like "Spanish stress is basically penultimate" conceal hard questions involving the most fundamental issues, such as the identification of units of computation, domains of scansion, and conditions on extrametricality. Small wonder that researchers find ample fuel here for extended controversies.

2   The Theoretical Framework

Following the tradition of Halle and Vergnaud (1987) and much related work, I take the position that metrical prominence (in particular, stress) is computed and represented on a special autosegmental plane – the "metrical grid" – as illustrated in (8a) with the word *è.le.gán.cia* "elegance":

(8)   (a)

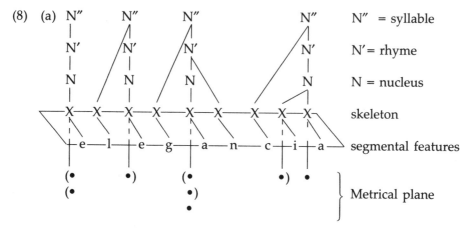

(b)   Prosodic Hierarchy

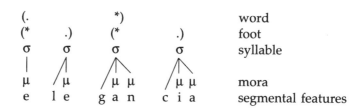

In the present context, the most important property of (8a) is that syllabic and metrical units are distributed on distinct, autonomous planes of representation. These two planes are autonomous in that X slots and N-bar structure are used in the expression of generalizations about segmental organization and are not elements of metrical structure, while grid marks and boundaries are used in the expression of generalizations about metrical organization and are not elements of syllable structure. For reasons that will become increasingly clear as the exposition proceeds, I explicitly reject the view of metrical structure illustrated in (8b), whereby the word (Wd), foot (F), syllable (σ), and mora (μ) levels constitute a single Prosodic Hierarchy.[13] As we will see below, it is not unusual for a given segmental string with a given syllabic organization in a given phonological environment to be systematically associated with different metrical structures in different morphological contexts. There is thus no otiose duplication of representational units in (8a).

The character and construction of the metrical plane is tightly constrained.[14] The vocabulary of elements that appear in metrical grids is limited to left and right boundaries "(", ")" and undifferentiated unit markers "•". Weight diacritics like H(eavy) versus L(ight), and their notational equivalents, are disallowed.[15] The projection of elements onto the grid is strictly "local": baseline (line-0) grid marks are projected only from the X-tier of segmental/syllabic structure; elements on grid line $n+1$ are projected only from line n. Projection of line-1 "accents" from syllable structure is disallowed.[16]

The projection of •s onto grid line 0 is executed by a parameter of universal grammar of the form shown in (9):

(9)   Project • for each X_m

where particular languages can choose from a small set of values for X_m, the metrically-relevant skeletal Xs; for example, X that is a syllable head, [-consonantal] X, all Xs dominated by N'.

Metrical boundaries may or may not be projected onto line 0 in accordance with a parameter of universal grammar of the form shown in (10):

(10)   Project (or) at the corresponding edge of Σ

where Σ stands for a small set of "closed" or "heavy" syllable types; for example, "$_\sigma[\ldots X_N X_{Son}]$" (an informal notation for a syllable containing a postnuclear sonorant). This parameter is inoperative in quantity-insensitive systems (where syllable-internal structure is metrically irrelevant).

After projection of • – and in some cases "(" or ")" – boundaries may be inserted under the control of two universal mechanisms. One is the Edge-Marking parameter shown in (11):[17]

(11)   Edge: place a {L(eft)/R(ight)} boundary to the {L/R} of the {L/R}-
       most •

The other boundary-inserting device is the so called Iterative Constituent Construction parameter (ICC), which particular languages may or may not set, shown in (12):

(12)   Iterative Constituent Construction (ICC): Insert a boundary every two
       •s starting from the {L/R}

The ICC (if employed) forms binary feet iteratively from an edge or an existing boundary; it inserts left parentheses when moving from right to left, and right parentheses when moving from left to right.

Languages sometimes disallow particular metrical configurations under special conditions. For example, it is well known that in Latin, complex rhymes contribute to metrical weight but not in word-final syllables. Metrical theory must therefore provide an appropriate filtering device for such cases. In Latin a filter with the effect shown in (13a) blocks operation of parameter (10) in word-final syllables (# = end of grid line 0):[18]

(13)   (a)   *(•#
       (b)   a.maa.bun.tur
             • (•   (•   •

Thus, as shown in (13b), of the three segmentally complex rhymes in a Latin word like *a.maa.bun.tur* "they will be loved", the first two but not the last project as metrically heavy. The eventual result is *a.maa.**bún**.tur* rather than **a.maa.bun.**túr**.

The parsing of a grid line is completed by application of the Head parameter, an instance of projection:

(14)   Head: Project the {L/R}-most • of each foot on line *n*
               (onto line *n+1*)

3   Parameter Settings in Spanish: Core Cases

I will now present basic examples in Spanish that exemplify the descriptive apparatus just sketched and provide primary evidence regarding language-particular settings of the various parameters. Refinements and extensions to more complex cases appear in subsequent sections.

The Spanish values for the projection parameter (9) are given in (15), and the setting for the boundary parameter (10) is shown in (16):

(15)   (a)   Project • for each syllable head in verbs
       (b)   Project • for each nuclear X elsewhere

(16)   Project (for $_\sigma$[... X$_N$X ...] in nonverbs

These two line-0 parameters together instantiate the claim that stress assignment is quantity insensitive in verbs but quantity sensitive in all other morphosyntactic categories. In verbs, syllables project exactly one • (15a) and no boundary (16), regardless of their internal structure. In nonverbs, simple and complex nuclei project • and ••, respectively (15b).[19] Furthermore, a left boundary is projected at the left edge of every syllable made heavy by a postnuclear segment (16).

In Spanish, complex rhymes in nouns/adjectives/adverbs do not project as metrically heavy (i.e., they do not attract stress) in word-final syllables. For example, words like *Ca.**rá**.cas*, *Gá.les* "Wales", *dé.fi.cit*, etc., have complex word-final rhymes that do not attract stress. The identical rhyme structure inexorably attracts stress to the penult; that is, it cannot be "ignored" by (10) = (16) in word-internal position: *car.**rás**.ca* "type of oak" (versus **cár.ras.ca*), *mo.**lés**.to* "annoyed" (versus **mó.les.to*), etc. Evidently then, Spanish, like Latin, utilizes filter (13a).

I show in (17) the Spanish settings for parameters that complete the construction of metrical grids:

(17) (a) Edge: RRR   cf. (11)
       (b) ICC: R to L   cf. (12)
       (c) Head: L   cf. (14)

Edge parameter (17a) places a right boundary ")" to the right of the rightmost • on line 0 of the grid; the ICC (17b) then parses binary feet leftward from the right edge; finally, Head parameter (17c) identifies the • on the immediate right of each "(" as the head of the foot by projecting a • onto line 1 of the grid.

The parameters discussed so far yield, for a given input, exactly one right boundary (at the right edge of line 0) but more than one left boundary in some cases, since (16b) and (17a) can both insert a "(" at more than one site. For example, every syllable but the last of *des.con.cer.tán.te* "disconcerting" is heavy and thus projects a "(" by (16b), and *pa.ra.le.le.pí.pe.do* "parallelepiped" has enough light syllables for two iterations of (17b) to the left of the syllable that bears main stress.[20] Unpaired left boundaries to the left of the rightmost foot obviously play no role in locating primary word stress; furthermore, they are irrelevant as well for the placement of secondary stress, which is assigned at the phrase level in Spanish after the operation of segmental rules at that level (Roca 1986; Harris 1991b). We can simply remove the irrelevant "("s from the grid by the following housekeeping operation:[21]

(18)   Delete unpaired (

Derivations are given in (19) that illustrate (15–18). The word *me.xi.cá.no* represents the huge class of words with "canonical" penult stress; this word also provides an example of an unpaired "(" inserted by (17b); *can.tán.tes* "singers" provides examples of internal and final syllables closed by a consonant.

(19)

		me.xi.ca.no	can.tan.tes
	(15b)	• • • •	• • •
	(16)		(• (• •
	(13a) blocks		. . . . . . (•
	(17a)	• • • •)	(• (• •)
	(17b)	(• •(• •)	
	(18)	• •(• •)	• (• •)
	(17c)	• •(• •)	• (• •)
		•	•

Given that postvocalic glides and consonants occupy the same position in syllable rhymes (8), the operation of (16) in *can.tán.tes* illustrates both of the window-narrowing cases (6b) *Ja.máy.ca* (*CV.CVG.CV) and (6c) *a.lár.ma* (*CV.CVC.CV). We proceed now to reconcile the apparent conflicts among descriptive generalizations sketched in section 1.

4   Elaboration

A significant metrical fault line bifurcates the vocabulary of Spanish. Verbs lie on one side; nouns, adjectives, and adverbs ("substantives") on the other. In verbs, each inflectional paradigm has a characteristic fixed stress pattern that admits no variation at all among individual lexical items. But in substantives the location of stress is subject to lexical idiosyncrasy within certain limits, as illustrated in section 1. Accordingly, I discuss verbs and substantives separately.[22]

4.1   *Verb Forms*[23]

We focus first on the claim that stress assignment in Spanish verb forms is quantity insensitive (QI): the only projection from segmental/syllabic structure onto grid line 0 is from X positions that are syllable heads, which project one •; parameter (10) does not operate in verbs.

Unmistakable positive evidence for QI is provided by the class of verbal inflectional morphemes that trigger antepenultimate stress, illustrated in (4b). In a subset of dialects scattered over both Spain and Latin America,[24] the present subjunctive marker belongs to this class: for example, subjunctive *cán.t+ E.+mos* "we sing" and *lím.py+E.+mos* "we clean" versus indicative *can.t+á.+mos* and *lim.py+á.+mos*.[25] Subjunctives like *lím.py+E.+mos* are the crucial examples since only a QI parse is possible for them:

(20)   (a)   Quantity insensitive   (b)   *Quantity sensitive
               lím.pye.mos   *lím.pye.mos
               (•   •) •   •• (••) •
                •   •

The conclusion that Spanish verb inflections entail QI does not rest solely on dialect-particular facts; it is supported as well by the following completely general, dialect-neutral argument. Consider the present indicative verb forms represented in (21), which are common to all dialects:

(21)   (a)   "(s)he cleans"   (b)   "we clean"
               lím.py+a   lim.py+á.+mos
               (•   •)   •   (•   •)
                •   •

(c)   "(s)he applauds"   (d)   "we applaud"
a.**pláw**.d+e   a.plaw.**d**+**í**.+mos
• (•   •)   •   •   (•   •)
      •   •

We see that the nonhead vocoids (glides) /y w/ and the rhyme consonant /m/ have no effect on stress placement, regardless of their position in the segmental string or the position on the grid they would occupy if projected. Now compare the representations in (22):

(22)   (a)   "(s)he continues"   (b)   "we continue"
con.ti.**nú**.+a   con.ti.nu.+**á**.+mos
•   • (•   •)   •   •   • (•   •)
         •   •

       (c)   "(s)he annoys"   (d)   "we annoy"
a.mo.**í**.n+a   a.mo.i.n+**á**.+mos
•   •(•   •)   •   •• (•   •)
        •   •

The morphological structures in (21) and (22) are parallel, and the grids are equivalent in that they all have a rightmost binary QI foot, as expected. The segmental representations, on the other hand, differ in that (22) has a nuclear vowel in every position where (21) has a glide. We thus learn from the comparison not only that glides and high vowels are lexically distinct (which we knew independently)[26] but also that the accentual contrasts *continúa* versus *límpia* and *amoína* versus *apláude* would be impossible to express in a quantity-sensitive system: if the penultimate *mora* (rhyme segment) rather than the penultimate *syllable* were stressed in every case, then **limpía*, **aplaúde*, etc., would be inevitable. The QI character of Spanish verb paradigms is thus securely established for all dialects.

Let us now look more closely at how antepenultimate stress is assigned in verbs. The special subset of triggering mood/aspect inflections contains those illustrated in (23), and a few others:

(23)   (a)   Nonfinal syllable
so.li.ci.**t**+**á**.+BA.+mos   "we solicited"   (imperfective)
so.li.**cí**.t+E.+mos   "we solicit"   (subjunctive)
       (b)   Final syllable
so.li.ci.**t**+**á**.+BA+s   "you solicited"   (imperfective)
so.li.**cí**.t+E+s   "you solicit"   (subjunctive)

As shown, these morphemes trigger antepenultimate stress when they are followed by another syllable but not when they are word final. Thus the inflectional morpheme itself does not exhibit the familiar syndrome of extrametricality. Rather, the trigger morpheme excludes from the line 0 parse the syllable to its right, if there is one, while allowing itself to be included in the parse. For example:

(24)   so.li.ci.t+á.BA   so.li.ci.t+á.BA.mos
   • • • (•   •)   • • • (•   •) •
        •   •

This pattern requires a very awkward formal statement in most accentual frameworks (cf. Den Os and Kager 1986, pp. 37–40; Harris 1987, p. 74), but finds a straightforward formalization in the theory sketched above:

(25)   Edge: RRR for specially marked morphemes

Edge Rule (25), followed by the ICC (17b), has exactly the effect shown in (24). Rule (25) stands in a disjunctive relationship with the general Edge Rule (17a), whose effect is illustrated in (19). In other words, (25) places a ")" at the right edge of an idiosyncratic triggering morpheme like imperfective *ba* and present subjunctive *e* (in some dialects) if such a morpheme is present; otherwise, the general rule (17a) places a ")" at the right edge of the word. The formal basis for the disjunctivity of these two rules can be brought out clearly in the restatement shown in (26):

(26)   Edge: $X\ (\ ]_{\mathscr{L}}\ )\ ]_{X}0$
                                 |
          $\emptyset\ \rightarrow\ )\ /\ \bullet\ \underline{\quad\quad}$

Let $\mathscr{L}$ (mnemonic for "leftward displacement" of accent) mark the morphological bracket at the right edge of the items that trigger insertion of a special right metrical foot boundary; $]_{X}0$ is the word edge. It is easy to see then that the observed disjunctivity follows in the normal way from proper inclusion of (17a) in (25).

   Spanish verb inflection also contains a subset of morphemes that trigger the metrical pattern illustrated in (27):

(27)   (a)   Final syllable
           com+e+ré   "I will eat"   (future)
           com+í   "I ate"   (preterit = past perfective)
   (b)   Nonfinal syllable
           com+e+ré+mos   "we will eat"   (future)
           com+í+mos   "we ate"   (preterit)

In a sense, these morphemes are the metrical converse of those illustrated in (23): the future and preterit morphemes trigger word-final stress when they themselves are in final position, but they allow canonical penultimate stress when they are followed by another syllable in the word. In other words, the peculiarity of the future and preterit morphemes is that they head a foot regardless of their position in the word. This is illustrated in (28):

(28)   co.**m+í**   co.**m+í+**.mos
   •   (•)   •   (•   •)
         •   •

The formal account of the future and preterit inflections is parallel to that of the set illustrated in (24): I propose that the final-stressing inflections are subject to the special rule (29):

(29)   Edge: $X]_{\mathfrak{R}}$
                                            |
                $\emptyset \rightarrow (/ \underline{\quad} \bullet$

Edge Rule (29) places "(" to the left of the rightmost • in morphemes whose right bracket is identified with the diacritic $\mathfrak{R}$ (mnemonic for "rightward displacement"). This rule and the general Edge Rule (17a) lead to the grids shown in (28). These two rules do not form a disjunctive pair, as do (25)/(17a). This is exactly the familiar disjunctivity syndrome: (25)/(17a) are incompatible in that they compete to place the rightmost ")" in the word (and are thus related by proper inclusion), while (29)/(17a) are compatible in that they insert different boundaries in different locations (thus neither is properly included in the other).

In short, a certain subset of verb inflections triggers rule (29), another subset triggers rule (25); otherwise, the general rules set out in section 3 apply. The characteristic fixed metrical patterns of verb paradigms follow from three independently determinable facts: (a) quantity insensitivity, (b) the location of inflectional morphemes in the outermost layer of suffixation in verb forms, and (c) the right word-edge orientation of the general metrification rules of Spanish.

To close this section, I observe that there seems to be no persuasive argument that stress assignment in verbs in Spanish is cyclic; more specifically, that a metrical grid is constructed and parsed in the domain of the verb stem alone prior to application of parsing rules to the entire word. I assume that noncyclic construction of the metrical plane is universally the default case: some positive evidence must be offered to support the claim that parsing operates cyclically. I therefore conclude that the metrical plane of Spanish verbs is parsed in a single pass, at the level of the word.

4.2   Substantives

4.2.1   Antepenult Stress

The set of special morphemes that trigger antepenult stress in Spanish nouns, adjectives, and adverbs ("substantives") constitutes only about 10 percent of the vocabulary but is composed of a variety of stems and derivational suffixes. For example:

(30)

Stems		Suffixes	
MISCELÁNE+o	"miscellaneous"	demó+CRAT+a	"democrat"
LIBÉLUL+a	"dragonfly"	kiló+METR+o	"kilometer"
CÉLEBR+e	"famous"	fonó+LOG+o	"phonologist"
SÁBAN+a	"sheet"	bené+FIC+o	"beneficial"
ÍDOL+o	"idol"	áwr+E+o	"golden"

I propose that rule (25) – collapsed with (17a) as (26) – is responsible for antepenult stress in substantives as well as in verb forms. Illustrative derivations are given in (31), where "canonical" *pe.rí.t+o* "expert" is shown together with special *MÉRIT+o* for contrast:

(31)

	[[pe.**rí**.t] o]	[[**mérit**]$_\mathscr{L}$ o]
(15b)	• • •	• • •
(26)	• • •)	• •) •
(17b)	•(• •)	(• •) •
(17c)	•(• •)	(• •) •
	•	•

Words like *IDÓL+ATR+a* "idolater", *demo+CRÁT+IC+o* "democratic", and many others, show that antepenult stress-triggering suffixes can attach both to triggering stems and to other triggering suffixes (as well as to ordinary nontriggering stems and affixes). Rule (25), as embodied in (26), handles such cases correctly: a ")" is projected for the *rightmost* trigger only, not for *every* trigger in the word. Therefore, no additional mechanism is needed to rectify derivational false starts of the sort shown in (32), which do not arise on our current analysis:[27]

(32)

	[[[idol]$_\mathscr{L}$ atr]$_\mathscr{L}$ a]
(15b)	• • • •
*(26)	• •) •) •

4.2.2   Quantity Sensitivity

A preliminary argument for quantity sensitivity (QS) in Spanish substantives is presented in sections 1 and 3, with illustrations in (6) and (19). To continue, unequivocal evidence for QS in Spanish substantives comes from the fact that strings of the form *X.CV.C(C)V* – that is, words with a single rhyme segment in the penult (followed by a complex onset or not) – permit stress on either the penult or the antepenult (*múl.ti.ple* "multiple" or *ma.nó.pla* "brass knuckles") while strings of the form *X.CVC.CV* and *X.CVG.CV* – that is, words with complex rhymes in the penult – allow only penultimate stress (*e.clíp.se* "eclipse" and *a.céy.te* "oil" versus *CV́.XVC.CV* and *CV́.XVG.CV*). These data are accounted for with the help of projection rule (16), as illustrated in (19) above.

As further illustration of (16), we may note that the current analysis solves the puzzle presented by words like *láwdano* and *terapéwtico* (cf. first long paragraph between (6) and (7)) without new mechanisms. This is shown in (33), where I include a derivation of *de.sa.ú.cyo* to illustrate the underlying contrast between /aw/ and /au/:[28]

(33)   [[**láw**.d a.n]_ℒ o]   [[de.sa.**ú**.cy]_ℒ o]

(15b)	•	•	•		•	• •	•	•	
(16)	(•	•	•						
(26)	(•	•)	•		•	• •	•)	•	
(17b)					•	•(•	•)	•	
(17c)	(•	•)	•		•	•(•	•)	•	
		•				•			

In words like *láw.da.no*, rules (16) and (25/26) insert the left and right boundaries, respectively, of the stressed foot, which therefore contains the fourth as well as the third vocoid from the right edge. Words like *de.sa.ú.cyo*, on the other hand, have no syllable with a postnuclear rhyme segment; thus (16) is inoperative and every vocoid projects •, with the result that the stressed foot contains the second and third vocoids from the end.

Spanish syllables may have complex nuclei as well as complex rhymes, as we have seen (note 19, (21), etc.). Complex nuclei also make heavy syllables. This fact is responsible for window-narrowing cases (6a) and (6d). Examples of (6a) are *a.dwá.na* "customs" and *an.cyá.no* "aged" versus *CV́.CGV.CV*; examples of (6d) are *ca.rí.cya* "caress" and *per.pé.two* "perpetual" versus *CV́.CV.CGV*. These data are accounted for with the help of projection rule (15b), as illustrated in the following derivations (ignore *pátria* "homeland" for a second):

(34)   [[a.**dw** á.n] a]   [[ca.**rí**.cy]_ℒ a]   [[**pá**.tri.]_ℒ a]

(15b)	•	• •	•		•	• •	•		•	•	•	
(26)	•	• •	•)		•	• •)	•		•	•)	•	
(17b)	(•	•(•	•)		•(•	•)	•		(•	•)	•	
(18)	•	•(•	•)									
(17c)	•	•(•	•)		•(•	•)	•		(•	•)	•̣	
		•				•				•		

Given that (15b) projects a • for each nuclear vocoid, including those of complex nuclei as in *dwa* and *cya*, there is no way that stress can be assigned leftward of the penultimate syllable in words like *a.dwá.na, ca.rí.cya*, etc.

An additional (desirable) consequence of this property of (15b) is that an underlying distinction can be maintained between the stem-final glide /y/ of substantives like *ca.rí.cya* versus the stem-final vowel /i/ of substantives like *pátr*/i/*a* – despite the fact that the latter, too, surfaces with a glide: *pá.trya*. As we saw in (21) and (22), underlying vowel versus glide contrasts play a crucial role in the QI stress placement in verb forms. And indeed present-tense verb forms with the same roots as *ca.rí.cya* and *pá.trya* reveal the contrast which remains covert in the substantives: *a.ca.rí.cya* "carresses" versus *re.pa.trí.a* "repatriates". In short, though QI (15a) projects only one • per syllable, (15b) reflects the makeup of complex nuclei, as we expect in a QS subsystem.[29]

We have now covered all of the puzzlements in section 1 except for those involving certain substantives that do not end in a vowel. We turn to these next.

4.2.3   Substantives with No Class Marker

I have given no explicit account yet of the accentual contrast between the very large "canonical" class of consonant-final words with final stress like *fis.tól* "tie pin", *ha.rén* "harem", *us.téd* "you", etc., versus the minority class of consonant-final words with penult stress like *a.pós.tol* "apostol", *Cár.men*, *wés.ped*, "guest", etc. All of these form a morphological natural class, as illustrated in (35):

(35)   Class A: aváro   pájaro   "stingy"   "bird"
       Class B: sabána   sábana   "savanna"   "sheet"
       Class C: (i)   jarábV   árabV   "syrup"   "Arab"
                             empátV   trámitV   "tie"   "transaction"
                  (ii)   animálV   caníbalV   "animal"   "canibal"

The stems of all native Spanish substantives belong to one of three declension classes, which we can label A, B, and C. These are identified by the class-marking vowels *o*, *a*, and *V*, respectively.[30] *V* is realized phonetically as [e] (the maximally underspecified, epenthetic vowel of Spanish) in all but one special context. The examples marked C(i) represent the general case; they are phonetically *jaráb*[e], *árab*[e], *empát*[e], *trámit*[e]. The examples marked C(ii), like those in the previous paragraph, illustrate the special context in which the class marker *V* has no phonetic realization: word-finally (i.e., in singulars) after unclustered voiced or continuant coronals – the only word-final codas allowed in Spanish. Thus phonetic *animál, caníbal, ustéd, wésped*, etc.

All morphological class marker vowels play the same role in stress assignment. This follows from the strict "locality" of projection, which can access only syllabified X positions and thus cannot in principle "know" or "care" about feature distinctions among nuclear vocoids. In particular, the grids for canonical *a.ni.má.lV*, *us.té.dV*, etc., and special *ca.ní.ba.lV*, *wés.pe.dV*, etc., are constructed exactly as illustrated for canonical *pe.rí.to* and special *mé.ri.to* in (31). The essential difference is that the class marker *-o* of *pe.rí.to* and *mé.ri.to* is realized phonetically while the *-V* of class C(ii) substantives is not, plus the fact that the segment preceding *-V* is incorporated into the rhyme on its left in phonetic representations. In short, the reason that the word-final consonants in class C(ii) substantives do not have the metrical properties of syllable codas is simply that they are onsets rather than codas in the phonological representations relevant to the construction of the metrical grid.

Words like *Pa.ra.gwáy*, *con.vóy*, *ma.méy*, etc., that illustrate the extreme window-narrowing case (6f) are also class C(ii) substantives (cf. plural *ma.mé.y[e]+s*, etc.) The metrically relevant phonological representations are thus essentially as in (35), that is, *ma.mé.yV*, etc., where *yV*, as always, is a complex nucleus. These words are thus the class C counterparts to class A words like *en.sá.yo* "essay" and class B words like *e.po.pé.ya* "epic poem", which systematically reject antepenult stress – there are no words like **én.sa.yo*, **e.pó.pe.ya*. Metrical grids for the words in question are identical in all relevant respects to those of *ca.rí.cya* and *pá.tri.a* in (34), as is shown in (36):

(36)   [[ma.**mé**.y]$_{\mathscr{L}}$ V]]

(15b)	•	• •	•	

(26)	•	• •)	•	

(17b)	•	(• •)	•	

(17c)	•(	• •)	•	
		•		

All substantives with stress on the penultimate vocoid in the stem belong to the special $\mathscr{L}$ class; *Pa.ra.gwáy*, *con.vóy*, *ma.méy*, etc., are no different. The unpredictable morphological property of such words is that they belong to class C, and their one relevant phonological peculiarity is that their stems end in the sequence *VG*. Given these properties, their stress contour could not be other than what it is, on our account. In other words, the seemingly odd window property (6a) requires no ad hoc addition to our proposals; it is a direct consequence of them.

We have now covered every detail of section 1 except for the marginal words like *me.nú* (5b). These are "marginal" in that they are few in number and not solidly integrated into native patterns. By this I mean that in addition to their unexpected final stress, their plurals show great intra- and inter-dialectal variation; for example, *me.nú.e+s* in competition with *me.nú+s*. Variants like *me.nú.(e+s)* can be analyzed as ordinary class C substantives, with the same metrical structure as, say, (class B) *ca.nó.a(+s)* "canoe(s)". But both these and the *me.nú(+s)*-type variants can also be handled as substantive stems with the same metrical properties as the future and preterit verb inflectional morphemes illustrated in (27) and (28), which trigger the special Edge Rule (29). I cannot devote more space to these forms.

5 Summary

For easy reference I place together in (37) the rules/parameters that determine the metrical grids that support the phonetic realization of primary word stress in Spanish:

(37)

	Substantives		Verbs
Projection:	• for nuclear Xs	• for syllable heads	(15)
	(for $_\sigma[\ldots X_N X \ldots]$		(16)

	General	
Edge:	LLL for $\mathfrak{R}$ class morphemes	(29)
	RRR for $\mathscr{L}$ class morphemes	(25)
	RRR	(17a)
Parsing:	ICC R to L	(17b)
	Delete unpaired (	(18)
	Head L	(17c)

Display (37) summarizes this study's endeavor to give an explanatory account of the metrical properties of Spanish words. The analysis entails recognition of interactive modules of lexical properties, syllabification, projection of baseline marks onto the metrical plane, and imposition of foot structure on this plane. Each of these modules is governed by autonomous and highly restrictive principles. In this framework, every Spanish word is associated with a metrical plane on which prominence is assigned to a single left-dominant foot formed by right-to-left scansion of undifferentiated baseline marks plus the boundaries supplied by (i) a general projection rule and (ii) one general and two lexically triggered Edge rules. No other information is necessary or allowed.

The one notable characteristic of (37) is that Spanish has separate projection subsystems for substantives (quantity sensitive) and verbs (quantity insensitive). Otherwise, (37) is quite unremarkable; all of its other properties are shared by numerous languages of the world. The apparent conundrums and complexities described in section 1, which have puzzled generations of scholars, arise out of the interactions among the component modules, each of which, like the metrical module, is basically unremarkable but has a particular quirk. For example, the morphological module houses several declension classes (an unremarkable fact), one of which, class C, provides a suffixal vowel with particular properties related to the fact that it is the default vocoid of Spanish; and the syllabification module offers the independently verifiable twist of complex nuclei with syllable-internal hierarchical structure distinct from that of complex rhymes. In many languages all vocoids project a • onto the grid, and in many languages complex rhymes project a boundary; Spanish happens to do both. In short, once these mild quirks are spotted and their interactions recognized, the apparent conundrums and complexities are unmasked as parts of a relatively simple and very orderly whole.

NOTES

1 This literature is "theoretically committed" in the sense that it has made direct and explicit ties with virtually every one of the general theoretical topics surveyed in this *Handbook* (the obvious exceptions being tone and manual signing).

 I hereby express deep gratitude for the generous advice and bibliographical help received from 31 knowledgeable participants in the field of Spanish phonology. Special thanks go to those who presciently warned me to narrow the focus radically, and to Tom Green, Morris Halle, José Ignacio Hualde, and Bill Idsardi for discussion of particular issues. I presented a version of some of this material at the 1992 Summer School in Linguistics, Universitat de Girona (Spain), and am indebted to the participants for numerous insights.

2 Substantial works published (or quasi-published by the Indiana University Linguistics Club) in the last decade of which I am aware are, in chronological order: Solan 1981 (A metrical analysis of Spanish stress); Harris 1983 (*Syllable Structure and Stress in Spanish*); Núñez Cedeño 1985 (Stress assignment in Spanish verb forms); Den Os and Kager 1986 (Extrametricality and stress in Spanish and Italian); Otero 1986 (A unified metrical account of Spanish stress); Roca 1986 (Secondary stress and metrical rhythm); Harris 1987 (The accentual patterns of verb paradigms in Spanish); Harris 1988/1992 (Spanish stress: The extrametricality issue); Roca 1988 (Theoretical implications of Spanish word stress); Harris 1989a (How different is verb stress in Spanish?); Harris 1989b (The Stress Erasure Convention and cliticization in Spanish); Farrell 1990 (Spanish stress: A cognitive analysis); Roca 1990a (Diachrony and synchrony in Spanish stress); Roca 1990b (Morphology and verbal stress in Spanish); Halle, Harris and Vergnaud 1991 (A reexamination of the Stress Erasure Convention and Spanish stress); Harris 1991b (With respect to accentual constituents in Spanish); Roca 1991 (Stress and syllables in Spanish); Roca 1992 (On the sources of word prosody).

3 As usual, I will draw on the variety of Spanish that I know best, educated central Mexican. Dialect variation will be pointed out where relevant.

4 For more detailed exposition of data, see the works listed in note 2, especially Harris (1988/1992).

5   Exact numbers depend on dialect and other factors.

6   I write these special morphemes in uppercase in (4) and subsequently where it will contribute to clarity.

7   An unexpected set of wellformed words of the form CV́.CGV.CVC in certain dialects is discussed in section 4.1.

8   For clarity I depart from standard orthography by using periods to indicate syllable breaks, by marking all primary stresses with an acute accent, by writing all glides (nonpeak high vocoids) as *y* and *w*, and by omitting "silent" (purely orthographic) *h* when it might be taken for a phonological segment.

9   It is not possible to make an end run around a potential window violation in words like *l*[**áw**.]*da.no* by deriving them from e.g., *l*[a.**ú**.]*da.no* by automatic contraction of *a.ú*. The reason is that there is a basic phonological contrast between *VH* (H a high vocoid) and *V́G*, even when these are the third and fourth vocoids from the end of the word (e.g., *v*[e.**í**]*culo* "vehicle, *des*[a.**ú**]*cyo* "dispossession, loss of hope", etc.).

10   These examples – like the preceeding note and much other evidence – also make it clear that the syllabicity of high vocoids is lexically contrastive in Spanish.

11   I henceforth enclose stems in { } and words in [ ] where this will contribute to clarity. The stem – or "derivational stem" as it is often called in the literature – is a familiar and indispensible unit in Spanish morphonology and phonology. Briefly, the stem consists of the root plus derivational affixes (if any are present) but not inflectional affixes. In the noun [{am+or}es] "loves", for example, *am* is the root and *am+or* is the stem (*es* is the inflection for plural nouns whose stem ends in a C); in the verb [{am+a}mos] "we love", *am* is the root and *am+a* is the stem (*mos* is the inflection for first person plural verbs). Both {amor} and {ama} – but not [amores] or [amamos] – can serve as input for further derivational affixation. Harris 1988/1992, section 2.4.1, and Harris 1991a provide detailed discussion.

12   Harris, 1988/1992, section 2.4.2, gives additional arguments that converge on the same conclusion.

13   Cf. McCarthy and Prince (1986, 1990) and much other current work, as well as Chapters 9 and 15, this volume.

14   The remainder of this subsection owes much to Idsardi (1992); see also chapter 11 of this volume.

15   Critical discussion can be found in Green (1991).

16   This device is utilized extensively in Halle and Vergnaud (1987), Halle, Harris, and Vergnaud (1991), and much other recent work, which must now be reexamined.

17   This parameter, which (among other things) can isolate a single peripheral grid element from inclusion in a metrical constituent, is the only implementation of extrametricality in the theory of Idsardi (1992).

18   The Latin setting of (10) is equivalent to "project (for $_{N'}[\ldots XX \ldots]$" (= any complex rhyme). Idsardi (1992) provides extensive motivation and exemplification for filters of the sort illustrated in (13a).

19   Prevocalic glides in Spanish are elements of complex nuclei while postvocalic glides occupy the same rhyme position, outside the nucleus, as coda consonants. For example, in words like *bwéy* and *cyén*, the nuclei are *wé* and *yé*, and the rhymes are

wéy and *yén*. Detailed arguments can be found in Harris (1989c) and Hualde (1991).

20 I assume that a general condition on wellformedness of grid representations prevents (16b) and (17b) from both inserting "("s at the same site.

21 This is the functional equivalent of the conflation operation of Halle and Vergnaud (1987); Halle, Harris, and Vergnaud (1991); and much other work.

22 Not accidentally, a morphological bifurcation parallels the metrical one: On one side, verbs are highly inflected, with affixation that manifests tense, mood, aspect, person, and number in finite forms. On the other side, substantives bear at most one specific inflectional affix (for number), but are distributed over several form classes similar to (and largely inherited from) the Latin declensional classes.

23 "Verb" and "verb form" are to be understood henceforth as "inflected verb form"; that is, as excluding infinitive, participle, and gerund, which lack inflections for tense/mood/aspect and person/number.

24 Cf. Harris (1987) and references therein for a review of the dialect situation.

25 Normative dialects have penultimate stress in subjunctives (*cantémos*, *limpiémos*) as in indicatives (*cantámos*, *limpiámos*).

These dialects are thus irrelevant to the issue at hand.

26 Any attempt to avoid this conclusion by deriving glides from high vowels via a syllable coalescence or mora deletion rule runs into an impasse: a lexically arbitrary set of exceptions to such rules would have to be marked. The attempt is thus empirically indistinguishable from an overt lexical glide/vowel distinction in any event.

27 The target of the comment is the Stress Erasure Convention (SEC) of Halle and Vergnaud (1987) and Halle, Harris, and Vergnaud (1991). The SEC can be dispensed with on the present proposals, which (unlike the SEC) explain the fact that the "erased" stresses have no known empirical consequences.

28 See notes 9 and 10.

29 "Canonical" substantives whose stems end in a high vowel are of course stressed on the penult as expected, like the corresponding verb forms with the same root; for example, *va.cí.o* "empty" (adjective), *va.cí.o* "I empty" (verb).

30 Cf. note 11 and for fully detailed discussion, Harris (1991a). Many readers will recognize in (35) the "epenthesis versus apocope" controversy of the late 60s and 70s, which is reviewed in Harris (1991a) in the light of current theories of morphology and syllabification.

Bibliography

Abaglo, P., and Diana Archangeli (1989). Language particular underspecification: Gengbe /e/ and Yoruba /i/. *LI* 20: 457–480.

Abraham, R. C. (1941). *A Modern Grammar of Spoken Hausa.* London: Crown Agents for the Colonies (published on behalf of the Nigerian Government).

Abraham, R. C. (1959). *Hausa Literature and the Hausa Sound System.* London: University of London Press.

Abu-Salim, I. M. (1980). Epenthesis and geminate consonants in Palestinian Arabic. *SLS* 10(2): 1–11.

Akinaga, K. (1960). Tokyo akusento hosoku ni tsuite [On the laws of Tokyo accent]. Appendix in H. Kindaichi (1960) *Neikai Nihongo Akusento Jiten* [Japanese accent dictionary] (pp. 1–68). Tokyo: Sanseido.

Akinlabi, A. (1993). Underspecification and the phonology of Yoruba /r/. *LI* 24: 139–160.

Al-Ani, Salman (1970). *Arabic phonology: An acoustic and physiological investigation.* The Hague: Mouton.

Al-Mozainy, H., R. Bley-Vroman, and J. McCarthy (1985). Stress shift and metrical structure. *LI* 16: 135–144.

Ali, H. L., T. Gallagher, J. Goldstein, and R. G. Daniloff (1971). Perception of coarticulated nasality. *JASA* 49: 538–540.

Allen, Margaret (1978). *Morphological investigations.* Doctoral dissertation, University of Connecticut.

Alpher, Barry (1973). *Son of ergative: The Yir Yoront language of North-Eastern Australia.* Doctoral dissertation, Cornell University.

Alpher, Barry (1988). Formalizing Yir-Yoront lenition. *Aboriginal Linguistics* 1: 188–197.

Alpher, Barry (1991). *Yir-Yoront Lexicon: Sketch and Dictionary of an Australian Language.* Berlin: Mouton de Gruyter.

Andersen, T. (1986a). The phonemic system of Madi. *AuU* 69: 193–207.

Andersen, T. (1986b). Verbal inflexion in Moru. *AuU* 69: 19–43.

Andersen, T. (1987). An outline of Lulubo phonology. *SAL* 18: 39–65.

Anderson, Janet (1987). The markedness differential hypothesis and syllable structure difficulty. In G. Ioup and S. H. Weinberger (eds.), *Interlanguage Phonology* (pp. 279–291). Cambridge: Newbury House.

Anderson, John (1969). Syllabic or non-syllabic phonology. *JL* 5: 136–143.

Anderson, John (1971). Dependency and grammatical functions. *FL* 7: 30–37.

Anderson, John (1977). *On Case Grammar*. London: Croom Helm.

Anderson, John (1986). Suprasegmental dependencies. In J. Durand (ed.), *Dependency and Non-Linear Phonology* (pp. 55–133). London: Croom Helm.

Anderson, John (1987). The limits of linearity. In J. M. Anderson and J. Durand (eds.), *Explorations in Dependency Phonology* (pp. 199–220). Dordrecht: Foris.

Anderson, John, and Jacques Durand (1988). Vowel harmony and non-specification in Nez Perce. In H. van der Hulst and N. Smith (eds.), *Features, Segmental Structure, and Harmony Processes* vol. 2 (pp. 1–18). Dordrecht: Foris.

Anderson, John, and Colin Ewen (1987). *Principles of Dependency Phonology*. Cambridge: CUP.

Anderson, John, Colin Ewen, and J. Staun (1985). Phonological structure: Segmental, suprasegmental and extrasegmental. *Phonology* 2: 203–224.

Anderson, John, and C. Jones (1974). Three theses concerning phonological representations. *JL* 10: 1–23.

Anderson, John, and C. Jones (1977). *Phonological Structure and the History of English*. Amsterdam: North-Holland.

Anderson, Lloyd (1975). *Phonetic and psychological explanations for vowel harmony, especially in Finnish*. Doctoral dissertation, University of Chicago.

Anderson, Lloyd (1980). Using asymmetrical and gradient data in the study of vowel harmony. In R. Vago (ed.), *Issues in Vowel Harmony* (pp. 271–340). Amsterdam: John Benjamins.

Anderson, Stephen R. (1972). On nasalization in Sundanese. *LI* 3: 253–268.

Anderson, Stephen R. (1974). *The Organization of Phonology*. New York: Academic Press.

Anderson, Stephen R. (1975). On the interaction of phonological rules of various types. *JL* 11: 39–62.

Anderson, Stephen R. (1976). Nasal consonants and the internal structure of segments. *Lg* 52: 326–344.

Anderson, Stephen R. (1978). Tone features. In V. Fromkin (ed.), *Tone: A Linguistic Survey* (pp. 133–176). New York: Academic Press.

Anderson, Stephen R. (1980). Problems and perspectives in the description of vowel harmony. In R. Vago (ed.), *Issues in Vowel Harmony* (pp. 1–48). Amsterdam: John Benjamins.

Anderson, Stephen R. (1981). Why phonology isn't "natural". *LI* 12: 493–539.

Anderson, Stephen R. (1982). The analysis of French schwa. *Lg* 58: 534–673.

Anderson, Stephen R. (1984). A metrical interpretation of some traditional claims about quantity and stress. In M. Aronoff and R. Oehrle (eds.), *Language Sound Structure*, Cambridge, MA: MIT Press.

Anderson, Stephen R. (1985). *Phonology in the Twentieth Century*. Chicago: University of Chicago Press.

Anderson, Stephen R. (1992). *A-Morphous Morphology*. Cambridge: CUP.

Angoujard, Jean-Pierre (1990). *Metrical Structure of Arabic*. Dordrecht: Foris.

Ann, Jean (1991). Constraining sign language handshapes: Toward a phonetically grounded account of handshapes in Taiwan Sign Language and American Sign Language. In K. Hunt, T. A. Perry, and V. Samiian (eds.), *Proceedings from the 1991 Western Conference on Linguistics* (pp. 1–13).

Aoki, H. (1968). Towards a typology of vowel harmony. *IJAL* 34: 142–145.

Applegate, R. (1971). Vowel harmony in Chumash. *Berkeley Papers in Linguistics* 1: 3–12.

Archangeli, Diana (1983). The root CV-template as a property of the affix: Evidence from Yawelmani. *NLLT* 1: 348–384.

Archangeli, Diana (1984). *Underspecification in Yawelmani phonology and morphology.* Doctoral dissertation, MIT. New York: Garland Press, 1988.

Archangeli, Diana (1985). Yokuts harmony: Evidence for coplanar representation in nonlinear phonology. *LI* 16: 335–372.

Archangeli, Diana (1986a). Extrametricality in Yawelmani. *LR* 4: 101–120.

Archangeli, Diana (1986b). The OCP and Nyangumarda buffer vowels. In *Proceedings of NELS 16* (pp. 34–46). Amherst: GLSA.

Archangeli, Diana (1988a). Aspects of underspecification theory. *Phonology* 5: 183–208.

Archangeli, Diana (1988b). Tiwi ghost consonants. MS, University of Arizona.

Archangeli, Diana (1991). Syllabification and prosodic templates in Yawelmani. *NLLT* 9: 231–283.

Archangeli, Diana, and Douglas Pulleyblank (1986). The content and structure of phonological representations. MS, University of Arizona and University of British Columbia.

Archangeli, Diana, and Douglas Pulleyblank (1987). Minimal and maximal rules: Effects of tier scansion. In J. McDough and B. Plunkett (eds.), *Proceedings of NELS 17* (pp. 16–35).

Archangeli, Diana, and Douglas Pulleyblank (1989). Yoruba vowel harmony. *LI* 20: 173–217.

Archangeli, Diana, and Douglas Pulleyblank (in press). *Grounded Phonology.* Cambridge, MA: MIT Press.

Ard, Joshua (1981). A sketch of vowel harmony in the Tungus languages. In B. Comrie (ed.), *Studies in the Languages of the USSR* (pp. 23–43). Edmonton: Linguistic Research.

Ard, Joshua (1984). Vowel harmony in Manchu: A critical overview. *JL* 20: 57–80.

Armstrong, L. E. (1934). The phonetic structure of Somali. *Mitteilungen des Seminars für Orientalische Sprachen zu Berlin* 37(3): 116–161.

Árnason, Kristján (1985). Icelandic word stress and metrical phonology. *Studia Linguistica* 39: 93–129.

Aronoff, Mark (1976). *Word Formation in Generative Grammar.* Cambridge, MA: MIT Press.

Aronoff, Mark (1988). Head operations and strata in reduplication: A linear treatment. *Yearbook of Morphology* 1: 1–15.

Aronoff, Mark, Azhar Arsyad, Hassan Basri, and Ellen Broselow (1987). Tier configuration in Makassarese reduplication. In A. Bosch, E. Schiller, and B. Need (eds.), *CLS 23: Parasession on Autosegmental and Metrical Phonology* (pp. 1–15). Chicago: CLS.

Aronoff, Mark, and S. N. Sridhar (1983). Morphological levels in English and Kannada; or, Atarizing Reagan. In J. Richardson, M. Marks, and A. Chukerman (eds.), *CLS 19: Parasession on the Interplay of Phonology, Morphology, and Synax* (pp. 16–35). Chicago: CLS.

Austerlitz, Robert (1956). Gilyak nursery words. *Word* 12: 260–279.

Austin, Peter (1981). *A Grammar of Diyari, South Australia.* Cambridge: CUP.

Austin, Peter (1986). Structural change in language obsolescence: Some eastern Australian examples. *AJL* 6: 201–30.

Austin, Peter (1988a). Phonological voicing contrasts in Australian Aboriginal languages. *La Trobe Working Papers in Linguistics* 1: 17–42.

Austin, Peter (1988b). Trill-released stops and language change in Central Australian languages. *AJL* 8: 219–244.

Austin, Peter, Ellis, R., and Hercus, Luise (1976). "Fruit of the eyes," semantic diffusion in the lakes languages of South Australia. *Papers in Australian Linguistics* 10: 57–77. Canberra: Pacific Linguistics.

Avanesov, R. I. (1968). *Russkoe literaturnoe proiznosenie* [Literary pronunciation of Russian]. Moscow: Izdatelstvo Prosvescenie.

Avery, P., and Keren Rice (1989). Segmental structure and coronal underspecification. *Phonology* 6: 179–200.

Avesani, Cinzia (1990). A Contribution to the Synthesis of Italian. MS, Scuola Normale di Pisa. Quaderni del Laboratorio di Linguistica 4.

Bagari, Dauda M. (1982). Some aspects of Guddiranci (the Guddiri dialect of Hausa). In H. Jungraithmayr (ed.), *The Chad Languages in the Hamitosemitic-Nigritic Border Area* (pp. 244–253). Marburger Studien zur Afrika- und Asienkunde, Serie A, Afrika, 27. Berlin: Dietrich Reimer.

Bagemihl, Bruce (1987). Tigrinya Speech Disguise and Constraints on Spreading Rules. In M. Crowhurst (ed.), *Proceedings of WCCFL 6* (pp. 1–15). Stanford: SLA.

Bagemihl, Bruce (1988a). *Alternate phonologies and morphologies.* Doctoral dissertation, University of British Columbia.

Bagemihl, Bruce (1988b). The morphology and phonology of Katajjait (Inuit throat games). *CJL* 33: 1–58.

Bagemihl, Bruce (1989). The Crossing Constraint and "backwards languages." *NLLT* 7: 481–549.

Bagemihl, Bruce (1991). Syllable structure in Bella Coola. *LI* 22: 589–646.

Bailey, C.-J. (1985). *English Phonetic Transcription.* Arlington: SIL.

Banner Inouye, Susan (1989). The phonological representation of flaps. Paper presented at the Second Annual Arizona Phonology Conference, Tucson.

Banti, G. (1988). Two Cushitic systems: Somali and Oromo nouns. In H. van der Hulst and N. Smith (eds.), *Autosegmental Studies on Pitch Accent Systems* (pp. 11–49). Dordrecht: Foris.

Bao, Zhi-ming (1990a). Fanqie languages and reduplication. *LI* 21: 317–350.

Bao, Zhi-ming (1990b). *On the nature of tone.* Doctoral dissertation, MIT.

Bao, Zhi-ming (1991). Tone and the geometry of laryngeal features. MS, University of Wisconsin, Madison.

Barker, C. (1989). Extrametricality, the cycle, and Turkish word stress. *Phonology at Santa Cruz* 1: 1–34.

Barker, M. A. R. (1963). *Klamath Dictionary.* Publications in Linguistics vol. 31. Berkeley: University of California Press.

Barker, M. A. R. (1964). *Klamath Grammar.* Publications in Linguistics 32. Berkeley: University of California Press.

Basbøll, Hans (1974). Structure consonantique du mot italien. *Revue Romane* 9: 27–40.

Basbøll, Hans (1977). The structure of the syllable and proposed hierarchy of phonological features. In W. Dressler et al. (eds.), *Phonologica 1976* (pp. 143–148). Innsbruck: Institut für Sprachwissenschaft.

Bat-El, Outi (1989). *Phonology and word structure in Modern Hebrew.* Doctoral dissertation, UCLA.

Bat-El, Outi (1992). Stem modification and cluster transfer in Modern Hebrew. MS, Tel-Aviv University.

Bates, Dawn, and Barry Carlson (1992). Simple syllables in Spokane Salish. *LI* 23: 653–659.

Battison, Robin (1978). *Lexical borrowing in American Sign Language.* Silver Spring: Linstok Press.

Battistella, Edward (1980). Igbo vowel harmony. In *Proceedings of NELS 9* (pp. 108–123).

Bauernschmidt, A. (1965). Amuzgo Syllable Dynamics. *Lg* 41: 471–483.

Bearth, T., and C. Link (1980). The tone puzzle of Wobe. *SAL* 11: 147–207.

Beckman, Mary (1982). Segmental duration and the "mora" in Japanese. *Phonetica* 39: 113–135.

Beckman, Mary (1986). *Stress and Non-Stress Accent.* Dordrecht: Foris.

Beckman, Mary, Kenneth de Jong, and Jan Edwards (1987). The surface phonology of stress clash in English. Presented at the LSA meeting.

Beckman, Mary, and Jan Edwards (1989). Lengthenings and shortenings and the nature of prosodic constituency. In J. Kingston and M. Beckman (eds.), *Papers in Laboratory Phonology 1:Between Grammar and the Physics of Speech* (pp. 152–178). Cambridge: CUP.

Beckman, Mary, and Janet Pierrehumbert (1986). Intonational structure in English and Japanese. *Phonology* 3: 255–309.

Beckman, Mary, and A. Shoji (1984). Spectral and perceptual evidence for CV coarticulation in devoiced /si/ and /syu/ in Japanese. *Phonetica* 41: 61–71.

Beckman, Mary, M. G. Swora, J. Rauschenberg, and K. De Jong (1991). Stress shift, stress clash and polysyllabic shortening in a prosodically annotated discourse. *Proceedings of the 1991 International Conference on Spoken Language Processing* 1: 5–8.

Bell, Alan (1978). Syllabic consonants. In J. H. Greenberg (ed.), *Universals of Human Language*, vol. 2, Phonology (pp. 153–201). Stanford: Stanford University Press.

Bell, Sarah (1983). Internal C reduplication in Shuswap. *LI* 14: 332–338.

Bender, M. Lionel, and Hailu Fulass (1978). *Amharic Verb Morphology*, vol. 7. East Lansing, MI: African Studies Center.

Bender, M. Lionel et al., eds. (1976) *Language in Ethiopia*. London: Oxford University Press.

Bendor-Samuel, J. (1970). Some Problems of Segmentation in the Phonological Analysis of Terena. In F. R. Palmer (ed.), *Prosodic Analysis* (pp. 214–221). London: OUP.

Berman, Arlene, and Michael Szamosi (1972). Observations on sentential stress. *Lg* 48: 304–325.

Bernard, C. (1957). *An Introduction to the Study of Experimental Medicine.* New York: Dover. First French edition, 1865.

Bickmore, Lee (1990). Branching nodes and prosodic categories. In S. Inkelas and D. Zec (eds.), *The Phonology-Syntax Connection* (pp. 1–17). Chicago: University of Chicago Press.

Bing, Janet (1979). *Aspects of English prosody.* Doctoral dissertation, University of Massachusetts, Amherst.

Bing, Janet (1980). Linguistic rhythm and grammatical structure in Afghan Persian. *LI* 11: 437–464.

Bird, Steven (1990). *Constraint base phonology.* Doctoral dissertation, Edinburgh University.

Birk, D. B. W. (1976). *The MalakMalak Language, Daly River (Western Arnhem Land).* Pacific Linguistics B-45. Canberra: Australian National University.

Black, H. Andrew (1991a). The optimal iambic foot and reduplication in Axininca Campa. *Phonology at Santa Cruz* 2: 1–18.

Black, H. Andrew (1991b). The phonology of the velar glide in Axininca Campa. *Phonology* 8: 183–217.

Black, Paul (1980). Norman Pama Historical Phonology. In B. Rigsby and P. Sutton (eds.), *Papers in Australian Linguistics* vol. 13 (pp. 181–239). Canberra: Australian National University.

Blanc, Haim (1970). The Arabic dialect of the Negev Bedouins. *Proceedings of the Israel Academy of Sciences and Humanities* 4, No. 7: 112–150. Jerusalem: Israel Academy of Sciences and Humanities.

Blevins, Juliette (1990). The independence of length and prosody in phonological representations. Paper presented at the Arizona Phonology Conference, Tucson.

Blevins, Juliette (1991). Evidence for the independent representation of length and weight. MS, Stanford University.

Blevins, Juliette (1992a). The nature of constraints on the non-dominant hand in ASL. In G. Coulter (ed.), *Current Issues in ASL Phonology* (pp. 43–62). San Diego: Academic Press.

Blevins, Juliette (1992b). Review of An Essay on Stress. *Lg* 68: 159–165.

Blevins, Juliette (1993a). A tonal analysis of Lithuanian nominal accent. *Lg* 69: 237–273.

Blevins, Juliette (1993b). Klamath laryngeal phonology. *IJAL* 59: 237–279.

Bliese, Loren F. (1981). *A Generative Grammar of Afar*. The Summer Institute of Linguistics, University of Texas at Arlington.

Bloch, Bernard (1950). Studies in Colloquial Japanese, IV: Phonemics. *Lg* 26: 86–125.

Blust, R. (1992). Obstruent epenthesis and the unity of phonological features. MS, University of Hawaii.

Boadi, L. (1963). Palatality as a factor in Twi vowel harmony. *JAL* 2: 133–138.

Boas, Franz, and Ella Deloria (1941). *Dakota Grammar*. Memoirs of the National Academy of Sciences 23. Washington, DC: US Govt. Printing Office.

Bogoras, V. (1922). Chukchee. In F. Boas (ed.), *Handbook of American Indian Languages*, vol. 2. Washington, DC: Smithsonian Institute.

Bolinger, Dwight (1958). A theory of pitch accent in English. *Word* 14: 109–149.

Bolinger, Dwight (1965). Pitch accent and sentence rhythm. In I. Abe and T. Kanekiyo (eds.), *Forms of English: Accent, Morpheme, Order*. Tokyo: Hokuou.

Bolinger, Dwight (1972). Accent is predictable (if you're a mind reader). *Lg* 48: 633–644.

Bolinger, Dwight (1982). *Intonation and Its Parts: The Melody of Speech*. Stanford: Stanford University Press.

Booij, Geert (1983). French C/Ø alternations, extrasyllabicity and lexical phonology. *LR* 3: 181–207.

Booij, Geert, and Jerzy Rubach (1984). Morphological and prosodic domains in lexical phonology. *Phonology* 1: 1–27.

Booij, Geert, and Jerzy Rubach (1987). Postcyclic versus postlexical rules in lexical phonology. *LI* 18: 1–44.

Borgstrøm, C. Hj. (1937). The Dialect of Barra in the Outer Hebrides. *Norsk Tidsskrift for Sprogvidenskap* 8: 71–242.

Borgstrøm, C. Hj. (1940). *A Linguistic Survey of the Gaelic Dialects of Scotland*, vol. 1: *The Dialects of the Outer Hebrides*. Norsk Tidsskrift for Sprogvidenskap, Suppl. Bind 1.

Borowsky, Toni (1986). *Topics in the lexical phonology of English*. Doctoral dissertation, University of Massachusetts.

Bosch, Anna (1988). VC syllable structure in Scottish Gaelic: Some implications for syllable theory. MS, University of Chicago.

Bosch, Anna (1991). *Phonotactics at the level of the phonological word*. Doctoral dissertation, University of Chicago.

Bourciez, E., and J. Bourciez (1967). *Phonétique française: Etude historique*. Paris: Editions Klincksieck.

Boxwell, H., and M. Boxwell (1966). Weri phonemes. In S. A. Wurm (ed.), *Papers in New Guinea Linguistics*, vol. 5. Linguistic Circle of Canberra Publications, Series A, no.7. Canberra: Australian National University.

Boyes-Braem, Penny (1981). *Distinctive features of the handshapes of American Sign Language.* Doctoral dissertation, University of California, Berkeley.

Boysson-Bardies, B. de (1993). Ontogeny of language-specific syllabic productions. In B. Boysson-Bardies et al. (eds.), *Developmental Neurocognition* (pp. 353–363). Dordrecht: Kluwer.

Bradley, D. (ed.) (1981). *Tonation.* Pacific Linguistics Series A. vol. 62. Canberra: Australian National University.

Bradlow, A. (1992). On the representation of clicks. In A. Bradlow (ed.), *Working Papers of the Cornell Phonetics Laboratory,* vol. 7 (pp. 83–102).

Braine, M. D. S. (1974). On what might constitute learnable phonology. *Lg* 50: 270–299.

Brame, Michael (1972). On the abstractness of phonology: Maltese ʕ. In M. Brame (ed.), *Contributions to Generative Phonology.* Austin: University of Texas Press.

Brame, Michael (1974). The cycle in phonology: Stress in Palestinian, Maltese and Spanish. *LI* 5: 39–60.

Brandenstein, C. G. von (1982). The secret respect language of the Pilbara (Western Australia). In W. Meid, H. Olberg and H. Schmeja (eds.), *Sprachwissenschaft in Innsbruck,* vol. 50 (pp. 33–52). IBK.

Breen, Gavan (1971). *A description of the Waluwara language.* MA dissertation, Monash University.

Breen, Gavan (1975). Innamincka talk. Unpublished MS.

Breen, Gavan (1976). An introduction to Gog-Naro. In P. Sutton (ed.), *Languages of Cape York* (pp. 243–259). Canberra: AIAS.

Breen, Gavan (1977). Antegerebenha vowel phonology. *Phonetica* 34: 371–391.

Breen, Gavan (1988). Arrernte phonology and antisyllables. Paper presented at Central Australian Linguistic Circle Mini-conference, Alice Springs.

Breen, Gavan (1991). The syllable in Arrernte phonology. MS, School of Australian Linguistics and Institute for Aboriginal Development.

Breen, Gavan (1992). Some problems in Kukatj phonology. *AJL* 12.1: 1–44.

Breen, Gavan (1991). Karrwa and Wanyi comparative notes. In N. Evans (ed.), *Studies in Comparative Non-Pama-Nyungan.*

Brentari, Diane (1990a). Licensing ASL handshape. In C. Lucas (ed.), *Sign Language Research: Theoretical Issues* (pp. 57–68). Washington, DC: Gallaudet University Press.

Brentari, Diane (1990b). *Theoretical foundations of American Sign Language phonology.* Doctoral dissertation, University of Chicago.

Brentari, Diane (1990c). Underspecification in American Sign Language phonology. In K. Hall, J.-P. Koenig, M. Meacham, S. Reinman, and L. Sutton (eds.), *Proceedings of BLS 16* (pp. 46–56). Berkeley: BLS.

Brentari, Diane (1993). Sonority and secondary movement in American Sign Language: Formal representation and phonetic realization. Paper presented at the Workshop on Phonology and Morphology, Amsterdam.

Brentari, Diane (1994). Establishing a sonority hierarchy in American Sign Language. *Phonology* 10(2).

Brentari, Diane, and Anna Bosch (1990). The mora: Autosegment or syllable constituent. In M. Ziolkowski, M. Noske, and K. Deaton (eds.), *CLS 26: Parasession on the Syllable in Phonetics and Phonology* (pp. 1–16). Chicago: CLS.

Brentari, Diane, and John Goldsmith (1993). Secondary licensing and the non-dominant hand in ASL phonology. In G. Coulter (ed.), *Current Issues in ASL Phonology* (pp. 19–41). San Diego: Academic Press.

Bresnan, Joan (1971). Sentence stress and syntactic transformations. *Lg* 47: 257–281.

Bresnan, Joan (1972). Stress and syntax: A reply. *Lg* 48: 325–342.

Bright, William (ed.) (1992). *International Encyclopedia of Linguistics.* Oxford: OUP.

Broadbent, S. M. (1964). *The Southern Sierra Miwok Language.* Berkeley and Los Angeles: University of California Press.

Bromberger, Sylvain, and Morris Halle (1988). Conceptual issues in morphology. MS, MIT.

Bromberger, Sylvain, and Morris Halle (1989). Why phonology is different. *LI* 20: 51–70.

Broselow, Ellen (1976). *The phonology of Egyptian Arabic.* Doctoral dissertation, University of Massachusetts, Amherst.

Broselow, Ellen (1979). Cairene Arabic syllable structure. *LA* 5: 345–382.

Broselow, Ellen (1982). On predicting the interaction of stress and epenthesis. *Glossa* 16: 115–132.

Broselow, Ellen (1983). Subjacency in morphology: Salish double reduplication. *NLLT* 1: 317–346.

Broselow, Ellen (1984). Default consonants in Amharic morphology. In M. Speas and R. Sproat (eds.), *Papers from the January 1984 MIT Workshop in Morphology* vol. 7 (pp. 15–32). Cambridge, MA: MIT Dept. of Linguistics.

Broselow, Ellen (1985). Amharic, automatic spreading, and the Obligatory Contour Principle. MS, SUNY at Stony Brook.

Broselow, Ellen (1992). Parametric variation in Arabic dialect phonology. In E. Broselow, M. Eid and J. McCarthy (eds.), *Perspectives on Arabic Linguistics,* vol. 4. Amsterdam and Philadelphia: John Benjamins.

Broselow, Ellen (in press). Transfixation. In G. Booij, C. Lehmann, and J. Mugdan (eds.), *Morphology: A Handbook on Inflection and Word Formation.* Berlin: Walter de Gruyter.

Broselow, Ellen, Marie Huffman, Su-I Chen, and Ruohmei Hsieh (in press). The timing of CVVC syllables. In Mushira Eid (ed.), Perspectives on Arabic Linguistics VIII. Amsterdam and Philadelphia: John Benjamins.

Broselow, Ellen, and John McCarthy (1983). A theory of internal reduplication. *LR* 3: 25–98.

Broselow, Ellen, and A. Niyondagara (1989). Feature geometry of Kirundi palatalization. *SLS* 20(1): 71–88.

Brosnahan, L. F., and Bertil Malmberg (1970). *Introduction to Phonetics.* Cambridge: CUP.

Browman, Catherine, and Louis Goldstein (1989). Articulatory gestures as phonological units. *Phonology* 6: 201–251.

Browman, Catherine, and Louis Goldstein (1992a). Articulatory phonology: An overview. *Phonetica* 49: 155–180.

Browman, Catherine, and Louis Goldstein (1992b). "Targetless" schwa: An articulatory analysis. In G. Docherty and R. Ladd (eds.), *Papers in Laboratory Phonology II: Gesture, Segment, Prosody* (pp. 26–56). Cambridge: CUP.

Bruce, Gösta (1970). Diphthongization in the Malmö dialect. *Working Papers in Linguistics* 3: 1–20. Lund University.

Bruce, Gösta (1977). *Swedish Word Accents in Sentence Perspective.* Lund: Gleerup.

Buckley, Eugene (1991). Kashaya closed-syllable shortening and prosodic syllabification. In D. Bates (ed.), *Proceedings of WCCFL 10* (pp. 65–74). Stanford: SLA.

Buckley, Eugene (1992). Kashaya laryngeal increments, contour segments, and the moraic tier. *LI* 23: 487–496.

Bullock, Barbara (1990). V/C planar segregation and the CVC syllable in Sierra Miwok nonconcatenative morphology. In M. Ziolkowski, M. Noske, and K. Deaton (eds.),

CLS 26: Parasession on the Syllable in Phonetics and Phonology (pp. 17–32). Chicago: CLS.

Burling, Robbins (1970). *Man's Many Voices*. New York: Holt, Reinhart and Winston.

Busby, Peter (1980). The distribution of phonemes in Australian Aboriginal languages. *Papers in Australian Linguistics* 14. Canberra: Pacific Linguistics, A-60.

Butcher, Andrew (to appear a). Phonetic correlates of some consonantal contrasts in Australian languages. In N. Evans (ed.), *Studies in Comparative Non-Pama-Nyungan*.

Butcher, Andrew (to appear b). *The Phonetics of Australian Languages*. Oxford: OUP.

Cairns, Charles (1969). Markedness, neutralization, and universal redundancy rules. *Lg* 45: 863–886.

Caisse, M. (1981). Cross-linguistic differences in fundamental frequency perturbation induced by voiceless aspirated stops. *JASA* 70: S76–S77.

Calabrese, A. (1986). Metaphony in Salentino. *Rivista di grammatica generativa* 9–10: 1–141.

Calabrese, A. (1987). The interaction of phonological rules and filters. In B. Plunkett and J. McDonough (eds.), *Proceedings of NELS 17* (pp. 79–99). Amherst: GSLA.

Calabrese, A. (1988). *Towards a theory of phonological alphabets*. Doctoral dissertation, MIT.

Camilli, A (1929). Il dialetto di Servigliano. *Archivum Romanicum* 13: 220–271.

Campbell, Lyle (1974). Phonological features: Problems and proposals. *Lg* 50: 52–65.

Campbell, Lyle (1980). The psychological and sociological reality of Finnish vowel harmony. In R. D. Vago (ed.), *Issues in Vowel Harmony* (pp. 245–270). Amsterdam: John Benjamins.

Campbell, Lyle (1986). Testing phonology in the field. In J. J. Ohala and J. J. Jaeger (eds.), *Experimental Phonology* (pp. 163–173). Orlando: Academic Press.

Capell, Arthur (1967). Sound systems in Australia. *Phonetica* 16: 85–110.

Capell, Arthur, and Heather Hinch (1970). *Maung Grammar, Texts and Vocabulary*. The Hague: Mouton.

Capo, H. B. (1989). L'assimilation d'arrondissement dans le redoublement des formes verbales en gbe. *Linguistique africaine* 3: 19–42.

Card, Elizabeth Ann (1983). *A phonetic and phonological study of Arabic emphasis*. Doctoral dissertation, Cornell University.

Carey, Susan (1985). *Conceptual Change in Childhood*. Cambridge, MA: The MIT Press.

Carlson, Lauri (1983). *Dialogue Games: An Approach to Discourse Analysis*. Dordrecht: Reidel.

Carlson, Lauri (1984). Focus and dialogue games: A game-theoretical approach to the interpretation of intonational meaning. In L. Vaina and J. Hintikka (eds.), *Cognitive Constraints on Communication* (pp. 259–333). Dordrecht: Reidel.

Carlson, R. (1983). Downstep in Supyire. *SAL* 14: 35–45.

Carnochan, J. (1970). Vowel Harmony in Igbo. In F. R. Palmer (ed.), *Prosodic Analysis* (pp. 222–229). Oxford: Basil Blackwell.

Caron, Bernard (1987). *Description d'un parler haoussa de l'Ader (République du Niger)*. Doctoral dissertation, Université de Paris 7.

Carrier, Jill (1979). *The interaction of phonological and morphological rules in Tagalog: A study in the relationship between rule components in grammar*. Doctoral dissertation, MIT.

Carrier-Duncan, Jill (1984). Some problems with prosodic accounts of reduplication. In M. Aronoff and R. Oehrle (eds.), *Language Sound Structure* (pp. 260–286). Cambridge, MA: MIT Press.

Carrington, J. F. (1949). *Talking Drums of Africa*. London: Harry Kingsgate Press.

Carter, Hazel (1971). Morphotonology of Zambian Tonga: Some developments of Meeussen's systems, part 1. *ALS* 12: 1–30.

Carter, Hazel (1972). Morphotonology of Zambian Tonga: Some developments of Meeussen's system, part 2. *ALS* 13: 52–97.

Casali, R. (1993a). Labial opacity and roundness harmony in Nawuri. In D. Silverman and R. Kirchner (eds.), *UCLA Occasional Papers in Linguistics*, no. 13 (pp. 1–19).

Casali, R. (1993b). On some uses of ATR. MS, UCLA.

Cassimjee, Farida, and Charles Kisseberth (1989). Shingazidja nominal accent. *SLS* 19.1: 33–61.

Catford, J. C. (1977). *Fundamental Problems in Phonetics*. Bloomington: Indiana University Press.

Chadwick, Neil (1975). *A Descriptive Study of the Djingili Language*. Canberra: AIAS.

Chafe, Wallace (1968). The ordering of phonological rules. *IJAL* 24: 115–136.

Chambers, Jack (1973). Canadian Raising. *CJL* 18: 113–135.

Chan, Marjorie (1988). An autosegmental analysis of Danyang tone sandhi: Some historical and theoretical issues. MS, International Conference on Wu Dialects, Chinese University of Hong Kong.

Chan, Marjorie (1991). Contour-tone spreading and tone sandhi in Danyang Chinese. *Phonology* 8: 237–259.

Chang, Kun (1953). On the tone system of the Miao-Yao languages. *Lg* 29: 374–378.

Chao, Y.-R. (1941). Distinctions within Ancient Chinese. *Harvard Journal of Asiatic Studies* 5: 203–233.

Chao, Y.-R. (1947). *Cantonese Primer*. Cambridge, MA: Harvard University Press.

Chao, Y.-R. (1968). *A Grammar of Spoken Chinese*. Berkeley: University of California Press.

Charette, Monik (1988). *Some constraints on governing relations in phonology*. Doctoral dissertation, McGill University.

Chen, Matthew (1985). Tianjin tone sandhi: Erratic rule application. MS, University of California, San Diego.

Chen, Matthew (1986). An overview of tone sandhi phenomena across Chinese dialects. In W. S.-Y. Wang (ed.), *Languages and Dialects of China* (pp. 113–158). Journal of Chinese Linguistics Monograph Series No. 3.

Chen, Matthew (1987). The syntax of Xiamen tone sandhi. *Phonology* 4: 109–150.

Chen, Matthew (1990). What must phonology know about syntax? In S. Inkelas and D. Zec (eds.), *The Phonology-Syntax Connection* (pp. 19–46). Chicago: University of Chicago Press.

Chen, Matthew (1991). Recent advances in tone sandhi studies. MS, LSA Institute, University of California, Santa Cruz.

Chen, Matthew, and William S.-Y. Wang (1975). Sound change: Activation and implementation. *Lg* 51: 228–281.

Cheng, C. C. (1973). A quantitative study of Chinese tones. *Journal of Chinese Linguistics* 1: 93–110.

Cheng, C. C., and William S.-Y. Wang (1977). Tone change in Chao-zhou Chinese: A study in lexical diffusion. In W. Wang (ed.), *The Lexicon in Phonological Change* (pp. 86–100). The Hague: Mouton.

Cheng, L. (1989). Feature geometry of vowels and co-occurrence restrictions in Cantonese. MS, MIT.

Cheung, Kwan-Hin (1986). *The phonology of present-day Cantonese*. Doctoral dissertation, University College, London.

Chi, M. (1976). Short term memory limitations in children: Capacity or processing deficits? *Memory and Cognition* 4: 559–572.

Chiang, Wen-yu (1992). *The prosodic morphology and phonology of affixation in Taiwanese and other Chinese languages.* Doctoral dissertation, University of Delaware.

Chiba, T., and M. Kajiyama (1941). *The Vowel: Its Nature and Structure.* Tokyo: Tokyo-Kaiseikan Publishing Co.

Chierchia, G. (1982). An autosegmental theory of Raddoppiamento. In J. Pustejovsky and P. Sells (eds.), *Proceedings of NELS 12.* Amherst: GLSA.

Chinchor, Nancy (1978). The syllable in American Sign Language. Paper presented at the MIT Sign Language symposium.

Cho, Young-mee Yu (1990a). *Parameters of consonantal assimilation.* Doctoral dissertation, Stanford University.

Cho, Young-mee Yu (1990b). Syntax and phrasing in Korean. In S. Inkelas and D. Zec (eds.), *The Phonology-Syntax Connection* (pp. 47–62). Chicago: University of Chicago Press.

Cho, Young-mee Yu (1992). A phonological constraint on the attachment of particles in Korean. In S. Kuno et al. (eds.), *Harvard Studies in Korean Linguistics,* vol. 4 (pp. 37–46). Seoul: Hanshin Publishing Company.

Choi, J. (1992). *Phonetic underspecification and target-interpolation: An acoustic study of Marshallese vowel allophony.* Doctoral dissertation, UCLA.

Chomsky, (Avram) Noam (1951). *Morphophonemics of Modern Hebrew.* MA dissertation, University of Pennsylvania. New York: Garland Press, 1979.

Chomsky, Noam (1965). *Aspects of the Theory of Syntax.* Cambridge, MA: MIT Press.

Chomsky, Noam (1967). Some general properties of phonological rules. *Lg* 43: 102–128.

Chomsky, Noam (1971). Deep structure, surface structure and semantic interpretation. In D. Steinberg and L. A. Jakobovits (eds.), *Semantics: An Interdisciplinary Reader* (pp. 183–216). Cambridge: CUP.

Chomsky, Noam (1981). *Lectures on Government and Binding.* Dordrecht: Foris.

Chomsky, Noam (1992). A minimalist programme for linguistic theory. *MIT Occasional Papers in Linguistics No. 1.*

Chomsky, Noam , and Morris Halle (1968). *The Sound Pattern of English.* New York: Harper and Row.

Chomsky, Noam, Morris Halle, and Fred Lukoff (1956). On accent and juncture in English. In *For Roman Jakobson* (pp. 65–80). The Hague: Mouton.

Christdas, Pratima (1988). *The phonology and morphology of Tamil.* Doctoral dissertation, Cornell University.

Chumbow, B. S. (1982). Ogori vowel harmony: An autosegmental perspective. *LA* 10: 61–93.

Chung, Gyeonghee (1991). Syllable structure in Tamazight Berber and its theoretical implications. MS, University of Texas at Austin.

Chung, Sandra (1983). Transderivational constraints in Chamorro phonology. *Lg* 59: 35–66.

Chung, Sandra, and Alan Timberlake (1985). Tense, aspect and mood. In T. Shopen (ed.), *Language Typology and Syntactic Description: Grammatical Categories in the Lexicon* (pp. 202–258). New York: CUP.

Churchyard, H. (1991). Compensatory lengthening and "gemination throwback" in Trukese and Puluwat as evidence for the rime in moraic theory. Paper presented at LSA Meeting, Chicago. MS, University of Texas.

Churma, Don G. (1979). *Arguments from external evidence in phonology.* Doctoral dissertation, Ohio State University. New York: Garland Press, 1985.

Cinque, Guglielmo (1993). A null theory of phrase and compound stress. *LI* 24: 239–398.

Clark, Mary (1990). *The Tonal System of Igbo*. Dordrecht: Foris.

Clements, G. N. (1976). Palatalization: Linking or assimilation? In S. S. Mufwene, C. A. Walker, and S. B. Steever (eds.), *Papers from CLS 12* (pp. 96–109). Chicago: CLS.

Clements, G. N. (1977). The autosegmental treatment of vowel harmony. In W. U. Dressler and I. E. Pfeiffer (eds.), *Phonologica 1976*. Innsbrucker Beitrage zur Sprachwissenschaft, vol. 19.

Clements, G. N. (1978). Tone and syntax in Ewe. In D. J. Napoli (ed.), *Elements of Tone, Stress, and Intonation* (pp. 21–99). Washington, DC: Georgetown University Press.

Clements, G. N. (1979). The description of terraced-level tone languages. *Lg* 55: 536–558.

Clements, G. N. (1980[1976]). *Vowel Harmony in Nonlinear Generative Phonology: An Autosegmental Model*. Bloomington: IULC.

Clements, G. N. (1981a). Akan vowel harmony: A nonlinear analysis. *Harvard Studies in Phonology* 2: 108–177.

Clements, G. N. (1981b). The hierarchical representation of tone features. In I. R. Dihoff (ed.), *Current Approaches to African Linguistics*, vol. 1 (pp. 145–176). Dordrecht: Foris.

Clements, G. N. (1983). A place for linking consonants in French. Paper presented at University of Southern California, October 13, 1983,

Clements, G. N. (1984). Principles of tone association in Kikuyu. In G. N. Clements and J. Goldsmith (eds.), *Autosegmental Studies in Bantu Tone* (pp. 281–339). Dordrecht: Foris.

Clements, G. N. (1985a). The geometry of phonological features. *Phonology* 2: 225–252.

Clements, G. N. (1985b). The problem of transfer in nonlinear morphology. *Cornell Working Papers in Linguistics* 7: 38–73.

Clements, G. N. (1986a). Compensatory lengthening and consonant gemination in Luganda. In L. Wetzels and E. Sezer (eds.), *Studies in Compensatory Lengthening* (pp. 37–77). Dordrecht: Foris.

Clements, G. N. (1986b). Syllabification and epenthesis in the Barra dialect of Gaelic. In K. Bogers, M. Maus, and H. van der Hulst (eds.), *The Phonological Representation of Suprasegmentals* (pp. 317–336). Dordrecht: Foris.

Clements, G. N. (1987). Phonological feature representation and the description of intrusive stops. In A. Bosch, B. Need, and E. Schiller (eds.), *CLS 23: Parasession on Autosegmental and Metrical Phonology* (pp. 29–50). Chicago: CLS.

Clements, G. N. (1988). Toward a substantive theory of feature specification. In J. Blevins and J. Carter (eds.), *Proceedings of NELS 18* (pp. 79–93). Amherst: GSLA.

Clements, G. N. (1989a). The representation of vowel height. Paper presented at the Conference on Features and Underspecification, MIT.

Clements, G. N. (1989b). A unified set of features for consonants and vowels. MS, Cornell University.

Clements, G. N. (1990). The role of the sonority cycle in core syllabification. In J. Kingston and M. Beckman (eds.), *Papers in Laboratory Phonology 1: Between the Grammar and Physics of Speech* (pp. 283–333). New York: CUP.

Clements, G. N. (1991a). Place of articulation in consonants and vowels: A unified theory. In *Working Papers of the Cornell Phonetics Laboratory*, vol. 5 (pp. 77–123). Ithaca: Cornell University. Presented at NELS 21, UQAM, Montreal.

Clements, G. N. (1991b). Vowel height assimilation in Bantu languages. In K. Hubbard (ed.), *BLS 17S: Proceedings of the Special Session on African Language Structures* (pp. 25–64). Berkeley: BLS.

Clements, G. N. (1992). Phonological primes: Features or gestures? *Phonetica* 49: 181–193.

Clements, G. N. (1993). Lieu d'articulation des consonnes et des voyelles: une théorie unifiée. In B. Laks and A. Rialland (eds.), *L'Architecture et la géometry des représentations phonologiques*. Paris: Editions du CNRS.

Clements, G. N., and K. C. Ford (1979). Kikuyu tone shift and its synchronic consequences. *LI* 10: 179–210.

Clements, G. N., and K. C. Ford (1981). On the phonological status of downstep in Kikuyu. In D. L. Goyvaerts (ed.), *Phonology in the 1980s* (pp. 309–357). Ghent: Story-Scientia.

Clements, G. N., and John Goldsmith (1984). Introduction. In G. N. Clements and J. Goldsmith (eds.), *Autosegmental Studies in Bantu Tone* (pp. 1–17). Dordrecht: Foris.

Clements, G. N., and S. Jay Keyser (1983). *CV Phonology: A Generative Theory of the Syllable*. Cambridge, MA: MIT Press.

Clements, G. N., and Engin Sezer (1982). Vowel and consonant disharmony in Turkish. In H. van der Hulst and N. Smith (eds.), *The Structure of Phonological Representations*, vol. 2 (pp. 213–255). Dordrecht: Foris.

Cohen, Marcel (1963). *Nouveaux regards sur la langue française*. Paris: Editions Sociales.

Cohn, Abigail (1989). Stress in Indonesian and bracketing paradoxes. *NLLT* 7: 167–216.

Cohn, Abigail (1990). *Phonetic and phonological rules of nasalization*. Doctoral dissertation, UCLA.

Cohn, Abigail (1992a). The consequences of dissimilation in Sundanese. *Working Papers of the Cornell Phonetics Laboratory* 7: 17–40. A revised version of this paper appeared as Cohn 1992b.

Cohn, Abigail (1992b). The consequences of dissimilation in Sundanese. *Phonology* 9: 199–220.

Cohn, Abigail (1993). The status of nasalized continuants. In M. Huffman and R. Krakow (eds.), *Nasality* (pp. 329–367). San Diego: Academic Press.

Cole, Jennifer (1987). *Planar phonology and morphology*. Doctoral dissertation, MIT.

Cole, Jennifer (1990). Arguing for the phonological cycle: A critical review. In D. Meyer, S. Tomioka, and L. Zidani-Eroglu (eds.), *Proceedings of the Formal Linguistics Society of Midamerica* (pp. 51–67). Madison: Linguistics Student Organization, University of Wisconsin.

Cole, Jennifer (1992). A reexamination of cyclicity in Catalan phonology. MS, University of Illinois, Urbana.

Cole, Jennifer (1993). A dynamic approach to rule ordering paradoxes in Klamath and Icelandic. MS, University of Illinois, Urbana.

Cole, Jennifer (in press). Eliminating cyclicity as a source of complexity in phonology. In J. Cole and C. Kisseberth (eds.), *Perspectives in Phonology*. Stanford: CSLI.

Cole, Jennifer, and John Coleman (1992). No need for cyclicity in generative grammar. In J. Denton, G. Chan, and C. Canakis (eds.), *CLS 28: Parasession on the Cycle in Linguistic Theory* (pp. 36–50). Chicago: CLS.

Cole, Jennifer, and L. Trigo (1989). Parasitic harmony. In H. van der Hulst and N. Smith (eds.), *Features, Segmental Structure and Harmony Processes* (pp. 19–38). Dordrecht: Foris.

Cole, Jennifer Fitzpatrick (1990). The minimal word in Bengali. In A. Halpern (ed.), *Proceedings of WCCFL 9* (pp. 157–170). Stanford: SLA.

Cole, Jennifer Fitzpatrick (1991). Phrasal reduplication in Bengali. In *Proceedings of the Third Leiden Conference of Junior Linguists*. Leiden: University of Leiden.

Coleman, Carolyn (1982). *A sketch grammar of Kunparlang, with particular reference to grammatical relations*. BA honors dissertation, Australian National University.

Coleman, John (1991). *Phonological representations – their names, forms, and powers*. Doctoral dissertation, University of York.

Collinder, B. (1960). *Comparative Grammar of the Uralic Languages*. Stockholm: Alqvist and Wiksell.

Collinge, N. E. (1985). *The Laws of Indo-European*. Amsterdam: John Benjamins.

Collins-Ahlgren, M. (1990). Word formation processes in New Zealand Sign Language. In S. Fischer and P. Siple (eds.), *Theoretical Issues in Sign Language Research*, vol. 1 (pp. 279–312). Chicago: University of Chicago Press.

Comrie, Bernard (1980). The sun letters in Maltese: Between morphophonemics and phonetics. *SLS* 10(2): 25–37.

Comrie, Bernard (1981). *The Languages of the Soviet Union*. Cambridge: CUP.

Condoravdi, C. (1990). Sandhi rules of Greek and prosodic theory. In S. Inkelas and D. Zec (eds.), *The Phonology-Syntax Connection* (pp. 63–83). Chicago: University of Chicago Press.

Conklin, H. (1956). Tagalog speech disguise. *Lg* 32: 136–139.

Conklin, H. (1959). Linguistic play in its cultural context. *Lg* 35: 631–636.

Conteh, P., E. Cowper, D. James, K. Rice, and M. Szamosi (1983). A reanalysis of tone in Mende. In J. Kaye, H. Koopman, D. Sportiche, and A. Dugas (eds.), *Current Approaches to African Linguistics*, vol. 2 (pp. 127–137). Dordrecht: Foris.

Cook, Antony (1987). *Wagiman Matyin*. Doctoral dissertation, Latrobe University.

Corazza, S. (1990). The morphology of classifier handshapes in Italian Sign Language (LIS). In C. Lucas (ed.), *Sign Language Research: Theoretical Issues* (pp. 71–82). Washington, DC: Gallaudet University Press.

Corina, David (1990). Reassessing the role of sonority in syllable structure: Evidence from a visual-gestural language. In M. Ziolkowski, M. Noske, and K. Deaton (eds.), *CLS 26: Parasession on Phonetics and Phonology* (pp. 33–44). Chicago: CLS.

Cornulier, Benoît de (1981). H-aspirée et la syllabation: Expressions disjonctives. In D. L. Goyvaerts (ed.), *Phonology in the 1980s* (pp. 183–230). Ghent: E. Story-Scientia.

Coupez, André (1969). Une leçon de linguistique. *Africa-Tervuren* 15: 33–37.

Cowan, J. Ronayne, and Russell Schuh (1976). *Spoken Hausa*. Ithaca: Spoken Language Services, Inc.

Cowan, N. (1989). Acquisition of Pig Latin: A case study. *Journal of Child Language* 16: 365–386.

Cowan, N., M. D. S. Braine, and L. A. Leavitt (1985). The phonological and metaphonological representation of speech: Evidence from fluent backward talkers. *Journal of Memory and Language* 24: 679–698.

Cowan, N., and L. A. Leavitt (1987). The developmental course of two children who could talk backward five years ago. *Journal of Child Language* 14: 393–395.

Cowell, M. (1965). *A Reference Grammar of Syrian Arabic*. Washington, DC: Georgetown University Press.

Cowper, Elizabeth, and Keren Rice (1987). Are phonosyntactic rules necessary? *Phonology* 4: 185–194.

Crothers, J. (1978). Typology and universals of vowel systems. In J. Greenberg (ed.), *Universals of Human Language*, vol. 2: Phonology. Stanford: Stanford University Press.

Crowhurst, Megan (1991a). Demorafication in Tübatulabal: Evidence from initial reduplication and stress. In T. Sherer (ed.), *Proceedings of NELS 21*. Amherst: GLSA.

Crowhurst, Megan (1991b). *Minimality and foot structure in metrical phonology and prosodic morphology*. Doctoral dissertation, University of Arizona, Tucson.

Crowhurst, Megan (1992a). Diminutives and augmentatives in Mexican Spanish: A prosodic analysis. *Phonology* 9: 221–253.

Crowhurst, Megan (1992b). The minimal foot and epenthesis in Sierra Miwok. MS, University of Texas, Austin.

Crowhurst, Megan (to appear). Foot extrametricality and template mapping in Cupeño. *NLLT*.

Crowhurst, Megan, and M. Hewitt (1993). Prosodic fusion and moonlightning feet in Yidiny. MS, University of Texas, Austin.

Crowley, Terry (1978). *The Middle Clarence Dialects of Bandjalang*. Canberra: AIAS.

Crowley, Terry (1980). Phonological targets and Northern Cape York Sandhi. In B. Rigsby and P. Sutton (eds.), *Contributions to Australian Linguistics* (pp. 241–257). Canberra: Pacific Linguistics.

Crowley, Terry (1981) The Mpakwithi dialect of Anguthimri. In R. M. W. Dixon and B. Blake (eds.), *The Handbook of Australian Languages,* vol. 2 (pp. 146–194). Melbourne: OUP Australia.

Crowley, Terry (1983). Uradhi. In R. M. W. Dixon and B. Blake (eds.), *The Handbook of Australian Languages,* vol. 3. Melbourne: OUP Australia.

Culicover, Peter, and Michael Rochemont (1983). Stress and focus in English. *Lg* 59: 123–165.

Czaikowska-Higgins, Ewa (1987). Characterizing tongue root behavior. MS, MIT.

Czaykowska-Higgins, Ewa (1993). Cyclicity and stress in Moses-Columbia Salish. *NLLT*.

D'urovic, L. (1975). Konsonanticky systém slovenciny [A consonantal system of Slovak]. *IJSLP* 19: 7–29.

Dalby, David (1970). Reflections on the classification of African languages. *ALS* 11: 147–171.

Darden, Bill (1971). A note on Sommer's claim that there exist languages without CV syllables. *IJAL* 37: 126–128.

Dart, S. (1991). *Articulatory and acoustic properties of apical and laminal articulations*. Doctoral dissertation, UCLA. UCLA Working Papers in Linguistics vol. 79.

Davis, Stuart (1985a). Syllable weight in some Australian languages. In M. Niepokuj, M. VanClay, V. Nikiforidou, and D. Feder (eds.), *Papers from BLS 11* (pp. 398–407). Berkeley: BLS.

Davis, Stuart (1985b). *Topics in syllable geometry*. Doctoral dissertation, University of Arizona.

Davis, Stuart (1988a). On the nature of internal reduplication. In M. Hammond and M. Noonan (eds.), *Theoretical Morphology: Approaches in Modern Linguistics* (pp. 305–323). San Diego: Academic Press.

Davis, Stuart (1988b). Syllable onsets as a factor in stress rules. *Phonology* 5: 1–19.

Davis, Stuart (1989). Location of the feature [continuant] in feature geometry. *Lingua* 78: 1–22.

Davis, Stuart (1990). Evidence for the full copy analysis of reduplication. MS, Indiana University.

Davis, Stuart (1992). The onset as a constituent of the syllable: Evidence from Italian. In M. Ziolkowski, M. Noske, and K. Deaton (eds.), *CLS 26: Parasession on Phonetics and Phonology* (pp. 71–80). Chicago: CLS.

De Chene, E. Brent, and Stephen R. Anderson (1979). Compensatory lengthening. *Lg* 55: 505–535.

De Jong, Daan (1988). *Sociolinguistic aspects of French liaison*. Doctoral dissertation, Vrije Universiteit Amsterdam.

De Jong, Daan (1990a). On floating consonants in French. In *Proceedings of the 21st Western Conference on Linguistics*. El Paso: University of Texas.

De Jong, Daan (1990b). The syntax-phonology interface and French liaison. *Linguistics* 28: 57–88.

Dell, François (1970). *Les règles phonologiques tardives et la morphologie dérivationnelle du français*. Doctoral dissertation, MIT.

Dell, François (1973). Two cases of exceptional ordering. In F. Kiefer and N. Ruwet (eds.), *Generative Grammar in Europe* (pp. 141–153). Dordrecht: Reidel.

Dell, François (1985). A propos de Svantesson, J.-O., Kammu Phonology and Morphology. *Cahiers de linguistique Asie Orientale* 14: 259–275.

Dell, François (1993). Assimilations supralaryngales dans deux parlers de la Chine méridionale. In B. Laks and A. Rialland (eds.), *L'Architecture et la géometrie des representations phonologiques*. Paris: Editions du C.N.R.S.

Dell, François, and Mohamed Elmedlaoui (1985). Syllabic consonants and syllabification in Imdlawn Tashlhiyt Berber. *JALL* 7: 105–130.

Dell, François, and Mohamed Elmedlaoui (1992). Quantitative transfer in the nonconcatenative morphology of Imdlawn Tashlhiyt Berber. *Journal of Afroasiatic Languages* 3: 89–125.

Demirdache, H. (1988). Transparent vowels. In H. van der Hulst and N. Smith (eds), *Features, Segmental Structure and Harmony Processes*, vol. 2 (pp. 39–76). Dordrecht: Foris.

Demisse, T., and M. L. Bender (1983). An Argot of Addis Ababa Unattached Girls. *LS* 12: 339–347.

Demolin, D. (1991). L'analyse des segments, de la syllabe et des tons dans un jeu de langage mangbetu. In M. Plénat (ed.), *Les javanais* (pp. 30–50). Paris: Larousse.

Den Os, E., and René Kager (1986). Extrametricality and stress in Spanish and Italian. *Lingua* 69: 23–48.

Dench, Alan (1981). *Panyjima phonology and morphology*. MA dissertation, Australian National University.

Dench, Alan (1990). Nyungar metathesis. Paper presented at Australian Linguistic Society, Macquarie University.

Denes, P. (1955). Effect of duration on the perception of voicing. *JASA* 27: 761–764.

Derbyshire, Desmond (1979). *Hixkaryana*. Lingua Descriptive Studies, no. 1. Amsterdam: North-Holland.

Derwing, B. L., and T. Nearey (1986). Experimental phonology at the University of Alberta. In J. J. Ohala and J. J. Jaeger (eds.), *Experimental Phonology* (pp. 187–209). Orlando: Academic Press.

Dickerson, W. B. (1975). Variable rules in the speech community. *SLS* 5: 41–68.

Diehl, R. (ed.) (1992). On the relation between phonetics and phonology. *Phonetica* 48(2–4): 77–278.

Diesing, Molly (1992). *Indefinites*. Cambridge, MA: MIT Press.

Dihoff, Ivan (1976). *Aspects of the tonal structure of Chori*. Doctoral dissertation, University of Wisconsin.

Dikken, M. den, and Harry van der Hulst (1988). Segmental hierarchitecture. In H. van der Hulst and N. Smith (eds.), *Features, Segmental Structure and Harmony Processes*, vol. 1 (pp. 1–78). Dordrecht: Foris.

Dimmendaal, Gerrit (1983). *The Turkana Language*. Dordrecht: Foris.

Dimmendaal, Gerrit, and Anneke Breedfeld (1986). Tonal influence on vocalic quality. In K. Bogers, H. van der Hulst, and M. Mous (eds.), *The Phonological Representation of Suprasegmentals* (pp. 1–33). Dordrecht: Foris.

Dineen, Anne (1989). *A comparative survey of reduplication in Australian languages*. MA dissertation, Australian National University.

Dinnsen, Daniel (1979). *Current Approaches to Phonological Theory*. Bloomington: Indiana University Press.

Dinnsen, Daniel (1992). Variation in developing and fully developed phonetic inventories. In C. Ferguson et al. (eds.), *Phonological Development* (pp. 191–210). Timonium, MD: York Press.

Dixon, Robert M. W. (1970a). Olgolo syllable structure and what they are doing about it. *LI* 1: 273–276.

Dixon, Robert M. W. (1970b). Proto-Australian laminals. *OL* 9: 79–103.

Dixon, Robert M. W. (1972). *The Dyirbal Language of North Queensland*. Cambridge: CUP.

Dixon, Robert M. W. (1977a). *A Grammar of Yidiny*. Cambridge: CUP.

Dixon, Robert M. W. (1977b). Some phonological rules in Yidiny. *LI* 8: 1–34.

Dixon, Robert M. W. (1980). *The Languages of Australia*. Cambridge: CUP.

Dixon, Robert M. W. (1981). Wargamay. In R. M. W. Dixon and B. J. Blake (eds.), *Handbook of Australian Language*, vol. 2. Amsterdam: John Benjamins.

Dixon, Robert M. W. (1988). *A Grammar of Boumaa Fijian*. Chicago: University of Chicago Press.

Dixon, Robert M. W. (1990). Compensating phonological changes: An example from the northern dialects of Dyirbal. *Lingua* 8: 1–34.

Dixon, Robert M. W. (1991). Mbabaram. In R. M. W. Dixon and B. Blake (eds.), *The Handbook of Australian Languages*, vol. 4. Melbourne: OUP Australia.

Doak, I. G. (1992). Another look at Coeur d'Alene harmony. *IJAL* 58: 1–35.

Dobson, E. J. (1968). *English Pronunciation 1500–1700*. Oxford: Clarendon Press.

Docherty, G. J., and D. R. Ladd (eds.) (1992). *Papers in Laboratory Phonology II: Gesture, Segment, Prosody*. Cambridge: CUP.

Dogil, Gregor (1988). Phonological configurations: Natural classes, sonority and syllabicity. In H. van der Hulst and N. Smith (eds.), *Features, Segmental Structure and Harmony Processes*, vol. 1 (pp. 79–103). Dordrecht: Foris.

Dogil, Gregor (1993). La phonologie peut-elle renoncer aux traits distinctifs de classe supérieur? In B. Laks and A. Rialland (eds.), *Architecture des représentations phonologiques*. Paris: Editions du CNRS.

Donaldson, Tamsin (1980). *Ngiyambaa: The Language of the Wangaaybuwan*. Cambridge: CUP.

Donegan, Patricia (1978). *The natural phonology of vowels*. Doctoral dissertation, Ohio State University. New York: Garland Press, 1985.

Doron, Edit (1981). Spirantization melodies: A prosodic treatment of Modern Hebrew spirantization. MS, University of Texas, Austin.

Douglas, Wilf (1964). *An Introduction to the Western Desert Language*. Oceania Linguistic Monographs No. 4. Sydney: Sydney University.

Downing, Laura (1990). *Problems in Jita tonology*. Doctoral dissertation, University of Illinois.

Dresher, B. Elan (1981). On the learnability of abstract phonology. In C. Baker and J. McCarthy (eds.), *The Logical Problem of Language Acquisition*. Cambridge, MA: MIT Press.

Dresher, B. Elan (1983). Postlexical phonology in Tiberian Hebrew. In M. Barlow, D. Flickinger, and M. Wescoat (eds.), *Proceedings of WCCFL 2* (pp. 67–78). Stanford: SLA.

Dresher, B. Elan (1985). Constraints on empty positions in tiered phonology. *Cahiers Linguistiques d'Ottawa* 14: 1–52.

Dresher, B. Elan (to appear). Acquiring Stress Systems. In E. Ristad (ed.), *Proceedings of the DIMACS Workshop on Human Language*. Providence, RI: American Mathematical Society Press.

Dresher, B. Elan, and Jonathan Kaye (1990). A computational learning model for metrical phonology. *Cognition* 34: 137–195.

Dresher, B. Elan, and A. Lahiri (1991). The Germanic foot: Metrical coherence in Old English. *LI* 22: 251–286.

Dressler, W. (1974). Diachronic puzzles for Natural Phonology. *CLS Parasession on Natural Phonology* (pp. 95–102). Chicago: CLS.

Dressler, Wolfgang (1985). *Morphophonology*. Ann Arbor: Karoma Press.

Duanmu, San (1990a). *A formal study of syllable, tone, stress and domain in Chinese languages*. Doctoral dissertation, MIT.

Duanmu, San (1990b). Phonetic correlates of register in Shanghai. Paper presented at LSA meeting.

Dunlop, Elaine (1991). *Issues in the moraic structure of Spanish*. Doctoral dissertation, University of Massachusetts, Amherst.

Durand, Jacques (1986). French liaison, floating segments and other matters in a dependency framework. In J. Durand (ed.), *Dependency and Non-Linear Phonology* (pp. 161–201). London: Croom Helm.

Durand, Jacques (1990). *Generative and Non-Linear Phonology*. London: Longman.

Durand, Jacques (to appear). In defense of dependency phonology. *Rivista di Linguistica*.

Duryea, David (1991). Issues in Thai template morphology: Word chains and word reversal. *Phonology at Santa Cruz* 2: 33–58.

Dvonc et al., L. (1966). *Morfológia slovenského jazyka* [Morphology of the Slovak language]. Bratislava: Vydavatel'stvo Slovenskej Akadémie Vied.

Dwyer, David (1978). What sort of tone language is Mende? *SAL* 9: 167–208.

Eades, Diana (1979). Gumbaynggir. In R. M. W. Dixon and B. Blake (eds.), *The Handbook of Australian Languages*, vol. 1 (pp. 244–361). Melbourne: OUP Australia.

Eather, Bronwyn (1990). *The grammar of Nakkara: A language of Arnhem Land*. Doctoral dissertation, Australian National University.

Ebeling, C. L. (1960). *Linguistic Units*. The Hague: Mouton.

Ebert, K.H. (1974). Partial vowel harmony in Kera. *SAL* Supplement 5: 75–80.

Ebert, K.H. (1979). *Sprache und Tradition der Kera Tschad. Teil III: Grammatik*. Berlin: Reimer.

Echeverría, Max S., and Heles Contreras (1965). Araucanian phonemics. *IJAL* 31: 132–135.

Edwards, Jan, and Mary Beckman (1988). Articulatory timing and the prosodic interpretation of the syllable. *Phonetica* 45: 156–174.

Edwards, M. L. and L. Shriberg. (1983). *Phonology: Applications in Communication Disorders*. San Diego: College-Hill Press.

Elmedlaoui, M. (1985). *Le parler berbère chleuh d'Imdlawn: Segments et syllabation*. 3rd cycle dissertation, Université de Paris VIII.

Elson, B. (1947). Sierra Popoluca syllable structure. *IJAL* 13: 13–17.

Emeneau, M. B. (1955). *Kolami: A Dravidian Language*. University of California Publications in Linguistics, vol. 12. Berkeley: University of California Press.

Encrevé, Pierre (1988). *La Liaison avec et sans enchainement: Phonologie tridimensionelle.* Paris: Seuil.

Esper, E. A. (1925). *A Technique for the Experimental Investigation of Associative Interference in Artificial Linguistic Material.* Language Monographs No. 1.

Evans, Nicholas (1988). Arguments for Pama-Nyungan as a genetic subgroup, with particular reference to initial laminalization. In N. Evans and S. Johnson (eds.), *Aboriginal Linguistics 1* (pp. 91–110). Armidale: Dept. of Linguistics, University of New England.

Evans, Nicholas (1991). A draft grammar of Mayali. MS.

Evans, Nicholas (in press). *A Grammar of Kayardild.* Berlin: Mouton.

Everett, Daniel, and K. Everett (1984). On the relevance of syllable onsets to stress placement. *LI* 15: 705–711.

Everett, Daniel, and Lucy Seki (1985). Reduplication and CV skeleta in Kamaiurá. *LI* 16: 326–330.

Ewen, Colin, and Harry van der Hulst (1985). Single-valued features and the non-linear analysis of vowel harmony. In H. Bennis and F. Beukema (eds.) *Linguistics in The Netherlands 1985*, 317–36. Dordrecht: Foris.

Ewen, Colin, and Harry van der Hulst (1987). Single-valued features and the distinction between [−F] and [0F]. In F. Beukema and P. Coopmans (eds.), *Linguistics in the Netherlands 1987* (pp. 51–60). Dordrecht: Foris.

Ewen, Colin, and Harry van der Hulst (1988). [high], [low] and [back], or [I], [A], and [U]. In P. Coopman and A. Hulk (eds.), *Linguistics in the Netherlands 1988.* Dordrecht: Foris.

Ewen, Colin, and Harry van der Hulst (forthcoming). *An Introduction to Nonlinear Phonology.* Cambridge: CUP.

Fabb, Nigel (1988). English suffixation is constrained only by selectional restrictions. *NLLT* 6: 527–539.

Fant, Gunnar (1960). *Acoustic Theory of Speech Production.* The Hague: Mouton.

Farina, Donna (1991). *Palatalization and yers in modern Russian phonology: An underspecification approach.* Doctoral dissertation, University of Illinois, Urbana.

Farkas, D. and P. Beddor (1987). Privative and equipollent backness in Hungarian. In *CLS 23 Parasession on Autosegmental and Metrical Phonology. Chicago: CLS.*

Farrell, P. (1990). Spanish stress: A cognitive analysis. *Hispanic Linguistics* 4: 21–56.

Farwaneh, Samira (1990). Well-formed associations in Arabic: Rule or condition? In M. Eid and J. McCarthy (eds.), *Perspectives on Arabic Linguistics,* vol. 2. Amsterdam: John Benjamins.

Fedson, Vijayarani (1981). *The Tamil serial or compound verb.* Doctoral dissertation, University of Chicago.

Ferguson, Charles (1975). "Short A" in Philadelphia English. In M. E. Smith (ed.), *Studies in Linguistics: In Honor of George L. Trager* (pp. 250–274). The Hague: Mouton.

Ferguson, Charles (1976). The Ethiopian language area. In M. L. Bender et al. (eds.), *Language in Ethiopia* (pp. 63–76). London: OUP.

Ferguson, Charles, L. Menn, and C. Stoel-Gammon (eds.) (1992). *Phonological Development.* Timonium, MD: York Press.

Féry, Caroline (1993). *German Intonational Patterns.* Tübingen: Max Niemayer Verlag.

Finer, Daniel (1978). Concrete vowel harmony in Manchu. *LA* 4: 263–275.

Finer, Daniel (1986). Reduplication and verbal morphology in Palauan. *LR* 6: 99–130.

Firth, J. R. (1948). Sounds and prosodies. *Transactions of the Philological Society* 127–152. Also in *Prosodic Analysis* (pp. 1–26), ed. F. R. Palmer. Oxford: OUP, 1970.

Firth, J. R. (1957). *Papers in Linguistics.* London: OUP.

Fischer, Susan, and Patricia Siple (eds.) (1990). *Theoretical Issues in Sign Language Research,* vol. 1, *Linguistics.* Chicago: University of Chicago Press.

Fleisch, Henri (1968). *L'arabe classique.* Beirut: Khayats.

Flemming, E. (1993). *The role of metrical structure in segmental rules.* MA dissertation, UCLA.

Flikeid, K. (1988). Unity and diversity in Acadian phonology: An overview based on comparisons among the Nova Scotia varieties. *Journal of the Atlantic Provinces Linguistic Association* 10: 64–110.

Foley, James (1977). *Foundations of Theoretical Phonology.* Cambridge: CUP.

Ford, Alan, and Rajendra Singh (1983). On the status of morphophonology. In J. Richardson, M. Marks, and A. Chukerman (eds.), *CLS 19: Papers from the Parasession on the Interplay of Phonology, Morphology, and Syntax.* Chicago: CLS.

Ford, Alan, and Rajendra Singh (1985). Towards a non-paradigmatic morphology. In M. Niepokuj, M. VanClay, V. Nikiforidou, and D. Feder (eds.), *Papers from BLS 11,* (pp. 87–95). Berkeley: BLS.

Ford, Kevin (1973). On the loss of cross-height vowel harmony. *Research Review Ghana, Supplement 4* (pp. 50–80).

Ford, Kevin, and Dana Ober (1985). Workbook practice in the autosegmental phonology of Kalaw Kawaw Ya, a dialect of the Western Torres Strait language, Australia. MS, School of Australian Linguistics.

Ford, Kevin, and Dana Ober (1986). Pragmatic conditioning of word-order in Kalaw Kawaw Ya (Western Torres Strait). *Language in Aboriginal Australia* 2: 29–33.

Foris, D. (1973). Sochiapan Chinantec syllable structure. *IJAL* 39: 232–235.

Fortescue, M. (1984). *West Greenlandic.* London: Croom Helm.

Foster, Michael K. (1982). Alternating weak and strong syllables in Cayuga words. *IJAL* 48: 59–72.

Fourakis, Marios, and Robert Port (1986). Stop epenthesis in English. *Journal of Phonetics* 14: 197–221.

Franks, Steven (1985). Extrametricality and stress in Polish. *LI* 16: 144–151.

Freeland, Lynn (1951). *The Language of Sierra Miwok.* Memoir 6 of the *International Journal of American Linguistics.* Bloomington: Indiana University.

French, Koleen (1988). *Insights Into Tagalog: Reduplication, Infixation, and Stress from Nonlinear Phonology.* Dallas: SIL and University of Texas at Arlington. MA thesis, University of Texas, Arlington.

Friedman, L. (1977). Formational properties of American Sign Language. In L. Friedman (ed.), *On the Other Hand: New Perspectives in American Sign Language* (pp. 13–56). New York: Academic Press.

Fries, C. C., and Kenneth Pike (1949). Coexistent phonemic systems. *Lg* 25: 29–50.

Fruchter, David (1988). Syllable structure in Efik. In J. Levin, D. Fruchter, and J. Lui (eds.), *Texas Linguistic Form 29* (pp. 79–96). Austin: Dept. of Linguistics, University of Texas at Austin.

Fu, G. T. (1984). Wuyi Fangyande Liandu Biandiao [Tone sandhi in the Wuyi dialect]. *Fangyan* 1984.2: 109–127.

Fudge, Erik (1969). Syllables. *JL* 5: 253–287.

Fudge, Erik (1987). Branching structure within the syllable. *JL* 23: 359–377.

Fujimura, Osamu (1979). An analysis of English syllables as cores and affixes. *Zeitschrift für Phonetik, Sprachwissenschaft und Kommunikationsforschung* 32: 471–476.

Fujimura, Osamu (1989). Demisyllables as sets of features: Comments on Clements' paper. In J. Kingston and M. Beckman (eds.), *Papers in Laboratory Phonology I: Between the Grammar and the Physics of Speech* (pp. 334–340). Cambridge: CUP.

Furby, Christine (1972). The pronominal system of Garawa. *OL* 9: 1–31.

Furby, Christine (1974). *Garawa Phonology*. Pacific Linguistics Series A #37. Canberra: Australian National University.

Gaatone, David (1978). Phonologie abstraite et phonologie concrete: A propos de h-aspiré en français. *Lingvisticae Investigationes* 2: 3–22.

Gandour, Jackson, and Richard Harshman (1978). Crosslanguage differences in tone perception: A multidimensional scaling investigation. *Language and Speech* 21: 1–33.

George, Isaac (1970). Nupe tonology. *SAL* 1: 100–122.

Geytenbeek, Brian (1992). Nyangumarta verbalisers – suffixes or separate forms? MS.

Geytenbeek, Brian, and H. Geytenbeek (1971). *Gidabal Grammar and Dictionary*. Canberra: AIAS.

Ghazeli, Salem (1977). *Back consonants and backing coarticulation in Arabic*. Doctoral dissertation, University of Texas, Austin.

Giegerich, H. (1981). Zero syllables in metrical theory. In W. U. Dressler, O. E. Pfeiffer, and J. R. Rennison (eds.), *Phonologica 1980* (pp. 153–160). Innsbruck: IBS.

Giegerich, H. (1985). *Metrical Phonology and Phonological Structure*. Cambridge: CUP.

Gil, David (1990). Speaking Backwards in Tagalog. Paper presented at 8th ASANAL International Conference, Kuala Lumpur.

Glasgow, K. (1981). Burarra phonemes. In B. Waters (ed.), *Australian Phonologies: Collected Papers* (pp. 91–101). Work papers of SIL-AAB, Series A, vol. 5. Darwin: SIL-AAB.

Glasgow, K. et al. (1984). *Papers in Australian Linguistics No. 16*. Pacific Linguistics, A-16. Canberra: Australian National University.

Gnanadesikan, A. E. (1993). The feature geometry of coronal subplaces. *University of Massachusetts Occasional Papers in Linguistics* 16: 27–67.

Goad, Heather (1991). [Atr] and [Rtr] are different features. In D. Bates (ed.), *Proceedings of WCCFL 11*, (pp. 163–173).

Goad, Heather (1992). *On the configuration of height features*. Doctoral dissertation, University of Southern California.

Goldsmith, John (1976a). *Autosegmental phonology*. Doctoral dissertation, MIT. New York: Garland Press, 1979.

Goldsmith, John (1976b). An overview of autosegmental phonology. *LA* 2: 23–68.

Goldsmith, John (1979). The aims of autosegmental phonology. In D. Dinnsen (ed.), *Current Approaches to Phonological Theory* (pp. 202–22). Bloomington: Indiana University Press.

Goldsmith, John (1981). Subsegmentals in Spanish phonology: An autosegmental approach. In W. W. Cressey and D. J. Napoli (eds.), *Linguistic Symposium on Romance Languages* no. 9 (pp. 1–16). Washington, DC: Georgetown University Press.

Goldsmith, John (1982). Accent systems. In H. van der Hulst and N. Smith (eds.), *The Structure of Phonological Representations*, vol. 1 (pp. 47–63). Dordrecht: Foris.

Goldsmith, John (1984a). Meeussen's rule. In M. Aronoff and R. Oehrle (eds.), *Language Sound Structure* (pp. 245–259). Cambridge, MA: MIT Press.

Goldsmith, John (1984b). Tone and accent in Tonga. In G. N. Clements and J. Goldsmith (eds.), *Autosegmental Studies in Bantu Tone* (pp. 19–51). Dordrecht: Foris.

Goldsmith, John (1985). Vowel harmony in Khalkha Mongolian, Yaka, Finnish and Hungarian. *Phonology* 2: 253–275.

Goldsmith, John (1986). Tone in KiHunde. *Wiener Linguistische Gazette* 5: 49–72.

Goldsmith, John (1987a). The rise of rhythmic structure in Bantu. In W. Dressler et al. (eds.), *Phonological 1984* (pp. 65–78). Cambridge: CUP.

Goldsmith, John (1987b). Tone and accent, and getting the two together. In J. Aske, N. Beery, L. Michaelis, and H. Filip (eds.), *Papers from BLS 13* (pp. 88–104). Berkeley: BLS.

Goldsmith, John (1987c). Vowel systems. In A. Bosch, B. Need, and E. Schiller (eds.), *CLS 23: Parasession on Autosegmental and Metrical Phonology* (pp. 116–133). Chicago: CLS.

Goldsmith, John (1989). Autosegmental licensing, inalterability, and harmonic application. In C. Wiltshire, R. Graczyk, and B. Music (eds.), *Papers from CLS 25* (pp. 145–156). Chicago: CLS.

Goldsmith, John (1990). *Autosegmental and Metrical Phonology*. Oxford and Cambridge, MA: Basil Blackwell.

Goldsmith, John (1991). Phonology as an intelligent system. In D. J. Napoli and J. A. Kegl (eds.), *Bridges between Psychology and Linguistics: A Swarthmore Festschrift for Lila Gleitman* (pp. 247–267). Hillsdale, NJ: Lawrence Erlbaum Associates.

Goldsmith, John (1992a). Local modeling in phonology. In S. Davis (ed.), *Connectionism: Theory and Practice* (pp. 229–246). Oxford: OUP.

Goldsmith, John (1992b). Tone and accent in Llogoori. In D. Brentari, G. Larson, and L. MacLeod (eds.), *The Joy of Syntax* (pp. 73–94). Philadelphia: John Benjamins.

Goldsmith, John (1993a). Harmonic phonology. In J. Goldsmith (ed.), *The Last Phonological Rule: Reflections on Constraints and Derivations* (pp. 21–60). Chicago: University of Chicago Press.

Goldsmith, John (ed.) (1993b). *The Last Phonological Rule: Reflections on Constraints and Derivations*. Chicago: University of Chicago Press.

Goldsmith, John (in press). A dynamic computational theory of accent systems. In J. Cole and C. Kisseberth (eds.), *Perspectives in Phonology*. Stanford: CSLI.

Goldsmith, John, and Gary Larson (1992). Using networks in a harmonic phonology. In C. Canakis, G. Chan, and J. Denton (eds.), *Papers from CLS 28* (pp. 94–125). Chicago: CLS.

Goldsmith, John, and Gary Larson (in prep). *Cognitive Neurophonology*.

Goldsmith, John, Karen Peterson, and Joseph Drogo (1989). Tone and accent in the Xhosa verbal system. In P. Newman and R. Botne (eds.), *Current Approaches to African Linguistics*, vol. 5 (pp. 157–178). Dordrecht: Foris.

Goldstein, Louis (1983). Vowel shifts and articulatory-acoustic relations. In A. Cohen and M. P. R. van der Broecke (eds.), *Abstracts of the Tenth International Congress of Phonetic Sciences* (pp. 267–273). Dordrecht: Foris.

Golston, Chris (1991). Minimal word, minimal affix. In T. Sherer (ed.), *Proceedings of NELS 21*, (pp. 95–110). Amherst, MA: GLSA.

Goodman, Beverly (1988). Takelma verbal morphology. In J. Blevins and J. Carter (eds.), *Proceedings of NELS 18* (pp. 156–174). Amherst, MA: GLSA.

Goodman, Beverly (1991). Ponapean labiovelarized labials: Evidence for internal segment structure. In T. Sherer (ed.), *Proceedings of NELS 21* (pp. 111–126). Amherst, MA: GLSA.

Goodman, Beverly (1993). *The integration of hierarchical features into a phonological system*. Doctoral dissertation, Cornell University.

Gordon, P. (1985). Level ordering in lexical development. *Cognition* 21: 73–93.

Gorecka, Alicja (1989). *Phonology of articulation*. Doctoral dissertation, MIT.

Gouffé, Claude (1968/1969). Deux notes grammaticales sur le parler haoussa de Dogondoutchi (République du Niger). *AuU* 52: 1–14.

Graaf, Tjeerd de, and Peter Tiersma (1980). Some phonetic aspects of breaking in West Frisian. *Phonetica* 37: 109–120.

Grammont, M. (1902). Observations sur le langage des enfants. In *Mélanges Linguistiques Offerts à M. Antoine Meillet* (pp. 61–82). Paris: Klincksieck.

Grammont, M. (1933). *Traité de phonétique*. Paris: Librairie Delagrave.

Green, Ian (1989). *Marrithiyel: A language of the Daly River region of Australia's Northern Territory*. Doctoral dissertation, Australian National University.

Green, T. (1991). Core syllabification and the grid: Explaining quantity sensitivity. In *Proceedings of NELS 22*. Amherst, MA: GLSA.

Greenberg, Joseph (1941). Some problems in Hausa phonology. *Lg* 17: 316–323.

Greenberg, Joseph (1950). The patterning of root morphemes in Semitic. *Word* 6: 162–181.

Greenberg, Joseph (1963). Vowel harmony in African languages. In *Actes du second colloque international de linguistique negro-africaine* (pp. 33–37).

Greenberg, Joseph (1966). Language universals. In T. Sebeok (ed.), *Current Trends in Linguistics*, vol. 3. The Hague: Mouton.

Greenberg, Joseph (1978). Some generalizations concerning initial and final consonant clusters. In J. Greenberg (ed.), *Universals of Human Language*, vol. 2: *Phonology* (pp. 243–280). Stanford: Stanford University Press.

Greenlee, M. and J. Ohala. (1980). Phonetically motivated parallels between child phonology and historical sound change. *Language Sciences* 2(2): 283–308.

Gregerson, J. (1976). Tongue-root and register in Mon-Khmer. In P. Jenner, L. Thompson, and S. Starosta (eds.), *Austro-Asiatic Studies*, vol. 1. Honolulu: University of Hawaii Press.

Gregerson, Kenneth J., and Kenneth D. Smith (1973). The development of Todrah register. In D. D. Thomas and N. Dinh-Hoa (eds.), *Mon-Khmer Studies 4* (pp. 143–184). Carbondale: Center for Vietnamese Studies and SIL.

Grimm, J. (1822). *Deutsche Grammatik*, vol. 1, 2nd edition. Göttingen: Dieterichschen Buchhandlung.

Gudschinsky, Sarah C., Harold Popovich, and Frances Popovich (1970). Native reaction and phonetic similarity in Maxakali phonology. *Lg* 46: 77–88.

Guerssel, Mohammed (1977). Constraints on phonological rules. *Lg* 3: 267–305.

Guerssel, Mohammed (1978). A condition on assimilation rules. *LA* 4: 225–254.

Guerssel, Mohammed (1986). Glides in Berber and syllabicity. *LI* 17: 1–12.

Gussenhoven, Carlos (1984). Testing the reality of focus domain. *Language and Speech* 26: 61–80.

Gussenhoven, Carlos (1991). The English rhythm rule as an accent deletion rule. *Phonology* 8: 1–35.

Gussenhoven, Carlos, and A. C. M. Rietveld (1992). Intonation contours, prosodic structure and preboundary lengthening. *JP* 20: 283–303.

Gussman, Edmund (1992). Resyllabification and delinking. *LI* 23: 29–56.

Guthrie, Malcolm (1970). *Comparative Bantu*, vol. 4. Farnborough, Hants: Gregg.

Haas, Mary (1946). A grammatical sketch of Tunica. In C. Osgood (ed.), *Linguistic Structures of Native America* (pp. 337–366). Viking Fund Publications in Anthropology, no. 6. New York: Viking Fund.

Haas, Mary (1967). A taxonomy of disguised speech. Paper presented at LSA meeting.

Haas, Mary (1977). Tonal accent in Creek. In L. M. Hyman (ed.), *Studies in Stress and Accent*, vol. 4. SCOPIL. Los Angeles: University of Southern California.

Haas, Wim de (1988). *A Formal Theory of Vowel Coalescence: A Case Study of Ancient Greek*. Publications in Language Sciences 30. Dordrecht: Foris.

Haden, E. F. (1938). *The Physiology of French Consonant Changes*. Language Dissertations, no. 26.

Hagman, R. (1977). *Nama Hottentot Grammar*. Bloomington: Indiana University Press.

Haiman, John (1980). *Hua: A Papuan Language of the Eastern Highlands of New Guinea*. Amsterdam: John Benjamins.

Hale, Kenneth (1962). Internal relationships in Arandic of Central Australia. In A. Capell (ed.), *Some Linguistic Types in Australia* (pp. 171–184). Oceania Linguistic Monograph No. 7. Sydney: University of Sydney.

Hale, Kenneth (1973). Deep-surface canonical disparities in relation to analysis and change: an Australian example. In T. Sebeok (ed.), *Current trends in Linguistics*, vol. 9: *Diachronic, Areal and Typological Linguistics* (pp. 401–458). The Hague: Mouton.

Hale, Kenneth (1976). Phonological developments in particular Northern Paman languages. In P. Sutton (ed.), *Languages of Cape York*. Canberra: AIAS.

Hale, Kenneth (1977). Elementary remarks on Walbiri orthography, phonology and allomorphy. MS, MIT.

Hale, Kenneth (1980). Remarks on creativity in Aboriginal verse. In J. C. Kassler and J. Stubington (eds.), *Problems and Solutions: Occasional Essays in Musicology Presented to Alice M. Moyle* (pp. 254–263). Sydney: Hale and Iremonger.

Hale, Kenneth (1985). A note on Winnebago metrical structure. *IJAL* 51: 427–429.

Hale, Kenneth, and Abanel Lacayo Blanco (1989). *Diccionario elemental del Ulwa (Sumu meridional)*. Cambridge, MA: Center for Cognitive Science, MIT.

Hale, Kenneth, and J. White Eagle (1980). A preliminary metrical account of Winnebago accent. *IJAL* 46: 117–132.

Hall, Beatrice, et al. (1974). African vowel harmony systems from the vantage point of Kalenjin. *AuU* 57: 241–267.

Hall, B. L. and R. M. R. Hall (1980). Nez Perce vowel harmony: An Africanist explanation and some theoretical questions. In R. M. Vago (ed.), *Issues in Vowel Harmony* (pp. 201–236). Amsterdam: John Benjamins.

Hall, Tracy Alan (1989). Lexical phonology and the distribution of German [ç] and [x]. *Phonology* 6(1): 1–18.

Halle, Morris (1959). *The Sound Pattern of Russian*. The Hague: Mouton.

Halle, Morris (1962). Phonology in generative grammar. *Word* 18: 54–72.

Halle, Morris (1983). On distinctive features and their articulatory implementation. *NLLT* 1: 91–105.

Halle, Morris (1988). The immanent form of phonemes. In W. Hurst (ed.), *Giving Birth to Cognitive Science: A Festschrift for George A. Miller* (pp. 167–83). Cambridge: CUP.

Halle, Morris (1989). The intrinsic structure of speech sounds. MS, MIT.

Halle, Morris (1990). Respecting metrical structure. *NLLT* 8: 149–176.

Halle, Morris (1991). Phonological features. In W. Bright (ed.), *Oxford International Encyclopedia of Linguistics* (pp. 207–212). N.Y.: OUP.

Halle, Morris, and G. N. Clements (1983). *Problem Book in Phonology: A Workbook for Introductory Courses in Linguistics and in Modern Phonology*. Cambridge, MA: MIT Press.

Halle, Morris, James W. Harris, and Jean-Roger Vergnaud (1991). A reexamination of the Stress Erasure Convention and Spanish stress. *LI* 22: 141–159.

Halle, Morris, and William Idsardi (1993). A Reanalysis of Indonesian Stress. MS, MIT and University of Delaware.

Halle, Morris, and Michael Kenstowicz (1991). The Free Element Condition and cyclic versus noncyclic stress. *LI* 22: 457–501.

Halle, Morris, and K. P. Mohanan (1985). Segmental phonology of Modern English. *LI* 16: 57–116.

Halle, Morris, and Kenneth Stevens (1969). On the feature "Advanced Tongue Root". *QPR* 94: 209–215. Research Laboratory of Electronics, MIT.

Halle, Morris, and Kenneth Stevens (1971). A note on laryngeal features. *QPR* 101: 198–213. Research Laboratory of Electronics, MIT.

Halle, Morris, and Jean-Roger Vergnaud (1978). Metrical structures in phonology. MS, MIT.

Halle, Morris, and Jean-Roger Vergnaud (1980). Three-dimensional phonology. *JLR* 1: 83–105.

Halle, Morris, and Jean-Roger Vergnaud (1981). Harmony processes. In W. Klein and W. Levelt (eds.), *Crossing the Boundaries in Linguistics* (pp. 1–22). Dordrecht: Reidel.

Halle, Morris, and Jean-Roger Vergnaud (1982). On the framework of autosegmental phonology. In H. van der Hulst and N. Smith (eds.), *The Structure of Phonological Representations*, vol. 1 (pp. 65–82). Dordrecht: Foris.

Halle, Morris, and Jean-Roger Vergnaud (1987a). *An Essay on Stress*. Cambridge, MA: MIT Press.

Halle, Morris, and Jean-Roger Vergnaud (1987b). Stress and the cycle. *LI* 18: 45–84.

Halpern, A. (1990). Phonological evidence for the surface (non)existence of empty categories. In P. Sells (ed.), *Proceedings of WCCFL 9* (pp. 233–248). Stanford: SLA.

Halpern, A. (1992). *Topics in the syntax and placement of clitics*. Doctoral dissertation, Stanford University.

Hamano, S. (1986). *The sound-symbolic system of Japanese*. Doctoral dissertation, University of Florida.

Hamans, C. (1985). Umlaut in a Dutch dialect. In H. van der Hulst and N. Smith (eds.), *Advances in Nonlinear Phonology* (pp. 381–396). Dordrecht: Foris.

Hamilton, Philip (1989). *Australian phonotactics and the internal structure of the place node*. MA dissertation, University of Toronto.

Hamilton, Philip (1992). Active articulators and the effect of multivalency in Australian phonotactics. Paper presented at Australian Linguistic Institute Workshop on Phonology in Australian Languages, University of Sydney.

Hamilton, Philip (1993). On the internal structure of the coronal node: Evidence from Australian languages. MS, University of Toronto.

Hammond, Michael (1982). Foot-domain rules and metrical locality. In D. T. Flickinger, M. Macken, and N. Wiegand (eds.), *Proceedings of WCCFL 1* (pp. 207–218). Stanford: GLSA.

Hammond, Michael (1984). *Constraining metrical theory: A modular theory of rhythm and destressing*. Doctoral dissertation, UCLA.

Hammond, Michael (1985). Main stress and parallel metrical planes. In M. Niepokuj, M. VanClay, V. Nikiforidou, and D. Jeder (eds.), *Proceedings of BLS 11: Parasession on Poetics, Metrics, and Prosody* (pp. 417–428). Berkeley: BLS.

Hammond, Michael (1986). The obligatory-branching parameter in metrical theory. *NLLT* 4: 185–228.

Hammond, Michael (1987). Accent, constituency, and lollipops. In A. Bosch, B. Need, and E. Schiller (eds.), *CLS 23: Parasession on Autosegmental and Metrical Phonology* (pp. 149–166). Chicago: CLS.

Hammond, Michael (1988a). On deriving the Well-formedness Condition. *LI* 19: 319–325.

Hammond, Michael (1988b). Templatic transfer in Arabic broken plurals. *NLLT* 6: 247–270.

Hammond, Michael (1989a). Cyclic stress and accent in English. In E. J. Fee and K. Hunt (eds.), *Proceedings of WCCFL 8* (pp. 139–153). Stanford: SLA.

Hammond, Michael (1989b). Lexical stresses in Macedonian and Polish. *Phonology* 6: 19–38.

Hammond, Michael (1990a). The "name game" and onset simplification. *Phonology* 7: 159–162.

Hammond, Michael (1990b). Metrical theory and learnability. MS, Department of Linguistics, University of Arizona, Tucson.

Hammond, Michael (1991a). Deriving the strict cycle condition. MS, University of Arizona.

Hammond, Michael (1991b). Morphemic circumscription. In Geert Booij and Jaap van Marle (eds.), *Yearbook of Morphology* (pp. 195–210). Dordrecht: Kluwer.

Hammond, Michael (1993). Language games and prosodic circumscription. MS., University of Arizona, Tucson.

Han, J.-I. (1992). On the Korean tensed consonants and tensification. In J. Denton, G. Chan, and C. Canakis (eds.), *Papers from CLS 28* (pp. 206–223). Chicago: CLS.

Handelsmann, Robert (1991). *Towards a descripton of Amurdak: A language of Northern Australia*. Honours dissertation, University of Melbourne.

Hankamer, Jorge, and Judith Aissen (1974). The sonority hierarchy. In M. W. LaGaly, R. A. Fox, and A. Bruck (eds.), *CLS 10: Parasession on Natural Phonology* (pp. 131–145). Chicago: CLS.

Hansen, K. C., and L. E. Hansen (1969). Pintupi phonology. *OL* 8: 153–170.

Haraguchi, Shosuke (1977). *The Tone Pattern of Japanese: An Autosegmental Theory of Tonology*. Tokyo: Kaitakusha.

Haraguchi, Shosuke (1992). *Nihongo no mora to onsetsukozo ni kansuru sogoteki kenkyu* [Research on the moraic and syllabic structure of Japanese]. Mombusho Research Report 03208104 (vol. 1). Tsukuba University.

Hardy, H. K., and T. R. Montler (1988). Imperfective gemination in Alabama. *IJAL* 54: 399–415.

Hargus, Sharon (1985). *The lexical phonology of Sekani*. Doctoral dissertation, UCLA.

Harris, Barbara, and Geoffrey O'Grady (1976). An analysis of the progressive morpheme in Umpila verbs: A revision of a former attempt. In P. Sutton (ed.), *Languages of Cape York*. Canberra: AIAS.

Harris, James (1969). *Spanish Phonology*. Cambridge, MA: MIT Press.

Harris, James (1983). *Syllable Structure and Stress in Spanish: A Nonlinear Analysis*. Cambridge, MA: MIT Press.

Harris, James (1985). Spanish diphthongization and stress: A paradox resolved. *Phonology* 2: 31–45.

Harris, James (1987). The accentual patterns of verb paradigms in Spanish. *NLLT* 5: 61–90.

Harris, James (1988). Spanish stress: The extrametricality issue. MS, distributed by IULC, 1992.

Harris, James (1989a). How different is verb stress in Spanish? *Probus* 1: 241–258.

Harris, James (1989b). Our present understanding of Spanish syllable structure. In P. Bjarkman and R. Hammond (eds.), *American Spanish Pronunciation* (pp. 151–169). Washington, DC: Georgetown University Press.

Harris, James (1989c). The stress erasure convention and cliticization in Spanish. *LI* 20: 339–363.

Harris, James (1991a). The exponence of gender in Spanish. *LI* 22: 27–62.

Harris, James (1991b). The form classes of Spanish substantives. *Yearbook of Morphology* 2: 65–88.

Harris, James (1991c). With respect to accentual constituents in Spanish. In H. Campos and F. Martínez-Gil (eds.), *Current Studies in Spanish Linguistics* (pp. 447–473). Washington, DC: Georgetown University Press.

Harris, James (1993). Integrity of prosodic constituents and the domain of syllabification rules in Spanish and Catalan. In K. Hale and S. J. Keyser (eds.), *The View from Building 20: Linguistic Essays in Honor of Sylvain Bromberger* (pp. 177–193). Cambridge, MA: MIT Press.

Harris, John (1987). Non-structure preserving rules in phonology. *Lingua* 72: 255–92.

Harris, John (1990). Segmental complexity and phonological government. *Phonology* 7: 255–300.

Harris, Zellig (1941). The linguistic structure of Hebrew. *JAOS* 61: 143–67.

Harris, Zellig (1942). The phonemes of Moroccan Arabic. *JAOS* 62: 309–318.

Harris, Zellig (1944). Simultaneous conponents in phonology. *Lg* 20: 181–205.

Harrison, Sheldon (1976). *Mokilese Reference Grammar*. Honolulu: University of Hawaii Press.

Hart, George (1981). Nasality and the organization of autosegmental phonology. Bloomington: IULC.

Harvey, Mark (1986). *Ngoni Waray Amungal-yang: The Waray language from Adelaide River*. MA dissertation, Australian National University.

Harvey, Mark (1991). Glottal stop, underspecification and syllable structure among the Top End languages. *AJL* 11: 67–105.

Harvey, Mark (to appear). Proto-Gunwinyguan phonology. In N. Evans (ed.), *Studies in Comparative Non-Pama-Nyungan*.

Hasegawa, N. (1979). Casual speech vs. fast speech. In P. Clyne, W. Hanks, and C. Hofbauer (eds.), *Papers from CLS 15* (pp. 126–137). Chicago: CLS.

Hattori, S. (1960). *Gengogaku no hoho* [Methods of linguistics]. Tokyo: Iwanami.

Hattori, S. (1982). Vowel harmonies of the Altaic languages, Korean, and Japanese. *Acta Orientalia Academiae Scientiarum Hungaricae* 36(1–3): 207–214.

Haugen, Einar (1956). The syllable in linguistic description. In M. Halle et al. (eds.), *For Roman Jakobson* (pp. 213–221). The Hague: Mouton.

Haviland, John (1979). Guugu Yimidhirr. In R. M. W. Dixon and B. Blake (eds.), *Handbook of Australian Languages* (pp. 27–182). Canberra: Australian National University Press.

Hayata, T. (1980). Non-abstract vowel harmony in Manchu. *Gengo Kenkyu* 77: 59–79.

Hayes, Bruce (1980). *A metrical theory of stress rules*. Doctoral dissertation, MIT. Distributed by the IULC. New York: Garland, 1985.

Hayes, Bruce (1982). Metrical structure as the organizing principle in Yidiny phonology. In H. van der Hulst and N. Smith (eds.), *The Structure of Phonological Representations*, vol. 1 (pp. 97–110). Dordrecht: Foris.

Hayes, Bruce (1984). The phonology of rhythm in English. *LI* 13: 227–276.

Hayes, Bruce (1985). Iambic and trochaic rhythm in stress rules. In M. Niepokuj, M. VanClay, V. Nikiforidou, and D. Jeder (eds.), *Proceedings of BLS 11: Parasession on Poetics, Metrics, and Prosody* (pp. 429–46). Berkeley: BLS.

Hayes, Bruce (1986a). Assimilation as spreading in Toba Batak. *LI* 17: 467–499.

Hayes, Bruce (1986b). Inalterability in CV phonology. *Lg* 62: 321–351.

Hayes, Bruce (1987). A revised parametric metrical theory. In J. McDonough and B. Plunkett (eds.), *Proceedings of NELS 17* (pp. 274–289). Amherst, MA: GLSA.

Hayes, Bruce (1989a). Compensatory lengthening in moraic phonology. *LI* 20: 253–306.

Hayes, Bruce (1989b). The prosodic hierarchy in meter. In P. Kiparsky and G. Youmans (eds.), *Rhythm and Meter* (pp. 201–260). Orlando: Academic Press.

Hayes, Bruce (1990). Diphthongization and coindexing. *Phonology* 7: 31–71.

Hayes, Bruce (1994). *Metrical Stress Theory: Principles and Case Studies*. Chicago: University of Chicago Press.

Hayes, Bruce (in press). Weight of CVC can be determined by context. In J. Cole and C. Kisseberth (eds.), *Perspectives in Phonology*. Stanford: CSLI.

Hayes, Bruce, and May Abad (1989). Reduplication and syllabification in Ilokano. *Lingua* 77: 331–374.

Hayes, Bruce, and Aditi Lahiri (1991). Bengali intonational phonology. *NLLT* 9: 47–96.

Hays, D. G. (1964). Dependency theory: A formalism and some observations. *Lg* 40: 511–525.

Hayward, K. M. , and R. J. Hayward (1989). "Guttural": Arguments for a new distinctive feature. *Transactions of the Philological Society* 87: 179–193.

Hayward, R. J. (1986a). *The Arbore Language*. Kuschitische Sprachstudien 2. Hamburg: Buske.

Hayward, R. J. (1986b). The high central vowel in Amharic: New approaches to an old problem. In J. A. Fishman et al. (eds.), *The Fergusonian Impact*, vol. 1 (pp. 301–325). Berlin: Mouton de Gruyter.

Hayward, R. J. (1988). In defense of the skeletal tier. *SAL* 19: 131–172.

Healey, P. M. (1960). *An Agta grammar*. Manila: SIL.

Heath, Jeffrey (1987). *Ablaut and Ambiguity: Phonology of a Moroccan Arabic Dialect*. Albany: State University of New York Press.

Henderson, E. J. A. (1949). Prosodies in Siamese. *Asia Major (n.s.)* 1: 189–215.

Hercus, Luise A. (1972). The prestopped nasal and lateral consonants of Arabana-Wangkanguru. *Anthropological Linguistics* 14: 293–304.

Hercus, Luise A. (1986). *Victorian Languages: A Late Survey*. Pacific Linguistics. Canberra: Australian National University.

Herzallah, R. (1990). *Aspects of Palestinian Arabic phonology: A nonlinear approach*. Doctoral dissertation, Cornell University. Distributed as Working Papers of the Cornell Phonetics Laboratory No. 4.

Hetzron, Robert (1964). La voyelle du sixième order en amharique. *JAL* 3: 179–190.

Hetzron, Robert (1972). *Ethiopian Semitic: Studies in Classification*, vol. 2. Journal of Semitic Studies Monograph. Manchester: University Press.

Hewitt, Mark, and Alan Prince (1989). OCP, locality and linking: The N. Karanga verb. In E. J. Fee and K. Hunt (eds.), *Proceedings of WCCFL 8* (pp. 176–191). Stanford: SLA.

Higurashi, Y. (1983). *The Accent of Extended Word Structures in Tokyo Standard Japanese*. Tokyo: Educa Inc.

Hill, Jane (1970). A peeking rule in Cupeño. *LI* 1: 534–539.

Hill, Jane, and Ofelia Zepeda (1992). Derived words in Tohono O'odham. *IJAL* 58: 355–404.

Hirschberg, L. K. (1913). "Dog Latin" and sparrow languages used by Baltimore children. *Pedagogical Seminar* 20: 257–258.

Hirst, Daniel (1977). *Intonative Features*. The Hague: Mouton.

Hirst, Daniel (1990). Detaching intonational phrases from syntactic structure. MS, CNRS, Université de Provence.

Hoard, James (1971). Aspiration, tenseness, and syllabication in English. *Lg* 47: 133–140.

Hoard, James (1978). Remarks on the nature of syllabic stops and affricates. In A. Bell and J. Hooper (eds.), *Syllables and Segments* (pp. 59–72). Amsterdam: North-Holland.

Hoard, James, and G. N. O'Grady (1976). Nyangumarda phonology, a preliminary report. In R. M. W. Dixon (ed.), *Grammatical Categories in Australian languages* (pp. 51–77). Canberra: AIAS.

Hoberman, Robert (1987). Emphasis (pharyngealization) as an autosegmental harmony feature. In A. Bosch, B. Need, and E. Schiller (eds.), *CLS 23: Parasession on Autosegmental and Metrical Phonology* (pp. 167–81). Chicago: CLS.

Hoberman, Robert (1988a). Emphasis harmony in Modern Aramaic. *Lg* 64: 1–26.

Hoberman, Robert (1988b). Local and long-distance spreading in Semitic morphology. *NLLT* 6: 541–549.

Hochberg, Judith (1988). Learning Spanish stress. *Lg* 64: 683–706.

Hock, Hans (1985). Regular metathesis. *Linguistics* 23: 529–546.

Hock, Hans (1986). Compensatory lengthening: In defense of the concept "Mora". *Folia Linguistica* 20: 431–460.

Hockett, Charles (1942). A system of descriptive phonology. *Lg* 18: 3–21.

Hockett, Charles (1947). Componential analysis of Sierra Popoluca. *IJAL* 13: 259–267.

Hockett, Charles (1955). *A Manual of Phonology.* IJAL Monograph Series, vol. 21, memoir 11.

Hoddinott, William, and Frances M. Kofod (1988). *The Ngankikurungkurr Language (Daly River area, Northern Territory).* Canberra: Pacific Lingusitics D-77.

Hodge, Carleton, and Helen Hause (1944). Hausa tone. *JAOS* 64(2): 51–52.

Hoeksema, Jack (1985). *Categorial Morphology.* New York: Garland.

Hoffman, Carl (1963). *A Grammar of the Margi Language.* London: OUP.

Hogg, R., and C. B. McCully (1987). *Metrical Phonology: A Coursebook.* Cambridge: CUP.

Hohepa, Patrick (1967). *A profile generative grammar of Maori.* IJAL Memoir 20. Bloomington: Indiana University.

Hoijer, Harry (1974). *A Navajo Lexicon*, vol. 78. University of California Publications in Linguistics. Berkeley: University of California Press.

Holden, K. (1976). Assimilation rates of borrowings and phonological productivity. *Lg* 52: 131–147.

Hollenbach, Barbara (1977). Phonetic vs. phonemic correspondence in two Trique dialects. In W. Merrifield (ed.), *Studies in Otomanguean Phonology* (pp. 35–68). Dallas: SIL.

Hollenbach, Barbara (1984). *The phonology and morphology of laryngeals in Copala Trique.* Doctoral dissertation, University of Arizona.

Hombert, Jean-Marie (1973). Speaking backwards in Bakwiri. *SAL* 4: 227–236.

Hombert, Jean-Marie (1975). The perception of contour tones. In C. Cogen, H. Thompson, G. Thurgood, K. Whistler, and J. Wright (eds.), *Proceedings from BLS 1* (pp. 221–232). Berkeley, CA: BLS.

Hombert, Jean-Marie (1977). A model of tone systems. *UCLA Working Papers in Phonetics* 36: 20–32.

Hombert, Jean-Marie (1986). Word games: Some implications for analysis of tone and other phonological constructs. In J. J. Ohala and J. J. Jaeger (eds.), *Experimental Phonology* (pp. 175–186). Orlando: Academic Press.

Hooper [Bybee], Joan. (1976). *An Introduction to Natural Generative Phonology.* New York: Academic Press.

Hooper [Bybee], Joan. (1979). Substantive principles in natural generative phonology. In D. Dinnsen (ed.), *Current Approaches to Phonological Theory* (pp. 106–125). Bloomington: Indiana University Press.

Hore, Michael (1981). Syllable length and stress in Nunggubuyu. In B. Waters (ed.), *Australian phonologies: Collected papers* (pp. 1–62). Work papers of SIL-AAB, Series A, vol. 5. Darwin: SIL-AAB.

Hosokawa, Komei (1991). *The Yawuru language of West Kimberley: A meaning-based description.* Doctoral dissertation, Australian National University.

Hou, J.-Y. (1980). Pingyao Fangyande Liandu Biandiao [Tone sandhi in the Pingyao dialect]. *Fangyan* 1980.1: 1–14.

Hou, J.-Y. (1983). Changzhi Fangyan Jilu [Notes on the Changzhi dialect]. *Fangyan* 1983.4: 260–274.

Howard, Irwin (1972). *A directional theory of rule application in phonology.* Doctoral dissertation, MIT.

Hualde, José (1988a). Affricates are not contour segments. In H. Borer (ed.), *Proceedings of WCCFL 7* (pp. 77–89). Stanford: SLA.

Hualde, José (1988b). *A lexical phonology of Basque.* Doctoral dissertation, University of Southern California.

Hualde, Jose (1989). The strict cycle condition and noncyclic rules. *LI* 20: 675–680.

Hualde, Jose (1991a). On Spanish syllabification. In H. Campos and F. Martínez-Gil (eds.), *Current Studies in Spanish Linguistics* (pp. 475–493). Washington, DC: Georgetown University Press.

Hualde, Jose (1991b). Unspecified and unmarked vowels. *LI* 22: 205–209.

Hudson, Grover (1974). The representation of non-productive alternation. In J. Anderson and C. Jones (eds.), *Historical Linguistics,* vol. 2 (pp. 203–229). Amsterdam: North Holland.

Hudson, Grover (1978). Lexical form of the Amharic reflexive-passive. In D. Farkas, W. Jacobsen, and K. Todrys (eds.), *CLS 14: Parasession on the Lexicon* (pp. 210–219). Chicago: CLS.

Hudson, Grover (1980). Automatic alternations in nontransformational phonology. *Lg* 56: 94–125.

Hudson, Grover (1985). The principled grammar of Amharic verb stems. *JALL* 7: 39–58.

Hudson, Grover (1986). Arabic root and pattern morphology without tiers. *JL* 22: 85–122.

Hudson, Grover (1991). A and B-type verbs in Ethiopian and Proto-Semitic. In A. S. Kaye (ed.), *Semitic Studies in Honor of Wolf Leslau* (pp. 678–689). Wiesbaden: Harrassowitz.

Hudson, Grover (1993). Evidence of an argot for Amharic and theoretical phonology. *JALL* 14: 47–60.

Hudson, Joyce (1977). *Five Papers in Australian Phonologies.* Work Papers of SIL-AAB, Series A, vol. 1. Darwin: SIL-AAB.

Huffman, Franklin (1972). The boundary between the monosyllable and the disyllable in Cambodian. *Lingua* 29: 54–66.

Hulst, Harry van der (1984). *Syllable Structure and Stress in Dutch.* Dordrecht: Foris.

Hulst, Harry van der (1985). Vowel harmony in Hungarian: A comparison of segmental and autosegmental approaches. In H. van der Hulst and N. Smith (eds.), *Advances in Nonlinear Phonology* (pp. 267–304). Dordrecht: Foris Publications.

Hulst, Harry van der (1988a). The geometry of vocalic features. In H. van der Hulst and N. Smith (eds.), *Features, Segmental Structure and Harmony Processes*, vol. 2 (pp. 77–125). Dordrecht: Foris.

Hulst, Harry van der. (1988b). The dual interpretation of |i|, |u| and |a|. *NELS* 18, pp. 208–22.

Hulst, Harry van der (1989). Atoms of segmental structure: Components, gestures and dependency. *Phonology* 6: 253–284.

Hulst, Harry van der (1990). The segmental spine and the non-existence of [ATR]. In J. Mascaró and M. Nespor (eds.), *Grammar in Progress* (pp. 247–257). Dordrecht: Foris.

Hulst, Harry van der (1991). The molecular structure of phonological segments [The Book of Segments]. MS, University of Leiden.

Hulst, Harry van der (1993). Radical CV phonology. MS, University of Leiden

Hulst, Harry van der, and Colin Ewen (1991). Major class and manner features. In P. M. Bertinetto, M. Kenstowicz, and M. Loporcaro (eds.), *Certamen Phonologicum 2: Papers from the 1990 Cortona Phonology Meeting* (pp. 19–41). Turin: Rosenberg and Sellier.

Hulst, Harry van der, M. Mous, and Norval Smith (1986). The autosegmental analysis of reduced vowel harmony systems: The case of Tunen. In F. Beukema and A. Hulk (eds.), *Linguistics in the Netherlands 1986* (pp. 105–122). Dordrecht: Foris.

Hulst, Harry van der, and Norval Smith (1982). Prosodic domains and opaque segments in autosegmental theory. In H. van der Hulst and N. Smith (eds.), *Structure of Phonological Representations*, vol. 2 (pp. 311–336). Dordrecht: Foris.

Hulst, Harry van der, and Norval Smith (1985). Vowel features and umlaut in Djingili, Nyangumarda and Warlpiri. *Phonology* 2: 277–303.

Hulst, Harry van der, and Norval Smith (1986). On neutral vowels. In K. Bogers, H. van der Hulst, and M. Mous (eds.), *The Representation of Suprasegmentals* (pp. 233–279). Dordrecht: Foris.

Hulst, Harry van der, and Norval Smith (1988). The varieties of pitch accent systems: Introduction. *Autosegmental Studies on Pitch Accent* (pp. 9–24). Dordrecht: Foris.

Hulst, Harry van der, and J. van de Weijer (1991). Topics in Turkish Phonology. In H. Boeschoten and L. Verhoeven (eds.), *Turkish Linguistics Today* (pp. 11–59). E. J. Brill.

Hume, Elizabeth (1990). Front vowels, palatal consonants and the rule of umlaut in Korean. In J. Carter, R.-M. Déchaine, B. Philip, and T. Sherer (eds.), *Proceedings of NELS 20* (pp. 230–243). Amherst, MA: GLSA.

Hume, Elizabeth (1991). Metathesis in Maltese: Implications for the Strong Morphemic Plane Hypothesis. In T. Sherer (ed.), *Proceedings of NELS 21* (pp. 157–172). Amherst, MA: GLSA.

Hume, Elizabeth (1992). *Front vowels, coronal consonants and their interaction in nonlinear phonology*. Doctoral dissertation, Cornell University.

Hung, Henrietta (1992). Relativized suffixation in Choctaw: A constraint-based analysis of the verb grade system. MS, Brandeis University.

Hutcheson, James (1973). Remarks on the nature of complete consonant assimilation. In C. Corum, T. C. Smith-Stark, and A. Weiser (eds.), *Papers from CLS 9*. Chicago: CLS.

Hyman, Larry (1973). *Consonant Types and Tone*. SCOPIL, no. 1. Los Angeles: University of Southern California.

Hyman, Larry (1975). *Phonology: Theory and Analysis*. New York: Holt, Rinehart, and Winston.

Hyman, Larry (1976). On some controversial questions in the study of consonant types and tone. In J.-M. Hombert (ed.), *Studies on Production and Perception of Tones* (pp. 90–98). UCLA Working Papers in Phonetics, vol. 33.

Hyman, Larry (1977). On the nature of linguistic stress. In L. Hyman (ed.), *Studies in Stress and Accent*, SCOPIL, no. 4. Los Angeles: University of Southern California.

Hyman, Larry (1978a). Historical tonology. In V. Fromkin (ed.), *Tone: A Linguistic Survey* (pp. 257–269). New York: Academic Press.

Hyman, Larry (1978b). Tone and/or accent. In D. J. Napoli (ed.), *Elements of Tone, Stress, and Intonation* (pp. 1–20). Washington, DC: Georgetown University Press.

Hyman, Larry (1981). Tonal accent in Somali. *SAL* 12: 169–203.

Hyman, Larry (1982a). Globality and the accentual analysis of Luganda tone. *JLR* 2(3): 1–40.

Hyman, Larry (1982b). Against asterisks in Luganda and Bantu tonology: A reply to Hyman (1982a). MS, USC.

Hyman, Larry (1985). *A Theory of Phonological Weight*. Dordrecht: Foris.

Hyman, Larry (1986). The Representation of multiple tone heights. In K. Bogers, H. van der Hulst, and M. Mous (eds.), *The Phonological Representation of Suprasegmentals* (pp. 109–152). Dordrecht: Foris Publications.

Hyman, Larry (1988a). Syllable structure constraints on tonal contours. *Linguistique Africaine* 1: 49–60.

Hyman, Larry (1988b). Underspecification and vowel height transfer in Esimbi. *Phonology* 5: 255–273.

Hyman, Larry M. (1989). Advanced Tongue Root in Kinande. MS, University of California in Berkeley.

Hyman, Larry (1990). Boundary tonology and the prosodic hierarchy. In S. Inkelas and D. Zec (eds.), *The Phonology-Syntax Connection* (pp. 109–125). Chicago: University of Chicago Press.

Hyman, Larry (1993a). Problems for rule ordering in phonology: Two Bantu test cases. In J. Goldsmith (ed.), *The Last Phonological Rule: Reflections on Constraints and Derivations* (pp. 195–222). Chicago: The University of Chicago Press.

Hyman, Larry (1993b). Register tones and tonal geometry. In K. Snider and H. van der Hulst (eds.), *The Phonology of Tone: The Representation of Tonal Register* (pp. 75–108). Berlin: Mouton de Gruyter.

Hyman, Larry, and Ernest Byarushengo (1980). Tonal accent in Haya: An autosegmental approach. MS, USC.

Hyman, Larry, and Ernest Byarushengo (1984). A model of Haya tonology. In G. N. Clements and J. Goldsmith (eds.), *Autosegmental Studies in Bantu Tone* (pp. 53–103). Dordrecht: Foris.

Hyman, Larry, Francis Katamba, and L. Walusimbi (1987). Luganda and the Strict Layer Hypothesis. *Phonology* 4: 87–108.

Hyman, Larry, and Russell Schuh (1974). Universals of tone rules: Evidence from West Africa. *LI* 5: 81–115.

Idsardi, William (1991). Stress in Interior Salish. In L. Dobrin, L. Nichols and R. Rodriguez (eds.), *Papers from CLS 27* (pp. 246–260). Chicago: CLS.

Idsardi, William (1992). *The computation of prosody*. Doctoral dissertation, MIT.

Idsardi, William (1993). Some properties of simplified bracketed grids. Paper presented at GLOW Workshop on Phonological Constituents.

Ingram, David (1974). Phonological rules in young children. *Journal of Child Language* 1: 49–64.

Ingram, David (1989). *First Language Acqusition*. Cambridge: CUP.

Ingria, Robert (1980). Compensatory lengthening as a metrical phenomenon. *LI* 11: 465–495.

Inkelas, Sharon (1988). Prosodic effects on syntax: Hausa fa. In H. Borer (ed.), *Proceedings of WCCFL 7* (pp. 375–88). Stanford: SLA.

Inkelas, Sharon (1989). *Prosodic constituency in the lexicon*. Doctoral dissertation, Stanford University. New York: Garland Press, 1990.

Inkelas, Sharon (1990). Prosodic replacement in Modern Hebrew. In M. Ziolkowski, M. Noske, and K. Deaton (eds.), *CLS 26: Parasession on the Syllable in Phonetics and Phonology* (pp. 197–212). Chicago: CLS.

Inkelas, Sharon (forthcoming). Nimboran position class morphology. *NLLT*.

Inkelas, Sharon, and Young-mee Cho (1993). Inalterability as prespecification. *LG* 69: 529–574.

Inkelas, Sharon, and Will Leben (1990). Where phonology and phonetics intersect: The case of Hausa intonation. In M. Beckman and J. Kingston (eds.), *Between the Grammar and the Physics of Speech* (pp. 17–34). New York: CUP.

Inkelas, Sharon, Will Leben, and M. Cobler (1987). The phonology of intonation in Hausa. In J. Blevins and J. Carter (eds.), *Proceedings of NELS 17* (pp. 327–341). Amherst, MA: GLSA.

Inkelas, Sharon, and Orhan Orgun (1993). Turkish coda devoicing: A prosodic constraint on extrametricality. MS., University of California, Berkeley. A version was presented at the 1993 LSA meeting, Los Angeles.

Inkelas, Sharon, and Draga Zec (1988). Serbo-Croatian pitch accent. *Lg* 64: 227–248.

Inkelas, Sharon, and Draga Zec (eds.) (1990). *The Phonology-Syntax Connection*. Chicago: University of Chicago Press.

Irshied, Omar, and Michael Kenstowicz (1984). Some phonological rules of Bani-Hassan Arabic: A Bedouin dialect. *SLS* 14: 109–147.

Isola, Akinwumi (1982). Ena: Code-talking in Yoruba. *Journal of West African Languages* 12: 43–51.

Itô, Junko (1985). Melodic dissimilation in Ainu. *LI* 15: 505–513.

Itô, Junko (1986). *Syllable theory in prosodic phonology*. Doctoral dissertation, University of Massachusetts, Amherst. New York: Garland Press, 1988.

Itô, Junko (1989). A prosodic theory of epenthesis. *NLLT* 7: 217–259.

Itô, Junko (1990). Prosodic minimality in Japanese. In K. Deaton, M. Noske, and M. Ziolkowski (eds.), *CLS 26: Parasession on the Syllable in Phonetics and Phonology* (pp. 213–239). Chicago: CLS.

Itô, Junko, and Jorge Hankamer (1989). Notes on monosyllabism in Turkish. *Phonology at Santa Cruz* 1: 61–70.

Itô, Junko, Yoshihisa Kitagawa, and R. Armin Mester (1992). Prosodic type preservation in Japanese: Evidence from zuuja-go. MS, Syntax Research Center, UC Santa Cruz. SRC-92–05. To appear in the *Journal of East Asian Linguistics*.

Itô, Junko, and R. Armin Mester (1986). The phonology of voicing in Japanese: Theoretical consequences of morphological accessibility. *LI* 17: 49–73.

Itô, Junko, and R. Armin Mester (1991). Linguistics 224: The Prosodic Phonology of Japanese. Lectures and handouts from LSA Linguistic Institute Course, UC Santa Cruz.

Itô, Junko, and R. Armin Mester (1992). Weak layering and word binarity. MS, UC Santa Cruz.

Itô, Junko, and R. Armin Mester (1993a). Sino-Japanese phonology: A preliminary study. MS, UC Santa Cruz. LRC-93–06, Linguistics Research Center.

Itô, Junko, and R. Armin Mester (1993b). Licensed segments and safe paths. In C. Paradis and D. LaCharité (eds.), *Constraint-based theories in multilinear phonology*, vol. 38 (pp. 197–213). Special issue of the *Canadian Journal of Linguistics*.

Itô, Junko, and R. Armin Mester (to appear). Weak Layering. *LI*.

Itô, Junko, R. Armin Mester, and J. Padgett (1993). Constraint ranking and underspecification. MS, UC Santa Cruz. LRC-93–08 Linguistic Research Center.

Iushmanov, N. V. (1938). Singarmonizm urmiiskogo narechiia. In *Pamiati akademika N. Ia. Marra* (pp. 295–314). Moscow and Leningrad: Akademiia Nauk S.S.S.R, Institut Iazyka i Myshleniia.

Iverson, Gregory (1974). *Ordering constraints in phonology*. Doctoral dissertation, University of Minnesota.

Iverson, Gregory (1989). On the category supralaryngeal. *Phonology* 6: 285–303.

Iverson, Gregory, and K.-H. Kim (1987). Underspecification and hierarchical feature representation in Korean consonantal phonology. In A. Bosch, B. Need, and E. Schiller (eds.), *CLS 23: Parasession on Autosegmental and Metrical Phonology* (pp. 182–198). Chicago: CLS.

Iverson, Gregory, and Deirdre Wheeler (1988). Blocking and the Elsewhere Condition. In M. Hammond and M. Noonan (eds.), *Theoretical Morphology: Approaches in Modern Linguistics* (pp. 325–338). San Diego: Academic Press.

Jackendoff, Ray (1972). *Semantics in Generative Grammar*. Cambridge, MA: MIT Press.

Jacobs, Haike (1990). On markedness and bounded stress systems. *LR* 7: 81–119.

Jacobson, Steven (1985). Siberian Yupik and Central Yupik prosody. In M. Krauss (ed.), *Yupik Eskimo Prosodic Systems: Descriptive and Comparative Studies*, (pp. 25–46). Alaska Native Language Center Research Papers No. 7. Fairbanks: Alaska Native Language Center, University of Alaska.

Jaeger, J. J. (1980). Testing the psychological reality of phonemes. *Language and Speech* 23: 233–253.

Jaeger, J. J. (1983). The fortis/lenis question: Evidence from Zapotec and Jawoñ. *JP* 11: 177–199.

Jaeger, J. J. (1986). Concept formation as a tool for linguistic research. In J. J. Ohala and J. J. Jaeger (eds.), *Experimental Phonology* (pp. 211–237). Orlando: Academic Press.

Jagst, Lothar (1975). Ngardilpa (Warlpiri) Phonology. In S. A. Wurm (ed.), *Papers in Australian Linguistics No. 8*, (pp. 21–58). Pacific Linguistics, A-39. Canberra: Australian National University.

Jakobson, Roman (1929). Remarques sur l'évolution phonologique du russe comparée à celle des autres langues slaves. *Travaux du Cercle linguistique de Prague 2*. Reprinted in *Selected Writings*, vol. 1.

Jakobson, Roman (1938). Observations sur le classement phonologique des consonnes. In N. Ruwet (ed.), *Essais de linguistique générale*, vol. 2. Paris: Editions de Minuit, 1973.

Jakobson, Roman (1941). *Child Language, Aphasia and Phonological Universals*. Translated into English by A. Keiler, 1968. The Hague: Mouton.

Jakobson, Roman (1957). Notes on Gilyak. In *Studies Presented to Yuen Ren Chao on his 65th Birthday*, vol. 29 (pp. 255–281). Academia Sinica.

Jakobson, Roman (1962). Typological studies and their contribution to historical comparative linguistics: Report in the first plenary session of the Eighth International Congress of Linguists, Oslo, 5 August 1957. In *Selected Writings 1: Phonological Studies*. The Hague: Mouton.

Jakobson, Roman, Gunnar Fant, and Morris Halle (1952). *Preliminaries to Speech Analysis*. Cambridge, MA: MIT Press.

Jakobson, Roman, and Morris Halle (1956). *Fundamentals of Language*. The Hague: Mouton.

Jakobson, Roman, and Linda Waugh (1979). *The Sound Shape of Language*. Bloomington: Indiana University Press.

Janda, Richard, and Brian Joseph (1986). One rule or many? Sanskrit reduplication as fragmented affixation. *Ohio State University Working Papers in Linguistics* 34: 84–107.

Jeanne, LaVerne (1982). Some phonological rules of Hopi. *IJAL* 48: 245–270.

Jensen, J. T. (1977). *Yapese Reference Grammar*. Honolulu: University Press of Hawaii.

Jensen, John T., and Margaret Stong-Jensen (1989). The strict cycle and epenthesis in Hungarian. In J. Carter and R.-M. Dechaine (eds.), *Proceedings of NELS 19* (pp. 223–235). Amherst, MA: GLSA.

Jespersen, Otto (1904). *Lehrbuch der Phonetik*. Leipzig and Berlin: B. G. Teubner.

Johnson, C. D. (1980). Regular disharmony in Kirghiz. In R. Vago (ed.), *Issues in Vowel Harmony* (pp. 89–99). Amsterdam: John Benjamins.

Johnson, Robert (1975). *The role of phonetic detail in Coeur D'Alene phonology*. Doctoral dissertation, Washington State University.

Johnson, Robert, and Scott Liddell (1984). Structural Diversity in American Sign Language. In J. Drogo, V. Mishra, and D. Testen (eds.), *CLS 20: Parasesssion on Lexical Semantics* (pp. 172–186). Chicago: CLS.

Johnson, Steve (1986). *Ngarrindjeri Dictionary*. Batchelor: SAL.

Jones, T., and L. M. Knudson (1977). Guelavía Zapotec phonemes. In W. Merrifield (ed.), *Studies in Otomanguean Phonology*. Dallas: SIL.

Joos, Martin (1942). A phonological dilemma in Canadian English. *Lg* 18: 141–144.

Jungraithmayr, H. (1971). The Tangale vowel system reconsidered. *JAL* 10: 28–33.

Kager, René (1989). *A Metrical Theory of Stress and Destressing in English and Dutch*. Dordrecht: Foris.

Kager, René (1991). The moraic iamb. In L. Dobrin, L. Nichols, and R. Rodriguez (eds.), *Papers from CLS 27* (pp. 291–306). Chicago: CLS.

Kager, René (1992a). Are there any truly quantity-insensitive systems? Paper presented at BLS.

Kager, René (1992b). Shapes of the generalized trochee. Paper presented at WCCFL 11.

Kager, René (1993). Alternatives to the iambic-trochaic law. *NLLT* II: 381–432.

Kager, René, and E. Visch (1988). Metrical constituency and rhythmic adjustment. *Phonology* 5(1): 21–72.

Kahn, Daniel (1976). *Syllable-based generalizations in English phonology*. Doctoral dissertation, MIT. New York: Garland Press, 1980.

Kaisse, Ellen (1983). The syntax of auxiliary reduction in English. *Lg* 59: 93–122.

Kaisse, Ellen (1985a). *Connected Speech: The Interaction of Syntax and Phonology*. San Diego: Academic Press.

Kaisse, Ellen (1985b). Some theoretical consequences of stress rules in Turkish. In W. Eilfort, P. Kroeber, and K. Peterson (eds.), *Papers from CLS 21* (pp. 199–209). Chicago: CLS.

Kaisse, Ellen (1992). Can [consonantal] Spread? *Lg* 68: 313–332.

Kaisse, Ellen, and Patricia Shaw (1985). On the theory of lexical phonology. *Phonology* 2: 1–30.

Kálmán, B. (1965). Das reduzierte Vokal-Phonem im Vogulischen. In E. Zwirner and W. Bethge (eds.), *Proceedings of the 5th International Congress of Phonetic Sciences*. Basel: S. Karger.

Kamprath, C. (1989). Patterns of vowel reduction. MS, University of Texas, Austin.

Kanerva, Jonni (1989). *Focus and phrasing in Chichewa phonology.* Doctoral dissertation, Stanford University.

Kanerva, Jonni (1990). Focusing on phonological phrases in Chichewa. In S. Inkelas and D. Zec (eds.), *The Phonology-Syntax Connection* (pp. 145–162). Chicago: University of Chicago Press.

Kao, Diana (1971). *Structure of the Syllable in Cantonese.* The Hague: Mouton.

Karlgren, B. (1954). Compendium of phonetics in Ancient and Archaic Chinese. *Bulletin of the Museum of Far Eastern Antiquities* 26: 211–367.

Karstrom, M. R., and E. V. Pike (1968). Stress in the phonological system of Eastern Popoloca. *Phonetica* 18: 16–30.

Karttunen, Lauri (1993). Finite-state constraints. In J. Goldsmith (ed.), *The Last Phonological Rule: Reflections on Constraints and Derivations* (pp. 173–194). Chicago: University of Chicago Press.

Katada, F. (1990). On the representation of moras: Evidence from a language game. *LI* 21: 641–646.

Katz, Graham (1991). A prosodic circumscription analysis of /gi/-words in Kannada. MS, LSA Linguistic Institute, UC Santa Cruz.

Kaun, A. (1993a). The coronal underspecification hypothesis. In D. Silverman and R. Kirchner (eds.), *UCLA Occasional Papers in Linguistics,* vol. 13 (pp. 69–108). Los Angeles: UCLA.

Kaun, A. (1993b). The typology of rounding harmony: An optimization approach. Doctoral dissertation, University of California, Los Angeles.

Kawasaki, H. (1982). *An acoustical basis for universal constraints on sound sequences.* Doctoral dissertation, University of California, Berkeley.

Kawasaki, H. (1986). Phonetic explanation for phonological universals: The case of distinctive vowel nasalization. In J. J. Ohala and J. J. Jaeger (eds.), *Experimental Phonology* (pp. 81–103). Orlando: Academic Press.

Kawasaki-Fukumori, H. (1992). An acoustical basis for universal phonotactic constraints. *Language and Speech* 35: 73–86.

Kaye, Jonathan (1982). Harmony processes in Vata. In H. van der Hulst and N. Smith (eds.), *The Structure of Phonological Representations,* vol. 2. Dordrecht: Foris.

Kaye, Jonathan (1988). On the interaction of theories of Lexical Phonology and theories of phonological phenomena. MS, SOAS.

Kaye, Jonathan (1990). "Coda" licensing. *Phonology* 7: 301–330.

Kaye, Jonathan, and Monik Charette (1981). Tone sensitive rules in Dida. In W. Leben (ed.), *Précis from the 12th Conference on African Linguistics,* Stanford University, April 10–12, 1981, (pp. 82–85). SAL Supplement 8. Los Angeles: UCLA.

Kaye, Jonathan, and Jean Lowenstamm (1984). De la syllabicité. In F. Dell, D. Hirst and J.-R. Vergnaud (eds.), *Forme sonore du language: Structure des représentations en phonologie* (pp. 123–159). Paris: Hermann.

Kaye, Jonathan, Jean Lowenstamm, and Jean-Roger Vergnaud (1985). The internal structure of phonological elements: A theory of charm and government. *Phonology* 2: 305–328.

Kaze, J. (1991). Metaphony and two models for the description of vowel systems. *Phonology* 8: 163–170.

Kean, Mary-Louise (1974). The strict cycle in phonology. *LI* 5: 179–203.

Keating, Patricia (1985). CV phonology, experimental phonetics and coarticulation. *UCLA Working Papers in Phonetics* 62: 1–13.

Keating, Patricia (1987). A survey of phonological features. *UCLA Working Papers in Phonetics* 66: 124–150. Distributed by the IULC.

Keating, Patricia (1988). Underspecification in phonetics. *Phonology* 5: 275–292.

Keating, Patricia (1990). Phonetic representation in a generative grammar. *JP* 18: 321–334.

Keating, Patricia (1991). Coronal places of articulation. In C. Paradis and F. Prunet (eds.), *The Special Status of Coronals: Internal and External Evidence* (pp. 29–48). San Diego: Academic Press.

Kegl, Judy, and Ronnie Wilbur (1976). When does structure stop and style begin? Syntax, morphology and phonology vs. stylistic variation in American Sign Language. In S. Mufwene, C. Walker and S. Steever (eds.), *Papers from CLS 12* (pp. 376–396). Chicago: CLS.

Kennedy, Rod J. (1981). Phonology of Kala Lagaw Ya in Saibai dialect. In B. Waters (ed.), *Australian Phonologies: Collected Papers* (pp. 103–137). Work papers of SIL-AAB, Series A, vol. 5. Darwin: SIL-AAB.

Kenstowicz, Michael (1971). Lithuanian phonology. *SLS* 2: 1–85.

Kenstowicz, Michael (1972). The morphophonemics of the Slovak noun. *Papers in Linguistics* 3: 550–567.

Kenstowicz, Michael (1979). Chukchee vowel harmony and epenthesis. In P. Clyne, W. Hanks, and C. Hofbauer (eds.), *CLS 15: The Elements: Parasession on Linguistic Units and Levels* (pp. 402–412). Chicago: CLS.

Kenstowicz, Michael (1982). Gemination and spirantization in Tigrinya. *SLS* 12: 103–122.

Kenstowicz, Michael (1983). Parametric variation and accent in the Arabic dialects. In A. Chukerman, M. Marks, and J. F. Richardson (eds.), *Papers from CLS 19* (pp. 205–213). Chicago: CLS.

Kenstowicz, Michael (1987). Tone and accent in Kizigua – a Bantu language. In P. M. Bertinetto and M. Loporcaro (eds.), *Certamen Phonologicum 1; Proceedings of the Cortona Phonology Conference.*

Kenstowicz, Michael (1993). *Phonology in generative grammar.* Oxford: Basil Blackwell.

Kenstowicz, Michael, and Charles Kisseberth (1971). Unmarked bleeding orders. *SLS* 1: 8–28.

Kenstowicz, Michael, and Charles Kisseberth (1977). *Topics in Phonological Theory.* New York: Academic Press.

Kenstowicz, Michael, and Charles Kisseberth (1979). *Generative Phonology: Description and Theory.* New York: Academic Press.

Kenstowicz, Michael, Emmanuel Nikiema, and Meterwa Ourso (1988). Tone polarity in two Gur languages. *SLS* 18(1): 77–103.

Kenstowicz, Michael, and Charles Pyle (1973). On the phonological integrity of geminate clusters. In M. Kenstowicz and C. Kisseberth (eds.), *Issues in Phonological Theory.* The Hague: Mouton.

Kenstowicz, Michael, and Jerzy Rubach (1987). The phonology of syllabic nuclei in Slovak. *Lg* 63: 463–497.

Kerek, Andrew (1971). *Hungarian Metrics: Some Linguistic Aspects of Iambic Verse.* Bloomington: Indiana University.

Key, Harold (1961). The phonotactics of Cayuvava. *IJAL* 27: 143–150.

Keyser, S. Jay, and Paul Kiparsky (1984). Syllable structure in Finnish phonology. In M. Aronoff and R. Oehrle (eds.), *Language Sound Structures* (pp. 7–31). Cambridge, MA: MIT Press.

Khumalo, J (1987). *An autosegmental account of Zulu phonology*. Doctoral dissertation, University of Witwatersrand.

Kidda, M. (1985). *Tangale phonology: A descriptive analysis*. Doctoral dissertation, University of Illinois, Champaign.

Kidima, L. (1990). Tone and syntax in Kiyaka. In S. Inkelas and D. Zec (eds.), *The Phonology-Syntax Connection* (pp. 195–216). Chicago: University of Chicago Press.

Kilham, Christine (1974). Compound words and close-knit phrases in Wik-Munkan. *Papers in Australian Linguistics* 7: 45–73.

Kim, Chin-Wu (1978). "Diagonal" vowel harmony? Some implications for historical phonology. In J. Fisiak (ed.), *Recent Developments in Historical Phonology* (pp. 221–236). The Hague: Mouton.

Kim, Kong-On, and Masayoshi Shibatani (1976). Syllabification phenomena in Korean. *Language Research* 12: 91–98.

Kim, S. (1990). *Phonologie des consonnes en coréen*. Doctoral dissertation, Ecole des hautes études en sciences humaines.

Kim, Young-Seok (1984). *Aspects of Korean morphology*. Doctoral dissertation, University of Texas, Austin.

Kim-Renaud, Young-Key (1977). Syllable boundary phenomena in Korean. *Korean Studies* 1: 243–273.

Kingdon, Roger (1958). *The Groundwork of English Intonation*. London: Longmans.

Kingston, John, and Mary Beckman (eds.) (1990). *Papers in Laboratory Phonology 1: Between the Grammar and the Physics of Speech*. Cambridge: CUP.

Kingston, John, and D. Solnit (1988). The tones of consonants. MS, Cornell University and the University of Michigan.

Kiparsky, Paul (1965). *Phonological Change*. Doctoral dissertation, MIT.

Kiparsky, Paul (1968a). How abstract is phonology? In O. Fujimura (ed.), *Three Dimensions of Linguistic Theory* (pp. 1–136). Tokyo: Taikusha.

Kiparsky, Paul (1968b). Linguistic universals and linguistic change. In E. Bach and R. Harms (eds.), *Universals in Linguistic Theory* (pp. 170–202). New York: Holt, Rinehart and Winston.

Kiparsky, Paul (1971). Historical linguistics. In W. O. Dingwall (ed.), *A Survey of Linguistic Science* (pp. 576–642). College Park: University of Maryland Linguistics Program.

Kiparsky, Paul (1973a). "Elsewhere" in phonology. In S. Anderson and P. Kiparsky (eds.), *A Festschrift for Morris Halle* (pp. 93–106). New York: Holt Rinehart and Winston.

Kiparsky, Paul (1973b). Abstractness, opacity and global rules. In O. Fujimura (ed.), *Three Dimensions of Linguistic Theory* (pp. 1–136). Tokyo: Taikusha.

Kiparsky, Paul (1974). A note on the vowel features. In E. Kaisse and J. Hankamer (eds.), *Proceedings of NELS 5* (pp. 162–171). Cambridge, MA: Harvard University Linguistics Department.

Kiparsky, Paul (1979). Metrical structure assignment is cyclic. *LI* 10: 421–441.

Kiparsky, Paul (1980). Concluding statement. In E. Traugott, R. Labrum, and S. Shepherd (eds.), *Papers from the 4th International Conference on Historical Linguistics* (pp. 409–417). Amsterdam: John Benjamins.

Kiparsky, Paul (1981a). Remarks on the metrical structure of the syllable. In W. Dressler et al. (eds.), *Phonologica*, vol. 3. Innsbrucker Beiträge zur Sprachwissenschaft. Innsbruck.

Kiparsky, Paul (1981b). Vowel harmony. MS, MIT.

Kiparsky, Paul (1982a). *Explanation in Phonology*. Dordrecht: Foris.

Kiparsky, Paul (1982b). From cyclic phonology to lexical phonology. In H. van der Hulst and N. Smith (eds.), *The Structure of Phonological Representations*, vol. 1 (pp. 131–175). Dordrecht: Foris.

Kiparsky, Paul (1982c). Lexical phonology and morphology. In I. S. Yang (ed.), *Linguistics in the Morning Calm*, vol. 2 (pp. 3–91). Seoul: Hanshin.

Kiparsky, Paul (1982d). The lexical phonology of Vedic accent. MS, MIT.

Kiparsky, Paul (1983). Word formation and the lexicon. In F. Ingemann (ed.), *Proceedings of the Mid-America Linguistics Conference* (pp. 3–29). Lawrence: University of Kansas.

Kiparsky, Paul (1985a). On the lexical phonology of Icelandic. In C. C. Elert, I. Johansson, and E. Stangert (eds.), *Nordic Prosody 3* (pp. 135–164). University of Umeå.

Kiparsky, Paul (1985b). Some consequences of lexical phonology. *Phonology* 2: 85–138.

Kiparsky, Paul (1986). The phonology of reduplication. MS, Stanford University.

Kiparsky, Paul (1988). Phonological change. In F. Newmeyer (ed.), *Linguistics: The Cambridge Survey*, vol. 1 (pp. 363–415). Cambridge: CUP.

Kiparsky, Paul (1992a). Catathesis. MS, Stanford University.

Kiparsky, Paul (1992b). In defense of the number two. MS, Stanford University.

Kiparsky, Paul (1993). Blocking in non-derived environments. In S. Hargus and E. Kaisse (eds.), *Studies in Lexical Phonology*. San Diego: Academic Press.

Kiparsky, Paul, and Morris Halle (1977). Towards a reconstruction of the Indo-European accent. In L. Hyman (ed.), *Studies in Stress and Accent* (pp. 209–238). SCOPIL, vol. 4. Los Angeles: USC.

Kiparsky, Paul, and Lise Menn (1977a). On the acquisition of morphology. In G. Ioup and S. Weinberger (eds.), *Interlanguage phonology* (pp. 23–52). Cambridge, MA: Newbury House.

Kiparsky, Paul, and Lise Menn. (1977b). On the acquisition of phonology. In J. Macnamara (ed.), *Language Learning and Thought*. New York: Academic Press.

Kirchner, Robert (1992). Lardil truncation and augmentation: A morphological account. MS, University of Maryland, College Park.

Kirchner, Robert (1993). Round and back vowel harmony and disharmony: an optimality theoretic account. MS, UCLA.

Kirshenblatt-Gimblett, B. (1976). Bibliographic survey of the literature on speech play and related subjects. In B. Kirshenblatt-Gimblett (ed.), *Speech Play* (pp. 179–223). Philadelphia: University of Pennsylvania Press.

Kirton, Jean, and Charlie Kirton (1979). Seven articulatory positions in Yanyuwa consonants. *Papers in Australian Linguistics* 11: 179–199.

Kisseberth, Charles (1970). On the functional unity of phonological rules. *LI* 1: 291–306.

Kisseberth, Charles (1971). Cyclic rules in Klamath phonology. *LI* 3: 3–33.

Kisseberth, Charles (1984). Digo Tonology. In G. N. Clements and J. Goldsmith (eds.), *Autosegmental Studies in Bantu Tone* (pp. 105–182). Dordrecht: Foris.

Kisseberth, Charles (1991). Metrical Structure in Chizigula tonology. MS, University of Illinois.

Kisseberth, Charles (in press). On domains. In J. Cole and C. Kisseberth (eds.), *Perspectives in Phonology*. Stanford: CSLI.

Kisseberth, Charles, and M. Abasheikh (1974). Vowel length in Chi Mwi:ni: A case study of the role of grammar in phonology. In M. LaGaly, A. Bruck, and R. Fox (eds.), *CLS 10: Parasession on Natural Phonology* (pp. 193–209). Chicago: CLS.

Klausenburger, Jürgen (1974). Rule inversion, opacity, conspiracies: French liaison and elision. *Lingua* 34: 167–179.

Klausenburger, Jürgen (1977). A non-rule of French: h-aspiré. *Linguistics* 192: 45–52.

Klausenburger, Jürgen (1978). French linking phenomena: A natural generative analysis. *Lg* 54: 21–40.

Klausenburger, Jürgen (1990). Topic . . . Comment. *NLLT* 8: 621–623.

Klavans, Judith (1983). The morphology of cliticization. In J. Richardson, M. Marks, and A. Chukerman (eds.), *CLS 19: Parasession on the Interplay of Phonology, Morphology, and Syntax* (pp. 103–21). Chicago: CLS.

Klavans, Judith (1985). The independence of syntax and phonology in cliticization. *Lg* 61: 95–120.

Klima, Edward, and Ursulla Bellugi (1979). *The Signs of Language*. Cambridge, MA: Harvard University Press.

Klokeid, Terry (1969). *Thagari Phonology and Morphology*. Pacific Linguistics B, no. 12. Canberra: Australian National University.

Klokeid, Terry (1976). *Topics in Lardil grammar*. Doctoral dissertation, MIT.

Koch, Harold (1980). Kaititj nominal inflection: some comparative notes. In B. Rigsby and P. Sutton (eds.), *Papers in Australian Linguistics*, vol. 13 (pp. 259–276). Canberra: Australian National University.

Kohler, K. (1966). Is the syllable a phonological universal? *JL* 2: 207–208.

Komatsu, H. (1981). *Nihongo no on'in* [Japanese phonology]. Tokyo: Chuokoronsha.

Korhonen, Mikko (1969). Die Entwicklung der morphologischen Methode im Lappischen. *Finnisch-Ugrische Forschungen* 37: 203–262.

Korn, D. (1969). Types of labial harmony in the Turkic languages. *AL* 11: 98–106.

Kornai, Andras (1987). Hungarian vowel harmony. MS, Stanford University.

Koutsoudas, Andreas, Gerald Sanders, and Craig Noll (1974). On the application of phonological rules. *Lg* 50: 1–28.

Kraft, Charles, and A. H. M. Kirk-Greene (1973). *Hausa*. Teach Yourself Books. London: Hodder and Stoughton.

Kratzer, Angelika (1991). The representation of focus. In A. v. Stechow and D. Wunderlich (eds.), *Semantik/Semantics: An International Handbook of Contemporary Research* (pp. 804–825). Berlin: de Gruyter.

Kratzer, Angelika (in press). Individual- and stage-level predicates. In G. Carlson et al. (eds.), *The Generic Book*. Chicago: University of Chicago Press.

Krause, S. (1980). *Topics in Chukchee phonology and morphology*. Doctoral dissertation, University of Illinois, Champaign-Urbana.

Krauss, Michael (1985). Yupik Eskimo Prosodic Systems: Descriptive and Comparative Studies. In *Alaska Native Language Center Research Papers 7*. Fairbanks, AL: Alaska Native Language Center, University of Alaska.

Kroch, Anthony (1978). Toward a theory of social dialect variation. *Language in Society* 7: 17–36. Reprinted in H. Allen and M. Linn, eds., *Dialects and Language Variation*. New York: Academic Press.

Kroeger, Paul (1989a). Discontinuous reduplication in vernacular Malay. In K. Hall, M. Meachum, and R. Shapiro (eds.), *Proceedings of BLS 15* (pp. 193–202). Berkeley: BLS.

Kroeger, Paul (1989b). On the nature of reduplicative templates. MS, Stanford University.

Kubozono, H. (1989a). Syntactic and rhythmic effects on downstep in Japanese. *Phonology* 6: 39–67.

Kubozono, H. (1989b). The mora and syllable structure in Japanese: Evidence from speech errors. *Language and Speech* 32: 249–278.

Kubozono, H. (1993). *The Organization of Japanese Prosody*. Tokyo: Kurosio.

Kuhl, P. (1987). Perception of speech and sound in early infancy. In P. Salapatek and L. Cohen (eds.), *Handbook of Infant Perception*, vol. 2 (pp. 275–382). New York: Academic Press.

Kuipers, Aert H. (1960). *Phoneme and Morpheme in Kabardian*. The Hague: Mouton.

Kumbarac, T. (1966). Consonantally conditioned alternation of vocalic morphophonemes in Turkish. *AL* 8: 11–24.

Kuroda, S.-Y. (1967). *Yawelmani Phonology*. Cambridge, MA: MIT Press.

Kurylowicz, J. (1948). Contribution à la théorie de la syllabe. *BPTJ* 8: 80–114.

Kuznecova, A. N., E. A. Xelimskij, and E. V. Gruškina (1980). *Očerki po sel'kupskomu jazyku*. Moscow: Isdatel'stvo Moskovskogo Universiteta.

Labov, William (1981). Resolving the neogrammarian controversy. *Lg* 57: 267–308.

Labov, William (1993). *Principles of Language Change*. Oxford: Basil Blackwell.

LaCharité, Darlene, and Carole Paradis (1993). The emergence of constraints in generative phonology and a comparison of three current constraint-based models. *CJL* 38: 127–153.

Ladd, D. Robert (1980). *The Structure of Intonational Meaning*. Bloomington: Indiana University Press.

Ladd, D. Robert (1983). Phonological features of intonational peaks. *Lg* 59: 721–759.

Ladd, D. Robert (1986). Intonational phrasing: The case for recursive prosodic structure. *Phonology* 3: 311–340.

Ladd, D. Robert (1988). Declination "reset" and the hierarchical organization of utterances. *JASA* 84: 530–544.

Ladefoged, Peter (1968). *A Phonetic Study of West African Languages*, 2nd ed. Cambridge: CUP.

Ladefoged, Peter (1971). *Preliminaries to Linguistic Phonetics*. Chicago: University of Chicago Press.

Ladefoged, Peter (1982). *A Course in Phonetics*. New York: Harcourt Brace Jovanovich.

Ladefoged, Peter (1989). *Representing Phonetic Structure*, vol. 73. UCLA Working Papers in Phonetics.

Ladefoged, Peter, and Morris Halle (1988). Some major features of the International Phonetic Alphabet. *Lg* 64: 577–582.

Ladefoged, Peter, and Ian Maddieson (1990). Vowels of the world's languages. *JP* 18: 93–122.

Ladefoged, Peter, and A. Traill (1984). Linguistic phonetic description of clicks. *Lg* 60:1: 1–120.

Lahiri, Aditi (1991). Anteriority in sibilants. In Comité d'Organisation du Congres (ed.), *Proceedings of the 12th International Congress of Phonetic Sciences*, vol. 1 (pp. 384–388). Aix-en-Provence, France: Université de Provence.

Lahiri, Aditi , and V. Evers (1991). Palatalization and coronality. In C. Paradis and J. F. Prunet (eds.), *The Special Status of Coronals* (pp. 79–100). San Diego: Academic Press.

Lahiri, Aditi, and W. D. Marslen-Wilson (1991). The mental representation of lexical form: A phonological approach to the recognition lexicon. *Cognition* 38: 245–294.

Lahiri, Aditi, and W. D. Marslen-Wilson (1992). Lexical processing and phonological representation. In D. R. Ladd and G. J. Docherty (eds.), *Papers in Laboratory Phonology: Gesture, Segment, Prosody* (pp. 229–254). Cambridge: CUP.

Laka, Itziar (1990). *Negation in syntax: On the nature of functional categories and projections*. Doctoral dissertation, MIT.

Lakoff, George (1993). Cognitive phonology. In J. Goldsmith (ed.), *The Last Phonological*

Rule: Reflections on Constraints and Derivations (pp. 117–145). Chicago: University of Chicago Press.

Lamontagne, Greg (1989). Suffix-triggered variation in Southern Sierra Miwok. MS, University of Massachusetts.

Lane, Harlan, P. Boyes-Braem, and Ursulla Bellugi (1976). Preliminaries to a distinctive feature analysis of handshapes in American Sign Language. *Cognitive Psychology* 8: 263–289.

Larsen, R. S., and E. V. Pike (1949). Huasteco intonations and phonemes. *Lg* 25: 268–277.

Larson, Gary (1992). *Dynamic computational models and the representation of phonological information.* Doctoral dissertation, University of Chicago.

Lass, Roger (1976). *English Phonology and Phonological Theory.* Cambridge: CUP.

Lass, Roger (1984). *Phonology: An Introduction to Basic Concepts.* Cambridge: CUP.

Laughren, Mary (1984). Warlpiri baby talk. *AJL* 4: 73–88.

Laughren, Mary (1990a). Another look at the stop (rt) versus flat (rd) contrast in Warlpiri. Paper presented at Central Australian Linguistic Circle Miniconference, Alice Spring.

Laughren, Mary (1990b). Tracking sound changes in Central Australian Languages in the light of recent developments in phonological theory. Paper presented at Australian Linguistic Society, Macquarie University.

Laycock, D. (1969). Sublanguages in Buin: Play, poetry, and preservation. *Pacific Linguistics* 22: 1–23.

Laycock, D. (1972). Towards a typology of ludlings or play-languages. *Linguistic Communications* 6: 61–113.

Leben, Will (1971). The morphophonemics of tone in Hausa. In C.-W. Kim and H. Stahlke (eds.), *Papers in African Linguistics* (pp. 201–218). Albert: Linguistic Research, Inc.

Leben, Will (1973). *Suprasegmental phonology.* Doctoral dissertation, MIT.

Leben, Will (1978). The representation of tone. In V. Fromkin (ed.), *Tone: A Linguistic Survey* (pp. 177–219). New York: Academic Press.

Leben, Will (1982). Metrical or autosegmental? In H. van der Hulst and N. Smith (eds.), *The Structure of Phonological Representations,* vol. 1 (pp. 177–190). Dordrecht: Foris.

Leben, Will (1985). Syllable and morpheme tone in Hausa. *JOLAN* 3: 39–52.

Leben, Will, Sharon Inkelas, and Mark Cobler (1989). Phrases and phrase tones in Hausa. In P. Newman and R. Botne (eds.), *Current Approaches to African Linguistics,* vol. 5 (pp. 45–61). Dordrecht: Foris.

Lee, Borim (1991). *Prosodic structures in Takelma phonology and morphology.* Doctoral dissertation, University of Texas, Austin.

Lee, Gregory (1975). Natural phonological descriptions, 1. *Working Papers in Linguistics* 7(5): 85–125. University of Hawaii.

Lee, J. F. (1989). The acquisition of syllable structure and stress patterns by monolingual Spanish-speaking children. *Hispanic Linguistics* 2: 229–252.

Lee, Jin-Seong, and Stuart Davis (1993). A prosodic analysis of infixing reduplication in Korean ideophones. MS, Indiana University.

Leer, Jeff (1985). Prosody in Alutiiq. In M. Kraus (ed.), *Yupik Eskimo Prosodic Systems: Descriptive and Comparative Studies* (pp. 77–133). Alaska Native Language Center Research Papers no. 7. Fairbanks: Alaska Native Language Center, University of Alaska.

Lees, Robert (1961). *The phonology of Modern Standard Turkish.* Uralic and Altaic Series, vol. 6. Bloomington: Indiana University Publications.

Lefkowitz, N. J. (1987). *Talking backwards and looking forwards: The French language game Verlan.* Doctoral dissertation, University of Washington.

Lehiste, Ilse (1970). *Suprasegmentals.* Cambridge, MA: MIT Press.

Lehiste, Ilse, and Pavle Ivic (1986). *Word and Sentence Prosody in Serbo-Croatian.* Cambridge, MA: MIT Press.

Lehn, Walter (1963). Emphasis in Cairo Arabic. *Lg* 39: 29–39.

Leopold, W. F. (1947). *Speech Development of a Bilingual Child,* vol. 2. New York: AMS Press.

Lerdahl, Fred, and Ray Jackendoff (1983). *A Generative Theory of Tonal Music.* Cambridge, MA: MIT Press.

Leslau, Wolf (1950). *Ethiopic documents: Gurage.* Viking Fund Publications in Anthropology 14. New York: Viking Fund.

Leslau, Wolf (1957). Une hypothèse sur la forme primitive du type B en amharique. *Word* 13: 479–488. Also in *Fifty Years of Research,* pp. 289–298. Wiesbaden: Otto Harrassowitz, 1988.

Leslau, Wolf (1964a). *Ethiopian Argots.* The Hague: Mouton.

Leslau, Wolf (1964b). The jussive in Chaha. *Lg* 40: 53–57.

Leslau, Wolf (1965). *An Annotated Bibliography of the Semitic Languages of Ethiopia.* The Hague: Mouton.

Leslau, Wolf (1971). Traces of the laryngeals in the Gurage dialect of Endegeñ. *JNES* 30: 218–224.

Leslau, Wolf (1988). Spirantization in the Ethiopian Languages. *Fifty Years of Research* (pp. 177–201). Wiesbaden: Otto Harrassowitz. Originally published in P. Fronzaroli (ed.), *Atti del Secondo Congresso Internazionale di Linguistica Camito-Semitica* (pp. 175–199). Quaderni di Semitistica 5. Florence: Instituto di Linguistica e di Linguae Orientali.

Letz, B. (1950). *Gramatika slovenského jazyka* [Grammar of the Slovak language]. Bratislava: Stáne Nakladatel'stvo.

Levelt, Clara (1990). Samoan reduplication. MS, University of Leiden.

Levergood, Barbara (1984). Rule governed vowel harmony and the strict cycle. In C. Jones and P. Sells (eds.), *Proceedings of NELS 14* (pp. 275–293). Amherst, MA: GSLA.

Levergood, Barbara (1987). *Topics in Arusa phonology and morphology.* Doctoral dissertation, University of Texas, Austin.

Levergood, Barbara (1989). Arusa (Maa) phrasal tonology. In P. Newman and R. Botne (eds.), *Current Approaches to African Linguistics,* vol. 5. Dordrecht: Foris.

Levin, Juliette (1983). Reduplication and prosodic structure. MS, MIT.

Levin, Juliette (1985a). *A metrical theory of syllabicity.* Doctoral dissertation, MIT.

Levin, Juliette (1985b). Reduplication in Umpila. *MIT Working Papers in Linguistics* 6: 133–59.

Levin, Juliette (1987a). Between epenthetic and excrescent vowels (or what happens after redundancy rules). In M. Crowhurst (ed.), *Proceedings of WCCFL 6* (pp. 187–202). Stanford: SLA.

Levin, Juliette (1987b). Constraints on rhyme-internal syllabification in French: Eliminating truncation rules. In D. Birdsong and J.-P. Montreuil (eds.), *Advances in Romance Linguistics.* Dordrecht: Foris.

Levin, Juliette (1987c). A place for lateral in the feature geometry. Paper presented at LSA meeting.

Levin, Juliette (1988a). Bidirectional stress assignment as a window on level ordering. In M. Hammond and M. Noonan (eds.), *Theoretical Morphology* (pp. 339–352). Orlando: Academic Press.

Levin, Juliette (1988b). Generating ternary feet. *Texas Linguistic Forum* 29: 97–113.

Levin, Juliette (1989). The autonomy of the skeleton: Evidence from Micronesian. MS, University of Texas, Austin.

Liberman, A. (1981). Review of Zinder 1979. *Lg* 57: 725–727.

Liberman, Mark (1975). *The intonational system of English*. Doctoral dissertation, MIT. Distributed by the IULC.

Liberman, Mark, and Alan Prince (1977). On stress and linguistic rhythm. *LI* 8: 249–336.

Lichtenberk, Frantisek (1983). *A grammar of Manam*. Honolulu: University of Hawaii Press.

Liddell, Scott (1984). THINK and BELIEVE: Sequentiality in American Sign Language. *Lg* 60: 372–392.

Liddell, Scott (1993). Conceptual and linguistic issues in spatial mapping: Comparing spoken and signed language. Paper presented at the Workshop on Phonology and Morphology. Amsterdam.

Liddell, Scott, and Robert Johnson (1986). American Sign Language compound formation processes, lexicalization, and phonological remnants. *NLLT* 4: 445–513.

Liddell, Scott, and Robert Johnson (1989). American Sign Language: The phonological base. *SLS* 64: 197–277.

Lieber, Rochelle (1980). *On the organization of the lexicon*. Doctoral dissertation, MIT.

Leiber, Rochelle (1987). Morphology and the Morphemic Tier Hypothesis. MS, University of New Harmpshire and MIT.

Lightner, Theodore (1965). *Segmental phonology of modern standard Russian*. Doctoral dissertation, MIT.

Lightner, Theodore (1972a). *Problems in the Theory of Phonology*, Vol 1: *Russian Phonology and Turkish Phonology*. Edmonton: Linguistic Research, Inc.

Lightner, Theodore (1972b). Some remarks on exceptions and on coexistent systems in phonology. In D. S. Worth (ed.), *The Slavic Word* (pp. 426–442). The Hague: Mouton.

Lindau, Mona (1975). A phonetic explanation to reduced vowel harmony systems *Working Papers (Lund University)* 11: 43–54.

Lindau, Mona (1978). Vowel Features. *Lg* 54: 541–563.

Lindblom, B. (1983). Economy of speech gestures. In P. MacNeilage (ed.), *The Production of Speech* (pp. 217–245). New York: Springer-Verlag.

Lindblom, B. (1984). Can the models of evolutionary biology be applied to phonetic problems? In M. P. R. van den Broeke and A. Cohen (eds.), *Proceedings of the Tenth International Congress of Phonetic Sciences* (pp. 67–81). Dordrecht: Foris.

Lindblom, B. (1986). Phonetic universals in vowel systems. In J. Ohala and J. Jaeger (eds.), *Experimental Phonology* (pp. 13–44). Orlando: Academic Press.

Lindblom, B. (1992). Phonological units as adaptive emergents of lexical development. In C. Ferguson et al. (eds), *Phonological Development* (pp. 131–163). Timonium, MD: York Press.

Lisker, Leigh (1957). Closure duration and the intervocalic voiced-voiceless distinction in English. *Lg* 33: 42–49.

Lisker, Leigh (1986). "Voicing" in English: A catalogue of acoustic features signaling /b/ versus /p/ in trochees. *Language and Speech* 29: 3–11.

Lisker, Leigh, and Arthur Abramson (1964). A cross-language study of voicing in initial stops: Acoustical measurements. *Word* 20: 384–422.

Lisker, Leigh, and Arthur Abramson (1967). Some effects of context on voice onset time in English stops. *Language and Speech* 10: 1–28.

Lisker, Leigh, and Arthur Abramson (1970). The voicing dimension: some experiments in comparative phonetics. In B. Hála, M. Romportl, and P. Janota (eds.), *Proceedings of the Sixth International Congress of Phonetic Sciences, Prague 1967* (pp. 563–567). Prague: Academia, Publishing House of the Czechoslovak Academy of Sciences.

Liu, F.-H. (1980). Mandarin tone sandhi: A case of interaction between syntax and phonology. Paper presented at summer meeting of the LSA, Albuquerque.

Lombardi, Linda (1990). The nonlinear organization of the affricate. *NLLT* 8: 375–425.

Lombardi, Linda (1991). *Laryngeal features and laryngeal neutralization.* Doctoral dissertation, University of Massachusetts, Amherst.

Lombardi, Linda, and John McCarthy (1991). Prosodic circumscription in Choctaw morphology. *Phonology* 8: 37–71.

Lotz, J., A. S. Abramson, L. Gerstman, F. Ingemann, and W. Nemser (1960). The perception of English stops by speakers of English, Spanish, Hungarian, and Thai: A tape-cutting experiment. *Word* 3: 71–77.

Lovins, Julie (1971). Melodic conspiracies in Lomongo tonology. In *Papers from CLS 7,* (pp. 469–478). Chicago: CLS.

Lowenstamm, Jean (1986). A propos d'une hypothèse sur la forme primitive du type B en amharique. *RQL* 16: 157–180.

Lowenstamm, Jean, and Jonathan Kaye (1986). Compensatory lengthening in Tiberian Hebrew. In L. Wetzels and E. Sezer (eds.), *Studies in Compensatory Lengthening* (pp. 97–146). Dordrecht: Foris.

Lowenstamm, Jean, and Jean-François Prunet (1986). Le Tigrinya et le principe du contour obligatoire. *RQL* 16: 181–207.

Lü, S.-X. (1980). Danyang Fangyande Shengdiao Xitong [The Tonal System of the Danyang Dialect]. *Fangyan* 1980.2: 85–122.

Lucas, C. (ed.) (1990). *Sign Language Research: Theoretical Issues.* Washington, DC: Gallaudet University Press.

Lucci, V. (1972). *Phonologie de l'Acadien.* Studia Phonetica 7. Ottawa: Didier.

Lunt, Horace (1973). Remarks on Nasality: The Case of Guaraní. In S. Anderson and P. Kiparsky (eds.), *A Festschrift for Morris Halle* (pp. 131–139). New York: Holt, Rinehart and Winston.

Lyman, L., and R. Lyman (1977). Choapan Zapotec Phonology. In W. Merrifield (ed.), *Studies in Otomangean Phonology.* Dallas: SIL.

Lynch, John (1974). *Lenakel phonology.* Doctoral dissertation, University of Hawaii. Also, University of Hawaii Working Papers in Linguistics vol. 7.1.

MacKay, Carolyn (1991). *A grammar of Misantla Totonac.* Doctoral dissertation, University of Texas at Austin.

Macken, Marlys (1987). Representation, rules and overgeneralization in phonology. In B. MacWhinney (ed.), *Mechanisms of Language Acquisition* (pp. 367–397). Hillsdale, NJ: Erlbaum.

Macken, Marlys (1992a). Lexical templates. In J. Denton, G. Chan, and C. Canakis (eds.), *Papers from CLS 28.* Chicago: CLS.

Macken, Marlys (1992b). Where's phonology? In C. Ferguson et al. (eds.), *Phonological Development.* Gimonium, MD: York Press.

Macken, Marlys, and D. Barton (1980). A longitudinal study of the acquisition of the voicing contrast in American-English word-initial stops, as measured by voice onset time. *J. Child Language* 7: 41–72.

Macken, Marlys, and Charles Ferguson (1983). Cognitive aspects of phonological development. In K. Nelson (ed.), *Children's Language.* Hillsdale, NJ: Erlbaum.

MacNeilage, Peter, and B. Davis (1993). Motor explanations of babbling and early speech patterns. In B. de Boysson-Bardies et al. (eds.), *Developmental Neurocognition* (pp. 341–352). Dordrecht: Kluwer.

Maddieson, Ian (1974). A note on tone and consonants. In I. Maddieson (ed.), *The Tone Tome: Studies on Tone from the UCLA Tone Project* (pp. 18–27). UCLA Working Papers in Phonetics, vol. 27. Los Angeles: UCLA.

Maddieson, Ian (1978). Universals of tone. In J. Greenberg (ed.), *Universals of Human Language*, vol. 2: *Phonology* (pp. 335–365). Stanford: Stanford University Press.

Maddieson, Ian (1984). *Patterns of Sounds.* Cambridge: CUP.

Maddieson, Ian (1987). Phonetic difficulty. MS, UCLA.

Maddieson, Ian (1990). Shona velarization: Complex consonants or complex onsets? *UCLA WPL* 74: 16–34.

Maddieson, Ian, and Peter Ladefoged (1985). "Tense" and "lax" in four minority languages in China. *JP* 13: 433–454.

Maddieson, Ian, and Peter Ladefoged (1988). Multiply articulated segments and the feature hierarchy. MS, UCLA. Expanded version of a paper presented at the 63rd Annual Meeting of the LSA, New Orleans, December 1988.

Maddieson, Ian, and Kristin Precoda (1992). Syllable structure and phonetic models. *Phonology* 9: 45–60.

Mahajan, G. (1993). Dissertation in progress, Brandeis University.

Manaster-Ramer, Alexis (1988). The phoneme in generative phonology and in phonological change. *Diachronica* 5: 109–139.

Mandel, M. (1981). *Phonotactics and morphophonology in American Sign Language.* Doctoral dissertation, University of California, Berkeley.

Marantz, Alec (1982). Re Reduplication. *LI* 13: 483–545.

Marantz, Alec (1984). *On the Nature of Grammatical Relations.* Cambridge, MA: MIT Press.

Marantz, Alec (1987). Phonologically induced bracketing paradoxes in full morpheme reduplication. In M. Crowhurst (ed.), *Proceedings of WCCFL 6* (pp. 203–212). Stanford: SLA.

Marlett, S., and Joseph Stemberger (1983). Empty consonants in Seri. *LI* 5: 617–639.

Marsack, C. C. (1962). *Teach Yourself Samoan.* London: Hodder and Stoughton.

Martin, Jack (1989). Infixation and extrametricality in prosodic morphology: Three rules from Creek. MS, University of North Texas.

Martin, Samuel (1951). Korean phonemics. *Lg* 27: 519–533.

Martin, Samuel (1952). *Morphophonemics of Standard Colloquial Japanese.* Language Dissertation No. 47. Linguistic Society of America.

Martin, Samuel (1975). *Reference Grammar of Japanese.* New Haven: Yale University Press.

Martin, Samuel (1987). *The Japanese Language through Time.* New Haven: Yale University Press.

Mascaró, Joan (1976). *Catalan phonology and the phonological cycle.* Doctoral dissertation, MIT.

Mascaró, Joan (1987). Place and voicing assimilation: A reduction and spreading account. MS, Universitat Autònoma de Barcelona.

Massamba, David (1982). *Aspects of accent and tone in Ci-ruri.* Doctoral dissertation, Indiana University.

Massamba, David (1984). Tone in Ci-Ruri. In G. N. Clements and J. Goldsmith (eds.), *Autosegmental Studies in Bantu Tone,* (pp. 235–254). Dordrecht: Foris.

Matteson, Esther (1965). *The Piro (Arawakan) Language.* Berkeley: University of California Press.

Matthews, P. 1972. *Morphology*. Cambridge: CUP.

May, Robert (1985). *Logical Form: Its Structure and Derivation*. Cambridge, MA: MIT Press.

McArthur, H., and L. McArthur (1956). Aguacatec (Mayan) phonemes in the stress group. *IJAL* 22: 72–76.

McCarthy, John (1979a). *Formal problems in Semitic phonology and morphology*. Doctoral dissertation, MIT. Garland Press, New York, 1985.

McCarthy, John (1979b). On stress and syllabification. *LI* 10: 443–466.

McCarthy, John (1981a). A prosodic theory of nonconcatenative morphology. *LI* 12: 373–418.

McCarthy, John (1981b). The role of the evaluation metric in the acquisition of morphology. In C. L. Baker and J. McCarthy (eds.), *The Logical Problem of Language Acquisition* (pp. 218–248). Cambridge, MA: MIT Press.

McCarthy, John (1982a). Prosodic organization in morphology. MS, University of Texas, Austin.

McCarthy, John (1982b). Prosodic templates, morphemic templates, and morphemic tiers. In H. van der Hulst and N. Smith (eds.), *The Structure of Phonological Representations*, vol. 1 (pp. 191–223). Dordrecht: Foris Publications.

McCarthy, John (1983a). Consonantal morphology in the Chaha verb. In M. Barlow, D. Flickinger and M. Wescoat (eds.), *Proceedings of WCCFL 2* (pp. 176–188). Stanford: SLA.

McCarthy, John (1983b). A prosodic account of Arabic broken plurals. In I. Dihoff (ed.), *Current Trends in African Linguistics*, vol. 1 (pp. 289–320). Dordrecht: Foris.

McCarthy, John (1984a). Speech disguise and phonological representation in Amharic. In H. van der Hulst and N. Smith (eds.), *Advances in Nonlinear Phonology* (pp. 305–312). Dordrecht: Foris.

McCarthy, John (1984b). Theoretical consequences of Montañes vowel harmony. *LI* 15: 291–318.

McCarthy, John (1984c). Prosodic structure in morphology. In M. Aronoff and R. Oehrle (eds.), *Language Sound Structure* (pp. 299–317). Cambridge, MA: MIT Press.

McCarthy, John (1985). Speech disguise and phonological representation in Amharic. In H. van der Hulst and N. Smith (eds.), *Advances in Nonlinear Phonology*, (pp. 305–312). Dordrecht: Foris.

McCarthy, John (1986a). Lexical phonology and nonconcatenative morphology in the history of Chaha. *RQL* 16: 209–228.

McCarthy, John (1986b). OCP Effects: Gemination and antigemination. *LI* 17: 207–263.

McCarthy, John (1988). Feature geometry and dependency: A review. *Phonetica* 43: 84–108.

McCarthy, John (1989a). Guttural Phonology. Paper presented at Conference on Features and Underspecification, MIT.

McCarthy, John (1989b). Linear order in phonological representation. *LI* 20: 71–99.

McCarthy, John (1991a). L'infixation reduplicative dans les langages secrets. In M. Plénat (ed.), *Les javanais* (pp. 11–29) (*Langages* 101). Paris: Larousse.

McCarthy, John (1991b). On gutturals. MS, U. Mass, Amherst.

McCarthy, John (1991c). Semitic gutturals and distinctive feature theory. In M. Eid and B. Comrie (eds.), *Perspectives on Arabic Linguistics*, vol. 3 (pp. 63–91). Philadelphia: John Benjamins.

McCarthy, John (1993). Template form in prosodic morphology. In L. Smith Stvan et al. (eds.), *Papers from the Third Annual Formal Linguistics Society of Midamerica Conference* (pp. 187–218). Bloomington: IULC.

McCarthy, John (in press). The Phonetics and Phonology of Semitic Pharyngeals. In P. Keating (ed.), *Papers in Laboratory Phonology*, vol. 3. Cambridge: CUP.

McCarthy, John, and Alan Prince (1986). Prosodic Morphology. MS, University of Massachusetts and Brandeis.

McCarthy, John, and Alan Prince (1988). Quantitative transfer in reduplicative and templatic morphology. In Linguistic Society of Korea (ed.), *Linguistics in the Morning Calm*, vol. 2 (pp. 3–35). Seoul: Hanshin Publishing Co.

McCarthy, John, and Alan Prince (1990a). Foot and word in prosodic morphology: The Arabic broken plural. *NLLT* 8: 209–283.

McCarthy, John, and Alan Prince (1990b). Prosodic morphology and templatic morphology. In M. Eid and J. McCarthy (eds.), *Perspectives on Arabic linguistics 2: Papers from the Second Annual Symposium on Arabic Linguistics* (pp. 1–54). Amsterdam: John Benjamins.

McCarthy, John, and Alan Prince (1991a). Linguistics 240: Prosodic Morphology. Material presented at 1991 LSA Linguistic Institute course.

McCarthy, John, and Alan Prince (1991b). Prosodic minimality. Paper presented at the conference on the Organization of Phonology, University of Illinois, Champaign.

McCarthy, John, and Alan Prince (1993a). Prosodic Morphology 1: Constraint interaction and satisfaction. MS, University of Massachusetts, Amherst and Rutgers University.

McCarthy, John and Alan Prince (1993b). Generalized alignment. *Yearbook of Morphology*.

McCarthy, John, and A. Taub (1992). Review of C. Paradis and J.-F. Prunet, eds., The Special Status of Coronals: Internal and External Evidence. *Phonology* 9: 363–370.

McCawley, James (1968). *The Phonological Component of a Grammar of Japanese*. The Hague: Mouton.

McCawley, James (1970). Some tonal systems that come close to being pitch accent systems but don't quite make it. In *Papers from CLS 6* (pp. 526–532). Chicago: CLS.

McCawley, James (1977). Accent in Japanese. In L. Hyman (ed.), *Studies in Stress and Accent*, (pp. 261–302). SCOPIL 4. Los Angeles: USC.

McCawley, James (1978). What is a tone language? In V. Fromkin (ed.), *Tone: A Linguistic Survey* (pp. 113–131). New York: Academic Press.

McConvell, P. (1988). Nasal cluster dissimilation and constraints on phonological variables in Gurindji and related languages. In N. Evans and S. Johnson (eds.), *Aboriginal Linguistics 1* (pp. 135–165). Armidale: Department of Linguistics, University of New England.

McCormick, S. (1981). A metrical analysis of umlaut. *Cornell Working Papers in Linguistics* 2: 127–137.

McDonough, Joyce (1990). *Topics in the phonology and morphology of Navajo verbs*. Doctoral dissertation, University of Massachusetts, Amherst.

McEachern, P. (1993). The effects of uvular consonants on vowels in Quechua. MS, UCLA.

McGregor, William (1988). On the status of the feature rhotic in some languages of the northwest of Australia. In N. Evans and S. Johnson (eds.), *Aboriginal Linguistics 1* (pp. 166–187). Armidale: Dept of Linguistics, University of New England.

McGregor, William (1990). *A Functional Grammar of Gooniyandi*. Amsterdam: John Benjamins.

McGregor, William (1993). Towards a systemic account of Gooniyandi segmental phonology. In P. Tench (ed.), *Studies in Systemic Phonology* (pp. 19–43). London and New York: Pinter.

McHugh, Brian (1990). The phrasal cycle in Kirunjo Chaga tonology. In S. Inkelas and

D. Zec (eds.), *The Phonology-Syntax Connection* (pp. 217–242). Chicago: University of Chicago Press.

McIntire, M. (1977). The acquisition of American Sign Language hand configurations. *SLS* 16: 247–266.

McKaughan, H. (1973). Introduction. In H. KcKaughan (ed.), *The Languages of the Eastern Family of the East New Guinea Highland Stock*. Seattle: University of Washington Press.

McKay, Graham (1975). *Rembarnga: A language of central Arnhem Land*. Doctoral dissertation, Australian National University.

McKay, Graham (1979). Djeebbana phonemic statement. MS, NT Department of Education. Darwin, Australia.

McKay, Graham (1980). Medial stop gemination in Rembarrnga: A spectrographic study. *Journal of Phonetics* 8: 343–352.

McKay, Graham (1984). Stop alternations in Ndjébbana (Kunibidji). In Glasgow et al. (eds.), *Papers in Australian Linguistics No. 16*. Canberra: Australian National University.

McKay, Graham, and Caroline Coleman (to appear). Ndjébbana. In R. M. W. Dixon and B. Blake (eds.), *Handbook of Australian languages*, vol. 5 Melbourne: OUP Australia.

McLemore, Cynthia (1991). *The pragmatic interpretation of English intonation: Sorority speech*. Doctoral dissertation, University of Texas, Austin.

McMahon, April M. S. (1991). Lexical phonology and sound change: The case of the Scottish vowel length rule. *JL* 27: 29–53.

McNally, Louise (1990). Multiplanar reduplication: Evidence from Sesotho. In A. Halpern (ed.), *Proceedings of WCCFL 9* (pp. 331–346). Stanford: SLA.

Meer, G. van der (1977). Frisian breaking: A hypothesis about its historical development. *Us Wurk* 26: 9–24.

Meeussen, Albert (1954). *Linguistische schets van het Bangubangu*. Annalen van het Koninklijk Museum van Belgisch Kong. Terveuren.

Melvold, Janis (1990). *Structure and stress in the phonology of Russian*. Doctoral dissertation, MIT.

Menn, L. (1971). Phonotactic rules in beginning speech. *Lingua* 26: 225–251.

Menn, L. (1977). Phonological units in beginning speech. In A. Bell and J. B. Hooper (eds.), *Syllables and Segments* (pp. 315–334). Amsterdam: North Holland.

Menn, L. (1980). Phonological theory and child phonology. In G. Yeni-Komshian et al. (eds.) *Child Phonology* (pp. 23–41). New York: Academic Press.

Meredith, Scott (1990). *Issues in the phonology of prominence*. Doctoral dissertation, MIT.

Merlan, Francesca (1982). *Mangarayi*. Lingua Descriptive Series. Amsterdam: North Holland.

Merlan, Francesca (1983). *Ngalakan grammar, texts and vocabulary*. Pacific Linguistics B-89. Canberra: Australian National University.

Merrifield, W. R. (1963). Palantla Chinantec Syllable Types. *AL* 5: 1–16.

Mester, R. Armin (1986). *Studies in tier structure*. Doctoral dissertation, University of Massachusetts, Amherst.

Mester, R. Armin (1988). Dependent tier ordering and the OCP. In H. van der Hulst and N. Smith (eds.), *Features, Segmental Structure and Harmony Processes*, vol. 2 (pp. 127–144). Dordrecht: Foris.

Mester, R. Armin (1990). Patterns of truncation. *LI* 21: 475–485.

Mester, R. Armin (in press). The quantitative trochee in Latin. *NLLT*.

Mester, R. Armin, and J. Itô (1989). Feature predictability and underspecification: Palatal prosody in Japanese mimetics. *Lg* 65: 258–293.

Michelson, Karin (1986). Ghost R's in Onondaga: An autosegmental analysis of *R-stems In L. Wetzels and E. Sezer (eds.), *Studies in Compensatory Lengthening* (pp. 147–166). Dordrecht: Foris.

Miller, W. (1965). *Acoma Grammar and Texts*. University of California Publications in Linguistics, vol. 40.

Miner, Kenneth (1989). Winnebago accent: The rest of the data. *AL* 31: 148–172.

Minor, Eugene (1956). Witoto vowel clusters. *IJAL* 22: 131–137.

Mithun, Marianne, and Hasan Basri (1986). The phonology of Selayarese. *OL* 25: 210–254.

Miyara, S. (1980). Phonological phrase and phonological reduction. *Papers in Japanese Linguistics* 7: 79–122.

Mohanan, K. P. (1982). *Lexical phonology*. Doctoral dissertation, MIT. Distributed by the IULC.

Mohanan, K. P. (1983). The structure of the melody. MS, MIT.

Mohanan, K. P. (1985). Syllable structure and lexical strata in English. *Phonology* 2: 139–155.

Mohanan, K. P. (1986). *The Theory of Lexical Phonology*. Dordrecht: Reidel.

Mohanan, K. P. (1989). Universal attractors in phonology. Paper presented at Berkeley Workshop on Rules and Constraints, Berkeley, CA, later published as Mohanan (1993).

Mohanan, K. P. (1991). On the bases of radical underspecification. *NLLT* 9: 285–325.

Mohanan, K. P. (1992). Emergence of complexity in phonological development. In C. Ferguson, C. Stoel-Gammon, and L. Menn (ed.), *Phonological Development*. York Press.

Mohanan, K. P. (1993). Fields of attraction in phonology. In J. Goldsmith (ed.), *The Last Phonological Rule: Reflections on Constraints and Derivations* (pp. 61–116). Chicago: University of Chicago Press.

Mohanan, K. P., and Tara Mohanan (1984). Lexical phonology of the consonant system in Malayalam. *LI* 15: 575–602.

Mohanan, Tara (1989). Syllable structure in Malayalam. *LI* 20: 589–625.

Mohanan, Tara (1990). *Arguments in Hindi*. Doctoral dissertation, Stanford University.

Mohanan, Tara (1993). Case OCP in Hindi. In M. Butt, T. King and G. Ramchand (eds.), *Word Order of South Asian Languages*. Stanford: CSLI.

Montler, Timothy (1989). Infixation, reduplication, and metathesis in the Saanich actual aspect. *Southwest Journal of Linguistics* 9.

Montler, Timothy, and Heather Hardy (1988). Imperfective gemination in Alabama. *IJAL* 54: 399–415.

Montler, Timothy, and Heather Hardy (1991). The phonology of negation in Alabama. *IJAL* 57: 1–23.

Moore, John (1989). Doubled verbs in Modern Standard Arabic. *Phonology at Santa Cruz* 1: 93–124.

Moore, Mary Jo (1968). *The ideophone in Hausa*. MA dissertation, Michigan State University.

Morais, J., L. Cary, J. Alegria, and P. Bertelson (1979). Does awareness of speech as sequence of phones arise spontaneously? *Cognition* 7: 323–331.

Moravcsik, Edith (1977). *On rules of infixing*. Bloomington: IULC.

Moravcsik, Edith (1978). Reduplicative constructions. In J. Greenberg (ed.), *Universals of Human Language*, vol 3: *Word Structure* (pp. 297–334). Stanford: Stanford University Press.

Morin, Yves-Charles (1974). Règles phonologiques à domaine indéterminé: Chute du cheva en français. *Cahiers de linguistique de l'Université du Québec* 4: 69–88.

Morin, Yves-Charles (1992a). Phonological interpretations of historical lengthening. Paper presented at Seventh International Phonology Meeting, Krems.

Morin, Yves-Charles (1992b). Un cas méconnu de la déclinaison de l'adjectif français: Les formes de liaison de l'adjectif antéposé. MS, Université de Montréal.

Morin, Yves-Charles, and Jonathan Kaye (1982). The syntactic bases for French liaison. *JL* 18: 291–330.

Morphy, Frances (1977). Language and moiety: Sociolectal variation in a Yu:lngu language of North-East Arnhem Land. *Canberra Anthropology* 1: 51–60.

Morphy, Frances (1983). Djapu. In R. M. W. Dixon and B. Blake (eds.), *Handbook of Australian Languages* vol. 3. Canberra: ANU Press.

Morris, Mitzi (1989). Swedish nickname formation. *Phonology at Santa Cruz* 1: 125–171.

Mors, Christina ter (1984). Empty V-nodes and their role in Klamath. In H. van der Hulst and N. Smith (eds.), *Advances in nonlinear phonology* (pp. 313–334). Dordrecht: Foris.

Moskowitz, A. (1970). The two-year-old stage in the acquisition of English phonology. *Lg* 46. 426–441.

Moskowitz, A. (1973). The acquisition of phonology and syntax. In J. Hintakka et al. (eds.) *Approaches to Natural Language* (pp. 48–84). Dordrecht: Reidel.

Moy, A. (1990). A psycholinguistic approach to categorizing handshapes in American Sign Language: Is [As] an allophone of /A/? In C. Lucas (ed.), *Sign Language Research: Theoretical Issues* (pp. 346–357). Washington, DC: Gallaudet University Press.

Mrayati, M., R. Carré, and B. Guérin (1988). Distinctive Regions and Modes: A New Theory of Speech Production. *Speech Communication* 7: 257–86.

Müller, J. (1848). *The Physiology of the Senses, Voice, and Muscular Motion with the Mental Faculties*. London: Walton and Maberly. W. Baly, translator.

Munro, Pamela, and P. Benson (1973). Reduplication and rule ordering in Luiseño. *IJAL* 39: 15–21.

Murray, R. W. (1982). Consonant cluster developments in Pali. *Folia Linguistica Historia* 3: 163–184.

Mutaka, N. (1991). Vowel harmony in Kinande. MS, University of Southern California.

Mutaka, Ngessimo, and Larry Hyman (1990). Syllable and morpheme integrity in Kinande reduplication. *Phonology* 7: 73–120.

Myers, Scott (1987a). *Tone and the structure of words in Shona*. Doctoral dissertation, Univ. of Massachusetts, Amherst.

Myers, Scott (1987b). Vowel shortening in English. *NLLT* 5: 485–518.

Myers, Scott (1991a). Persistent rules. *LI* 22: 315–344.

Myers, Scott (1991b). Structure Preservation and the Strong Domain Hypothesis. *LI* 22: 379–385.

Myers, Scott (1992). The morphology and phonology of INFL in Bantu. MS, University of Texas, Austin.

Nagano-Madsen, Y. (1992). *Mora and prosodic coordination: A prosodic study of Japanese, Eskimo, and Yoruba*. Travaux de l'Institut de Linguistique de Lund, 27. Lund: Lund University Press.

Nash, David (1979a). Warlpiri vowel assimilations. *MIT Working Papers in Linguistics* 1: 12–24.

Nash, David (1979b). Yidiny stress: A metrical account. *CUNY Forum* 7/8: 112–30.

Nash, David (1980). *Topics in Warlpiri grammar*. Doctoral dissertation, MIT. New York: Garland Press, 1986.

Nash, David, and Ken Hale (1987). Lardil and Damin Phonotactics. Paper presented at Australian Linguistics Society,

Navarro Tomás, T., et al. (1970). *Spanische Aussprachlehre*. Munich: Max Huber Verlag.

Nemer, Julie, and Keith Mountford (1984). The interaction of segmental and tonal levels: The case of [ʍ] in Temne. *SAL* 15: 107–161.

Nespor, Marina, and Irene Vogel (1982). Prosodic domains of external sandhi rules. In H. van der Hulst and N. Smith (eds.), *The Structure of Phonological Representations*, vol. 1 (pp. 222–255). Dordrecht: Foris.

Nespor, Marina, and Irene Vogel (1986). *Prosodic Phonology*. Dordrecht: Foris.

Nessly, L. (1971). Anglicization in English phonology. In *Papers from CLS 7* (pp. 499–510). Chicago: CLS.

Newkirk, D. (1981). On the Temporal Segmentation of Movement in American Sign Language. MS, Salk Institute of Biological Studies.

Newman, Paul (1972). Syllable weight as a phonological variable. *SAL* 3: 301–323.

Newman, Paul (1974). *The Kanakuru Language*. West African Language Monographs, 9. Leeds: Institute of Modern English Language Studies, University of Leeds and West African Linguistic Society.

Newman, Paul (1979). The historical development of medial /ee/ and /oo/ in Hausa. *JALL* 1: 172–188.

Newman, Paul (1986a). Contour tones as phonemic primes in Grebo. In K. Bogers, H. van der Hulst and M. Mous (eds.), *The Phonological Representation of Suprasegmentals* (pp. 175–193). Dordrecht: Foris.

Newman, Paul (1986b). Tone and affixation in Hausa. *SAL* 17: 249–267.

Newman, Paul (1991). Historical decay and growth in the Hausa lexicon. In A. Kaye (ed.), *Semitic Studies in Honor of Wolf Leslau* (pp. 1131–1139). Wiesbaden: Harrassowitz.

Newman, Paul, and Roxana Ma Newman (1981). The question morpheme q in Hausa. *AuU* 64: 35–46.

Newman, Roxanne (1977). Y-prosody as a morphological process in Ga'anda. In P. Newman and R. M. Newman (eds.), *Papers in Chadic linguistics – Papers from the Leiden Colloqium on the Chadic Language Family* (pp. 121–130). Leiden: Afrika-Studiecentrum.

Newman, Stanley (1944). *Yokuts Language of California*. Viking Fund Publications in Anthropology 2. New York.

Newton, B. (1972). *The Generative Interpretation of Dialect: A Study of Modern Greek Phonology*. Cambridge: CUP.

Ní Chiosáin, M. (1991). *Topics in the phonology of Irish*. Doctoral dissertation, University of Massachusetts, Amherst.

Ní Chiosáin, M., and J. Padgett (1993). Consonant-vowel interactions and "cross tier" effects. Paper presented at LSA annual meeting, Los Angeles.

Nibert, H. (1991). Processes of vowel harmony in the Italian dialect of Servigliano: an analysis of data using various models of vowel representation. MS, Dept. of Spanish, Italian, and Portuguese, University of Illinois.

Nicklas, Thurston (1974). *The elements of Choctaw*. Doctoral dissertation, University of Michigan.

Nicklas, Thurston (1975). Choctaw morphophonemics. In J. Crawford (ed.), *Studies in Southeastern Indian Languages* (pp. 237–250). Athens GA: University of Georgia Press.

Nicholson, R. and R. Nickolson (1962). Fore phonemes and their interpretation. Oceanic Linguistic Monographs No. 6. University of Sydney.

Nivens, Richard (1992). A lexical phonology of West Tarangan. In D. Burquest and W. Laidig (ed.), *Phonological Studies in Four Languages of Maluku*, (pp. 127–227). Dallas: SIL.

Noske, Manuela (1990). Vowel harmony in Turkana. *SLS* 17(1): 123–134.

Noske, Manuela (1991). Metrical structure and reduplication in Turkana. In M. L. Bender (ed.), *Proceedings of the Fourth Nilo-Saharan Linguistics Colloquium*, (pp. 245–262). Hamburg: Helmut Buske Verlag.

Noske, Manuela (1993). Tucano nasal harmony: Evidence for a ternary contrast in the feature [nasal]. In K. Beals et al. (eds.), *Papers from CLS 29*. Chicago: CLS.

Noske, Roland (1982). Syllabification and syllable changing rules in French. In H. van der Hulst and N. Smith (eds.), *The Structure of Phonological Representations*, vol. 2. Dordrecht: Foris.

Noske, Roland (1984). Syllabification and syllable changing processes in Yawelmani. In H. van der Hulst and Norval Smith (eds.), *Advances in Non-Linear Phonology* (pp. 335–362). Dordrecht: Foris.

Noye, D. 1975. Langages secrets chez les Peul. *African Languages* 1: 81–95.

Nuñez-Cedeño, Rafael (1985). Stress assignment in Spanish verb forms. In F. Nuessel (ed.), *Current Issues in Hispanic Phonology and Morphology* (pp. 55–76). Bloomington: IULC.

Nuñez-Cedeño, Rafael (1986). La /s/ ultracorrectiva en dominicano y la estructura silábica. In J. G. Moreno de Alba (ed.), *Actas del 2 Congreso International sobre el Español de América* (pp. 337–347). Mexico: Universidad Autónoma de México.

Nykiel-Herbert, B. (1984). *Phonological and morphological analysis of prefixation in Polish and English*. Doctoral dissertation, Adam Mickiewicz University.

O'Connor, J. D., and G. F. Arnold (1973). *Intonation of Colloquial English*. 2nd Edition. London: Longmans.

O'Grady, G. N. (1977). Proto-Ngayarda phonology. *OL* 4: 71–130.

Oates, Lynette (1988). *The Muruwari language*. Pacific Linguistics. Canberra: Australian National University.

Oates, William (1967). Syllable patterning and phonetically complex consonants in some Australian languages. *Papers in Australian Linguistics* 1: 29–52.

Odden, David (1978). Abstract vowel harmony in Manchu. *LA* 4: 149–165.

Odden, David (1979). Principles of stress assignment: A crosslinguistic view. *SLS* 9: 157–175.

Odden, David (1980). Associative tone in Shona. *JLR* 1: 37–51.

Odden, David (1981). *Problems in tone assignment in Shona*. Doctoral dissertation, University of Illinois.

Odden, David (1982a). Separating tone and accent: The case of Kimatuumbi. In D. Flickinger, M. Macken, and N. Wiegand (eds.), *Papers from WCCFL 1* (pp. 219–230). Stanford: SLA.

Odden, David (1982b). Tonal phenomena in Kishambaa. *SAL* 13: 177–208.

Odden, David (1984). Stem tone assignment in Shona. In G. N. Clements and J. Goldsmith (eds.), *Autosegmental Studies in Bantu Tone* (pp. 255–280). Dordrecht: Foris.

Odden, David (1985). An accentual approach to tone in Kimatuumbi. In D. Goyvaerts (ed.), *African Linguistics: Studies in Memory of M. W. K. Seminenke* (pp. 345–419). Amsterdam: John Benjamins.

Odden, David (1986a). On the Obligatory Contour Principle. *Lg* 62: 353–383.

Odden, David (1986b). Review of L. Hyman, A Theory of Phonological Weight. *Lg* 62: 669–673.

Odden, David (1987a). Dissimilation as Deletion in Chukchi. In A. Miller and J. Power (eds.), *Proceedings from ESCOL 3* (pp. 235–246). Columbus, OH: Ohio State University.

Odden, David (1987b). Kimatuumbi phrasal phonology. *Phonology* 4: 13–36.

Odden, David (1987c). Predicting tone in Kikuria. In D. Odden (ed.), *Current Approaches to African Linguistics*, vol. 5 (pp. 311–326). Dordrecht: Foris.

Odden, David (1988). AntiAntigemination and the OCP. *LI* 19: 451–475.

Odden, David (1989a). Kimatuumbi phonology and morphology. MS, Ohio State University.

Odden, David (1989b). Predictable tone systems in Bantu. In H. van der Hulst and N. Smith (eds.), *Autosegmental Studies on Pitch Accent Systems* (pp. 225–251). Dordrecht: Foris.

Odden, David (1990a). Syntax, lexical rules, and postlexical rules in Kimatuumbi. In S. Inkelas and D. Zec (eds.), *The Phonology-Syntax Connection* (pp. 259–278). Chicago: University of Chicago Press.

Odden, David (1990b). Tone in the Makonde dialects: Chimaraba. *SAL* 21(1): 61–105.

Odden, David (1991). Vowel geometry. *Phonology* 8: 261–289.

Odden, David (1994). Adjacency parameters in phonology. *Lg* 70: 289–330.

Odden, David, and Mary Odden (1985). Ordered reduplication in Kihehe. *LI* 16: 497–503.

Ohala, John J. (1978). The production of tone. In V. Fromkin (ed.), *Tone: A Linguistic Survey* (pp. 5–39). New York: Academic Press.

Ohala, John J. (1983). The origin of sound patterns in vocal tract constraints. In P. MacNeilage (ed.), *The Production of Speech* (pp. 189–216). New York: Springer Verlag.

Ohala, John J. (1986a). Consumer's Guide to Evidence in Phonology. *Phonology* 3: 3–26.

Ohala, John J. (1986b). Phonological evidence for top-down processing in speech perception. In J. S. Perkell and D. H. Klatt (eds.), *Invariance and Variability in Speech Processes* (pp. 386–397). Hillsdale, NJ: Lawrence Erlbaum Associates.

Ohala, John J. (1989). Sound change is drawn from a pool of synchronic variation. In L. E. Breivik and E. H. Jahr (eds.), *Language Change: Contributions to the Study of its Causes* (pp. 173–198). Berlin: Mouton de Gruyter.

Ohala, John J. (1990). The phonetics and phonology of aspects of assimilation. In J. Kingston and M. Beckman (eds.), *Papers in Laboratory Phonology*, vol. 1 (pp. 258–275). Cambridge: CUP.

Ohala, John J. (1992). What's cognitive, what's not, in sound change. In G. Kellerman and M. D. Morrissey (eds.), *Diachrony within Synchrony: Language History and Cognition* (pp. 309–355). Frankfurt/M.: Peter Lang Verlag. Reprinted in *Lingua e Stile* (1992) 27: 321–362.

Ohala, John J. (1993). The phonetics of sound change. In C. Jones (ed.), *Historical Linguistics: Problems and Perspectives* (pp. 237–278). London: Longman Academic.

Ohala, John J., and J. J. Jaeger (eds.) (1986). *Experimental Phonology*. Orlando: Academic Press.

Ohala, John, and Manjari Ohala (1993). Speech perception and lexical representation: The role of vowel nasalization. Paper presented at 4th Conference on Laboratory Phonology, August 11–14, University of Oxford.

Ohala, Manjari, and John J. Ohala (1987). Psycholinguistic probes of native speakers' phonological knowledge. In W. U. Dressler, H. C. Luschützky, O. E. Pfeiffer, and J. R. Rennison (eds.), *Phonologica 1984* (pp. 227–233). Cambridge: CUP.

Orgun, C. Orhan, and Sharon Inkelas (1992). Turkish prosodic minimality. Paper presented at 6th International Conference on Turkish Linguistics, Anadolu University, Eskisehir, Turkey.

Osborn, Henry (1966). Warao I: Phonology and morphophonemics. *IJAL* 32: 108–123.

Osborne, Charles (1974). *The Tiwi Language.* Canberra: AIAS.

Otake, T., G. Hatano, A. Cutler, and J. Mehler (to appear). Mora or syllable? Speech segmentation in Japanese. *Journal of Memory and Language.*

Otero, Carlos (1986). A unified metrical account of Spanish stress. In M. Brame, H. Contreras and F. Newmeyer (eds.), *A Festschrift for Sol Saporta* (pp. 299–332). Seattle: Noit Amrofer.

Otsikrev, A. (1963). *Play Languages and Language Play.* Hillsboro, Oregon: Esperanto.

Owens, Jonathan (1988). *The Foundations of Grammar: An Introduction to Medieval Arabic Grammatical Theory.* Amsterdam: Benjamins.

Padden, Carol (1990). The Relation Between Space and Grammar in ASL Verb Morphology. In C. Lucas (ed.), *Sign Language Research: Theoretical Issues* (pp. 103–188). Washington, DC: Gallaudet University Press.

Padden, Carol, and David Perlmutter (1987). American Sign Language and the architecture of phonological theory. *NLLT* 5: 335–375.

Padgett, J. (1991). *Stricture in feature geometry.* Doctoral dissertation, MIT.

Painter, Colin (1971). Vowel harmony in Anum. *Phonetica* 23: 239–248.

Painter, Colin (1973). Cineradiographic data on the feature "Covered" in Twi vowel harmony. *Phonetica* 28: 97–120.

Palmer, F. R. (1962). Gemination in Tigrinya. In Philological Society of Great Britain (ed.), *Studies in Linguistic Analysis* (pp. 139–149). Oxford: Basil Blackwell.

Palmer, F. R. (ed.) (1970) *Prosodic Analysis.* London: OUP.

Palmer, Harold (1939). *A Grammar of Spoken English on a Strictly Phonetic Basis.* Cambridge: Heffer. 2nd edition revised.

Paradis, Carole (1984). Le comportement tonal des constructions associatives en mobé. *JALL* 6: 147–171.

Paradis, Carole (1988). On constraints and repair strategies. *LR* 6: 71–97.

Paradis, Carole, and Fatimazohra El Fenne (1992). L'alternance C/Ø des verbes français: Une analyse par contraintes et stratégies de réparation. *RQL* 21: 107–140.

Paradis, Carole, and Darlene LaCharité (eds.) (1993). *Constraint-based Theories in Multilinear Phonology.* Special issue, CJL 39(2).

Paradis, Carole, and Jean-François Prunet (1989). On coronal transparency. *Phonology* 6: 317–348.

Paradis, Carole, and Jean-François Prunet (1991). Introduction: asymmetry and visibility in consonant articulations. In C. Paradis and J.-F. Prunet (eds.), *The Special Status of Coronals: Internal and External Evidence* (pp. 1–28). San Diego: Academic Press.

Park, H. (1992). *External evidence for representations, rules, and constraints in Korean and Japanese.* Doctoral dissertation, SUNY at Stony Brook.

Parkinson, F. (1993). The feature pharyngeal in Rwaili Arabic. Paper presented at LSA Annual Meeting, Ohio State University.

Parodi, I. G. (1923). Questioni teoriche: Le leggi fonetiche. *NSM* 1: 263–282. Reprinted in his *Lingua e Letteratura.* Venice: Neri Pozza, 1957.

Parsons, F. W. (1955). Abstract nouns of sensory quality and their derivatives in Hausa.

In J. Lukas (ed.), *Afrikanistische Studien [Festschrift Westermann]* (pp. 373–404). Berlin: Akademie-Verlag.

Parsons, F. W. (1960). The verbal system in Hausa. *AuU* 44: 1–36.

Patz, Elisabeth (1982). *A grammar of the Kuku-Yalanji language of North Queensland.* Doctoral dissertation, Australian National University.

Paul, H. (1886). *Principien der Sprachgeschichte,* 2nd edition. Halle: Niemeyer.

Pauliny, E. (1979). *Slovenska fonologia* [Slovak phonology]. Bratislava: Slovenské Pedagogické Nakladatel'stvo.

Payne, David L. (1981). *The Phonology and Morphology of Axininca Campa.* SIL and University of Texas at Arlington.

Perlmutter, David (1989). A moraic theory of American Sign Language syllable structure. MS, University of California, San Diego.

Perlmutter, David (1990). On the segmentation of transitional and bidirectional movements in ASL phonology. In S. Fischer and P. Siple (eds.), *Theoretical Issues in Sign Language Research,* vol. 1, *Linguistics* (pp. 67–80). Chicago: University of Chicago Press.

Perlmutter, David (1991). The role of the syllable in prosodic representations. Paper presented at WECOL, Simon Fraser University.

Perlmutter, David (1992a). Pervasive word formation patterns in a grammar. Paper presented at BLS, Berkeley, CA.

Perlmutter, David (1992b). Sonority and syllable structure in American Sign Language. *LI* 23: 407–442.

Perlmutter, David (1993). Sonority and syllable structure in American Sign Language. In G. Coulter (ed.), *Current Issues in ASL Phonology* (pp. 227–261). Phonetics and Phonology vol. 3. San Diego: Academic Press.

Pesetsky, David (1979). Russian morphology and lexical theory. MS, MIT.

Pesetsky, David (1985). Morphology and logical form. *LI* 16: 193–246.

Peters, Ann (1973). A new formalization of downdrift. *SAL* 4: 139–154.

Peterson, Karen (1989). A comparative look at Nguni verbal tone. In I. Haïk and L. Tuller (eds.), *Current Approaches to African Linguistics,* vol. 6 (pp. 115–137). Dordrecht: Foris.

Pierrehumbert, Janet (1980). *The phonetics and phonology of English intonation.* Doctoral dissertation, MIT.

Pierrehumbert, Janet, and Mary Beckman (1988). *Japanese Tone Structure.* LI Monograph Series No. 15. Cambridge, MA: MIT Press.

Pierrehumbert, Janet, and Julia Hirschberg (1990). The meaning of intonational contours in the interpretation of discourse. In P. R. Cohen, J. Morgan, and M. E. Pollock (eds.), *Intentions in Communication* (pp. 271–311). Cambridge, MA: MIT Press.

Piggott, Glyne (1987). On the autonomy of the feature Nasal. In A. Bosch, B. Need, and E. Schiller (eds.), *Parasession on Autosegmental and Metrical Phonology* (pp. 223–239). Chicago: CLS.

Piggott, Glyne (1988a). A parametric approach to nasal harmony. In H. van der Hulst and N. Smith (eds.), *Features, Segmental Structure and Harmony Processes,* vol. 1 (pp. 131–167). Dordrecht: Foris.

Piggott, Glyne (1988b). Prenasalization and Feature Geometry. In *Proceedings of NELS 19,* (pp. 345–352). Amherst, MA: GLSA.

Piggott, Glyne (1991). Empty onsets: Evidence for the skeleton in prosodic phonology. MS, McGill University.

Piggott, Glyne (1992a). Satisfying the minimal word. MS, McGill University.

Piggott, Glyne (1992b). Variability in feature dependency: The case of nasality. *NLLT* 10: 33–78.

Piggott, Glyne, and Rajendra Singh (1985). The phonology of epenthetic segments. CJL 30: 415–451.

Pike, Kenneth (1948). *Tone languages.* Ann Arbor: University of Michigan Press.

Pike, Kenneth (1962). Practical phonetics of rhythm waves. *Phonetica* 8: 9–30.

Pike, Kenneth (1967). Tongue root position in practical phonetics. *Phonetica* 17: 129–140.

Pike, Kenneth, and E. Pike (1947). Immediate constituents of Mazatec syllables. *IJAL* 13: 78–91.

Plénat, Marc (1984). Toto, fanfan, totor et même guiguitte sont des anars. In F. Dell, D. Hirst, and J.-R. Vergnaud (eds.), *Forme sonore du langage* (pp. 161–182). Paris: Hermann.

Plénat, Marc (1985). Morphologie du Largonji des loucherbems. *Langages* 78: 73–122.

Plénat, Marc (1987). On the structure of rime in Standard French. *Linguistics* 25: 867–887.

Podolsky, Baruch (1980). Morphophonology of Amharic verbs. In G. Goldenberg and B. Podolsky (eds.), *Ethiopian Studies* (pp. 447–454). Rotterdam: Balkema.

Poizner, Howard, Edward Klima, and Ursula Bellugi (1987). *What the Hands Reveal about the Brain.* Cambridge, MA: MIT Press.

Pollock, J.-Y. (1989). Verb movement, universal grammar, and the structure of IP. *LI* 20: 365–378.

Poppe, N. (1962). *Bashkir Manual.* Uralic and Altaic series, vol. 36. Bloomington: Indiana University.

Port, Robert, Jonathan Dalby, and Michael O'Dell (1987). Evidence for mora timing in Japanese. *JASA* 81: 1574–1585.

Poser, William (1982a). Phonological representations and action-at-a-distance. In H. van der Hulst and N. Smith (eds.), *The Structure of Phonological Representations*, vol. 2 (pp. 121–158). Dordrecht: Foris.

Poser, William (1982b). Why cases of syllable reduplication are so hard to find. MS, MIT.

Poser, William (1984a). Hypocoristic formation in Japanese. In M. Cobler, S. MacKaye, and M. Wescoat (eds.), *Proceedings of WCCFL 3* (pp. 218–229). Stanford: SLA.

Poser, William (1984b). *The phonetics and phonology of tone in Japanese.* Doctoral dissertation, MIT.

Poser, William (1986a). Japanese evidence bearing on the compensatory lengthening controversy. In L. Wetzels and E. Sezer (eds.), *Studies in Compensatory Lengthening.* Dordrecht: Foris.

Poser, William (1986b). Yidiny stress, metrical structure assignment, and the nature of metrical representation. In J. Goldberg, S. MacKaye, and M. Wescoat (eds.), *Papers from WCCFL 4* (pp. 178–91). Stanford: SLA.

Poser, William (1988). Glide formation and compensatory lengthening in Japanese. *LI* 19: 494–502.

Poser, William (1989). The metrical foot in Diyari. *Phonology* 6: 117–148.

Poser, William (1990). Evidence for foot structure in Japanese. *Lg* 66: 78–105.

Poser, William (1992). The structural typology of phonological writing. MS, Stanford University.

Postal, Paul (1968). *Aspects of Phonological Theory.* New York: Harper and Row.

Prentice, D. J. (1971). *The Murut languages of Sabah.* Pacific Linguistics, Series C, no. 18. Canberra: Australian National University.

Price, Patti, Mari Ostendorf, Stephanie Shattuck-Hufnagel, and G. Fong (1991). The use of prosody in syntactic disambiguation. *JASA* 90: 2956–2970.

Prideaux, G. D., B. L. Derwing, and W. J. Baker (1980). *Experimental Linguistics: Integration of Theories and Applications*. Ghent: E. Story-Scientia.

Priestly, T. (1977). One idiosyncratic strategy in the acquisition of phonology. *Journal of Child Language* 4: 45–66.

Prietze, Rudolf (1908). Die spezifischen Verstärkungsadverbien im Hausa und Kanuri. *Mitteilungen des Seminars für Orientalische Sprachen* 11: 307–317.

Prince, Alan (1975). *The phonology and morphology of Tiberian Hebrew*. Doctoral dissertation, MIT.

Prince, Alan (1976). "Applying" stress. MS, University of Massachusetts, Amherst.

Prince, Alan (1980). A metrical theory for Estonian quantity. *LI* 11: 511–562.

Prince, Alan (1983). Relating to the grid. *LI* 14: 19–100.

Prince, Alan (1984). Phonology with tiers. In M. Aronoff and R. Oehrle (eds.), *Language Sound Structure* (pp. 234–244). Cambridge, MA: MIT Press.

Prince, Alan (1985). Improving tree theory. In M. Niepokuj, M. VanClay, V. Nikiforidou, and D. Jeder (eds.), *Proceedings of BLS 11* (pp. 471–490). Berkeley: BLS.

Prince, Alan (1987). Planes and copying. *LI* 18: 491–510.

Prince, Alan (1990). Quantitative consequences of rhythmic organization. In M. Ziolkowski, M. Noske, and K. Deaton (eds.), *Parasession on the Syllable in Phonetics and Phonology* (pp. 355–398). Chicago: CLS.

Prince, Alan, and Paul Smolensky (1991a). Connectionism and harmony theory in linguistics. Technical report CU-CS-533-91. MS, Dept of Computer Science, University of Colorado, Boulder.

Prince, Alan, and Paul Smolensky (1991b). Optimality. Paper presented at the Arizona Phonology Conference.

Prince, Alan, and Paul Smolensky (1992). Optimality: Constraint interaction in generative grammar. Paper presented at WCCFL 12, Los Angeles.

Prince, Alan, and Paul Smolensky (1993). Optimality theory: Constraint interaction in generative grammar. MS, Rutgers University and University of Colorado, Boulder.

Prunet, Jean-François (1986). *Spreading and locality domains in phonology*. Doctoral dissertation, McGill University.

Puech, Gilbert (1978). A cross-dialectal study of vowel harmony in Maltese. In D. Farkas, W. Jacobsen, and K. Todrys (eds.), *Papers from CLS 14* (pp. 377–390). Chicago: CLS.

Pukui, Mary Kawena, and Samuel H. Elbert (1986). *Hawaiian Dictionary*. Honolulu: University of Hawaii Press.

Pulleyblank, Douglas (1983a). Extratonality and polarity. In *Proceedings from WCCFL 2* (pp. 204–216). Stanford: SLA.

Pulleyblank, Douglas (1983b). Accent in Kimatuumbi. In J. Kaye, H. Koopman, D. Sportiche, and A. Dugas (eds.), *Current Approaches to African Linguistics*, vol. 2. Dordrecht: Foris.

Pulleyblank, Douglas (1984). Autosegmental accent. In *Proceedings of NELS 14*, Amherst, MA: GSLA.

Pulleyblank, Douglas (1986a). *Tone in Lexical Phonology*. Dordrecht: D. Reidel.

Pulleyblank, Douglas (1986b). Underspecification and low vowel harmony in Yoruba. *SAL* 17: 119–153.

Pulleyblank, Douglas (1988a). Underspecification, the feature hierarchy and Tiv vowels. *Phonology* 5: 299–326.

Pulleyblank, Douglas (1988b). Vocalic underspecification in Yoruba. *LI* 19: 233–270.

Pulleyblank, Douglas (1992). Feature geometry and underspecification. In J. Durand and F. Katamba (eds.), *New frontiers in phonology*. Longmans.

Pulleyblank, E. G. (1989). The role of coronal in articulator based features. In C. Wiltshire, R. Graczyk, and B. Music (eds.), *Papers from CLS 25* (pp. 379–393). Chicago: CLS.

Pullum, Geoffrey, and Arnold Zwicky (1988). The Syntax-Phonology Interface. In F. Newmeyer (ed.), *Linguistics: The Cambridge Survey*, vol. 1 (pp. 255–280). Cambridge: CUP.

Pye, C., D. Ingram, and H. List. (1987). A comparison of initial consonant acquisition in English and Quiche. In K. E. Nelson and A. van Kleek (eds.), *Children's Language*, vol. 6 (pp. 175–190). Hillsdale, NJ: Erlbaum.

Pym, Noreen, with Bonnie Larrimore (1979). *Papers on Iwaidja Phonology and Grammar*. Darwin: SIL-AAB.

Quicoli, A. C. (1990). Harmony, lowering, and nasalization in Brazilian Portuguese. *Lingua* 80: 295–331.

Raphael, L. (1972). Preceding vowel duration as a cue to the perception of the voicing characteristic of word-final consonants in American English. *JASA* 51: 1296–1303.

Rappaport, Malka (1981). The phonology of gutterals in Biblical Hebrew. In J. Aoun and H. Borer (eds.), *Theoretical Issues in Semitic Linguistics* (pp. 101–127). Cambridge, MA: MIT.

Rappaport, Malka (1984). *Issues in the phonology of Tiberian Hebrew*. Doctoral dissertation, MIT.

Rask, R. K. (1818). *Undersögelse om det gamle Nordiske eller Islandske Sprogs Oprindelse*. Copenhagen: Gyldendalske Boghandlings Forlag.

Raum, O. (1937). Language Perversions in East Africa. *Africa* 10: 221–226.

Raz, Shlomo (1983). *Tigre Grammar and Texts*. Afroasiatic Dialects, vol. 4. Malibu, CA: Undena.

Read, C., Z. Yun-fei, N. Hong-yun, and D. Bao-qing (1986). The ability to manipulate speech sounds depends on knowing alphabetic writing. *Cognition* 24: 31–44.

Rehg, Kenneth, and Damien Sohl (1981). *Ponapean Reference Grammar*. Honolulu: University of Hawaii Press.

Reid, Nicholas (1990). *Grammar of Ngan'gityemerri*. Doctoral dissertation, Australian National University.

Reighard, John (1972). Labiality and velarity in consonants and vowels. In *Papers from CLS 6* (pp. 533–43). Chicago: CLS.

Rennison, John (1986). On tridirectional feature systems for vowels. In J. Durand (ed.), *Dependency and Nonlinear Phonology* (pp. 281–303). London: Croom Helm.

Rensch, C. R. (1978). Ballistic and controlled syllables in Otomanguean languages. In A. Bell and J. Hooper (eds.), *Syllables and Segments* (pp. 85–92). Amsterdam: North Holland.

Repetti, L. D. (1989). *The Bimoraic Norm of Tonic Syllables in Italo-Romance*. Los Angeles: University of California.

Reuse, Willem de (n.d.). The derivation of Spanish hypocoristics in a nonconcatenative theory of morphology. MS, University of Texas, Austin.

Riad, Tomas (1992). *Structures in Germanic prosody*. Stockholm: Dept. of Scandinavian Languages, Stockhom University.

Rialland, Annie (1993). L'allongement compensatoire: nature et modèles. In B. Laks and A. Rialland (eds.), *L'architecture des représentations phonologiques*. Paris: Editions du CNRS.

Rialland, Annie, and R. Djamouri (1984). Harmonie vocalique, consonantique et structure de dépendence dans le mot en Mongol Khalkha. *Bulletin de la societé de linguistique de Paris* 79: 333–383.

Rice, Keren (1987). On defining the intonational phrase: Evidence from Slave. *Phonology* 4: 37–59.

Rice, Keren (1989). On eliminating resyllabification into onsets. In E. Fee and K. Hunt (eds.), *Proceedings of WCCFL 8.* Stanford: SLA.

Rice, Keren (1990a). Blocking and privative features: A prosodic account. MS, University of Toronto.

Rice, Keren (1990b). Predicting rule domains in the phrasal phonology. In S. Inkelas and D. Zec (eds.), *The Phonology-Syntax Connection* (pp. 289–312). Chicago: University of Chicago Press.

Rice, Keren (1992). On deriving sonority: A structural account of sonority relationships. *Phonology* 9: 61–99.

Rice, Keren, and Peter Avery (1989). On the interaction between sonority and voicing. *Toronto Working Papers in Linguistics* 10: 65–92.

Rich, F. (1963). Arabela phonemes and high-level phonology. In B. Elson (ed.), *Studies in Peruvian Indian Languages*, vol. 1 (pp. 193–206). Norman OK: SIL/University of Oklahoma.

Ringen, Catherine (1975). *Vowel harmony: Theoretical implications*. Doctoral dissertation, Indiana University.

Ringen, Catherine (1979). Vowel harmony in Igbo and Diola Fogny. *SAL* 10: 247–259.

Ringen, Catherine (1988). Transparency in Hungarian vowel harmony. *Phonology* 5: 327–342.

Ringen, Catherine (1989). Vowel harmony in Kalenjin. In H. van der Hulst and N. Smith (eds.), *Features, Segmental Structure and Harmony Processes* (pp. 145–160). Dordrecht: Foris.

Rischel, Jørgen (1962). Stress, Juncture, and Syllabification in Phonemic Description. In H. G. Lunt (ed.), *Proceedings of the Ninth International Congress of Linguists*, Cambridge, MA., August 27–31, 1962 (pp. 85–93). The Hague: Mouton.

Rischel, Jørgen (1968). Diphthongization in Faroese. *Acta Linguistica Hafniensa* 11.

Robbins, F. E. (1961). Quiotepec Chinantec Syllable Patterning. *IJAL* 27: 237–250.

Roberts, R. Ruth (1991). A non-metrical theory of Sukuma tone. In E. Hume (ed.), *Papers in Phonology (OSU Working papers in Linguistics* 41) (pp. 135–148).

Robinson, J. J. (1970). Dependency relations and transformational rules. *Lg* 46: 259–285.

Roca, I. (1986). Secondary stress and metrical rhythm. *Phonology* 3: 341–370.

Roca, I. (1988). Theoretical implications of Spanish word stress. *LI* 19: 393–423.

Roca, I. (1990a). Diachrony and synchrony in Spanish stress. *JL* 26: 133–164.

Roca, I. (1990b). Morphology and verbal stress in Spanish. *Probus* 2: 321–350.

Roca, I. (1991). Stress and syllables in Spanish. In H. Campos and F. Martínez-Gil (eds.), *Current Studies in Spanish Linguistics* (pp. 599–635). Washington, DC: Georgetown University Press.

Roca, I. (1992). On the sources of word prosody. *Phonology* 9: 267–287.

Rochemont, Michael (1986). *Focus in Generative Grammar*. Amsterdam/Philadelphia: John Benjamins.

Rooth, Mats (1985). *Association with focus*. Doctoral dissertation, University of Massachusetts, Amherst.

Rooth, Mats (1992). A theory of focus interpretation. *Natural Language Semantics* 1: 75–116.

Rosenthall, Sam (1988). The representation of prenasalized consonants. In H. Borer (ed.), *Proceedings of WCCFL 7* (pp. 277–291). Stanford: SLA.

Rosenthall, Sam (1992a). The intonation of simple sentences in Hungarian. In *Proceedings of the Formal Linguistics Society of Mid-America*, vol. 3.

Rosenthall, Sam (1992b). Prenasalized Stops and Feature Geometry. In W. Dressler et al. (eds.), *Phonologica 1988: Proceedings of the 6th International Phonology Meeting* (pp. 249–58). Cambridge: CUP.

Rotenberg, Joel (1978). *The syntax of phonology*. Doctoral dissertation, MIT.

Rousselot, P.-J. (1891). *Les modifications phonétiques du langage, étudiées dans le patois d'une famille de Cellefrouin (Charente)*. Paris: H. Welter.

Rubach, Jerzy (1981). *Cyclic Phonology and Palatalization in Polish and English*. Warsaw: Wydawnictwa Uniwersytetu Warszawskiego.

Rubach, Jerzy (1984). *Cyclic and Lexical Phonology: The Structure of Polish*. Dordrecht: Foris.

Rubach, Jerzy (1985). Lexical phonology: Lexical and postlexical derivations. *Phonology* 2: 157–172.

Rubach, Jerzy (1986). Abstract vowels in three-dimensional phonology: The yers. *LR* 5: 247–280.

Rubach, Jerzy (1990). Final devoicing and cyclic syllabification in German. *LI* 21: 79–94.

Rubach, Jerzy (1993). *The Lexical Phonology of Slovak*. Oxford: OUP.

Rubach, Jerzy (forthcoming). Skeletal versus moraic representations in Slovak.

Rubach, Jerzy, and Geert Booij (1990). Syllable structure assignment in Polish. *Phonology* 7: 121–158.

Ruhlen, Merritt (1978). Nasal vowels. In J. Greenberg (ed.), *Universals of Human Language*, vol. 2, *Phonology* (pp. 203–242). Stanford: Stanford University Press.

Sabol, J. (1989). *Synteticka fonologia slovenskeho jazyka* [Synthetic phonology of the Slovak language]. Bratislava: Slovenska Akademia Vied.

Saciuk, B. (1969). The stratal division of the lexicon. *Papers in Linguistics* 1: 464–532.

Sadock, Jerrold (1985). Autolexical syntax: A proposal for the treatment of noun incorporation and similar phenomena. *NLLT* 3: 379–439.

Sadock, Jerrold (1991). *Autolexical Syntax*. Chicago: University of Chicago Press.

Sadtano, E. (1971). Language games in Javanese. In J. Sherzer et al. (eds.), *A Collection of Linguistic Games*. Austin: University of Texas.

Sagey, Elizabeth (1986a). On the representation of complex segments and their formation in Kinyarwanda. In E. Sezer and L. Wetzels (eds.), *Studies in Compensatory Lengthening*. Dordrecht: Foris Publications.

Sagey, Elizabeth (1986b). *The representation of features and relations in nonlinear phonology*. Doctoral dissertation, MIT. New York: Garland Press, 1991.

Sagey, Elizabeth (1988). On the ill-formedness of crossing association lines. *LI* 19: 109–118.

Sagey, Elizabeth (1989). Degree of closure in complex segments. In H. van der Hulst and N. Smith (eds.), *Features, Segmental Structure, and Harmony Processes*, vol. 1 (pp. 169–208). Dordrecht: Foris Publications.

Saib, J. (1978). Segment organization and the syllable in Tamazight Berber. In A. Bell and J. Hooper (eds.), *Syllables and Segments* (pp. 93–104). Amsterdam: North Holland.

Sainz, Susana (1992). *A noncyclic approach to the lexical phonology of English*. Doctoral dissertation, Cornell University.

Samek-Lodovici, Vieri (1992). Universal constraints and morphological gemination: A crosslinguistic study. MS, Brandeis University.

Samek-Lodovici, Vieri (1993). A unified analysis of crosslinguistic morphological gemination. MS, Rutgers University.

Sampson, Geoffrey (1985). *Writing Systems*. Stanford: Stanford University Press.

Sampson, Rodney (1992). Le status phonologique de la nasal vélaire en français contemporain. *Le Français moderne* 60: 82–96.

Sanders, Gerald (1974). Precedence relations in language. *FL* 11: 361–400.

Sandler, Wendy (1986). The spreading hand autosegment of American Sign Language. *SLS* 50: 1–28.

Sandler, Wendy (1987). Assimilation and feature hierarchy in American Sign Language. In A. Bosch, B. Need, and E. Schiller (eds.), *CLS 23: Parasession on Autosegmental and Metrical Phonology* (pp. 266–278). Chicago: CLS.

Sandler, Wendy (1989). *Phonological Representation of the Sign*. Dordrecht: Foris.

Sandler, Wendy (1990). Temporal aspects and ASL phonology. In S. Fischer and P. Siple (eds.), *Theoretical Issues in Sign Language Research*, vol. 1: *Linguistics* (pp. 7–36). Chicago: University of Chicago Press.

Sandler, Wendy (1992). Phonological tier conflation and the ASL lexicon. In G. Coulter (ed.), *Current Issues in ASL Phonology*, vol. 3 (pp. 103–129). San Diego: Academic Press.

Sansom, George (1928). *An Historical Grammar of Japanese*. Oxford: Clarendon Press.

Sapir, Edward (1922). The Takelma language of southwestern Oregon. *Bulletin of American Ethology* 40(2): 1–296.

Sapir, J. D. (1965). *A Grammar of Diola-Fogny*. Cambridge: CUP.

Saxton, Dean (1963). Papago phonemics. *IJAL* 29: 29–35.

Sayers, Barbara (1974). *Interpenetration of stress and pitch in Wik-Munkan.*, vol. 1. SIL.

Sayers, Barbara (1976). The relevance of stress and pitch in the grammatical hierarchy of Wik-Mungkan (Wik-Munkan). In P. Sutton (ed.), *Languages of Cape York* (pp. 284–298). Canberra: AIAS.

Sayers, Barbara (1977). What are contrastive syllables? The Wik-Munkan picture. In J. Hudson (ed.), *Five Papers in Australian Phonologies*. Working Papers of the SIL-AAB, Series A, vol. 1. Darwin: SIL-AAB.

Sayers, Barbara, and Noreen Pym (1977). Notes on rhythmic patterning in Iwaidja. In J. Hudson (ed.), *Five Papers in Australian Phonologies*. Working Papers of SIL-AAB, Series A, vol. 1. Darwin: SIL-AAB.

Shane, Sanford (1968). *French Phonology and Morphology*. Cambridge, MA: MIT Press.

Schane, Sanford (1971). The phoneme revisited. *Lg* 47: 503–521.

Schane, Sanford (1973). The treatment of phonological exceptions: The evidence from French. In B. Kachru et al (eds.), *Issues in Linguistics* (pp. 822–835). Urbana: University of Illinois.

Schane, Sanford (1978a). L'emploi des frontières de mots en français. In B. de Cornulier and F. Dell (eds.), *Etudes de phonologie française* (pp. 133–147). Paris: Editions du CNRS.

Schane, Sanford (1978b). Syllable versus word boundary in French. In M. Suñer (ed.), *Contemporary Issues in Romance Linguistics* (pp. 302–315). Washington, DC: Georgetown University Press.

Schane, Sanford (1984a). The fundamentals of particle phonology. *Phonology* 1: 129–155.

Schane, Sanford (1984b). Two English vowel movements: A particle analysis. In M. Aronoff and R. Oehrle (eds.), *Language Sound Structure* (pp. 32–51). Cambridge, MA: MIT Press.

Schane, Sanford (1987). The resolution of hiatus. In A. Bosch, B. Need, and E. Schiller (eds.), *CLS 23: Parasession on Autosegmental and Metrical Phonology* (pp. 279–90). Chicago: CLS.

Schane, Sanford (1989). Diphthongs and monophthongs in Early Romance. In C. Kirschner and J. DeCesaris (eds.), *Current Studies in Romance Linguistics* (pp. 365–376). Amsterdam: John Benjamins.

Schebeck, B. (n.d.). The glottal stop in north-east Arnhem Land. MS, PMs 1529. Canberra: AIAS.

Schebeck, B. (1974). *Texts on the social system of the atʸnʸamaṭaṇa people with grammatical notes.* Canberra: AIAS.

Schein, Barry (1981). Spirantization in Tigrinya. In H. Borer and J. Aoun (eds.), *Theoretical Issues in the Grammars of Semitic Languages* (pp. 32–42). Cambridge, MA: MIT Dept of Linguistics.

Schein, Barry, and Donca Steriade (1986). On geminates. *LI* 17: 691–744.

Schindler, J (1976). Diachronic and synchronic remarks on Bartholomae's and Grassman's laws. *LI* 7: 622–637.

Schlegel, G. (1891). Secret languages in Europe and China. *T'oung Pao* 2: 161.

Schlindwein, Deborah (1987). P-bearing units: A study of Kinande vowel harmony. In B. Plunkett and J. McDonough (eds.), *Proceedings of NELS 17* (pp. 551–568). Amherst, MA: GSLA.

Schlindwein, Deborah (1988). *The phonological geometry of morpheme concatenation.* Doctoral dissertation, University of Southern California.

Schlindwein, Deborah (1991). Reduplication in lexical phonology: Javanese plural reduplication. *LR* 8: 97–106.

Schmerling, Susan (1976). *Aspects of English Sentence Stress.* Austin: University of Texas Press.

Schourup, Lawrence (1973). A cross-linguistic study of vowel nasalization. *Ohio State University Working Papers in Linguistics* 15: 190–221.

Schuchardt, Hugo (1885). *Über die Lautgesetze. Gegen die Junggrammatiker.* Berlin.

Schuh, Russell (1978a). Bade/Ngizim vowels and syllable structure. *SAL* 9: 247–283.

Schuh, Russell (1978b). Tone rules. In V. Fromkin (ed.), *Tone: A Linguistic Survey* (pp. 221–256). New York: Academic Press.

Schultz-Lorentzen, C. W. (1945). *A Grammar of the West Greenlandic Language.* Meddelelser om Grønland 129.

Schütz, Albert J. (1980). A reanalysis of the Hawaiian vowel system. *OL* 20: 1–43.

Schütz, Albert J. (1985). *The Fijian Language.* Honolulu: University of Hawaii Press.

Scobbie, James (1991). *Attribute value phonology.* Doctoral dissertation, University of Edinburg.

Scobbie, James (1992). Licensing and inalterability in Tiberian Hebrew. In C. Canakis, G. Chan, and J. Denton (eds.), *Papers from CLS 28* (pp. 457–471). Chicago: CLS.

Sebeok, Thomas, and Frances Ingemann (1961). *An Eastern Cheremis Manual.* Indiana University Publications, Uralic and Altaic Series, no. 5. Bloomington: Indiana University.

Selkirk, Elisabeth (1972). *The phrase phonology of English and French.* Doctoral dissertation, MIT.

Selkirk, Elisabeth (1974). French liaison and the X' notation. *LI* 5: 573–590.

Selkirk, Elisabeth (1978). On prosodic structure and its relation to syntactic structure. In T. Fretheim (ed.), *Nordic Prosody*, vol. 2 (pp. 111–140). Trondheim: TAPIR.

Selkirk, Elisabeth (1980a). Prosodic domains in phonology: Sanskrit revisited. In M. Aronoff and M.-L. Kean (eds.), *Juncture* (pp. 107–129). Saratoga, CA: Anma Libri.

Selkirk, Elisabeth (1980b). The role of prosodic categories in English word stress. *LI* 11: 563–605.

Selkirk, Elisabeth (1981a). Epenthesis and degenerate syllables in Cairene Arabic. In H. Borer and J. Aoun (eds.), *Theoretical Issues in the Grammar of the Semitic Languages* (pp. 111–140). Cambridge, MA: MIT.

Selkirk, Elisabeth (1981b). On prosodic structure and its relation to syntactic structure. In T. Fretheim (ed.), *Nordic Prosody 2*, (pp. 111–140). Trondheim: Tapir. Circulated in 1978.

Selkirk, Elisabeth (1981c). On the nature of phonological representation. In J. Anderson, J. Laver and T. Meyers (eds.), *The Cognitive Representation of Speech*. Amsterdam: North Holland.

Selkirk, Elisabeth (1982). Syllables. In H. van der Hulst and N. Smith (eds.), *The Structure of Phonological Representations*, vol. 2 (pp. 337–383). Dordrecht: Foris.

Selkirk, Elisabeth (1984a). On the major class features and syllable theory. In M. Aronoff and R. T. Oehrle (eds.), *Language Sound Structures* (pp. 107–136). Cambridge, MA: MIT Press.

Selkirk, Elisabeth (1984b). *Phonology and Syntax: The Relation between Sound and Structure.* Cambridge, MA: MIT Press.

Selkirk, Elisabeth (1986). On derived domains in sentence phonology. *Phonology* 3: 371–405.

Selkirk, Elisabeth (1988a). Dependency, adjacency, and secondary articulation. Paper presented at 63rd Annual Meeting of the LSA, New Orleans.

Selkirk, Elisabeth (1988b). Dependency, place and the notion "tier". MS, University of Massachusetts, Amherst.

Selkirk, Elisabeth (1990). A two-root theory of length. MS, University of Massachusetts, Amherst.

Selkirk, Elisabeth (1993). [Labial] relations. MS, University of Massachusetts, Amherst.

Selkirk, Elisabeth, and T. Shen (1990). Prosodic domains in Shanghai Chinese. In S. Inkelas and D. Zec (eds.), *The Phonology-Syntax Connection* (pp. 313–337). Chicago: University of Chicago Press.

Selkirk, Elisabeth, and Koichi Tateishi (1988). Minor phrase formation in Japanese. In L. Macleod et al. (eds.), *Papers from CLS 24* (pp. 316–336). Chicago: CLS.

Selkirk, Elisabeth, and Koichi Tateishi (1991). Syntax and downstep in Japanese. In C. Georgopoulos and R. Ishihara (eds.), *Interdisciplinary Approaches to Language: Essays in Honor of S.-Y. Kuroda* (pp. 519–544). Dordrecht: Kluwer.

Selkirk, Elisabeth, and Jean-Roger Vergnaud (1973). How abstract is French phonology? *FL* 10: 249–254.

Seppänen, J. (1982). *Computing Families of Natural Secret Languages: An Exercise in Functional Linguistics.* Helsinki: Helsinki University of Technology Computing Centre.

Sezer, Engin (1983). On non-final stress in Turkish. *Journal of Turkish Studies* 5: 61–69.

Sharp, Janet (1986). Spreading in Nyangumarta: A non-linear analysis. MS, University of Arizona.

Sharpe, Margaret (1972). *Alawa Phonology and Grammar.* No. 37. Canberra: AIAS.

Shattuck-Hufnagel, Stefanie, Mari Ostendorf, and Ken Ross (in press). Pitch accent placement within lexical items in American English. *JP.*

Shaw, Patricia (1980). *Dakota Phonology and Morphology.* New York: Garland.

Shaw, Patricia (1987). Non-conservation of melodic structure in reduplication. In A. Bosch, B. Need, and E. Schiller (eds.), *CLS 23: Parasession on Autosegmental and Metrical Phonology* (pp. 291–306). Chicago: CLS.

Shaw, Patricia (1989). The complex structure of complex segments in Dakota. Paper presented at Theoretical Perspectives on Native American Languages, Albany.

Shaw, Patricia (1991). Consonant harmony systems: The special status of coronal harmony. Paper presented at The Special Status of Coronals, San Diego.

Shaw, Patricia (1992). Templatic evidence for the syllable nucleus. Paper presented at NELS 23, University of Ottawa.

Sherzer, Joel (1970). Talking backwards in Cuna: The sociological reality of phonological descriptions. *Southwestern Journal of Anthropology* 26: 343–353.

Sherzer, Joel (1975). A problem in Cuna phonology. *The Journal of the Linguistic Association of the Southwest* 1: 45–53.

Sherzer, Joel (1982). Play languages: With a note on ritual languages. In L. K. Obler and L. Menn (eds.), *Exceptional Language and Linguistics* (pp. 175–199). New York: Academic Press.

Shibatani, M. (1990). *The Languages of Japan*. Cambridge: CUP.

Shih, Chi-Lin (1985). *The prosodic domain of tone sandhi in Chinese*. Doctoral dissertation, University of California, San Diego.

Shih, Chi-Lin (1991). Mandarin third-tone sandhi and prosodic structure. Paper presented at Studies in Chinese Phonology,

Shipley, W. (1956). The phonemes of Northeastern Maidu. *IJAL* 22: 233–237.

Siegel, Dorothy (1974). *Topics in English morphology*. Doctoral dissertation, MIT.

Sietsema, Brian (1988). Reduplication in Dakota. Paper presented at CLS 24, Chicago.

Sietsema, Brian (1989). *Metrical dependencies in tone assignment*. Doctoral dissertation, MIT.

Sievers, E. (1881). *Grundzüge der Phonetik*. Leipzig: Breitkopf and Hartel.

Silverman, Daniel (1991). The asymmetrical application of phonology and morphological principles in reduplication. MS, UCLA.

Simpson, Jane (1992). Reduplication in Warumungu. Paper presented at University of Melbourne Linguistics Dept,

Simpson, Jane, and Jeffrey Heath (1982). Warumungu sketch grammar. MS.

Simpson, Jane, and Margaret Withgott (1986). Pronominal clitic clusters and templates. In H. Borer (ed.), *The Syntax of Pronominal Clitics* (pp. 149–174). New York: Academic Press.

Singh, Rajendra (1987). Well-formedness conditions and phonological theory. In W. Dressler et al. (eds.) *Phonologica 1984*. Cambridge: CUP.

Singh, Rajendra (in press). Natural phono(morpho)logy: A view from the outside. In B. Hurch and R. Rhodes (eds.), *Natural Phonology: The State of the Art*. Berlin: Mouton.

Singler, John (1983). Vowel harmony in Klao: Linear and nonlinear analyses. *SAL* 14: 1–33.

Singler, John (1984). On the underlying representation of contour tones in Wobe. *SAL* 15: 59–75.

Singler, John (1985). The status of lexical associations and the obligatory contour principles in the analysis of tone languages. In D. L. Goyvaerts (ed.), *African Linguistics: Studies in the Memory of M. W. K. Semikenke* (pp. 491–508). Amsterdam: John Benjamins.

Sloan, Kelly (1988). Bare consonant reduplication: Implications for a prosodic theory of reduplication. In H. Borer (ed.), *Proceedings of WCCFL 7* (pp. 319–330). Stanford: SLA.

Sloan, Kelly (1991). *Syllables and templates: Evidence from Southern Sierra Miwok*. Doctoral dissertation, MIT.

Sluyters, W. (1988). Vowel harmony, underspecification and rule mechanisms: The dialect of Francavilla-Fontana. In H. van der Hulst and N. Smith (eds.), *Features, Segmental Structure and Harmony Processes*, vol. 2 (pp. 161–184). Dordrecht: Foris.

Smeets, R. (1984). *Studies in West Circassian Phonology and Morphology*. Leiden: The Hakuchi Press.

Smith, I., and S. Johnson (1985). The syntax of clitic cross-referencing pronouns in Kugu Nganhcara. *AL* 27: 102–111.

Smith, I., and S. Johnson (n.d.). *A grammar of Kugu Nganhcara*.

Smith, Kenneth D. (1979). *Sedang Grammar*. Pacific Linguistics B-50. Canberra: Australian National University.

Smith, Neilson V. (1973). *The Acquisition of Phonology, A Case Study*. Cambridge: CUP.

Smith, Norval (1985). Spreading, reduplication, and the default option in Miwok non-concatenative morphology. In H. van der Hulst and N. Smith (eds.), *Advances in Nonlinear Phonology* (pp. 363–380). Dordrecht: Foris.

Smith, Norval (1986). Reduplication, spreading, and/or empty suffix slots in Sierra Miwok associative morphology. In H. Bennis and F. Beckema (eds.), *Linguistics in the Netherlands 1986* (pp. 235–243). Dordrecht: Foris.

Smith, Norval (1988). Consonant place features. In H. van der Hust and N. Smith (eds.), *Features, Segmental Structure and Harmony Processes*, vol. 1 (pp. 209–235). Dordrecht: Foris.

Smith, Norval, and Ben Hermans (1982). Nonconcatenatieve woordvorming in het Sierra Miwok. *Glot* 5: 263–284.

Smith, Norval, et al. (1988). Yurok retroflex harmony. MS, University of Amsterdam.

Snider, K. (1990a). *Studies in Guang phonology*. Doctoral dissertation, University of Leiden.

Snider, Keith (1990b). Tonal upstep in Krachi: Evidence for a register tier. *Lg* 66: 453–474.

Solan, L. (1981). A metrical analysis of Spanish stress. In W. Cressey and D. J. Napoli (eds.), *Linguistic Symposium on Romance Languages*, vol. 9 (pp. 90–104). Washington, DC: Georgetown University Press.

Sommer, Bruce (1969). *Kunjen Phonology: Synchronic and Diachronic*. Pacific Linguistics B-11. Canberra: Australian National University.

Sommer, Bruce (1970). An Australian language without CV syllables. *IJAL* 36: 57–58.

Sommer, Bruce (1976). A problem of metathesis. In P. Sutton (ed.), *Languages of Cape York*, (pp. 139–43). Canberra: AIAS.

Sommer, Bruce (1981). The shape of Kunjen syllables. In D. L. Goyvaerts (ed.), *Phonology in the 1980s* (pp. 231–44). Ghent: Story-Scientia.

Sommerstein, Alan (1974). On phonotactically motivated rules. *JL* 10: 71–94.

Sommerstein, Alan (1977). *Modern Phonology*. London: Arnold.

Sosa, Juan Manuel (1991). *Fonetica y fonología de la entonación del español hispano-americano*. Doctoral dissertation, University of Massachusetts, Amherst.

Spelke, E. S. (1990). Principles of object perception. *Cognitive Science* 14: 29–56.

Spelke, E. S., R. Kestenbaum, D. Simons, and D. Wein (in press). Spatio-temporal continuity, smoothness of motion, and object identity in infancy. *British Journal of Developmental Psychology*.

Spencer, Andrew (1986). Towards a theory of phonological development. *Lingua* 68: 3–38.

Spencer, Andrew (1991). *Morphological Theory*. Oxford: Basil Blackwell.

Spotts, H. (1953). Vowel harmony and consonant sequences in Mazahua Otomí. *IJAL* 19: 253–259.

Spring, Cari (1990a). How many feet per language? In A. Halpern (ed.), *Proceedings of WCCFL 9*, (pp. 493–508). Stanford: SLA.

Spring, Cari (1990b). *Implications of Axininca Campa for prosodic morphology and reduplication*. Doctoral dissertation, University of Arizona.

Spring, Cari (1990c). Unordered morphology: The problem of Axininca reduplication. In D. Costa (ed.), *Proceedings of BLS 16* (pp. 137–157). Berkeley: BLS.

Spring, Cari (1992). Maximization as association. MS, Ohio State University. To appear as "'Maximization' explains minimal word variability" in *Papers from NELS 22*.

Sproat, Richard (1985). *On deriving the lexicon*. Doctoral dissertation, MIT.

Sproat, Richard (1986). Malayalam compounding: A non-stratum ordered account. In *Proceedings of WCCFL 5*. Stanford: SLA.

Sproat, Richard (1993). Looking into words. In S. Hargus and E. Kaisse (eds.), *Lexical Phonology*. San Diego: Academic Press.

Sproat, Robert, and Osamu Fujimura (1993). Allophonic variation in English /l/ and its implications for phonetic implementation. *JP* 21.

Stahlke, Herbert (1971). The noun prefix in Ewe. *SAL* Supplement 2: 141–159.

Stampe, David (1969). The acquisition of phonemic representation. *Papers from CLS 5* (pp. 433–444). Chicago: CLS.

Stampe, David (1972). *How I Spent My Summer Vacation [A dissertation on Natural Phonology]*. Doctoral dissertation, University of Chicago. New York: Garland, 1980.

Stanley, Richard (1967). Redundancy rules in phonology. *Lg* 43: 393–436.

Steedman, Mark (1991). Structure and intonation. *Lg* 67: 260–296.

Stemberger, Joseph P. (1988). Between word processes in child phonology. *Journal of Child Language* 15: 39–62.

Stemberger, Joseph P. (1991). Radical underspecification in language production. *Phonology* 8: 73–112.

Stemberger, Joseph P. (1992a). A connectionist view of child phonology. In C. Ferguson et al. (eds.), *Phonological Development* (pp. 165–189). Timonium, MD: York Press.

Stemberger, Joseph P. (1992b). Vocalic underspecification in language production. *Lg* 68: 492–524.

Stemberger, Joseph P. (1993). Glottal transparancy. *Phonology*.

Steriade, Donca (1979). Vowel harmony in Khalkha Mongolian, including as an appendix: The input representations to Warlpiri's vowel assimilation rules. In K. Safir (ed.), *Papers on Syllable Structure, Metrical Structure, and Harmony Processes* (pp. 43–48). MIT Working Papers in Linguistics. Cambridge, MA: MIT Dept. of Linguistics.

Steriade, Donca (1981). Certain parameters of metrical harmony. Paper presented at GLOW 5.

Steriade, Donca (1982). *Greek prosodies and the nature of syllabification*. Doctoral dissertation, MIT.

Steriade, Donca (1984). Glides and Vowels in Romanian. In *Papers from BLS 10*. Berkeley: BLS.

Steriade, Donca (1986a). A note on coronal. MS, MIT.

Steriade, Donca (1986b). Yokuts and the vowel plane. *LI* 17: 129–146.

Steriade, Donca (1987a). Locality conditions and feature geometry. In *Papers of NELS 17* (pp. 595–617). Amherst, MA: GLSA.

Steriade, Donca (1987b). On class nodes. MS, MIT.

Steriade, Donca (1987c). Redundant Values. In A. Bosch, B. Need, and E. Schiller (eds.), *CLS 23: Parasession on Autosegmental and Metrical Phonology* (pp. 339–362). Chicago: CLS.

Steriade, Donca (1988a). Greek accent: A case for preserving structure. *LI* 19: 271–314.

Steriade, Donca (1988b). Reduplication and syllable transfer in Sanskrit and elsewhere. *Phonology* 5: 73–155.

Steriade, Donca (1988c). Review article on G. N. Clements and S. J. Keyser (1983). *Lg* 64: 118–129.

Steriade, Donca (1990). Gestures and autosegments: Comments on Browman and Goldstein's paper. In J. Kingston and M. Beckman (eds.), *Papers in Laboratory Phonology*. Cambridge: CUP.

Steriade, Donca (1991). Moras and other slots. In *Proceedings of the Formal Linguistics Conference of the Midwest*.

Steriade, Donca (1993a). Closure, release and nasal contours. In M. Huffman and R. Krakow (eds.), *Nasality*. San Diego: Academic Press.

Steriade, Donca (1993b). Orality and markedness. In B. Keyser and J. Guenther (eds.), *Papers from BLS 19*. Berkeley: BLS.

Steriade, Donca (in press). Complex onsets as single segments. In J. Cole and C. Kisseberth (eds.), *Perspectives in Phonology*. Stanford: CSLI.

Stevens, Kenneth (1972). The quantal nature of speech: Evidence from articulatory-acoustic data. In E. E. David and P. B. Denes (eds.), *Human Communication: A Unified View* (pp. 51–66). New York: McGraw Hill.

Stevens, Kenneth (1989). On the quantal nature of speech. *JP* 17: 3–45.

Stevens, Kenneth, and Arthur House (1955). Development of a quantitative description of vowel articulation. *JASA* 27: 484–493.

Stevens, Kenneth, and S. J. Keyser (1989). Primary features and their enhancements in consonants. *Lg* 65: 81–106.

Stevens, Kenneth, S. J. Keyser, and H. Kawasaki (1986). Toward a phonetic and phonological theory of redundant features. In J. Perkell and D. Klatt (eds.), *Invariance and Variability in Speech Processes* (pp. 426–449). Hillsdale, NJ: Lawrence Erlbaum.

Stevick, Earl (1969). Tone in Bantu. *IJAL* 35: 330–341.

Stewart, John (1967a). A theory of the origin of Akan vowel harmony. In *Proceedings of the 6th International Congress of Phonetic Sciences* (pp. 863–865). Prague: Czechoslovak Academy of Sciences.

Stewart, John (1967b). Tongue Root position in Akan vowel harmony. *Phonetica* 16: 185–204.

Stewart, John (1971). Cross-height vowel harmony in the Kwa languages. Paper presented at Proceedings of the 8th West African Languages Congress.

Stockwell, Robert (1978). Perseverance in the English vowel shift. In J. Fisiak (ed.), *Recent Developments in Historical Phonology*. Trends in Linguistics: Studies and Monographs, vol. 4. The Hague: Mouton.

Stokes, Bronwyn (1982). *A description of Nyigina, a language of the West Kimberley, Australia.* Doctoral dissertation, Australian National University.

Stokes, Judith (1981). Anindilyakwa phonology from phoneme to syllable. In B. Waters (ed.), *Australian Phonologies: Collected Papers* (pp. 139–182). Work papers of SIL-AAB, Series A, vol. 5. Darwin: SIL-AAB.

Stokoe, William (1960). *Sign Languge Structure: An Outline of the Visual Communication Systems of the American Deaf.* Studies in Linguistics, Occasional Papers 8. Silver Spring, MD: Linstock Press.

Stokoe, William, Dorothy Casterline, and C. Croneberg (1965). *A Dictionary of American Sign Language on Linguistic Principles.* Silver Spring, MD: Linstok Press.

Stonham, John (1990). *Current issues in morphological theory*. Doctoral dissertation, Stanford University.

Straight, H. Stephen (1976). *The Acquisition of Maya Phonology: Variation in Yucatec Child Language*. New York: Garland Press.

Strauss, Steven (1982). *Lexicalist Phonology of English and German*. Dordrecht: Foris.

Street, Chester S., and Gregory Mollinjin (1981). The phonology of Murinbata. In B. Waters (ed.), *Australian Phonologies: Collected Papers* (pp. 183–244). Work papers of SIL-AAB, Series A, Vol. 5. Darwin: SIL-AAB.

Street, J. C. (1963). *Khalkha Structure*. Bloomington: Indiana University Press.

Strehlow, T. G. H. (1942–44). *Aranda Phonetics and Grammar*. Oceania Monograph No. 7. Sydney: Sydney University.

Sundberg, Johan (1979). Maximum speed of pitch changes in singers and untrained subjects. *JP* 7: 71–79.

Suomi, K. (1983). Palatal vowel harmony: A perceptually motivated phenomenon? *Nordic Journal of Linguistics* 6: 1–35.

Supalla, Ted (1982). *Structure and acquisition of verbs of motion and location in American Sign Language*. Doctoral dissertation, University of California, San Diego.

Supalla, Ted (1985). The classifier system of American Sign Language. In C. Craig (ed.), *Noun Classification: Proceedings of a Symposium on Categorization and Noun Classification* (pp. 181–214). Philadelphia: John Benjamins.

Supalla, Ted, and Elissa Newport (1978). How many seats in a chair? The derivation of nouns and verbs in American Sign Language. In P. Siple (ed.), *Understanding Language through Sign Language Research* (pp. 91–133). New York: Academic Press.

Surintramont, A. (1973). Some aspects of underlying syllable structure in Thai: Evidence from Khampuan–A Thai word game. *SLS* 3: 121–142.

Svantesson, Jan-Olof (1985). Vowel harmony shift in Mongolian. *Lingua* 67: 283–327.

Svantesson, Jan-Olof (1989). Tonogenetic mechanisms in northern Mon-Khmer. *Phonetica* 46: 60–79.

Swingle, K. (1993). The role of prosody in Right Node Raising. Paper presented at LSA Meeting, Los Angeles.

Szpyra, Jolanta (1989). *The Phonology-Morphology Interface: Cycles, Levels and Words*. London: Routledge.

Szpyra, Jolanta (1992). Ghost segments in nonlinear phonology: Polish yers. *Lg* 68: 277–312.

Talmy, Leonard (1972). *Semantic structure in English and Atsugewi*. Doctoral dissertation, University of California, Berkeley.

Tateishi, Koichi (1989a). Phonology of Sino-Japanese morphemes. *University of Massachusetts Occasional Papers in Linguistics* 13.

Tateishi, Koichi (1989b). Theoretical implications of the Japanese musician's language. In E. J. Fee and K. Hunt (eds.), *Proceedings of WFFCL 8* (pp. 384–398). Stanford: SLA.

Tateishi, Koichi (1991). Les implications théoriques du langage des musiciens japonais. In M. Plénat (ed.), *Les javanais* (pp. 51–72). Paris: Larousse.

Taylor, P., and J. Taylor (1971). A tentative statement of Kitja phonology. In B. J. Blake (ed.), *Papers on the languages of the Australian Aborigines*, (pp. 100–109). Canberra: AIAS.

Teshome, Demisse, and M. Lionel Bender (1983). An argot of Addis Ababa unattached girls. *LS* 12: 339–347.

Thráinsson, H. (1978). On the phonology of Icelandic preaspiration. *Nordic Journal of Linguistics* 1: 3–54.

Thumb, A., and K. Marbe (1901). *Experimentelle Untersuchungen über die Psychologischen Grundlagen der Sprachlichen Analogiebildung*. Leipzig: Wilhelm Englemann.

Togeby, K. (1951). *Structure immanente de la langue française*. Copenhagen: Nordisk *Sprog-og* Kulturforlag.

Tohsaku, Y.-H. (1983). *A formal theory of vowel harmony*. Doctoral dissertation, UC San Diego.

Topping, D. (1968). Chamorro vowel harmony. *OL* 7: 67–79.

Traill, A (1985). *Phonetic and Phonological Studies of !Xóõ Bushman*. Hamburg: Helmut Buske.

Tranel, Bernard (1974). *The phonology of nasal vowels in Modern French*. Doctoral dissertation, UC San Diego.

Tranel, Bernard (1981a). *Concreteness in Generative Phonology: Evidence from French*. Berkeley: University of California Press.

Tranel, Bernard (1981b). The treatment of French liaison: Descriptive, methodological, and theoretical implications. In H. Contreras and J. Klausenberger (eds.), *Proceedings of the Tenth Anniversary Symposium on Romance Linguistics (Papers in Romance, Volume 3, Supplement 2)* (pp. 261–281). Seattle: University of Washington.

Tranel, Bernard (1986). French liaison and extrasyllabicity. In O. Jaeggli and C. Silva-Corvalan (eds.), *Studies in Romance Linguistics* (pp. 283–395). Dordrecht: Foris.

Tranel, Bernard (1987a). French schwa and non-linear phonology. *Linguistics* 25: 845–866.

Tranel, Bernard (1987b). *The Sounds of French*. Cambridge: CUP.

Tranel, Bernard (1988a). Floating consonants and ghost consonants: French versus Tiwi. MS, University of California, Irvine.

Tranel, Bernard (1988b). A propos de l'ajustement de E en français. In S. P. Verluyten (ed.), *La Phonologie du schwa français* (pp. 89–131). Amsterdam: John Benjamins.

Tranel, Bernard (1990). On suppletion and French liaison. *Probus* 2: 169–208.

Tranel, Bernard (1991a). CVC light syllables, geminates and moraic theory. *Phonology* 8: 291–302.

Tranel, Bernard (1991b). Moraic theory and French liaison. In W. Ashby, M. Mithun, G. Perissinotto, and E. Raposo (eds.), *Linguistic Perspectives on Romance Languages* (pp. 97–112). Amsterdam: John Benjamins.

Tranel, Bernard (1992). The representations of French final consonants and related issues. In *Proceedings of the 22nd Linguistics Symposium on Romance Languages*. University of Texas at El Paso.

Tranel, Bernard (1993). French final consonants and nonlinear phonology. MS, University of California, Irvine.

Trefry, D. (1983). Discerning the back vowels /u/ and /o/ in Burarra, a language of the Australian Northern Territory. *Working Papers of the Speech and Language Research Centre, Macquarie University* 3: 19–51.

Trefry, D. (1984). Diari segmental phonology. In K. Glawgow et al. (eds.), *Papers in Australian Linguistics*, vol. 16 (pp. 171–327). Canberra: Australian National University.

Treiman, Rebecca (1983). The structure of spoken syllables: Evidence from novel word games. *Cognition* 15: 49–74.

Trigo, L. (1988). *On the phonological derivation and behavior of nasal glides*. Doctoral dissertation, MIT.

Trigo, L. (1991). On pharynx-larynx interactions. *Phonology* 8: 113–136.

Trigo, L. (1993). The inherent structure of nasal segments. In M. Huffman and R. Krakow (eds.), *Nasality*. San Diego: Academic Press.

Trubetzkoy, N. (1939). *Grundzüge der Phonologie*. Güttingen: Vandenhoeck and Ruprecht. Citations from the English translation by C. A. M. Baltaxe, (Berkeley: University of California Press, 1969); see also the French edition, *Principes de phonologie*, translated by J. Cantineau (Paris: Klincksieck, 1964).

Truckenbrodt, H. (1991). Taiwanese tone sandhi and the theory of underspecification. MS, Brandeis University and MIT.

Tryon, D. T. (1970). *An Introduction to Maranungku (Northern Australia)*. Pacific Linguistic Series B, no. 14. Canberra: Australian National University.

Tsay, Jane (1990). Tone alternation in Taiwanese and its diachronic implications. MS, University of Arizona.

Tschenkeli, K. 1958. *Einführung in die Georgische Sprache*. Band 1: Theoretischer Teil. Zurich: Amirani Verlag.

Tsunoda, T. (1981). Interaction of phonological, grammatical and semantic factors: An Australian example. *OL* 20: 45–92.

Tucker, A. N. (1940). *The Eastern Sudanic Languages*, vol. 1. London: Dawsons.

Tucker, A. N. (1962). The syllable in Luganda: A prosodic approach. *JAL* 1: 122–166.

Turner, M., and Gavan Breen (1984). Akarre rabbit talk. *Language in Central Australia* 1: 16–22.

Turtle, Nancy (1977). Alyawarra phonology. In J. Hudson (ed.), *Five Papers in Australian Phonologies* (pp. 1–56). Working Papers of SIL-AB, Series A, vol. 1. Darwin: SIL AAB.

Tyler, S. A. (1969). *Koya: An Outline Grammar*. University of California Publications in Linguistics no. 54.

Uhmann, Susanne (1987). *Fokussierung und Intonation*. Doctoral dissertation, University of Konstanz.

Uhrbach, Amy (1987). *A formal analysis of reduplication and its interaction with phonological and morphological processes*. Doctoral dissertation, University of Texas, Austin.

Ulrich, Charles (1986). *Choctaw morphophonology*. Doctoral dissertation, UCLA.

Ulrich, Charles (1992). A unified account of Choctaw intensives. Paper presented at 1992 Canadian Linguistic Association Annual Conference.

Ultan, Russell (1973). Some reflections on vowel harmony. *Working Papers on Language Universals* 12: 37–67.

Ultan, Russell (1978). A typological view of metathesis. In J. Greenberg (ed.), *Universals of Human Language* (pp. 367–402). Stanford: Stanford University Press.

Unseth, Peter (1990). *Bibliography of the Non-Semitic Languages of Ethiopia*. East Lansing, MI: African Studies Center, Michigan State University.

Urbanczyk, Suzanne (1992). Infixing and melodic circumscription. MS, University of Massachusetts, Amherst.

Vago, Robert (1973). Abstract vowel harmony systems in Uralic and Altaic languages. *Lg* 49: 579–605.

Vago, Robert (1976). Theoretical implications of Hungarian vowel harmony. *LI* 7: 242–263.

Vago, Robert (1980a). *Issues in Vowel Harmony*. Amsterdam: John Benjamins.

Vago, Robert (1980b). *The Sound Pattern of Hungarian*. Washington, DC: Georgetown University Press.

Vago, Robert (1985). The treatment of long vowels in word games. *Phonology* 2: 327–342.

Vago, Robert (1988). Underspecification in the height harmony system of Pasiego. *Phonology* 5: 343–362.

Vago, Robert, and H. Leder (1987). On the autosegmental analysis of vowel harmony in Turkana. In D. Odden (ed.), *Current Approaches to African Linguistics*, vol. 4 (pp. 383–393). Dordrecht: Foris.

Vallduví, Enric (1990). *The informational component*. Doctoral dissertation, University of Pennsylvania.

Van Haitsma, J. D., and W. Van Haitsma (1976). *A Hierarchical Sketch of Mixe as Spoken in San José El Paraíso*. SIL Publications 44. Norman, OK: SIL.

Vance, T. J. (1987). *An Introduction to Japanese Phonology*. SUNY Press.

Velten, H. V. (1943). The growth of phonemic and lexical patterns in infant language. *Lg* 19: 281–292.

Vennemann, Theo (1972). On the theory of syllabic phonology. *LB* 18: 1–18.

Vennemann, Theo (1984). The rule dependence of syllable structure. MS, Fifth International Phonology Meeting, Eisenstadt, Austria.

Vergnaud, Jean-Roger (1976). Formal properties of phonological rules. In R. Butts and J. Hintikka (ed.), *Basic Problems in Methodology and Linguistics* (pp. 299–318). Dordrecht: Reidel.

Vergnaud, Jean-Roger (1980). A formal theory of vowel harmony. In R. Vago (ed.), *Issues in Vowel Harmony* (pp. 49–62). Amsterdam: John Benjamins.

Vergnaud, Jean-Roger (1982). Paper presented at GLOW, and reported in Encrevé (1988) and Kaye (1988).

Vihman, M. (1978). Consonant harmony: Its scope and function in child language. In J. Greenberg et al. (eds.), *Universals of Human Language* (pp. 403–442). Stanford: Stanford University Press.

Vihman, M. M., M. A. Macken, R. Miller, H. Simmons, and J. Miller (1985). From babbling to speech: A re-assessment of the continuity issue. *Lg* 61: 397–445.

Voegelin, C. (1935). *Tübatulabal Grammar*. University of California Publications in American Archeology and Ethnology no. 34.2. Berkeley: University of California Press.

Vogel, Irene, and Istvan Kenesei (1990a). Focus and phonological structure. Paper presented at GLOW 13, Cambridge.

Vogel, Irene, and Istvan Kenesei (1990b). Syntax and semantics in phonology. In S. Inkelas and D. Zec (eds.), *The Phonology-Syntax Connection* (pp. 339–364). Chicago: University of Chicago Press.

von Stechow, Arnim (1989). Focus and background operators. MS, Technical Report 6, Fachgruppe Sprachwissenschaft, Universität Konstanz.

von Stechow, Arnim (1991). Current issues in the theory of focus. In A. v. Stechow and D. Wunderlich (eds.), *Semantik/Semantics: An International Handbook of Contemporary Research* (pp. 804–825). Berlin: deGruyter.

Walker, Alan, and R. David Zorc (1981). Austronesian loanwords in Yolngu-Matha of northeast Arnhem Land. *Aboriginal History* 4: 109–134.

Walker, Douglas (1975). Lexical stratification in French phonology. *Lingua* 37: 177–196.

Walker, Richard (1979). Central Carrier phonemics. In D. Zimmerly (ed.), *Contributions to Canadian Linguistics*, (pp. 93–107). Canadian Ethnology Service Paper No. 50, National Museum of Man Mercury Series. National Museums of Canada, Ottawa.

Wallace, Karen (1988). Parsing Quechua morphology for syntactic analysis. In K. Wallace (ed.), *Morphology as a Computational Problem*, vol. 7 (pp. 145–161). Los Angeles: UCLA Dept of Linguistics.

Wallin, Lars (1990). Polymorphemic Predicates in Swedish Sign Language. In C. Lucas (ed.), *Sign Language Research: Theoretical Issues* (pp. 133–148). Washington, DC: Gallaudet University Press.

Walsh, Michael (1979). Recent research in Australian linguistics. In S. A. Wurm (ed.), *Australian Linguistic Studies* (pp. 1–72). Pacific Linguistics C-54. Canberra: Australian National University.

Walter, H. (1983). La nasal vélaire /ŋ/: un phonème du français? *Langue française* 60: 14–29.

Wang, H. S., and B. L. Derwing (1986). More on English vowel shift: The back vowel question. *Phonology* 3: 99–116.

Wang, Hong-jun (1991). On the base form of tone sandhi pattern of Danyang. MS, Linguistic Institute, UC Santa Cruz.

Wang, William S.-Y. (1967). Phonological features of tone. *IJAL* 33: 93–105.

Wanner, Dieter, and Thomas Cravens (1980). Early intervocalic voicing in Tuscan. In E. Traugott, R. Labrum, and S. Shepherd (eds.), *Papers from the 4th International Conference on Historical Linguistics* (pp. 339–347). Amsterdam: John Benjamins.

Ward, Gregory, and Julia Hirschberg (1985). Implicating uncertainty: The pragmatics of fall-rise intonation. *Lg* 61: 747–776.

Ward, Ida (1952). *An Introduction to the Yoruba Language*. Cambridge: CUP.

Waters, Bruce (1980). Djinang phonology. *Papers in Australian Linguistics* 14.

Waterson, N. (1987). *Prosodic Phonology: The Theory and its Application to Language Acquisition and Speech Processing*. Newcastle upon Tyne: Grevatt and Grevatt.

Weeda, Donald (1987). Formal properties of Madurese final syllable reduplication. In A. Bosch, B. Need, and E. Schiller (eds.), *CLS 23: Parasession on Autosegmental and Metrical Phonology* (pp. 403–417). Chicago: CLS.

Weeda, Donald (1992). *Word truncation in prosodic morphology*. Doctoral dissertation, University of Texas, Austin.

Wehr, Hans (1971). *A Dictionary of Modern Written Arabic*. Ithaca: Spoken Language Service.

Weidert, Alfons (1987). *Tibeto-Burman Tonology*, vol. 54. Current Issues in Linguistic Theory. Amsterdam: John Benjamins.

Welmers, William (1959). Tonemics, morphotonemics, and tonal morphemes. *General Linguistics* 4: 1–9.

Welmers, William (1962). The phonology of Kpelle. *JAL* 1: 69–93.

Welmers, William, and Zellig Harris (1942). The phonemes of Fanti. *JAOS* 62: 318–33.

Westbury, J. R. (1979). *Aspects of the temporal control of voicing in consonant clusters in English*. Doctoral dissertation, University of Texas, Austin.

Westley, D. O. (1971). The Tepetotutla Chinantec stressed syllable. *IJAL* 37: 160–163.

Wetzels, Leo (1986). Phonological timing in ancient Greek. In L. Wetzels and E. Sezer (eds.), *Studies in Compensatory Lengthening* (pp. 279–344). Dordrecht: Foris.

Wetzels, Leo (1987). The timing of latent consonants in Modern French. In C. Neidle and R. Nuñez Cedeño (eds.), *Studies in Romance Languages* (pp. 283–317). Dordrecht: Foris.

Wetzels, Leo (1993). Mid vowel alternations in Brazilian Portuguese. MS, Free University of Amsterdam and University of Nijmegen.

Wetzels, Leo, and Engin Sezer (1986). *Studies in Compensatory Lengthening*. Dordrecht: Foris.

Wheeler, A., and M. Wheeler (1963). Siona phonemics. In B. Elson (ed.), *Ecuadorian Indian Languages*, vol. 1 Norman, OK: SIL and University of Oklahoma.

Wheeler, Deirdre (1980). A metrical analysis of stress and related processes in Southern

Paiute and Tübatulabal. In J. Lowenstamm (ed.), *University of Massachusetts Occasional Papers in Linguistics 5* (pp. 145–175). Amherst, MA: University of Massachusetts.

Wheeler, Deirdre, and David Touretzky (1991). The role of the syllabifier in Modern Icelandic phonology. MS, School of Computer Science, Carnegie Mellon University.

Wheeler, Deirdre, and David Touretzky (1993). A connectionist implementation of cognitive phonology. In J. Goldsmith (ed.), *The Last Phonological Rule: Reflections on Constraints and Derivations* (pp. 146–172). Chicago: University of Chicago Press.

White, C. (1955). Backwards languages in Africa. *Man* 55: 96.

Whitney, W. D. (1889). *Sanskrit Grammar*. Cambridge, MA: Harvard University Press.

Wilbur, Ronnie (1974). *The phonology of reduplication*. Doctoral dissertation, University of Illinois.

Wilbur, Ronnie (1985). Towards a theory of "syllable" in signed languages: Evidence from the numbers of Italian Sign Language. In W. Stokoe and V. Volterra (eds.), *Sign Language Research '83* (pp. 160–174). Linstok Press.

Wilbur, Ronnie (1987). *American Sign Language: Linguistic and Applied Dimensions*, 2nd ed. Boston: Little, Brown.

Wilbur, Ronnie (1990). Why syllables? What the notion means for ASL research. In S. Fischer and P. Siple (eds.), *Theoretical Issues in Sign Language Research*, vol. 1: *Linguistics* (pp. 81–108). Chicago: University of Chicago Press.

Wilkins, David (1983). Nominal reduplication in Mpartnwe Arrernte. *Language in Central Australia* 1: 16–22.

Wilkins, David (1989). *Mparntwe Arrernte (Aranda): Studies in the structure and semantics of grammar*. Doctoral dissertation, Australian National University.

Wilkinson, Karina (1988). Prosodic structure and Lardil phonology. *LI* 19: 25–34.

Williams, A., and E. Pike (1973). The phonology of Western Popoluca. *Linga* 20: 368–380.

Williams, Edwin (1976). Underlying tone in Margi and Igbo. *LI* 7: 463–484.

Williams, Edwin (1980). Remarks on stress and anaphora. *Journal of Linguistic Research* 1: 1–16.

Williams, Jeffrey (1984). Phonological conditioning in Nakanai reduplication. *LA* 14: 173–190.

Williams, Jeffrey (1991). A note on echo word morphology in Thai and the languages of South and South-East Asia. *AJL* 11: 107–112.

Williams, S., and Gavan Breen (1984). The alphabet in Arrernte. *Language in Central Australia* 2: 21–22.

Williamson, Kay (1973). Some reduced harmony systems. *Research Notes* [from the Dept. of Linguistics and Nigerian Languages, University of Ibadan] 6, No. 1–3: 145–169.

Williamson, Kay (1983). Vowel merger in harmony languages. *JOLAN* 2: 61–82.

Wiltshire, Caroline (1991a). Appendices, structure preservation, and the Strong Domain Hypothesis. In B. A. Chae and H. R. Chae (eds.), *Proceedings of ESCOL 8*. Columbus: The Ohio State University Press.

Wiltshire, Caroline (1991b). On syllable structure at two levels of analysis. In L. Dobrin, L. Nicholls, and R. Rodriguez (eds.), *Papers from CLS 27* (pp. 476–491). Chicago: CLS.

Wiltshire, Caroline (1992). *Syllabification and rule application in harmonic phonology*. Doctoral dissertation, University of Chicago.

Withgott, Mary Margaret (1982). *Segmental evidence for phonological constituents*. Doctoral dissertation, University of Texas, Austin.

Woo, Nancy (1969). *Prosody and phonology*. Doctoral dissertation, MIT.

Wood, Ray (1977). Some aspects of Galpu phonology. *Talanya* 4: 24–29.

Wood, Ray (1978). Some Yuulngu phonological patterns. *Papers in Australian Linguistics* 11: 53–117.

Wood, S. (1981). Tense and lax vowels – degree of constriction or pharyngeal volume? *Working Papers in Linguistics* 1: 109–134. Lund University.

Wood, S. (1982). X-Ray and model studies of vowel articulation. *Working Papers in Linguistics* 23: Lund University.

Woodbury, Anthony (1985). Meaningful phonological processes: A consideration of Central Alaskan Yupik Eskimo prosody. MS, University of Texas, Austin. A revised version of this paper appeared as Woodbury (1987).

Woodbury, Anthony (1987). Meaningful phonological processes: A study of Central Alaskan Yupik Eskimo prosody. *Lg* 63: 685–740.

Woodrow, Herbert (1951). Time perception. In S. S. Stevens (ed.), *Handbook of Experimental Psychology*. New York: Wiley.

Wordick, Frank (1982). *The Yindjibarndi Language*. Pacific Linguistics C-71. Canberra: Australian National University.

Wright, J. T. (1986). The behavior of nasalized vowels in the perceptual vowel space. In J. J. Ohala and J. J. Jaeger (eds.), *Experimental Phonology* (pp. 45–67). Orlando: Academic Press.

Xu, B.-H., Z.-Z. Tang, and N.-R. Qian (1981–1983). Xingpai Shanghai Fangyande Liandu Biandiao [Tone Sandhi in New Shanghai]. *Fangyan* 1981.2: 145–155; 1982.2: 115–128; 1983.3: 197–201.

Yallop, Colin (1977). *Alyawarra: An Aboriginal language of Central Australia*. Canberra: AIAS.

Yallop, Colin (1982). *Australian Aboriginal Languages*. London: Andre Deutsch.

Yatabe, S. (1991). Verbal compounding in Malayalam. MS, Stanford University.

Ye, Xiangling (1983). Wujiang Fangyan Shengdiao Zai Diaocha [Tones of the Wujiang dialect]. *Fangyan* 1983.1: 32–35.

Yeni-Komshian, G., J. Kavanaugh, and C. Ferguson (eds.) (1980). *Child Phonology*, vols. 1 and 2. New York: Academic Press.

Yin, Yuen-Mei (1989). *Phonological aspects of word formation in Mandarin Chinese*. Doctoral dissertation, University of Texas, Austin.

Yip, Moira (1980a). Scanian is not a case of multivalued features. *LI* 11: 432–436.

Yip, Moira (1980b). *The tonal phonology of Chinese*. Doctoral dissertation, MIT. New York: Garland Press, 1991.

Yip, Moira (1982). Reduplication and C-V skeleta in Chinese secret languages. *LI* 13: 637–661.

Yip, Moira (1983a). Redundancy and the CV-skeleton. MS, Brandeis University.

Yip, Moira (1983b). Some problems of syllable structure in Axininca Campa. In P. Sells and C. Jones (eds.), *Proceedings of NELS 13* (pp. 243–251). Amherst, MA: GLSA.

Yip, Moira (1988a). The Obligatory Contour Principle and phonological rules: A loss of identity. *LI* 19: 65–100.

Yip, Moira (1988b). Template morphology and the direction of association. *NLLT* 6: 551–577.

Yip, Moira (1989a). Contour tones. *Phonology* 6: 149–174.

Yip, Moira (1989b). Feature geometry and co-occurrence restrictions. *Phonology* 6: 349–374.

Yip, Moira (1990). Tone, phonation, and intonation register. In J. Carter, R.-M. Déchaine,

B. Philip, and T. Sherer (eds.), *Proceedings of NELS 20* (pp. 487–501). Amherst, MA: GLSA.

Yip, Moira (1991). Prosodic morphology of four Chinese dialects. *Journal of East Asian Linguistics* 1: 1–35.

Yip, Moira (1992). Reduplication with fixed melodic material. In *Proceedings of NELS 22*. Amherst, MA: GLSA.

Zaria, Ahmadu Bello (1982). *Issues in Hausa dialectology*. Doctoral dissertation, Indiana University.

Zec, Draga (1988). *Sonority constraints on prosodic structure*. Doctoral dissertation, Stanford University.

Zec, Draga (1993). Rule domains and phonological change. In S. Hargus and E. Kaisse (eds.), *Studies in Lexical Phonology* (pp. 365–405). San Diego: Academic Press.

Zec, Draga, and Sharon Inkelas (1990). Prosodically constrained syntax. In S. Inkelas and D. Zec (eds.), *The Phonology-Syntax Connection* (pp. 365–378). Chicago: University of Chicago Press.

Zec, Draga, and Sharon Inkelas (1991). The place of clitics in the prosodic hierarchy. In D. Bates (ed.), *Proceedings of WCCFL 10*. Stanford: SLA.

Zee, E., and Ian Maddieson (1979). Tones and tone sandhi in Shanghai: Phonetic evidence and phonological analysis. In *UCLA Working Papers in Phonetics* (pp. 93–129).

Zhang, H.-N. (1985). Zhenjiang Fangyande Liandu Biandiao [Tone sandhi in the Zhenjiang dialect]. *Fangyan* 1985.3: 191–204.

Zhengzhang, S.-F. (1964). Wenzhou Fangyande Liandu Biandiao [Tone sandhi in the Wenzhou dialect]. *Zhongguo Yuwen* 106–152.

Zimmer, Karl (1969). Psychological correlates of some Turkish morpheme structure conditions. *Lg* 45: 309–321.

Zubizarreta, M.-L. 1987. *Levels of Representation in the Lexicon and in Syntax*. Dordrecht: Foris.

Zwicky, Arnold (1988). Morphological rules, operations and operation types. In *Papers from ESCOL 4* (pp. 318–334).

Names Index

Subject Index

Language Index